ACCOUNTANCY

CBSE

ACCOUNTANCY
FOR CLASS XI

B.K. BANERJEE
Faculty Member
Durgapur Government College
Durgapur (West Bengal)

PHI Learning Private Limited

New Delhi-110001
2010

Rs. 350.00

ACCOUNTANCY for Class XI—CBSE
B.K. Banerjee

ISBN-978-81-203-3948-4

The export rights of this book are vested solely with the publisher.

Published by Asoke K. Ghosh, PHI Learning Private Limited, M-97, Connaught Circus, New Delhi-110001 and Printed by Mohan Makhijani at Rekha Printers Private Limited, New Delhi-110020.

To
My Parents
Smt. Bidyut Rani and Shri Ananda Gopal Banerjee
for
Their Love, Support and Blessings

Contents

Preface

Accountancy involves systematically identifying, recording, measuring, summarizing, interpreting and communicating financial information. This book offers detailed coverage of the principles and underlying concepts of financial accounting and their applications. The focus of this book is on developing the interest of students in the field of accountancy, enhancing their skill and building their confidence.

The initial chapters of the book provide an extensive overview of the field of accountancy. Chapter 1 provides a brief introduction to the field. Chapter 2 makes the readers familiar with the major terms in accountancy. The theoretical basis of accounting and the various accounting standards are explained in Chapter 3. The process of accounting is elaborated in Chapter 4. Chapters 5 and 7 present the various methods of recording the accounting transactions, while Chapter 6 discusses the accounting equations.

Chapters 8 to 10 provide detailed expositions of the various books of original entry. Chapter 8 presents the journal and the ledger, Chapter 9 presents the cash book, and Chapter 10 covers the special purpose books.

The bank reconciliation statement is presented in Chapter 11. Some useful ways of presenting disagreements and the effects of particular mistakes are discussed in this chapter. Chapters 12 and 13 cover the trial balance of errors and the rectification of errors respectively.

The accounting procedures for dealing with depreciation, provisions and reserves, bills of exchange, and incomplete records are covered in Chapters 14, 15, 16 and 19 respectively. In the chapter on bills of exchange, all the procedures for calculation of dates as well as for dealing with discounting and dishonour of bills are explained.

The financial statements and various related adjustments are covered in Chapters 17 and 18. It is expected that the students, after reading these chapters, will understand the importance of financial statements and attain the ability to prepare them with practical adjustments.

The importance of the application of information technology in modern accountancy cannot be overemphasized. The final chapters of this book (20 and 21) are devoted to the role of computers and database management in accounting.

The application of Accounting Standards (AS) in general has been highlighted in various chapters of the book.

The concepts discussed in this book are illustrated with the help of numerous examples, figures and tables. Plenty of graded numerical problems are provided at the end of each chapter. Many of these problems, based on current trends, are provided with appropriate notes and hints for solution.

More than 450 objective-type and short-answer type questions with answers are provided in the book, along with their answers, to reinforce the readers' grasp of the underlying theoretical concepts.

I wish to thank my wife Smt. Chandrani Banerjee for her active co-operation and valuable suggestions for preparing this book. My son Sri Soham Banerjee also deserves great appreciation for inspiring me to complete this book at the earliest. I also wish to convey my deep gratitude to the staff of PHI Learning for their wholehearted efforts towards shaping the book into its present form.

In spite of all efforts to the contrary, some errors might have crept into the book. I shall remain grateful to all readers who point out such mistakes. Constructive and notable suggestions by the readers for the improvement of the contents of the book are most welcome.

It would be a great source of pleasure for me if this book is found useful by the teachers as well as the students of accountancy.

B.K. Banerjee

1

Introduction to Accounting

CONTENTS

INTRODUCTION

An enterprise or a business is an economic unit, engaged in selling goods or services to its customers. Accountancy is a very old discipline and is the language of business. All business transactions are recorded with the help of accounting and at the end of a financial year the results of all the business transactions are assessed in the form of final accounts on the basis of some accepted principles, rules and guidelines.

Bookkeeping is the process of recording financial transactions and keeping financial records. *Accounting,* on the other hand, includes the design of an accounting information system that meets the user's needs. The major goals of accounting are analysis, interpretation, and use of information.

Accounting consists of a series of activities such as collecting, recording, analyzing and finally communicating information to its users. Data itself is simply a collection of facts expressed as symbols and characters which are unable to influence decisions until transformed into information. The task of an accountant is transformation. The term system is now commonly used to refer to a set of elements based on some accepted principles which operate together in order to attain some desired objectives or common goals.

Thus, the final accounts of an enterprise are prepared with the help of a series of accounting systems through which the financial position of the enterprise is presented. From there the position of assets, liabilities, net worth of the business and the result, (i.e., profit or loss) are reflected through the income statement. Accountancy is an evolving subject, and is being improved regularly by professional accountants for the benefit of the users of the financial statements.

1.1 ACCOUNTING

Accounting is primarily concerned with recording the transactions affecting a business, as well as the preparation of the income statement and the balance sheet. According to the Committee on Terminology of American Institute of Certified Public Accountants (AICPA):

1

Accounting is the art of recording, classifying and summarizing, in a significant manner and in terms of money, transactions and events which are in part at least, of a financial character, and interpreting the results thereof.

American Accounting Association, on the other hand defines Accounting as the process of identifying, measuring and communicating economic information to permit informed judgements and decisions by the users of the information.

Thus, accounting is an information system that measures, processes and communicates financial information about an identifiable economic entity. On the basis of the above definitions, the salient features of accounting may be summarized as follows:

1. *Art of recording business transactions.* Here, the term **art** refers to the style and technique of recording financial transactions in the books of accounts in a systematic manner. The way the transactions are recorded is the art or the style of presentation in the books of accounts as per the requirement of the owner. It is done in such a way that it helps fulfil the objectives of the enterprise.

2. *Accounting is a process.* All the transactions are recorded regularly in a chronological manner by applying different rules, principles, judgements, skills and expertise. It involves the task of classifying, summarizing and analyzing all the business transactions.

3. *Accounting records transactions which are measurable in terms of money.* This means that events or transactions which are recorded in the books of accounts must be measurable in terms of money. Those events which are not measurable in terms of money need not be recorded though for such an event the business may suffer a loss. For example, if the General Manager of a company meets with an accident, the incident amounts to a great loss for the company, but it cannot be measurable in terms of money and hence, need not be recorded in the books of accounts.

4. *Accounting is a means and not an end.* Accounts are maintained to protect the assets and the interest of the business. By recording and classifying the business data, accounting provides a vital service by supplying the information to the decision makers in the form of financial statements together with its interpretation through reporting. Keeping the accounts is not the basic objective of an entity. Thus, it can be said that accounting is a means and not an end in itself.

5. *Accounting is an information system.* Accounting is an information system that measures, processes, and communicates financial information about an identifiable economic entity. It provides an important service by supplying the information to the decision makers. Thus, accounting is an essential link between the business activities and the decision makers.

6. *Accounting is a medium for communicating financial position.* Accounts are used as a medium for communicating financial transactions and their interpretations. The basic objective of accounting is to provide necessary information to owners and users in a systematic and consistent manner.

1.1.1 Functions

The chief functions of accounting are as follows:

1. **Identification.** The primary function of accounting is to identify the financial transactions or the economic activities which are measurable in terms of money.

2. **Recording.** After the economic activities have been identified as business transactions, recording of the said transactions (i.e., deals with financial transactions) is done systematically and in a consistent way in the books of original entries or in subsidiary books through journal.

3. **Classifying.** It is related to the task of grouping the transactions of similar nature or identical transactions in a particular place or in one place. Classifying is done in the book known as **ledger**. It helps one in knowing the total amount involved in a particular account or head

which in turn helps one to get an idea about the net position of a party's account (i.e., net amount payable to a party or receivable from a party).

4. **Summarizing.** It involves the preparation of trial balance, income statement and balance sheet through classified data on the basis of the accepted accounting principles. Summarizing is a continuous process.

5. **Analysing and interpreting.** After the preparation of the financial statements, the net result of an enterprise is ascertained and the financial position is then analyzed and interpreted in such a way which could meet the user's needs. The goal of the accounting system is to provide information which meets the needs of its users, i.e., to the people or groups of people who have vested interests in a business organization—managers, shareholders, employees, customers, and creditors.

6. The accounting information is communicated to interested parties or groups.

7. The accounting helps in protecting the interest and the assets of the business.

8. According to the provisions of the different laws, the legal requirements of the business are to be fulfilled.

1.1.2 Objectives

The main objectives of accounting are as follows:

1. To ascertain the results of business transactions (profit or loss) within a given period.

2. To ascertain the true financial position of a concern on a certain date, i.e., at the end of the financial period.

3. To provide necessary information to the users, namely, different interested parties of accounting information.

In addition to the above stated objectives some other purposes are also fulfilled through accounting information by preparation data in respect of future plans regarding the use of the funds in the best possible way. Accounting helps the organization to increase the net worth of its business considering the present economic condition globally.

1.2 ACCOUNTING CYCLE

Accounting cycle includes the following:

1. Recording all transactions in a journal or in its subsidiary books.

2. Posting data under different heads to different accounts, i.e., posting in ledger.

3. Preparation of the final accounts after closing the accounts in ledger.

The above steps are followed during each accounting period.

1.3 BOOKKEEPING

According to R.N. Carter, "Bookkeeping is the science and art of correctly recording in the books of accounts all those business transactions that result in the transfer of money or money's worth."

Bookkeeping is the science of recording transactions in money or money's worth in such a manner that, at any subsequent day, the nature and effect of each transaction, and the combined effect of the transactions may be clearly understood so that the accounts prepared at any time from the records thus kept may show the owner of the books his true financial position.
                          —L.C. Cropper

Bookkeeping is chiefly concerned with recording the financial data or events measurable in terms of money. Thus, it helps to keep a complete record of business transactions in a systematic manner through which the financial position of a concern for a certain period may be ascertained.

1.4 ACCOUNTING AND BOOKKEEPING

People often fail to understand the difference between accounting and bookkeeping. *Bookkeeping* is the process of recording financial transactions and keeping financial records. Mechanical and repetitive bookkeeping is only a small, but important, part of accounting. *Accounting*, on the other hand, includes the design of an information system that meets the user's needs. The major goals of accounting are the analysis, interpretation and use of information. The basic differences between accounting and bookkeeping are given in Table 1.1.

TABLE 1.1   Differences between Bookkeeping and Accounting

	Bookkeeping	Accounting
Scope or area	The primary function is to identify the financial transactions and then record the said transactions systematically in the books of original entries or in the subsidiary books through journal.	It involves the preparation of trial balance, income statement and balance sheet through classified data on the basis of the accepted accounting principles. It is a continuous process.
Objective	Bookkeeping is mainly concerned with the recording of the financial data or events measurable in terms of money.	It includes the design of an information system that meets the user's needs. The major goals of accounting are analysis, interpretation and use of information.
Performer of the job	It may be performed by a mere clerk having no skilled knowledge of accounting.	It is performed by skilled persons having knowledge of accounting.
Stage	It is the primary stage.	Accountancy begins where Bookkeeping ends.
Nature of job	It is a clerical job done regularly and chronologically.	It is an analytical and a systematic job done in a consistent manner.
Skills used	It does not require any special skill. It is a mechanical regular job.	It requires special skills and knowledge of accounting and concerned accepted rules.

1.5   ACCOUNTING VS ACCOUNTANCY

Accountancy is the art as well as the science of recording, classifying, and summarizing the business transactions in terms of money within an accounting or financial year, with the help of principles and techniques. On the other hand, **accounting** is a systematic process by which transactions are recorded on the basis of accepted principles and techniques developed for accountancy to represent the financial results thereof.

1.6   USES OF ACCOUNTING

The following are important uses of a good accounting system:

1. It helps to assess the present position or the results, i.e., profit or loss of a business.
2. Accounting helps in representing the financial stability of a business by stating the position of its assets and liabilities.
3. It helps to ascertain the profitability and solvency of the business.
4. Account data are presented in such a way that it helps to prepare a comparative analysis of the financial results, and the position of the trading and non-trading concerns.
5. It helps the management in taking decisions in adverse situations.
6. Accounting helps the management in taking decisions in respect of declaring dividend, change in capital, price fixation, and so on.
7. Government is also benefited by accounting data for selecting tax rate, subsidies, etc.
8. The present and future earning capacity of the business.
9. Accounting helps in taking the required measures or steps to overcome future uncertainties.
10. It helps to estimate or assess the amount of income tax, sales tax, etc.
11. Accounting helps in taking decisions regarding whether to manufacture a product or to divert the production structure or to buy the same from the market.

1.7 LIMITATIONS OF ACCOUNTING

The main limitations of accounting are as follows:

1. It does not disclose the present value of all the assets of the business. Actually accounts are maintained on historical cost basis.
2. Non-monetary factors are not considered in accounting.
3. Impact of inflation is not properly assessed.
4. Sometimes it is influenced by personal judgments or biases.
5. Alternative methods can be developed for some transactions or events and consequently it will influence the profit or loss of the business.
6. Managerial performances can not be measured properly on the basis of the profits earned by the enterprise as there is ample scope to increase profits by manipulation of accounts.
7. It ignores the qualitative aspects within an enterprise.

1.8 BRANCHES OF ACCOUNTING

Accounting has the following branches:

1. Financial accounting
2. Cost accountancy
3. Management accounting

Financial accounting generates reports and communicates them to external decision makers so that they can evaluate the extent to which the business has achieved its goals. These reports to the external users are called **financial reports**.

Cost accountancy according to ICMA London, is

The application of costing and cost accounting principles, methods and techniques to the science, art and practice of cost control and the ascertainment of profitability. It includes the presentation of information derived therefrom for the purpose of managerial decision-making.

Cost Accounting has developed primarily because of the limitations of financial accounting.

Management accounting includes the methods/systems which help management to predict the future and formulate future policies in due time by presenting the accounting data in a systematic manner after its proper evaluation and analytical interpretation. Since business is becoming complex with each day, management needs more information in a systematic manner to face the new challenges. In order to meet these needs, the other branches of accounts have developed from financial accounting, but here, we are concerned only with financial accounting. Before going into further details, we may look into the history of evolution of accountancy in brief.

1.9 SYSTEM OF BOOKKEEPING

Recording of day-to-day transactions are made through the following systems:

1. Single entry system
2. Double entry system

1.9.1 Single Entry System

The single entry system is nothing but a limited form of the double entry system. In other words, single entry system is an unscientific method of record keeping which does not follow the accepted accounting rules. It maintains only a few accounts, and records according to the desire of the proprietors. There does not exist any particular system which may be called a single entry system. However, **single entry system** may be thus defined as an incomplete record of business transactions which does not follow the general accounting principles and procedures, and is done according to the desires of the trader or the owner.

1.9.2 Double Entry System

This system has a two-fold effect or a dual aspect. We know that any business transaction affects the two accounts in the opposite direction. Double entry system is based on the principle that there can be no giving without a receiving. The receiving aspect is known as **debit** and the giving aspect is called **credit**. Thus, every debit must have a corresponding credit. On the basis of the dual aspect concept, the accounting equation under the double entry system is as follows:

Owner's Equity + Outsider's Equity = Total Assets

or, Capital + Liabilities = Total Assets

Basic features of double entry system

1. Every transaction has a two-fold effect or a dual aspect a receiving aspect and a corresponding giving aspect.
2. The receiving aspect is known as debit and the giving aspect is called credit.
3. In every transaction, there must be two parties—the receiving side and the giving side.
4. The amount which is paid by the giving side is being received by the acceptor side.
5. In every transaction, the total of the debit side and the credit side is always equal.
6. Any transaction of a business affects the two accounts in the opposite directions.

Advantages of double entry system

1. This method helps to record the transactions perfectly. According to the double entry system, every debit must have a corresponding credit. Thus, when one account is debited, the other account must be credited. As a result, total debit is always equal to total credit.
2. It is a highly scientific method. It helps to detect the errors and also in the rectification of the said errors.
3. It helps to ensure the arithmetical accuracy of the accounts.
4. This system is applicable to all types of firms or organizations.
5. As accounts are maintained scientifically, the closing balance of all accounts can be obtained whenever required. This is helpful at the time of taking important decisions.
6. It helps to ascertain the profits or losses of a firm at the end of the financial year.
7. It helps to ascertain the balance of closing assets and liabilities of a firm at the end of the financial year.
8. The books maintained under the double entry system are accepted by different authorities like Income Tax Department and Sales Tax Department.
9. It helps to maintain the books of accounts perfectly.
10. This system facilitates the comparison of the results of the business of different years while taking managerial decisions.

Disadvantages of double entry system

1. This system requires effective control over accounts, or else it will develop a lot of problems.
2. When a transaction is missing (i.e., omitted from the books), it cannot be detected through this system.
3. The book-maintaining costs are so high that small businesses cannot afford to maintain double entry books.
4. Without having any accounting knowledge, books cannot be maintained perfectly.
5. In some cases, it depends on the personal judgement of the accountant or the owner to keep the books.
6. When a particular transaction is recorded wrongly in the books of original entry, it becomes very difficult to detect the said error.
7. According to the double entry system, all recorded transactions are based on historical records. Hence, the effect of inflation gets ignored. As a result, a question may arise regarding whether it is representing the true and fair view of the business or not.

1.10 A BRIEF HISTORY OF DEVELOPMENT OF ACCOUNTANCY

In India, **Chanakya** is famous for his book *Arthashastra* where he defined the existence and the need of accounting and its auditing. In *Manusanhita*, the preparation of accounting and the determination of profit were emphasized. In England and in Europe, *Stewardship* accounting was followed for a long time for keeping household accounts. The Double Entry System of Bookkeeping was first developed by the famous Italian mathematician, scholar and philosopher Fra Luca Bartolo meo de Pacioli in 1494. Pacioli published his most important work, *Summa de Arithmetica, Geometrica, Proportioniet Proportionalita,* which contained a detailed description of accounting as practised in that age. This book became the most widely read book on mathematics in Italy and firmly established Pacioli as the Father of Accounting.

The Industrial Revolution brought considerable economic change to society which, in turn, enhanced the importance of accounting. But in recent years, considerable changes have taken place in science technology and which have brought about a remarkable change in the field of accounting. The growth of business resulted in the introduction of Joint Stock Company, where ownership was separated from management. It developed different parties or users like investors, customers, suppliers, owners, the Government, employees, etc., and with a view of making the accounting language a standard language, i.e., practicable and understandable to all, different accounting principles, concepts, and conventions have been developed. To remove the drawbacks of the conventional accounting system a new method of accounting known as **inflation accounting** has been developed which takes into account the present trend of rising prices/continuous inflation.

In the present time accounting undertakes a responsibility of measuring, interpreting and communicating the results of different economic activities systematically. In recent times, a new specialized branch of accounting, known as **human resource accounting**, has developed.

In the late 1960s the importance of establishing certain generally accepted principles was felt by the accounting bodies of some of the developed countries. Accordingly, on 20th June, 1973, the International Accounting Standard Committee (IASC) was set up with 16 accounting bodies from nine nations. At present, the Institute of Chartered Accountants of India (ICAI) and the Institute of Cost and Works Accountants of India (ICWAI) are members of the IASC. It may be mentioned here that the IASC has teen reconstituted as the International Accounting Standards Board (IASB).

After a long chase, interactions and development, we have reached the age of computer. The computer is an electronic tool that is used to collect, organize, and communicate vast amount of information with great speed. Accountants were among the earliest and most enthusiastic users of computers and today they use microcomputers in all aspects of their work. With the widespread use of the computer today, business information needs are organized into a system called **Management Information System (MIS)**. An MIS consists of the interconnected subsystems that provide the information needed to run a business. It plays the key role of managing the flow of data to all parts of the business and to the interested parties outside the business. A useful information must have the following qualities:

1. Relevance
2. Understandability
3. Verifiability
4. Neutrality
5. Comparability
6. Completeness.

1. *Relevance*: Accounting information must provide those data and facts which are relevant to the financial statements, and which at the same time, serve the purpose of the users. Irrelevant and unnecessary information must not be provided to the users. Thus, management must provide and prepare the contents of the accounting information in such a way that all data must be relevant to the users in all respects. For example, while presenting the debtors schedule of an enterprise, it is advisable that the break-up of the total amount of debtors must be disclosed considering its period of outstanding along with the amount of provision for bad debts made during the current year. For example, suppose total debtors is Rs. 374,000, then the break-up may be given as follows:

(a) Out of the debtors Rs. 40,000 is six months old
(b) Rs. 100,000 is one year old
(c) Rs. 234,000 is two years old and above, and so on.

Thus the management of an account must provide relevant information considering the possible needs of the users based on justice and values.

2. *Understandability*: It means that all the information provided through the financial and other statements must be presented in such a way that all classes of users may understand the contents as they actually are without the need to passes any special skill or knowledge in accounting. Thus, to make the financial statements more convincing and useful to the users, detailed explanatory notes and analyses of different items must be given by the accountant. Otherwise, they will not serve the purpose for which they are prepared.

3. *Verifiability*: Accounting information should provide only that information which are based on the facts and figures prepared with the help of reliable documents. After preparation of financial statements, if any doubt or question is raised in respect of any figure or data, then there must be some provision or arrangement to verify the said or figure data from the documents preserved for the said purpose. Here lies the importance of accounting information. Suppose, when a land is purchased, then the cost of the said land may be verified from the deed of the land. Thus, verifiability ensures the truthfulness of the facts and figures presented in financial statements. It gives the users confidence and satisfaction from the information provided through the financial statements.

4. *Neutrality*: Appropriate steps should be taken to refine the presentation of the financial statements and the relate data because, wherever human action and effort are involved, there may be some amount of biasness or manipulation of data. However, by these implementation and imposition of new laws and restrictions, these shortcomings can bere moved to a great extent. Thus, steps should be taken to present the financial statements free of any kind of biasness from the parties involved.

5. *Comparability*: A characteristic that increases the usefulness of accounting information to its users is called **comparability**. Information about a ccompany is more useful if it can be compared with similar facts of other companies over the same period. Comparability means that the information is presented in such a way that a decision-maker can recognize similarities, dissimilarities and trends over different time periods and between different companies.

Thus, to maintain the quality of comparability, accounts are maintained and prepared on the basis of the accepted accounting principles and guidelines. In this way the users will be benefited more and the enterprise objectives will also be achieved.

The information contained in the financial statement is so important to it susers that without it, they would have to take decisions in different matters under a considerable degree of uncertainty.

6. *Completeness*: It is desirable that all information must be clearly and completely presented through the financial statements so that their users can get better insight about the financial strengths and weaknesses of the firm.

1.11 ACCOUNTING AS AN INFORMATION SYSTEM

There are three basic forms of business enterprise—the corporate form, the sole proprietorship form and the partnership form. No matter which form of business enterprise is involved, a business should be viewed for accounting purposes as a separate entity and the reports should be developed separately from those of its owners. All business transactions are economic events recorded in terms of money which affect the financial position of a business entity. Money is the only factor that is common to all business transactions, and thus it is the only practical unit of measure that can produce the financial data or the raw materials of accounting reports.

All businesses pursue their goals by engaging in similar activities. Generally at *first*, each business enterprise engages in financing activities to obtain adequate funds or capital to begin and to continue operating activities. *Second*, each of them then engages in investing activities to spend the capital. It includes buying land, building, equipments and other resources that are needed in the operation of the business and *third*, engages in operating activities. In addition to selling goods and services to customers, business activities include such actions as employing managers and workers, buying and producing services, and paying taxes to the Government.

Accounting is an information system that measures, processes, and communicates financial information about an identifiable economic entity. Accounting provides a vital service by supplying the information to the decision-makers, and acts as a link between business activities and the decision-makers. Through accounting,

1. The business activities are measured by recording data for future reference,
2. The data are stored and then processed with the help of some accepted guidelines to become useful information, and
3. The information is communicated through reports to the decision-makers.

We may thus say that the data about the business activities is the *input* to the accounting system and the useful information for decision-makers is the *output*. As defined earlier, the term **system** is commonly used today to refer to a set of elements based on some accepted principles, which operate together in order to attain some desired objectives or common goals. Generally, a system may be seen as consisting of three activities—input, i.e., collection of data, processing of input and the result, i.e., the output.

Thus, accounting consists of a series of activities such as collecting, recording, analyzing and finally communicating this information to its users. Data itself is simply a collection of facts expressed as symbols and characters which are unable to influence decisions until transformed into information. The task of an accountant is to bring about this transformation. We may say that the selected data forms the input for the processing system which provides accounting information. This information output is used by decision-makers, which are identifiable. Thus it is evident that a decision-oriented information system should produce information which meets the needs of its users. Bookkeeping is the process of recording financial transactions and keeping financial records. Accounting, on the other hand, includes the design of an accounting information system that meets the user's needs. The major goals of accounting are analysis, interpretation and use of information. Accounting as an information system is shown in Figure 1.1 with the help of a chart.

The goal of the accounting system is to provide information which meets the needs of its users, i.e., to several groups of people who have vested interests in a business organization—managers, shareholders, employees, customers, and creditors.

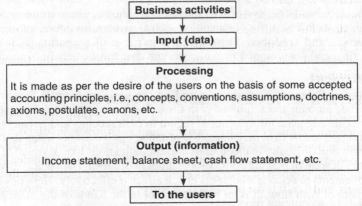

FIGURE 1.1 Accounting as an information system.

The accounting information system is the most important element of an organization's information system for the following reasons:

1. The accounting information system enables the management and the external information users to get a picture of the whole organization.
2. It links other information systems such as marketing, personnel, R & D, stores and purchases, and production, so that the information produced by these systems can be expressed in financial terms for planning suitable strategies to attain organizational goals.

With the wide spread use of computer today, the information needs of a business are organized into a **Management Information System (MIS)**. An MIS consists of the inter connected subsystems that provide the information needed to run a business. The accounting information system is the most important subsystem because it plays the key role of managing the flow of economic data to all parts of a business and to the interested parties outside the business.

1.12 THE OUTPUT

Accounting consists of a series of activities such as collecting, recording, analyzing and finally communicating this information to its users. This information output is used by different groups of decision-makers, and meets the needs of its users.

The output, i.e., accounting information is explained below in brief.

Income statement

An income statement is a measure of the financial performance of a firm in an accounting year. Generally, an Income Statement is divided into two parts. The *first part* is called the **Trading Account**. Trading Account is prepared to represent the trading results of a firm, i.e., gross profit or gross loss. The *second part* of the Income Statement is called **Profit and Loss Account**. It is opened with gross profit or gross loss transferred from the Trading Account. All incomes and expenses which are not considered in Trading Account (i.e., indirect incomes and expenses), and all loses are taken into account in the Profit and Loss Account. While preparing the Income Statement, Accrual concept is followed to ascertain the true profit or loss of a business. The net result of a profit and loss account is called **net profit** or **net loss** and the said amount is transferred to the Capital Account in case of proprietary business and to the Profit and Loss Appropriation Account in case of partnership firm sand companies.

Balance sheet

It is a statement prepared at the end of a financial year to represent the true financial position of a firm or a business. It is not an account but is only a statement representing the closing assets and liabilities of a firm on a certain date. On the left hand side, liabilities (owner's equity and outsiders' equity)are shown while on the right hand side, assets of the business are shown. There are several groups of people who have vested interests in a business organization such as owners, investors, managers, shareholders, employees, customers and creditors. Therefore, the purpose of preparing a Balance Sheet is to represent the true financial position of a firm on a certain date for the benefit of its users.

Cash flow statement

Income Statement and Balance Sheet are prepared on the basis of Accrual System which does not reflect the appropriate amount and timing of cash flow. The basic objective of preparing a Cash Flow Statement is to provide adequate information in regard to cash receipts and payments of an enterprise within an accounting period. A firm may operate profitably, but it does not mean that it's cash position is very sound. It may find difficulty in meeting its current obligations like payment of taxes, dividends, loans, interests, etc., in spite of making considerable amount of profit. Hence, it is essential to know the details of cash movements to operate a business efficiently and effectively. Here lies the importance of preparing a statement of cash flow. It is an important tool in the hands of the management to assess a firm's cash liquidity in an accounting year.

1.12.1 The Users of Accounting Information

The people who use accounting information to make decisions can be grouped into three categories:
1. Those who manage a business
2. Those outside a business enterprise who have a direct financial interest in the business
3. The people, organizations, and agencies that have an indirect financial interest in the business.

They are shown in Figure 1.2.

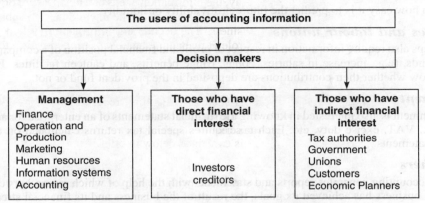

FIGURE 1.2 The users of accounting information.

An information management system captures data about all aspects of the company's operations, organizes the data into usable information, and provides reports to the internal managers and the appropriate outside parties. Accounting plays a key role in this function.

Users of financial statements fall into two broad categories: internal and external. Management is the main internal user. On the other hand, investors and creditors are the chief external users.

Internal users

Management and the owners are the main internal user. The owners invest their resources within the business and remain very much interested in the financial information. On the other hand, the management is the caretaker of the resources invested by the owners. They provide financial information to the owners to assess the business stability and its performance.

Thus, these groups are directly connected with the preparation of the financial statements and are also responsible for operating the business and its profitability. Financial information is very important to this group for the effective running of the business and for taking important business decisions. For example, they would want to know whether the present profitability is enough for the business or not? Is the liquidity position of the company satisfactory? Which product is more profitable among the different products? Thus, a number of decisions are taken by this group on the basis of the accounting data, and hence they are the most important users of accounting information.

Investors and creditors

Investors and creditors are the chief external users. Generally, they use the financial statement to judge the current position compared to past performance and the future potential, and the risk connected with the potential.

Creditors make loans in the form of trade accounts, notes or bonds, on which they receive interest. A loan is expected to be repaid according to its terms. On the other hand, investors buy capital stock from which they expect to receive dividends and an increase in value. Both creditors and investors face risks. For both these groups, the common goal is to achieve a return that makes up for the risk. In general, greater the risk taken, greater is the return required as compensation.

Past performance is often a good indicator of future performance. Therefore, an investor or a creditor looks at the trend of past sales, expenses, net income, cash flow, and return on investment not only as a means for judging a management's past performance but also as a possible indicator of its future performance.

Information about the past and present is useful only to the extent to which it bears on decisions about the future. An investor judges the potential earning ability of a company as this ability will affect the market price of the company's stock and dividends that the company will pay. A creditor on the contrary judges the potential debt-paying ability of the company. The risk of an investment or loan depends on how easy it is to predict the future profit ability or liquidity.

Employees and labour unions

These groups also require information in respect of profit and financial position of a company to realize their demands, (e.g., increase in salaries, bonus, fringe benefits, and canteen facilities. It also helps them to know whether their contributions are deposited in the provident fund or not.

Government

The Government is also interested in knowing the financial statements of an enterprise for assessing the income tax, VAT, excise duty, etc. Each tax requires special tax returns calculated on the basis of financial statements.

Researchers

Financial accounting generates reports and statements with the help of which researchers can evaluate how well a business has achieved its goals, the result of the business and its financial strength. These reports and statements help them prepare different advance accounting techniques and case studies for the benefit of future generations.

1.13 THE PRESENT FORM OF BUSINESS

The present form of business is shown in Figure 1.3. Stockholders, Board of Directors and the Management form the three components of today's business.

FIGURE 1.3   Present form of business.

1.13.1 Shareholders

A person who purchases a share is called shareholder. The shareholders are the proprietors of a company.

1.13.2 Board of Directors

The shareholders of a company are numerous, scattered and unorganized. Therefore, they elect and select some representatives called directors to manage the company owned by them. These directors act with collective responsibility and are jointly known as the board. The Board of Directors constitutes the top administrative organ of the company. The Board is the highest body as far as management of day-to-day affairs of the company is concerned. From legal point of view they can be treated as agents or as trustees because they have to perform acts on behalf of the company using the resources of the company which they have to hold and protect.

1.13.3 Management

The Board of Directors appoints managers to carry out the corporation's policies and run the day-to-day operations. The management consists of the operating officers, who are generally the president, vice-presidents, controller, treasurer, and secretary. Besides being responsible for running the business, a management has the duty of reporting the financial results of its administration to the board of directors and the stockholders. Companies are owned by shareholders but they are not managed by them directly. The management of companies is entrusted to the representatives of shareholders and the Board of Directors. Every human group activity consists of some objectives. Management is an intangible but distinct process by which such objectives are realized. Without the help of management 'the resources of production' remain resources and never become products. For this purpose, management organizes, plans, directs and controls an enterprise.

The pattern of the company management as discussed above may be presented in the form of a chart as given in Fig. 1.4 below.

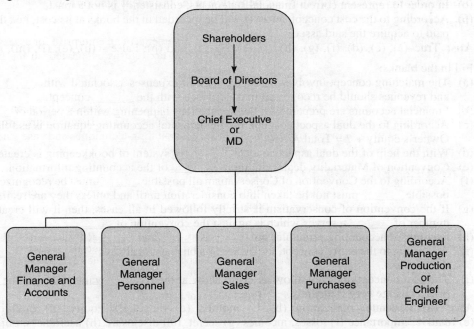

FIGURE 1.4 Pattern of Company Management.

EXERCISES

I. *Objective Type Questions*

1. State whether each of the following statement is true or false:
   (a) Bookkeeping is the science and art of recording business transactions in a systematic manner.
   (b) Accounting is the valuation of transactions in terms of money.
   (c) The main objective of accounting is to ascertain the results of the business transactions within a certain period.
   (d) The accounting information is to be communicated to the different interested parties or groups.

(e) Financial accounting is concerned with top management only.

(f) Accounting cycle deals with recording of all transactions in journal, ledger and final accounts.

(g) Good accounting system helps to know the true financial position of a firm.

(h) Non-monetary factors are not considered in conventional accounting system.

(i) Out of the limitations of accounting, the most important one is the impact of inflation, is not properly assessed.

(j) Accountancy is the method by which all business decisions are taken.

(k) Double entry system of bookkeeping was first introduced by F. Luca Paciori.

(l) Accounting principles are universal like other natural science.

(m) According to the entity concept, the owner of a firm/business and the business is the same.

(n) According to the assumptions of the going concern concept, it is assumed that the business enterprise will exist indefinitely for a long period of time in future.

(o) In order to represent correct financial statements, consistency is not a must.

(p) According to the cost concept, an asset will be recorded in the books at its cost, i.e., the price paid to acquire the said asset.

Ans: True–(a), (c), (d), (f), (g), (h), (i), (k), (l), (n), and (p); False – (b), (e), (j), (m), and (o).

2. Fill in the blanks:

(a) The matching concept involves the recognition of expenses associated with _____ earned and revenues should be recognized in accordance with the _____ concept.

(b) Financial accounts are prepared for the transactions happening within a period of _____.

(c) According to the dual aspect concept, the fundamental accounting equation is as follows: Owner's equity + ? = Total Assets.

(d) With the help of the dual aspect concept ___ _____ system of bookkeeping is created.

(e) Convention of Materiality deals with the ___ _____ of the accounting information.

(f) According to the Convention of Conservatism all possible _____ must be recognize and all possible _____ must not be taken into consideration until and unless they are realized.

(g) If the convention of conservatism is strictly followed in all cases, then it will create large number of _____ reserves which is against the convention of _____ _____ .

(h) Features of accounting principles are _____, _____ and _____ .

(i) According to the entity concept, the owner of a business is always _____ and _____ from the business.

(j) The cost concept does not allow assets to show at their _____ value, because the market prices change very frequently.

Ans: (a) Revenue, realization (b) 12 months (c) outsider's equity (d) double entry (e) relative, importance (f) losses, incomes (g) secret, full disclosure (h) usefulness, objectivity and feasibility (i) separated, distinct (j) present.

3. Choose the correct alternative from the following cases:

(a) In the entity concept, ownership is
  (i) separated from the business.
  (ii) not separated from the business.

(b) According to the cost concept, an asset will be recorded
  (i) at the price actually paid by the enterprise.
  (ii) at its present value.

(c) According to the matching concept
  (i) balance sheet is prepared.
  (ii) income statement is prepared.

(d) Under the realization concept, the revenue is deemed to be earned when
  (i) cash is actually received.
  (ii) the goods have been sold/transferred or the services rendered.

(e) According to the money measurement concept, all transactions are to be recorded in the financial accounts which
    (i) are measurable in terms of money.
    (ii) are acceptable to the owner.

(f) According to the convention of disclosure
    (i) all the transactions are to be valued on the basis of the current price.
    (ii) all the material facts regarding the business activites must be disclosed in financial accounts.

(g) Accounting principles are
    (i) not universal like other natural sciences.
    (ii) universal like other natural sciences.

(h) In accounting principles,
    (i) some standards are applied to measure the economic activites of a firm to ensure uniformity.
    (ii) some rules are framed according to Companies Act to measure the economic activities.

Ans: a. (i) b. (i) c. (ii) d. (ii) e. (i) f. (ii) g. (i) and h. (i).

II. *Short Answer Type Questions (with answers)*

1. Who first developed the double entry system and what was his main contribution in this respect?
Ans: The **double entry system of bookkeeping** was first developed by famous Italian mathematician, scholar and philosopher **Fra Luca Pacioli, in 1494**. Pacioli published his most important work, *Summa de Arithmetica, Geometrica, Proportioniet Proportionalita,* which contained a detailed description of accounting as practiced in that age. This book became the most widely read book on mathematics in Italy and firmly established Pacioli as the "**father of accounting**".

2. What do you mean by bookkeeping?
Ans: *Bookkeeping* is the process of recording financial transactions and keeping financial records. Mechanical and repetitive, bookkeeping is only a small, but important, part of accounting. It helps to keep a complete record of business transactions in a systematic manner and by which the financial position of a concern for a certain period may be ascertained.

3. What do you mean by Accounting?
Ans: Accounting is primarily concerned with the recording of transactions affecting the business and the preparation of income statement and balance sheet. "Accounting is the art of recording, classifying and summarizing—in a significant manner and in terms of money, transactions and events which are, in part at least, of a financial character—and interpreting the results thereof" (given by AICPA committee on terminology). So, accounting is an information system that measures, processes and communicates financial information about an identifiable economic entity.

4. What do you mean by the term 'Accountancy'?
Ans: *Accountancy* is the art as well as science of recording, classifying and summarizing of the business transactions in terms of money within an accounting or financial year, with the help of principles and techniques.

5. What is the main objective of accounting?
Ans: The main objectives are as follows:
(a) To ascertain the result of the business transactions within a given period, i.e., profit or loss.
(b) To ascertain the true financial position of the concern on a certain date, i.e., at the end of the financial period.

6. What are the basic forms of business enterprise?
Ans: There are three basic forms of business enterprise. Beside the corporate form, there are the sole proprietorship form and the partnership form.

7. Why is it said that accounting is an information system?

   Ans: Accounting is an information system that measures, processes and communicates financial information about an identifiable economic entity. Accounting provides a vital service by supplying the information to decision makers. Accounting is a link between business activities and decision makers. Through accounting.

   (a) Business activities are measured by recording data for future reference.

   (b) The data are stored and then processed with the help of some accepted guidelines to become useful information.

   (c) The information is communicated through reports to the decision makers.

   We might say that data about the business activities are the inputs to the accounting system and that useful information for decision makers is the output.

8. How is the term 'system' related with accounting?

   Ans: The term *system* is commonly used today as a set of elements based on some accepted principles, which operate together in order to attain some desired objectives or of some common goals. Generally, a system may be seen as consisting of three activities—input, i.e., collection of data, processing of input and the result, i.e., the output.

   So, accounting consists of a series of activities such as collecting, recording, analyzing and finally communicating information to its users.

9. Why the accounting information system is the most important element for an enterprise?

   Ans: The accounting information system is the most important element of an organization's information system for the following reasons:

   (a) The accounting information system enables management and external information users to get a picture of the whole organization.

   (b) The accounting information system links other information systems such as marketing, personnel, research and development, stores and purchases and production in that the information produced by these system can be expressed in financial terms in planning strategy to attain organizational goals.

III. *Long Answer Type Questions*

1. Define bookkeeping and accountancy. What are the objectives of accounting?

2. State the relation between bookkeeping and accountancy. What are the advantages of accounting?

3. Briefly describe the history of Evolution of accounting.

4. What do you mean by accounting? What are the different branches of accounting? How will you distinguish between accounting and accountancy?

5. What do you mean by accounting cycle? Explain the chief functions of accounting.

6. What do you mean by financial accounting? What are its main advantages and limitations?

7. What is double entry system of bookkeeping? Explain its chief features.

8. Briefly explain the advantages and disadvantages of the double entry system of bookkeeping.

9. How could you explain the phase "accounting as an information system"?

10. Discuss the qualitative characteristics of accounting information.

Basic Accounting Terms

CONTENTS

2.1 ASSETS

The term 'assets' denotes the resources acquired by a business to get some benefit in the future. Any capitalized expenditure can be treated as an asset. An expenditure is capitalized when it is not charged against the revenue earned in the accounting or financial period in which it is incurred. As a result, the balance of the said expenditure is carried forward to the next financial year at the end of the current financial year, and these assets are usually represented by debit balances. Land and buildings, plant and machinery, investments, etc., are some such examples.

2.1.1 Classification of Assets

Assests can be classified into following categories:

1. *Fixed assets or block capital*

Fixed assets are those assets which are purchased to be used in the business for a long duration and are not meant for resale. These assets do not change their form like the current assets do. They may be divided into two types—tangible and intangible.

(a) *Tangible assets*: These assets can be touched and seen, and are purchased for earning revenue. Land and building, plant and machinery, motor vans, etc., are such examples. They may further be subdivided as under:

    (i) *Wasting assets*: There are some assets which are exhausted completely by their use and cannot be replaced by new ones within the same place. These assets are known as **wasting assets**. Mines, queries, and oil are some such examples.

    (ii) *Non-wasting assets*: These assets are neither exhausted by their continued usage nor their value is reduced due to their extensive use. Freehold land is such an example.

(b) *Intangible assets*: These assets have no physical existence and as such, cannot be touched or seen. They are of two types **identifiable intangible assets** and **unidentifiable intangible assets**.

Trademark and patents are examples of *identifiable intangible assets,* whereas goodwill is an example of *unidentifiable intangible assets.*

2. *Current assets or floating assets or circulating assets*

Current assets are those assets which are acquired with the intention of converting them into cash in the ordinary course of business of an enterprise, usually within an year. Cash and bank balance, stock in trade, debtors, bills receivable, and investments (short term) are some examples.

3. *Fictitious assets*

There are some expenditures which are not charged to the Profit and Loss Account within the year in which they actually take place but are written off gradually in the subsequent years. As long as those items of expenditures are not written off completely they are shown as **fictitious assets**. For example discount on issue of shares and debenture, Profit and Loss Account (Dr.) balance, underwriting commission, and preliminary expenses.

4. *Contingent assets*

There are some assets whose ownerships or titles may or may not be achieved in future, depending on the occurrence or non-occurrence of some future *uncertain* event(s). Hence, the ownership of a particular asset will be achieved only when the said uncertain event occurs in favour of the enterprise in future. Such assets are called **contingent assets**. Suppose, a case is pending in a court of law in respect of the title of a patent; however, the ownership of the said patent will be achieved only when the judgement goes in favour of the enterprise. As long as the case is pending in the court, it may be mentioned in the footnote as a contingent asset only, but cannot be mentioned in the Balance Sheet as an asset.

2.2 LIABILITY OR EQUITY

A claim against the assets of a business that can be enforced by law is called an equity or a liability. Liabilities are promises in favour of different persons for money, goods, and/or services, e.g., sundry creditors, bills payable, debentures, share capital and outstanding expenses. Any amount received in advance for goods to be supplied in future are example of promises for goods. On the other hand incomes received in advance are examples of promises for services. The amount of claim for which a business is liable to pay to its owner is called an **internal liability** or an **owner's equity**, whereas the one which is payable to outsiders is called **external liability**. Capital, profits and reserves are the examples of promises in favour of owners.

Liabilities shown in the Balance Sheet may be classified as under:

1. **Long-term or fixed liability:** These liabilities are payable over a period exceeding one year. They are of two types—payable to outsiders, (e.g., debentures, bonds, fixed deposits received, etc.), and payable to owners.
2. **Current liability:** These liabilities are payable within a year or within a very short period. Sundry creditors, bills payable, bank overdraft, and outstanding expenses are some examples of current liabilities.
3. **Contingent liability:** These liabilities are not the actual liabilities of a business on the date of the Balance Sheet, but may become liabilities in future based on the occurrence of any uncertain event. For example, a guarantor's liability is a contingent liability because a guarantor is liable only when the principal debtor fails to pay his loan.

2.3 CAPITAL

The general idea of capital is what the owner or the proprietor of a business has invested in his business. But, in fact, the capital of a business is its stock of resources that can be utilized for the purpose of earning or generating income. Capital is required to increase income, and money can perform this role. In this sense, one may assume that capital and money are the same. However, when money is invested into business for earning, or for increasing income or resources, then it may be considered as capital. From the point of view of a balance sheet, we can simply say that the excess of assets over liabilities (i.e., obligations to the creditors and others) is called **capital** also known as **net worth**. The balance of capital is shown on the liability side of a balance sheet. It indicates how much capital is received from the owner or how much the business entity is liable to pay to its owner.

2.4 INCOME

Here, income means the income of an enterprise. The financial health of a business or an enterprise should be tested at regular intervals. To attain this objective, we should assess the income of the said enterprise. Now, the question will arise regarding determining the meaning of the term 'income' or 'business income'.

For a business firm, income is the excess of the price ultimately paid by individual and other entities for the output of the firm over the expenses incurred by the firm.   —Vernon Kam

Since the inception of the GAAP (**Generally Accepted Accounting Principles**), the chief function of accounting is to calculate or measure the business income because it is the ultimate goal that encourages the entrepreneurs to enter into business. Without knowing the income, running a business is just like driving a car without fuel. Hence, it is essential to know the meaning of business income in financial accounting. We may simply say that in accounting, the term 'income' is used as 'net income' or 'profit'.

Accountants prefer to use the term 'net income', which can be precisely defined from an accounting viewpoint. Net income is reported on the income statement of an enterprise and is used by the management, owners and others to assess the performance (i.e., to know the strengths and weaknesses) of the business. Thus, net income, in its simplest form, may be expressed as follows:

Net income = Revenues – Expenses

Strictly specking a business entity cannot have its own income. Whatever is reported as income, belongs to the business owners because the net income or profits earned by an enterprise is actually the amount of reward which goes to its owner for taking risk in the business (i.e., investment in business) and for the services given as an entrepreneur. So, the net income or profit earned is a promise made by an enterprise to its owners, and, therefore, it is shown as a credit item or liability in accounts. The accounting income or net profit of an enterprise is the excess of revenue and gains from other sources over the expenses incurred to earn such revenue and loss suffered. Thus, from the accounting viewpoint, we can say that the net profit is the surplus which arises by comparing expired costs and other losses of a particular period against the revenue and other gains realized during the said period.

2.5 EXPENSES OR EXPIRED COSTS

Expenses are the costs of the goods and services used up in the course of earning revenues while performing the commercial activities of an enterprise. Generally, expenses include the cost of sales, other costs for running the business, and the costs of attracting and serving customers. Fixed assets such as plant and machinery are fully consumed during their lifetime (which is fixed). Hence, as their usefulness expires or gets consumed in the operation of the business, their proportionate cost (i.e., depreciation) is allocated to the expenses. If they lose their ability to generate revenue in future, then the concerned portion/value will be treated as **expired costs**. We may say that all the costs, the benefits of which have been exhausted during the accounting year, are known as **expenses**.

Generally, the cost is distinguished as expired and unexpired. Expired costs are the ones which help produce revenues. They are recognized as expenses.

The expenses are classified mainly under two broad headings—direct expenses and indirect expenses. The expenses which are related to purchase or provide service to the customers for sale or produce goods for sale are known as **direct expenses** and the other costs which are incidental to run or promote the business are called **indirect expenses**. Hence, expired costs or expenses are the outflow of funds in the process of earning revenue for a particular accounting period.

2.6 REVENUE

It results from selling goods, rendering services, performing other business or trading activities of the business. In the simplest case, revenues equal the price of goods sold and services rendered over a specific period of time. Generally, when an enterprise delivers goods or provides service to a customer, it usually receives either cash or a promise to pay cash in the near future. The promise to pay cash is recorded in the accounts, either as accounts receivable or notes receivable. We know that the trading activity of a business is a continuous process, and the assets within the business are changed continuously. Increase in the total assets volume of the business results, in the net worth of the business getting increased. When the closing net worth is greater than the opening net worth, the surplus is called **profit** or **net income**.

For example, when an enterprise receives cash of Rs. 14,000 as an advance from a customer for supplying goods in future, it will increase the cash balance of the said enterprise by Rs. 14,000 and at the same time, will also increase the liability to deliver goods of worth Rs. 14,000 in future. At this point of time, no revenue has resulted, but the moment the goods are delivered, revenue is realized. It will increase the owner's equity on one hand and on the other hand, will decrease the liability to deliver the goods, which is the outcome of this resulted revenue. Thus, we may say that when revenue arises, it increases the owner's equity.

Hence, when inflow of assets is greater than their outflow resulting from a particular transaction, it may be considered as revenue. It is the major source of income for an enterprise. It may also arise from the supply of resources to others, resulting in the receipt of interest, dividends, rents, royalties, commission and fees.

2.7 DEBTORS

The customers' accounts total or accumulated figure is generally shown as Debtors or Sundry Debtors. Usually the realizable value of the Sundry Debtors is shown in the Balance Sheet. It is based on the conservative principle. For this reason, some adjustments are made like provision for bad debts, provision for discount, and so on with Sundry Debtors in the Balance Sheet.

2.8 CREDITORS

The suppliers' accounts total or accumulated figure is generally shown as Creditors or Sundry Creditors. The total amount payable to the suppliers for goods or services supplied by them is shown in the Balance Sheet as liability under the head 'Sundry Creditors'.

2.9 GOODS

The term 'goods' include those items which are purchased by the business/firm for resale. For example, when furniture is purchased for resale, it will be considered as goods and when it is purchased for use, it will be considered as an asset.

Purchases A/c, Sales A/c, Purchases Returns A/c, Sales Returns A/c, Stock A/c and goods sent on consignment A/c are examples of goods account.

2.10 COST

The term 'cost' has a variety of meanings depending on the context. Cost means expenditure incurred on, or attributable to, a given thing. Some people use this term as a price paid for something, but in management terminology, cost refers to expenditure and not to price. In case of a manufacturing concern, cost means total expenses incurred to produce an item or article. The various elements of cost are illustrated in Figure 2.1.

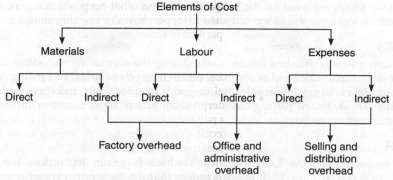

FIGURE 2.1 Elements of cost.

2.11 GAIN

The term 'gain' is used to express the amount of profit earned through a transaction, i.e., by selling an asset or goods. Thus, it is the positive result of a transaction, i.e., the excess amount earned over the investment or cost incurred. For example, a land costing Rs. 100,000 is sold at Rs. 155,000. Here, gain or profit by selling the plot of land is Rs. 55000.

2.12 CLOSING STOCK

Stock includes stock of raw materials, finished and partly finished goods (or work in progress). Here, stock means unused materials or unsold or unfinished goods. Trading Account is credited for these goods. Also, there are some other types of stock like stock of stationery, stock of postage, stock of factory consumables, etc., which are not to be considered as closing stock of goods. While valuing the closing stock, conservative accounting practice is generally followed. Under the conservative accounting practice, cost or market price, whichever is lower should be taken into consideration. For example, if on the date of the balance sheet (i.e., on the closing date of the year), the market price of the inventory becomes lower than its cost, then the possible loss that may arise on sale of the same should be provided for and accordingly, the inventory should be valued at the market price instead of at cost. On the other hand, if the market price of the inventory becomes higher than its cost, the inventory should be valued at cost price.

Regarding the valuation of closing stock, there are a number of methods of which any one can be followed based on the nature of goods used. A particular method of valuation of stock might not be suitable for all types of firms. Thus, before selecting a particular method of valuation of stock, a number of factors should be considered.

In order to ascertain the true profit of the business to represent its precise position, it is essential to determine the value of closing stock at the end of the financial or accounting period correctly.

While valuing the inventories, the components like net purchases or the cost of goods sold must be considered carefully, otherwise it will badly affect the financial statements. A number of items have to be taken into account for calculating the net purchases or the cost of goods sold, e.g., trade discount, quantity discount for bulk purchase, freight and carriage including insurance, duties, dock charges, import duties, and so on. In order to consider these factors on the basis of accepted accounting principles, we must follow the guidelines of **Accounting Standard (AS) 2.**

2.13 PURCHASES

Here, the term purchase' stands for goods or raw materials purchased during the period. It includes cash purchases, credit purchases and import of goods from foreign countries. In Trading Account the net purchases are shown. To get the net purchases, goods returned to suppliers (or Purchase Returns or Return Outwards) are deducted from gross purchases. In some cases, goods that are distributed as free samples or those which are used by the proprietors for personal purposes (i.e., not sold during the period but used for some purposes) are deducted from purchases or opening stock.

2.14 SALES

Here sales means goods or finished products sold during the accounting period/the financial year. It includes cash sales, credit sales and export of goods to foreign countries. In Trading Account, the net sales are shown. Hence, to get the net sales figure, goods returned from customers (or Sales Returns or Return Inwards) are deducted form gross sales. Sales of any fixed assets or other items wrongly included in sales are eliminated.

2.15 LOSS

It may be expressed in two ways. Loss arises when outflow is greater than inflow. For example, when an item of Rs. 15 was sold at Rs. 12, it indicates a loss of Rs. 3. Generally expenditures are incurred to earn revenue, but when revenue earned is less than expenditure, it amounts to a loss. Alternatively, it arises due to loss of business assets, e.g., goods lost by fire/theft, cash stolen and business vehicle met with an accident.

2.16 PROFIT

Generally, the term 'profit' represents the surplus revenue realized over the expenditure incurred to earn revenue. Thus, excess of income over expenditure is **profit**. It is of two types—gross profit and net profit.

  Gross profit is the difference between the cost of goods sold and the net sales proceeds. When net sales proceeds exceed the cost of goods sold, the difference is known as **gross profit**. Here, sales stand for, goods sold during the financial year.

  Net profit is the difference between gross profit minus all operating expenses, selling and distribution expenses, depreciation and losses.

2.17 VOUCHER

It is a document prepared for future reference. It records the basis on which a transaction took place. Voucher is a document prepared to record a business transaction and is kept for future reference. Hence, it is a proof or a supporting document of a transaction. Generally, invoice, cash memo, debit note, credit note, etc., are used as vouchers. There is no fixed form of a voucher and it varies from enterprise to enterprise.

2.18 DISCOUNT

Generally two types of discounts are used in purchase and sale transactions. To increase the volume of sales, trade discounts are allowed and to increase the flow of cash, cash discounts are allowed.

2.18.1 Trade Discount

This discount is given by manufacturers or the whole salers to their customers on a percentage basis on the list price of the goods. It is used to increase the sales volume. After charging this discount, the net sale price or the net amount payable by the customer is calculated. Accounts are recorded on the basis of this net sale price. Trade discount is given to all types of customers, i.e., both on cash sales and credit sales.

2.18.2 Cash Discount

Generally, a cash discount is allowed to encourage debtors for making prompt payment. It is given only when a debtor pays his debt within or before the due date, i.e., cash within the credit period. Cash discount is calculated on percentage basis on the total amount payable by the debtor/customer. Thus, when goods are sold on cash basis, a customer will enjoy both trade discount and cash discount. The mode of calculation of the cash discount is shown as follows:

List price of the goods (Rs. 40 per set)	
Units sold	50 units
Rate of trade discount	10%
Rate of cash discount	10%
List price of goods sold Rs. 40 × 50	Rs. 2,000
Less: Trade discount 10 %	Rs. 200
Net Selling price (amount payable)	Rs. 1,800
Less: Cash discount 10%	Rs. 180
Net amount payable	Rs. 1,620

Hence, if the customer pays his dues within the due date or specified date, then he has to pay only Rs. 1,620 instead of Rs. 1,800.

2.19 TRANSACTION

An event measurable in terms of money, and which has occurred within an accounting year and by which the financial position of a firm/person has changed is called a **transaction**. Hence, any event which indicates the change in the financial condition or position of a person or a firm or an enterprise can be considered as a transaction. Such changes may improve or decline the financial condition of a person or a firm or an enterprise.

Thus, whenever an event capable a changing the financial condition of a firm/person and measurable in terms of money occurs can be considered as a transaction.

Suppose Mr. Sharma, senior manager of M/s Bright India Bros., met with an accident on December 7, 2009. Now, this event will surely affect the functioning of M/s Bright India Bros., and consequently may change the financial condition of the firm. But the said event cannot be considered as a transaction because we cannot measure the loss suffered by the firm in terms of money.

Generally, transactions are of two types—external and internal.

External transactions

For these transactions a second party is involved, such as cash paid to Ram or, cash received from Ram or sold goods to Ram, etc. So, there must be two or more parties involved for these transactions.

External transactions may be further subdivided into two types—cash and credit transactions.

Cash transaction: The transaction which is related to cash/cheque received or paid for any purpose is called **cash transaction.**

Credit transaction: The external transaction which is not related to cash payment or receipt forthwith is called **credit transaction** such as goods sold on credit to M/s D.D. Bros.

Internal transaction

In this type of transaction, a second party is not involved but due to some incident, the financial position of the firm changes or has to be changed, e.g., depreciation charged on fixed assets, obsolete item of assets to be written off, and so on.

2.19.1 Features of a Transaction

1. It is an event which is measurable in terms of money.
2. It may occur in a particular financial year or in any subsequent period or in any previous period or both in subsequent and previous periods.
3. It always indicates a change in the financial condition of a firm or a person.
4. The change in the financial condition is not always visible, but has to be considered as a transaction, e.g., depreciation charged on fixed assets.
5. It is not only related to exchange of properties, but includes exchange of services also.
6. In every transaction there must be two parties, and every party gets some return which he parts with.

7. Generally, transactions are of two types—external and internal.
8. Every transaction wiil directly affect the asset or liability of the firm because either it will increase one asset and decrease the other, or will increase liability and asset both or will decrease liability and asset both.

2.20 DRAWINGS

When cash or goods are withdrawn by the proprietor from a business for personal use, the amount involved is recorded in the books as **drawings**. If any personal expenditure of the proprietor is incurred from the business as cash then it is also known as drawings. It will be deducted from the capital account of the proprietor. Proprietor's house rent/electric charges/telephone bill/income tax/children's school fees paid, etc., are some such examples.

EXERCISES

I. *Objective Type Questions*

1. Fill in the blanks:
   (a) A claim against the assets of the business that can be enforced by law is called _____ or _____.
   (b) Any capitalized expenditure is treated as an _____.
   (c) Assets which are exhausted completely by use and cannot be replaced by new ones within the same place are known as _____.
   (d) _____ _____ have no physical existence and as such, cannot be touched or seen.
   (e) The capital of a business firm is its stock of resources which can be utilized for the purpose of _____ or _____ income.
   (f) Expired costs are the ones which have helped to produce _____.
   (g) Expired costs are recognized as _____.
   (h) When inflow of assets is greater than their outflow resulting from a particular transaction, it may be considered as _____.
   (i) Trade discount is allowed by the manufacturer or the wholesaler to their customers on a percentage basis on the _____ _____ of the goods.
   (j) Cash discount is calculated on a percentage basis on the total amount _____ by the _____.

   Ans: (a) equity or liability (b) asset (c) wasting assets (d) Intangible assets (e) earning or generating (f) revenues (g) expenses (h) revenue (i) list price (j) payable, debtor/customer.

2. Choose the best alternative from the options:
   (a) Assets are usually represented by
      (i) Debit balances.
      (ii) Credit balances.
   (b) Intangible assets include
      (i) Goodwill and trademark.
      (ii) Quarries and oil.
      (iii) Machinery and motor vans.
   (c) We know that
      (i) Expired costs are recognized as expenses.
      (ii) Unexpired costs are recognized as expenses.
   (d) In respect of owner's equity we may say that
      (i) when revenue arises, it increases the owner's equity.
      (ii) when a sale arises, it increases the owner's equity.

(e) In respect of purchase, we may say that
    (i) Purchase means assets purchased during the period for production.
    (ii) Purchase means goods or raw materials purchased during the period.

(f) The term 'goods' include those items
    (i) Which are purchased by the business/firm for consumption.
    (ii) Which are purchased by the business/firm for resale.

(g) The discount allowed on list price is known as
    (i) Trade discount.
    (ii) Cash discount.

(h) Depreciation charged on fixed assets is an example of
    (i) External transaction.
    (ii) Internal transaction.

(i) Expenditure incurred for proprietor's foreign travel to attend a trade fair is a
    (i) Business expenditure.
    (ii) Personal expenditure (drawings).

Ans: a. (i) b. (i) c. (i) d. (i) e. (ii) f. (ii) g. (i) h. (ii) i. (i).

II. *Short Answer Type Questions*

1. What do you mean by tangible assets?
2. Define contingent assets.
3. What are wasting assets?
4. What do you understand by fictitious assets?
5. What is meant by contingent liability?
6. What do you mean by goods?
7. What is transaction?
8. How are transactions classified?
9. What do you mean by drawings?

III. *Long Answer Type Questions*

1. What do you mean by the term 'asset'? How are assets classified? Give an example of each type of asset.
2. What do you mean by the term 'liability'? How are liabilities classified? Give an example of each type of liability.
3. What do you mean by capital and income? Explain the relationship between them.
4. Distinguish between capital and revenue.
5. What do you meant by revenue and expenses or expired costs?
6. What is meant by the term cost? How are costs classified? Explain with example.
7. What do you mean by the term 'transaction'? How are transactions classified? Explain with example.
8. Write short notes on the following:
    (a) Closing stock
    (b) Capital
    (c) Internal transaction
    (d) Goods
    (e) Income
    (f) Drawings
    (g) Cash discount.

3

Theory Base of Accounting and Accounting Standards

3.1 ACCOUNTING PRINCIPLES

Generally, some accepted guidelines or standards are followed while preparing the financial statements which are known as **accounting principles**. These guidelines or principles have been developed for accounting on the basis of past experiences, customs, conventions and necessities depending on the practical situations. Hence, the term 'principle' means rule of action or conduct or basis of conduct. It may also be termed as general or fundamental truth. Accounting principles are not universal like those of natural sciences, but they are evolving rapidly. They are used to measure the economic activities of a firm and to ensure a uniformity in character in a simplified manner with the help of some established standards. These standards are generally known as **Generally Accepted Accounting Principles (GAAP).**

Accounting principles are based on conventions, customs, laws, usages, and the fast changing business environment. There is no fixed universally acceptable set of principles. However, some standards have been set by FASB (Financial Accounting Standards Board) to harmonize the diversified policies in order to ensure uniformity and reliability of accounting statements/information, because there should not be any kind of personal biasness or influence; it must be supported by the accepted facts and figures.

3.2 NATURE OR CHARACTERISTICS OF ACCOUNTING PRINCIPLES

The chief characteristics of accounting principles are as follows:

1. They have been developed to ensure uniformity and understandability among the business community for preparing financial statements.

2. These principles have been developed by accountants and academicians on the basis of periodic observations to stress on the importance of the accounting information in the existing economic condition. Their motto is to select some universal rules and regulations for the accountants.

3. These principles are the best possible suggestions for accounting prepared on the basis of facts and figures.

4. These principles should be accepted by all universally. To be universal in character, following three basic criteria or norms should be fulfilled:
   (a) Usefulness,
   (b) Objectivity, and
   (c) Feasibility.
   In other words, they must be very useful, free from personal biasness and applicable without complexity.

5. These principles are flexible in nature. They are continuously evolving with respect to the fast changing business environment.
   Dynamic discussions are always going on for selecting fruitful and effective principles for the business community to protect the interest of shareholders and the economy as a whole.

3.3 NEED FOR ACCOUNTING PRINCIPLES

The objective of accounting is to convey information about the economic activity of an enterprise to all its users. It is made through financial statements which are prepared on the basis of facts and figures compiled by the accountants. Here lies the problem, because facts and figures may vary from accountant to accountant due to their biasness and difference of opinion. Hence, in order to remove these practical problems, it becomes essential to prepare the financial statements of different enterprises on the basis of some universally accepted guidelines. These guidelines are used for sound accounting practices. For fair presentation of financial statement and for ensuring uniformity in character, accepted accounting principles must be followed with the help of some standard guidelines. Without having any accepted accounting principles, a fair presentation of financial statements by the enterprise as a whole is impossible and here lies the importance of the accounting principles. These principles have been developed through the passage of time and are replaced by new ones in place of old principles.

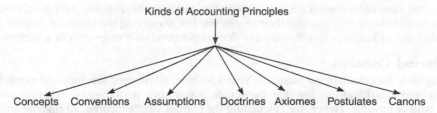

Kinds of Accounting Principles

Concepts   Conventions   Assumptions   Doctrines   Axiomes   Postulates   Canons

3.4 ACCOUNTING CONCEPTS OR ASSUMPTIONS

Accounting principles have been developed over the years from practical experiences, usage, requirements and the related problems. The International Accounting Standards Committee or IASC (the Predecessor body of IASB) and the Institute of Chartered Accountants of India (ICAI) have formulated the following assumptions for the preparation and presentation of financial statements:

3.4.1 Going Concern Concept

Generally, it is assumed that a business enterprise will exist for a long period of time. That means that it will not wound up in the immediate future, and as such, it is expected to be able to meet its contractual obligations according to the desired plans and procedures. By taking into consideration this assumption, the assets and liabilities are valued on the basis of historical costs, and on that basis, the balance sheet represents the true and fair view of the state of affairs of a concern on a particular date. This concept may be termed as **continuity concept.**

According to this concept, it is assumed that the business will continue in future, though there is a chance of cessation of its life due to liquidation, dissolution, insolvency, etc. When there is no certainty of dissolution or liquidation of a business, we may assume that it will continue its operation for a long time. If this is not assumed, then it will convey the message that the business will not be able to meet its obligations in future. As a result, investors will not be interested to invest their money, suppliers will not supply their goods and services, and providers and employees will not provide their services freely and so on. The natural activity of the business or business dealings will then collapse or jeopardize. On the basis of this continuity concept, costs are generally distinguished as expired and unexpired costs. **Expired costs** are the ones which have helped to produce revenues. They are recognized as expenses. **Unexpired costs** are those costs which will help to produce revenue in future. Such costs are recognized as assets to be shown in the balance sheet.

3.4.2 Entity Concept

According to this concept, the owner or the proprietor of a business is always separate and distinct from the business or enterprise. Business is treated here as a separate 'unit' or 'entity'. All business transactions are recorded in the books of such an 'entity' or an artificial body, i.e., the legal entity. For accounting purpose, a business is generally treated as a separate entity, distinct not only from its debtors and creditors but also from its owners or proprietors. All business records and reports should be developed separately and must be separate from their owners. It is applicable to all forms of business organizations. Generally there are three basic forms of business enterprises—sole proprietorship, partnership and corporate form. For example, P. Gills started his business with cash of Rs. 50,000. This will increase the business cash (assets) by Rs. 50,000. At the same time, it will also increase its liability of Rs. 50,000, which is recognizing its indebtedness to P. Gills (the owner) in respect of his capital, that he has invested therein. Through this convention, a clear distinction has been made between P. Gills's private affairs and business affairs. *But legally, there is no economic separation between the owners and the business entity in case of a sole proprietorship and partnership business.* However, in case of a corporate form of business, a legal distinction has been made between the owners and the business entity, (i.e., the shareholders and the enterprise). The shareholders are not liable for the enterprise's debts beyond the capital. In other words, their risk of loss is limited to the amount they paid for their shares. Here, the shareholders elect a Board of Directors to run the business on their behalf and for their benefit. The shareholders may transfer their shares without dissolving the business. Hence, the life of the corporate form of business is unlimited and does not depend on a proprietor or a partner.

3.4.3 Accrual Concept

Under this system, for calculating a particular year's income, all revenue incomes and expenditures are to be taken into consideration for that particular accounting period only, whether received or receivable, paid or payable. Hence, for calculating the current year's income, all revenue incomes and expenditures of the previous year and for the coming year are not taken into account. The transactions are recorded within the accounts of an enterprise in the periods in which these transactions actually occurred rather than only in the periods in which cash was received or paid by the enterprise. This convention makes a distinction between the receipts of cash and the right to receive cash, and the payment of cash and the legal obligation to pay cash.

Let us examine the manner in which the accrual convention applies to revenues and expenditures under the following cases:

1. In case of revenue, cash receipts may occur under the following ways:
    (a) Cash received with sale
    (b) Cash received as an advance, i.e., before the right to receive arises
    (c) Cash received after the right to receive has been matured or established

2. In case of expenditures, cash payments may occur under the following ways:
   (a) Cash paid at the time of purchase
   (b) Cash paid as an advance, i.e., before an obligation for payment arises
   (c) Cash paid after the due date, i.e., after the payment has been matured.

Accrual convention provides guidelines regarding how to treat these receipts or payments and rights or obligations, as the case may be. In case of revenue, it must be earned, i.e., goods are sold (ownership of the goods has been transferred), or the services performed. Thus, it is not essential to receive cash immediately after the sale because cash may be received in three ways as stated above.

Through accounting treatment, the effects of the above three cases are shown below:

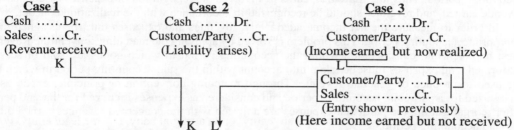

As per accrual convention, income/revenue has been earned under the two different situations shown above (when cash is received for sale **and** for credit sale).

In the case of expenses, it must be taken into account within the said accounting period in which they are used to produce or generate revenue (i.e., the period when ownership of the goods has been transferred from seller to buyer or the services accepted/enjoyed). Here also, it is not essential to make payment of the cash immediately after the purchase or the services accepted because the cash may be paid in three ways as stated above. Through accounting treatment, the effects of the above three cases are shown below:

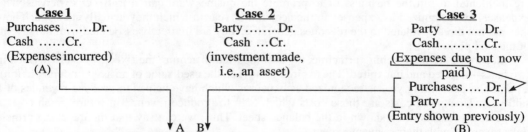

As per accrual convention, expenses/expired cost has been incurred, i.e., ownership of the goods received or the services enjoyed under the two different situations are shown above (A and B).

3.4.4 Dual-Aspect Concept

Generally, assets or goods are purchased or acquired with the help of the funds provided by the owners and the outside parties, e.g., creditors, banks, and financial institutions. These funds are called **equities** and are of two types—inside or owner's equity (or capital) and outsider's equity (creditors, bank loan, etc.).

The following fundamental accounting equation may be drawn from the above discussion:

$$\text{Owners' Equity + Outsiders' Equity = Total Assets}$$
$$\text{or, Capital + Liabilities = Total Assets}$$

The above equation is based on the principle of dual-aspect (or duality) concept which is the basis of our accountancy. According to the duality concept, every transaction will affect at least two items and the outcome of such transaction will be the total assets [owner's equity (capital) + liabilities]. The double entry system of book keeping is created with the help of this concept.

3.4.5 Matching Concept

An income statement is prepared on the basis of the matching concept. Income arises when revenue income exceeds revenue expenses. In simple words, an expense is the cost of earning revenue. According to this concept, matching of expenses with revenue is based on accrual system of accounting. Revenue is earned when goods or services are sold, and expenses are recognized not only when cash is paid, but also when services or assets have been used to produce such revenues in an accounting period. Thus, the **matching concept** involves the recognition of expenses associated with revenue earned, and revenues should be recognized in accordance with the realization concept.

In order to measure the net income adequately, revenues and expenses must be assigned to the appropriate accounting period. This problem is solved by applying the matching convention. Revenues must be taken into consideration within the accounting period in which goods are sold or services performed, and expenses must be taken into account within the said accounting period in which they are used to produce or generate revenue. Through matching convention or principle, expenses are recognized for a particular accounting period and considered as **expenses incurred** for the said period. After reorganization, the particular expenses are adjusted with the concerned revenues earned during the said accounting period.

As defined by the 1964 American Accounting Association (AAA) Committee on the matching concept, matching is the process of reporting expenses on the basis of a cause-and-effect relationship with reported revenues. A proper matching is assumed to occur only when a reasonable association is found between the revenues and expenses. The timing of expenses, therefore, requires (i) association with revenue, and (ii) reporting in the same period as the related revenue is reported. The expenses are classified mainly into two broad categories—direct expenses and indirect expenses. The expenses which are related to purchase or service to the customers for sale or production of the goods for sale are known as **direct expenses**. These are directly related to the generation of revenues. Other costs which are incidental to run the business or to promote the business are called **indirect expenses**. These expenses are recognized as expenses in the accounting year in which they actually incurred. Though they are not directly related to the revenues generated, they are indirectly associated with the revenues of the said period.

According to the matching principle, the cost incurred to acquire the fixed assets are divided into two parts—expired and unexpired. The expired costs (i.e., the used value of an asset or depreciation) of a particular accounting year is recognized as expenses which have helped to produce revenues of the said year. Unexpired costs are those costs which help to produce revenue in future. Such costs are recognized as assets to be shown in the balance sheet. Thus, we can say that the matching principle links revenues with their relevant expenses.

3.4.6 Cost Concept

Under this concept, an asset will be recorded in the books at its cost, i.e., the price paid or to be paid to acquire the asset. The acquisition cost of the asset may be greater or lesser than the fair market price, but it has to be recorded at the price actually paid by the buyer/enterprise. As the asset is used in the process of creating goods and services, its cost expires. The expired cost, known as **depreciation**, is deducted from the asset cost and thus, the cost of an asset is allocated over the estimated economic life of the asset. The cost concept does not allow assets to be shown at their present value because the market prices of the assets keep changing very frequently. However, it is still used as it satisfies the criteria of objectivity and feasibility. This concept is closely related to going concern concept.

3.4.7 Realization Concept or Revenue Recognition Concept

According to this concept, revenue is deemed to be earned when goods have been transferred (when the title of the goods is transferred according to the Sale of Goods Act, 1930), or services rendered to a customer and it does not matter when cash is actually received or realized. For instance, if an advance of Rs. 500 is received in May and goods are supplied in July, then Rs. 500 will be recognized as revenue only in July.

The realization concept reflects the historical origin of accounting as a method of recording the results of transactions. The revenue is recorded in the books as earned or recognized as received on the basis of realization concept. According to this concept, there cannot be any revenue or profit until or unless a sale has been made. Hence, there cannot be any revenue or profit which has not been realized even though there is actual increase in the value of certain assets. In this connection, it may be mentioned that unrealized gains in value are widely accepted/recognized by non-accountants.

According to realization concept, two classes of gains may be distinguished—**holding gains**, which have resulted in an increase in value of an asset from holding (but not selling), and **trading or operating gains**, which have resulted by actual selling of the assets/goods. Hence, as per this concept, the reported profits or operating gains earned within an accounting period are recorded in the books of accounts as revenue. In case of *contract jobs,* there can be cases where contracts are not completed within the accounting year. *For example,* in shipbuilding contracts, large civil engineering contracts and large Government contracts, the timings of the realizations (i.e., rights to payment) are mentioned in the original agreement or contract. Under the situations stated, accountants have to follow the law, and the timing of the right to receive cash is to be determined on the basis of the agreement between the contractor and the contractee. There are some specific guidelines in the Accounting Standard (AS)7 for its treatment under different situations.

Revenue recognition is mainly concerned with the timing of recognition of revenue in the statement of profit and loss of an enterprise. The amount of revenue arising on a transaction is usually determined by an agreement between the parties involved in the transaction. When uncertainties exist regarding the determination of the amount, or its associated costs, they may influence the timing of revenue recognition. The revenue is earned in the accounting period in which it accrues, and thus, it is treated as realized though not actually received in cash.

In order to recognize revenue within an accounting period, the following points are to be considered:

In case of sale of goods

1. In a transaction involving sale of goods, revenue should normally be recognized when the seller of goods has transferred to the buyer the goods for a price, or all significant risks and rewards of ownership have been transferred to the buyer and the seller retains no effective control of the goods transferred to a degree usually associated with ownership, and no significant uncertainty exists regarding the amount of the consideration that will be derived from the sale of the goods.

2. There are some cases where goods are sold subject to conditions like approval, installation and inspection. Under such circumstances, revenue should normally be recognised when goods are duly accepted by the buyer or the buyer accepts the delivery and installation and inspection. If the goods are sold subject to conditions like cash on delivery, then revenue should be recognised only after the receipt of cash by the seller or his agent. In case of consignment sale revenue should not be recognized until the goods are sold to a third party.

3. In case of instalment sales, when consideration is receivable in instalments, revenue attributable to the sales price exclusive of interest should be recognized on the date of sale. The interest element should be recognized as revenue, proportionate to the unpaid balance due to the seller.

4. There are some cases where goods are sold subject to warranties, and generally, sellers give guarantee to repair goods free of cost during the warranty period. Under such circumstances, it may be appropriate to recognize the sale, but a suitable provision for repairs must be made based on previous experience. Actual expenses incurred are to be adjusted against the said provision.

5. At certain stages in specific industries, such as when agricultural crops have been harvested or mineral ores extracted, performance may be substantially completed prior to the execution of the transaction generating revenue. In such cases, when sale is assured under a forward contract or a Government guarantee or where market exists and there is a negligible risk of failure to sell, the goods involved are often valued at net realizable value.

Rendering of services

Revenue from service transactions is usually recognized as the service performed, either by proportionate completion method or by completed service contract method.

1. **Proportionate completion method:** Performance consists of the execution of more than one act. Revenue is recognized proportionately by reference to the performance of each act. The revenue recognized under this method will be determined on the basis of contract value, associated costs, number of acts or some other suitable basis. For all practical purposes, when services are provided by an indeterminate number of acts over a specific period of time, revenue is recognized on a straight line basis over the specific period unless there is evidence that some other method represents the pattern of performance in a better way.

2. **Completed service contract method:** Performance consists of the execution of a single act. Alternatively, services are performed in more than a single act, and the services yet to be performed are so significant in relation to the transaction taken as a whole that performance cannot be deemed to have been completed until the execution of those acts. The completed service contract method is relevant to these patterns of performance and accordingly revenue is recognised when the sole or final act takes place and the service becomes chargeable.

By the use by other enterprise resources yielding interest, royalties and dividends

Revenue arising from the use of other enterprise resources yielding interest, royalties and dividends should be recognized only when no significant uncertainty as to its measurability or collectibility exists. These revenues are recognized on the following bases:

1. **Interest:** On a time proportion basis, taking into account the amount outstanding and the rate applicable.
2. **Royalties:** On an accrual basis in accordance with the terms of the relevant agreement.
3. **Dividends from investments in shares:** When the owner's right to receive payment is established.

3.4.8 Accounting Period Concept

Financial accounts are prepared for the transactions occurring within a specific period, i.e., for a year, and at the end of such period, financial statements are prepared to ascertain the results of a business. Thus, the above-stated period with a span of 12 months is known as the **accounting period**. We do not know how long a business entity may last. Many enterprises may be liquidated within a few years. To prepare an income statement, accountants assume that a business will continue to operate for an indefinite period because of the going concern concept. Now, the question arises when and for what period the income statement be prepared to know the result of the business because the owners, management, investors and the other users will not wait for an indefinite period to know the result or growth of the enterprise. Hence, it becomes essential to measure the financial health of a business or an enterprise at regular intervals. To attain this objective, we have to assess the income of the said enterprise periodically. It is essential to measure the progress of an enterprise for a particular period. Generally, to make comparisons easier, the time periods taken are of equal duration and the said time periods should be noted in the income statements. The 12 month accounting period used by an enterprise is called its **financial**, **fiscal** or **accounting year**.

Since all assets are considered as 'costs' in accounting, and assets such as building, plant and machinery have a useful life of more than one year, the entire cost of the fixed assets cannot be considered as an expenditure of the business. In order to represent the true income and the financial position, it is advisable to distribute the value of these assets, i.e., the expired costs over the period of their effective lives on an yearly basis. On the basis of the convention of periodicity, the accounting income or profit is the result of the entire transaction during an accounting period. The convention of periodicity has now been established by laws for preparing reports such as the Income Statement and the Balance Sheet.

3.4.9 Money Measurement Concept

Under this concept, all the events, facts or transactions occurring within an accounting period, causing a change in the financial position of a business or company and which are measurable in terms of money, should be recorded in the financial accounts. In other words, events/facts, which have a direct effect on the business but cannot be measured in terms of money, should not be considered in the financial accounts. Suppose, if the General Manager of a company meets with an accident and remains absent from his duties for a long period, it amounts to a great loss for the company, but it is not to be considered in the financial accounting. Thus, it indicates that accounting records entertain only those facts which can be expressed in terms of money. It is the best means of measuring different transactions in homogeneous terms (units) which can be added and subtracted.

3.4.10 Verifiability and Objectivity Concept

The term 'verifiability' means that accounting data are subject to verification by any person in future and the data are the proof or evidence of a specific transaction. Hence, for the best interest of the business, there must be some documentary evidence for each and every transaction of an enterprise for future reference and only then, those data can be considered as dependable or reliable.

Here, the term 'objectivity' means that all facts, depending on financial transactions, must be impartially determined and presented. All the techniques and principles followed for recording and analyzing the accounting data must be free from any personal biasness of the concerned person.

In accounting practice, personal opinions and judgements of an accountant may play an important role while preparing the financial statements of an enterprise. Hence, accounting data should be supported by documentary evidence and must be free from personal biasness to prove its worthiness, reliability, verifiability and dependability. Only then the data furnished in the financial statements would represent the true state of affairs of an enterprise.

3.5 ACCOUNTING CONVENTIONS

3.5.1 Convention of Full Disclosure

According to this convention, all the material facts regarding business activities must be disclosed in the financial accounts and statements. The Companies Act also has provisions for fair disclosure of all related facts and figures regarding the financial position of a company. Thus, to protect the interest of the shareholders, owners, creditors, investors and the Government, necessary steps must be taken to disclose all possible material facts and pertinent information while presenting financial statements to maintain their reliability.

The convention of full disclosure requires that financial statements and their notes present all possible information relevant to the users' understanding of the statements. Hence, the disclosure of the information in the financial statements is presumed to be sufficiently adequate so that a user can make an informed judgement or decision. To meet the requirements of full disclosure, the enterprise must add notes to the financial statements to help its users interpret some of the most complex items of transactions. The notes are considered an integral part of the financial statements. However, here disclosure does not include disclosure of all business secrets and such other information which can be used by the rival firms against the firm. Instead, a fair disclosure of relevant information means all essential and significant information regarding the method of valuation of different assets, investments, big commercial transactions, remarkable decisions taken during the period, and so on. The main objective of fair disclosure is to represent a transparent financial statement to its users.

3.5.2 Convention of Conservatism

This convention is generally used in case of uncertainties in respect of some business incidents or economic events that may happen in future. According to this convention, all possible losses must be recognized but all possible incomes must not be taken into consideration until and unless they are realized. However, if this convention is strictly followed in all cases, then it will create a large number of secret reserves, which is against the convention of full disclosure. Hence, this principle must be applied cautiously, taking into consideration the interest of the investors, Government, creditors and the other related parties. Thus, the main objective of this convention is to give the most pessimistic view of an enterprise while presenting the financial statements. An enterprise has to work in an uncertain and ever changing environment. Generally, the convention of conservatism is applied in case of making provisions for bad and doubtful debts, making provisions for discount on debtors, valuing stock at market price or cost whichever is lower, and creating provisions against fluctuations in the market price of investments.

3.5.3 Convention of Materiality

It deals with the *relative importance* of the accounting information. The state of *relative importance* may vary from one accountant to another, or one firm to another. The material facts are disclosed in financial accounting or the statements. An item or information may be important for a particular situation, but may be immaterial for another situation or environment. Hence, importance of an information depends on a number of factors closely associated with the firm and is a matter of judgement and knowledge of the particular situation or environment of the business.

Convention of materiality also depends on the nature of the item, and not just its value. For example, in a big company, mistake in recording an item of expenditure of Rs. 3,000 may not be important, but the discovery of a bribe or theft of a sum of Rs. 2,000 can be very important. A large company may decide that consumable items of less than Rs. 1,000 should be considered as revenue expenses. On the other hand, under the same situation, another company may consider the consumable items as revenue expenditure on the basis of its actual consumption, and the unused portion may be shown as closing asset. Thus, we may conclude that materiality is dependent on some allied or incidental factors which help to evaluate a particular expenditure or an event as being material or immaterial. Practically, an event or transaction may be considered as material if it has sufficient grounds to influence the quality of the periodical financial statements. The main objective of recording the material information is to avoid unnecessary wastage of time in unimportant matters.

3.5.4 Convention of Consistency

In order to represent clear and correct interpretation of the financial statements and results, consistency is essential. For preparing financial accounts, a number of concepts and principles are followed and if frequent changes are made regarding the principles and policies for a particular transaction/event, the comparison of the financial statements from one period to the next would become a meaningless job. Inconsistency in principles and policies will develop a misleading interpretation, and consequently, some misjudgments might occur while deciding future courses of action. Thus, consistent use of accounting measures and procedures is important in achieving comparability. **Comparability** means the presentation of information in such a way that decision-makers or the users of accounting information can recognize similarities, differences, and trends over different time periods or between different enterprises. It is essential to evaluate the realistic position and performance of an enterprise from different angles to identify the true financial position (i.e., weak and strong areas), profitability and the degree of risk for business forecasting in a situation where economy is unstable and there is inflationary tendencies. The consistency convention requires that an accounting procedure, once adopted by an enterprise, remains in use from one period to the next unless the users are informed of the change. Thus, without a notice to the contrary, the users of financial statements can assume that there has been no arbitrary change in the treatment of a particular transaction, account or item that would affect the interpretation of the statements. If the management decides that a certain procedure is no longer appropriate and should be changed, then the justification for the change should be explained clearly regarding why the newly adopted accounting principle is preferable.

3.6 ACCOUNTING STANDARDS

The Companies (Amendment) Act, 1999, has empowered the Central Government to constitute an advisory committee to advice the Government on the formulation and laying down of accounting policies and standards for adoption by companies or class of companies. Till the time an advisory committee is constituted, the standards of accounting specified by the Institute of Chartered Accountants of India (ICAI) shall be deemed to be the accounting standards. This will continue until new accounting standards are prescribed by the Central Government. The proposed accounting standards will be in tune with the emerging globalization and competitiveness of the Indian economy (PIB Press Release, New Delhi, dated 6th August, 1999).

According to Section 211(3C) of Companies Act by the expression 'accounting standards' it is meant that the standards of accounting recommended by the ICAI constituted under the Chartered Accountants Act, 1949 (38 of 1949), as may be prescribed by the Central Government in consultation with the National Advisory Committee on Accounting Standards established under sub-section (I) of section 210A.

The various accounting standards issued by ICAI are listed in Table 3.1.

3.6.1 Nature and Scope of Accounting Standards

In order to represent true financial position of a firm, accounting standards were introduced. In India ASB has been given the power to formulate accounting standards on behalf of ICAI on April 21, 1977. Accounting standards are set by ASB to harmonize the diverse accounting policies and practices in India. While formulating the accounting standards, relevant International Accounting Standard/ International Financial Reporting Standard are also considered. The main function of ASB is to formulate accounting standards so that such standards may be established by the ICAI in India.

The ASB has also been entrusted with the responsibility of propagating the accounting standards and persuading the concerned parties to adopt them in preparation and presentation of financial statements. ASB also reviews the accounting standards periodically and, if necessary, revises the same.

Accounting standards are designed for appling to general purpose financial statements and other financial reports. Accounting standards apply in respect of any enterprise engaged in commercial, industrial or business activities, irrespective of whether it is profit oriented or established for charitable purposes.

The date from which a particular standard comes into effect as well as the class of enterprises to which it will apply, will be specified by the ICAI. Efforts will be made to issue accounting standards which are in conformity with the provisions of the applicable laws, customs, usages and business environment in India.

Accounting standards are a set of guidelines or norms to be followed while preparing financial statement of an enterprise to protect the interest of shareholders and the stake-holders, i.e., the government, customers, creditors, investors, employees, and the society as a whole. These guidelines or standards are set or prepared in such a way that financial results of different enterprises can be compared or analyzed on a common platform, because if different standards are used for an identical situation by the enterprises as per their own interest or biasness, then the financial statement published by them will not represent the true financial position of an enterprise. Thus, in order to overcome these difficulties, a set of principles and guidelines, known as **standards**, have been introduced based on the usage, practical experiences, conventions and necessities depending on the practical situations to ensure uniformity in character. These standards help us to reduce and eliminate the problems arising while preparing the financial statements.

These standards have been framed considering the existing laws, customs, conventions and the fast changing business environment. They have been developed through various periods; considering all social and economical factors and are replaced by a new one rejecting an old.

It is expected that when a financial statement is prepared in compliance with the Companies Act to give a true and fair picture of an enterprise to satisfy the reasonable expectations of its users, it should be prepared in accordance with the accepted accounting concepts and standards. Only then the data furnished in the financial statements would represent the true state of affairs of an enterprise.

3.6.2 Utility of Accounting Standards

Accounting standards have the following utility:

1. With the help of accounting standards, the published accounting statements or information have achieved their reliability and are acceptable nationally and internationally.
2. Accounting standards help one compare financial statements of different firms effectively, provided all the firms have followed the accounting standards.
3. If the accounting standards are followed strictly, chances of manipulation and fraud within the accounts will reduce. They are used for sound accounting practices and to ensure uniformity in character for fair presentation of financial statements.
4. While preparing the financial statements, there should not be any kind of personal biasness or influence for which accounting standards have to be followed. Otherwise financial statements will represent conflicting results and would not be able to protect the interest of shareholders and stakeholders. Therefore, to remove these practical problems, accounting standards are used.
5. They help ensure uniformity and reliability in character.
6. It is the responsibility of the management of an enterprise to comply with the accounting standards while preparing the financial statements, and as a result, it becomes helpful for an auditor to execute his job in an efficient manner.

3.6.3 List of Accounting Standards Issued by the Institute of Chartered Accountants of India (ICAI)

Table 3.1 lists all the accounting standards and the date from which it became mandatory

TABLE 3.1 Accounting Standards

Sl. no.	AS no.	Title	Date from which it commenced/became mandatory
1.	AS 1	Disclosure of accounting policies	01.04.1991 01.04.1993
2.	AS 2 (Revised)	Valuation of inventories	01.04.1999
3.	AS 3 (Revised)	Cash flow statements	01.04.2001
4.	AS 4	Contingencies and events occurring after the balance sheet date.	01.04.1995
5.	AS 5 (Revised)	Net profit or loss for the period, prior period items and changes in accounting policies	01.04.1996
6.	AS 6 (Revised)	Depreciation accounting	01.04.1995
7.	AS 7	Accounting for construction contracts	As in case of AS 1 above
8.	AS 8	Accounting for research and development	As in case of AS 1 above
9.	AS 9	Revenue recognition	As in case of AS 1 above
10.	AS 10	Accounting for Fixed Assets	As in case of AS 1 above
11.	AS 11 (Revised)	Accounting for the effects of changes in foreign exchange rates	01.04.1995
12.	AS 12	Accounting for Government grants	01.04.1994

(Contd.)

13.	AS 13	Accounting for investments	01.04.1995
14.	AS 14	Accounting for amalgamations	01.04.1995
15.	AS 15	Accounting for retirement benefits in the financial statements of employers	01.04.1995
16.	AS 16	Borrowing costs	01.04.2000
17.	AS 17	Segment reporting	01.04.2001
18.	AS 18	Related party disclosures	01.04.2001
19.	AS 19	Leases	In respect of all assets leased during accounting periods commencing on or after 01.04.2001
20.	AS 20	Earning per share	01.04.2001
21.	AS 21	Consolidated financial statements	01.04.2001
22.	AS 22	Accounting for taxes on income	01.04.2001
23.	AS 23	Accounting for investments in associates in consolidated financial statements	01.04.2002
24.	AS 24	Discontinuing operations recommendatory	01.04.2002
25.	AS 25	Interim financial reporting	01.04.2002
26.	AS 26	Intangible assets	01.04.2003
27.	AS 27	Financial reporting of interests in joint ventures	01.04.2002
28.	AS 28	Impairment of assets	2004-05 2005-06
29.	AS 29	Provisions, contingent liabilities and contingent assets	01.04.2004

EXERCISES

I. *Objective Type Questions*

1. Fill in the blanks:

    (a) Matching concept involves the recognition of expenses associated with _____ earned and revenues should be recognized in accordance with the _____ concept.

    (b) Financial accounts are prepared for the transactions happening within a period of _____ _____ .

    (c) According to dual-aspect concept, the fundamental accounting equation is as follows:

    Owner's Equity + = Total Assets

    (d) With the help of dual-aspect concept, _____ _____ system of book keeping is created.

    (e) Convention of materiality deals with the _____ _____ of the accounting information.

    (f) According to the convention of conservatism, all possible _____ must be recognized and all possible _____ must not be taken in to consideration until and unless they are realized.

    (g) If the convention of conservatism is strictly followed in all cases then it will create large number of _____ reserves which is against the convention of _____ _____.

    (h) Features of accounting principles are _____, _____ and _____.

    (i) In entity concept, the owner of a business is always _____ and _____ from the business.

    (j) The cost concept does not allow assets to show at their _____ value, because the market prices change very frequently.

Ans: (a) revenue, realization (b) 12, months (c) Outsiders equity (d) double entry (e) relative, importance (f) losses, incomes (g) secret, full disclosure (h) usefulness, objectivity and feasibility (i) separated, distinct (j) present.

2. Choose the best alternative from the options:
   (a) In entity concept, ownership is
       (i) separated from the business.
       (ii) not separated from the business.
   (b) According to cost concept, an asset will be recorded
       (i) at the price actually paid by the enterprise.
       (ii) at it's present value.
   (c) According to matching concept,
       (i) balance sheet is prepared.
       (ii) income statement is prepared.
   (d) Under realization concept, the revenue is deemed to be earned when
       (i) cash is actually received.
       (ii) the goods have been sold/transferred or the services rendered.
   (e) According to money measurement concept, all transactions are to be recorded in the financial accounts which
       (i) are measurable in terms of money.
       (ii) are acceptable to the owner.
   (f) According to convention of disclosure,
       (i) all the transactions are to be valued on the basis of current price.
       (ii) all the material facts regarding the business activities must be disclosed in financial statements.
   (g) Accounting principles are
       (i) not universal like other natural sciences.
       (ii) universal like other natural sciences.
   (h) In accounting principles,
       (i) some standards are applied to measure the economic activites of a firm to ensure uniformity.
       (ii) some rules are framed according to Companies Act to measure the economic activities.
   Ans: (a) i (b) i (c) ii (d) ii (e) i (f) ii (g) i and (h) i.

II. *Short Answer Type Questions with Answers*

1. What do you mean by accounting principles?
   Ans: The term 'principle' means rule of action or conduct or basis of conduct or it may be termed as a general or fundamental truth. Accounting principles are not universal like other natural science but, they are evolving rapidly. It is applied to measure the economic activities of a firm and to ensure uniformity in character with the help of some standards. These standards are generally known as Generally Accepted Accounting Principles (GAAP).

   Accounting principles are based on conventions, customs, laws, usages, and the fast changing business environment. There is no fixed universally acceptable set of principles, but some standards are set (by ASB) to harmonise the diversified policies, and ensure uniformity and reliability of accounting statements/information because there should not be any kind of personal biasness or influence, and it must be supported by the accepted facts and figures.

2. What are the main features of accounting principles?
   Ans: Accounting principles are acceptable only when the following three basic criteria are fulfilled:
   (a) Usefulness (b) Objectivity (c) Feasibility.

3. What problem will be faced by a business unit or an enterprise if the going concern concept is not considered?

Ans: If the assumption that a business will continue is not considered, then it will convey a message that the business will not be able to meet its obligations in future. As a result, investors will not be interested in investing their money, suppliers will not supply their goods and services, and employees will not provide their services and so on. The natural activity of the business or business dealings will, thus, collapse or jeopardize.

4. How are costs recorded in accounts on the basis of continuity concept?

Ans: On the basis of the continuity concept, costs are generally distinguished as expired and unexpired costs. Expired costs are the ones which help to produce revenues. They are recognized as expenses. Unexpired costs are those costs which help to produce revenue in future. Such costs are recognized as assets to be shown in the balance sheet.

5. What is the object of accepting the consistency assumption?

Ans: In order to represent a clear and correct interpretation of the financial statements and results, consistency is a must. Consistent use of accounting measures and procedures is important in achieving comparability. For preparing financial accounts, a number of concepts and principles are followed and if frequent changes are made regarding the principles and policies for a particular transaction/event, the comparison of the financial statements from one period to the next would become meaningless. Inconsistency in principles and policies will develop misleading interpretations and as a result, some misjudgments may occur while deciding some future course of actions.

6. What do you mean by accrual system in accounting?

Ans: Under the accrual system in accounting, for calculation of a particular year's income all revenue incomes and expenditures are to be taken into consideration for that particular accounting period only, whether received or receivable and paid or payable. Hence, for calculating the current year's income, all revenue incomes and expenditures of previous year and for the coming year are not taken into account.

According to this system, transactions are recorded in the accounts of an enterprise in the periods in which the transactions occur rather than only in the periods in which cash is received or paid by the enterprise.

7. What do you mean by entity concept?

Ans: According to this concept, the owner or the proprietor of a business is always separate and distinct from the business or enterprise. Business is treated here as a separate 'unit' or 'entity'. All business transactions are recorded in the books of such an 'entity' or an artificial body, i.e., the legal entity.

8. How is income considered in realization concept?

Ans: According to this concept revenue is deemed to be earned when goods are transferred (when the title of the goods is transferred according to the Sale of Goods Act), or services rendered to a customer and it does not matter when cash is actually received or realized. For instance, if an advance of Rs. 500 is received in May and goods supplied in July, then Rs. 500 will be recognized as revenue only in July.

9. What do you mean by accounting period concept and why is this concept applied?

Ans: Financial Accounts are prepared for the transactions taking place within a specific period, i.e., for 12 months/one year. At the end of such period, financial statements are prepared to ascertain the results of the business. Thus, the above stated period of 12 months is known as **accounting period**.

It is essential to measure the financial health of a business or an enterprise for a particular period, and hence it should be tested at regular intervals. In order to attain this objective, we should assess the income of the said enterprise periodically. The 12 months accounting period used by an enterprise is called its **financial year** or **fiscal year** or **accounting year**.

10. What do you mean by money measurement concept?

   Ans: Under this concept, all the events or transactions occurring within an accounting period, which results in the change of financial position of a business or company and which are measurable in terms of money are to be recorded in the financial accounts.

11. What do you mean by the fundamental accounting equation based upon the principle of dual-aspect concept?

   Ans: The following fundamental accounting equation may be drawn on the basis of the principle of dual-aspect concept which is the basis of accountancy:

$$\text{Owner's Equity} + \text{Outsiders Equity} = \text{Total Assets}$$
$$\text{or, } \text{Capital} + \text{Liabilities} = \text{Total Assets}$$

   Thus, according to duality concept, every transaction will affect at least two items and the outcome of such transaction will be

$$\text{Total Assets} = \text{Owner's Equity (Capital)} + \text{Liabilities}$$

   Double entry system of book keeping is created with the help of this concept.

12. What do you mean by the convention of full disclosure and why is it made?

   Ans: According to this convention, all material facts regarding business activities must be disclosed in the financial accounts and statements. The Companies Act also makes it essential by it's provisions for fair disclosure of all related facts and figures regarding the financial position of a company. Hence, to protect the interest of the shareholders, owners, creditors, investors and the Government, necessary steps must be taken to disclose all possible material facts and pertinent information in presenting the financial statements to maintain its reliability.

13. What is the implication of the convention of materiality?

   Ans: It deals with the *relative importance* of the accounting information. The state of *relative importance* may vary from one accountant to another or one firm to another. The material facts are to be disclosed in the financial statements. An item or information may be material for a particular situation, but may be immaterial for another situation or environment. Thus, materiality is depends on a number of factors closely associated with it and is a matter of judgement and knowledge of the particular situation or environment of the business. Materiality also depends on the nature of the item, not on just its value.

14. What do you mean by the Convention of Conservatism? Is there any negative or adverse effect of this convention?

   Ans: According to this convention, all possible losses must be recognized and all possible incomes must not be taken into consideration until and unless they are realized. Hence, the chief objective of this convention is to give the most pessimistic view of an enterprise while presenting the financial statements.

   However, if this convention is strictly followed in all cases, then it will create a large number of secret reserves which is against the convention of full disclosure. Hence, this principle must be applied cautiously taking into consideration the interest of the investors, Government, creditors and other interested parties.

III. *Long Answer Type Questions*

1. What do you mean by Generally Accepted Accounting Principles (GAAP)? What are the basic features of accounting principles?

2. What are the accounting assumptions formulated by the Institute of Chartered Accountants of India (ICAI) for the preparation and presentation of financial statements?

3. What is the importance of following the convention of consistency and conservatism to an enterprise?

4. "A business unit is distinct from its owners". Evaluate.

5. Briefly explain the chief characteristics and importance of accounting principles.

6. On the basis of revenue recognition concept, how is revenue recognized in case of sale of goods and rendering of services?
7. What is accounting standards? Explain the nature and scope of accounting standards.
8. What is the utility of accounting standards while preparing the financial statements of a firm? How many accounting standards have been issued by the ICAI till date?
9. Write short notes on:
   (a) Going concern concept
   (b) Consistency
   (c) Accrual assumptions
   (d) Entity concept
   (e) Matching concept
   (f) Realization concept
   (g) Convention of Conservatism
   (h) Dual-aspect concept
   (i) Accounting standard.

4

Process and Bases of Accounting

CONTENTS

- Process of Accounting
- Bases of Accounting
  - Cash Basis of Accounting
- Accrual Basis
- Hybrid System of Accounting

4.1 PROCESS OF ACCOUNTING

Accounting is the process of identifying, measuring and communicating economic information to permit informed judgements and decisions by users of the information.

—American Accounting Association

Generally, a system may be considered as consisting of three activities: input, processing of input, and output. If we consider the definition of 'accounting' according to the American Accounting Association and analyse the said definition, we find that accounting is a series of activities which are linked and from a chain of steps, beginning with observing, then collecting, recording, analyzing and finally communicating information to the users.

Thus, accounting is the *process of recording* the financial transactions chronologicaly in a regular manner. It involves the task of identifying, classifying, summarizing and analysing all those business transactions which are measurable in terms of money. It is the primary duty of an accountant to identify the financial transactions or economic activities which can be measurable in terms of money. Those events which are not measurable in terms of money need not be recorded, even if the business suffers a loss for such an event.

After identifying the economic activities as business transactions, recording of the said transactions are made systematically through journal in the books of original entries or subsidiary books. Then, classifying and summarizing the financial transactions are done. It involves the grouping of transactions of similar nature in a particular place known as **ledger,** and then preparation of Trial Balance, Income Statement and Balance Sheet through classified data is done on the basis of accepted accounting principles. Hence, it is a continuous process.

The process of accounting is depicted in Figure 4.1 and is explained below (starting from recording of business transactions to the preparation of Trial Balance)

1. *Identification of financial transactions*: Whenever there is a transaction, it needs to be recorded in the books on the basis of accepted accounting principles and rules, but before recording it must be observed whether there is any documentary evidence in support of the transaction or not. Here, documentary evidence means invoices, cash memos, pass books, pay-in-slips, cheques, debit notes, credit notes, etc. After considering the documentary evidences if it is confirmed by the concerned person that those documents are dependable or reliable and measurable in terms of money, only then that particular transaction may be identified as a financial transaction. After proper identification of a financial transaction, the recording of the transaction has to be made.

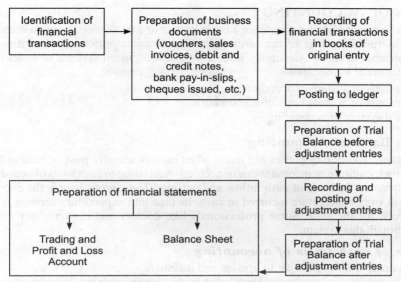

FIGURE 4.1 Process of accounting.

2. *Preparation of business documents*: Accounting entries are made in the books of original entry or Journal on the basis of the vouchers prepared on the basis of the documentary evidences in support of the transaction. All firms or business houses print vouchers in their own business names. Generally for each financial transaction a separate voucher is prepared and the specific account to be debited or credited with account code (if any) are clearly mentioned in the said voucher. Vouchers are maintained serially for future reference and the concerned documentary evidences are also attached with the voucher.

3. *Recording of financial transactions in books of original entry*: Daily transactions of a firm are recorded chronologically under the double entry system of book keeping. All the transactions are first recorded in the journal book or book of original entry. After preparing a voucher, a journal entry is passed in the book of original entry in respect of a particular transaction. When the volume of transactions becomes huge, subdivision of journal may be made on the basis of the nature of transaction. Due to this subdivision, a particular day book will record transactions of similar nature and as such its volume will be limited. Thus, it will help easy detection of detection errors and frauds.

4. *Posting to ledger*: After preparing journal entries for all transactions, they are at first transferred to the ledger book under different heads of accounts to know the net or final position of a particular account at the end of a certain period. The process or techniques of recording the transactions from the journal to the ledger is called **posting**. Ledger is a set of accounts or a book where different types of accounts are maintained. It is the principal book of accounts.

5. *Preparation of trial balance before adjustment entries*: The last but one step in this process is the preparation of Trial Balance before adjustment entries. To know the net or final position of a particular account at the end of a certain period, balancing is made for all accounts and then Trial Balance is prepared with the help of the said balances. All debit balances of accounts are shown on the debit side of the trial balance and credit balances are shown on the credit side. The total of both the sides of the trial balance must be equal. It is prepared to check the arithmetical accuracy of the book keeping entries.

6. *Preparation of financial statements*: The last and the final step in this process is the preparation of financial statements. After preparing of Trial Balance, the financial statements are prepared with the help of the ledger account balances. The final account is prepared to know the financial position of a firm, but before that the necessary adjustment entries are made at the end of an accounting period.

4.2 BASES OF ACCOUNTING

At the end of a financial period if a trader or a businessman or a professional person wants to know the financial results (profit or loss or net earnings) of his business/profession, recording of financial transactions becames essential. Generally, there are three recognized systems or bases of accounting for recording financial transactions.

1. Cash basis or system of accounting
2. Mercantile or accrual basis of accounting
3. Hybrid system of accounting

4.2.1 Cash Basis of Accounting

Under this system, accounting entries are made when cash is actually paid or received. No entry is shown when an expenditure or income is due or accrued. According to cash basis of accounting system, profit is calculated on the basis of cash inflow and outflow. Thus, profit here is the excess of income received in cash over expenditure incurred in cash. Income and expenditure account is prepared for calculating profit for the year. Some professionals like doctors and lawyers keep record of their transactions through this system.

Advantages of cash basis of accounting

1. This method is very simple to operate and maintain.
2. It does not require any special knowledge or skill for maintaining the accounts and the related records.
3. It is effective and suitable for those small firms where goods are sold or services provided on cash basis, i.e., where cash transactions are the mainstay of the business.
4. It is helpful for the professionals like doctors and lawyers for keeping records of their transactions.

Disadvantages of cash basis of accounting

1. Here, accounts are not maintained on the basis of accepted accounting principles and conventions.
2. The system fails to represent the true picture of the firm as accepted accounting principles, standards and conventions are not followed.
3. No discrimination is made in respect of capital expenditure and revenue expenditure. Thus, effective comparison is not possible in respect of past profits and hence, important decisions taken for the future period may not prove beneficial for the firm.
4. This method is not recognized by the Companies Act.
5. There is no provision for adjustment and recording of outstanding, prepaid and accruals.
6. Changes in resources and liabilities are not measured properly through this method.

4.2.2 Accrual Basis

According to this system, every transaction or event which changes the financial position of a firm within an accounting period must be taken into consideration, whether cash is received or not, paid or not. It means that not only the cash transactions are to be taken into account, but other transactions such as outstanding expenditures, accrued incomes, prepaid expenditures or pre-received incomes also need to be considered.

Under the accrual system, for calculating a particular year's income, all revenue incomes and expenditures are taken into consideration for that particular accounting period only, whether received or receivable and paid or payable. Hence, for calculating the current year's income, all revenue incomes and expenditures of the previous year and for the coming year are not taken into account. According to this system, transactions are recorded in the accounts of an enterprise in the periods in which the transactions occurred rather than only in the periods in which cash is received or paid by the enterprise. Accrual convention is applied here. This convention makes distinction between the receipts of cash and the right to receive cash, and the payment of cash and the legal obligation to pay cash.

Let us examine the manner in which the accrual convention applies to revenues and expenditures under the following cases:

1. Cash received as an advance from a customer: It is not an income, but a liability.
2. Rent paid during the current year for nine months: It is an expenditure.
3. Rent outstanding for remaining three months: Here three months' rent is an expenditure while the amount payable (not yet paid) is a liability.
4. Interest on fixed deposits due but not received: Here interest is an income (though not received) and the amount receivable (due but not received) is an asset.
5. Suppose, rent is paid in advance for the next period for two months. It is not an expenditure, because it is not paid for the current year and as such it will be treated as an asset.

It is essential to measure the financial health of a business or an enterprise at regular intervals. In order to attain this objective, we have to assess the income of the said enterprise periodically. To measure the net income adequately through accrual basis, revenues and expenses must be assigned to the appropriate accounting period. This problem is solved by applying the matching convention. Revenues must be taken into consideration within the accounting period in which goods are sold or services performed, and expenses must be taken into account within the said accounting period in which they are used to produce or generate revenue.

Through the matching convention, expenses are recognized for a particular accounting period and considered as expenses incurred for the said period. After reorganization, the particular expenses are adjusted with the concerned revenues earned during the said accounting period.

Thus, the accrual system of accounting is the most systematic method for ascertaining true result (profit or loss) of an enterprise and helps to know the true financial position.

Advantages of accrual basis

1. All accepted accounting principles, standards and conventions are followed. As a result, accounts maintained through this system represent the true and fair state of affairs of an enterprise.
2. This method is recognized by the Companies Act.
3. Proper analysis of revenues capitals, incomes and expenditures are made through this system.
4. Profit disclosed through this method is acceptable to all trading concerns.
5. It helps in taking decision for the future on the basis of past performances because it may be assumed that financial results are properly calculated.

In accounting practice, personal opinions and judgements of an accountant may play an important role in the preparation of the financial statements of an enterprise. However, if it is free from any personal bias of the concerned person, then it is the best method for assessing a firm's financial health.

Disadvantages of accrual basis

1. We know that personal opinions and judgements of an accountant may play an important role in the preparation of the financial statements of an enterprise. Thus, until and unless it is free from personal biasness, its worthiness and reliability cannot be established.
2. It is not simple like cash basis in operating and maintaining the accounts properly.
3. It requires specialized person for preparing the annual accounts and as such book-maintaining cost is very high.
4. Financial result of the business cannot be calculated easily and quickly like that in cash basis.

The distinction between cash basis and accrual basis of accounting is given in Table 4.1.

4.2.3 Hybrid System of Accounting

Under this system, incomes are measured on the basis of cash basis while expenditures are measured on the basis of mercantile system. This system is followed by a few professionals only.

TABLE 4.1 Distinction between Cash Basis and Accrual Basis

Cash basis	Accrual basis
1. It is simple and easy to maintain.	1. It is not so easy like cash basis. It requires specialized skill and knowledge.
2. Only cash transactions are recorded.	2. Both cash and credit transactions are recorded.
3. Outstanding, prepaid and accruals are not considered here.	3. Outstanding, prepaid and accruals are considered here.
4. It is not applicable for going concerns.	4. It is perfectly applicable for going concerns.
5. Matching concept is not followed.	5. Matching concept is followed.
6. Accepted accounting principles and concepts are not followed.	6. Accepted accounting principles and concepts are followed.
7. It is suitable for professionals.	7. It is suitable for big business houses.
8. Final account cannot be prepared.	8. Final account can be prepared.
9. It fails to represent the true financial position of a firm.	9. It helps to represent the true financial position of a firm.
10. Double entry system is not followed.	10. Double entry system is followed here.
11. No discriminations are being made in respect of capital expenditure and revenue expenditures.	11. Capital expenditure and revenue expenditures are properly analysed.

The difference between cash basis and accrual basis of accounting is shown below (Illustration 4.1) through the computation of net income as under:

ILLUSTRATION 4.1 From the following particulars, calculate the net income of Dr. Rajiv Sen for the year ending December 31, 2008 under (i) cash basis and (ii) accrual basis:

	Rs.
Fees received in cash during the year (Gross)	190,700
Fees earned in 2008 but not received	8,400
Received interest from bank	4,800
Interest on fixed deposit due but not received	2,300
Fees for the year 2007 received	3,500
Fees for the year 2007 still to be collected	1,600
Fees received in advance	2,900
Total chamber rent paid during the year	8,700
Chamber rent outstanding for the year 2008	1,100
Last year's outstanding chamber rent paid	1,600
Telephone bill paid	3,500
Staff salaries paid (Gross)	14,100
Staff salaries paid in advance	2,000
Lighting of the chamber paid	3,900
Miscellaneous office expenses paid	4,100
Newspaper and magazine	2,700

Solution

(i) **Computation of net income of Dr. Rajiv Sen under cash basis for the year 2008:**

	Rs.	Rs.
Income received in 2008:		
Fees received	190,700	
Received interest from bank	4,800	195,500
Less: Expenses paid in 2008:		
Total chamber rent paid during the year	8,700	
Telephone bill paid	3,500	
Staff salaries paid (Gross)	14,100	
Lighting of the chamber paid	3,900	
Miscellaneous office expenses paid	4,100	
Newspaper and magazine	2,700	37,000
Net income		158,500

(ii) **Computation of net income of Dr. Rajiv Sen under accrual basis for the year 2008:**

	Rs.	Rs.	Rs.
Income for the year 2008:			
Fees received	190,700		
Add: Fees earned in 2008 but not received	8,400		
	199,100		
Less: Fees for the year 2007 received	3,500		
	195,600		
Less: Fees received in advance	2,900	192,700	
Received interest from bank	4,800		
Add: Interest on fixed deposit due but not received	2,300	7,100	199,800
Total Income for the year 2008			
Less: Expenses for the year 2008:			
Total chamber rent paid during the year	8,700		
Add: Rent outstanding for the year 2008	1,100		
	9,800		
Less: Last year's outstanding rent paid	1,600	8,200	
Telephone bill paid		3,500	
Staff salaries paid (Gross)	14,100		
Less: Staff salaries paid in advance	2,000	12,100	
Lighting of the chamber paid		3,900	
Miscellaneous office expenses paid		4,100	
Newspaper and magazine		2,700	34,500
Net income			165,300

EXERCISES

I. *Short Answer Type Questions*

1. What is process of accounting?
2. What do you mean by bases of accounting?
3. What is cash basis?
4. What is meant by accrual basis?
5. Explain the advantages of accrual basis.
6. Discuss the disadvantages of cash basis of accounting.

II. *Long Answer Type Questions*

1. What is process of accounting? Explain the process of accounting starting from identification of financial transactions to preparation of financial statements.
2. What do you mean by bases of accounting? What are the different bases of accounting?
3. Define accrual basis. Also, explain the advantages of this system. How does it differ from cash basis of accounting?
4. What do you mean by cash basis of accounting? Discuss the advantages and disadvantages of this system.

5

Recording of Business Transactions: Vouchers

CONTENTS

- Source Documents
- Voucher

- Types of Vouchers

5.1 SOURCE DOCUMENTS

In accounting practice, an accounting data should be supported by documentary evidence and must be free from personal biasness to prove its worthiness, reliability, verifiability and dependability. Only then the data furnished in the financial statements would represent the true state of affairs of an enterprise.

All transactions are recorded in the books of accounts on the basis of some documentary evidence or supporting papers. Cash receipts, invoices, bills, debit notes, credit notes, cheques, and pay-in-slips are generally used as documentary evidences or supporting papers. On the basis of these documents, primary entries are made within a Journal and a Ledger. These documents contain the nature of transaction, date, amount, name of parties, etc., in support of the respective transaction. These documents are known as **source documents**. Without source documents, no transaction can be recorded in the books of accounts because that would amount to the violation of the accounting principle of objectivity and *verifiability*. All accounting data are subject to verification by anyone in future and the data are the proof or evidence of the specific transaction. Thus, for the best interest of the business there must be some documentary evidence for each and every transaction of an enterprise for future reference and only then, such data may be considered to be dependable or reliable.

Brief ideas about some common source of documents are given below:

1. *Cash memos*

When goods are purchased from a trader in cash then the seller of the said goods gives a cash memo to the buyer as a document of purchase. It contains the details about the goods sold, i.e., the name of the seller's firm, purchaser's name and address, quantity, price of each unit, total value, date and other related terms and conditions.

It is an important document in the hands of the purchaser in support of his purchase. The specimen of a cash memo is given it following tabulated form.

CASH MEMO

IAC Electricals (An ISO 9001 company)

9/1 S.B.Road, Kolkata – 700 014

Ph.No. 2287-9867

e.Mail: info@IACelect.com

Website: www.infoiacelect.com

No. R/D/K/102   Dated: 12.12.08

Quantity	Description	Rate (Rs.)	Amount (Rs.)
24	11 KV Disc insulator	95.00	2,280.00
	Add: VAT 4%		91.20
	Add: Education cess 3%		68.40
	Total		2,439.60
	(Two thousand four hundred thirty nine only)		2,439.00

Note:

Goods once sold are not taken back.

Stamp OF IAC Electricals

For IAC Electricals

Senior Executive (Sales)

2. Invoice or bill

When goods are sold on credit, the seller prepares a sale invoice for the purchaser. It contains the name of the purchaser, cost of the goods, quantity, tax/duty if any, and the detailed description of the goods sold. The original copy of the invoice is sent to the purchaser and the duplicate copy is kept for office use of the seller. In some cases, in addition to the original copy, a duplicate copy is also sent to the purchaser. The specimen of an invoice or bill is given in the following tabulated form.

Dhanraj & Bipco Ltd.

Plot No.24, Block No.D/56,

Daria Ganj, New Delhi- 100 007

Tel.No.2256-9980/81/82/83.

Fax No. 091-2256-9980

Website: www.dh.bip.com

INVOICE

Ref. No. GH/RE/ kp/ 304 Date: 12.12.08

SD. Bros. ...Dr.

Plot No. 234, City Centre,

Durgapur – 713 202

Ref.: Your P.O. No. S/D/STORAGE/145/08-09 Dated 24.11.08

No. R/D/K/102   Dated: 12.12.08

Quantity	Description	Rate (Rs.)	Amount (Rs.)
10	Washing machine—Model No. G 7	3,980	39,800
5	Microwave open—Model No. 156	4,000	20,000
			59,800
	Add: VAT 4%		2,392
		Total	62,192
	(Sixty two thousand one hundred ninety two only)		

E. & O.E.   Terms: 7.5 % cash at two months

Yours faithfully,

For Dhanraj & Bipco Ltd.

xxx

Area Sales Manager

Stamp of the company/seller

[**E. & O.E.:** It is an abbreviated term used in invoice. It means 'Errors and Omissions Excepted', i.e., if any error is detected in the invoice, which may result in an increase or decrease in value may be adjusted subsequently/accordingly.

7.5% cash at two months: It means a cash discount is allowed @ 7.5% on the net sale price, if payment is being made within two months.]

3. *Debit note*

Generally, goods are returned to suppliers for being defective or not being according to the sample or quality. These types of transactions are recorded like the ruling of the purchase day book. A note or a letter, known as **debit note**, is given to the supplier, together with the returned goods, stating that their account has been debited for the goods returned. It contains the date of return, quantity and value, supplier's name and the reasons for such return. After recording the transaction in the return outward book or purchase return book, the creditor's account will be debited (for each return) and at the end of the period, return outward account or purchase return account will be credited for the total returns. A specimen of a debit note is given in box 5.1.

BOX 5.1   Debit Note

Telegram _____	No. _____
Telephone _____	Place _____
From:	Date _____
Name and address (of the sender)	
_____	
_____	

To,
Name and address (of the person to whom it is sent) _____

We are debiting your account with value of under mentioned materials returned to you for the reasons stated below. Meanwhile, we await your instructions.

Description	Specification	Price	Amount

Reasons:

Ref. _____ Invoice No. _____ etc.

Signature

4. *Credit note*

Here also, goods are returned by customers for being defective or for not being according to the sample or quality. These types of transactions are also recorded like the ruling of the sales day book. A debit note is also received together with the goods returned by the customers or purchasers. Thus, it is a claim raised by the purchaser and when such a claim is accepted by the seller, another note is sent to the purchaser known as **credit note**. Through the credit note, the seller informs his acceptance of the goods and also certifies that the customer has been given the due credit for such return. After recording the transaction in the return inward book or sales return book, the Debtor's A/c will be credited (for each return) and at the end of the period, the Return Inward A/c or Sales Return A/c will be debited for the total returns. A specimen of a credit note is given in Box 5.2.

BOX 5.2   Credit Note

Telegram _____

Telephone _____

From:

Name and address (of the sender)

No . _____

Place _____

Date _____

_____

To,

Name and address (of the person to whom it is sent)

We are crediting your account with the value of under mentioned materials received from you, for the reasons stated as in your Debit Note No. _____

Description	Specification	Price	Amount
Reasons:			

Ref._____

Signature

5. *Pay-in-slip*

It is a special type of printed form supplied by the bank to their customers/account holders for depositing cash and cheque in the bank. It has two parts the left hand side and the right hand side. The left hand side is used as a counterfoil and the other part is kept for the banker's use. When cash or cheque is deposited by a customer in his bank account, the cashier puts his signature and the bank's stamp on both the parts, and returns the counterfoil to the customer. It is a document for depositing cash or cheque in the hands of a customer. It shows the details of cash or cheque deposited. A specimen of a Pay-in-slip is given in Box 5.3.

BOX 5.3   Pay-in-slip

6. *Cheque*

A cheque book is supplied by the bank to their customers/account holders for withdrawing cash from the bank. A cheque is used as a future document of payment or withdrawing cash from the bank. It is drawn on a specified banker and is always payable on demand. A specified amount is paid by the bank to the bearer or to the person whose name is written on the cheque. Like pay-in-slips, each cheque has a counterfoil and is signed by the drawer with date and amount. The data recorded in the cheque is also recorded in the counterfoil. A specimen of a cheque is given in Box 5.4.

BOX 5.4   A cheque

Date...................

Pay To ....

.... Or Bearer

Rupees ....

Rs.

A/c No.		LF		INTLS

UNITED BANK OF INDIA
Address:
EIH/SBF IFSC: UTBIOCOK231

II*271568II* 713027203 10

7. *Receipt*

At the time of receiving cash from a customer, a receipt of the said cash is issued by the trader/firm to the customer as an acknowledgement. It contains the name of the person/firm from whom cash is received, date, amount and the reference for which cash is received. It is prepared in duplicate. The original is handed over to the party making payment and the duplicate is kept for future reference. A specimen of a Receipt is given in Box 5.5.

BOX 5.5   A Receipt

The D.D. Manufacturers and Suppliers
26, City Centre, Durgapur – 713 216
West Bengal

No. 4/1256   Date: 23.12.08

Received with thanks from .... a sum of Rs. ....
(in words...) in cash/cheque No. ....Dated ....Drawn on ....
.... on account of Invoice No. .... Dated ....

For D.D. Manufacturers and Suppliers
Authorized Signatory

Note: Cheques are subject to realization.

5.2   VOUCHER

It is a document prepared on the basis of supporting documents like cash receipts, invoices, bills, debit notes, credit notes, cheques, pay-in-slips, and so on. On the basis of a voucher, primary entries are made in Journal and Ledger. Thus, it acts as documentary evidence in support of a transaction recorded in the books of accounts. Generally, a separate voucher is prepared for each business transaction where the account to be debited or credited is clearly mentioned. Vouchers are printed in the name of the firm it belongs. For example, when vouchers are printed for S.S. Traders, it means that S.S. Traders must be printed on all vouchers. It is prepared by an accountant or a senior employee of the accounts department, and after its preparation the voucher is certified by the concerned person or officer in charge.

Usually, a number is used serially for each voucher and is preserved chronologically for future reference. When vouchers are preserved chronologically, it helps the auditor at the time of vouching. Differences between source documents and vouchers are shown in Table 5.1.

TABLE 5.1 Distinction between Source Documents and Vouchers

Source documents	Vouchers
1. It is a supporting paper or documentary evidence for preparing a voucher.	1. It is prepared on the basis of supporting documents.
2. It is prepared as an evidence of the transaction.	2. It is prepared to record the transaction.
3. Details of transaction are available, but not the analysis of accounts.	3. Account to be debited or credited is clearly mentioned in a voucher.
4. It is a must for future reference, otherwise the respective transaction may not be considered as reliable.	4. Without supporting documents, a voucher may not be acceptable or reliable.

5.2.1 Types of Vouchers

Vouchers may be classified as follows:

1. Source vouchers or source documents or supporting vouchers
2. Accounting vouchers.

Account vouchers may be further subdivided as follows:

(a) Cash vouchers: Cash vouchers may be classified as under:
    (i) Debit vouchers: For cash payment.
    (ii) Credit vouchers: For cash receipts.
(b) Non-cash vouchers or transfer vouchers.

Source vouchers or source documents or supporting vouchers

Whenever there is a transaction, it must be recorded in the books of accounts on the basis of some documentary evidence or supporting papers, known as **source vouchers** or **source documents** or **supporting vouchers**. Cash receipts, invoices, bills, debit notes, credit notes, cheques, pay-in-slips, etc., are generally used as documentary evidences or supporting vouchers. Without these documents, no transaction can be recorded in the books of accounts.

However, there are some cases where a supporting voucher is not available, but transaction has occurred. Under such circumstances, a supporting voucher is prepared. For example, cash is paid for office water pump repair, but no receipt is available from the mechanic. In this case, a supporting voucher is prepared by the concerned person or the person in charge and the said voucher must be countersigned by the authorized person/officer.

Features of source vouchers

1. It is a written document prepared on the basis of actual business transaction.
2. The details of the transaction are available from this document.
3. It must be signed by the person preparing it and then countersigned by the authorized person/officer.
4. It is prepared only after for the business transactions has occurred.

Accounting voucher

All transactions are recorded in the books of accounts on the basis of some documentary evidence or supporting vouchers. Before recording any transaction in the books of accounts, the supporting vouchers are analysed on the basis of its character and only then it is determined which account (or accounts) is to be debited or credited. After completing the analysis of transaction, the decision is recorded by the accountant in a printed format mentioning the account to be debited or credited is known as **accounting voucher**. It must be signed by the accountant and then countersigned by authorized person/officer. These vouchers are used for future reference, and on the basis of these vouchers, accounts are audited by the auditor.

Features/elements of accounting vouchers

1. These printed vouchers are prepared by an accountant.
2. These vouchers are prepared on the basis of supporting vouchers.
3. It a document recording the analysis of transaction mentioning the account to be debited or credited along with necessary details.
4. It is generally signed by an accountant and then countersigned by an authorized person.

Types of accounting vouchers

Different types of accounting vouchers are shown in Figure 5.1.

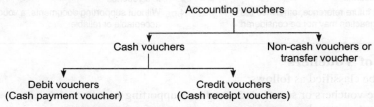

FIGURE 5.1 Types of accounting vouchers.

Cash vouchers: It refers to those vouchers which are prepared for cash transactions. Thus, when cash (including cheque) is received or paid for a transaction, these vouchers are prepared. Cash voucher is of two types and may be classified as follows:

1. Debit Vouchers for cash payment
2. Credit Vouchers for cash receipts

Debit vouchers: These accounting vouchers are prepared for all types of cash payments. Generally, cash payment may be made for the following:

1. Cash paid for any expenses
2. Cash paid for purchase of goods
3. Payment made to suppliers or creditors
4. Cash deposited into bank
5. Repayment of loans
6. Cash withdrawn by the proprietor (Drawings)
7. Cash paid for purchase of any asset.

The person concerned receiving the net amount must put his signature on the space provided on the receipt. When payment is made for more than Rs. 5,000, a revenue stamp of Re. 1 must be affixed on it.

The following information may be obtained from a debit voucher:

1. The date of preparing the voucher
2. The voucher number
3. The name of the account debited
4. A brief description of the transaction, i.e., narration
5. Net amount paid for the transaction
6. Signature of the accountant preparing it
7. Countersignature of the authorized person/officer
8. Source document number (for example, cash memo no.)

A specimen of a debit voucher is given in Box 5.6.

BOX 5.6   Debit Voucher

Received Rs._____	XYZ Pvt. Ltd. Connaught Circus, New Delhi-110 001.		
	Voucher No. _____		Date _____
Affix revenue stamp _____ _____ _____	**Debit:** **Computer A/c** (Computer purchased for cash vide cash memo No.1234)		Amount (Rs.) 34,000
	Total		34,000
	Sd. Manager		Sd. Accountant

Credit vouchers: These accounting vouchers are prepared for all types of cash receipts. Cash may be received for the following:

1. Cash received for sale of goods
2. Cash received for any incomes
3. Cash received from customers or debtors
4. Cash withdrawn from bank
5. Loan taken
6. Cash invested by the proprietor (Fresh capital)
7. Sale of investments.

The format of a credit voucher is given in Box 5.7.

BOX 5.7   Credit Voucher

XYZ Ltd.		
Connaught Circus, New Delhi-110 001		
Voucher No. _____		Date _____
Credit:		Amount (Rs.)
Sales A/c (Sale of goods for cash vide cash memo No.137)		52,000
Total		52,000
Sd. Manager		Sd. Accountant

The following information may be obtained from a credit voucher:

1. The date of preparing the voucher
2. The voucher number
3. The name of the account credited
4. A brief description of the transaction, i.e., narration
5. Net amount received for the transaction
6. Signature of the accountant preparing it
7. Countersignature of the authorized person/officer
8. The source document number (e.g., cash memo no.)

Non-cash vouchers or transfer vouchers: It refers to the vouchers prepared for non-cash transactions. Generally, non-cash vouchers are prepared for the following:

1. Credit purchase and sale of goods
2. Credit purchase and sale of assets

3. For goods returned to suppliers or by the customers
4. For charging depreciation
5. Rectification of errors
6. Adjustment entries (e.g., writing off bad debts).

Specimens of transfer vouchers is given in Box 5.8(a) and Box 5.8(b).

BOX 5.8(a) Transfer Voucher

XYZ Pvt. Ltd.

Connaught Circus, New Delhi-110001

Voucher No. B2/156		Dated. _____	
Debit: M/s G.P. Bros		A/c	Amount (Rs.)
			56,000
		Total	56,000
Credit: Sales A/c			56,000
(Goods sold on credit vide bill No. 02/ 97)			
		Total	56,000
Sd. Manager			Sd. Accountant

BOX 5.8(b) Transfer Voucher

XYZ Pvt. Ltd.

Connaught Circus, New Delhi-110001

Voucher No. B7/ 78		Dated _____	
Debit: Office equipments	A/c		Amount (Rs.)
	Two computers @ Rs. 21,800 each		43,600
	Two printer machine @ Rs.10,200 each		20,400
(Office equipment purchased on credit vide bill No. 7/37)			
		Total	64,000
Credit: M/S S.K. Traders		A/c	64,000
		Total	64,000
Sd. Accounts Manager			Sd. Accountant

The following information may be obtained from a transfer voucher:

1. The date of preparing the voucher
2. The voucher number
3. The name of the account credited
4. A brief description of the transaction, i.e., narration
5. Net amount receivable or payable for the transaction
6. Signature of the accountant preparing it
7. Countersignature of the authorized person/officer
8. Source document number (for example, sales invoice no.).

EXERCISES

I. Short Answer Type Questions

1. What do you mean by source of documents?
2. What is an invoice?
3. What is pay-in-slip?
4. What are cash receipts?
5. Define a cheque and give a specimen of a cheque.
6. What is debit note?
7. What is credit note?
8. What do you mean by voucher?
9. What is a supporting voucher?
10. Define an accounting voucher and transfer vouchers.
11. What do you mean by debit voucher?
12. What do you mean by credit voucher?

II. Long Answer Type Questions

1. What do you mean by source of documents and a voucher? Distinguish between them.
2. What is an accounting voucher? What are its types? Give a specimen of an accounting voucher.
3. "Source of documents is the basis of a voucher." Do you agree with this? Give reasons in support of your answer.

III. Problems

1. Prepare debit Voucher from the following particulars in the books of M/s S. P. Syndicate:
   (a) On 12.12.08, purchased furniture in cash Rs. 14,600 (Cash memo no. E/34).
   (b) On 21.12.08, paid shop rent Rs. 7,000(Cash memo no. D/67).
2. Prepare credit voucher from the following particulars in the books of M/s S. P. Syndicate:
   (a) On 05.12.08, sold old machine at Rs. 14,600 in cash (cash memo no. F/14).
   (b) On 24.12.08, sold goods for cash Rs. 37,000(cash memo no. D/67).
3. Prepare transfer voucher from the following particulars in the books of M/s S. P. Syndicate:
   (a) On 05.12.08 purchased furniture on credit from M/s GT. Bros at Rs. 14,600 (bill no. K/23).
   (b) On 20.12.08, sold goods on credit to Mr. KL. Das for Rs. 12,000 (bill no. D/12).

6

Accounting Equation

CONTENTS

- Accounting Equation
  - Presentation of Accounting Equation
- General Guidelines for the Accounting Equation
- Effect of Transactions on Accounting Equation

6.1 ACCOUNTING EQUATION

The accounting equation is based on the principle of dual-aspect (or duality) concept which is the basis of our accountancy. The double entry system of book keeping is created with the help of this concept. The **accounting equation** represents the equality which exists between the resources owned by an enterprise and the claims against the enterprise in relation to those resources. One side of the accounting equation expresses the amount of resources held by an enterprise while the other side shows how the acquisition of the said assets has been financed by the owner (through capital contribution) and from borrowed funds(through loans).

The following fundamental accounting equation may be drawn from the above discussion:

$$\text{Owner's Equity + Outsiders' Equity = Total Assets}$$

or

$$\text{Capital + Liabilities = Total Assets}$$

The concept underlying the accounting equation is that the enterprise itself is a vehicle, and transactions keep this entity running. Accounting records these transactions, measures their impacts on the assets and liabilities, and ultimately prepares financial statements for various groups of users.

6.1.1 Presentation of Accounting Equation

Generally, assets or goods are purchased or acquired with the help of the funds provided by the owners and outside parties, i.e., creditors, banks, and financial institutions. These funds are called **equities** and are of two types—inside or owner's equity (or capital + profit) and outsider's equity (creditors, bank loan, etc.). Thus, according to the duality concept, every transaction will affect at least two items and the outcome of such a transaction will be equal to the total assets [owner's equity (capital + profit) + Liabilities].

It follows from this discussion that the balance sheet indicates the financial position of an enterprise at a given point in time, i.e., a list of assets and liabilities, and according to our fundamental accounting equation stated above, both lists will be equal in total.

6.1.2 General Guidelines for the Accounting Equation

$$\text{Capital + Outside Liabilities = Total Assets}$$

or

$$\text{Capital = Total Assets – Outside Liabilities}$$

or

$$\text{Owner's Equity (Capital + Profit) = Total Assets – Outside Liabilities}$$

Accounting equation
Total Liabilities(Owner's Equity + Outside Liabilities) = Total Assets

Herd of different liabilities	Herd of different assets
Owner's equity (Capital + Profit)	Fixed assets
+	+
Creditors	Debtors
+	+
Loan received	Investments
+	+
Bills payable	Stock in hand
+	+
Outstanding expenses	Cash in hand and at bank
=	=
Total liabilities	Total assets

6.1.3 Effect of Transactions on Accounting Equation

The general guidelines for assessing the impact and effect of transactions on total assets and liabilities as per accounting equation are given below:

1. *For all incomes*
   (a) *When received in cash:* Total assets and capital will increase.
   (b) *When due but not received:* Total assets and capital will increase.
2. *For all expenses*
   (a) *When paid in cash:* Total assets and capital will decrease.
   (b) *When due but not paid:* Capital will decrease and liabilities will increase.
3. *For purchasing fixed assets on credit:* Capital will remain intact, and total assets and liabilities will increase.
4. *For purchasing fixed assets in cash:* Capital and total assets will remain intact.
5. *When capital is withdrawn:* Both capital and total assets will decrease.
6. *When capital is introduced:* Both capital and total assets will increase.
7. *For taking loan:* Both outside liabilities and total assets will increase.
8. *For repayment of loan:* Both outside liabilities and total assets will decrease.
9. *For loss of assets or stock:* Both capital and total assets will decrease.

The above-stated impact and effect of transactions on total assets and liabilities as per the accounting equation are shown in Table 6.1 through imaginary figures:

TABLE 6.1 Accounting Equation

Sl. No.	Transactions	Capital + Outside Liabilities = Total Liabilities			Total Assets
		Rs.	Rs.	Rs.	Rs.
1.	Mr. X started his business with Cash Rs. 75,000. [both Cash and Capital will increase by Rs. 75,000]	+75,000	0	75,000	75,000
2.	Purchased goods for Cash Rs. 8,000. [Stock will increase by Rs. 8,000 and Cash will decrease by Rs. 8,000]	0	0	75,000	+8,000 −8,000 75,000
3.	Opened a Bank A/c with Cash Rs. 30,000. [Bank balance will increase by Rs. 30,000 and Cash will decrease by Rs. 30,000]	0	0	75,000	+30,000 −30,000 75,000
4.	Paid for Advertisement Rs. 700. [Cash and Capital both will decrease by Rs. 700]	−700 74,300	0	74,300	−700 74,300

(Contd.)

Sl. no.	Transactions	Capital + Outside Liabilities = Total Liabilities			Total Assets
		Rs.	Rs.	Rs.	Rs.
5.	Purchased office furniture in Cash Rs. 1,800. [Furniture to be shown as Rs. 1,800 and Cash will decrease by Rs. 1,800]	0	0	74,300	+1,800 −1,800 74,300
6.	Proprietor's house Rent paid Rs. 900. [Cash and Capital both will decrease by Rs. 900]	−900 73,400	0	73,400	−900 73,400
7.	Sold goods of Rs. 4,500 at Rs. 6,500 in Cash. [Stock will decrease by Rs. 4,500; Cash will increase by Rs. 6,500; and Capital will increase by Rs. 2,000 for profit]	+2,000 75,400	0	75,400	−4,500 +6,500 75,400
8.	Purchased goods on credit from Q & Co. for Rs. 9,000. [Stock and Creditors(Q & Co.) both will increase by Rs.9,000]	0	+9,000 Creditors (Q & Co.) 84,400		+9,000 84,400
9.	Carriage paid on goods purchased Rs. 400. [Cash and Capital both will decrease by Rs. 400]	−400 75,000		84,000	−400 84,000
10.	Purchased machinery and paid by Cheque of Rs. 8,000. [Machinery to be shown as Rs. 8,000 and Cash will decrease by Rs. 8,000]	0	0	84,000	+8,000 −8,000 84,000
11.	Commission received Rs. 1,200. [Cash and capital both will increase by Rs. 1,200]	+1,200 76,200	0	85,200	+1,200 85,200
12.	Sold goods to K.K. Traders for Rs. 7,500 (cost of goods sold Rs. 5000). [Debtors will increase by Rs. 7,500; Stock will reduce by Rs. 5,000; and Capital will increase by Rs. 2,500]	+2,500 78,700	0	87,700	+7,500 −5,000 87,700
13.	Interest on fixed deposits due but not received Rs. 1,500. [Accrued interest of Rs. 1,500 to be shown as an asset and Capital will increase by Rs. 1,500]	+1,500 80,200	0	89,200	+1,500 89,200
14.	Life insurance premium of proprietor paid by Cheque Rs. 1,200. [Bank balance and Capital both will decrease by Rs. 1,200]	−1,200 79,000	0	88,000	−1,200 88,000
15.	Paid to Q & Co. Rs. 3,000. [Cash and Q & Co.'s balance will reduce by Rs. 3,000]	0	−3,000 6,000	85,000	−3,000 85,000

The effect of each individual transaction in comparison to the previous one on total assets and liabilities as per accounting equation is shown through a statement to show the net financial position (on the basis of previous example):

1. Mr. X started his business with Cash Rs.75,000.

Financial Position

Liabilities	Rs.	Assets	Rs.
Capital	75,000	Cash in hand	75,000
	75,000		75,000

2. Purchased goods for Cash Rs. 8,000.

Financial Position (Revised after item No.2.)

Liabilities	Rs.	Assets	Rs.
Capital	75,000	Cash in hand (Rs. 75,000 − Rs. 8,000) Stock in hand	67,000 8,000
	75,000		75,000

3. Opened a Bank A/c with Cash Rs. 30,000.

Financial Position (Revised after item No. 3.)

Liabilities	Rs.	Assets	Rs.
Capital	75,000	Cash in hand (Rs. 67,000 – Rs. 30,000)	37,000
		Cash in at bank	30,000
		Stock in hand	8,000
	75,000		75,000

4. Paid for advertisement Rs. 700.

Financial Position (Revised after item No. 4.)

Liabilities	Rs.	Assets	Rs.
Capital (Rs. 75,000 – Rs. 700)	74,300	Cash in hand (Rs. 37,000 – Rs. 700)	36,300
		Cash in at bank	30,000
		Stock in hand	8,000
	74,300		74,300

5. Purchased office furniture in Cash Rs. 1,800.

Financial Position (Revised after item No. 5.)

Liabilities	Rs.	Assets	Rs.
Capital	74,300	Furniture	1,800
		Cash in hand (Rs. 36,300 – Rs. 1,800)	34,500
		Cash at bank	30,000
		Stock in hand	8,000
	74,300		74,300

6. Proprietor's house rent paid Rs. 900.

Financial Position (Revised after item No. 6.)

Liabilities		Rs.	Assets	Rs.
Capital	74,300		Furniture	1,800
Less: Drawing	900	73,400	Cash in hand (Rs. 34,500 – Rs. 900)	33,600
			Cash at bank	30,000
			Stock in hand	8,000
		73,400		73,400

7. Sold goods of Rs. 4,500 at Rs. 6,500 in cash.

Financial Position (Revised after item No. 7.)

Liabilities		Rs.	Assets	Rs.
Capital	73,400		Furniture	1,800
Add: Profit on sale	2,000	75,400	Cash in hand (Rs. 33,600 + Rs. 6,500)	40,100
			Cash at bank	30,000
			Stock in hand (Rs. 8,000 – Rs. 4,500)	3,500
		75,400		75,400

8. Purchased goods on credit from Q & Co. for Rs. 9,000.

Financial Position (Revised after item No. 8.)

Liabilities	Rs.	Assets	Rs.
Capital	75,400	Furniture	1,800
Creditors	9,000	Cash in hand (Rs. 33,600 + Rs. 6,500)	40,100
(Q & Co.)		Cash at bank	30,000
		Stock in hand (Rs. 3,500 + Rs. 9,000)	12,500
	84,400		84,400

9. Carriage paid on goods purchased Rs. 400.

Financial Position (Revised after item No. 9.)

Liabilities	Rs.	Assets	Rs.
Capital (Rs. 75,400 – Rs. 400)	75,000	Furniture	1,800
Creditors	9,000	Cash in hand (Rs. 40,100 – Rs. 400)	39,700
(Q & Co.)		Cash at bank	30,000
		Stock in hand	12,500
	84,000		84,000

10. Purchased machinery and paid by cheque of Rs. 8,000.

Financial Position (Revised after item No. 10.)

Liabilities	Rs.	Assets	Rs.
Capital	75,000	Furniture	1,800
Creditors	9,000	Machinery	8,000
(Q & Co.)		Cash at bank (Rs. 30,000 – Rs. 8,000)	22,000
		Cash in hand	39,700
		Stock in hand	12,500
	84,000		84,000

11. Commission received Rs. 1,200.

Financial Position (Revised after item No. 11.)

Liabilities	Rs.	Assets	Rs.
Capital (Rs. 75,000 + Rs. 1,200)	76,200	Furniture	1,800
Creditors	9,000	Machinery	8,000
(Q & Co.)		Cash at bank	22,000
		Cash in hand (Rs. 39,700 + Rs. 1,200)	40,900
		Stock in hand	12,500
	85,200		85,200

12. Sold goods to K.K. Traders for Rs. 7,500 (Cost of goods sold Rs. 5000).

Financial Position (Revised after item No. 12.)

Liabilities	Rs.	Assets	Rs.
Capital (Rs. 76,200 + Rs. 2,500)	78,700	Furniture	1,800
Creditors	9,000	Machinery	8,000
(Q & Co.)		Debtors	7,500
		Cash at bank	22,000
		Cash in hand (Rs. 40,900)	40,900
		Stock in hand (12,500 – 5,000)	7,500
	87,700		87,700

13. Interest on fixed deposits due but not received Rs. 1,500.

Financial Position (Revised after item No. 13.)

Liabilities	Rs.	Assets	Rs.
Capital (Rs. 78,700 + Rs. 1,500)	80,200	Furniture	1,800
Creditors	9,000	Machinery	8,000
(Q & Co.)		Debtors	7,500
		Cash at bank	22,000
		Accrued interest on fixed deposit	1,500
		Cash in hand	40,900
		Stock in hand	7,500
	89,200		89,200

14. Life insurance premium of proprietor paid by Cheque Rs. 1,200.

Financial Position (Revised after item No. 14.)

Liabilities	Rs.	Assets	Rs.
Capital (Rs. 80,200 – Rs. 1,200)	79,000	Furniture	1,800
Creditors	9,000	Machinery	8,000
(Q & Co.)		Debtors	7,500
		Cash at bank (Rs. 22,000 – Rs. 1,200)	20,800
		Accrued interest on fixed deposit	1,500
		Cash in hand	40,900
		Stock in hand	7,500
	88,000		88,000

15. Paid to Q & Co. Rs. 3,000.

Financial Position (Revised after item No. 15.)

Liabilities	Rs.	Assets	Rs.
Capital	79,000	Furniture	1,800
Creditors (Rs. 9,000 – Rs. 3,000)	6,000	Machinery	8,000
(Q & Co.)		Debtors	7,500
		Cash at bank	20,800
		Accrued interest on fixed deposit	1,500
		Cash in hand (Rs. 40,900 – Rs. 3,000)	37,900
		Stock in hand	7,500
	85,000		85,000

ILLUSTRATION 6.1 On the basis of guidelines of accounting equation, the effect of a transaction on total assets and liabilities is shown in the following table.

	Transactions	Total assets Rs.	=	Total liabilities Rs.	+	Capital Rs.
1.	Mr. A started business with Cash Rs. 75,000	75,000	=		+	75,000
2.	Purchased goods for cash Rs. 8,000 (Cash – 8,000 and Stock + 8,000)	(–) 8,000 (+) 8,000				
	Net Position	**75,000**	=		+	**75,000**
3.	Opened a Bank A/c with Cash Rs. 30,000 (Cash – 30,000 and Bank + 30,000)	(–) 30,000 (+) 30,000				
	Net Position	**75,000**	=		+	**75,000**
4.	Paid for advertisement Rs. 700	(–) 700				(–) 700
	Net Position	**74,300**	=		+	**74,300**
5.	Purchased office furniture in Cash Rs. 1,800	(–) 1,800 (+) 1,800				
	Net Position	**74,300**	=		+	**74,300**
6.	Proprietor's house rent paid Rs. 900 (Drawings)	(–) 900				(–) 900
	Net Position	**73,400**	=		+	**73,400**
7.	Sold goods for Cash Rs. 6,500 (Cost of goods sold = Rs. 4,500)	(+) 6,500 (–) 4,500				(+) 2,000 (profit)
	[Assets + Cash – Goods 73,400 + 6,500 – 4,500 = 75,400 Capital + Profit = 73,400 + 2000 = 75,400	(–) 4,500				(–) 4,500
	Net Position	75,400	=			75,400
8.	Purchased goods on credit from X & Co. Rs. 9,000	(Goods) (+) 9,000		(X & Co.) (+) 9,000		
	Net Position	**84,400**	=	**9,000**	+	**75,400**
9.	Carriage paid on goods purchased Rs. 400.	(–) 400			+	(–) 400
	Net Position	**84,000**	=	**9,000**	+	**75,000**
						(Contd.)

	Transactions	Total assets Rs.	=	Total liabilities Rs.	+	Capital Rs.
10.	Purchased machinery and paid by Cheque Rs. 8,000	(−) 8,000 (+) 8,000				
	Net Position	**84,000**	=	**9,000**	+	**75,000**
11.	Fresh Capital paid by Mr. A Rs. 9,000	(+) 9,000				(+) 9,000
	Net Position	**93,000**	=	**9,000**	+	**84,000**
12.	Purchased furniture for Rs. 6,000	(+) 6,000 (−) 6,000				
	Net Position	**(+) 93,000**	=	**9,000**	+	**84,000**
13.	Commission received Rs. 1,200	(+) 1,200			+	(+) 1,200
	Net Position	**94,200**	=	**9,000**	+	**85,200**
14.	Cash paid to X and Co. Rs. 3,000	(−) 3,000	=	(−) 3,000		
	Net Position	**91,200**	=	**6,000**	+	**85,200**
15.	Sold goods to K.K. Traders for Rs. 7,500 (Cost of goods sold Rs. 5,000)	(−) 5,000 (+) 7,500				(Profit) (+) 2,500
	Net Position	**93,700**	=	**6,000**	+	**87,700**
16.	Loan taken from P.K. Bose Rs. 8,000	(+) 8,000		(+) 8,000		
	Net Position	**101,700**	=	**14,000**	+	**87,700**
17.	Furniture of the book value of Rs. 500 sold at Rs. 300	(+) 300 (−) 500				(−) 200 (Loss on sale)
	Net Position	**101,500**	=	**14,000**	+	**87,500**
18.	Received interest from Bank Rs. 400	(+) 400				(+) 400
	Net Position	**101,900**	=	**14,000**	+	**87,900**

ILLUSTRATION 6.2 Mr. P started his business with cash of Rs. 60,000 and at the end of the year, his position was as follows:

1. Cash Rs. 26,700
2. Stock Rs. 8,000
3. Furniture Rs. 10,000
4. Machinery Rs. 28,000
5. Bank Balance Rs. 23,600
6. Loan Rs. 9,000.

Calculate the following on the basis of Accounting Equation:

1. Owner's Equity
2. Total Liabilities
3. Profit
4. Show the closing position with the help of on equation.

Solution

As per Accounting Equation

Total Assets = Total Liabilities

or Owner's Equity (Capital + Profit) = Total Assets – Outside Liabilities

Here, Total Assets at the end of the year = Rs. 26,700 (Cash) Rs. 8,000 (Stock) Rs. 10,000 (Furniture) Rs. 28,000 (Machinery) Rs. 23,600 (Bank Balance) = Rs. 96,300.

Total Assets = Total Liabilities

Thus, Total Liabilities = Rs.96,300.

Total Liabilities = Owner's Equity (Capital + Profit) + Outside Liabilities

Hence, Total Liabilities (Rs. 96,300) = Owner's Equity (Capital + Profit) + Loan (Rs. 9,000)

Owner's Equity (Capital + Profit) = Rs. 96,300 – Rs. 9,000 = Rs. 87,300

Profit = Closing Capital – Opening Capital

= Closing Owner's Equity – Opening Owner's Equity

= Rs. 87,300 – Rs. 60,000 = Rs. 27,300.

Liabilities	Rs.	Assets	Rs.
Capital	60,000	Machinery	28,000
Add: Profit	27,300	Furniture	10,000
Owner's Equity	87,300	Stock	8,000
Loan	9,000	Bank Balance	23,600
		Cash	26,700
	96,300		96,300

ILLUSTRATION 6.3   Mr. GG started his business with cash of Rs. 59,000 on January 2009, and during the month, the following transactions took place:

1. Goods purchased on credit for Rs. 18,000.
2. Salary paid Rs. 6,000
3. Paid for advertisement Rs. 4,500
4. LIP of proprietor paid Rs. 3,000
5. Goods sold on credit at Rs. 14,000 (Cost Rs. 8,000)
6. Commission received Rs. 2,500
7. Goods sold in cash at Rs. 11,000 (Cost Rs. 6,000)
8. Goods purchased in cash Rs. 12,000
9. Computer purchased at Rs. 16,000
10. Received loan from Mr. X Rs. 10,000

Represent the above transactions in a tabular form showing closing position of Mr. GG as per Accounting Equation.

Solution

Sl. No.	Transactions	Assets					Liabilities			
		Cash	Debtors	Stock	Computer	Total	Capital	Creditors	Loan-X	Total
	Business started with cash	+59,000					+ 59,000			
	Net Position	**59,000**	**0**	**0**	**0**	**59,000**	**59,000**	**0**	**0**	**59,000**
1.	Goods purchased			+18,000				+18,000		
	Net Position	**59,000**	**0**	**18,000**	**0**	**77,000**	**59,000**	**18,000**	**0**	**77,000**
2.	Salary paid	−6,000					−6,000			
	Net Position	**53,000**	**0**	**18,000**	**0**	**71,000**	**53,000**	**18,000**	**0**	**71,000**
3.	Advertisement paid	−4,500					−4,500			
	Net Position	**48,500**	**0**	**18,000**	**0**	**66,500**	**48,500**	**18,000**	**0**	**66,500**
4.	LIP of proprietor paid	−3,000					−3,000			
	Net Position	**45,500**	**0**	**18,000**	**0**	**63,500**	**45,500**	**18,000**	**0**	**63,500**
5.	Goods sold on credit (Cost Rs. 8,000)		+14,000	−8,000			+6,000 (Profit)			
	Net Position	**45,500**	**14,000**	**10,000**	**0**	**69,500**	**51,500**	**18,000**	**0**	**69,500**
6.	Commission received	+2,500					+2,500			
	Net Position	**48,000**	**14,000**	**10,000**	**0**	**72,000**	**54,000**	**18,000**	**0**	**72,000**
7.	Goods sold in cash (Cost Rs. 6,000)	+11,000		−6,000			+5,000 (Profit)			
	Net Position	**59,000**	**14,000**	**4,000**	**0**	**77,000**	**59,000**	**18,000**	**0**	**77,000**
8.	Goods purchased	−12,000		+12,000						
	Net Position	**47,000**	**14,000**	**16,000**	**0**	**77,000**	**59,000**	**18,000**	**0**	**77,000**

(Contd.)

Sl. no.	Transactions	Assets					Liabilities			
		Cash	Debtors	Stock	Computer	Total	Capital	Creditors	Loan-X	Total
9.	Computer purchased	−16,000			+16,000					
	Net Position	**31,000**	**14,000**	**16,000**	**16,000**	**77,000**	**59,000**	**18,000**	**0**	**77,000**
10.	Loan received	+10,000							+10,000	
	Net Position	**41,000**	**14,000**	**16,000**	**16,000**	**87,000**	**59,000**	**18,000**	**10,000**	**87,000**

ILLUSTRATION 6.4 Prepare a statement in a tabular form showing the closing position of Mr. K K as per Accounting Equation on the basis of following transactions:

1. Mr. KK started his business with cash Rs. 68,000
2. Purchased machinery in cash Rs. 21,000
3. Goods purchased on credit for Rs. 15,000
4. Goods costing Rs. 12,000 sold on credit at a profit of 30% on cost.
5. Received loan from Mr. X Rs. 15,000
6. Cash received from debtors Rs. 6,000
7. Travelling expenses paid Rs. 2,500
8. Goods purchased on credit for Rs. 10,000
9. Proprietor's house rent paid Rs. 2,000 (Drawings)
10. Goods sold on credit for Rs. 10,000 at a profit of 25% on cost.

Solution

Sl. no.	Transactions	Assets					Liabilities			
		Cash	Debtors	Stock	Machinery	Total	Capital	Creditors	Loan-X	Total
1.	Business started with cash	+ 68,000					+68,000			
	Net Position	**68,000**	**0**	**0**	**0**	**68,000**	**68,000**	**0**	**0**	**68,000**
2.	Machinery purchased	−21,000			+ 21,000					
	Net Position	**47,000**	**0**	**0**	**21,000**	**68,000**	**68,000**	**0**	**0**	**68,000**
3.	Goods purchased			+ 15,000				+ 15,000		
	Net Position	**47,000**	**0**	**15,000**	**21,000**	**83,000**	**68,000**	**15,000**	**0**	**83,000**
4.	Goods sold (profit Rs.3,600)		+ 15,600	−12,000			+ 3,600			
	Net Position	**47,000**	**15,600**	**3,000**	**21,000**	**86,600**	**71,600**	**15,000**	**0**	**86,600**
5.	Loan from-X	+ 15,000							+ 15,000	
	Net Position	**62,000**	**15,600**	**3,000**	**21,000**	**101,600**	**71,600**	**15,000**	**15,000**	**101,600**
6.	Cash received from debtors	+ 6,000	−6,000							
	Net Position	**68,000**	**9,600**	**3,000**	**21,000**	**101,600**	**71,600**	**15,000**	**15,000**	**101,600**
7.	Travelling expenses paid	−2,500					−2,500			
	Net Position	**65,500**	**9,600**	**3,000**	**21,000**	**99,100**	**69,100**	**15,000**	**15,000**	**99,100**
8.	Goods purchased			+ 10,000				+10,000		
	Net Position	**65,500**	**9,600**	**13,000**	**21,000**	**109,100**	**69,100**	**25,000**	**15,000**	**109,100**
9.	Proprietor's house rent paid	−2,000					−2,000			
	Net Position	**63,500**	**9,600**	**13,000**	**21,000**	**107,100**	**67,100**	**25,000**	**15,000**	**107,100**
10.	Goods sold (Profit = 25/125 × 10,000 = 2,000)		+ 10,000	−8,000			+ 2,000			
	Net Position	**63,500**	**19,600**	**5,000**	**21,000**	**109,100**	**69,100**	**25,000**	**15,000**	**109,100**

ILLUSTRATION 6.5 Mr. SS started his business with cash of Rs. 36,000 and the following transactions took place during the previous month:

1. Purchased goods from Kartic for Rs. 9,000 on credit
2. Paid carriage on purchase Rs. 300
3. Goods costing Rs. 1,200 were sold to Pradip at Rs. 1,800 on credit
4. Purchased furniture for Rs. 6,000 in cash
5. Paid salary to a staff member as an advance Rs. 2,000
6. Shop rent outstanding Rs. 2,100
7. Cash received from a customer Rs. 3,000 as an advance.
8. Old furniture of Rs. 2,400 sold at Rs. 1,900
9. Sold goods for cash Rs. 9,000(goods are sold at a profit of 25% on selling price).
10. Goods costing Rs. 500 were used by Mr. SS for personal purpose.

Show his closing position as per Accounting Equation. Also, show the effect of a transaction on Total Assets and Liabilities.

Solution

Sl. No.	Transactions	Assets					Liabilities			
		Cash + Debtors + Stock + Furniture = Total Assets					Capital + Creditors + Outstanding = Total Liabilities			
		Cash	Debtors	Stock	Furniture and advance salary	Total Assests	Capital	Creditors	Outstanding and advance received	Total Liabilities
	Business started with cash	+ 36,000					+36,000			
	Net Position	**36,000**	**0**	**0**	**0**	**36,000**	**36,000**	**0**	**0**	**36,000**
1.	Goods purchased on credit			+ 9,000				+9,000		
	Net Position	**36,000**	**0**	**9,000**	**0**	**45,000**	**36,000**	**9,000**	**0**	**45,000**
2.	Carriage paid	−300					−300			
	Net Position	**35,700**	**0**	**9,000**	**0**	**44,700**	**35,700**	**9,000**	**0**	**44,700**
3.	Goods sold on credit. Profit is Rs. 600		+1,800	−1,200			+600			
	Net Position	**35,700**	**1,800**	**7,800**	**0**	**45,300**	**36,300**	**9,000**	**0**	**45,300**
4.	Purchased furniture	−6,000			+6,000					
	Net Position	**29,700**	**1,800**	**7,800**	**6,000**	**45,300**	**36,300**	**9,000**	**0**	**45,300**
5.	Paid advance salary	−2,000			+2,000					
	Net Position	**27,700**	**1,800**	**7,800**	**8,000**	**45,300**	**36,300**	**9,000**	**0**	**45,300**
6.	Shop rent outstanding						−2,100		+2,100	
	Net Position	**27,700**	**1,800**	**7,800**	**8,000**	**45,300**	**34,200**	**9,000**	**2,100**	**45,300**
7.	Advance received from a customer	+3,000							+3,000	
	Net Position	**30,700**	**1,800**	**7,800**	**8,000**	**48,300**	**34,200**	**9,000**	**5,100**	**48,300**
8.	Old furniture sold (Loss on sale=500)	+1,900			−2,400		−500			
	Net Position	**32,600**	**1,800**	**7,800**	**5,600**	**47,800**	**33,700**	**9,000**	**5,100**	**47,800**
9.	Goods sold (Profit= 25/100 × 9,000 = 2,250)	+9,000		−6,750			+ 2,250			
	Net Position	**41,600**	**1,800**	**1,050**	**5,600**	**50,050**	**35,950**	**9,000**	**5,100**	**50,050**
10.	Personal use of goods (Drawings)			−500			−500			
	Net Position	**41,600**	**1,800**	**550**	**5,600**	**49,550**	**35,450**	**9,000**	**5,100**	**49,550**

Note:
1. Due to shortage of column, Advance salary shown in 'Furniture' column.
2. Outstanding expenses and advance received from customer, both are liability and shown in a single column (Due to shortage of column).

ILLUSTRATION 6.6 Calculate the missing figure from the table given below:

Sl No.	Total Assets (Rs.)	Incomes Received (Rs.)	Expenses Paid (Rs.)	Other Liabilities (Rs.)	Owner's Equity (Capital + Profit)		
					Owner's Equity	Capital (Rs.)	Profit/(Loss) (Rs.)
1.	95,000	18,700	11,200	21,000	?	?	?
2.	?	37,600	41,200	32,000	?	80,000	?
3.	87,400	?	27,600	18,500	?	65,000	3,900

Solution

Sl. No.	Total Assets = Total Liabilities Total Liabilities = Owner's Equity + Other Liabilities Incomes Received – Expenses paid = Profit/(Loss) Owner's Equity = Capital + Profit /(– Loss)
1.	Total Liabilities – Other Liabilities = Owner's Equity Rs. 95,000 – 21,000 = Rs. 74,000 Incomes Received – Expenses Paid = Profit Rs. 18,700 – 11,200 = Rs. 7,500 Owner's Equity – Profit = Capital Rs. 74,000 – 7,500 = Rs. 66,500 **Ans:** Owner's Equity Rs. 74,000; Capital Rs. 66,500; Profit Rs. 7,500.
2.	Expenses Paid – Incomes Received = Loss Rs. 41,200 – 37,600 = Rs. 3,600 Here, Owner's Equity = Capital – Loss Rs. 80,000 – 3,600 = Rs. 76,400 Total Liabilities = Owner's Equity + Other Liabilities Rs. 76,400 + 32,000 = Rs. 1,08,400 **Ans:** Total Assets Rs. 108,400; Owner's Equity Rs. 76,400; Loss Rs. 3,600.
3.	Incomes Received = Expenses Paid + Profit Rs. 27,600 + 3,900 = Rs. 31,500 Owner's Equity = Capital + Profit Rs. 65,000 + 3,900 = Rs. 68,900 **Ans:** Incomes Received Rs. 31,500; Owner's Equity Rs. 68,900.

ILLUSTRATION 6.7 Calculate the missing figure from the table given below:

Sl No.	Total Assets (Rs.)	Incomes Received (Rs.)	Expenses Paid (Rs.)	Other Liabilities (Rs.)	Owner's Equity (Capital + Profit)		
					Owner's Equity	Capital (Rs.)	Profit/(Loss) (Rs.)
1.	94,900	43,700	?	30,000	?	69,400	(4,500)
2.	?	45,300	34,800	34,000	87,800	?	?
3.	132,000	46,200	34,000	?	?	99,800	?

Solution

1.	Expenses Paid = Incomes Received + Loss Rs. 43,700 + 4,500 = Rs. 48,200 Owner's Equity = Capital – Loss Rs. 69,400 – 4,500 = Rs. 64,900 **Ans:** Expenses Paid Rs. 48,200; Owner's Equity Rs.64,900.

(Contd.)

2.	Profit = Incomes Received – Expenses Paid

Rs. 45,300 – 34,800 = Rs. 10,500
Capital = Owner's Equity – Profit
Rs. 87,800 – 10,500 = Rs. 77,300
Total Assets = Owner's Equity + Other Liabilities
Rs. 87,800 + 34,000 = Rs. 121,800
Ans: Profit Rs. 10,500; Capital Rs. 77,300; Total Assets Rs. 121,800.

3.	Profit = Incomes Received – Expenses Paid

Rs. 46,200 – 34,000 = Rs. 12,200
Owner's Equity = Capital + Profit. Rs. 99,800 + 12,200 = Rs. 112,000
Other Liabilities = Total Assets – Owner's Equity
Rs. 132,000 – 112,000 = Rs. 20,000
Ans: Profit Rs. 12,200; Owner's Equity Rs. 112,000; Other Liabilities Rs. 20,000.

EXERCISES

I. Short Answer Type Questions

1. What do you mean by Accounting Equation?
2. What is Owner's Equity?
3. What is Outsider's Equity?
4. What is the effect of profit on sale of goods on Owner's Equity?
5. What is the effect of loss on sale of goods on Owner's Equity?

II. Long Answer Type Questions

1. What do you mean by Accounting Equation? On the basis of some imaginary transactions, show the effect of a transaction on Total Assets and Liabilities as per the guidelines of Accounting Equation.
2. How can you establish that the Accounting Equation (Assets = Liabilities) is true under all circumstances? Prove the validity of your answer with imaginary transactions.

III. Problems

1. Give the missing figures from the table shown below:

	Total Assets (Rs.)	Total Liabilities (Rs.)	Owner's Equity or Capital (Rs.)
(a)	29,000	9,000	?
(b)	42,000	?	31,000
(c)	?	10,500	32,500
(d)	58,000	0	?
(e)	50,000	25,000	?

Ans: (a) Rs. 20,000 (b) Rs. 11,000 (c) Rs. 43,000 (d) Rs. 58,000 (e) Rs. 25,000

2. Calculate the missing figures from the table given below:
Adjusted with assets only

	Total Assets Rs.	Expenses Paid in Cash Rs.	Incomes Received in cash Rs.	Liabilities Rs.	Capital Rs.
(a)	34,000	4,000	6,000	11,000	?
(b)	42,000	—	3,000	9,000	?
(c)	51,000	8,000	—	8,000	?
(d)	45,000	2,000	?	4,000	43,000
(e)	39,000	?	4,800	5,600	29,400
(f)	?	3,000	4,000	8,000	40,000
(g)	41,000	2,800	3,900	?	31,000
(h)	50,000	3,000	?	6,000	42,000

[**Hint:** Total Assets = Capital Net + Liabilities

Capital – Expenses + Income = Capital Net]

Ans: (a) Rs. 21,000 (b) Rs. 30,000 (c) Rs. 51,000 (d) Rs. 0 (e) Rs. 800 (f) Rs. 49,000 (g) Rs. 8,900 (h) Rs. 5,000.

3. With the help of Accounting Equation and the data mentioned below, describe the possible transactions for the items (a) to (g):

	Cash	+	Goods	+	Fixed assets	=	Capital	+	Liabilities
	b/f 25,000	+	8,000	+	17,000	=	45,000	+	5,000
(a)	(+) 4,000	+	(–) 3,000	+	—	=	(+) 1,000	+	—
(b)	(–) 3,000	+	(+) 7,000	+	—	=	—	+	(+) 4,000
(c)	(+) 5,000	+			(–) 6,000	=	(–) 1,000	+	—
(d)	—		(+) 6,000		—	=	—		(+) 6,000
(e)	(–) 1,000		(+) 5,000		—	=	—		(+) 4,000
(f)	(+) 9,000		(–) 6,000		—	=	(+) 3,000		—
(g)	(–) 4,000		—		(+) 8,000	=	—		(+) 4,000

Ans: (a) Goods of Rs. 3,000 sold at Rs. 4,000 (b) Goods of Rs. 3,000 purchased in cash and Rs. 4,000 on Credit (c) Fixed assets of Rs. 6,000 sold at Rs. 5,000 (d) Goods of Rs. 6,000 purchased on credit (e) Goods of Rs. 1,000 purchased in cash and Rs. 4,000 on credit (f) Goods of Rs. 6,000 sold at Rs. 9,000 (g) Fixed assets of Rs. 8,000 purchased on credit but out of that paid in cash Rs. 4,000 only.

4. Prove that the Accounting Equation is satisfied in all the following transactions of Ramesh:
   (a) Commenced business with cash Rs. 60,000
   (b) Rent paid in advance Rs. 500
   (c) Purchased goods for Cash Rs. 30,000 and for credit Rs. 20,000
   (d) Sold goods costing Rs. 20,000, for Cash Rs. 30,000
   (e) Paid Salary Rs. 500 and Salary outstanding Rs. 100
   (f) Bought Motorcycle for personal use Rs. 5,000.
   [All India Higher Secondary Examination, adapted]

   Ans: Rs. 84,500 (Assets) = Rs. 64,400 (Capital) + Rs. 20,100 (Liabilities).

5. Sunil had the following transactions. Use Accounting Equation to show their effects on his Assets, Liabilities and Capital.
   (a) Commenced business with Cash Rs. 50,000
   (b) Purchased goods for Cash Rs. 20,000 and for Credit Rs. 30,000
   (c) Sold goods costing Rs. 30,000 for Cash Rs. 40,000
   (d) Rent paid Rs. 500
   (e) Rent outstanding Rs. 100
   (f) Bought furniture Rs. 5,000 on Credit
   (g) Bought refrigerator for personal use of Sunil Rs. 5,000
   (h) Purchased building for Cash Rs. 20,000
   [All India Higher Secondary Examination, adapted]

   Ans: Assets Rs. 89,500; Liabilities Rs. 35,100; Owner's Equity Rs. 54,400).

6. Ravindranath had the following transactions. Use Accounting Equation to show their effects on his Assets, Liabilities and Capital:
   (a) Investment Rs. 15,000 in Cash
   (b) Purchases securities for Cash Rs. 7,500
   (c) Purchased a building for Rs. 15,000 giving Rs. 5,000 in Cash and the balance being treated as loan
   (d) Sold securities costing Rs. 1,000 for Rs. 1,500
   (e) Purchased an old car for Rs. 2,800 in Cash

(f) Received Cash as Salary Rs. 3,600
(g) Paid Cash Rs. 500 for loan and Rs. 300 for interest
(h) Paid cash for household Expenses Rs. 300
(i) Received Cash for dividend on securities Rs. 200.

(All India Higher Secondary Examination)

Hint: [Liabilities + Capital = Total assets]
Assets = Rs. 28,200; Liabilities = Rs. 9,500; Capital = Rs. 18,700

Ans: (a) Assets, Cash Rs. 15,000 and Owner's Equity Rs. 15,000 (b) Assets, securities Rs. 7,500 and Cash Rs. 7,500 etc.

7. Find out the missing figure from the table given below on the basis of the equation (Total Assets = Capital + Liabilities)
   (a) Cash Rs. 18,000; Loan from Mr. X Rs. 10,000, Machinery Rs. 20,000; Patent Rs. 5,000; and Capital Rs.?
   (b) Capital Rs. 60,000; Loan to Mr. Y Rs. 4,000; Bank Overdraft Rs. 5,000; Goodwill Rs. 6,000, Machinery Rs. 40,000; and Cash Rs.?
   (c) Reserves Rs. 5,000; Trade Creditors Rs. 12,000; Advance given Rs. 2,000, Prepaid Expenses Rs. 1,000, Investment Rs. 10,000, Cash Rs. 21,000, Fixed Assets Rs. 30,000 and Capital Rs. ?
   (d) Sundry Debtors Rs. 9,000; Closing Stock Rs. 5,000; Trade Mark Rs. 3,000; Outstanding Expenses Rs. 2,000; loan Rs. 6,000; Cash Rs. 18,000 and Capital Rs.?
   Ans: (a) Rs. 33,000 (b) Rs. 15,000 (c) Rs. 47,000 (d) Rs. 27,000.

8. The summary data of Sarkar & Co. are given below in the equation form. Describe the possible transactions for entries (a) to (f).

	Cash	+	Goods	+	Machine	=	Liability	+	Capital
	Balance = 10,000		6,000		5,000	=	6,000		15,000
(a)	−5,000	+	5,000			=			
(b)		+	4,000			=	4,000		
(c)	−1,000	+	2,000			=	+1,000		
(d)	+1,800	−	1,000			=		+	800
(e)	−4,000					=	−4,000		
(f)	−800					=		−	−800

(CBSE)

Ans: (a) Goods purchased for cash (b) Good purchased on credit (c) Goods purchased for cash Rs. 1,000 and on credit Rs. 1,000 (d) Sale of goods for cash Rs. 1,000, capital introduction Rs. 800 (e) Liabilities paid off in cash Rs. 4,000 (f) Drawings in cash Rs. 800.

9. Prepare Accounting Equation of Mr. D.D. on the basis of the following transactions:
   (a) Started business with cash Rs. 54,000
   (b) Purchased furniture for cash Rs. 5,000
   (c) Purchased goods on credit from Mr. G Rs. 8,000
   (d) Sold goods costing Rs. 4,200 at Rs. 5,600
   (e) Purchased a Computer in cash Rs. 15,000
   (f) Paid shop rent Rs. 900
   (g) House rent of Mr. D.D. paid Rs. 2,400
   (h) Loan taken from Mr. R Rs. 10,000

Ans: Owner's Equity Rs. 52,100; Loan Rs. 10,000; Mr. G Rs. 8,000; Total Liabilities/Assets Rs. 70,100; Cash Rs. 46,300; Computer Rs. 15,000; Furniture Rs. 5,000 and Goods Rs. 3,800 (8,000 − 4,200).

10. On July 1, 2008, the position of Assets and Liabilities were as follows:

Liabilities	Rs.	Assets	Rs.
Capital	113,000	Building	60,000
Creditors	7,000	Machinery	31,000
Loan	10,000	Furniture	11,000
		Debtors	9,000
		Closing Stock	3,000
		Cash in hand	16,000
	130,000		130,000

The following transactions took place during the month of July 2008:
(a) Goods purchased on credit Rs. 9,000 and in cash Rs. 4,000
(b) Goods of Rs. 6,000 sold at Rs. 10,900 in cash
(c) Cash realized from Debtors Rs. 4,100 and discount allowed Rs. 200
(d) Loan paid Rs. 4,000 and paid interest Rs. 200
(e) Proprietor's house rent paid Rs. 600
(f) Miscellaneous expenses paid Rs. 900
(g) Machinery purchased on credit Rs. 4,000
(h) Cash paid to creditors Rs. 1,900 and discount allowed by them Rs. 100.
Show the effects of the above transactions on Assets, Liabilities and Capital.
Ans: Position on July 31, 2008: Capital Rs. 116,100; Loan Rs. 6,000; Creditors Rs. 18,000; Total Liabilities/Assets Rs. 140,100; Cash Rs. 23,400; Stock Rs. 6,000; Debtors Rs. 4,700; Machinery Rs. 35,000; Furniture Rs. 11,000; Building Rs. 60,000.

7

Recording of Business Transactions: Rules of Debit and Credit

CONTENTS

- Meaning of Debit and Credit
- Rules of Debit and Credit

• Accounts

7.1 MEANING OF DEBIT AND CREDIT

Transactions are usually recorded in the books of accounts on the basis of the rules of **debit** and **credit**. In Italian, the term 'Credit' (Cr.) means to give and the term 'Debit' (Dr.) means to to owe. In practice, the left hand side of an account is the debit side, while the right hand side is the credit side.

Any transaction of a business affects these two accounts in the opposite directions. It is based on the principles of the double entry system which states that there can be no giving without a receiving. The receiving aspect is known as debit and the giving aspect is known as credit. Hence, every debit must have a corresponding credit.

7.2 RULES OF DEBIT AND CREDIT

To understand the rules of debit and credit, it is essential to know accounts, because accounts are the medium for recording transactions in the books on the basis of the rules of debit and credit.

7.2.1 Account

It is a statement prepared in a special format in the ledger where summarized records of transactions affecting a particular person, asset, income or any other subject are shown, the benefits received being on one side and the benefits given on the other side. Examples of accounts are Machinery Account, Ram Account, Rent Account, Debtor's Account, and so on.

Different types of accounts are shown in Table 7.1. In Table 7.2. rules for debiting or crediting an account are listed.

TABLE 7.1   Classifications of Accounts Made on the basis of Modern Approach

Capital Accounts	Assets Accounts	Liabilities Accounts	Revenue/Income Accounts	Expenses Accounts
Examples: The amount contributed by the owner or owners or partners to the firm.	Examples: Goodwill, cash, trademarks, debtors or customers (for sale of goods), patents, buildings, machinery, bank balances, furniture, investments, etc.	Examples: Moneylender's accounts, loans, creditors or suppliers of goods, creditors for expenses, bank overdrafts, etc.	Examples: Sale of goods, rent received, interest received, commission received, dividend received, discount received, etc.	Examples: Purchase of goods, rent paid, salaries, wages, carriage, freight, discount allowed, interest paid, advertisement, etc.

TABLE 7.2 Rules for Debiting or Crediting an Account

	Debit (Dr.)	Credit (Cr.)
	(Respective account will be debited)	(Respective account will be credited)
Capital Accounts	For decrease in Capital	For increase in Capital
Assets Accounts	Increase in Assets	For decrease in Assets
Liabilities Accounts	For decrease in Liabilities	For increase in Liabilities
Revenue/Income Accounts	For decrease in Incomes or Profits	For increase in Incomes or Profits
Expenses Accounts	For increase in Expenses and Losses	For decrease in Expenses and Losses

Classifications of accounts may be made on the basis of *Traditional Approach* and are shown in Table 7.3.

TABLE 7.3 Classification of Accounts on the basis of Traditional Approach

Personal A/c			Real (Assets) A/c		Nominal A/c	
Natural persons	Artificial persons	Representative persons	Tangible	Intangible	Expenses	Incomes
The receiver is Debit A/c The giver is Credit A/c			Increase in Assets Debit A/c Decrease in Assets Credit A/c		All Expenses/Losses Debit A/c All Incomes/Profits Credit A/c	

Some other types of accounts are listed below:

Natural person's account: The transactions concerning an individual person are recorded under the category of natural person's account such as Rohim's A/c and Madhu's A/c.

Artificial person's account: Accounts of firms, companies, clubs, institutions, etc., are known as artificial person's account.

Representative personal account: These accounts represent a certain person or group of persons. Examples are Capital A/c (represents the proprietor for his investments/contributions, Drawings A/c (represents the proprietor for his drawings), Outstanding Rent A/c (represents the Landlord's A/c who will receive the rent in future), Income Received in Advance A/c, accrued Incomes A/c, and so on.

Tangible real accounts: The items of asset which can be touched and felt come under tangible real assets like buildings, machinery, cash, furniture, etc.

Intangible real accounts: These assets cannot be touched, for example, goodwill, trademarks and patents.

Nominal accounts: These accounts include all incomes, profits, gains, losses and expenses.

Goods accounts: The term 'goods' include those items which are purchased by the business/firm for resale. For example when furniture is purchased for resale, it will be considered as goods; however, when purchased for use, it will be considered as an asset. Purchases A/c, Sales A/c, Purchases Returns A/c, Sales Returns A/c, Stock A/c and goods sent on Consignment A/c are examples of goods account.

Analysis of rules for debiting or crediting an account

In earlier sections, the different types of accounts and the governing rules for debiting or crediting an account have been explained. For recording a transaction in the books, it is essential to know the rules for debiting or crediting an account. The applications of rules for debiting or crediting an account are explained below:

1. *Capital accounts:* When capital is contributed or brought in by the owner or a partner of a firm, Capital Account will be *credited* and for withdrawing capital from the business, it will be debited. For example, Mr. K started his business with cash of Rs. 80,000. Here, Capital Account will be credited by Rs. 80,000 and debited (as increase in assets) by Rs. 80,000.

2. *Assets accounts:* When an asset is purchased or brought in by a partner/owner of a firm, the respective asset account will be debited. If an asset is sold or taken over by a partner/owner of a firm, the respective asset account will be credited. Hence, for increase in assets the respective asset account will be debited, whereas for decrease in assets the respective asset account will be credited.

For example

(a) Purchased machinery for Rs. 24,000 in cash. Here, Machineries Account will be debited (as increased) by Rs. 24,000 and Cash Account will be credited by Rs. 24,000 (for decrease in cash). If the said machinery was purchased on credit from Machine Tools Ltd., then Machineries Account will be debited as before but Machine Tools Ltd. account will be credited.

(b) A car was sold at Rs. 35,000 and the payment was received through a cheque. The Bank Account will be debited (as it will increase) by Rs. 35,000, whereas the car account will be credited (as decrease in asset) by Rs. 35,000.

3. *Liabilities accounts:* When a loan is received or taken from a party the Respective Loan Account will be credited, while for repayment of the said loan the Respective Loan Account will be debited. For example,

(a) Purchased good from X Bros. on credit for Rs. 12,000. Here loan is taken from X Bros. and as such X Bros. Account will be credited by Rs. 12,000. For receiving goods from X Bros., Goods/Purchases Account will be debited by Rs. 12,000.

(b) Taken a loan of Rs. 15,000 from bank and the amount was deposited into bank immediately or credited by the bank to the trader's account. Here, Bank Account will be debited (for increase in asset) by Rs. 15,000, and Bank Loan Account will be credited by Rs. 15,000.

(c) Cash paid to X Bros. (previously goods were purchased from them) Rs. 5,000. Here, X Bros. Account will be debited (decrease in liability) by Rs. 5,000 and Cash Account will be credited (decrease in asset) by Rs. 5,000. Alternatively, according to the traditional approach, the receiver will be debited. Since here X Bros. is the receiver of cash, its Account will be debited.

4. *Revenue/income accounts:* By revenue, we mean flow of funds, i.e., money or rights to money, which have resulted from the trading activities of a business, but it is distinct from the funds (capital) invested by the owner or loans made by the creditors and others. When any amount is received or receivable from the revenue or income account, the respective income account will be credited. Thus, for increase in income the respective income account will be credited and for decrease, the respective income account will be debited. For example,

(a) Sale of goods for cash of Rs. 7,000. Here, Sales Account will be credited by Rs. 7,000 and Cash Account will be debited (as increase in assets) by an equal amount.

(b) Received interest from bank Rs. 900. Here, Interest Received Account (increase in income) will be credited by Rs. 900 and Bank Account will be debited (as increase in assets) by the same amount.

5. *Expenses accounts:* Expenses may be defined as the cost of running a business during the accounting period. It can also be defined as all costs, the benefit of which has been exhausted during the current year. Hence, for increase in expenses the respective expenses account will be debited while for decrease in expenses the respective expenses account will be credited. For example:

(a) Paid salary to the staff Rs. 3,000. Here Salary Account (as increase in expenditure) will be debited by Rs. 3,000 and Cash Account will be credited by Rs. 3,000.

(b) Paid rent by a cheque of Rs. 1,500. Here, Rent Account (as increase in expenditure) will be debited by Rs. 1,500 and Bank Account will be credited by the same amount.

If we consider the net effect of point (4) and (5) on capital, we will find that for incomes and profits the capital balance will increase and as such the respective income account will be credited. On the other hand, for expenses and losses, the capital balance will decrease and hence, the respective expenditure account will be debited.

Table 7.4 lists the rules required to debit or credit an account. An analysis of business transactions on the basis of rules for debiting or crediting an account is depicted in Table 7.5.

TABLE 7.4 Applications of Rules for Debiting or Crediting an Account

Name of the Account	Nature of Account	When it will be Debited	When it will be Credited
Capital	Representative personal account	For decrease	For increase
Cash	Real/asset	For increase	For decrease
Bank Balance	Real/asset	For increase	For decrease
Machinery	Real/asset	For increase	For decrease
Wages	Expenditure/nominal	For increase	For decrease
Carriage	Expenditure/nominal	For increase	For decrease
Rent	Expenditure/nominal	For increase	For decrease
Salary	Expenditure/nominal	For increase	For decrease
Interest Received	Income/nominal	For decrease	For increase
Interest Paid	Expenditure/nominal	For increase	For decrease
Discount Received	Income/nominal	For decrease	For increase
Discount Given	Expenditure/nominal	For increase	For decrease
Goodwill	Real/asset	For increase	For decrease
Patent	Real/asset	For increase	For decrease
Furniture	Real/asset	For increase	For decrease
Advertisement	Expenditure/nominal	For increase	For decrease
Suppliers' Account	Liability	For decrease	For increase
Customers' Account	Real/asset	For increase	For decrease
Loan	Liability	For decrease	For increase
Insurance	Expenditure/nominal	For increase	For decrease
Drawings	Representative personal account	For increase	For decrease
Sales	Income/nominal	For decrease	For increase
Purchases	Expenditure/nominal	For increase	For decrease
Dividend Received	Income/nominal	For decrease	For increase

TABLE 7.5 Analysis of Business Transactions on the basis of the Rules for Debiting or Crediting an Account

Transactions	Event	Accounts Involved	Nature of Account	Account to be Debited	Account to be Credited
1. Business started with cash	Increase in cash Increase in capital	Cash Capital	Asset Representative personal	Cash	Capital
2. Purchased goods	Increase in goods Decrease in cash	Goods/purchase Cash	Nominal Real	Purchases	Cash
3. Purchase of Furniture	Increase in asset Decrease in asset	Furniture Cash	Real Real	Furniture	Cash
4. Opened a Bank A/c	Increase in bank Decrease in cash	Bank Cash	Real Real	Bank	Cash
5. Sold goods in cash	Increase in cash Sale of goods	Cash Sales	Real Nominal	Cash	Sales
6. Sold goods to K	Amount receivable from K Sale of goods	K Sales	Personal Nominal	K	Sales

(Contd.)

7. Paid for advertisement	Expenditure paid Decrease in Cash	Advertisement Cash	Nominal Real	Advertisement	Cash
8. Salaries paid	Expenditure paid Decrease in Cash	Salaries Cash	Nominal Real	Salaries	Cash
9. Wages paid	Expenditure paid Decrease in Cash	Wages cash	Nominal Real	Wages	Cash
10. Rent paid	Expenditure paid Decrease in Cash	Rent Cash	Nominal Real	Rent	Cash
11. Purchased computer	Increase in asset Decrease in Cash	Computer Cash	Real Real	Computer	Cash
12. Proprietor's house rent paid	Personal expenditure Decrease in Cash	Drawings Cash	Representative personal Real	Drawings	Cash
13. Carriage paid	Expenditure paid Decrease in Cash	Carriage Cash	Nominal Real	Carriage	Cash
14. Machinery purchased from TK Bros.	Increase in asset Increase in liabilities/ loan given by TK Bros.	Machinery TK Bros.	Real Personal	Machinery	TK Bros.
15. Received interest from bank	Increase in bank balance Increase in income	Bank Interest received	Real Nominal	Bank	Interest Received

EXERCISES

I. *Objective Type Questions (With Answers)*

A. Tick (í) the correct answer from the brackets to complete the following statements:

1. Increase in assets shows (Debit Balance/Credit Balance/none).
2. Decrease in assets shows (Debit Balance/Credit Balance/none).
3. All expenses are (Debit Balance/Credit Balance/none).
4. All incomes are (Debit Balance/Credit Balance/none).
5. For personal accounts, receiver is (Debit/Credit).
6. For personal accounts, giver is (Debit/Credit).
7. Capital is a (Real Account/Representative Personal Account/none).
8. Proprietor's personal expenses are known as (Drawings/Miscellaneous Expenses).
9. Proprietor's personal property brought into the business will (decrease his Drawings/ increase his Capital/none).
10. Private loan collected through business will (increase Capital/decrease Loan or Cash/none).
11. Personal NSC cashed and brought that money into the business will increase (Capital/Capital and Cash/Drawings/none).
12. Goods purchased in the last month and the payment made on the next month by debiting (Supplier's A/c/Purchases A/c/Inward Invoice A/c).
13. Machine purchased on credit and payment is made by debiting (Machinery A/c/Purchases A/c/Supplier's A/c).
14. Discount allowed by suppliers is to be recorded in the books by (debiting Discount Allowed A/c/crediting Discount Received A/c).
15. Carriage paid for purchase of machinery is to be shown by debiting (Carriage/Carriage Inward/Machinery A/c).
16. Income tax paid by the proprietor is a/an (office expense/business expense/personal expense).

Ans: 1. Debit Balance **2.** Credit Balance **3.** Debit Balance **4.** Credit Balance **5.** Debit **6.** Credit **7.** Representative Personal Account **8.** Drawings A/c **9.** Increase in Capital **10.** Increase in Capital **11.** Capital **12.** Supplier's A/c **13.** Supplier's A/c **14.** Crediting Discount Received A/c **15.** Machinery A/c **16.** Personal expense.

B. You are required to form a transaction with the help of the guidelines mentioned below:
1. It will increase an asset and will also increase a liability.
2. It will decrease a liability and will also decrease an asset.
3. It will increase an asset and will decrease another asset.
4. It will decrease the capital and an asset.
5. It will decrease an asset but will increase another asset and capital.
6. It will decrease an asset and capital but will increase another asset.
7. It will increase a liability and an asset, but, at the same time, will reduce an asset.
8. It will increase an asset and, at the same time, will reduce two assets.
9. It will increase two assets and the capital.
10. Proprietor's personal expenses paid through the business.
11. Cash not withdrawn from the business but due to some event, Drawings A/c is opened.
12. It will decrease proprietor's drawings and will increase a fixed asset of the business.
13. It will decrease only a fixed asset.
14. It will decrease only current asset.
15. Goods not lost or sold, but used for the purpose of the business.

Ans:
1. Fixed asset purchased on credit.
2. Loan or any liability paid.
3. Fixed asset purchased in cash or by cheque.
4. Capital withdrawn from the business through cash, cheque or other assets.
5. Fixed asset sold at a profit.
6. Fixed asset sold at a loss.
7. An asset purchased on credit but out of the total purchase price, some amount has already been paid.
8. A fixed asset is purchased with cash and cheque, or a fixed asset is purchased in exchange of another asset and the balance is paid by cash/cheque.
9. Two assets brought in as capital.
10. Rent includes proprietor's house rent.
11. Goods used by the proprietor for personal purposes.
12. Out of the total cash withdrawn from the business for personal use, some is paid for purchasing a fixed asset for the business.
13. Depreciation charged on a fixed asset or a fixed asset is lost by fire/stolen/others.
14. A debtor became insolvent (i.e., bad debts) or goods lost by fire or stolen.
15. Goods distributed as free sample (i.e. for advertisement).

C. Identify the correct nature of account (personal/real/nominal/liability):
1. Purchase of goodwill.
2. Salary paid to manager.
3. Salary paid in advance.
4. Rent from sub-letting.
5. Rent received in advance.
6. Subscriptions paid to Trade Protection Society.
7. Subscriptions received in advance by Star Club.
8. Subscriptions receivable by Star Club.
9. Patent purchased.
10. Paid for neon sign.
11. When furniture is purchased by a dealer of furniture.
12. When furniture is purchased for the business.
13. When stationery is purchased by a retailer of stationeries.

14. When stationery is purchased for the business.
15. Goods distributed as free sample.

Ans: 1. Real 2. Nominal 3. Real 4. Nominal 5. Real 6. Nominal 7. Liability 8. Real 9. Real 10. Real 11. Nominal (here, furniture is considered goods) 12. Real (here, furniture is considered an asset) 13. Nominal 14. Nominal 15. Nominal (It is an advertisement expenditure).

II. *Short Answer Type Questions*

1. What is the meaning of debit and credit?
2. What do you mean by representative personal account?
3. What do you mean by tangible and intangible real accounts? Give example.

III. *Long Answer Type Questions*

1. What is the meaning of debit and credit? Explain the rules of Debit and Credit.
2. What do you mean by the term 'account'? How are Accounts classified as per modern approach and traditional approach?
3. What do you mean by representative personal account? Give three examples of representative personal account.
4. How can you analyse the rules for debiting or crediting an account? Explain with example.
5. What do you mean by the golden rule of accounts?

IV. *Problems*

1. With the help of the following guidelines prepare a transaction:
   (a) It will increase an asset and also increase liability.
   (b) It will decrease an asset and also decrease a liability.
   (c) It will decrease an asset and also increase another asset.
   (d) It will increase an asset and increase capital.
   (e) It will decrease an asset and decrease capital.
   Ans: (a) Purchase furniture on credit (b) Repayment of loan (c) Purchase of an asset in cash (d) Fresh capital introduced into business (e) Capital withdrawn by the proprietor or drawings made by the owner.

2. Correct the following:
   (a) Patent is a nominal account.
   (b) Neon sign is a personal account.
   (c) Manager's salary is a personal account.
   (d) Return Inward is a real account.
   (e) Return Outward is a nominal account.
   (f) Goodwill is a personal account.
   (g) Capital is an asset account.
   (h) Drawings are nominal account.
   (i) Carriage Inward is a real account.
   (j) House Rent is a personal account.
   Ans: (a) Real account (b) Real account (c) Nominal account (d) Nominal account (e) Nominal account (f) Real account (g) Liability (Representative personal account) (h) Representative personal account (i) Nominal account (j) Nominal account.

3. Classify the following items into assets and liabilities:
   (a) Goodwill (b) Mr. X(Supplier of goods) (c) Mr. Z (Customer) (d) Cash received an advance (from customer) (e) Trademark (f) Bank Overdraft (g) Outstanding Expenses (h) Freehold Premises (i) Investment (j) Loan to Mr. H.
   Ans: Assets: (a); (c) ; (e); (h) ; (i) ; (j) Liabilities: (b); (d); (f) ; (g).

4. Fill in the blanks by applying the rules for debiting or crediting an account:

Name of the account	Nature of account	When it will be debited	When it will be credited
Goodwill	---		
Drawings	---		
Commission paid	---		---
Patent	---		---
Wages	---		
Freight	---		
General expenses	---		---
Bad debts	---		
Discount received	---		
Fire insurance	---	---	
Capital	---	---	
Depreciation	---		---
Sales	---	---	
Bonus	---		---
Furniture	---		---

5. Fill in the blanks by applying the rules for debiting or crediting an account:

Name of the account	Nature of account	When it will be debited	When it will be credited
Fuel	---	---	
Customs duty	---	---	
Royalty on production	---	---	
Advertisement	---	---	
Bank interest	---	---	---
Rent from sub-letting	---	---	---
Travelling expenses	---	---	---
Samples	---		---
Export duty	---		---
Audit fees	---		---
Motor van	---		---
Machinery	---		---
Cash at bank	---		---
Investment	---		---
Trademark	---		---

6. Analyse the following business transactions on the basis of the rules for debiting or crediting an account:

Transactions	Event	Accounts involved	Nature of account	Account to be debited	Account to be credited
1. Sold old furniture	---	---	---	---	---
2. Cash withdrawn by Proprietor	---	---	---	---	---
3. Purchased machinery on credit	---	---	---	---	---
4. Paid wages	---	---	---	---	---
5. Received interest	---	---	---	---	---
6. Advertisement paid	---	---	---	---	---
7. Discount Allowed to X	---	---	---	---	---
8. Loan given to Z	---	---	---	---	---
9. Loan received from S	---	---	---	---	---
10. Capital withdrawn	---	---	---	---	---

7. Analyse the following business transactions on the basis of the rules for debiting or crediting an account:

Transactions	Event	Accounts involved	Nature of account	Account to be debited	Account to be credited
1. Furniture purchased	---	---	---	---	---
2. Stationery purchased	---	---	---	---	---
3. Rent paid	---	---	---	---	---
4. Loan paid	---	---	---	---	---
5. Interest received	---	---	---	---	---
6. Salary paid	---	---	---	---	---
7. Dividend Received	---	---	---	---	---
8. Cash deposited into fixed deposit account	---	---	---	---	---
9. Law charges paid	---	---	---	---	---
10. Audit fees paid	---	---	---	---	---

8

Books of Original Entry: Journal and Ledger

CONTENTS

- Journal
  - Types of Journal
  - Features of Journal
  - Advantages of a Journal
  - Presentation of Journal Entries
  - Guidelines for Double Entry System and the Necessary Journal Entries
- Special Instructions in Respect of some Specific Transactions
- Ledger

- Subdivision of Ledger
- Features of Ledger
- Advantages of Ledger
- Relation Between Journal and Ledger
- Posting
  - Techniques of Posting in a Ledger
- Balancing of an Account
- Trial Balance
  - Objectives of a Trial Balance
  - Methods of Preparing a Trial Balance

INTRODUCTION

The primary duty of an enterprise is to record its day-to-day transactions in journals or in its subsidiary books. The next step is posting the data under different heads to different accounts, i.e., posting in ledger, and thereafter, the income statement or the final accounts are prepared. The above steps should be followed during each accounting period. To record the transactions and maintain the records, a particular system is followed about which we will study in subsequent sections.

8.1 JOURNAL

The term **journal** has been derived from the French word *Jour* which means a diary. It is a subsidiary book in which daily transactions of a firm are recorded chronologically under the double entry system of book keeping. All transactions are first recorded in the journal book and thus, it is called the **book of original entry**. In other words, the book in which transactions are primarily recorded in a chronological order after the proper analysis of debit and credit followed by a brief description is known as a **journal**. As the transactions are primarily recorded, the book is also known as the **book of primary entry** or the **book of prime entry** or the **book of original entry** or the **book of first entry**. Due to huge volume of transactions it becomes impossible to record all the transactions of a given financial year efficiently in a single book because its use would become difficult, especially in case of a big concerns. If all the transactions are recorded in a single book, the distribution of work among the employees regarding the recording of the transactions would became a very difficult task. Thus for proper recording of the transactions, a journal is subdivided into a number of sub-journals. A person specialized in recording the transactions is employed to get the highest productivity. However, it will not be possible if the journal is not subdivided on the basis of the nature of transactions.

8.1.1 Types of Journal

Journals are divided into two types:
1. General journal
2. Special journal.

General journal: There are some transactions which take place only occasionally and are thus not recorded in special journals. Such transactions are recorded in a separate book known as a **journal proper**. The following transactions are recorded in a journal proper:
1. Opening entries
2. Closing entries
3. Transfer entries
4. Credit purchase and sale of fixed assets
5. Adjustment entries
6. Rectification of errors.

Special journal: It can be further subdivided into the following types:
1. Cash book
2. Purchase day book
3. Sales day book
4. Purchase return book
5. Sales return book
6. Bills receivable book
7. Bills payable book.

8.1.2 Features of Journal
1. The first step of applying the double entry system is the journal entry.
2. After a transaction has taken place, it is first recorded in the journal and as such the book is known as the book of prime entry or the book of original entry or the book of first entry.
3. As daily transactions are recorded chronologically, it is also known as a **chronological book**.
4. After recording the transactions a brief note known as **narration** is added to each journal entry.
5. The entire matter about each transaction is recorded in the journal.
6. It records both debit and credit aspects of a transaction through double entry system.
7. Ledger folio of each journal entry is noted in the book for further reference.

8.1.3 Advantages of Journal
1. As the date, amount and a brief description of each transaction are recorded in the journal, the entire matter about the respective transaction is available, whenever required subsequently.
2. It records all the daily transactions chronologically. Thus, it helps to detect any particular transaction or the details of the said transaction which were not recorded in the journal for further necessary action in the ledger or others.
3. Since all the daily transactions are recorded chronologically, the risk of missing an entry is very low.
4. It helps to identify and prevent errors.
5. As both debit and credit aspects of a transaction are recorded in the journal after their proper analysis, it helps in recording the debit and credit accounts in the ledger.

8.1.4 Presentation of Journal Entries

Generally, a journal is divided into five columns and each transaction is recorded in the said columns chronologically. The columns are shown within the journal as shown in Table 8.1.

TABLE 8.1 Journal Entries

Date	Particulars	L. F.	Amount Dr. (Rs.)	Amount Cr. (Rs.)

Date column: It is the first column. The date of the transaction is to be recorded here.

Particulars column: It is the second column and the detail of the transaction (a particular account is to be debited and other account is to be credited) is recorded here with narration. The method of recording is explained below:

While recording the journal entries, the rules regarding debit and credit must be taken into consideration. For example, on August 3, 2008, Mr. Y sold goods to Mr. X for Rs. 1,000. As per the double entry system and according to our golden rules of accounts the transaction has to be analyzed as under:

It is a credit transaction. So, Mr. X's account is to be recorded for further (future) transactions. Here, Mr. X is the receiver of the goods, and thus his account will be debited (as per personal account rules, receiver is debited) while sales is the income account, and hence it will be credited (as per nominal account rules, incomes and profits are credited). After selecting the debit and the credit account, a brief description about the transaction is also noted in the journal entry as shown in Table 8.2.

TABLE 8.2 Journal (In the books of Y).

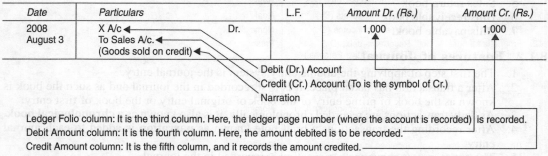

Date	Particulars	L.F.	Amount Dr. (Rs.)	Amount Cr. (Rs.)
2008 August 3	X A/c Dr.		1,000	1,000
	To Sales A/c.			
	(Goods sold on credit)			

Debit (Dr.) Account
Credit (Cr.) Account (To is the symbol of Cr.)
Narration

Ledger Folio column: It is the third column. Here, the ledger page number (where the account is recorded) is recorded.
Debit Amount column: It is the fourth column. Here, the amount debited is to be recorded.
Credit Amount column: It is the fifth column, and it records the amount credited.

Simple journal entries: In every transaction, at least two accounts are affected for which one account is debited while the other is credited. These types of transactions require simple journal entries. For example, sold goods for cash Rs. 400, for which a simple journal entry will be as under:

Cash A/c   Dr. 400
To Sales A/c 400

Compound journal entries: There are some cases where more than two accounts are affected for a transaction. In such cases, compound journal entries are shown. For example, cash received from Ram Rs. 3,150 and allowed discount to him Rs. 50. Compound journal entry for the said transaction will be as under:

Cash A/c Dr. 3,150
Discount Allowed A/c Dr. 50
To Ram A/c 3,200

8.1.5 Guidelines for Double Entry System and the Necessary Journal Entries

Transactions	What has happened	Nature of Account	Journal Entries	Amount (Rs.) Dr.	Cr.
1. Mr. X started his business with cash Rs. 50,000	Increase in cash (Dr.) Giver is credit (Cr.)	Real Representative personal	Cash A/c Dr. To capital A/c*	50,000	50,000

* It will represent the properietor (giver).

(Contd.)

2.	Opened a bank account with cash Rs. 20,000	Increase in bank balance (Dr.) Decrease in cash (Cr.)	Real Real	Bank A/c	Dr.	20,000	
				To Cash A/c			20,000
3.	Purchased goods from Mr. Z for Rs. 6,000	Increase in expenditure (Dr.) Giver is credit (Cr.)	Nominal Personal	Purchases A/c	Dr.	6,000	
				To Z A/c			6,000
4.	Paid carriage on purchase Rs. 1,200	Increase in expenditure (Dr.) Decrease in cash (Cr.)	Nominal Real	Carriage Inward A/c	Dr.	1,200	
				To Cash A/c			1,200
5.	Paid for advertisement Rs. 2,000.	Increase in expenditure (Dr.) Decrease in cash (Cr.)	Nominal Real	Advertisement A/c	Dr.	2,000	
				To Cash A/c			2,000
6.	Bought furniture for office use at Rs. 3,500	Increase in assets (Dr.) Decrease in cash (Cr.)	Real Real	Furniture A/c	Dr.	3,500	
				To Cash A/c			3,500
7.	Paid insurance premium by cheque Rs. 750	Increase in expenditure (Dr.) Decrease in bank balance (Cr.)	Nominal Real	Insurance Premium A/c	Dr.	750	
				To Bank A/c			750
8.	Issued a cheque of Rs. 5,800 to Mr. Z in full settlement of his account Rs. 6,000	Receiver is debit (Dr.) Decrease in bank balance (Cr.) Receiver is debit (Dr.) Increase in income (Cr.)	Personal Real Personal Nominal	Z A/c To Bank A/c Z A/c	Dr. Dr.	5,800 200	5,800
				To Discount Received A/c			200
9.	Sold goods to Mr. G Rs. 8,300	Receiver is debit (Dr.) Increase in income (Cr.)	Personal Nominal	G A/c	Dr.	8,300	
				To Sales A/c			8,300
10.	Paid carriage on sales Rs. 650	Increase in expenditure (Dr.) Decrease in cash (Cr.)	Nominal Real	Carriage Outward A/c	Dr.	650	
				To Cash A/c			650
11.	Sold goods for cash Rs. 5,400	Increase in assets (Dr.) Increase in income (Cr.)	Real Nominal	Cash A/c	Dr.	5,400	
				To Sales A/c			5,400
12.	Proprietor's house rent paid Rs. 1,600	Receiver is debit (Dr.) (Representative Personal) Decrease in cash (Cr.)	Personal Real	Drawings A/c**	Dr.	1,600	
				To Cash A/c			1,600
13.	Cash deposited in bank Rs. 2,500	Increase in bank balance (Dr.) Decrease in cash (Cr.)	Real Real	Bank A/c	Dr.	2,500	
				To Cash A/c			2,500
14.	Paid salary to manager Mr. D Rs. 2,400	Increase in expenditure (Dr.) Decrease in cash (Cr.)	Nominal Real	Salary A/c	Dr.	2,400	
				To Cash A/c			2,400
15.	Received cash from Mr. G Rs. 2,500 and allowed him discount Rs. 50	Increase in assets (Dr.) Giver is credit (Cr.) Increase in expenditure (Dr.) Decrease in debtors (G) (Cr.)	Real Personal Nominal Personal	Cash A/c To G A/c Discount Allowed A/c	Dr. Dr.	2,500 50	2,500
				To G A/c			50
16.	Paid Trade subscription Rs. 250	Increase in expenditure (Dr.) Decrease in cash (Cr.)	Nominal Real	Trade Subscription A/c	Dr.	250	
				To Cash A/c			250
17.	Cash withdrew from bank for office use Rs. 2,000	Increase in cash (Dr.) Decrease in bank balance (Cr.)	Real Real	Cash A/c	Dr.	2,000	
				To Bank A/c			2,000
18.	Cash withdrew from bank for personal use Rs. 1,500	Receiver is debit (Dr.) (Representative Personal) Decrease in bank balance (Cr.)	Personal Real	Drawings A/c	Dr.	1,500	
				To Bank A/c			1,500
19.	Machinery purchased from Machine Tools Ltd Rs. 5,000	Increase in assets (Dr.) Giver is credit (Cr.)	Real Personal	Machinery A/c	Dr.	5,000	
				To Machine Tools Ltd. A/c			5,000
20.	Paid godown rent by cheque Rs. 550	Increase in expenditure (Dr.) Decrease in bank balance (Cr.)	Nominal Real	Godown Rent A/c	Dr.	550	
				To Bank A/c			550
21.	Goods returned by Mr. G Rs. 400	Increase in expenditure (Dr.) Giver is credit (Cr.)	Nominal Personal	Sales Return/Return Inward A/c To G	Dr.	400	400

(Contd.)

** It will represent the proprietor (receiver).

Transactions	What has happened	Nature of Account	Journal Entries	Amount (Rs.) Dr.	Cr.
22. Mr. X, the proprietor cashed his personal NSC and brought that amount into the business Rs. 4,000	Increase in cash (Dr.) Giver is credit (Cr.)	Real Representative Personal	Cash A/c Dr. To Capital A/c***	4,000	4,000
23. Paid telephone rent Rs. 450	Increase in expenditure (Dr.) Decrease in cash (Cr.)	Nominal Real	Telephone rent A/c Dr. To cash A/c	450	450
24. Purchased a computer for office use from Sup. Tech. Rs. 12,000	Increase in assets (Dr.) Giver is credit (Cr.)	Real Personal	Computer A/c Dr. To Sup. Tech. A/c	12,000	12,000
25. Received interest from bank Rs. 350	Increase in assets (bank) (Dr.) Increase in income (Cr.)	Real Nominal	Bank A/c Dr. To Interest Received A/c	350	350

*** It will represent the proprietor (giver).

8.2 SPECIAL INSTRUCTIONS IN RESPECT OF SOME SPECIFIC TRANSACTIONS

1. In case of purchase and sale transactions if the name of the purchaser or seller is not mentioned, the respective transaction is considered as cash transaction. For example, sold goods for Rs. 2,000. It should be treated as a cash transaction.

2. Again in case of purchase and sale transactions, if the name of the purchaser or seller is given but *for cash* or *in cash* is not mentioned, then the respective transaction is to be considered as a credit transaction. For example, sold goods to Pranjal for Rs. 2,000. It should be treated as a credit transaction. On the other hand, if it is given that goods are sold to Ratan for Rs. 2,000 in cash, then it is to be treated as a cash transaction.

3. When cash or an asset is brought in by the proprietor, then it should be recorded in the books as his Capital for which the Capital A/c is credited and the cash or asset A/c is debited correspondingly.

4. When cash/goods is withdrawn by the proprietor from the business, or any personal expenses of the proprietor is paid from the business cash/bank, then it is considered as a drawing. For such a transaction, the Drawings A/c is debited and the Cash/Stock/Purchases A/c is credited. Entry for the same will be as under:

    Drawings A/c   Dr.
        To Purchase or Opening Stock A/c
        To Cash/Bank A/c

5. In case of payment or receipt of any expenditure or income from a person, the name of the person to whom the cash is paid or received should not be recorded. For example, rent or salary paid to Rahul is Rs. 2,500. Here Rent/Salary A/c is debited, but not Rahul A/c. Similarly, Cash received from Madhu Rs. 3,000 for interest. Here, Interest A/c is credited, but not Madhu's A/c.

6. Generally, goods are sold on credit to increase the volume of sales. Out of all customers (debtors), some fail to pay the whole or a part of their dues or obligations in future which becomes a business loss. These types of losses are known as **bad debts**. When a debt (a customer) is declared bad or irrecoverable, then such an amount is written off from the debtors as bad debts. For such an incident, the Bad Debts A/c is debited and the Customers (debtors) A/c is credited.

    Entry for the same will be as under:
    Bad Debts A/c   Dr.
        To Debtor's A/c

7. When a debt becomes irrecoverable, it is written off as bad debt, but sometimes a portion or the whole of the said bad debts is recovered from the concerned debtor. It is then known as **Bad Debts Recovered**. Entry for the same will be as under:

When cash is realized

Cash/Bank A/c   Dr.(Increase in asset—to be debited)

To Bad Debts Recovery A/c (Increase in profit—to be credited)

For bad debts, Profit and Loss Account is debited as loss, so the bad debts recovery should be considered profit.

8. Goods lost by fire or stolen:

   (a) Goods lost by Fire/Stolen A/c   Dr.

        To Purchases/Trading A/c

        (For the original/gross loss)

   (b) Admitted Insurance Claim A/c   Dr.

        To goods lost by Fire/Stolen A/c

        (When fully admitted by the insurance company)

        Or,

        Admitted Insurance Claim A/c   Dr. (Admitted portion)

        Profit and Loss A/c   Dr. (Net loss)

        To Goods lost by Fire/Stolen A/c

        Or,

        Profit and Loss A/c   Dr.

        To Goods Lost by Fire/Stolen A/c

        (When not admitted by the Insurance Company)

   (c) When cash is realized from the Insurance Company

        Bank A/c   Dr.

        To Admitted Insurance Claim A/c

9. Goods distributed as charity

        Charity A/c   Dr.

        To Opening Stock or Purchase A/c

10. Sales tax:

   (a) When Sales Tax is collected from the debtors at the time of sale

        Cash/Bank A/c   Dr.

        To Sales Tax A/c

   (b) (i) When Sales Tax is charged to debtors (not received)

        Debtors A/c   Dr.

        To Sales Tax A/c

        (ii) When cash is received or collected from the debtors

        Cash/Bank A/c   Dr.

        To Debtors A/c

   (c) When Sales Tax is deposited into Government Account

        Sales Tax A/c   Dr.

        To Cash/Bank A/c

11. VAT (Value Added Tax)

Sales tax has now been replaced by VAT. Generally, accounting treatment for VAT is identical to sales tax, however, when VAT is paid at the time of purchasing goods, the said amount may be adjusted against the amount payable as VAT for selling goods. Suppose, VAT paid at the time of purchasing goods is Rs. 600 while that for selling goods is Rs. 900, then the net amount payable for VAT would be Rs. 300 (900 – 600) only. Entry for the same will be as under:

(a) When VAT is paid at the time of purchasing goods
Purchases A/c   Dr.
VAT A/c   Dr. 600 (Assumed)
    To Bank A/c

(b) When VAT is colleted from the customers at the time of sale of goods
Bank/Cash A/c   Dr.
    To Sales A/c
    To VAT Collected A/c   Dr. 900(Assumed)

(c) For payment of net VAT to the Government (after adjustment of VAT paid on purchase and payable for sale)
VAT Collected A/c   Dr. 900
    To VAT A/c (Paid)   Dr. 600
    To Cash/Bank A/c   Dr. 300

12. Goods distributed as free samples
Advertisement A/c   Dr.
    To Opening Stock or Purchases A/c

13. Wages paid for installation of plant
Plant A/c   Dr.
    To Cash/Bank A/c

14. Wages paid for construction of building
Building A/c   Dr.
    To Cash/Bank A/c

15. Depreciation charged on fixed assets
Depreciation A/c   Dr.
    To Assets A/c

16. Carriage paid for carrying fixed assets
Asset A/c   Dr.
    To Cash A/c

ILLUSTRATION 8.1   Give necessary journal entries for the following transactions in the books of Mr. D. Srivastava for the month of January 2008:

2008	**Transactions**
Jan.1	Mr. D. Srivastava started business with cash Rs. 65,000
2	Opened a bank account with cash Rs. 34,000
3	Goods purchased from M/s D. Bros. for Rs. 12,600 and paid carriage on it Rs. 800
4	Paid shop rent Rs. 1,800
5	Paid for advertisement by a cheque of Rs. 2,100
6	Sold goods for cash Rs. 4,600
7	Sold goods to Mr. H. Samanta for Rs. 9,800 and paid carriage on it Rs. 540
8	Issued a cheque of Rs. 5,600 in favour of M/s D. Bros
8	Trade subscription paid by cheque Rs. 750
9	Received interest from bank Rs. 210
10	Purchased furniture from Durgapur Timber Suppliers Rs. 7,500
11	Purchased computer from M/s Rick Tech in cash Rs. 9,000
12	Paid cash Rs. 6,500 to M/s D. Bros. in full settlement of their account and received discount Rs. 500
13	Goods returned by Mr. H. Samanta amounting to Rs. 760 and received cash from him Rs. 3,600
14	Cash withdrawn from bank for office use Rs. 5,000
15	Cash withdrawn from bank for personal use Rs. 1,500

Solution

In the books of Mr. D. Srivastava
Journal

Date	Particulars	L.F.	Amount Dr. (Rs.)	Amount Cr. (Rs.)
2008 January 1	Cash A/c Dr. To Capital A/c (Being the business started with cash)		65,000	65,000
2	Bank A/c Dr. To Cash A/c (Being the bank account opened)		34,000	34,000
3	Purchases A/c Dr. To M/s D. Bros. (Being the goods purchased on credit)		12,600	12,600
3	Carriage Inward A/c Dr. To Cash A/c (Being the carriage paid on purchases)		800	800
4	Shop Rent A/c Dr. To Cash A/c (Being the shop rent paid)		1,800	1,800
5	Advertisement A/c Dr. To Bank A/c (Being advertisement paid by cheque)		2,100	2,100
6	Cash A/c Dr. To Sales A/c (Being the goods sold for cash)		4,600	4,600
7	H. Samanta A/c Dr. To Sales A/c (Being the goods sold on credit)		9,800	9,800
7	Carriage Outward A/c Dr. To Cash A/c (Being the carriage paid on sales)		540	540
8	M/s D. Bros. A/c Dr. To Bank A/c (Being the cheque issued to M/s D. Bros.)		5,600	5,600
8	Trade subscription A/c Dr. To Bank A/c (Being Trade subscription paid by cheque)		750	750
9	Bank A/c Dr. To Interest Received A/c (Being the interest received from bank)		210	210
10	Furniture A/c Dr. To Durgapur Timber Suppliers A/c (Being the furniture purchased on credit)		7,500	7,500
11	Computer A/c Dr. To Cash A/c (Being the computer purchased)		9,000	9,000

12	M/s D. Bros. A/c Dr.
	   To Cash A/c
	   To Discount Received A/c
	(Being cash paid in full settlement and received discount.)
			7,000	6,500
				500

13	Sales Returns A/c Dr. To H. Samanta A/c (Being goods returned by H. Samanta)		760	760
	Cash A/c Dr. To H. Samanta A/c (Being cash received from H. Samanta)		3600	3,600

(Contd.)

Date	Particulars		L.F.	Amount Dr. (Rs.)	Amount Cr. (Rs.)
14	Cash A/c	Dr.		5,000	
	To Bank A/c				5,000
	(Being cash withdrawn from bank)				
15	Drawings A/c	Dr.		1,500	
	To Bank A/c				1,500
	(Being cash withdrawn from bank for personal use)				
		Total		172,160	172,160

ILLUSTRATION 8.2 Journalize the following transactions in the books of Mr. S. Manikchand:

2008	Transactions
March 16	Trade subscription paid by cheque Rs. 560

      17   Paid cash to Ratan Rs. 6,400 and received discount Rs. 350

      19   Goods returned by M/s G. Bros. Rs. 1,700

      21   Sold old furniture Rs. 2,460

      22   Life insurance premium of the proprietor paid Rs. 750

      24   Received interest from bank Rs. 450

      25   Paid for advertisement Rs. 1,650

      25   Received cash from Mr. D Rs. 6,500 out of which cash deposited into bank Rs. 4,500

      26   Received a cheque from Mr. G Rs. 2,900

      27   Goods returned to M/s P. Suppliers Rs. 2,400.

Solution

In the books of Mr. S. Manikchand
Journal

Date	Particulars		L.F.	Amount Dr. (Rs.)	Amount Cr. (Rs.)
2008 March 16	Trade subscription A/c	Dr.		560	
	To Cash A/c				560
	(Being the trade subscription paid)				
17	Ratan A/c	Dr.		6,400	
	To Cash A/c				6,400
	(Being cash paid to Ratan)				
	Ratan A/c	Dr.		350	
	To Discount Received A/c				350
	(Being discount received from Ratan)				
19	Sales Returns A/c	Dr.		1,700	
	To M/s G. Bros. A/c				1,700
	(Being the goods returned by M/s G. Bros.)				
21	Cash A/c	Dr.		2,460	
	To Furniture A/c				2,460
	(Being an old furniture sold)				
22	Drawings A/c	Dr.		750	
	To Cash A/c				750
	(Being life insurance premium of the proprietor paid)				
24	Bank A/c	Dr.		450	
	To Interest Received A/c				450
	(Being the interest received from bank)				
25	Advertisement A/c	Dr.		1,650	
	To Cash A/c				1,650
	(Being the advertisement paid)				
25	Cash A/c	Dr.		6,500	
	To D A/c				6,500
	(Being the cash received from Mr. D)				

(Contd.)

Date	Particulars		L.F.	Amount Dr. (Rs.)	Amount Cr. (Rs.)
	Bank A/c	Dr.		4,500	
	To Cash A/c				4,500
	(Being the cash deposited into bank)				
26	Bank A/c	Dr.		2,900	
	To G A/c				2,900
	(Being the cheque received from Mr. G)				
27	M/s P. Suppliers. A/c	Dr.		2,400	
	To Return Outwards A/c				2,400
	(Being the goods returned)				
		Total		30,620	30,620

ILLUSTRATION 8.3   Enter the following transactions in the books of Mr. N. Roy:

2008   **Transactions**
April 3   Travelling expenses paid Rs. 1,400
      5   Received a cheque of Rs. 4,500 from Mridul in full settlement of his account Rs. 4,600
      6   Bank credited for interest Rs. 240 and debited for bank charge Rs. 70
      7   Received a loan of Rs. 20,000 from Mr. S. Bali
      9   Paid salary to manager Mr. G. Kumar Rs. 6,000
     11   Proprietor's house rent paid by cheque Rs. 2,500
     13   Purchased goods from Mr. P Rs. 10,000
     15   Goods returned to Mr. P Rs. 1,500
     17   Received cash from D. Dutta Rs. 1,710 and allowed 5% discount
     19   Cash withdrawn from bank for personal use Rs. 3,000
     21   Purchased shares of D&D Company at Rs. 10,000 and payment was made by a cheque.

Solution

In the books of Mr. N. Roy
Journal

Date	Particulars		L.F.	Amount Dr. (Rs.)	Amount Cr. (Rs.)
April 3	Travelling Expenses A/c	Dr.		1,400	
	To Cash A/c				1,400
	(Being travelling expenses paid)				
5	Bank A/c	Dr.		4,500	
	Discount Allowed A/c	Dr.		100	
	To Mridul A/c				4,600
	(Being cheque received from Mridul and allowed him discount)				
6	Bank A/c	Dr.		240	240
	To Interest Received A/c				
	(Being the interest received from bank)				
	Bank Charge A/c	Dr.		70	
	To Bank A/c				70
	(Being bank charge charged by the bank)				
7	Cash A/c	Dr.		20,000	
	To Loan (T. S. Bali) A/c				20,000
	(Being loan received from Mr. T. S. Bali)				
9	Salary A/c	Dr.		6,000	
	To Cash A/c				6,000
	(Being salary paid to manager)				
11	Drawings A/c	Dr.		2,500	
	To Bank A/c				2,500
	(Being house rent of the proprietor paid)				

(Contd.)

Date	Particulars	L.F.	Amount Dr. (Rs.)	Amount Cr. (Rs.)
13	Purchases A/c Dr.		10,000	
	To P A/c			10,000
	(Being goods purchased on credit)			
15	P A/c Dr.		1,500	
	To Return Outwards A/c			1,500
	(Being the goods returned)			
17	Cash A/c Dr.		1,710	
	Discount Allowed A/c Dr.		90	
	To D. Dutta A/c			1,800
	(Being cash received and allowed 5% discount)			
19	Drawings A/c Dr.		3,000	
	To Bank A/c			3,000
	(Being cash withdrawn from bank for personal use)			
21	Investments A/c Dr.		10,000	
	To Bank A/c			10,000
	(Being investments made in shares of D&D Company)			

Working Note

Calculation of discount allowed on April 17:

Received cash from D. Dutta Rs. 1,710 and allowed 5% discount, i.e., out of Rs. 100 discount allowed is Rs. 5 cash paid by D. Dutta is 95%, i.e., Rs. 1,710. Hence, the amount of discount allowed = 1,710/95 × 5 = Rs. 90.

ILLUSTRATION 8.4 Journalize the following transactions for the month of May, 2008:

2008	Transactions

May 1 Issued a cheque of Rs. 2,700 to M/s Supply Syndicate
2 Paid for advertisement by a cheque of Rs. 2,700
4 Received cash Rs. 2,600 and a cheque of Rs. 4,000 from M/s D. Bros. and allowed discount Rs. 300
5 Paid cash Rs. 9,500 to M/s S.P. Bros. in full settlement of their account and received discount Rs. 450
7 The cheque which was issued to M/s Supply Syndicate on May 1 became dishonoured
8 Proprietor's house rent paid by a cheque of Rs. 4,500
9 Paid cash to Mr. S Rs. 4,100 and received discount Rs. 200 from him
11 Cash paid to petty cashier Rs. 1,200
14 An old machinery was sold Rs. 2,400
15 Sold goods to Mr. N. Bedi (as per list price) for Rs. 4,000, subject to trade discount 5% and allowed 3% cash discount if payment is made within a week
17 Commission received Rs. 670
19 Travelling expenses paid Rs. 2,300
20 Cash withdrawn from bank Rs. 15,000 to pay the salary of the office staff and it was paid on the next day
28 Cash Rs. 4,750 paid to D. Dhoni and received 5% discount from him
30 H. Sinha's account of Rs. 6,000 was settled in cash and received 5% discount
31 Interest on loan paid Rs. 450 and loan refunded Rs. 8,000.

Solution

In the Books of ...
Journal

Date	Particulars	L.F.	Amount Dr. (Rs.)	Amount Cr. (Rs.)
2008 May 1	M/s Supply Syndicate A/c Dr.		2,700	
	To Bank A/c			2,700
	(Being cheque issued)			
2	Advertisement A/c Dr.		2,700	
	To Bank A/c			2,700
	(Being advertisement paid by cheque)			
4	Cash A/c Dr.		2,600	
	Bank A/c Dr.		4,000	
	Discount allowed A/c Dr.		300	
	To M/S D. Bros. A/c			6,900
	(Being cash and cheque received from M/S D. Bros. and allowed discount)			
5	M/s S.P. Bros. A/c Dr.		9,950	
	To Cash A/c			9,500
	To Discount Received A/c			450
	(Being cash received and discount received)			
7	Bank A/c Dr.		2,700	
	To M/s Supply Syndicate A/c			2,700
	(Being the cheque issued on May 1 became dishonoured)			
8	Drawings A/c Dr.		4,500	
	To Bank A/c			4,500
	(Being house rent of the proprietor paid)			
9	S A/c Dr.		4,300	
	To Cash A/c			4,100
	To Discount Received A/c			200
	(Being cash paid and received discount)			
11	Petty Cashier A/c Dr.		1,200	
	To Cash A/c			1,200
	(Being cash paid to petty cashier)			
14	Cash A/c Dr.		2,400	
	To Machinery A/c			2,400
	(Being an old machinery sold)			
15	N. Bedi A/c Dr.		3,800	
	To Sales A/c			3,800
	[Being the Goods sold on credit at list price less 5% T.D. (4,000 − 200 = 3,800)]			
17	Cash A/c Dr.		670	
	To Commission Received A/c			670
	(Being commission received)			
19	Travelling Expenses A/c Dr.		2,300	
	To Cash A/c			2,300
	(Being travelling expenses paid)			
20	Cash A/c Dr.		15,000	
	To Bank A/c			15,000
	(Being cash withdrawn from bank)			
21	Salary A/c Dr.		15,000	
	To Cash A/c			15,000
	(Being salary paid to staff)			
28	D. Dhoni A/c Dr.		5,000	
	To Cash A/c (95% = 4,750)			4,750
	To discount received A/c (4,750/95 x 5)			250
	(Being cash paid and received discount 5 %)			

(Contd.)

Date	Particulars		L.F.	Amount Dr. (Rs.)	Amount Cr. (Rs.)
30	H. Sinha A/c	Dr.		6,000	
	To Cash A/c (95% of 6,000 = 5,700)				5,700
	To Discount Received A/c (5% of 6,000)				300
	(Being cash paid and received discount 5%)				
31	Interest on Loan A/c	Dr.		450	
	To Cash A/c				450
	(Being interest on loan paid)				
	Loan A/c	Dr.		8,000	
	To Cash A/c				8,000
	(Being loan repaid/refunded)				

ILLUSTRATION 8.5   Enter the following transactions in the books of a firm:

1.   Purchased building materials for Rs. 23,800 and the payment was made by a cheque
2.   Goods distributed as free samples amounting to Rs. 5,400
3.   Sold goods for Rs. 18,000 in cash and collected VAT @ 4 % for the same from the customer
4.   Sold goods to M/s Das Bros. for Rs. 12,000 as per list price, less Trade Discount 10% and 7.5% Cash at seven days. M/s Das Bros. settled their account immediately
5.   Goods lost by fire amounting to Rs. 6,400
6.   A Plant purchased from Super Machine Ltd. at Rs. 38,900 by a draft. Paid carriage on it Rs. 3,400
7.   Wages paid for installation of a plant Rs. 9,800
8.   Received an advance of Rs. 7,000 from a customer Mr.K. Kulkarni.

Solution

In the Books of ...
Journal

Date	Particulars		L.F.	Amount Dr. (Rs.)	Amount Cr. (Rs.)
1.	Buildings A/c	Dr.		23,800	
	To Bank A/c				23,800
	(Being building materials purchased)				
2.	Advertisement A/c	Dr.		5,400	
	To Opening Stock or Purchases A/c				5,400
	(Being the goods distributed as free samples)				
3.	Cash A/c	Dr.		18,720	
	To Sales A/c				18,000
	To VAT Collected A/c				720
	(Being the goods sold and collected VAT @ 4%)				
4.	Cash A/c	Dr.		9,990	
	Discount Allowed A/c	Dr.		810	
	To Sales A/c				10,800
	(Being the goods sold at 10 % T.D. and allowed 7.5% cash discount)				
5.	Goods Lost by Fire A/c	Dr.		6,400	
	To Purchases A/c or Stock A/c				6,400
	(Being the goods lost by fire)				
6.	Plant A/c	Dr.		38,900	
	To Bank A/c				38,900
	(Being a plant purchased and payment was made by a draft)				
	Plant A/c	Dr.		3,400	
	To Cash A/c				3,400
	(Being carriage paid for carrying the plant)				

(Contd.)

Date	Particulars	L.F.	Amount Dr. (Rs.)	Amount Cr. (Rs.)
7.	Plant A/c Dr.		9,800	
	To Cash A/c			9,800
	(Being wages paid for installation of a plant)			
8.	Cash A/c Dr.		7,000	
	To K. Kulkarni A/c			7,000
	(Being an advance received from a customer)			

ILLUSTRATION 8.6 Give necessary journal entries for the following transactions:
1. Goods distributed as charity for a sum of Rs. 2,600
2. Cash realized from the Insurance Company Rs. 2,900 for goods lost during the last month
3. Sales Tax for the month deposited into Government Account amounting to Rs. 4,600
4. Sold goods to D.F. Traders for Rs. 25,000 and charged sale tax @ 5%
5. An advance of Rs. 3,000 paid to an employee against his salary
6. Debtors include Rs. 700 due from a customer Mr. G. Guha who has became insolvent and nothing could be realized from his estate
7. Depreciate Machinery @ 10% and Machinery A/c appears in the books as Rs. 45,000.

Solution

In the Books of ...
Journal

Date	Particulars	L.F.	Amount Dr. (Rs.)	Amount Cr. (Rs.)
1.	Charity A/c Dr.		2,600	
	To Opening Stock or Purchase A/c			2,600
	(Being the Goods distributed as charity)			
2.	Bank A/c Dr.		2,900	
	To Admitted Insurance Claim A/c			2,900
	(Being cash realized from the Insurance Company)			
3.	Sales Tax A/c Dr.		4,600	
	To Cash/Bank A/c			4,600
	(Being sales tax for the month deposited into Government Account)			
4.	D.F. Traders A/c Dr.		26,250	
	To Sales A/c			25,000
	To Sales Tax A/c			1,250
	(Being the Goods sold and sales tax is charged @ 5%)			
5.	Advance Salary A/c Dr.		3,000	
	To Cash A/c			3,000
	(Being advance salary paid to Mr. ... {employee No.})			
6.	Bad Debts A/c Dr.		700	
	To G. Guha A/c			700
	(Being G. Guha's account written off as bad debt due to insolvency)			
7.	Depreciation A/c Dr.		4,500	
	To Machinery A/c			4,500
	(Being depreciation charged @ 10% on Machinery)			

ILLUSTRATION 8.7 Journalize the following transactions in the books of a firm:
1. A horse purchased for business use Rs. 7,600
2. Cash received from a debtor Rs. 1,600, whose account was written off as bad debt during the last month
3. Received an order for 230 tonnes of goods @ Rs. 450 per tonne from X Bros
4. Purchased a three kottahs of land @ Rs. 60,000 per kottah (*kottah is a unit for measurement of land*) and paid registration charges @ 7.1%. Paid Rs. 6,000 to a land broker for the said purchase of land

5. Goods costing Rs. 16,000 sold at a profit of 20% on sales price to Mr. S. Hamid and allowed 10% discount for immediate payment
6. Sold old papers and periodicals amounting to Rs. 380
7. Income Tax paid Rs. 5,800.

Solution

In the Books of ...
Journal

Date	Particulars	L.F.	Amount Dr. (Rs.)	Amount Cr. (Rs.)
1.	Live Stock A/c Dr.		7,600	
	To Cash A/c			7,600
	(Being a horse purchased for business use)			
2.	Cash A/c Dr.		1,600	
	To Bad Debts Recovery A/c			1,600
	(Being cash received against bad debts)			
3.	No entry is required. It is not a transaction.			
4.	Land A/c Dr.		198,780	
	To Cash A/c (180,000 + 12,780 + 6,000)			198,780
	(Being purchased three kottahs of land @Rs. 60,000 per kottah and paid registration charges @ 7.1% and brokerage Rs. 6,000)			
5.	Mr. S. Hamid A/c[1] Dr.		20,000	
	To Sales A/c			20,000
	(Being the goods sold at profit of 20% on sales price)			
	Cash A/c Dr.		18,000	
	Discount Allowed A/c Dr.		2,000	
	To Mr. S. Hamid A/c			20,000
	(Being cash received and allowed 10% discount)			
6.	Cash A/c Dr.		380	
	To Miscellaneous Receipts A/c or Sundry Receipts A/c			380
	(Being sale of old papers and periodicals)			
7.	Drawings A/c[2] Dr.		5,800	
	To Bank A/c			5,800
	(Being income tax paid)			

Working Notes

1. *Calculation of selling price for item No. 5*:
   Goods were sold @ 20% profit on sale price. Thus, when selling price is Rs. 100 then cost would be Rs. 80 (100 – 20). Hence, profit percentage on cost = 20/80 × 100 = 25%.

	Rs.
Cost of the goods	16,000
Add: 25% profit on cost	4,000
Selling Price	20,000

2. It has been assumed here that income tax was paid for the proprietor, as it is not a company. Hence, it is treated as drawings of the proprietor.

ILLUSTRATION 8.8 Enter the following transactions in the books of a firm:

1. A machine which stood in the books for Rs. 8,500 on January 1, 2007, was sold for Rs. 5,100 in exchange for a new machine costing Rs. 17,600 on June 1, 2007, supplied by D K. Suppliers
2. Received Rs. 2,700 of a bad debts written off during the last month

3. Cash of Rs. 24,000 invested in shares of SAIL and payment was made through bank
4. Sold goods to Mr. R. Vharaj for Rs. 24,000 and charged sales tax @ 5% and freight Rs. 700
5. Bought from M/s Kamath Bros. 200 cases of goods @ Rs. 350 per case less trade discount 10%; purchase terms provide that 15% cash discount will be allowed provided the payment is made within 15 days of purchase, 60% of the invoice was paid immediately
6. Received interest from bank Rs. 2,500 on fixed deposits
7. Municipal tax paid Rs. 1,900.

Solution

In the Books of ...
Journal

Date	Particulars		L.F.	Amount Dr. (Rs.)	Amount Cr. (Rs.)
1.	D.K. Suppliers A/c	Dr.		5,100	
	Loss on Sale of Machine A/c	Dr.		3,400	
	To Machinery A/c				8,500
	Machinery A/c	Dr.		17,600	
	To D.K. Suppliers A/c				17,600
	(Being an old machine of Rs. 8,500 sold at Rs. 5,100 in exchange for a new machine costing Rs. 17,600)				
	Or				
	Machinery A/c (New Machine No.)	Dr.		17,600	
	Loss on Sale of Machine A/c	Dr.		3,400	
	To Machinery A/c (Old Machine No.)				8,500
	To D.K. Suppliers A/c (Net invoice)				12,500
	(Being an old machine of Rs. 8,500 sold at Rs. 5,100 in exchange for a new machine costing Rs. 17,600)				
2.	Cash A/c	Dr.		2,700	
	To Bad Debts Recovery A/c				2,700
	(Being cash received against bad debts)				
3.	Investment A/c	Dr.		24,000	
	To Bank A/c				2,400
	(Being investment made in shares of SAIL)				
4.	R. Vharaj A/c	Dr.		25,900	
	To Sales A/c				24,000
	To Sales tax A/c				1,200
	To Freight A/c				700
	(Being the goods sold on credit and charged sales tax @ 5% and freight)				
5.	Purchases A/c	Dr.		63,000	
	To M/s Kamath Bros.				63,000
	(Being 200 cases of Goods @ Rs. 350 per case purchased less Trade Discount 10%.)				
	M/s Kamath Bros. A/c	Dr.		37,800	
	To Cash A/c				32,130
	To Discount Received A/c[1]				5,670
	(Being 60% of invoice of Rs. 63,000 paid and received 15% cash discount)				
6.	Bank A/c	Dr.		2,500	
	To Interest on Fixed Deposits A/c				2,500
	(Being interest received from bank on A/c)				
7.	Municipal Taxes A/c	Dr.		1,900	
	To Cash A/c				1,900
	(Being municipal tax paid)				

Working Note

1. *Calculation of invoice price and cash discount received for item No. 5*

M/s Kamath Bros.	Rs.
200 cases of goods @ Rs. 350 per case	70,000
Less: Trade Discount 10%	7,000
Invoice Price	63,000
60% of invoice price (60/100 × 63,000) =	37,800
Less: Cash Discount 15%	5,670
Amount paid	32,130

8.3 LEDGER

It is a set of accounts or a book where different types of accounts are maintained. After recording all the transactions in a journal, posting is made for all the transactions from journal to the ledger. It is a process of posting figures, and entries are made from one account to another in the ledger book under different heads of accounts to know the net or the final position of a particular account at the end of a certain period. It is the main or the principal book of accounts. Though the transactions are first recorded in the journal and are then posted to the ledger, it is not possible to calculate or estimate the business performance or the result from the journal. The final account is prepared from the ledger account balances to know the financial position of a firm. Without taking the help of the ledger account balances, the financial position or the performance of the business cannot be measured. Due to this reason, ledger is called the **main book of accounts**.

8.3.1 Subdivision of Ledger

General or impersonal ledger: It contains all types of accounts except debtors and creditors. For example, capital and drawings accounts, assets accounts, goods accounts, liabilities accounts (excluding creditors) and all nominal accounts.

Debtors' ledger: It contains all the accounts of those persons or firms to whom goods are sold on credit.

Creditors' ledger: It contains all the accounts of those persons or firms from whom goods are purchased on credit.

8.3.2 Features of Ledger

1. It is prepared with the help of the data (i.e., respective account's debit or credit position) provided by the journal.
2. It shows the present and the closing position of all accounts.
3. It is the principal book of accounts.
4. Trial balance is prepared with the help of the closing balance of all accounts maintained under the ledger.
5. A particular account in the ledger represents the details of the transaction occurring during the period concerning the said account and its closing balance.
6. At the end of the period, all nominal accounts' balances are transferred to the trading/profit and loss account.
7. The balances of the real and the personal accounts are shown in the balance sheet and carried forward to the next year.
8. Summarized form of all the accounts are shown in the ledger.
9. All accounts along with their details are maintained in the ledger.

8.3.3 Advantages of Ledger

1. Perfect application of double entry system is made through the ledger.
2. Trial balance is prepared with the help of the closing balances of all the accounts maintained under the ledger. Thus, it helps to check the accuracy of the transactions recorded in the ledger.
3. As all the accounts of different persons or organizations are recorded separately, it helps to calculate the exact figure of the amount receivable from the debtors and payable to the creditors.
4. It helps to prepare the balance sheet as all real accounts, liabilities accounts and personal accounts are maintained separately.
5. It helps in preparing the trading and profit and loss accounts with the help of the nominal accounts' balances.
6. It is the main source of information for the management or the owner, and helps in taking necessary action.
7. It helps in detecting errors and frauds, and reduces the chances of probable errors.
8. Cash is the blood of any business and hence it is essential to monitor the cash position of the firm. The details of all cash transactions along with the closing balance of the cash account can be ascertained in the ledger whenever required.
9. Without ledger account balances, a financial statement cannot be prepared.

8.4 RELATION BETWEEN JOURNAL AND LEDGER

1. All transactions are first recorded in the journal and then posted to the ledger.
2. Journal is a subsidiary book, while ledger is the main book of accounts.
3. Transactions are recorded chronologically in the journal, whereas in the ledger, they are recorded (posted) analytically.
4. Detailed descriptions of the transactions are found in the journal rather than in the ledger.
5. The process of recording the transactions in the journal is called **journalizing,** while that in the ledger is called **posting.**
6. Financial position of a business or a firm is measured with the help of the ledger account balances only.

Table 8.3 lists the differences between a journal and ledger.

TABLE 8.3 Differences between Journal and Ledger

Journal	Ledger
1. It is known as the **book of primary entry** or **original entry.**	1. It is the principal book of accounts.
2. Transactions are recorded in detail.	2. Summarized form of all transactions are recorded in it.
3. Narrations are used in journals.	3. No narrations are used in ledgers.
4. There are two columns in a journal and they are totalled at the end of the day or a certain period.	4. There are two sides of each account in a ledger and the balancing of each account is made at the end of a certain period.
5. Transactions are recorded chronologically.	5. Transactions are recorded (posted) analytically in a ledger.
6. There is no scope of carrying forward to the next year in a journal.	6. The balances of real and personal accounts are carried forward to the next year.
7. Trading and Profit & Loss Accounts cannot be prepared through a journal.	7. It helps to prepare Trading and Profit & Loss Accounts with the help of nominal accounts' balances.
8. Ledger folio is mentioned in it.	8. Journal folio is mentioned in a ledger.
9. Generally, entries are made in a journal on the basis of vouchers.	9. Here, entries are made on the basis of records maintained in a journal.
10. It helps to prepare a ledger.	10. It helps in preparing the financial statements and represent the financial position of a firm or an enterprise.

8.5 POSTING

The process or technique of recording the transactions from a journal to a ledger is called **posting**. The concerned account which has been debited in the journal should also be debited in the ledger (left hand side), stating or putting the other account's name (with the same account). Similarly, the concerned account which has been credited in the journal should also be credited in the ledger (right hand side), putting the other account's name.

8.5.1 Techniques of Posting in a Ledger

Journal

Date	Particulars	L.F.	Amount Dr. (Rs.)	Amount Cr. (Rs.)
2008 August 1	Cash A/c Dr.		60,000	
	To Capital A/c			60,000
	(Being the business started with cash)			

Ledgers

Cash Account

Dr.   Cr.

Date	Particulars	J.F.	Amount (Rs.)	Date	Particulars	J.F.	Amount (Rs.)
2008 August 1	To Capital A/c		60,000	2008 August 31	By Balance c/d		60,000
			60,000				60,000
September 1	To Balance b/d		60,000				

Capital Account

Dr.   Cr.

Date	Particulars	J.F.	Amount (Rs.)	Date	Particulars	J.F.	Amount (Rs.)
2008 August 31	To Balance c/d		60,000	2008 August 1	By Cash A/c		60,000
			60,000	September 1	By Balance b/d		60,000
							60,000

This is called balancing

If we consider the above presentation, we will find that for posting the journal entries in the ledger the following steps need to be taken:

1. The account debited in the journal is posted on the credit side of the other/opposite account in the ledger. Here, cash account is debited in the journal and is shown on the credit side of the capital A/c in the ledger.
2. The account credited in the journal is posted on the debit side of the other/opposite account in the ledger. Here, capital accounts is credited in the journal and is shown on the debit side of the cash account in the ledger.
3. This procedure is to be followed in every transaction.
4. After recording all the transactions in the ledger, balancing of all the accounts are to made as shown above.

8.6 BALANCING OF AN ACCOUNT

To determine the net or final position of a particular account at the end of a certain period, balancing is made. At first, the two sides (debit and credit) are added up, and if they are not equal, the difference is ascertained or calculated. This difference is put on the smaller side written as 'To Balance c/d' or 'By Balance c/d' (carried down) and in the subsequent period, it is known as 'Balance b/d' (brought down), shown on the opposite side of the c/d Balance (i.e., on the heavier side).

ILLUSTRATION 8.9   Give necessary journal entries of the following transactions and prepare ledger accounts, and ascertain the balances in the books of Mr. N. Bharati for the month of August, 2008:

2008	**Transactions**
August 1	Mr. N. Bharati started business with cash Rs. 60, 000
2	Opened a bank account with cash Rs. 20,000
3	Trade subscription paid by a cheque of Rs. 1,200
4	Sold goods to Mr. T. Bhatt for Rs. 6,500 and paid carriage on it Rs. 800
5	Paid for advertisement by a cheque of Rs. 2,500
6	Sold goods for cash Rs. 5,900
7	Goods purchased from M/s G.H. Bros. for Rs. 10,000 and paid carriage on it Rs. 700
8	Issued a cheque of Rs. 4,750 in favour of M/s G.H. Bros
8	Paid shop rent Rs. 2,400
9	Received interest from bank Rs. 640
10	Purchased furniture from Calcutta Furniture for Rs. 9,000
11	Cash withdrawn from bank for personal use Rs. 2,500
12	Paid cash Rs. 5,000 to M/s G.H. Bros. in full settlement of their account and received discount of Rs. 250
13	Purchased Computer from M/s P.P. Syndicate in cash Rs. 16,000
14	Cash withdrawn from bank for office use Rs. 3,000
15	Goods returned by Mr. T. Bhatt amounting to Rs. 900 and received cash from him Rs. 4,000.

Solution

In the Books of Mr. N. Bharati
Journal

Date	Particulars		L.F.	Amount Dr. (Rs.)	Amount Cr. (Rs.)
2008 August 1	Cash A/c To Capital A/c (Being the business started with cash)	Dr.		60,000	60,000
2	Bank A/c To Cash A/c (Being the bank account opened)	Dr.		20,000	20,000
3	Trade subscription A/c To Bank A/c (Being trade subscription paid by cheque)	Dr.		1,200	1,200

4	T. Bhatt A/c
	    To Sales A/c
	(Being the Goods Sold on Credit)
	Carriage Outward A/c
	    To Cash A/c
	(Being the carriage paid on sales)
		Dr.
		
		Dr.
				6,500
				
				800
					6,500
					
					800

5	Advertisement A/c To Bank A/c (Being advertisement paid by cheque)	Dr.		2,500	2,500
6	Cash A/c To Sales A/c (Being the goods sold for cash)	Dr.		5,900	5,900

7	Purchases A/c
	    To M/s G.H. Bros.
	(Being the Goods Purchased on Credit)
	Carriage Inward A/c
	    To Cash A/c
	(Being the carriage paid on purchases)
		Dr.
		
		Dr.
				10,000
				
				700
					10,000
					
					700

(Contd.)

Date	Particulars		L.F.	Amount Dr. (Rs.)	Amount Cr. (Rs.)
8	M/s G.H. Bros A/c	Dr.		4,750	
	To Bank A/c				4,750
	(Being cheque issued to M/s G.H.Bros.)				
8	Shop Rent A/c	Dr.		2,400	
	To Cash A/c				2,400
	(Being the shop rent paid)				
9	Bank A/c	Dr.		640	
	To Interest Received A/c				640
	(Being the interest received from bank)				
10	Furniture A/c	Dr.		9,000	
	To Calcutta Furniture A/c				9,000
	(Being the furniture purchased on credit)				
11	Drawings A/c	Dr.		2,500	
	To Bank A/c				2,500
	(Being cash withdrawn from bank for personal use)				
12	M/s G.H. Bros. A/c	Dr.		5,250	
	To Cash A/c				5,000
	To Discount Received A/c				250
	(Being cash paid in full settlement and received discount)				
13	Computer A/c	Dr.		16,000	
	To Cash A/c				16,000
	(Being the computer purchased)				
14	Cash A/c	Dr.		3,000	
	To Bank A/c				3,000
	(Being cash withdrawn from bank for office use)				
15	Sales Returns A/c	Dr.		900	
	To T. Bhatt A/c				900
	(Being goods returned by T. Bhatt)				
	Cash A/c	Dr.		4,000	
	To T. Bhatt A/c				4,000
	(Being cash received from T. Bhatt)				

Ledger

Cash Account

Dr.   Cr.

Date	Particulars	J.F.	Amount (Rs.)	Date	Particulars	J.F.	Amount (Rs.)
2008 August 1	To Capital A/c		60,000	2008 August 2	By Bank A/c		20,000
6	To Sales A/c		5,900	5	By Carriage Outward A/c		800
14	To Bank A/c		3,000	7	By Carriage Inward A/c		700
15	To T. Bhatt A/c		4,000	8	By Shop rent A/c		2,400
				12	By M/s G.H. Bros. A/c		5,000
				13	By Computer A/c		16,000
				31	By Balance c/d		28,000
			72,900				72,900
September 1	To Balance b/d		28,000				

Capital Account

Dr.   Cr.

Date	Particulars	J.F.	Amount (Rs.)	Date	Particulars	J.F.	Amount (Rs.)
2008 August 31	To Balance c/d		60,000	2008 August 1	By Cash A/c		60,000
			60,000				60,000
				September 1	By Balance b/d		60,000

Dr.   **Bank Account**   Cr.

Date	Particulars	J.F.	Amount (Rs.)	Date	Particulars	J.F.	Amount (Rs.)
2008 August 2	To Cash A/c		20,000	2008 August 3	By Trade Subscription A/c		1,200
9	To Interest Received A/c		640	8	By M/s G.H. Bros A/c		4,750
				11	By Drawings A/c		2,500
				14	By Cash A/c		3,000
				31	By Balance c/d		9,190
			20,640				20,640
September 1	To Balance b/d		9,190				

Dr.   **Trade Subscription**   Cr.

Date	Particulars	J.F.	Amount (Rs.)	Date	Particulars	J.F.	Amount (Rs.)
2008 August 3	To Bank A/c		1,200	2008 August 31	By Balance c/d		1,200
			1,200				1,200
September 1	To Balance b/d		1,200				

Dr.   **T. Bhatt's Accounts**   Cr.

Date	Particulars	J.F.	Amount (Rs.)	Date	Particulars	J.F.	Amount (Rs.)
2008 August 4	To Sales A/c		6,500	2008 August 15	By Sales return A/c		900
					By Cash A/c		4,000
				31	By Balance c/d		1,600
			6,500				6,500
September 1	To Balance b/d		1,600				

Dr.   **Sales Accounts**   Cr.

Date	Particulars	J.F.	Amount (Rs.)	Date	Particulars	J.F.	Amount (Rs.)
2008 August 31				2008 August 4	By T. Bhatt A/c		6,500
	By Balance c/d		12,400	6	By Cash A/c		5,900
			12,400				12,400
				September 1	By Balance b/d		12,400

Dr.   **Carriage Outward Accounts**   Cr.

Date	Particulars	J.F.	Amount (Rs.)	Date	Particulars	J.F.	Amount (Rs.)
2008 August 5	To Cash A/c		800	2008 August 31	By Balance c/d		800
			800				800
September 1	To Balance b/d		800				

Dr.   **Purchases Accounts**   Cr.

Date	Particulars	J.F.	Amount (Rs.)	Date	Particulars	J.F.	Amount (Rs.)
2008 August 7	To M/s G.H. Bros		10,000	2008 August 31	By Balance c/d		10,000
			10,000				10,000
September 1	To Balance b/d		10,000				

Dr. | | | | Carriage Inward Accounts | | | | Cr.

Date	Particulars	J.F.	Amount (Rs.)	Date	Particulars	J.F.	Amount (Rs.)
2008 August 7	To Cash A/c		700	2008 August 31	By Balance c/d		700
			700				700
September 1	To Balance b/d		700				

Dr. | | | | M/s G.H. Bros. Account | | | | Cr.

Date	Particulars	J.F.	Amount (Rs.)	Date	Particulars	J.F.	Amount (Rs.)
2008 August 8	To Bank A/c		4,750	2008 August 7	By Purchases A/c		10,000
12	To Cash A/c		5,000				
	To Discount Received A/c		250				
			10,000				10,000

Dr. | | | | Shop Rent Account | | | | Cr.

Date	Particulars	J.F.	Amount (Rs.)	Date	Particulars	J.F.	Amount (Rs.)
2008 August 8	To Cash A/c		2,400	2008 August 31	By Balance c/d		2,400
			2,400				2,400
September 1	To Balance b/d		2,400				

Dr. | | | | Interest Received Account | | | | Cr.

Date	Particulars	J.F.	Amount (Rs.)	Date	Particulars	J.F.	Amount (Rs.)
2008 August 31	To Balance c/d		640	2008 August 9	By Bank A/c		640
			640				640
				September 1	By Balance b/d		640

Dr. | | | | Furniture Account | | | | Cr.

Date	Particulars	J.F.	Amount (Rs.)	Date	Particulars	J.F.	Amount (Rs.)
2008 August 10	To Calcutta Furniture A/c		10,000	2008 August 31	By Balance c/d		10,000
			10,000				10,000
September 1	To Balance b/d		10,000				

Dr. | | | | Calcutta Furniture Account | | | | Cr.

Date	Particulars	J.F.	Amount (Rs.)	Date	Particulars	J.F.	Amount (Rs.)
2008 August 31	To Balance c/d		10,000	2008 August 10	By Furniture A/c		10,000
			10,000				10,000
				September 1	By Balance b/d		10,000

Dr. | | | | Drawing Account | | | | Cr.

Date	Particulars	J.F.	Amount (Rs.)	Date	Particulars	J.F.	Amount (Rs.)
2008 August 11	To Bank A/c		2,500	2008 August 31	By Balance c/d		2,500
			2,500				2,500
September 1	To Balance b/d		2,500				

Dr.			Discount Received Account					Cr.
Date	Particulars	J.F.	Amount (Rs.)	Date	Particulars	J.F.	Amount (Rs.)	
2008 August 31	To Balance c/d		250	2008 August 12	By G.H. Bros. A/c		250	
			250				250	
				September 1	By Balance b/d		250	

Dr.			Computer Account					Cr.
Date	Particulars	J.F.	Amount (Rs.)	Date	Particulars	J.F.	Amount (Rs.)	
2008 August 13	To Cash A/c		16,000	2008 August 31	By Balance c/d		16,000	
			16,000				16,000	
September 1	To Balance b/d		16,000					

Dr.			Sales Returns Account					Cr.
Date	Particulars	J.F.	Amount (Rs.)	Date	Particulars	J.F.	Amount (Rs.)	
2008 August 15	To T. Bhatt A/c		900	2008 August 31	By Balance c/d		900	
			900				900	
September 1	To Balance b/d		900					

Note

To judge the arithmetical accuracy of the ledger accounts, the following statement (Trial Balance) may be prepared with the help of the closing balances of all the accounts. If the total of both the amount columns in the statement are equal (identical), then we may assume that the journal entries are correctly posted in the ledger.

Closing Balances of All Accounts	Amount (Dr.) Rs.	Amount (Cr.) Rs.
Cash Account	28,000	
Capital Account		60,000
Bank Account	9,190	
Trade Subscription	1,200	
T. Bhatt's Account	1,600	
Sales Account		12,400
Carriage Outward Account	800	
Purchases Account	10,000	
Carriage inward Account	700	
Shop Rent Account	2,400	
Interest Received Account		640
Furniture Account	10,000	
Calcutta Furniture Account		10,000
Drawings Account	2,500	
Discount Received Account		250
Computer Account	16,000	
Sales Returns Account	900	
	83,290	83,290

8.7 TRIAL BALANCE

At the end of an accounting period or a certain period, when all the accounts of a firm are closed or balanced, then with the help of those account balances, a statement is prepared known as a **Trial Balance**. All debit balances of accounts are shown on the debit side of the trial balance and the credit balances are shown on the credit side. The total of both the sides of the trial balance must be equal, because it is based on the double entry system according to which every debit must have a corresponding credit. It is prepared to check the arithmetical accuracy of the book keeping entries.

8.7.1 Objectives of Trial Balance

The following are the objectives of maintaining a trial balance:

1. Arithmetical accuracy of accounting entries is checked.
2. It helps to prepare final accounts.
3. The entire ledger account balances are summarized with a list.
4. Comparisons may be made with different account balances of different years.

8.7.2 Methods of Preparing Trial Balance

It is prepared generally under the following two methods:

1. Total method
2. Balance method

Trial balance with totals: According to this method, a trial balance is prepared with the help of the total of each of the accounts (without taking the balancing figure of each account). The debit total and the credit total are shown in two different columns, and at the end both, the total will be found to be equal.

Trial balance with balances: According to this method, a Trial Balance has to be prepared with the help of the balancing figures of each of the accounts. The debit balances and the credit balances are shown in two different columns, and it will be seen that at the end both the totals be equal.

If we consider the nature of the accounts showing debit balance or credit balance, we will find the following differences (Table 8.4) between the accounts having debit and credit balances.

TABLE 8.4   Differences between the Accounts Having Debit Balances and Those Having Credit Balances

Accounts having debit balances	Accounts having credit balances
The items which are to be considered in the debit side of the *Trial Balance:*	The items which are to be considered in the credit side of the *Trial Balance:*
1. All asset account balances	1. All incomes and profits
2. All expenses and Losses	2. All liabilities
3. All personal accounts having debit balances (representing assets).	3. All personal accounts having credit balances (representing liabilities).

ILLUSTRATION 8.10   Journalize the following transactions and post them in ledger accounts and balance them:

2008	Transactions

April 1 Mr. R.P. Singh started his business with capital of Rs. 124,000. His capital consists of stock Rs. 21,000; furniture Rs. 28,000, machinery Rs. 30,000; and the balance in cash.

3 Purchased a computer for office use from M/s Machino Make at Rs. 21,200.

7 Paid rent Rs. 2,600 and Rs. 3,600 for advertisement.

11 Personal NSC of Mr. N. Roy was cashed and brought that amount into the business Rs. 16,000.

14 Opened a bank account with UBI in cash Rs. 28,000.

17 Purchased goods from Ratan for Rs. 12,700.

19 Goods returned to Ratan Rs. 1,900.

23 Sold goods to Mahim for Rs. 17,800.

26 Miscellaneous expenses paid Rs. 750.

28 Cash paid to petty cashier Rs. 1,200.

29 Issued a cheque of Rs. 14,000 to M/s Machino Make.

Solution

In the Books of Mr. R.P. Singh
Journal

Date	Particulars	L.F.	Amount Dr. (Rs.)	Amount Cr. (Rs.)
April 1	Stock A/c Dr.		21,000	
	Machinery A/c Dr.		30,000	
	Furniture A/c Dr.		28,000	
	Cash A/c Dr.		45,000	
	To Capital A/c			124,000
	(Being the business started with the above assets)			
3	Computer A/c Dr.		21,200	
	To Machino Make A/c			21,200
	(Being the computer purchased on credit)			
7	Rent A/c Dr.		2,600	
	To Cash A/c			2,600
	Advertisement A/c Dr.		3,600	
	To Cash A/c			3,600
	(Being rent and advertisement paid)			
11	Cash A/c Dr.		16,000	
	To Capital A/c			16,000
	(Being NSC of the proprietor cashed and brought that amount into the business)			
14	Bank A/c Dr.		28,000	
	To Cash A/c			28,000
	(Being the bank account opened)			
17	Purchases A/c Dr.		12,700	
	To Ratan A/c			12,700
	(Being goods purchased on credit)			
19	Ratan A/c Dr.		1,900	
	To Return Outwards A/c			1,900
	(Being goods returned)			
23	Mahim A/c Dr.		17,800	
	To Sales A/c			17,800
	(Being the goods sold on credit)			
26	Miscellaneous expenses A/c Dr.		750	
	To Cash A/c			750
	(Being miscellaneous expenses paid)			
28	Petty Cashier A/c Dr.		1,200	
	To Cash A/c			1,200
	(Being cash paid to petty cashier)			
29	M/s Machino Make A/c Dr.		14,000	
	To Bank A/c			14,000
	(Being cheque issued to M/s Machino Make)			

Ledger
Cash Account

Dr.								Cr.
Date	Particulars	J.F.	Amount (Rs.)	Date	Particulars	J.F.	Amount (Rs.)	
2008 April 1	To Capital A/c		45,000	2008 April 7	By Rent A/c		2,600	
11	To Capital A/c		16,000	7	By Advertisement A/c		3,600	
				14	By Bank A/c		28,000	
				26	By Miscellaneous Expenses A/c		750	
				28	By Petty Cashier A/c		1,200	
				30	By Balance c/d		24,850	
			61,000				61,000	
May 1	To Balance b/d		24,850					

Dr.   **Stock Account**   Cr.

Date	Particulars	J.F.	Amount (Rs.)	Date	Particulars	J.F.	Amount (Rs.)
2008 April 1	To Capital A/c		21,000	2008 April 30	By Balance c/d		21,000
			21,000				21,000
May 1	To Balance b/d		21,000				

Dr.   **Machinery Account**   Cr.

Date	Particulars	J.F.	Amount (Rs.)	Date	Particulars	J.F.	Amount (Rs.)
2008 April 1	To Capital A/c		30,000	2008 April 30	By Balance c/d		30,000
			30,000				30,000
May 1	To Balance b/d		30,000				

Dr.   **Furniture Account**   Cr.

Date	Particulars	J.F.	Amount (Rs.)	Date	Particulars	J.F.	Amount (Rs.)
2008 April 1	To Capital A/c		28,000	2008 April 30	By Balance c/d		28,000
			28,000				28,000
May 1	To Balance b/d		28,000				

Dr.   **Capital Account**   Cr.

Date	Particulars	J.F.	Amount (Rs.)	Date	Particulars	J.F.	Amount (Rs.)
2008 April 30	To Balance c/d		140,000	2008 April 1	By Stock A/c		21,000
					By Machinery A/c		30,000
					By Furniture A/c		28,000
					By Cash A/c		45,000
				11	By Cash A/c		16,000
			140,000				140,000
				May 1	By Balance b/d		140,000

Dr.   **Bank Account**   Cr.

Date	Particulars	J.F.	Amount (Rs.)	Date	Particulars	J.F.	Amount (Rs.)
2008 April 14	To Cash A/c		28,000	2008 April 29	By M/s Machino Make A/c		14,000
				30	By Balance c/d		14,000
			28,000				28,000
May 1	To Balance b/d		14,000				

Dr.   **Computer Account**   Cr.

Date	Particulars	J.F.	Amount (Rs.)	Date	Particulars	J.F.	Amount (Rs.)
2008 April 3	To Machino Make A/c		21,200	April 30	By Balance c/d		21,200
			21,200				21,200
May 1	To Balance b/d		21,200				

Dr.   **Machino Make Account**   Cr.

Date	Particulars	J.F.	Amount (Rs.)	Date	Particulars	J.F.	Amount (Rs.)
2008 April 29	To Bank A/c		14,000	2008 April 3	By Computer A/c		21,200
30	To Balance c/d		7,200				
			21,200				21,200
				May 1	By Balance b/d		7,200

Dr.   **Sales Account**   Cr.

Date	Particulars	J.F.	Amount (Rs.)	Date	Particulars	J.F.	Amount (Rs.)
2008 June 30	By Balance c/d		17,800	2008 April 23	By Mahim A/c		17,800
			17,800				17,800
				May 1	By Balance b/d		17,800

Dr.   **Advertisement Account**   Cr.

Date	Particulars	J.F.	Amount (Rs.)	Date	Particulars	J.F.	Amount (Rs.)
2008 April 7	To Cash A/c		3,600	2008 April 30	By Balance c/d		3,600
			3,600				3,600
May 1	To Balance b/d		3,600				

Dr.   **Rent Account**   Cr.

Date	Particulars	J.F.	Amount (Rs.)	Date	Particulars	J.F.	Amount (Rs.)
2008 April 7	To Cash A/c		2,600	2008 April 30	By Balance c/d		2,600
			2,600				2,600
May 1	To Balance b/d		2,600				

Dr.   **Purchases Account**   Cr.

Date	Particulars	J.F.	Amount (Rs.)	Date	Particulars	J.F.	Amount (Rs.)
2008 April 17	To Ratan A/c		12,700	2008 June 30	By Balance c/d		12,700
			12,700				12,700
May 1	To Balance b/d		12,700				

Dr.   **Return Outwards Account**   Cr.

Date	Particulars	J.F.	Amount (Rs.)	Date	Particulars	J.F.	Amount (Rs.)
2008 April 30	By Balance c/d		1,900	2008 April 19	By Ratan A/c		1,900
			1,900				1,900
				May 1	By Balance b/d		1,900

Dr.   **Ratan Account**   Cr.

Date	Particulars	J.F.	Amount (Rs.)	Date	Particulars	J.F.	Amount (Rs.)
2008 April 19	Return Outwards A/c		1,900	2008 April 17	By Purchases A/c		12,700
30	By Balance c/d		10,800				
			12,700				12,700
				May 1	By Balance b/d		10,800

Dr.   **Mahim Account**   Cr.

Date	Particulars	J.F.	Amount (Rs.)	Date	Particulars	J.F.	Amount (Rs.)
2008 April 23	To Sales		17,800	2008 April 30	By Balance c/d		17,800
			17,800				17,800
May 1	To Balance b/d		17,800				

Dr.			Miscellaneous Expenses Account					Cr.
Date	Particulars	J.F.	Amount (Rs.)	Date	Particulars	J.F.	Amount (Rs.)
2008 April 26	To Cash A/c		750	2008 April 30	By Balance c/d		750
			750				750
May 1	To Balance b/d		750				

Dr.			Petty Cashier Account					Cr.
Date	Particulars	J.F.	Amount (Rs.)	Date	Particulars	J.F.	Amount (Rs.)
2008 April 28	To Cash A/c		1,200	2008 April 30	By Balance c/d		1,200
			1,200				1,200
May 1	To Balance b/d		1,200				

Trial Balance prepared with the help of the closing balances of all the accounts as under:

Trial Balance for the period ended ...

Closing Balances of All Accounts	Amount (Dr.) Rs.	Amount (Cr.) Rs.
Cash Account	24,850	
Capital Account		140,000
Stock Account	21,000	
Machinery Account	30,000	
Furniture Account	28,000	
Bank Account	14,000	
Computer Account	21,200	
Advertisement Account	3,600	
Purchases Account	12,700	
Mahim Account	17,800	
Miscellaneous Expenses Account	750	
Petty Cashier Account	1,200	
Machino Make Account		7,200
Sales Account		17,800
Ratan Account		10,800
Return Outwards Account		1,900
Rent Account	2,600	
	177,700	177,700

ILLUSTRATION 8.11   Pass necessary journal entries and post them in the appropriate ledger accounts of Mr. T. K. Basant for the month of June, 2008:

2008 June 1   Started business with cash in hand Rs. 48,000 and Rs. 50,000 at bank

3   Paid wages to staff Rs. 5,600

7   Purchased stationery Rs. 1,300 in cash

9   Paid insurance premium by a cheque of Rs. 2,100

11   Bought goods from Sindh & Co. Rs. 18,700

14   Paid electricity bill Rs. 900

17   Purchased office equipment Rs. 7,600

19   Goods returned to Sindh & Co. Rs. 1,300

23   Sold goods to Saha Bros. for Rs. 16,500

24   Issued a cheque of Rs. 17,000 to Sindh & Co. in full settlement of their account

27   Received a cheque of Rs. 7,600 from Saha Bros. and allowed them discount Rs. 200

28   Received interest from bank Rs. 280

29   Delivery van purchased on credit from G.P. Suppliers Rs. 24,000

Solution

In the books of Mr. T.K. Basant
Journal

Date	Particulars		L.F.	Amount Dr. (Rs.)	Amount Cr. (Rs.)
2008 June 1	Cash A/c	Dr.		48,000	
	Bank A/c	Dr.		50,000	
	To Capital A/c				98,000
	(Being the business started with cash and bank balances)				
3	Wages A/c	Dr.		5,600	
	To Cash A/c				5,600
	(Being wages paid to staff)				
7	Stationery A/c	Dr.		1,300	
	To Cash A/c				1,300
	(Being stationery purchased)				
9	Insurance Premium A/c	Dr.		2,100	
	To Bank A/c				2,100
	(Being insurance premium paid)				
11	Purchases A/c	Dr.		18,700	
	To Sindh & Co. A/c				18,700
	(Being goods purchased on credit)				
14	Electric Charges A/c	Dr.		900	
	To Cash A/c				900
	(Being electric charges paid)				
17	Office Equipments A/c	Dr.		7,600	
	To Cash A/c				7,600
	(Being office equipments purchased)				
19	Sindh & Co. A/c	Dr.		1,300	
	To Purchase Returns A/c				1,300
	(Being goods returned)				
23	Saha Bros. A/c	Dr.		16,500	
	To Sales A/c				16,500
	(Being goods sold on credit)				
24	Sindh & Co A/c	Dr.		17,400	
	To Bank A/c*				17,000
	To Discount Received A/c				400
	(Being final payment made to Sindh & Co and received discount)				
27	Bank A/c	Dr.		7,600	
	Discount Allowed A/c	Dr.		200	
	To Saha Bros. A/c				7,800
	(Being cheque received and allowed discount)				
28	Bank A/c	Dr.		280	
	To Interest Received A/c				280
	(Being the interest received from bank)				
29	Delivery van A/c	Dr.		24,000	
	To G.P. Suppliers A/c				24,000
	(Being the delivery van purchased on credit)				

	Rs.
*Total goods purchased from Sindh & Co.	18,700
Less: Goods returned to them	1,300
	17,400
Less: Issued cheque	17,000
Hence, Discount received	400

Ledger

Dr.   **Cash Account**   **Cr.**

Date	Particulars	J.F.	Amount (Rs.)	Date	Particulars	J.F.	Amount (Rs.)
2008 June 1	To Capital A/c		48,000	2008 June 3	By Wages A/c		5,600
				7	By Stationery A/c		1,300
				9	By Insurance Premium A/c		2,100
				14	By Electric Charges A/c		900
				17	By Office Equipments A/c		7,600
				30	By Balance c/d		30,500
			48,000				48,000
July 1	To Balance b/d		30,500				

Dr.   **Capital Account**   **Cr.**

Date	Particulars	J.F.	Amount (Rs.)	Date	Particulars	J.F.	Amount (Rs.)
2008 June 30	To Balance c/d		98,000	2008 June 1	By Cash A/c		48,000
					By Bank A/c		50,000
			98,000				98,000
				July 1	By Balance b/d		98,000

Dr.   **Purchases Account**   **Cr.**

Date	Particulars	J.F.	Amount (Rs.)	Date	Particulars	J.F.	Amount (Rs.)
2008 June 11	To Sindh & Co. A/c		18,700	2008 June 30	By Balance c/d		18,700
			18,700				18,700
July 1	To Balance b/d		18,700				

Dr.   **Sales Account**   **Cr.**

Date	Particulars	J.F.	Amount (Rs.)	Date	Particulars	J.F.	Amount (Rs.)
2008 June 30	By Balance c/d		16,500	2008 June 23	By Saha Bros. A/c		16,500
			16,500				16,500
				July 1	By Balance b/d		16,500

Dr.   **Bank Account**   **Cr.**

Date	Particulars	J.F.	Amount (Rs.)	Date	Particulars	J.F.	Amount (Rs.)
2008 June 1	To Capital A/c		50,000	2008 June 24	By Sindh & Co. A/c		17,000
27	To Saha Bros. A/c		7,600	30	By Balance c/d		40,880
28	To Interest Received A/c		280				
			57,880				57,880
July 1	To Balance b/d		40,880				

Dr.   **Wages Account**   **Cr.**

Date	Particulars	J.F.	Amount (Rs.)	Date	Particulars	J.F.	Amount (Rs.)
2008 June 3	To Cash A/c		5,600	2008 June 30	By Balance c/d		5,600
			5,600				5,600
July 1	To Balance b/d		5,600				

Dr.   **Stationery Account**   Cr.

Date	Particulars	J.F.	Amount (Rs.)	Date	Particulars	J.F.	Amount (Rs.)
2008 June 7	To Cash A/c		1,300	2008 June 30	By Balance c/d		1,300
			1,300				1,300
July 1	To Balance b/d		1,300				

Dr.   **Insurance Premium Account**   Cr.

Date	Particulars	J.F.	Amount (Rs.)	Date	Particulars	J.F.	Amount (Rs.)
2008 June 9	To Cash A/c		2,100	2008 June 30	By Balance c/d		2,100
			2,100				2,100
July 1	To Balance b/d		2,100				

Dr.   **Sindh & Co. Account**   Cr.

Date	Particulars	J.F.	Amount (Rs.)	Date	Particulars	J.F.	Amount (Rs.)
2008 June 19	To Purchase returns A/c		1,300	2008 June 11	By Purchases A/c		18,700
24	To Bank A/c		17,000				
24	To Discount received A/c		400				
			18,700				18,700

Dr.   **Electric Charges Account**   Cr.

Date	Particulars	J.F.	Amount (Rs.)	Date	Particulars	J.F.	Amount (Rs.)
2008 June 14	To Cash A/c		900	2008 June 30	By Balance c/d		900
			900				900
May 1	To Balance b/d		900				

Dr.   **Office Equipment Account**   Cr.

Date	Particulars	J.F.	Amount (Rs.)	Date	Particulars	J.F.	Amount (Rs.)
2008 June 17	To Cash A/c		7,600	2008 June 30	By Balance c/d		7,600
			7,600				7,600
July 1	To Balance b/d		7,600				

Dr.   **Purchase Returns Account**   Cr.

Date	Particulars	J.F.	Amount (Rs.)	Date	Particulars	J.F.	Amount (Rs.)
2008 June 30	To Balance c/d		1,300	2008 June 19	By Sindh & Co. A/c		1,300
			1,300				1,300
				July 1	By Balance b/d		1,300

Dr.   **Saha Bros. Account**   Cr.

Date	Particulars	J.F.	Amount (Rs.)	Date	Particulars	J.F.	Amount (Rs.)
2008 June 23	To Sales A/c		16,500	2008 June 27	By Bank A/c		7,600
					By Discount Allowed A/c		200
				30	By Balance c/d		8,700
			16,500				16,500
July 1	To Balance b/d		8,700				

Dr.   **Discount Received Account**   Cr.

Date	Particulars	J.F.	Amount (Rs.)	Date	Particulars	J.F.	Amount (Rs.)
2008 June 30	To Balance c/d		400	2008 June 24	By Sindh & Co. A/c		400
			400				400
				July 1	By Balance b/d		400

Dr.   **Discount Allowed Account**   Cr.

Date	Particulars	J.F.	Amount (Rs.)	Date	Particulars	J.F.	Amount (Rs.)
2008 June 27	To Saha Bros. A/c		200	2008 June 30	By Balance c/d		200
			200				200
July 1	To Balance b/d		200				

Dr.   **Interest Received Account**   Cr.

Date	Particulars	J.F.	Amount (Rs.)	Date	Particulars	J.F.	Amount (Rs.)
2008 June 30	To Balance c/d		280	2008 June 24	By Bank A/c		280
			280				280
				July 1	By Balance b/d		280

Dr.   **Delivery Van Account**   Cr.

Date	Particulars	J.F.	Amount (Rs.)	Date	Particulars	J.F.	Amount (Rs.)
2008 June 29	To G.P. Suppliers A/c		24,000	2008 June 30	By Balance c/d		24,000
			24,000				24,000
July 1	To Balance b/d		24,000				

Dr.   **G.P. Suppliers Account**   Cr.

Date	Particulars	J.F.	Amount (Rs.)	Date	Particulars	J.F.	Amount (Rs.)
2008 June 30	To Balance c/d		24,000	2008 June 29	By Delivery Van A/c		24,000
			24,000				24,000
				July 1	By Balance b/d		24,000

Trial Balance for the period ended ...

Closing balances of all accounts	Amount (Dr.) Rs.	Amount (Cr.) Rs.
Cash Account	30,500	
Capital Account		98,000
Bank Account	40,880	
Stationery Account	1,300	
Wages Account	5,600	
Insurance Premium Account	2,100	
Electric Charges Account	900	
Office Equipments Account	7,600	
Purchases Account	18,700	
Purchase Returns Account		1,300
Saha Bros. Account	8,700	
Discount Allowed Account	200	
Delivery Van Account	24,000	
Sales Account		16,500
Discount Received Account		400
Interest Received Account		280
G.P. Suppliers Account		24,000
	140,480	140,480

EXERCISES

I. *Objective Type Questions (With Answers)*

Fill in the blanks:

1. When an asset is brought in by the proprietor for business use, _____ A/c will be credited.
2. When Goods are distributed as charity, _____ A/c will be debited.
3. When goods are withdrawn by the proprietor from the business for personal use, _____ A/c will be debited
4. For Salary paid to Shyam, _____ A/c will be debited.
5. Interest received from Gupta, _____ A/c will be credited.
6. Rent paid to D'Silva, _____ A/c will be debited.
7. For payment of net VAT to the Government (after adjustment of VAT paid on purchase and payable for sale), _____ A/c will be debited and _____ A/c will be credited.
8. When a debt (a customer) is declared bad, _____ A/c will be debited and _____ A/c will be credited.
9. When Sales Tax is charged to debtors (not received), _____ A/c will be debited and _____ A/c will be credited.
10. When Sales Tax is collected from the debtors at the time of sale, _____ A/c will be debited and _____ A/c will be credited.
11. When VAT is paid at the time of purchasing goods, _____ and _____ A/c's will be debited and _____ A/c will be credited.
12. For wages paid for installation of plant, _____ A/c will be debited.
13. For carriage paid for carrying fixed assets, _____ A/c will be debited.
14. When VAT is collected from the customers at the time of sale of goods: _____ and _____ A/c's will be credited.
15. For goods distributed as free samples, _____ A/c will be debited and _____ A/c will be credited.

   Ans: 1. Capital A/c; 2. Charity A/c; 3.Drawings A/c; 4.Salary A/c; 5. Interest Received A/c; 6. Rent A/c; 7. VAT Collected A/c will be debited and VAT A/c(paid) and Cash/Bank A/c will be credited; 8. Bad Debts A/c will be debited and Debtors A/c will be credited; 9. Debtors A/c and Sales Tax A/c; 10. Cash/Bank A/c and Sales Tax A/c; 11. Purchases and VAT A/c will be debited and Bank A/c will be credited; 12. Plant A/c will be debited; 13. Fixed Asset A/c will be debited; 14. Sales and VAT Collected A/c will be credited; 15. Advertisement A/c will be debited and Opening Stock/Purchases A/c will be credited.

II. *Short Answer Type Questions*

1. What do you mean by double entry system?
   Ans: This system has two-fold effect or dual aspect. Any transaction of a business affects two accounts in the opposite directions. According to the principle of double entry system, there can be no giving without a receiving. The receiving aspect is known as **debit** and the giving aspect is known as **credit**. So every debit must have a corresponding credit.

2. What are the different types of accounting methods or systems used in accounting?
   Ans: Generally, there are three recognized systems of accounting. They are as follows:
   (a) Mercantile or accrual system of accounting
   (b) Cash system or method of accounting
   (c) Hybrid system of accounting.

3. What do you mean by mercantile or accrual system of accounting?
   Ans: According to this system, every transaction or an event which has changed the financial position of a firm within an accounting period must be taken into consideration, whether cash is received or not, paid or not. It means that not only the cash transactions are to

be taken into account, but other transactions such as outstanding expenditures, accrued incomes, prepaid expenditures or pre-received incomes are also to be taken into account.

4. **What do you mean by cash system or method of accounting?**

   Ans: Under this system, accounting entries are made when actual cash is paid or received. No entry is required to be shown when any expenditure or income is due or accrued. Some professionals keep record of their transactions through this system.

5. **What do you mean by transaction and how is it classified?**

   Ans: An event which is measurable in terms of money, has happened within an accounting year and by which the financial position of a firm/person has been changed is called a transaction. Generally transactions are of two types—external and internal transactions.

6. **What do you mean by internal transactions?**

   Ans: Within this type of transaction, a second party is not involved but due to some incident the financial position of the firm has been changed or has to be changed. For example, depreciation charged on fixed assets, obsolete item of assets to be written off, etc.

7. **How are external transactions classified?**

   Ans: External transactions may be further sub-divided into two types—cash transactions and credit transactions. The transactions which are related in cash/cheque received or paid for any purpose are called cash transaction. Those external transactions which are not related in cash payment or receipt forthwith are called credit transactions. Such as goods sold on credit to M/s. D.D. Bros.

8. **What do you mean by 'Accounts'?**

   Ans: It is a statement prepared in a special form in the ledger where summarized record of transactions affecting to a particular person, asset, income or any other subject are shown. The benefits received being on the one side and benefits given on the other side, such as Machinery A/c, Ram A/c, Rent A/c, etc.

9. **How are accounts classified?**

   Ans: Accounts are classified into three types which are shown below:

	Accounts (A/c)				
	Personal A/c		Real (Assets) A/c		Nominal A/c
Natural Persons	Artifical Persons	Representative Personal	Tangible	Intangible	Expenses	Incomes

10. **What do you mean by representative personal account?**

    Ans: These accounts represent a certain person or group of persons. For Example, capital A/c (Which represent the proprietor for his investments/contributions), drawings A/c (which represent the proprietor for his drawings), outstanding Rent A/c (which represent the Landlord's A/c who will receive the rent in future), income received in advance A/c, accrued incomes A/c, etc.

11. **What do you mean by artificial person's account?**

    Ans: Any firm's A/c, company's A/c, club's A/c, institution's A/c, etc. are known as artificial person's A/c.

12. **How are Real Accounts classified? Explain in brief.**

    Ans: Generally, real accounts are classified into two types—tangible and intangible. They are explained in brief below:

    Tangible real accounts. The items of assets which can be touched and felt are called tangible real assets such as buildings, machinery, cash, furniture, etc.

    Intangible real accounts. The kinds of assets which cannot be touched are called intangible real assets, for example, goodwill, trademarks, patents, etc.

13. What do you mean by goods?
   Ans: The term *goods* include those items which are purchased by a business/firm for resale. So when a furniture is purchased for resale, it will be considered goods and when it is purchased for use, it will be considered an asset.

14. How are goods accounts classified?
   Ans: The division of goods account is given below:
   Purchases A/c, Sales A/c, Purchases Returns A/c, Sales Returns A/c, Stock A/c and Goods Sent on Consignment A/c.

15. What do you mean by journal?
   Ans: The word *journal* has been derived from the French word *jour* which means a diary. It is a subsidiary book where daily transactions of a firm are recorded chronologically under the double entry system of book keeping. All the transactions are first recorded in the journal book and as such, it is called a book of original entry.

16. How is journal classified? Explain in brief them.
   Ans: Generally, journals are divided into two types as given below:
   (i) General journal
   (ii) Special journal
       Special journals can be further sub-divided into the following types:
       Cash Book, Purchase Day Book, Sales Day Book, Purchase Return Book, Sales Return Book, Bills Receivable Book and Bills Payable Book.

       There are some transactions which occasionally happen and are not recorded in special journals. Such type of transactions are recorded in a separate book known as **journal proper.** The following types of transactions are recorded in journal proper:
   1. Opening entries
   2. Closing entries
   3. Transfer entries
   4. Credit purchase and sale of fixed assets
   5. Adjustment entries
   6. Rectification of errors.

17. How is ledger classified? Explain in brief.
   Ans: Ledgers may be classified as follows:
   (a) *General or impersonal ledger.* It contains all types of accounts except debtors and creditors, for example, capital and drawings accounts, assets accounts, goods accounts, liabilities accounts (excluding creditors) and all nominal accounts.
   (b) *Debtors ledger.* It contains all the accounts of those persons or firms to whom goods are sold on credit.
   (c) *Creditors ledger.* It contains all the accounts of those persons or firms from whom goods are purchased on credit.

18. What do you mean by balancing of an account?
   Ans: At the end of a certain period, to know the net or final position of a particular account, balancing is made. At first, two sides (debit and credit) are added up and if they are not equal, then the difference is ascertained or calculated. The difference is put on the smaller side written as To Balance c/d or By Balance c/d (carried down) and in the subsequent period, it is known as Balance b/d (brought down), shown on the opposite side of the c/d balance (i.e. on the heavier side).

19. What do you mean by trial balance?
   Ans: Trial balance is prepared to check the arithmetical accuracy of the book-keeping entries. At the end of accounting period or at the end of a certain period, when all the accounts of a firm are closed or balanced, then with the help of those balances, a list or statement is

prepared, which is known as **Trial Balance**. All debit balances of accounts are shown on the debit side of the trial balance and credit balance on the credit side. The total of both the sides of the trial balance must be equal, because it is based on the double entry system that every debit must have a corresponding credit.

III. *Long Answer Type Questions*

1. "Every transaction in a double entry book keeping must have a double entry". Evaluate.
2. How are transactions recorded through the double entry system?
3. State the rules of journalising with respect to each class of accounts.
4. What do you mean by a journal? Give the subdivisions of journals.
5. Briefly explain the chief features and advantages of a journal.
6. What is a ledger? Explain the relation between a journal and a ledger.
7. Distinguish between a journal and a ledger
8. What do you mean by a Trial Balance? Explain the objectives of preparing a Trial Balance.
9. Write short notes on the following:
    (a) Accounts
    (b) Transaction
    (c) Internal transaction
    (d) Methods of preparing Trial Balance
    (e) Representative Personal Account
    (f) Balancing of an Account
    (g) Posting.

IV. *Problems*

1. Give necessary Journal Entries for the following transactions in the books of Mr. K. Sen for the month of April, 2008:

2008	Transactions
April 1	Started business with cash Rs. 78, 000.
4	Goods purchased from Mukesh Rs. 11,900.
5	Paid carriage on purchase Rs. 780.
9	Purchased furniture for Rs. 4,100.
11	Paid shop rent Rs. 1,300.
16	Sold goods to Suvir Rs. 3,700.
19	Goods returned to Mukesh Rs. 600.
22	Commission received Rs. 950.
26	Goods returned by Suvir Rs. 500.
28	Opened a bank account with cash Rs. 26, 000.
29	Paid for advertisement Rs. 1,500.
30	Paid wages Rs. 3,100.

2. Enter the following transactions in the books of Mr. Naveen Kurla:

2008	Transactions
May 1	Started business with cash Rs. 65, 000.
3	Purchased furniture Rs. 2,490.
5	Purchased goods from Kumar Rs. 8,700.
8	Purchased machinery in cash Rs. 12,800.
10	Travelling expenses paid Rs. 800.
12	Cash paid to petty cashier Rs. 500.
16	Commission received Rs. 750.
19	Proprietor's house rent paid 1,600.
22	Sold goods to Mr. D.P. Guha Rs. 15,200.

25 Paid carriage on sales Rs. 700.

29 Sold goods for cash Rs. 8,000.

30 Paid salary to manager Mr. Sunil Das Rs. 3,000.

3. Give necessary Journal Entries for the following transactions in the books of Mr. P. Sinha for the month of April, 2008:

2008	Transactions
April 1	Started business with cash Rs. 91,000.
2	Purchased goods for cash Rs. 6,900.
4	Purchased goods from Raj Rs. 7,400.
7	Goods returned to Raj Rs. 1,100.
10	Sold goods for cash Rs. 6,700.
13	Opened a bank account with cash Rs. 31,000.
15	Purchased computer Rs. 10,300.
18	Wages paid for installation of computer Rs. 700.
23	Paid for advertisement Rs. 2,600.
25	Paid shop rent Rs. 1,400.
27	Sold goods for cash Rs. 6,000.
29	Paid salary to manager Mr. Yadav Rs. 2,900.

4. Journalize the following transactions in the books of S.P. Dutta:

2008	Transactions
July 1	Started business with cash Rs. 115, 000.
3	Purchased machinery for cash Rs. 21,000.
5	Wages paid for installation of new machinery Rs. 1,100.
8	Purchased goods from Nirmal for Rs. 9,300.
11	Opened a bank account with cash Rs. 31, 000.
14	Sold goods for cash Rs. 7,100.
16	Proprietor's house rent paid Rs. 1,600.
19	Trade subscription paid by a cheque of Rs. 500.
24	Received interest from bank Rs. 710.
27	Paid for advertisement Rs. 2,600.
29	Purchased stationery Rs. 320.
30	Cash paid to petty cashier Rs. 700.

5. Pass Journal Entries for the following transactions in the books of Mr. S. Khanna:

2008	Transactions
July 1	Travelling expenses paid Rs. 800.
4	Cash paid to petty cashier Rs. 500.
5	Commission received Rs. 750.
9	Proprietor's house rent paid 1,600.
11	Trade subscription paid by a cheque of Rs. 500.
16	Received interest from bank Rs. 710.
19	Paid for advertisement Rs. 2,600.
22	Paid shop rent Rs. 1,400.
26	Sold goods for cash Rs. 6,000.
28	Paid salary to manager Mr. Sunil Das Rs. 3,000.
29	Received interest on fixed deposits from bank Rs. 1,400.
30	Sold goods to Mr. D. Rum for Rs. 14,300.

6. Give necessary Journal Entries of the following transactions in the books of Mr. K. Gilani for the month of January, 2008:

2008	Transactions
January 1	Started business with cash Rs. 124,000.
3	Paid to Sudhir as an advance Rs. 750.
5	Purchased office equipments for cash Rs. 2,300.
8	Purchased goods from Nikhil for Rs. 5,600.
10	Opened a bank account with cash Rs. 41,000.
12	Received rent from Tapas Rs. 1,200.
16	Cash deposited into bank Rs. 1,700.
19	Paid Nikhil on account Rs. 1,400.
22	Paid electric charges Rs. 340.
25	Received interest from bank Rs. 210.
29	Cash withdrawn from bank for personal use Rs. 1,800.
30	Life insurance premium of the proprietor paid Rs. 1,700.

7. Enter the following transactions in the books of Mr. Shaidh Bala:

2008	Transactions
May 1	Started business with cash Rs. 110,000.
3	Purchased furniture from Durgapur Furniture for Rs. 3,000.
5	Goods purchased from M/s Ghosh Bros. for Rs. 10,800 and paid carriage on it Rs. 500.
8	Sold goods to Mr. Mukesh Rs. 11,650 and paid carriage on it Rs. 300.
10	Cash received from Mukesh Rs. 6,500.
12	Discount allowed to Mukesh Rs. 240.
16	Paid sundry expenses Rs. 350.
19	Paid coolie charges Rs. 120.
22	Repair charges for computer paid Rs. 300.
25	Received a loan of Rs. 4,000 from Sunil.
29	Cash withdrawn from business account for personal use Rs. 750
30	Paid wages Rs. 2,500.

8. Journalize the following transactions in the books of Mr. C.P. Sen:

1997	Transactions
March 1	Sri Sen started his business with capital of Rs. 60,000 which consist of machinery worth Rs. 15,000, furniture worth Rs. 10,000 and balance in cash.
4	Opened a Bank A/c with cash Rs. 10,000.
5	Purchase office stationery for Rs. 600.
7	Purchased goods from D.K. Brothers for Rs. 8,000 and paid carriage on it Rs. 300.
12	Sold goods to P. Sen for Rs. 3,200.
13	Received a cheque of Rs. 1,900 from Mr. P. Sen.
15	Paid Life Insurance premium of Rs. 650.
18	Paid cash to D.K. Brothers Rs. 6,000.
21	Sold goods for Rs. 3,900 in cash and out of that, deposited Rs. 2,500 in cash into bank.
24	Paid shop rent of Rs. 460.
25	Drew from bank Rs. 300 for personal use.
27	Paid salary of Rs. 1,800 to the manager Mr. A. Bose.
29	Received interest of Rs. 250 from bank.
30	Paid telephone charges of Rs. 170.
31	Sold old furniture for Rs. 6,900.

9. Enter the following transactions in the books of T.T. Traders:

1997	Transactions
April 1	Rs. 6,000 cash withdrawn from bank.
3	Rs. 4,600 salary paid to workers.
4	Purchased goods from M.K. Brothers for Rs. 7,000.
7	Purchased furniture for office use for Rs. 2,800.
9	Paid Rs. 750 for advertisement.
12	Received a cheque of Rs. 2,500 from A.B. Kar.
14	Bank notified that A.B. Kar's cheque became dishonoured.
15	Paid Rs. 750 towards repairs charges.
18	Loan of Rs. 6,000 taken from D.K. finance.
21	Issued a cheque of Rs. 1,250 in favour of G.R. Dhar.
24	Paid customs duty of Rs. 900 by cheque.
26	Mr. T. Das settled his account of Rs. 1,800 in cash and was allowed a discount of Rs. 100.
28	Rs. 950 in cash paid to N. Mukherjee and received a discount of Rs. 50.
29	Received commission of Rs. 450.
30	Deposited Rs. 2,750 in cash into bank.

10. Journalize the following transactions:

1997	Transactions
May 1	Paid for postage and stationery Rs. 350.
3	Purchased old furniture for Rs. 2,100.
5	Cash withdrawn from bank for petty expenses Rs. 500.
6	Paid rent to landlord Rs. 1,500.
8	Mr. X settled his A/c of Rs. 650 by paying cash Rs. 620.
10	Proprietor's house rent paid Rs. 1,500.
12	Cash withdrawn from bank for payment of salary of the office staff Rs. 4,500.
15	Bought a typewriter for Rs. 5,000.
16	Paid for advertisement by cheque Rs. 950.
18	Withdrawn from bank for household purpose Rs. 1,500.
21	Purchase stationery worth Rs. 260.
22	Sold goods to P. Kumar for Rs. 5,000 and was allowed 5% trade discount.
25	Paid interest on loan Rs. 850.
26	Purchase household furniture for Rs. 2,500.
28	Bank collected dividend Rs. 1,600.
30	Paid subscription Rs. 350.

11. Journalize the following transactions in the books of Sri Arup Ganguly:

1997	Transactions
January 1	Started business with capital Rs. 80,000.
2	Purchased office furniture for Rs. 9,000.
3	Purchased goods from Raha Bros. Rs. 11,200.
5	Sold goods to Prakash for Rs. 3,000.
7	Goods return to Raha Bros. for Rs. 700.
8	Paid subscription Rs. 650.
10	Paid salary to manager Rs. 4,000.
13	Goods returned by Prakash Rs. 300.
15	Donation to Prime Minister's Flood Relief Fund Rs. 2,000.
18	Received commission Rs. 1,500.
19	Proprietor's house rent paid Rs. 1,200.

22 Sold goods Rs. 4,000.
24 Paid telephone rent by cheque Rs. 750.
25 Paid godown rent Rs. 630.
28 Prakash settled his account by cheque and was allowed a discount of Rs. 130.
29 Paid Raha Bros. Rs. 4,600.
29 Received interest from bank Rs. 500.
30 Paid repairs to building Rs. 1,500.
31 Cash deposited into bank Rs. 10,000.

12. From the information given below, give the Journal Entries and show the Ledger Accounts in the books of Mr. Mahima Prakash:

1997	Transaction

May 1 Mr. Mahima Prakash started his business with cash Rs. 50,000, furniture worth Rs. 10,000, machinery worth Rs. 30,000 and stock worth Rs. 9,000.
2 Opened a bank account with cash Rs. 30,000.
3 Purchased goods from Hindustan Traders for Rs. 9,550 and paid carriage on it Rs. 630.
5 Sold goods to Vikram Bros. for Rs. 6,610 and paid carriage on it Rs. 220.
7 Paid van driver's wages Rs. 950.
8 Goods returned to Hindustan Traders Rs. 780 and paid Rs. 9,000 by cheque in full settlement of their account.
10 Issued a cheque in favour of Vikram Bros. for Rs. 5,600.
11 Salary paid to Kuntal Roy Rs. 2,000.
12 Sold goods for cash Rs. 3,100.
14 Purchased shares of X Ltd. for Rs. 2,600 by cheque.
17 Purchased office stationery for Rs. 520.
19 Loan given to Sri P. Sen Rs. 4000.
20 Paid repairs charges Rs. 430.
22 Paid for advertisement by cheque Rs. 1,660.
23 Paid godown rent by cheque Rs. 920.
25 Trade subscription paid by bank Rs. 450.
30 Paid repairs charges of proprietor's car Rs. 1,580.

13. From the following Ledger Account, show the necessary Journal Entries:

Dr.　　　　　　　　　　　　　　　　　**Cash Account**　　　　　　　　　　　　　　　　Cr.

Date	Particulars	J.F.	Amount (Rs.)	Date	Particulars	J.F.	Amount (Rs.)
1997				1997			
January 1	To Capital A/c		18,000	January 3	By Purchases A/c		9,000
6	To Sales A/c		5,000	8	By Rent A/c		700
10	To Rabin A/c		3,000	10	By Wages A/c		500
16	To P. Bros. A/c		6,000	15	By Advertisement A/c		900
21	To Machinery A/c		4,200	18	By X & Co. A/c		2,000
				24	By Drawings A/c		600
				30	By Machinery A/c		2,800
				31	By Balance c/d		19,700
			36,200				36,200
Febuary 1	To Balance b/d		19,700				

Ans: Jan. 1: Cash A/c Dr., Capital A/c Cr.; Jan. 3: Purchase A/c Dr. and Cash A/c Cr.; Jan. 6: Cash A/c Dr. and Sales A/c Cr.; Jan. 8. Rent A/c Dr. and Cash A/c Cr.; Jan. 10: Wages A/c Dr. and Cash A/c Cr.; Jan. 10: Cash A/c Dr., Rabin A/c Cr.; Jan. 15: Advertisement A/c Dr. and Cash A/c Cr.; Jan. 16: Cash A/c Dr., and P. Bros. A/c Cr.; Jan. 18: X & Co. A/c Dr.

and Cash A/c Cr.; Jan. 21: Cash A/c Dr. and Machinery A/c Cr.; Jan. 24: Drawings A/c Dr. and Cash A/c Cr.; Jan. 30: Machinery A/c Dr. and Cash A/c Cr.

14. From the following two accounts, give the necessary Journal Entries:

Dr.   **Cash Account**   Cr.

Date	Particulars	J.F.	Amount (Rs.)	Date	Particulars	J.F.	Amount (Rs.)
1997				1997			
January 1	To Balance b/d		16,900	January 5	By Bank A/c		4,000
3	To P. Kumar A/c		6,000	12	By Purchase A/c		3,900
12	To Sales A/c		7,200	17	By Furniture A/c		2,500
18	To Bank A/c		3,000	21	By S. Kar A/c		3,400
				31	By Balance c/d		19,300
			33,100				33,100
Febuary 1	To Balance b/d		19,300				

Dr.   **Bank Account**   Cr.

Date	Particulars	J.F.	Amount (Rs.)	Date	Particulars	J.F.	Amount (Rs.)
1997				1997			
January 1	To Balance b/d		12,500	January 10	By Roy Bros. A/c		6,100
5	To Cash A/c		4,000	18	By Cash A/c		3,000
16	To Interest A/c		300	31	By Balance c/d		10,400
23	To Sen Bros. A/c		2,700				
			19,500				19,500
Febuary 1	To Balance b/d		10,400				

Ans: Jan. 3: Cash A/c Dr. and P. Kumar A/c Cr.; Jan. 5: Bank A/c Dr. and Cash A/c Cr.; Jan. 10: Roy Bros. A/c Dr. and Bank A/c Cr.; Jan. 12: Cash A/c Dr. and Sales A/c Cr.; Jan. 12: Purchases A/c Dr. and Cash A/c Cr.; Jan. 16: Bank A/c Dr. and Interest A/c Cr.; Jan. 17: Furniture A/c Dr. and Cash A/c Cr.; Jan. 18: Cash A/c Dr. and Bank A/c Cr.; Jan. 21: S. Kar A/c Dr. and Cash A/c Cr.; Jan. 23: Bank A/c Dr. and Sen Bros. A/c Cr.

15. Give the correct Journal Entries on the basis of the narrations stated below:

Date	Particulars	L.F.	Amount Dr. (Rs.)	Amount Cr. (Rs.)
2008 January 1	Bank A/c Dr.		10,000	
	To Cash A/c			10,000
	(Being the cash withdrawn from the bank)			
4	M. Sen A/c Dr.		3,000	
	To Cash A/c			3,000
	(Being the salary paid to M. Sen)			
6	Purchases A/c Dr.		2,800	
	To Cash A/c			2,800
	(Being machinery purchased for cash)			
8	B. Das A/c Dr.		6,000	
	To Purchases A/c			6,000
	(Being the goods purchased from B. Das on credit)			
12	Cash A/c Dr.		700	
	To Drawings A/c			700
	(Being cash withdrawn from business for personal use)			
18	X A/c Dr.		600	
	To Sales Return A/c			600
	(Being the goods returned by X)			

(Contd.)

Date	Particulars		L.F.	Amount Dr. (Rs.)	Amount Cr. (Rs.)
22	A. Roy A/c To Discount A/c (Being discount allowed to A. Roy)	Dr.		100	100
25	Cash A/c To Sales A/c (Being furniture sold in cash)	Dr.		900	900
28	Furniture A/c To Depreciation A/c (Being depreciation charged on furniture)	Dr.		800	800

Ans: Jan. 1: Cash Dr. and Bank Cr; Jan. 4: Salary A/c Dr. and Cash A/c Cr.; Jan. 6: Machinery A/c Dr. and Cash A/c Cr.; Jan. 8: Purchases A/c Dr. and B. Das A/c Cr.; Jan. 12: Drawings A/c Dr. and Cash A/c Cr.; Jan. 18: Sales Return A/c Dr. and X A/c Cr.; Jan. 22: Discount A/c Dr. and A. Roy A/c Cr.; Jan. 25: Cash A/c Dr. and Furniture A/c Cr.; Jan. 28: Depreciation A/c Dr. and Furniture A/c Cr.

16. From the following information, prepare A. Roy's Account in the books of P. Sen:

> **1998** **Transactions**
>
> March 1 Sold goods to A. Roy Rs. 8,000.
>   4 Cash received from A. Roy Rs. 2,500.
>   7 Goods returned by A. Roy Rs. 160.
>   9 Received a cheque of Rs. 500 from A. Roy.
>   12 Sold goods worth Rs. 12,000 to A. Roy and paid carriage on it Rs. 200.
>   18 Received cash Rs. 6,500 from A. Roy and allowed him discount Rs. 150.
>   24 Received a cheque of Rs. 3,500 from A. Roy.
>   28 Received cash from A. Roy Rs. 700.

Ans: A. Roy's A/c showing a Closing Debit Balance of Rs. 5,990.

17. Cash A/c of Rabi Das for January 1998 is given below, in which some entries have been wrongly posted. You are required to correct those errors and close the accounts:

In the Books of Rabi Das

Dr. **Cash Account** Cr.

Date	Particulars	J.F.	Amount (Rs.)	Date	Particulars	J.F.	Amount (Rs.)
1998 January 1	To Balance b/d		21,600	**1998** January 5	By Sales A/c		7,000
7	To Purchases A/c		3,000	6	By Rent A/c		800
18	To Drawings A/c		1,000	8	By Wages A/c		900
21	To B. Roy's A/c (Creditor)		4,000	12	By Purchase Return A/c		1,200
				15	By Bad Debts A/c		700
26	To Sales Return		400	19	By Y's A/c (Debtor)		1,900
				31	By Balance c/d		17,500
			30,000				30,000

Ans: Cash A/c Closing Balance on January 31, 1998 Rs. 20,800. Purchase Return, Sales Return and Bad Debt will not be included in this account.

18. Give necessary Journal Entries and Ledger Accounts for the following transactions and trial balance in the books of Mr. K.K. Krishnamurti for the month of January, 2008:

> **2008** **Transaction**
>
> January 1 Mr. K.K.Krishnamurti started business with cash Rs. 95,000.
>   3 Purchased furniture from Durgapur Suppliers for Rs. 4,000.
>   5 Goods purchased from M/s T.G. Bros. for Rs. 15,800 and paid carriage on it Rs. 600.

6   Opened a bank account with cash Rs. 24,000.
10   Sold goods to Mr. D.P. Dhara for Rs. 12,800 and paid carriage on it Rs. 700.
13   Sold goods for cash Rs. 8,000.
15   Paid for advertisement by a cheque of Rs. 1,600.
18   Purchased computer from M/s Durgapur Syndicate in cash Rs. 11,000.
20   Trade subscription paid by a cheque of Rs. 800.
21   Goods returned by Mr. D.P. Dhara amounting to Rs. 1,200 and received cash from him Rs. 4,000.
25   Paid cash Rs. 3,700 to Durgapur Suppliers in full settlement of their account and received discount of Rs. 300.
26   Cash withdrawn from bank for office use Rs. 1,000.
27   Cash withdrawn from bank for personal use Rs. 1,400.
29   Issued a cheque of Rs. 3,900 in favour of M/s T.G. Bros.
30   Paid shop rent Rs. 2,100.
30   Received interest from bank Rs. 140.

Ans: Trial Balance Total Rs. 128,140.

19. Give necessary Journal Entries and Ledger Accounts of the following transactions in the books of Mr. R.P. Jalal for the month of March, 2008:

2008	Transactions
March 3	Paid cash to Suresh Rs. 5,900 and received discount Rs. 230.
4	Goods returned by M/s R.E Bros. Rs. 2,300.
7	Sold old furniture Rs. 1,670.
9	Received a cheque from Mr. G.S. Dutta Rs. 2,900.
11	Goods returned to M/s G. D. Suppliers Rs. 1,750.
13	Sold goods to Mr. T. Samanta for Rs. 6,700 and paid carriage on it Rs. 400.
15	Proprietor's house rent paid by a cheque of Rs. 3,100.
17	Trade subscription paid by a cheque of Rs. 500.
19	Received interest from bank Rs. 430.
20	Cash withdrawn from bank for personal use Rs. 2,800.
24	Travelling expenses paid Rs. 1,700.
25	Received a cheque of Rs. 5,100 from Mr. D. Ghosh in full settlement of his account of Rs. 5,300.
27	Cash paid to petty cashier Rs. 960.
28	Sold goods to Mr. S. Dutta (as per list price) for Rs. 6,000, subject to trade discount 5% and allowed 3% cash discount if payment is made within a week.
30	Commission received Rs. 1,600.

20. Enter the following transactions in the books of Mr. S.K. Setty:

2008	Transactions
May 1	Paid for advertisement by a cheque of Rs. 2,100.
3	Purchased computer from M/s Rick Bros. in cash Rs. 12,500.
5	Goods purchased from M/s G. Bros. for Rs. 12,600.
7	Cash withdrawn from bank for office use Rs. 3,700.
8	Trade subscription paid by cheque of Rs. 360.
10	Life insurance premium of the proprietor paid Rs. 1,200.
11	Paid for advertisement Rs. 2,600.
13	Bank credited for interest Rs. 310 and debited for bank charge Rs. 110.
15	Issued a cheque of Rs. 3,700 to M/s Durgapur Syndicate.
17	Goods returned by Mr. D. Ghosh amounting to Rs. 800 and received cash from him Rs. 2,300.

20   Received cash from Mr. P. Sen Rs. 7,500 out of which cash deposited into bank Rs. 3,500.

23   Received a loan of Rs. 10,000 from Mr. G. Seni.

25   Paid shop rent Rs. 2,800.

27   Sold goods for cash Rs. 5,700.

29   The cheque issued to M/s Durgapur Syndicate on May 15 became dishonoured.

30   Paid salary to manager Mr. N. Roy Rs. 5,000.

21. Give necessary Journal Entries and ledger accounts of the following transactions in the books of Mr. K. Lahari for the month of April, 2008:

2008	Transactions
April 4.	Issued a cheque of Rs. 2,600 in favour of M/s P. Bros.
6.	Paid cash Rs. 4,500 to Mr. D. Kamath in full settlement of their account and received discount of Rs. 300.
7.	Purchased furniture from Durgapur Timber Suppliers for Rs. 6,500.
9.	Received cash from Mr. K.G. Das Rs. 3,800 and allowed 5 % discount.
10.	Purchased goods from Mr. D.P. Khan for Rs. 13,000.
12.	Goods return to Mr. D.P. Khan Rs. 2,500.
15.	Purchased shares of G.P. & Co. at Rs. 8,000 and payment was made by a cheque.
17.	Proprietor's house rent paid by a cheque of Rs. 3,300.
19.	An old machinery was sold at Rs. 3,100.
22.	Travelling expenses paid Rs. 1,600.
23.	Interest on loan paid Rs. 650.
25.	Cash withdrawn from bank for personal use Rs. 3,000.
25.	Paid for advertisement by a cheque of Rs. 4,700.
26.	Cash Rs. 5,700 paid to Mr. D. Dhara and received 5 % discount from him.
27.	Cash withdrew from bank Rs. 7,500 to pay the salary of the office staff and it was paid on the next day.
29.	Received cash Rs. 4,200 and a cheque of Rs. 3,000 from Mr. S. Bhowmik and allowed discount Rs. 400.
30.	Loan refunded Rs. 4,000.

22. Enter the following transactions in the books of a firm:

1. Sold old papers and periodicals amounting to Rs. 610.
2. Received an advance of Rs. 3,000 from a customer Mr. H. Hundai.
3. Income tax paid Rs. 7,600.
4. A machine which stood in the books for Rs. 12,800 on January 1, 2007, was sold for Rs. 7,400 in exchange for a new machine costing Rs. 22,500 on June 1, 2007, supplied by M.P. Suppliers.
5. Purchased a plot of land at Rs. 230,000 and paid registration charges @ 8%, and paid Rs. 4,000 to a land broker for the said purchase of land
6. Cash received from a debtor Rs. 650, whose account was written off as bad debt in the last month.
7. Cash realized from the Insurance Company Rs. 4,700 for goods lost during the last month.
8. Municipal Tax Paid Rs. 2,900.

23. Enter the following transactions in the books of M/s Sahara Traders and also show the Ledger Accounts:

1. Purchased building materials for Rs. 51,500 and the payment was made by a cheque.
2. A horse purchased for business use Rs. 16,200.
3. Received an order for 450 tonnes of goods @ Rs. 250 per tonne from H.H. Bros.

4. Goods lost by fire amounting to Rs. 3,700
5. Goods costing Rs. 12,000 were sold at a profit of 20% on sale price to Mr. K. Sen and allowed 10% discount for immediate payment.
6. Debtors include Rs. 1,800 due from a customer Mr. N. Das who had become insolvent and nothing could be realized from his estate.
7. Received an advance of Rs. 5,000 from a customer Mr. C. Thakur.
8. Received Rs. 900 of a bad debts written off in the last month.

24. Give necessary Journal Entries and Ledger Accounts of the following transactions in the books of Mr. G. Naval for the month of May, 2008:

2008	Transactions

May 1. Goods distributed as free samples amounting to Rs. 3,000.
2. Sales Tax for the month deposited into Government account amounting to Rs. 2,900.
3. An advance of Rs. 2,500 paid to an employee against his salary.
4. Sold goods to M/s C.P. Bros. for Rs. 10,000 as per list price, less trade discount 10% and 8 % Cash at seven days; M/s C.P. Bros. settled their account immediately.
5. Sold goods to D.F. Traders for Rs. 25,000 and charged sale tax @ 5%
6. Depreciate machinery @ 10% and machinery account appears in the books as Rs. 60,000.
7. A plant purchased from Hard Machine Ltd. at Rs. 52,600 by a draft and paid carriage on it Rs. 5,800.
8. Wages paid for installation of a plant Rs. 6,400.
9. Received interest from bank Rs. 1,700 on fixed deposits.

9

Books of Original Entry: Cash Book

CONTENTS

- Special Purpose Subsidiary Books
  - Advantages of Special Purpose Subsidiary Books
- Cash Book
  - Features of a Cash Book
  - Similarities between a Cash Book and a Journal
  - Is Cash Book a Journalised Ledger?
  - Procedure for Writing a Cash Book
  - Advantages of a Cash Book
  - Verification of Cash Book Balance
  - Types of Cash Book
- Single Column Cash Book
  - Points to be Noted While Preparing a Single Column Cash Book
- Cash book with cash and bank columns (Double Column Cash Book)
  - Contra Entry
  - General Guidelines to Solve Problems
- Discount
  - Distinction between Cash Discount and Trade Discount
- Three Column Cash Book/Triple Column Cash Book
- Petty Cash Book
  - Advantages of Petty Cash Book
  - Simple Petty Cash Book
  - Imprest System of Petty Cash
  - Analytical Petty Cash Book

9.1 SPECIAL PURPOSE SUBSIDIARY BOOKS

Daily transactions are supposed to be recorded first through journal entries and then in the principal book, i.e., the ledger. When daily transactions are large in number, this process of recording the transactions is highly time consuming and it results in an increase of overhead costs. In case of a big concern if all the transactions are recorded in a single book, then its volume and size will become very large and its use would become a difficult task. Again when all the transactions are recorded in a single book, the distribution of work among the employees regarding the recording of the transactions would be a tough task. Thus, it becomes more convenient and economical to keep records for a particular class or group of transactions in separate books. These books are generally known as **sub-journal** or **subsidiary books**.

In view of the facts stated above, it is clear that if a separate book is maintained for each particular class of transactions, it becomes highly economical and helpful for the bookkeepers. It also reduces the overhead cost and labour for recording the transactions. These books can be subdivided into the following types:

1. Cash book
2. Purchase day book
3. Sales day book
4. Purchase return book
5. Sales return book
6. Bills receivable book
7. Bills payable book.

9.1.1 Advantages of Special Purpose Subsidiary Books

1. In case of a big concern if all the transactions are recorded in a single book, then its volume and size will become very large. As a result, its use would become a very difficult task.
2. If all transactions are recorded in a single book, the distribution of work among the employees will become a very difficult task regarding the recording of the transactions.
3. The present age is the age of specialization. Hence, a specialized person must be selected for a specific job to get the highest productivity, but it will not be possible if the journal is not subdivided on the basis of its nature of transaction (shown in Section 8.1.1)
4. Due to subdivision, a particular day book will record transactions of similar nature and as such its volume will be limited. It will help in easy detection of errors and frauds and will also be helpful for collecting any information in respect of a particular transaction.
5. When cash and credit transactions are recorded separately, it becomes very helpful for getting any information whenever needed regarding cash balance, total credit sales, and total credit purchases. Otherwise, it would become very difficult in big business houses to obtain such information.
6. Due to the subdivision, posting of different entries in the ledger would become easy and chances of mistakes would be highly limited.
7. In big business houses, subdivision of journal must be made, otherwise it would be an impossible task to record all the transactions in a single journal book.
8. It helps to keep the records up-to-date as different journal books are maintained by different employees separately and independently.

9.2 CASH BOOK

According to the double entry system, all transactions are first recorded in a subsidiary book and then the accounts are posted in the ledger. Here, a deviation of the said rule is seen because a cash book serves the dual role of a journal as well as a ledger. We all know that cash transactions are usually large in volume in almost all business houses. Therefore, if a cash book is not opened then all the cash transactions are first passed through the subsidiary book and then posted in the ledger which would be a highly laborious job. Moreover, there would be every possibility of mistakes. When a cash book is opened, maintaining cash and bank accounts in the ledger is not required. At the same time, it is also a book of original entry as cash receipts and payments are not generally entered in the subsidiary books. All cash and bank transactions (receipts and payments) are recorded in the cash book chronologically. Receipts (cash and cheques) are recorded on the debit side while payments are recorded on the credit side with due narrations. As the cash book serves the purpose of both journal and ledger, it is often said that a cash book is a journalised ledger.

9.2.1 Features of a Cash Book

1. All types of cash transactions are recorded in the cash book.
2. A cash book serves the purpose of both journal and ledger, and as such, it is often said that a cash book is a journalised ledger.
3. The debit side of a cash book records all cash receipts while the credit side records all cash payments.
4. The total of the debit side will always be greater than that of the credit side. As a result, it always shows surplus debit balance.
5. The difference between the total of both the sides is known as **cash in hand** or **closing cash balance**.
6. All cash and bank transactions (receipts and payments) are recorded in the cash book chronologically.

9.2.2 Similarities between a Cash Book and a Journal

It has the following similarities with a journal:

1. Cash book is a part of the subsidiary books like a journal.
2. All transactions are recorded chronologically like that in a journal.
3. At the end of each transaction, narration is written similar to that in a journal.
4. After recording all transactions in a cash book, all accounts are posted in the ledger like that in a journal.
5. A ledger folio (L.F.) is maintained just like that in a journal.

9.2.3 Is Cash Book a Journalized Ledger?

A cash book serves the dual role of a journal as well as a ledger. When a cash book is opened, maintaining cash and bank accounts in the ledger is not required any more. Thus, it is an important account and a part of the ledger accounts also. As the numbers of transactions recorded in the cash book are too many compared to other accounts, a specific system/guideline is followed for recording the transactions.

Thus, a cash book has a number of similarities with a journal at one hand while on the other hand, it acts as an important account also. As the cash book serves the purpose of both a journal and a ledger, a cash book is also formed a journalised ledger.

9.2.4 Procedure for Writing a Cash Book

A cash book is the main and very important book. The procedures for writing a cash book are given below:

1. Generally, all cash transactions are recorded chronologically. All collections/receipts are recorded the debit side (left side) and all payments on the credit side (right side).
2. All transactions are recorded with due narrations.

A specimen of a cash book is given below.

Dr. (Double Column) Cash Book Cr.

Date	Particulars	L.F.	V.N.	Cash (Rs.)	Bank (Rs.)	Date	Particulars	L.F.	V.N.	Cash (Rs.)	Bank (Rs.)
	To						By				

The procedures of filling up the above columns while recording the transactions are described below:

1. In the Date column, dates of different transactions are recorded chronologically. Transactions relating to receipts are shown on the debit side and payments on the credit side.
2. In the Particulars column, transactions are recorded as under:
   In the debit side: Suppose, cash received from Ram is Rs. 300. It is to be recorded as 'To Ram A/c' and then the narration (brief descriptions of the transaction) within a bracket is to be given. For the above example the narration may be written/recorded as (Being cash received/ For cash received).
   In the credit side: Suppose, cash paid to Madhu is Rs. 600. It is to be recorded as By 'Madhu A/c' and then the narration is written. The narration may be written as '(Being Cash paid/For cash paid)'. Suppose, cash paid to the manager Mr. X is Rs. 1,000. It is to be written as 'By Salary A/c' and the narration is written as '(Being salary paid to the manager Mr. X)'.
3. In the ledger folio (L.F.) column, the page number of the concerned account in the ledger is recorded. As per the example given for the debit side, suppose Ram's account is opened or written on page number 6 in the ledger, then, page number 6 has to be mentioned in the L.F. column.

4. In the V.N. column, the voucher number is noted or recorded. Voucher here stands for the documents accepted in support of a particular transaction. Suppose, a payment is made to a supplier for Rs. 500. A document must be taken from the said supplier stating that he has received a sum of Rs. 500 from the business. In the said document he must clearly mention the details of the transaction. He can also use a printed voucher filling the concerned portion duly. These documents or vouchers are kept chronologically and a number is given to each voucher for future reference. This number has to be mentioned in the V.N. column.
5. In the amount column, the amount of cash received or paid is written.

9.2.5 Advantages of a Cash Book

1. It helps in calculating the closing cash balance as and when required by the business management or the owner.
2. Since a Cash Book serves the purposes of both Journal and Ledger, no further cash account is required to be opened in the ledger.
3. As all cash transactions are recorded in the cash book, it helps to control the cash expenditures of a business.
4. Cash Book helps in verifying the physical cash balances on any particular day.
5. It helps the trader in taking important business decisions on the basis of the data provided by the Cash Book in respect of cash movements.
6. Cash Book helps the traders prepare budget estimates regarding the proposed cash transactions for the subsequent years.

9.2.6 Verification of Cash Book Balance

A Cash Book is a vital account of a business. It can be considered the blood of the business. Thus, special attention should always be given on recording transactions in the Cash Book. If all transactions are recorded properly in it, the closing cash balance of any day would be equal to the actual physical cash balance of the business. Generally, the physical cash balance and the cash in hand as per Cash Book should not differ, but if they differ, as it may happen, in some cases it may be due to a loss of cash or fraud or mistake while recording the transactions. Hence there are a number of reasons for the difference in the two balances (physical cash balance and the cash in hand as per Cash Book). The chief reasons for such differences in the two balances are given below:

1. Recording of wrong opening balance or closing balance
2. Receipts showing shortage or excess in figure
3. Payments showing shortage or excess in figure
4. Recording of any receipt or payment made twice
5. Any income recorded as expenditure or an item of expenditure recorded as an income
6. Error in counting at the time of balancing the Cash Book
7. Error in counting of physical cash in hand
8. Loss of cash.

At the end of a certain period, the cash balance can be obtained from the Cash Book balance, but to make it true, actual counting of cash in hand is essential. If proper attention is paid to the reasons sated above, it can be expected that the physical cash balance and the cash in hand as per Cash Book would be equal. However, to avoid fraud and manipulation all receipts of the day should be banked in full, either at the end of the day or on the next day. The minimum and maximum amount of cash that can be held by the cashier in his safe under ordinary circumstances should be fixed. Failure to verify the cash on hand may constitute gross negligence on the part of the management or owner of the business. For counting physical cash balance, a statement may be prepared as under:

Statement showing the details of cash in hand on ... (Date)

Denomination × abstract	Number	Amount (Rs.)	
Rs.	Currency notes		
Rs. 1,000	10	10,000	
Rs. 500	30	15,000	
Rs. 100	200	20,000	
Rs. 50	150	7,500	
Rs. 20	100	2,000	
Rs. 10	400	4,000	
Rs. 5	100	500	
Rs. 2	50	100	
Re. 1	100	100	59,200
	Coins		
Rs. 5	200	1,000	
Re. 1	400	400	
Re. 0.50	200	100	1,500
	Postal stamps		
Rs. 20	100	2,000	
Rs. 10	80	800	
Rs. 5	200	1,000	
Rs. 3	100	300	
Re. 1	150	150	4,250
	Bank drafts		
Rs. 1,000	20	20,000	
Rs. 100	24	2,400	
Rs. 50	45	2,250	24,650
	Postal orders		
Rs. 100	20	2,000	
Rs. 50	25	1,250	3,250
	Cash in hand on ...(Date)		92,850

Note: Postal stamps, Bank drafts, Postal orders, etc., are to be considered as part of cash balances.

9.2.7 Types of Cash Book

1. Single column or simple cash book
2. Cash book with cash and bank columns
3. Cash book with bank and discount columns
4. Petty cash book:
   (a) Simple petty cash book
   (b) Imprest system of petty cash
   (c) Analytical petty cash book
5. Multi-Columnar Cash book.

9.3 SINGLE COLUMN CASH BOOK

Generally, small business owner use this cash book. All cash transactions are recorded here chronologically excluding the transactions relating to cheque issued or received from the customer. In this cash book, single amount column is opened on both the sides where cash receipts and payments are recorded. Due to this reason, cash book is known as Single Column Cash Book. The procedure for writing a Cash Book has already been explained in Section 9.5. The specimen of a single column cash book is shown as follows.

Dr.				Cash Book					Cr.
Date	Particulars	L.F.	V.N.	Cash (Rs.)	Date	Particulars	L.F.	V.N.	Cash (Rs.)
	To					By			

9.3.1 Points to be Noted While Preparing a Single Column Cash Book

1. Only cash transactions are to be recorded, i.e., only cash receipts and cash payments.
2. No entry is required to be shown in respect of cheques received or issued and discounts received or allowed.
3. No further Cash Account is required to be opened in the ledger.
4. It is balanced like other accounts of ledger.
5. It always shows a debit balance.

ILLUSTRATION 9.1 From the following transactions, prepare Single Column Cash Book of Mr. D. Gokhle for May, 2008:

2008	**Transactions**
May 1	Cash in hand Rs. 31,700.
3	Sold goods for cash Rs. 8,900.
7	Paid carriage on sales Rs. 740.
9	Received commission Rs. 900.
12	Proprietor's house rent paid Rs. 2,300.
15	Sold old furniture at Rs. 3,100.
18	Sold goods for cash Rs. 4,100.
21	Purchased goods for cash Rs. 5,400.
24	Paid for advertisement Rs. 1,250.
25	Cash withdrawn for personal use Rs. 1,400.
27	Paid salary to staff Rs. 3,200.
29	Purchased furniture for Rs. 4,500.

Solution

In the Books of Mr. D. Gokhle

Dr.				Cash Book					Cr.
Date	Particulars	L.F.	V.N.	Cash (Rs.)	Date	Particulars	L.F.	V.N.	Cash (Rs.)
2008					2008				
May 1	To Balance b/d			31,700	May 7	By Carriage Outward A/c (Being carriage paid)			740
3	To Sales A/c (Being goods sold)			8,900	12	By Drawings A/c (Being proprietor's house rent paid)			2,300
9	To Commission A/c (Being commission received)			900	21	By Purchases A/c (For purchase of goods)			5,400
15	To Furniture A/c (For sale of furniture)			3,100	24	By Advertisement A/c (Being advertisement paid)			1,250
18	To Sales A/c (Being goods sold)			4,100	27	By Drawings A/c (Being cash withdrawn for personal use)			1,400
					29	By Salary A/c (Being salary paid)			3,200
					29	By Furniture A/c (For furniture purchase)			4,500
					31	By Balance c/d			29,910
				48,700					48,700
June 1	To Balance b/d			29,910					

ILLUSTRATION 9.2 From the following transactions, prepare Single Column Cash Book of Mr. Niraj Kumar for the month of July, 2008, and post them in ledger accounts:

2008	Transactions
July 1	Started business with cash Rs. 55,000.
3	Trade subscription paid Rs. 600.
4	Purchased stationery Rs. 250.
7	Purchased goods for cash Rs. 7,200.
9	Wages paid to workers Rs. 2,400.
13	Office equipments purchased Rs. 3,500.
15	Sold goods for cash Rs. 6,300.
19	Paid carriage on purchase Rs. 700.
21	Purchased machinery for cash Rs. 14,500.
25	Travelling expenses paid Rs. 900.
28	Paid salary to manager Mr. P. Sen Rs. 2,500, sold goods for cash Rs. 13,600.
29	Paid shop rent Rs 1,200.
30	Cash paid to petty cashier Rs. 400.

Solution

In the Books of Mr. Niraj Kumar

Dr.   **Cash Book**   Cr.

Date	Particulars	L.F.	V.N.	Cash (Rs.)	Date	Particulars	L.F.	V.N.	Cash (Rs.)
2008					2008				
July 1	To Capital A/c (Being the business started)			55,000	July 3	By Trade Subscription A/c (Being trade subscription paid)			600
15	To Sales A/c (Being goods sold)			6,300	4	By Stationery A/c (Being stationery purchased)			250
28	To Sales A/c (Being goods sold)			13,600	7	By Purchases A/c (For purchase of goods)			7,200
					9	By Wages A/c (Being wages paid)			2,400
					13	By Office equipments A/c (Being equipments purchased for office)			3,500
					19	By Carriage inward A/c (Being carriage paid)			700
					21	Machinery A/c (Being machinery purchased)			14,500
					25	By Travelling expenses A/c (Being travelling expenses paid)			900
					28	By Salary A/c (Being salary paid to manager)			2,500
					29	By Shop rent (Being shop rent paid)			1,200
					30	By Petty cashier A/c (Being cash paid)			400
					31	By Balance c/d			40,750
				74,900					74,900
August 1	To balance b/d			40,750					

Ledger

Dr. **Capital Account** **Cr.**

Date	Particulars	J.F.	Amount (Rs.)	Date	Particulars	J.F.	Amount (Rs.)
				2008 July 1	By cash A/c		55,000

Dr. **Sales Account** **Cr.**

Date	Particulars	J.F.	Amount (Rs.)	Date	Particulars	J.F.	Amount (Rs.)
				2008 July 15	By cash A/c		6,300
				28	By cash A/c		13,600

Dr. **Trade Subscription** **Cr.**

Date	Particulars	J.F.	Amount (Rs.)	Date	Particulars	J.F.	Amount (Rs.)
2008 July 3	To cash A/c		600				

Dr. **Stationery Account** **Cr.**

Date	Particulars	J.F.	Amount (Rs.)	Date	Particulars	J.F.	Amount (Rs.)
2008 July 4	To cash A/c		250				

Dr. **Purchases Account** **Cr.**

Date	Particulars	J.F.	Amount (Rs.)	Date	Particulars	J.F.	Amount (Rs.)
2008 July 7	To cash A/c		7,200				

Dr. **Wages Account** **Cr.**

Date	Particulars	J.F.	Amount (Rs.)	Date	Particulars	J.F.	Amount (Rs.)
2008 July 9	To cash A/c		2,400				

Dr. **Office Equipment Account** **Cr.**

Date	Particulars	J.F.	Amount (Rs.)	Date	Particulars	J.F.	Amount (Rs.)
2008 July 13	To cash A/c		3,500				

Dr. **Carriage Inward Account** **Cr.**

Date	Particulars	J.F.	Amount (Rs.)	Date	Particulars	J.F.	Amount (Rs.)
2008 July 19	To cash A/c		700				

Dr. **Travelling Expenses Account** **Cr.**

Date	Particulars	J.F.	Amount (Rs.)	Date	Particulars	J.F.	Amount (Rs.)
2008 July 25	To cash A/c		900				

Dr. **Salary Account** **Cr.**

Date	Particulars	J.F.	Amount (Rs.)	Date	Particulars	J.F.	Amount (Rs.)
2008 July 28	To cash A/c		2,500				

Dr.   **Shop Rent Account**   Cr.

Date	Particulars	J.F.	Amount (Rs.)	Date	Particulars	J.F.	Amount (Rs.)
2008 July 29	To cash A/c		1,200				

Dr.   **Petty Cashier Account**   Cr.

Date	Particulars	J.F.	Amount (Rs.)	Date	Particulars	J.F.	Amount (Rs.)
2008 July 30	To cash A/c		400				

9.4 CASH BOOK WITH CASH AND BANK COLUMNS (DOUBLE COLUMN CASH BOOK)

In a Double Column Cash Book, cash and bank transactions are recorded. Recording of transactions in this book is done in the same way as in single column cash book, but some specific guidelines are required to be followed for bank transactions or transactions made through cheques. The said guidelines are given in Section 9.4.2.

When a bank account is opened with any bank, the banker will provide the following documents to their customers/account holders for making their transactions and for future reference:

1. *Passbook:* This book is a copy of bank transactions. It is given by a banker to the account holders and the banker records/copies the transactions made by them from time to time. To get these opportunities, the said book has to be deposited by the account holder with the bank for necessary posting of transactions (i.e., for updating the passbook). This book is kept by the account holder, but recording of the transactions are made by the Bank only. It is an important document of the bank transactions in the hands of an account holder.

2. *Cheque book:* It is also supplied by the bank to its customers/account holders for withdrawing cash from the bank. An account holder issues a cheque to his suppliers/parties for payment of business liabilities and for withdrawing cash for business/personal purposes. The specimen of a cheque is given in the Box 9.1.

Box 9.1 A cheque

Date...................

Pay To ....

.... Or BEARER

RUPEES ....   Rs.

A/c No.   LF   INTLS

UNITED BANK OF INDIA
Address:
EIH/SBF   **IFSC: UTBIOCOK231**

II*271568II* 713027203   10

3. *Pay-in-slip Book:* This book is also supplied by the bank to its customers/account holders for depositing cash and cheque in the bank.

9.4.1 Contra Entry

A particular type of transaction when recorded on both sides of the cash book on the same day is known as **contra entry**. Contra entries are made under the following circumstances:

1. Cash or cheque
    deposited in the bank
    (which was received earlier)

    On debit side:
    To Cash A/c
    (Amount in bank column)
    On credit side:
    By Bank A/c (Amount in cash column)

2. Cash withdrawn from bank

    on debit side:
    To Bank A/c
    (Amount in cash column)
    On credit side:
    By Cash A/c (Amount in bank column)

9.4.2 General Guidelines to Solve Problems

1. All receipts should be on the debit side of the cash book.
2. All payments should be on the credit side of the cash book.
3. Contra entries:
    (a) Cash
        or cheque deposited in the bank
        (Received earlier)

        On debit side:
        To Cash A/c (Amount in bank column)
        On credit side:
        By Bank A/c (Amount in cash column)

    (b) Cash withdrawn from bank

        On debit side:
        To Bank A/c (Amount in cash column)
        On credit side:
        By Cash A/c (Amount in bank column)

4. For cheque received from debtors/parties:
    (a) Cheque received and deposited the same in the bank immediately:
        To Party's A/c (At bank column Dr.)
    (b) Cheque received and deposited the same in the bank on subsequent dates:
        (i) The date when received: To party's A/c (At cash column Dr.)
        (ii) The date when sent to bank for collection: Contra entry [3.(a) above]
    (c) Received bearer cheque and cashed at bank counter subsequently:
        (i) The date when received: To party's A/c (At cash column Dr.)
        (ii) The date when cashed: No entry required
    (d) Cheque received and endorsed to some other party:
        (i) The date when received: To party's A/c (At cash column Dr.)
        (ii) The date when endorsed: By party's A/c (At cash column Cr.)
    (e) When cheque received and the problem remains silent: It may be assumed that the cheque was received and deposited into bank immediately:
        To party's A/c (At bank column Dr.)
5. As per instruction if bank has
    (a) collected some incomes/receipts: To Income A/c/from whom received (At bank column Dr.)
    (b) Made a payment: By expenses A/c/to whom payment was made (At bank column Cr.)
6. Amount deposited by a debtor/customer directly into Bank A/c:
    To party's A/c (At bank column Dr.)
7. Discounted bills receivable dishonoured:
    By acceptor's/party's A/c (At bank column Cr.)
8. Cash withdrawn by the proprietor for personal use:
    (a) From cash: By Drawing (At cash column)
    (b) From bank: By Drawing (At bank column)

9. Bank interest:
    (a) On deposits: To interest (At bank column Dr.)
    (b) On overdraft: By interest (At bank column Cr.)
10. Bank charges/commission: By Bank Charge A/c (At bank column)
11. Cheque dishonoured:
    (a) Received cheque: By party's A/c (At bank column)
    (b) Endorsed cheque: No entry in the cash book
    (c) Issued cheque: To party's A/c (At bank column)
12. For discounting bill: To bills receivable A/c (in debit side bank column, net amount received) or on the debit side of bills receivable A/c full value and on the credit side by discount on bills A/c (discount charges only) may be shown.

ILLUSTRATION 9.3 From the following transactions prepare a Double Column Cash Book of Mr. N Sarkhel for the month of May, 2008:

2008	Transactions
May 1	Cash in hand Rs. 24,200 and Bank Rs. 34,700.
2	Sold goods for cash Rs. 4,600.
4	Paid salary to staff Rs. 2,300.
6	Purchased furniture for Rs. 2,600 and paid by a cheque.
9	Purchased goods for cash Rs. 3,100.
12	Paid for advertisement Rs. 750.
15	Cash withdrew from bank for office use Rs. 1,700.
17	Paid shop rent Rs. 760.
19	Proprietor's house rent paid Rs. 1,500.
22	Issued a cheque to Dulal Rs. 1,900.
23	Received commission Rs. 1,650.
25	Bank credited interest Rs. 340 and debited bank charges Rs. 70.
25	Sold old computer Rs. 2,900.
26	Cash withdrew from bank for personal use Rs. 1,600.
27	Paid to Hiran on account by a cheque of Rs. 2,300.
29	Sold goods for cash Rs. 4,100.
30	Paid carriage on sales Rs. 470.

Solution

In the Books of Mr. N. Sarkhel

Dr.   **Cash Book (Double Column)**   Cr.

Date	Particulars	L.F.	Cash (Rs.)	Bank (Rs.)	Date	Particulars	L.F.	Cash (Rs.)	Bank (Rs.)
2008					2008				
May 1	To Balance b/d		24,200	34,700	May 4	By Salary A/c		2,300	
2	To Sales A/c		4,600			(Being salary paid)			
	(Being goods sold)				6	By Furniture A/c			2,600
15	To Bank A/c	C	1,700			(For furniture purchase)			
	(Being cash withdrawn from bank)				9	By Purchases A/c (For purchase of goods)		3,100	
23	To Commission A/c		1,650		12	By Advertisement A/c			
	(Being commission received)					(Being advertisement paid)		750	
25	To Interest Received A/c			340	15	By Cash A/c	C		1,700
	(Being interest credited by bank)					(Being cash withdrawn from bank)			
25	To Computer A/c		2,900		17	By Shop Rent		760	
	(For sale of computer)					(Being shop rent paid)			

(Contd.)

Date	Particulars	L.F.	Cash (Rs.)	Bank (Rs.)	Date	Particulars	L.F.	Cash (Rs.)	Bank (Rs.)
29	To Sales A/c (Being goods sold)		4,100		19	By Drawings A/c (Being proprietor's house rent paid)		1,500	
					22	By Dulal's A/c (Being cheque issued)			1,900
					25	By Bank Charge A/c (Being bank charge debited by bank)			70
					26	By Drawings A/c (Being cash withdrawn for personal use)			1,600
					27	By Hiran A/c (Being cheque issued)			2,300
					30	By Carriage Outward A/c (Being carriage paid)		470	
					31	By Balance c/d		30,270	24,870
			39,150	35,040				39,150	35,040
June 1	To Balance b/d		30,270	24,870					

ILLUSTRATION 9.4   Enter the following transactions in the double column cash book of Mr. N.K. Mallik for the month of April, 2008:

2008   **Transactions**

April 1   Cash in hand Rs. 31,700 and Bank Rs. 45,100.
  2   Sold goods for cash Rs. 12,700 and out of that deposited cash into bank Rs. 7,500.
  4   Travelling expenses paid Rs. 800.
  6   Cash paid to petty cashier Rs. 500.
  9   Commission received Rs. 750.
  12   Proprietor's life insurance premium paid by a cheque of Rs. 1,600.
  15   Paid carriage on sales Rs. 700.
  17   Sold goods for cash Rs. 8,000.
  19   Paid salary to manager Mr. Sunil Das Rs. 3,000.
  20   Issued a cheque of Rs. 1,950 to Nilay.
  22   Purchased furniture Rs. 2,490.
  23   Wages paid to workers Rs. 700.
  25   Paid for advertisement Rs. 2,600.
  25   Paid shop rent Rs. 1,400.
  28   Issued a cheque of Rs. 2,500 to B.P. Traders.

Solution

In the Books of Mr. N. K. Mallik

Dr.   Cr.

Cash Book (Double Column)

Date	Particulars	L.F.	Cash (Rs.)	Bank (Rs.)	Date	Particulars	L.F.	Cash (Rs.)	Bank (Rs.)
2008					2008				
April 1	To Balance b/d		31,700	45,100	April 4	By Travelling expenses A/c (Being travelling expenses paid)		800	
2	To Sales A/c (Being goods sold)		5,200	7,500					
9	To Commission A/c (Being commission received)		750		6	By Petty Cashier A/c (Being cash paid)		500	
17	To Sales A/c (Being goods sold)		8,000		12	By Drawings A/c (Being proprietor's LIP paid)			1,600

(Contd.)

Date	Particulars	L.F.	Cash (Rs.)	Bank (Rs.)	Date	Particulars	L.F.	Cash (Rs.)	Bank (Rs.)
					15	By Carriage Outward A/c (Being carriage paid)		700	
					19	By Salary A/c (Being salary paid to manager)		3,000	
					20	By Nilay's A/c (Being cheque issued)			1,950
					22	By Furniture A/c (Being furniture purchased)		2,490	
					23	By Wages A/c (Being wages paid)		700	
					25	By Advertisement A/c (Being advertisement paid)		2,600	
					25	By Shop Rent (Being shop rent paid)		1,400	
					28	By B.P.Traders A/c (Being cheque issued)			2,500
					31	By Balance c/d		33,460	46,550
			45,650	52,600				45,650	52,600
May 1	To Balance b/d		33,460	46,550					

Working Note

1. Any expenditure incurred for personal use or proprietor's use will be treated as *Drawings*.

ILLUSTRATION 9.5 From the following transactions, prepare double column cash book of Mr. Sujay Giri for the month of July, 2008:

2008	**Transactions**
July 1	Started business with cash Rs. 75,000.
3	Purchased machinery for cash Rs. 21,000.
5	Wages paid for installation of new machinery Rs. 1,100.
8	Opened a bank account with cash Rs. 31, 000.
11	Issued a cheque of Rs. 2,300 to X & Co.
14	Sold goods for cash Rs. 7,100.
16	Received a cheque of Rs. 2,600 from Suresh.
19	Trade subscription paid by a cheque of Rs. 500.
20	Deposited Suresh's cheque of Rs. 2,600 into bank.
24	Received interest from bank Rs. 710.
27	Paid for advertisement Rs. 850.
28	Received a cheque of Rs. 3,560 from M & Co.
29	Purchased stationery Rs. 320.
30	Office equipment purchased Rs. 2,800.

Solution

In the Books of Mr. Sujay Giri

Dr.   **Cash Book (Double Column)**   Cr.

Date	Particulars	L.F.	Cash (Rs.)	Bank (Rs.)	Date	Particulars	L.F.	Cash (Rs.)	Bank (Rs.)
2008 July 1	To Capital A/c		75,000		2008 July 3	Machinery A/c (Being machinery purchased)		21,000	
8	To Cash A/c (Being bank account opened)	C		31,000	5	By Machinery A/c			1,100

(Contd.)

Date	Particulars	L.F.	Cash (Rs.)	Bank (Rs.)	Date	Particulars	L.F.	Cash (Rs.)	Bank (Rs.)
14	To Sales A/c (Being goods sold)		7,100			(Being Wages paid for installation of machine)			
16	To Suresh's A/c (Being cheque received)		2,600		8	By Bank A/c	C	31,000	
					11	By X & Co. A/c (Being cheque issued)			2,300
20	To Cash A/c (Being Suuresh's cheque paid into bank)	C		2,600	19	By Trade Subscription A/c (Being trade subscription paid)			500
24	To Interest Received A/c (Being interest credited by bank)			710	20	By Bank A/c	C	2,600	
					27	By Advertisement A/c (Being advertisement paid)		850	
28	To M & Co. A/c (Being cheque received)			3,560	29	By Stationery A/c (Being stationery purchased)		320	
					30	By Office Equipments A/c (Being equipments purchased for office)		2,800	
					31	By Balance c/d		25,030	35,070
			84,700	37,870				84,700	37,870
August 1	To balance b/d		25,030	35,070					

ILLUSTRATION 9.6 From the following transactions, prepare double column cash book of Mr. Rupak Sen for the month of March, 2008:

2008   **Transactions**

March 1   Cash in hand Rs. 21,350 and bank Rs. 61,200.

3   Issued a cheque to Machine Tools Ltd. Rs. 5,400.

4   Received a cheque from Anil Rs. 3,700.

5   Cash withdrew from bank for office use Rs. 3,200.

9   Sold goods for cash Rs. 4,900.

11   Computer purchased by a cheque of Rs. 12,500.

14   Endorsed Anil's cheque to Nilesh.

16   Received interest from bank Rs. 540.

17   Received a cheque from Vikram Rs. 2,550 and deposited the said cheque in the bank on March 19.

19   Purchased stationery Rs. 640.

24   Cash withdrew from bank for personal use Rs. 2,100.

26   Sold goods for cash Rs. 6,000.

28   Paid salary to manager Mr. Sunil Das by a cheque of Rs. 3,000.

29   Received interest on fixed deposits from bank Rs. 1,400.

30   Deposited D. Roy's cheque of Rs. 1,200 into bank which was received during the last month.

Solution

In the Books of Mr. Rupak Sen

Dr.   **Cash Book (Double Column)**   Cr.

Date	Particulars	L.F.	Cash (Rs.)	Bank (Rs.)	Date	Particulars	L.F.	Cash (Rs.)	Bank (Rs.)
2008 Mar. 1	To Balance b/d		21,350	61,200	2008 Mar. 3	By Machine Tools Ltd. A/c (Being cheque issued)			5,400
4	To Anil's A/c (Being cheque received)		3,700		5	By Cash A/c (Being cash withdrawn from bank)	C		3,200
5	To Bank A/c (Being cash withdrawn from bank)	C	3,200		11	By Computer A/c (Being Computer purchased)			12,500
9	To Sales A/c (Being goods sold)		4,900						

(Contd.)

Date	Particulars	L.F.	Cash (Rs.)	Bank (Rs.)	Date	Particulars	L.F.	Cash (Rs.)	Bank (Rs.)
16	To Interest Received A/c (Being interest credited by bank)			540	14	By Nilesh A/c (Endorsed Anil's cheque)		3,700	
17	To Vikram A/c (Being cheque received)		2,550		19	By Stationery A/c (Being stationery purchased)		640	
19	To Cash A/c (Being Vikram's cheque paid into bank)	C		2,550	19	By Bank A/c (Being Vikram's cheque paid into bank)	C	2,550	
26	To Sales A/c (Being goods sold)		6,000		24	By Drawings A/c (Being cash withdrawn for personal use)			2,100
29	To Interest received A/c (Being interest on F/D received from bank)			1,400	28	By Salary A/c (Being salary paid to manager)			3,000
30	To Cash A/c (Being D. Roy's cheque paid into bank)	C		1,200	30	By Bank A/c (Being D.Roy's cheque paid into bank)	C	1,200	
					31	By Balance c/d		33,610	40,690
			41,700	66,890				41,700	66,890
April 1	To balance b/d		33,610	40,690					

Working Note

1. Vikram's cheque deposited on 19.03.08 and D. Roy's cheque deposited on 30.03.08 were treated as contra entry as the said cheques were kept within the business cash.

ILLUSTRATION 9.7 Enter the following transactions in the double column cash book of Mr. Navin Singh for the month of May, 2008:

2008	Transactions
May 1	Cash in hand Rs. 17,400 and bank Rs. 49,700.
3	Purchased furniture from Durgapur furniture for Rs. 3,000.
5	Received a cheque from K. Lahari Rs. 2,450 and deposited the same in the bank immediately.
8	Sold goods to Mr. Manoj for Rs. 11,500.
10	Cash received from Manoj Rs. 2.500 and a cheque of Rs. 3,000.
12	Received a loan of Rs. 4,000 from Sunil.
14	Deposited Manoj's cheque of Rs. 3,000 in the bank.
16	K. Lahari's cheque deposited in the bank on May 5 became dishonoured.
19	Issued a cheque to Sanjay Rs. 1,750.
22	Repair charges for computer paid Rs. 300.
25	The cheque issued to Sanjay on May 19 became dishonoured.
29	Cash withdrawn from business accoiunt for personal use Rs. 750.
30	Paid wages Rs. 2,500.

Solution

In the Books of Mr. Navin Singh

Dr. **Cash Book (Double Column)** Cr.

Date	Particulars	L.F.	Cash (Rs.)	Bank (Rs.)	Date	Particulars	L.F.	Cash (Rs.)	Bank (Rs.)
2008					2008				
May 1	To balance b/d		17,400	49,700	May 14	By Bank A/c (Being Manoj's cheque paid into bank)	C	3,000	
5	To K. Lahari's A/c (Being cheque received and deposited into bank)			2,450	16	By K. Lahari's A/c (Being K. Lahari's cheque dishonoured)			2,450

(Contd.)

Date	Particulars	L.F.	Cash (Rs.)	Bank (Rs.)	Date	Particulars	L.F.	Cash (Rs.)	Bank (Rs.)
10	To Manoj's A/c (Being cash Rs. 2,500 and cheque of Rs. 3,000 received)		5,500		19	By Sanjay's A/c (Being cheque issued)			1,750
12	To Loan A/c (Being loan received from Sunil)		4,000		22	By Repairs A/c (Being repairs charges paid for computer)		300	
14	To Cash A/c (Being Manoj's cheque deposited into bank)	C		3,000	29	By Drawings A/c (Being cash withdrawn for personal use)		750	
25	To Sanjay's A/c (Being the issued cheque became dishonoured)			1,750	30	By Wages A/c (Being wages paid)		2,500	
					31	By Balance c/d		20,350	50,250
			26,900	54,450				26,900	54,450
June 1	To Balance b/d		20,350	50,250					

Working Notes

1. No entry is required for purchase of furniture on May 3 as it is a credit transaction.
2. No entry is required for sale of goods on May 8 as it is a credit transaction.

ILLUSTRATION 9.8 From the following transactions, prepare Double Column Cash Book of Mr. K. Arora for the month of June, 2008:

2008	Transactions
July 1	Cash in hand Rs. 18,250 and overdraft balance at bank Rs. 12,800.
3	Paid salary to staff Rs. 2,900.
7	Paid for advertisement Rs. 1.600.
8	Received two cheques of Rs. 2,600 and Rs. 1,400 from M. Roy. First one is crossed cheque and the other is bearer.
10	Received interest on fixed deposits from bank Rs. 900.
13	Sold goods for cash Rs. 5,600.
14	Sold old furniture at Rs. 900.
19	Endorsed M. Roy's cheque of Rs. 1,400 to Sailesh.
20	Received a cheque of Rs. 1,900 from GT & Co.
21	Receive a cheque of Rs. 2,780 from Mukesh.
23	Endorsed GT & Co.'s cheque of Rs. 1,900 to M. Lal.
26	Cash withdrew from Bank for office use Rs. 2,400.
30	Dividend collected by Bank Rs. 3,600.

Solution

In the Books of Mr. K. Arora

Dr.   Cash Book (Double Column)   Cr.

Date	Particulars	L.F.	Cash (Rs.)	Bank (Rs.)	Date	Particulars	L.F.	Cash (Rs.)	Bank (Rs.)
2008					2008				
July 1	To Balance b/d		18,250		July 1	By Balance b/d			12,800
8	To M. Roy's A/c (Being two cheques received)		1,400	2,600	3	By Salary A/c (Being salary paid)		2,900	
10	To Interest Received A/c (Being interest on F/D received from bank)			900	7	By Advertisement A/c (Being advertisement paid)		1,600	
13	To sales A/c (Being goods sold)		5,600		19	By Sailesh A/c (Endorsed M. Roy's cheque)		1,400	

(Contd.)

Date	Particulars	L.F.	Cash (Rs.)	Bank (Rs.)	Date	Particulars	L.F.	Cash (Rs.)	Bank (Rs.)
14	To Furniture A/c (Being old furniture sold)		900		23	By M. Lal A/c (Endorsed GT & Co.'s cheque)		1,900	
20	To GT & Co. A/c		1,900						
21	To Mukesh A/c (Being cheque received) and deposited into bank)			2,780	26	By Cash A/c (Being cash withdrawn from bank)	C		2,400
26	To Bank A/c (Being cash withdrawn from bank)	C	2,400						
30	To Dividend A/c (Being dividend collected by bank)			3,600					
31	To Balance c/d			5,320	31	By Balance c/d		22,650	
			30,450	15,200				30,450	15,200
Aug. 1	To Balance b/d		22,650		Aug. 1	To Balance b/d			5,320

Working Note

Overdraft balance at Bank

Generally, cash is withdrawn from bank by traders from their deposited balances, but there are some cases where they are allowed to draw cash from the bank to a certain amount (limit is fixed by the bank) without having any bank balances. This facility is known as **overdraft facility** by the bank, and the excess amount withdrawn from the bank is called **overdraft (loan).** The trader is liable to pay the withdrawn amount, i.e., the overdraft within the stipulated time fixed by the bank. Hence, it is a liability of the firm or the business owner. The opening balance of overdraft is shown on the credit side of the Cash Book as 'By Balance b/d'. Since overdraft is a liability, the interest charged by the bank on such balances is expenditure to the business. When interest is charged by the bank on such amount, it is shown on the credit side of the Cash Book as 'By Interest A/c' and the amount is shown in the bank column.

ILLUSTRATION 9.9 From the following transactions, prepare a double column cash book of Sri W.W. Dan for the month of December, 2007:

2007	Transactions
December 1	Cash in hand Rs. 12,190 and Bank Rs. 19,950.
3	Fresh capital introduced amounting to Rs. 9,000.
5	Proprietor's house rent paid Rs. 1,750.
9	Paid for advertisement Rs. 940 and received commission Rs. 750.
13	Cash withdrawn from bank for office use and personal use Rs. 3,100 and Rs. 900 respectively.
18	Received a cheque of Rs. 1,900 from X & Co.
19	Deposited M.K. Roy's cheque of Rs. 960 in the Bank which was received during the last month.
21	Endorsed X & Co.'s cheque of Rs. 1,900 to K. Sen.
23	Dividend collected by bank Rs. 1,400.
25	Bank credited interest Rs. 730 and debited bank charges Rs. 90.
27	Drew cheque for petty cash Rs. 600.
28	M.K. Roy's cheque of Rs. 1,900 was returned by the bank marked 'return to drawer'.
29	Received two cheques of Rs. 1,900 and Rs. 1,500 from A.B. Puri. The first one is crossed cheque while the other is bearer.
30	Cashed the bearer cheque of Rs. 1,500 over bank counter received from A.B. Puri.
31	It was reported that X & Co.'s cheque of Rs. 1,900 endorsed to K. Sen became dishonoured: deposited cash in the bank in excess of Rs. 9,000 in hand.

Solution

In the Books of Sri W.W Dan

Dr.   **Cash Book (Double Column)**   Cr.

Date	Particulars	L.F.	Cash (Rs.)	Bank (Rs.)	Date	Particulars	L.F.	Cash (Rs.)	Bank (Rs.)
2007					2007				
December 1	To Balance b/d		12,190	19,950	December 5	By Drawings A/c (Being proprietor's house rent paid)		1,750	
3	To Capital A/c (Being capital introduced)		9,000		9	By Advertisement A/c (Being advertisement paid)		940	
9	To Commission A/c (Being commission received)		750		13	By Cash A/c (Being cash withdrawn from bank)	C		3,100
13	To Bank A/c (Being cash withdrawn from bank)	C	3,100		13	By Drawings A/c (Being withdrawn for personal use)			900
18	To X & Co. A/c (Being cheque received)		1,900		19	By Bank A/c (Being M.K. Roy's cheque deposited)	C	960	
19	To Cash A/c (Being M.K. Roy's cheque deposited)	C		960	21	By K. Sen A/c (Being X & Co.'s cheque endorsed)		1,900	
23	To Dividend A/c (Being dividend collected by bank)			1,400	25	By Bank Charge A/c (Being bank charged educted)			90
25	To Interest A/c (Being interest received)			730	27	By Petty Cash A/c (Being cash withdrawn for petty cash)			600
29	To A.B. Guha A/c (Being two cheques received and crossed cheque deposited)		1,500	1,900	28	By M.K. Roy A/c (Being deposited cheque dishonoured)			1,900
31	To Cash A/c (Being cash deposited into bank)	C		13,890	31	By Bank A/c (Being cash deposited into bank)	C	13,890	
					31	By Balance c/d		9,000	32,240
			28,440	38,830				28,440	38,830
2008 January 1	To Balance b/d		9,000	32,240					

Working Notes

1. Any expenditure incurred for personal use or proprietor's use will be treated as Drawings.
2. M.K. Roy's cheque deposited on 19.12.07 was treated as contra entry as the said cheque was kept within the business cash.
3. On 28.12.07, M.K. Roy's cheque was dishonoured.
4. No entry is required for the bearer cheque of Sri A.B. Puri cashed over bank counter.
5. No entry is required in the cash book for the dishonoured cheque of X & Co. endorsed to K. Sen.
6. On 31.12.07, actual cash in hand was Rs. 22,890, but out of that after keeping Rs. 9,000 in hand, balance was deposited in the bank by passing a contra entry.

ILLUSTRATION 9.10 Enter the following transactions in the double column cash book of Sri B. Srivastava:

2008	**Transactions**
March 1	Started business with cash Rs. 90,000.
2	Opened a bank account with cash Rs. 56,000

3   Interest on fixed deposit credited by bank Rs. 930.
5   Purchases goods for Rs. 14,600 from P.P. Bros. and purchased furniture for Rs. 3,800.
9   Sold goods to M.R. Traders for Rs. 8,300 and paid carriage on it Rs. 160.
10 Received cash Rs. 3,100 and a cheque of Rs. 2,800 from M.R. Traders.
13 Deposited M.R. Trader's cheque in the bank.
15 As per bank statement, M.R. Trader's cheque became dishonoured.
18 Cash withdrawn from bank Rs. 3,900 for payment of salaries of the office staff, which was paid on the next day.
21 Issued a cheque in favour of G. Sen Rs. 750.
23 Proprietor's LIC paid by cheque Rs. 900.
26 Discounted a bill of Rs. 4,600 with the bank at Rs. 4,450.
27 As per instruction, bank honoured a bill of Rs. 2,600.
28 Received a cheque of Rs. 1,930 from K.S. Bros. and deposited the same into Bank immediately.
29 A discounted bill of Rs. 2,460 during the last month became dishonoured and noting charge incurred Rs. 40.
30 Sold old furniture for Rs. 2,100 and paid trade subscriptions Rs. 370. Banked all cash, keeping a balance of Rs. 18,000 in hand.

Solution

In the Books of Sri B. Srivastava

Dr.   Cash Book (Double Column)   Cr.

Date	Particulars	L.F.	Cash (Rs.)	Bank (Rs.)	Date	Particulars	L.F.	Cash (Rs.)	Bank (Rs.)
2008					2008				
March 1	To Capital A/c (Business started)		90,000		March 2	By Bank A/c	C	56,000	
2	To Cash A/c (Bank A/c opened)	C		56,000	5	By Furniture A/c (Purchase of furniture)		3,800	
3	To Interest A/c (Interest of F/D received)			930	9	By Carriage Outward A/c (Carriage on sales paid)		160	
10	To M.R. Traders A/c (Cash Rs. 3100 and cheque Rs. 2,800 received)		5,900		13	By Bank A/c (Deposited M.R. Traders cheque)	C		2,800
13	To Cash A/c (Deposited M.R. Traders cheque)	C		2,800	15	By M.R. Traders A/c (Cheque dishonoured)			2,800
18	To Bank A/c (Cash withdrawn from bank)	C	3,900		18	By Cash A/c (Cash withdrawn from Bank)	C		3,900
26	To Bills Receivable A/c (Bills receivable of Rs. 4600 discounted)			4,450	19	By Salaries A/c (Salaries paid)		3,900	
28	To K.S. Bros. A/c (Cheque received and deposited)			1,930	21	By G. Sen A/c (Cheque issued)			750
30	To Furniture A/c (Sold old furniture)		2,100		23	By Drawing A/c (Proprietor's LIP paid)			900
30	To Cash A/c (Cash deposited in bank)	C		16,870	27	By Bills Payable A/c (Bills payable paid)			2,600
					29	By Acceptor's A/c (Bills receivable of Rs. 2,460 dishonoured and noting charge Rs. 40)			2,500
					30	By Trade Subscription A/c (Trade subscription paid)		370	
					30	By Bank A/c (Cash deposited)	C	16,870	
					31	By Balance c/d		18,000	69,530
			101,900	82,980				101,900	82,980
April 1	To Balance b/d		18,000	69,530					

Working Notes

1. Goods purchased on March 5 are a credit transaction and as such not taken into account here.
2. Goods sold on March 9 are also a credit transaction and not taken into account here.
3. Bank honoured a bill, i.e., made a payment against a bill on March 27.
4. In case of bills discounted and dishonoured, acceptor's A/c (from whom the said bill was received) will be debited and bank A/c will be credited including the noting charges.
5. On March 30 actual cash in hand was Rs. 34,870, which was deposited in bank after keeping Rs. 18,000 in hand.

ILLUSTRATION 9.11 From the following transactions, prepare double column cash book of Sri P.K. Roy for the month of July, 2008.

2008	Transactions
July 1	Cash in hand Rs. 9,850.
	Cash at bank Rs. 17,250.
3	Received a cheque of Rs. 1,900 from Ashim Dev.
	Sold goods for cash Rs. 8,200, out of which deposited Rs. 5,000 into Bank.
4	Deposited Ashim Dev's cheque in bank.
7	Purchased office stationery for cash Rs. 700 and paid godown rent by cheque Rs. 2,000.
9	Received two cheques for Rs. 1,200 and Rs. 1,600 from Ashok Solankey.
12	Endorsed Ashok Solankey's cheque of Rs. 1,200 to Pravir Dutta.
14	Received interest from bank Rs. 80 (as per bank statement).
15	Issued a cheque of Rs. 1,250 in favour of Pratul Kar.
18	Cash withdrawn from bank for personal use Rs. 1,800.
21	Cheque issued to Pratul Kar became dishonoured.
23	Purchased Office furniture for Rs. 1,850 in Cash.
24	Ashim Dev's cheque became dishonoured.
27	Discounted a bill of Rs. 880 with the bank at Rs. 845.
29	Cash withdrawn from bank Rs. 3,000 for payment of salary of the office staff, which was paid on the next day.

Solution

In the Books of Sri P.K. Roy
Cash Book (Double Column)

Dr.   Cr.

Date	Particulars	L.F.	Cash (Rs.)	Bank (Rs.)	Date	Particulars	L.F.	Cash (Rs.)	Bank (Rs.)
2008					2008				
July 1	To Balance b/d		9,850	17,250	July 4	By Bank A/c	C	1,900	
3	To Ashim Dev A/c (Cheque received)		1,900		7	By Stationary A/c (Purchased in Cash)		700	
	To Sales A/c (Goods sold for cash and out of that deposited cash in bank)		3,200	5,000		By godown rent A/c (Paid by cheque)			2,000
					12	By Pravir Dutta A/c (Endorsed Ashok Solankey's cheque)		1,200	
4	To Cash A/c (Ashim Dev's cheque deposited)	C		1,900	15	By Pratul Kar A/c (Cheque issued)			1,250
9	To Ashok Solankey A/c (Received two cheques)		1,200	1,600	18	By Drawings A/c (Withdrawn cash from bank for personal use)			1,800
14	To Interest A/c (Received from Bank)			780	23	By Furniture A/c (Cash purchase)		1,850	
21	To Pratul Kar A/c (Issued cheque dishonoured)			1,250	24	Ashim Dev A/c (Deposited cheque is dishonoured)			1,900
27	To Bills Receivable A/c (Discounted with the bank)			880					

(Contd.)

Date	Particulars	L.F.	Cash (Rs.)	Bank (Rs.)	Date	Particulars	L.F.	Cash (Rs.)	Bank (Rs.)
29	To Bank A/c (Cash withdrawn)	C	3,000		27	By Discount A/c (Discounting charges on bills discounted)			35
					29	By Cash A/c (Cash withdrawn)	C		3,000
					30	By Salaries A/c (Salaries paid)		3,000	
					31	By Balance c/d		10,500	18,675
			19,150	28,660				19,150	28,660
August 1	To Balance b/d		10,500	18,675					

Working Notes

1. It is assumed that the cheque of Rs. 1,600 of Ashok Solankey received on 09.07.08 was deposited in the bank immediately.

2. Discount charged by bank on discounted bill shown on the credit side. It should not be shown in the discount column of cash book because it is different from cash discount allowed to a party.

ILLUSTRATION 9.12 Enter the following transactions in the cash book of Sri M. Sen in cash and bank columns (without narration).

2008	**Transactions**
May 1	Cash in hand Rs. 11,680.
	Cash at bank Rs. 27,480.
3	Sold goods to P.Q. Traders for Rs. 9,800 and paid carriage on it Rs. 340.
4	Purchased goods from Roy Bros. for Rs. 5,850 and paid carriage on it Rs. 150.
6	Purchased goods for Rs. 450 in cash.
9	P.Q. Traders settled their account by cheque of Rs. 9,720 and was allowed a discount of Rs. 80.
10	A cheque of 3,860 drawn in favour of Roy Bros.
12	Proprietor's house rent paid by cheque Rs. 750.
14	Dividend collected by bank for Rs. 1,840.
17	Bank credited interest Rs. 1,920 and debited bank charge Rs. 40.
19	Received cheque for Rs. 1,920 from X and Co., and deposited the same in the bank immediately.
20	Received a cheque of Rs. 1,340 from Y Traders and it was deposited in the bank on the next day.
24	Drew cheque for petty cash Rs. 650.
25	Drew cheque for office use Rs. 1,800.
28	Fresh capital introduced amounting to Rs. 7,000.
30	Y Traders' cheque was returned by the bank marked 'return to drawer'.
31	Deposited cash in the bank in excess of Rs. 5,000 in hand.

Solution

In the Books of Sri M. Sen

Dr. **Cash Book (Double Column)** Cr.

Date	Particulars	L.F.	Cash (Rs.)	Bank (Rs.)	Date	Particulars	L.F.	Cash (Rs.)	Bank (Rs.)
2008					2008				
May 1	To Balance b/d		11,680	27,480	May 3	By Carriage Outward A/c			340
9	To P.Q. Traders A/c			9,720	4	By Carriage Inward A/c			150
14	To Dividend A/c			1,840	6	By Purchase A/c			450

(Contd.)

Date	Particulars	L.F.	Cash (Rs.)	Bank (Rs.)	Date	Particulars	L.F.	Cash (Rs.)	Bank (Rs.)
17	To Interest A/c			1,920	10	By Roy Bros. A/c			3,860
19	To X & Co.			1,920	12	By Drawings A/c			750
20	To Y Traders A/c		1,340		17	By Bank charge A/c			40
21	To Cash A/c	C		1,340	21	By Bank A/c	C	1,340	
25	To Bank A/c	C	1,800		24	By Petty cash A/c			650
28	To Capital A/c		7,000		25	By Cash A/c	C		1,800
31	To Cash A/c	C		14,540	30	By Y Traders A/c			1,340
					31	By Bank (Balancing)		14,540	
					31	By Balance c/d		5,000	50,320
			21,820	58,760				21,820	58,760
June 1	To Balance b/d		5,000	50,320					

Working Notes

1. Goods sold on 3.5.08 was on credit, hence it is not taken here.
2. Goods purchased on 4.5.08 were on credit, and thus it is not taken here.
3. The cheque received from P.Q. Traders on 9.5.08 is considered here as deposited into Bank immediately.
4. Any expenditure incurred for proprietor's personal expenses will be treated as drawing. Thus, proprietor's house rent paid on 12.5.08 is posted to drawings account.

9.5 DISCOUNT

Generally, two types of discounts are used in purchase and sale transactions. To increase the volume of sales, trade discounts are allowed while to increase the flow of cash, cash discounts are allowed. They are explained below.

Trade discount

This discount is allowed by manufacturers or wholesalers to their customers on a percentage basis on the list price of the goods. It is used to increase the sales volume. After charging this discount, the net sale price or the net amount payable by a customer is calculated. Accounts are recorded on the basis of this net sale price. Trade discount is allowed to all types of sales, i.e., both on cash sales and on credit sales.

Cash discount

A cash discount is allowed to encourage debtors in making prompt payment. It is allowed only when a debtor pays his debt within or before the due date, i.e., within the credit period. It is calculated on percentage basis on the total amount payable by the debtor/customer. Hence, when goods are sold on cash basis, a customer will enjoy both trade discount and cash discount. The mode of calculation of cash discount is shown below:

	(Rs.)
List price of the goods	40 per set
Units sold	50 units
Rate of trade discount	10%
Rate of cash discount	10%
List price of goods sold (Rs. 40 × 50)	Rs. 2,000
Less: Trade discount 10 %	Rs. 200
Net selling price (Amount payable)	Rs. 1,800
Less: Cash discount (10%)	Rs. 180
Net amount payable	Rs. 1,620

Hence, if the customer pays his dues within the due date or specified date, then he has to pay only Rs. 1,620 instead of Rs. 1,800.

9.5.1 Distinction between Cash Discount and Trade Discount

Cash discount	Trade discount
It is given to encourage customers for prompt payment.	It is allowed to increase the sales volume.
It is given by the creditors to their debtors	It is given by the manufacturers or the wholesalers to their retailers.
It is calculated on the net sales price/amount due.	It is calculated on the list price/catalogue price of the goods.
The amount of cash discount allowed/received is recorded in the books.	Generally, the amount of trade discount is not recorded in the books of accounts.
The rate of discount may vary from customer to customer depending on the period of prompt payment.	Usually, the rate of discount is fixed.
It is conditional.	It is unconditional.
It is deducted from the net sale price/amount due.	It is deducted from the list price/ catalogue price of goods.

ILLUSTRATION 9.13 Enter the following transactions in the double column cash book (without narration) of Mr. B. Mukherjee:

2008	Transactions

June 1 Cash in hand Rs. 17,200 and at bank Rs. 16,500.

3 P.K. Sen settled his account of Rs. 7,800 by a cheque of Rs. 7,650.

7 Cash paid to D.K. Roy Rs. 1,780 and received discount Rs. 30.

9 M.R. Basu settled his account of Rs. 4,900 by cheque subject to 5% discount.

12 A.B. Khan settled his account by a cheque of Rs. 3,950 and was allowed a discount of Rs. 50.

14 M.R. Basu's cheque was endorsed to S.S. Dhar in full settlement of his account of Rs. 4,700.

18 Cash paid to Sri M. Ram Rs. 1,980 and issued a cheque of Rs. 2,800 to him, and received discount from him Rs. 190.

21 Sold goods for cash Rs. 21,000, out of which deposited cash in bank Rs. 8,400.

22 B.K. Roy's account of Rs. 3,950 was settled by issuing a cheque of the Rs. 3,900, goods purchased from X & Co. for Rs. 7,200.

24 The cheque which was issued to B.K. Roy on 22.6.08 returned dishonoured, and as such cash was paid to him for the same amount.

25 Sri P.U. Gupta deposited cash in bank Rs. 2,750.

26 Cash Rs. 3,800 paid to N. Sen and received 5% discount from him.

27 M.P. Dhara's account of Rs. 3,600 was settled by a cheque and received 5% discount.

29 Proprietor's house rent paid Rs. 750.

30 Bank credited for interest Rs. 1,300 and debited Rs. 75 for their charges. A.B. Khan's cheque of Rs. 3,950 became dishonoured (received on June 12).

Solution

In the Books of Mr. B. Mukherjee

Dr. **Cash Book (Double Column)** Cr.

Date	Particulars	L.F.	Cash (Rs.)	Bank (Rs.)	Date	Particulars	L.F.	Cash (Rs.)	Bank (Rs.)
2008					2008				
June1	To Balance b/d		17,200	16,500	June 7	By D.K. Roy A/c		1,780	
3	To P.K. Sen A/c			7,650	14	By S.S. Dhar A/c		4,655	
9	To M.R. Basu A/c		4,655		18	By M. Ram A/c		1,980	2,800
12	To A.B. Khan A/c			3,950	22	By B.K. Roy A/c			3,900
21	To Sales A/c		12,600	8,400	24	By B.K. Roy A/c		3,900	
24	To B.K. Roy A/c			3,900	26	By N. Sen A/c		3,800	
25	To P.K. Gupta A/c			2,750	27	By M.P. Dhara A/c			3,420
30	To Interest A/c			1,300	29	By Drawings A/c		750	
					30	By Bank Charge			75
						By A.B. Khan A/c			3,950
					30	By Balance c/d		17,590	30,305
				34,455	44,450			34,455	44,450
July 1	To Balance b/d		17,590	30,305					

Working Notes

1. Goods purchased on June 22 are credit transactions and as such not taken into account.
2. Discount was allowed to A.B. Khan on June 12 but was cancelled on June 30 due to dishonour of Khan's cheque.
3. Cash paid to N. Sen Rs. 3,800 and received 5% discount. Hence, 95% of Rs. 3,800 is the total claim and as such discount (3,800/95 × 5) comes out to be Rs. 200.

ILLUSTRATION 9.14 Enter the following transactions in the double column cash book (without narration) of Mr. Sunil Khandola:

2008	Transactions
December 1	Cash in hand Rs. 32,700 and bank Rs. 54,250.
3	Received cash Rs. 3,980 and a cheque of Rs. 2,500 from M/s R.P. Bros. and allowed discount Rs. 250.
5	Paid for rent Rs. 650.
9	Cash Rs. 2,850 paid to S. Nigam and received 5% discount from him.
13	Cash withdrew from bank for office use Rs. 2,700.
18	Received a cheque from Nakul Rs. 2,900.
19	Sold goods for cash Rs. 7,100.
21	Endorsed Nakul's cheque to Pratik in full settlement of his account of Rs. 3,000.
23	D. Konar's account of Rs. 4,000 was settled in cash and received 7.5 % discount.
25	Issued a cheque of Rs. 3,100 to Mr. Sharma and received discount Rs. 260.
27	Dividend collected by bank Rs. 660.
28	Paid for advertisement Rs. 900.
31	Banked all cash, keeping a balance of Rs. 21,000 in hand.

Solution

In the Books of Mr. Sunil Khandola

Dr.   **Cash Book (Double Column)**   Cr.

Date	Particulars	L.F.	Cash (Rs.)	Bank (Rs.)	Date	Particulars	L.F.	Cash (Rs.)	Bank (Rs.)
2008 December					2008 December				
1	To Balance b/d		32,700	54,250	7	By Rent		650	
3	To M/s R.P. Bros. A/c		3,980	2,500	9	By S. Nigam A/c		2,850	
13	To Bank A/c	C	2,700		13	By Cash A/c	C		2,700
18	To Nakul A/c		1,800		21	By Pratik A/c		2,900	
19	To Sales A/c		7,100		23	By D. Konar A/c		3,700	
27	To Dividend A/c			660	25	By Sharma			3,100
31	To Cash A/c	C		16,280	28	By Advertisement		900	
					31	By Bank A/c	C	16,280	
						By Balance c/d		21,000	67,890
			48,280	73,690				48,280	73,690
2009 January 1	To Balance b/d		21,000	67,890					

9.6 THREE COLUMN CASH BOOK/TRIPLE COLUMN CASH BOOK

Triple column cash book is prepared to record transactions regarding discount allowed and received during a particular period in addition to the cash and bank transactions. To record the transactions regarding discount, two columns are opened on both the sides. The debit side records the discount allowed while the credit side records the discount received during the period. Here, cash and bank transactions are recorded like that in a double column cash book.

[It is not covered within the syllabus, hence not discussed here.]

9.7 PETTY CASH BOOK

Big business houses have large number of small or petty cash transactions. If all the transactions were recorded in the main cash book, the chief cashier would have to forgo a number of important business works. This would affect the business. Thus, to relieve the him from the burden of recording all the petty transactions like postage, carriage, collie charges, travelling charges, purchase of stationery etc. a separate cash book is opened where all petty expenses are recorded, and the said cash book is known as a Petty cash book. The petty cashier is given a certain amount of money as per the business requirements at the beginning of each month or week, and he pays all petty expenses from the said sum or amount. When the said sum is fully expended or after keeping some minimum amount in hand, he submits his accounts before the chief cashier. The Chief Cashier then examines the accounts and after being satisfied pays the expended amount to the petty cashier for the next period. This procedure is followed throughout the year. Generally, the procedure is of three types:

1. Simple Petty Cash Book
2. Imprest System of Petty Cash Book
3. Analytical Petty Cash Book.

9.7.1 Advantages of Petty Cash Book

1. It helps the chief cashier in disbursement of small or petty expenses. Hence, this system saves his valuable time.
2. A small amount is allotted in favour of the petty cashier for necessary petty expenses. Hence, there is little chance of fraud, because the petty cashier is personally responsible for the accounts maintained by him.
3. It helps to control petty expenses.
4. Petty cash book reduces the volume of transactions to be recorded in the main Cash Book, because petty expenses are huge in number and are not considered in the main Cash Book.
5. It is very simple to operate and does not require any specialized knowledge or skill.
6. According to this system, the total amount of each petty expense is transferred to the ledger and hence it saves a lot of space in the ledger.

9.7.2 Simple Petty Cash Book

It is prepared like a single column cash book. The petty cashier is given a certain amount of money as per the business requirements at the beginning of each month or week, from which he pays all petty expenses. When the said sum is fully expended or after a minimum amount is kept in hand, he submits his accounts before the chief cashier. When cash is received from the chief cashier, it is debited on the left hand side while all expenses credited on the right hand side. This is shown below with the help of an example.

ILLUSTRATION 9.15 Enter the following transactions in a simple petty cash book:

2008	Transactions
March 1	Received cash from the chief cashier Rs. 450.
2	Paid for newspaper and magazines Rs. 64.
2	Carriage and coolie hire Rs. 45.
3	Taxi fares to cashier Rs. 15.
3	Paid for postage and stamp Rs. 24.
4	Paid for STD Rs. 12.
4	Repair to typewriter Rs. 55.
5	Bus fares to peons Rs. 18.
5	Registration of letters Rs. 35.
6	Paid for Thumps Up and Coca Cola Rs. 22.
6	Cost of pins and clips Rs. 11.

7 Postage stamps Rs. 18.
7 Purchased a bottle of glue Rs. 21.

Solution

Dr.   **Simple Petty Cash Book**   Cr.

Amount Received (Rs.)	C.B. Folio	Date		Particulars	V.N.	Total Payment (Rs.)
450		2008	1	To Cash A/c		
		March	2	By Newspaper and Magazines		64
			2	By Carriage and coolie hire		45
			3	By Taxi Fares		15
			3	By Postage Stamps		24
			4	By STD Charges		12
			4	By Repair to Typewriter		55
			5	By Bus Fares		18
			5	By Registration Charges		35
			6	By Cold Drinks		22
			6	By Pins and Clips		11
			7	By Postage Stamps		18
			7	By Glue		21
				By Balance c/d		110
450						450
110			8	To Balance b/d		

9.7.3 Imprest System of Petty Cash

The best method for maintaining petty cash is the imprest system. Under this system, at the beginning, a fixed amount is given to the petty cashier who makes payment out of the said amount. At the end of the period (week, fortnight or month), an amount equal to the amount of total expenditure is again given to the petty cashier. The next period will begin with the same fixed sum of money. This procedure is to be followed for the next period and so on.

ILLUSTRATION 9.16 Suppose the imprest amount is Rs. 450 and previous Illustration 9.15 is solved here under imprest system to show the amount the petty cashier would receive from the chief cashier at the beginning of the next week.

Solution

Dr.   **Simple Petty Cash Book**   Cr.

Amount Received (Rs.)	C.B. Folio	Date		Particulars	V.N.	Total Payment (Rs.)
450		2008	1	To Cash A/c		
		March	2	By Newspaper and Magazines		64
			2	By Carriage and coolie hire		45
			3	By Taxi Fares		15
			3	By Postage and Stamp		24
			4	By STD Charges		12
			4	By Repair to Typewriter		55
			5	By Bus Fares		18
			5	By Registration Charges		35
			6	By Cold Drinks		22
			6	By Pins and Clips		11
			7	By Postage Stamps		18
			7	B Glue		21
				By Balance c/d		110
450						450
110			8	To Balance b/d		
340				To Cash A/c**		

** Here, total petty expenses are Rs. 340 and hence, Petty Cashier would receive Rs. 340 from the Chief Cashier at the beginning of the next week.

ILLUSTRATION 9.17 Record the following transactions in analytical petty cash book under imprest system and show how much will be paid to the petty cashier on March 16, 2008:

Date	Particulars	Rs.
2008 March 1	Balance in hand	34
1	Received cash from the Chief Cashier to make up the required balance	366
2	Bought Envelops and Gum	27
3	Paid Bus Fair	19
5	Postage and Stamp	35
7	Paid STD Charges	28
	Local travelling by the office clerk	22
8	Paid coolie charges for shifting of furniture	20
9	Paid washing charges of office equipments and other materials	21
11	Paid repair charges of Delivery Van	35
12	Purchase of Pen and Pencils	20
13	Paid for Xerox charges	15
15	Speed Post charges	27
	Paid to D. Sharma	100

Also, show the Journal Entries and Ledger Accounts.

Solution

In the Books of ...
Analytical Petty Cash Book

Dr.   Cr.

Cash Received (Rs.)	C.B. Folio	Date 2005	Particulars	Petty Cash (V.N.) Rs.	Total Pay-ment Rs.	Sta-tionery Rs.	Post-age Stamp Rs.	Travel-ling Rs.	Coolie & Clean ing Charges Rs.	Repairs Rs.	Misc-ellane-ous Rs.	Ledger Rs.
34		March 1	To Balance b/d									
366		1	To Cash A/c									
		2	By Stationery A/c		27	27						
		3	By Travelling A/c		19			19				
		5	By Postage A/c		35		35					
		7	By Postage A/c		28		28					
			By Travelling A/c		22			22				
		8	By Coolie charges A/c		20				20			
		9	By Cleaning charges A/c		21				21			
		11	By Repairs charges A/c		35					35		
		12	By Stationery A/c		20	20						
		13	By Miscellaneous charges A/c		15						15	
		15	By Postage A/c		27		27					
			By D. Sharma A/c		100							100
			Total		369	47	90	41	41	35	15	100
			By Balance c/d		31							
400					400							
31		16	To Balance b/d									
369		16	To Cash A/c									

Notes:

    1. The above total will be posted to the debit of respective nominal accounts in the ledger.

    2. The above amount will be shown in the debit side of D. Sharma's Account in creditors' ledger.

Journal Entry and Posting into Ledger

Journal

Date	Particulars	L.F.	Amount Dr. (Rs.)	Amount Cr. (Rs.)
2005 March 1	Petty Cash A/c Dr.		366	
	To Cash A/c			366
	(Being cash paid to petty cashier)			

(Contd.)

Date	Particulars		L.F.	Amount Dr. (Rs.)	Amount Cr. (Rs.)
15	Stationery A/c	Dr.		47	
	Postage A/c	Dr.		90	
	Travelling Expenses A/c	Dr.		41	
	Coolie & Cleaning charges A/c	Dr.		41	
	Repairs A/c	Dr.		35	
	Miscellaneous Expenses A/c	Dr.		15	
	D. Sharma A/c	Dr.		100	
	To Petty Cash A/c				369
	(Being account balances transferred to the respective accounts)				
16	Petty Cash A/c	Dr.		369	
	To Cash A/c				369
	(Being cash paid to petty cashier)				

Ledger

Dr.   **Stationery Account**   Cr.

Date	Particulars	J.F.	Amount (Rs.)	Date	Particulars	J.F.	Amount (Rs.)
2008 March 15	To Petty Cash A/c		47				

Dr.   **Postage Account**   Cr.

Date	Particulars	J.F.	Amount (Rs.)	Date	Particulars	J.F.	Amount (Rs.)
2008 March 15	To Petty Cash A/c		90				

Dr.   **Travelling Expenses Account**   Cr.

Date	Particulars	J.F.	Amount (Rs.)	Date	Particulars	J.F.	Amount (Rs.)
2008 March 15	To Petty Cash A/c		41				

Dr.   **Coolie and Cleaning Charges Account**   Cr.

Date	Particulars	J.F.	Amount (Rs.)	Date	Particulars	J.F.	Amount (Rs.)
2008 March 15	To Petty Cash A/c		41				

Dr.   **Repairs Account**   Cr.

Date	Particulars	J.F.	Amount (Rs.)	Date	Particulars	J.F.	Amount (Rs.)
2008 March 15	To Petty Cash A/c		35				

Dr.   **Miscellaneous Expenses Account**   Cr.

Date	Particulars	J.F.	Amount (Rs.)	Date	Particulars	J.F.	Amount (Rs.)
2008 March 15	To Petty Cash A/c		15				

Dr.   **D. Sharma Account**   Cr.

Date	Particulars	J.F.	Amount (Rs.)	Date	Particulars	J.F.	Amount (Rs.)
2008 March 15	To Petty Cash A/c		100				

9.7.4 Analytical Petty Cash Book

The recording procedure of an Analytical Petty Cash Book is similar to that of a Simple Petty Cash Book. However, the basic difference is that in analytical petty cash book all expenditures are first recorded in the total amount column and they are again recorded in the respective expenditure column. Suppose, cash paid for purchase of postage stamp is Rs. 30. First, Rs. 30 is shown in the Total Amount column and then again it is shown in the Postage Stamp column.

ILLUSTRATION 9.18   Enter the following transactions in an analytical petty cash book:

1998		Transactions
January	1	Received a cheque from the chief cashier Rs. 600.
	1	Paid for postage and stamp Rs. 12.
	1	Repair to typewriter Rs. 22.
	2	Bus fares to peons Rs. 8.
	2	Paid for newspaper and magazines Rs. 32.
	2	Paid for telegram Rs. 16.
	3	Cost of pins and clips Rs. 6.
	3	Carriage and coolie hire Rs. 36.
	3	Registration of letters Rs. 12.
	4	Taxi fares to cashier Rs. 15.
	4	Postage stamps Rs. 18.
	4	Paid for Thumps Up and Coca Cola Rs. 22.
	5	Purchase of stationery for personal use Rs. 21.
	5	Purchase of a typewriter cover Rs. 50.
	5	Purchase of a bottle of glue Rs. 11.
	6	Polishing of table and chairs Rs. 36.
	6	Tram and bus fares of office staffs Rs. 19.
	6	Advances to peon K. Kar Rs. 25, Sale of old papers Rs. 40.
	7	Cost of papers and pencils Rs. 26, Purchase of file rack Rs. 60.

Balance the petty cash book on January 7 and also show the amount of the cheque to be received by the petty cashier again on January 8.

Solution

Analytical Petty Cash Book of M/s K

Amount received	C.B.F.	Date	Particulars	V.N.	Total (Rs.)	Postage & Telegrams (Rs.)	Printing & Stationery (Rs.)	Carriage & Coolie Charge (Rs.)	Travelling & Conveyance (Rs.)	Papers & Magazines (Rs.)	Repairs & Others (Rs.)	Misc. Exp. (Rs.)	L.F.	Amount (Rs.)	Remarks
															Ledger A/c
600		1998 Jan.1	To Bank												
		1	By Postage Stamps		12	12									
		1	By Repairs		22						22				
		2	By Bus Fares		8				8						
		2	By Newspapers & Magazines		32					32					
		2	By Telegram		16	16									
		3	By Pins & Clips		6		6								
		3	By Carriage & Coolie Hire		36			36							
		3	By Registration of letters		12	12									

(Contd.)

Amount received	C.B.F.	Date	Particulars	V.N.	Total (Rs.)	Postage & Telegrams (Rs.)	Printing & Stationery (Rs.)	Carriage & Coolie Charge (Rs.)	Travelling & Conveyance (Rs.)	Papers & Magazines (Rs.)	Repairs & Others (Rs.)	Misc. Exp. (Rs.)	L.F.	Amount (Rs.)	Remarks
		4	By Taxi Fares to cashier		15				15						
		4	By Postage Stamps		18	18									
		4	By Cold Drinks		22							22			
		5	By Drawings		21									21	Drawings A/c
		5	By Typewriter Cover		50									50	Fittings
		5	By Glue		11		11								
		6	By Polishing of tables and chairs		36						36				
		6	By Tram & Bus Fares		19				19						
		6	By K. Kar A/c		25									25	K.K. A/c
		7	By Papers & Pencils		26		26								
		7	By File Rack		60									60	
					447	58	43	36	42	32	58	22		156	
		7	By Balance c/d		153										
600					600										
153		8	To Balance b/d												
447			To Bank												

Working Note

1. No entry is required for the sale of old papers on January 6, 1998 because it should have been recorded in the cash book.

EXERCISES

I. Objective Type Questions

A. Fill up the correct word in the blanks:

- (a) All _____ transactions are recorded. (cash/credit)
- (b) Cash deposited into bank is a _____ entry. (contra/single)
- (c) Cash withdrawn from bank is a _____ entry. (contra/single)
- (d) Interest _____ by bank is shown on the debit side of the cash book. (credited/debited)
- (e) Bank charge _____ by the bank is shown on the credit side of the cash book. (credited/debited)
- (f) Cheque issued to a party is to be shown on the _____ side of the cash book. (debit/credit)
- (g) The deposited cheque which has become dishonoured is to be shown on the _____ side of the cash book. (debit/credit)
- (h) Cheque endorsed to a party (received previously) is to be in _____ coloumn. (cash/bank)
- (i) The issued cheque which has become dishonoured is to be shown on the _____ side of the cash book. (debit/credit)
- (j) Dishonoured endorsed cheque is _____ shown in the cash book. (not to be/to be)
- (k) Discount recorded on the debit side of the cash book represents _____ (discount allowed/discount received).
- (l) The closing balance of the cash book indicates _____ (cash in hand/closing capital)
- (m) Cash withdrawn from bank for personal use is _____ entry. (a contra/not a contra)

Ans: (a) Cash (b) Contra (c) Contra (d) Credited (e) Debited (f) Credit (g) Credit (h) Cash (i) Debit (j) not to be (k) discount allowed (l) Cash in hand (m) Not a contra.

B. Choose the correct answer from the options given within the brackets:
  (a) Cash withdrawn from bank for office use: (is a contra entry/is a drawing)
  (b) Cash withdrawn from bank for personal use: (is a drawing/is a contra entry)
  (c) Cheque deposited into bank received earlier is a: (contra entry/personal entry)
  (d) Received a bearer cheque and cashed at bank counter and the data when cashed: (a contra entry is required/no entry is required)
  (e) Received interest from bank: (credited by bank/debited by bank)
  (f) Bank charge and interest on overdraft is shown in the cash book on: (debit side/credit side)
  (g) If an endorsed cheque is dishonoured, then in the cash book: (no entry is required/entry is required)
  (h) Proprietor's Life Insurance Policy matured and collected by bank is to be shown in the cash book: (To Drawings A/c/To Capital A/c)
  (i) For incomes collected by bank, the banker will: (debit the business A/c/credit the business A/c)
  (j) A Trader's cheque when returned by the bank marked 'Return to drawer': (dishonoured entry is required/contra entry is required)

  Ans: (a) Contra entry (b) Drawings (c) Contra entry (d) No entry is required (e) Credited by bank (f) Credit side (g) No entry is required (h) To Capital A/c (i) Credit the business A/c (j) Dishonoured entry is required.

C. Choose the Correct alternative:
  (a) In the cash book, Cash A/c always shows
      (i) Debit balance
      (ii) Credit balance
      (iii) Either debit or credit balance
  (b) In the cash book, Bank A/c shows
      (i) Debit balance
      (ii) Credit balance
      (iii) Either debit or credit balance
  (c) The Imprest System is followed in
      (i) Double column cash book
      (ii) Petty cash book
      (iii) Triple column cash book
  (d) Petty cash book is prepared to record the
      (i) Personal expenses
      (ii) Petty office expenses
      (iii) Administrative expenses
  (e) For interest on overdraft balance, the bank
      (i) Charges the Trader's A/c
      (ii) Deducts interest from the bank balance
      (iii) Deducts from interest receivables
  (f) For bank commission
      (i) Bank balance is increased
      (ii) Bank balance is decreased
  (g) Received cheque when endorsed, it decreases
      (i) The cash balance of the cash book
      (ii) The bank balance of the cash book
  (h) Cash withdrawn from bank for personal use will
      (i) Decrease the bank balance only
      (ii) Decrease the bank balance and increase the cash balance
      (iii) Have no effect on the bank balance

   (i) A cheque when received and nothing is mentioned about the cheque, then
   (i) No entry is required
   (ii) Contra entry is required
   (iii) It is to be assumed that the cheque was deposited into bank immediately.

Ans: (a) i, (b) iii, (c) ii, (d) ii, (e) i, (f) ii, (g) i, (h)i, (i) iii.

II. *Short Answer Type Questions*

   (a) Mr. X settled his account of Rs. 3,000 by cheque and was allowed 5% discount. Calculate the amount of discount.
   (b) Mr. Y settled his account by a cheque of Rs. 4,275 and was allowed 5% discount. Calculate the amount of discount.
   (c) Discount received @ 4%, i.e. Rs. 300 and the account was settled by issuing a cheque in favour of M/S Z. Calculate the amount of cheque issued.
   (d) Mr. Q's A/c of Rs. 4,000 was settled by a cheque and received 3% discount. Calculate the amount of discount.
   (e) A party's cheque is returned dishonoured marked 'Refer to drawer'. How is it to be dealt with in the cash book?

   Ans: (a) Rs. 150 (b) Rs. 225 (c) Rs. 7,200 (d) Rs. 120 (e) Party's A/c will be credited in the cash book (bank column).

III. *Long Answer Type Questions*

1 What is special purpose subsidiary books? Explain their chief advantages.
2 What is a Cash Book? What are its functions? Name the different classes of Cash Book.
3 What are the features and advantages of a Cash Book?
4 "The actual amount of cash in hand can never be accurately determined without the actual counting of cash in the Cash Box." Evaluate the statement.
5 "A Cash Book is a Journalized Ledger". Give your opinion on this statement.
6 What is a Double Column Cash Book? State the procedure for writing a Double Column Cash Book.
7 What is Contra Entry? What are the transactions for which such entry is required to be made?
8 "The Cash Book always shows a debit balance." Justify this statement.
9 Is it necessary to open a separate Discount Account in the Ledger when discount column is provided in both sides of a Cash Book.?
10 What do you understand by Petty Cash Book? Is it essential to maintain it? What is the relation between a main Cash Book and a Petty Cash Book?
11 What do you mean by Imprest System of Petty Cash Book?
12 What is multi-columnar Cash Book? Who are the users of this cash book?

IV. *Problems*

Single Column Cash Book

1. Record the following transactions in a Single Column Cash Book of Sri N.G. Das:

1991	Transactions
Jan. 1	Started business with cash Rs. 62,000.
2	Purchased goods from P.K. Traders Rs. 9,200 and paid carriage on it Rs. 360.
3	Paid for advertisement Rs. 600.
6	Paid salary to manager Rs. 1,200.
9	Sold goods for cash Rs. 2,900.
11	Travelling expenses paid Rs. 590.
13	Purchased furniture for Rs. 5,200.
18	Purchased machineries for Rs. 11,000.
21	Sold goods to M.G. Bros. Rs. 7,200.

24   Cash paid to P.K. Traders Rs. 5,900.

26   Paid proprietor's house rent Rs. 1,250.

29   Paid bonus to staff Rs. 4,000.

30   Commission received Rs. 750.

Ans: Cash in hand Rs. 35,550 on 31.1.91. Purchase ans sales on 2nd Jan and on 21st Jan. are credit transactions.

2.   Draw up a Single Column Cash Book from the following:

1993   Transactions

March 1   Cash in hand Rs. 21,200.

3   Cash deposited into Bank Rs. 3,000.

6   Paid carriage for goods purchased Rs. 700.

9   Paid electric charges Rs. 270.

11   Proprietor's L.I.P. paid Rs. 940.

13   Sold old furniture Rs. 630.

18   Lent to P.K. Das Rs. 3,000.

22   Paid shop rent Rs. 600.

24   Cash withdrawn from business for private use Rs. 900.

25   Cash received from A. Kar Rs. 5,900.

27   Repairs of typewriter paid Rs. 260.

28   Purchased postage and stationery Rs. 400.

30   Q. Sen repaid his loan with interest Rs. 1,600 (Rs. 1,500 + Rs. 100).

31   Deposited excess cash into Bank after keeping Rs. 9,000 in hand.

Ans: Cash deposited into Bank on 31st March Rs. 10,260.

3.   Enter the following transactions in a Single Column Cash Book:

1995   Transactions

April 1   Cash in hand Rs. 21,650.

3   Sold goods for cash Rs. 7,200.

5   Cash paid to petty cashier Rs. 600.

6   Telephone bill paid Rs. 150.

9   Loan to B. Mukherjee Rs. 3,000.

12   Paid insurance premium Rs. 760.

13   Paid wages Rs. 2,100.

18   Purchased a typewriter Rs. 3,000.

21   Goods purchased for Rs. 5,900.

24   Cashed N.S.C. and brought that amount into business Rs. 4,000.

27   Cash withdrew from business for private use Rs. 650.

29   Cash paid to G. Ram Rs. 1,600.

30   Paid godown rent Rs. 1,350.

Ans: Closing cash in hand Rs. 13,740.

Double Column Cash Book

4.   From the following transactions prepare a Double Column Cash Book of Sri D.K. Dey for the month of January 1996:

1996   Transactions

Jan. 1   Cash in hand Rs. 16,600. Cash at Bank Rs. 28,200.

3   Sold goods for cash Rs. 8,900 and out of that deposited cash into Bank Rs. 5,000.

5   Issued a cheque of Rs. 3,200 to Roy Bros.

7   Paid salary by cheque Rs. 2,600.

9   Received a cheque of Rs. 2,750 from Dhar Bros.

12   Dhar Bros., cheque deposited into Bank.

18 Purchased office furniture for Rs. 1,800.
21 Cash withdrawn from Bank for office use Rs. 4,000.
24 Cash withdrawn from Bank for personal use Rs. 750.
26 Received interest from Bank Rs. 950.
27 Paid trade subscription by cheque Rs. 640.
29 Sold old furniture Rs. 840.
30 Paid for advertisement Rs. 980.
Ans: Closing cash in hand Rs. 22,560 and cash at Bank Rs. 25,710.

5. Write up the Double Column Cash Book of Mr. M. Sen from the following transactions:

1996   **Transactions**

April 1 Cash in hand Rs. 19,600. Cash at Bank Rs. 24,700.
4 Received two cheques for Rs. 1,250 and Rs. 1,500 from S.K. Roy.
6 Endorsed S.K. Roy's cheque of Rs. 1,500 to T.R. Sen.
8 Deposited S.K. Roy's cheque of Rs. 1,250 into Bank.
11 Cash withdrawn from Bank Rs. 1,800 to pay the salary of the office staff, which was paid on the next day.
14 Sold goods for cash Rs. 8,900 and paid Rs. 6,000 out of that into Bank on the next day.
18 Bank collected dividend Rs. 850.
21 S.K. Roy's cheque of Rs. 1,250 became dishonoured.
24 Received a cheque of Rs. 650 from Amit Dhar.
25 Endorsed Amit Dhar's cheque to Kamal Sarkar.
27 Received a cheque of Rs. 1,800 from P. Bros.
29 Purchased machinery for Rs. 8,000 from Machine & Tools Ltd. and out of that issued a cheque of Rs. 4,000 to them.
30 Paid Rs. 600 for installation of machine.
Ans: Closing cash in hand Rs. 21,900 and cash at Bank Rs. 27,550.

6. Enter the following transactions in the Cash Book with Cash and Bank column:

1994   **Transactions**

May 1 Cash in hand Rs. 13,600 and Cash at Bank Rs. 19,850.
2 Introduced further capital Rs. 15,000 and out of that paid into Bank Rs. 6,000.
4 Drew cheque for personal use Rs. 800.
6 Drew cheque for petty cash Rs. 1,100.
9 Drew cheque for office use Rs. 900.
12 Received a cheque of Rs. 1,750 from C. Chanda.
15 Paid advance salary to manager Rs. 2,500.
21 C. Chanda's cheque became dishonoured.
23 Sold goods for cash Rs. 7,200.
23 Paid godown rent Rs. 850.
26 Received a cheque of Rs. 1,650 from D. Khan.
28 Endorsed D. Khan's cheque to G. Karmakar.
29 The cheque which was endorsed to G. Karmakar became dishonoured (received from D. Khan).
30 Deposited A. Kumar's cheque into Bank Rs. 2,100, received during the last month.
31 Received interest from Bank Rs. 1,850 and Bank debited for charges Rs. 160.
Ans: Closing cash in hand Rs. 25,250 and at Bank Rs. 26,840. No entry is required in the cash book on 29.5.94. A. Kumar's cheque paid into Bank on 30.5.94 treated contra entry.

7. Record the following transactions in the Cash Book of Sri Rahaman and show the closing balances of Cash and Bank Accounts:

1988	Transactions
Mar. 22	He had cash in hand Rs. 35,000.
23	Opened a Bank Account Rs. 28,000.
24	Received from Sri Munshi Rs. 9,000 Paid to Sri Nariwal in cheque Rs. 6,000.
25	Purchases made in cash Rs. 4,000. Paid Rent Rs. 500. Withdrawn from Bank Rs. 8,000.
26	Received a cheque from Sri Gupta Rs. 12,000.
27	Paid Salaries Rs. 3,000.
28	Purchased a typewriting machine and paid in cheque Rs. 5,000. Purchases in cash Rs. 1,500.
29	Sent to Bank a cheque received from Sri Mishra Rs. 5,600. Paid electric bill Rs. 400.
30	Cash Sales Rs. 9,800.
	Purchases from Sri N. Roy Rs. 2,500.
31	Sold to Sri Bhalotia Rs. 6,800.
	Purchases stationery Rs. 200.
	Deposit in Bank Account Rs. 5,500.

(W.B.H.S. Examination, 1988)

Ans: Closing cash in hand Rs. 18,700 and at Bank Rs. 32,100; Purchases on 30th March and sales on 31st March are credit transactions.

8. From the following transactions prepare a Double Column Cash Book of Sri M.M. Rudra for the month of April 1996:

1996	Transactions
April 1	Cash in Hand Rs. 19,650.
	Cash at Bank Rs. 27,680.
3	Sale of old furniture and payment received in cheque Rs. 1,700, immediately banked.
6	Received interest from Bank on Fixed Deposits Rs. 1,950.
8	Sold goods for Rs. 8,200 and out of that paid into Bank Rs. 3,900.
11	Mr. Khan settled his Account of Rs. 3,600 by a cheque of Rs. 3,500.
13	Deposited Khan's cheque into Bank.
14	Received a crossed cheque of Rs. 1,900 from P. Kumar.
15	Received a bearer cheque of Rs. 1,400 from P. Kar.
16	Cashed the bearer cheque of Rs. 1,400 over Bank counter.
22	Paid Rs. 950 to Mr. A.B. Some in full settlement of his A/c of Rs. 1,000.
26	Purchased goods Rs. 6,200. Paid for Stationery Rs. 560.
30	L.I.P. of Mr. M.M. Rudra paid Rs. 750.

Ans: Closing cash in hand Rs. 16,890 and at Bank Rs. 40,630. No entry is required for bearer cheque cashed over Bank counter on 16th April.

9. Write up the Double Column Cash/Book of sri P.P. Tony from the following transactions:

1994	Transactions
June 1	Balance at Bank Rs. 17,600 and in hand Rs. 8,500.
2	Sold goods for cash Rs. 9,200.
4	Received a cheque of Rs. 1,480 from G. Bros, for goods sold to them during the last month.
5	As per instruction Bank paid a Bills Payable of Rs. 1,900.
7	Cashed N.S.C of the proprietor and brought that amount into the business Rs. 6,000.
9	G. Bros.'s cheque became dishonoured.
13	Cash deposited into Bank in excess of Rs. 9000 in hand.
18	Trade subscriptions paid Rs. 630.

19 Commission received Rs. 1,450.
23 A bill of Rs. 3,800 discounted with the Bank at Rs. 3,705.
28 Settled P. Basu Roy's A/c of Rs. 2,600 by a cheque of Rs. 2,520.
29 Draw cheque for petty cash Rs. 600.
30 Banked all cash, keeping a balance of Rs. 5,000.
Ans: Closing cash in hand Rs. 5,000 and at Bank Rs. 35,805 on 13.6.94 cash deposited into Bank Rs. 14,700 and Rs. 4,820 on 30.6.94.

10. Write up the following transactions in a Double Column Cash Book:

1997   **Transactions**
May 1 Cash in hand Rs. 19,860. Cash at bank Rs. 26,720.
   4 Deposited C. Bishayee's cheque of Rs. 850 into Bank, received on 28th April.
   7 A cheque of Rs. 1,350 issued to A. Das.
   8 Counter manded the payment of cheque issued to A. Das on 7th May by order to Bank.
  11 A crossed cheque of Rs. 1,590 received from M. Chatterjee and paid to him a similar amount in cash.
  16 Bank honoured a bill of Rs. 1,700.
  18 Bank collected a sum of Rs. 4,980 from the Insurance Co.
  20 Received interest from Bank Rs. 2,100.
  23 A discounted bill of Rs. 3.100 became dishonoured.
  25 Sold goods for cash Rs. 7,200 and paid into Bank Rs. 5,000 on the next day.
  27 Cash withdrew from Bank for personal use Rs. 1,700.
  29 Invested a sum of Rs. 2,500 in N.S.C.
  30 C. Bishyaee's cheque was returned by the Bank marked "Refer to Drawer".
Ans: Closing Cash in hand Rs. 17,120 and at Bank Rs. 33,890.

11. The following are the receipts and payments of Bidhan Memorial Hospital for the month of October 1989. Draw up a suitable Cash Book and carry down the balances on 31st October, 1989 :

1989   **Transactions**
Oct. 1 Cash in hand (Dr.) Rs. 1,380. Cash at bank (Cr.) Rs. 6,000.
   3 Received subscription and paid into Bank Rs. 320.
   4 Paid for stationary articles purchased Rs. 40.
   6 Paid for staff salary Rs. 400.
   7 received subscription Rs. 300.
  10 Paid for medicines purchased by a cheque Rs. 125.
  12 Received interest on Government securities Rs. 200.
  14 Paid for patients' diets Rs. 145.
  17 Received corporation grant by an A/c Payee cheque Rs. 250.
  18 Paid for medicines Rs. 130.
  19 Received donation Rs. 400.
  22 Paid for patients' diets Rs. 180.
  24 Received one cheque for Govt. grant Rs. 250.
  25 Paid in Bank Rs. 600.
  27 Paid for stationery Rs. 20.
  30 Withdrew from Bank Rs. 500.
  30 Paid for diets Rs. 175.
  30 Received from patients Rs. 130.
  31 Paid wages Rs. 80.
  31 Paid telephone bill by a cheque Rs. 30.

(W.B.H.S., Adapted)

Ans: Cash in hand Rs. 1,140 and Bank (Cr.) Rs. 5,235.

12. Record the following transactions in Double Column Cash book with Cash and Bank Columns and balance the book on 30th June 1984:

1984	Transactions
June 1	Cash in hand Rs. 550. Cash at bank Rs. 12,480.
3	Paid salary to staff by cheques Rs. 4,200.
5	Interest paid by Bank on Bank balance Rs. 100.
5	Received from Gora cash Rs. 60 and cheque for Rs. 300 and the cheque was sent to Bank.
8	Withdrawn cash from Bank for office use Rs. 4,500.
12	Purchased furniture in cash Rs. 3,800.
16	Paid Pal & Co. by cheque Rs. 2,300.
23	The proprietor withdrew from office cash for his personal use Rs. 300.
27	Sold goods to Mahabir for cash Rs. 3,400.
30	Deposited office cash into Bank Rs. 2,500.

    (W.B.H.S.)

    Ans: Cash in hand Rs. 1,910; Cash at Bank Rs. 4,380.

13. The following are the Cash and Bank transactions of Mr. P. Singh, owner of 'Santipur Stationery House':

1993	Transactions
May 1	Cash in hand Rs. 2,400. Cash at Bank Rs. 3,500.
3	Purchased goods from M/s Jhunjhunwala and paid by cheque Rs. 700.
9	Cash purchases Rs. 800. Less Trade Discount 5%.
10	Purchased stamps etc. Rs. 50.
12	Cash sales and banked the same Rs. 2,000.
14	Drew cash for personal use Rs. 160.
15	Received from Abdul Hamid cash deposited into Bank Rs. 300.
15	Received from Abdul Hamid cheque deposited into Bank Rs. 500.
15	Withdrawn from Bank for office use Rs. 800.
16	Paid wages Rs. 300.
16	Paid rent Rs. 500.
19	Paid M/S Milly & Co. by cheque Rs. 2,400.
23	Received a cheque from Manab for sale of old goods Rs. 800.
25	Paid M/s Jhunjhunwala cash Rs. 750.
25	Paid M/s Jhunjunwala cheque Rs. 360.
26	Dolly a customer, deposited into Bank Rs. 600.
29	Withdrew from Bank for personal use Rs. 200.
31	Bank charged for commission Rs. 100.

    (W.B.H.S.)

    Ans: Cash in hand Rs. 680 and cash at Bank Rs. 3,140.

14. Sri P operates two Bank Accounts both of which are maintained in the Three Column Cash Book itself. You are required to draw up a proforma of the Cash Book, show how the following transactions related to 28th February 1987, will appear therein and close the Cash Book for the day:

    (i) Opening Balance

    Cash Rs. 100.

    State Bank (overdraft) Rs. 10,000.

    United Bank Rs. 30,000.

    (ii) Received a cheque of Rs. 1,000 in respect of Sales for realising which State Bank charged Rs. 2 and credited the balance,

(iii) Purchased goods for Rs. 13,000 and a cheque issued on the United Bank.

(iv) Paid office expenses Rs. 45 and Rs. 15 for stationery.

(v) Out of cash sales of Rs. 13,000, a sum of Rs. 10,000 was deposited in the State Bank.

(vi) Credit purchases of Rs. 15,000 was made from Q who sent the documents relating to the goods through the United Bank for 90% of their values. The Bank charged Rs. 100 for releasing the documents.

(vii) Deposited Rs. 5,000 to State Bank.

(viii) A "B/R" for Rs. 10,000 was discounted with the United Bank, which charges 1% towards discounting.

(ix) Withdrew Rs. 5,000 from United bank.

(x) A Demand draft was purchased for Rs. 3,000 from a Bank after paying Rs. 2 towards charges.

[C.U., B. Com. (Hons.)]

Ans: Cash in hand Rs. 38; Cash at United Bank Rs. 8,300 and at State Bank Rs. 5,998.

15. Prepare a Double Column Cash Book from the following informations:

1997 **Transactions**

June 1 Cash in hand Rs. 21,200 and at Bank Rs. 19,000.

3 Issued a cheque of Rs. 3,100 in favour of P.P. Traders.

4 Personal N.S.C. cashed and brought that amount into the business Rs. 4,000.

6 The cheque which was issued to P.P. Traders returned dishonoured and as such issued a fresh cheque to them.

9 Cash withdrew from Bank for personal use Rs. 750 and for office use Rs. 1,850.

11 Received cash Rs. 3,000 and a cheque of Rs. 4,100 from T.Y. Bros.

14 Endorsed T.Y. Bros's cheque to Rama Traders.

16 Rama Traders informed that T.Y. Bros.,'s cheque became dishonoured and as such similar amount was paid to them in cash.

18 Sold goods for cash Rs. 6,600.

19 Paid for advertisement Rs. 750 and Godown rent Rs. 1,650.

23 Interest on Fixed deposit credited by Bank Rs. 880.

25 As per Bank statement Roy Bros. paid directly into Bank Rs. 1,900.

27 Investment in shares Rs. 2,600.

29 Purchased books for Rs. 900.

30 Banked Rs. 4,200 in cash.

Ans: Closing cash in hand Rs. 22,450 and at Bank Rs. 20,280.

Notes: 1. No entry is required in cash book for cheque dishonoured on June 16.

2. The cheque which was issued on June 3 is to be cancelled on June 6 and then a new cheque of similar amount is to be issued.

16. Enter the following transactions in the Cash Book with Cash & Bank Columns:

1996 **Transactions**

Oct. 1 Cash in hand Rs. 13,200.

Overdraft balance at Bank Rs. 5,900.

3 Received two cheques for Rs. 1,400 and Rs. 1,600 from G.C. Saha.

6 Endorsed G.C. Saha's cheque of Rs. 1,600 to Mr. Rudra.

9 A cheque of Rs. 1,920 issued in favour of C.K. Traders.

11 Deposited G.C. Saha's cheque of Rs. 1,400 into bank.

13 Cash withdrawn from Bank for personal use Rs. 700.

14 Interest charged by Bank Rs. 580.

15 It was reported that both the cheques of G.C. Saha became dishonoured.

20   The cheque which was issued to C.K. Traders became dishonoured.
23   A bill of Rs. 2,100 was discounted with the Bank became dishonoured.
26   Cashed personal N.S.C. of the proprietor and brought that amount into the business Rs. 8,000.
30   Deposited cash into Bank Rs. 4,500.
Ans: Closing cash in hand Rs. 16,700 and overdraft balance at Bank Rs. 4,780.

17. Enter the following transactions in Double Column Cash Book:

1997   **Transactions**
May 1   Cash in hand Rs. 18,260 and at Bank Rs. 21,900.
   2   Goods purchased from B. Bose for Rs. 8,000.
   3   Paid Rs. 3,000 by cheque to Sri N. Sarkar in full settlement of his account of Rs. 3,200.
   5   Received Rs. 3,850 from D. Dutta on full settlement of his account of Rs. 3,950.
   6   K. Ram settled his account of Rs. 3,800 by cheque and was allowed discount Rs. 150.
   7   A. Roy settled his account by a cheque of Rs. 2,950 and was allowed a discount of Rs. 50.
   8   Sold goods for cash Rs. 9,000 and out of that deposited cash into Bank Rs. 6,000.
   9   Purchased furniture for Rs. 2,600.
  10   Cash withdrew from bank for Petty Cash Rs. 700.
  13   Cash paid to C. Kumar Rs. 810 and received discount Rs. 40.
Ans: Closing cash balance Rs. 21,700 and at bank Rs. 30,850 as on 15th May.

18. Write up the following transactions in Double Column Cash Book of Sri N. Saha:

1997   **Transactions**
Feb. 21   Cash in hand Rs. 12,600. Overdraft balance at Bank Rs. 3,910.
  22   Issued a cheque of Rs. 1,950 to Sri T.K. Sinha and received a discount of Rs. 50.
  23   Received a cheque of Rs. 3,160 from R.K. Thakur and allowed a discount of Rs. 90.
  24   The cheque which was issued to T.K. Sinha on 22nd Feb. returned dishonoured and as such cash was paid to him for the said amount.
  25   Endorsed R.K. Thakur's cheque to Sri Pradip Sen in full settlement of his account of Rs. 3,200.
  26   Interest debited by Bank Rs. 460.
  27   Mr. Arun Roy deposited cash directly into Bank Rs. 850.
  28   Paid for advertisement Rs. 900. Paid Trade subscription Rs. 460. Dividend collected by Bank Rs. 1,250.
Ans: Cash in hand Rs. 9,290 and overdraft balance at Bank Rs. 2,270.

19. From the following particulars prepare a Double Column Cash Book:

1995   **Transactions**
Jan. 1   Cash in hand Rs. 2,500. Cash at bank Rs. 12,600.
   2   Received cash from Roy Rs. 2,900. Allowed him discount Rs. 100.
   7   Purchased goods for cash Rs. 2,000.
  12   Received from Sen Rs. 3,000 and Allowed discount Rs. 120.
  14   Paid Shyam by cheque Rs. 4,000. Received discount Rs. 230.
  16   Jadu settled his A/c for (less 5% discount) in cash Rs. 5,000.
  20   Paid salary to domestic servant in cash Rs. 300.
  21   Purchased furniture in cash Rs. 600.
  22   Paid Madhu in cash Rs. 2,500. Received discount Rs. 200.
  24   Withdrew from Bank for office use Rs. 3,000.
  25   Repaid loan from Paritosh (including interest Rs. 250) Rs. 5,500.
  28   Withdrew from Bank and paid tution fees for children Rs. 500.
  29   Sold goods for cash Rs. 5,600. Paid carriage thereon Rs. 60.

(W.B.H.S.)

Ans: Cash in hand Rs. 10,790 and Cash at bank Rs. 5,100.

20. Prepare a Double Column Cash Book from the following transactions and post them to the appropriate ledger accounts:

1996   **Transactions**

March 1   Cash in hand Rs. 7,000. Bank Balance (Dr.) Rs. 1,00,000.

     3   Cash Sales Rs. 60,000.

     6   Rent paid by cheque Rs. 24,000.

     8   Cash deposited into Bank Rs. 60,000.

    10   Wages paid Rs. 1,000.

    10   Rent paid Rs. 1,800.

    12   Received cheque from Mohan Rs. 7,800. Discount allowed Rs. 200.

    14   Goods purchased Rs. 4,000.

    16   Withdrawn from bank for office use Rs. 20,000.

    18   Issued cheque to Hari Rs. 13,400. Discount received Rs. 600.

    20   Withdrawn cash for personal use Rs. 4,000.

    22   Received cheque from Sriram and deposited into the Bank Rs. 10,000.

    24   Sriram's cheque dishonoured Rs. 10,000.

    26   Furniture purchased and issued cheque Rs. 6,000.

    29   Received interest on investment and deposited in the Bank Rs. 3,000.

    30   Paid Salaries Rs. 4,800.

(H.S. Central Board)

Ans: Cash in hand Rs. 11,400, Cash at bank Rs. 107,400.

21. Write up the following transactions in a Double Column Cash Book and bring down the balance:

1978   **Transactions**

Dec. 1   Cash balance in hand Rs. 200. Cash at Bank Rs. 1,800.

     4   Received cash from Ram Rs. 95. Allowed him discount Rs. 5.

     6   Purchased stationery for cash Rs. 20.

     7   Paid Shyam by cheque Rs. 330. Received discount Rs. 10.

    12   Rahim settled his account for Rs. 500. Less 5% discount by cheque.

    18   Paid Sundry Expenses in cash Rs. 30.

    23   Paid Jadu in cash Rs. 190. Received discount Rs. 10.

    24   Withdrew from Bank for office cash Rs. 100.

    28   Withdrew from Bank for personal use Rs. 150.

    29   Bought goods by cheque Rs. 500.

    31   Sold goods for cash Rs. 200.

(W.B.H.S.)

Ans: Cash in hand Rs. 355 and Cash at Bank Rs. 1,195.

22. Enter the following transactions in the Cash Book with cash, discount and bank columns:

1987   **Transactions**

June 1   Balance of cash in hand Rs. 400. Balance at bank (overdraft) Rs. 5,000.

     4   Invested further capital of Rs. 10,000 out of which Rs. 6,000 deposited in the Bank.

     5   Sold goods for cash Rs. 3,000.

     6   Collected from debtors of last year Rs. 8,000 and discount allowed to him Rs. 200.

    10   Purchased goods for cash Rs. 5,500.

    11   Paid Ramvilas, our creditor Rs. 2,500. Discount allowed Rs. 65.

    13   Commission paid to our agent Rs. 530.

    14   Office furniture purchased from Keshav Rs. 200.

    14   Rent paid Rs. 50.

    14   Electric charges paid Rs. 10.

    16   Drew cheque for personal use Rs. 700.

17 Cash sales Rs. 2,500.
18 Collection from Atul Rs. 4,000; deposited into the Bank next day.
22 Drew cheque for petty cash Rs. 150.
24 Dividend received by cheque Rs. 50; deposited in the Bank on the same day.
25 Commission received by the cheque Rs. 230; deposited into the Bank on 28th.
29 Paid from Bank, salary of the office staff Rs. 1,500.
29 Paid salary of the manager by cheque Rs. 500.
30 Deposited cash into Bank Rs. 1,000.

(Company Secretary Ship Examination)

Ans: Cash in hand Rs. 8,310 and at Bank Rs. 3,430.

23. From the following particulars prepare a Cash Book with proper columns and bring down the balances:

1984	**Transactions**

Jan. 1 Cash in hand Rs. 1,200.
   5 Deposited cash into Bank Rs. 600.
   6 Paid a cheque to H. James Rs. 200 and Received discount from him Rs. 4.
   8 Cheque drawn for trade expenses Rs. 120.
  15 Issued a cheque to T. Bush Rs. 100. Deposited S. Mitra's cheque into Bank Rs. 150.
  22 Issued a cheque to K. Roy and received discount from him Rs. 8.
  25 Received a cheque from V.K. Rao (paid into Bank) Rs. 300 and allowed him discount Rs. 15.
  29 Drew a cheque for office use Rs. 50.
  31 Drew a cheque for personal use Rs. 40.

(Tripura H.S. Exam)

Ans: Cash in hand Rs. 500 and Cash at Bank Rs. 400.

24. Prepare a Cash Book with the appropriate number of columns from the following information for the month of December, 1992 in the books of Rahaman:

1992	**Transactions**

Dec. 1 Cash in hand Rs. 2,780. Bank overdraft Rs. 3,125.
   2 Cheque worth Rs. 400 issued to the petty cashier.
   5 Rs. 350 was paid to Rabin and Sons, for the supply of stationary on these days.
   7 Received a cheque worth Rs. 600 from Krishna against sale of goods.
  10 Received Rs. 1,200 for sale of goods.
  11 The cheque which was received from Krishna on 7th December 1992 was endorsed in favour of Morgan together with Rs. 1,400 in cash.
  15 Received Rs. 950 from Rohini after allowing a rebate of Rs. 20 on account of retiring a bill of exchange.
  20 The cheque that was endorsed in favour of Morgan on 11th December, 1992 was returned dishonoured and therefore returned to the drawer.
  23 Murarilal paid Rs. 2,000 in cash and Rs. 3,000 in cheque after receiving a discount of Rs. 200 for goods sold to him in November, 1992. The cheque was immediately deposited into the bank.
  26 Bought goods worth Rs. 1,700 from Keshavan and paid by cheque after receiving a discount of Rs. 170.
  30 Interest on overdraft Rs. 50 was charged by the Bank.
  30 Cash in excess of Rs. 1,000 was deposited into Bank.

(Delhi I.S.C.,H.S.)

Ans: Closing cash in hand Rs. 1,000 and at Bank Rs. 2,075.

25. Draw up a Double Column Cash book of Sri Amit Sen from the following particulars:

1996	Transactions
Mar. 21	Cash in hand Rs. 19,200 and cash at Bank Rs. 26,900.
22	Rupak Sen settled his account of Rs. 3,000 in cash less 5% discount.
23	G. Guha settled his account of Rs. 2.500 by cheque subject to 5% discount.
24	Cheque drawn in favour of P.K. Sinha Rs. 1,250 and received discount Rs. 80.
25	Cash Rs. 2,850 paid to Karuna Dutta and received 5% discount.
26	Cash withdrew from Bank for office use Rs. 1,750.
27	Sold old furniture Rs. 980.
28	Purchased stationery for Rs. 320.
29	Endorsed M. Kumar's cheque of Rs. 1,750 to K. Khan.
30	Rupak Sengupta was paid a cheque of Rs. 1,900.
31	Countermanded the payment of cheque drawn in favour of Rupak Sengupta on 30th March by order to Bank.

Ans: Cash in hand Rs. 19,860 and at Bank Rs. 26,275.

Petty Cash Book

26. Rule a suitable Petty Cash Book and enter the following items showing/balance in hand on 31st March 1991:

1991	Transactions
March 1	Balance in hand Rs. 32.
1	Received from cashier Rs. 68.
3	Postage Rs. 9.
4	Telephone charges Rs. 7.
6	Cleaning charges Rs. 12.
9	Taxi charges Rs. 18.
11	Paper and ink Rs. 8.
12	Bus fare Rs. 6.
13	Telegram to Kolkata Rs. 18.
14	Postage Rs. 7.
15	Sundry Expenses Rs. 6. Gum Rs. 3

Ans: Balance in hand Rs. 6, Carriage or travelling Rs. 24, Postage Rs. 16, Telephone and Telegram Rs. 25, Stationery Rs. 11, Sundries Rs. 18.

27. Prepare a Petty Cash Book kept on Imprest System from the following transactions:

1992	Transactions
May 1	Cash in hand Rs. 43. Cash received from cashier Rs. 132.
2	Postage Stamps Rs. 8.50.
3	Bus fares to peon Rs. 6.
5	Newspapers Rs. 32.
6	A bottle of glue Rs. 11.
7	Papers and pencils Rs. 13.
9	Carriage and coolie hire Rs. 21.
11	Repairs to type writer Rs. 15.
12	Pins and clips Rs. 9.
13	Stamps Rs. 10.50.
14	Telegram charges Rs. 9.
15	Advance to peon Rs. 10. Periodicals Rs. 25.

Ans: Balance in hand Rs. 5, Re-imbursement Rs. 170, Postage and Telegram Rs. 28, Stationery Rs. 33, Travelling Rs. 27, Sundries Rs. 15, Newspapers and periodicals Rs. 57.

28. Enter the following transactions in an Analytical Petty Cash Book:

1997	Transactions
June 1	Received a cheque from chief cashier Rs. 400. Polishing of table and chairs Rs. 39.
2	Coolie charges Rs. 13.
3	Taxi fare Rs. 18.
4	Electric bill Rs. 31.
5	Blotting paper Rs. 7. Pins and clips Rs. 18.
6	Duster (cloth) Rs. 21.
7	Postage Rs. 20.
9	Thumps Up and Coca Cola Rs. 18.
10	Bus fares Rs. 22.
11	Fill rack Rs. 90.
12	Papers and Inks Rs. 8.
13	Taxi fare Rs. 19.
14	Office cleaning Rs. 20. Tea and others Rs. 6

Ans: Closing balance on 15th June Rs. 40, Reimbursement Rs. 360, Travelling and coolie Rs. 72, Postage Rs. 20, Stationery Rs. 64, Misc. Exp. Rs. 90, Entertainment Rs. 24, File rack is to be shown in the ledger A/c column.

29. Rule a Petty Cash Book with four analysis columns for Postage and Stationery, Travelling Expenses, Carriage and Office Expenses and enter in it the following transactions. The book is kept on Imprest System, the imprest amount being Rs. 75 only:

1980	Transactions
Jan. 4	Petty cash in hand Rs. 1.60.
	Received cash to make up the interest from head cashier Rs ____.
5	Bought stamps Rs. 6.20. Paid bus fares Re. 0.50 p.
6	Paid Railways fares Rs. 21.75 Paid Telegram charges Rs. 4.90.
7	Paid carriage on parcels Rs. 5.20.
8	Bought shorthand notebook Rs. 2.25. Paid for repairs to typewriters Rs. 6.80.
9	Paid for cart hire Rs. 16.35.
10	Paid office expenses Rs. 10.70.

(Tripura H.S.)

Ans: Closing cash in hand Re. 0.35, Reimbursement Rs. 74.65. Cash received on Jan, 4 is 73.40 (75 – 1.60).

30. Prepare a Petty Cash Book with suitable rulings and enter the following transactions showing the balance in hand on 30th November 1984 and opening entries on 1st December 1984:

1984	Transactions
Nov. 1	Received cash Rs. 100.
4	Paid for postage and stamps Rs. 6.40.
6	Paid for conveyance Rs. 2.30.
9	Paid for Taxi fare Rs. 6.84.
13	Paid for cartage Rs. 6.
14	Paid for puja subscription Rs. 10.
15	Wages account overdrawn and deposited to petty cashier Rs. 20.
22	Paid for electric bill Rs. 14.75.
30	Paid for purchase of papers for office use Rs. 25.25.

(W.B.H.S.)

Ans: Closing balance Rs. 48.46.

[Hint: Entry on 15th—is to be shown as "To Wages A/c" amount in the Debit side.]

31. Enter the following transactions in an analytical Petty Cash Book and also show the cash to be received by the Petty cashier on 16.3.97.

1997	Transactions
March 1	Received cash from chief cashier Rs. 400.
2	Purchase of stationery for personal use Rs. 60.
3	Advances to Head clerk Rs. 30.
4	Stationery Rs. 16.
5	Bus fare Rs. 10.
6	Sale of old papers Rs. 31.
7	Purchase of Telephone rack Rs. 75.
8	Postage Rs. 19.
9	Telegram to Delhi Rs. 22.
10	Taxi fare Rs. 26.
11	Telephone bill Rs. 16.
12	Cost of glue Rs. 15.
13	Pens and clips Rs. 24.
14	Registration charges Rs. 19.
15	Telephone charges Rs. 15.

Ans: Closing cash in hand Rs. 84, Reimbursement Rs. 316.

10

Books of Original Entry:
Special Purpose Books

CONTENTS

- Utility of Subdivision of Journals
- Trade Discount
  - Advantages of Trade Discount
- Cash Discount
  - Advantages of Cash Discount
- Purchase Day Book
- Sales Day Book
- Purchase Return Book
- Sales Return Book
- Bills Receivable Book
- Bills Payable Book
- Journal Proper
  - Uses of the Journal Proper
  - Opening Entries
  - Closing Entries
  - Transfer Entries
  - Credit Sale and Credit Purchase of Assets
  - Adjustment Entries

INTRODUCTION

To keep records of a particular class or group of transactions in a separate book, the books are subdivided into seven heads. These books are generally known as **sub-journal** or **subsidiary books.** The different types of Cash Book have been explained in detail in Chapter 9. The rest of the books and the special journals or journal proper will be discussed in this chapter.

10.1 UTILITY OF SUBDIVISION OF JOURNALS

1. It helps in recording transactions efficiently and at the same time, increases the productivity of the concerned person engaged in recording the transactions in different books.
2. It helps in saving time in recording the transactions.
3. It helps in promoting effective internal check system.
4. It helps to provide information about a particular class of transactions, and their present position and trends within a very short period. As a result, it helps in taking quick decision, by the management.
5. It helps the auditor and his team in conducting their audit.

TABLE 10.1   Distinction between Day Book and Ledger

Day book	Ledger
1. Here transactions are recorded on regular basis, i.e., daily basis.	1. Here journal entries are recorded on regular basis, but at the end of a certain period.
2. It is a book of original entry or subsidiary book.	2. It is a principal book.
3. It helps in saving time in recording the transactions.	3. No such saving is possible.
4. At the end of a certain period, all the transactions are added and the accumulated figure is transferred to a particular account.	4. At the end of a certain period, balancing of all accounts are made.

(Contd.)

Day book	Ledger
5. Generally, it records credit transactions only.	5. It records both cash and credit transactions.
6. Through day books ledger accounts are prepared.	6. Through ledger accounts final account is prepared.
7. It provides detailed data about a transaction.	7. It provides basic data of a transaction in brief.
8. It helps to provide information about a particular class of transactions.	8. It helps to provide information about all types of transactions.

10.2 TRADE DISCOUNT

This discount is allowed by the manufacturer or the wholesaler to their customers on a percentage basis on the list price of the goods. It is employed to increase the sales volume. After charging this discount, the net sale price or the net amount payable by the customer is calculated. Accounts are recorded on the basis of this net sale price. Trade discount is allowed on all types of sales, i.e. both on cash sales and credit sales.

10.2.1 Advantages of Trade Discount

1. It helps to increase total volume of sales.
2. In case of stiff competition it helps in maintaining profit volume as per a desired target by changing the rate of trade discount.
3. It helps to encourage all types of customers.

10.3 CASH DISCOUNT

Usually a cash discount is employed to encourage debtors in making prompt payment. It is allowed only when a debtor pays his debt within or before the due date, i.e. within the credit period. It is calculated on a percentage basis on the total amount payable by the debtor/customer. Hence, when goods are sold on cash basis, a customer will enjoy both trade discount and cash discount. The mode of calculation of the cash discount is shown below:

List price of the goods	Rs. 40 per set
Units sold	50 units
Rate of trade discount	10%
Rate of cash discount	10%
List price of goods sold (Rs. 40 × 50)	2,000
Less: Trade discount (10%)	Rs. 200
Net Selling Price (Amount payable)	Rs. 1,800
Less: Cash discount (10%)	Rs. 180
Net amount payable	Rs. 1,620

Hence, if the customer pays his dues within the due date or specified date, then he has to pay only Rs. 1,620 instead of Rs. 1,800.

10.3.1 Advantages of Cash Discount

1. Cash discount is given to encourage customers for prompt payment. Consequently, it helps to improve the cash or liquidity position of a firm.
2. It helps to reduce uncertainty in respect of debt realization.
3. It reduces the chances of bad debts of a firm.
4. It helps to increase sales volume of a firm.
5. Since it helps to improve the cash or liquidity position of the firm, the profit or revenue of a firm increases.

The basic differences between the trade discount and cash discount are given in Table 10.2.

TABLE 10.2 Distinction between Cash Discount and Trade Discount

Cash discount	Trade discount
1. It is given to encourage customers for making prompt payment.	1. It is allowed to increase the sales volume.
2. It is given by a creditor to his debtors.	2. It is given by manufacturers or wholesalers to their retailers.
3. It is calculated on net sale price/amount due.	3. It is calculated on the list price/catalogue price of the goods.
4. The amount of cash discount allowed/received is recorded in the books.	4. The amount of trade discount is generally not recorded in the books of accounts.
5. The rate of discount may vary from customer to customer depending on the period of prompt payment.	5. The rate of discount is usually fixed.
6. It is conditional.	6. It is unconditional.
7. It is deducted from the net sale price/amount due.	7. It is deducted from the listprice/ catalogue price of the goods.

10.4 PURCHASE DAY BOOK

This book is used to record the credit transactions for goods purchased. Daily transactions are recorded chronologically. Credit purchase of fixed assets cannot be recorded in this book. Detailed particulars about the purchase of goods are recorded through this book. For example, cost of goods, packing charges, freight charges, excise duty, VAT or sales tax, and cost of containers, if any. Excise duty is calculated on the list price, but sales tax or VAT is calculated on the net price (i.e., after deducting trade discount).

Generally, entries are made on the basis of inward invoice received from the suppliers and are totalled at the end of a day or a week or a month, depending on the volume of transactions.

The following points are recorded in the purchase day book:

1. **Date:** The date of purchase.
2. **Particulars:** The details of suppliers, goods, rate, quantity, charges to be considered or to be included, etc.
3. **Invoice No.:** Invoice numbers given by the sellers are recorded for future reference. In case of credit sale, a statement is sent by the seller to the customers stating the details of the products or goods. This statement is known as **invoice**. The specimen of an invoice is given below.

Invoice
X & Bros.
Address.

To ZV & Co.   Dr.
Address.

	Rs.	Rs.
To cost 300 cases of goods @ Rs. 240 per case	72,000	
Less: Trade discount 10%	7,200	
	64,800	
Add: Packing charges	460	65,260
		65,260

Invoice No. P/D/234
Date: August 12, 2008

Terms: 7.5 % Cash at two months
E. & O.E.
For ZV & Co.
P. Kumar
Senior Manager

4. **Ledger folio:** The Ledger folio number is recorded with the transaction in the ledger.
5. **Details:** Within this column, the amounts deducted and added are shown clearly.
6. **Amount:** The net amount payable by the purchaser is recorded in this column.

E. & O.E.: It stands for Errors and Omissions Excepted, i.e., if any error is detected in the invoice, which may result in the increase or decrease in value, may be adjusted subsequently/accordingly.

Terms: 7.5 % Cash at two months means cash discount is allowed @ 7.5 % on net sale price, if payment is made within two months.

Differences between purchase day book and purchase account are listed in Table 10.3.

TABLE 10.3 Differences between Purchase Day Book and Purchase Account

Purchase day book	Purchase account
1. All credit purchase of goods are recorded here.	1. All cash and credit purchase of goods are recorded.
2. It is a part of sub-journal or subsidiary books.	2. It is a part of ledger.
3. It has no debit and credit column like a ledger because its format is different from that of a ledger.	3. It has debit and credit columns as it is a part of a ledger.
4. Purchase day book's total amount is transferred to purchases account.	4. Purchase account's total is transferred to trading account.
5. Details of credit purchases are written in the purchase day book.	5. Only total credit purchases are written in the purchase account.

ILLUSTRATION 10.1 Enter the following transactions in the Purchase Day Book of M/s T.K. Bros. and show the ledger posting.

2008	**Transactions**

April 7 Bought from M/s Gupta Bros. 650 cases of goods @ Rs. 200 per case less trade discount 10%, plus Packing charges Rs. 2,100, cost of containers Rs. 6,500, Forwarding charges Rs. 600, Postage Rs. 100, Excise Duty 5% and Sales Tax/VAT 5%.

21 Bought from M/s Blue Star & Co. 250 cases of goods @ Rs. 140 per case less trade discount 12½%, plus packing charges Rs. 650, forwarding charges Rs. 150, excise duty 8% and sales tax 6%.

Solution

In the Books of M/s T. K. Bros.
Purchase Day Book

Date	Particulars	Invoice no.	L.F.	Details (Rs.)	Amount (Rs.)	Remarks
2008 April 7	**M/s Gupta Bros.**					
	650 cases of goods @ Rs. 200 per case			130,000		
	Less: Trade discount 10%			13,000		
				117,000		
	Add: Packing charges			2,100		
	Add: Cost of containers			6,500		
	Add: Forwarding charges			600		
	Add: Postage			100		
	Add: Excise Duty 5% 6,000 (on Rs. 130,000)			6,500		
	Add: Sales Tax / VAT 5% (on Rs. 117,000)			5,850	138,650	
21	**M/s Blue Star & Co.**					
	250 cases of goods @ Rs. 140 per case			35,000		
	Less: Trade discount 10%			3,500		
				31,500		
	Add: Packing charges			650		

(Contd.)

Date	Particulars	Invoice no.	L.F.	Details (Rs.)	Amount (Rs.)	Remarks
	Add: Forwarding charges			150		
	Add: Excise Duty 8%			2,800		
	6,000 (on Rs. 35,000)					
	Add: Sales Tax/Vat 6%			1,890	36,990	
	(on Rs. 31,500)					
					175,640	

Notes:

1. Excise duty is calculated on list price.
2. Sales tax is calculated on net price (after deducting trade discount).

In Creditors Ledger
M/s Gupta Bros. Account

Dr.   Cr.

Date	Particulars	J.F.	Amount (Rs.)	Date	Particulars	J.F.	Amount (Rs.)
2008 April 30	To Balance c/d		138,650	2008 April 7	By Purchases A/c		138,650
			138,650				138,650
				May 1	By Balance b/d		138,650

M/s Blue Star & Co. Account

Dr.   Cr.

Date	Particulars	J.F.	Amount (Rs.)	Date	Particulars	J.F.	Amount (Rs.)
2008 April 30	To Balance c/d		36,990	2008 April 21	By Purchases A/c		36,990
			36,990				36,990
				May 1	By Balance b/d		36,990

In the General Ledger
Purchases Account

Dr.   Cr.

Date	Particulars	J.F.	Amount (Rs.)	Date	Particulars	J.F.	Amount (Rs.)
2008 April 30	To Sundries (Purchases for the month)		175,640	2008 April 30	By Balance c/d		175,640
			175,640				175,640
May 1	To Balance b/d		175,640				

ILLUSTRATION 10.2   Enter the following transactions in the purchase day book of M/s Bright & Blue Suppliers and show the ledger posting.

2008	**Transactions**

April 19   Bought from M/s Kamath Bros. 260 cases of goods @ Rs. 350 per case, less Trade Discount 10%, plus packing charges Rs. 900, forwarding charges Rs. 240, excise duty 6% and Sales Tax/VAT 7%.

     23   Bought from M/s P.P. Traders 190 cases of goods @ Rs. 300 per case, less Trade Discount 10%, plus packing charges Rs. 650, forwarding charges Rs. 150 and Sales Tax VAT 7%.

     26   Bought from M/s Tiny Bros. 270 cases of goods @ Rs. 240 per case, less Trade Discount @ 10%, plus Packing charges Rs. 580, cost of containers Rs. 2,160 and Sales Tax/VAT 7%.

Solution

In the Books of M/s Bright and Blue Suppliers
Purchase Day Book

Date	Particulars	Invoice no.	L.F.	Details (Rs.)	Amount (Rs.)	Remarks
2008 April 19	**M/s Kamath Bros.**					
	260 cases of goods @ Rs. 350 per case			91,000		
	Less: Trade discount 10%			9,100		
				81,900		
	Add: Packing charges			900		
	Add: Forwarding charges			240		
	Add: Excise Duty 6% (on Rs. 91,000)			5,460		
	Add: Sales Tax/VAT 7 % (on Rs. 81,900)			5733	94,233	
23	**M/s P.P.Traders**					
	190 cases of goods @ Rs. 300 per case			57,000		
	Less: Trade discount 10%			5,700		
				51,300		
	Add: Packing charges			650		
	Add: Forwarding charges			150		
	Add: Sales Tax/Vat 7 % (on Rs. 51,300)			3,591	55,691	
26	**M/s Tiny Bros.**					
	270 cases of goods @ Rs. 240 per case			64,800		
	Less: Trade discount 10%			6,480		
				58,320		
	Add: Packing charges			580		
	Add: Cost of containers			2,160		
	Add: Sales Tax/VAT 7 % (on Rs. 58,320)			4,082	65,142	
					215,066	

Notes:
1. Excise Duty is calculated on List Price.
2. Sales Tax is calculated on net price (after deducting trade discount).

In Creditors Ledger

Dr.   **M/s Kamath Bros. Account**   Cr.

Date	Particulars	J.F.	Amount (Rs.)	Date	Particulars	J.F.	Amount (Rs.)
2008 April 30	To Balance c/d		94,233	2008 April 19	By Purchases A/c		94,233
			94,233				94,233
				May 1	By Balance b/d		94,233

Dr.   **M/s P.P. Traders Account**   Cr.

Date	Particulars	J.F.	Amount (Rs.)	Date	Particulars	J.F.	Amount (Rs.)
2008 April 30	To Balance c/d		55,691	2008 April 23	By Purchases A/c		55,691
			55,691				55,691
				May 1	By Balance b/d		55,691

Dr.   **M/s Tiny Bros. Account**   Cr.

Date	Particulars	J.F.	Amount (Rs.)	Date	Particulars	J.F.	Amount (Rs.)
2008 April 30	To Balance c/d		65,142	2008 April 26	By Purchases A/c		65,142
			65,142				65,142
				May 1	By Balance b/d		65,142

In the General Ledger

Dr.   **Purchases Account**   Cr.

Date	Particulars	J.F.	Amount (Rs.)	Date	Particulars	J.F.	Amount (Rs.)
2008 April 30	To Sundries (Purchases for the month)		215,066	2008 April 30	By Balance c/d		215,066
			215,066				215,066
May 1	To balance b/d		215,066				

ILLUSTRATION 10.3   From the following particulars, write up the purchase day book in the books of Pritam Bros.

2008   **Transactions**

June 4   Purchased from M/s S. K. Bros., Kolkata 250 shirts (cotton) @ Rs. 30 per shirt, 150 pants (cotton) @ Rs. 40 per pant, less trade discount 5%.

   9   Purchased from M/s Dutta Bros., Asansol, 250 silk sarees @ Rs. 225 per saree, less 8% trade discount.

   13   Purchased from M/s T. T. Traders, Bombay, 100 woollen jackets @ Rs. 300 per jacket, less trade discount 5%.

   20   Purchased from G.K. Bros., Dhanbad, 100 cotton shirts @ Rs. 120 per piece, less trade discount 5%.

   24   Purchased from Mallik Bros., Burdwan, 120 silk sarees @ Rs. 310 per piece, less trade discount 10%.

   Sales Tax charged on all the items @ 8%.

Solution

In the Books of M/s Pritam Bros.
Purchase Day Book

Date	Particulars	Invoice no.	L.F.	Details (Rs.)	Cotton shirt and pants (Rs.)	Silk sarees (Rs.)	Wollen items (Rs.)	Remarks
2008 June 4	**M/s. S. K. Bros.**							
	150 pants @ Rs. 40			6,000				
	250 shirts @ Rs. 30			7,500				
				13,500				
	Less: Trade discount 5%			675				5 % Trade discount
				12,825				
	Add: Sales Tax 8%			1,026	13,851			8% Sales tax
9	**M/s Dutta Bros.**							
	250 Silk sarees @ Rs. 225			56,250				
	Less: Trade discount 8%			4,500				8% Trade discount

(Contd.)

Date	Particulars	Invoice no.	L.F.	Details (Rs.)	Cotton shirt and pants	Silk sarees (Rs.)	Wollen items (Rs.)	Remarks
				51,750				
	Add: Sales Tax 8%			4,140		55,890		8% Sales Tax
13	M/s T. T. Traders							
	100 woollen jackets			30,000				
	@ Rs. 300 per piece							
	Less: Trade discount 5%			1,500				5% Trade Discount
				28,500				
	Add: Sales Tax 8%			2,280			30,780	8% Sales Tax
20	M/s G. K. Bros.							
	100 cotton shirts			12,000				
	@ Rs. 120 per piece							
	Less: Trade discount 5%			600				5% Trade discount
				11,400				
	Add: Sales Tax 8%			912	12,312			8% Sales Tax
24	M/s Mallik Bros.							
	120 silk sarees			37,200				
	@ Rs. 310 per piece							
	Less: Trade discount 10%			3,720				10% Trade discount
				33,480				
	Add: Sales Tax 8%			2,678		36,158		8% Sales Tax
					26,163	92,048	30,780	

10.5 SALES DAY BOOK

This book is particularly used to record the credit transactions for goods sold. Daily transactions are also recorded here chronologically. Credit sale of fixed assets cannot be recorded in this book. Detailed particulars about the sale of goods are recorded through this book. The calculations of excise duty, VAT or sales taxes are to be made like that of Purchase Day Book.

Table 10.4 shows the differences between a sales day book and sales account.

TABLE 10.4 Differences between a Sales Day Book and a Sales Account

Sales day book	Sales account
1. All credit sale of goods are recorded here.	1. All cash and credit sale of goods are recorded.
2. It is a part of sub-journal or subsidiary books.	2. It is a part of ledger.
3. It has no debit and credit column like a ledger because its format is different from a ledger.	3. It has debit and credit columns as it is a part of a ledger.
4. Sales day book's total amount is transferred to sales account.	4. Sales account's total is transferred to trading account.
5. Details of credit sales are available here.	5. Only total credit sales are available here.

ILLUSTRATION 10.4 Enter the following transactions in a suitably ruled Sales Day Book of M/s Dhara Bros.:

2008	**Transactions**
May 4	Sold to Roy & Co. 550 cases of goods @ Rs. 150 each, less trade discount 5%, excise duty 10%, packing charges Rs. 380; and freight charges Rs. 450.
21	Sold to Biswas Bros. 600 cases of goods @ Rs. 150 each, less trade discount 5%, excise duty 10%, packing charges Rs. 400, and coolie charges Rs. 250.

All sales are subject to 8% VAT/Sales Tax.

Solution

In the Books of M/s Dhara Bros.
Sales Day Book

Date	Particulars	Invoice no.	L.F.	Details (Rs.)	Amount (Rs.)	Remarks
2008 May 4	**M/s Roy & Co.** 550 cases of goods @ Rs. 150 per case *Less:* Trade discount 5%			82,500 4,125		
				78,375		
	Add: Packing charges *Add:* Freight charges *Add:* Excise duty 10% (on Rs. 82,500) *Add:* Sales tax/VAT 8% (on Rs. 78,375)			380 450 8,250 6,270	93,725*	
21.	**M/s Biswas Bros.** 600 cases of goods @ Rs. 150 per case *Less:* Trade discount 5 %			90,000 4,500		
				85,500		
	Add: Packing charges *Add:* Coolie charges *Add:* Excise duty 10 % (on Rs. 90,000) *Add:* Sales tax / VAT 8 % (on Rs. 85,500)			400 250 9,000 6,840	101,990*	
					195,715**	

* These amounts are to be transferred to the debit of Customers account.

** This amount is to be posted to the credit of Sales account periodically.

Working Notes
1. Excise duty is calculated on list price.
2. Sales Tax/VAT is calculated on net price (after deducting trade discount).

Ledger
M/s Roy and Co. Account

Dr.   Cr.

Date	Particulars	J.F.	Amount (Rs.)	Date	Particulars	J.F.	Amount (Rs.)
2008 May 4	To Sales A/c		93,725	2008 May 31	By Balance c/d		93,725
			93,725				93,725
June 1	To Balance b/d		93,725				

M/s Biswas Bros. Account

Dr.   Cr.

Date	Particulars	J.F.	Amount (Rs.)	Date	Particulars	J.F.	Amount (Rs.)
2008 May 4	To Sales A/c		101,990	2008 May 31	By Balance c/d		101,990
			101,990				101,990
June 1	To Balance b/d		101,990				

Sales Account

Dr.   Cr.

Date	Particulars	J.F.	Amount (Rs.)	Date	Particulars	J.F.	Amount (Rs.)
2008 May 31	To Balance c/d		195,715	2008 May 31	To Sundries (Sales for the month)		195,715
			195,715				195,715
				June 1	By Balance b/d		195,715

ILLUSTRATION 10.5   Enter the following transactions in a suitable ruled Sales Day Book of M/s XYZ:

2005	**Transactions**
February 2	Sold to Ratanlal & Bros. nine T.V. sets @ Rs. 3,900 each, less trade discount 10 % Sales Tax 8%. Freight and packing charges Rs. 720.
16	Sold to D.D. Kar & Co. five T.V. sets @ Rs. 3,900 each, less trade discount 10 % sales tax 8%, freight and packing charges Rs. 470.
25	Sold to M.M. & Suppliers 14 T.V. sets @ Rs. 3,900 each, less trade discount 10 % Sales Tax 8%, freight and packing charges and Rs. 980.

Post the above transactions to respective ledger accounts.

Solution

In the books of XYZ
Sales Day Book

Date	Particulars	Invoice no.	L.F.	Details (Rs.)	Total Amount (Rs.)	Net Sales (Rs.)	Sales tax (Rs.)	Freight and packing (Rs.)
2005 February 2	**Ratan Lal & Bros.**							
	9 T.V. Sets @ Rs. 3,900			35,100				
	Less: 10 % trade discount			3,510				
				31,590		31,590		
	Add: Sales Tax 8 %			2,527			2,527	
				34,117				
	Add: Packing and freight			720				720
				34,837	34,837			
16	**D.D. Kar & Co.**							
	5 T.V. sets @ Rs. 3,900			19,500				
	Less: 10% trade discount			1,950				
				17,550		17,550		
	Add: Sales Tax 8%			1,404			1,404	
				18,954				
	Add: Packing and freight			470				470
				19,424	19,424			
25	**M.M. & Suppliers**							
	14 T.V. sets @ Rs. 3,900			54,600				
	Less: 10 % trade discount			5,460				
				49,140		49,140		
	Add: Sales Tax 8 %			3,931			3,931	
				53,071				
	Add: Packing and freight			980				980
				54,051	54,051			
					108,312	98,280	7,862	2,170

In the General Ledger

Dr.   **Sales Account**   Cr.

Date	Particulars	J.F.	Amount (Rs.)	Date	Particulars	J.F.	Amount (Rs.)
				2005 Feb. 28	By Sundry debtors		98,280

Dr.   **Sales Tax Account**   Cr.

Date	Particulars	J.F.	Amount (Rs.)	Date	Particulars	J.F.	Amount (Rs.)
				2005 Feb. 28	By sundry debtors		7,862

| Dr. | | | | | | Freight and Packing Account | | | Cr. |
Date	Particulars	J.F.	Amount (Rs.)	Date	Particulars		J.F.	Amount (Rs.)
				2005 Feb. 28	By Sundry Debtors			2,170

In the Debtors' Ledger
Ratan Lal and Bros. Account

| Dr. | | | | | | | | Cr. |
Date	Particulars	J.F.	Amount (Rs.)	Date	Particulars	J.F.	Amount (Rs.)
2005 Feb. 2	To Sales A/c To Sales Tax A/c To Freight and Packing		31,590 2,527 720				

D.D. Kar and Co. Account

| Dr. | | | | | | | | Cr. |
Date	Particulars	J.F.	Amount (Rs.)	Date	Particulars	J.F.	Amount (Rs.)
2005 Feb. 16	To Sales A/c To Sales Tax A/c To Freight and Packing		17,550 1,404 470				

M.M. and Suppliers Account

| Dr. | | | | | | | | Cr. |
Date	Particulars	J.F.	Amount (Rs.)	Date	Particulars	J.F.	Amount (Rs.)
2005 Feb. 25	To Sales A/c To Sales Tax A/c To Freight and Packing		49,140 3,931 980				

10.6 PURCHASE RETURN BOOK

This book records the goods returned to suppliers. Generally, goods are returned to suppliers due to being defective or not being according to the sample or quality. These types of transactions are recorded like the ruling of the purchase day book. A note or a letter, known as **debit note**, is given to the supplier together with the returned goods, stating that their account has been debited for the goods returned. It contains the date of return, quantity and value, supplier's name and the reasons for such return. After recording the transaction in the return outward book or purchase return book, the creditor's account will be debited (for each return) and at the end of the period, return Outward account or purchase return account will be credited for the total returns.

The specimen of a debit note is given in Box 10.1.

Box 10.1 Debit Note

Telegram _____

Telephone _____

From:

Name and address (of the sender)

_____

_____

No. _____

Place _____

Date _____

To,

Name and address (of the person to whom it is sent) _____

We are debiting your account with value of under mentioned materials returned to you for the reasons stated below. Meanwhile, we await your instructions.

Description	Specification	Price	Amount

Reasons:

Ref. _____ Invoice No. _____

Signature

ILLUSTRATION 10.6 Prepare the returns outward book from the following particulars:

2008	**Transactions**
June 11	Returned to K. K. Traders 15 cases of goods @ Rs. 200 per case, less 10% trade discount due to bad quality.
17	Returned to M.R. Basu & Co. 18 cases of goods @ Rs. 150 per case, plus Packing charges Rs. 190 due to damaged goods.
23	Returned to S. Bros. 10 cases of goods @ Rs. 100 per case, plus freight Rs. 75 due to goods not being in accordance with their order.
29	Sent to debit note for Rs. 300 to Gupta Traders, who overcharged the invoice by mistake and which they accepted duly.

Solution

In the Books of ...
Returns Outward Book

Date	Particulars	Debit note no.	L.F.	Details (Rs.)	Amount (Rs.)	Remarks
2008 June 11	**K. K. Traders** 15 cases @ Rs. 200 *Less:* 10% trade discount			3,000 300	2,700	Bad quality
17	**M. R. Basu & Co.** 18 cases @ Rs. 150 *Add:* Packing charges			2,700 190	2,510	Damaged goods
23	**S. Bros.** 10 cases @ Rs. 100 *Add:* Freight			1,000 75	1,075	Not accordance with the order
29	**Gupta Traders** Regarding adjustment of overcharge				300	Over charged
					6,585	

In the General Ledger
Returns Outward Account

Dr.   Cr.

Date	Particulars	J.F.	Amount (Rs.)	Date	Particulars	J.F.	Amount (Rs.)
				June 30	By Sundry Creditors		6,585

In the Creditors' Ledger
K. K. Traders Account

Dr.   Cr.

Date	Particulars	J.F.	Amount (Rs.)	Date	Particulars	J.F.	Amount (Rs.)
2008 June 11	To Return Outward A/c		2,700				

M. R. Basu and Co. Account

Dr.   Cr.

Date	Particulars	J.F.	Amount (Rs.)	Date	Particulars	J.F.	Amount (Rs.)
2008 June 17	To Return Outward A/c		2,510				

S. Bros. Account

Dr.   Cr.

Date	Particulars	J.F.	Amount (Rs.)	Date	Particulars	J.F.	Amount (Rs.)
2008 June 23	To Return Outward A/c		1,075				

Dr. **Gupta Traders Account** Cr.

Date	Particulars	J.F.	Amount (Rs.)	Date	Particulars	J.F.	Amount (Rs.)
2008 June 29	To Return outward A/c		300				

10.7 SALES RETURN BOOK

Sales return book records the goods returned by customers. Here again, goods are returned by customers for being defective or not being according to the sample or quality. These types of transactions are also recorded like the ruling of the sales day book. A debit note is also received together with the goods returned by the customers or purchasers. Thus, it is a claim raised by the purchaser and when such a claim is accepted by the seller, then another note is sent to the purchaser known as a **credit note**. Through a credit note the seller informs his acceptance of the goods and also certifies that the customer has been given the due credit for such return. After recording the transaction in the return inward book or sales return book, the debtor's account will be credited (for each return) and at the end of the period, the return inward account or the sales return account will be debited for the total returns.

A specimen of a credit note is given below:

Box 10.2   Credit Note

Telegram _____

Telephone _____

From:

Name and address (of the sender)

_____

_____

No . _____

Place _____

Date _____

To,

Name and address (of the person to whom it is sent)

_____

_____

We are crediting your account with the value of under mentioned materials received from you, for the reasons stated as in your D.N. No. _____

Description	Specification	Price	Amount

Reasons:

Ref. _____

Signature

ILLUSTRATION 10.7   Enter the following transactions in a Returns Inward Book:

2008   **Transaction**

March 9   Returned by P. K. Traders 15 cases @ Rs. 150 due to goods not being in accordance with their order, credit note no. 36A, plus freight changes Rs. 70.

13   Returned by M/s R. P. Singh 12 cases @ Rs. 125 due to inferior quality, credit note no. 27B, less trade discount 5%.

19   Return from Mukherjee Bros. 18 cases @ Rs. 190, less trade discount 5% being out of size, credit note no. 39B.

26   Dalal Bros. returned 21 cases of goods @ Rs. 136 due to Damaged goods, packing charges Rs. 170 and credit note no. 50B.

Solution

In the Books of ...
Returns Inward Book

Date	Particulars	Credit note no.	L.F.	Details (Rs.)	Amount (Rs.)	Remarks
2008 March 9	**P.K. Traders** 15 cases @ Rs. 150 *Add:* Freight charges (Not accordance with the order)	36A		2,250 70	2,320	
13	**M/s R.P. Singh** 12 cases @ Rs. 125 *Less:* 5% trade discount (Inferior quality)	27B		1,500 75	1,425	
19	**Mukherjee Bros.** 18 cases @ Rs. 190 *Less:* 5% trade discount	39B		3,420 171	3,249	(Out of size)
26	**Dalal Bros.** 21 cases @ Rs. 136 *Add:* Packing charges	50B		2,856 170	3,026 10,020	(Damaged goods)

10.8 BILLS RECEIVABLE BOOK

This book is maintained to record transactions regarding the bills received from the customers who purchase goods on credit. The customers promise to pay their debt through this bill within the credit period. The bills receivable book keeps the records of the bills receivable received within a certain period and provides the following information:

1. Name of the acceptor
2. From received
3. Date of the bill
4. Term (i.e., the period)
5. Date of maturity
6. Amount and remarks, if any, or how dealt with it.

10.9 BILLS PAYABLE BOOK

Bills payable book records transactions regarding the bills accepted and issued in favour of the suppliers from whom goods are purchased on credit. It is maintained like the bills receivable book and also provides the same information as is given by the Bills Receivable book.

ILLUSTRATION 10.8 Record the following transactions in the Bills Receivable and Bills Payable books of a trader:

1996   **Transactions**

March 11   Acceptance given to Mr. Ambuja at three months for Rs. 6,200.

     16   Received acceptances from Mr. Pillai of three months for Rs. 5,000.

     19   Received from Mr. Saraf as acceptance for two months for Rs. 6,500.

     24   Acceptance given to Mr. Kumar at two months for Rs. 3,900.

     27   Acceptance given to Mr. Kartik at four months for Rs. 4,000.

     29   Endorsed Pillai's acceptance to Mr. Rajan.

     29   Acceptance renewed to Mr. Ambuja by issuing a new bill for Rs. 6,600 for four months including interest Rs. 300.

     31   Discounted Saraf's acceptance at Rs. 6,250 with the Bank.

     31   Received an acceptance from Mr. Ram for two months for Rs. 4,000.

Solution

Bills Receivable Book

Sl. no.	No. of the bill	Name of the acceptor	Received from	Date of the bill	Term (months)	Date of Maturity	Amount (Rs.)	Remarks
1.		Mr. Pillai	Mr. Pillai	16.3.96	3	19.6.96	5,000	Endorsed
2.		Mr. Saraf	Mr. Saraf	19.3.96	2	22.5.96	6,500	Discounted
3.		Mr. Ram	Mr. Ram	31.3.96	2	3.6.96	4,000	

Bills Payable Book

Sl. no.	No. of the bill	Name of the Drawer	Payee	Date of the bill	Term (months)	Date of Maturity	Amount (Rs.)	Remarks
1.		Mr. Ambuja	Mr. Ambuja	11.3.96	3	14.6.96	6,200	Renewal
2.		Mr. Kumar	Mr. Kumar	24.3.96	2	27.5.96	3,900	
3.		Mr. Kartik	Mr. Kartik	27.3.96	4	30.7.96	4,000	
4.		Mr. Ambuja	Mr. Ambuja	29.3.96	4	2.8.96	6,600	

10.10 JOURNAL PROPER

Generally, most transactions of a business are recorded in a cash book, purchase day book, sales day book, returns outward book, returns inward book, bills receivable book and bills payable book. But there are some other transactions also which take place occasionally and are not recorded in the above books. Such transactions are recorded in a special book known as a **Journal Proper**. The following types of transactions are recorded in a journal proper:

1. Opening entries
2. Closing entries
3. Transfer entries
4. Credit purchase and sale of assets
5. Adjustment entries
6. Rectification entries.

10.10.1 Uses of the Journal Proper

1. The transactions which are not recorded in special journals or which occasionally take place and no special journals are maintained for them, are recorded in the Journal Proper.
2. It helps to close the nominal accounts by transferring them to Trading or Profit and Loss Account.
3. It helps to apply the accrual system of accounting, i.e., by adjusting the prepaid, outstanding, received in advance, etc.
4. Credit purchase and sales of fixed assets are recorded here.
5. It helps to rectify the errors occurred during the financial year.
6. It acts as a link between the two periods through opening and closing entries.
7. It helps to transfer a particular amount from one account to another for adjustment of the balance.
8. It helps to represent the true financial position of a firm.

Table 10.5 shows the differences between special journal and journal proper.

TABLE 10.5 Distinction between Special Journal and Journal Proper

	Journal proper		*Special journal*
1.	The transactions which are not recorded in special journals are recorded in journal proper.	1.	Special types of transactions are recorded here, like credit purchase and sale of fixed assets, rectification entries, etc.
2.	The format of a journal proper is like a journal and does not vary in character.	2.	The format of a special journal is like a statement and it varies depending the on transactions.

(Contd.)

Journal proper	Special journal
3. The mistakes of special journals are rectified in journal proper.	3. There is no scope of rectification of errors in special journals.
4. Generally, transactions are recorded at the end of the year.	4. Here, transactions are recorded throughout the year.
5. The number of transactions recorded are very few.	5. Huge number of transactions can be recorded in special journal.
6. Both internal and external transactions are recorded in it.	6. Internal transactions are not recorded here.
7. Double entry system is followed in journal proper.	7. Double entry system is not followed here, as they are prepared in the form of a statement.
8. This book is not maintained for credit transactions only. It also helps to record the transactions which are not recorded in special journals.	8. Special journals are developed chiefly due to the presence of similar types of credit transactions.

10.10.2 Opening Entries

These entries are made for opening accounts in the beginning of a financial year in respect of assets and liabilities of a firm.

ILLUSTRATION 10.9   The balance sheet of XYZ Ltd. is shown below:

XYZ Ltd.
Balance Sheet as on December 31, 2007

Liabilities	Rs.	Rs.	Assets	Rs.	Rs.
Capital		1,00,000	Land and Buildings		60,000
Reserve		18,000	Plant and Machinery		28,000
Loan		30,000	Furniture		12,000
Bills Payable		9,000	Investment		20,000
Sundry Creditors		16,000	Stock in Trade		19,000
Outstanding Expenses		2,000	Sundry Debtors	26,000	
Income Received in Advance		1,000	*Less:* Provision for Bad Debts	3,000	23,000
			Prepaid Expenses		1,000
			Cash at Bank		10,000
			Cash in Hand		3,000
		176,000			176,000

The opening entries in the journal proper as on January 1, 2008 are shown below:

Solution

In the Books of XYZ Ltd.
Journal Proper

Date	Particulars		L.F.	Amount Dr. (Rs.)	Amount Cr. (Rs.)
2008 Jan. 1	Land and Building A/c	Dr.		60,000	
	Plant and Machinery A/c	Dr.		28,000	
	Furniture A/c	Dr.		12,000	
	Investments A/c	Dr.		20,000	
	Stock in Trade A/c	Dr.		19,000	
	Prepaid Expenses A/c	Dr.		1,000	
	Sundry Debtors A/c	Dr.		26,000	
	Cash at Bank A/c	Dr.		10,000	
	Cash in Hand A/c	Dr.		3,000	
	To Sundry Creditors A/c				16,000
	To Bills Payable A/c				9,000
	To Loan A/c				30,000
	To Outstanding Expenses A/c				2,000
	To Income Received in Advance A/c				1,000

(Contd.)

Date	Particulars	L.F.	Amount Dr. (Rs.)	Amount Cr. (Rs.)
	To Provision for Bad Debts A/c			3,000
	To Reserve A/c			18,000
	To Capital A/c			100,000
	(Being last year's balance of assets and liabilities brought forward)			

10.10.3 Closing Entries

At the end of a financial year, all nominal accounts are transferred to trading accounts (direct incomes and expenditures only), and profit and loss account (indirect incomes, expenditures and losses) to ascertain the net profits earned or net losses suffered during the period. The net result is then transferred to capital account. All the entries are passed through the journal proper. They are shown in Table 10.6.

TABLE 10.6 Journal Proper Entries for Closing Entries

Date	Particulars	L.F.	Amount Dr. (Rs.)	Amount Cr. (Rs.)
2007 Dec. 31	Trading A/c Dr.			
	To Opening Stock A/c			
	To Purchases A/c			
	To Sales Return A/c			
	To Carriage Inward A/c			
	To Import Duty A/c			
	To Wages A/cTo Freight A/c			
	To Motive Power A/c			
	(Being transfer of the above items to trading A/c to ascertain gross profit)			
	Sales A/c Dr.			
	Purchase Return A/c Dr.			
	Closing Stock A/c Dr.			
	To Trading A/c			
	(Being transfer of the above items to Trading A/c to ascertain gross profit)			
	Trading A/c Dr.			
	To Profit and loss A/c			
	(Being the gross profit transferred)			
	Profit and Loss A/c Dr.			
	To Salaries A/c			
	To Rent A/c			
	To Insurance A/c			
	To Advertisement A/c			
	To Bad Debts A/c			
	To Carriage Outwards A/c			
	To Discount Allowed A/c			
	To Repairs A/c			
	To Depreciation A/c			
	(Being transfer of the above items to profit and loss A/c)			
	Discount Received A/c Dr.			
	Interest Received A/c Dr.			
	Commission Received A/c Dr.			
	Rent Received A/c Dr.			
	Bad Debts Recovered A/c Dr.			
	Miscellaneous Receipts A/c Dr.			
	To Profit and Loss A/c			
	(Being transfer of the above items to profit and loss A/c)			
	Profit and Loss A/c Dr.			
	To Capital A/c			
	(Being net profit transferred to capital A/c)			

ILLUSTRATION 10.10 From the following data, pass necessary closing entries for the year ended December 31, 2007, in the books of M/s. C.P. Traders:

Particulars	(Rs.)
Opening Stock	8,400
Purchases	41,700
Carriage Inward	2,800
Purchase Return	2,500
Wages	4,900
Carriage Outwards	2,600
Salaries	6,700
Discount Allowed	2,400
Rent	4,400
Insurance	3,200
Advertisement	2,600
Discount Received	2,700
Rent Received	3,100
Depreciation	6,000
Bad Debts	2,100
Sales	97,200
Closing Stock	8,900
Sales Return	3,100

Solution

In the Books of M/s. C.P. Traders
Journal Proper

Date	Particulars		L.F.	Amount Dr. (Rs.)	Amount Cr. (Rs.)
2007 Dec. 31	Trading A/c	Dr.		60,900	
	To Opening Stock A/c				8,400
	To Purchases A/c				41,700
	To Sales Return A/c				3,100
	To Carriage Inward A/c				2,800
	To Wages A/c				4,900
	(Being transfer of the above items to trading A/c to ascertain gross profit)				
	Sales A/c	Dr.		97,200	
	Purchase Return A/c	Dr.		2,500	
	Closing Stock A/c	Dr.		8,900	
	To Trading A/c				108,600
	(Being transfer of the above items to trading A/c to ascertain gross profit)				
	Trading A/c	Dr.		47,700	
	To Profit and Loss A/c				47,700
	(Being the gross profit transferred)				
	Profit and Loss A/c	Dr.		30,000	
	To Salaries A/c				6,700
	To Rent A/c				4,400
	To Insurance A/c				3,200
	To Advertisement A/c				2,600
	To Bad Debts A/c				2,100
	To Carriage Outwards A/c				2,600
	To Discount Allowed A/c				2,400
	To Depreciation A/c				6,000
	(Being transfer of the above items to profit and loss A/c)				
	Discount Received A/c	Dr.		2,700	
	Rent Received A/c	Dr.		3,100	
	To Profit and Loss A/c				5,800
	(Being transfer of the above items to profit and loss A/c)				
	Profit and Loss A/c	Dr.		23,500	
	To Capital A/c				23,500
	(Being net profit transferred to capital A/c)				

ILLUSTRATION 10.11 From the following Trial Balance and the additional information, pass necessary closing entries for the year ended December 31, 2007:

Dr.		Trial Balance as on December 31, 2007	Cr.
Particulars	Amount (Rs.)	Particulars	Amount (Rs.)
Opening Stock	8,600	Rent Received	4,300
Purchases	67,300	Capital	78,000
Wages	4,800	Sundry Creditors	28,400
Return Inwards	2,900	Sales	132,600
Drawings	3,500	Discount Received	5,800
Salaries	5,100		
Carriage Inwards	2,600		
Machinery	42,800		
Discount Allowed	2,400		
Cash at Bank	21,900		
Insurance Premium	2,400		
Depreciation	9,000		
Advertisement	3,700		
Sundry Debtors	39,500		
General Expenses	1,600		
Buildings	31,000		
	249,100		249,100

Additional information:

Closing Stock Rs. 32,700.

Solution

In the Books of ...
Journal Proper

Date	Particulars		L.F.	Amount Dr. (Rs.)	Amount Cr. (Rs.)
2007 Dec. 31	Trading A/c	Dr.		86,200	
	To Opening Stock A/c				8,600
	To Purchases A/c				67,300
	To Sales Return A/c				2,900
	To Carriage Inward A/c				2,600
	To Wages A/c				4,800
	(Being transfer of the above items to trading A/c to ascertain gross profit)				
	Sales A/c	Dr.		132,600	
	Closing Stock A/c	Dr.		32,700	
	To Trading A/c				165,300
	(Being transfer of the above items to trading A/c to ascertain gross profit)				
	Trading A/c	Dr.		79,100	
	To Profit and Loss A/c				79,100
	(Being the gross profit transferred)				
	Profit and Loss A/c	Dr.		24,200	
	To Salaries A/c				5,100
	To Insurance Premium A/c				2,400
	To Advertisement A/c				3,700
	To Discount Allowed A/c				2,400
	To General Expenses A/c				1,600
	To Depreciation A/c				9,000
	(Being transfer of the above items to profit and loss A/c)				
	Discount Received A/c	Dr.		5,800	
	To Profit and Loss A/c				5,800
	(Being transfer of the above items to profit and loss A/c)				
	Profit and Loss A/c	Dr.		60,700	
	To Capital A/c				60,700
	(Being net profit transferred to capital A/c)				

10.10.4 Transfer Entries

When a transfer is made from one account to another, then such entry is passed through the journal proper.

ILLUSTRATION 10.12 Prepare a journal proper based on the following information:

1. Transferred Rs. 30,000 to reserve fund from profit.
2. K. Sen, a customer, agreed to pay Rs. 3,000 to G. Roy, a creditor.
3. Drawings of Rs. 15,000 transferred to Capital Account.
4. Transferred Rs. 4,000 from Stock Account to Drawings Account.
5. Debtors include Rs. 1,000 due from a customer, Mr. P. Kar, and creditors include Rs. 1,500 due to Mr. P. Kar.
6. Bad debts of Rs. 1,600 transferred to Provision for Bad and Doubtful Debts Account.
7. Net profit of Rs. 50,000 transferred to Capital Account.
8. Transferred from Rs. 3,000 Debtor's Account to Drawings Account.

Solution

In the Books of ...
Journal Proper

Date	Particulars	L.F.	Amount Dr. (Rs.)	Amount Cr. (Rs.)
1.	Profit and Loss A/c Dr.		30,000	
	To Reserve Fund A/c			30,000
	(Being the profit transferred)			
2.	G. Roy A/c Dr.		3,000	
	To K. Sen A/c			3,000
	(Being the payment made by K. Sen to G. Roy as per agreement)			
3.	Drawings A/c Dr.		15,000	
	To Capital A/c			15,000
	(Being drawings account balance transferred to capital account)			
4.	Drawings A/c Dr.		4,000	
	To Stock A/c			4,000
	(Being a portion of stock account transferred to drawings account)			
5.	Creditor's A/c (P. Kar) Dr.		1,000	
	To Debtors A/c (P. Kar)			1,000
	(Being the set off made)			
6.	Provision for bad and doubtful debts A/c Dr.		1,600	
	To Bad Debts A/c			1,600
	(Being transfer to provision for bad and doubtful debts account)			
7.	Profit and Loss A/c Dr.		50,000	
	To Capital A/c			50,000
	(Being the net profit transferred to capital A/c)			
8.	Drawings A/c Dr.		3,000	
	To Debtors A/c			3,000
	(Being the transfer from debtors A/c to drawings A/c)			

10.10.5 Credit Sale and Credit Purchase of Assets

When assets are purchased or sold in cash, they are passed through the Cash Book. When assets are purchased/sold on credit, they are passed through the journal proper.

ILLUSTRATION 10.13 Prepare necessary entries in the journal proper based on the following information:

1. Purchased machinery from Machine & Tools Ltd. for Rs. 60,000.
2. Purchased furniture from Godrej Co. for Rs. 8,000.

3. Sold old furniture to Mr. M. Das for Rs. 3,000.
4. Purchased office equipments from M/s Raj & Raj for Rs. 6,200.
5. Sold obsolete machinery to Rupkar Traders for Rs. 2,800.

Solution

In the Books of ...
Journal Proper

Date	Particulars	L.F.	Amount Dr. (Rs.)	Amount Cr. (Rs.)
1.	Machinery A/c Dr.		60,000	
	To Machine & Tools Ltd. A/c			60,000
	(Being machinery purchased on credit)			
2.	Furniture A/c Dr.		8,000	
	To Godrej Co. A/c.			8,000
	(Being furniture purchased on credit)			
3.	M. Das A/c Dr.		3,000	
	To old furniture A/c			3,000
	(Being old furniture sold)			
4.	Office equipment A/c Dr.		6,200	
	To M/s Raj & Raj A/c			6,200
	(Being office equipment purchased on credit)			
5.	Rupkar traders A/c Dr.		2,800	
	To machinery A/c			2,800
	(Being obsolete machinery sold)			

10.10.6 Adjustment Entries

In order to ascertain the exact financial position of a firm or a concern, some adjustments are required to be made in respect of certain incomes, expenditures or assets and liabilities at the end of a financial period. Adjustment means recording the current year's transactions which were omitted from the books, rectification of errors, recording the internal transactions not yet recorded and adjustments regarding prepaid, accrued, received in advance, and outstanding. Thus, if adjustments are not made regarding the said items, the actual income and expenditure cannot be ascertained on the basis of the accepted accounting principles. As a result, the Balance Sheet will not represent the true financial position of the firm.

Therefore, in order to represent the true financial position, some necessary adjustments have to be made in the Income Statement and the Balance Sheet of a firm on the basis of the accepted accounting principles. Otherwise, the Final Accounts cannot reveal the true state of affairs of the firm. Hence, appropriate adjustments are made while preparing the Final Accounts. Without these adjustments, the actual net profits cannot be ascertained.

Some examples of such adjustments are given below:

1. **Closing Stock**
   Closing Stock A/c   Dr.
      To Trading A/c
2. **Accrued Income (due but not received)**
   Accrued Income A/c   Dr.
      To Particular Income A/c
3. **Outstanding or Unpaid Expenses**
   Particular Expenses A/c   Dr.
      To Outstanding Expenses A/c
4. **Prepaid or Unexpired Expenses**
   Prepaid Expenses A/c   Dr.
      To Particular Expenses A/c
5. **Income Received in Advance**
   Particular Income A/c   Dr.
      To Income Received in Advance A/c

(Contd.)

6. **Goods Used by Proprietor for Personal Purposes**
   Drawings A/c   Dr.
      To Purchase or Opening stock A/c

7. **Goods Distributed as Free Samples**
   Advertisement A/c   Dr.
      To Opening Stock or Purchase A/c

8. **Asset Purchased but Wrongly Included in Purchase A/c**
   Asset A/c   Dr.
      To Purchase A/c

9. **Goods Purchased on Credit but not Recorded in the Books**
   Purchase A/c   Dr.
      To Creditors A/c

10. **Wages Include Wages Paid for Installation of Plant**
    Plant A/c   Dr.
       To Wages A/c

11. **Wages Include Wages Paid for Construction of Building**
    Building A/c   Dr.
       To Wages A/c

12. **Depreciation Charged on Assets**
    (i) Depreciation A/c   Dr.
       To Assets A/c
    (ii) Profit and Loss A/c   Dr.
       To Depreciation A/c

13. **Bad Debts to be Written Off**
    (i) Bad Debts A/c   Dr.
       To Debtor's A/c
    (ii) Profit and Loss A/c   Dr.
       To Bad Debt A/c

14. **Sales Include Sale of Assets**
    Sales A/c   Dr.
       To Assets A/c

15. **For Creating Provision for Doubtful Debts**
    Profit and Loss A/c   Dr.
       To Provision for Doubtful Debts A/c

16. **For Creating Provision for Discount on Debtors**
    Profit and Loss A/c   Dr.
       To Provision for Discount on Debtors A/c

17. **Proprietors Life Insurance Premium Included in Insurance Account**
    Drawings A/c   Dr.
       To Insurance A/c

18. **Carriage Includes Carrying of an Asset**
    Asset A/c   Dr.
       To Carriage A/c

19. **Set Off—A Person When Both as a Debtor and a Creditor**
    Creditors A/c   Dr.
       To Debtors A/c
    (Entry is for the smaller of the two amounts.)

20. **Bills receivable include a dishonoured bill**
    Debtors A/c   Dr.
       To Bills Receivable A/c

21. **Goods lost by fire**
    (a) Goods Lost by Fire A/c   Dr.
       To Trading A/c
       (For the Original/Gross Loss)
    (b) Admitted Insurance Claim A/c   Dr.
       To Goods Lost by Fire A/c
       (When Fully Admitted by the Insurance Company)
            Or
    Admitted Insurance Claim A/c   Dr. (Admitted Portion)
    Profit and Loss A/c   Dr. (Net Loss)
    To Goods Lost by Fire A/c

(Contd.)

Or

Profit and Loss A/c		Dr. (When Not Admitted by the Insurance Company)
To Goods Lost by Fire A/c		

22. **Interest on Capital**

Profit and Loss Appropriation A/c	Dr.
To Interest on Capital A/c	

23. **Interest on Drawings**

Interest on Drawings A/c	Dr.
To Profit and Loss Appropriation A/c	

Generally, the following differences as given in Table 10.7 are observed in respect of adjustment entries and rectification entries:

TABLE 10.7 Distinction between Adjustment Entries and Rectification Entries

	Adjustment Entries		*Rectification Entries*
1.	Here, though the accounting entries are made correctly, yet some adjustment is required at the end of the year to represent the correct financial statements.	1.	Since accounting entries are made incorrectly here, corrections are made to show the correct financial statements.
2.	Generally, it affects two accounts.	2.	It may be restricted to one account or to two or even more accounts.
3.	These entries are made before preparing the Final Accounts.	3.	These entries may be made at any point of time. Usually, it is made before or after the preparation of a trial balance and before the Final Accounts.
4.	It must be made where the mercantile system of Accounts is followed.	4.	It is always essential when an error is detected.
5.	Places where adjustments are to be made are clearly mentioned in the accounting principles and concepts.	5.	Places where rectifications are made depend on the nature of errors detected.

ILLUSTRATION 10.14 *Pass* the necessary adjustment entries from the following information for the year ended March 31, 2008:

1. Interest on investment due but not received Rs. 1,260.
2. Rent outstanding Rs. 950.
3. Insurance premium paid in advance amounting to Rs. 750.
4. Goods distributed as free samples amounting to Rs. 1,650.
5. Wages include wages paid for installation of plant Rs. 2,400.
6. Proprietors life insurance premium included in Insurance Premium Account Rs. 1,700.
7. Carriage includes carrying of furniture Rs. 800.
8. Debtors include Rs. 2,600 due from Mr. Sirkar and creditors include Rs. 1,200 due to Mr. Sirkar

Solution

Journal Proper

Date	Particulars		L.F.	Amount Dr. (Rs.)	Amount Cr. (Rs.)
2008 March 31					
1	Accrued Interest A/c	Dr.		1,260	
	To Interest on Investment A/c				1,260
	(Being interest on due but not received adjusted)				
2	Rent A/c	Dr.		950	
	To Outstanding Rent A/c				950
	(Being outstanding rent adjusted.)				
3	Prepaid Insurance A/c	Dr.		750	
	To Insurance Premium A/c				750
4	Advertisement A/c	Dr.		1,650	
	To Opening Stock or Purchases A/c				1,650
	(Being goods distributed as free samples adjusted.)				

(Contd.)

Date	Particulars	L.F.	Amount Dr. (Rs.)	Amount Cr. (Rs.)
5	Plant A/c .... Dr.		2,400	
	To Wages A/c.			2,400
	(Being the wages paid for installation of plant adjusted)			
6	Drawings A/c .... Dr.		1,700	
	To Insurance A/c			1,700
	(Being life insurance of proprietor included in insurance premium A/c adjusted)			
7	Furniture A/c .... Dr.		800	
	To Carriage A/c			800
	(Being carriage includes carrying of furniture adjusted)			
8	Creditors A/c (Mr. Sirkar) .... Dr.		1,200	
	To Debtors A/c(Mr. Sirkar)			1,200
	(Being entry for 'Set off' made)			

ILLUSTRATION 10.15 Pass the necessary adjustment entries from the following information for the year ended March 31, 2008:

1. Goods costing Rs. 2,000 used by the proprietor as personal gifts to some relatives.
2. Insurance premium included Rs. 1,800 annual insurance premium paid commencing from July 1, 2007.
3. Bills receivable include a dishonoured bill of Rs. 1,400.
4. Furniture of book value of Rs. 1,600 sold for Rs. 1,050 and the sale proceeds credited to furniture account.
5. Debtors include Rs. 700 due from a customer who has become insolvent and nothing could be realized from his estate.
6. Depreciate machinery by 10% and the machinery account shows a balance of Rs. 65,000.

Solution

Journal Proper

Date	Particulars	L.F.	Amount Dr. (Rs.)	Amount Cr. (Rs.)
2008 March 31				
1	Drawings A/c .... Dr.		2,000	
	To Purchases A/c			2,000
	(Goods used by the proprietor for personal purposes)			
2	Prepaid insurance A/c .... Dr.		450	
	To Insurance Premium A/c			450
	(Insurance premium paid in advance for three months adjusted)			
3	Debtors A/c .... Dr.		1,400	
	To Bills Receivable A/c			1,400
	(Being bills receivable include a dishonoured bill adjusted)			
4	Loss on sale A/c .... Dr.		550	
	To Furniture A/c			550
	(Being loss on sale of furniture adjusted)			
5	Bad Debts A/c .... Dr.		700	
	To Debtors A/c			700
	(Bmeing bad debts written off)			
6	Depreciation A/c .... Dr.		6,500	
	To Machinery A/c (10% of Rs. 65,000)			6,500
	(Depreciation provided on machinery by 10%)			

ILLUSTRATION 10.16 Give the necessary adjustment entries (without narration) from the following for the year ended December 31, 2007:

1. Goods lost by fire amounting to Rs. 2,650 but insurance company admitted the claim to the extent of Rs. 1,400 only.

2. For creating provision for doubtful debts @ 5% on Debtors of Rs. 42,000.
3. Unexpired rent Rs. 600.
4. Bonus declared but not paid amounting to Rs. 2,700.
5. Accrued interest on bank deposit Rs. 900.

Solution

Journal Proper

Date	Particulars		L.F.	Amount Dr. (Rs.)	Amount Cr. (Rs.)
2007 Dec. 31					
1	(a) Goods Lost by Fire A/c	Dr.		2,650	
	To Trading A/c				2,650
	(Goods lost by fire)				
	(b) Admitted Insurance Claim A/c	Dr.		1,400	
	(Admitted Portion)				
	Profit and Loss A/c (Net Loss)	Dr.		1,250	
	To Goods Lost by Fire A/c				2,650
	(Being goods lost by fire amounting to Rs. 2,650 and insurance company admitted the claim to the extent of Rs. 1,400 adjusted)				
2	Profit and Loss A/c	Dr.		2,100	
	To Provision for Doubtful Debts A/c				2,100
	(Being provision for doubtful debts @ 5% on debtors of Rs. 42,000 created)				
3	Prepaid Rent A/c	Dr.		600	
	To Rent A/c				600
	(Being prepaid rent adjusted)				
4	Bonus A/c	Dr.		2,700	
	To Outstanding Bonus A/c				2,700
	(Being bonus declared but not paid adjusted)				
5	Accrued Interest A/c	Dr.		900	
	To Interest A/c				900
	(Being accrued interest on bank deposit adjusted)				

ILLUSTRATION 10.17 Pass the necessary adjustment entries (without narration) from the following for the year ended December 31, 2007:

1. Subscription received in advance Rs. 1,400
2. Rent paid Rs. 2,400 out of which one-fourth is to be carried forward to the next year .
3. The manager is to get a commission of 10% on net profits after charging his commission, while the net profit before charging manager's commission was Rs. 11,000.
4. Unexpired Insurance on December 31, 2007 was Rs. 600.
5. Investment was made on April 1, 2007 Rs. 20,000. The rate of interest on investment was 12% p.a. During the year, no interest was received.

Solution

Journal Proper

Date	Particulars		L.F.	Amount Dr. (Rs.)	Amount Cr. (Rs.)
2007 Dec. 31					
1	Subscription A/c	Dr.		1,400	
	To Subscription Received in Advance A/c				1,400
2	Prepaid Rent A/c	Dr.		600	
	To Rent A/c				600
3	Commission A/c	Dr.		1,000	
	To Manager's commission payable A/c				
	(10/110 × 11,000)				1,000

(Contd.)

Date	Particulars	L.F.	Amount Dr. (Rs.)	Amount Cr. (Rs.)
4	Prepaid Insurance A/c Dr.		600	
	To Insurance Premium A/c			600
5	Accrued Interest on Investment A/c Dr.		1,800	
	To Interest A/c			1,800
	[Interest accrued for nine months, i.e., Rs. 1,800 (12/100 20,000 × 9/12)]			

ILLUSTRATION 10.18 Give the necessary adjustment entries (without narration) from the following:

1. Wages paid during the year Rs. 4,200, two-thirds of which were for preparing goods for sale.
2. Commission paid in advance Rs. 550.
3. Subscription due but not received Rs. 650.
4. Closing valued at Rs. 21,800.
5. Debtors include Rs. 2,500 due from the proprietor.

Solution

Journal Proper

Date	Particulars	L.F.	Amount Dr. (Rs.)	Amount Cr. (Rs.)
1	Indirect Wages A/c Dr.		1,400	
	To Wages A/c			1,400
	[2/3 was for preparing goods, so 1/3rd was for other than production, i.e., indirect wages]			
2	Commission Paid in Advance A/c Dr.		550	
	To Commission A/c			550
3	Subscription Receivable A/c Dr.		650	
	To Subscriptions A/c			650
4	Closing Stock A/c Dr.		21,800	
	To Trading A/c			21,800
5	Drawings A/c Dr.		2,500	
	To Debtors A/c			2,500

ILLUSTRATION 10.19 Enter the following transactions in the proper books of the Hotco Brothers:

Date 1997	Transactions
January 1	Assets: Building Rs. 50,000, Machinery Rs. 30,000, Furniture Rs. 10,000, Stock Rs. 12,000, Sen Brothers (debtors) Rs. 18,000, Cash in hand Rs. 6,200, Cash at bank Rs. 18,500.
	Liabilities: Kar Brothers (creditors) Rs. 12,000, Loan from Gupta Brothers Rs. 10,000.
1	Paid fire insurance premium of Rs. 600.
2	Purchased goods from Saha Brothers: 350 cases @ Rs. 150 per case. Less: 5% trade discount, plus packing charges of Rs. 80.
4	Received a cheque of Rs. 8,000 from Sen Bros.
5	Issued a cheque of Rs. 7,500 in favour of Kar Bros.
8	Paid Rs. 750 for advertisement.
10	Sold goods to Rupa Traders: 200 cases @ Rs. 225.
	Less: 5% Trade Discount, packing charge Rs. 110.
12	Sen Brothers settled their account fully by paying a cheque of Rs. 9,700.
15	Interest of Rs. 1,250 received from bank.
18	Paid Rs. 600 towards repairs to furniture.

20   Goods returned to Saha Brothers: 10 cases.

22   Goods returned by Rupa Traders: 12 cases.

23   Paid salary of Rs. 3,000 to the staff.

24   Sold goods for Rs. 18,000 in cash.

25   Proprietor's house rent of Rs. 1,200 paid.

27   Sold old furniture for Rs. 1,600.

28   Deposited Rs. 6,000, in cash into bank.

29   Paid Rs. 600 in cash to petty cashier.

30   Rs. 24,000 in cash received from Rupa Traders.

31   Issued a cheque of Rs. 15,000 to Saha Brothers. Goods worth Rs. 1,600 distributed as free samples. Depreciation of Rs. 300 charged on the furniture sold.

Solution

In the Books of Hotco Brothers

Dr.   **Cash Book**   Cr.

Date	Receipts	L.F.	Disc.	Cash (Rs.)	Bank (Rs.)	Date	Payments	L.F.	Disc.	Cash (Rs.)	Bank (Rs.)
1997						1997					
January 1	To Balance b/d			6,200	18,500	January 1	By Insurance Prem.			600	
4	To Son Bros.				8,000	5	By Kar Bros.				7,500
12	To Sen Bros.		300		9,700	8	By Advertisement			750	
15	To Interest				1,250	18	By Repairs			600	
24	To Sales			18,000		23	By Salary			3,000	
27	To Furniture			1,600		25	By Drawings			1,200	
28	To Cash	C			6,000	28	By Bank	C		6,000	
30	To Rupa Traders			24,000		29	By Petty Cash			600	
						31	By Saha Bros.				1,5000
						31	By Balance c/d			37,050	20,950
			300	49,800	43,450				–	49,800	43,450
February 1	To Balance b/d			37,050	20,950						

Journal Entries

Date	Particulars		L.F.	Amount Dr. (Rs.)	Amount Cr. (Rs.)
1997 January 1	Building A/c	Dr.		50,000	
	Machinery A/c	Dr.		30,000	
	Stock A/c	Dr.		12,000	
	Sen Bros. (Debtor's) A/c	Dr.		18,000	
	Cash in Hand A/c	Dr.		6,200	
	Cash at Bank A/c	Dr.		18,500	
	Furniture A/c	Dr.		10,000	
	To Kar Bros. (Creditor's) A/c				12,000
	To Loan (Gupta Bros.) A/c				10,000
	To Capital A/c				122,700
	(Being the opening balances of assets and liabilities brought into accounts)				
31	Advertisement A/c	Dr.		1,600	
	To Purchases A/c				1,600
	(Being the goods distributed as free sample)				
31	Depreciation A/c	Dr.		300	
	To Furniture A/c				300
	(Being the depreciation charged on the furniture sold)				
				146,600	146,600

Purchase Day Book

Date	Particulars	L.F.	Amount (Rs.)	Amount (Rs.)
1997 January 2	Saha Bros. 350 cases @ Rs. 150 per case *Less:* 5% Trade Discount		52,500 2,625	
			49,875	
	Add: Packing Charges		80	
				49,955
				49,955

Sales Day Book

Date	Particulars	L.F.	Amount (Rs.)	Amount (Rs.)
1997 January 10	Rupa Traders 200 cases @ Rs. 225 per case *Less:* 5% Trade Discount		45,000 2,250	
			42,750	
	Add: Packing Charges		110	
				42,860
				42,860

Return Outward Book

Date	Particulars	L.F.	Amount (Rs.)	Amount (Rs.)
1997 January 20	Saha Bros. 10 cases @ Rs. 150 *Less:* Trade Discount 5%		1,500 75	
	(Goods received as per invoice no. ...			1,425
	dated ...... returned. Our Debit Note No.			1,425
	dt. .... sent)			

Return Inward Book

Date	Particulars	L.F.	Amount (Rs.)	Amount (Rs.)
1997 January 22	Rupa Traders 12 cases @ Rs. 225 per case *Less:* Trade Discount 5%		2,700 135	
				2,565
				2,565

Ledger

Capital Account

Dr.   Cr.

Date	Particulars	Folio	Amount (Rs.)	Date	Particulars	Folio	Amount (Rs.)
				1997 January 1	By Balance b/d		122,700

Building Account

Dr.   Cr.

Date	Particulars	Folio	Amount (Rs.)	Date	Particulars	Folio	Amount (Rs.)
1997 January 1	To Balance b/d		50,000				

Dr.   **Machinery Account**   Cr.

Date	Particulars	Folio	Amount (Rs.)	Date	Particulars	Folio	Amount (Rs.)
1997 January 1	To Balance b/d		30,000				

Dr.   **Stock Account**   Cr.

Date	Particulars	Folio	Amount (Rs.)	Date	Particulars	Folio	Amount (Rs.)
1997 January 1	To Balance b/d		12,000				

Dr.   **Sen Brothers Account**   Cr.

Date	Particulars	Folio	Amount (Rs.)	Date	Particulars	Folio	Amount (Rs.)
1997 January 1	To Balance b/d		18,000	Jan. 4	By Bank		8,000
				12	By Bank		9,700
				12	By Discount Allowed		300

Dr.   **Kar Brothers Account**   Cr.

Date	Particulars	Folio	Amount (Rs.)	Date	Particulars	Folio	Amount (Rs.)
1997 January 5	To Bank		7,500	1997 January 1	By Balance b/d		12,000

Dr.   **Furniture Account**   Cr.

Date	Particulars	Folio	Amount (Rs.)	Date	Particulars	Folio	Amount (Rs.)
1997 January 1	To Balance b/d		10,000	1997 January 27	By Cash		1,600
				31	By Depreciation		300

Dr.   **Saha Brothers Account**   Cr.

Date	Particulars	Folio	Amount (Rs.)	Date	Particulars	Folio	Amount (Rs.)
1997 Jan. 20	To Return Outward		1,425	1997 January 2	By Purchases A/c		49,955
31	To Bank		15,000				

Dr.   **Advertisement Account**   Cr.

Date	Particulars	Folio	Amount (Rs.)	Date	Particulars	Folio	Amount (Rs.)
1997 January 8	To Cash		750				

Dr.   **Insurance Premium Account**   Cr.

Date	Particulars	Folio	Amount (Rs.)	Date	Particulars	Folio	Amount (Rs.)
1997 January 1	To Cash		600				

Dr.   **Interest Received Account**   Cr.

Date	Particulars	Folio	Amount (Rs.)	Date	Particulars	Folio	Amount (Rs.)
				1997 Jan. 15	By Bank		1,250

Dr.				Repairs Account				Cr.
Date	Particulars	Folio	Amount (Rs.)	Date	Particulars	Folio	Amount (Rs.)
1997 January 18	To Cash		600				

Dr.				Salary Account				Cr.
Date	Particulars	Folio	Amount (Rs.)	Date	Particulars	Folio	Amount (Rs.)
1997 January 23	To Cash		3,000				

Dr.				Rupa Trader Account				Cr.
Date	Particulars	Folio	Amount (Rs.)	Date	Particulars	Folio	Amount (Rs.)
1997 January 10	To Sales		42,860	1997 January 22 30	By Return Inward By Cash		2,565 24,000

Dr.				Drawings Account				Cr.
Date	Particulars	Folio	Amount (Rs.)	Date	Particulars	Folio	Amount (Rs.)
1997 January 25	To Cash		1,200				

Dr.				Purchases Account				Cr.
Date	Particulars	Folio	Amount (Rs.)	Date	Particulars	Folio	Amount (Rs.)
1997 January 31	To Sundries (as per purchase day book)		49,955				

Dr.				Sales Account				Cr.
Date	Particulars	Folio	Amount (Rs.)	Date	Particulars	Folio	Amount (Rs.)
				1997 January 31	By Sundries (as per Sales Day Book)		42,860

Dr.				Return Outward Account				Cr.
Date	Particulars	Folio	Amount (Rs.)	Date	Particulars	Folio	Amount (Rs.)
				1997 January 31	By Sundries (as per return outward Book)		1,425

Dr.				Return Inward Account				Cr.
Date	Particulars	Folio	Amount (Rs.)	Date	Particulars	Folio	Amount (Rs.)
1997 January 31	To Sundries (as per Return Inward Book)		2,565				

Dr. **Petty Cash Account** Cr.

Date	Particulars	Folio	Amount (Rs.)	Date	Particulars	Folio	Amount (Rs.)
1997 January 29	To Cash		600				

Dr. **Loan (Gupta Brothers) Account** Cr.

Date	Particulars	Folio	Amount (Rs.)	Date	Particulars	Folio	Amount (Rs.)
				1997 January 1	By Balance b/d		10,000

EXERCISES

I. *Multiple Choice Type Questions*

1. Choose the correct alternative from the following:

(a) The term 'goods' include
- (i) all high value items.
- (ii) those items which are purchased for resale.
- (iii) assets purchased on credit.

(b) Trade discount is allowed to
- (i) credit customers only.
- (ii) cash customers only.
- (iii) All types of customers(both for cash and credit transactions).

(c) Invoice is prepared by
- (i) the seller/supplier.
- (ii) the purchaser.
- (iii) the retailer.

(d) The transactions recorded in the Sales Day Book are
- (i) all cash sale of assets.
- (ii) all credit sale of goods.
- (iii) all credit sale of assets.

(e) The transactions recorded in the Purchases Day Book are
- (i) all cash purchases of assets.
- (ii) all credit purchases of goods.
- (iii) all credit purchases of assets.

(f) From Purchases Day Book
- (i) all individual purchases will be debited to Purchases Account.
- (ii) with the total amount of periodical purchases, Purchases Account will be debited.

(g) From Sales Day Book
- (i) all individual sales will be credited to Sales Account.
- (ii) with the total amount of periodical sales, the Sales Account will be credited.

(h) For charging Sales Tax to customers for sales
- (i) Customer's account will be debited for individual sales.
- (ii) Sales tax account will be debited.
- (iii) Cash account will be credited.

(i) Sales Tax is calculated on
- (i) the list price.
- (ii) the net price (list price – T.D.)
- (iii) the gross price.

(j) Periodical total Sales Tax is
    (i) Credited to Sales Tax A/c.
    (ii) Credited to Customer's A/c.
    (iii) Credited to Cash A/c .
(k) When actual Sales Tax is paid
    (i) Sales Tax A/c is debited and Cash A/c is credited.
    (ii) Customer's A/c is debited and Cash A/c is credited.
    (iii) Sales A/c is debited and Cash A/c is credited.
(l) Debit Note is issued by
    (i) the supplier.
    (ii) the purchaser.
    (iii) the retailer.
(m) Credit Note is issued by
    (i) the supplier/seller.
    (ii) the purchaser.
    (iii) the retailer.
(n) Debit Note is issued for
    (i) purchases return.
    (ii) sales return.
    (iii) purchases.
(o) Credit Note is issued for
    (i) purchases return.
    (ii) sales return.
    (iii) purchases.
Ans: (a) ii; (b) iii; (c) i; (d) ii; (e) ii; (f) ii; (g) ii; (h) i; (i) ii; (j) i; (k) i; (l) ii; (m) i; (n) i; and (o) ii.

II. *Short Answer Type Questions (with answers)*

1. What are Subsidiary Books?
Ans: The transactions which are regular and frequent in nature are generally recorded in a Subsidiary Book. A particular group/nature of transactions are recorded in a separate book of original entry known as **Subsidiary Books** or **Sub-Journal.**

2. What do mean by the term 'Goods'?
Ans: The term 'goods' include those items which are purchased by a Business/Firm for resale at a profit. Thus, when a furniture is purchased for resale then it will be considered goods and when it is purchased for use, it will be considered an asset.

3. What are the divisions of Subsidiary Books?
Ans: The divisions of Subsidiary Books usually maintained by a firm are as follows:
1. Cash book, 2. Purchases Book, 3. Sales Day Book, 4. Purchases Return Book, 5. Sales Return Book, 6. Bills Receivable Book, 7. Bills Payable Book 8. Journal Proper.

4. What are the divisions of goods account ?
Ans: Purchases account, sales account, purchases returns account, sales returns account, stock account and goods sent on consignment account are the divisions of goods account.

5. What do you mean by Trade Discount?
Ans: It is an allowance given by the supplier/manufacture/wholesaler to their retailers. It is generally calculated on the list/catalogue/invoice price, and is deducted from the list price. Trade discount is allowed to all types of transactions i.e., both on cash and credit transactions.

6. What do you mean by invoice?
Ans: Generally, when goods are purchased, a statement is given by the supplier/seller to the buyer about the goods supplied by him which is called Invoice. It contains the price, quantity,

value, make/group of the goods supplied and additional charges charged for carriage, insurance and cost of containers, if any.

7. What type of transactions are recorded in the Sales and Purchases Day Book?

Ans: Sales Day Book is used for recording all transactions regarding credit sale of goods, while Purchases Day Book is used for recording all transactions regarding credit purchases of goods.

8. How is posting made in the Ledger from Purchases Day Book?

Ans: The net amount of invoice (List price–Trade Discount + other charges and Duties) will be posted in the Ledger as follows:

1. Purchases accounts will be debited with the total amount of periodical purchases 2. The total of Packing and Forwarding Charges will also be debited to Packing and Forwarding Charges Account 3. The personal account of the Suppliers will be credited for the total of the above two items.

9. How is posting made in the Ledger from Sales Day Book?

Ans: The net amount of invoice (List price –Ttrade Discount + Other Charges and Duties) will be posted in the Ledger as follows:

1. Sales account will be credited with the total amount of periodical sales 2. Sales Tax Account will be credited by the total of periodical Sales Tax 3. Freight and Packing Charges will also be credited by the total of periodical Freight and Packing Charges 4. The personal account of the customers will be debited by the total of above three items.

10. How is Sales Tax / VAT treated in the books of Accounts?

Ans: Sales Tax/VAT is charged upon the net price (List Price – Trade Discount) as per the government rate and is collected by the Seller from the Customer. At the end of a particular period, the total of Sales Tax column is credited to Sales Tax Account. When it is paid, the Sales Tax Account will be debited for the actual amount paid and Bank Account will be credited. If there is any balance in Sales Tax Account, it will be treated as a Liability and will be shown in the Balance Sheet .

11. What is Debit Note?

Ans: Whenever some goods are returned by a Purchaser to the Supplier, a letter, is sent with it known as **Debit Note,** stating that their account is debited for the goods returned. It contains the date of return, quantity, value, supplier's name and the reasons for such return.

12. What is Credit Note?

Ans: Whenever some goods are returned by a Purchaser to the Supplier, a Debit Note is sent together with the goods. It is a claim raised by the purchaser and when such claim is accepted by the seller, another note is sent to the purchaser known as **Credit Note.** Through a Credit Note, the seller informs his acceptance of the goods and also certifies that customer has been given the due credit for such return.

13. How is posting made in the Ledger from the purchases return book?

Ans: After recording the transaction in the Return Outward Book or Purchases Return Book, Creditor's Account will be debited (for each return) and at the end of the period, Return Outward Account or Purchases Return Account will be credited for the total returns.

14. How is posting made in the Ledger from the Sales Return Book?

Ans: After recording the transaction in the return Inward Book or Sales Return Book, Debtor's Account will be credited (for each return) and at the end of the period, return inward account or Sales Return Account will be debited for the total returns.

III. *Long Answer Type Questions*

1. What do you mean by Subsidiary Books? Name the principal subsidiary books used for recording different transactions and give a brief note of each book.

2. What is the advantage or Utility of subdivision of Journals?

3. What do you understand by Purchase Day Book? Give draft ruling for a Purchase Day Book and enter therein three imaginary entries.

4. What do you understand by Sales Day Book? Give draft ruling for a Sales Day Book and enter therein three imaginary entries.

5. Differentiate between:
   (a) Cash Discount and Trade Discount
   (b) Purchase Day Book and Purchase Account
   (c) Sales Day Book and Sales Account

6. What is a Journal Proper? What types of transactions are recorded through this book? How does it differ from Special Journals?

7. What is the importance of Journal Proper?

8. What are Adjustment Entries? What are the objects of Adjustment Entries? If Adjustment entries are not made, then how does it affect the final accounts of a firm?

9. How do Adjustment Entries differ from Rectification Entries?

IV. *Problems*

Purchase Day Book

1. From the following transactions, prepare Purchase Day Book and close the books at the end of May, 2008:

2008	Transactions

   May 9   Bought from M/s S.D. Traders 12 chests of tea @ Rs. 1,050 per chest, less Trade Discount 5%, plus freight Rs. 780 (as per invoice no. K/09).

   16   Purchased from M/s T.T. Suppliers 16 chests of tea @ Rs. 1,200 per chest, less Trade Discount 6%, plus freight Rs. 960, and excise duty 2% (as per invoice no. MP/12).

   21   Purchased from M/s M.S. & Co. 11 chests of tea @ Rs. 980 per chest less Trade discount 5%, plus freight Rs. 650, and VAT 3 % (as per invoice no. GT/26).

   28   Bought from M/s G.P. Suppliers & Co. 18 chests of tea @ Rs. 1,160 per chest, less Trade Discount 5%, plus forwarding charges Rs. 850, Sales Tax 4% and excise duty 3% (as per invoice no. 12T/GT/10).

   Ans: Total of Purchase Day Book Rs. 65,445.

2. Enter the following credit transactions in the appropriate Day Books of M/s D.K. Enterprise and also close books at the end of the month:

2008	Transactions

   June 7   Purchased from Star Techno ten computer sets @ Rs. 16,300 per set, less Trade Discount 5%, plus freight Rs. 730, and excise duty 4%.

   16   Purchased from K.B.L. Ltd. six computer sets @ Rs. 18,100 per set less Trade Discount 6%, plus Packing Charges Rs. 560, Carriage Rs. 390, VAT 5%.

   22   Purchased from Dark Horse Bros. 11 computer sets @ Rs. 19,200 per set, less Trade Discount 10%, plus freight Rs. 680, Sales Tax 3% and Packing Charges Rs. 50 per set.

   28   Purchased from K.B.L. Ltd. nine computer sets @ Rs. 15,600 per set, less Trade Discount 8%, plus freight Rs. 460, Sales Tax 5% and excise duty 3%.

   Also, show the ledger account postings.

   Ans: Total of Purchase Day Book Rs. 607,548.

3. From the following transactions, prepare a multi-columnar Purchase Day Book:

2008	Transactions

   July 3   Purchased from G.S. Electronics 10 calculators @ Rs. 160 each less Trade Discount 10%, plus freight Rs. 80 and Packing Charges Rs. 30.

11 Purchased 15 albums @ Rs. 120 each, less Trade Discount 5%, plus Sales Tax 2% from B.C. Bros.

15 Purchased from Roy Traders ten tea sets @ Rs. 360 per set, less Trade Discount 5%, plus Carriage Rs. 280 and special Packing Charges Rs. 300.

24 Purchased from B.K. Plastics 15 dozen plastic jars @ Rs. 180 per dozen, less Trade Discount 10%, plus carriage Rs. 180 and Sales Tax 4%.

28 Purchased five electric irons @ Rs. 310 each, less Trade Discount 5%, plus Sales Tax 5%, Packing and freight Rs. 150 from G.C. Electricals.

Ans: Total of Purchase Day Book Rs. 12,243.

4. Record the following transactions in the Purchase Day Book of M/S K.K. Traders and post them in Ledger Accounts:

2008   **Transactions**

Aug. 4 Purchased from Khanna & Sons 150 bags of cement @ Rs. 180 per bag, less Trade Discount 5%, plus Coolie charges Rs. 5 per bag, Carriage Rs. 480 and Sales Tax 3%.

10 Purchased from Sunrise Traders 220 bags of cement @ Rs. 190 per bag, less Trade Discount 10%, plus Coolie charges Rs. 4 per bag, Carriage Rs. 600 and Sales Tax 3%.

19 Purchased 300 bags of cement @ Rs. 210 per bag, less trade discount 5%, plus Coolie charges Rs. 600, Freight Rs. 900 and Sales Tax 4% from P.P.L. & Sons.

26 Purchased from S.K. Suppliers 250 bags of cement @ Rs. 190 per bag, less Trade Discount 10%, plus Freight charges Rs. 5 per bag, Excise duty 2% and Sales Tax 5%.

31 Purchased 110 bags of cement @ Rs. 195 per bag, less Trade Discount 10%, plus Forwarding charges Rs. 600, and Sales Tax 3% from M/s Camak & Sons.

Ans: Total of Purchase Day Book Rs. 195,919.

5. Enter the following transactions in the Purchase Day Book:

1997   **Transactions**

Mar. (a) 9.3.97 purchased from Biswas Bros. 350 cases of goods @ Rs. 100 per case less Trade Discount 10%, plus Packing Charges Rs. 280, Sates Tax 5%.

(b) 18.3.97 purchased from Roy Bros. 190 cases of goods @ Rs. 150 per case less Trade Discount 10%, plus Cost of Containers Rs. 950, Forwarding Charges Rs. 220 and Excise Duty 5%.

(c) 27.3.97 purchased from Das & Co. 300 cases of goods @ Rs. 200 per case, less Trade Discount 10%, plus Freight Rs. 350. Postage Rs. 25 and Sales Tax 5%.

Ans: Purchase Day Book Total Rs. 118,675.

6. Write up the Purchase Day Book of Mr. Roy from the following particulars and show their postings into the ledger:

1979   **Transactions**

Jan. 2 Bought from Simla Plastic Co. Ltd. 12 dozens of plastic tubes @ Rs. 7 per dozen.

5 Bought from Bharat Glass Works 25 table glasses @ Rs. 15 each.

10 Bought from Ramkrishna Ltd. 33 mahagony tables @ Rs. 82 each and 5 chairs @ Rs. 63 each.

12 Bought from Sri Ramkrishna & Sons. 11 chairs @ Rs. 30 each less 15% Trade Discount plus Freight Charges Rs. 40.

(Tripura H.S.)

Ans: Total of Purchase Day Book Rs. 3,800.50.

7. From the following particulars prepare Multi-Columnar Purchase Day Book:

1998   **Transactions**

Jan. 7 Purchased from Dutta & Co. 200 kg A-l Tea @ Rs. 160 per kg, less 5% Trade Discount plus Freight Rs. 260 and Sales Tax 5%.

19 Purchased from Khan & Co. 260 Kg A-3 Tea @ Rs. 120 per kg, less 5% Trade Discount plus Forwarding Charges Rs. 230 and Sales Tax 5%.

21 Purchased powder milk from Mother Dairy, 150 kg @ Rs. 80 per kg, less 10% Trade Discount plus Freight Rs. 175 and Sales Tax 5%.

28 Purchased from Roy Bros. 180 kg A-2 tea @ Rs. 140 per kg, less 5% Trade Discount, plus Packing Charges Rs. 240 and Sales Tax 5%.

Ans: Total Purchase Day Book Rs. 100,424.

8. Prepare a Purchase Day Book from the following particulars:

1998	Transactions

Feb. 2 Bought 150 electric fans @ Rs. 300 each from M.S. Traders, less 5% Trade Discount, plus Freight Rs. 390.

7 Bought 200 tubelights @ Rs. 30 each from Bright Electricals, less 5% Trade Discount, plus Sales Tax 5%.

19 Bought 100 fan motors @ Rs. 75 each from R.K. Electricals, plus Forwarding Charges Rs. 150.

Ans: Total of Purchase Day Book Rs. 56,775.

9. Enter the following transactions in the Purchase Day Books of M/s Saha Bros. and Ledger Accounts:

1998	Transactions

Mar. 3 Purchased from Sharma Traders 150 silk sarees @ Rs. 450 each, less 10% Trade Discount, plus Packing Charges Rs. 450 and Sales Tax 5%.

10 Purchased from Mohini Mills 200 pieces of Dhotis @ Rs. 150 each, less 10% Trade Discount, plus Forwarding Charges Rs. 350, Excise Duty 5% and Sales Tax 5%.

19 Purchased from Roy & Co. 200 cotton printed sarees @ Rs.125 each, less 5% Trade Discount, plus Packing Charges Rs. 460, Freight Rs. 250 and Sales tax 5%.

27 Purchased from M/s N. S. Bros. 100 pieces of bed covers @ Rs. 175 each, less 10% Trade Discount, plus Freight Rs. 460 plus Sales Tax 8%.

Ans: Purchase Day Book Total Rs. 137,555.

10. Record the following transactions in the Purchase Day Book:

1998	Transactions

Apr. 5 Bought 150 cases of green tea @ Rs. 120 each from Tata Tea & Co. less 10% Trade Discount, plus cost of containers Rs. 600, Freight Rs. 460, Sales Tax 5% and Excise Duty 8%.

11 Purchased from Nirmal Tea & Co. 125 packets of half dust tea @ Rs.100 per packet, less 5% Trade Discount, plus Forwarding charges Rs. 360 and Sales Tax 5%.

19 Purchased from Asha Tea & Co. 100 kg golden dust tea @ Rs. 95, less 5% Trade Discount, plus Packing Charges Rs. 490, Excise Duty 5% and Sales Tax 5%.

26 Purchased from Saha Bros. 100 cases of green tea @ Rs. 105 each, less 10% Trade Discount, plus Freight Rs. 420, Cost of containers Rs. 400 and Sales Tax 5%.

Ans: Purchase Day Book Total Rs. 53,522.50.

Sales Day Book

11. Dharam Das used to sell his goods @ Rs. 20 per unit on the basis of the trade discount chart mentioned below:

Volume of Sales	Trade Discount Percentage
Up to 100 units	12
101 to 400	15
401 to 1,000	20
1,001 to 2,000	25
2,001 to 4,000	30
4,001 and above	35

His transactions for the month of April, 2008 were as under:

2008   **Transactions**

April 1   Sold to K.K. Bros. 350 units, Freight and Packing Charges Rs. 360.

6   Sold goods to S.S. Suppliers 3,000 units and charged for packing Rs. 600.

11   Sold goods to Dhumal Bros. 900 units, with freight and Packing Charges Rs. 900.

19   Sold goods to Kamath Trading 5,000 units with Packing and Coolie Charges Rs. 1,200.

24   Sold goods to M.G. Khan 1,800 units. Freight and Packing Charges Rs. 690.
Record the above transactions in the appropriate books.

12. From the following particulars of the business of P.P. Traders, record the transactions in the Sales Day Book and post them in the ledger:

Transactions

July 4   Asansol Electrical 2,500 pieces of 100 watt bulbs @ Rs. 9 per piece, less Trade Discount 5%.

12   Sold to Dhar & Sons. 3,000 pieces of 200 watt bulbs @ Rs. 15 per piece, less Trade Discount 10% and cash discount 5%.

20   Sold to Durgapur Electrical 1,500 pieces of 100 watt bulbs @ Rs.8 per piece, less trade discount 7.5% and carrying charges Rs. 300.

[W.B.H.S. Adapted]

Ans: Total of Sales Day Book Rs.73,275.

13. Enter the following credit transactions in the appropriate Day Books of M/s Desai & Sons:

May 1   Sold 20 almirahs at Rs. 3,600 to Howrah Furniture, Trade Discount 5%, Carriage paid Rs. 600.

10   Returned by M/s Pal Bros. two tables at Rs. 2,050 each, Trade Discount at 5% and Freight Charges Rs. 200.

22   Sold ten sofa sets for Rs. 5,200 each to Sarada Furniture, less Trade Discount at 10% and Carriage Charges Rs. 1,000.

30   Sold eight showcase for Rs. 7,500 to Roy & Co., less Trade Discount 5% and Freight Charges Rs. 500.

Ans: Total of Sales Day Book Rs. 174,300 and sales return book Rs. 4,095.

14. From the following transactions prepare a Sales Day Book:

1997   **Transactions**

Mar. 7   Sold to M.S. Traders 125 kg coffee @ Rs. 250, less 10% Trade Discount, plus Packing Charges Rs. 250, Forwarding Charges Rs.175 and Sales Tax 5%.

12   Sold to Sen Bros. 100 Kg of Tea @ Rs. 110 per kg, less 10% Trade Discount plus Packing Charges Rs. 290, Sales Tax 5% and Excise Duty 2%.

19   Sold to S. S. Traders 125 kg of powder milk @ Rs. 75 per kg, less 5% Trade Discount, plus Freight Rs. 250 and Sales Tax 5%.

Ans: Sales Day Book Total Rs. 50,462.81.

15. Enter the following transactions in a suitably ruled Sales Day Book of M/s Sinha Bros.:

1998   **Transactions**

Jan. 8   Sold to Gupta Traders 90 cases of goods @ Rs. 150 each, less 5% Trade Discount plus Freight Charges Rs. 170, Packing Charges Rs. 200 and Sales Tax 5%.

16   Sold to S.K. Constructions 120 cases of goods @ Rs. 180 each, less 8% Trade Discount, plus Forwarding Charges Rs. 400 and Sales Tax 7½%.

27   Sold to M.K. Traders 125 cases of goods @ Rs. 160 each, Less 8% Trade Discount, plus Packing Charges Rs. 340, Freight Rs. 150 and Sales Tax 10%.

29   Sold to Das Bros. 100 cases of goods @ Rs. 200 each, less 5% Trade Discount, plus Coolie Charges Rs. 85, Freight Rs. 360 and Sales Tax 5%.

Ans: Sales Day Book Total Rs. 76,723.65.

16. Enter the following transactions in the Sales Day Book of M/s Kar & Co.:

    1983   **Transactions**

Sept. 1   Sold to Madhusudan & Sons 40 bags of sugar @ Rs. 560 per bag, less Trade Discount @ 5%, paid Freight Rs. 5 per bag as per Invoice no. K/305/83.

    15   Sold to Dock & Co. 120 quintals of molasses @ Rs. 325 per quintal, less Trade Discount @ 10% as per Invoice No. K/218/83, paid Packing Charges Rs. 3,000.

    28   Sold to Khemka Bros. 90 bags of cement @ Rs. 65 per bag, less Trade Discount @ 7½%, paid Coolie Charges Rs. 2 per bag Invoice no. K/405/83.   (W.B.H.S.)

Ans: Sales Day Book total Rs. 62,171.25.

17. Enter the following Credit Sales in a Sales Day Book of a business firm:

    1977   **Transactions**

Dec. 8   Sold 600 sarees to Ghosh & Sons @ Rs. 32 per piece, less Trade Discount 4%.

    15   Sold 1,400 silk shirts to Bharat Bastralaya @ Rs. 37 each, less Trade Discount 4%.

    21   Sold 7 dozens cotton trousers to Gupta & Co. @ Rs. 96 per dozen, less Trade Discount 5%.

    27   Sold 5 dozen handkerchiefs to K. Banerjee @ Rs.18 per dozen, less Trade Discount 5%.

                                                 (Tripura H.S.)

Ans: Sales Day Book total Rs. 68,883.90.

18. Record the following Credit Sales in an Analytical Sales Day Book and also show the Ledger Accounts:

    1998   **Transactions**

April 7   Sold 36 dozen steel jugs @ Rs. 800 per dozen to Ruma Traders, less 10% Trade Discount plus Packing Charges Rs. 190.

    11   Sold 15 dozen steel trays @ Rs. 360 per dozen to Dhar Bros. less 10% Trade Discount, plus Freight Rs. 180.

    19   Sold 25 dozens steel spoons (big) @ Rs. 140 per dozen to Sharma & Sons, less 5% Trade Discount, plus Packing Charges Rs. 120.

    23   Sold 12 dozens steel tiffin boxes @ Rs. 350 per dozen to Biswas & Co. less 5% Trade Discount, plus Freight charges Rs. 320.

    27   Sold 8 dozen steel trays @ Rs. 370 per dozen to Kar Bros. less 10% Trade Discount, plus Packing Charges Rs. 160.

Ans: Sales Day Book total Rs. 41,729.

Retun Outward Book

19. From the following particulars make out the Return Outward Book:

    1998   **Transactions**

Mar. 6   Returned goods to Roy & Co. 30 cases @ Rs. 160 per case, less 5% Trade Discount, for defect.

    11   Returned to Sen Bros. 11 cases @ Rs. 100 per case, *less* 8% Trade Discount for damaged in transit.

    19   Returned to Saha Bros. 16 cases @ Rs. 110 per case, less 10% Trade Discount, goods being not as per sample.

    27.   Returned to Mukti Bros. 9 cases @ Rs. 150 per case, less 10% Trade Discount for goods being of inferior quality.

Ans: Return Outward Book total Rs. 8,371.

20. Enter the following transactions in the Purchase Return Book:

    1998   **Transactions**

Jan. 3   Returned to Sima Electrics 30 pieces of tubelights @ Rs. 31 per piece being defective, less 5% Trade Discount.

11 Returned to Dhar Electrics 18 pieces of fan regulators @ Rs. 50 per piece being not as per sample, less 8% Trade Discount.

17 Returned to Kar Bros. 14 pieces of light brackets @ Rs. 40 each being of inferior quality, less 10% Trade Discount.

24 Returned to Saha Electricals 21 pieces of wooden boards @ Rs. 50 each being damaged in transit, less 10% Trade Discount.

Ans: Return Outward Book total Rs. 3,160.50.

21. From the following particulars make out the Purchase Returns Book:

1998   **Transactions**

Mar. 7 Returned to Gupta Bros. 30 pieces of cotton shirts @ Rs. 90 each, less 5% Trade Discount.

14 Returned to Roy Bros. 25 pieces of cotton sarees @ Rs. 120 each, less 10% Trade Discount, plus Packing charges Rs. 130.

22 Returned to Mukherjee & Sons 40 pieces of terry-cotton garments @ Rs. 180 each, less 10% Trade Discount, plus Freight Charges Rs. 150.

27 Sent a Debit Note for Rs. 210 to Ritz Bros. who overcharged the invoice by mistake.

Ans: Return Outward Book total Rs. 12,235.

Return Inward Book

22. Enter the following transactions in Return Inward Book:

1998   **Transactions**

April 3 Returned from M/s S. S. Bros. 30 shirts (cotton) @ Rs. 60 each, less 5% Trade Discount, plus Packing Charges Rs. 90.

10 Returned from M/s Dutta Traders 26 (cotton) pants @ Rs. 40 each, less 10% Trade Discount.

17 Returned from M/s K.K. Bros. 28 silk sarees @ Rs. 440 each, less 10% Trade Discount, plus Freight Rs. 170.

28 Returned from M/s Mukti Bros. 15 shirts (woollen) @ Rs.190 each, less 10% Trade Discount, plus Packing Charges Rs. 120.

Ans: Return Inward Book total Rs. 16,679.

23. Prepare a Returns Inward Book from the following particulars:

1998   **Transactions**

April 4 Returned by Rupa Traders 18 cases @ Rs. 130 each due to inferior quality, less 5% Trade Discount.

11 Returned by M/s Sakti Traders 12 cases @ Rs. 100 each being out of size, less 2% Trade Discount.

19 Returned by S.S. Traders 90 cases @ Rs. 120 each being damaged in transit, less 5% Trade Discount, plus Packing Charges Rs. 160.

29 Returned by M. K. Bros. 15 cases @ Rs. 90 each due to not being in accordance with their order, less 4% Trade Discount.

Ans: Return Inward Book total Rs. 15,115.

With Multiple Day Books

24. Enter the following transactions in appropriate day books of M/s H.K. Khan:

2009   **Transactions**

Mar. 5 Sold goods to Rupen for Rs. 8,000 and Paid Freight Rs. 240.

13 Purchased goods from S.G. Trader for Rs. 4,800, less Trade Discount 10%.

19 Goods returned by Rupen for Rs. 800.

22 Sold goods to B. Sharma for Rs. 6,400, less Trade Discount 10%.

25 Goods returned to Satyen for Rs. 650.

28   Bought goods from M/s G. Lal for Rs. 6,600, less Trade Discount 10%.

Ans: Total of Sales Day Book Rs. 14,000; Purchase Day Book Rs. 10,260; Sales Return Book Rs. 800 and Purchase Return Book Rs. 650.

25. Enter the following transactions in the respective day book of M/s D.P. Bros.:

2009   **Transactions**

Feb. 11   Bought from M/s S.P. Bros. 340 cases of goods @ Rs. 250 per case less Trade Discount 10%, plus Packing Charges Rs. 900, cost of containers Rs. 1,500, Sales Tax 10% and Excise Duty 5%.

    17   Returned to B.K. Sharma & Co. 20 cases of goods @ Rs. 240 per case, plus Packing Charges Rs. 300 due to damaged goods.

    21   Sold to Jibandas Bros. 12 T.V. sets @ Rs. 4,600 each, less Trade Discount 10% Freight and Packing Charges Rs. 1,600, plus VAT 10%.

    24   Returned by N.P. Traders 25 cases @ Rs. 210 due to goods not being in accordance with their order, Credit Note no. 65C, plus Freight Rs. 120.

    27   Sold to A.G. Bhadra & Sons 22 T.V. sets @ Rs. 4,800 each, less Trade Discount 10% Freight and Packing Charges Rs. 1,400, plus VAT 10%.

Ans: Total of Sales Day Book Rs. 162,192; Purchase Day Book Rs. 90,800; Sales Return Book Rs. 5,370; Purchase Return Book Rs. 5,100.

26. Enter the following transactions in the respective Day Book of M/s Niladri & Sons:

2009   **Transactions**

Mar. 4   Returned to G. Sen 30 cases of goods @ Rs. 360 per case, plus packing charges Rs. 450, due to damaged goods.

    12   Purchased from G.K. Bros. 200 cotton shirts @ Rs. 225 per piece, less Trade Discount 5%, Freight and Packing Charges Rs. 900 and Sales Tax 12%.

    18   Returned by M/s D.P. Jadab 25 cases @ Rs. 140 due to inferior quality, Credit Note no. 41E, less Trade Discount 10%.

    22   Bought from M/s N.K. Saha 350 cases of goods @ Rs. 420 per case, less Trade Discount 10%, plus Packing Charges Rs. 800, Forwarding Charges Rs. 250 and Sales Tax 12%.

    28   Sold to Chattula Bros. 400 cases of goods @ Rs. 450 each, less trade discount 10%, excise duty 5%, packing charges Rs. 650, coolie charges Rs. 150 and sales tax 12%.

Ans: Total of sales day book Rs. 191,240; Purchase day book Rs. 198,006; sales return book Rs. 3,150; and Purchase return book Rs.11,250.

27. Prepare appropriate day books in the books of M/s Sukhram & Co. for recording transactions from the following particulars:

2009   **Transactions**

March 9   Purchased fromD.K. Bros. 240 silk sarees @ Rs.300 per piece, less trade discount 10%, plus VAT 10%.

    15   Returned to S.Hauk 30 cases of goods @ Rs.320 per case, plus packing charges Rs. 800, due to damaged goods.

    23   Returned by Prokash Traders 22 cases @ Rs. 540 due to goods not being in accordance with their order, credit note no. 54D, plus freight charge Rs. 220.

    26   Sold to Roy & Co. 250 cases of goods @ Rs. 400 each, less trade discount 10%, excise duty 5%, packing charges Rs. 450, freight charges Rs. 650 and VAT 10%.

    29   Bought from M/s G.L. Dhara 410 cases of goods @ Rs. 280 per case, less trade discount 10%, plus packing charges Rs. 900, cost of containers Rs. 2,500, forwarding charges Rs. 600, and sales tax/VAT 10%.

Ans: Total of sales day book Rs. 105,100; Purchase day book Rs. 188,932; Sales return book Rs. 12,100 and Purchase return book Rs. 10,400.

Bills Receivable Book

28. Record the following transactions in the Bills Receivable Book:

1998	Transactions
May 1	Received acceptance from Samir for Rs. 9,000 at 3 months.
18	Received acceptance from Anup at 2 months for Rs. 7,000.
21	Received acceptance from Subhas at 4 months for Rs. 4,000.
27	Received acceptance from Nobin at 3 months for Rs. 3,000.

29. S. Sen received the following bills duly accepted during the month of March,1998:

1998	Transactions
Mar. 4	Received a bill from S. Roy at 2 months after date Rs. 5,200.
11	Received a bill from P. Das at 3 months for Rs. 6,000.
17	Endorsed S. Roy's acceptance to G. Dhar.
22	Discounted P. Das's acceptance with the Bank at Rs. 5,850.
26	Received a bill from N. Kar at 4 months for Rs. 3,700.

Biils Payable Book

30. During May 2009 Mr. K. Sen accepted the following bills:

May 5	Acceptance given to Mr. Sujoy Das at 4 months for Rs. 7,000.
11	Accepted a 3 months bill drawn by Mr. D. Gupta for Rs. 4,700.
18	Accepted a bill of exchange of Rs. 5,300 for 4 months in favour of Mr. R. Rudra.
21	Acceptance given to Mr. Sukla at 2 months for Rs. 6,100.
27	Accepted a 3 months bill drawn by Mr. M. Notia for Rs. 3,800.

Record the above transactions in the Bills Payable book of Mr. K. Sen.

31. Record the following transactions in the Bills Payable book of a trader:

2009	Transactions
June 12	Accepted a 4 months bill drawn by Mr. S. Baxi for Rs. 6,700.
19	Acceptance given to Mr. Nilamoy at 3 months for Rs. 5,400.
24	Accepted a bill of exchange of Rs. 3,600 for 2 months in favour of Mr. Prabhu.
27	Accepted a 3 months bill drawn by Mr. G. R. Khan for Rs. 4,500.

32. Record the following transactions regarding bills of exchange issued by Mr. P Some to his suppliers during the month of July, 2009:

2009	Transactions
July 5	Acceptance given to Mr. Kamal at 2 months after date for Rs. 4,800.
14	Accepted a 3 months bill drawn by Mr.R. Raja for Rs. 6,400.
17	Accepted a bill of exchange of Rs. 3,900 for 2 months in favour of Mr. Bhar.
20	A promissory note is given to Mr. Ram for Rs. 2,400 for 90 days.
25	Acceptance given to Mr. Sarkar at 3 months after date for Rs. 5,300.
29	Accepted a 4 months bill drawn by Mr. Suresh for Rs. 5,500 payable at Durgapur.

33. Record the following transactions in the Bills Payable Book of a trader:

2009	Transactions
June 10	Accepted a 3 months bill drawn by Mr. Sundaram for Rs. 4,900.
14	Acceptance given to Mr.Sudip at 2 months after date for Rs. 6,700.
21	Accepted a bill of exchange of Rs. 4,300 for 90 days in favour of Mr. Khan.
28	Accepted a 3 months' after sight bill drawn by Mr. Prasad for Rs. 5,100.

34. Enter the following transactions in the Bills Payable Book of Mr. G. Karmakar:

2009	Transactions
Apr. 9	Accepted a 3 months after sight bill drawn by Mr. Banerjee for Rs. 4,200.
16	Acceptance given to Mr. Nilamoy at 3 months for Rs. 5,900.
23	Accepted a bill of exchange of Rs. 8,500 for 90 days in favour of Mr. Darsan.
28	Accepted a 3 months after date bill drawn by Mr. Sunil for Rs. 7,500.

35. Record the following transactions regarding bills of exchange issued by Mr. Protap to his suppliers during the month of August, 2009:

2009	Transactions
Aug. 15	Accepted a 3 months after date bill drawn by Mr. Jugnu for Rs. 4,900.
20	Acceptance given to Mr. Sen at 2 months' after sight for Rs. 6,800.
26	Accepted a bill of exchange of Rs. 5,200 for 2 months in favour of Mr. Soham.
30	Accepted a 2 months bill drawn by Mr. Darshan for Rs. 7,200.

Problems on opening entries

36. Give Journal Entries for opening of the books from the following information:

Building Rs. 80,000, Machinery Rs. 31,000, Sundry Debtors Rs. 36,000, Sundry Creditors Rs. 27,000, Bills Receivable Rs. 18,000, Bills Payable Rs. 9,000, Cash in hand Rs. 21,300, Cash at Bank Rs. 17,700 and Capital Rs. 168,000.

37. From the following particulars pass the necessary Journal Entries in order to open the books of Roy Bros. as on 1.1.98:

Bank Overdraft Rs. 21,000, Cash in hand Rs. 31,000, Stock in trade Rs. 13,400, Debtors Rs. 27,900, Creditors Rs. 18,200, Furniture Rs. 16,200, Machinery Rs. 26,000 and Capital Rs. 75,300.

38. The Balance Sheet of K.K. Traders as on 31.12.96 is given below:

Liabilities	Rs.	Assets	Rs.
Capital	70,000	Machinery	27,200
Sundry Creditors	22,600	Investment	15,000
Bills Payable	12,400	Debtors	28,900
Outstanding Expenses	2,000	Cash in hand	12,700
		Stock	23,200
	107,000		107,000

Show the Opening Entries as on 1.1.97.

39. From the following Balance Sheet pass the Journal Entries in order to open the books on 1.1.98:

Balance Sheet as at 31.12.97

Liabilities		Rs.	Assets		Rs.
Capital		110,600	Machinery		39,000
Reserve Fund		15,000	Furniture		16,000
Creditors		16,400	Investment		24,000
Outstanding Expenses:			Stock in trade		19,700
Salary	1,700		Debtors	34,000	
Rent	1,300	3,000	*Less:* Reserve		
			for Bad Debt	2,000	32,000
			Cash at Bank		14,300
		145,000			145,000

40. The following is the Balance Sheet of M. Kar as at 31.12.96:

Balance Sheet as at 31.12.96

Liabilities		Rs.	Assets		Rs.
Capital	84,100		Machinery	40,000	
Add: Net profit	28,000		*Less:* Depreciation	2,000	38,000
	112,100		Furniture	21,000	
Less: Drawings	8,000	104,100	*Less:* Depreciation	1,800	19,200
Creditors		19,700	Investment		18,000
Bank Loan		10,000	Closing Stock		17,300
Outstanding Expenses:			Debtors	32,400	
Insurance	1,600		*Less:* Provision		
Rent	1,800	3,400	for Bad Debts	1,600	30,800
			Prepaid Expenses		700
			Cash in hand		13,200
		137,200			137,200

Show the Opening Entries on 1.1.97.

Problems on closing entries

41. From the following Ledger Balances pass the Closing Entries:
Purchases Rs. 48,000, Sales Rs. 72,000, Closing Stock Rs. 18,000, Opening Stock Rs. 13,000, Wages Rs. 4,000, Carriage Inward Rs.3,200, Carriage Outward Rs. 1,700, Advertisement Rs. 1,200, Rent Rs. 4,200, Salaries Rs. 3,600, Debtors Rs. 18,900, Creditors Rs. 9,000, Cash in hand Rs. 15,600, and Capital Rs. 32,400.

42. From the following information prepare Closing Entries for the year ended 31st December, 1988:

	Rs.		Rs.
Advertisement	12,000	Wages	7,500
Purchases	150,000	Commission Paid	4,500
Discount Allowed	1,500	Sales Return	6,000
Opening Stock	30,000	Interest Paid	6,000
Salaries	36,000	Carriage Inward	1,500
Discount Received	4,500	Sales	300,000
Purchase Returns	3,000	Depreciation	10,500
Rent Received	1,500	Closing Stock	45,000

(W.B.H.S.)

43. From the following Ledger Account balances show the closing entries: Opening Stock Rs. 18,000, Purchases Rs. 62,000, Purchase Returns Rs. 1,800, Sales Rs. 116,000, Sales Return Rs. 1,900, Wages Rs. 2,800, Freight Rs. 1,700, Carriage inward Rs. 2,100, Carriage Outward Rs. 1,900, Rent Rs. 2,300, Advertisement Rs. 2,400, Insurance Rs. 900, Discount Allowed Rs. 1,400, Discount Received Rs. 1,800, Commission Received Rs. 1,600, Interest paid Rs. 700, Depreciation Rs. 2,600, Closing Stock Rs. 9,600, Bad debts Rs. 600, Drawings Rs. 2,600 and General Expenses Rs. 840.

Problems on transfer entries

44. Show the Transfer Entries from the following information:
(a) Transfer from Stock A/c Rs. 1,800.
(b) Transfer Rs. 4,000 to Reserve Fund from Profit.
(c) Bad Debts of Rs. 1,900 transferred to provision for Bad and Doubtful Debts.
(d) Debtors include Rs. 700 due from a customer Mr. K. and Creditors include amount due to Mr. K. Rs. 900.
(e) Gross profit transferred to P/L A/c Rs. 48,000.
(f) Drawings of Rs. 6,200 transferred to Capital A/c.
(g) Transfer Rs. 1,200 from K. Roy's A/c to P. Das's A/c.
(h) Net profit transferred to Capital A/c Rs. 31,200.
(i) Mr. X a Debtor agreed to pay Rs. 1,600 to Mr. Y a Creditor.
(j) Transfer from Debtors A/c to Drawings A/c Rs. 3,000.

Problems on credit sale and purchase of assets

45. Give the Journal Entries from the following particulars:
(a) Purchased furniture from Raj & Raj Co. for Rs. 18,000.
(b) Purchased machinery from Kar Bros. for Rs. 26,000.
(c) Sold old furniture to M. Sen for Rs. 2,900.
(d) Sold obsolete machineries to K.K. Traders for Rs. 8,000.
(e) Purchased printing machine from Taru Bros, for Rs. 18,000.
(f) Purchased typewriter from Godrej Co. for Rs. 16,000.
(g) Purchased sheet cabinets from Steel Co. for Rs. 13,200.

Problems on adjustment entries

46. Pass the necessary Adjustment Entries from the following information for the year ended 31.12.96:
  (a) Outstanding Wages Rs. 700.
  (b) Prepaid Rent Rs. 1,600.
  (c) Goods used by proprietor for personal use Rs. 1,400.
  (d) Wages paid includes wages paid for installation of plant Rs. 2,600.
  (e) Depreciation charged on machinery Rs. 2,900.
  (f) Goods distributed as free sample Rs. 670.

47. Give the necessary Adjustment Entries from the following :
  (a) Accrued interest on Investment Rs. 1,900.
  (b) Bad debts to be written off Rs. 640.
  (c) Insurance premium includes proprietor's life insurance premium Rs. 630.
  (d) Sales includes sale of furniture Rs. 2,300.
  (e) Interest on Capital Rs. 680.
  (f) Create provision for bad and doubtful debts Rs. 940.
  (g) Carriage includes carriage paid for purchase of furniture Rs. 600.

48. Pass the necessary Adjustment Entries from the following (year closes on 31.12.78):
  (a) Salary Rs. 1,000 for December 1978 outstanding.
  (b) Interest accrued on investment Rs. 200.
  (c) Rent received in advance Rs. 400.
  (d) Insurance Prepaid Rs. 300.
  (e) Closing Stock Rs. 10,000.
  (f) Depreciate furniture by Rs. 800.

(W.B.H.S.)

49. How would you deal with the following in accounting of a going concern?
  (a) Rent amounting to Rs. 5,000 paid in advance for the next financial year and total rent paid Rs. 20,000.
  (b) Outstanding wages for current year amounted to Rs. 15,000.
  (c) Rs. 2,000 due from Sri Basu, a debtor, is unrealisable from him. Pass Journal Entries to record the above.

(W.B.H.S.)

50. Give the Adjustment Entries of the following items in the Journal of the year ending 31.12.97:
  (a) Insurance premium paid in advance Rs. 750.
  (b) Interest receivable Rs. 480.
  (c) Prepaid Rent Rs. 1,850.
  (d) Charge 10% interest on Capital of Rs. 68,000.
  (e) Bad debts to be written off Rs. 520.
  (f) Depreciation on Machinery Rs. 1,750.

51. Give the Adjustment Entries of the following items for the year ended 31.12.96.
  (a) Closing Stock Rs. 13,200.
  (b) Provide interest on loan @12% p.a. on Rs. 16,000.
  (c) Uninsured goods lost by fire Rs. 3,000.
  (d) Interest on Drawings Charged Rs. 160.
  (e) Carriage includes carrying of machinery Rs. 340.
  (f) Sales includes sale of old machinery Rs. 1,800.

52. Pass the necessary Adjustment Entries of the following:
  (a) Goods costing Rs. 850 distributable as free sample.
  (b) Goods costing Rs. 1,900 destroyed by fire and insurance company admitted a claim of Rs. 1,250 finally.

(c) Repairs charges of building debited to Building A/c Rs. 980.

(d) Outstanding interest on loan Rs. 1,950.

(e) Provide 10% depreciation on typewriter of Rs. 18,000.

53. Make Adjustment Entries for the following:

 (a) Bad debts to be written off Rs. 790.

 (b) Provide Provision for Bad and Doubtful debts @5% on Debtors of Rs. 24,000.

 (c) Provide Provision for Discount on Debtors @2% on Debtors of (b) above.

 (d) Provide Provision for Discount on Creditors @2% on Creditors of Rs. 19,200.

 (e) Commission earned but not received Rs. 640.

54. Journalize the following for necessary adjustment:

 (a) The manager is entitled to a commission of 10% on Net Profit after charging his commission. Net Profit before charging commission was Rs. 18,900.

 (b) Annual insurance premium paid Rs. 2,400 commencing from 1.4.96 (Accounts closed on 31.12.96).

 (c) Rent paid for 15 months Rs. 3,000 upto 31.5.98 (Accounts closed on 31.12.97).

 (d) Rent from sub-letting due but not received Rs. 1,600.

55. Make necessary Adjustment Entries on 31.12.96:

 (a) Mr. X was declared insolvent, Rs. 900 was due from him and dividend realised Rs. 320 only.

 (b) Goods used by proprietor for personal use Rs. 650.

 (c) Unexpired insurance Rs. 610.

 (d) Write off 20% of Goodwill. Goodwill appears in the book Rs. 31,000.

 (e) Closing Stock Rs. 17,000.

56. Pass the necessary Adjustment Entries for the following:

 (a) Travelling Expenses includes proprietor's personal travelling for which he is to be charged Rs. 780.

 (b) Sundry Creditors included a sum of Rs. 900 recovered from a Debtor whose A/c was written off as bad in the previous year.

 (c) Debtors include Rs. 1,300 due from the proprietor.

 (d) An amount of Rs. 1,200 received from Debtor was wrongly credited to Sales A/c.

 Ans: (i) Drawings A/c Dr. and Travelling Expenses A/c Cr. (ii) S/c A/c Dr. and Bad Debts Recovery A/c Cr. (iii) Drawings A/c Dr. and Debtors A/c Cr. (iv) Sales A/c Dr. and Debtors A/c Cr.)

57. Pass the necessary Adjustment Entries for the following:

 (a) A Plant which stood in the books at Rs. 8,000 on 1.1.96 was sold for Rs. 4,900 in exchange for a new machine costing Rs. 7,800 on 1.4.96. The net invoice of Rs. 2,900 was posted through the Purchase Day Books. Depreciate Machinery by 10%. Machinery A/c shows a balance of Rs. 34,000 on 1.1.96.

 Ans: Depreciation on Machinery charged Rs. 3,380; Loss on sale of Machine Rs. 3,100.

58. Give Journal Entries for the following:

 (a) Depreciation on Motor Car whose cost is Rs. 58,000 with accumulated Depreciation Reserve of Rs. 11,600 at 20% p.a. on the diminishing balance.

 (b) Closing Stock in trade Rs. 1,95,000.

 (c) Present Provision of Rs. 7,500 for Doubtful Debts at 5% of Sundry Debtors to be enhanced to 7½%.

 (d) Rs. 750 worth goods drawn by the proprietor from the stocks in the business for his personal use.

 (C.A. Entrance)

11

Bank Reconciliation Statement

CONTENTS

INTRODUCTION

All closing balances of cash in hand and cash at bank are shown in a cash book. Likewise, for the benefit of customers a bank also provides a book or a statement to its customers showing all bank transactions and the resulting closing balance on a certain date. The said book or statement is known as a **Bank Pass Book.** It is a copy of the ledger account of a customer in the bank books. For the cash deposited by a customer and for all the incomes or receipts collected by the bank on behalf of the customer, the respective customer's account is credited by the bank. Similarly, for cash withdrawn by a customer and for all payments made by the bank on behalf of the customer, the respective customer's account is debited by the bank. At the end of a certain period, the trader or the account holder tallies this Pass Book with the Cash Book from where he is able to understand the effect and position of all bank transactions. If all bank transactions recorded in the cash book are equally recorded in the bank pass book, then both the books will represent identical closing balances. But in practice on a particular date, the balances in both the books are not identical or they do not tally. There are various reasons which cause the difference in the bank balances between these two books on a particular date. Thus, it is the duty of an accountant on behalf of a trader to sort out the causes and identify them for their early settlement. They are explained in detail in the subsequent sections.

11.1 BANK RECONCILIATION STATEMENT

All transactions made through cash or cheques are not recorded simultaneously in the Cash Book and the Pass Book regularly. Some transactions are recorded in the Cash Book first and in the Pass Book later, while others are recorded in the Pass Book first and then in the Cash Book. The causes of differences between these two books have been explained in Section 11.1.1. Hence, on a particular date, both the books do not show identical balances. Therefore, the transactions which appear in any one of the books are actually the main causes of differences/discrepancies. or disagreements. Here lies the problem which a trader or a business has to face. In order to reconcile those differences/ disagreements with the cash book balance or the pass book balance on a particular date, a statement is prepared. This is known as the **Bank Reconciliation Statement.**

To prepare a Bank Reconciliation Statement with the help of the balance of a particular book, the following disagreements have to be considered:

Suppose, the balance of a Cash Book is given and for a particular disagreement (or mistake), if the said balance is

1. less than the Pass Book balance, then the difference is added to the Cash Book balance.
2. greater than the Pass Book balance, then the difference is to be deducted from the Cash Book balance.

All the disagreements are considered as stated above. By preparing a bank reconciliation statement, it is generally confirmed that there are no other undetected causes of differences. This is because when this statement is prepared by taking one of the book's balances as the basis, the result which will be derived after the adjustment of the disagreements will be the other book's balance. But if the resultant balance does not tally with the original balance of the said book, then it indicates that there are still some undetected causes of difference or disagreements or mistakes which are yet to be found out. Here lies the importance of preparing a bank reconciliation statement.

11.1.1 Causes of Differences

The following are the causes of differences between a cash book balance and a pass book balance:

1. **Cheques deposited but not collected or credited by the bank:** When a cheque is paid or deposited in a bank, it is recorded immediately in the cash book, but the bank will credit the customer's account only when the said cheque is actually collected by the bank and not before that. Due to this reason, both the books will not represent identical closing balances, i.e., a difference in the balances between these two books will develop.

2. **Cheques issued but not cashed:** When a cheque is issued or given to a supplier, it is immediately recorded in the cash book but the bank will debit the customer's account only when the said cheque is actually paid to the supplier and not before that. As a result, a difference in the balances between these two books develops.

3. **Bank interest and bank charges not reflected in the cash book:** Interest on bank deposits and commission are first calculated by the bank and then charged by it to the customer's account. Thus, there does not arise any possibility to record these two transactions in the cash book in advance or at the same time. Hence, there is always a gap in recording these two types of transactions in these two books as they are recorded on different dates.

4. **Direct collections or payments on behalf of customers made by the bank:** Due to agency functions different payments are made by a bank on behalf of the customers. Likewise, different receipts/incomes are also collected by the bank as per the standing instructions of the customers. After these transactions/events take place, the bank records these transactions first in it's books and then informs the matter to the customers or sends bank statements to them. After the said information or the statements are received, the transactions are then recorded by the trades in the cash books. Therefore, a difference in the balances between these two books develop due to the recording of transactions at two different times/dates. For example:
   (a) As per instructions bank collected dividend and insurance claims.
   (b) As per instructions bank paid godown rent and insurance premium of the business.
   (c) As per instructions bank honoured a bill.

5. **Errors while recording of transactions in the cash book or the pass book:** In some cases, a difference in balances between the two books arises due to mistakes or errors while recording a particular transaction in any one of the books. For example,
   (a) Debit side of the cash book bank column undercasted by Rs. 100.
   (b) Cheque drawn by another customer but wrongly charged to Trader's Account.
   (c) Credit side of the cash book bank column overcasted by Rs. 100.
   (d) A cheque of Rs. 370 issued and cashed but shown in the cash book as Rs. 730.
   (e) A cheque of Rs. 680 issued and cashed but wrongly shown in the cash book's cash column.
   (f) A cheque paid in the bank but was debited in the pass book.

(g) A cheque of Rs. 150 paid in the bank, duly collected by it but recorded in the cash book as Rs. 510.

(h) An outgoing cheque of Rs. 840 recorded twice in the cash book.

6. **For direct deposits in the bank made by customers or debtors:** There are some cases when cash is deposited by the debtors directly in the bank. For those deposits, the bank balances will increase immediately, but will be reflected in the traders' account only after the bank statement is received. This will develop the difference in the balances between the two books.

11.2 BANK CHARGES

Banks charge a certain amount to their customers' account for the services rendered to them. It is charged through incidental charges, collection charges or as service charges for which the customer's account is debited. This will reduce his account balance or increase the overdraft balance at the bank. Usually, entries are made in the cash book for bank charges after the bank statement is received.

11.3 BANK PASS BOOK/BANK STATEMENT

It is prepared and provided by a bank to its customers (a firm or an individual) regarding the transactions recorded by the bank for a certain period. The book pass book or statement is the identical copy of the transactions recorded by the bank in their own books which are supplied to their customers according to their desires/demands. It shows a customer's account balance on a particular date. The specimen of a bank pass book is given below.

UNITED BANK OF INDIA
(Name of Branch)..........BRANCH
PASS BOOK

ACCOUNT NO. ....
NAME ....
ADDRESS ....

Date	Particulars	Cheque No.	Cheque Date	Withdrawals	Deposits	Balance	Officers' Initials

11.4 ADVANTAGES OF PREPARING BANK RECONCILIATION STATEMENT

1. It helps to control all bank transactions which are not transacted as per requirement or direction. Here, control means follow-up actions to be taken for the said transactions made by the bank.

2. Book Reconciliation Statement helps to calculate the actual cash at bank balance after considering both cash at bank Cash Book and Pass Book.

3. There are a number of cases where cheques are deposited but not collected by the bank, or when cheques are dishonoured but no entry made in the cash book for such dishonours or no steps taken for the uncredited cheques. A Bank Reconciliation Statement helps to highlight such transactions/incidents which help to take appropriate action in due time.

4. In case of issued cheques, there are some creditors or suppliers who fail to cash their cheques in due time. These cheques are identified at the time of preparing the Bank Reconciliation Statement. This helps a trader in taking appropriate action and build a good trade relationship.

5. Bank Reconciliation Statements help to detect the missing transactions and errors while recording the transactions in both the cash book and Pass book.
6. Since the preparation of a Bank Reconciliation Statement is a routine matter, it helps to prevent fraud or misappropriation of cash.
7. At the time of preparing a Bank Reconciliation Statement the names of default customers are identified and highlighted. It helps the management in taking important business decisions in respect of such customers for future transactions

11.5 IS BANK RECONCILIATION STATEMENT AN ACCOUNT?

A Bank Reconciliation Statement is chiefly, prepared to reconcile the differences or disagreements with the cash book or the Pass book balance on a particular date, but it is not an account. The reasons for not considering this statement as an account are listed below:

1. A Bank Reconciliation Statement is prepared at the end of a period or on a particular date as per the desire of the users, but an account is opened and prepared for recording the transactions in a financial year.
2. In order to reconcile the differences or disagreements with a cash book or a Pass book balance on a particular date, a Bank Reconciliation Statement is prepared.
3. The preparation of an account within a ledger is essential, but the preparation of a Bank Reconciliation Statement is not essential.
4. All accounts are part of a ledger which is the principal book of an enterprise, but a Bank Reconciliation Statement is not any part of any ledger.
5. A Bank Reconciliation Statement is only a statement where there is no debit side or credit side like that of an account. Transactions are recorded in an account as per the golden rules of accounting, whereas no transactions are recorded in a Bank Reconciliation Statement. Only the differences, discrepancies or disagreements between a cash book and a Pass book are recorded in a Bank Reconciliation Statement.

11.6 RULES FOR FINDING OUT DISCREPANCIES

When cash book and Pass book balances are given for the same period

In order to prepare a bank reconciliation statement, first the disagreements or differences between a cash book or a Pass book balance on a particular date are found out. Then with the help of the said disagreements or differences, a bank reconciliation statement is prepared. For example,

Cash Book (Bank Columns Only)

Dr.   Cr.

Date	Particulars		Amount (Rs.)	Date	Particulars		Amount (Rs.)
April 1	To Balance b/d		12,800	April 3	By M.F. Rahman	×	3,700
4	To Gupta Bros.	✓	5,000	5	By H.P. Roy	✓	4,800
9	To S.S. Traders	×	6,300	6	By Insurance Premium	✓	5,900
13	To D.G. Basak	✓	4,200	9	By Cash	✓	6,200
19	To Syndicate Co.	×	7,500	11	By Simphony Bros.	×	2,100
26	To Commission	✓	600	17	By A.B. Singhania	✓	3,700
27	To Cash	✓	5,500	21	By N.N. Dhiman	×	4,600
29	To Wall Cat Traders	×	6,400	24	By D.F. Khurana	✓	2,900
				28	By M.L. Khan	×	4,600
				30	By Balance c/d		9,800
			48,300				48,300

UNITED BANK OF INDIA
PASS BOOK

Date	Particulars		Cheque No.	Cheque Date	Withdrawals (Rs.)	Deposits (Rs.)	Balance (Rs.)	Officers Initials
2008 April 1	Opening Balance						12,800	
6	By Gupta Bros.	✓	32678			5,000	17,800	
	To H.P. Roy	✓	54780		4,800		13,000	
9	By F.D. Das	×	81237			6,300	19,300	
	To Insurance Co.	✓	54781		5,900		13,400	
12	To Self	✓	54782		6,200		7,200	
21	By D.G. Basak	✓	61703			4,200	11,400	
	To A.B. Singhania	✓	54784		3,700		7,700	
28	By Commission	✓				600	8,300	
	To D.F. Khurana	✓	54786		2,900		5,400	
	By Interest	×				740	6,140	
	By Dividend	×				4,500	10,640	
	By Cash	✓				5,500	16,140	
29	To Bank Charge	×			50		16,090	
30	To Bills Payable	×			2,500		13,590	

When both the cash book and the bank statement/pass book are given for the same period, the causes of discrepancies are found out first with the help of the list of 'causes of differences'. Then the bank reconciliation statement is prepared. The transactions which appear in both the books are not the causes of differences/discrepancies, but those which appear only in one of the books are the main causes of difference/discrepancies. In the above example tick mark (✓) have been put against the figures which agree in both the books and cross mark (×) against those which do not agree.

List of causes of difference:

1.	Cheques deposited but not credited by bank		
	S. S. Traders	Rs. 6,300	
	Syndicate Co.	Rs. 7,500	
	Wall Cat Traders	Rs. 6,400	Rs. 20,200
2.	Cheques issued but not cashed		
	M.F. Rahman	Rs. 3,700	
	Simphony Bros.	Rs. 2,100	
	N.N. Dhiman	Rs. 4,600	
	M.L. Khan	Rs. 4,600	Rs. 15,000
3.	Debtors deposited directly into bank		
	F.D.Das	Rs. 6,300	
4.	Amount debited by bank		
	Bank Charge	Rs. 50	
	Bills payable	Rs. 2,500	
5.	Amount credited by bank		
	Interest	Rs. 740	
6.	Bank collected dividend as per instruction	Rs. 4,500	

With the help of the above stated causes of difference (1–6), a Bank Reconciliation Statement is prepared as under.

Bank Reconciliation Statement as on April 30, 2008

		Rs.	Rs.
	Bank balance as per cash book		9,800
Add: 2.	Cheques issued but not presented for payment	15,000	
3.	A debtor deposited cash directly into bank	6,300	
5.	Bank interest not shown in the cash book	740	
6.	Bank collected dividend as per instruction	4,500	26,540
			36,340
Less: 1.	Cheques deposited but not collected by bank	20,200	
4.	Amount debited by bank as bank charge and Bills Payable	2,550	22,750
	Balance as per Pass Book		13,590

If we consider the nature of causes/disagreements, we will find that the cash book balance has been reduced for the above stated four items(2, 3, 5 and 6) and hence, has to be added to *make the cash book's balance equal to the Pass book balance.* On the other hand the cash book balance has been increased by two remaining items (1 and 4) and thus has to be deducted to *make the cash book's balance equal to the Pass book balance.*

Guidelines for preparing bank reconciliation statement: The following statement shows the procedure for preparing a Bank Reconciliation Statement and is prepared with the help of the above stated 'List of Causes of Difference' (1 – 6).

Sl. No.	What has happened and what is to be done *As cash book balance is given, all adjustments are made in such a way* *that it would make the cash book's balance equal to the Pass book balance.*	Cash book (Rs.)	Pass book (Rs.)
1.	Present position after this disagreement	+20,200	0
	Due to this disagreement, the cash book balance is greater than the Pass book balance by Rs. 20,200 which is to be deducted.	−20,200	
	Net position after deduction	0	0
2.	Present position after this disagreement	−15,000	0
	Due to this disagreement, the cash book balance is less than the Pass book balance by Rs. 15,000 and hence, it is has to be increased.	+15,000	
	Net position after increase	0	0
3.	Present position after this disagreement	0	+6,300
	Due to this disagreement, the cash book balance has become less than the Pass book balance by Rs. 6,300. The amount was deposited in the bank directly and Thus Rs. 6,300, has to be added to the cash book balance.	+6,300	
	Net position after addition	+6,300	+6,300
4.	Present position after this disagreement	0	−2,550
	Due to this disagreement, the cash book balance has become more than the Pass book balance by Rs. 2,550. Actually the amount was debited by the bank for bank charge and bills payable. Hence, Rs. 2,550 has to be deducted from the cash book balance.	−2,550	
	Net position after deduction	−2,550	−2,550
5.	Present position after this disagreement	0	+740
	Due to this disagreement the cash book balance has become less than the Pass book balance by Rs. 740. Thus, Rs. 740 has to be added to the cash book balance.	+740	
	Net position after the addition	+740	+740
6.	Present position after this disagreement	0	+4,500
	Due to this disagreement, the cash book balance has become less than the Pass book balance by Rs. 4,500. Therefore, Rs. 4,500 has to be added to the cash book balance.	+4,500	
	Net position after the addition.	+4,500	+4,500

The above statement shows the items which are added or deducted from the cash book balance and the reasons for such additions or deductions while preparing a Bank Reconciliation Statement.

When cash book and pass book balances are given for successive periods

Dr.						**Cash Book (Bank Columns Only)**		Cr.
Date	Particulars		Amount (Rs.)	Date	Particulars			Amount (Rs.)
April 1	To Balance b/d		18,700	April 3	By N.P. Saha (976)			5,700
6	To Mohan & Co. (574)		3,900	7	By G.R. Ram (977)			4,800
9	To S.P. Jain (923)		4,500	11	By Gupta Bros. (978)			6,400
15	To Cash		5,100	14	By Tilak Sharma (979)	×		3,800
19	To N. Mukhati (321)	×	2,700	18	By Madhu Talwar (980)			9,100
23	To D. Thakkar (638)		4,500	21	By Bittu Raj (981)	×		2,600
28	To S. J. Bros. (476)	×	2,800	27	By Suresh Kumar (982)	×		1,900
	To M. Sharma (989)	×	3,000	30	By Balance c/d			10,900
			45,200					45,200

UNITED BANK OF INDIA
PASS BOOK

Date	Particulars		Cheque No.	Cheque Date	Withdrawals (Rs.)	Deposits (Rs.)	Balance (Rs.)	Officers Initials
May 1	Opening Balance						13,700	
3	By N. Mukhati	×	321			2,700	16,400	
6	To Tilak Sharma	×	979		3,800		12,600	
9	To Rahul Gupta		983		1,500		11,100	
13	By S. J. Bros.	×	476			2,800	13,900	
17	By M. Sharma	×	989			3,000	16,900	
19	To Pratap Sen		984		2,700		14,200	
23	To Suresh Kumar	×	982		1,900		12,300	
25	By D. Lalit		418			11,000	23,300	
26	To Bittu Raj	×	981		2,600		20,700	
28	To Bank Charge				105		20,595	
30	By Interest					940	21,535	

When both the cash book and the bank statement/pass book are given for successive periods, then the causes of discrepancies are found out first with the help of the list of 'causes of differences'. Then the bank reconciliation statement is prepared. The transactions, which appear in both the books, are the main causes of differences/discrepancies. Cross marks (×) are put against the figures which agree in both the books.

List of causes of difference:

1.	Cheques deposited but not credited by bank		
	N.N. Mirja (3421)	Rs. 2,700	
	Syndicate Bros.(476)	Rs. 2,800	
	Mukul Sharma(989)	Rs. 3,000	Rs. 8,500
2.	Cheques issued but not cashed		
	Tilak Sharma (979)	Rs. 3,800	
	Bittu Raj (981)	Rs. 2,600	
	Suresh Kumar (982)	Rs. 4,900	Rs. 11,300

Bank Reconciliation Statement as on May 31, 2008

	Rs.	Rs.
Bank balance as per cash book		10,900
Add: 2. Cheques issued but not presented for payment	11,300	11,300
		22,200
Less: 1. Cheques deposited but not collected by bank	8,500	8,500
Balance as per Pass book		13,700

ILLUSTRATION 11.1 Prepare a Bank Reconciliation Statement from the following particulars as on March 31, 2008:

1. Bank balance as per Cash Book as on March 31, 2008 Rs. 15,800.
2. Cheques amounting to Rs. 3,900 deposited in the bank but bank collected Rs. 2,700 only.
3. Cheques amounting to Rs. 2,800 issued to the creditors out of which Rs. 2,100 only presented for payment.
4. A debtor deposited cash directly in the bank Rs. 900.
5. Bank credited Rs. 1,400 for interest, but not yet entered in the Cash Book.
6. Credit side of the Cash Book bank column undercasted by Rs. 100.
7. As per instruction, bank collected a dividend of Rs. 700.
8. Cheque of Rs. 850 drawn by another customer but wrongly charged to trader's account.
9. An outgoing cheque of Rs. 610 recorded twice in the Cash Book.

Solution

Bank Reconciliation Statement as on March 31, 2008

		Rs.	Rs.
	Bank balance as per cash book		15,800
Add: 3.	Cheques issued but not presented for payment	700	
4.	A debtor deposited cash directly in the bank	900	
5.	Bank interest not shown in the cash book	1,400	
7.	Bank collec.. d dividend as per instruction	700	
9.	One outgoing cheque recorded twice in the cash book	610	4,310
			20,110
Less: 2.	Cheques deposited but not collected by bank (Rs. 3,900 – Rs. 2,700)	1,200	
6.	Credit side of the cash book bank column undercast	100	
8.	Cheque drawn by another customer but wrongly charged to trader's account	850	2,150
	Balance as per pass book		17,960

If we consider the nature of causes/disagreements, we will find that cash book balance has been reduced for the above stated five items (3, 4, 5, 7 and 9) and hence, added to *make the cash book's balance equal to the pass book balance*. On the other hand, the cash book balance has been increased by three remaining items (2, 6 and 8) and hence, deducted.

The following statement shows the treatments (add or less) of various disagreements within the Bank Reconciliation Statement and the reasons for such treatments:

Sl. No.	What has happened and what is to be done (As cash book balance is given, all adjustments are made in such a way that it would make the cash book's balance equal to the pass book balance)	Cash book (Rs.)	Pass book (Rs.)
2.	Present position after this disagreement Due to this disagreement, the cash book balance has become greater than the pass book balance by Rs. 1,200 which is to be deducted.	+3,900 −1,200	+2,700
	Net position after deduction	+2,700	+2,700
3.	Present position after this disagreement Due to this disagreement, the cash book balance has become less than the pass book balance by Rs. 700 and hence, it has to be increased.	−2,800 +700	−2,100
	Net position after the increase	−2,100	−2,100
4.	Present position after this disagreement Due to this disagreement, the cash book balance has become less than the pass book balance by Rs. 900. The amount was deposited in the bank directly for which Rs. 900 has to be added to the cash book balance.	0 +900	+900
	Net position after the addition	+900	+900
5.	Present position after this disagreement Due to this disagreement, the cash book balance has become less than the pass book balance by Rs. 1,400. The amount was credited by the bank for interest. Thus, Rs. 1,400 has to be added to the cash book balance.	0 +1,400	+1,400
	Net position after the addition	+1,400	+1,400
6.	Present position after this disagreement Due to this disagreement, the cash book balance has become greater than the pass book balance by Rs. 100. Thus, Rs. 100 has to be deducted from the cash book balance.	+100 −100	0
	Net position after deduction	0	0
7.	Present position after this disagreement Due to this disagreement, the cash book balance has become less than the pass book balance by Rs. 700. Hence, the cash book balance has to be increased by Rs. 700.	0 +700	+700
	Net position after the increase	+700	+700
8.	Present position after this disagreement Due to this disagreement, the Pass book balance has become less than the cash book balance by Rs. 850. Hence, Rs. 850 has to be deducted from the cash book balance.	0 −850	−850
	Net position after deduction	−850	−850

(Contd.)

Sl. No	What has happened and what is to be done (As cash book balance is given, all adjustments are made in such a way that it would make the cash book's balance equal to the pass book balance)	Cash book (Rs.)	Pass book (Rs.)
9.	Present position after this disagreement Due to this disagreement, the cash book balance has become less than the pass book balance by Rs. 610. Therefore, the cash book balance has to be increased by Rs. 610.	– 1,220 + 610	– 610
	Net position after the increase	– 610	– 610

ILLUSTRATION 11.2 Gupta Traders submits the following particulars for preparing their Bank Reconciliation Statement as on January 31, 2008:

1. Bank balance as per Cash Book as on January 31, 2008 Rs. 28,400.
2. Cheques of Rs. 700, Rs. 800, Rs. 1,200 and Rs. 1,600 paid to the bank, out of which the bank collected the cheques of Rs. 800 and Rs. 1,600 only.
3. Cheques amounting to Rs. 2,850 drawn in favour of suppliers, out of which a creditor presented a cheque of Rs. 980 for payment on February 4, 2008.
4. Credit side of the Cash Book bank column overcast by Rs. 200.
5. As per instructions, the bank collected a claim of Rs. 900 from the insurance company.
6. A periodic payment of Rs. 750 made by the bank under standing instructions not entered in the cash book.
7. A cheque of Rs. 450 deposited in the bank and duly credited it but not recorded in the cash book.
8. A party's cheque of Rs. 570 returned dishonoured as per bank statement but not reflected in the cash book.
9. A cheque of Rs. 650 drawn on the trader's Personal Savings A/c but was wrongly shown in the cash book.
10. A cheque of Rs. 750 issued and cashed but was wrongly shown in the cash book as Rs. 570.
11. A cheque of Rs. 20,350 issued and cashed but was omitted to be recorded in the cash book.

Solution

In the Books of Gupta Traders
Bank Reconciliation Statement as on January 31, 2008

		Rs.	Rs.
Bank balance as per cash book			28,400
Add: 3.	Cheque issued but not presented for payment till January 31, 2008	980	
4.	Credit side of the Cash Book bank column overcasted	200	
5.	Insurance claim collected by bank	900	
7.	Cheque deposited and duly credited by bank, but not shown in the cash book	450	
9.	Cheque drawn on trader's Personal Savings A/c but wrongly shown in the cash book.	650	3,180
			31,580
Less: 2.	Cheques deposited but not collected by bank	1,900	
6.	A periodic payment made by bank under standing instruction	750	
8.	A deposited cheque became dishonoured, but not shown in the cash book	570	
10.	An issued cheque of Rs. 750 shown in the cash book as Rs. 570	180	
11.	Cheque issued and cashed but omitted to be recorded in the cash book.	20,350	23,750
	Balance as per Pass Book		7,830

The following statement shows the treatments (Add or Less) of various disagreements within the Bank Reconciliation Statement and the reasons for such treatments:

Sl. No.	What has happened and what is to be done (As the cash book balance is given, all adjustments are to be made in such a way that it would make the cash book's balance equal to the Pass book balance)	Cash book (Rs.)	Pass book (Rs.)
2.	Present position after this disagreement Due to this disagreement, the cash book balance has become move than the pass book balance by Rs. 1,900 which has to be deducted.	+4,300 –1,900	+2,400
	Net position after the deduction	+2,400	+2,400

(Contd.)

Sl. No.	What has happened and what is to be done (As the cash book balance is given, all adjustments are to be made in such a way that it would make the cash book's balance equal to the Pass book balance)	Cash book (Rs.)	Pass book (Rs.)
3.	Present position after this disagreement Due to this disagreement, the cash book balance has been reduced by Rs. 2,850, but the pass book balance was reduced by Rs. 1,870 (Rs. 2,850 − Rs. 980) only. Thus, the cash book balance is actually less than the pass book balance by Rs. 980 and hence it has to be increased.	−2,850 +980	−1,870
	Net position after the increase	−1,870	−1,870
4.	Present position after this disagreement Due to this disagreement, the cash book balance has become less than the Pass book balance by Rs. 200 at the time of casting. Thus, Rs. 200 has to be added to the cash book balance.	−200 +200	0
	Net position after the addition	0	0
5.	Present position after this disagreement Due to this disagreement, the cash book balance becomes less than the Pass book balance by Rs. 900. The amount was credited by the bank after collecting insurance claim from the Insurance Co. Hence, Rs. 900 has to be added to the cash book balance.	0 +900	+900
	Net position after the addiiton	+900	+900
6.	Present position after this disagreement Due to this disagreement, the cash book balance is greater than the Pass book balance by Rs. 750. Hence, Rs. 750 has to be deducted from the cash book balance.	0 −750	−750
	Net position after deduction	−750	−750
7.	Present position after this disagreement Due to this disagreement, the cash book balance became lesser than the pass book balance by Rs. 450. Thus, the cash book balance has to be increased by Rs. 450.	0 +450	+450
	Net position after the increase	+450	+450
8.	Present position after this disagreement Due to this disagreement, the cash book balance was increased than the pass book balance by Rs. 570. Thus, the cash book balance has to be reduced by Rs. 570.	+570 −570	0
	Net position after the reduction	0	00
9.	Present position after this disagreement Due to this disagreement, the cash book balance was reduced by Rs. 650 than the pass book balance. Hence, the cash book balance has to be increased by Rs. 650.	−650 +650	0
	Net position after the increase	0	0
10.	Present position after this disagreement Due to this disagreement, the cash book balance was increased by Rs. 180 (Rs. 750 − Rs. 570) than the pass book balance. Hence, the cash book balance has to be reduced by Rs. 180.	−570 −180	−750
	Net position after the reduction	−750	−750
11.	Present position after this disagreement Due to this disagreement, the cash book balance was increased by Rs. 20,350 than the pass book balance. Hence, the cash book balance has to be reduced by Rs. 20,350.	0 −20,350	−20,350
	Net position after the reduction	−20,350	−20,350

ILLUSTRATION 11.3 From the following information, prepare a Bank Reconciliation Statement of Mr. M. Chadda as on June 30, 2008:

1. Balance as per pass book as on June 30, 2008 Rs. 16,200.
2. Debit side of the cash book bank column overcasted by Rs. 100.
3. Bank credited Mr. M. Chadda's account by error Rs. 690.
4. A cheque of Rs. 600 deposited in the bank and duly credited, but shown in the cash book as Rs. 60 only.
5. A cheque of Rs. 390 shown in the cash book as deposited in the bank, but was wrongly kept inside the cash box.

6. As per instructions bank honoured a bill of Rs. 740.
7. Bank charge Rs. 75 recorded twice in the cash book.

Solution

Bank Reconciliation Statement of Mr. M. Chadda as on June 30, 2008

	Rs.	Rs.
Balance as per pass book as on June 30, 2008		16,200
Add: 2. Debit side of the cash book bank column overcast	100	
5. A cheque of Rs. 390 shown in the cash book as deposited into bank, but not sent to bank	390	
6. As per instructions bank honoured a bill.	740	1,230
		17,430
Less: 3. Bank credited trader's account wrongly	690	
4. A deposited cheque of Rs. 600 recorded in the cash book as Rs. 60	540	
7. Bank charge Rs. 75 recorded twice in the cash book.	75	1,305
Bank balance as per Cash Book		16,125

ILLUSTRATION 11.4 Prepare a Bank Reconciliation Statement from the following information as on March 31, 2008:

1. Balance as per pass book as on March 31, 2008 Rs. 21,700.
2. Cheques of Rs. 1,900 drawn but presented for encashment after March 31, 2008.
3. A party's cheque of Rs. 1,700 returned dishonoured as per bank statement, but not reflected in the cash book.
4. A cheque of Rs. 650 issued and cashed duly, but was not recorded in the cash book.
5. Uncredited cheques amounted to Rs. 1,400.
6. A bill of Rs. 1,500 discounted with the bank at Rs. 1,430, but shown in the cash book without deducting the discount charge.
7. A cheque of Rs. 670 issued and cashed duly, but shown in the cash book as paid into bank.
8. Credit side of the cash book bank column undercast by Rs. 200.

Solution

Bank Reconciliation Statement as on March 31, 2008

	Rs.	Rs.
Balance as per pass book as on March 31, 2008		21,700
Add: 3. Deposited cheque became dishonoured, but not reflected in the cash book	1,700	
4. An issued cheque cashed duly, but not recorded in the cash book	650	
5. Cheques deposited but not credited by the bank	1,400	
6. A discounted bill recorded in the cash book without deducting the discount charge (Rs. 1,500 – Rs. 1,430)	70	
7. An issued cheque of Rs. 670 recorded in the cash book as deposited into bank wrongly (Rs. 670 + Rs. 670)	1,340	
8. Credit side of the cash book bank column undercasted.	200	5,360
		27,060
Less: 2. Cheques drawn but presented for encashment after March 31.	1,900	1,900
Bank balance as per Cash Book		25,160

ILLUSTRATION 11.5 From the following information, prepare a Bank Reconciliation Statement of Mr. Vishal Roy as on May 31, 2008:

1. Balance as per pass book as on May 31, 2008 Rs. 18,400.
2. A debit of Rs. 90 entered in the bank statement but does not appear in the cash book.
3. A cheque of Rs. 375 issued and cashed but wrongly shown in the cash book cash column.
4. A credit note for Rs. 920 received from the bank was wrongly recorded in the cash book debit side as Rs. 290.

5. Cheques drawn but presented for encashment after May 31, 2008 Rs. 1,900.
6. Uncredited cheques amounted to Rs. 3,100.
7. Interest on bank deposits not shown in the cash book Rs. 230.

Solution

Bank Reconciliation Statement of Mr. Vishal Roy as on May 31, 2008

	Rs.	Rs.
Balance as per Pass Book as on May 31, 2008		18,400
Add: 2. A debit of Rs. 90 entered in the bank statement but does not appear in the cash book	90	
3. A cheque of Rs. 375 issued and cashed but wrongly shown in the cash book cash column	375	
6. Uncredited cheques amounted to Rs. 3,100	3,100	3,565
		21,965
Less: 4. A credit note received for Rs. 920 from the bank but wrongly recorded in the cash book debit side as Rs. 290 (Rs. 920 – Rs. 290)	630	
5. Unpresented cheques amounted to Rs. 1,900	1,900	
7. Interest on bank deposits not shown in the cash book.	230	2,760
Bank balance as per Cash Book		19,205

ILLUSTRATION 11.6 Prepare a Bank Reconciliation Statement from the following information as on March 31, 2008:

1. Bank balance as per Cash Book as on March 31, 2008 Rs. 31,600.
2. A party's cheque of Rs. 750 was returned by the bank marked as 'insufficient funds, return to drawer', but no correction had been made in the cash book.
3. A debtor settled his account of Rs. 980 by paying cash of Rs. 950 which was deposited into bank immediately, but was shown in the cash book without deducting the discount charges.
4. Bank commission Rs. 60 debited in the cash book wrongly.
5. A cheque of Rs. 760 deposited and duly credited by bank, but shown in the cash book as Rs. 670.
6. Cheque amounting to Rs. 550 drawn by a customer but wrongly charged to the trader's account .
7. Bank interest Rs. 320 and bank charge Rs. 40 not shown in the cash book.
8. Cheques amounting to Rs. 5,800 deposited in the bank but bank failed to collect Rs. 1,400.

Solution

Bank Reconciliation Statement as on March 31, 2008

	Rs.	Rs.
Bank balance as per Cash Book as on March 31, 2008		31,600
Add: 5. Deposited cheque of Rs. 760 recorded in the cash book as Rs. 670	90	
7. Bank interest not shown in the cash book.	320	410
		32,010
Less: 2. Deposited cheque became dishonoured, but not shown in the cash book	750	
3. Discount allowed to a debtor Rs. 30, but shown in the cash book without deducting the discount charges	30	
4. Bank commission Rs. 60 debited in the cash book wrongly (Rs. 60 + Rs. 60)	120	
6. Cheque drawn by another customer but wrongly charged to trader's account	550	
7. Bank charge not shown in the cash book	40	
8. Uncredited cheques amounted to Rs 1,400.	1,400	2,890
Balance as per Pass Book		29,120

ILLUSTRATION 11.7   The following are the causes of discrepancies between cash book balance and pass book balance as on May 31, 2008:

Prepare a statement on that day reconciling the discrepancies.

1. A bill of Rs. 2,400 discounted with the bank at Rs. 2,150, but shown in the cash book without deducting the discount.
2. A cheque of Rs. 650 deposited into bank, but wrongly debited by bank.
3. As per instructions, bank honoured a bill of Rs. 950 and paid godown rent of Rs. 550.
4. An issued cheque of Rs. 650 became dishonoured, but recorded in the cash book that a deposited cheque became dishonoured.
5. An outgoing cheque of Rs. 450 recorded twice in the cash book.
6. A cheque of Rs. 700 issued and cashed but not to be recorded in the cash book.
7. Credit side of the cash book bank column overcast by Rs. 200.
8. A cheque of Rs. 850 deposited and credited by bank duly, but shown in the cash book as Rs. 580.
9. Balance as per Cash Book as on May 31, 2008 Rs. 24,800.

Solution

Bank Reconciliation Statement as on May 31, 2008

	Rs.	Rs.
Bank balance as per Cash Book as on May 31, 2008		24,800
Add: 4. An issued cheque of Rs. 650 became dishonoured, but recorded in the cash book as deposited cheque became dishonoured (Rs. 650 + Rs. 650)	1,300	
5. An outgoing cheque of Rs. 450 recorded twice in the cash book	450	
7. Credit side of the cash book bank column overcasted by Rs. 200	200	
8. A cheque of Rs. 850 deposited and credited by bank duly, but shown in the cash book as Rs. 580 (Rs. 850 – Rs. 580).	270	2,220
		27,020
Less: 1. A bill of Rs. 2,400 discounted with the bank at Rs. 2,150, but shown in the cash book without deducting the discount (Rs. 2,400 – Rs. 2,150)	250	
2. Deposited cheque debited by bank (Rs. 650 + Rs. 650)	1,300	
3. As per instructions, bank honoured a bill of Rs. 950 and paid go-down rent of Rs. 550 (Rs. 950 + Rs. 550)	1,500	
6. A cheque of Rs. 700 issued and cashed but not recorded in the cash book.	700	3,750
Balance as per pass book		23,270

ILLUSTRATION 11.8   Prepare a Bank Reconciliation Statement from the following information as on March 31, 2008:

1. Balance as per pass book as on March 31, 2008 Rs. 23,600.
2. A cheque of Rs. 580 issued and cashed, but wrongly shown in the cash book cash column.
3. An issued cheque of Rs. 550 became dishonoured but the cash book record shows that a deposited cheque had become dishonoured.
4. A debit balance of Rs. 10,400 for the month of February, 2008 was shown in the cash book as a credit balance on March 1, 2008.
5. A debtor deposited cash of Rs. 3,100 directly in the bank.
6. Cheques for Rs. 600, Rs. 850 and Rs. 1,250 paid to the bank, but bank credited the cheque of Rs. 1,250 on April 3, 2008.
7. Interest on investment of Rs. 750 c llected by bank, but not shown in the cash book.
8. Debit side of the cash book bank column overcast by Rs. 100.
9. A bill of Rs. 2,600 receivable due on March 27, 2008 was sent to bank for collection on March 24, 2008 and was entered in the cash book forthwith, but the proceeds were not credited in the bank pass book till July 2, 2008.

Solution

Bank Reconciliation Statement as on March 31, 2008

	Rs.	Rs.
Balance as per Pass Book as on March 31, 2008		23,600
Add: 2. A cheque of Rs. 580 issued and cashed, but wrongly shown in the cash book cash column	580	
6. Cheque deposited but not credited by bank	1,250	
8. Debit side of cash book bank column overcast by Rs. 100.	100	1,930
		25,530
Less: 3. A dishonoured issued cheque shown in the Cash Book as deposited cheque dishonoured (Rs. 550 + Rs. 550)	1,100	
4. A debit balance of Rs. 10,400 for the month of February, 2008 was shown in the cash book as a credit balance on March 1, 2008	20,800	
5. A debtor deposited cash of Rs. 3,100 directly into bank	3,100	
7. Interest on investment collected by bank, but not shown in the cash book	750	
9. Bills receivable not collected by bank.	2,600	28,350
Overdraft balance as per Cash Book		2,820

ILLUSTRATION 11.9   Prepare a Bank Reconciliation Statement from the following information as on March 31, 2008:

1. Bank balance as per Cash Book as on March 31, 2008 Rs. 24,980.
2. A party's cheque of Rs. 1,200 was returned by bank marked as 'insufficient funds, return to drawer', but no correction had been made in the cash book.
3. An issued cheque of Rs. 650 duly cashed, but shown in the cash book as Rs. 1,650.
4. A cheque amounting to Rs. 3,700 paid to the bank but bank collected Rs. 2,100 on April 2, 2008.
5. Bank interest and bank charge of Rs. 560 and Rs. 120, respectively, not shown in the cash book.
6. A cheque of Rs. 370 drawn by another customer but wrongly charged to Traders A/c.
7. As per instructions, the bank honoured a bill of Rs. 900 and collected a claim of Rs. 2,600 from the Insurance company.
8. Debit side of the cash book bank column overcast by Rs. 100.

Solution

Bank Reconciliation Statement as on March 31, 2008

	Rs.	Rs.
Bank balance as per Cash Book as on March 31, 2008		24,980
Add: 3. An issued cheque of Rs. 650 shown as Rs. 1,650 in the cash book	1,000	
5. Bank interest not shown in the cash book	560	
7. As per instructions, bank collected a claim from the Insurance company.	2,600	4,160
		29,140
Less: 2. Deposited cheque became dishonoured, but not corrected in the cash book	1,200	
4. Cheque deposited but not collected by the bank within March 31, 2008	2,100	
5. Bank charge not shown in the cash book	120	
6. Wrongly charged by the bank to Traders A/c	370	
7. As per instructions, bank honoured a bill	900	
8. Debit side of the cash book bank column overcast.	100	4,790
Overdraft balance as per Pass Book		24,350

When overdraft/overdrawn balance as per cash book or pass book is given

Overdraft/Overdrawn means excess amount withdrawn over the amount deposited in a bank. Thus, it is a liability of a trader which is required to be paid as per the terms of the bank. For preparing a Bank Reconciliation Statement in case of an overdraft balance at bank, the impact of all disagreements or differences or discrepancies or mistakes are considered as following:

1. Suppose, a cheque of Rs. 500 is deposited in a bank, but is not credited by it. In case of favourable balance at bank, the cash book balance is greater than the pass book balance by Rs. 500 due to this disagreement. On the other hand, in case of overdraft balance at bank, the cash book balance would be less than the pass book balance due to this disagreement, i.e., the pass book overdraft balance would be greater than the cash book overdraft balance. This is because when a cheque/cash is deposited into bank it is assumed that it will reduce the customer's liability at bank. Hence, the overdraft balance as per cash book will reduce by Rs. 500, but the liability as per pass book will remain as before, i.e., there will be no change. As a result, the pass book's liability or balance would be greater than that of cash book's.

2. A debtor deposited cash of Rs. 600 directly in a bank. Normally, it would have increased his bank balance. But in case of an overdraft balance, it will reduce the liability at bank and as such the overdraft balance as per cash book would be greater than the pass book balance.

Under such circumstances, adjustments are made as under.

		Cash book overdraft balance is given (Rs.)	Pass Book overdraft balance is given (Rs.)
1.	Suppose, a cheque of Rs. 500 deposited in the bank, but not credited by the it.	*Add:* Rs. 500 (As cash book overdraft balance is less than the pass book balance)	*Less:* Rs. 500 (As pass book overdraft balance is greater than the cash book balance)
2.	A debtor deposited cash of Rs. 600 directly to the bank, but not recorded in the cash book.	*Less:* Rs. 600 (As cash book overdraft balance is greater than the pass book balance)	*Add:* Rs. 600 (As pass book overdraft balance is less than the cash book balance)

11.7 GENERAL GUIDELINES TO SOLVE THE PROBLEMS

For preparing the Bank Reconciliation Statement, the treatment of different mistakes or disagreements in the Cash Book and Pass Book are to be made as follows:

Nature of the items or disagreements	In case of favourable balances			In case of overdraft balances		
	Effects of disagreements or mistakes (Rs.)	*Cash book Dr. bal. is given* (Rs.)	*Pass book Cr. bal. is given*	*Effects of disagreements or mistakes* (Rs.)	*Cash book Cr. bal. is given* (Rs.)	*Pass book Dr. bal. is given*
1. A debtor deposited cash directly into bank, not recorded in the cash book.	Pass Book balance is greater than the cash book balance.	Add	Less	It has decreased the pass book balance than the cash book balance.	Less	Add
2. Cheques deposited or paid into bank but not collected by the bank (or not credited by the bank).	Cash book balance is greater than the pass book balance.	Less	Add	Cash book balance is less than the pass book balance.	Add	Less
3. Cheques issued but not cashed or presented for payment.	Cash book balance is less than the pass book balance.	Add	Less	Cash book balance is greater than the pass book balance.	Less	Add

(Contd.)

Nature of the items or disagreements	In case of favourable balances			In case of overdraft balances		
	Effects of disagreements or mistakes (Rs.)	Cash book Dr. bal. is given (Rs.)	Pass book Cr. bal. is given	Effects of disagreements or mistakes (Rs.)	Cash book Cr. bal. is given (Rs.)	Pass book Dr. bal. is given
4. As per instruction, bank collected dividend but not recorded in the cash book.	Pass book balance is greater than the cash book balance.	Add	Less	Pass book balance is less than the cash book balance.	Less	Add
5. Credit side of the cash book bank column undercasted by some amount.	Cash book balance is greater than the pass book balance.	Less	Add	Cash book balance is less than the cash book balance.	Add	Less
6. A periodic payment understanding instruction not recorded in the cash book.	Pass book balance is less than the cash book balance.	Less	Add	Pass book balance is greater than the cash book balance.	Add	Less
7. A cheque deposited and credited by bank but not recorded in the cash book.	Cash book balance is less than the pass book balance.	Add	Less	Cash book balance is greater than the pass book balance.	Less	Add
8. A party's cheque (deposited cheque) returned dishonoured but not reflected in the cash book.	Cash book balance is greater than the pass book balance.	Less	Add	Cash book balance is less than the pass book balance.	Add	Less
9. A cheque issued and cashed but omitted to be recorded in the cash book.	Cash book balance is greater than the pass book balance.	Less	Add	Cash book balance is less than the pass book balance.	Add	Less
10. As per instruction, bank honoured a bill (payment of a bill made by the bank).	Pass book balance is less than the cash book balance.	Less	Add	Pass book balance is greater than the cash book balance.	Add	Less
11. A cheque shown in the cash book as deposited into the bank but was wrongly kept inside the cash box.	Cash book balance is greater than the pass book balance.	Less	Add	Cash book balance is less than the pass book balance.	Add	Less
12. A cheque issued and cashed but shown in the cash column wrongly.	Cash book balance is greater than the pass book balance.	Less	Add	Cash book balance is less than the pass book balance.	Add	Less
13. A bill of Rs. 520 discounted with the bank at Rs. 490 recorded in the book without deducting the discount.	Cash book balance is greater than the pass book balance by Rs. 30.	Less 30	Add 30	Cash book balance is less than the pass book balance by Rs. 30.	Add 30	Less 30
14. A bill of Rs. 950 discounted with the bank at Rs. 910 became dishonoured but not reflected in the cash book. Noting charge incurred Rs. 20.	Cash book balance is greater than the pass book balance by Rs. (950 + 20) = Rs. 970.	Less 970	Add 970	Cash book balance is less than the pass book balance by Rs. 970.	Add 970	Less 970

(Contd.)

Nature of the items or disagreements	In case of favourable balances			In case of overdraft balances		
	Effects of disagreements or mistakes (Rs.)	Cash book Dr. bal. is given (Rs.)	Pass book Cr. bal. is given	Effects of disagreements or mistakes (Rs.)	Cash book Cr. bal. is given (Rs.)	Pass book Dr. bal. is given
15. A cheque drawn by another customer but wrongly charged to Trader's A/c.	Pass book balance is less than the cash book balance.	Less	Add	Pass book balance is greater than the cash book balance.	Add	Less
16. Interest on bank deposits credited in the pass book but not reflected in the cash book.	Pass book balance is greater than the cash book balance.	Add	Less	This item does not arise for overdraft balance.		
17. Interest on overdraft balance debited in the pass book but not shown in the cash book.	This item does not arise for favourable balances.			Pass book balance is greater than cash book balance.	Add	Less
18. Bank charge not recorded in the cash book.	Cash book balance is greater than the Pass book balance.	Less	Add	Cash book balance is less than the pass book balance.	Add	Less
19. A cheque of Rs. 650 deposited into bank but recorded in the cash book as Rs. 560.	Cash book balance is less than the pass book balance by Rs. 90.	Add 90	Less 90	Cash book balance is greater than the the pass book balance by Rs. 90.	Less 90	Add 90
20. An issued cheque became dishonoured not reflected in the cash book.	Cash book balance is less than the pass book balance.	Add	Less	Cash book balance is greater than the pass book balance.	Less	Add

ILLUSTRATION 11.10   Prepare a Bank Reconciliation Statement from the following information as on March 31, 2008:

1. Overdraft balance as per Cash Book as on March 31, 2008 Rs. 14,800.
2. A periodic payment of Rs. 1,400 under standing instructions by bank not entered in the cash book.
3. Bank charge of Rs. 75 recorded twice in the cash book.
4. A cheque of Rs. 650 deposited in the bank and duly credited by it, but not recorded in the cash book.
5. As per instructions bank honoured a bill of Rs. 1,600.
6. A cheque of Rs. 440 drawn by another customer but wrongly charged to trader's account.
7. Cheques amounting to Rs. 2,800 issued to the creditors, out of which only Rs. 2,100 presented for payment.
8. Credit side of the Cash Book bank column undercast by Rs. 100.

Solution

Bank Reconciliation Statement as on March 31, 2008

	Rs.	Rs.
Overdraft balance as per Cash Book as on March 31, 2008		14,800
Add: 2. A periodic payment made by bank as per standing instructions	1,400	
5. As per instructions bank honoured a bill	1,600	
6. Cheque drawn by another customer but wrongly charged to trader's account Rs. 440	440	
8. Credit side of the Cash Book bank column undercast.	100	3,540
		18,340

	Rs.	Rs.
Less: 3. Bank charge recorded twice in the cash book	75	
4. Cheque deposited in the bank and duly credited by it, but not recorded in the cash book	650	
7. Cheques issued but not presented for payment (Rs. 2,800 – Rs. 2,100).	700	1,425
Overdraft balance as per Pass Book		16,915

Working guidelines for preparing the above Bank Reconciliation Statement:

2. This transaction will increase the overdraft balance at bank. As a result, the overdraft balance as per cash book would be less than the pass book balance. Hence, Rs. 1,400 is added.
3. It has increased the overdraft balance of the cash book as compared the pass book balance. Hence, Rs. 75 is deducted.
4. Deposited cheque not recorded in the cash book. Thus, overdraft balance as per cash book is greater than the pass book balance. Hence, Rs. 650 is deducted.
5. As payment has been made by bank, it has increased the overdraft balance of the pass book as compared to that of the cash book. For this reason, the cash book balance is less than the pass book balance. Hence, Rs. 1,600 is added.
6. Trader's account is wrongly charged by the bank. As a result, it has increased the overdraft balance of the pass book. Hence, the cash book balance is less than the pass book balance. Therefore Rs. 440 is added.
7. When a cheque is issued, it will increase the overdraft balance of the cash book automatically and if the said cheque is not presented for payment, then the overdraft balance as per cash book will be greater than the pass book balance. Hence, Rs. 700 is deducted.
8. For this mistake, the overdraft balance of the cash book has been reduces by Rs. 100. As a result, the overdraft balance as per cash book would be less than the pass book balance. Hence, Rs. 100 is added.

ILLUSTRATION 11.11 The following are the causes of discrepancies between the cash book balance and the pass book balance as on July 31, 2008. Prepare a statement on that day reconciling the discrepancies.

1. Overdraft balance as per Pass Book as on July 31, 2008 Rs. 21,700.
2. Cheques of Rs. 500, Rs. 900, Rs. 1,500 and Rs. 1,800 paid to the bank, out of which bank collected cheques of Rs. 1,500 and Rs. 900 only.
3. As per instructions bank collected an insurance claim of Rs. 1,250
4. A cheque of Rs. 390 shown in the cash book as deposited in the bank, but was wrongly kept inside the cash box.
5. Cheques amounting to Rs. 1,900 drawn in favour of suppliers, out of which a creditor of Rs. 650 presented for payment on August 7, 2008.
6. A cheque of Rs. 750 deposited in the bank and also duly credited by it but shown in the cash book as Rs. 705 only.
7. Debit side of the cash book bank column overcast by Rs. 200.
8. A cheque of Rs. 2,700 issued and cashed, but not recorded in the cash book.
9. Interest on overdraft of Rs. 280 not shown in the cash book.

Solution

Bank Reconciliation Statement as on July 31, 2008

	Rs.	Rs.
Overdraft balance as per Pass Book as on July 31, 2008		21,700
Add: 3. As per instructions bank collected an insurance claim	1,250	
5. A cheque issued, but not presented within July 31, 2008	650	
6. A deposited cheque of Rs. 750 shown in the cash book as Rs. 705.	45	1,945
		23,645

(Contd.)

		Rs.	Rs.
Less: 2.	Cheques deposited but not collected by the bank (Rs. 500 + Rs. 1,800)	2,300	
4.	A cheque recorded in the cash book as deposited into bank, but was wrongly kept inside the cash box	390	
7.	Debit side of the cash book bank column overcast	200	
8.	A cheque of Rs. 2,700 issued and cashed but was omitted to be recorded in the cash book	2,700	
9.	Interest on overdraft not shown in the cash book.	280	5,870
	Overdraft balance as per Cash Book		17,775

Working guidelines for preparing the above Bank Reconciliation Statement:

2. Overdraft balance as per Pass Book is greater than the cash book balance. This is because any deposit in the bank will reduce the overdraft balance of the cash book.
3. As bank has collected the claim from the insurance company, it will reduce the overdraft balance at bank. For this reason, the pass book balance is less than the cash book balance. Thus, Rs. 1,250 is added.
4. For this error, the overdraft balance of the cash book has been reduced by Rs. 390 and as a result, the overdraft balance as per pass book would be greater than the cash book balance. Hence, Rs. 390 is to be deducted (Less).
5. When a cheque is issued, it will increase the overdraft balance of the cash book automatically and if the said cheque is not presented for payment, then the overdraft balance as pass book would be less than the cash balance. Hence, Rs. 650 is added.
6. A deposited cheque shown short in the cash book by Rs. 45. As a result, it will increase the overdraft balance of the cash book. For this reason, the pass book overdraft balance would be less than the cash book balance. Thus, Rs. 45 is added.
7. For this error, the overdraft balance of the cash book has been reduced by Rs. 200 and consequently, the overdraft balance as per pass book would be greater than the cash book balance. Hence, Rs. 200 is deducted (Less).
8. An issued cheque not shown in the cash book, but is cashed. It will consequently increase the overdraft balance of the pass book only. Hence, Rs. 2,700 is deducted.
9. It has increased the overdraft balance of the pass book as compared to the cash book balance. Hence, Rs. 280 is deducted.

ILLUSTRATION 11.12   A.B. Roy of Kolkata furnished the following information in order to prepare his bank reconciliation statement as on March 31, 2008:

1. Overdraft balance as per Cash Book as on March 31, 2008 Rs. 19,700.
2. An outgoing cheque of Rs. 850 recorded twice in the Cash Book.
3. As per instructions, the bank collected a dividend of Rs. 1,100.
4. A party's cheque of Rs. 650 returned dishonoured as per bank statement, but not reflected in the cash book.
5. A cheque of Rs. 900 drawn on trader's Personal Savings A/c but was wrongly shown in the cash book.
6. A cheque of Rs. 950 deposited in the bank and duly credited by it but shown in the cash book as Rs. 590 only.
7. Interest on overdraft of Rs. 180 charged by bank, but recorded in the cash book as interest received from bank.
8. A cheque of Rs. 1,350 issued and cashed but wrongly shown in the cash book cash column.
9. An issued cheque of Rs. 450 became dishonoured but shown in the cash book as deposited cheque became dishonoured.

Solution

Bank Reconciliation Statement as on March 31, 2008

			Rs.	Rs.
Overdraft balance as per Cash Book as on March 31, 2008				19,700
Add:	4.	Deposited cheque became dishonoured, but not shown in the cash book	650	
	7.	Interest on overdraft charged by bank, but recorded in the cash book as interest received from bank (Rs. 180 + Rs. 180)	360	
	8.	A cheque issued and cashed but wrongly shown in the cash book cash column.	1,350	2,360
				22,060
Less:	2.	One outgoing cheque recorded twice in the Cash Book	850	
	3.	As per instructions, bank collected dividend	1,100	
	5.	A cheque drawn on trader's personal savings A/c, but wrongly shown in the cash book	900	
	6.	Deposited cheque shown short in the cash book (Rs. 950 – Rs. 590)	360	
	9.	An issued cheque of Rs. 450 became dishonoured but shown in the cash book as deposited cheque became dishonoured (450 + 450).	900	4,110
Overdraft balance as per Pass Book				17,950

ILLUSTRATION 11.13 Prepare a bank reconciliation statement from the following information as on June 30, 2008:

1. Overdraft balance as per Cash Book as on June 30, 2008 Rs. 12,400.
2. Credit balance of Rs. 1,320 for the month of May, 2008 was shown as debit balance on June 1 (in the cash book).
3. Bank interest on overdraft and bank charge of Rs. 410 and Rs. 120, respectively, not shown in the cash book.
4. A cheque of Rs. 1,450 paid to the bank but was wrongly debited in the pass book.
5. Cheques amounting to Rs. 1,870 drawn in favour of suppliers out of which a supplier's cheque of Rs. 900 became dishonoured and another supplier's cheque of Rs. 370 was lost due to pick-pocketing (not cashed).
6. Uncredited cheques amounted to Rs. 1,400.
7. Credit transfer of Rs. 600 not recorded in the cash book.
8. Mr. D. Deol settled his account of Rs. 3,800 by paying a cheque of Rs. 3,730, and it was recorded in the cash book bank column without charging discount.
9. A bill of Rs. 2,980 receivable due on June 27, 2008 was sent to the bank for collection on June 26, 2008 and was entered in the cash book forthwith, but the proceeds were not credited in the bank pass book till July 3, 2008.

Solution

Bank Reconciliation Statement as on June 30, 2008

			Rs.	Rs.
Overdraft balance as per Cash Book as on June 30, 2008				12,400
Add:	2.	Credit balance of Rs. 1,320 for the month of May ,2008 was shown as debit balance on June 1 (Rs. 1,320 + Rs. 1,320)	2,640	
	3.	Interest on overdraft and bank charge not shown in the cash book	530	
	4.	A cheque deposited, but was debited in the pass book (Rs. 1,450 + Rs. 1,450)	2,900	
	6.	Uncredited cheques	1,400	
	8.	Discount allowed to Mr. D. Deol but not deducted (Rs. 3,800 – Rs. 3,730)	70	
	9.	A bill sent for collection, but wrongly entered in the cash book.	2,980	10,520
				22,920
Less:	5.	Cheques issued but not cashed (Rs. 900 + Rs. 370)	1,270	
	7.	Credit transfer of Rs. 600 not recorded in the cash book.	600	1,870
Overdraft balance as per Pass Book				21,050

ILLUSTRATION 11.14 The following are the entries recorded in the bank column of the cash book of Mr. Satish Kashyap for the month of March 31, 2008:

Dr.			Cash Book (Bank Column)			Cr.
Date	Particulars	Amount (Rs.)	Date	Particulars		Amount (Rs.)
2008			2008			
March 4	To Mr. Kumar	1,700	March 1	By Balance b/d		13,900
9	To Mr. B.R. Rakshit	3,600	7	By Mr. Murali		950
14	To Mr. Rohani	2,700	12	By Mr. C.K. Dhoon		1,800
19	To Mr. Chandra	4,500	15	By Mr. M.M. Bhimani		3,400
26	To Mr. Rubal	2,900	21	By Bills Payable		4,650
31	To Balance c/d	14,100	28	By Mr. Ashoke Ray		5,000
		29,500				29,500

On March 31, 2008, Mr. Satish Kashyap received the bank statement from UBI. On perusal of the statement, he ascertained the following information:

1. Cheques issued to Mr. M.M. Bhimani and Mr. Murali during March not yet cashed.
2. Cheques of Mr. B.R. Rakshit and Mr. Chandra deposited but not yet credited by the bank.
3. Insurance claim collected by the bank but not shown in the cash book Rs. 900.
4. Interest on overdraft Rs. 240 and bank charge Rs. 130 not shown in the cash book.
5. Credit side of the cash book bank column undercasted by Rs. 200.

From the above information, prepare a Bank Reconciliation Statement to ascertain the balance as per the bank statement.

Solution

Bank Reconciliation Statement as on March 31, 2008

	Rs.	Rs.
Overdraft balance as per Cash Book as on March 31, 2008		14,100
Add: 2. Cheques deposited but not yet credited by the bank (Rs. 3,600 + Rs. 4,500)	8,100	
4. Interest on overdraft and bank charge not shown in the cash book.	370	
5. Credit side of the cash book bank column undercasted (Note.)	200	8,670
		22,770
Less: 1. Cheques issued but not yet cashed (Rs. 3,400 + Rs. 950)	4,350	
3. Insurance claim collected by the bank.	900	5,250
Overdraft balance as per Pass Book		17,520

Working Notes
1. Actual total of cash book credit side would be Rs. 29,700, but was shown as 29,500. Thus, actual closing balance on March 31 would be Rs. 14,300, but was shown as Rs. 14,100. Consequently, it has reduced the closing balance on March 31 by Rs. 200 and so it has to be added.

ILLUSTRATION 11.15 The pass book of a trader showed a debit balance of Rs. 5,400 on April 30, 2008, which does not tally with the bank balance of the cash book. On scrutiny, the following disagreements are noticed:

1. A cheque of Rs. 710 issued and cashed but shown in the cash column of the cash book.
2. A cheque of Rs. 3,400 was issued to a creditor on April 25, but was not recorded in the cash book. The cheque was, however, duly encashed till April 30.
3. A credit note for Rs. 450 received from bank but recorded in the cash book credit side as Rs. 540.
4. A party's cheque for Rs. 2,550 had been returned by the bank marked 'refer to drawer', but no entry had been made in the cash book for such an event.

5. On instructions from the proprietor, the bank had transferred interest of Rs. 2,900 from his deposits account to his current account, recording the transfer on May 3, 2008. This amount had, however, been debited in the cash book on April 28, 2008.
6. The bank had credited the Trader's Account with Rs. 2,350 being the proceeds of a foreign bill. No entry had been made in the cash book.
7. A cheque of Rs. 750 paid to the bank but was debited in the pass book.
8. An outgoing cheque of Rs. 850 recorded twice in the cash book.

Solution

Bank Reconciliation Statement as on April 30, 2008

		Rs.	Rs.
Overdraft balance as per Pass Book as on April 30, 2008			5,400
Add: 3. A credit note received for Rs. 450 from bank but recorded in the cash book credit side as Rs. 540 (Rs. 450 + Rs. 540)		990	
6. The bank had credited the Trader's Account, but no entry had been made in the cash book.		2,350	
8. An outgoing cheque was recorded twice in the cash book.		850	4,190
			9,590
Less: 1. An issued cheque shown in the cash column of the cash book		710	
2. An issued cheque not shown in the cash book		3,400	
4. Deposited cheque became dishonoured, but not corrected in the cash book		2,550	
5. The bank had transferred interest on deposits to current account on May 3, but was debited in the cash book as on April 28, 2008		2,900	
7. Cheque deposited but wrongly debited in the pass book (Rs. 750 + Rs. 750)		1,500	11,060
Bank balance as per Cash Book (Note)			1,470

Working Note

1. As the total of the *less amounts* is greater than that of the *add amounts,* the resulting figure would be a reverse balance. Thus, instead of overdraft balance, the cash book will show favourable balance (Dr.).

11.8 PREPARATION OF BANK RECONCILIATION STATEMENT WITH ADJUSTED CASH BOOK BALANCE

When a trader wants to adjust his cash book before preparing the Bank Reconciliation Statement, the following steps are to be taken:

1. Identify those causes or disagreements which are not entered in the cash book but are required to be shown in the cash book (bank column only). For example, bank interest and bank charges, direct deposits and payment made by the bank, etc.
2. Rectifications are to be made in the cash book for those errors which are committed in the cash book only.

After considering the above two steps, the bank reconciliation statement is prepared with the help of the remaining disagreements, i.e., cheques issued but not presented, uncredited cheques and those errors which are committed in the pass book only. But under such circumstances, the bank reconciliation statement will be started by taking the cash book-adjusted bank balance as the basis.

ILLUSTRATION 11.16   From the following information, prepare a Bank Reconciliation Statement of Mr. G.R. Gupta as on January 31, 2008, after making necessary corrections in the Cash Book:

1. Bank balance as per Cash Book Rs. 19,800 as on January 31, 2008.
2. Cheques issued but not presented for payment amounting to Rs. 1,800.
3. Cheques paid to the bank but not credited amounting to Rs. 900.
4. A cheque of Rs. 750 deposited in the bank but wrongly debited by it.
5. As per instructions bank honoured a bill of Rs. 740 and paid godown rent Rs. 380.

6. A cheque of Rs. 440 shown in the cash book as deposited in the bank, but was wrongly kept inside the cash box.
7. Bank interest of Rs. 390 and bank charge of Rs. 70 not shown in the cash book.
8. Credit side of the cash book bank column undercast by Rs. 100.
9. A cheque of Rs. 950 deposited in the bank and credited by the bank duly, but shown in the cash book as Rs. 590.
10. A cheque of Rs. 345 issued and cashed, but shown in the cash book cash column wrongly.
11. A debtor deposited cash directly in the bank Rs. 740.
12. Cheque drawn by another customer but wrongly charged to Trader's Account Rs. 920.
13. A cheque of Rs. 420 issue and cashed but wrongly credited in the pass book.

Solution

In the books of Mr. G. R Gupta

Dr.   **Cash Book (Bank Column)**   Cr.

Date	Particulars		Amount (Rs.)	Date	Particulars		Amount (Rs.)
2008 Jan. 31	To Balance b/d		19,800	2008 Jan. 31	By Bills Payable	(5)	740
	To Interest	(7)	390		By Godown Rent	(5)	380
	To Debtor's A/c	(9)	360		By Bank Charge	(7)	70
	To Debtor's A/c	(11)	740		By Error	(8)	100
					By Creditor's	(10)	345
					By Balance c/d		19,655
			21,290				21,290
Feb. 1	To Balance b/d		19,655				

Bank Reconciliation Statement as on January 31, 2008

		Rs.	Rs.
Bank balance as per Cash Book (adjusted or amended)			19,655
Add: 2. Cheques issued but not presented for payment		1,800	
13. A cheque issued and cashed but wrongly credited in the pass book (Rs. 420 + Rs. 420)		840	2,640
			22,295
Less: 3. Cheques paid to the bank but not credited		900	
4. A cheque of Rs. 750 deposited in the bank but wrongly that was debited by it (Rs. 750 + Rs. 750).		1,500	
6. A cheque shown in the cash book as deposited in the bank, but was wrongly kept inside the cash box		440	
12. Cheque drawn by another customer but wrongly charged to Trader's Account		920	3,760
Balance as per Pass Book			18,535

ILLUSTRATION 11.17 From the following particulars, prepare a Bank Reconciliation Statement of Mr. M.K. Kulkarni as on June 30, 2008, after making the necessary corrections in the Cash Book:

1. Overdraft balance as per Cash Book Rs. 3,750.
2. Unpresented cheques amounted to Rs. 7,100.
3. Uncredited cheques amounted to Rs. 8,700.
4. Bank collected a dividend of Rs. 780 as per standing instructions.
5. Interest on overdraft debited in cash book Rs. 390.
6. An issued cheque of Rs. 810 became dishonoured but recorded in the cash book as deposited cheque dishonoured.
7. Bank wrongly credited Trader's Account Rs. 600.
8. A deposited cheque of Rs. 920 became dishonoured but not reflected in the cash book.
9. A cheque of Rs. 640 issued and cashed duly, but not recorded in the cash book.

10. An outgoing cheque of Rs. 450 to Mr. Y recorded twice in the cash book.
11. Debit balance for the month of May, 2008 was shown in the cash book as credit balance on June 1, 2008 Rs. 420.
12. A bank commission of Rs. 40 debited in the cash book wrongly.

Solution

In the Books of Mr. G.R. Gupta

Dr.   **Cash Book (Bank Column)**   Cr.

Date	Particulars		Amount (Rs.)	Date	Particulars		Amount (Rs.)
2008				2008			
June 30	To Dividend	(4)	780	June 30	By Balance b/d		3,750
	To Creditor's A/c	(6)	1,620		By Interest	(5)	780
	[Rs. 810 + Rs. 810]				[Rs. 390 + Rs. 390]		
	To Y's A/c	(10)	450		By Debtor's A/c	(8)	920
	To Balance Adjusted	(11)	840		By Creditor's A/c	(9)	640
	[Rs. 420 + Rs. 420]				By Bank Commission	(12)	80
	To Balance c/d		2,560				
			6,250				6,250
				July 1	By Balance b/d		2,560

Bank Reconciliation Statement as on June 30, 2008

	Rs.	Rs.
Overdraft balance as per Cash Book (adjusted or amended)		2,560
Add: 3. Uncredited cheques	8,700	8,700
		11,260
Less: 2. Unpresented cheques	7,100	
7. Wrongly credited by Bank	600	7,700
Overdraft balance as per Pass Book		3,560

ILLUSTRATION 11.18 From the following information, prepare a Bank Reconciliation Statement of Mr. Ritesh Ambani as on March 31, 2008, after making the necessary corrections in the cash book:

1. Bank balance as per the cash book Rs. 21,890.
2. A cheque of Rs. 1,200 paid to the bank but was debited in the pass book.
3. A cheque of Rs. 950 issued and cashed but shown in the cash book as Rs. 590.
4. Debit side of the cash book bank column overcasted by Rs. 100.
5. Bank wrongly credited Mr. Ritesh Ambani's A/c by Rs. 540.
6. A debtor deposited Rs. 560 cash directly in the bank.
7. A cheque of Rs. 710 drawn by another customer but was wrongly charged to Traders A/c.
8. Cheque amounting to Rs. 4,100 paid to the bank but only Rs. 850 was collected by bank on April 2, 2008.
9. A cheque of Rs. 750 deposited in the bank but not recorded in the cash book.
10. As per instructions, bank honoured a bill of Rs. 2,700 and collected a claim of Rs. 2,500 from the insurance company.
11. Bank interest and bank charge of Rs. 450 and Rs. 110, respectively, not shown in the cash book.
12. A deposited cheque of Rs. 850 became dishonoured but not shown in the cash book.

Solution

In the Books of Mr. Ritesh Ambani

Dr.   **Cash Book (Bank Column)**   Cr.

Date	Particulars		Amount (Rs.)	Date	Particulars		Amount (Rs.)
2008 March 31	To Balance b/d		21,890	2008 March 31	By Supplier's A/c (Rs. 950 – Rs. 590)	(3)	360
	To Debtor's A/c	(6)	560		By Error	(4)	100
	To Error	(9)	750		By Bills Payable	(10)	2,700
	To Insurance claim	(10)	2,500		By Bank charge	(11)	110
	To Interest	(11)	450		By Customer's A/c	(12)	850
					By Balance c/d		22,030
			26,150				26,150
April 1	To Balance b/d		22,030				

Bank Reconciliation Statement as on March 31, 2008

		Rs.	Rs.
	Bank balance as per Cash Book (adjusted or amended)		22,030
Add: 5.	Wrongly credited by Bank	540	540
			22,570
Less: 2.	A cheque deposited in the bank but was debited in the pass book (Rs. 1,200 + Rs. 1,200)	2,400	
8.	Cheques deposited but collected after date	850	
7.	Cheque drawn by another customer but wrongly charged to Trader's A/c	710	3,960
	Balance as per Pass Book		18,610

ILLUSTRATION 11.19 The following is the cash book (bank column) and the bank statement of Mr. A.S. Sen:

Dr.   **Cash Book (Bank column only)**   Cr.

Date	Particulars	Amount (Rs.)	Date	Particulars	Amount (Rs.)
1997 April 1	To Balance b/f	8,400	1997 April 3	By C.K. Roy (712)	900
6	To P.G. Das (6111)	1,700	9	By M.M. Das (713)	1,200
18	To M.R. Basu (7120)	2,100	15	By P.M. Kar (714)	2,300
21	To A.B. Dhar (3217)	2,400	19	By B.B. Karmakar (715)	1,350
25	To C.C. Sen (2418)	1,300	21	By S.K. Sen (716)	2,800
29	To D.D. Bose (3417)	3,200	27	By L.R. Ram (717)	1,750
			29	By F.M. Munna (718)	2,450
			30	By Balance c/d	6,350
		19,100			19,100

Bank Statement/Pass Book

Date	Particulars	Withdrawals (Rs.)	Deposited amount (Rs.)	Balance amount (Rs.)
1997 April 1	By Balance	—	—	8,400
9	To M.M. Das (713)	1,200	—	7,200
15	To P.M. Kar (714)	2,300	—	4,900
18	By M.R. Basu (7120)	—	2,100	7,000
21	By A.B. Dhar (3214)	—	2,400	9,400

(Contd.)

Date	Particulars	Withdrawals (Rs.)	Deposited amount (Rs.)	Balance amount (Rs.)
22	By G.K. Roy	—	2,150	11,550
25	By C.C. Sen (2418)	—	1,300	12,850
25	By Interest	—	700	13,550
26	To Bank Charge	150	—	13,400
27	To L.R. Ram (717)	1,750	—	11,650
29	By A. Banerjee	—	1,800	13,450
30	To Subscription	600	—	12,850

You are required to prepare a bank reconciliation statement as on April 30, 1997.

Solution

Note for the Students: When both the cash book and the bank statement/pass book are given for the same period then the causes of discrepancies are to be searched out first with the help of the list of 'causes of differences'. Then the bank reconciliation statement is prepared.

The transactions which appear in both the books are not the causes of differences/discrepancies, but those which appear in any one of the books only are the main causes of difference/discrepancies. Put tick marks (√) against those figures which agree in both the books and similarly put cross mark (×) against those items which do not agree.)

Cash Book (Bank Column Only)

Dr.   Cr.

Date	Particulars		Amount (Rs.)	Date	Particulars		Amount (Rs.)
1997				1997			
April 1	To Balance b/f		8,400	April 3	By C.K. Roy (712)	(×)	900
6	To P.G. Das (6111)	(×)	1,700	9	By M.M. Das (713)	(√)	1,200
18	To M.R. Basu (7120)	(√)	2,100	15	By P.M. Kar (714)	(√)	2,300
21	To A.B. Dhar (3217)	(√)	2,400	19	By B.B. Karmakar (715)	(×)	1,350
25	To C.C. Sen (2418)	(√)	1,300	21	By S.K. Sen (716)	(×)	2,800
29	To D.D. Bose (3417)	(×)	3,200	27	By L.R. Ram (717)	(√)	1,750
				29	By F.M. Munna (718)	(×)	2,450
				30	By Balance c/d		6,350
			19,100				19,100

Bank Statement/Pass Book

Date	Particulars		Withdrawals amount (Rs.)	Debit amount (Rs.)	Credit (Rs.)
1997					
April 1	By Balance		—	—	8,400
9	To M.M. Das (713)	(√)	1,200	—	7,200
15	To P.M. Kar (714)	(√)	2,300	—	4,900
18	By M.R. Basu (7120)	(√)	—	2,100	7,000
21	By A.B. Dhar (3214)	(√)	—	2,400	9,400
22	By G.K. Roy	(×)	—	2,150	11,550
25	By C.C. Sen (2418)	(√)	—	1,300	12,850
25	By Interest	(×)	—	700	13,550
26	To Bank charge	(×)	150	—	13,400
27	To L.R. Ram (717)	(√)	1,750	—	11,650
29	By A. Banerjee	(×)	—	1,800	13,450
30	To Subscription	(×)	600	—	12,850

List of Causes of difference:

(a) Cheques deposited but not credited by bank:

	Rs.	Rs.
P.G. Das	1,700	
D.D. Bose	3,200	4,900

(b) Cheques issued but not cashed:

	Rs.	Rs.
C.K. Roy	900	
B.B. Karmakar	1,350	
S.K. Sen	2,800	
F.M. Munna	2,450	7,500

(c) Debtors deposited directly into bank:

	Rs.	Rs.
G.K. Roy	2,150	
A. Banerjee	1,800	3,950

(d) Amount debited by bank:

	Rs.
Subscription	600
Bank charge	150

(e) Amount credited by bank:

	Rs.
Interest	700

Bank Reconciliation Statement as on April 30, 1997

	Rs.	Rs.
Bank balance as per the cash book		6,350
Add: Cheques issued but not cashed	7,500	
Interest not entered in the cash book	700	
Debtors deposited directly into bank	3,950	12,150
		18,500
Less: Cheques deposited but not credited by bank	4,900	
Amount debited by bank:		
Subscription	600	
Bank charge	150	5,650
Balance as per the pass book		12,850

ILLUSTRATION 11.20   D.D. Guha of Kolkata furnished the following information in order to prepare his Bank Reconciliation Statement as on March 31, 2008, after making the necessary corrections in the cash book:

1. Balance as per pass book as on March 31, 2008 Rs. 12,100.
2. Cheques amounting to Rs. 4,820 paid into bank but bank failed to collect Rs. 1,930.
3. Cheques totaling Rs. 3,290 issued to creditors, out of which creditors presented only Rs. 1,320 for payment on April 2.
4. Credit side of the cash book bank column overcast by Rs. 100.
5. Bank interest of Rs. 1,260 recorded twice in the cash book.
6. A bill of Rs. 2,580 discounted with bank at Rs. 2,495 became dishonoured and noting charge of Rs. 20 incurred but no entry had been made in the cash book for such dishonour.
7. As per instructions, bank collected a claim of Rs. 1,750 from the insurance company.
8. Bank wrongly credited D. D. Guha's A/c for Rs. 210.
9. A cheque of Rs. 370 issued and cashed but shown in the cash book as Rs. 730.
10. Bank charge of Rs. 90 entered in the bank statement but does not appear in the cash book.
11. Mr. X settled his account of Rs. 670 by paying a cheque of Rs. 650 and it was deposited in the bank immediately, but was shown in the cash book as a cheque of Rs. 670 deposited in the bank.

Solution

When a pass book balance is given, then it is essential to prepare a Bank Reconciliation Statement to know the cash book bank balance and then the cash book is prepared for necessary corrections. After preparing the cash book, the Bank Reconciliation Statement is prepared.

Bank Reconciliation Statement as on March 31, 2008

	Rs.	Rs.
Balance as per the pass book		12,100
Add: 2. Cheques deposited but not collected by bank	1,930	
5. Bank interest recorded twice in the cash book	1,260	
6. Discounted bill became dishonoured but not shown in the cash book	2,600	
10. Bank charge debited in the pass book but not shown in the cash book	90	
11. A cheque of Rs. 650 deposited in the bank but shown in the cash book as Rs. 670.	20	5,900
		18,000
Less: 3. Cheques issued but cashed on April 2	1,320	
4. Credit side of the cash book bank column overcasted by Rs. 100	100	
7. As per instructions, the bank collected a claim from the insurance company	1,750	
8. Wrongly credit by bank to Trader's A/c	210	
9. A cheque of Rs. 370 cashed but shown in the cash book as Rs. 730.	360	3,740
Bank balance as per the cash book		14,260

Dr. **Cash Book (Bank Column)** Cr.

Date	Particulars		Amount (Rs.)	Date	Particulars		Amount (Rs.)
2008				2008			
March 31	To Balance b/d		14,260	March 31	By Bank interest	(5)	1,260
	To Error	(4)	100		(Bank interest recorded		
	To Insurance Claim	(7)	1,750		twice adjusted)		
	To Error	(9)	360		By Acceptor's A/c	(6)	2,600
	(An issued cheque of				(B/R dishonoured)		
	Rs. 370 shown in the				By Bank charge	(10)	90
	cash book as Rs. 730)				By Mr. X	(11)	20
					By Balance c/d		12,500
			16,470				16,470

Bank Reconciliation Statement as on March 31, 2008

	Rs.	Rs.
Bank balance as per Cash Book (adjusted or amended)		12,500
Add: 3. Cheques issued but cashed on April 2	1,320	
8. Wrongly credit by bank to trader's A/c	210	1,530
		14,030
Less: 2. Cheques deposited but not collected by bank.	1,930	1,930
Balance as per the pass book		12,100

Correction of Bank Reconciliation Statement

ILLUSTRATION 11.21 Redraft the following Bank Reconciliation Statement which was prepared by an accountant of M/s M.M. Sharma assuming that the bank balance as per cash book and the narrations given within the statement are correct.

Bank Reconciliation Statement as on January 31, 2008

	Rs.	Rs.
Bank balance as per cash book		15,700
Add: 3. Cheque issued but not presented for payment within January 31, 2008	4,900	
6. A periodic payment made by bank under standing instruction	750	

(Contd.)

		Rs.	Rs.
7.	Cheque deposited and duly credited by bank , but not shown in the cash book	1,400	
8.	A deposited cheque became dishonoured, but not shown in the cash book	1,450	
11.	Cheque issued and cashed but not recorded in the cash book.	800	9,300
			25,000
Less: 2.	Cheques deposited but not collected by bank	4,550	
4.	Credit side of the Cash Book bank column overcasted	2,600	
5.	Insurance claim collected by bank	500	
9.	Cheque drawn on trader's Personal Savings A/c but was wrongly shown in the cash book.	2,500	
10.	An issued cheque of Rs. 750 shown in the cash book as Rs. 570	1,320	11,470
	Balance as per Pass Book		13,530

Solution

Bank Reconciliation Statement as on January 31, 2008

		Rs.	Rs.
Bank balance as per cash book			15,700
Add: 3.	Cheque issued but not presented for payment within January 31, 2008	4,900	
4.	Credit side of the Cash Book bank column overcasted	2,600	
5.	Insurance claim collected by bank	500	
7.	Cheque deposited and duly credited by bank , but not shown in the cash book	1,400	
9.	Cheque drawn on trader's Personal Savings A/c but was wrongly shown in the cash book.	2,500	11,900
			27,600
Less: 2.	Cheques deposited but not collected by bank	4,550	
6.	A periodic payment made by bank under standing instructions	750	
8.	A deposited cheque became dishonoured, but not shown in the cash book	1,450	
10.	An issued cheque of Rs. 750 shown in the cash book as Rs. 570	180	
11.	Cheque issued and cashed but not recorded in the cash book.	800	7,730
	Balance as per Pass Book		19,870

EXERCISES

I. *Objective Type Questions (with answers)*

A. Choose the correct alternative:

(a) A bank statement is a copy of
    (i) Cash A/c balance
    (ii) Bank A/c balance
    (iii) Trader's transaction record in the bank book

(b) A bank reconciliation statement (BRS) is prepared
    (i) To know the bank balances
    (ii) To know the bank transactions
    (iii) To reconcile the bank balance as per the cash book with the pass book balance

(c) A bank reconciliation statement is prepared when
    (i) Cash book, cash and bank balances are different
    (ii) Cash book, bank balance and pass book balance are same
    (iii) Cash book bank balance is not tallying with the pass book balance

(d) The main causes of difference/disagreements are due to
    (i) Shortage of funds
    (ii) Lack of accounting knowledge
    (iii) Nonavailability of information
    (iv) None of these

(e) Bank Reconciliation is not required to prepare when
   (i) Cash book bank balance and pass book balance are identical
   (ii) Cash book bank balance and pass book balance are not identical
   (iii) None of these

(f) Those transaction which are omitted from both the books are
   (i) Not to be considered in the BRS
   (ii) To be considered in BRS
   (iii) None of these

(g) Standing instructions for any payments or receipts are recorded generally
   (i) First in pass book and then in cash book
   (ii) In both the books simultaneously
   (iii) In the cash book first

Ans: (a) (iii), (b) (iii), (c) (iii), (d) (iii), (e) (i), (f) (i), (g) (i).

B. A trader's pass book balance is given which is not tallying with his cash book bank balance due to the following disagreements or mistakes. Choose the correct correction.

(a) A cheque of Rs. 750 issued and cashed but recorded in the cash book as Rs. 570.
   (i) Add Rs. 180
   (ii) Add Rs. 750
   (iii) None of these

(b) A cheque of Rs. 680 issued and cashed but recorded in the cash book as Rs. 860 in the cash column.
   (i) Add Rs. 680
   (ii) Add Rs. 860
   (iii) None of these

(c) A cheque of Rs. 890 issued and cashed but recorded in the cash book as cheque deposited into bank.
   (i) Add Rs. 980
   (ii) Add Rs. 1,780
   (iii) Not affected

(d) A cheque of Rs. 460 deposited and become dishonoured but recorded in the cash book as issued cheque dishonoured.
   (i) Add Rs. 460
   (ii) Add Rs. 920
   (iii) None of these

(e) A bill of Rs. 820 discounted with the bank at Rs. 790 became dishonoured and noting charge of Rs. 20 incurred. No entry has been made in the cash book for such dishonoured.
   (i) Add Rs. 840
   (ii) Add Rs. 810
   (iii) Add Rs. 800

(f) One outgoing cheque of Rs. 750 recorded twice in the cash book.
   (i) Less Rs. 1,500
   (ii) Less Rs. 750
   (iii) None of these

(g) Discount allowed of Rs. 50 has been entered by mistake with the cheque in the bank column in the cash book.
   (i) Add Rs. 50
   (ii) Add Rs. 100
   (iii) No effect

(h) Cheque of Rs. 150 drawn by another customer but wrongly charged to Trader's A/c.
   (i) Add Rs. 150
   (ii) Less Rs. 150
   (iii) None of these

(i) Uncredited cheques amounted to Rs. 600.
   (i) Add Rs. 600
   (ii) Less Rs. 600
   (iii) None of these

(j) Bank credited the Trader's A/c in error for Rs. 500.
   (i) Add Rs. 500
   (ii) Less Rs. 500
   (iii) None of these

(k) A cheque of Rs. 950 recorded in the cash book as Rs. 590, deposited into bank and was credited by the bank into another customer's A/c.
   (i) Add Rs. 590
   (ii) Less Rs. 360
   (iii) Add Rs. 360

Ans: (a) (i), (b) (i), (c) (ii), (d) (ii), (e) (i), (f) (ii), (g) (i), (h) (i), (i) (i), (j) (ii), (k) (i).

II. *Short Answer Type Questions*

1. What is a Bank Reconciliation Statement?
2. Is it necessary for a trade to prepare a Bank Reconciliation Statement?
3. How is a Bank Reconciliation Statement prepared?
4. Give five causes of disagreements that increase the Pass Book balance in comparison to the Cash Book balance.
5. Give five causes of disagreements that increase the Cash Book overdraft balance in comparison to the Pass Book balance.

III. *Long Answer Type Questions*

1. What is a Bank Reconciliation Statement? When and how is it prepared?
2. What are the causes of disagreements between bank balance as per cash book and the pass book ?
3. What purpose does a Bank Reconciliation Statement serve?
4. What is a Pass Book? How does it differ from a Cash Book?

IV. *Problems on Bank Reconciliation Statement*

A. With Cash Book/Pass Book Favourable Balance

1. K.K. Banerjee of Durgapur submits the following particulars for preparing his Bank Reconciliation Statement as on 31st January, 1997:
   (a) Bank Balance as per Cash Book Rs. 17,500.
   (b) Cheques for Rs. 700, Rs. 800, Rs, 900 and Rs. 1,100 deposited into Bank, but out of that Bank collected Rs. 800 and Rs. 900 only.
   (c) Cheques amounting to Rs. 4,700 issued to the suppliers, but out of that presented for payment Rs. 3,900 only.
   (d) A debtor deposited cash directly into Bank Rs. 780.
   (e) As per instruction, Bank collected dividend Rs. 750.
   (f) Debit side of the Cash Book Bank column undercast by Rs. 100.
   (g) Bank Interest Rs. 1,050 and Bank Charge Rs. 75 not entered in the Cash book.

Ans: Balance as per Pass Book Rs. 19,105.

2. From the following information prepare a Bank Reconciliation Statement as at 30th April, 1998:
   (a) Bank balance as per Cash Book Rs. 16,500.
   (b) Cheques amounting to Rs. 3,850 paid into Bank, but out of that Bank credited Rs. 2,170 only.
   (c) Cheques for Rs. 1,200, Rs. 750, Rs. 1,150 and Rs. 950 drawn in favour of Creditors, but out of that presented for payment after 30th April Rs. 750 and Rs. 950 respectively.
   (d) Bank honoured a bill of Rs. 1,750 as per standing instruction.
   (e) Interest on investment collected by Bank Rs. 840 not shown in the Cash Book.
   (f) Credit side of the Cash Book undercast by Rs. 100.
   (g) Interest on Bank deposits recorded twice in the Cash Book Rs. 175.

   Ans: Balance as per Pass Book Rs. 15,335.

   [**Hint:** For the following item numbers:
   (b) To be deducted by Rs. 1,680, because Bank failed to collect Rs. 1,680 (Rs.3,850 – Rs. 2,170)
   (c) To be added by Rs. 1,700, because Bank paid cheques for Rs. 750 and Rs. 950 after 30.4.96.
   (d) To be deducted by Rs. 1,750 because Bank paid a bill.
   (e) To be deducted by Rs. 100. Total of the payment side shown short of Rs. 100. As a result it has increased the Cash Book bank balance.]

3. Mr. M.K. Sen submits the following information for preparing his Bank Reconciliation Statement as on 30th June, 1996:
   (a) Balance as per Pass Book Rs. 8,900.
   (b) Uncredited cheques amounted to Rs. 740.
   (c) Unpresented cheques amounted to Rs. 900.
   (d) A deposited cheque became dishonoured but not entered in the Cash Book Rs. 450.
   (e) A cheque of Rs. 810 shown in the Cash Book as deposited into Bank, but it was wrongly kept inside the cash box.
   (f) Bank interest of Rs. 350 shown in the Cash Book as Rs. 530.
   (g) A debtor deposited cash directly into Bank Rs. 720.

   Ans: Bank balance as per Cash Book Rs. 9,460.

4. Prepare the Bank Reconciliation Statement from the following information as on 31st March, 1997:
   (a) Bank balance as per Pass Book Rs. 18,300.
   (b) Cheque drawn by another customer but wrongly charged to Trader's A/c Rs. 320.
   (c) One outgoing cheque recorded twice in the Cash Book Rs. 170.
   (d) Bank collected insurance claim of Rs. 1,750 as per standing instructions.
   (e) Cheques totalling Rs. 3,900 paid into Bank but Bank collected Rs. 1,780 on 2nd April, 1997.
   (f) A cheque drawn and cashed but not entered in the Cash Book Rs. 210.
   (g) Bank commission Rs. 175 shown in the Cash Book debit side.

   Ans: Bank balance as per Cash Book Rs. 19,040.

   [**Hint:** For the following item number:
   (g) To be added by Rs. 350, because Bank commission is a charge but it was shown in the Cash Book as income. Hence 175 + 175 = Rs. 350 is to be added.]

5. From the following particulars prepare a Bank Reconciliation Statement of P.K. Bros, as on 31st December, 1996:

(a) Cheques amounting to Rs. 4,800 drawn in favour of suppliers, but a supplier's cheque of Rs. 600 became dishonoured and another supplier's cheque of Rs. 700 was lost due to pick-pocketing (not yet cashed by others).

(b) A cheque of Rs. 570 issued and cashed but recorded in the Cash Book as Rs. 750.

(c) A bill of Rs. 2,800 discounted with the Bank as Rs. 2,650 but shown in the Cash Book without deducting the discount charges.

(d) Bank interest of Rs. 210 shown in the Cash Book as Bank Charge wrongly.

(e) Debit side of the Cash Book overcast by Rs. 100.

(f) Trade subscription paid by Bank Rs. 600 as per standing instruction.

(g) Bank balance as per Cash Book Rs. 15,900.

Ans: Balance as per Pas Book Rs. 16,950.

[**Hint:** For the following item numbers:

(a) To be added Rs. 1,300. Two cheques for Rs. 600 and Rs. 700 not yet cashed and as such Cash Book balance is less than the Pass Book.

(d) To be added Rs. 420, because of income of Rs. 210 shown as expenses in the Cash Book and as such Cash Book balance is less than the Pass Book balance by Rs. 210 + 210]

6. You are required to prepare a Bank Reconciliation Statement as on 31st March, 1997 from the following informations:

(a) Balance as per Pass Book Rs. 7,100.

(b) A bill of Rs. 1,960 discounted with the Bank at Rs. 1,810, but became dishonoured. No entry has been made in the Cash Book for such dishonour.

(c) A cheque of Rs. 610 issued and cashed but shown in the Cash Book's Cash column wrongly.

(d) A cheque of Rs. 720 paid into Bank and duly credited in the Pass Book, but this was not recorded in the Cash Book.

(e) Cheques for Rs. 7,000 drawn but Bank debited Rs. 6,100 within 31st March, 1997.

(f) A party's cheque paid into Bank Rs. 300, but became dishonoured. Not yet reflected in the Cash Book (for such dishonour).

(g) A debit of Rs. 360 entered in the Bank Statement but not entered in the Cash book.

Ans: Bank balance as per Cash Book Rs. 8,710.

[**Hint:** For the following item numbers:

(b) To be added Rs. 1,960. Bank deducted Rs. 1,960 for Bill receivable dishonoured but not shown in the Cash Book.

(g) To be added Rs. 360. Bank balance is less than the Cash Book balance for expenses/payment.]

7. Prepare a Bank Reconciliation Statement of Mr. S. Tendulkar as on 31st December, 1992 from the following particulars:

(i) Bank balance as per Cash Book Rs. 12,500.

(ii) During the month of December, cheques for Rs. 3,000 were issued to M/s Dutson & Co., but encashed after 31st December, 1992.

(iii) On December 20, 1992 a cheque for Rs. 2,000 was deposited into Bank which had been entered in the Pass Book on January 16, 1993 Another cheque for Rs. 1,500 debited in the Cash Book, but omitted to be sent to the Bank.

(iv) During the month the cheque for Rs. 1,000 was received from his employer and sent to the Bank without recording in the Cash Book.

(v) Bank charges for Rs. 100 were debited in the Pass Book, but not entered in the Cash Book.

(vi) On 31st December, 1992 Bank credited the Pass Book with Rs. 350 as interest, but no entry for this was made in the Cash Book.

(vii) Dividend of Rs. 750 were collected by the Bank and credited in the Pass Book but not debited in the Cash Book.

(viii) Insurance premium of Rs. 400 was paid by the Bank on 28th December, 1992 but no entry for this was made in the Cash Book.

(ix) A cheque for Rs. 900 received from m/s Power & Co. was dishonoured, but it was not entered in the Cash Book.

(x) As per instruction given by Mr. Tendulkar, *the bank met* a liability for Rs. 300 and debited in the Pass Book, but not entered in the Cash Book.

(W.B.H.S.)

Ans: Bank balance as per Pass Book Rs. 12,400.

8. Prepare a Bank Reconciliation Statement as on 31st December, 1996 from the following particulars:

(i) On 31st December, 1996, the Cash Book of Iqbal showed an overdraft of Rs. 22,050.

(ii) On 29th December, 1996, cheques amounting to Rs. 6,000, Rs. 12,000 and Rs. 15,000 were deposited into the Bank, but the cheque for Rs. 12,000 was collected by the Bank on 5th January 1997.

(iii) It is learnt that out of the cheques for Rs. 2,500, Rs. 4,500, Rs. 7,800 and Rs. 11,000 issued on 25th December, 1996, only first two cheques were presented to the Bank in December, 1996.

(iv) On 31st December, 1996, the Pass Book of Iqbal has been debited with Rs. 1,800 for interest on overdraft, but the same was not entered in his Cash Book within 31st December 1996.

(v) A debtor directly deposited a cheque of Rs. 2,500 into the Bank of Iqbal, but the same was not recorded in the Cash Book.

(W.B.H.S.)

Ans: Pass Book balance (overdraft) Rs. 14,550.

9. The following are the causes of discrepancy between Cash Book balance and Pass book balance as on 31st March, 1994. Prepare the statement on that day reconciling the discrepancies,

(i) Bank balance as per Pass Book Rs. 2,400.

(ii) Cheques totalling Rs. 10,000 were deposited into Bank on 27th March, but they were collected and credited by Bank on 6th April.

(iii) A cheque for Rs. 5,400 issued to Ashok Roy was dishonoured on 28th March, but no entry has been made in Cash Book to record the dishonour,

(iv) A customer deposited Rs. 6,000 directly into Bank on 29th March, but it was not recorded in the Cash Book within 31st March.

(v) A cheque of Rs. 1,800 was deposited into Bank, but wrongly debited in Cash column of Cash Book.

(vi) Bank charges amounting to Rs. 200 was credited twice in Cash Book.

(W.B.H.S.)

Ans: Bank balance as per Cash Book Rs. 1,000.

10. From the following information prepare a Bank Reconciliation Statement as at 31st December, 1982:

(i) Bank balance as per Cash Book Rs. 1,250.

(ii) Cheques of Rs. 8,600 deposited on 26th December, 1982, but the same collected by Bank on 4th January, 1983.

(iii) Cheque of Rs. 650 issued on 29th December, 1982, but not presented for payment till 31st December, 1982.

(iv) Insurance Premium amounting to Rs. 900 and subscription Rs. 700 paid by Bank, but not recorded in cash book.

(v) Bank charges debited in pass book, but not recorded in cash book Rs. 150.

(vi) Dividend collected by Bank, but not entered in cash book Rs. 1,200.

(vii) Sri Sukumar Sen, a customer, paid Rs. 1,400 directly into Bank on 27th December, 1982 and the Bank entered the information on 6th January, 1983.

(W.B.H.S.)

Ans: Overdraft balance as per Pass Book Rs. 5,850.

11. Mr. Kumar submits the following particulars for preparing his Bank Reconciliation Statement as on December 31, 2007:

(a) Bank balance as per cash book as on December 31, 2007: Rs. 22,500.

(b) During the month of December, cheques for Rs. 3,000 were issued to M/S Duston & Co. but cashed after December 31, 2007.

(c) On December 20, 2007, a cheque of Rs. 2,000 was deposited in the bank which had been entered in the pass book on January 16, 2008. Another cheque for Rs. 1,500 was debited in the cash book but was not sent to bank.

(d) During the month, a cheque for Rs. 1,000 was received from his employer and sent to bank without being recorded in the cash book.

(e) Bank charges of Rs. 100 debited in the pass book but not reflected in the cash book.

(f) A cheque of Rs. 660 was drawn by another customer but was wrongly charged to Mr. Kumar's account.

(g) As per instructions, bank honoured a bill for Rs. 900 and collected dividend of Rs. 1,500.

Ans: Balance as per Pass Book Rs. 22,840.

12. From the following information, prepare a Bank Reconciliation Statement as on March 31, 2008:

(a) Bank balance as per cash book as on March 31, 2008 Rs. 9,940.

(b) A cheque of Rs. 1,960 issued and cashed but wrongly credited in the pass book.

(c) A debtor deposited cash of Rs. 1,290 directly in the bank.

(d) Credit side of the cash book bank column overcast by Rs. 100.

(e) A bill of Rs. 3,900 discounted with the bank at Rs. 3,640, but shown in the cash book without deducting the discount.

(f) Bank charge of Rs. 190 recorded twice in the cash book.

(g) A credit note received for Rs. 1,250 from the Bank but recorded in the cash book debit side as Rs. 2,150.

(h) Cheque of Rs. 390 drawn by another customer but wrongly charged to Trader's Account.

Ans: Balance as per Pass Book Rs. 13,890.

[**Hint:** To item numbers (b) add Rs. 1960 + Rs. 1,960. To item no. (e) less Rs. 260]

13. Prepare a Bank Reconciliation Statement as on March 31, 2008 from the following particulars:

(a) Cheques deposited and credited by bank but not recorded in the Cash Book Rs. 13,600.

(b) During March, 2008, cheques amounting to Rs. 8,000 were issued to creditors, out of which one creditor for Rs. 500 encashed his cheque on April 5, 2008, whereas the other creditor for Rs. 700 had not encashed his cheque till then.

(c) A cheque issued to M/s Roy & Co. amounting to Rs. 800 was recorded twice in the Cash Book.

(d) On March 31, 2008, bank credited the Pass Book with Rs. 1,000 as interest on deposit but no entry had been made in the Cash Book.

(e) A bill for Rs. 1,000, discounted with the Bank at a discount of 10%, was entered in the Cash Book without recording the discount charges.

(f) A debtor deposited cash directly in the bank Rs. 290 on March 25, 2008, but the same had been recorded in the Cash Book on March 30, 2008.

(g) Debit side of the Cash Book bank column was undercast by Rs. 400.

(h) Bank met a bill payable for Rs. 1,000 on March 30, 2008, under advice to a business man on April 5, 2008.

(i) Bank balance as per Pass Book (Cr.) Rs. 4,000.

[Tripura H.S. (Adapted)]

Ans: Overdraft balance as per Cash Book Rs. 11,900.

[**Hint:** The item Number (f) is to be ignored, because there is no effect on the bank balance on March 31.]

B. Overdraft or (Cr. Balance) as per Cash Book

14. Sri M.D. Das of Calcutta furnished the following information in order to prepare his Bank Reconciliation Statement as on 31st October, 1996:

(a) Overdraft balance as per Cash Book Rs. 18,900.

(b) A periodic payment by Bank Rs. 390 under standing instructions not entered in the Cash Book.

(c) A cheque drawn on Trader's Savings A/c (Personal) Rs. 700, but it was shown in the Cash book wrongly.

(d) Bank credited Sri. M.D. Das's A/c wrongly Rs. 340.

(e) A cheque of Rs. 700 deposited and duly credited by Bank but recorded in the Cash Book as deposited into Bank Rs. 70 only.

(f) A cheque of Rs. 820 issued and cashed but recorded in the Cash Book as deposited into bank.

(g) Cheques drawn but cashed after 31st October, 1996 Rs. 790.

(h) Cheques totalling Rs. 3,940 paid into Bank but out of that credited by Bank Rs. 2,860 only.

Ans: Overdraft balance as per Pass Book Rs. 19,550.

[**Hint:** For the following item numbers:]

(c) To be deducted by Rs. 700. Here Cash Book liabilities is greater than the Pass Book liabilities.

(f) To be added by Rs. 1,640. Issued cheque shown in the Cash Book as deposited. As such Cash book liabilities is less than the Pass Book liabilities.]

15. From the following particulars, prepare the Bank Reconciliation Statement as on 30th April, 1996:

(a) Overdraft balance as per Cash Book Rs. 7,200.

(b) One outgoing cheque recorded twice in the Cash Book Rs. 640.

(c) Credit balance for the month of March 1996 was shown in the Cash Book as debit balance on 1st April, 1996 Rs. 900.

(d) Interest on overdraft Rs. 170 recorded in the Cash Book as deposited Rs. 710 on the debit side.

(e) A cheque of Rs. 510 issued and cashed but recorded in the Cash Book as deposited Rs. 150.

(f) Discount allowed to a debtor Rs. 60 for a cheque received from him and it was duly credited in the Pass Book, but of the amount of discount was included with the amount of cheque in the Cash Book.

(g) A bill of Rs. 800 discounted with the Bank at Rs. 710, but became dishonoured. No entry has been made in the Cash Book for such dishonour.

(h) A customer's cheque recorded in the Cash Book, duly but not banked Rs. 600.

Ans: Overdraft balance as per Pass Book Rs. 11,360.

[**Hint:** For the following item numbers:

(c) To be added Rs. 1,800. Credit balance shown as Debit balance. As a result it has decreased the liabilities of Cash Book by Rs. 900 + 900 = Rs. 1,800.

(g) To be added by Rs. 60. Discount allowed but wrongly included with the amount of cheque received; as such, Cash Book liabilities are less than the Pass Book liabilities.

(h) To be added by Rs. 600. Received cheque not sent to Bank. As such Cash Book liabilities are less than the Pass Book liabilities.]

16. From the following information you are required to prepare a Bank Reconciliation Statement as on 31st March, 1997:

(a) Bank balance as per Cash Book (Cr.) Rs. 3,425.

(b) Uncredited cheques amounting to Rs. 2,120.

(c) Unpresented cheques totalling Rs. 1,650.

(d) Interest on fixed deposits accrued and as such recorded in the Cash Book only in advance Rs. 400.

(e) Bank charge Rs. 100 recorded as interest received in the Cash Book.

(f) Bank statement shows that the debtor deposited cash directly into Bank Rs. 820 and Bank debited Rs. 950 for trade subscription.

(g) A cheque of Rs. 820 deposited and duly credited by the Bank but recorded in the Cash Book as Rs. 280.

(h) Credit side of the Cash Book Bank column undercast by Rs. 150.

Ans: Overdraft balance as per Pass Book Rs. 4,235.

17. From the following information you are required to prepare a Bank Reconciliation Statement of Sri B. Mehta as on 31st March, 1996:

(a) Bank balance as per Cash Book (Cr.) Rs. 9,525.

(b) A cheque of Rs. 930 issued to a supplier and duly cashed but shown in the Cash Book as Rs. 390.

(c) Debit balance of the Cash Book on 31st January, 1996 was recorded as credit balance on 1st Febuary, 1996 Rs. 535.

(d) Bank interest on overdraft recorded twice in the Cash Book Rs. 380.

(e) A party's cheque of Rs. 540 has been returned by the Bank remarked "refer to drawer", but no entry has been made in the Cash Book for such an event.

(f) A cheque of Rs. 220 drawn by another customer but wrongly charged to Trader's A/c (by the bank).

(g) A cheque of Rs. 150 issued and became dishonoured but shown in the Cash Book as deposited cheque became dishonoured.

(h) A cheque of Rs. 205 paid into Bank and was dully collected by Bank, but shown as Rs. 502 in the Bank statement.

Ans: Overdraft balance as per Pass Book Rs. 8,778.

[**Hint:** For the following item numbers:

(c) To be deducted Rs. 1,070.

(g) To be deducted Rs. 300.]

18. (i) On 31st December, 1980, the Cash Book of Iqbal showed an overdraft of Rs. 22,050.

(ii) On 29th December, 1980, cheque 6 amounting to Rs. 6,000, Rs. 12,000 and Rs. 15,000 were deposited into the Bank, but the cheque for Rs. 12,000 was collected by the Bank on 5th January, 1981.

(iii) It is learnt that out of the cheques for Rs. 2,500, Rs. 4,500, Rs. 7,800 and Rs. 11,000 issued on 25th December, 1980, only first two cheques (for Rs. 2,500 and Rs. 4,500) were presented to Bank in December, 1980.

(iv) On 31st December, 1980, the Pass Book of Iqbal has been debited with Rs. 1,800 for interest on overdraft, but the same was not entered in the Cash Book within 31st December, 1980.

(v) A debtor directly deposited a cheque of Rs. 2,500 into the Bank of Iqbal, but the same was not recorded in the Cash Book. From the above particulars, prepare the Bank Reconciliation Statement as on 31st December, 1980.

(W.B.H.S.)

Ans: Bank overdraft as per Pass Book Rs. 14,550.

19. From the undermentioned particulars of a business prepare the Bank Reconciliation Statement as on 31st December, 1985:

(i) Bank overdraft as per Cash Book Rs. 1,410.

(ii) During the month the total amount of cheques for Rs. 2,700 was deposited into Bank, but of those one cheque of Rs. 480 has been recorded in the Pass Book on 4th January.

(iii) During the month, cheques amounting to Rs. 3,470 were drawn in favour of creditors — of them one creditor for Rs. 1,440 encashed his cheque on 8th January, whereas the other for Rs. 660 has not encashed his cheque yet.

(iv) As per order, the Bank on 28th December 1985, has paid out Rs. 400 to a creditor, but by mistake the same has not yet been entered in the Cash Book.

(v) According to agreement, on 30th December 1985, a debtor has deposited directly into the Bank Account Rs. 295, but the same has not been recorded in the Cash Book.

(vi) In the month of December, the Bank has without any intimation debited the account of the businessman for Rs. 50 as Bank charges and credited the same for Rs. 120 as interest for the previous year.

(W.B.H.S. Exam)

Ans: Bank balance as per Pass Book Rs. 175.

20. From the undermentioned particulars of a businessman prepare the Bank Reconciliation Statement as on 31st Dec. 1996:

(i) Bank overdraft as per Cash Book Rs. 11,410.

(ii) During the month of December, the total amount of cheques for Rs. 12,700 was deposited into Bank, but, out of those, one cheque for Rs. 1,480 was recorded in the Pass Book on 4th January next,

(iii) During December, 1996 cheques amounting to Rs. 13,470 were drawn in favour of creditors — of them one creditor for Rs. 1,400 encashed his cheque on 8th of January, 1997 whereas the other for Rs. 1,600 has not encashed his cheque yet.

(iv) As per order, the Bank on 28th December 1996 had paid out Rs. 1,400 to a creditor, but by mistake the same has not yet been entered in Cash Book,

(v) According to agreement, a debtor had deposited directly into the Bank Account Rs. 1,290 on 30th December 1996 but the same has not been recorded in the Cash Book.

(vi) In the month of December, the Bank without any intimation had debited the account of the businessman for Rs. 150 as Bank charges and credited the same for Rs. 1,120 as interest for the last year.

Ans: Balance as per Pass Book Rs. 9,030 (Cr.).

21. On 31st December, 1996 the Cash Book of Jain Iron Works showed an overdraft of Rs. 6,000. From the following particulars make out a Bank Reconciliation Statement:

(i) Cheques drawn but not cashed before 31st December, 1996 amounting to Rs. 4,000.

(ii) Cheques paid into bank but not collected and credited before 31st December, 1996 amounted to Rs. 4,800.

(iii) A bill receivable for Rs. 500 previously discounted with the Bank had been dishonoured and debited in the Pass Book.

(iv) Debit is made in the Pass Book for Rs. 150 on account of interest on overdraft and Rs. 50 on account of charges for collecting bills,

(v) The Bank has collected interest on investment and credited Rs. 800 in the Pass Book.

(H.S.—Delhi Board)

Ans: Balance as per Pass Book Rs. 6,700 (Dr.).

22. The Cash book of Gupta showed an overdraft of Rs. 30,000 on 31st December 1986. The scrutiny of the entries in the Cash Book and the Pass Book revealed that:

(a) On 22nd December cheques totalling Rs. 6,000 were sent to bankers for collection; out of this, a cheque for Rs. 1,000 was wrongly recorded in the credit side of the Cash Book and cheques amounting to Rs. 300 could not be collected by the Bank within the year.

(b) A cheque for Rs. 4,000 was issued to a supplier on 28th December on line 1986. The cheque as presented to Bank on 4th January 1987.

(c) There was debit in the Pass Book for interest Rs. 2,000 on overdraft and Bank charges Rs. 600 not recorded in the Cash Book.

(d) The credit side of the Bank column of the Cash Book was undercast by Rs. 100.

(e) A cheque for Rs. 1,000 was issued to a creditor on 27th December, but unfortunately the same was not recorded in the Cash Book. The cheque was however duly encashed within 31st December.

(f) As per standing instructions the bank collected dividend of Rs. 500 on behalf of Gupta and credited the same to his account within 31st December 1986. The fact was however intimated to Gupta on 3rd January 1987.

You are required to prepare a Bank Reconciliation Statement as on 31st December 1986.

[C.U., B.Com (Hons.)]

Ans: Overdraft balance as per Pass Book Rs. 27,500.

[**Hint:** For the following item numbers:

(a) Rs. 300 is to be added and Rs. 2,000 (1,000 + 1,000) is to be deducted.

(c) Rs. 2,000 + Rs. 600 = Rs. 2,600 to be added.]

23. From the following information, prepare a Bank Reconciliation Statement on March 31, 2008:

(a) Bank balance as per Cash Book (Cr.) as on March 31, 2008 Rs. 5,950.

(b) A cheque of Rs. 674 deposited in the bank and duly credited by it but recorded in the Cash Book as Rs. 764.

(c) Interest on fixed deposits accrued Rs. 820 and as such recoded in the Cash Book in advance.

(d) Uncredited cheques amounting to Rs. 4,780.

(e) Cheques drawn but encashed after March 31, 2008 Rs. 1,000.

(f) Bank statement shows that a debtor deposited cash directly into bank Rs. 550 and bank debited Rs. 650 for trade subscriptions.

(g) Unpresented cheques amounted to Rs. 1,250.

(h) Credit side of the Cash Book bank column undercast by Rs. 240.

Ans: Balance as per Pass Book (overdraft) Rs. 10,030.

24. From the following information, prepare a Bank Reconciliation Statement of Mr. R. Das as on December 31, 2007:

(a) On December 31, 2007, Mr. Das had an overdraft of Rs. 17,000 as shown by the bank column of his Cash Book.

(b) Cheques amounting to Rs. 5,000 had been paid to the bank, but of these only Rs. 2,200 had been credited in the Pass Book within that date.

(c) Another cheque of Rs. 3,000 had been debited to the bank column of the Cash Book, but this cheque had not been deposited to the bank by mistake.

(d) During the month, three cheques amounting to Rs. 8,000 were issued, but a cheque for Rs. 2,000 was encashed after December 31, 2007.

(e) A debtor of Mr. Das directly deposited Rs. 8,560 in the bank account of Mr. Das, but there was no record of the same in his Cash Book.

(f) Bank charges of Rs. 240 were debited in the Pass Book, but not entered in the Cash Book.

(g) On December 31, 2007 dividends of Rs. 900 were collected by the bank and credited in the Pass Book, but it was not debited in the Cash Book.

(h) A cheque for Rs. 1,600 received from Suresh was dishonoured, but it was not recorded in the Cash Book.

(i) The Pass Book was debited with Rs. 2,050 for interest on overdraft, but the same was not entered in the Cash Book within December 31, 2007.

(j) Mr. R. Das withdrew Rs. 2,000 from bank for his personal use, but it was not recorded in the Cash Book.

Ans: Balance as per Pass Book (overdraft) Rs. 17,230.

Overdraft or (Dr. Balance) as per Pass Book

25. You are required to prepare a Bank Reconciliation Statement from the following particulars:

(a) Overdraft balance as per Pass Book Rs. 13,300.

(b) Unpresented cheques amounted to Rs. 1,740.

(c) Cheques paid into Bank but not credited Rs. 1,990.

(d) Interest on investment credited in the Pass book Rs. 710 but not entered in the cash book.

(e) A party's cheque of Rs. 800 was returned by the Bank marked as "insufficient funds returned to drawer", but no correction has been made in the Cash Book.

(f) As per instructions Bank honoured a bill of Rs. 1,400.

(g) Interest on overdraft debited in the Cash Book Rs. 720.

(h) A debtor deposited cash directly into Bank Rs. 930.

Ans: Overdraft balance as per Cash Book Rs. 11,050.

[**Hint:** For the following item numbers:

(e) To be deducted by Rs. 800. Deposited cheque dishonoured but no correction has been made in the Cash Book. As a result it has made the Pass Book liabilities greater than the Cash Book liabilities.

(g) To be deducted Rs. 1,440. Interest on overdraft is an expenditure but shown in the Cash Book as an income (debited). As such Pass Book liabilities are greater than the Cash Book liabilities.]

26. On 31st December, 1996, the Bank Pass Book of Rahim showed an overdraft of Rs. 3,000. It is learnt that out of the cheques amounting to Rs. 8,000, Rs. 9,000 and Rs. 10,000 issued on 28th December 1996 the cheque for Rs. 9,000 was presented to the Bank on 4th January, 1997. Rahim had deposited cheques amounting to Rs. 12,000, Rs. 15,000, Rs. 3,000 and Rs. 10,000 in the last week of December, 1996. The first two cheques were duly collected within December, 1996 while the other two cheques were collected in January, 1997. The Pass Book of Rahim showed a debit of Rs. 1,000 for interest, but the same was not entered into his Cash Book within 31st December, 1996. (W.B.H.S.)

Ans: Bank balance as per Cash Book Rs. 2,000.

27. On June 30, 1996, the Pass Book of Moon Moon showed a debit balance of Rs. 8,000. On verification the following errors were discovered:

(i) Cheques deposited in Bank but not recorded in Cash Book Rs. 500.

(ii) Cheque received and recorded in the Bank column, but not sent to Bank for collection Rs. 1,000.

(iii) Chamber of commerce fee Rs. 250 was paid by the Bank and recovered in Cash column of Cash Book.

(iv) In the Cash Book a Bank charge of Rs. 50 was recorded twice.

(v) On 20th June 1996 the credit side of Cash Book was cast Rs. 1,500 short and on 25th June 1996 the credit balance of Rs. 3,000 was brought forward on 26th June 1996 as debit balance of Rs. 3,000. (H.S.—Central Board)

Ans: Bank balance as per Cash Book Rs. 200.

28. From the following particulars a Bank Reconciliation Statement for A/c no. 1 as on 31st December 1986.
  (i) Bank balance of A/c no. 1 as per Cash Book Rs. 1,000.
  (ii) Cheques deposited and credited by Bank but omitted to be recorded in Cash book Rs. 1,700,
  (iii) Cheques issued but not presented Rs. 300.
  (iv) Cheques against A/c no. 1 but wrongly charged by Bank to A/c no. 2 Rs. 200.
  (v) Dividend collected by Bank but not recorded in Cash Book Rs. 250.
  (vi) Insurance premium paid and debited by Bank but no entry was made in Cash Book Rs. 400.
  (vii) Interest on Bank deposit credited by bank on 26th December, but recorded in Cash Book as on 31st December Rs. 150.
  (viii) Debit side of Cash Book was undercast by Rs. 100.
  (ix) Cheques issued and paid by bank but wrongly entered in cash column of Cash Book Rs. 800.
  (x) An entry of Rs. 500 being payment by a customer directly into the Bank but no entry was made in the Cash Book. (B.U., B.Com.)

Ans: Balance as per Pass Book Rs. 2,850.
[Hint: For the following item number:
(viii) No effect on Cash Book or Pass book.]

29. The following information are available from the books of M/s Lakshmi Agency, Agartala. Prepare a Bank Reconciliation Statement on March 31st, 2008:
  (a) Debit balance as per Pass Book Rs. 6,950.
  (b) Cheques for Rs. 650 were issued during March, 2008, but were enchased in April, 2008.
  (c) Cheques for Rs. 1,550 were deposited on March 29, 2008 but were credited by the bank in April, 2008.
  (d) Bank charged interest of Rs. 150 on overdraft.
  (e) A customer directly deposited Rs. 1,500 in the bank account on March 27, 2008, but was not recorded in the cash book of the business before April 3, 2008.
  (f) The bank debited the business account of Rs. 500 for a dishonoured bill and Rs. 150 for insurance premium paid on behalf of the business but these are not recorded in the Cash Book. [Tripura H.S. (Adapted)]

Ans: Bank Balance as per Cash Book (overdraft) Rs. 6,750.

30. While examining the bank Pass Book balance of Mr. G.S. Bose, it was found that the balance shown on May 31, 2008, differed from the bank balance as per Cash Book. Overdraft balance as per Pass Book as on that date was Rs. 14,600. With the help of the following particulars, prepare a Bank Reconciliation Statement as on May 31, 2008:
  (a) Cash withdrawn from bank for personal use Rs. 1,680 not reflected in the Cash Book.
  (b) A debtor deposited cash directly in the bank Rs. 950.
  (c) A cheque of Rs. 1,480 paid to the bank became dishonoured, but no entry was made in the Cash Book for such dishonoured cheque.
  (d) A bill of Rs. 3,800 discounted with the bank at Rs. 3,650 but shown in the Cash Book without deducting the discount.
  (e) As per standing instructions, the bank made a payment of Rs. 1,950, but the matter was informed by the bank on June 3, 2008.

(f)   Credit side of bank column of the Cash Book undercasted by Rs. 400.

(g)   Bank interest on overdraft Rs. 480 and bank commission Rs. 320 debited in the Cash Book.

Ans: Bank Balance as per Cash Book (overdraft) Rs. 9,090.

Where There are two Bank Accounts

31.   D.K. Traders has two bank accounts with SBI Coke Oven Branch, Durgapur. On March 31, 2008, their cash book balances of account No. 1 and No. 2 showed Rs. 18,400 and Rs. 13,200 respectively. On verification with the respective bank statements, the following mistakes were noticed:

(a)   Dividend collected by bank (A/c No. 1) Rs. 1,250 but recorded in the cash book A/c No. 2.

(b)   A transfer of Rs. 5,000 from A/c No. 2 to A/c No. 1 was made by the bank as per advice, but was not reflected in the cash book.

(c)   A cheque of Rs. 2,500 issued on A/c No. 2 and duly cashed, but shown in the cash book A/c No. 1 wrongly.

(d)   A cheque of Rs. 1,750 deposited in the bank A/c No. 2 wrongly credited by bank to A/c No. 1.

(e)   Bank interest of Rs. 780 and Rs. 1,250 credited by the bank in A/c No.1 and A/c No. 2, respectively, but not reflected in the cash book.

(f)   Bank commission of Rs. 170 charged by bank in A/c No. 1 but no information had been given by the bank.

(g)   A debtor deposited cash of Rs. 1,340 directly in the bank A/c No. 1.

Prepare a Bank Reconciliation Statement as on March 31, 2008 for the above two accounts.

Ans: Balance as per Pass Book A/c (a) Rs. 30,850 and A/c (b) Rs. 3,950.

32.   Mr. K. Desai had two bank accounts with Canara Bank, City Centre Branch and their respective account numbers were 201 and 204. On April 30, 2008, his cash book showed a balance of Rs. 11,600 and Rs. 19,000, respectively, in the said two bank accounts. On scrutiny, the following discrepancies were noticed:

(a)   A debtor deposited cash directly in the bank A/c No. 204 Rs. 1,980 but it was not shown in the cash book.

(b)   A cheque of Rs. 1,850, deposited in the bank A/c No. 201, became dishonoured but shown in the cash book A/c No. 204 for such dishonour.

(c)   Unpresented cheques amounted to Rs. 2,870 and Rs. 3,100 (A/c Nos. 201 & 204).

(d)   A transfer of Rs. 3,800 from A/c No. 201 had not been reflected in cash book.

(e)   Bank interest of Rs. 1,420 credited in A/c No. 201 and bank commission of Rs. 70 debited in A/c No. 204 not shown in the cash book.

(f)   Dividend of Rs. 890 was collected by bank and was credited in A/c No. 204 but was debited in the cash book in A/c No. 201.

(g)   A deposited cheque of Rs. 1,850 was duly credited by bank in A/c No. 201 but was wrongly debited in A/c No. 204 in the cash book.

Prepare a Bank Reconciliation Statement for the said two accounts as on April 30, 2008.

Ans: Balance as per Pass Book A/c 201 Rs. 18,800 and A/c 204 Rs. 21,200.

33. Prepare a Bank Reconciliation Statement for the said two accounts as on May 31, 2008, with the help of the following data:

		Bank A/c No. 304. (Rs.)	Bank A/c No. 305 (Rs.)
(a)	Balance as per pass book as on May 31, 2008	18,900	10,200
(b)	Unpresented cheques	—	3,200
(c)	Uncredited cheques	4,500	—
(d)	Interest on bank deposit not reflected in cash book	750	410
(e)	A debtor deposited cash directly in the bank	1,900	—
(f)	Bank collected dividend as per instruction	—	1,750
(g)	Wrongly debited by bank	505	

Ans: Balance as per Pass Book A/c 304 Rs. 21,255 and A/c 305 Rs. 7,440.

Correction of Bank Reconciliation Statement

34. The following Bank Reconciliation Statement was prepared by an accountant of Dhara Bros. as on July 31, 2008. The bank balance shown in the bank statement does not agree with the balance shown in the cash book. Correct the Bank Reconciliation Statement assuming that the descriptions given in the statement about all the events and overdraft balance as per pass book are correctly recorded.

Bank Reconciliation Statement as on July 31, 2008

	Rs.	Rs.
Overdraft balance as per Pass Book as on July 31, 2008		21,700
Add:		
5. A cheque issued, but not presented within July 31, 2008	650	
2. Cheques deposited but not collected by the bank	2,300	
4. A cheque recorded in the cash book as deposited in the bank, but was wrongly kept inside the cash box	390	
7. Debit side of the cash book bank column overcasted	200	
8. A cheque of Rs. 2,700 issued and cashed but not recorded in the cash book.	2,700	6,240
		27,940
Less:		
3. As per instructions bank collected an insurance claim	1,250	
6. A deposited cheque of Rs. 750 shown in the cash book as Rs. 705	1,455	
9. Interest on overdraft not shown in the cash book.	280	2,985
Overdraft balance as per cash Book		24,955

Ans: Overdraft balance as per Cash Book Rs. 17,775.

35. The following Bank Reconciliation Statement was prepared by the accountant of Dulal Bros. as on March 31, 2008. The bank balance shown in the statement does not agree with the balance shown in the one cash book. Correct the Bank Reconciliation Statement assuming that the descriptions given within the statement about all the events and the balance as per pass book are correctly recorded.

Bank Reconciliation Statement as on March 31, 2008

	Rs.	Rs.
Balance as per Pass Book	18,600	
Add: A debtor deposited cash directly in the bank	1,700	
Bank interest shown in the cash book	1,450	
Cheques deposited but not collected by bank	4,100	
Wrongly debited by the bank.	700	7,950
		26,550

(Contd.)

	Rs.	Rs.
Less: Cheques issued but not cashed	3,900	
Bank honoured a bill as per instruction	2,500	
Bank collected dividend.	3,400	9,800
Bank balance as per cash book		16,750

Ans: Corrected Balance as per Cash Book Rs. 15,450.

Reconciliation after Amendments in cash book when cash book balance is given

36. From the following information you are required to prepare a Bank Reconciliation Statement of Sri M.R. Basu as on 31st March, 1997, after making necessary corrections in the Cash Book:

(a) Bank balance as per Cash Book Rs. 18,100.
(b) As per instruction Bank honoured a bill of Rs. 1,700 and collected a dividend Rs. 700.
(c) Bank interest Rs. 175 not yet reflected in the Cash Book.
(d) Debit side of the Cash book Bank column undercasted by Rs. 100.
(e) A cheque of Rs. 720 issued and cashed but not shown in the Cash Book.
(f) Cheque drawn by another customer wrongly charged to Trader's A/c Rs. 390.
(g) A cheque of Rs. 195 deposited and credited by Bank but recorded in the Cash Book as Rs. 519.
(h) Uncredited cheques amounted to Rs. 1,800.
(i) Cheques drawn but not cashed Rs. 1,100.

Ans: Adjusted Bank balance as per Cash book Rs. 16,331; Bank balance as per Pass Book Rs. 15,241.

37. From the following information you are required to prepare a Bank Reconciliation Statement as on 30th April, 1997 after making necessary corrections in the Cash Book:

(a) Bank balance as per Cash Book Rs. 21,400.
(b) Cheques drawn amounting to Rs. 8,100 in favour of suppliers but out of that suppliers for Rs. 790 presented for payment on 4th May.
(c) Cheques for Rs. 900, Rs. 1,200 and Rs. 1,400 paid into Bank but Bank credited Rs. 2,100 within 30th April.
(d) Interest on Bank deposit recorded twice in the Cash book Rs. 210.
(e) A party's cheque became dishonoured but not reflected in the Cash Book Rs. 860.
(f) A cheque of Rs. 990 issued and cashed but shown in the Cash Book Cash column wrongly.
(g) A cheque of Rs. 630 recorded in the Cash Book as deposited into Bank but wrongly it was kept by the cashier.

Ans: Adjusted Bank balance as per Cash Book Rs. 19,340; Balance as per Pass Book Rs. 18,100.

38. The following particulars are furnished by P.K. Kumar. Prepare Bank Reconciliation Statement after making necessary corrections in the Cash Book.

(a) Bank balance as per Cash Book (Cr.) Rs. 4,280 on 31st March, 1997.
(b) Trade subscription Rs. 350 and insurance premium Rs. 490 paid by Bank as per standing instruction.
(c) Interest on overdraft not entered in the Cash Book Rs. 325.
(d) A debtor deposited cash directly into Bank Rs. 1,850.
(e) An issued cheque of Rs. 925 became dishonoured but recorded in the Cash Book as a deposited cheque became dishonoured.
(f) Cheque of Rs. 650 paid into Bank and duly credited in the Pass Book but recorded in the Cash Book as Rs. 560.

(g) A bill of Rs. 1,250 discounted with the Bank at Rs. 1,150 became dishonoured but no entry has been made in the Cash Book for such dishonour.

(h) A cheque of Rs. 450 issued but cashed on 3rd April,

(i) Cheques paid into Bank but credited by Bank on 2nd April Rs. 780.

Ans: Adjusted Bank balance as per Cash Book Rs. 2,905; Balance as per Pass Book Rs. 3,235.

39. You are required to prepare a Bank Reconciliation Statement as on 30th April, 1997 after necessary adjustments in the Cash Book:

(a) Overdraft balance as per Cash Book Rs. 4,500.

(b) Bank debited Trader's A/c wrongly Rs. 750.

(c) Cheques totalling Rs. 3,100 drawn but cashed Rs. 1,900 within 30th April.

(d) Interest on overdraft Rs. 550 and Bank charge Rs. 80 not yet considered in the Cash Book.

(e) Credit balance on 28th February Rs. 350 shown in the Cash Book on 1st March as debit balance.

(f) A cheque issued and cashed but omitted to be recorded in the Cash Book Rs. 570.

(g) One outgoing cheque recorded twice in the Cash Book Rs. 420.

Ans: Adjusted Bank balance as per Cash Book Rs. 5,980; Balance as per Pass Book Rs. 5,530.

40. The following particulars are supplied by Mr. S. Thakkar. Prepare a Bank Reconciliation Statement after making necessary corrections in the cash book as on April 30, 2008:

(a) Bank balance as per cash book as on April 30, 2008 Rs. 15,600.

(b) A debtor deposited cash directly in the bank Rs. 1,750.

(c) A cheque of Rs. 750 recorded in the cash book as paid to the bank but not sent to it.

(d) Cheques amounting to Rs. 1,840 issued but not presented for payment.

(e) Bank interest and bank charges Rs. 350 and Rs. 70, respectively, not reflected in the cash book.

(f) As per instructions bank honoured a bill of Rs. 1,990.

(g) Cheque amounting to Rs. 860 drawn by another customer wrongly charged to trader's account.

Ans: Adjusted cash book balance (Dr.) Rs. 15,640 and balance as per pass book Rs. 15,870.

41. From the following information prepare a Bank Reconciliation Statement as on May 31, 2008, after making necessary corrections in the cash book:

(a) Bank balance as per cash book as on May 31, 2008 Rs. 21,500.

(b) Debit side of the cash book bank column undercasted by Rs. 200.

(c) A deposited cheque of Rs. 780 became dishonoured but no entry had been made in the books for such dishonour.

(d) As per instructions, bank collected dividend of Rs. 1,850.

(e) A cheque of Rs. 1,300 issued and cashed but not shown in the cash book.

(f) Wrongly debited by bank Rs. 780.

(g) Unpresented cheques amounted to Rs. 970.

(h) Uncredited cheques amounted to Rs. 1,780.

(i) Bank interest Rs. 170 recorded twice in the cash book.

Ans: Adjusted cash book balance (Dr.) Rs. 21,300 and balance as per pass book Rs. 19,710.

42. From the following particulars, prepare a Bank Reconciliation Statement as on March 31, 2008, after making necessary corrections in the cash book:

(a) Bank balance as per cash book (Cr.) as on March 31, 2008 Rs. 6,430.

(b) A cheque of Rs. 740 paid to the bank and duly credited by it but recorded in the cash book as Rs. 470.

(c) A cheque of Rs. 520 issued but cashed on April 3.

(d) Trade subscription Rs. 450 and insurance premium Rs. 620 paid by the bank as per standing instructions.

(e) Cheques paid to the bank but credited by it only on April 2.

(f) Interest on overdraft not reflected in the cash book Rs. 240.

(g) A cheque of Rs. 820 issued and cashed but shown in the cash book as Rs. 280.

(h) An issued cheque of Rs. 775 became dishonoured but shown in the cash book as a deposited cheque becoming dishonoured.

(i) A debtor deposited cash directly in the bank Rs. 660.

Ans: Adjusted cash book balance (Cr.) Rs. 5,800 and balance as per pass book (Dr.) Rs. 5,950.

43. According to the Cash Book of Gopi, there was a balance of Rs. 44,500 standing to his credit in bank on June 30, 1993. On investigation, it was found that:

(a) Cheques amounting to Rs. 60,000 issued to creditors have not been presented for payment till that date.

(b) Cheques amounting to Rs. 105,000 paid to the bank out of which only cheques amounting to Rs. 55,000 collected by the bank up to June 30, 1996.

(c) A dividend of Rs. 4,000 and rent amounting to Rs. 6,000 received by the bank and entered in the pass book but not recorded in the cash book.

(d) Insurance Premium of Rs. 2,700 (up to December 31, 1996) paid by the bank, is not entered in the cash book.

(e) The payment side of the cash book had been undercast by Rs. 50.

(f) Bank charges of Rs. 50 shown in the pass book had not been entered in the cash book.

(g) A bill payable for Rs. 2,000 has been paid by the bank but is not entered in the cash book and a bill receivable for Rs. 6,000 has been discounted with the bank at a cost of Rs. 100 has also not been recorded in the cash book.

You are required:

(a) to make the appropriate adjustments in the cash book, and

(b) to prepare a statement reconciling it with the bank pass book.

[C.A. (Foundation), Adapted]

Ans: Adjusted cash book balance (Dr.) Rs. 55,600; Balance as per the pass book Rs. 65,600.

44. On March 31, 2004, the bank account of Mr. X according to the bank column of cash book was overdrawn to the extent of Rs. 4,500. On the same date, the bank statement showed a balance of Rs. 880 in favour of Mr. X. An examination of the cash book and bank statement revealed the following:

(a) A cheque of Rs. 1,200 deposited on March 29, 2004 was credited by the bank only on April 3, 2004.

(b) A payment by cheque for Rs. 150 has been entered twice in the cash book.

(c) On March 29, 2004, the bank credited an amount of Rs. 1,700 received from a customer of Mr. X, but the advice was not received by Mr. X until April 1, 2004.

(d) Bank charge of Rs. 70 had not been entered in the cash book.

(e) On March 10, 2004, the bank credited Rs. 2,500 to Mr. X in error.

(f) A bill of exchange of Rs. 1,200 was discounted by Mr. X with his bank. This bill was dishonoured on March 28, 2004, but no entry had been made in the books of Mr. X.

(g) Cheque issued up to March 31, 2004 Rs. 6,000 but not presented for payment up to that date totalled Rs. 3,500.

You are required to:
(a) show appropriate rectifications required in the cash book of Mr. X to arrive at the correct balance on March 31, 2004, and
(b) prepare a Bank Reconciliation Statement as on that date.

[C.A. Entrance, Adapted]

Ans: Adjusted cash book balance (Cr.) Rs. 3,920 and Balance as per the pass book Rs. 880.

When Pass Book Balance is given

45. The following data are supplied by Rup Ram Bros.:
    (a) Balance as per pass book as on May 31, 2008 Rs. 14,200.
    (b) Cheques amounting to Rs. 5,800 paid to the bank, out of which bank credited Rs. 3,400 only.
    (c) Cheques drawn in favour of suppliers totalling Rs. 4,500 but presented for payment Rs. 2,900 only.
    (d) A debtor deposited cash directly in the bank Rs. 1,730.
    (e) Bank interest Rs. 380 and bank commission Rs. 80 not reflected in the cash book.
    (f) Debit side of the cash book bank column undercast by Rs. 300.
    (g) As per instructions Bank collected a claim of Rs. 2,400 from Insurance Company.
    (h) Wrongly credited by Bank Rs. 550.
    Prepare a Bank Reconciliation Statement after necessary adjustments in the Cash Book.
    Ans: Cash Book balance before amendments (F) Rs. 9,720 and after amendments (F) Rs. 14,450.

46. On June 30, 2008, Mr. S. Sain's book showed that he had an overdraft balance of Rs. 11,900. On checking the Cash Book with the Bank Statement, following were found:
    (a) Cheques paid into bank but not credited by it Rs. 2,900.
    (b) Unpresented cheques up to June 30 amounting to Rs. 2,000.
    (c) Bank charge Rs. 95 not reflected in the cash book.
    (d) Interest on overdraft debited in the cash book Rs. 590.
    (e) Credit side of the cash book column undercasted by Rs. 300.
    (f) As per instructions, bank collected dividend Rs. 1,950.
    (g) Wrongly debited to Mr. Sain's A/c by bank Rs. 1,600.
    (h) Cash withdrawn by Mr. Sain from the bank for his personal use Rs. 2,500 but not recorded in the cash book.
    Prepare a Bank Reconciliation Statement after making necessary adjustments in the cash book.
    Ans: Cash Book balance before amendments (Cr.) Rs. 7,275 and after amendments (Cr.) Rs. 9,400.

47. Pink Pond Ltd. have a current account with National Bank Ltd. The following are all extracts from the bank's books of account for the last week of June, 2008:

Account of Pink Pond Ltd.

Favouring/Particulars	Cheque No.	Rs.	Clearing etc.	Rs.
Gupta Bros.	322	4,000	Balance b/d	21,000
Steelcon Traders	323	7,200	Cheque of Madhav Industries	5,000
Gupta Bros.	325	4,100	Cheque of Chandra Bros.	7,500
Ourselves	326	2,400	Dividend Warrants	500
Incidental Charges		10		
Interest on loan		900		
Lal Chand	327	1,000		
Balance c/d		14,390		
		34,000		34,000

It is understood that:

(a) Cheque No. 314 drawn in favour of M.P. Bros. for Rs. 2,100 was not yet presented to the bank.

(b) Advice regarding incidental charges, interest on loan and dividend warrants, reached Pink Pond Ltd. only in July.

(c) Cheque favouring Lal Chand was towards rent for the month of June.

From the above data, prepare a Cash Book (Bank column only) of Pink Pond Ltd. for the above period and a Bank Reconciliation Statement in their books at the end of the month.

[C.A. Entrance, Adapted]

Ans: Cash Book balance before amendments (F) Rs. 12,700 and after amendments (F) Rs. 12,290.

When Cash Book and Pass Book are given

(i) Where the books relate to the same period

48. The following are the Cash Book and the Pass Book of Sri P.K. Sen:

Dr.   **Cash Book (Bank Column only)**   Cr.

Date	Particulars	Amount (Rs.)	Date	Particulars	Amount (Rs.)
1997			1997		
Mar. 1	To Balance b/f	18,950	March 6	By S.K. Ghosh (3940)	3,500
3	To M.G. Kar (7345)	6,100	11	By D.D. Gupta (3941)	2,450
8	To K.K. Kumar (9217)	3,200	14	G.G. Dhara (3942)	1,860
12	To P.K. Das (6327)	2,350	18	By B.K. Roy (3943)	2,350
18	To L.K. Dhar (5281)	1,850	24	By N.N. Mukui (3944)	1,890
23	To N.K. Sen (4987)	2,250	27	By O.P. Khanna (3945)	2,640
26	To A.K. Runu (8910)	1,150	30	By G.K. Sarkar (3946)	1,950
			31	By Balance c/d	19,210
		35,850			35,850

Bank Statement/Pass Book

Date	Particulars	Withdrawals (Rs.)	Debit Amount (Rs.)	Credit Amount (Rs.)
1997 1	By Balance			18,950
March 6	By M.G. Kar		6,100	25,050
7	To S.K. Ghosh (3940)	3,500		21,550
11	To D.D. Gupta (3941)	2,450		19,100
14	By P.K. Das (6327)		2,350	21,450
18	To B.K. Roy (3940)	2,350		19,100
22	By L.K. Dhar (5281)		1,850	20,950
28	To O.P. Khanna (3945)	2,640		18,310
28	To Bills Payable	3,000		15,310
29	By Dividend		2,800	18,110
29	By Interest		560	18,670
30	By M. Mukherjee		3,100	21,770
31	By A.K. Runu (8910)		1,150	22,920

You are required to prepare a Bank Reconciliation Statement as on 31st March, 1997 from the above informations.

49. The Cash Book and Pass Book of P.K. Das & Bros. are given below. Prepare a Bank. Reconciliation Statement as at 31st March, 1998.

Dr.   **Cash Book (Bank Column only)**   Cr.

Date	Particulars	Amount (Rs.)	Date	Particulars	Amount (Rs.)
1997			1997		
March 1	To Balance b/d	18,200	March 3	By C. Dhar	2,130
7	To P & Co.	3,600	8	By D. Das	3,870
12	To Roy. Bros.	2,700	10	By M. Kumar	4,100
16	To M.M. Traders	4,900	12	By P. Mukherjee	2,650
19	To K.K. Bros.	3,750	18	By G. Ghatak	3,980
26	To Sen Bros.	2,850	27	By Singha & Co.	6,200
			30	By Balance c/d	13,070
		36,000			36,000

Bank Statement/Pass Book

Date	Particulars	Withdrawals (Rs.)	Debit Amount (Rs.)	Credit Amount (Rs.)
1997 March 1	By Balance			18,200
3	To C. Dhar	2,130		16,070
10	By P & Co.		3,600	19,670
11	To M. Kumar	4,100		15,570
14	By Roy Bros.		2,700	18,270
15	By A. San		6,900	25,170
20	To G. Ghatak	3,980		21,190
22	By K.K. Bros.		3,750	24,940
30	By Interest		930	25,870
	To Bank Charges	170		25,700
31	To Bills Payable	2,400		23,300

50. From the following entries in the Cash Book of Mr. G. Saxena and corresponding Bank Pass Book, prepare a Bank Reconciliation Statement as on March 31, 2008:

Dr.   **Cash Book (Bank column)**   Cr.

Date	Particulars	Amount (Rs.)	Date	Particulars	Amount (Rs.)
2008			2008		
March 1	To Balance b/d	18,900	March 4	By Shop Rent (716)	4,900
9	To D.K. Roy	3,400	12	By P.P. Dhar (717)	3,100
16	To M.R. Basu	2,600	18	By G.V. Ram (718)	4,200
19	To N.N. Das	1,700	21	By Drawings (719)	900
23	To Cash	2,800	24	By Salary (720)	6,000
29	To Sales	4,500	31	By Balance c/d	14,800
		33,900			33,900

Bank Statement/Pass Book

Date	Particulars	Cheque No.	Dr. Withdrawals (Rs.)	Cr. Deposits (Rs.)	Balance (Rs.)
2008 March 1	By Balance b/d				18,900
4	To Cheque	716	4,900		14,000
9	By Cheque			3,400	17,400
11	By Cheque (Dividend)			2,660	20,060

(Contd.)

Date	Particulars	Cheque No.	Dr. Withdrawals (Rs.)	Cr. Deposits (Rs.)	Balance (Rs.)
18	To Cheque	718	4,200		15,860
21	To Cheque	719	900		14,960
23	By Cash			2,800	17,760
24	To Cheque	720	6,000		11,760
25	To Bills Payable		3,000		8,760
29	By Deposits			4,500	13,260
31	By Interest			640	13,900

Ans: List of causes of difference: (a) Cheques deposited but not credited by bank Rs. 4,300 (b) Cheques issued but not cashed Rs. 3,100 (c) Amount credited by bank Rs. 3,300 (2,660 + 640) (d) Amount debited by bank: Rs. 3,000.

51. The following are the Cash Book (Bank column) and Pass Book of Mr. K.K. Kumar as on May 31, 2008:

Dr. **Cash Book (Bank column)** Cr.

Date	Particulars	Amount (Rs.)	Date	Particulars	Amount (Rs.)
2008			2008		
May 1	To Balance b/d	21,400	May 3	By Salary (243)	4,800
7	To Sales	5,900	9	By Subscriptions (244)	2,100
12	To A.B. Sen	4,400	14	By D.D. Dhara (245)	3,200
18	To C.R. Roy	3,750	19	By B.K. Sen (246)	2,950
22	To Cash	4,000	21	By T.T. Bros. (247)	4,300
24	To M.M. Das	2,800	25	By Godown Rent (248)	3,250
27	To U.V. Kar	3,450	31	By Balance c/d	25,100
		45,700			45,700

Bank Statement/Pass Book

Date	Particulars	Cheque No.	Dr. Withdrawals Rs.	Cr. Deposits Rs.	Balance Rs.
2008 May 1	By Balance b/d				21,400
3	To Cheque	243	4,800		16,600
7	By Deposits			5,900	22,500
12	By Cheque			4,400	26,900
19	To Cheque	246	2,950		23,950
22	By Cash			4,000	27,950
25	To Cheque	248	3,250		24,700
27	To Interest			1,300	26,000
27	To Bank Charge		180		25,820
31	By Balance c/d				25,820

Prepare a Bank Reconciliation Statement as on May 31, 2008.
Ans: List of causes of difference: (a) Cheques deposited but not credited by bank Rs. 10,000 (b) Cheques issued but not cashed Rs. 9,600 (c) Amount credited by bank Rs. 1,300 (d) Amount debited by bank Rs. 180.

52. The Cash Book (Bank column) and Pass Book of Mr. P. Ghatak are given below:

Dr. **Cash Book (Bank column)** Cr.

Date	Particulars	Amount (Rs.)	Date	Particulars	Amount (Rs.)
2008			2008		
April 1	To Balance b/d	16,200	April 2	By A.K. Banerjee (720)	2,100
7	To Sales	3,600	9	By G.D. Sen (721)	3,450

Date	Particulars	Amount (Rs.)	Date	Particulars	Amount (Rs.)
12	To A.B.Sen	4,100	16	By K.M. Sinha (722)	4,210
18	To C.R.Roy	2,300	19	By Rent (723)	3,340
24	To Cash	4,600	25	By Salary (724)	4,600
26	To M.M.Das	5,800	28	By L.M. Prasad (725)	1,400
			30	By Balance c/d	17,500
		36,600			36,600

Bank Statement/Pass Book

Date	Particulars	Cheque No.	Dr. Withdrawals (Rs.)	Cr. Deposits (Rs.)	Balance (Rs.)
2008					
April 1	By Balance b/d				16,200
7	By D.S. Bros.			3,600	19,800
9	To G.D. Sen	721	3,450		16,350
16	To K.M. Sinha	722	4,210		12,140
18	By C.R. Roy			2,300	14,440
24	By Cash			4,600	19,040
25	To Cheque	724	4,600		14,440
30	To Bank Charge		210		14,230
	To Bills Payable		2,100		12,130
	By Interest			970	13,100

Prepare a Bank Reconciliation Statement as on April 30, 2008.

Ans: List of causes of difference: (a) Cheques deposited but not credited by bank Rs. 9,900 (b) Cheques issued but not cashed Rs. 6,840 (c) Amount credited by bank: Rs. 970 (d) Amount debited by bank Rs. 2,310.

(ii) When Pass book is given for the following period

53. On May 31, 2008 bank account balance as per Cash Book of Mr. S.R. Tandon did not agree with the Pass Book balance as on that date. Prepare a Bank Reconciliation Statement with the help of the following data:

Dr. **Cash Book (Bank column)** Cr.

Date	Particulars	Amount (Rs.)	Date	Particulars	Amount (Rs.)
2008			2008		
May 1	To Balance b/d	11,300	May 3	By G.K. Bros. (1105)	3,600
4	To P.P. Bros.	1,400	8	By C.M. Kar (1106)	2,400
7	To S.V. Ram	2,800	12	By Rent (1107)	4,300
16	To K.K. Gupta	3,600	19	By K.G. Bros. (1108)	2,900
21	To N.S. Sarma	2,900	23	By D. Sarkar (1109)	1,700
23	To A.B. Das	3,100	27	By M.K. Basu (1110)	2,300
28	To L.M. Dey	4,200	31	By Balance c/d	12,100
		29,300			29,300

Bank Statement/Pass Book

Date	Particulars	Cheque No.	Dr. Withdrawals (Rs.)	Cr. Deposits (Rs.)	Balance (Rs.)
2008					
June 1	By Balance b/d				10,600
4	By S. V. Ram			2,800	13,400
9	By M.S. Bros.			3,450	16,850

(Contd.)

Date	Particulars	Cheque No.	Dr. Withdrawals (Rs.)	Cr. Deposits (Rs.)	Balance (Rs.)
12	To C.M. Kar	1106	2,400		14,450
16	To D. Sarkar	1109	1,700		12,750
18	To Cheque	1107	4,300		8,450
21	By N.S. Sarma			2,900	11,350
22	By L.M. Dey			4,200	15,550
25	By Cash			2,700	18,250
30	By Interest			750	19,000

Ans: Uncredited cheques: Rs. 2,800, Rs. 2,900 and Rs. 4,200; Unpresented cheques: Rs. 2,400, Rs. 4,300 and Rs. 1,700. Prepare Bank Reconciliation Statement by taking Cash Book balance Rs. 12,100 and answer would be Pass Book balance Rs. 10,600.

54. The Cash Book (Bank column) and Pass Book of Mr. G. Chowla are given below:

Dr.   **Cash Book (Bank column)**   Cr.

Date	Particulars	Amount (Rs.)	Date	Particulars	Amount (Rs.)
2008			2008		
April 1	To Balance b/d	15,900	April 5	By K.G. Bros. (804)	2,450
3	To M.P. Sons.	3,250	8	By M. Kanti (805)	3,160
10	To Raj & Raj	4,150	16	By S. Kumar (806)	4,050
14	To S. Sharma	2,200	20	By P.K. Sons. (807)	1,850
20	To P. Bagchi	3,350	25	By S.K. Saxena (808)	2,160
25	To M. Dhar	1,500	27	By L. Tewari (809)	3,240
28	To B. Gupta	1,650	29	By A. Gupta (810)	3,090
			30	By Balance c/d	12,000
		32,000			32,000

Bank Statement/Pass Book

Date	Particulars	Cheque No.	Dr. Withdrawals (Rs.)	Cr. Deposits (Rs.)	Balance (Rs.)
2008					
May 1	By Balance b/d				12,560
4	By Raj & Raj			4,150	16,710
6	To M. Kanti	805	3,160		13,550
10	To N.N. Roy	812	2,240		11,310
14	To S.K. Saxena	808	2,160		9,150
19	To L. Tewari	809	3,240		5,910
21	By S. Sharma			2,200	8,110
21	By B. Gupta			1,650	9,760
25	By C.R. Darbar			6,400	16,160
28	To D.D. Bros.	816	4,100		12,060
31	To T.K. Roy	819	2,600		9,460

Prepare a Bank Reconciliation Statement as on April 30, 2008.

Ans: Uncredited Cheques: Rs. 4,150, Rs. 2,200 and Rs. 1,650; Unpresented cheques: Rs. 3,160, Rs. 2,160 and Rs. 3,240. Prepare Bank Reconciliation Statement by taking Cash Book balance Rs. 12,000 and answer would be Pass Book balance Rs. 12,560.

Miscellaneous Problems [Selected Problems for Revision]

55. From the following particulars, prepare a Bank Reconciliation Statement as on April 30, 2008:
   (a) Overdraft balance as per Cash Book on April 30, 2008 Rs. 9,540.
   (b) A cheque of Rs. 750 issued and encashed but recorded in the Cash Book as deposited Rs. 570.

(c) A cheque of Rs. 360 drawn by another customer but wrongly charged to trader's account (by the bank).

(d) A customer's cheque of Rs. 440 recorded in the Cash Book duly, but not banked.

(e) An outgoing cheque of Rs. 520 recorded twice in the Cash Book.

(f) Discount of Rs. 100 allowed to a debtor for a cheque received from him and was duly credited in the Pass Book, but the amount of discount was included with the amount of cheque in the Cash Book.

(g) Interest on overdraft Rs. 250 recorded in the Cash Book as deposited Rs. 520 on the debit side.

(h) A bill of Rs. 880 discounted with the bank at Rs. 750, but became dishonoured. No entry was made in the Cash Book for such dishonour.

(i) Credit balance of Rs. 720 for March, 2008, was shown in the Cash Book debit side on April 1, 2008.

(j) An issued cheque of Rs. 800 became dishonoured but was recorded in the Cash Book that a deposited cheque became dishonoured.

Ans: Balance as per Pass Book (overdraft) Rs. 12,730.

56. The Cash Book of Mr. T. Gupta showed an overdraft balance of Rs. 23,400 as on March 31, 2008. Scrutiny of the entries in the Cash Book and the Pass Book revealed that:

(a) As per instructions, bank collected dividend of Rs. 1,750 and paid Godown rent Rs. 900, but the fact was intimated to Mr. Gupta on April 3, 2008.

(b) A bill receivable of Rs. 3,100 due on March 29, 2008 was sent to Bank for collection on March 27, 2008 and was entered in the Cash Book forthwith, but the proceeds were not credited in the Pass Book till April 1, 2008.

(c) Interest debited by the bank Rs. 710, but it was debited in the cash book as Rs. 170.

(d) A cheque of Rs. 1,790 issued and cashed but wrongly shown in the cash book cash column.

(e) A party's cheque of Rs. 1,900 was returned by the banker marked as 'insufficient funds, return to drawer', but no correction had been made in the cash book.

(f) A bill receivable of Rs. 2,400 collected by Bank, but recorded in the Cash Book as bill honoured by bank.

(g) A credit note received for Rs. 850 from the bank but recorded in the cash book credit side as Rs. 580.

(h) Debit balance of the Cash Book bank column on March 1, 2008 was recorded as credit balance on March 1, 2008 Rs. 950.

Prepare a Bank Reconciliation Statement as on March 31, 2008.

Ans: Balance as per Pass Book (overdraft) Rs. 23,790.

57. On June 30, 1987, Mr. C. Chandra's cash book showed that he had an overdraft of Rs. 300 on his current account at the bank. On checking the cash book with the bank statement, you found the following:

(a) Cheque drawn amounting to Rs. 500 had been entered in the cash book but has not presented.

(b) Cheque received amounting to Rs. 400 had been entered in the cash book but not credited by the bank.

(c) On instructions from Mr. C. Chandra, the bank had transferred interest of Rs. 60 from his deposits account to his current account, recording the transfer on July 5, 1987. This amount had, however, been credited in the cash book as on June 30, 1987.

(d) Bank charges of Rs. 35 shown in the bank statement had not been entered in the cash book.

(e) The payment side of the cash book had been undercasted by Rs. 10.

(f) Dividend amounting to Rs. 200 had been paid directly to the bank and not entered in the cash book.

(g) A cheque of Rs. 50 drawn on deposit account had been shown in the cash book as drawn on current account.

(h) A cheque issued to B. Banerjee for Rs. 25 was replaced when out of date. It was entered again in the cash book, no other entry being made. Both cheques were included in the total of unpresented cheques shown above.

You are required:

(a) to indicate the appropriate adjustments in the cash book, and

(b) to prepare a statement reconciling the amended balance with that shown in the bank statement.

[ICWA (Intermediate)]

Ans: Adjusted cash book bank balance (Dr.) Rs. 50; Pass Book balance (Cr.): Rs. 65.

[**Hint:** For item (c), interest of Rs. 120 (60 + 60) is to be shown in the cash book (Dr.) and in the Bank Reconciliation Statement, Rs. 60 is to be deducted for interest not recorded till June 30, 1987.]

58. The following are the entries recorded in the bank column of the cash book of Mr. X for the month of March 31, 1997:

Dr.					Cash Book (Bank Column)			Cr.
Date	Particulars			Amount (Rs.)	Date	Particulars		Amount (Rs.)
1997					1997			
March 15	To Cash			36,000	1	By Balance b/d		40,000
20	To Roy			24,000	4	By John		2,000
22	To Kapoor			10,000	6	By Krishnan		400
31	To Balance c/d			7,640	15	By Kailash		240
					20	By Joshi		35,000
				77,640				77,640
					31	By Balance b/d		7,640

On March 31, 1997, Mr. X received the bank statement. On perusal of the statement, he ascertained the following information:

(a) Cheques of Rs. 10,000 deposited but not credited by the bank.

(b) Rs.1,080 interest on securities collected by the bank but not recorded in the cash book.

(c) Credit transfer of Rs. 200 not recorded in the cash book.

(d) Dividend of Rs. 1,000 collected by the bank directly but not recorded in the cash book.

(e) Cheques of Rs. 37,400 issued but not presented for payment.

(f) Rs. 1,000 interest debited by the bank but not recorded in the cash book.

(g) Bank charges of Rs. 340 not recorded in the cash book.

From the above information, prepare a Bank Reconciliation Statement to ascertain the balance as per the bank statement.

[CA (Foundation), Adapted]

Ans: Balance as per the pass book (Cr.) Rs. 20,700.

59. Redraft the following Bank Reconciliation Statement prepared by an accountant of M/s P.P. Suppliers. Assume that the bank balance as per Cash Book and the descriptions given within the statement are correct.

Bank Reconciliation Statement as on March 31, 2008

	Rs.	Rs.
Balance as per Cash Book		18,340
Add: Bank honoured a bill as per instruction	2,400	
Deposited cheque became dishonoured but not shown in the Cash Book	1,900	
Bank commission debited in the Cash Book wrongly	180	
Unpresented cheques	1,600	
Debit side of the Cash Book cash column undercasted	100	6,180
		24,520
Less: A debtor deposited cash into bank directly	1,700	
Bank interest not shown in the Cash Book	700	
An outgoing cheque recorded twice in the Cash Book	700	
(Original cheque amount Rs. 700)		
Uncredited cheques	2,400	5,500
		19,020

Ans: Corrected Pass Book balance Rs. 16,780.

Trial Balance and Errors

CONTENTS

12.1 TRIAL BALANCE

At the end of an accounting period or a certain period, when all the accounts of a firm are closed or balanced, a statement is prepared with the help of these account balances which is known as **trial balance**. All debit balances of accounts are shown on the debit side of the trial balance and credit balances are shown on the credit side. The total of both the sides of the trial balance must be equal, as it is based on double entry system according to which every debit must have a corresponding credit. Trial balance is prepared to check the arithmetical accuracy of the book keeping entries.

12.1.1 Advantages of Preparing Trial Balance

1. Arithmetical accuracy of accounting entries is checked.
2. It helps to prepare final accounts.
3. The entire ledger account balances are summarized with a list.
4. Comparisons may be made with different account balances of different years.

12.1.2 Features of Trial Balance

1. It is a statement, and not an account.
2. It is prepared in a separate sheet and is not a part of the ledger accounts.
3. Trial balance is prepared to examine the arithmetical accuracy of accounts.
4. It is a list of accounts opened/maintained in a ledger.
5. It helps to prepare final accounts of a firm.
6. It is not essential to prepare a Trial Balance unless required.
7. Trial balance is prepared at the end of a certain period.

12.1.3 Necessity of Trial Balance

1. When a trial balance agrees, it may be assumed that the accounts are arithmetically correct.
2. The ledger accounts balances can be collected at a glance from the Trial Balance.
3. Trial balance helps to prepare the final accounts of a firm.
4. It helps to rectify the errors detected before the preparation of final accounts.
5. It helps to assess/estimate the present position of a business on the basis of the closing balances of the different accounts shown in the Trial Balance.

12.2 IS TRIAL BALANCE AN ACCOUNT?

Trial Balance is prepared to examine the arithmetical accuracy of the accounts maintained in a ledger within a certain period. It is not essential to prepare a Trial Balance, but it preparing has certain benefits. It is prepared in a separate sheet and is not a part of the ledger accounts. If an accountant is satisfied with his accounts, he may prepare the final accounts without preparing the Trial Balance. The basic differences between a Trial Balance and an account are given below:

1. A Trial Balance is prepared with the help of the balances of different accounts maintained in a ledger. An account, on the other hand, is prepared with the help of the journal entries, prepared for each transaction.
2. An account is a statement prepared in a special form in the ledger where summarized records of transactions affecting a particular person, asset, income or any other subject are shown. Trial Balance is a statement prepared with account balances on a separate sheet to examine the arithmetical accuracy of accounts.
3. It is not necessary to prepare a Trial Balance, but preparation of an account is essential.
4. The appearance of a Trial Balance is different from that of an account.

In view of the facts stated above, we may conclude that a Trial Balance is not an account and it is different in character.

12.3 IS PREPARATION OF TRIAL BALANCE INDISPENSABLE?

A Trial Balance is chiefly prepared to examine the arithmetical accuracy of accounts. We have read that if an accountant is satisfied with his accounts, then he may prepare the final accounts without preparing the Trial Balance. Thus, if we stick to this point, then we may say that a Trial Balance is not indispensable.

However, it has been observed that an accountant always prepares a Trial Balance, not only for the arithmetical accuracy of accounts but also for other advantages (Section 12.1.1). A Trial Balance is the most useful document for an accountant or a businessman.

Hence, it may not be indispensable/essential, but from practical point of view, it is indispensable.

12.3.1 Errors Disclosed by Trial Balance

1. Wrong totalling or casting
2. Posting of wrong amount
3. Posting of an amount on the wrong side
4. Incomplete double entry
5. Error in balancing of an account
6. Error in carrying forward the total of one page to the next page
7. Wrong preparation of debtors/creditors' schedule
8. Omission of an account balance while preparing the trial balance.

12.3.2 Errors Not Disclosed by Trial Balance or Limitations of the Trial Balance

1. Errors of omission
2. Errors of commission
3. Errors of principle
4. Compensating errors
5. A wrong entry in the subsidiary book.

12.3.3 Classification of Errors

There are many types of errors as shown in Figure 12.1.

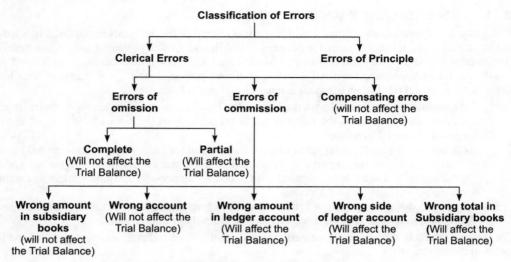

FIGURE 12.1 Classification of errors.

Errors of principle

Errors of principle occur when a transaction is recorded in the books without following our generally accepted accounting principles. For example, capital expenditures considered as revenue expenditures or a delivery van purchased for the business use shown in the books as delivery expenses. These types of errors will not affect the trial balance, but will affect the profits of the business.

Clerical errors

These types of errors are generally subdivided as follows:

1. **Errors of omission:** When a transaction is omitted completely or partially from the books, then the errors which are found are known as **errors of omission**. Generally, these types of errors arise when a transaction is not recorded in the books of original entry, i.e., in journals. It is very difficult to locate these types of errors. When a transaction is completely omitted from the books, then it will not affect the trial balance.

2. **Errors of commission:** These errors arise due to wrong posting, wrong balancing of an account, wrong totalling, wrong carrying forward, wrong calculations, etc. Some of these errors will affect the trial balance while the others will not. For example, cash paid to Madhu Rs. 700, but shown as Rs. 70 only, is an error of commission.

3. **Compensating errors:** When the effect of a particular error is compensated (i.e., corrected) with the help of another error or errors, then such type of error is called **compensating errors**. For example, cash paid to R.R. Rs. 860 but only Rs. 800 debited to his account. On the other hand, cash received from K.K. Rs. 460 but credited to his account Rs. 400 only. Here, R. R.'s shortage of Rs. 60 (Dr.) is compensated by K. K.'s credit shortage of Rs. 60. Such errors will not affect the trial balance.

4. **Errors of casting:** When the total of any book or an account is wrong, then trial balance will not tally. For example, Cash Book bank column's total of Rs. 34,200 shown as 35,200; it will increase Cash Book bank balance by Rs. 1,000. As a result, Trial Balance debit side total will also increase by Rs. 1,000.

5. **Errors of balancing of an account:** While balancing a particular account within the Ledger, there might occur some mistake. For example, the total of credit side of Protap's account is Rs. 36,400 and the debit side total is Rs. 21,900. Here, balancing figure would be Rs. 14,500, but recorded as Rs. 15,400. Hence, it will increase Protap's account balance(Cr.) and the total of Trial Balance credit side by Rs. 900.

6. **Errors while carrying forward:** At the end of a certain period, balancing is made and the closing balance (Balance c/d) is considered as the opening balance (Balance b/d) for the next period. For example, closing balance for the month of March 2008 of Cash Book (Cash Column) shown as Rs. 24,600 instead of actual balance of Rs. 26,400. It will reduce both the Cash Book (Cash Column) debit balance and the total of Trial Balance debit side by Rs. 1,800.

7. **Wrong totalling in the subsidiary books:** Suppose, Purchase Day Book's total for the month March is shown as Rs. 34,500 instead of actual amount of Rs. 32,500. As per practice Purchase Day Book's total amount is transferred to Purchases Account in the Ledger. It will increase the Purchase Account balance as well as the total of Trial Balance debit side by Rs. 2,000.

8. **Errors of posting to wrong account:** Suppose, cash received from P.K. Dhara Rs. 3,000. It was correctly recorded in the Journal and posted to P.K. Dua's Account in the Ledger. It will affect P.K. Dhara and P.K. Dua's Account both in the Ledger.

9. **Errors of posting of wrong amount in ledger:** Suppose, cash received from G. Guha Rs. 3,000. It was correctly recorded in the Cash Book, but posted to G. Guha's Account Rs. 3,300. For this mistake cash balance will increase by Rs. 3,000, whereas debtor's account (G.Guha's) will reduce by Rs. 3,300. It will affect the Trial Balance.

10. **Errors of posting in the wrong side of ledger accounts:** Suppose, cash received from G. Guha Rs. 3,000. It was correctly recorded in the Cash Book, but posted to the debit of G. Guha's Account (instead of credit side). For this mistake, cash balance will increase by Rs. 3,000. At the same time Debtor's Account (G. Guha's) will also increase by Rs. 3,000 (instead of decreasing). It will affect the Trial Balance and will increase the debit total by Rs. 6,000.

Errors affecting one account only

1. Errors of casting
2. Errors of balancing of an account
3. Errors while carrying forward
4. Omission from the trial balance
5. Wrong totalling in the subsidiary books.

Errors affecting two or more accounts

1. Errors of omission
2. Errors of principles
3. Errors of posting to wrong account
4. Errors of posting of wrong amount in ledger
5. Errors of posting on the wrong side of ledger accounts.

12.4 SUSPENSE ACCOUNT

Generally, final accounts are prepared after the preparation of trial balance. But when a Trial Balance disagrees due to some errors, it may delay the preparation of the final accounts. Hence, to avoid the said delay in the preparation of the final accounts, the difference in the trial balance is replaced by a new account known as **suspense account.** Subsequently, when all the errors are rectified, the suspense account will automatically close.

12.5 STEPS TO BE TAKEN WHEN A TRIAL BALANCE DISAGREES

The following steps may be taken to find out the causes of disagreements:

1. Check the totals of both sides of a Trial Balance.
2. Check the totals and the balances of the different accounts opened in the ledger.
3. Check whether the balances of the different accounts are properly taken in the Trial Balance or not. Suppose cash balance of Rs. 4,170 is shown in the Trial Balance as Rs. 4,710, rent of Rs. 3,570 is shown as Rs. 3,750 and so on.

4. Check the posting of the different accounts from the journal to the ledger.

It is expected that if the above steps are properly followed, we will be able to find the mistakes or the disagreements.

12.6 PREPARATION OF A TRIAL BALANCE

It is prepared generally under the following two methods:

1. Total method
2. Balance method.

12.6.1 General Rules for Preparing Trial Balance

1. **Trial Balance with Total:** According to this method, Trial Balance has to be prepared with the help of the total of each of the accounts (without taking the balancing figure of each account). The debit total and the credit totals are shown in two different columns and it will be seen at the end that both the totals are equal.

2. **Trial balance with balances:** In this method, Trial Balance is prepared with the help of the balancing figures of each of the accounts. The debit balances and the credit balances are to be shown in two different columns and it will be seen at the end that both the totals are equal.

The different items which come under debit side and credit side of the trial balance are listed in Table 12.1.

TABLE 12.1 Items shown under Debit Balance and Credit Balance

Accounts having debit balances	Accounts having credit balances
The items which are to be considered in debit side of the *Trial Balance*:	The items which are to be considered in credit side of the *Trial Balance*:
1. All Asset Account balances	1. All Incomes and Profits
2. All Expenses and Losses	2. All Liabilities
3. All Personal Accounts having debit balances (representing assets)	3. All Personal Accounts having credit balances (representing liabilities)

Different account balances and their positions in Trial Balance are shown in Table 12.2 for preparing a Trial Balance at a glance.

In the Books of Sri/M/s. ....
Trial Balance for the year ended...
Or
Trial Balance for the period ended ...

Dr. **TABLE 12.2** Positions of Account Balances in Trial Balance Cr.

Particulars	Amount (Rs.)	Particulars	Amount (Rs.)
Opening Stock		Sales:	
Raw Materials		Local	
Finished Goods		Export	
Work in Progress		Purchases Returns (Return Outwards)	
Purchases:		Capital	
Local		Sundry Creditors	
Import		Bills Payable	
Carriage Inward		Bank Overdraft	
Freight		Loan	
Import Duty		Discount Received	
Dock Dues		Commission Received	
Motive Power		Dividend Received	
Carriage Outward		Interest Received	
Sales Returns (Return inwards)		Reserve	

(Contd.)

Particulars	Amount (Rs.)	Particulars	Amount (Rs.)
Wages		Miscellaneous Receipts	
Rent		Bad Debts Recovered	
Salaries		Advance from Mr. Y (Loan)	
Insurance		Rebates Received	
Bad Debts		Rent from Subletting	
Discount Allowed		Apprenticeship Premium Received	
Rebate Allowed		Provision for Bad and Doubtful Debts	
Packing Charges			
Petty Expenses			
Trade Expenses			
Repairs			
Building and Land			
Drawings			
Plant and Machinery			
Furniture and Fittings			
Sundry Debtors			
Bills Receivable			
Cash in Hand			
Cash at Bank			
Investment			
Goodwill			
Freehold Premises			
Bank Charges			
Patent			
Audit Fees			
Advertisement			
Miscellaneous Expenses			
Advance to Mr. X (Investment)			
Trademark			
Octroy			
Travelling Expenses			
Apprenticeship Premium (Paid)			
Rates and Taxes			
Depreciation			
Coke, Coal and Gas			
Printing and Stationery			

Note Regarding Adjusted Purchases and Closing Stock

Here, Adjusted Purchases means 'Opening Stock + Purchases – Closing Stock' i.e., cost of goods used or sold during the period. It is a general rule that *total stocks* are to be shown in the Trial Balance. Hence, it may be shown either as 'Opening Stock + Purchases' in Debit side of the Trial Balance or as 'Adjusted purchases' (used goods) + closing stock (unused goods)' in Debit side of the Trial Balance. Thus, when Opening Stock and Purchases are shown in the Trial Balance, then *Closing Stock is not required to be shown* in it, because it is already included in the opening stock and/or purchases. In other words, when Adjusted Purchases (used goods) is shown in the Trial Balance, then *closing stock (unused goods)* is *also to be shown* in the Trial Balance (because used goods + unused goods = Total goods or stocks, i.e., Opening Stock + Purchases). If the Trial Balance is prepared after preparing the Trading A/c, then closing stock is to be shown in the debit side of the Trial Balance.

ILLUSTRATION 12.1   Journalize the following transactions and post them in Ledger Accounts and prepare Trial Balance:

2008

April 1   Mr. R.P. Singha started his business with capital of Rs. 124,000. His capital consists of stock Rs. 21,000; Furniture Rs. 28,000; Machinery Rs. 30,000; and balance in cash.

3   Purchased a Computer for office use from M/s Machino Make at Rs. 21,200.
7   Paid rent Rs. 2,600 and Rs. 3,600 for advertisement.
11 Personal NSC of Mr. N. Roy was cashed and brought that amount into the business Rs. 16,000.
14 Opened a bank account with UBI in cash Rs. 28,000.
17 Purchased goods from Ratan for Rs. 12,700.
19 Goods returned to Ratan Rs. 1,900.
23 Sold goods to Mahim for Rs. 17,800.
26 Miscellaneous expenses paid Rs. 750.
28 Cash paid to petty cashier Rs. 1,200.
29 Issued a cheque of Rs. 14,000 to M/s Machino Make.

Solution

In the Books of Mr. R.P. Singha
Journal

Date	Particulars		L.F.	Amount Dr. (Rs.)	Amount Cr. (Rs.)
2008 April 1	Stock A/c	Dr.		21,000	
	Machinery	Dr.		30,000	
	Furniture	Dr.		28,000	
	Cash A/c	Dr.		45,000	
	To Capital A/c				124,000
	(Being the business started with the above assets)				
3	Computer A/c	Dr.		21,200	
	To Machino Make A/c				21,200
	(Being the computer purchased on credit)				
7	Rent A/c	Dr.		2,600	
	To Cash A/c				2,600
	Advertisement A/c	Dr.		3,600	
	To Cash A/c				3,600
	(Being rent and advertisement paid)				
11	Cash A/c	Dr.		16,000	
	To Capital A/c				16,000
	(Being NSC of the proprietor cashed and brought that amount into the business)				
14	Bank A/c	Dr.		28,000	
	To Cash A/c				28,000
	(Being the bank account opened)				
17	Purchases A/c	Dr.		12,700	
	To Ratan A/c				12,700
	(Being goods purchased on credit)				
19	Ratan A/c	Dr.		1,900	
	To Return Outwards A/c				1,900
	(Being goods returned)				
23	Mahim A/c	Dr.		17,800	
	To Sales A/c				17,800
	(Being the goods sold on credit)				
26	Miscellaneous expenses A/c	Dr.		750	
	To Cash A/c				750
	(Being miscellaneous expenses paid)				
28	Petty Cashier A/c	Dr.		1,200	
	To Cash A/c				1,200
	(Being cash paid to petty cashier)				
29	M/s Machino Make A/c	Dr.		14,000	
	To Bank A/c				14,000
	(Being cheque issued to M/s Machino Make)				

Ledger

Dr. **Cash Account** **Cr.**

Date	Particulars	J.F.	Amount (Rs.)	Date	Particulars	J.F.	Amount (Rs.)
2008 April 1	To Capital A/c		45,000	2008 April 7	By Rent A/c		2,600
11	To Capital A/c		16,000	7	By Advertisement A/c		3,600
				14	By Bank A/c		28,000
				26	By Miscellaneous expenses A/c		750
				28	By Petty Cashier A/c		1,200
				30	By Balance c/d		24,850
			61,000				61,000
May 1	To Balance b/d		24,850				

Dr. **Stock Account** **Cr.**

Date	Particulars	J.F.	Amount (Rs.)	Date	Particulars	J.F.	Amount (Rs.)
2008 April 1	To Capital A/c		21,000	2008 April 30	By Balance c/d		21,000
			21,000				21,000
May 1	To Balance b/d		21,000				

Dr. **Machinery Account** **Cr.**

Date	Particulars	J.F.	Amount (Rs.)	Date	Particulars	J.F.	Amount (Rs.)
2008 April 1	To Capital A/c		30,000	2008 April 30	By Balance c/d		30,000
			30,000				30,000
May 1	To Balance b/d		30,000				

Dr. **Furniture Account** **Cr.**

Date	Particulars	J.F.	Amount (Rs.)	Date	Particulars	J.F.	Amount (Rs.)
2008 April 1	To Capital A/c		28,000	2008 April 30	By Balance c/d		28,000
			28,000				28,000
May 1	To Balance b/d		28,000				

Dr. **Capital Account** **Cr.**

Date	Particulars	J.F.	Amount (Rs.)	Date	Particulars	J.F.	Amount (Rs.)
2008 April 30	To Balance c/d		140,000	2008 April 1	By Stock A/c		21,000
					By Machinery A/c		30,000
					By Furniture A/c		28,000
					By Cash A/c		45,000
				11	By Cash A/c		16,000
			140,000				140,000
				May 1	By Balance b/d		140,000

Dr. **Bank Account** **Cr.**

Date	Particulars	J.F.	Amount (Rs.)	Date	Particulars	J.F.	Amount (Rs.)
2008 April 14	To Cash A/c		28,000	2008 April 29	By M/s Machino Make A/c		14,000
				30	By Balance c/d		14,000
			28,000				28,000
May 1	To Balance b/d		14,000				

Dr. **Computer Account** Cr.

Date	Particulars	J.F.	Amount (Rs.)	Date	Particulars	J.F.	Amount (Rs.)
2008 April 3	To Machino Make A/c		21,200	April 30	By Balance c/d		21,200
			21,200				21,200
May 1	To Balance b/d		21,200				

Dr. **Machino Make Account** Cr.

Date	Particulars	J.F.	Amount (Rs.)	Date	Particulars	J.F.	Amount (Rs.)
2008 April 29	To Bank A/c		14,000	2008 April 3	By Computer A/c		21,200
30	To Balance c/d		7,200				
			21,200				21,200
				May 1	By Balance b/d		7,200

Dr. **Sales Account** Cr.

Date	Particulars	J.F.	Amount (Rs.)	Date	Particulars	J.F.	Amount (Rs.)
2008 April 30	By Balance c/d		17,800	2008 April 23	By Mahim A/c		17,800
			17,800				17,800
				May 1	By Balance b/d		17,800

Dr. **Advertisement Account** Cr.

Date	Particulars	J.F.	Amount (Rs.)	Date	Particulars	J.F.	Amount (Rs.)
2008 April 7	To Cash A/c		3,600	2008 April 30	By Balance c/d		3,600
			3,600				3,600
May 1	To Balance b/d		3,600				

Dr. **Rent Account** Cr.

Date	Particulars	J.F.	Amount (Rs.)	Date	Particulars	J.F.	Amount (Rs.)
2008 April 7	To Cash A/c		2,600	2008 April 30	By Balance c/d		2,600
			2,600				2,600
May 1	To Balance b/d		2,600				

Dr. **Purchases Account** Cr.

Date	Particulars	J.F.	Amount (Rs.)	Date	Particulars	J.F.	Amount (Rs.)
2008 April 17	To Ratan A/c		12,700	2008 April 30	By Balance c/d		12,700
			12,700				12,700
May 1	To Balance b/d		12,700				

Dr. **Return Outwards Account** Cr.

Date	Particulars	J.F.	Amount (Rs.)	Date	Particulars	J.F.	Amount (Rs.)
2008 April 30	By Balance c/d		1,900	2008 April 19	By Ratan A/c		1,900
			1,900				1,900
				May 1	By Balance b/d		1,900

Dr.   **Ratan Account**   Cr.

Date	Particulars	J.F.	Amount (Rs.)	Date	Particulars	J.F.	Amount (Rs.)
2008 April 19 30	Return outwards A/c By Balance c/d		1,900 10,800	2008 April 17	By Purchases A/c		12,700
			12,700				12,700
				May 1	By Balance b/d		10,800

Dr.   **Mahim Account**   Cr.

Date	Particulars	J.F.	Amount (Rs.)	Date	Particulars	J.F.	Amount (Rs.)
2008 April 23	To Sales		17,800	2008 April 30	By Balance c/d		17,800
			17,800				17,800
May 1	To Balance b/d		17,800				

Dr.   **Miscellaneous Expenses Account**   Cr.

Date	Particulars	J.F.	Amount (Rs.)	Date	Particulars	J.F.	Amount (Rs.)
2008 April 26	To Cash A/c		750	2008 April 30	By Balance c/d		750
			750				750
May 1	To Balance b/d		750				

Dr.   **Petty Cashier Account**   Cr.

Date	Particulars	J.F.	Amount (Rs.)	Date	Particulars	J.F.	Amount (Rs.)
2008 April 28	To Cash A/c		1,200	2008 April 30	By Balance c/d		1,200
			1,200				1,200
May 1	To Balance b/d		1,200				

Preparation of Trial Balance

1. *Trial Balance with totals*

Heads of Accounts	Debit totals (Rs.)	Credit totals (Rs.)
Cash Account	61,000	36,150
Capital Account		140,000
Bank Account	28,000	14,000
Stock Account	21,000	
Machinery	30,000	
Sales Account		17,800
Furniture	28,000	
Purchases Account	12,700	
Return Outward Account		1,900
Ratan Account	1,900	12,700
Mahim Account	17,800	
Miscellaneous Expenses	750	
Computer Account	21,200	
Machino Make Account	14,000	21,200
Rent Account	2,600	
Petty Cashier	1,200	
Advertisement Account	3,600	
	243,750	243,750

2. *Trial balance with balances*

Closing balances of all accounts	Amount (Dr.) (Rs.)	Amount (Cr.) (Rs.)
Cash Account	24,850	
Capital Account		140,000
Bank Account	14,000	
Stock Account	21,000	
Machinery	30,000	
Sales Account		17,800
Furniture	28,000	
Purchases Account	12,700	
Return Outward Account		1,900
Ratan Account		10,800
Mahim Account	17,800	
Miscellaneous Expenses	750	
Computer Account	21,200	
Machino Make Account		7,200
Rent Account	2,600	
Petty Cashier	1,200	
Advertisement Account	3,600	
	177,700	177,700

ILLUSTRATION 12.2   From the following balances, prepare a Trial Balance:

Particulars	Rs.	Particulars	Rs.
Rates and Taxes	4,500	Audit Fees	3,900
Travelling Expenses	2,800	Advertisement	4,700
Investment	20,000	Salaries	6,500
Commission Received	3,600	Insurance	2,700
Interest Received	2,300	Bad Debts	1,800
Goodwill	25,000	Printing and Stationery	900
Cash in Hand	18,700	Discount Allowed	1,900
Sundry Creditors	32,000	Capital	110,900
Bills Receivable	16,900	Commission Received	1,400
Purchases Return	2,600	Purchases	67,000
Sales	167,000	Opening Stock	13,100
Loan to Mr. X	10,000	Plant and Machinery	34,000
Loan from Mr. D	12,000	Buildings	65,000
Sundry Debtors	43,000	Sales Returns	2,000

Solution

In the Books of ...

Dr.   **Trial Balance for the period ended ...**   Cr.

Particulars	Rs.	Particulars	Rs.
Rates and Taxes	4,500	Commission Received	3,600
Travelling Expenses	2,800	Interest Received	2,300
Investment	20,000	Sundry Creditors	32,000
Goodwill	25,000	Purchases Return	2,600
Cash in Hand	18,700	Sales	167,000
Bills Receivable	16,900	Loan from Mr. D	12,000
Sundry Debtors	43,000	Purchases Return	2,600
Audit Fees	3,900	Capital	110,900
Advertisement	4,700	Commission Received	1,400
Salaries	6,500		
Insurance	2,700		
Sales Returns	2,000		
Bad Debts	1,800		

(Contd.)

Particulars	Rs.	Particulars	Rs,
Printing and Stationery	900		
Discount Allowed	1,900		
Purchases	67,000		
Opening Stock	13,100		
Buildings	65,000		
Plant and Machinery	34,000		
	334,400		334,400

ILLUSTRATION 12.3   The following Trial Balance was wrongly drawn by an accountant. Redraft the following Trial Balance correctly.

In the Books of ...

Dr.   **Trial Balance for the year ended March 31,2008**   Cr.

Particulars	Rs.	Particulars	Rs.
Insurance	2,400	Sales	113,400
Furniture and Fittings	14,000	Bad Debts	1,900
Opening Stock	10,800	Sundry Debtors	29,000
Bad Debts Recovered	1,400	Bills Receivable	15,600
Wages	12,800	Discount Received	2,700
Rent	3,600	Commission Received	1,500
Salaries	5,700	Capital	43,800
Carriage Inward	1,600	Miscellaneous Receipts	2,400
Bank Overdraft	27,000	Suspense Account	27,600
Cash in Hand	21,700		
Purchases	65,000		
Bills Payable	10,300		
Purchases Returns	1,800		
Sundry Creditors	19,800		
Plant and Machinery	40,000		
	237,900		237,900

Solution

In the Books of ...

Dr.   **Trial Balance for the year ended March 31,2008**   Cr.

Particulars	Rs.	Particulars	Rs.
Wages	12,800	Discount Received	2,700
Rent	3,600	Commission Received	1,500
Salaries	5,700	Capital	43,800
Carriage Inward	1,600	Miscellaneous Receipts	2,400
Insurance	2,400	Bad debts Recovered	1,400
Bad Debts	1,900	Sales	113,400
Opening Stock	10,800	Sundry Creditors	19,800
Cash in Hand	21,700	Bills Payable	10,300
Purchases	65,000	Bank Overdraft	27,000
Plant and Machinery	40,000	Purchases Returns	1,800
Furniture and Fittings	14,000		
Sundry Debtors	29,000		
Bills Receivable	15,600		
	224,100		224,100

Working Note

It is to be noted here that if the Trial Balance is prepared correctly, then suspense account will automatically vanish, i.e., there would be no balance in suspense account.

ILLUSTRATION 12.4 From the following balances, prepare a Trial Balance for the year ended March 31, 2008:

Particulars	Rs.	Particulars	Rs.
Sales	143,000	Freight	3,100
Furniture and Fittings	26,000	Import Duty	3,600
Dividend Received	3,400	Capital	65,000
Interest Received	2,700	Bad Debts	1,700
Sundry Creditors	21,600	Discount Allowed	2,100
Bills Payable	13,500	Rebate Allowed	1,900
Rebates Received	1,700	Plant and Machinery	50,000
Purchases	66,500	Bills Receivable	18,700
Cash in Hand	23,600	Carriage Inward	2,600
Import	18,900	Drawings	8,000
Rent from Subletting	4,300	Sundry Debtors	31,200
Apprenticeship Premium Received	2,700		

Solution

In the Books of ...

Dr.   **Trial Balance for the year ended March 31, 2008**   Cr.

Particulars	Rs.	Particulars	Rs.
Plant and Machinery	50,000	Sundry Creditors	21,600
Furniture and Fittings	26,000	Bills Payable	13,500
Sundry Debtors	31,200	Capital	65,000
Bills Receivable	18,700	Rent from Subletting	4,300
Bad Debts	1,700	Apprenticeship Premium Received	2,700
Discount Allowed	2,100	Rebates Received	1,700
Rebate Allowed	1,900	Dividend Received	3,400
Purchases	66,500	Interest Received	2,700
Cash in Hand	23,600	Sales	143,000
Import	18,900		
Carriage Inward	2,600		
Freight	3,100		
Import Duty	3,600		
Drawings	8,000		
	257,900		257,900

ILLUSTRATION 12.5 From the following Ledger Balances of Durgapur Diamond Club, prepare a Trial balance as on December 31, 2007: Cash in hand Rs. 18,100; Staff salaries Rs. 3,000; Travelling Expenses Rs. 1,700; Investment Rs. 8,000; Interest on Investment Rs. 800; Donation Received Rs. 9,000; Entrance Fees Received Rs. 3,400; Subscription from members Rs. 30,080; Grants from Government Rs. 900; Donation for building Rs. 9,200; Sale of Old Papers Rs. 320; Subscription received in Advance for 1998 Rs. 700; Outstanding subscription for 1997 Rs. 930; General Fund (or Accumulated Fund) Rs. 21,200; Sale of furniture Rs. 700; Newspapers and periodicals Rs. 640; Charities Rs. 960; Tournament Expenses Rs. 3,400; Printing and Stationery Rs. 390; Tournament Fund Receipts Rs. 4,000; Audit Fees Rs. 700; Ground Rent Rs. 1,200; Grants from Local Authorities Rs. 4,600; Sports Materials Rs. 3,100; Entertainments Rs. 2,100; Library books Rs. 3,200; Locker rent received Rs. 3,100; Curtains Rs. 900; Building Rs. 30,000; Upkeep of Grounds Rs. 2,230; Electric Installation Rs. 3,000; Crockery Rs. 1,000; Advertisements Rs. 900; Advance for Construction of Building Rs. 5,100; Legacies Rs. 1,000; Endowment Fund Receipts Rs. 6,000; Advertisement in the 'Year Book' Rs. 900; Proceeds on Concerts Rs. 2,100; Depreciation on furniture Rs. 450 and Furniture Rs. 7,000.

Solution

Dr.   **Durgapur Diamond Club Trial Balance as on December 31, 2007**   Cr.

Particulars	Amount (Rs.)	Particulars	Amount (Rs.)
Cash in Hand	18,100	Interest on Investment	800
Staff Salaries	3,000	Donation Received	9,000
Investment	8,000	Entrance Fees Received	3,400
Travelling Expenses	1,700	Subscription from Members	30,080
Outstanding Subscriptions for 1997	930	Grants from Government	900
Furniture	7,000	Donation on Furniture	4,500
Newspapers and Periodicals	640	Donation from Building	9,200
Charities	960	Sale of Old Papers	320
Tournament Expenses	3,400	Subscription Received Inadvance for 1998	700
Printing and Stationery	390	General Fund (or Accumulated Fund)	21,200
Audit Fees	700	Sale of Furniture	700
Ground Rent	1,200	Tournament Fund Receipts	4,000
Sports Material	3,100	Grants from Local Authorities	4,600
Entertainments	2,100	Locker Rent Received	3,100
Library Books	3,200	Endowment Fund Receipts	6,000
Curtains	900	Legacies	1,000
Building	30,000	Advertisement in the 'Year Book,	900
Upkeep of Grounds	2,230	Proceeds of Concerts	2,100
Electric Installation	3,000		
Crockery	1,000		
Advertisement	900		
Advance for Construction of Building	5,100		
	98,000		98,000

ILLUSTRATION 12.6 The total of the Trial Balance of a firm as on December 31, 2007 is Rs. 178,300 on the debit side and Rs. 152,800 on the credit side. After scrutiny, the following mistakes were found:

Items	Original amount (Rs.)	Actual amount shown in the Trial Balance (Rs.)	
Opening Stock	13,500	15,300	
Closing Stock	11,200	11,200	(debit side)
Provision for Bad Debts	1,900	1,900	(debited)
Outstanding Wages	700	900	(debited)
Discount Received	2,100	1,200	(debited)
Salaries	6,200	2,600	(credited)
Bank Overdraft	7,000	7,800	(debited)
Commission Received	1,800	1,000	(debited)
Advertisement	2,500	2,500	(credited)

Calculate the correct total of the Trial Balance.

Solution

Statement showing the calculation of correct total of the Trial Balance as on 31st December, 2007:

Items	Debit Balance (Rs.)	Credit Balance (Rs.)
Present balance as per Trial Balance	178,300	152,800
Opening Stock shown excess on the debit side Rs. (15,300 – 13,500)	(–) 1,800	
	176,500	152,800
Closing Stock wrongly debited	(–) 11,200	

(Contd.)

Items	Debit Balance (Rs.)	Credit Balance (Rs.)
Provision for Bad Debts to be shown on the credit side instead of the debit side	165,300 (−) 1,900	152,800 (+) 1,900
Outstanding wages to be shown on the credit side instead of the debit side	163,400 (−) 900	154,700 (+) 700
Discount received to be shown on the credit side instead of the debit side	162,500 (−) 1,200	155,400 (+) 2,100
Salaries to be shown on the debit side instead of the credit side	161,300 (+) 6,200	157,500 (−) 2,600
Bank Overdraft to be shown on credit side instead of the debit side	167,500 (−) 7,800	154,900 (+) 7,000
B/F	159,700 (−) 1,000	161,900 (+) 1,800
Commission received to be shown on the credit side instead of the debit side	158,700 (+) 2,500	163,700 (−) 2,500
Advertisement to be shown on the debit side instead of the credit side		
Correct Trial Balance total	161,200	161,200

EXERCISES

I. *Short Answer Type Questions (with answers)*

1. What do you mean by trial balance?

    Ans: Trial balance is prepared to check the arithmetical accuracy of the book keeping entries. At the end of accounting period or at the end of a certain period, when all the accounts of a firm are closed or balanced, then with the help of these balances, a list or statement is prepared known as **trial balance**. All debit balances of accounts are shown on the debit side and credit balance on the credit side of the trial balance. The total of both the sides of the trial balance must be equal as it is based on the double entry system according to which every debit must have a corresponding credit.

2. Identify the errors which are not disclosed by the trial balance.

    Ans: Errors which are not disclosed by the trial balance or limitations of the trial balance are given below:
    (a) Errors of omission
    (b) Errors of commission
    (c) Errors of principle
    (d) Compensating errors
    (e) A wrong entry in the subsidiary book.

3. What do you mean by suspense account?

    Ans: Generally, final accounts are prepared after the preparation of trial balance. However, due to some errors which affect the agreement of the trial balance and to avoid delay in the preparation of final accounts, the difference in the trial balance is replaced by a new account know as **suspense account**. Subsequently, when all the errors are rectified, the suspense account will automatically close.

4. What are the errors disclosed by Trial Balance?
    (a) Wrong totalling or casting
    (b) Posting of wrong amount
    (c) Posting of an amount on the wrong side
    (d) Incomplete double entry
    (e) Error in balancing of an account
    (f) Error in carrying forward the total of one page to the next page

(g) Wrong preparation of debtors/creditors' schedule

(h) Omission of an account balance while preparing the trial balance.

5. What do you mean by Errors of Principle?

Ans: Errors of principle occur when a transaction is recorded in the books without following generally accepted accounting principles. For example, capital expenditures considered as revenue expenditures or a delivery van purchased for the business use shown in the books as delivery expenses. These types of errors will not affect the trial balance. However, will affect the profits of the business.

6. What do you mean by Errors of omission?

Ans: When a transaction is omitted completely or partially from the books, then the errors which are found are known as **errors of omission**. Generally, these types of errors arise when a transaction is not recorded in the books of original entry, i.e. in journals. It is very difficult to locate these types of errors. When a transaction is completely omitted from the books, then it will not affect the trial balance.

7. What do you mean by Errors of commission?

Ans: These errors arise due to wrong posting, wrong balancing of an account, wrong totalling, wrong carrying forward, wrong calculations, and so on. Some of these errors will affect the trial balance while the others will not. For example, cash paid to Madhu Rs. 700, but shown a Rs. 70 only, is an error of commission.

8. What do you mean by Compensating errors?

Ans: When the effect of a particular error is compensated (i.e., corrected) with the help of other error or errors. For example, cash paid to R.R. Rs. 860 but only Rs. 800 debited to his account. On the other hand, cash received from K.K. Rs. 460 but credited to his Rs. 400 only. Here, R. R.'s shortage of Rs. 60 (Dr.) is compensated by his credit shortage of Rs. 60. Such errors will not affect the trial balance.

II. *Very Short Answer Type Questions*

1. What is Trial Balance?
2. What are the objectives of preparing a Trial Balance?
3. What are the chief features of a Trial Balance?
4. Can Trial Balance be considered an Account?
5. Is the preparation of Trial Balance indispensable?
6. What are the limitations of a Trial Balance?
7. What do you mean by errors of principle?
8. What are clerical errors?
9. What is meant by errors of commission?
10. What do you mean by clerical errors?
11. Define suspense account?
12. What are compensating errors?

III. *Long Answer Type Questions*

1. What is trial balance? What are the objectives of preparing a Trial Balance?
2. Identify the errors disclosed and those not disclosed by a Trial Balance.
3. What do you mean by errors in accounts? How are they classified?
4. What are errors of commission? How are they classified? Which will of them will affect the Trial Balance?
5. How could you classify the errors
   (a) affecting one account only, and
   (b) affecting two or more accounts?
6. Explain in brief the effect of errors in final accounts.
7. What are the steps to be taken when a Trial Balance disagrees?

IV. *Problems*

1. Pass necessary journal entries and post them in the appropriate ledger accounts of Mr. D. K. Juneja for June, 2008, and prepare Trial Balance as on June 30, 2008:

2008	Transactions
June 1	Started business with cash in hand Rs. 48,000 and Rs. 50,000 at bank.
3	Paid wages to staff Rs. 5,600.
7	Purchased stationery Rs. 1,300 in cash.
9	Paid insurance premium by a cheque of Rs. 2,100.
11	Bought goods from Sindh & Co. Rs. 18,700.
14	Paid electric bill Rs. 900.
17	Purchased office equipments Rs. 7,600.
19	Goods returned to Sindh & Co. Rs. 1,300.
23	Sold goods to Saha Bros. for Rs. 16,500.
24	Issued a cheque of Rs. 17,000 to Sindh & Co. in full settlement of their account.
27	Received a cheque of Rs. 7,600 from Saha Bros. and allowed them discount Rs. 200.
28	Received interest from bank Rs. 280.
29	Delivery van purchased on credit from G.P.Suppliers Rs. 24,000.

2. Give necessary journal entries of the following transactions in the books of Mr. G.D. Neogi for the month of January, 2008, and prepare Trial Balance on January 31, 2008:

2008	Transactions
Jan. 1	Mr. G.D. Neogi started business with cash Rs. 106,000.
2	Opened a bank account with cash Rs. 45, 000.
3	Goods purchased from M/s D. Bros. for Rs. 12, 600 and paid carriage on it Rs. 800.
4	Paid shop rent Rs. 1,800.
5	Paid for advertisement by a cheque of Rs. 3,500.
6	Sold goods for cash Rs. 4,600.
7	Sold goods to Mr. H. Samanta for Rs. 9,800 and paid carriage on it Rs. 540.
8	Issued a cheque of Rs. 5,600 in favour of M/s D. Bros.
8	Trade subscription paid by a cheque of Rs. 750.
9	Received interest from bank Rs. 210.
10	Purchased furniture from Durgapur Timber Suppliers for Rs. 7,500.
11	Purchased computer from M/s Rick Tech in cash Rs. 9,000.
12	Paid cash Rs. 6,500 to M/s D. Bros. in full settlement of their account and received discount of Rs. 500.
13	Goods returned by Mr. H. Samanta amounting to Rs. 760 and received cash from him Rs. 3,600.
14	Cash withdrawn from bank for office use Rs. 5,000.
15	Cash withdrawn from bank for personal use Rs. 1,500.

3. From the following Ledger a Account balances of a household as on 31st December, 1998, prepare a Trial Balance as on that date:

Particulars	Rs.	Particulars	Rs.
Income from Salaries	17,200	Interest from Fixed Deposits	3,100
Income from House Property	4,600	Income from Lottery	5,000
Dividends from Shares	1,300	Income from Agriculture	2,400
Cash in Hand	1,550	Newspapers & periodicals	600
Cash at Bank	2,200	Expenses for foodgrains	6,200
Furniture	4,900	Fish, Meat, Egg, etc.	2,100
Fixed Deposits	1,000	Expenses for Oil & Spices	3,200
Shares	2,000	Vegetables & Fruits	2,300

(Contd.)

Particulars	Rs.	Particulars	Rs.
Educational Expenses	1,900	Travelling Expenses	2,400
Club Subscriptions	250	Donations	600
Repairs	300	Corporation Tax	400
Servant's Salary	1,200	Income Tax	500

Ans: Trial Balance Total Rs. 33,600.

4. From the following Ledger Account balances of a household as on 31st December, 1985, prepare the Trial Balance as on that date:

Particulars	Rs.	Particulars	Rs.
Cash in Hand	100	Income from House Property	2,500
Expenses for Foodgrains	975	Income from Agriculture	1,500
Newspaper Subscription	25	Dinner Table	1,325
Expenses for Vegetables	275	Almirah	1,800
Expenses for Fish, Meat, Egg, etc	475	Expenses for Pulse	100
Travelling Expenses	250	Expenses for Oil	100
Tiffin Expenses	475	Expenses for Spices	100
Income from salary	2,000		

(W.B.H.S.)

Ans: Trial Balance Total Rs. 6,000.

5. From the following Ledger Account balances of Kolkata 'Amra Kajan Club', prepare a Trial Balance as on 31st March, 1999:

Particulars	Rs.	Particulars	Rs.
Admission Fees Received	2,100	Capital Fund (or General Fund)	19,200
Donation Received	6,400	Sale of Old Papers	600
Subscription from Members	9,800	Donation for Books	4,700
Interest Received	1,700	Tournament Fund	3,900
Library Books	8,400	Sports Materials	7,100
Entertainment	2,300	Cash in Hand & at Bank	7,800
Newspappers & Periodicals	700	Travelling Expenses	4,600
Furniture	1,600	Advertisement	900
Interest on Investment	2,500	Accrued Interest on Investment	1,200
Outstanding Subscription	700	Printing & Stationery	600
10% Govt. Bonds	10,000	Curtains	600
Audit Fees	900	Grants from KMDA	1,000
Subscription Received in Advance	500	Tournament Expenses	5,000

Ans: Trial Balance Total Rs. 52,400.

6. Draw up a Trial Balance of Burdwan 'Toofan Society' as on 31st December, 1998, from the following Ledger Account balances:

Particulars	Rs.	Particulars	Rs.
Salaries and Wages	7,600	Advertisement	700
Maintenance of Grounds	1,300	Advertisement in "Year Book"	4,800
Sports Materials	3,800	Entrance Fees	2,700
Electric Installation	1,500	Donations	4,300
Crockery	400	Subscriptions from Members	9,800
Proceed of Concerts	1,600	Interest from Bank	1,300
Cash in Hand	700	Bank Deposits	16,800
Papers and Periodicals	1,500	Construction of Building	8,000
Accumulated Fund	13,200	Furniture	3,700
Tournament	4,400	Charities	900
Depreciation on Furniture	300	Postage and Telegram	400
Legal Charges	500	Tournament Expenses	2,700
Rent Paid	1,300		

Ans: Trial Balance Total Rs. 52,100.

7. Correct the following Trial Balance:

Particulars	Debit (Rs.)	Particulars	Credit (Rs.)
Return Outward	16,000	Debtors	15,000
Opening Stock	34,200	Carriage Outward	5,000
Salaries	12,000	Capital	55,200
Creditors	28,000	Machinery	18,000
Bank	45,000	Return Inward	3,000
Carriage Inward	6,000	Discount Received	4,000
Rent Received	3,000	Trade Expenses	6,000
Discount Allowed	2,000	Sales	140,000
Purchases	100,000	Building	20,000
Bills Payable	20,000		
	266,200		266,200

(W.B.H.S.)

Ans: Correct Trial Balance Total Rs. 266,200.

8. The following Trial Balance for the year ended 31st December, 1980 has been prepared by a novice of a trader. Redraft the same and mention the nature of mistakes in each case:

Particulars	Debit (Rs.)	Credit (Rs.)
Closing Stock	10,100	
Capital Accounts:		
A (Overdrawn)		3,300
B	5,450	
Cash in hand	1,400	
Bank Overdraft	9,320	
Sales		126,400
Purchases	76,400	
Return Inward		3,400
Return Outward	2,900	
Carriage	2,300	
Discount Allowed		4,200
Salary	9,540	
Wages	3,720	
Sundry Debtors	16,500	
Sundry Creditors		26,500
Opening Stock		12,120
Land and Buildings	20,000	
Machinery	15,900	
Trade Expenses	2,090	
	175,620	175,620

(Tripura H.S.)

Ans: Correct Trial Balance Total Rs. 170,570.

9. Prepare the Trial Balance of S. Kumar as on 31.3.1997.

Particulars	Rs.	Particulars	Rs.
Discount (Dr.)	700	Discount (Cr.)	1,200
Commission Received	900	Opening Stock	3,400
Purchases	51,000	Sales	93,000
Debtors	21,000	Creditors	14,600
Loan	9,000	Bills Payable	8,000
Bills Receivable	12,000	Salary and Wages	6,000
Travelling Expenses	1,200	Machinery	31,000
Horses and Carts	12,000	Capital	56,000
Interest Received	2,300	Closing Stock	7,000

(Contd.)

Particulars	Rs.	Particulars	Rs.
Bad Debts	700	Insurance	900
Rent from Subletting	2,000	Cash in Hand	16,000
Cash at Bank	11,000	Carriage Inward	900
Return Inward	700	Furniture and Fittings	18,500

Ans: Correct Trial Balance Total Rs. 187,000.

10. The following are the balances extracted from the books of B.B. Gupta as on 31.12.96.

Particulars	Rs.	Particulars	Rs.
Capital	50,000	Furniture	12.000
Motor Car	16,000	Adjusted Purchases	72,000
Closing Stock	15,000	Discount Received	1,600
Commission Allowed	2,100	Debtors	24,100
Creditors	19,600	Provision for Bad Debts	2,200
Loan to Mr. X	18,000	Loan from Mr. Y	10,000
Carriage	1,400	Rent and Rates	2,500
Sales	105,000	Genera! Expenses	1,200
Bad Debts	500	Cash in Hand and at Bank	14,900
Return Inward	1,100	Wages	3,200
Advertisement	1,900	Taxes	900
Duty on Purchase	1,400		

Ans: Correct Trial Balance Total Rs. 187,000.

11. Prepare the Trial Balance of H. Sen as on 31.3.1997

Particulars	Rs.	Particulars	Rs.
Goodwill	12,000	Investment	18,000
Patent	7,000	Trade Mark	8,000
Closing Stock	12,000	Sundry Debtors	14,000
Rent	6,000	Prepaid Rent	1,000
Salaries	5,400	Outstanding Salaries	600
Advance given to X. Bros.	2,000	Provision for Bad debts	1,600
Bad Debt	600	Reserves	4,000
Rebates Received	1,500	Bad Debts Recovered	900
Petty Expenses	200	Depreciation	4,000
Carriage	1,700	Import Duty	600
Plant and Machinery	36,000	Cash in Hand	5,900
Cash at Bank	11,200	Apprenticeship Premium	1,800
Audit Fees	400	Insurance	700
Creditors	14,500	Sales	86,000
Capital	85,000	Interest Received	1,500
Octroy	700	Purchases	59,000

Ans: Correct Trial Balance total Rs. 195,600.

12. From the following list of balances prepare a Trial Balance:

Particulars	Rs.	Particulars	Rs.
Capital A/c	100,000	Debtors A/c	20,000
Fixed Assets A/c	92,000	Sales A/c	110,000
Returns Outward A/c	1,000	Bills Payable A/c	8,000
Bank Overdraft A/c	11,000	Opening Stock A/c	15,000
Creditors A/c	20,000	Purchases A/c	70,000
Returns Inward A/c	2,000	Wages and Salaries A/c	30,000
Bills Receivable A/c	15,000	Rent A/c	6,000

(W.B.H.S.)

Ans: Trial Balance Total of Rs. 250,000.

13. A businessman wrongly prepared the following Trial Balance. You are required to prepare the Trial Balance, correctly stating reasons for errors in brief:

Dr.   **Trial Balance for the year ended 31.12.89**   Cr.

Particulars	Rs.	Particulars	Rs.
Opening Stock of Materials	10,000	Capital	30,000
Opening Stock of finished Goods	15,000	Sales	130,000
		Returns Inward	5,000
Wages	30,000	Bills Receivable	12,000
Salaries	20,000	Creditors	5,000
Purchases	80,000	Discount Allowed	3,000
Returns Outward	1,000	Carriage Outward	500
Debtors	20,000	Fixed Assets	15,000
Bills Payable	8,000	Closing Stock of Materials	500
Discount Received	6,000	Closing Stock of Finished Goods	1,500
Carriage Inward	3,000		
Fuel	1,500		
Accrued Wages	1,000		
Cash in Hand	2,000		
Bank Overdraft	5,000		

(W.B.H.S.)

Ans: Correct Trial Balance Total Rs. 217,000; Suspense A/c Rs. 31,000 Cr.

14. The clerk of a businessman wrongly prepared the following Trial Balance:

	Dr. (Rs.)	Cr. (Rs.)
Capital		80,000
Stock at the commencement of the year	25,000	
Discount allowed		500
Commission received		700
Fixed Assets		60,000
Sales	90,000	
Purchases		50,000
Return Outward		1,000
Return Inward	2,000	
Carriage Inward		600
Carriage Outward		700
Wages and Salaries	27,000	
Bills receivable	5,000	
Sundry Debtors	10,000	
Bills payable		8,000
Accrued rent	3,000	
Interest paid		2,000
Cash	800	
Sundry Creditors	6,900	
Stock at the end	33,800	
	203,500	203,500

You are required to draw up the Trial Balance correctly stating reasons in brief.

(W.B.H.S.)

Ans: Total of corrected Trial Balance Rs. 186,600.

15. The undermentioned Trial Balance of M/s Putriram & Co. has been wrongly drawn, you are to redraft the same correctly:

Ledger Balances	Dr. (Rs.)	Cr. (Rs.)
Stock on 1.4.92		70,000
Stock on 31.3.93	80,000	
Carriage Inward	21,200	

(Contd.)

Ledger Balances	Dr. (Rs.)	Cr. (Rs.)
Accrued Municipal tax	3,000	
Machinery	17,000	
Land and Building	114,000	
Bills receivable		40,000
Capital A/c		170,000
Furniture	19,000	
Salaries	37,300	
Purchase	240,000	
Sales		426,000
Carriage Outward		8,000
Payment on Suspense A/c	600	
Labour charges	33,500	
Bills payable	48,400	
Balance of customers A/c	82,000	
Cash in hand	1,800	
Drawings A/c		10,000
Balance on suppliers A/c		48,000
Provision for Doubtful debts		3,600
Reserve for discount on creditors		1,600
Suspense A/c (Difference in Trial Balance)	79,400	
	777,200	777,200

(H.S. 1994, W.B.)

Ans: Trial Balance Total Rs. 699,000, Suspense A/c (Debit) Rs. 3,000.

16. The following Trial Balance has been prepared by a novice. You are asked to correct it.

	Dr. (Rs.)		Cr. (Rs.)
Returns Outward	16,000	Debtors	15,000
Opening Stock	34,200	Carriage Outward	5,000
Salaries	12,000	Capital	55,200
Creditors	28,000	Machinery	18,000
Bank	45,000	Return Inward	3,000
Carriage Inward	6,000	Discount Received	4,000
Rent Received	3,000	Trade Expenses	6,000
Discount Allowed	2,000	Sales	140,000
Purchases	100,000	Building	20,000
Bills Payable	20,000		
	266,200		266,200

(H.S.)

Ans: Total Rs. 266,200.

17. The undermentioned Trial Balance of M/s Karim Bros. has been wrongly prepared. You are to redraft the same correctly.

Trial Balance for the year ended 31st December, 1995

	Dr. (Rs.)	Cr. (Rs.)
Rent, rates and taxes	41,850	
Bills receivable		26,640
Trade Expenses	43,920	
Bills Payable	9,000	
Salary and Wages	53,820	
Cash in hand	12,780	
Stock in trade		26,760
Drawings Account	50,760	

(Contd.)

	Dr. (Rs.)	Cr. (Rs.)
Capital Account		140,040
Closing Stock	26,640	
Trade Creditors	47,520	
Leasehold premises	66,690	
Sales		248,040
Purchase return	23,760	
Dues from customers		47,700
Bank Loan		4,500
Purchases	114,120	
Reserve fund		18,000
Sales return		8,820
	490,860	517,500

(W.B.H.S. 1995)

Ans: Correct Trial Balance Total Rs. 490,860.

18. The following Trial Balance of Md. Jamal of Ranaghat was wrongly prepared by an accountant. You are required to draw a correct Trial Balance stating reasons:

Ledger Accounts	Dr. (Rs.)	Cr. (Rs.)
Capital		250,000
Purchases	700,000	
Opening Stock	225,000	
Bills Payable		150,000
Wages	7,500	
Sales		800,000
Advertisement	6,250	
Closing Stock		592,500
Bills Receivable	300,000	
Debtors		325,000
Creditors	675,000	
Bank Balance	155,000	
General Expenses	1,500	
Bad Debt	1,000	
Building	125,000	
Income Tax		50,000
Loan Taken		25,000
Interest on Loan Taken		3,750
Sales Return		1,500
Rent from Subletting	1,500	
Total	21,97,750	21,97,750

(W.B.H.S.)

Ans: Correct Trial Balance Total Rs. 19,01,500.

19. The following Trial Balance of Mr. Anil Roy of Rajnagar was drafted by his Accountant. But due to imperfect knowledge in the subject, it has been done incorrectly. You are now asked to redraft it.

Trial Balance
for the year ended December 31, 1986

Ledger Balances	Dr. (Rs.)	Cr. (Rs.)
Opening Stock	49,770	
Closing Stock		61,740
Capital		300,000
Fixed Assets	237,000	

(Contd.)

Ledger Balances	Dr. (Rs.)	Cr. (Rs.)
Sundry Creditors		37,500
Sundry Debtors	62,010	
Return Inwards	7,200	
Sales		307,800
Purchases	182,760	
Discount Allowed		2,280
Rates and Taxes	21,390	
Commission Received		2,610
Cash in Hand	1,140	
Bank Overdraft	33,000	
Interest Paid		3,300
Rent Received	11,400	
Bills Payable		24,000
Wages and Salaries	94,200	
Bills Receivable	45,000	
Export Duty		2,400
Return Outwards		3,690
Carriage Inwards	2,400	
Import Duty	3,600	
Carriage Outwards		5,550
	750,870	750,870

Ans: Correct Trial Balance Total Rs. 720,00.   (W.B.H.S., 1987)

20. The total of the debit side of the Trial Balance of a large boot and shoe repairing firm as on December 31, 1987 is Rs. 166,590 and that of the credit side is Rs. 42,470.

After several checking and rechecking, the following mistakes are discovered:

Items of Accounts	Correct Figure as it should be (Rs.)	Figure as it appears to the Trial Balance (Rs.)
Opening Stock	14,900	14,800
Repairs	61,780	61,780 (appears on the debit side)
Rent and Rates	2,160	2,400
Sundry Creditors	6,070	5,900
Sundry Debtors	8,060	8,310
Ascertain the correct total of the Trial Balance.		

[Calcutta University, B.Com. (Hons.)]

Ans: Correct Total of Trial Balance Rs. 104,420.

Note: Here repairs is an item of income but wrongly shown on the debit side instead of the credit side.

21. The total of the Trial Balance of a firm as on December 31, 1996 is Rs. 115,390 on the debit side and Rs. 109,500 on the credit side. After a thorough scrutiny, the following errors are discovered:

Items	Correct Amount (Rs.)	Amount shown in the Trial Balance (Rs.)
Sundry Debtors	21,300	23,100
Salaries	6,900	6,090
Cash at Bank	18,000	16,500
Discount Received	1,900	1,400
Closing Stock	9,500	5,900 (Debit)

Calculate the correct total of the Trial Balance.
Ans: Correct Trial Balance Total Rs. 110,000.

22. The following Trial Balance was prepared by Mr. M. Sen as on December 31, 1997.

Dr.   *Cr.*

	Rs.		Rs.
Machinery	31,000	Capital	66,400
Opening Stock	9,000	Sales	78,000
Sundry Debtors	24,000	Sundry Creditors	16,000
Investment	19,000	Discount Received	4,300
Purchases	46,000	Rent Received	3,400
Commission	3,800	Closing Stock	20,000
Carriage	2,600		
Cash in Hand	16,300		
Wages	4,900		
Drawings	6,200		
Sundry Expenses	5,300		
	168,100		188,100

Subsequently, the following errors were noticed:

(a) A machine purchased on credit for Rs. 3,000 shown as goods purchased on credit.

(b) Furniture purchased on credit for Rs. 900 not taken into account.

(c) Rent receivable Rs. 600 not yet considered.

(d) Cash withdrawn for personal use Rs. 750 included in the Sundry Expenses A/c.

(e) Goods sold for Rs. 4,500 on credit not reflected in the books.

Considering the above errors, draw up the correct Trial Balance.

Ans: Correct Total of Trial Balance Rs. 174,100.

Note: There is no effect in the Trial Balance due to the errors (a) and (d).

23. Following is the Trial Balance of M.M. Traders as on December 31, 1997:

Dr.   *Cr.*

	Rs.		Rs.
Purchases	56,000	Sales	82,000
Machinery	25,000	Creditors	9,500
Wages	3,000	Bad Debts	500
Carriage	2,500	Capital	36,000
Debtors	21,700	Rent	2,000
Cash	14,400	Suspense	3,700
Discounts	1,600		
Bad Debts Recovered	2,100		
Sundry Expenses	4,400		
Salaries	3,000		
	133,700		133,700

After preparing the Trial Balance, the following errors were detected:

(a) Sales Day Book undercasted by Rs. 1,100.

(b) Purchase Day Book overcasted by Rs. 200.

(c) Goods sold on credit for Rs. 1,600 not recorded in the books.

(d) Stationery purchased for Rs. 600 shown in the books as "Goods Purchased".

(e) Proprietor's house rent paid Rs. 1,200, recorded as Sundry Expenses.

(f) Discount appearing in the Trial Balance should have been recorded as Discount Received.

(g) Rent paid wrongly recorded in the Trial Balance as Rent received.

Ans: Correct Trial Balance Total Rs. 133,900.

Note: There is no effect in the Trial Balance due to the errors (d) and (e).

13

Rectification of Errors

CONTENTS

13.1 RECTIFICATION OF ERRORS

An error can creep in the accounting process at any time. It may be due to carelessness or lack of accounting knowledge, or due to some other errors. If the errors are not detected in due time and are not corrected accordingly, it will lead to problems and confusions in running the business. Therefore, steps must be taken to identify the errors at the earliest and then necessary rectification entries be made for the same. Trial Balance is prepared to check the arithmetical accuracy of the book keeping entries and when Trial Balance disagrees, it indicates that there are some mistakes or undetected errors. At the some time, even if the Trial Balance agrees, there might be a possibility that some errors may still exist in the accounting records. A particular error can be rectified either before preparing the trial balance, after preparing the trial balance but before preparing the final account, or after preparing the final account. In the subsequent sections, different types of errors and the method(s) to rectify them have been explained.

13.1.1 Objectives of Rectifying Errors

1. Errors affecting nominal accounts will result in either increase or decrease in the profits of the business. As a result, the true profits of the business cannot be ascertained. Thus, it becomes essential to rectify these errors.
2. Errors affecting personal accounts, real accounts and the profits of the business will result in either increase or decrease in assets or liabilities of the business. Hence, to represent the true financial position of a concern, it is essential to rectify the detected errors as early as possible.
3. If the errors are not detected in due time and are not corrected accordingly, it will lead to problems and confusions in running the business.

13.2 TYPES OF ERRORS

The different types of errors are explained below (see Figure 13.1)

13.2.1 Errors of Principle

When a transaction is recorded in the books without following generally accepted accounting principles, errors of principle occur. For example, Capital expenditures considered as Revenue expenditures;

a delivery van purchased for business use shown in the books as delivery expenses. Errors of principle will not affect the trial balance, but will affect the profits of the business.

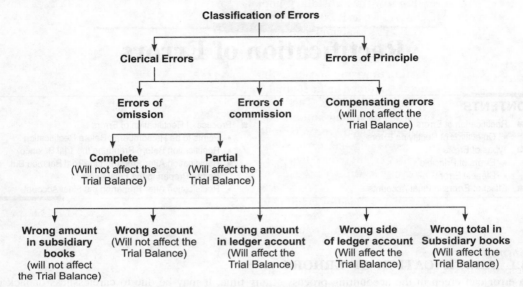

FIGURE 13.1 Classification of errors.

13.2.2 Clerical Errors

These type of errors are generally subdivided as follows:

Errors of omission

When a transaction is omitted completely or partially from the books, then the errors which are found are known as errors of omission. Generally, these types of errors arise when a transaction is not recorded in the books of original entry, i.e., in journals. It is very difficult to locate errors of omission. When a transaction is completely omitted from the books, then it will not affect the trial balance.

Errors of commission

These errors arise due to wrong posting, wrong balancing of an account, wrong totalling, wrong carrying forward, wrong calculation, etc. Some of these errors will affect the trial balance while the others will not. For example, cash paid to Jadu Rs. 700, but shown as Rs. 70 only.

1. **Errors of casting:** When the total of any book or an account is wrong, then trial balance will not tally. For example, Cash Book bank column's total of Rs. 34,200 shown as Rs. 35,200, it will increase Cash Book bank balance by Rs. 1,000. As a result, Trial Balance debit side total will also increase by Rs. 1,000.

2. **Errors of balancing an account:** While balancing a particular account in the Ledger, there may occur some mistakes. For example, the total of credit side of Protap's account is Rs. 36,400 and the debit side total is Rs. 21,900. Here balancing figure would be Rs. 14,500, but recorded as Rs. 15,400. Hence, it will increase Protap's account balance(Cr.) by Rs. 900 and the total of Trial Balance credit side by Rs. 900.

3. **Errors while carrying forward:** At the end of a certain period balancing is done and the closing balance (Balance c/d) is considered as the opening balance (Balance b/d) for the next period. For example, closing balance for the month of March 2008 of Cash Book (Cash Column) shown as Rs. 24,600 instead of actual balance of Rs. 26,400. It will reduce

Cash Book (Cash Column) debit balance by Rs. 1,800 and the total of Trial Balance debit side by Rs. 1,800.

4. **Wrong totalling in the subsidiary books:** Suppose, Purchase Day Book's total for the month March is shown as Rs. 34,500 instead of actual amount of Rs. 32,500. As per practice, Purchase Day Book's total amount is transferred to Purchases Account in the Ledger. It will increase the Purchase Account balance by Rs. 2,000 and the total of Trial Balance debit side by Rs. 2,000.

5. **Errors of posting to wrong account:** Suppose, cash received from P.K. Dhara is Rs. 3,000 and it is correctly recorded in the Journal, posted to P.K. Dua's Account in the Ledger. It will affect both P.K. Dhara and P.K. Dua's Account in the Ledger.

6. **Errors of posting of wrong amount in ledger:** Suppose, cash received from G. Guha is Rs. 3,000 and it is correctly recorded in the Cash Book, but posted to G.Guha's Account as Rs. 3,300. For this mistake, cash balance will increase by Rs. 3,000, whereas Debtor's Account (G.Guha's) will reduce by Rs. 3,300. It will affect the Trial Balance.

7. **Errors of posting in the wrong side of ledger accounts:** Suppose, cash received from G.Guha is Rs. 3,000 and is correctly recorded in the Cash Book, but posted to the debit of G.Guha's Account (instead of credit side). For this mistake, cash balance will increase by Rs. 3,000, whereas Debtor's Account (G.Guha's) will increase by Rs. 3,000 (instead of decreasing). It will affect the Trial Balance and will increase the debit total by Rs. 6,000.

Compensating errors

Compensating errors arise when the effect of a particular error is compensated (i.e., corrected) with the help of other error or errors. For example, cash paid to R.R. Rs. 860 but debited to his account Rs. 800 only. On the other hand cash received from K.K. Rs. 460 but credited to his account Rs. 400 only. Here, R.R.'s shortage of Rs. 60 (Dr.) is compensated by K.K.'s credit shortage of Rs. 60. These errors will not affect the Trial balance.

Miscellaneous errors

There are some errors which cannot be classified under any of the above headings, but have some effect on the books of accounts.

The errors may be further classified into heads as given below:

Errors affecting one account only

1. Errors of casting
2. Errors of balancing an account
3. Errors while carrying forward
4. Omission from the Trial Balance
5. Wrong total in the Subsidiary books.

Errors affecting two or more accounts

1. Errors of omission
2. Errors of principles
3. Errors of posting to wrong account
4. Errors of posting of wrong amount in Ledger
5. Errors of posting in the wrong side of Ledger Accounts.

13.3 EFFECT OF ERRORS IN FINAL ACCOUNTS

Errors effecting profit and loss account

The items which are generally considered in trading and profit and loss accounts have a direct effect on the profits or losses of the firm. These items are generally nominal in nature, e.g., expenses, losses, incomes and profit items. Hence, any error affecting these items or accounts will result in either an increase or a decrease in profits of the business. Hence, in order to ascertain the true profits of the business, necessary corrections are made regarding the detected errors. For example, wages paid for installation of a plant Rs. 3,000, but wrongly debited to wages account instead of the plant account. This will result in reduction of the company's profit by Rs. 3,000, and at the same time, the company's plant account will show a decrease in value by Rs. 3,000.

Errors affecting the balance sheet

Generally, personal and real accounts are considered while preparing the balance sheet. Any error affecting the personal or real accounts will directly affect the balance sheet of the firm. The net profit or loss is shown in the balance sheet. Hence, if there is any error (in nominal accounts) which results in reduction of the business profit, it will ultimately affect the balance sheet. Thus, unless and until the above errors are duly corrected, the balance sheet will not represent the true and fair view of the state of affairs (financial position) of a business enterprise.

13.4 PROCESS OF RECTIFICATION OF ERRORS

A particular error can be rectified through the journal proper in the following three different stages:
- Before preparing the trial balance
- After preparing the trial balance but before preparing the final account
- After preparing the final account.

13.4.1 Points to be Remembered Before Rectification

1. Identify the area where the error has taken place because it gives us the way to rectify the errors. If the area is not properly identified, the rectification entry will definitely be wrong. Thus, we must be very particular at this point because the error might have been committed either during the recording of the transaction in the Journal or Subsidiary Books or during the process of posting to Ledger.
2. Here the term 'recorded' means we may assume that the particular transaction has been recorded in the Journal or Subsidiary Books.
3. The term 'posted' means we may assume that the particular transaction has been recorded in the Journal or Subsidiary Books and the process of posting to Ledger has been done.
4. The term 'shown' means the error occurred at the time of making entries in the Journal or Subsidiary Books.
5. Sometimes it is said that 'Suppose, debited to X's account instead of Y's account. It means the error was made at the time of making postings to Ledger.

13.4.2 Rectification Before Preparing the Trial Balance

Rectification of double-sided errors

First, the error is cancelled and then the actual effect is made. For example, in case of goods sold to Ram but debited to Y, the entry will be as follows:

Ram A/c   Dr.
    To Y A/c

The following steps are to be considered for making rectification entry in case of double-sided errors:
1. The mistakes that have taken place in a transaction: The wrong entry made.
2. The correct entry: The correct entry required to be shown, but not shown.
3. To rectify the errors: The rectification entry required to be made to give the correct effect.

For example

1. Carriage paid for the carriage of machinery but wrongly debited to Carriage Inward account.

   Wrong entry actually made: Carriage Inward A/c   Dr.
             To Cash/Bank A/c

   Correct entry required to be shown, but not shown: Machinery A/c   Dr.
             To Cash/Bank A/c

   Rectification Entry: Machinery A/c   Dr.
             To Carriage Inward A/c

   [For rectification: Carriage Inward Account wrongly debited, it is now credited. Machinery account should have been debited but not debited, and thus is now debited.]

2. Salary paid to G. Ganapati but debited to G. Ganapati's A/c

   Wrong entry actually made: G. Ganapati's A/c   Dr.
             To Cash/Bank A/c

   Correct entry required to be shown, but not shown: Salary A/c   Dr.
             To Cash/Bank A/c

   Rectification Entry: Salary A/c   Dr.
             To G. Ganapati's A/c

   [For rectification: G. Ganapati's account wrongly debited, it is now credited. Salary account should have been debited but not debited, and thus is now debited.]

3. Cash withdrawn by the proprietor for personal use debited to trade expenses account

   Wrong entry actually made: Trade Expenses A/c   Dr.
             To Cash/Bank A/c

   Correct entry required to be shown, but not shown: Drawings A/c   Dr.
             To Cash/Bank A/c

   Rectification entry: Drawings A/c   Dr.
             To Trade Expenses A/c

   [For rectification: Trade expenses account wrongly debited, it is now credited. Drawings account should have been debited but not debited, and thus has now debited.]

4. Sold goods to Mr. S.S. for Rs. 900, but recorded in the books as goods purchased from Mr. S.S.

   Wrong entry actually made: Purchases A/c   Dr.
             To Mr. S.S. A/c

   Correct entry required to be shown, but not shown: Mr. S.S. A/c   Dr.
             To Sales A/c

   Rectification entry: Mr. S.S. A/c (900 + 900) Dr. 1,800
             To purchases A/c 900
             To Sales A/c 900

   [For rectification: Purchases account was wrongly debited, so it is now credited. Sales account not yet credited now credited. Mr. S.S. was wrongly credited but normally to be debited, so he is now debited by double amount.]

Rectification of single-sided errors

In case of single-sided errors, no entry is required but necessary posting is made by debiting/crediting the particular account. For example,

1. If a sales day book is overcasted by Rs. 100, then the Sales A/c is to be debited by Rs. 100.
2. If a Purchase day book is overcasted by Rs. 300, then the Purchases A/c is to be credited by Rs. 300.
3. If a Sales Return book is undercasted by Rs. 400, then the Sales Return A/c is to be debited by Rs. 400.

4. Discount amounting to Rs. 430 received and entered in the cash book was not posted to the ledger, then the Discount Received A/c is to be credited by Rs. 430.
5. Cash paid to P. Hari Rs. 530 but posted to P. Hari's A/c Rs. 350, then P. Hari's A/c is to be debited by Rs. 180.
6. Discount allowed Rs. 250 but debited to Discount A/c Rs. 520, then Discount Allowed A/c is to be credited by Rs. 270.

Single-sided Errors

ILLUSTRATION 13.1 Pass necessary Journal Entries rectifying the following errors which were detected before the preparation of Trial Balance:

1. Sales day book overcasted by Rs. 100.
2. Purchase day book undercasted by Rs. 300.
3. Sales day book on a folio was carried forward to the next page aᶜ Rs. 450 instead of Rs. 540.
4. Depreciation charged on Machinery, but not posted to Depreciation on Machinery A/c Rs. 4,500.
5. Cash book debit side discount account total transferred to Discount A/c as Rs. 750 instead of Rs. 570.
6. Cash received from Mr. G. Lalit Rs. 350, but posted to the debit of Mr.Lalit's A/c.
7. Sold goods to D. Raja for Rs. 4,300, but posted to his account Rs. 3,400.
8. Interest received from bank Rs. 240 has duly been shown in the Cash Book, but not posted to Interest Received A/c.

Solution

1. The general rule is that the total of Sales Day Book is credited to Sales A/c. Sales day book is overcast by Rs. 100. Thus, Sales A/c is overcast by Rs. 100 which needs to be reduced/ rectified by debiting the Sales A/c by the entry as under:
   "To overcasting of Sales Day Book for the month of … Rs. 100."
2. The general rule is that the total of Purchase Day Book is debited to Purchases A/c. Here, Purchase Day Book is undercast by Rs. 300. Thus, Purchases A/c is undercast by Rs. 300 which needed to be increased/rectified by debiting the Purchases A/c by the entry as under:
   "To undercasting of Purchases Day Book for the month of … Rs. 300."
3. For this mistake, Sales A/c is shown short by Rs. 90 (540 – 450), and hence, to be increased/ rectified by crediting Sales A/c as under:
   " By mistake in posting the wrong amount from Sales Day Book on … Rs. 90."
4. Though depreciation on Machinery has been charged, but not posted to Depreciation on Machinery A/c Rs. 4,500. Hence, Depreciation on Machinery A/c is to be debited by Rs. 4,500 as under:
   " To omission of posting on … Rs. 4,500"
5. Due to this mistake, Discount Allowed A/c has been debited by excess Rs. 180 (750 – 570)and hence, to be credited for rectification as under:
   " By Excess debit posted on … Rs. 180."
6. Mr. G.Lalit's A/c should be credited by Rs. 350, but wrongly debited. Hence, Mr. G. Lalit's A/c should be credited by Rs. 700 (350 + 350) as under:
   " By wrong posting on … adjusted Rs. 700."
7. For this mistake, D. Raja'a A/c is debited by Rs. 3,400 instead of Rs. 4,300. Thus, D. Raja'a A/c should be debited by a further sum of Rs. 900 (4,300 – 3,400) for rectification as under:
   " To wrong amount posted on … adjusted Rs. 900."
8. Due to this omission or mistake, Interest Received A/c has not been credited by Rs. 240. Hence, to be credited as under:
   " By omission of posting on … Rs. 240."

ILLUSTRATION 13.2 Pass necessary Journal Entries rectifying the following errors which were detected before the preparation of Trial Balance:

1. Salary paid to D. Roy Rs. 2,400, but debited to Salary A/c twice.
2. Return Inward Book undercasted by Rs. 450.
3. Cash received from Mr. P. Sohal Rs. 1,200, but posted to the credit of is A/c Rs. 2,100.
4. Cash paid to Mr. N. Kumar Rs. 1,750, but debited to his account as Rs. 1,570.
5. Cash paid to Mr. S.R. Bhaduri Rs. 2,350, but credited to his account as Rs. 350.
6. The total of Bills Payable Book Rs. 12,500 posted to Bills Payable A/c Rs. 1,250.
7. Brokerage paid Rs. 550 and duly entered in the Cash Book, but not posted to Brokerage A/c.
8. Cash Book credit side discount account total not transferred to Discount A/c Rs. 650.

Solution

1. Due this mistake, Salary A/c was debited by excess Rs. 2,400. Hence, it is to be credited by Rs. 2,400 as under:
   " By mistake in debiting the account twice on … Rs. 2,400."
2. For this mistake, Sales Return/Return Inward A/c was shown short by Rs. 450 and hence, is required to be increased for rectification by debiting Return Inward A/c as under:
   "To undercasting of Return Inward Book on … Rs. 450".
3. Due to this mistake, P. Sohal's A/c was credited in excess of Rs. 900 (2,100 – 1,200). Thus, to rectify the error, P. Sohal's A/c should be debited by Rs. 900 as under:
   " To excess amount posted on … Rs. 900.''
4. Due to this mistake, N. Kumar's A/c was shown short by Rs. 180 (1,750 – 1,570). Thus, to rectify the error, N. Kumar's A/c should be further debited by Rs. 180 as under:
   " To shortage amount posted on … Rs. 180."
5. Due to this mistake, S.R. Bhaduri's A/c was credited by Rs. 350, instead of debiting the account Rs. 2,350. Thus, to rectify the error, S.R. Bhaduri's A/c should be further debited by Rs. 2,700 (2,350 + 350) as under:
   " To amount posted on reverse side on … Rs. 2,700."
6. For this mistake, Bills Payable A/c was shown short by Rs. 11,250 (12,500 – 1,250). Hence, to increase the balance of Bills Payable A/c, it is to be credited by further Rs. 11,250 as under:
   " By wrong amount posted on … adjusted Rs. 11,250."
7. Due to this omission or mistake, Brokerage A/c has not been debited by Rs. 550. Hence, to be debited as under:
   " To omission of posting on … Rs. 550."
8. Due to this omission or mistake, Discount Received A/c has not been credited by Rs. 650. Hence, to be credited as under:
   " By omission of posting on … Rs. 650."

Double-sided Errors

ILLUSTRATION 13.3 Pass necessary Journal Entries rectifying the following errors which were detected before the preparation of Trial Balance:

1. Bad debt amounting to Rs. 900 recovered, but credited to Personal Account of the customer.
2. Annual whitewashing of Rs. 4,100 was debited to Building A/c.
3. Sale worth Rs. 2,500 to M/s. D.D. Bros. wrongly passed through the purchase day book.
4. A credit sale of Rs. 3,200 to P. Rohit was debited to P. Rudra.
5. Sale worth Rs. 3,900 to M/s Singhania Bros., but recorded in the day book as Rs. 1,900.
6. An old furniture (book value Rs. 6,900) was sold for Rs. 4,600, but the proceeds had been wrongly credited to Sales A/c.
7. Wages paid for installation of machine Rs. 3,900, but debited to wages A/c.
8. A credit purchases of Rs. 2,900 had been passed twice through the purchase day book.

Solution

Journal Proper
Rectification Entries

Date	Particulars		L.F.	Amount Dr. (Rs.)	Amount Cr. (Rs.)
1.	Customer's Personal A/c	Dr.		900	
	To Bad Debts Recovered A/c				900
	(Being bad debt recovered, but credited to personal account of the customer, now rectified)				
2.	Whitewashing A/c	Dr.		4,100	
	To Building A/c				4,100
	(Being annual whitewashing charges was debited to Building A/c, now rectified)				
3.	M/s. D.D. Bros. A/c	Dr.		5,000	
	To Purchase A/c				2,500
	To Sales A/c				2,500
	(Being the goods sold but passed through the purchase day book, now rectified)				
4.	P. Rohit A/c	Dr.		3,200	
	To P. Rudra A/c				3,200
	(Being a credit sale to P. Rohit was debited to P. Rudra, now rectified)				
5.	M/s. Singhania Bros. A/c	Dr.		2,000	
	To Sales A/c				2,000
	(Being goods sold but shown short, now rectified)				
6.	Sales A/c	Dr.		4,600	
	Loss on Sale A/c (Rs. 6,900 – Rs. 4,600)	Dr.		2,300	
	To Furniture A/c				6,900
	(For sale of an old furniture and sale proceeds credited to Sales A/c, now corrected)				
7.	Machinery A/c	Dr.		3,900	
	To Wages A/c				3,900
	(Being wages paid for installation of machine debited to Wages A/c, now rectified)				
8.	Creditors A/c	Dr.		2,900	
	To Purchases A/c				2,900
	(Being a purchase recorded twice in the books, now rectified)				

ILLUSTRATION 13.4 Pass necessary Journal Entries rectifying the following errors which were detected before the preparation of Trial Balance:

1. Cash paid to G. Kar Rs. 3,400, but debited to G. Kiron's A/c
2. Purchased goods from S.P. Roy for Rs. 2,800, but credited to S.P.Raina's A/c
3. Purchased goods from R. Singha for Rs. 5,700, but recorded in the books as goods sold to him.
4. Purchased goods from K. Lakhani for Rs. 4,200, but recorded in the books as Rs. 3,600.
5. Sold an old computer at Rs. 3,100, but credited to Sales A/c.
6. Goods used by the proprietor for Rs. 2,200, but not recorded in the books.
7. Goods returned by D. Ghosh worth Rs. 1,600, but recorded in the books as goods returned to him.
8. Registration charges of a land debited to Office Expenses A/c Rs. 4,600.

Solution

Journal Proper
Rectification Entries

Date	Particulars	L.F.	Amount Dr. (Rs.)	Amount Cr. (Rs.)
1.	G. Kar A/c Dr. To G. Kiron A/c (Being Cash paid to G. Kar but debited to G. Kiron's A/c, now rectified)		3,400	3,400
2.	S.P. Raina's A/c Dr. To S.P. Roy A/c (Being goods purchased from S.P. Roy but credited to S.P. Raina's A/c, now rectified)		2,800	2,800
3.	Purchases A/c Dr. Sales A/c Dr. To R. Singha A/c (Being goods purchased, but recorded as sales, now rectified)		5,700 5,700	11,400
4.	Purchases A/c Dr. To K. Lakhani A/c (Being goods purchased for Rs. 4,200, but recorded in the books as Rs. 3,600, now rectified)		600	600
5.	Sales A/c Dr. To Computer A/c (Being sale of computer shown as goods sold, now rectified)		3,100	3,100
6.	Drawing A/c Dr. To Purchases A/c (Being the goods taken over by proprietor omitted from the books, now rectified)		2,200	2,200
7.	Returns Inward A/c Dr. Returns Outward A/c Dr. To D. Ghosh A/c (Being sales return recorded as purchased return, now rectified)		1,600 1,600	3,200
8.	Land A/c Dr. To Office Expenses A/c (Being Registration charges of land debited to Office Expenses A/c, now rectified)		4,600	4,600

ILLUSTRATION 13.5 Give the necessary Journal Entries to rectify the following errors (after preparation of the Trial Balance but before preparation of the final account):

1. Salary paid to manager Rs. 4,000, but debited to manager's personal A/c.
2. Rs. 12,500 paid for purchase of a computer, was charged to Office Expenses A/c.
3. A sale of Rs. 750 to Mr. D. Sharma was entered in the sales book as Rs. 570.
4. Bad debt amounting to Rs. 650 recovered, but credited to Personal Account of the customer.
5. Wages paid for installation of machine Rs. 2,800, but debited to Wages A/c.
6. Annual whitewashing of Rs. 2,700 was debited to Building A/c.

Solution

Journal Proper
Rectification Entries

Date	Particulars	L.F.	Amount Dr. (Rs.)	Amount Cr. (Rs.)
1.	Salary A/c Dr. To Manager's Personal A/c (Being salary paid to manager, but debited to manager's personal A/c, now rectified)		4,000	4,000

(Contd.)

Date	Particulars	L.F.	Amount Dr. (Rs.)	Amount Cr. (Rs.)
2.	Computer A/c Dr. To Office Expenses A/c (Being computer purchased, but was charged to Office Expenses A/c, now corrected)		12,500	12,500
3.	D. Sharma A/c Dr. To Sales A/c (Being a sale of Rs. 750 entered in the sales book as Rs. 570, now corrected)		180	180
4.	Customer's Personal A/c Dr. To Bad Debts Recovered A/c (Being bad debt recovered, but credited to personal account of the customer, now rectified)		650	650
5.	Machinery A/c Dr. To Wages A/c (Being wages paid for installation of machine, but debited to Wages A/c, now rectified)		2,800	2,800
6.	Whitewashing A/c Dr. To Building A/c (Being annual whitewashing charges was debited to Building A/c, now rectified)		2,700	2,700

13.4.3 Rectification After Preparing the Trial Balance But Before Preparing the Final Account

In case of double-sided errors, the same procedure is followed as in the case of rectification before preparing the trial balance. In case of single-sided errors, the affected account is debited/credited, as the case may be, and the other side A/c (in journal entries) is shown in suspense A/c. For example, if a sales day book is overcast by Rs. 100, then the entry will as follows:

    Sales A/c   Dr. 100
        To Suspense A/c   100

Suspense account

Generally, final accounts are prepared after the preparation of trial balance. However, when a Trial Balance disagrees due to some errors, it may delay the preparation of the final accounts. Thus, to avoid the said delay in the preparation of the final accounts the difference in the trial balance is replaced by a new account known as **suspense account**. Subsequently, when all the errors are rectified, the suspense account will automatically get closed.

ILLUSTRATION 13.6 Pass necessary Journal Entries rectifying the following errors which were detected before the preparation of Trial Balance:

1. Sales day book overcasted by Rs. 100.
2. A sum of Rs. 670 received from a debtor was debited to his account.
3. Return outward book overcast by Rs. 300.
4. Bad debts written off amounting to Rs. 600, but not posted to Bad Debts A/c.
5. Cash Book debit side discount account total transferred to Discount A/c as Rs. 620 instead of Rs. 1,620.
6. Return Inward Book overcast by Rs. 500.
7. Rent paid Rs. 650, but debited to Rent A/c twice.
8. Purchase Day Book on a folio was carried forward to the next page as Rs. 860 instead of Rs. 680.

Solution

Journal Proper
Rectification Entries

Date	Particulars	L.F.	Amount Dr. (Rs.)	Amount Cr. (Rs.)
1.	Sales A/c Dr.		100	
	To Suspense A/c			100
	(Being Sales day book overcast, now corrected)			
2.	Suspense A/c Dr.		1,340	
	To Debtor's A/c (Rs. 670 + Rs. 670)			1,340
	(Being a sum of Rs. 670 received from a debtor			
	was debited to his account, now rectified)			
3.	Return Outward A/c Dr.		300	
	To Suspense A/c			300
	(Being Return outward book overcast, now rectified)			
4.	Bad Debts A/c Dr.		600	
	To Suspense A/c			600
	(Being Bad debts written off but not posted to			
	Bad Debt's A/c, now rectified)			
5.	Discount Allowed A/c Dr.		1,000	
	To Suspense A/c			1,000
	(Being discount allowed not posted to			
	Discount Allowed A/c, now rectified)			
6.	Suspense A/c Dr.		500	
	To Return Inward A/c			500
	(Being Return Inward Book overcast, now adjusted)			
7.	Suspense A/c Dr.		650	
	To Rent A/c			650
	(Being Rent A/c debited twice, now rectified)			
8.	Suspense A/c Dr.		180	
	To Purchases A/c			180
	(Being excess debited to Purchases A/c, now rectified)			

ILLUSTRATION 13.7 Pass Journal Entries (without narration) to rectify the following errors (after preparation of the trial balance but before preparing the final account).

1. Goods purchased for Rs. 920 had been posted to the credit of the Supplier's A/c as Rs. 290.
2. Goods worth Rs. 550 returned by a customer were taken into stock but no entry made in the books.
3. Sale worth Rs. 4,700 to M/s. R.K. Bros. wrongly passed through the purchase day book.
4. Discount allowed of Rs. 720 was credited to Discount Received A/c.
5. Cash sale of Rs. 2,600 to M. Singha debited to his account in the ledger.
6. A credit sale of Rs. 1,600 to T. Sharma was debited to T. Shandilya.
7. Cash received from Mr. Sekhar Dalal Rs. 540, but credited to him Rs. 450.
8. Cash received from Mr. F.M. Chatalia Rs. 780, but debited to him Rs. 870.

Solution

Journal Proper

Date	Particulars	L.F.	Amount Dr. (Rs.)	Amount Cr. (Rs.)
1.	Suspense A/c Dr.		630	
	To Supplier's A/c			630
2.	Return Inward A/c Dr.		550	
	To Customer's A/c			550

(Contd.)

Date	Particulars		L.F.	Amount Dr. (Rs.)	Amount Cr. (Rs.)
3.	M/s. R.K. Bros. A/c	Dr.		9,400	
	To Purchase A/c				4,700
	To Sales A/c				4,700
4.	Discount Received A/c	Dr.		720	
	Discount Allowed A/c	Dr.		720	
	To Suspense A/c				1,440
5.	Suspense A/c	Dr.		5,200	
	To Sales A/c				2,600
	To M. Singha A/c				2,600
6.	T. Sharma A/c	Dr.		1,600	
	To T. Shandilya A/c				1,600
7.	Suspense A/c	Dr.		90	
	To Sekhar Dalal A/c				90
8.	Suspense A/c	Dr.		1,650	
	To F.M. Chatalia A/c (Rs. 780 + Rs. 870)				1,650

ILLUSTRATION 13.8 Give the necessary Journal Entries (without narration) to rectify the following errors (after preparation of the trial balance but before preparing the final account). Also, show the Suspense Account.

1. Cash of Rs. 900 withdrawn by the proprietor for personal use debited to Trade Expenses A/c.
2. Sale worth Rs. 3,900 to M/s. Grasim Bros. wrongly passed through the purchase day book.
3. A sales return of Rs. 830 from Mr. D. Dogra entered in the sales book.
4. A purchase of Rs. 650 posted to the debit of suppliers Mr. P. Sundaram's A/c as Rs. 560.
5. Goods purchased for Rs. 4,100 from L.K. Traders, but wrongly credited Rs. 1,400 to L.K. Traders A/c and debited to Purchase A/c Rs. 410 only.
6. Rs. 1,500 paid to the landlord for rent wrongly debited to Landlord's Personal A/c.
7. An item of Rs. 170 was posted as Rs. 710 in the Sales A/c.
8. Return Inwards book overcasted by Rs. 200.

Solution

Journal Proper

Date	Particulars		L.F.	Amount Dr. (Rs.)	Amount Cr. (Rs.)
1.	Drawings A/c	Dr.		900	
	To Trade Expenses A/c				900
2.	M/s. Grasim Bros. A/c	Dr.		7,800	
	To Purchase A/c				3,900
	To Sales A/c				3,900
3.	Sales Return A/c	Dr.		830	
	Sales A/c	Dr.		830	
	To D. Dogra A/c				1,660
4.	Suspense A/c	Dr.		1,210	
	To P. Sundaram A/c (Rs. 650 + Rs. 560)				1,210
5.	Purchase A/c (Rs. 4,100 – Rs. 410)	Dr.		3,690	
	To L.K. Traders A/c (Rs. 4,100 – Rs. 1,400)				2,700
	To Suspense A/c (balancing figure)				990
6.	Rent A/c	Dr.		1,500	
	To Landlord's Personal A/c				1,500
7.	Sales A/c (Rs. 710 – Rs. 170)	Dr.		540	
	To Suspense A/c				540
8.	Suspense A/c	Dr.		200	
	To Return Inwards A/c				200

Dr.		Suspense Account				Cr.
Date	Particulars	Amount (Rs.)	Sl.No.	Particulars		Amount (Rs.)
	To Balance b/d (balancing figure)	120	5.	By Purchase A/c		990
4.	To P. Sundaram A/c	1,210	7.	By Sales A/c		540
8.	To Return Inwards A/c	200				
		1,530				1,530

ILLUSTRATION 13.9 Pass necessary Journal Entries rectifying the following errors which were detected after the preparation of Trial Balance:

1. A credit purchases of Rs. 700 had been passed twice through the purchase day book.
2. Sales Day Book undercasted by Rs. 200.
3. Cash of Rs. 1,350 paid to Mr. N. Singhania, but credited to his account.
4. Cash of Rs. 1,100 paid to Mr. G. D. Dua, but debited to his account Rs. 100 only.
5. An old furniture (of book value Rs. 4,900) was sold for Rs. 3,050, but the proceeds had been wrongly credited to Sales A/c
6. Rs. 750 due from a customer omitted, to be taken in the schedule of sundry debtors.
7. Rs. 560, being the total of the discount column on the credit side of the Cash Book, was not posted in General Ledger.
8. Sales Day Book on a folio was carried forward to the next page as Rs. 450 instead of Rs. 540.

Solution

Journal Proper

Date	Particulars		L.F.	Amount Dr. (Rs.)	Amount Cr. (Rs.)
1.	Creditors A/c	Dr.		700	
	To Purchases A/c				700
	(For a purchase recorded twice in the books, now rectified)				
2.	Suspense A/c	Dr.		200	
	Sales A/c				200
	(Being Sales Day Book undercasted, now rectified)				
3.	N. Singhania's A/c (Rs. 1,350 + Rs. 1,350)	Dr.		2,700	
	To Suspense A/c				2,700
	(Being Mr. N. Singhania's A/c was credited instead of debit, now rectified)				
4.	G. D. Dua A/c	Dr.		1,000	
	To Suspense A/c				1,000
	(Being Mr. G.D. Dua's A/c was debited by Rs. 100 instead of Rs. 1,100, now rectified)				
5.	Sales A/c	Dr.		3,050	
	Loss on Sale A/c (Rs. 4,900 – Rs. 3,050)	Dr.		1,850	
	To Furniture A/c				4,900
	(For sale of an old furniture and sale proceeds credited to Sales A/c, now corrected)				
6.	Sundry Debtors A/c	Dr.		750	
	To Suspense A/c				750
	(Being due from a customer was omitted to be taken in the schedule of sundry debtors, now rectified)				
7.	Suspense A/c	Dr.		560	
	To Discount Received A/c				560
	(Being discount received was not posted to Discount Received A/c in the ledger, now rectified)				
8.	Suspense A/c	Dr.		90	
	To Sales A/c				90
	(Being the total of one page of Sales Day Book was carried forward to the next page as Rs. 450 instead of Rs. 540, now rectified)				

ILLUSTRATION 13.10 Mr. Avtar Singh noticed that his Trial Balance on December 31, 2007 did not agree, and as such the difference (excess debit) Rs. 3,000 was carried to the Suspense Account and the books were closed. On going through the records, the following errors were detected:

1. A sales return of Rs. 750 from Mr. Kuntal Sen was entered in the Sales Book.
2. Bad debt amounting to Rs. 900 recovered, but credited to Personal Account of the customer.
3. Wages paid for installation of machine Rs. 2,100, but debited to Wages A/c.
4. Sale worth Rs. 3,600 to M/s. G.M. Bros. wrongly passed through the Purchase Day Book.
5. Rs. 1,700 paid to the landlord for rent wrongly debited to Landlord's Personal A/c.
6. Discount allowed of Rs. 450 was credited to Discount Received A/c.
7. Cash of Rs. 2,400 withdrawn by the proprietor for personal use debited to Trade Expenses A/c.
8. Sales Day Book undercast by Rs. 1,000.
9. Rs. 700 due from a customer omitted, to be taken in the schedule of Sundry Debtors.
10. Cash sale of Rs. 1,800 to M/s. P. Traders debited to M/s. P. Traders's A/c in the Ledger.

Give necessary Journal Entries (without narration) necessary to correct the above errors and prepare the Suspense Account.

Solution

In the Books of Mr. Avtar Singh
Journal Proper

Date	Particulars		L.F.	Amount Dr. (Rs.)	Amount Cr. (Rs.)
1.	Sales Return A/c	Dr.		750	
	Sales A/c	Dr.		750	
	To Kuntal Sen A/c				1,500
2.	Customer's Personal A/c	Dr.		900	
	To Bad Debts Recovered A/c				900
3.	Machinery A/c	Dr.		2,100	
	To Wages A/c				2,100
4.	M/s. G.M. Bros. A/c	Dr.		7,200	
	To Purchase A/c				3,600
	To Sales A/c				3,600
5.	Rent A/c	Dr.		1,700	
	To Landlord's Personal A/c				1,700
6.	Discount Received A/c	Dr.		450	
	Discount Allowed A/c	Dr.		450	
	To Suspense A/c				900
7.	Drawings A/c	Dr.		2,400	
	To Trade Expenses A/c				2,400
8.	Suspense A/c	Dr.		1,000	
	Sales A/c				1,000
9.	Sundry Debtors A/c	Dr.		700	
	To Suspense A/c				700
10.	Suspense A/c	Dr.		3,600	
	To Sales A/c				1,800
	To M/s. P. Traders A/c				1,800

Dr.			Suspense Account			Cr.
Date	Particulars	Amount (Rs.)	Date	Particulars		Amount (Rs.)
	To Sales A/c	1,000		By Balance b/d		3,000
	To Sales A/c	1,800		By Discount Received A/c		450
	To M/s. P. Traders A/c	1,800		By Discount Allowed A/c		450
				By Sundry Debtors A/c		700
		4,600				4,600

13.4.4 Rectification After Preparing the Final Account

After preparing the final accounts, all the nominal accounts are closed by transferring them to Trading Account or to Profit and Loss Account. The balances of assets, liabilities, personal accounts and Suspense Account (if any) are left and carried forward to the next year. At this stage, for rectifying a particular error, nominal accounts are replaced by Profit and Loss Adjustment A/c.

In this case, for both double-and single-side errors, the same steps are followed for rectification, after preparing the trial balance but before the final account. Here, the only difference is that, for any nominal accounts, the Profit and Loss Adjustment Account is to be replaced.

For example, in case of salary paid to manager, Mr. X, but debited to his account, the rectification entry will be as follows:

Profit and Loss Adjustment A/c   Dr. (in place of Salary A/c)
    To X A/c

ILLUSTRATION 13.11   Rectify the following errors in three different stages:
- (a) Paid Rs. 1,000 for installation of Machinery debited to Wages A/c.
- (b) Carriage paid Rs. 700 for carriage of Machinery but wrongly debited to Carriage Inward A/c.
- (c) Salary paid to P. Sen Rs. 1,800 but debited to P. Sen's A/c.
- (d) Sold old Furniture for Rs. 900 passed through the Sales Day Book.
- (e) Discount amounting to Rs. 650 received and entered in the Cash Book was not posted to the Ledger.
- (f) Paid Rs. 630 towards the repairs to motor van but debited to Motor Van A/c.
- (g) The purchase of Machinery for Rs. 3,800 was entered in the Purchases A/c.
- (h) Cash Rs. 600 paid to D. Sen but debited to P. Sen A/c.
- (i) Cash Rs. 980 received from M. Kumar but credited to N. Ram A/c.
- (j) Sales day book undercast by Rs. 100.
- (k) Purchase day book overcast by Rs. 100.
- (l) Sold goods to R. Das for Rs. 1,750 but debited to P. Das.
- (m) Goods returned by M. Kar for Rs. 640 but recorded in the books as goods purchased from M. Kar.
- (n) Sold goods to A. Nath for Rs. 740 but recorded in the books as goods purchased from A. Nath.
- (o) Cash paid to P. Hari Rs. 640 but posted to P. Hari's A/c Rs. 460.
- (p) Discount allowed Rs. 150 but debited to Discount A/c Rs. 510.

Solution

Before preparation of the Trial Balance	After preparation of the Trial Balance but before preparation of the Final A/c	After preparation of the Final A/c

(a) Machinery A/c Dr. 1,000
    To Wages A/c 1,000
	(a) Machinery A/c Dr. 1,000
	    To Wages A/c 1,000
		(a) Machinery A/c Dr. 1,000
		    To P & L Adjustment A/c 1,000

(b) Machinery A/c Dr. 700
    To Carriage Inward A/c 700
	(b) Machinery A/c Dr. 700
	    To Carriage Inward A/c 700
		(b) Machinery A/c Dr. 700
		    To P & L Adjustment A/c 700

(c) Salary A/c Dr. 1,800
    To P. Sen A/c 1,800
	(c) Salary A/c Dr. 1,800
	    To P. Sen A/c 1,800
		(c) P&L Adjustment A/c Dr. 1,800
		    To P. Sen A/c 1,800

(d) Sales A/c Dr. 900
    To Furniture A/c 900
	(d) Sales A/c Dr. 900
	    To Furniture A/c 900
		(d) P&L Adjustment A/c Dr. 900
		    To Furniture A/c 900

(e) Discount A/c will be credited by Rs. 650.	(e) Suspense A/c Dr. 650
	    To Discount Received A/c 650
		(e) Suspense A/c Dr. 650
		    To P & L Adjustment A/c 650

(f) Repairs A/c Dr. 630
    To Motor Van A/c 630
	(f) Repairs A/c Dr. 630
	    To Motor Van A/c 630
		(f) P&L Adjustment A/c Dr. 630
		    To Motor Van A/c 630

(g) Machinery A/c Dr. 3,800
    To Purchases A/c 3,800
	(g) Machinery A/c Dr. 3,800
	    To Purchase A/c 3,800
		(g) Machinery A/c Dr. 3,800
		    To P & L Adjustment A/c 3,800

(h) D. Sen A/c Dr. 600
    To P. Sen A/c 600
	(h) D. Sen A/c Dr. 600
	    To P. Sen A/c 600
		(h) D. Sen A/c Dr. 600
		    To P. Sen A/c 600

(i) N. Ram A/c Dr. 980
    To M. Kumar A/c 980
	(i) N. Ram A/c Dr. 980
	    To M. Kumar A/c 980
		(i) N. Ram A/c Dr. 980
		    To M. Kumar A/c 980

(Contd.)

Before preparation of the Trial Balance	After preparation of the Trial Balance but before preparation the Final A/c	After preparation of the Final A/c

(j) Sales A/c will be credited by Rs. 100.	(j) Suspense A/c Dr. 100
	  To Sales A/c 100
		(j) Suspense A/c Dr. 100
		  To P & L Adjustment A/c 100

(k) Purchases A/c will be credited by Rs. 100.	(k) Suspense A/c Dr. 100
	  To Purchases A/c 100
		(k) Suspense A/c Dr. 100
		  To P&L Adjustment A/c 100

(l) R. Das A/c Dr. 1,750
  To P. Das A/c 1,750
	(l) R. Das A/c Dr. 1,750
	  To P. Das A/c 1,750
		(l) R. Das A/c Dr. 1,750
		  To P. Das A/c 1,750

(m) Return Inward A/c Dr. 640
  To Purchases A/c 640
	(m) Return Inward A/c Dr. 640
	  To Purchases A/c 640
		(m) To P&L Adjustment A/c Dr.
		  To P&L Adjustment A/c
		  As such no entry is required.

(n) A. Nath A/c Dr. 1,480
  To Purchases A/c 740
  To Sales A/c 740
	(n) A. Nath A/c Dr. 1,480
	  To Purchases A/c 740
	  To Sales A/c 740
		(n) A. Nath A/c Dr. 1,480
		  To P/L Adjustment A/c 1,480

(o) P. Hari's A/c will be debited by Rs. 180	(o) P. Hari's A/c Dr. 180
	  To Suspense A/c 180
		(o) P. Hari's A/c Dr. 180
		  To Suspense A/c 180

(p) Discount Allowed A/c will be credited by Rs. 360.	(p) Suspense A/c Dr. 360
	  To Discount Allowed 360
		(p) Suspense A/c Dr. 360
		  To P/L Adjustment A/c 360

ILLUSTRATION 13.12   The following errors were disclosed in the books of Mr. N. Kumar on December 31, 2008. The difference in the Trial Balance has been transferred to a Suspense A/c. On correction of errors, the Suspense A/c was eliminated.

(a) Rs. 790 cash received from D. Dutta was debited to D. Domani.

(b) Goods bought from a trader amounting to Rs. 750 had been posted to the credit of his account as Rs. 570.

(c) The total of the Discount column in the Cash Book on the debit side was Rs. 650 on one page but was carried forward to the next page as Rs. 560.

(d) An old Machinery (of book value Rs. 6,300) was sold for Rs. 4,670 but the proceeds had been wrongly credited to Sales A/c.

(e) Discount allowed of Rs. 620 was credited to Discount Received A/c.

(f) Bad debts amounting to Rs. 650 recovered, but credited to Personal A/c of the customer.

(g) A purchase of Rs. 980 had been posted to the debit of Mr. K. Reddy's A/c as Rs. 890.

(h) While carrying forward the total of one page of the Sales Book to the next, the amount of Rs. 4,370 was written as Rs. 3,470.

(i) Rs. 1,250 due from a customer was omitted, to be taken in the schedule of Sundry Debtors.

(j) Sales to Mr. Kaul of Rs. 580 credited to Mr. Khurana's A/c as Rs. 850.

Pass necessary Rectification Entries and close the Suspense A/c. Give necessary Journal Entries if corrections are made after preparation of Final Accounts and show the effect of the corrections on the profits of the firm.

Solution

In the Books of ...

Journal Proper

Date	Particulars	L.F.	Amount Dr. (Rs.)	Amount Cr. (Rs.)

2008 Dec. 31 1.	Suspense A/c Dr.
	  To D. Dutta A/c
	  To D. Domani A/c
	(Being cash received from D. Dutta, debited to
	D. Domani's A/c, now corrected)
			1,580	790
				790

2.	Suspense A/c Dr. To Supplier's A/c (Being Supplier's A/c credited Rs. 570 instead of Rs. 750, now rectified)		180	180

(Contd.)

Date	Particulars	L.F.	Amount Dr. (Rs.)	Amount Cr. (Rs.)
3.	Discount Allowed A/c Dr. To Suspense A/c (Being Discount Allowed column in the Cash Book, carried forward to the next page as Rs. 560 instead of Rs. 650, now corrected)		90	90
4.	Sales A/c Dr. Loss on Sale A/c (6,300 – 4,670) Dr. To Machinery A/c (For sale of an old machinery and sale proceeds credited to Sales A/c, now corrected)		4,670 1,630	6,300
5.	Discount Received A/c Dr. Discount Allowed A/c Dr. To Suspense A/c (Being discount allowed of Rs. 620, credited to Discount Received A/c, now corrected)		620 620	1,240
6.	Customer's Personal A/c Dr. To Bad Debts Recovered A/c (Being bad debt recovered, but credited to Personal Account of the customer, now rectified)		650	650
7.	Suspense A/c Dr. To K. Reddy's A/c (980 + 890) (Being a purchase of Rs. 980, posted previously to the debit of Supplier's A/c as Rs. 890, now rectified)		1,870	1,870
8.	Suspense A/c Dr. To Sales A/c (Being Sales Book shown short, now rectified)		900	900
9.	Sundry Debtors A/c Dr. To Suspense A/c (Being Rs. 1,250 due from a customer, omitted and to be taken in the schedule of sundry debtors, now corrected)		1,250	1,250
10.	Khurana's A/c Dr. Kaul's A/c Dr. To Suspense A/c (Being sales to Mr. Kaul of Rs. 580 credited to Mr. Khurana's A/c as Rs. 850, now rectified)		850 580	1,430

Dr.   **Suspense Account**   **Cr.**

Date	Particulars	Amount (Rs.)	Date	Particulars	Amount (Rs.)
2008 Dec. 31	To D. Dutta A/c	790	2008 Dec. 31	By Balance b/d (balancing figure —difference in Trial Balance)	520
31	To D. Domani A/c	790	31	By Discount Allowed A/c	90
31	To Supplier's A/c	180	31	By Discount Received A/c	620
31	To K. Reddy's A/c	1,870	31	By Discount Allowed A/c	620
31	To Sales A/c	900	31	By Sundry Debtors A/c	1,250
			31	By Khurana's A/c	850
			31	By Kaul's A/c	580
		4,530			**4,530**

When rectification of errors is made after preparation of Final Accounts:

Journal Proper

Date	Particulars	L.F.	Amount Dr. (Rs.)	Amount Cr. (Rs.)
2008 Dec. 31				
1.	Suspense A/c Dr.		1,580	
	To D. Dutta A/c			790
	To D. Domani A/c			790
	(Being cash received from D. Dutta debited to D. Domani's A/c, now corrected)			
2.	Suspense A/c Dr.		180	
	To Supplier's A/c			180
	(Being Supplier's A/c credited Rs. 570 instead of Rs. 750, now rectified)			
3.	Profit and Loss Adjustment A/c Dr.		90	
	To Suspense A/c			90
	(Being Discount Allowed column in the cash book carried forward to the next page as Rs. 560 instead of Rs. 650, now corrected)			
4.	Profit and Loss Adjustment A/c (4,670 + 1,630) Dr.		6,300	
	To Machinery A/c			6,300
	(For sale of an old machinery and sale proceeds credited to Sales A/c, now corrected)			
5.	Profit and Loss Adjustment A/c Dr.		1,240	
	To Suspense A/c			1,240
	(Being Discount allowed of Rs. 620 credited to Discount Received A/c, now corrected)			
6.	Customer's Personal A/c Dr.		650	
	To Profit and Loss Adjustment A/c			650
	(Being bad debt recovered, but credited to Personal A/c of the customer, now rectified)			
7.	Suspense A/c Dr.		1,870	
	To K. Reddy's A/c (980 + 890)			1,870
	(Being a purchase of Rs. 980 posted to the debit of supplier's A/c as Rs. 890, now rectified)			
8.	Suspense A/c Dr.		900	
	To Profit and Loss Adjustment A/c			900
	(Being sales book shown short, now rectified)			
9.	Sundry Debtors A/c Dr.		1,250	
	To Suspense A/c			1,250
	(Being Rs. 1,250 due from a customer omitted, to be taken in the schedule of sundry debtors, now corrected)			
10.	Khurana's A/c Dr.		850	
	Kaul's A/c Dr.		580	
	To Suspense A/c			1,430
	(Being sales to Mr. Kaul of Rs. 580 credited to Mr. Khurana's A/c as Rs. 850, now rectified)			

Dr.   **Suspense Account**   Cr.

Date	Particulars	Amount (Rs.)	Date	Particulars	Amount (Rs.)
2008 Dec. 31	To D. Dutta A/c	790	2008 Dec. 31	By Balance b/d (balancing figure —difference in Trial Balance)	520
31	To D. Domani A/c	790			
31	To Supplier's A/c	180	31	By Profit and Loss Adjustment A/c	90
31	To K. Reddy's A/c	1,870	31	By Profit and Loss Adjustment A/c	1,240
31	To Profit and Loss Adjustment A/c	900	31	By Sundry Debtors A/c	1,250
			31	By Khurana's A/c	850
			31	By Kaul's A/c	580
		4,530			4,530

Effect of Rectification of Errors on Net Profit

Sl. No.	Items	Effect	
		Increase in profit (Rs.)	Decrease in profit (Rs.)
1.	No effect	—	—
2.	No effect	—	—
3.	Decrease	—	90
4.	Decrease	—	6,300
5.	Decrease	—	1,240
6.	Increase	650	—
7.	No effect	—	—
8.	Increase	900	—
9.	No effect	—	—
10.	No effect	—	—
		1,550	7,630
	Net decrease in profit	6,080	
		7,630	7,630

Working Note

For calculating effect on profits, only nominal accounts are to be considered from the Rectification Entries. When the nominal account are debited, it indicates a decrease in profit, and when the nominal account are credited, it indicates an increase in profit. Here, all nominal accounts are replaced by Profit and Loss Adjustment A/c.

ILLUSTRATION 13.13   There was a difference in Trial Balance of Mr. K. Sen, a trader, on 31.12.2008 and the difference in books was carried to a Suspense Account and the books were closed. Subsequently, on going through the books, the following errors were located:

1. Rs. 2,296 paid for repairs to motor car was debited to Motor Car Account as Rs. 696.
2. A sale of Rs. 1,400 to D. Konar entered in Sales Book as Rs. 2,120.
3. A cash discount of Rs. 800 received was entered in the cash book but was not posted in the ledger.
4. Rs. 400 being purchase returns posted to the debit of Purchases Account.
5. The purchase of a machine on 1.4.2008 for Rs. 24,000 was entered in the purchase book.
6. While carrying forward the total of one page in P. Guha's Account, the amount of Rs. 1,000 was written on the credit side instead of the debit side.
7. A cheque of Rs. 6,192 received from R. Dhar (after allowing a discount of Rs. 92) was endorsed to S. Kar in full settlement for Rs. 7,000. The cheque was finally dishonoured, but no entry was passed in the books.

Give Journal Entries to rectify the above errors and prepare the Suspense Account.

[C.U. B. Com.(Hons.), 1993—Modified]

Solution

In the books of ...

Journal Entries

Date	Particulars	L.F.	Amount Dr. (Rs.)	Amount Cr. (Rs.)

2008 Dec. 31 1.	Profit and Loss Adjustment A/c Dr.
	   To Motor Car A/c
	   To Suspense A/c
	(Being repairs to motor car Rs. 2,296, was debited to Motor Car Account as Rs. 696, now rectified)
			2,296	696
				1,600

(Contd.)

Date	Particulars	L.F.	Amount Dr. (Rs.)	Amount Cr. (Rs.)
2.	Profit and Loss Adjustment A/c Dr. To D. Konar A/c (Being sale of Rs. 1,400 entered in Sales Book as Rs. 2,120, now rectified)		720	720
3.	Suspense A/c Dr. To Profit and Loss Adjustment A/c (Being cash discount received was entered in the cash book but was not posted in the Ledger, now rectified)		800	800
4.	Suspense A/c Dr. To Profit and Loss Adjustment A/c (Being purchase returns posted to the debit of Purchases Account, now rectified)		800	800
5.	Machinery A/c Dr. To Profit and Loss Adjustment A/c (Being purchase of a machine was entered in the Purchase Book, now rectified)		24,000	24,000
6.	P. Guha's A/c Dr. To Suspense A/c (Being debit balance carried forward as credit balance, now rectified)		2,000	2,000
7.	R. Dhar A/c (6,192 + 92) Dr. Profit and Loss Adjustment A/c Dr. To S. Kar A/c (Being endorsed cheque dishonoured and discount allowed and received both to be cancelled, but no entry was passed, now rectified)		6,284 716	7,000

Dr.   **Suspense Account**   Cr.

Date	Particulars	Amount (Rs.)	Date	Particulars	Amount (Rs.)
2008 Dec. 31	To Balance b/d (balancing figure)	2,000	2008 Dec. 31	By Profit and Loss Adjustment A/c	1,600
31	To Profit and Loss Adjustment A/c	800	31	By P. Guha's A/c	2,000
31	To Profit and Loss Adjustment A/c	800			
		3,600			3,600

EXERCISES

I. *Choose the correct alternative*

1. Which of the following errors will not affect the Trial Balance?
   (a) Wrong amount in Ledger A/c
   (b) Wrong amount in subsidiary books
   (c) Wrong side of Ledger A/c
   (d) Wrong total in subsidiary books.

2. 'Cash paid to Mr. X is Rs. 700 but shown as Rs. 70' is an example of
   (a) Error of omission
   (b) Error of commission
   (c) Compensating error
   (d) None of these.

3. The effect of an error affecting nominal accounts is
   (a) Increase in profit of the business
   (b) Decrease in profit of the business
   (c) Either increase or decrease in profit of the business
   (d) Neither increase nor decrease in profit of the business.

4. Which of the following errors will affect only one account?
   (a) Error of principle
   (b) Error of posting to wrong account
   (c) Error of casting
   (d) Error of omission.

5. Which of the following errors will affect two or more accounts?
   (a) Error occurred while carrying forward
   (b) Error of posting of wrong amount in Ledger
   (c) Wrong total in subsidiary books
   (d) Error of balancing of an account.

6. Errors of omission will affect
   (a) Only one account
   (b) Two accounts
   (c) Two or more accounts
   (d) None of these.

7. Error affecting personal acccounts will
   (a) Directly affect the balance sheet
   (b) Directly affect the Profit and Loss A/c
   (c) Directly affect the profits of the business
   (d) None of these.

8. Suspense Account is opened to
   (a) Prepare the final accounts
   (b) To avoid delay in preparation of the final accounts.
   (c) For correcting the errors
   (d) None of these.

9. One-sided error arises if
   (a) There is a double A/c mistake in posting or at the time of totalling
   (b) There is a single A/c mistake in posting or at the time of totalling
   (c) There is either double A/c or single A/c mistake in posting or at the time of totalling
   (d) None of these.

10. When rectification of errors is made after the preparation of Final Accounts and, in that case, if the errors involving both the accounts are nominal in nature, then for rectification
    (a) Profit and Loss A/c will be debited
    (b) Profit and Loss Adjustment A/c will be debited
    (c) No entry is required to be shown.

11. When rectification of errors is made after the preparation of Final Accounts, Profit and Loss Adjustment A/c balance is closed
    (a) By transferring it to Suspense A/c
    (b) By transferring it to Capital A/c
    (c) By transferring it to Profit and Loss A/c.

12. When all the detected errors are rectified, the Suspense A/c will
    (a) Be closed by transferring the balance to Capital A/c
    (b) Be closed by transferring the balance to Profit and Loss Adjustment A/c
    (c) Be automatically closed.

13. When all the detected errors are rectified and the Suspense A/c still shows some balance, it indicates that
    (a) There still are some undetected errors
    (b) There is some error in the balance sheet
    (c) There is some error in the Profit and Loss Adjustment A/c.

14. Salary was paid to D. Ratan, but D. Ratan's A/c was wrongly credited in the Ledger. For rectification
    (a) D. Ratan's A/c will be debited
    (b) Salary A/c will be debited
    (c) Both Salary A/c and D. Ratan's A/c will be debited.

15. Cash was withdrawn by the proprietor for personal use but was debited to Trade Expenses A/c. For rectification
    (a) Cash A/c will be debited and Trade Expenses A/c will be credited
    (b) Drawings A/c will be debited and Trade Expenses A/c will be credited
    (c) Drawings A/c will be debited and Suspense A/c will be credited
    (d) Cash A/c will be credited and Trade Expenses A/c will be debited.

16. Purchase of furniture was passed through the Purchase Day Book. It is
    (a) An error of principle
    (b) A compensating error
    (c) A clerical error
    (d) An error of omission.

17. In compensating errors, it is generally seen that
    (a) One debit shortage is compensated by another debit shortage
    (b) One debit shortage is compensated by another credit shortage
    (c) None of these.

18. Omission from the trial balance will affect
    (a) One account only
    (b) Two accounts
    (c) Suspense A/c only
    (d) None of these.

19. Wrong total in a Subsidiary book will affect
    (a) One account only
    (b) Two accounts
    (c) Suspense A/c only.

20. Any error affecting personal accounts will directly affect
    (a) The balance sheet
    (b) The profit/loss of the firm
    (c) The Capital A/c
    (d) None of these.

    Ans: 1. (b), 2. (b), 3. (c), 4. (c), 5. (b), 6. (b), 7. (a), 8. (b), 9. (b), 10. (c), 11. (b), 12. (c), 13. (a), 14. (c), 15. (b), 16. (a), 17. (b), 18. (a), 19. (a), 20. (a).

II. *Short Answer Type Questions (with answers)*

1. What are the different types of errors that are found in accounts?
   Ans: Generally, the errors found in accounts are classified into two categories—**clerical errors** and **errors of principle.** Clerical errors may further be sub-divided into three categoreis—**errors of omission, errors of commission** and **compensating errors.**

2. What is error of principle?
   Ans: When a transaction is recorded in the books without following the generally accepted accounting principles, the error of principle occurs. For example, capital expenditure is considered as revenue expenditure.These types of errors will not affect the trial balance.

3. What is error of commission?
   Ans: Errors of commission arise due to wrong posting, balancing of account, totalling, carrying forward, calculation, etc. Some of these errors will not affect the trial balance while others will affect. For example, cash paid to Shyam was Rs. 600, but was shown as Rs. 60 only.

4. What is compensating error?

   Ans: An error whose effect is compensated (i.e. corrected) with the help of other error (s) is called a compensating error. Such errors will not affect the trial balance. For example, cash paid to K is Rs. 460, but debited to K A/c Rs. 400. On the other hand, cash received from G is Rs. 660, but credited to G A/c Rs. 600. Here, K's debit shortage of Rs. 60 is compensated by G's credit shortage of Rs. 60.

5. Identify the errors affecting only one account.

   Ans: Errors affecting one account only are as follows:
   (a) Errors of casting
   (b) Errors of balancing of an account
   (c) Errors occurred while carrying forward
   (d) Omission from the trial balance
   (e) Wrong total in subsidiary books

6. Identify the errors affecting two or more accounts.

   Ans: Errors affecting two or more accounts are as follows:
   (a) Errors of omission
   (b) Errors of principles
   (c) Errors of posting to wrong A/c
   (d) Errors of posting to wrong amount in the ledger
   (e) Errors of posting in wrong side of the ledger accounts

7. What is the effect of an error affecting nominal acccounts?

   Ans: The items which are nominal in nature (such as expenses, losses, incomes and profits) has a direct effect on the profit or loss of the firm. Hence, any error affecting these items or accounts will result in either increase or decrease in profits of the business.

8. What is the effect of an error affecting personal and real acccounts?

   Ans: Generally, personal and real accounts are considered while preparing the balance sheet. So, any error affecting these accounts will directly affect the balance sheet and it will not represent the true and fair view of the state of affairs (financial position) of a business enterprise.

9. What are the different ways of correcting errors?

   Ans: The different ways of correcting errors are as follows:
   (a) Rectification of errors **before** preparing the trial balance.
   (b) Rectification of errors **after** preparing the trial balance but before preparing the final account.
   (c) Rectification of errors **after** preparing the final account.

10. When can the errors be detected?

    Ans: The errors may be detected in different situations as follows:
    (a) **Before** or at the time of preparing the trial balance.
    (b) **Ater** preparing the trial balance but before preparing the final accounts.
    (c) **After** preparing the final accounts.

11. What is suspense account?

    Ans: Generally, after the preparation of trial balance, final accounts are prepared. But due to some errors which affect the agreement of trial balance and to avoid delay in preparation of final accounts, the difference in the trial balance is replaced by a new account known as Suspense A/c. Subsequently, when all the errors are rectified, the Suspense A/c will automatically be closed.

III. *Long Answer Type Questions*

1. Give the classification of errors with example. What are the objectives of rectification of errors?

2. What do you mean by single-sided errors and double-sided errors? Explain with example.

3. What is the effect of errors in Final Accounts?
4. What are compensating errors? Explain with the help of two examples. Also, give the name of the errors which will not affect the trial balance.
5. Give the name and nature of the errors which will affect one account only and those which affect two or more accounts.
6. What steps would you take for rectification of errors after preparing the trial balance but before preparing the final accounts in case of single-sided error? Explain with example.

IV. *Problems on Rectification of Errors*

A. **Errors Detected before preparation of the Trial Balance**

Single-sided Errors

1. Pass necessary Journal Entries rectifying the following errors which were detected before the preparation of Trial Balance:
   (a) Sales day book overcasted by Rs. 100.
   (b) Purchase day book undercasted by Rs. 300.
   (c) Sales Day Book on a folio was carried forward to the next page as Rs. 450 instead of Rs. 540.
   (d) Depreciation charged on Machinery, but not posted to depreciation on machinery account Rs. 4,500.
   (e) Cash Book debit side discount account total transferred to Discount A/c as Rs. 750 instead of Rs. 570.
   (f) Cash received from Mr. G. Lalit Rs. 350, but posted to the debit of Mr. Lalit's account.
   (g) Sold goods to D. Raja for Rs. 4,300, but posted to D. Raja's account Rs. 3,400.

2. Pass necessary Journal Entries rectifying the following errors which were detected before the preparation of Trial Balance:
   (a) Cash paid to Mr. H. Hundai Rs. 4,400, but credited to his account as Rs. 1,400.
   (b) Commission paid Rs.1,200 and duly entered in the Cash Book, but not posted to commission account.
   (c) Cash received from Mr. N. Bhimani Rs. 3,100, but credited to his account Rs. 1,300.
   (d) Cash received from Mr. N. Bhimani Rs. 3,100 but debited to his account Rs. 1,300.
   (e) Rent paid Rs. 1,700, but debited to rent account twice.
   (f) Purchase Day Book on a folio was carried forward to the next page as Rs. 760 instead of Rs. 700.
   (g) Sold goods to M. Khan for Rs. 5,600, but posted to H. Khan's account Rs. 6,500.
   (h) Sales day book undercasted by Rs. 300.

3. Pass necessary Journal Entries rectifying the following errors which were detected before the preparation of Trial Balance:
   (a) Insurance premium paid Rs. 1,240 and duly entered in the Cash Book, but not posted to insurance premium account.
   (b) Cash Book debit side discount account total has been transferred to discount account as Rs. 440 instead of Rs. 1,440.
   (c) Return inward book overcasted by Rs. 700.
   (d) Interest received from bank Rs. 950 duly shown in the Cash Book, but not posted to interest received account.
   (e) Cash paid to Mr. Sunil Das Rs. 2,600, but debited to his account as Rs. 260
   (f) The total of bills receivable book Rs. 4,300 was posted to Bills Receivable A/c Rs. 3,400.
   (g) Return inward book undercasted by Rs. 200.
   (h) Cash paid to Mr. D. Routh Rs. 1,870, but credited to his account as Rs. 1,070.

4. Give necessary Journal Entries rectifying the following errors which were detected before the preparation of Trial Balance:
   (a) Return outward book overcasted by Rs. 100.
   (b) Bad debts written off amounting to Rs. 560, but not posted to bad debts account.
   (c) Depreciation charged on machinery, but not posted to machinery account Rs. 3,100.
   (d) Cash received from Mr. Mohim Kapadia Rs. 4,350, but posted to the debit of Mr. Mohim Kapadia's account.
   (e) Purchased goods to Sunil for Rs. 2,700, but posted to his account Rs. 3,700.
   (f) Discount allowed Rs. 250, but debited to discount account Rs. 50.

Double-sided Errors

5. Pass necessary Journal entries to rectify the following errors detected before preparation of Trial Balance:
   (a) Cash paid Rs. 750 to N. Roy but debited to K. Roy A/c.
   (b) Cash received from M. Kar Rs. 950 but credited to N. Kar A/c.
   (c) Cash paid Rs. 350 to A. Das but shown as paid Rs. 530.
   (d) Paid repairs to typewriter Rs. 630 debited to Typewriter A/c.
   (e) Paid salary to B. Dhar, the Manager. Rs. 1,250 debited to B. Dhar's A/c.

6. Rectify the following errors:
   (a) The purchase of Machinery for Rs. 7,200 was entered in the Purchase Day Book.
   (b) Sold old furniture for Rs. 3,100 credited to Sales A/c,
   (c) Wages paid for installation of Machinery debited to Wages A/c. Rs. 780.
   (d) Carriage paid for purchase of Machinery debited to Carriage Inward A/c Rs. 390.
   (e) Sold goods to A. Khan for Rs. 2,300 but debited to B. Khan.

7. Give necessary Journal entries to rectify the following errors:
   (a) Sales Day Book was overcast by Rs. 100.
   (b) Sales Return Book undercast by Rs. 200.
   (c) Purchase Day Book undercast by Rs. 100.
   (d) Goods returned by M. Das for Rs. 750 but recorded in the books as goods purchased from him.
   (e) Discount allowed Rs. 510 but debited to Discount A/c Rs. 150.

8. Rectify the following errors:
   (a) Rs. 7,800 paid for purchase of Typewriter was charged to Office expenses A/c.
   (b) Rs. 1,850 paid to landlord for Rent but wrongly debited to landlord's Personal A/c.
   (c) Bad Debt recovered Rs. 780 from Mr. P. Sen but credited to P. Sen's A/c.
   (d) A sale of Rs. 650 to Mr. N. Saha was entered in the Sales Book as Rs. 560.
   (e) Cash withdrawn by the proprietor Rs. 1,750 for personal use debited to Trade Expenses A/c.

9. The following errors are detected before opening a Suspense A/c. Give Journal entries for rectification:
   (a) A cheque of Rs. 950 received from Prabir but posted to Pratap's A/c.
   (b) Repair charges for Building Rs. 1,920 debited to Building A/c.
   (c) A credit sale of Rs. 280 to Mr. K. Rudra has been wrongly passed through the Purchase Day Book.
   (d) Wages paid for installation of Machinery Rs. 4,200, wrongly debited to Wages A/c.
   (e) A sale of old furniture to Mr. D. Sen was passed through the Sales Day Book Rs. 1,740.

10. Rectify the following errors:
    (a) A cheque of Rs. 1,780 issued to S. Roy but wrongly debited to Purchase A/c.
    (b) Salary paid to Manager. Mr. A. B. Mukherjee Rs. 2,600 but debited to Manager's A/c.
    (c) Discount received Rs. 720 but wrongiy debited to Discount Allowed A/c.

    (d) Cash withdrawn from Bank Rs. 680 for personal use but wrongly debited Office expenses A/c.

    (e) Proprietor's Life Insurance premium paid Rs. 920 debited to Insurance Premium A/c.

11. Pass the necessary rectification entries for the following:

    (a) Cash paid to Ram Rs. 530 but wrongly shown as paid Rs. 350.

    (b) Cash paid to N. Sen Rs. 780 but posted to N. Sen's A/c Rs. 870.

    (c) Cash paid to G. Das Rs. 550 but posted to the debit of G. Das's A/c.

    (d) Cash received Rs. 570 from K. Kundu but posted to the debit of K. Kumar's A/c Rs. 750.

    (e) A sum of Rs. 950 was written off from Machinery A/c has not been posted to Depreciation A/c.

    (f) Sales Day Book overcasted by Rs. 100.

    (g) A cash sale of Rs. 3,800 duly entered in the Cash Book but not posted to Sales A/c.

    (h) Office stationery purchased for Rs. 820 debited to Office expenses A/c.

B. Errors Detected After preparation of the Trial Balance but before Final Accounts

12. Rectify the following errors by way of Journal Entries:

    (a) Bills payable issued to P. Kumar Rs. 950 shown as cheque issued to him.

    (b) Sales Day Book undercast by Rs. 200.

    (c) A purchase made for Rs. 900 was posted to the Purchase A/c Rs. 90.

    (d) Cash paid to S.S. Das Rs. 780 but debited to Das's A/c Rs. 80.

    (e) Bills Payable honoured for Rs. 1,500 shown in the Books as Bills Receivable received Rs. 1,500.

    (f) Sales return of Rs. 250 from a customer has not been posted to that A/c. but the customer's A/c has been credited.

13. Pass the Journal Entries to rectify the following errors and then prepare a Suspense A/c in the books of Bachhan:

    (a) Rs. 3,000 spent on repairs of Building but posted to the credit side of the Building A/c from the Cash Book.

    (b) Return Outward book was overcasted by Rs. 4,000.

    (c) Rs. 6,500 received from Aloke was debited to his A/c with Rs. 1,500.

    (d) A discount of Rs. 250 allowed to Aniket has not been posted to his A/c.

    (e) A commission of Rs. 1,520 paid to an agent was posted to the Commission Received A/c (credit side) from the Cash Book.   (Delhi I.S.C. H.S.)

14. There was an error in the Trial Balance of Mr. Arora on 31st December, 1986 and the difference in the books was carried to Suspense A/c. On going through the books you find that:

    (a) Rs. 5,400 received from Mr. Rajiv was posted to the debit of his A/c.

    (b) Rs. 1,000 being purchases return were posted to the debit of Purchase A/c.

    (c) Discount of Rs. 2,000 received were posted to the debit of Discount Received A/c.

    (d) Rs. 2,740 paid for repairs to motor cars was debited to Motor Car A/c as Rs. 1,740.

    (e) Rs. 4,000 paid to R. Sanjay Das debited to S. Sanjoy A/c.

Give Journal entries to rectify the above errors and ascertain the amount transferred to Suspense A/c on 31st December. 1986 by showing the Suspense A/c, assuming that the Suspense A/c is balanced after the above corrections.   (C.A. (Entrance))

Ans: Suspense A/c Opening Balance Rs. 15,800 (Cr.).

15. The Trial Balance as on 31.12.82 of Moon Light Pvt. Ltd. showed a difference and the T.B. was made agreed with the help of Suspense A/c. The following errors were detected afterwards:

    (a) The Sales Day Book was overcast by Rs. 3,000.

    (b) A sum of Rs. 1,000 received from R. Bose was wrongly credited to B. Bose.

(c) A creditors balance was extracted as Rs. 1,345 instead of Rs. 345.

(d) A sale bill for Rs. 9,289 was wrongly debited to Customer's A/c as Rs. 9,810.

(e) The Purchase Day Book was undercast by Rs. 1,000.

(f) An invoice of Rs. 2,000 for purchase of a typewriter was debited to Purchase A/c.

Pass Journal Entries to rectify the above errors and show the Suspense A/c.

(B.U. B.Com. (Pass))

Ans: Suspense A/c opening Balance Rs. 4,479 (Dr.).

16. Rectify the following errors found in the books of Mr. S.K. Sharma. The Trial Balance had Rs. 1,860 excess credit. The difference had been posted to a Suspense A/c:

(a) The total of Return Inwards Book has been cast Rs. 2,000 short.

(b) The purchase of an office table costing Rs. 6,000 has been passed through the Purchase Day Book.

(c) Rs. 7,500 paid for wages to workman for making showcases had been charged to wages A/c.

(d) A purchase of Rs. 1,340 had been posted to the Creditor's A/c as Rs. 600.

(e) A cheque of Rs. 4,000 received from Mr. P.C. Joshi had been dishonoured and was passed to the debit of "Allowances A/c".

After rectification reflect the transactions in the Suspense A/c. (C.A. Entrance)

17. Show how will you rectify the following:

(a) Discount allowed Rs. 135, but not posted to the Discount A/c.

(b) The Returns Inward book showed Rs. 100 less in totals.

(c) A purchase of Rs. 390 had been posted to the debit of supplier Mr. X as Rs. 930.

(d) A sale of Rs. 760 to Mr. Y was credited to his A/c wrongly.

(e) An item of purchase of Rs. 760 was entered in the Purchase Day Book as 60 and posted to the Suppliers A/c as Rs. 670.

(f) Goods returned by Mr. Z Rs. 750 were entered in the Sales Day Book.

18. Rectify the following errors found in the books of Mr. X:

The Trial Balance had Rs. 1,900 excess debit. The difference has been posted to a Suspense A/c.

(a) A credit sale of Rs. 1,900 to Mr. N. Gupta was debited to P. Gupta.

(b) Cash Sale of Rs. 1,750 to CR. Chanda debited to R. Chanda's A/c Rs. 750.

(c) Goods purchased from D. Dhar for Rs. 1,800 but posted to D. Dhar's A/c debit Rs. 800.

(d) Discount allowed Rs. 125 was credited to Discount Received A/c.

(e) Cash withdrawn by Proprietor for personal expenses debited to Trade Expenses A/c. Rs. 640.

(f) Bad debt recovered Rs. 390 but credited to customer Mr. K. Sukul's A/c.

(g) Sold goods to S. Soney for Rs. 1,200 but not posted to his A/c. Give Journal Entries and the Suspense A/c.

19. Rectify the following errors and also show the Suspense A/c:

(a) Wages paid for installation of Machinery Rs. 1,790 debited to Wages A/c.

(b) Sales Day Book overcast by Rs. 100.

(c) Purchase return Book undercast by Rs. 200.

(d) Discount Rs. 750 received, entered in the Cash Book was not posted to the Ledger.

(e) Cash paid to M. Sen Rs. 130 but debited to N. Sen Rs. 310.

(f) Discount allowed Rs. 120 but credited to discount Received A/c.

20. Pass Journal Entries to rectify the following errors and show the Suspense A/c:

(a) An item of Sales for Rs. 187 was posted as Rs. 78 in the Sales A/c.

(b) A sum of Rs. 380 written off fixtures as depreciation has not been posted to Depreciation A/c.

(c) A Bills Receivable for Rs. 450 was passed through Bills Payable Book. This bill was given by Y.

(d) Licence fee for Proprietor' Radio Rs. 125 has been debited to General Expenses A/c.

(e) Purchase Day Book undercast by Rs. 200.

(f) Return Inward Book overcast by Rs. 100.

(g) Rs. 700 received from Q was posted to the debit of his A/c.

21. Pass rectification entries for the following transactions:

(a) Interest paid to Mr. A by cheque was wrongly entered into the Cash column as interest received Rs. 1,250.

(b) Rs. 300 salary paid to Mr. N stands wrongly debited to his Personal A/c.

(c) Goods sold Mr. R for Rs. 475 has been wrongly entered in the Sales Book as Rs. 745.

(d) An amount of Rs. 900 received for commission has been wrongly entered in the Cash Book as received on dividend.

(e) Discount allowed by Mr. T of Rs. 60 on payment to him of Rs. 740 has not been entered in the books of accounts at all.

Find out the difference in Trial Balance arising out of the above errors.

(C.A. Entrance)

14

Depreciation

CONTENTS

INTRODUCTION

The part of the fixed asset used up in an accounting year in course of its use is known as **depreciation**. The fixed assets are entirely consumed the over the years due their continuous use. The economic potential so consumed represents the expired cost or utility of these fixed assets. It is the expired cost of a fixed asset considered as expenditure in the process of its useful life in an accounting year. Therefore, depreciation is the permanent decrease in the value of a fixed asset and represents a part of the total cost of fixed asset used/consumed in an accounting period. It is a charge against profit. When it actually arises, an amount equal to it (the depreciation) has to be charged to the profit and loss account of a firm.

14.1 NATURE OF DEPRECIATION

Generally, every fixed asset excluding land has a certain specific number of years of useful life. In the process of business operations, almost the entire asset value is consumed during the lifetime of the said asset. Therefore, the historical cost of the asset is spread over its effective life in a systematic and rational manner. Thus, depreciation becomes a part of the total historical cost of a fixed asset, which is allocated to periodic revenues over a number of accounting periods. Hence, we can say that the historical cost of the fixed asset is spread over its effective life based on some accepted rules or methods by way of depreciation and is charged against the revenue of each financial year.

It may be interpreted as an expiration of the capital outlay in respect of a fixed asset used by an enterprise in the process of its economic activities to earn revenues. According to this concept, depreciation is a part of the capital outlay in respect of a fixed asset which has expired and which is equal to its loss of service capacity. In fact, it is the expired cost of the capital outlay in respect of a fixed asset charged against revenues for a particular financial year as an expense in the name of depreciation.

Depreciation may be further interpreted as the means of maintenance of nominal capital invested in the fixed assets. According to this concept, the amount of nominal capital invested in the fixed assets is consumed during the effective lifetime of the concerned assets, and thus, the part of the nominal capital expired in an accounting year is recovered by way of depreciation, by charging it against the revenues of the respective financial year. This process of recovery of the historical cost of a fixed asset by way of depreciation helps to maintain the nominal capital, and hence, it may be considered as maintenance of nominal capital(but not the real capital) of an enterprise.

14.2 CAUSES OF DEPRECIATION

The chief causes of depreciation are as follows:

1. *Wear and tear* (**Deterioration**): During the life time of a fixed asset, its value decreases naturally due to natural elements like gas, heat, rain, etc., which results in corrosion, rust, and decay from its constant use. Therefore, depreciation arises due to normal wear and tear when a fixed asset is engaged in production.

2. *Obsolescence*: Some assets are discarded due to new inventions, though their economic potential might not have been fully consumed. For example, a new machine replaces an old one though the old machine works properly because the new machine is more economical and efficient than the old one.

3. *Efflux of time:* With time, value of some assets is decreased even if they are not used. For example, patents, copyrights, etc., may be purchased or acquired for a fixed period and after the expiry of this period, the said assets become valueless. Thus, considering the cost incurred in purchasing the rights and the period for which they were acquired, a part of the said assets should be written off yearly by way of depreciation.

4. *Accidents:* Due to some accident, an asset's value may be decreased or depreciated.

5. *Exhaustion:* It is applicable to mineral mines, oil wells, etc. Due to continuous extraction of minerals, a stage comes when the mines and oil wells get completely exhausted or out of use. Thus, to calculate the true profit of the business, necessary provisions should be made to reduce the value of a particular asset of a wasting character during the said process of extraction. The said provision can be termed as 'depreciation by exhaustion'.

14.3 CHARACTERISTICS OF DEPRECIATION

The following are the important characteristics of depreciation:

1. Depreciation accounting is a process of allocation of expired cost of a fixed asset.
2. It is calculated based on some accepted principles of accounting.
3. It results from a permanent decrease in the value of fixed assets.
4. It is a charge against revenues earned by a firm.
5. Depreciation indicates the gradual deterioration of working efficiency, service potentiality and effective life of a fixed asset.
6. It may be physical (due to natural wear and tear, exhaustion, efflux of time, etc.) or functional (due to obsolescence, inadequacy, etc.).
7. Market fluctuations should not affect the amount of depreciation.
8. It is charged as long as the fixed asset functions, and its effective live losts.
9. Depreciation arises due to the use of the fixed asset engaged in business for earning revenues.

14.4 OBJECTIVES OF PROVIDING DEPRECIATION

1. **To ascertain true profits of the business:** If depreciation was not charged, then the resultant profit would be the inflated profit, which would not be true. It is because of the fact that if the expired cost is not considered, then it is not possible to derive a realistic measure of income and net worth of a business enterprise.

2. **To show the true financial position:** According to the objectives of accounting, a balance sheet must represent a 'true and fair view' of its state of affairs as at the end of the accounting period. If depreciation is not provided, then the asset will show the overstated value in the balance sheet. Hence, without charging depreciation on the fixed assets, the balance sheet cannot reveal the true state of affairs of the firm.

3. **For replacement of assets:** Depreciation is not an outflow of fund. If a provision is made for depreciation, the amount so saved every year may be utilized for replacing or purchasing a new asset at the end of the commercial life of the old asset.

4. **To follow the Companies Act:** According to the Companies Act, a joint stock company is bound to provide for depreciation on fixed assets before distributing dividends.

5. **To keep the nominal capital invested in different fixed assets intact:** By providing depreciation, the consumed capital(expired cost of the fixed assets) will be recovered and retained within the business. However, if this is not done, the business will have to be closed down for want of capital in the future.

14.5 ACCOUNTING STANDARDS (AS) 6

Depreciation is a measure of the wearing out, consumption or other loss of value of a depreciable asset arising from use, efflux ion of time or obsolescence through technology and market changes. Depreciation is allocated to charge a fair proportion of the depreciable amount in each accounting period during the expected useful life of the asset. Depreciation includes amortization of assets whose useful life is predetermined.

The *useful life* of a depreciable asset should be estimated after considering the following factors:

1. Expected physical wear and tear
2. Obsolescence
3. Legal or other limits on use of the asset.

The useful life of major depreciable assets or classes of depreciable assets may be reviewed periodically. Where there is a revision of the estimated useful life of an asset, the unamortized depreciable amount should be charged over the revised useful life.

Depreciable amount of a depreciable asset is its historical cost, or other amount substituted for historical cost in the financial statements, less the estimated residual value.

14.5.1 Assessment of Depreciation

Assessment of depreciation and the amount to be charged in respect thereof in an accounting period are usually based on the following three factors:

1. Historical cost or other amount substituted for the historical cost of the depreciable asset when the asset has been revalued;
2. Expected useful life of the depreciable asset; and
3. Estimated residual value of the depreciable asset.

Historical cost of a depreciable asset represents its money outlay or its equivalent in connection with its acquisition, installation and commissioning as well as for additions to or improvement thereof. The historical cost of a depreciable asset may undergo subsequent changes arising due to increase or decrease in long-term liability because of exchange fluctuations, price adjustments, changes in duties or similar factors. Any addition or extension to an existing asset, which is of capital nature and which becomes an integral part of the existing asset, is depreciated over the remaining useful life of that asset. As a practical measure, however, depreciation is sometimes provided on such addition or extension at the rate that is applied to an existing asset. Any addition or extension, which retains a separate identity and is capable of use even after the existing asset is disposed of, is depreciated independently based on an estimate of its own useful life.

There are several methods of allocating depreciation over the useful life of the assets. Two such methods most commonly employed in industrial and commercial enterprises are the **straight-line method** and the **reducing balance method**. The management of a business selects the most appropriate method(s) based on various important factors such as type of asset, the nature of the use of such asset and the circumstances prevailing in the business. A combination of more than one method is sometimes used. In respect of depreciable assets that do not have material value, the depreciation is often allocated fully in the accounting period in which they are acquired.

The statute governing an enterprise may provide the basis for computation of the depreciation. For example, the **Companies Act, 1956** lays down the rates of depreciation in respect of various assets. If any depreciable asset is disposed of, discarded, demolished or destroyed, then the net surplus or deficiency, if material, should be disclosed separately.

14.6 RELATION BETWEEN DEPRECIATION AND MAINTENANCE

Maintenance expenditure on a machine or a motor is necessary. Without proper maintenance, a machine cannot function properly. Thus, in order to maintain its productivity and efficiency, it is essential to regularly take proper maintenance according to the nature of the machine. It is recurring in nature and is revenue expenditure. On the other hand, depreciation is the expired cost of an asset. Thus, the total cost of an asset is written off within the period of its effective life. Hence, there is no direct relationship between maintenance and depreciation. Depreciation is required to maintain the nominal capital intact, whereas maintenance is essential or desirable to run the machine properly.

14.7 BASIC FACTORS IN CALCULATING THE AMOUNT OF DEPRECIATION OF AN ASSET

For calculating the amount of depreciation in a financial year, the following factors should be taken into consideration:

1. **Cost of the asset:** It includes the invoice price of the asset, less the trade discount, plus all other costs incurred to bring the asset to a usable condition. For example, freight charges, transit insurance charges, repair costs, installation charges, and so on. It should be noted that financial charges such as interest on money borrowed for the purchase of an asset should not be included in the cost of the asset.
2. **Estimated useful life or economic life:** The estimated life of an asset may be measured in terms of months, years, hours, units or outputs and mileage (in case of a vehicle).
3. **Estimated scrap value or turn-in value:** The scrap value (also known as **residual** or **salvage value**) of an asset is an estimated sale value of the asset at the end of its economic life. While calculating the scrap value, the cost incurred for removing the said asset should be deducted out of the total or original realizable value.
4. **The mode of use:** The working hours of the fixed assets engaged in the production or utilized.
5. **The legal provisions:** The provisions of Companies Act, Income Tax Act, etc., applicable in respect of depreciation should be taken into consideration.

14.8 METHODS OF DEPRECIATION

The following are the various methods for providing depreciation:

1. Fixed installment or straight-line method
2. Diminishing balance method
3. Depreciation fund method
4. Annuity method
5. Insurance policy method
6. Machine hour rate method
7. Sum of years digit method
8. Double declining method
9. Depletion method
10. Repairs, maintenance and depreciation fund method.

14.8.1 Guidelines for Selecting Methods for Charging Depreciation on Different Assets

The following observations are to be followed for selecting the method of depreciation on different fixed assets:

1. **Free-hold land:** No depreciation is required to be charged on these assets.
2. **Free-hold buildings, plant and machineries, ships, etc.:** Straight-line method and diminishing balance method may be followed for charging depreciation on these assets. The main object of accepting these methods is to write off the asset within its effective lifetime. When plant and machinery are used on shifting basis (i.e., extensive use), machine hour rate method may be used.
3. **Patents, trademarks, leasehold lands and buildings:** The lives of these assets are fixed as per agreement. Thus, straight-line method may be followed for charging depreciation on these assets.
4. **Loose tools, jigs, livestock, hand tools, etc.:** Inventory or revaluation system of depreciation is generally adopted for these assets. This method is suitable for those assets which are of small value and whose life cannot be ascertained properly or correctly.
5. Mines, oil wells, quarries, etc.: Depletion method is suitable for charging depreciation on these assets.
6. **Goodwill:** Generally, no depreciation is charged on goodwill. However, it is better to write off goodwill completely within a reasonable time.
7. **Free-hold buildings, plant and machinery, ships, leasehold land and buildings, etc.:** Depreciation fund method, insurance policy method and annuity method may be followed for charging depreciation on these assets.

14.8.2 Purchase of Fixed Assets during the Year

Generally, fixed assets are purchased during the financial year, but the question arises about the period to be considered for charging depreciation on the additions made during the year. The following points are to be considered for calculating the period for charging depreciation:

1. **When specific guidelines are given in the problem:** As per the directions of the problem depreciation is to be charged. Suppose, it is mentioned in the problem that it was the practice to charge full year's depreciation on all additions made during the year at any time and ignore depreciation on any machinery sold during the year, then depreciation is to be charged on all additions for full year.
2. **When no specific guidelines are given in the problem:** Under such circumstances, the following steps are to be followed:
   (a) *When no date of purchase is given.* It is advisable to charge half year's depreciation on the additions made during the year.
   (b) When an asset is purchased within the first half of the month, then it is advisable to charge depreciation for full month. For example, an asset is purchased on 7th April and the firm follows the calendar year (January 1 to December 31), then depreciation is to be charged for nine months, i.e., April to December.
   (c) When an asset is purchased within the last half of the month, then it is advisable not to charge any depreciation for the said month. For example, an asset is purchased on 17th April and the firm follows the calendar year (January 1 to December 31), then depreciation is to be charged for eight months, i.e., May to December.

14.8.3 Sale of Fixed Assets during the Year

It is generally seen that an asset is sold in an accounting or financial year due to some defect or for becoming obsolete or scrapped. When an asset is sold, then it is essential to calculate the profit or loss on sale of the said asset. In order to calculate the profit or loss on sale of an asset the following steps are to be taken:

	Rs.
Cost price or book value of the asset sold	...
Less: Depreciation** from the date of purchase to the date of sale	...
Value on the date of sale	...
Sale proceeds	...
Profit on sale (When sale proceeds is greater than the value on the date of sale)/Loss on sale (When sale proceeds is less than the value on the date of sale)	

**While calculating depreciation if it is noticed that the asset is sold during the first half of the month, then depreciation for the said month may be ignored. On the other hand, if the asset is sold during the last half of the month, then the depreciation for the said month should be considered. For example, an asset is sold on 7th April and the firm follows the calendar year (January 1 to December 31), then depreciation is to be charged for three months, i.e., January to March. On the other hand, if the asset is sold on 17th April and the firm follows the calendar year (January 1 to December 31), then depreciation is to be charged for 4 months, i.e., January to April.

These guidelines should be followed only when no specific direction in this respect is given in the problem.

14.8.4 Fixed Instalment Method

This method is also known as **straight-line** or **original cost method**. Under this method, depreciation is charged evenly every year during the economic or effective life of the asset. Thus, the amount of depreciation is fixed for each financial year and the value of the fixed asset reduces evenly until it reaches its scrap value. This method is suitable for those assets, which are expected to render equal or uniform services during their effective lives.

The amount of depreciation is calculated as follows:

$$\text{Depreciation} = \frac{\text{Original cost of the asset} - \text{Estimated scrap value}}{\text{Estimated (useful) life of the asset in years or hours}}$$

Or,

$$D = \frac{C - S}{N}$$

where,

D = Amount of yearly depreciation
C = Cost of the asset
S = Estimated scrap value
N = Estimated (useful) life of the asset expressed in years or hours

For example, if a machine was purchased for Rs. 25,000, it will have a scrap value of Rs. 5,000 at the end of its useful life of 5 years and the depreciation will be as under:

$$\text{Depreciation} = \frac{(\text{Rs. } 25,000 - \text{Rs. } 5,000)}{5 \text{ (years)}}$$
$$= \text{Rs. } 4,000 \text{ each year}$$

The percentage of depreciation may be calculated as under:

$$\text{Percentage of depreciation} = \frac{\text{Amount of depreciation}}{(\text{Original cost of the asset} - \text{Estimated Scrap value})} \times 100$$

Considering the previous example, percentage of depreciation will be as under:

$$\text{Percentage of depreciation} = \frac{\text{Rs. } 4,000}{\text{Rs. } 20,000} \times 100$$
$$= 20\%$$

While calculating the depreciation, if the amount of estimated scrap value is negligible or very small as compared to its original cost, then the said small amount of scrap value may be ignored. Under such circumstances, the amount of depreciation will calculated as under:

$$\text{Depreciation} = \frac{\text{Original cost of the asset}}{\text{Estimated (useful) life of the asset in years or hours}}$$

Advantages of straight-line method

The important advantages of this method are as under:

1. It is an extremely simple method to operate.
2. Small business owners favour this method because of its simplicity.
3. Straight-line method is suitable for those assets whose effective lives can easily be estimated.
4. It suitable for calculating depreciation of patents, leases, copyrights, etc.
5. As the amount of depreciation is fixed for each financial year, it helps to calculate the reasonable and fair closing values of the fixed assets easily.

Disadvantages of straight-line method

The important disadvantages of this method are as under:

1. An asset renders more useful and effective services during the initial periods of its effective life. However, this practical point is ignored under this method because depreciation is fixed for each financial year.
2. It is not suitable for all types of fixed assets.
3. According to straight-line method, depreciation is fixed for each financial year, but the annual repair and maintenance costs increase during the latter periods of the effective lives of these assets. The early years of the effective lives of these assets show considerable amount of profits, but during the latter periods, profits reduce remarkably. Thus, more and more amount is charged to the profit and loss account as depreciation, repair and maintenance during the latter periods of the effective lives (because service-rendering capacity decreases gradually). As a result, the reasonability between expenditure and revenue of a financial year is not maintained considering the effective service rendering capacity of an asset.
4. This method ignores the working capacity of an asset and the actual work performed by the concerned asset.
5. For each item of fixed asset, depreciation should be calculated separately.
6. As the amount of depreciation of an asset is fixed for each financial year, the amount of depreciation during the earlier periods of its effective life is not fair (when an asset renders more useful and effective services). Thus, the closing value of the concerned fixed asset cannot be considered as reasonable and fair.
7. Straight-line method fails to consider the loss of interest on the amount invested for purchasing an asset.

Accounting entries

Depreciation of an asset can be recorded by any of the following two methods:

Sl. No.	When no provision for depreciation is maintained		When provision for depreciation is maintained	
1.	For providing or charging depreciation:			
	Depreciation A/c	Dr.	Depreciation A/c	Dr.
	To Asset A/c		To Provision for Depreciation A/c	
2.	When the annual depreciation is transferred to profit and loss account			
	Profit and Loss A/c	Dr.	Profit and Loss A/c	Dr.
	To Depreciation A/c		To Depreciation A/c	

(Contd.)

3.	When an asset is sold			
	Cash/Bank A/c	Dr.	Cash / Bank A/c	Dr.
	To Asset A/c		To Asset A/c	
4.	For transferring the accumulated depreciation of the asset sold to asset A/c			
	(Here, accumulated depreciation = Total depreciation from the date of purchase to the date of sale of the asset sold)			
	No Entry		Provision for Depreciation A/c	Dr.
			To Asset A/c	
5.	When profit is earned on sale of an asset			
	Asset A/c	Dr.	Asset A/c	Dr.
	To Profit & Loss A/c		To Profit & Loss A/c	
	(For transfer of profit on sale of the asset)		(For transfer of profit on sale of the asset)	
6.	When loss is occurred on sale of an asset			
	Profit & Loss A/c	Dr.	Profit & Loss A/c	Dr.
	To Asset A/c		To Asset A/c	
	(For transfer of loss on sale of the asset)		(For transfer of loss on sale of the asset)	

When provision for depreciation is maintained and an 'Asset Disposal Account' is opened, the entries for sale of an asset and the profit or loss on sale may be recorded alternatively as under (Sl. No. 3 to 6):

1.	When an asset is sold	
	Cash/Bank A/c	Dr.
	To Asset Disposal A/c	
2.	For transferring the original cost of the asset sold	
	Asset Disposal A/c	Dr.
	To Asset A/c	
3.	For transferring the accumulated depreciation of the asset sold	
	to Asset Disposal A/c	
	(Here, accumulated depreciation = Total depreciation from the date	
	of purchase to the date of sale of the asset sold)	
	Provision for Depreciation A/c	Dr.
	To Asset Disposal A/c	
4.	When profit is earned on sale of an asset	
	Asset Disposal A/c	Dr.
	To Profit and Loss A/c	
	(For transfer of profit on sale of the asset)	
5.	When loss is occurred on sale of an asset	
	Profit and Loss A/c	Dr.
	To Asset Disposal A/c	
	(For transfer of loss on sale of the asset)	

Differences between depreciation account and provision for depreciation are listed in Table 14.1.

TABLE 14.1 Distinction between Depreciation Account and Provision for Depreciation Account

	Depreciation account		*Provision for depreciation account*
1.	It is a nominal account in nature.	1.	It is not a nominal account in nature. It is created to show the accumulated figure of the depreciation.
2.	At the end of the financial year, the balance of this account is transferred to the profit and loss account, and the account is closed.	2.	At the end of the year, the balance of this account is carried forward to the next year, but not transferred to the profit and loss account.
3.	Depreciation account is opened by crediting the asset account to reduce the asset value.	3.	Provision for depreciation account is opened by debiting depreciation account.
4.	It always shows a debit balance.	4.	It always shows a credit balance.

(Contd.)

	Depreciation account		*Provision for depreciation account*
5.	This account is not reflected in the balance sheet.	5.	This account is reflected in the balance sheet and shown either on the liability side or on the asset side, and the balance is deducted from the respective asset.
6.	When depreciation account is opened, asset account is shown at its depreciated value, i.e., written down value.	6.	When provision for depreciation account is opened, asset account is shown at its original cost.

Tables 14.2, 14.3(a) and 14.3(b) show the position of balance sheet after charging depreciation.

TABLE 14.2 When No Provision for Depreciation is Maintained

Balance Sheet as at ... (includes)

Liabilities	*Rs.*	*Assets*	*Rs.*
		Fixed Asset (Book Value – Depreciation, i.e., Written Down Value of the asset)	—

TABLE 14.3 When Provision for Depreciation is Maintained

(a) Balance Sheet as at ... (includes)

Liabilities	*Rs.*	*Assets*	*Rs.*
Provision for Depreciation Account	—	Fixed Asset (at original cost)	—

Or

(b) Balance Sheet as at ... (includes)

Liabilities	*Rs.*	*Assets*	*Rs.*
	—	Fixed Asset (At original cost) Less: Provision for Depreciation Account	—

ILLUSTRATION 14.1 On April 1, 2006, a machinery costing Rs. 60,000 was purchased and carriage of Rs. 1,200 and installation charges of Rs. 4,800 were paid. It was estimated that a scrap value of Rs. 8,000 would be realized at the end of its useful life of eight years. Depreciation was charged on straight-line method.

Show the necessary entries in the books of Mr. T. Sharma for two years ending on March 31, 2007 and 2008. Also, show the depreciation account and the machinery account for the said period.

Solution

$$\text{Annual depreciation} = \frac{(\text{Rs. } 60,000 + \text{Rs. } 1,200 + \text{Rs. } 4,800) - \text{Rs. } 8,000}{8 \text{ (years)}} = \text{Rs. } 7,250$$

In the Books of Mr. T. Sharma

Journal Entries

Date	Particulars		L.F.	Amount Dr. (Rs.)	Amount Cr. (Rs.)
2006 April 1	Machinery A/c To Cash/Bank A/c (Being the machine purchased)	Dr.		60,000	60,000
1	Machinery A/c To Cash/Bank A/c (Being carriage of Rs. 1,200 and installation charges of Rs. 4,800 paid for the new machine)	Dr.		6,000	6,000
2007 March 31	Depreciation A/c To Machinery A/c (Being the annual depreciation charged on machinery)	Dr.		7,250	7,250

(Contd.)

Sl.No.	Particulars		L.F.	Amount Dr. (Rs.)	Amount Cr. (Rs.)
	Profit and Loss A/c	Dr.		7,250	
	To Depreciation A/c				7,250
	(Being the depreciation transferred to profit and loss account)				
2008 March 31	Depreciation A/c	Dr.		7,250	
	To Machinery A/c				7,250
	(Being the annual depreciation charged on machinery)				
	Profit and Loss A/c	Dr.		7,250	
	To Depreciation A/c				7,250
	(Being the depreciation transferred to profit and loss account)				

Dr.   **Machinery Account**   Cr.

Date	Particulars	Amount (Rs.)	Date	Particulars	Amount (Rs.)
2006 April 1	To Bank A/c	60,000	2007 March 31	By Depreciation A/c	7,250
	To Cash/Bank A/c	6,000		By Balance c/d	58,750
		66,000			66,000
2007 April 1	To Balance b/d	58,750	2008 March 31	By Depreciation A/c	7,250
				By Balance c/d	51,500
		58,750			58,750
2008 April 1	To Balance b/d	51,500			

Dr.   **Depreciation Account**   Cr.

Date	Particulars	Amount (Rs.)	Date	Particulars	Amount (Rs.)
2007 March 31	To Machinery A/c	7,250	2007 March 31	By Profit and Loss A/c	7,250
		7,250			7,250
2008 March 31	To Machinery A/c	7,250	2008 March 31	By Profit and Loss A/c	7,250
		7,250			7,250

ILLUSTRATION 14.2   On January 1, 2006, machinery costing Rs. 90,000 was purchased, and Rs. 3,000 was paid for its carriage and installation. It was estimated that a scrap value of Rs. 6,000 might be realized at the end of its useful life of 12 years. Another machine was purchased for Rs. 50,000 and Rs. 4,000 was spent on its installation on April 1, 2007. The estimated life of the said machine was 10 years and its scrap value would be Rs. 8,000 at the end of its effective life. Depreciation was charged on straight-line method.

Give the necessary entries in the books of Mr. Bijlani for the year ending December 31, 2006 and 2007.

Solution

In the Books of Mr. Bijlani
Journal Entries

Date	Particulars		L.F.	Amount Dr. (Rs.)	Amount Cr. (Rs.)
2006 January 1	Machinery A/c	Dr.		90,000	
	To Cash/Bank A/c				90,000
	(Being the machine purchased)				
1	Machinery A/c	Dr.		6,000	
	To Cash A/c				6,000
	(Being carriage and installation charges paid for the new machine)				
December 31	Depreciation A/c	Dr.		7,250	
	To Machinery A/c				7,250
	(Being the annual depreciation charged on machinery)				

(Contd.)

Date	Particulars		L.F.	Amount Dr. (Rs.)	Amount Cr. (Rs.)
	Profit and Loss A/c	Dr.		7,250	
	To Depreciation A/c				7,250
	(Being the depreciation transferred to profit and loss account)				
2007 April 1	Machinery A/c	Dr.		50,000	
	To Cash/Bank A/c				50,000
	(Being the machine purchased)				
	Machinery A/c	Dr.		4,000	
	To Cash A/c				4,000
	(Being installation charges paid for machine)				
December 31	Depreciation A/c	Dr.		10,700	
	To Machinery A/c				10,700
	(Being the annual depreciation charged on machinery)				
	Profit and Loss A/c	Dr.		10,700	
	To Depreciation A/c				10,700
	(Being the depreciation transferred to profit and loss account)				

Working Notes

1. Calculation of depreciation for the year 2006:

$$\text{Annual depreciation} = \frac{(\text{Rs. } 90,000 + \text{Rs. } 3,000) - \text{Rs. } 6,000}{12 \text{ (years)}} = \text{Rs. } 7,250 \text{ p.a.}$$

2. Calculation of depreciation for the year 2007:
Depreciation for the first machine = Rs. 7,250
Depreciation for the second machine:

$$\text{Annual depreciation} = \frac{(\text{Rs. } 50,000 + \text{Rs. } 4,000) - \text{Rs. } 8,000}{10 \text{ (years)}} = \text{Rs. } 4,600 \text{ p.a.}$$

Depreciation for nine months for the first year = $(4,600/12) \times 9$ = Rs. 3,450
Hence, depreciation for the year 2007 = Rs. 7,250 + Rs. 3,450 = Rs. 10,700.

ILLUSTRATION 14.3 On January 1, 2006 the machinery account of Mr. D. Shukla shows a balance of Rs. 64,000 (original cost Rs. 80,000). On April 1, 2006, machinery costing Rs. 40,000 was purchased, and Rs. 8,000 was incurred for its freight and installation. On May 1, 2007 another new machine was purchased for Rs. 40,000 by cheque, but the machine started functioning from June 1, 2007. Depreciation was charged @ 10% p.a. on straight-line method.

Give the necessary entries in the books of Mr. D. Shukla and show the machinery account for two years ending December 31, 2006 and 2007.

Solution

In the Books of Mr. D. Shukla
Journal Entries

Date	Particulars		L.F.	Amount Dr. (Rs.)	Amount Cr. (Rs.)
2006 April 1	Machinery A/c	Dr.		40,000	
	To Cash/Bank A/c				40,000
	(Being the machine purchased)				
1	Machinery A/c	Dr.		8,000	
	To Cash A/c				8,000
	(Being freight and installation charges paid for purchasing machinery)				

(Contd.)

Date	Particulars		L.F.	Amount Dr. (Rs.)	Amount Cr. (Rs.)
2006 Dec. 31	Depreciation A/c To Machinery A/c (Being the annual depreciation charged on machinery)	Dr.		11,600	11,600
	Profit and Loss A/c To Depreciation A/c (Being the depreciation transferred to profit and loss account)	Dr.		11,600	11,600
2007 May 1	Machinery A/c To Bank A/c (Being the machine purchased)	Dr.		40,000	40,000
December 31	Depreciation A/c To Machinery A/c (Being the annual depreciation charged on machinery)	Dr.		15,133	15,133
	Profit and Loss A/c To Depreciation A/c (Being the depreciation transferred to profit and loss account)	Dr.		15,133	15,133

Working Notes

1. Calculation of depreciation for the year 2006:
   Annual depreciation for the first machine = Rs. 80,000 × 10% = Rs. 8,000
   Depreciation for the second machine:
   Annual depreciation = (Rs. 40,000 + Rs. 8,000) × 10 % = Rs. 4,800 p.a.
   Depreciation for 9 months for the first year = (4,800/12) × 9 = Rs. 3,600
   Hence, total depreciation for the year 2006 = Rs. 8,000 + Rs. 3,600 = Rs. 11,600.

2. Calculation of depreciation for the year 2007:
   Annual depreciation for the first machine = Rs. 8,000
   Annual depreciation for the second machine = Rs. 4,800
   Annual depreciation for the third machine = Rs. 40,000 × 10 % = Rs. 4,000
   Depreciation for seven months for the first year = (4,000/12) × 7 = Rs. 2,333
   (Machine started functioning from June 1, 2007, so depreciation will be charged for the period from June to December = 7 months)
   Hence, total depreciation for the year 2007 = Rs. 8,000 + Rs. 4,800 + Rs. 2,333 = Rs. 15,133.

14.8.5 Diminishing Balance Method

This method is also known as **written down value** or **reducing installment method**. Under this method, depreciation is charged on the book value of an asset every year and as a result, depreciation goes on decreasing every year. This method is suitable for those assets whose repair costs increase when the asset becomes older like machinery. An asset renders services that are more useful during the earlier periods of its effective life, Thus, it is quite reasonable to charge the annual depreciation at a higher amount during the said periods.

For example, if machinery is purchased at Rs. 80,000 and the rate of depreciation is 10% p.a., then depreciation for the first year is Rs. 8,000 (10% of Rs. 80,000); for second year, it is Rs. 7,200 [10% of (Rs. 80,000 – 8,000)]; for third year, Rs. 6,480 [10% of (Rs. 72,000 – 7,200)], and so on.

Thus, according to this method depreciation is charged at a fixed percentage on the book value (b/f balance) of the asset, and as a result, in the initial years (when an asset renders more useful and effective services) the repair costs are less and the amount of depreciation is greater than these in the latter periods. When the asset becomes older, repairs costs increase, but the amount of depreciation decreases.

Diminishing balance method maintains a good uniformity regarding the total cost (repair cost + depreciation) incurred for maintaining an asset and the amount charged to profit and loss account. For example,

Year	Asset value (Rs.)	Depreciation @ 10 % p.a. (Rs.)	Repairs (Rs.)	Total cost of maintaining an asset (Rs.)	Asset value after charging depreciation (Rs.)
1	100,000	10,000	2,000	12,000	100,000 – 10,000 = 90,000
2	90,000	9,000	3,000	12,000	90,000 – 9,000 = 81,000
3	81,000	8,100	4,000	12,100	81,000 – 8,100 = 72,900
4	72,900	7,290	5,000	12,290	72,900 – 7,290 = 65,610

The fixed rate of depreciation under diminishing balance method can be calculated as follows:

$$R = 1 - \sqrt[n]{\frac{S}{C}}$$

where,

R = Rate of depreciation
n = Estimated (useful) life of the asset
S = Scrap value of the asset
C = Original cost of the asset

For example, a plant costing Rs. 2,000 was purchased on January 1, 1980. Its expected life is three years and its turn-in value is Rs. 128. Rate of depreciation is:

$$R = 1 - \sqrt[3]{\frac{128}{2000}} = 0.6 = 60\%$$

Advantages of diminishing balance method

The chief advantages of this method are as under:

1. This method maintains a good uniformity regarding the total cost (repair and maintenance cost + depreciation) incurred for maintaining an asset. It means the total cost charged to profit and loss account for maintaining an asset each year is more or less equal or reasonable.
2. Diminishing balance method is very simple to understand and its application is very easy.
3. As the repair and maintenance cost plus depreciation are charged equitably during the effective life of an asset, it helps to ascertain the true profit of the business.
4. It helps to represent the real cost of an asset in the balance sheet considering its useful and effective services.
5. Income tax officials prefer this method for charging depreciation.
6. In this method, repairs cost increases as the asset becomes older. However, it is compensated by charging less depreciation during the latter periods.

Disadvantages of diminishing balance method

The major disadvantages of diminishing balance method are as under:

1. According to this method, either the closing value of an asset cannot be brought down to zero or it takes very long to write off an asset completely, unless the rate of depreciation is very high.
2. The method for calculating the rate of depreciation under this method is not very simple.
3. For assets having very short lives, the amount of depreciation charged in the early years is very high.
4. Diminishing is not applicable for those assets whose closing values at the end of their lives is balance method zero. For example, copyrights, patents, and leasehold properties.
5. This method also does not consider the loss of interest on tne amount invested for purchasing an asset.
6. When depreciation is charged at a fixed percentage at a higher rate on any asset during the earlier periods of its effective life, the amount of depreciation actually charged is higher than the actual depreciation suffered by the concerned asset.

The differences between straight-line method and diminishing line method are listed in Table 14.4.

TABLE 14.4 Difference between Straight-line Method and Diminishing Balance Method

Straight-line method	Diminishing balance method
1. Depreciation is always charged on the original cost of an asset.	1. Under this method, depreciation is charged on the book value of an asset every year, i.e., on the last year's closing balance.
2. Depreciation charged on a particular asset is fixed for all the years.	2. Depreciation charged on a particular asset goes on decreasing every year.
3. Calculation of depreciation is easy and simple under straight-line method.	3. Calculation of depreciation is not simple like that in the straight-line method.
4. It is applicable for those assets whose closing values at the end of their lives is zero.	4. Diminishing balance method is not applicable for those assets whose closing values at the end of their lives is zero.
5. Total cost, i.e., depreciation and repairs charges, charged to profit and loss account for maintaining an asset is less in the early years and very high in the subsequent years.	5. Total cost, i.e., depreciation and repairs charges, charged to profit and loss account for maintaining an asset each year is more or less equal or reasonable.
6. The income tax department does not prefer this method for charging depreciation.	6. The income tax department prefers this method for charging depreciation.
7. The book value of an asset may be zero at the end of its effective life.	7. The book value of an asset may never be zero at the end of its effective life.

ILLUSTRATION 14.4 On January 1, 2006, machinery costing Rs. 120,000 was purchased and Rs. 18,000 was paid for its carriage and installation. It was estimated that a scrap value of Rs. 14,000 would be realized at the end of its useful life. Another machine was purchased on May 1, 2007, at Rs. 70,000 and its installation charge was Rs. 6,000. The estimated scrap value would be Rs. 6,000 at the end of its effective life. Depreciation is to be provided @ 10% p.a. on diminishing balance method.

Give necessary entries in the books of Mr. Karunanidhi for the year ended December 31, 2006 and 2007.

Solution

In the Books of Mr. Karunanidhi
Journal Entries

Date	Particulars	L.F.	Amount Dr. (Rs.)	Amount Cr. (Rs.)
2006 January 1	Machinery A/c Dr. To Cash/Bank A/c (Being the machine purchased)		120,000	120,000
1	Machinery A/c Dr. To Cash A/c (Being carriage and installation charges paid for the new machine)		18,000	18,000
December 31	Depreciation A/c Dr. To Machinery A/c (Being the annual depreciation charged on machinery)		13,800	13,800
	Profit and Loss A/c Dr. To Depreciation A/c (Being the depreciation transferred to profit and loss account)		13,800	13,800
2007 May 1	Machinery A/c Dr. To Cash/Bank A/c (Being the machine purchased)		70,000	70,000
	Machinery A/c Dr. To Cash A/c (Being installation charges paid for the new machine)		6,000	6,000

(Contd.)

Date	Particulars	L.F.	Amount Dr. (Rs.)	Amount Cr. (Rs.)
December 31	Depreciation A/c Dr. To Machinery A/c (Being the annual depreciation charged on machinery)		17,487	17,487
	Profit and Loss A/c Dr. To Depreciation A/c (Being the annual depreciation transferred to profit and loss account)		17,487	17,487

Working Note

1. Calculation of depreciation for the year 2006 and 2007:

	First machine purchased on January 1, 2006	Second machine purchased on May 1, 2007	Total depreciation (Rs.)
Original cost of the machine *Less:* Depreciation for the year 2006 @ 10%	138,000 13,800	76,000	13,800
	124,200	76,000	
Less: Depreciation for the year 2007 @ 10%	12,420	5,067*	17,487
	111,780	70,933	

* (Depreciation charges for eight months)

ILLUSTRATION 14.5 On April 1, 2005, the machinery account of Mr. H. Khanna shows a balance of Rs. 98,000. On September 1, 2005, a machine costing Rs. 60,000 was purchased, and Rs. 4,000 was incurred for its freight and installation. On June 1, 2006, another new machine was purchased at Rs. 80,000. Depreciation was charged @ 10% p.a. on diminishing balance method.

Show the machinery account for two years ending March 31, 2006 and 2007.

Solution

In the Books of Mr. H. Khanna

Machinery Account

Dr.   Cr.

Date	Particulars	Amount (Rs.)	Date	Particulars	Amount (Rs.)
2005 April 1 September 1	To Balance b/d To Bank A/c To Cash A/c	98,000 60,000 4,000	2006 March 31	By Depreciation A/c By Balance c/d	13,533 148,467
		162,000			162,000
2006 April 1 June 1	To Balance b/d To Bank A/c	148,467 80,000	2007 March 31	By Depreciation A/c By Balance c/d	21,514 206,953
		228,467			228,467
2007 April 1	To Balance b/d	206,953			

Working Note

1. Calculation of depreciation for two years:

	Old machine purchased on April 1, 2005	Machine purchased on September 1, 2005	Machine purchased on June 1, 2006	Total depreciation (Rs.)
Balance/cost of the machine *Less:* Depreciation on 31.03.06 @ 10%	98,000 9,800	64,000 3,733*	80,000	13,533
	88,200	60,267	80,000	
Less: Depreciation on 31.03.07 @ 10%	8,820	6,027	6,667**	21,514
	79,380	54,240	73,333	

*(Depreciation charged for seven months)
**(Depreciation charged for ten months)

ILLUSTRATION 14.6 On January 1, 2005 the machinery account of Mr. S.P. Dutta shows a balance of Rs. 46,000 (original cost Rs. 68,000). On April 1, 2005, a new machine was purchased at Rs. 18,000 and Rs. 4,000 was incurred for its installation. On August 1, 2005, an old machinery was sold at Rs. 9,200, which was installed on May 1, 2003, costing Rs. 16,500. Depreciation was charged @ 10% p.a. on straight-line balance method.

Show the machinery account and depreciation account in the books of Mr. S. P. Dutta for the year ending December 31, 2005.

Solution

In the Books of Mr. S.P. Dutta

Dr. **Machinery Account** Cr.

Date	Particulars	Amount (Rs.)	Date	Particulars	Amount (Rs.)
2005 Jan. 1	To Balance b/d	46,000	2005 August 1	By Bank A/c—sale proceeds	9,200
April 1	To Bank A/c	18,000		By Depreciation A/c	963
	To Cash A/c	4,000		By Profit and Loss A/c (Loss on sale transferred)	3,587
			Dec. 31	By Depreciation A/c	6,800
				By Balance c/d	47,450
		68,000			68,000

Dr. **Depreciation Account** Cr.

Date	Particulars	Amount (Rs.)	Date	Particulars	Amount (Rs.)
2005 August 1	To Machinery A/c	963	2005 Dec. 31	By Profit and Loss A/c (Transferred)	7,763
December 31	To Machinery A/c	6,800			
		7,763			7,763

Working Notes

1. Calculation of profit or loss on sale of machine on 1.8.05:

		Rs.
01.05.03	Purchased	16,500
31.12.03	*Less:* Depreciation @ 10 % p.a. for eight months	1,100
01.01.04	Book Value	15,400
31.12.04	*Less:* Depreciation @ 10 % p.a. on Rs. 16,500	1,650
01.01.05	Book Value	13,750
01.08.05	*Less:* Depreciation @ 10 % p.a. for seven months on Rs. 16,500	963
	Value on the date of sale	12,787
	Sale Proceeds	9,200
	Loss on sale	3,587

2. Calculation of depreciation on the remaining machineries:

	Rs.
Machinery A/c balance on 1.1.04 (Original cost)	68,000
Less: Original cost of the machine sold on 1.8.05	16,500
Original cost of the remaining old machineries	51,500
Depreciation on the remaining old machineries of Rs. 51,500 @ 10 % p.a.	5,150
Depreciation on the machine purchased on 1.4.05 @ 10 % p.a. on Rs. 22,000 for nine months	1,650
	6,800

ILLUSTRATION 14.7   On April 1, 2006, the machinery account of Mr. Khurana shows a balance of Rs. 67,800 (original cost Rs. 98,600). On July 1, 2006, a new machine was purchased at Rs. 26,500 and Rs. 3,500 was incurred for its installation. On November 30, 2006, an old machinery was sold at Rs. 18,400, which was installed on June 1, 2004, costing Rs. 31,000. It was the practice of Mr. Khurana's business to charge full year's depreciation on all additions made during the year at any time and to ignore depreciation on any machinery sold during the year. Depreciation was charged @ 15% p.a. on straight-line balance method.

Show the machinery account in the books of Mr. Khurana for the year ending March 31, 2007.

Solution

In the Books of Mr. Khurana

Dr.   **Machinery Account**   Cr.

Date	Particulars	Amount (Rs.)	Date	Particulars	Amount (Rs.)
2006 April 1	To Balance b/d (Original cost Rs. 98,600)	67,800	2006 Nov. 30	By Bank A/c—sale proceeds	18,400
July 1	To Bank A/c	26,500		By Profit & Loss A/c (loss on sale transferred)	3,300
	To Cash A/c	3,500	2007 March 31	By Depreciation A/c	14,640
				By Balance c/d	61,460
				Old machinery Rs. 67,600 + New machinery Rs. 30,000	
		97,800			97,800

Working Notes

1. Calculation of profit or loss on sale of machine on 30.11.06:

		Rs.
01.06.04	Purchased	31,000
31.03.05	*Less:* Depreciation @ 15 % p.a. on Rs. 31,000 for full year	4,650
01.04.05	Book Value	26,350
31.03.06	*Less:* Depreciation @ 15 % p.a. on Rs. 31,000	4,650
01.04.06	Book Value	21,700
30.11.06	*Less:* Depreciation (to ignore depreciation on machinery sold during the year)	Nil
	Value on the date of sale	21,700
	Sale proceeds	18,400
	Loss on sale	3,300

2. Calculation of depreciation on the remaining machineries:

	Rs.
Machinery A/c balance on 1.1.06 (Original cost)	98,600
Less: Original cost of the machine sold on 30.11.06	31,000
Original cost of the remaining old machineries	67,600
Depreciation on the remaining old machineries of Rs. 67,600 @ 15 % p.a.	10,140
Depreciation on the machine purchased on 1.07.06 @ 15 % p.a. on Rs. 30,000 for full year	4,500
	14,640

ILLUSTRATION 14.8   A firm purchases two machines for Rs. 36,000 and Rs. 56,000 on January 1, 2004. It charges depreciation @ 15 % p.a. on diminishing balance method. The machine costing at Rs. 36,000 was sold at Rs. 17,400 on October 1, 2007. The accounts are closed on December 31 every year.

Give necessary entries for the year ended December 31, 2004 to December 31, 2007. Also, give the machinery account of the said period.

Solution

In the Books of ...
Journal Entries

Date	Particulars	L.F.	Amount Dr. (Rs.)	Amount Cr. (Rs.)
2004 January 1	Machinery A/c Dr. To Cash/Bank A/c (Being two machines for Rs. 36,000 and Rs. 56,000, respectively purchased)		92,000	92,000
December 31	Depreciation A/c Dr. To Machinery A/c (Being the annual depreciation charged on machinery)		13,800	13,800
	Profit and Loss A/c Dr. To Depreciation A/c (Being the depreciation transferred to profit and loss account)		13,800	13,800
2005 Dec. 31	Depreciation A/c Dr. To Machinery A/c (Being the annual depreciation charged on machinery)		11,730	11,730
	Profit and Loss A/c Dr. To Depreciation A/c (Being the depreciation transferred to profit and loss account)		11,730	11,730
2006 Dec. 31	Depreciation A/c Dr. To Machinery A/c (Being the annual depreciation charged on machinery)		9,971	9,971
	Profit and Loss A/c Dr. To Depreciation A/c (Being the depreciation transferred to profit and loss account)		9,971	9,971
2007 October 1	Cash A/c Dr. To Machinery A/c (Being the machine purchased on January 1, 2004 at Rs. 36,000 sold)		17,400	17,400
	Depreciation A/c Dr. To Machinery A/c (Being depreciation charged on machine sold)		2,487	2,487
	Profit and Loss A/c Dr. To Machinery A/c (Being loss on sale transferred)		2,221	2,221
December 31	Depreciation A/c Dr. To Machinery A/c (Being the annual depreciation charged on machinery)		5,159	5,159
	Profit and Loss A/c Dr. To depreciation A/c (Being the depreciation transferred to profit and loss account)		5,159	5,159

Dr.   **Machinery Account**   Cr.

Date	Particulars	Amount (Rs.)	Date	Particulars	Amount (Rs.)
2004 Jan. 1	To Bank A/c	92,000	2004 Dec. 31	By Depreciation A/c By Balance c/d	13,800 78,200
		92,000			92,000
2005 Jan. 1	To Balance b/d	78,200	2005 Dec. 31	By Depreciation A/c By Balance c/d	11,730 66,470
		78,200			78,200
2006 Jan. 1	To Balance b/d	66,470	2006 Dec. 31	By Depreciation A/c By Balance c/d	9,971 56,499
		66,470			66,470

(Contd.)

Date	Particulars	Amount (Rs.)	Date	Particulars	Amount (Rs.)
2007 Jan. 1	To Balance b/d	56,499	2007 Oct. 1	By Bank A/c—sale proceeds	17,400
				By Depreciation A/c	2,487
				By Profit and Loss A/c	
				(Loss on sale transferred)	2,221
			2007 Dec. 31	By Depreciation A/c	5,159
				By Balance c/d	29,232
		56,499			56,499

Working Note

		Machine 1 (Rs.)	Machine 2 (Rs.)	Total depreciation (Rs.)
01.01.04	Purchased	36,000	56,000	
31.12.04	*Less:* Depreciation @ 15 % p.a.	5,400	8,400	13,800
01.01.05	Book Value	30,600	47,600	
31.12.05	*Less:* Depreciation @ 15 % p.a.	4,590	7,140	11,730
01.01.06	Book Value	26,010	40,460	
31.12.06	*Less:* Depreciation @ 15 % p.a.	3,902	6,069	9,971
01.01.07	Book Value	22,108	34,391	
01.10.07	*Less:* Depreciation @ 15 % p.a. for nine months	2,487		2,487
	Value on the date of sale	19,621		
	Sale Proceeds	17,400		
	Loss on sale	2,221		
31.12.07	*Less:* Depreciation @ 15 % p.a.		5,159	5,159
01.01.08	Book Value		29,232	

ILLUSTRATION 14.9 On January 1, 2004, the machinery account of a trader shows a balance of Rs. 58,000. On May 1, 2004, a machine costing Rs. 18,000 was purchased, and Rs. 6,000 was incurred for its freight and installation. The said machine started functioning from June 1, 2004. On July 31, 2004, an old machinery was sold at Rs. 8,300, which was installed on March 1, 2002 at a cost of Rs. 19,100. Depreciation is charged @ 10% p.a. on diminishing balance method.

Show the machinery account for the year ending December 31, 2004. Also, show the position of machinery account in the balance sheet.

Solution

In the Books of ...

Dr. **Machinery Account** Cr.

Date	Particulars	Amount (Rs.)	Date	Particulars	Amount (Rs.)
2004 Jan. 1	To Balance b/d	58,000	2004 July 31	By Bank A/c—sale proceeds	8,300
May 1	To Bank A/c	18,000		By Depreciation A/c	919
	To Cash A/c	6,000		By Profit and Loss A/c	6,538
	(Started functioning			(Loss on sale transferred)	
	from June 1)		2004 Dec. 31	By Depreciation A/c	5,624
				By Balance c/d	60,619
		82,000			82,000

Working Notes

1. Calculation of profit or loss on sale of machine on 31.7.04:

		Rs.
01.03.02	Purchased	19,100
31.12.02	*Less:* Depreciation @ 10 % p.a. for ten months	1,592
01.01.03	Book Value	17,508
31.12.03	*Less:* Depreciation @ 10 % p.a.	1,751
01.01.04	Book Value	15,757
31.07.04	*Less:* Depreciation @ 10 % p.a. for seven months	919
	Value on the date of sale	14,838
	Sale Proceeds	8,300
	Loss on sale	6,538

2. Calculation of depreciation on the remaining machineries:

	Rs.
Machinery A/c balance on 1.1.04	58,000
Less: Book Value of the machine sold on 1.1.04 (as per working note 1)	15,757
Book value of the remaining old machine	42,243
Depreciation on the remaining old machine of Rs. 42,243 @ 10 % p.a.	4,224
Depreciation on the machine purchased on 1.5.04 @ 10 % p.a. on Rs. 24,000 for seven months *	1,400
	5,624

* The machine purchased on May 1, 2004, started functioning from June 1, 2004. Hence, depreciation is to be charged for the period from June 1, 2004 to December 31, 2004 i.e., for seven months.

Balance Sheet as at December 31, 2004(includes)

Liabilities	Amount (Rs.)	Amount (Rs.)	Assets	Amount (Rs.)	Amount (Rs.)
			Machinery Account		60,619

ILLUSTRATION 14.10 On January 1, 2006, the machinery account of Mr. Ambani shows a balance of Rs. 92,000. On April 1, 2006 a machinery costing Rs. 60,000 was purchased and Rs. 5,000 was incurred for its freight and installation. The said machine started functioning from June 1, 2006. On July 31, 2006, an old machinery was sold at Rs. 24,500, which was installed on May 1, 2004 at a cost of Rs. 39,000. On October 1, 2006, an old machinery was purchased at Rs. 26,400 and Rs. 12,800 was paid for its immediate repairs, and Rs. 3,800 towards the installation charges. Depreciation is charged @ 10% p.a. on diminishing balance method. Show the machinery account for the year ending December 31, 2006.

Solution

In the Books of Mr. Ambani

Dr. **Machinery Account** Cr.

Date	Particulars	Amount (Rs.)	Date	Particulars	Amount (Rs.)
2006 Jan. 1	To Balance b/d	92,000	2006 July 31	By Bank A/c—sale proceeds	24,500
April 1	To Bank A/c	60,000		By Depreciation A/c	1,911
	To Cash A/c	5,000		By Profit and Loss A/c	6,349
	(Started functioning			(Loss on sale transferred)	
	from June 1)		December 31	By Depreciation A/c	10,791
October 1	To Bank A/c	26,400		By Balance c/d	156,449
	To Cash A/c	16,600			
	(12,800 + 3,800)				
		200,000			200,000

Working Notes

1. Calculation of profit or loss on sale of machine on 31.7.06:

		Rs.
01.05.04	Purchased	39,000
31.12.04	*Less:* Depreciation @ 10 % p.a. for eight months	2,600
01.01.05	Book Value	36,400
31.12.05	*Less:* Depreciation @ 10 % p.a.	3,640
01.01.06	Book Value	32,760
31.07.06	*Less:* Depreciation @ 10 % p.a. for seven months	1,911
	Value on the date of sale	30,849
	Sale Proceeds	24,500
	Loss on sale	6,349

2. Calculation of depreciation on the remaining machineries:

	Rs.
Machinery A/c balance on 1.1.06	92,000
Less: Book Value of the machine sold on 1.1.06 (as per working note 1)	32,760
Book value of the remaining old machineries	59,240
Depreciation on the remaining old machineries of Rs. 59,240 @ 10 % p.a.	5,924
Depreciation on the machine purchased on 1.4.06 @ 10 % p.a. on Rs. 65,000 for seven months *	3,792
Depreciation on the machine purchased on 1.10.06 @ 10 % p.a. on Rs. 43,000 for three months **	1,075
	10,791

* The machine purchased on April 1, 2006 started functioning from June 1, 2006. Hence, depreciation is to be charged for the period from June 1, 2006 to December 31, 2006, i.e., for seven months.

** An old machinery was purchased on October 1, 2006 and Rs. 12,800 was paid for its immediate repairs, and Rs. 3,800 towards the installation charges. Here, immediate repairs of Rs. 12,800 have been considered as capital expenditure because it is assumed here that the said expenditure has been made to increase the working capacity of the old machine. Thus, depreciation has been charged on the total expenditure of Rs. 43,000 (26,400 + 12,800 + 3,800).

When Provision for Depreciation Account is Maintained

ILLUSTRATION 14.11 A firm purchases two machines for Rs. 18,000 and Rs. 28,000 respectively, on January 1, 2002. The firm charges depreciation @ 15 % p.a. on diminishing balance method. The machine bought for Rs. 18,000 was sold at Rs. 8,850 on October 1, 2005. Accounts are closed on December 31 every year.

Give the necessary entries for the year ended December 31, 2005, assuming that the provision for depreciation account is maintained.

Solution

In the Books of ...
Journal Entries

Date	Particulars		L.F.	Amount Dr. (Rs.)	Amount Cr. (Rs.)
2002 Jan. 1	Machinery A/c To Bank A/c (Being two machines purchased for Rs. 18,000 and Rs. 28,000 respectively)	Dr.		46,000	46,000
2002 Dec. 31	Depreciation A/c To Provision for Depreciation A/c (Being the annual depreciation charged on machinery @15% p.a.)	Dr.		6,900	6,900

(Contd.)

Date	Particulars		L.F.	Amount Dr. (Rs.)	Amount Cr. (Rs.)
	Profit and Loss A/c	Dr.		6,900	
	To Depreciation A/c				6,900
	(Being the depreciation transferred to profit and loss account)				
2003 Dec. 31	Depreciation A/c	Dr.		5,865	
	To Provision for Depreciation A/c				5,865
	(Being the annual depreciation charged on machinery @15% p.a.)				
	Profit and Loss A/c	Dr.		5,865	
	To Depreciation A/c				5,865
	(Being the depreciation transferred to profit and loss account)				
2004 Dec. 31	Depreciation A/c	Dr.		4,985	
	To Provision for Depreciation A/c				4,985
	(Being the annual depreciation charged on machinery @15% p.a.)				
	Profit and Loss A/c	Dr.		4,985	
	To Depreciation A/c				4,985
	(Being the depreciation transferred to profit and loss account)				
2005 Oct. 1	Bank A/c	Dr.		8,850	
	To Machinery A/c				8,850
	(Being the sale proceeds of an old machine received)				
	Depreciation A/c	Dr.		1,244	
	To Provision for Depreciation A/c				1,244
	(Being the depreciation charged on machinery @15% p.a. for nine months on the machine sold)				
	Provision for Depreciation A/c	Dr.		8,190	
	To Machinery A/c				8,190
	(Being the accumulated depreciation of the machine sold transferred to machinery A/c)				
	Profit and Loss A/c	Dr.		960	
	To Machinery A/c				960
	(Being the loss on sale transferred)				
2005 Dec. 31	Depreciation A/c	Dr.		2,579	
	To Provision for Depreciation A/c				2,579
	(Being the annual depreciation charged on machinery @15% p.a.)				
	Profit and Loss A/c	Dr.		3,823	
	To Depreciation A/c				3,823
	(Rs. 1,244 + Rs. 2,579) (Being the depreciation transferred to profit and loss account)				

Working Note

		Machine 1 (Rs.)	Machine 2 (Rs.)	Total depreciation (Rs.)
01.01.02	Purchased	18,000	28,000	
31.12.02	Less: Depreciation @ 15 % p.a.	2,700	4,200	6,900
01.01.03	Book Value	15,300	23,800	
31.12.03	Less: Depreciation @ 15 % p.a.	2,295	3,570	5,865
01.01.04	Book Value	13,005	20,230	
31.12.04	Less: Depreciation @ 15 % p.a.	1,951	3,034	4,985
01.01.05	Book Value	11,054	17,196	
01.10.05	Less: Depreciation @ 15 % p.a. for nine months	1,244		1,244
	Value on the date of sale	9,810		
	Sale Proceeds	8,850		
	Loss on sale	960		
31.12.05	Less: Depreciation @ 15 % p.a.		2,579	2,579
01.01.06	Book Value		14,617	

ILLUSTRATION 14.12   A firm purchased a machine for Rs. 68,000 on January 1, 2003 and incurred Rs. 6,000 for its freight and installation. On April 1, 2004, another new machine was purchased for Rs. 56,000. The firm charges depreciation @ 10 % p.a. on diminishing balance method. The machine installed on January 1, 2003, was sold at Rs. 46,600 on September 30, 2005. The accounts are closed on December 31 every year.

Show machinery account, provision for depreciation account, depreciation account and machine disposal account for the period from January 1, 2003 to December 31, 2005.

Solution

In the Books of ...

Dr. **Machinery Account** Cr.

Date	Particulars	Amount (Rs.)	Date	Particulars	Amount (Rs.)
2003 Jan. 1	To Bank A/c	68,000	2003 Dec. 31	By Balance c/d	74,000
	To Bank A/c	6,000			
		74,000			74,000
2004 Jan. 1	To Balance b/d	74,000	2004 Dec. 31	By Balance c/d	130,000
April 1	To Bank A/c	56,000			
		130,000			130,000
2005 Jan. 1	To Balance b/d	130,000	2005 Sep. 30	By Machine Disposal A/c	74,000
			Dec. 31	By Balance c/d	56,000
		130,000			130,000

Dr. **Depreciation Account** Cr.

Date	Particulars	Amount (Rs.)	Date	Particulars	Amount (Rs.)
2003 Dec. 31	To Provision for Depreciation A/c	7,400	2003 Dec. 31	By Profit and Loss A/c	7,400
		7,400			7,400
2004 Dec. 31	To Provision for Depreciation A/c	10,860	2004 Dec. 31	By Profit and Loss A/c	10,860
		10,860			10,860
2005 Sep. 30	To Provision for Depreciation A/c	4,496	2005 Dec. 31	By Profit and Loss A/c	9,676
Dec. 31	To Provision for Depreciation A/c	5,180			
		9,676			9,676

Dr. **Provision for Depreciation Account** Cr.

Date	Particulars	Amount (Rs.)	Date	Particulars	Amount (Rs.)
2003 Dec. 31	To Balance c/d	7,400	2003 Dec. 31	By Depreciation A/c	7,400
		7,400			7,400
2004 Dec. 31	To Balance c/d	18,260	2004 Jan. 1	By Balance b/d	7,400
			Dec. 31	By Depreciation A/c	10,860
		18,260			18,260
2005 Sep. 30	To Machine Disposal A/c*	18,556	2005 Jan. 1	By Balance b/d	18,260
Dec. 31	To Balance c/d **	9,380	Sep. 30	By Depreciation A/c	4,496
			Dec. 31	By Depreciation A/c	5,180
		27,936			27,936

* Accumulated depreciation balance of the first machine (sold) transferred from provision for depreciation account to machine disposal account (Rs. 7,400 + Rs. 6,660 + Rs. 4,496 = 18,556).

** Provision for depreciation account's balance on December 31, 2005, represents the total or accumulated depreciation of the second machine (Rs. 4,200 + Rs. 5,180 = Rs. 9,380).

Dr.   **Plant Disposal Account**   Cr.

Date	Particulars	Amount (Rs.)	Date	Particulars	Amount (Rs.)
2005 Sep. 30	To Machinery A/c	74,000	2005 Sep. 30	By Bank A/c—sale proceeds	46,600
				By Provision for Depreciation A/c	18,556
				By Profit and Loss A/c (loss on sale transferred)	8,844
		74,000			74,000

Working Note

		Machine 1 (Rs.)	Machine 2 (Rs.)	Total depreciation (Rs.)
01.01.03	Purchased (Rs. 68,000 + Rs. 6,000)	74,000		
31.12.03	Less: Depreciation @ 10 % p.a.	7,400		7,400
01.01.04	Book Value	66,600		
01.04.04	Purchased		56,000	
31.12.04	Less: Depreciation @ 10 % p.a.	6,660	4,200	10,860
01.01.05	Book Value	59,940	51,800	
30.09.05	Less: Depreciation @ 10 % p.a. for nine months	4,496		4,496
	Value on the date of sale	55,444		
	Sale Proceeds	46,600		
	Loss on sale	8,844		
31.12.05	Less: Depreciation @ 10 % p.a.		5,180	5,180
01.01.06	Book Value		46,620	9,676

ILLUSTRATION 14.13 On January 1, 2004, the machinery account(cost) and provision for depreciation account of Mr. K. Siddhant shows a balance of Rs. 72,000 and Rs. 28,700, respectively. On May 31, 2004, a machine costing Rs. 48,000 was purchased, and for its freight and installation Rs. 9,000 was incurred. On August 31, 2004, an old machinery was sold at Rs. 18,700, which was installed on April 1, 2002, at a cost of Rs. 31,400. Depreciation is charged @ 10% p.a. on diminishing balance method.

Show the machinery account, provision for depreciation account and depreciation account for the year ending December 31, 2004. Also, show the position of machinery account in the balance sheet.

Solution

In the Books of Mr. K. Siddhant

Dr.   **Machinery Account**   Cr.

Date	Particulars	Amount (Rs.)	Date	Particulars	Amount (Rs.)
2004 Jan. 1	To Balance b/d	72,000	2004 Aug. 31	By Bank A/c—sale proceeds	18,700
May 31	To Bank A/c	48,000		By Provision for	
	To Cash A/c	9,000		Depreciation A/c	7,003
				By Profit and Loss A/c	5,697
				(Loss on sale transferred)	
				By Balance c/d	97,600
		129,000			129,000

Dr.   **Depreciation Account**   Cr.

Date	Particulars	Amount (Rs.)	Date	Particulars	Amount (Rs.)
2004 Aug. 31	To Provision for Depreciation A/c	1,743	2004 Dec. 31	By Profit and Loss A/c—transferred	6,784
Dec. 31	To Provision for Depreciation A/c	5,041			
		6,784			6,784

Dr.   **Provision for Depreciation Account**   Cr.

Date	Particulars	Amount (Rs.)	Date	Particulars	Amount (Rs.)
2004 Aug. 31	To Machinery A/c*	7,003	2004 Jan. 1	By Balance b/d	28,700
Dec. 31	To Balance c/d	28,481	Aug. 31	By Depreciation A/c	1,743
			Dec. 31	By Depreciation A/c	5,041
		35,484			35,484

Balance Sheet as at December 31, 2004(includes)

Liabilities	Amount (Rs.)	Amount (Rs.)	Assets	Amount (Rs.)	Amount (Rs.)
			Machinery Account	97,600	
			Less: Provision for depreciation	28,481	69,119

Working Notes

1. Calculation of profit or loss on sale of machine on 31.8.04:

		Rs.
01.04.02	Purchased	31,400
31.12.02	Less: Depreciation @ 10 % p.a. for nine months	2,355
01.01.03	Book Value	29,045
31.12.03	Less: Depreciation @ 10 % p.a.	2,905
01.01.04	Book Value	26,140
31.08.04	Less: Depreciation @ 10 % p.a. for eight months	1,743
	Value on the date of sale	24,397
	Sale Proceeds	18,700
	Loss on sale	5,697

2. Calculation of depreciation on the remaining machines:

	Rs.
Written down value of machinery A/c balance on 1.1.04	43,300
(Rs. 72,000 – Rs. 28,700)	
Less: Book value of the machine sold on 1.1.04	26,140
(as per working note 1)	
Book value of the remaining old machineries	17,160
Depreciation on the remaining old machineries of	1,716
Rs.17,160 @ 10 % p.a.	
Depreciation on the machine purchased on 31.5.04 @ 10 % p.a. on	3,325
Rs. 57,000 for seven months	5,041

* Accumulated depreciation balance of the machine sold transferred from provision for depreciation account to machinery account (Rs. 2,355 + Rs. 2,905 + Rs. 1,743 = Rs. 7,003).

ILLUSTRATION 14.14 On January 1, 2008, the machinery account and provision for depreciation account of Mr. *Nirmal Kumar* shows a balance of Rs. 94,000 and Rs. 37,400, respectively. On April 30, 2008, a machine costing Rs. 56,000 was purchased, and paid for its freight and installation Rs. 12,000. On September 30, 2008, an old machinery was sold at Rs. 23,600, which was installed on June 1, 2006 at a cost of Rs. 45,100. Depreciation is charged @ 10% p.a. on diminishing balance method.

Show the machinery account, provision for depreciation account, plant disposal account and depreciation account for the year ending December 31, 2008. Also, show the position of machinery account in the balance sheet.

Solution

In the Books of Mr. Nirmal Kumar

Dr.   **Machinery Account**   Cr.

Date	Particulars	Amount (Rs.)	Date	Particulars	Amount (Rs.)
2008 Jan. 1	To Balance b/d	94,000	2008 Sep. 30	By Plant Disposal A/c	45,100
April 30	To Bank A/c	56,000		By Balance c/d	116,900
	To Cash A/c	12,000			
		162,000			162,000

Dr.   **Depreciation Account**   Cr.

Date	Particulars	Amount (Rs.)	Date	Particulars	Amount (Rs.)
2008 Sep. 30	To Provision for Depreciation A/c	2,867	2008 Dec. 31	By Profit and Loss A/c —transferred	9,237
Dec. 31	To Provision for Depreciation A/c	6,370			
		9,237			9,237

Dr.   **Provision for Depreciation Account**   Cr.

Date	Particulars	Amount (Rs.)	Date	Particulars	Amount (Rs.)
2008 Sep. 30	To Plant Disposal A/c*	9,740	2008 Jan. 1	By Balance b/d	37,400
Dec. 31	To Balance c/d	36,897	Sep. 30	By Depreciation A/c	2,867
			Dec. 31	By Depreciation A/c	6,370
		46,637			46,637

Dr.   **Plant Disposal Account**   Cr.

Date	Particulars	Amount (Rs.)	Date	Particulars	Amount (Rs.)
2008 Sep. 30	To Machinery A/c	45,100	2008 Sep. 30	By Bank A/c— sale proceeds	23,600
			30	By Provision for Depreciation A/c	9,740
			30	By Profit and Loss A/c (loss on sale transferred)	11,760
		45,100			45,100

Balance Sheet as at December 31, 2008 (includes)

Liabilities	Amount (Rs.)	Amount (Rs.)	Assets	Amount (Rs.)	Amount (Rs.)
			Machinery Account	116,900	
			Less: Provision for depreciation	36,897	80,003

Working Notes

1. Calculation of profit or loss on sale of machine on 30.9.08:

		Rs.
01.06.06	Purchased	45,100
31.12.06	*Less:* Depreciation @ 10 % p.a. for seven months	2,625
01.01.07	Book Value	42,475
31.12.07	*Less:* Depreciation @ 10 % p.a.	4,248
01.01.08	Book Value	38,227
30.09.08	*Less:* Depreciation @ 10 % p.a. for nine months	2,867
	Value on the date of sale	35,360
	Sale Proceeds	23,600
	Loss on sale	11,760

* Accumulated depreciation balance of the machine sold transferred from Provision for Depreciation account to machine disposal account (Rs. 2,625 + Rs. 4,248 + Rs. 2,867 = Rs. 9,740).

2. Calculation of depreciation on the remaining machineries:

	Rs.
Written down value of machinery A/c balance on 1.1.08	56,600
(Rs. 94,000 – Rs. 37,400)	
Less: Book value of the machine sold on 1.1.08 (as per working note 1)	38,227
Book value of the remaining old machineries	18,373
Depreciation on the remaining old machineries of Rs. 18,373 @ 10 % p.a.	1,837
Depreciation on the machine purchased on 30.4.08 @ 10 % p.a. on	4,533
Rs. 68,000 for eight months	6,370

14.9 IS DEPRECIATION A SOURCE OF FUND?

Sometimes, depreciation is considered to be a source of fund. Depreciation is a charge against revenues such as other revenue expenses (both direct and indirect expenses), however it is not an outflow of funds such as other expenses. Considering this particular point (regarding outflow of fund as expenses), some amount of the revenues are kept within the business through depreciation (without making any payment in an accounting year) because of the expired cost of an asset without making any immediate payment. Thus, the amount of depreciation may be considered as a fund.

On the other hand, it has been observed that by providing depreciation, the volume of net profit is reduced, especially for a big concern, and consequently, corporate tax, rate of dividend and amount of bonus are reduced. The reduced amount of corporate tax, dividend, bonus, etc., may be considered as savings of funds, which are retained within the business. However, we must not consider this point of thinking as valid and acceptable. If depreciation is not charged against the revenue of an enterprise, the true profit of the concern cannot be established or it will not represent the true picture of the business because it is against the accepted accounting principles.

In fact, provision for depreciation helps to recover the *nominal capital* of a firm invested in the business by way of fixed assets. We know that by rendering services, the fixed assets are entirely consumed over the years and depreciation represents a part of the total cost of fixed asset used/consumed in an accounting period. Therefore, it is a means of recovering (maintenance) the nominal capital, but not a source of fund.

EXERCISES

I. *Objective Type Questions (with answers)*

1. Fill in the blanks:
    (a) Depreciation is the gradual _____ in the value of an asset.
    (b) Depreciation, in its broadest sense, is _____ of the value of an asset during the period of its effective life from any cause.

(c) Depreciation should be charged and is to _____ over during the effective commercial life of an asset for the purpose of _____ determination.

(d) Depreciation should be charged to find out the _____ for the year.

(e) Depreciation is charged to show the _____ position of the business.

(f) Decrease in the value of a fixed asset due to its economic use during the period of effective life is called _____.

(g) The term depreciation is used when the _____ utility of a physical asset is taken into consideration.

(h) Depreciation arises directly through _____ or indirectly by _____ .

(i) Depreciation is charged to _____ the required amount in replacing the asset when it is _____ worn out or has become obsolete.

(j) The amount of depreciation is considered in the cost sheet or the manufacturing account to ascertain the _____ of production.

(k) Depreciation is charged or considered to keep the owner's capital _____ .

(l) The expired cost of an asset is known as _____ and must be recovered from the _____ to ascertain the true income of a business.

(m) Depreciation is a _____ profit.

(n) The term depletion is used to refer to the _____ utility of a wasting asset.

(o) 'Wear and tear' is an important cause of _____ in case of tangible fixed assets.

Ans. (a) decrease (b) diminution (c) spread, income (d) correct/true profit (e) correct/true financial (f) depreciation (g) expired (h) deterioration, obsolescence (i) accumulate, completely (j) correct cost (k) intact (l) depreciation, revenue (m) charge against (n) expired (o) depreciation.

2. Choose the correct alternative:

(a) Under straight-line method, depreciation is charged:
   (i) properly every year.
   (ii) evenly every year.
   (iii) not evenly every year.

(b) Under straight-line/fixed instalment method, at the end of the effective life of an asset, its book value is reduced to:
   (i) residual value.
   (ii) zero.
   (iii) residual value or zero.

(c) Under diminishing balance method,
   (i) an asset is reduced to zero.
   (ii) an asset is never reduced to zero.
   (iii) an asset is reduced consistently.

(d) Written down value method should be applied for those assets on which
   (i) the expenses for repairs increase with the passage of time or as the asset gets older.
   (ii) no repairs or maintenance costs are involved.
   (iii) repair charges are fixed.

Ans: (a) (iii), (b) (iii), (c) (ii) and (d) (i).

II. *Short Answer Type Questions (with answers)*

1. What do you mean by depreciation?

Ans: Depreciation is the permanent decrease in the value of a fixed asset. It represents a part of the total cost of the fixed asset used/consumed in an accounting period. Thus, the part of the fixed asset (i.e., claims to service) consumed during a particular accounting period within its effective life in course of its use is considered depreciation. It is an expired cost of a fixed asset considered as an expenditure in the process of its useful life in an accounting year.

2. Depreciation as an expiration of the capital outlay. Evaluate.
   Ans: Depreciation may be interpreted as an expiration of the capital outlay in respect of a fixed asset used by an enterprise in the process of its economic activities to earn revenues. Depreciation is the capital outlay in respect of a fixed asset which has expired and which is equal to its loss of service capacity. In other words, it is the expired cost of the capital outlay in respect of a fixed asset charged against revenues for a particular financial year as an expense in the name of depreciation.

3. Briefly explain depreciation can be considered as means of maintenance of nominal capital.
   Ans: Depreciation may be interpreted as means of maintenance of nominal capital invested in fixed assets. According to this concept, the amount of nominal capital invested in the fixed assets is consumed during the effective lifetimes of the concerned assets, and thus, the part of the nominal capital expired in an accounting year is recovered by way of depreciation by charging it against the revenues of the respective financial year. This process of recovering the historical cost of a fixed asset by way of depreciation helps to maintain the nominal capital. Thus, it may be considered as maintenance of nominal capital (but not the real capital) of an enterprise.

4. Which Accounting Standard (AS) provides the guidelines for estimation of depreciation and its basis?
   Ans: In case of companies, the amount of depreciation and its basis with accounting must be made according to the guidelines of Accounting Standard (AS) 6, but in *other cases*, if those guidelines were followed, the result would be the most practicable and acceptable to all.

5. What are the factors which are considered for the estimation of useful life of a depreciable asset as per (AS) 6?
   Ans: The useful life of a depreciable asset should be estimated after considering the following factors:
   (a) Expected physical wear and tear
   (b) Obsolescence
   (c) Legal or other limits on the use of the asset.

6. What are the factors to be considered before selecting the most appropriate method of depreciation?
   Ans: The management of a business selects the most appropriate method(s) based on various important factors, e.g., type of asset, the nature of the use of such asset and circumstances prevailing in the business. A combination of more than one method is sometimes used. In respect of depreciable assets which do not have material value, depreciation is often allocated fully in the accounting period in which they are acquired.

7. What do you mean by cost of an asset?
   Ans: Cost of an asset includes the invoice price of the asset, less the trade discount, plus all other costs incurred to bring the asset to a usable condition such as freight charges, transit insurance charges, repair costs, installation charges, and so on. It may be noted here that financial charges such as interest on money borrowed for the purchase of an asset, should not be included in the cost of the asset.

8. Depreciation and maintenance expenses are both revenue expenditures and related to fixed assets. Are these two terms complementary to each other?
   Ans: Maintenance expenditure on a machine or a motor is essential. Without proper maintenance, a machine cannot function properly. Thus, to maintain its productivity and efficiency, it is essential to take proper maintenance regularly according to the nature of the machine. It is recurring in nature and is revenue expenditure. On the other hand, depreciation is the expired cost of an asset. Thus, total cost of an asset is written off in the period of its effective life.

Hence, there is no direct relationship between maintenance and depreciation. Depreciation is required to maintain the nominal capital intact, whereas maintenance is essential or desirable to run the machine properly.

III. *Long Answer Type Questions*

1. Define depreciation. Is depreciation an expense, a provision, or both?
2. Why is depreciation charged on fixed assets? What are the chief causes of depreciation?
3. Explain the following two methods for estimating depreciation on fixed assets:
   (a) Fixed installment method
   (b) Diminishing balance method
4. Discuss the different methods of accounting depreciation. How depreciation account is maintained through provision for depreciation account?
5. Why is it necessary to charge depreciation? Explain the important characteristics of depreciation.
6. What are the basic factors to be considered while calculating the amount of depreciation of an asset?
7. What are the points to be considered for selecting the method of depreciation on different fixed assets?
8. Write short notes on the following:
   (a) Annuity method of depreciation
   (b) Depreciation fund method.
   How does the later differ from the former?

IV. *Problems*

1. On May 2004, Mr. D. Saxena purchased a machine from Machine & Tools Ltd. in cash for Rs. 80,000. He paid freight and installation charges for Rs. 4,200 on it immediately. Its expected life is six years. The estimated scrap value at the end of its effective life is Rs. 3,200. Usually, the accounts are closed on December 31, each year.

   Calculate the amount of depreciation to be charged each year. Also, show the machinery account.

   Ans: Depreciation for each year Rs. 13,500; Depreciation for 2004 Rs. 9,000.

2. S.K. Traders purchased a new machine on January 1, 2003, for Rs. 68,000, and paid for its installation and carriage Rs. 6,800. The machine started functioning from February 1, 2006. Depreciation is to be charged @ 10% p.a. on straight-line method.

   Show the machinery account and depreciation account for the first two years. The accounts are closed on December 31, each year.

   Ans: Machinery account balance on December 31, 2004, Rs. 60,463; Depreciation for the year 2003 Rs. 6,857 and for 2004 Rs. 7,480.

3. On January 1, 2004, a machinery acccunt shows a balance of Rs. 58,800 (original cost Rs. 84,000). On March 1, 2004, new machinery was purchased at Rs. 24,000 and Rs. 2,800 was paid for its installation charges. Depreciation is provided on fixed installation method @ 10% p.a.

   Show machinery account and depreciation account for the year ending December 31, 2004.

   Ans: Machinery account balance on December 31, 2004 Rs. 74,967 and depreciation for 2004 Rs. 10,633.

4. On January 1, 2007, the machinery account of Modern Tiles Ltd. shows a balance of Rs. 50,400 (original cost Rs. 72,000). On May 1, 2007, a new machine was purchased at Rs. 32,000, and Rs. 4,600 was paid for carriage and installation charges. On September 1, 2007, the old machinery was sold completely at Rs. 39,800. Depreciation is generally provided on straight-line basis @ 10 % p.a.

Show machinery account and depreciation account for the year ending December 31, 2007.

Ans: Loss on sale Rs. 5,800; Machinery account balance on December 31, 2007 Rs. 34,160; Depreciation Rs. 4,800 and Rs. 2,440, respectively.

5. B. M. Bros. purchased a new machine on January 1, 2007, at Rs. 79,000, and paid for its installation and carriage Rs. 4,200. The machine started functioning from March 1, 2007. Depreciation is to be charged @ 10% p.a. on diminishing method.

Show machinery account and depreciation account for the year ending December 31, 2007.

Ans: Machinery account balance on December 31, 2007 Rs. 76,267 and Rs. 6,933 (for 10 months).

6. On January 1, 2006, a machinery account shows a balance of Rs. 65,000. On April 1, 2006, new machinery was purchased at Rs. 32,500 and paid for its installation Rs. 3,100. Depreciation is provided based on reducing balance method @ 10% p.a. The accounting year ends on December 31, every year.

Show machinery account and depreciation account for the year 2006.

Ans: Machinery account balance on December 31, 2006 Rs. 91,430; Depreciation Rs. 9,170 (6,500 + 2,670).

7. On January 1, 2005, the depreciated value of the machinery of Mr. Rakshit was Rs. 7,000. On June 1, 2005, Mr. Rakshit purchased another machine for Rs. 12,000 and spent Rs. 1,000 for its installation. He charges depreciation @ 10% under diminishing balance method.

Show machinery account and depreciation account for three years including the year ending on December 31, 2005. [Tripura H.S., Adapted]

Ans: Machinery account balance on December 31, 2007 Rs. 15,019; Depreciation for the year 2005 Rs. 1,458; for 2006 Rs. 1,854; for 2007 Rs. 1,669.

8. Based on the information given below, prepare a machinery account for 2006 and 2007 based on straight-line method, and diminishing balance method:

T.D. Traders purchased a machine on January 1, 2006 for Rs. 80,500. They purchased another machine on September 1, 2006 for Rs. 50,000. They decided to charge depreciation @ 7.5 % p.a. on original cost or on diminishing balance as the case may be.

[W.B.H.S., adapted]

Ans: Machinery account balance on December 31, 2006 Rs. 113,424 (straight-line method) and Rs. 113,971 (diminishing balance method).

9. Hind Motors Ltd. paid Rs. 87,000 for a fixed asset, which is expected to last for seven years. It is to be written off on the straight-line basis assuming ultimate salvage proceeds of Rs. 3,000. Calculate the amount of annual depreciation of the asset and ascertain the profit or loss on disposal, if the asset is actually sold for
(a) Rs. 45,000 at the end of the fourth year.
(b) Rs. 25,000 at the end of the fifth year.
State how the asset would be shown at the end of the third year.

[W.B.H.S., adapted]

Ans: Annual depreciation Rs. 12,000; Profit on sale Rs. 6,000 at the end of 4th year and loss on sale Rs. 2,000 at the end of 5th year.

10. The following information relates to Tewari Industries Machinery Account: Balance of machinery account as an January 1, 2007, Rs. 60,000. Machine purchased on July 1, 2007, Rs. 25,000. On October 1, 2007, a machine, the original cost of which was Rs. 8,000 (which was purchased on April 1, 2007) was sold for Rs. 6,000. Assume that depreciation was charged @ 10% p.a. on diminishing balance method.

Show the machinery account in the books of Tewari Industries for the year ending on December 31, 2007. Also, show the position of the balance sheet with respect to the asset.

[W.B.H.S., adapted]

Ans: Machinery account balance on December 31, 2007 Rs. 71,090; Loss on sale Rs. 845.

11. On January 1, 2004, the machinery account of S.S. Traders showed a balance of Rs. 59,700. On May 1, 2004, a new machine was purchased at Rs. 28,400 and Rs. 2, 600 was paid for its installation. On August 1, 2004, an old machine was sold at Rs. 19,200 whose original cost was Rs. 28,700 (installed on April 1, 2002). Depreciation is charged @ 10% p.a. on diminishing balance method.
   Show machinery account for the year ending on December 31, 2004.
   Ans: Machinery account balance on December 31, 2004 Rs. 61,159. Loss on sale Rs. 2,067; Depreciation on the asset sold Rs. 1,394 and on the remaining Rs. 5,648 (3,581 + 2,067).

12. The machinery account of Sri. G. D. Khan shows a balance of Rs. 64,400 (original cost Rs. 92,000) on January 1, 2004. On May 1, 2004, a new machine was purchased at Rs. 36,000 and installed at Rs. 2,900. On August 1, 2004, an old machine costing Rs. 28,000 was sold at Rs. 18,700 (installed on January 1, 2002). Depreciation is charged @ 10% p.a. on fixed installment basis.
   Show machinery account and depreciation account as it would appear in the books of Sri. G.D. Khan on December 31, 2004.
   Ans: Machinery account balance on December 31, 2004 Rs. 71,907; Loss on sale Rs. 2,067; Depreciation on the asset sold Rs. 1,633 and on the remaining assets Rs. 8,993 (6,400 + 2,593).

13. A machine was purchased on 1.1.1978 for Rs. 50,000. On 1.1.1978 another machine was purchased for Rs. 30,000. Depreciation is to be provided @ 10% p.a. on the machine under the Reducing Balance System.
   (i) Show the Machine A/c for 1978 and 1979. The accounting period is from 1st January to 31st December.
   (ii) Show how the Machine A/c appeared in the Balance Sheet at the end of 1979.
   (iii) Pass the necessary Journal Entries.

(W.B.H.S. Exam. 1980)

Ans: Depreciation for 1978—Rs. 6,500 and for 1979—Rs. 7,350; Machinery A/c balance on 31.12.79 Rs. 66,150.

14. Fill up the blank:
   Purchase price of a machine Rs. 30,000; wages paid for installing the machine at the factory Rs. 2,000; charge for repairing in a year (approximately) Rs. 1,000; Scrap value (estimated by an expert) Rs. 7,000; Productivity life of Machine (estimated by an expert) 10 years; Annual Depreciation_____?

(W.B.H.S. Exam. 1980)

Ans: Annual depreciation = 30,000 + 2,000 – 7,000 = Rs. 25,000/10 = Rs. 2,500.

15. Show the Journal Entries of the following adjustments at the time of preparation of Final Accounts at 31st December, 1986 and also show the Assets Accounts:
   (i) Plant and machinery costing Rs. 60,000, purchased on 1st July, 1986 and depreciation @ 20% per annum was to be provided.
   (ii) Building which was constructed on 1st January 1986, amounting to Rs. 200,000 was to be depreciated @ 5% per annum.

(W.B.H.S. Exam. 1987)

Ans: Depreciation on Machinery Rs. 6,000 and on Building Rs. 10,000.

16. On 1st January 1990, Basak & Co. purchased a machine for Rs. 100,000. It purchased another machine for Rs. 60,000 on 1st June 1990. On 1st March 1991, the firm bought a new machine costing Rs. 54,000 on the same date.
    Basak and Co. charges depreciation @ 20% p.a. on the diminishing balance method. Show the Machinery A/c for the two years 1990 and 1991.
    (W.B.H.S. Exam. 1992)
    Ans: Depreciation on 31.12.90 Rs. 27,000, on 1.3.91 Rs. 1,767, on 31,12.91 Rs. (16,000 + 9,000) 25,000. Machine A/c balance on 31.12.91 Rs. 1,09,000

17. The machinery account of Rama Prasad shows the following:
    (a) Machinery purchased on April 1, 2005 at Rs. 36,000
    (b) Machinery purchased on July 1, 2006 at Rs. 48,000
    (c) Machinery purchased on May 1, 2007 at Rs. 62,000.
    Depreciation was provided @ 15% p.a. on reducing installment basis. The machinery installed on April 1, 2005 was sold at Rs. 15,900 on October 1, 2007.
    Show machinery account for the last three years ending on December 31, 2007.
    Ans: Loss on sale Rs. 8,202; Depreciation: 2005 Rs. 4,050, 2006 Rs. 8,393 (4,793 + 3,600) and 2007 Rs. 12,860 (6,660 + 6,200); Depreciation on the asset sold Rs. 3,055; Machinery account balance on December 31, 2007 Rs. 93,540.

18. An old machinery was purchased on April 1, 2003 at Rs. 31,900. Rs. 8,200 was paid for its thorough repair and Rs. 2,900 for its installation charges. On October 1, 2003, another new machine was purchased at Rs. 24,500, and Rs. 2,100 was paid for its carriage and installation. Due to some mechanical trouble, the old machine installed on April 1, 2003, was sold at Rs. 22,700 on August 1, 2004. Depreciation was provided @ 10% p.a. on diminishing balance method.
    Show machinery account for two years ending on December 31, 2004.
    Ans: Depreciation: 2003 Rs. 3,890 (3,225 + 665) and 2004 Rs. 2,594; Depreciation on the asset sold Rs. 2,320; Loss on sale Rs. 14,750; Machinery account balance on December 31, 2004 Rs. 23,341.

19. X Ltd. purchased two assets whose particulars are mentioned below:

Assets	Cost	Turn-in value	Estimated life
	Rs.	Rs.	
Machinery	80,000	16,000	12 yr
Furniture	21,000	3,000	7 yr

Calculate the amount of depreciation to be written off in each case and assume that the company has adopted the Straight-Line Method of depreciation.
Ans: Annual depreciation on Machinery = 80,000 − 16,000

$$= \frac{64,000}{12} = \text{Rs. } 5,333$$

Annual depreciation on Furniture = 21,000 − 3,000

$$= \frac{18,000}{7} = \text{Rs. } 2,571$$

20. A company, whose accounting year is the calendar year, purchased machineries on 1st April, 1994 costing Rs. 50,000. It further purchased a machine costing Rs. 20,000 on 1st October, 1994 and another machine costing Rs. 10,000 on 1st July 1995. On 1st January, 1996, of the machineries which were purchased on 1st April, 1994, one machine costing Rs. 10,000 became obsolete and was sold for Rs. 3,500. Show how the Machinery Account would appear

for all the 3 years in the books of the company after charging depreciation at 10% p.a. on Written Down Value Method. (C.A. Entrance)

Ans: Loss on sale Rs. 4,825: Depreciation for 1996 Rs. 6,868; Machinery A/c balance— 1994 — Rs. 65,750, 1995 — Rs. 68,675, 1996 — Rs. 53,482.

21. On 1.1.1984, A purchased roasting machine for Rs. 60,000 and grinding machine for Rs. 40,000. On 1.1.1985 he purchased an oil expeller for Rs. 100,000. On 1.1.1986 the roasting machine got out of order and a new roaster was purchased costing Rs. 120,000 after surrendering the old one and paying cash Rs. 90,000. On 1.1.1987, the oil expeller purchased on 1.1.1985 was destroyed by fire and the insurance company paid Rs. 60,000 only.

Show Machinery Account for 1984, 1985, 1986 and 1987. Charge depreciation at 10% p.a. on the Written Down Value Method. (C.A. Entrance)

Ans: Machinery A/c balance on 31.12.87 Rs. 123,444. Loss due to exchange of old roaster Rs. 18,600 (48,600 – 30,000) Loss by fire (81,000 – 60,000) = Rs. 21,000)

[**Hint:** Calculation of depreciation on W.D.V Method below:

	Roaster Rs.	Grinder Rs.	Oil Expl. Rs.	New Roaster Rs.	Total Dep. Rs.
Cost on 1.1.84	60,000	40,000			
Less: depreciation for	6,000	4,000			10,000
On 1.1.85	54,000	36,000			
Purchased on 1.1.85			100,000		
Less: depreciation for 1985	5,400	3,600	10,000		
On 1.1.86	48,600	32,400	90,000		
Less: Machine Surrender	48,600				
Purchased on 1.1.86				120,000	
Less: depreciation for 1986		3,240	9,000	12,000	24,240
On 1.1.87		29,160	81,000	108,000	
Loss by fire		2,916	81,000	10,800	13,716
Depreciation for 1987		26,244		97,200	

22. On 1st January, 1992 Nabin Company purchased a machine for Rs. 200,000 and paid Rs. 40,000 for installation charge. On 30th June, 1994, the machine was sold for Rs. 120,000 and purchase another machine for Rs. 250,000 and paid Rs. 50,000 for installation charge. The residual value of the first machine was Rs. 20,000 and the estimated life was 10 years. Depreciation on the machine was charged on a Straight Line Basis. In the case of the second machine, depreciation is to be provided @10% per annum on Reducing Balance Basis. Show the Machinery Account for 3 years. [W.B.H.S.]

Ans: Machinery A/c balance on 31.12.94 Rs. 285,000; Loss on Sale of Machinery Rs. 65,000).

23. A company purchased machinery costing Rs. 50,000 on 30th June, 1993. It further purchased machinery costing Rs. 30,000 on 1.4.94. Company made another purchase of Rs. 20,000 on 30th June, 1994. On 1.4.95 company sold 1/5th of the machinery (purchased on 30.6.93) at Rs. 2,000 and again 2/3rds of the machinery purchased on 1.4.94 was sold on the same date for Rs. 10,000. Rate of depreciation is 10% (under Written Down Value Method). Company closes its accounts on 31st March every year.

Give journal entries and Ledger Accounts for the period 1.4.93 to 31st March 1996.

(Central Board—H.S.)

Ans: Machinery A/c balance on 31.3.94 Rs. 46,250, on 31.3.95 Rs. 87,125 and on 31.3.96 Rs. 58,320. Loss on Sale of Machinery Rs. 6,325 (purchased on 30.6.93) and Rs. 4,000 (purchased on 1.4.94); Depreciation for 1995-96 Rs. 6,480.

24. On 1st January, 1993, Shyambazar Company purchased a machine for Rs. 500,000 and paid Rs. 100,000 for installation charge. On 30th September, 1995, the machine was sold for Rs. 300,000 and purchased another machine for Rs. 600,000 and paid 150,000 for installation charge. The estimated residual value of the first machine was Rs. 30,000 and the estimated life was 10 years. Depreciation on the machine was charged on a Straight-Line Basis. In the case of the second machine, depreciation is to be provided @ 10% p.a. on the Reducing Balance Basis. Show the Machinery Account for 3 years.

(W.B.H.S.)

Ans: Machinery A/c balance on 31.12.95 Rs. 731,250. Loss on Sale of Machinery Rs. 143,250. Depreciation for 1993 Rs. 57,000, for 1994 Rs. 57,000, for 1995 Rs. 61,500 (42,750 + 18,750)

25. XYZ & Co. closes its accounts on 31st March every year. On 1.7.1989 machineries costing Rs. 60,000 were purchased. Further on 1.1.1990 a machinery costing Rs. 60,000 was purchased and another machinery costing Rs. 10,000 was purchased on 1.10.1990.

Out of the machineries which were purchased on 1.7.89, one machinery costing Rs. 20,000 became obsolete and was sold for Rs. 6,000 on 1.4.91.

On 1.1.92 a new machinery costing Rs. 30,000 was purchased.

Show how the Machinery Account would appear for the all the three years in the books

of XYZ & Co. after charging depreciation at $33\frac{1}{3}\%$ on written down value method.

While preparing the Machinery Account you are required to observe the following notes:

(i) Calculate the amount of depreciation to the nearest rupee.

(ii) Provide depreciation for the full year even if the machinery has been used for a part of the year. (C.A. Entrance)

Ans: Machinery A/c balance on 31.3.92 Rs. 54,074.

Provision of Depreciation

26. The ledger accounts of Dalmia Bros. shows the following:
Machinery purchased on May 1, 2002 at Rs. 50,500
Machinery purchased on June 1, 2003 at Rs. 62,000
Machinery purchased on August 1, 2004 at Rs. 75,400
Depreciation was provided @ 10 % p.a. on reducing installment basis. The machine installed on June 1, 2003 was sold at Rs. 41,200 on July 1, 2004.
Show machinery account, provision of depreciation account and machine disposal account for the last three years ending on December 31, 2004.

Ans: Loss on sale Rs. 14,364; Depreciation: 2002 Rs. 3,367, 2003 Rs. 8,330 and 2004 Rs. 7,384; Accumulated depreciation on the asset sold Rs. 6,536; Machinery account balance on December 31, 2004 Rs. 125,900; Provision of depreciation account balance Rs. 15,464.

27. Machinery account and provision of depreciation account of Mr. Tripathi shows a balance of Rs. 68,200 (cost) and Rs. 19,700, respectively, on April 1, 2003. On September 1, 2003, an old machinery costing Rs. 21,600 was sold at Rs. 12,900, installed on June 1, 2001. On October 1, 2003, a new machinery was purchased at Rs. 26,400. Depreciation is charged @ 10% on diminishing balance method.

Show machinery account and provision of depreciation account for the year ending March 31, 2004.

Ans: Accumulated depreciation on the asset sold Rs. 4,523; Machinery account balance on March 31, 2004 Rs. 73,000. Provision of depreciation account balance on March 31, 2004 Rs. 20,308; Loss on sale Rs. 4,117; Depreciation on the asset sold Rs. 743 and on the remaining assets Rs. 4,388.

28. On January 1, 1982, machinery account shows a balance of Rs. 64,800 (cost) and provision for depreciation account stood at Rs. 15,200 on that date. On April 1, 1982, a new machine was purchased for Rs. 30,000 and Rs. 1,200 was paid towards the carriage on it. It started functioning on June 1, 1982. On May 1, 1983, an old machine, installed on January 1, 1981, costing Rs. 40,000, was then sold for Rs. 27,600. Depreciation is charged @ 15% p.a. on reducing installment basis.

   Show machinery account, provision for depreciation account and machinery disposal account for the year ending December 31, 1983.

   Ans: Profit on sale of machine: Rs. 145

Depreciation charged for 1982:	Rs.
On Rs. 64,800 – Rs. 15,200 = Rs. 49,600 × 15/100 =	7,440
On Rs. 31,200 × 15/100 × 7/12 =	2,730
	10,170
For 1983:	
On Rs. 28,900 × 15/100 × 4/12 =	1,445
On Rs. 41,730 × 15/100 = Rs. 6,259.50 =	6,260
	7,705

Provision for depreciation account balance on December 31, 1983 = Rs. 20,530; Provision for depreciation account balance transferred to plant disposal account: Rs. 12,545 (Rs. 6,000 + 5,100 + 1,445) for the plant sold on May 1, 1983.

<big><big><big>**15**</big></big></big>

Provisions and Reserves

CONTENTS

15.1 PROVISION

A *provision* is a charge against income, and it is immaterial whether there is profit or not. A provision or a specific reserve is created against a loss, a liability or a contingency, which is known to a firm and will occur in future. According to the conservative principle, making a provision for an expected loss or expense is a common practice for firms. Provision usually means an amount written off or retained by way of providing depreciation, renewals or retained by way of providing for any known liability of which the amount cannot be determined with substantial accuracy. (It has been defined in Part III of Schedule VI of the Companies Act, 1956). The amount of a known liability which can be estimated with reasonable accuracy should be treated as current liability, but not as a provision. As it is a charge against profit and as such, for creating provisions, profit and loss account is debited. Provisions are made for bad and doubtful debts, discount on debtors, repairs and renewals, provision for taxation, and so on.

15.1.1 Characteristics of Provision

The following are the chief features of a provision:

1. It is a charge against profit and not an appropriation of the profits.
2. It is generally created without depending on the volume of profits, i.e., it is created even though there is a loss or insufficient profit.
3. Provision is not an asset. On the contrary, it will reduce the net assets of a firm.
4. It is not created for any unknown liability. In fact, it is provided for known or expected contingencies which may occur in future.

15.1.2 Importance of Provisions

1. It helps to follow the *matching convention*, i.e., all the actual and the estimated current year's losses are to be adjusted from the current year's revenues or profits.
2. It helps to represent the true financial position of an enterprise by creating a provision based on the accepted accounting principles.
3. Provisions help to assess or estimate the true current year's profit of an enterprise.

361

4. An important example of a conservative accounting practice is the use of the provisions. The convention of conservatism is generally used in cases of uncertainties in respect of some business incidents or economic events that may happen in future. For example, it is applied in case of making provisions for bad and doubtful debts, and for discount on debtors.

5. If a provision is not created to meet a specific or a known liability (whose amount or volume cannot be estimated accurately), it will increase the volume of the current year's profit and asset position. As a result, true financial position of a firm cannot be presented.

6. Provisions help to create secret reserve of a firm.

15.2 PROVISION FOR BAD AND DOUBTFUL DEBTS

Bad and doubtful debts are irrecoverable debts whose recovery is doubtful in future. The provision for them safeguards the business from likely future loss. Thus, this loss is always anticipated, though its amount cannot be ascertained accurately in the current year; it can only be estimated on the basis of past experiences. With the help of this estimated amount, a provision is created out of the current year's profit or revenue known as the **provision for bad and doubtful debts**.

It is a practice that all the actual and estimated current year's losses should be adjusted from the current year's revenues. In order to follow this practice, a provision for bad and doubtful debts is created. When the actual loss arises in future as bad debts, the same should be adjusted against the 'provision for bad and doubtful debts'. If this procedure is not followed or an inadequate provision is made in this regard, then the profit and loss account will not show the true profit or the balance sheet will not represent the true financial position of the business. An inadequate provision for bad and doubtful debts has the twin effect of overstating profit and also overstating the net amount of debtors after deduction of the provision.

15.2.1 Necessity for Creating Provision for Bad Debts

1. It is a practice that all the actual and estimated current year's losses are adjusted from the current year's revenues. To follow this principle, a provision for bad and doubtful debts is created.

2. If provision for bad and doubtful debts is not created, then it will increase the current year's profit volume which is not justifiable.

3. If provision for bad and doubtful debts is not created or a less amount is considered, then it will increase the net amount of debtors (shown in the balance sheet) after deduction of the provision.

4. To represent the true financial position of an enterprise, a provision for bad and doubtful debts is created based on the accepted accounting principles.

5. In order to follow the matching convention, a provision for bad and doubtful debts is created. Through matching convention, principal expenses are recognized for a particular accounting period and are considered as expenses incurred for the said period. After recognition, the particular expenses are adjusted with the concerned revenues earned during the said accounting period.

6. The convention of conservatism is generally used in case of uncertainties in respect of some business incidents or economic events that may happen in future, and is applied in case of making provision for bad and doubtful debts, for discount on debtors, etc. Thus, to follow this principles, provision for bad and doubtful debts needs to be created properly.

The differences between bad debts and doubtful debts are shown in Table 15.1, while Table 15.2 differentiates between bad debts and provision for doubtful debts.

TABLE 15.1   Distinction between Bad Debts and Doubtful Debts

Bad debts	Doubtful debts
These are the debts which cannot be recovered in future.	Doubtful debts mean irrecoverable debts whose recovery is doubtful in future.
It is an actual loss.	This loss is always anticipated.
It is a loss based on actual facts and figures.	This anticipated loss cannot be ascertained accurately in the current year, but can only be estimated on the basis of past experiences.
Because of this loss, a particular debtor's account is removed or closed permanently.	For this loss, a particular debtor's account is not removed. It is an estimated amount calculated on total debtors on the basis of past experiences.
After writing off bad debts, the actual book debts are shown.	After adjustment of doubtful debts, the estimated realizable value of debtors are shown.
Bad debts are adjusted against the provision for bad and doubtful debts or profit and loss account.	A provision is created based on this amount.

TABLE 15.2   Distinction between Bad Debts and Provision for Doubtful Debts

Bad debts	Provision for doubtful debts
These are the debts which cannot be recovered in future.	It is estimated on doubtful debts.
It is a loss based on actual facts and figures.	It is an anticipated loss estimated on the basis of past experiences.
This account is shown on the debit side of the trial balance.	This account is shown on the credit side of the trial balance.
Due to this loss, a particular debtor's account is removed or closed permanently.	Due to this provision, the net realizable value of the debtors is shown.
It is shown or recorded when it actually occurred.	Provision for doubtful debts is estimated and shown at the end of the year.
This account is transferred to the provision for bad and doubtful debts account or to the profit and loss account.	This account is created by charging profit and loss account.
Before making provisions for doubtful debts, it must be deducted from the debtors.	After deducting the bad debts from the debtors, the provision for doubtful debts is estimated and then deducted from the debtors.

15.3   PROVISION FOR DISCOUNT ON DEBTORS

Cash discount is allowed to encourage debtors if the debts are paid within the credit period. The total goods sold in an accounting period cannot be realized within the said period because a part of the debtors are realized in the next accounting period and at the same time, a cash discount is allowed. Though the discount is allowed in the next year, it is, in fact, the expenditure of the previous year, i.e., the discount allowed should be charged to the period in which the related sales were actually achieved. Hence, considering this point, a provision is created on the basis of the past experience at a fixed percentage on the debtors. This provision is known as the **provision for discount on debtors**.

It is desirable that the debtors should appear in the balance sheet as the net amount (not as the gross figure) which is expected to be realized in future. In the balance sheet, the 'provision for discount on debtors' should be deducted from the gross figure of the debtors to show the net realizable value, or else the balance sheet will not represent the true financial position of an enterprise.

15.3.1   Accounting Treatments regarding Provision for Bad and Doubtful Debts and Provision for Discount on Debtors

Method I: According to this method, the actual amount of total bad debts is transferred to the provision for bad and doubtful debts account at the end of the year, and required amount is taken from the profit and loss account for creating new provision for the next year. It involves following steps:

Step 1: Estimate the total amount of the current year's bad debts and find out whether it is written off or not. If not, then the part of the bad debt which is not written off has to be written off as follows:

        Bad Debts A/c   Dr. (New bad debts to be written off)
          To Sundry Debtors A/c

Step 2: Now, the total bad debts are to be adjusted as follows (i.e., at the end of the year, the bad debts account's balance is closed by transferring it to the following accounts as under):

(a) When the total bad debts amount is less than the provision for doubtful debts account balance

        Provision for Doubtful Debts A/c   Dr.
          To Bad Debts A/c (Total bad debts)

                            Or

(b) When provision for doubtful debts account balance is less than the total bad debts amount

        Provision for doubtful debts A/c   Dr. (Opening balance)
           Profit and Loss A/c*   Dr. (Shortage amount)

(*When the old provision for bad debts is less than the total bad debts, then the shortage amount is to be adjusted through profit and loss account)

          To Bad Debts A/c   (Total bad debts)

Step 3: After adjustment of bad debts, the new provision for bad debts for the next period is created or adjusted through the profit and loss account as follows:

(a) When the old provision is greater than total bad debts but less than the new provision or when there is no balance in the old provision account

        Profit and Loss A/c **   Dr.
          To Provision for Bad Debts A/c
    (Net amount to be taken from the profit and loss account)

Note: Calculation of net amount required to be taken from the profit and loss account for creating new provision for bad debts for the next period would be as under:

First, select or calculate the amount of actual closing debtors and then calculate the amount of new provision on such debtors with the help of the given percentage. Then, follow the following steps:

	Rs.
New provision for bad debts	...
Less: Remaining part of old provision after adjustment of bad debts	...
Net amount required to be taken from the profit and loss account	**

                            Or

(b) When old provision is greater than the bad debts plus new provision for bad debts, then entry for transferring the surplus provision to profit and loss account

        Provision for Bad Debts A/c   Dr.
           To Profit and Loss A/c ***
        (Surplus provision A/c balance transferred)

	Rs.
Old provision for bad debts (opening balance)	...
Less: Bad debts	...
	...
Less: New provision for bad debts	...
Surplus of provision for bad debts account balance transferred to profit and loss A/c	***

Step 4: Regarding the discount allowed and provision for discount on debtors:

(a) If discount is allowed to the debtors but no entry has been made in the books, then the entry would be as under:

Discount Allowed A/c   Dr.
    To Debtors A/c

(b) The total discount allowed to debtors is to be adjusted through provision for discount on debtors account as follows:

(i) When amount of total discount allowed is less than the provision for discount on debtors account balance

Provision for Discount on Debtors A/c   Dr.
    To Discount Allowed A/c (Total discount)

Or

(ii) When amount of provision for discount account balance is less than the total discount allowed or where there is no provision for discount account balance, then discount is to be transferred to profit and loss account:

Provision for Discount on Debtors A/c   Dr.
Profit and Loss A/c (Shortage portion)   Dr.
    To Discount Allowed A/c (Total discount)

Step 5: After adjustment of 'discount allowed' the new provision for discount on debtors for the next period is to be created or adjusted through the profit and loss account as follows:

(a) When the old provision for discount on debtors is greater than the total discount allowed but less than the new provision for discount on debtors or when there is no balance in the old provision for discount on debtors account:

Profit and Loss A/c **   Dr.
    To Provision for Discount on Debtors A/c
(Net amount to be taken from the profit and loss account)

Note: Calculation of net amount required to be taken from the profit and loss account for creating new provision for discount on debtors for the next period would be as under:

First, select or calculate the amount of actual closing debtors (debtors' account closing balance — new provision for bad debts), and then calculate the amount of new provision for discount on such debtors with the help of the given percentage. Then, follow the following steps:

	Rs.
New provision for discount on debtors	...
Less: Remaining portion of old provision after adjustment of discount allowed	
(Old provision – Discount allowed)	...
Net amount required to be taken from the profit and loss A/c	**

Or

(b) When old provision for discount on debtors is greater than the discount allowed plus new provision for discount on debtors, then entry for transferring surplus provision for discount on debtors account balance to profit and loss account:

    Provision for Discount on Debtors A/c   Dr.
        To Profit and Loss A/c ***
    (Surplus provision account balance transferred)

	Rs.
Old provision for discount on debtors (opening balance)	...
Less: Total discount allowed	...
	...
Less: New provision for discount on debtors	...
Surplus of provision for discount on debtors account balance transferred to profit and loss account	***

Alternative Method: According to this method, actual amount of total bad debts is transferred to the profit and loss account directly at the end of the year. Provision for bad and doubtful debts account is adjusted on the basis of old and new provision, and the shortage or surplus is transferred to profit and loss account.

(a) For writing off the bad debts:

    Bad Debts A/c   Dr.
        To Debtor's/Customer's A/c

(b) For transferring bad debts account to profit and loss account at the end of the year:

    Profit and Loss A/c   Dr.
        Bad Debts A/c

(c) For new provision for bad debts for the next period is to be created or adjusted through the profit and loss account as follows:

 (i) When the old provision is less than the new provision

    Profit and Loss A/c (New provision – Old provision)   Dr.
        To Provision for Bad and Doubtful Debts A/c
    (Net amount to be taken from the profit and loss A/c)

 (ii) When the old provision is greater than the new provision

    Provision for Bad and Doubtful Debts A/c   Dr.
        To Profit and Loss A/c (Old provision – New provision)
    (Surplus amount of old provision is transferred to profit and loss A/c)

ILLUSTRATION 15.1   On December 31, 2007, debtors account shows a balance of Rs. 82,000. Bad debts already written off during the year amount to Rs. 2,100. Bad debts to be written off amount to Rs. 900. Provision for bad and doubtful debts account balance on January 1, 2007 was Rs. 3,300. Provision for bad and doubtful debts is always made on debtors @ 5%.

Give necessary journal entries and relevant ledger accounts.

Solution

In the Books of ...
Journal

Date	Particulars	L.F.	Amount Dr. (Rs.)	Amount Cr. (Rs.)
2007 Dec. 31	Bad Debts A/c **Dr.**		900	
	To Debtors A/c			900
	(Being the amount written off as bad debts)			
	Provision for Bad and Doubtful Debts A/c **Dr.**		3,000	
	To Bad Debts A/c			3,000
	(Being the bad debts transferred to provision for bad debts A/c)			
	Profit and Loss A/c **Dr.**		3,755	
	To Provision for Bad and Doubtful Debts A/c			3,755
	(Being the provision for bad and doubtful debts provided on debtors of Rs. 81,100 @ 5%)			

Ledger Accounts

Bad Debts Account

Dr. | | | | | | Cr.

Date	Particulars	Amount (Rs.)	Date	Particulars	Amount (Rs.)
2007 Dec. 31	To Debtors (already written off) To Debtors	2,100 900	2007 Dec. 31	By Provision for bad and doubtful debts A/c	3,000
		3,000			3,000

Debtors Account

Dr. | | | | | | Cr.

Date	Particulars	Amount (Rs.)	Date	Particulars	Amount (Rs.)
2007 Dec. 31	To Balance b/f	82,000	2007 Dec. 31	By Bad Debts A/c By Balance c/d	900 81,100
		82,000			82,000
2008 Jan. 1	To Balance b/d	81,100			

Provision for Bad and Doubtful Debts Account

Dr. | | | | | | Cr.

Date	Particulars	Amount (Rs.)	Date	Particulars	Amount (Rs.)
2007 Dec. 31	To Bad Debts A/c To Balance c/d	3,000 4,055	2007 Jan. 1 Dec. 31	By Balance b/d By Profit and Loss A/c	3,300 3,755
		7,055			7,055
			2008 Jan. 1	By Balance b/d	4,055

Working Notes

Calculation for new provision for bad and doubtful debts:

	Rs.
Provision @ 5% on closing debtors of Rs. 81,100	4,055
Less: Remaining portion of provision for bad debt A/c (Rs. 3,300 – Rs. 3,000)	300
Further amount required to be charged to profit and loss A/c	3,755

Second Method [*Alternatively the problem may be solved as under*]

Journal

Date	Particulars		L.F.	Amount Dr. (Rs.)	Amount Cr. (Rs.)
2007 Dec. 31	Bad Debts A/c	Dr.		900	
	To Debtors A/c				900
	(Being the amount written off as bad debts)				
	Profit and Loss A/c	Dr.		3,000	
	To Bad Debts A/c				3,000
	(Being the bad debts transferred to profit and loss A/c)				
	Profit and Loss A/c	Dr.		755	
	To Provision for Bad and Doubtful Debts A/c				755
	(Being the provision for bad and doubtful debts provided on debtors of Rs. 81,100 @ 5%)				

Working Note

Calculation for new provision for bad and doubtful debts:

	Rs.
Provision @ 5% on closing debtors of Rs. 81,100	4,055
Less: Provision for bad and doubtful debts A/c balance on 1.1.07	3,300
Further amount required to be charged to profit and loss A/c	755

Note: Profit and loss A/c is debited by Rs. 3,755 (as a whole) in both the methods.

ILLUSTRATION 15.2 Provision for bad and doubtful debts account shows a (Cr.) balance of Rs. 2,700 on January 1, 2007. Bad debts already written off amounted to Rs. 2,600. Bad debts to be written off amount to Rs. 700. Debtors on December 31, 2007 were Rs. 56,700. Provision for bad and doubtful debts is to be created @ 5% on debtors.

Pass necessary journal entries.

Date	Particulars		L.F.	Amount Dr. (Rs.)	Amount Cr. (Rs.)
2007 Dec. 31	Bad Debts A/c	Dr.		700	
	To Debtors A/c				700
	(Being the amount written off as bad debts)				
	Provision for Bad and Doubtful Debts A/c	Dr.		2,700	
	Profit and Loss A/c	Dr.		600	
	To Bad Debts A/c				3,300
	(Being the bad debts for the year transferred to provision for bad debts A/c, and the shortage portion to profit and loss A/c)				
	Profit and Loss A/c	Dr.		2,800	
	To Provision for Bad and Doubtful Debts A/c				2,800
	(Being the provision for bad and doubtful debts provided on debtors of Rs. 56,000 @ 5%)				

Second Method [*Alternatively the problem may be solved as under*]

Journal

Date	Particulars	L.F.	Amount Dr. (Rs.)	Amount Cr. (Rs.)
2007 Dec. 31	Bad Debts A/c Dr. To Debtors A/c (Being the amount written off as bad debts)		700	700
	Profit and Loss A/c Dr. To Bad Debts A/c (Being the bad debts transferred to profit and loss A/c)		3,300	3,300
	Profit and Loss A/c Dr. To Provision for Bad and Doubtful Debts A/c (Being the provision for bad and doubtful debts provided on debtors of Rs. 56,000 @ 5%)		100	100

Working Note

Calculation for new provision for bad and doubtful debts:

	Rs.
Provision @ 5% on closing debtors of Rs. 56,000	2,800
Less: Provision for Bad and Doubtful Debts A/c balance on 1.1.07	2,700
Further amount required to be charged to Profit and Loss A/c	100

ILLUSTRATION 15.3   The following balances are extracted from the trial balance of Mr. M. Roy on December 31, 2007:

> Debtors Rs. 43,000
> Bad debts Rs. 1,850
> Provision for bad and doubtful debts Rs. 4,500 (Cr.)

Provision for bad and doubtful debts is to be created @ 5% on the debtors. Give necessary journal entries and draw up the bad debts account and provision for bad and doubtful debts account.

Solution

Journal Entries

Date	Particulars	L.F.	Amount Dr. (Rs.)	Amount Cr. (Rs.)
2007 Dec. 31	Provision for Bad and Doubtful Debts A/c Dr. To Bad Debts A/c (Being the bad debts for the year transferred to provision for bad and doubtful debts account)		1,850	1,850
	Provision for Bad and Doubtful Debts A/c Dr. To Profit and Loss A/c (Being the surplus of provision for bad and doubtful debts account transferred after providing Rs. 2,150 as new provision on debtors of Rs. 43,000)		500	500

Ledger Accounts

Bad Debts Account

Dr.   Cr.

Date	Particulars	Amount (Rs.)	Date	Particulars	Amount (Rs.)
2007	To Debtors (already written off)	1,850	2007 Dec. 31	By Provision for bad and doubtful debts A/c	1,850
		1,850			1,850

Dr.   **Provision for Bad and Doubtful Debts Account**   Cr.

Date	Particulars	Amount (Rs.)	Date	Particulars	Amount (Rs.)
2007 Dec. 31	To Bad Debts A/c	1,850	2007 Jan. 1	By Balance b/d	4,500
	To Profit and Loss A/c	500			
Dec. 31	To Balance c/d	2,150			
		4,500			4,500
			2008 Jan. 1	By Balance b/d	2,150

Working Notes:

1. Calculation of the amount to be transferred to profit and loss account from provision for bad and doubtful debts account:

	Rs.
Provision for bad and doubtful debts A/c balance on 1.1.07	4,500
Less: Bad debts adjusted	1,850
	2,650
Less: New provision for bad and doubtful debts	2,150*
Surplus transferred to profit and loss A/c	500

*5% provision on remaining debtors of Rs. 43,000 = Rs. 2,150.

ILLUSTRATION 15.4 On December 31, 2007, debtors account of S. Bose shows a balance of Rs. 72,000. Bad debts written off during the year amounted to Rs. 1,900. Discount allowed during the period is Rs. 1,300. Provision for bad and doubtful debts account shows a balance of Rs. 3,800 on January 1, 2007, and provision for discount on debtors Rs. 1,900 as on that date. Provision for bad and doubtful debts is always made on debtors @ 5%, and provision for discount on debtors @ 2% on debtors.

Pass necessary entries and relevant ledger accounts. Also, show the balance sheet as on December 31, 2007.

Solution

Journal

Date	Particulars	L.F.	Amount Dr. (Rs.)	Amount Cr. (Rs.)
2007 December 31	Provision for Bad and Doubtful Debts A/c Dr.		1,900	
	To Bad Debts A/c			1,900
	(Being the bad debts for the year transferred to provision for bad and doubtful debts account)			
	Provision for Discount on Debtors A/c Dr.		1,300	
	To Discount Allowed A/c			1,300
	(Being the transfer of discount allowed during the period to provision for discount on debtor's account)			
	Profit and Loss A/c Dr.		1,700	
	To Provision for Bad and Doubtful Debts A/c			1,700
	(Being the provision for bad and doubtful debts provided on debtors of Rs. 72,000 @ 5%)			
	Profit and Loss A/c Dr.		768	
	To Provision for Discount on Debtors A/c			768
	(Being provision for discount on debtors created @ 2% on debtors of Rs. 68,400)			

Ledger Accounts

Bad Debts Account

Dr.						Cr.
Date	Particulars	Amount (Rs.)	Date	Particulars		Amount (Rs.)
2007	To Balance B/f	1,900	2007 Dec. 31	By Provision for bad and doubtful debts A/c		1,900
		1,900				1,900

Debtors Account

Dr.					Cr.
Date	Particulars	Amount (Rs.)	Date	Particulars	Amount (Rs.)
2007 Dec. 31	To Balance b/f	72,000	2007 Dec. 31	By Balance c/d	72,000
		72,000			72,000
2008 Jan. 1	To Balance b/d	72,000			

Provision for Bad and Doubtful Debts Account

Dr.					Cr.
Date	Particulars	Amount (Rs.)	Date	Particulars	Amount (Rs.)
2007 Dec. 31	To Bad Debts A/c	1,900	2007 Jan. 1	By Balance b/d	3,800
	To Balance c/d	3,600	Dec. 31	By Profit and Loss A/c	1,700
		5,500			5,500
			2008 Jan. 1	By Balance b/d	3,600

Discount Allowed Account

Dr.					Cr.
Date	Particulars	Amount (Rs.)	Date	Particulars	Amount (Rs.)
2007	To Debtors (already deducted)	1,300	2007 Dec. 31	By Provision for Discount on Debtors A/c	1,300
		1,300			1,300

Provision for Discount on Debtors Account

Dr.					Cr.
Date	Particulars	Amount (Rs.)	Date	Particulars	Amount (Rs.)
2007 Dec. 31	To Discount Allowed A/c	1,300	2007 Jan. 1	By Balance b/d	1,900
	To Balance c/d	1,368	Dec. 31	By Profit and Loss A/c	768
		2,668			2,668
			2008 Jan. 1	By Balance b/d	1,368

Balance Sheet as on December 31, 2007 (includes)

Liabilities	Amount (Rs.)	Amount (Rs.)	Assets	Amount (Rs.)	Amount (Rs.)
			Debtors	72,000	
			Less: Provision for bad and doubtful debts	3,600	
				68,400	
			Less: Provision for Discount on Debtors	1,368	67,032

Working Notes

1. Calculation for new provision for bad and doubtful debts:

	Rs.
Provision @ 5% on closing debtors of Rs. 72,000	3,600
Less: Remaining portion of Provision for Bad and Doubtful Debts A/c (Rs. 3,800 – Rs. 1,900)	1,900
Further amount required to be charged to profit and loss A/c	1,700

2. Calculation of amount to be charged to profit and loss account for provision for discount on debtors:

	Rs.
Closing debtors after adjustment of new provision for bad debts (Rs.72,000 – Rs. 3,600)	68,400
2% Provision for discount on debtors of Rs. 68,400	1,368
Less: Remaining balance for provision for discount A/c (Rs. 1,900 – Rs. 1,300)	600
Net amount to be charged to profit and loss A/c	768

ILLUSTRATION 15.5 During the year 2007, Mr. Sen sold goods on credit for Rs. 218,600. During the year, his business transactions with his debtors were as under:

		Rs.
1.	Cash realized from debtors	164,900
2.	Goods received on returns from the debtors	4,700
3.	Bad debts during the year amounted to (written off)	2,440
4.	Bad debts recovered	780
5.	Discount allowed	1,760

On January 1, 2007, there was a provision for doubtful debts of Rs. 3,150. On December 31, 2007, provision for doubtful debts was to be made @ 5% on debtors.

Prepare the sundry debtors account, bad debts account, provision for doubtful debts account and bad debts recovered account for the year ending December 31, 2007, in the books of Mr. Sen for the above transactions and the adjustment entries regarding provision for doubtful debts.

Solution

In the Books of Mr. Sen
Ledger Accounts

Dr.   **Debtors Account**   Cr.

Date	Particulars	Amount (Rs.)	Date	Particulars	Amount (Rs.)
2007	To Sales A/c	218,600	2007 Dec. 31	By Bank A/c	164,900
				By Discount Allowed A/c	1,760
				By Return Inwards A/c	4,700
				By Bad Debts A/c	2,440
				By Balance c/d	44,800
		218,600			218,600
2008 Jan. 1	To Balance b/d	44,800			

Dr.   **Bad Debts Account**   Cr.

Date	Particulars	Amount (Rs.)	Date	Particulars	Amount (Rs.)
2007	To Debtors A/c	2,440	2007 Dec. 31	By Provision for bad	2,440
		2,440		and doubtful debts A/c	2,440

Dr.   **Provision for Bad and Doubtful Debts Account**   Cr.

Date	Particulars	Amount (Rs.)	Date	Particulars	Amount (Rs.)
2007 Dec. 31	To Bad Debts A/c	2,440	2007 Jan. 1	By Balance b/d	3,150
	To Balance c/d (5% of 44,800)	2,240	Dec. 31	By Profit and Loss A/c (balancing figure)	1,530
		4,680	2008		4,680
			Jan. 1	By Balance b/d	2,240

Dr.   **Bad Debts Recovery Account**   Cr.

Date	Particulars	Amount (Rs.)	Date	Particulars	Amount (Rs.)
2007 Dec. 31	To Profit and Loss A/c	780	2007	By Bank A/c	780
		780			780

ILLUSTRATION 15.6 From the following information, calculate the amount of provision for bad and doubtful debts to be made at the end of the year. Closing debtors is Rs. 82,000. Debtors include the following:

1. Amount due from Mr. X: Rs. 5,000 (considered definitely good).
2. Amount due from Mr. Y: Rs. 2,000 (considered definitely bad).
3. Amount due from Mr. Z: Rs. 2,500 (considered very much doubtful).

Make provision for bad and doubtful debts @ 5% on debtors.

Solution
Calculation of the amount to be charged to profit and loss account for provision for bad and doubtful debts:

	Rs.
Closing debtors	82,000
Less: Due from Mr. X (good debtors—normally no provision is required)	5,000
	77,000
Less: Due from Mr. Y (bad debt)	2,000
	75,000
Less: Due from Mr. Z (very much doubtful debts—100% provision is required)	2,500
Remaining debtors (whose financial position is not known, i.e., doubtful debts)	72,500
5% provision on the remaining debtors of Rs. 72,500	3,625
Add: 100% provision for the amount due from Mr. Z	2,500
Total provision for bad and doubtful debts for the current year	6,125

Hence, for the purpose of Final Accounts, provision for bad and doubtful debts would be Rs. 6,125.

ILLUSTRATION 15.7

		Case I	Case II	Case III
1.	Bad debts already written off	700	1,300	1,400
2.	Bad debts to be written off	900	—	800
3.	Debtors at the closing of the year	30,400	40,000	36,900
4.	Provision for bad and doubtful debts at the beginning (January 1, 2007)	2,000	1,000	4,500
5.	Provision for discount on debtors at the beginning (January 1, 2007)	900	1,500	1,000
6.	Discount allowed during the period	700	600	1,500

Provision for bad and doubtful debts to be provided @ 5% and provision for discount on debtors to be provided @ 2% on debtors. Give necessary journal entries and show the relevant ledger accounts and the balance sheet as on December 31, 2007 (Case I only).

Solution
Case I

Journal Entries

Date	Particulars	L.F.	Amount Dr. (Rs.)	Amount Cr. (Rs.)
2007 Dec. 31	Bad Debts A/c Dr. 　To Debtors A/c (Being the amount written off as bad debts)		900	900
	Provision for Bad and Doubtful Debts A/c Dr. 　To Bad Debts A/c (Being the bad debts transferred to provision for bad debts account)		1,600	1,600
	Profit and Loss A/c Dr. 　To Provision for Bad and Doubtful Debts A/c (Being the provision for bad and doubtful debts provided on debtors)		1,075	1,075
	Provision for Discount on Debtors A/c Dr. 　To Discount Allowed A/c (Being the transfer of discount allowed during the period to provision for discount on debtor's account)		700	700
	Profit and Loss A/c Dr. 　To Provision for Discount on Debtors A/c (Being provision for discount on debtors created)		361	361

Dr.　　　　　　　　　**Provision for Bad and Doubtful Debts Account**　　　　　　　　　Cr.

Date	Particulars	Amount (Rs.)	Date	Particulars	Amount (Rs.)
2007 Dec. 31	To Bad Debts A/c	1,600	2007 Jan. 1	By Balance b/d	2,000
	To Balance c/d	1,475	Dec. 31	By Profit and Loss A/c	1,075
		3,075			3,075
			2008 Jan. 1	By Balance b/d	1,475

Dr.　　　　　　　　　　　　　　　**Bad Debts Account**　　　　　　　　　　　　　　　Cr.

Date	Particulars	Amount (Rs.)	Date	Particulars	Amount (Rs.)
2007	To Debtors (already written off)	700	2007 Dec. 31	By Provision for bad and doubtful debts	1,600
2007 Dec. 31	To Debtors	900			
		1,600			1,600

Dr.   **Debtors Account**   Cr.

Date	Particulars	Amount (Rs.)	Date	Particulars	Amount (Rs.)
2007	To Balance b/d	30,400	2007 Dec. 31	By Bad Debts A/c	900
				By Balance c/d	29,500
		30,400			30,400
2008 Jan. 1	To Balance b/d	29,500			

Dr.   **Discount Allowed Account**   Cr.

Date	Particulars	Amount (Rs.)	Date	Particulars	Amount (Rs.)
2007	To Debtors (already charged)	700	2007 Dec. 31	By Provision for discount on debtors	700
		700			700

Dr.   **Provision for Discount on Debtors Account**   Cr.

Date	Particulars	Amount (Rs.)	Date	Particulars	Amount (Rs.)
2007 Dec. 31	To Discount Allowed A/c	700	2007 Jan. 1	By Balance b/d	900
	To Balance c/d	561	Dec. 31	By Profit and Loss A/c	361
		1,261			1,261
			2008 Jan. 1	By Balance b/d	561

Balance Sheet as on December 31, 2007 (includes)

Liabilities	Amount (Rs.)	Amount (Rs.)	Assets	Amount (Rs.)	Amount (Rs.)
			Debtors	29,500	
			Less: Provision for bad and doubtful debts	1,475	
				28,025	
			Less: Provision for discount on debtors	561	27,464

Working Notes

1. Calculation for new provision for bad and doubtful debts:

	Rs.
Provision @ 5% on closing debtors of Rs. 29,500	1,475
Less: Remaining portion of provision for bad debt A/c (Rs. 2,000 – Rs. 1,600)	400
Further amount required to be charged to profit and loss A/c	1,075

2. Calculation of amount to be charged to profit and loss account for provision for discount on debtors:

	Rs.
Closing debtors after adjustment of new provision for bad debts (Rs. 29,500 – Rs. 1,475)	28,025
2% Provision for discount on debtors of Rs. 28,025(560.50) (approx.)	561
Less: Remaining balance for provision for discount A/c (Rs. 900 – Rs. 700)	200
Net amount to be charged to profit and loss A/c	361

Case II

Journal Entries

Date	Particulars		L.F.	Amount Dr. (Rs.)	Amount Cr. (Rs.)
2007 Dec. 31	Provision for Bad and Doubtful Debts A/c	Dr.		1,000	
	Profit and Loss A/c	Dr.		300	
	To Bad Debts A/c				1,300
	(Being the bad debts transferred to provision for bad debts account)				
	Profit and Loss A/c	Dr.		2,000	
	To Provision for Bad and Doubtful Debts A/c				2,000
	(Being the provision for bad and doubtful debts provided on debtors)				
	Provision for Discount on Debtors A/c	Dr.		600	
	To Discount Allowed A/c				600
	(Being the transfer of discount allowed during the period to provision for discount on debtor's account)				
	Provision for Discount on Debtors A/c	Dr.		140	
	To Profit and Loss A/c				140
	(Being surplus provision transferred)				

Dr. **Provision for Bad and Doubtful Debts Account** Cr.

Date	Particulars	Amount (Rs.)	Date	Particulars	Amount (Rs.)
2007 Dec. 31	To Bad Debts A/c	1,000	2007 Jan. 1	By Balance b/d	1,000
	To Balance c/d	2,000	Dec. 31	By Profit and Loss A/c	2,000
		3,000			3,000
2008 Jan. 1	By Balance b/d	2,000			

Dr. **Bad Debts Account** Cr.

Date	Particulars	Amount (Rs.)	Date	Particulars	Amount (Rs.)
2007	To Debtors (already written off)	1,300	2007 Dec. 31	By Provision for bad and doubtful debts	1,000
				By Profit and Loss A/c	300
		1,300			1,300

Dr. **Discount Allowed Account** Cr.

Date	Particulars	Amount (Rs.)	Date	Particulars	Amount (Rs.)
2007	To Debtors (already charged)	600	2007 Dec. 31	By Provision for discount on debtors	600
		600			600

Dr. **Provision for Discount on Debtors Account** Cr.

Date	Particulars	Amount (Rs.)	Date	Particulars	Amount (Rs.)
2007 Dec. 31	To Discount Allowed A/c	600	2007 Jan. 1	By Balance b/d	1,500
	To Profit and Loss A/c	140			
	To Balance c/d	760			
		1,500			1,500
			2008 Jan. 1	By Balance b/d	760

Working Notes

1. Calculation of amount to be charged to profit and loss account for provision for bad debts:

   5% on closing debtors of Rs. 40,000 — Rs. 2,000

   There is no balance in the provision for bad and doubtful debts account.

   Hence, to create new provision, the entire amount is to be charged to profit and loss account, i.e., Rs. 2,000.

2. Calculation of the amount to be charged to profit and loss account for provision for discount on debtors:

	Rs.
Closing debtors after adjustment of new provision for bad debt (Rs. 40,000 – Rs. 2,000)	38,000
2% Provision for discount on debtors of Rs. 38,000	760
On January 1, 2007, provision for discount account balance	1,500
Less: Discount allowed adjusted	600
Balance remaining	900
Less: Balance to be maintained for new provision	760
Surplus amount to be transferred to profit and loss A/c	140

Case III

Journal Entries

Date	Particulars		L.F.	Amount Dr. (Rs.)	Amount Cr. (Rs.)
2007 Dec. 31	Bad Debts A/c	Dr.		800	
	To Debtors A/c				800
	(Being the amount written off as bad debts)				
	Provision for Bad and Doubtful Debts A/c	Dr.		2,200	
	To Bad Debts A/c				2,200
	(Being the bad debts transferred to provision for bad debts account)				
	Provision for Bad and Doubtful Debts A/c	Dr.		495	
	To Profit and Loss A/c				495
	(Being the surplus of Provision for bad and doubtful debts account transferred)				
	Provision for Discount on Debtors A/c	Dr.		1,000	
	Profit and Loss A/c	Dr.		500	
	To Discount Allowed A/c				1,500
	(Being the transfer of discount allowed during the period to provision for discount on debtor's account)				
	Profit and Loss A/c	Dr.		686	
	To Provision for Discount on Debtors A/c				686
	(Being provision for discount on debtors created)				

Working Notes

1. Ledger accounts are not shown here because they are to be prepared like Cases I and II.
2. Calculation of new provision for doubtful debts:

	Rs.
5% provision on closing debtors of Rs. 36,100 (Rs. 36,900 – Rs 800)	1,805
Provision for bad and doubtful debts account balance on January 1, 2007	4,500
Less: Current years' bad debts adjusted	2,200
	2,300
Less: Balance to be maintained for new provision on December 31, 2007	1,805
Surplus transferred to profit and loss A/c	495

3. Calculation of amount to be charged to profit and loss account for provision for discount:

Rs.

Closing debtors after adjustment of new provision for bad debts
(Rs. 36,100 – Rs. 1,805)

34,295

2% provision for discount on debtors Rs. 34,295 (Rs. 685.9)

686 (approx.)

There is no balance remaining on December 31, 2007 after adjustment of current year's discount. Hence, full amount of Rs. 686 is to be charged to the profit and loss account to create a new provision.

15.4 RESERVES

Reserve is an appropriation of profit but not a charge against profit. It is created not to cover any approved liability or shrinkage in the value of assets. Reserve is created out of profits as a future security to meet certain unforeseen contingencies. Thus, creation of provisions decreases proprietor's fund or owner's equity. On the other hand, creation of reserves increases proprietor's fund or owner's equity.

Hence, **Reserves** are undistributed profits set aside to meet future contingencies, whether known or unknown, and also for certain specific needs. It helps to strengthen the financial soundness of a firm or an enterprise.

TABLE 15.3 Distinctions between Provisions and Reserves

Reserve	Provisions
It is an appropriation of profit.	It is a charge against profit.
It is created for meeting some unknown future needs.	Provision is created to provide for known liabilities, commitments, etc.
Reserve is created by means of an appropriation of profit.	It is created irrespective of whether there is any profit or not.
It is created to strengthen the financial position of the business.	Generally, it is created to meet losses and expenses.
It is always shown on the liability side of the balance sheet.	Some of the provisions are shown on the assets side by way of deductions from some assets and others are shown on the liability side of the balance sheet.
In some cases, the creation of reserve is more or less discretionary and is depends on the management policy.	As per the required amount, provision is created and the making of provision is never discretionary.
It can not be created if there is no net profit.	It can be created even if there is no net profit or there is loss.
Reserve may be created for redemption of capital or debentures.	Provisions cannot be created for any such purpose.

15.4.1 Characteristics of Reserve

1. It is created out of the net profits of the business and/or out of surplus created by an enterprise.
2. It is created by an appropriation of profit but not a charge against profit.
3. Reserve is not created to meet any known liability or contingency.
4. It helps to increase proprietor's fund.
5. It helps to strengthen the financial position of a firm.

15.4.2 Types of Reserves

Reserves may be classified into three categories—revenue, capital and secret. The classification of reserves is shown below through Figure 15.1.

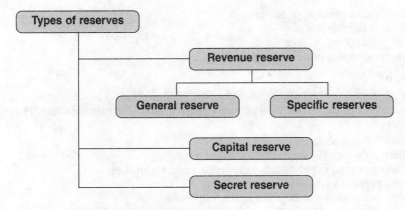

FIGURE 15.1 Types of reserve.

Revenue reserves

These reserves are created out of the revenue profit. These include specific reserves, like general reserves, dividend equalization reserves, investment fluctuation reserve, and dividend redemption reserve, for which the financial position of a firm is strengthened.

General reserve: It is created out of profit not for some specific purpose, but for future security to strengthen the financial position of a firm. It is a revenue reserve in nature. Thus, general reserve is simply an accumulation of profit by appropriation. Though it is not created for specific purpose, the motive behind the creation of this reserve may be depicted as under:

1. To absorb future operating loss.
2. To meet any unforeseen contingency.
3. To provide working capital for the firm.
4. To provide funds for the acquisition of capital assets.
5. To provide funds for payment of long-term liabilities.

Specific reserves: It is a revenue reserve created out of a profit to cater future needs and is utilized for a specific purpose, for which it is created. Specific reserve strengthens the financial soundness of a firm. The following are some examples of specific reserves:

1. Investment fluctuation reserve
2. Dividend equalization reserve
3. Capital redemption reserve
4. Contingencies reserve
5. Special depreciation reserve
6. Debentures redemption reserve
7. Development rebate reserve
8. Taxation equalization reserve
9. Staff gratuity reserve.

Capital reserves

These reserves are created out of the capital profit. Some examples of capital reserves are given below:

1. Profit on sale of fixed assets
2. Profit on revaluation of fixed assets
3. Profit on reissue of forfeited shares

4. Profit on redemption of debentures
5. Profit prior to incorporation
6. Capital redemption reserve
7. Premium on shares or debentures.

Secret reserves

These reserves are found in the balance sheet but are hidden. Due to these reserves, the position of assets of a business is stronger so that their position as disclosed in the balance sheet. These reserves are created as follows:

1. By undervaluing an asset
2. By charging excessive depreciation on the assets
3. By treating capital expenditures as revenue expenditures, etc.
4. Ignoring prepaid expenses
5. Ignoring permanent appreciation in the value of assets
6. Ignoring accrued incomes
7. Understatement of goodwill
8. Providing higher amount of bad debt provisions
9. Overstating liabilities and provision.

Objects behind secret reserve

1. To strengthen the financial position of the business by undisclosed amount of net worth.
2. To reduce the amount of income tax by showing lesser amount of profit.
3. To absorb future losses.
4. To keep aside competition by showing low profit.

Dangers of secret reserve

1. The balance sheet fails to represent true state of affairs of the firm.
2. The secret reserve can be misused for personal gains.
3. The owners are deprived from getting the actual profits of the firm.
4. Where an asset is totally omitted from the books, the auditor may not have the opportunity to verify the asset.
5. Where assets are undervalued and in case of an accident/damage caused by fire or otherwise, the insurance company will entertain only the book value, and as a result, the firm has to suffer.
6. The value of shares is allowed to fall.

Distinguish between revenue reserves and capital reserves

1. Revenue reserves are created by means of an appropriation of profit, whereas capital reserves are created out of the capital profit.
2. Revenue reserves are available for dividends. Capital reserves on the other hand, are not freely available for dividends, can be distributed subject to law and Articles.
3. Revenue reserve is created for meeting some unknown future needs and to strengthen the financial position of the business, whereas capital reserve is created for meeting future capital losses, or may be utilized as per the provisions of the Companies Act.

EXERCISES

I. *Short Answer Type Questions (with answers)*

1. Define reserve.

   Ans: Reserve is an appropriation of profits. It is not a charge against profits. Reserve is not created to cover any approved liability or shrinkage in the value of assets. It is created out of profits as a future security to meet certain unforeseen contingencies. Creation of reserves increases the proprietor's fund or the owner's equity.

2. How are reserves classified?

   Ans: Reserves are classified into three categories—revenue reserves, capital reserves and secret reserves.

3. Give the general features of reserves.

   Ans: 1. Reserves are provided for meeting certain unforeseen contingencies or for future security.
   2. It is not a charge against profit but is an appropriation of profits.
   3. It is provided out of profits of the firm.

4. Give some examples of revenue reserves.

   Ans: Revenue reserves are created out of revenue profits. Some examples of revenue reserves are general reserve, dividend equalization reserve, contingencies reserve, and investment fluctuation reserve.

5. Give some sources from where capital reserves are created.

   Ans: Capital reserves are created out of capital profits. Some of its sources are as follows:
   1. Profit on sale of fixed assets
   2. Profit on revaluation of fixed assets
   3. Profit on reissue of forfeited shares
   4. Capital redemption reserves
   5. Premium on issue of shares/debentures
   6. Profit on redemption of debentures
   7. Profit prior to incorporation.

6. Why and how secret reserves are created?

   Ans: Secret reserves are not shown in the balance sheet but are hidden. These are created to strengthen the financial position of a firm. Due to these reserves, the asset position of a firm is stronger than that disclosed in the balance sheet. Generally, these reserves are created as follows:
   1. By undervaluation of assets
   2. By charging excessive depreciation on assets
   3. By treating capital expenditure as revenue expenditure
   4. By overstating liabilities
   5. By including fictitious liability
   6. By suppressing revenue incomes.

7. Define provisions.

   Ans: Provision usually means an amount written off or retained by way of providing depreciation, renewals or retained by way of providing for any known liability of which the amount cannot be determined with substantial accuracy (Part III of Schedule VI, Companies Act).

   According to conservative principle, making a provision for an expected loss is a common practice for an enterprise/firm. Provision is a charge against profit and as such, for creating provision, the profit and loss account is debited.

8. Give some examples of provisions.

   Ans: Provision for doubtful debts, provision for discount on debtors, provision for repairs and renewals, provision for depreciation, provision for taxations, etc., are some examples of provisions.

9. Give the general features of provisions.

   Ans: 1. It is provided for certain known liability.
   2. It is a charge against profit.
   3. It is provided without depending on the profit or loss of the firm.
   4. The amount of provision cannot be calculated with substantial accuracy.

10. What are bad debts?

    Ans: Generally, goods are sold on credit to increase the volume of sales. Out of these debtors, some fail to pay the whole or a part of their dues in future which becomes a business loss. These types of losses are known as bad debts. When a debt is declared as bad, then that amount is to be written off from the debtors by debiting the bad debts account and crediting the debtors account.

11. What is provision for bad and doubtful debts?

    Ans: Generally, debtors are of three types—good, bad and doubtful. A portion of doubtful debts may or may not be realized in future (i.e., recovery of debts is not certain), and if not realized, that amounts to a loss. A provision is created to meet such a loss. This provision is known as provision for bad and doubtful debts. It is created regularly irrespective of profit and loss earned by the concern.

12. Why is provision for bad and doubtful debts created?

    Ans: The amount of bad debts cannot be ascertained or anticipated accurately in the current year; it can only be estimated on the basis of past experiences. With the help of this estimation, the amount of provision for bad debt is created out of the current year's profit. It is our practice to adjust all the actual and estimated current year's losses from the current year's revenues (based on the matching concept).

13. If provision for bad and doubtful debts is not created, in what ways will it then affect the business?

    Ans: It is a standard practice to adjust all the actual and estimated current year's probable losses from the current year's revenues (based on the matching concept). If this procedure is not followed or an inadequate provision is made, then the current year's profit and loss account will not show the true profit, or the balance sheet will not represent the true financial position of the business. On the other hand, in the subsequent year, when the actual bad debt will occur, the profits of the subsequent year will decline due to the last year's loss. Thus, provision must be created properly to represent the true financial position of the firm.

14. What is provision for discount on debtors?

    Ans: In order to encourage debtors to make prompt payments, cash discounts are generally allowed which are regular in nature. To meet these types of losses or expenditures, a provision is created known as **provision for discount on debtors**. It is a charge against profit.

15. Why is provision for discount on debtors created?

    Ans: The cost of total goods sold in an accounting period cannot be fully realized within the said period, because a part of the debtors is realized only in the next accounting period and a cash discount is allowed at that time. Though the discount is allowed in the next year, it is actually the expenditure of the previous year. Thus, it should be charged to the period in which the related sales were achieved. Considering this point of view, a provision for discount on debtors is created on the basis of the past experience at a fixed percentage on the debtors.

16. How is provision for discount on debtors shown in the balance sheet and why?

Ans: It is desirable that the debtors should appear in the balance sheet as the net amount (and not as the gross figure) which is expected to be realized in future. That is why in the balance sheet, the provision for discount on debtors should be deducted from the debtors after deducting provision for bad and doubtful debts to show the net realizable value. Otherwise, the balance sheet will not represent the true financial position of the business.

II. *Long Answer Type Questions*

1. Is reserve a charge against profit or an appropriation of profit? Discuss.
2. How do you classify reserves? Give three examples of each group.
3. What is a secret reserve? How is it created? Give justification for the creation of this reserve.
4. What is the difference between reserve and provision? How is a capital reserve created?
5. What do you mean by bad debts? Distinguish between bad debts, and bad and doubtful debts.
6. What is provision for bad and doubtful debts? Why is it created? Will it depend on the volume of profit of the business?
7. Distinguish between:
   (a) Bad debts, and provision for bad and doubtful debts.
   (b) Revenue reserves and capital reserves.
8. What are the objects behind creation of secret reserve? What are the risks of secret reserve?
9. Explain the important characteristics of a provision.
10. Write a short notes on general reserve.

III. *Problems*

1. On 31.12.96 Debtors A/c shows a balance of Rs. 68,000. Bad Debts written off during the year Rs. 1,600. Bad Debts to be written off Rs. 300. Provision for Bad and Doubtful Debts A/c balance on 1.1.96 was Rs. 2,000. Provision for Bad and Doubtful Debts is always made on Debtors @5%.

   Give necessary Journal entries.

   Ans: New Provision for Bad and Doubtful Debts would be Rs. 3,385 (5% of Rs. 67,700) and to be charged to P/L A/c Rs. 3,285; Total Bad Debt Rs. 1,900.

2. Provision for Bad and Doubtful Debts A/c shows a Cr. balance of Rs. 3,100 on 1.1.97. Bad Debts written off Rs. 2,600. Debtors on 31.12.97 were Rs. 46,600. Provision for Bad and Doubtful Debts is to be created @5% on Debtors.

   Pass necessary Journal entries.

   Ans: New Provision Rs. 2,330, Charged to P/L A/c for Provision Rs. 1,830.

3. The following balances are extracted from the Trial Balance of M. Roy on 31.12.96:

   Debtors Rs. 68,000, Bad Debts Rs. 2,700, Provision for Bad and Doubtful Debts Rs. 2,400 (Cr.), Provision for Bad and Doubtful Debts is to be created @5% on Debtors.

   Draw up the Bad Debts A/c and Provision for Bad and Doubtful Debts A/c.

   Ans: Shortage of Old Provision for Bad Debts would be adjusted fromP/L A/c, i.e., Rs. 300 and for New Provision P&L A/c would be charged for Rs. 3,400.

4. On 31.12.90 Debtors A/c of S. Bose shows a balance of Rs. 72,000. Bad Debts written off during the year Rs. 1,900. Provision for Bad and Doubtful Debts A/c shows a balance of Rs. 5,800 on 1.1.90. Provision for Bad and Doubtful Debts is always made on Debtors @5%.

   Pass necessary entries.

   Ans: New Provision for Bad and Doubtful Debts would be Rs. 3,600. After adjustment of Bad debts and New Provision, surplus amount of Old Provision would be transferred to be Profit & Loss A/c i.e. Rs. 300. The entry is Provision for Bad and Doubtful Debts A/c debit and Profit & Loss A/c credit Rs. 300.

5. The Debtors balance as at 1.1.1978 was Rs. 2,000 and at 31.12.78 Rs. 2,500. Provision is always made for Doubtful Debts at 5% on Debtors. Bad Debts written off during the year amounted to Rs. 200. Show separately the Bad Debt and the Provision for Bad Debts Account. (W.B.H.S.)

6. How would you deal with the following in accounting for a going concern?
   Amount due from Mr. X Rs. 3,000—considered definitely good.
   (i) Rs. 1,000 is due from A. Nothing is realisable from him.
   (ii) Out of the total Sundry Debtors of Rs. 45,000 (including A's balance) $2\frac{1}{2}\%$ is considered doubtful.
   (iii) It is anticipated that discount at 2% on the remaining Debtors may have to be allowed.
   Pass suitable entries to record the above and show relevant entries in Profit & Loss A/c and Balance Sheet. (W.B.H.S.)
   Ans: (i) Bad Debt A/c Dr. and A A/c Cr., P/L A/c Dr. and Bad Debt A/c Cr. Rs. 1,000.
   (ii) P/L A/c Dr. and Provision for Doubtful Debts A/c Cr. Rs. 1,100. (iii) P/L A/c Dr. and Provision for Discount on Debt A/c Cr. Rs 858.

7. On 1st January, 1982 the balance of Provision for Doubtful Debts was Rs, 3,500. Bad Debts during the year were Rs. 1,500. Sundry Debtors as on 31st December, 1982 stood at Rs. 50,600. Out of these Debtors Rs. 600 are bad and cannot be realised. The Provision for Doubtful Debts is to be raised to 5% on Sundry debtors.
   Show the relevant accounts and show how Bad Debts and Provision for Doubtful Debts will appear in the Profit & Loss A/c and Balance Sheet as at 31st December, 1982. (W.B.H.S.)
   Ans: New Bad Debts to be written off Rs. 600; New Provision is Rs. 2,500. Net amount to be charged to P/L A/c Rs. 1,100 for New Provision.

8. On 1.1.95 Provision for Doubtful Debts Account shows a balance of Rs. 9,270. Bad Debts during the year were Rs. 10,120. At the end of 1995 Debtors amounted to Rs. 2,57,000. Provision for Doubtful Debts to be made at 5%.
   In 1996 actual Bad Debts amounted to Rs. 8,000 only. Out of the dues from a Debtor Rs. 2,250 which was written off as Bad Debt in 1995, Rs. 1,250 was received in Cash in 1996. At the end of 1996 Provision for Doubtful Debts is made to the extent of Rs. 800. Show Provision for Doubtful Debts Account, Bad Debt Account and Profit & Loss A/c for the years 1995 and 1996. (W.B.H.S.)
   Ans: For Bad Debts Rs. 850 to be charged to P & L A/c. New Provision for Bad Debts on 31.12.95 Rs. 12,850. It is assumed here that in addition to the remaining balance of Old Provision, further Provision of Rs. 800 is to be made in 1996. For Bad Debt recovery P/L A/c is to be credited for Rs. 1,250.

9. On 1st January, 1985, the balance of Provision for Doubtful Debts was Rs. 3,000. The Bad Debt during the year was Rs. 2,500. The Sundry debtors as on 31st December, 1985, stood at Rs. 80,000. A new provision of 5% is required. Show Journal entries and necessary Ledger Accounts. (W.B.H.S.)
   Ans: New Provision for Bad Debts Rs. 4,000, Net amount to be charged to P/L A/c Rs. 3,500 for New Provision.

10. The figure of Sundry Debtors in a Trial Balance is Rs. 70,000. You are required to write off Rs. 500 as Bad Debts and make a Provision for Doubtful Debts @ 10% on Sundry Debtors. Pass the necessary Journal entries. (W.B.H.S.)
    Ans: Bad Debts to be written off Rs. 500 and to be transferred to P/L A/c. New Provision would be Rs. 6,950.

11. On 1st January, 1995, the balance in the account of Provision for Doubtful Debts of Shankar Ltd. of Jaipur was Rs. 34,000. During 1995, Bad Debt written off was Rs. 27,500. On 31st December, 1995. the balance of Sundry Debtors stood at Rs.8,00,000, on which a Provision for Doubtful Debts @ 15% was to be made.

Prepare Journal entries and relevant Ledger Accounts as on 31.12.95. Also show how these would appear in the Profit and Loss Account and in the Balance Sheet.

(W.B.H.S.)

Ans: Amount to be charged to P/L A/c for New Provision Rs. 1,13,500. New Provision Rs. 1,20,000.

12. Trial Balance of Sri B. Basu shows the following balances as on 31.12.95:

	Rs.	Rs.
Provision for Bad Debts (1.1.95) Cr.		2,500
Provision for Discount (1.1.95) Cr.		1,400
Sundry Debtors	30,200	
Bad Debts	2,300	
Discount Allowed	1,100	

You are required to keep a Provision for Bad Debts @ 10% on Sundry Debtors and a Provision for Discount @ 5%. Show the Ledger Accounts and show also how Sundry Debtors will appear in the Balance Sheet for Sri Basu as on 31.12.95.

(W.B.H.S.)

Ans: Amount to be charged to P/L for new Provision for Bad Debts Rs.2,820. New Provision Rs. 3,020 charged to P/L for New Provision for Discount Rs. 1,059. Sundry Debtors in Balance Sheet Rs. 25,821.

13. On 1st January,. 1994, the Balance of Provision for Doubtful debts was Rs. 15,000. The Bad Debts during the year was Rs. 10,000. Debtors as on 31st December, 1994 was Rs. 2,00,000. A New Provision of 5% is required for Doubtful Debts.
    (i) Show entries in the Journal.
    (ii) Show also how they appear in Profit & Loss Account and Balance Sheet.

(W.B.H.S.)

Ans: Amount to be charged to P/L A/c for new provision Rs. 5,000.

14. On 1st January, 1995 the Provision for Doubtful Debts Account in the books of a firm which maintains it at 5% has a credit balance of Rs. 1,100. During the year Bad Debts amounted to Rs. 800 and the Debtors at the end of the year were Rs. 20,000. Show Provision for Doubtful Debts Account and Bad Debt Account for the year 1995.

(Central Board)

Ans: Amount to be charged to P/L A/c for New Provision Rs. 700.

15. Balmiki, a trader, had incurred a loss of Rs. 2,500 as a Bad Debt during the year 1990 and then decided to create a Provision for Doubtful Debts at 5% on the good debtors amounting to Rs. 75,000 on 31st December,1990.

During the year ended 31st December, 1991 his debtors worth Rs. 1,500 failed to pay their dues on 31st December, 1991. His good debtors amounted to Rs. 40,000 and he decided to maintain the Provision for Doubtful Debt at 4% on debtors.

During 1992 his Bad Debts amounted to Rs. 3,000. He decided to increase the Provision for Doubtful Debts to 5% on the good debtors, which amounted to Rs. 80,000 on 31st December, 1992. Show the Bad Debts A/c, Provision for Doubtful Debts A/c and also the appropriate entries in the Profit and Loss A/c and Balance Sheet of 1990, 1991 and 1992.

(Delhi I.S.C. Examination.)

Ans: Amount charged to P/L A/c: In 1990 Rs. 6,250 and in 1992 Rs. 5,400. In 1991 amount to be credited to P/L A/c Rs. 650. Provision for Bad debt: 1990—Rs. 3,750, 1991—Rs. 1,600 and 1992—Rs. 4,000.

16. Rectify the following Journal entries assuming that the narrations are correct:

  (i) Sundry Debtors A/c   Dr.
        To Bad Debt A/c
        (Being the amount of Bad Debts written off)

  (ii) Provision for Bad Debts A/c   Dr.
        To Profit & Loss A/c
        (Being the amount of Provision for Bad and Doubtful Debts created @)

  (iii) Bad Debts A/c   Dr
        To Profit & Loss A/c
        (Being the balance of Bad Debts Account transferred)

  (iv) Bank A/c   Dr.
        To Sundry Debtors A/c
        (Being the amount recovered previously written off as Bad Debts)

  (v) Sundry Debtors A/c   Dr.
        To Profit & Loss A/c
        (Being the amount of Bad Debt recovery transferred)

                                                             (W.B.H.S.)

Ans: (iv) Bank A/c Dr. and Bad Debt Recovery A/c (v) Bad Debt Recovery A/c Dr. and P/L A/c Cr. For item nos. (i) to (iii), correct entry is just the opposite.

17. Blackstone Ltd. had (a) Sundry Debtors worth Rs. 68,000, Rs. 48,000 and Rs. 92,000 and (b) Sundry Creditors worth Rs. 38,000, Rs. 45,000 and Rs. 55,000 as on 31st December, 1990, 1991 and 1992 respectively. Show from the following data the Provision for Doubtful Debts A/c, Provision for Discount on Debtors A/c and Provision for Discount on Creditors A/c at 5%, 2% and 2% respectively, for the years 1990, 1991 and 1992 respectively.

During the year	Bad Debts written off Rs.	Discount Allowed Rs.	Discount Received Rs.
1990	3,000	1,000	700
1991	1,800	500	880
1992	2,900	1,200	620

All the provisions were created for the first time on 31st December, 1990 and maintained accordingly in the following years.   (Delhi I.S.C. Examination)

Ans: Provision for Bad Debts 1990 — Rs. 3,400, 1991 — Rs. 2,400 and 1992 — Rs.4,600, Provision for Discount (on Debtors) 1990 — Rs. 1,292, 1991 — Rs. 912 and 1992 — Rs. 836, Provision for Discount on Creditors 1990 — Rs. 760, 1991 — Rs. 900, 1992 — Rs. 1,100

18. During the year 1979, S. Roy Chowdhury sold goods on credit by Rs. 150,000. During the same year his business had the following transactions with the debtors:

		Rs.
(i)	Cash realised from the Debtors	1,05,000
(ii)	Goods received on returns from the Debtors	5,000
(iii)	Bad Debt during the year amounted to	1,000

On 1.1.79 there was a Provision for Doubtful Debts of Rs. 2,500. For 1979 Provision for Doubtful Debts was to be made @ 5% on Debtors. You are to prepare the Sundry Debtors Account showing the closing balance and make entries in the journal for the Provision for Doubtful Debts.   (C.U. B.Com.)

Ans: Sundry Debtors closing balance Rs. 39,000. Amount charged to P/L A/c for new provision Rs. 450

16

Bills of Exchange

INTRODUCTION

In India, negotiable instruments are regulated by the Negotiable Instruments Act, 1881. According to Section 13 of the Negotiable Instruments Act, 'A negotiable instrument means a promissory note, a bill of exchange or a cheque payable either to order to bearer.' The term 'negotiable' means transferable and the term 'instrument' means a written document by which a right is created in favour of some person. From the definition it appears that the Act exclusively applies to promissory note, bill of exchange and cheque. Here, all discussions are to be made in respect of bill of exchange only considering its application as per law and accounting aspects.

16.1 PROMISSORY NOTE

Section 4 of the Negotiable Instruments Act defines a promissory note as "an instrument in writing (not being a bank note or a currency note) containing an unconditional undertaking, signed by the maker, to pay a certain some of money only to, or to the order of, a certain person, or to the bearer of the instrument." A specimen of a promissory note is given in Box 16.1.

16.1.1 Parties to a Promissory Note

1. The maker, who makes writes the promise to pay, i.e., the debtor or the buyer of the goods.
2. The payee, to whom the amount is promised to be paid.

16.1.2 Characteristics of a Promissory Note

1. It must be in writing.
2. It must contain an express undertaking to pay.
3. The promise to pay must be unconditional.

4. The instrument must be signed by the maker.
5. The maker must be a certain and definite person.
6. The payee must be certain and definite person.
7. The amount payable must be certain.
8. It may be payable on demand or on a specified date (after a specified period).
9. Payment must be made in legal tender money of India.
10. It can be endorsed.
11. Here acceptance is not required.

BOX 16.1   The Specimen form of a promissory note

Rs. 80,000	Durgapur
Stamp	August 18, 2000

Two months after data, I promise to pay to P.K. Das or order the sum of Rupees Eighty thousand only, for value received.

To
P.K. Das
18 C.R. Road   D.P. Dua
Kolkata-7

16.2   BILL OF EXCHANGE

A bill of exchange is an instrument in writing containing an unconditional order, signed by the maker, directing a certain person to pay a certain sum of money only to, or to the order of, a certain person, or to the bearer of the instrument (Section 5 of the Negotiable Instruments Act). A specimen of a bill of exchange is given in Box 16.2. The differences between promissory note and bill of exchange is mentioned in Table 16.1.

16.2.1   Parties to a Bill of Exchange

1. Drawer: The person who draws or writes or makes the bill, i.e., the creditor or the seller.
2. Drawee: The person on whom the bill is drawn or the person who is directed to pay the bill, i.e., the debtor or the buyer.
3. Payee: The person who will receive the money or to whom the payment is to be made.

BOX 16.2   Specimen of bill of exchange

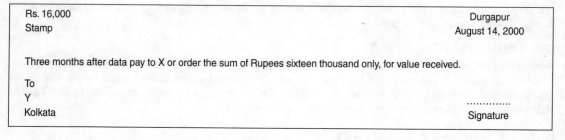

Rs. 16,000	Durgapur
Stamp	August 14, 2000

Three months after data pay to X or order the sum of Rupees sixteen thousand only, for value received.

To
Y   ....
Kolkata   Signature

16.2.2   Salient Features of a Bill of Exchange

1. The instrument must be in writing.
2. The instrument must contain an express order to pay, money and money alone. A mere request to pay on account will not amount to an order.
3. The order to pay must be unconditional.
4. It must be duly signed by the drawer.

5. The parties of the bill must be definite and certain persons.
6. The amount of money to be paid must be certain.
7. The money must be paid to a bearer on demand.
8. It is payable on demand or on a specified date or written for specified period of time.
9. The payment must be made in legal tender money of India.

16.2.3 Parts of a Bill of Exchange (or The Essentials of a Bill)

1. The date: It is the date on which the bill is drawn.
2. The amount: The amount must be mentioned both in figures and in words.
3. Stamp: The stamp is to be affixed on a bill and a promissory note, depending on the amount of the bill or promissory note.
4. The term: It is the period of the bill by which the due date of the bill is calculated.
5. Parties: There are three parties—drawer, drawee and payee.
6. For value received: These words must be mentioned in the bill.
7. The acceptance: The bill must be accepted by the drawee.

TABLE 16.1 Difference between Promissory Note and Bill of Exchange

	Points of difference	Promissory note	Bill of exchange
1.	Number of parties	Two parties–the maker and the payee.	Three parties—the drawee, the drawer and the payee.
2.	Promise or order	There is a promise.	There is an order.
3.	Acceptance	No acceptance is required.	Acceptance is required.
4.	Liability	The maker is primarily liable.	Drawer is liable only when the drawee fails to meet his obligation.
5.	Relationship	The maker stands in an immediate relationship to the payee.	The drawer stands in an immediate relationship with the acceptor.
6.	Notice	Notice of dishonour to the maker is not necessary.	Notice must be given to all persons liable to pay.
7.	Protest	Not necessary.	Incase of dishonour of a foreign bill, it must be protested according to the law of the place where it is drawn.

16.2.4 Acceptance of a Bill of Exchange

A bill is complete lawfully when it is duly accepted by the drawee. Acceptance means writing/putting of signature by the drawee, that is the drawee has accepted the liability. Before acceptance, a bill is called a **draft.** A draft when accepted is called a **bill.** A bill of exchange can be accepted in two ways—general and qualified.

General acceptance: When an acceptor or a drawee puts his/her signature on the bill without any condition.

Qualified acceptance: When a bill is accepted by the drawee by adding some conditions or fulfillment of some conditions or qualifications. The types of qualifications are as follows:

1. Conditional
2. Qualified as to time
3. Partial or qualified as to amount
4. Qualified as to place of payment
5. Qualified as to parties.

A bill of exchange may be accepted by any one of the following:

1. Drawee
2. All or some of the drawee
3. Drawee in case of need (Section 7 of the Negotiable Instruments, Act)
4. Acceptor for honour (Section 108 of the Negotiable Instruments, Act).

16.2.5 Types of Bill of Exchange

1. Inland bill: This bill is drawn and payable within India, or when both the drawer and the drawee belong to the same country.

2. Foreign bill: When both the drawer and the drawee belong to different countries, the bill is referred to as a foreign bill.

3. Bill in sets: Generally, a foreign bill is drawn in sets of three, each being called **via**, so that if one is paid, the other becomes ineffective.

4. Documentary bill: It is prepared by an exporter to the importer which is accompanied by shipping documents to be handed over to the importers on his acceptance or payment of the bill. Documentary bills are of two types—D/A bill and D/P bill, i.e., documentary bill against acceptance or payment.

5. Demand or sight bill: It is a type of bill which is payable on demand.

6. Term bill: This type of bill is payable after some period, after date or after sight.

7. Trade bill: It is a bill of exchange drawn in the ordinary course of a business, i.e., when a bill is drawn by a creditor on his/her debtor for the goods sold on credit.

8. Accommodation bill: It is the bill drawn by a party without receiving any goods or services, but for the temporary financial benefit of the drawer or the drawee or both. Generally, it is drawn for the accommodation of drawer only, or drawer and drawee both.

16.3 DAYS OF GRACE

A bill or note which is not payable on demand becomes mature on the third day after the day on which it is expressed to be payable. These three days are known as the days of grace.

16.3.1 Date of Maturity or Due Date

The **maturity** of a bill or note is the date on which it falls due. A bill which is **payable on demand** becomes mature or due immediately on presentation for payable. A bill which is not payable on demand becomes mature on the third day after the day on which it is expressed to be payable . The following points are to be considered while calculating the due date/maturity date:

1. In case the bill is drawn 'after date':

Date of drawing the bill:	January 1, 2000 (say)
Bill period (days or months)	+ 3 months (say)
Days of grace	+ 3 days
Date of maturity	**April 4, 2000**

2. In case the bill is drawn 'after sight':

Date of acceptance of the bill:	January 2, 2000 (say)
Bill period (days or months)	+ 3 months (say)
Days of grace	+ 3 days
Date of maturity	**April 5, 2000**

3. In case the date of maturity is a holiday: If the due date or the maturity date happens to be a public holiday or Sunday, the due date shall be the day earlier (i.e., the day before maturity), and if that is also a holiday or a Sunday, the next day after the counted day of maturity shall be the due date or the date of maturity.

Suppose, the due date of a bill is January 26 (being a public holiday), the instrument shall fall due for payment on January 25 (Section 25 of the Negotiable Instruments Act). Again, if the Government declares January 25 as a holiday on account of the death of an important leader, the instrument shall fall due for payment on January 27.

Public Holiday: The expression 'public holiday' includes Sundays and any other days declared by the Central Government by notification in the official Gazette, to be a public holiday.

16.4 TRANSACTIONS REGARDING BILLS OF EXCHANGE

Generally, after acceptance of the drawee (or acceptor), a bill becomes an important asset in the hands of a drawer, and therefrom, the said bill is known as **bills receivable** in the hands of the drawer. At the same time, the bill creates a liability to its acceptor and is called **bills payable** to him. Where the volume of transactions is numerous through bills, special subsidiary books are opened known as **bills receivable book** and **bills payable book**. The specimen of a bills receivable book and Bills payable book are given in Box 16.3 and Box 16.4, respectively.

BOX 16.3   Bills receivable book

S. No.	No. of the bill	Name of the acceptor	Received from	Date of the bill	Term (Months)	Date of maturity	Amount (Rs.)	Remarks or how dealt with
1.		Mr. Pradip	Mr. Pradip	16.3.08	3	19.6.08	5,000	Endorsed
2.		Mr. Sanjay	Mr. Sanjay	19.3.08	2	22.5.08	4,000	Discounted
3.		Mr. Ram	Mr. Ram	31.3.08	2	3.6.08	3,000	

BOX 16.4   Bills payable book

S.No.	No. of the bill	Date of the bill	Name of the drawer	Payee	Term (Months)	Date of maturity	Amount (Rs.)	Remarks or how disposed of
1.		11.3.96	Mr. Kumar	Mr. Kumar	3	14.6.96	7,000	
2.		24.3.96	Mr.Roy	Mr.Roy	2	27.5.96	5,000	Renewed
3.		27.3.96	Mr.Sen	Mr.Sen	4	30.7.96	4,500	

When the bill is retained by the drawer till maturity, the transactions are recorded in the book of drawer and drawee as shown in Table 16.2.

TABLE 16.2   Recording of the Transactions

Transactions	In the books of Drawer		In the books of Drawee/Acceptor	
When goods are sold on credit	Drawee/Customer's A/c To Sales A/c	Dr.	Purchases A/c To Drawer's A/c	Dr.
When bill is drawn and accepted by drawee	Bills Receivable A/c To Drawee/Customer's A/c	Dr.	Drawer's A/c To Bills Payable A/c	Dr.
At maturity, when cash is received by the drawer (honoured)	Cash/Bank A/c To Bills Receivable A/c	Dr.	Bills Payable A/c To Cash/Bank A/c	Dr.

In the previous section, it has been stated that after a bill is drawn and duly accepted by the drawee, the said bill is retained by the drawer till maturity. At maturity or on the due date, the said bill is honoured. This is the most simple incident or transaction. However, a number of incidents/transactions may happen in respect of bills, which are as under:

1. After receiving a bill, the drawer may choose to accept any one of the following:
   (Thus, *any one of the following transactions may take place*)
   (a) When the bill is retained by the drawer till maturity
   (b) When endorsed to a creditor
   (c) When the bill is discounted with the bank
   (d) When the bill is sent to bank for collection.
2. At maturity (i.e., on the due date), the bill may be honoured.
3. At maturity, the bill may be dishonoured.
4. Retirement of a bill.
5. Renewal of a bill.

In the subsequent sections, the above stated transactions and their implications are explained.

16.5 ENDORSEMENT OF A BILL

Endorsement means signature of the holder or maker made with the purpose of transferring the document, i.e., the bill. The person who makes the endorsement is called the **endorser**, and the person to whom it is endorsed or given is called the **endorsee**. Types of endorsement are briefly discussed below.

1. Blank or general endorsement: The endorsement made when the endorser merely signs his/her name on the back or front of an instrument, then it is called a **blank endorsement**. In such an endorsement, the endorser does not make any mention of the name of the endorsee.

2. Special or full endorsement: If, with the signature, the endorser writes name of a specified person to whom, or to whose order, the instrument will be payable, then the endorsement made is called a **special endorsement**.

3. Restrictive endorsement: The endorsement made in such a manner so as to restrict the right of the endorsee to negotiate the instrument is called a **restrictive endorsement**.

4. Partial endorsement: An endorsement for transferring only a part of the amount due in a negotiable instrument is invalid. However, when an instrument has been partly paid, it can be negotiated for the balance after mentioning on the instrument the fact of part payments. Such endorsement is called **partial endorsement**.

5. Conditional or qualified endorsement: When an endorsement limits or increases the liability of the endorser, it is called conditional endorsement (or qualified).

6. Negotiation back endorsement: When, by a circular action, an endorser who has negotiated an instrument again becomes its holder by further negotiation, then, the endorsement made in such a fashion is known as **negotiation back endorsement**. Sometimes it may happen that during the course of negotiation the instrument may come back to the same person who had endorsed it previously. This is termed as "negotiation back". For example, P, the holder of bill, endorses it to Q. Q endorses it to R, R to S, S to T and T endorses it to P again.

When a bill is endorsed to a creditor, the drawer makes the following entry:

     Creditor's A/c   Dr.
         Bills Receivable A/c

Note: No entry is required in the books of the drawee/acceptor for such endorsement.

ILLUSTRATION 16.1 Anup sold goods to Kamal on January 1, 2008, for Rs.7,000. On that date, Anup drew a bill for Rs.7,000 on Kamal for three months after date and the said bill was duly accepted on January 2, 2008. On January 14, 2008, the bill was endorsed to Subhas who retained the bill till maturity. At maturity, the bill was honoured.

Show the necessary journal entries in the books of all the parties.

Solution

In the Books of Anup

Date	Particulars		L.F.	Amount Dr. (Rs.)	Amount Cr. (Rs.)
2008 Jan. 1	Kamal's A/c To Sales A/c (Being the goods sold on credit)	Dr.		7,000	7,000
2	Bills Receivable A/c To Kamal's A/c (Being the acceptance received for three months)	Dr.		7, 000	7,000
14	Subhas A/c To Bills Receivable A/c (Being the bill endorsed)	Dr.		7, 000	7,000
April 4	No entry is required at maturity				

In the Books of Subhas

Date	Particulars	L.F.	Amount Dr. (Rs.)	Amount Cr. (Rs.)
2008 Jan. 14	Bills Receivable A/c Dr. To Anup A/c (Being the bill received duly endorsed by Anup)		7,000	7,000
April 4	Cash/Bank A/c Dr. To Bills Receivable A/c [Being the bill honoured (i.e., cash received) at maturity]		7,000	7,000

In the Books of Kamal

Date	Particulars	L.F.	Amount Dr. (Rs.)	Amount Cr. (Rs.)
2008 Jan. 1	Purchases A/c Dr. To Anup A/c (Being the goods purchased on credit)		7,000	7,000
2	Anup A/c Dr. To Bills Payable A/c (Being the acceptance given for three months)		7,000	7,000
April 4	Bills Payable A/c Dr. To Cash/Bank A/c (Being the bill paid at maturity)		7,000	7,000

Working Note

Here, the bill is drawn 'after date'. As such, the period is calculated or counted from the date of drawing the bill. Thus, the three-month period is calculated here from January 1. Hence, the date of maturity is three months + three days from January 1, i.e., April 4.

16.6 DISCOUNTING OF BILL

When a bill is taken to a bank before its maturity for immediate payment, cash is credited by the bank after deducting their discount charges. This act is known as **discounting of bill**. The bank will deduct a small amount as discount charges on the basis of the rate of interest charged for the period from the date of discounting to the date of maturity of the bill.

In case of discounting of a bill, the following entry is required to be shown in the books of the drawer only:

Bank A/c   Dr. (For actual amount received)
Discount A/c   Dr. (For the amount of discount charges)
    To Bills Receivable A/c   (Original amount of the bill)

Note:

No entry is required to be shown in the books of the drawee for the above discounting. Here, discount charges are to be calculated as under:

$$\text{Discount charges} = \frac{(\text{Amount of bill}) \times \left(\begin{array}{c}\text{Rate of}\\\text{interest charged}\end{array}\right) \times \left(\begin{array}{c}\text{Period from the date}\\\text{of discounting to the date}\\\text{of maturity of bill}\end{array}\right)}{365}$$

ILLUSTRATION 16.2 On January 1, 2008, Mr. Gills drew a bill for Rs. 5,000 on Mr. Katkar for three months after sight and the said bill was duly accepted on January 3, 2008. On January 15, 2008, the bill was discounted with the bank at 12 % p.a. At maturity, the bill was honoured.

Show the necessary journal entries in the books of both the parties.

Solution

In the Books of Mr. Gills

Date	Particulars	L.F.	Amount Dr. (Rs.)	Amount Cr. (Rs.)
2008 Jan. 3	Bills Receivable A/c Dr.		5,000	
	To Katkar's A/c			5,000
	(Being the acceptance received for three months)			
Feb. 1	Bank A/c Dr.		4,866	
	Discount A/c Dr.		134	
	To Bills Receivable A/c			5,000
	(Being the bill discounted with the bank @ 12 % p.a.)			
April 6	No entry is required at maturity			

In the Books of Mr. Katkar

Date	Particulars	L.F.	Amount Dr. (Rs.)	Amount Cr. (Rs.)
2008 Jan. 3	Gills A/c Dr.		5,000	
	To Bills Payable A/c			5,000
	(Being the acceptance given for three months)			
April 6	Bills Payable A/c Dr.		5, 000	
	To Cash/Bank A/c			5, 000
	(Being the bill paid at maturity)			

Working Notes

1. Here, the bill is drawn 'after sight'. For calculating the due date or maturity date, the period is to be counted from the date of acceptance of the bill. Hence, the due date for the present bill is three months + three days from January 3, i.e., April 6.

2. Calculation of discount charges:
   Bill is discounted on January 15. Thus, discount charges to be paid for the following days:

January	16 days
February	29 days
March	31 days
April	6 days
Total	82 days

   The bill was discounted with the bank 82 days before the date of maturity at 12% p.a.

   Discount charges = $(12/100 \times 5,000) \times (82/366)$ = Rs. 134.42 = Rs. 134 (approx.)

16.7 SENDING BILL TO BANK FOR COLLECTION

When it is not possible for the holder of a bill to collect the bill on the due date, he/she may send the bill to the bank with the instruction that whenever it becomes due, its amount may be collected on behalf of the holder and the proceeds credited into his/her account. This is known as **bill sent to bank for collection** and it is done before the due date of a bill.

When the bill is sent to bank for collection, the following entry is required to be shown in the books of drawer only:

Bill for Collection/Bank for Collection A/c   Dr.
        To Bills Receivable A/c

Here, bank account is not debited immediately though the bill is deposited in the bank as the payment of the bill will be collected by the bank subsequently. Thus, when the bank realizes the proceeds of the bill from the acceptor on behalf of customer, it informs the matter to the customer or the drawer accordingly. However, the bank charges certain amount for this service. On receipt of the said information, the drawer makes the following entry:

Bank A/c   Dr.
     To Bill for Collection/Bank for Collection A/c

ILLUSTRATION 16.3 On March 1, 2008, Mr. Dhar drew a bill for Rs. 8,000 on Mr. Kanoria for two months and the said bill was duly accepted on the same date. On April 29, 2008, the bill was sent to bank for collection. At maturity the bill was honoured.

Give the necessary journal entries in the books of Mr. Dhar.

Solution

In the Books of Mr. Dhar

Date	Particulars		L.F.	Amount Dr. (Rs.)	Amount Cr. (Rs.)
2008 March 1	Bills Receivable A/c To Kanoria's A/c (Being the acceptance received for two months)	Dr.		8,000	8,000
April 29	Bill for Collection A/c To Bills Receivable A/c (Being the bill sent to bank for collection)	Dr.		8,000	8,000
May 4	Bank A/c To Bill for Collection A/c (Being the bill collected by the bank)	Dr.		8,000	8,000

ILLUSTRATION 16.4 Rahul drew a bill for three months on Pritam for Rs. 4,000 on January 1, 2008. Pritam accepted the bill duly on that date. Give the necessary journal entries in the books of Rahul under each of the following cases:

1. The bill was retained by Rahul till maturity and was duly honoured.
2. The bill was endorsed to Latif in full settlement of his account of Rs. 4,100.
3. The bill was sent to bank for collection and was honoured at maturity.
4. The bill was discounted with the bank immediately at Rs. 3,750 and was duly honoured.

Solution

In the Books of Rahul

Date	Particulars		L.F.	Amount Dr. (Rs.)	Amount Cr. (Rs.)
2008 Jan. 1	Bills Receivable A/c To Pritam's A/c (Being the acceptance received for three months) [The above entry is required for all four cases]	Dr.		4,000	4,000
April 4	Case 1 Cash/Bank A/c To Bills Receivable A/c (Being the bill realized at maturity)	Dr.		4,000	4,000

?	Case 2
	Latif's A/c
	   To Bills Receivable A/c
	   To Discount Received A/c
	(Being the bill endorsed)
		Dr.		4,100	4,000
					100

(Contd.)

Date	Particulars		L.F.	Amount Dr. (Rs.)	Amount Cr. (Rs.)
4	No entry is required at maturity				
?	Case 3				
	Bill for Collection A/c	Dr.		4,000	
	To Bills Receivable A/c				4,000
	(Being the bill sent to bank for collection)				
4	Bank A/c	Dr.			
	To Bill for Collection A/c				
	(Being the bill collected by the bank)				
January 1	Case 4				
	Bank A/c	Dr.		3,750	
	Discount A/c	Dr.		250	
	To Bills Receivable A/c				4,000
	(Being the bill discounted with the bank)				
April 4	No entry is required at maturity				

16.8 RETIREMENT OF A BILL

The act of payment of a bill by the acceptor before its maturity with the consent of the drawer is known as **retirement of a bill**. Under such circumstances, the drawer allows some amount of rebate for the period from the date of retirement to the date of maturity of the bill to encourage the acceptor for premature payment.

The following are the accounting entries required to be shown in the books of drawer and drawee at maturity:

In the books of drawer:

Bank/Cash A/c	Dr. (Actual amount received)
Rebate A/c	Dr. (Rebate allowed)
To Bills Receivable A/c	(Original amount of the bill)

In the books of drawee:

Bills Payable A/c	Dr. (Original amount of the bill)
To Bank/Cash A/c	(Actual amount paid)
To Rebate A/c	(Rebate received)

ILLUSTRATION 16.5 John drew a bill for Rs. 6,000 on Robin on January 1, 2008, for three months. The said bill was duly accepted by Robin immediately. One month before maturity, Robin informed John that he wanted to make payment of the bill immediately and acted accordingly. John allowed him a rebate @ 12 % p.a.

Give the necessary journal entries in the books of both the parties.

Solution

In the Books of John

Date	Particulars		L.F.	Amount Dr. (Rs.)	Amount Cr. (Rs.)
2008 Jan. 1	Bills Receivable A/c	Dr.		6,000	
	To Robin's A/c				6,000
	(Being the acceptance received for three months)				
March 4	Bank A/c	Dr.		5,940	
	Rebate Allowed A/c	Dr.		60	
	To Bills Receivable A/c				6,000
	(Being the bill retired by Robin one month before maturity and was allowed a rebate @ 12 % p.a.)				
April 4	No entry is required at maturity				

In the Books of Robin

Date	Particulars		L.F.	Amount Dr. (Rs.)	Amount Cr. (Rs.)
2008 Jan. 1	John A/c	Dr.		6,000	
	To Bills Payable A/c				6,000
	(Being the acceptance given for three months)				
March 4	Bills Payable A/c	Dr.		6,000	
	To Cash/Bank A/c				5,940
	To Rebate Received A/c				60
	(Being the bill retired one month before maturity and received a rebate @ 12% p.a.)				
April 4	No entry is required at maturity				

16.9 DISHONOUR OF A BILL OF EXCHANGE

A bill may be dishonoured for the following two reasons:

Dishonoured by non-acceptance: When after due presentation, a bill is not accepted by the drawee, the bill is said to be dishonoured.

Dishonoured by non-payments: When at maturity, the acceptor refuses to make payment of a bill, the bill is dishonoured.

Here, accounting treatment is required to be made for dishonour by non-payments only in the books of drawer and drawee both. The entries for dishonour of a bill is generally fixed in the books of a drawee, but in case of a drawer, it depends on as to how he has used the bill previously, and on that basis, entries are required to be shown in the books of the drawer.

16.9.1 Noting and Protesting

When a bill of exchange or a promissory note has been dishonoured by non-acceptance or non-payment, the holder may cause such dishonour to be noted by a notary public. This is known as **noting**. The noting must be done within a reasonable time after the dishonour, and the date of dishonour must specifically mention the reason for such dishonour and the notary's charges for noting. Noting is the authentic and official proof of presentment and dishonour of a negotiable instrument.

When a promissory note or a bill of exchange has been dishonoured, the holder may, within a reasonable time, get such dishonour noted by a notary public and receive a certificate for the same. Such certificate is known as **protesting**.

Distinction between noting and protesting

Noting means mere recording of the fact of dishonour by a notary public, whereas protesting is a certificate issued by the notary public after noting has been done.

Notary public

A **notary public** is an officer appointed by the Government to perform the functions such as noting, protesting, etc., as given under the Negotiable Instrument Act. The Notaries Act, 1952, regulates the functions of a notary public.

Noting charge

When noting is done through a notary public for recording the fact of dishonour, an amount is charged by the notary public as his/her fee known as **noting charge**. At first, it is paid by the holder of the bill; subsequently, it is to be borne by the acceptor. Hence, noting charge is not the expense of the holder; it is the expenditure of the acceptor.

Table 16.3 shows the accounting entries when a bill is dishonoured at maturity.

TABLE 16.3 Accounting Entries in Case of Dishonour of a Bill at Maturity

Transactions: How the bill was used by the drawer previously	In the books of drawer		In the books of drawee/Acceptor	
When no noting charge is paid:				

1. When the bill is retained by the drawer till maturity	Acceptor's A/c
	    To Bills Receivable A/c
		Dr.	Bills Payable A/c
			    To Drawer's A/c
				Dr.

2. When the bill is discounted with the bank	Acceptor's A/c
	    To Bank A/c
		Dr.	Bills Payable A/c
			    To Drawer's A/c
				Dr.

3. When endorsed to a creditor	Acceptor's A/c
	    To Creditor's A/c
		Dr.	Bills Payable A/c
			    To Drawer's A/c
				Dr.

4. When sent to bank for collection	Acceptor's A/c
	    To Bill for Collection A/c
		Dr.	Bills Payable A/c
			    To Drawer's A/c
				Dr.

When noting charge is paid:				

1. When the bill is retained by the drawer till maturity	Acceptor's A/c
	    To Bills Receivable A/c
	    To Cash A/c (Noting charge)
		Dr.	Bills Payable A/c
			Noting Charge A/c
			    To Drawer's A/c
				Dr.
				Dr.

2. When the bill is discounted with with the bank	Acceptor's A/c
	    To Bank A/c
	    (Bill amount + Noting charge)
		Dr.	Bills Payable A/c
			Noting Charge A/c
			    To Drawer's A/c
				Dr.
				Dr.

3. When endorsed to a creditor	Acceptor's A/c
	    To Creditor's A/c
	    (Bill amount + Noting charge)
		Dr.	Bills Payable A/c
			Noting Charge A/c
			    To Drawer's A/c
				Dr.
				Dr.

4. When sent to bank for collection	Acceptor's A/c
	    To Bill for Collection A/c
	    To Bank A/c (Noting charge)
		Dr.	Bills Payable A/c
			Noting Charge A/c
			    To Drawer's A/c
				Dr.
				Dr.

ILLUSTRATION 16.6 On April 1, 2008, Milind drew three bills for Rs. 3,000, Rs. 5,000 and Rs. 2,500 for three months, two months and one month, respectively, on Pratap. On that date, the above bills were accepted by Pratap. On April 12, 2008, the first bill was endorsed to Manas. On May 1, 2008, the second bill was discounted with the bank at Rs.4,750. The third bill was retained by the drawer till maturity.

At maturity, all the bills were dishonoured. Give necessary journal entries in the books of all the parties.

Solution

In the Books of Milind

Date	Particulars		L.F.	Amount Dr. (Rs.)	Amount Cr. (Rs.)

2008 April 1	Bills Receivable A/c
	    To Pratap's A/c
	    (Being the acceptance received for three months)
		Dr.		3,000	3,000

1	Bills Receivable A/c
	    To Pratap's A/c
	    (Being the acceptance received for two months)
		Dr.		5,000	5,000

1	Bills Receivable A/c
	    To Pratap's A/c
	    (Being the acceptance received for one month)
		Dr.		2,500	2,500

	Or, Instead of above three entries a single entry may be shown as below				

(Contd.)

Date	Particulars		L.F.	Amount Dr. (Rs.)	Amount Cr. (Rs.)
1	Bills Receivable A/c	Dr.		10,500	
	To Pratap's A/c				10,500
	(Being three acceptances received for Rs. 3,000, Rs. 5,000 and Rs. 2,500 for three months, two months and one month, respectively)				
April 12	Manas A/c	Dr.		3,000	
	To Bills Receivable A/c				3,000
	(Being the bill endorsed)				
May 1	Bank A/c	Dr.		4,750	
	Discount A/c	Dr.		250	
	To Bills Receivable A/c				5,000
	(Being the bill discounted with the bank)				
4	Pratap's A/c	Dr.		2,500	
	To Bills Receivable A/c				2,500
	(Being the third bill dishonoured at maturity)				
June 4	Pratap's A/c	Dr.		5,000	
	To Bank A/c				
	(Being the discounted bill dishonoured at maturity)				5,000
July 4	Pratap's A/c	Dr.		3,000	
	To Manas A/c				3,000
	(Being the endorsed bill dishonoured at maturity)				

In the Books of Manas

Date	Particulars		L.F.	Amount Dr. (Rs.)	Amount Cr. (Rs.)
2008 April 12	Bills Receivable A/c	Dr.		3,000	
	To Milind A/c				3,000
	(Being the bill received duly endorsed by Milind)				
July 4	Milind A/c	Dr.		3,000	
	To Bills Receivable A/c				3,000
	(Being the bill dishonoured at maturity)				

In the Books of Pratap

Date	Particulars		L.F.	Amount Dr. (Rs.)	Amount Cr. (Rs.)
2008 April 1	Milind A/c	Dr.		3,000	
	To Bills Payable A/c				3,000
	(Being the acceptance given for three months)				
1	Milind A/c	Dr.		5,000	
	To Bills Payable A/c				5,000
	(Being the acceptance given for two months)				
1	Milind A/c	Dr.		2,500	
	To Bills Payable A/c				2,500
	(Being the acceptance given for one month)				
	Or, instead of above three entries, a single entry may be shown as below.				
1	Milind A/c	Dr.		10,500	
	To Bills Payable A/c				10,500
	(Being the acceptance given for three bills for Rs. 3,000, Rs. 5,000 and Rs. 2,500 for three months, two months and one month, respectively)				
May 4	Bills Payable A/c	Dr.		2,500	
	To Milind A/c				2,500
	(Being the third bill dishonoured at maturity)				

(Contd.)

Date	Particulars		L.F.	Amount Dr. (Rs.)	Amount Cr. (Rs.)
June 4	Bills Payable A/c To Milind A/c (Being the second bill dishonoured at maturity)	Dr.		5,000	5,000
July 4	Bills Payable A/c To Milind A/c (Being the first bill dishonoured at maturity)	Dr.		3,000	3,000

ILLUSTRATION 16.7 Anupam sold goods to Mahim for Rs. 8,100 on credit on January 12, 2008. On January 15, 2008, Anupam drew two bills for Rs. 4,500 and Rs. 3,600, respectively, for three months on Mahim. Mahim duly accepted the same on that date. On January 21, 2008, Anupam discounted the first bill with his bank at 10% p.a. On February 2, 2008, he endorsed the second bill to Gopi in full settlement of his account of Rs. 3,500. At maturity, the second bill was honoured but the first bill was dishonoured and noting charge incurred Rs. 40.

Give necessary entries in the books of Anupam, Gopi and Mahim. Show the necessary ledger accounts in the books of Anupam and Anupam's Account in the books of Mahim.

Solution

In the Books of Anupam

Date	Particulars		L.F.	Amount Dr. (Rs.)	Amount Cr. (Rs.)
2008 Jan. 12	Mahim A/c To Sales A/c (Being the goods sold on credit)	Dr.		8,100	8,100
15	Bills Receivable A/c To Mahim's A/c (Being two acceptances of Rs. 4,500 and 3,600 received for three months)	Dr.		8,100	8,100
21	Bank A/c Discount A/c To Bills Receivable A/c (Being the bill discounted with the bank at 10% p.a. 88 days before maturity)	Dr. Dr.		4,392 108	4,500
February 2	Interest A/c To Gopi's A/c [Being the interest charged by Gopi (Rs. 3,600 – Rs. 3,500) Rs. 100]	Dr.		100	100
2	Gopi's A/c To Bills Receivable A/c (Being the bill endorsed to Gopi in full settlement of his claim)	Dr.		3,600	3,600
April 18	Mahim A/c To Bank A/c (Being the discounted bill dishonoured and noting charge paid Rs.40)	Dr.		4,540	4,540

Ledger Accounts

Dr.   **Mahim's Account**   Cr.

Date	Particulars	Amount (Rs.)	Date	Particulars	Amount (Rs.)
2008 Jan. 12	To Sales A/c	8,100	2008 Jan. 15	By Bills Receivable A/c	8,100
April 18	To Bank A/c	4,540			

Dr.   **Sales Account**   Cr.

Date	Particulars	Amount (Rs.)	Date	Particulars	Amount (Rs.)
2008			Jan. 12	By Mahim A/c	8,100

Dr.   **Bills Receivable Account**   Cr.

Date	Particulars	Amount (Rs.)	Date	Particulars	Amount (Rs.)
2008 Jan. 15	To Mahim A/c	8,100	2008 Jan. 21	By Bank A/c	4,392
			21	By Discount A/c	108
			February 2	By Gopi's A/c	3,600
		8,100			8,100

Dr.   **Discount Account**   Cr.

Date	Particulars	Amount (Rs.)	Date	Particulars	Amount (Rs.)
2008 Jan. 21	To Bills Receivable A/c	108	2008		

Dr.   **Bank Account**   Cr.

Date	Particulars	Amount (Rs.)	Date	Particulars	Amount (Rs.)
2008 Jan. 21	To Bills Receivable A/c	4,392	2008		

Dr.   **Interest Account**   Cr.

Date	Particulars	Amount (Rs.)	Date	Particulars	Amount (Rs.)
2008 Feb. 2	Gopi's A/c	100	2008		

Dr.   **Gopi's Account**   Cr.

Date	Particulars	Amount (Rs.)	Date	Particulars	Amount (Rs.)
2008 Feb. 2	Bills Receivable A/c	3,600	2008	By Balance B/d	3,500
			February 2	By Interest A/c	100
		3,600			3,600

In the Books of Gopi

Date	Particulars	L.F.	Amount Dr. (Rs.)	Amount Cr. (Rs.)
2008 Feb. 2	Anupam A/c Dr.		100	
	To Interest Received A/c			100
	(Being the interest charged on the outstanding balances)			
2	Bills Receivable A/c Dr.		3,600	
	To Anupam A/c			3,600
	(Being the bill received duly endorsed by Anupam)			
April 18	Bank A/c Dr.		3,600	
	To Bills Receivable A/c			3,600
	(Being the bill honoured at maturity)			

In the Books of Mahim

Date	Particulars	L.F.	Amount Dr. (Rs.)	Amount Cr. (Rs.)
2008 Jan. 12	Purchases A/c Dr.		8,100	
	To Anupam A/c			8,100
	(Being the goods purchased on credit)			
Jan. 15	Anupam's A/c Dr.		8,100	
	To Bills Payable A/c			8,100
	(Being the acceptance given for two bills of Rs. 4,500 and Rs. 3,600 respectively, for three months)			
April 18	Bills Payable A/c Dr.		4,500	
	Noting Charge A/c Dr.		40	
	To Anupam's A/c			4,540
	(Being the first bill dishonoured at maturity and noting charge being Rs. 40)			
18	Bills Payable A/c Dr.		3,600	
	To Bank A/c			3,600
	(Being the second bill honoured at maturity)			

Dr.					**Anupam's Account**		Cr.
Date	Particulars	Amount (Rs.)		Date	Particulars		Amount (Rs.)
2008 Jan. 15	To Bills Payable A/c	8,100		2008 Jan. 12	By Purchases A/c		8,100
				April 18	By Bills Payable A/c		4,500
					Noting Charge A/c		40

Working Notes

1. Calculation of discount charges:

   Bill is discounted on January 21. Thus, discount charges are to be paid for the following days:

January	10 days
February	29 days
March	31 days
April	18 days
Total	88 days

   The bill was discounted with the bank 88 days before the date of maturity at 10 % p.a.

   Discount charges = $(10/100 \times 4,500) \times (88/366)$ = Rs. 108.20 = Rs. 108 (approx.)

2. It is assumed here that the second bill was retained by Gopi till maturity.

ILLUSTRATION 16.8   On January 15, 2008, Mr. Lakhani drew two bills for Rs. 6,000 and Rs. 4,000, respectively, for three months on Mr. Bhatia and the bills were duly accepted. On January 25, 2008, Mr. Lakhani endorsed the first bill to Mr. Singhania in full settlement of his account of Rs. 6,200. The second bill was retained by Mr. Lakhani till maturity. At maturity, both the bills were dishonoured and noting charges incurred Rs. 40 and Rs. 30, respectively.

Give necessary entries in the books of Mr. Lakhani, Mr. Singhania and Mr. Bhatia.

Solution

In the Books of Mr. Lakhani

Date	Particulars		L.F.	Amount Dr. (Rs.)	Amount Cr. (Rs.)
2008 Jan. 15	Bills Receivable A/c	Dr.		10,000	
	To Bhatia's A/c				10,000
	(Being two acceptances of Rs.6,000 and 4,000 for three months received)				
25	Singhania's A/c	Dr.		6,200	
	To Bills Receivable A/c				6,000
	To Discount Received A/c				200
	(Being the bill of Rs.6,000 endorsed to Mr. Singhania in full settlement of his claim of Rs. 6,200)				
April 18	Bhatia's A/c	Dr.		6,040	
	Discount Received A/c	Dr.		200	
	To Singhania's A/c				6,240
	(Being Mr. Bhatia's acceptance of Rs.6,000 endorsed to Mr. Singhania dishonoured at maturity and the discount received from him cancelled, and noting charge incurred Rs. 40)				
April 18	Bhatia's A/c	Dr.		4,030	
	To Bills Receivable A/c				4,000
	To Cash A/c				30
	(Being Mr. Bhatia's acceptance of Rs.4,000 dishonoured at maturity, and noting charge incurred Rs. 30)				

In the Books of Mr. Singhania

Date	Particulars		L.F.	Amount Dr. (Rs.)	Amount Cr. (Rs.)
2008 Jan. 25	Bills Receivable A/c	Dr.		6,000	
	Discount Allowed A/c	Dr.		200	
	To Lakhani A/c				6,200
	(Being the bill received duly endorsed by Mr.Lakhani and allowed discount Rs. 200)				
April 18	Lakhani 's A/c	Dr.		6,240	
	To Bills Receivable A/c				6,000
	To Discount Allowed A/c				200
	To Cash A/c				40
	(Being the bill of Rs.6,000 endorsed by Mr. Lakhani dishonoured at maturity, discount allowed to him cancelled and noting charge incurred Rs. 40)				

In the Books of Mr. Bhatia

Date	Particulars		L.F.	Amount Dr. (Rs.)	Amount Cr. (Rs.)
2008 Jan. 15	Lakhani's A/c	Dr.		10,000	
	To Bills Payable A/c				10,000
	(Being the acceptance given for two bills of Rs.6,000 and Rs. 4,000, respectively, for three months)				
April 18	Bills Payable A/c	Dr.		6,000	
	Noting Charge A/c	Dr.		40	
	To Lakhani's A/c				6,040
	(Being the first bill dishonoured at maturity and noting charge being Rs.40)				
18	Bills Payable A/c	Dr.		4,000	
	Noting Charge A/c	Dr.		30	
	To Lakhani's A/c				4,030
	(Being the bill dishonoured at maturity and noting charge being Rs.30)				

Working Note

It is assumed here that the first bill was retained by Mr. Singhania till maturity.

ILLUSTRATION 16.9 On January 4, 2008, Mr. Hiralal accepted two bills for Rs. 9,000 and Rs. 7,000 for two months and three months, respectively, drawn by Mr. Khanna. On January 16, 2008, Mr. Khanna endorsed the first bill to Mr. Dalvir in full settlement of his Account of Rs. 12,000 and a cheque of Rs. 2,800. Mr. Dalvir discounted the bill immediately with his bank at Rs. 8,910. The second bill was sent to bank for collection by Mr. Khanna on April 3. At maturity, the second bill was dishonoured and noting charge incurred Rs. 50.

Give necessary entries in the books of Mr. Khanna, Mr. Hiralal and Mr. Dalvir.

Solution

In the Books of Khanna

Date	Particulars		L.F.	Amount Dr. (Rs.)	Amount Cr. (Rs.)
2008 Jan. 4	Bills Receivable A/c	Dr.		16,000	
	To Hiralal's A/c				16,000
	(Being two acceptances of Rs. 9,000 and 7,000 for two months and three months, respectively, received)				
16	Dalvir's A/c	Dr.		12,000	
	To Bills Receivable A/c				9,000
	To Bank A/c				2,800
	To Discount Received A/c				200
	(Being the bill of Rs. 9,000 and a cheque of Rs. 2,800 endorsed to Dalvir in full settlement of his account of Rs. 12,000, and received discount Rs. 200)				
April 3	Bill for Collection A/c	Dr.		7,000	
	To Bills Receivable A/c				7,000
	(Being the bill sent to bank for collection)				
7	Hiralal's A/c	Dr.		7,050	
	To Bill for Collection A/c				7,000
	To Bank A/c				50
	(Being Hiralal's acceptance of Rs. 7,000 dishonoured at maturity, and noting charge incurred Rs. 50)				

In the Books of Dalvir

Date	Particulars		L.F.	Amount Dr. (Rs.)	Amount Cr. (Rs.)
2008 Jan. 16	Bills Receivable A/c	Dr.		9,000	
	Bank A/c	Dr.		2,800	
	Discount Allowed A/c	Dr.		200	
	To Khanna's A/c				12,000
	(Being the bill of Rs.9,000 and a cheque of Rs.2,800 received and allowed discount Rs. 200)				
16	Bank A/c	Dr.		8,910	
	Discount A/c	Dr.		90	
	To Bills Receivable A/c				9,000
	(Being the bill discounted with the bank)				

In the Books of Hiralal

Date	Particulars		L.F.	Amount Dr. (Rs.)	Amount Cr. (Rs.)
2008 Jan. 15	Khanna's A/c To Bills Payable A/c (Being acceptance given for two bills of Rs. 9,000 and Rs. 7,000 for two months and three months respectively)	Dr.		16,000	16,000
March 7	Bills Payable A/c To Bank A/c (Being payment of bill made at maturity)	Dr.		9,000	9,000
April 7	Bills Payable A/c Noting Charge A/c To Khanna's A/c (Being the second bill dishonoured at maturity and noting charge being Rs. 50)	Dr. Dr.		7,000 50	7,050

16.10 RENEWAL OF BILL

Sometimes, it is not possible for an acceptor to make payment of a bill (accepted by him/her) in due time. Considering this difficulty, he/she may request the drawer for renewal of the bill by cancellation of the old bill and drawing a new one to replace the old. If it is accepted by the drawer, then it is known as **renewal of bill**. Under this arrangement, the drawee is liable to pay some amount of interest at a fixed rate on the outstanding balances for the extended period. The interest so charged may be paid in cash, or it may be included with the new bill (i.e., Outstanding amount + Interest = Amount of New Bill).

Table 16.4 shows the accounting entries recorded in the book of drawer and drawee in case of renewal of a bill.

TABLE 16.4 Accounting Entries on the Renewal of Bill

Transactions	In the books of drawer		In the books of drawee/acceptor	
Cancellation of old bill (i.e., dishonour entry)	Acceptor's A/c To Bills Receivable A/c	Dr.	Bills Payable A/c To Drawer's A/c	Dr.
For any part payment received/made	Cash/Bank A/c To Acceptor's A/c	Dr.	Drawer's A/c To Cash/Bank A/c	Dr.
For charging interest on the outstanding balances for the extended period :				
When interest is received in cash	Cash A/c To Interest Received A/c	Dr.	Interest A/c To Cash A/c	Dr.
When interest is not received in cash	Acceptor's A/c To Interest A/c	Dr.	Interest A/c To Drawer's A/c	Dr.
When the new or renewed bill is accepted	Bills Receivable A/c To Acceptor's A/c	Dr.	Drawer's A/c To Bills Payable A/c	Dr.

Here, new or renewed bill amount = Old Bill or Outstanding Amount (Old Bill – Cash Received (if any) + Interest (if not paid in cash).

ILLUSTRATION 16.10 Mr. Sitaram received a bill for Rs. 11,000 for three months on January 7, 2008, from Mr. Reshmia, the acceptor. At maturity, Mr. Reshmia requests Mr. Sitaram to cancel the above bill and draw a new bill for two months including interest at 12% p.a. for the extended period. Mr. Sitaram acts accordingly. At maturity, the new bill was duly honoured.

Show necessary entries in the books of Mr. Sitaram and Mr. Reshmia.

Solution

In the Books of Sitaram

Date	Particulars		L.F.	Amount Dr. (Rs.)	Amount Cr. (Rs.)
2008 Jan. 7	Bills Receivable A/c	Dr.		11,000	
	To Reshmia's A/c				11,000
	(Being the acceptance received from Reshmia payable after three months)				
April 10	Reshmia's A/c	Dr.		11,000	
	To Bills Receivable A/c				11,000
	(Being Reshmia's acceptance of Rs.11,000 cancelled)				
10	Reshmia's A/c	Dr.		220	
	To Interest A/c				220
	(Being the interest charged @ 12 % p.a. on Rs.11,000 for two months)				
10	Bills Receivable A/c	Dr.		11,220	
	To Reshmia's A/c				11,220
	(Being the acceptance received from Reshmia payable after two months)				
June 13	Bank A/c	Dr.		11,220	
	To Bills Receivable A/c				11,220
	(Being the renewed bill honoured at maturity)				

In the Books of Mr. Reshmia

Date	Particulars		L.F.	Amount Dr. (Rs.)	Amount Cr. (Rs.)
2008 Jan. 7	Sitaram's A/c	Dr.		11,000	
	To Bills Payable A/c				11,000
	(Being the acceptance given for three months)				
April 10	Bills Payable A/c	Dr.		11,000	
	To Sitaram's A/c				11,000
	(Being the acceptance cancelled at maturity for renewal)				
April 10	Interest A/c	Dr.		220	
	To Sitaram's A/c				220
	(Being the interest charged @ 12 % p.a. on Rs.11,000 for two months)				
April 10	Sitaram's A/c	Dr.		11,220	
	To Bills Payable A/c				11,220
	(Being the acceptance given for two months)				
June 13	Bills Payable A/c	Dr.		11,220	
	To Bank A/c				11,220
	(Being payment of the renewed bill made at maturity)				

ILLUSTRATION 16.11 Mr. Pathan received a bill for Rs. 8,000 for three months on January 12, 2008, from Mr. Dhali, the acceptor. At maturity, Mr. Dhali informed Mr. Pathan that he is not in a position to pay the bill, but was ready to pay Rs. 3,000 in cash and requested him to draw a fresh bill for three months for the balance amount due together with an interest @18% p.a. Mr. Pathan acted accordingly. He then discounted the new bill immediately with the bank at 12% p.a. At maturity, the new bill was duly honoured.

Give necessary entries in the books of Mr. Pathan and Mr. Dhali.

Solution

In the Books of Mr. Pathan

Date	Particulars		L.F.	Amount Dr. (Rs.)	Amount Cr. (Rs.)
2008 Jan. 12	Bills Receivable A/c	Dr.		8,000	
	To Dhali's A/c				8,000
	(Being the acceptance received from Mr. Dhali payable after three months)				
April 15	Dhali 's A/c	Dr.		8,000	
	To Bills Receivable A/c				8,000
	(Being Dhali 's acceptance of Rs.8,000 cancelled)				
15	Cash A/c	Dr.		3,000	
	To Dhali's A/c				3,000
	(Being cash paid by Mr. Dhali)				
15	Dhali's A/c	Dr.		225	
	To Interest A/c				225
	(Being the interest charged @ 18 % p.a. on Rs.5,000 for three months)				
15	Bills Receivable A/c	Dr.		5,225	
	To Dhali's A/c				5,225
	(Being the acceptance received from Dhali payable after three months)				
15	Bank A/c	Dr.		5,068	
	Discount A/c	Dr.		157	
	To Bills Receivable A/c				5,225
	(Being the bill discounted with the bank @ 12% p.a. three months before maturity)				

In the Books of Mr. Dhali

Date	Particulars		L.F.	Amount Dr. (Rs.)	Amount Cr. (Rs.)
2008 Jan. 12	Pathan's A/c	Dr.		8,000	
	To Bills Payable A/c				8,000
	(Being the acceptance given for three months)				
April 15	Bills Payable A/c	Dr.		8,000	
	To Pathan 's A/c				8,000
	(Being the acceptance cancelled at maturity for renewal)				
15	Pathan's A/c	Dr.		3,000	
	To Cash A/c				3,000
	(Being cash paid to Mr. Pathan)				
15	Interest A/c	Dr.		225	
	To Pathan's A/c				225
	(Being the interest charged @12 % p.a. on Rs.5,000 for three months)				
15	Pathan's A/c	Dr.		5,225	
	To Bills Payable A/c				5,225
	(Being the acceptance given for three months)				
July 18	Bills Payable A/c	Dr.		5,225	
	To Bank A/c				5,225
	(Being payment of the renewed bill made at maturity)				

ILLUSTRATION 16.12 On March 15, 2008, Mr. D'Souza discounted a bill for Rs. 5,000 with his bank at 18% p.a. maturing on May 15. At maturity, the bill was dishonoured and noting charge incurred Rs. 50. On the due date, Mr. Shetti, the acceptor of the above bill, paid Rs. 1,200 in cash plus discount charges in cash and accepted a new bill of Rs. 3,950 for the balance amount due for three months to Mr. D'Souza.

Give necessary journal entries in the books of Mr. D'Souza and Mr. Shetti.

Solution

In the Books of Mr. D'Souza

Date	Particulars	L.F.	Amount Dr. (Rs.)	Amount Cr. (Rs.)
2008 March 15	Bank A/c Dr.		4,850	
	Discount A/c Dr.		150	
	To Bills Receivable A/c			5,000
	(Being the bill discounted with the bank @ 18% p.a. two months before maturity)			
May 15	Shetti's A/c Dr.		5,050	
	To Bank A/c			5,050
	(Being the discounted bill dishonoured and noting charge being Rs. 50)			
15	Cash A/c Dr.		1,350	
	To Shetti's A/c			1,200
	To Discount Charges A/c			150
	(Being cash received from Mr. Shetti on account and received discount charges)			
15	Shetti's A/c Dr.		100	
	To Interest A/c			100
	(Being the interest charged for the extended period)			
15	Bills Receivable A/c Dr.		3,950	
	To Shetti's A/c			3,950
	(Being the renewed bill received from Mr. Shetti payable after three months)			

In the Books of Mr. Shetti

Date	Particulars	L.F.	Amount Dr. (Rs.)	Amount Cr. (Rs.)
2008 May 15	Bills Payable A/c Dr.		5,000	
	Noting Charge A/c Dr.		50	
	To D'Souza's A/c			5,050
	(Being the acceptance dishonoured at maturity)			
15	D'Souza's A/c Dr.		1,200	
	Discount Charges A/c Dr.		150	
	To Cash A/c			1,350
	(Being cash paid to Mr. D'Souza on account and paid discount charges)			
15	Interest A/c Dr.		100	
	To D'Souza's A/c			100
	(Being the interest charged on the renewed bill)			
15	D'Souza's A/c Dr.		3,950	
	To Bills Payable A/c			3,950
	(Being the acceptance given for three months)			

Working Note

Calculation of interest on the renewed bill.

	Rs.
Original bill amount	5,000
Add: Noting charge	50
Total amount receivable	5,050
Less: Cash received	1,200
Net amount receivable	3,850
New bill accepted	3,950
Net amount receivable	3,850
Excess amount included	100

Here, the excess amount included within the new bill is to be considered as interest charged.

16.11 INSOLVENCY OF ACCEPTOR

When an acceptor is declared insolvent or if he/she becomes insolvent (before or at maturity), it is confirmed that he/she would not be able to meet his/her acceptance at maturity. The acceptance should be treated as dishonoured and the necessary entries are to be made accordingly.

Subsequently, when the final dividend is received or realized from the acceptor's estate, necessary entries are to be shown and the unrealized portion of the debt would be considered as bad debt.

Table 16.5 shows the accounting entries recorded in the book of drawer and drawee in case of insolvency.

TABLE 16.5 Accounting Entries in Case of Insolvency

Transactions	In the books of drawer	In the books of drawee/acceptor

When an acceptor is declared as insolvent, the bill accepted by him should be treated as dishonoured and dishonoured entry for the said bill should be shown immediately	Acceptor's A/c Dr.
	  To Bills Receivable A/c (if retained)
	Or
	  To Bank (if discounted)
	Or
	  To Endorsee (if endorsed)
	Or
	  To Bill for Collection (if sent for collection)
		Bills Payable A/c Dr.
		  To Drawer's A/c

The date when the final dividend or cash is realized from the estate of the Acceptor	Cash /Bank A/c Dr. (amount received)
	Bad Debt A/c Dr. (Unrealized amount)
	  To Acceptor's A/c (Total amount due)
		Drawer's A/c Dr.(Total amount due)
		  To Cash/Bank A/c (Amount paid)
		  To Deficiency A/c (Amount failed to Pay)

ILLUSTRATION 16.13 Mr. K. Mukherjee accepted a bill of Rs. 12,000 for four months on January 1, 2008, drawn by Mr. D. Kulkarni. Mr. D. Kulkarni endorsed the same to Mr. H. Thapar on January 18, 2008. At maturity, the bill was dishonoured due to insolvency of Mr. K. Mukherjee and noting charge of Rs.70 was paid. Fifteen days after maturity, a final dividend of 30 paise in a rupee was realized from his estate.

Pass necessary journal entries in the books of Mr. K. Mukherjee and Mr. D. Kulkarni.

Solution

In the Books of Mr. D. Kulkarni

Date	Particulars		L.F.	Amount Dr. (Rs.)	Amount Cr. (Rs.)
2008 Jan. 1	Bills Receivable A/c To K. Mukherjee A/c (Being the acceptance received, payable after four months)	Dr.		12,000	12,000
18	H. Thapar A/c To Bills Receivable A/c (Being the bill endorsed)	Dr.		12,000	12,000
May 4	K. Mukherjee A/c To H. Thapar A/c (Being K. Mukherjee's acceptance dishonoured due to insolvency and noting charge being Rs.70)	Dr.		12,070	12,070
19	Bank A/c (30% of Rs. 12,070) Bad Debt A/c (70% of Rs. 12,070) To K. Mukherjee A/c (Being final dividend received @ 30 paise in a rupee)	Dr. Dr.		3,621 8,449	12,070

In the Books of Mr. K.Mukherjee

Date	Particulars	L.F.	Amount Dr. (Rs.)	Amount Cr. (Rs.)
2008 Jan. 1	D. Kulkarni A/c Dr.		12,000	
	To Bills Payable A/c			12,000
	(Being the acceptance given for four months)			
May 4	Bills Payable A/c Dr.		12,000	
	Noting Charge A/c Dr.		70	
	To D. Kulkarni A/c			12,070
	(Being the acceptance dishonoured at maturity due to insolvency)			
19	D. Kulkarni A/c Dr.		12,070	
	To Bank A/c (30% of Rs. 12,070)			3,621
	To Deficiency A/c (70% of Rs. 12,070)			8,449
	(Being the final dividend paid @ 30 paise in a rupee)			

ILLUSTRATION 16.14 On January 15, 2008, Mr. Akram discounted a bill for Rs.10,000 with his bank at 18% p.a. by paying discount charges of Rs. 300. At maturity, the bill was dishonoured and noting charge incurred Rs.150. On the due date, Mr.Vilash, the acceptor of the above bill, paid Rs. 3,000 in cash and accepted a new bill for the balance amount due together with interest at 20 % p.a. for three months to Mr. Akram.

The new bill was discounted by Mr. Akram immediately with his bank at 10% p.a. On May 28, 1993, Mr. Vilash was declared insolvent and on July 11, 2008, a final dividend of 20 paise in a rupee was realized from his estate.

Give journal entries in the books of Mr. Akram and Vilash. Also, show ledger accounts in the books of Akram and Akram's Account in the books of Vilash.

Solution

In the Books of Mr. Akram

Date	Particulars	L.F.	Amount Dr. (Rs.)	Amount Cr. (Rs.)
2008, Jan. 15	Bank A/c Dr.		9,700	
	Discount A/c Dr.		300	
	To Bills Receivable A/c			10,000
	(Being the bill discounted with the bank two months before maturity @ 18 % p.a.)			
March 15	Vilash A/c Dr.		10,150	
	To Bank A/c			10,150
	(Being the discounted bill dishonoured at maturity and noting charge being Rs.150)			
15	Cash A/c Dr.		3,000	
	To Vilash A/c.			3,000
	(Being cash received from Vilash on account)			
15	Vilash A/c Dr.		358	
	To Interest A/c			358
	(Being the interest charged @ 20% p.a. on the outstanding balance of Rs. 7,150 for three months)			
15	Bills Receivable A/c Dr.		7,508	
	To Vilash A/c			7,508
	(Being the acceptance received for three months)			
15	Bank A/c Dr.		7,320	
	Discount A/c Dr.		188	
	To Bills Receivable A/c			7,508
	(Being the bill discounted with the bank three months before maturity @ 10% p.a.)			

(Contd.)

Date	Particulars		L.F.	Amount Dr. (Rs.)	Amount Cr. (Rs.)
May 28	Vilash A/c	Dr.		7,508	
	To Bank Suspense A/c				7,508
	(Being Mr. Vilash, the acceptor of a discounted bill debited due to his insolvency)				
June 18	Bank Suspense A/c	Dr.		7,508	
	To Bank A/c				7,508
	(Being Mr. Vilash's acceptance taken up from the bank on its maturity)				
July 11	Bank A/c (20% of Rs. 7,508)	Dr.		1,502	
	Bad Debt A/c (80% of Rs. 7,508)	Dr.		6,006	
	To Vilash's A/c				7,508
	(Being final dividend received @ 20 paise in a rupee from Mr. Vilash's estate and the balance written off as bad debt)				

Ledger Accounts

Vilash's Account

Dr.   Cr.

Date	Particulars	Amount (Rs.)	Date	Particulars	Amount (Rs.)
2008	To Balance B/d / Sales A/c	10,000	2008	By Bills Receivable A/c	10,000
March 15	To Bank A/c	10,150	March 15	By Cash A/c	3,000
15	To Interest A/c	358	15	By Bills Receivable A/c	7,508
May 28	To Bank Suspense A/c	7,508	July 11	Bank A/c	1,502
				Bad Debt A/c	6,006
		28,016			28,016

Bills Receivable Account

Dr.   Cr.

Date	Particulars	Amount (Rs.)	Date	Particulars	Amount (Rs.)
2008	To Vilash A/c	10,000	2008 Jan. 15	By Bank A/c	9,700
March 15	To Vilash A/c	7,508		By Discount A/c	300
			March 15	By Bank A/c	7,320
				By Discount A/c	188
		17,508			17,508

Discount Account

Dr.   Cr.

Date	Particulars	Amount (Rs.)	Date	Particulars	Amount (Rs.)
2008 Jan. 15	To Bills Receivable A/c	300	2008		

Bank Account

Dr.   Cr.

Date	Particulars	Amount (Rs.)	Date	Particulars	Amount (Rs.)
2008 Jan. 15	To Bills Receivable A/c	9,700	2008 March 15	By Vilash A/c	10,150
July 11	To Vilash A/c	1,502			

Cash Account

Dr.   Cr.

Date	Particulars	Amount (Rs.)	Date	Particulars	Amount (Rs.)
2008 March 15	To Vilash A/c	3,000	2008		

Dr.   **Interest Account**   Cr.

Date	Particulars	Amount (Rs.)	Date	Particulars	Amount (Rs.)
2008			2008 March 15	By Vilash A/c	358

Dr.   **Bank Suspense Account**   Cr.

Date	Particulars	Amount (Rs.)	Date	Particulars	Amount (Rs.)
2008 June 18	To Bank A/c	7,508	2008 May 28	By Vilash A/c	7,508
		7,508			7,508

Dr.   **Bad Debt Account**   Cr.

Date	Particulars	Amount (Rs.)	Date	Particulars	Amount (Rs.)
2008 July 11	To Vilash A/c	6,006	2008		

In the Books of Mr. Vilash

Date	Particulars	L.F.	Amount Dr. (Rs.)	Amount Cr. (Rs.)
2008 March 15	Bills Payable A/c	Dr.	10,000	
	Noting Charge A/c	Dr.	150	
	To Akram's A/c			10,150
	(Being the acceptance dishonoured at maturity)			
15	Akram's A/c	Dr.	3,000	
	To Cash A/c			3,000
	(Being cash paid to Mr. Akram's on account)			
15	Interest A/c	Dr.	358	
	To Akram's A/c			358
	(Being the interest charged on the renewed bill)			
15	Akram's A/c	Dr.	7,508	
	To Bills Payable A/c			7,508
	(Being the acceptance given for three months)			
May 28	Bills Payable A/c	Dr.	7,508	
	To Akram's A/c			7,508
	(Being the acceptance cancelled due to insolvency)			
July 11	Akram's A/c	Dr.	7,508	
	To Bank A/c (20% of Rs. 7,508)			1,502
	To Deficiency A/c (80% of Rs. 7,508)			6,006
	(Being the final dividend paid @ 20 paise in a rupee)			

Ledger Accounts

Dr.   **Akram's Account**   Cr.

Date	Particulars	Amount (Rs.)	Date	Particulars	Amount (Rs.)
2008 March 15	To Cash A/c	3,000	2008 March 15	By Bills Payable A/c	10,000
	To Bills Payable A/c	7,508	15	By Noting Charge A/c	150
July 11	To Bank A/c	1,502	15	By Interest A/c	358
	To Deficiency A/c	6,006	May 28	By Bills Payable A/c	7,508
		18,016			18,016

Working Note

Calculation of the date of maturity:

Discount charges on Rs.10,000 @ 18% for full year is Rs.1,800 , i.e. for 12 months.

Hence, Rs. 300 is paid for two months (12 /1,800 × 300 = 2). The bill was discounted two months before maturity. Thus, date of maturity = January 15 + 2 months = March 15.

ILLUSTRATION 16.15 Mr. Desai received a bill for Rs.9,000 for three months on January 1, 2008, from Mr. Pandey, the acceptor. At maturity, the bill was dishonoured and noting charge incurred Rs.100. One month after maturity, Mr. Pandey requests Mr. Desai to draw a new bill for two months including interest at 15% p.a. for the extended period. Mr. Desai acted accordingly.

One month before maturity, Mr. Pandey paid the fresh bill and was allowed a rebate of 20 % p.a. Show necessary entries in the books of Mr. Desai and Mr. Pandey.

Solution

In the Books of Mr. Desai

Date	Particulars	L.F.	Amount Dr. (Rs.)	Amount Cr. (Rs.)
2008 Jan. 1	Bills Receivable A/c Dr.		9,000	
	To Pandey A/c			9,000
	(Being acceptance received for three months)			
April 4	Pandey A/c Dr.		9,100	
	To Bills Receivable A/c			9,000
	To Cash A/c			100
	(Being the bill dishonoured at maturity and noting charge being Rs. 150)			
May 4	Pandey A/c Dr.		341	
	To Interest A/c			341
	(Being interest charged @ 15% p.a. on the outstanding balance of Rs. 9,100 for three months)			
4	Bills Receivable A/c Dr.		9,441	
	To Pandey A/c			9,441
	(Being the acceptance received for two months)			
June 7	Bank A/c Dr.		9,284	
	Rebate Allowed A/c Dr.		157	
	To Bills Receivable A/c			9,441
	(Being the bill retired by Mr. Pandey one month before maturity and was allowed a rebate @ 20% p.a.)			
July 7	No entry is required at maturity			

In the Books of Mr. Pandey

Date	Particulars	L.F.	Amount Dr. (Rs.)	Amount Cr. (Rs.)
2008 Jan. 1	Desai A/c Dr.		9,000	
	To Bills Payable A/c			9,000
	(Being the acceptance given for three months)			
April 4	Bills Payable A/c Dr.		9,000	
	Noting Charge A/c Dr.		100	
	To Desai's A/c			9,100
	(Being the acceptance dishonoured at maturity and noting charge being Rs. 100)			
May 4	Interest A/c Dr.		341	
	To Desai's A/c			341
	(Being interest charged @ 15% p.a. for three months on the outstanding balance for the renewed bill)			

(Contd.)

Date	Particulars		L.F.	Amount Dr. (Rs.)	Amount Cr. (Rs.)
4	Desai's A/c	Dr.		9,441	
	To Bills Payable A/c				9,441
	(Being acceptance given for three months)				
June 7	Bills Payable A/c	Dr.		9,441	
	To Cash / Bank A/c				9,284
	To Rebate Received A/c				157
	(Being the bill retired one month before maturity and received a rebate @ 20 % p.a.)				
July 7	No entry is required at maturity				

Working Notes

1. Calculation of interest on the outstanding balance of the bill dishonoured at maturity:
   The bill was dishonoured on April 4 and one month later, the new bill was accepted for two months. Thus, the new bill was accepted on May 4 for two months. Interest is to be charged @ 15% p.a. for the period from April 4 to July 4, i.e. for three months on the outstanding balance of Rs. 9,100. Interest amount = Rs. 341 (15/100 × 9,100 × 3/12).

2. Calculation of the amount of fresh bill drawn on renewal:

	Rs.
Original bill amount	9,000
Add: Noting charge	100
Outstanding amount	9,100
Add: Interest charged	341
Amount of fresh bill	9,441

ILLUSTRATION 16.16 Mukesh accepted a bill of Rs. 15,000 for two months on March 1, 2008, drawn by Paresh. Paresh discounted the same with his bank on March 4, 2008, at 12% p.a. At maturity, the bill was dishonoured and noting charge of Rs.120 was paid. One month after maturity, Mukesh paid Rs. 4,000 to Paresh and accepted a fresh bill for three months for the outstanding amount including interest at 12% p.a. on the outstanding period.

Give the necessary journal entries in the books of Mukesh and Paresh.

Solution

In the Books of Paresh

Date	Particulars		L.F.	Amount Dr. (Rs.)	Amount Cr. (Rs.)
2008 March 1	Bills Receivable A/c	Dr.		15,000	
	To Mukesh A/c				15,000
	(Being the acceptance received for two months)				
4	Bank A/c	Dr.		14,700	
	Discount A/c	Dr.		300	
	To Bills Receivable A/c				15,000
	(Being the bill discounted with the bank two months before maturity @ 12% p.a.)				
May 4	Mukesh A/c	Dr.		15,120	
	To Bank A/c				15,120
	(Being the discounted bill dishonoured at maturity and noting charge being Rs. 120.)				

(Contd.)

Date	Particulars		L.F.	Amount Dr. (Rs.)	Amount Cr. (Rs.)
June 4	Cash A/c	Dr.		4,000	
	To Mukesh A/c				4,000
	(Being cash received from Mukesh on account)				
4	Mukesh A/c	Dr.		485	
	To Interest A/c				485
	(Being interest charged @ 12 % p.a. on the outstanding balance)				
4	Bills Receivable A/c	Dr.		11,605	
	To Mukesh A/c				11,605
	(Being the acceptance received for three months)				

In the Books of Mukesh

Date	Particulars		L.F.	Amount Dr. (Rs.)	Amount Cr. (Rs.)
2008 March 1	Paresh A/c	Dr.		15,000	
	To Bills Payable A/c				15,000
	(Being the acceptance given for two months)				
May 4	Bills Payable A/c	Dr.		15,000	
	Noting Charge A/c	Dr.		120	
	To Paresh's A/c				15,120
	(Being the acceptance dishonoured at maturity and noting charge being Rs. 120)				
June 4	Paresh A/c	Dr.		4,000	
	To Cash A/c				4,000
	(Being the cash paid to Paresh on account)				
June 4	Interest A/c	Dr.		485	
	To Paresh 's A/c				485
	(Being interest charged @ 12 % p.a. on the outstanding balance for the renewed bill)				
June 4	Paresh 's A/c	Dr.		11,605	
	To Bills Payable A/c				11,605
	(Being the acceptance given for three months)				

Working Notes

1. Calculation of interest on the outstanding balance of the bill dishonoured at maturity:

   The bill was dishonoured on May 4 and one month later, the new bill was accepted for three months. Thus, the new bill was accepted on June 4 for three months. Interest is to be charged @ 12 % p.a. for the period from May 4 to September 4 on the outstanding balances as under:

	Rs.
On Rs. 15,120 for one month @ 12% (15,120 × 12/100 × 1/12)	151.20
On Rs. 11,120 (15,120 – 4,000) for three months @ 12%	
= (11,120 × 12/100 × 3/12)	333.60
Total interest charged	484.80

   Hence, total interest to be charged Rs. 485 (approx.).

2. Calculation of the amount of fresh bill drawn on renewal:

	Rs.
Original bill amount	15,000
Add: Noting charge	120
	15,120
Less: Cash received	4,000
Outstanding amount	11,120
Add: Interest charged	485
Amount of fresh bill	11,605

16.12 DRAWEE IN CASE OF NEED

When in the bill or any endorsement thereon, the name of any person is given in addition to the drawee to be resorted to in case of need, such person is called a **drawee in case of need** (under Section 7 of the Negotiable Instruments Act).

16.13 HOLDER AND HOLDER IN DUE COURSE (SECTIONS 8 AND 9 OF NEGOTIABLE INSTRUMENTS ACT)

The holder of a negotiable instrument is any person entitled in his/her own name to the possession thereof and to receive or recover the amount due thereon from the parties thereto. Only the person legally entitled to receive the money due on the instrument is the holder.

The holder in due course is a particular kind of holder. The holder of a negotiable instrument is called the **holder in due course** if he/she satisfies the following conditions:

1. has obtained the instrument for valuable consideration.
2. has become holder of the instrument before its maturity.
3. has no cause to believe that any defect existed in the title of the person from whom he/she derived his/her title.

Table 16.6 gives difference between Bill of exchange and Cheque.

TABLE 16.6 Differences between Bill of Exchange and Cheque

Bill of exchange	Cheque
It can be drawn on any person including a banker. Thus, so every bill of exchange is not a cheque.	It can be drawn only on a banker. Thus, every cheque is a bill of exchange.
It requires acceptance, unless under special circumstances.	It does not require acceptance.
A bill of exchange has no provision for crossing.	A cheque can be crossed.
A bill of exchange has to be stamped.	It need not be stamped.
It may be paid by instalments.	It can not be paid by instalments.
A grace period of three days is allowed in case of a bill.	No days of grace is allowed in case of a cheque.
In case of bill of exchange, notice of dishonour is necessary (except in some special circumstances).	It is not necessary to give notice of dishonour to the drawer. (Notice is required to be given under clause (b) of the proviso to Section 138.)
The payment of a bill of exchange, cannot be countermanded.	The payment of a cheque can be countermanded.
Noting and protesting is necessary for dishonour of a bill of exchange.	In case of dishonour of a cheque it is not required to be noted or protested.

16.14 ACCOMMODATION BILL (MUTUAL ACCOMMODATION)

An accommodation bill is one which is drawn and accepted without any consideration, with a view to oblige some person, i.e., to provide him with funds. Thus, a bill drawn and accepted not for a genuine trade transaction but to provide only financial help to some party is termed as an **accommodation bill**.

For example, Mr. Q is in need of Rs. 3,000 and approaches his friend Mr. G for the said fund. Mr. G is not in a position to lend the money, but suggests Mr. Q to draw a bill on him that he could accept. Mr. Q acts accordingly and collects the desired amount from bank by discounting the bill. Mr. Q then has to repay Rs. 3,000 to Mr. G on the due date or before maturity of the bill who would meet the said bill. This type of bill is known as an accommodation bill.

In its form and in all other respects, an accommodation bill is quite similar to an ordinary bill of exchange. There is nothing on the face of an accommodation bill to distinguish it from an ordinary trade bill. Thus, for temporary financial help, this type of bill is drawn for the accommodation of the drawer only, or for both the drawer and the drawee. At maturity, the drawer remits the amount of the bill or remits his share (when it is drawn for the accommodation of the drawer and the drawee both) to the acceptor before the due date.

Section 43 of the Negotiable Instruments Act provides that "a negotiable instrument made, drawn, accepted, endorsed or transferred without consideration, or for a consideration which fails, creates no obligation of payment between the parties to the transaction. But if any such party has transferred the instrument with or without endorsement to the holder for consideration, such holder, and every subsequent holder deriving title from him, may recover the amount due on such instrument from the transferor for consideration or any prior party thereto."

The general accounting entries of accommodation bills are the same as shown in case of trade bills in the previous sections.

Table 16.7 lists the differences between trade bill and accomodation bill.

TABLE 16.7   Distinction between Trade Bill and Accommodation Bill

Trade bill	Accommodation bill
Trade bill is drawn for the settlement of a claim/obligation arising out of a business transaction.	An accommodation bill is one which is drawn and accepted without any consideration, with a view to oblige some person, i.e., to provide him with funds.
It is drawn against some specific consideration already enjoyed by the drawee.	It is drawn without having any consideration.
When a trade bill is discounted, the entire proceeds are enjoyed by the drawer only.	When this bill is discounted, the proceeds may be enjoyed by both the drawer and the drawee.
This bill is a proof of debt/obligation.	These bills are not a proof of debt/obligation.
If the bill is retained by the drawer till maturity, the drawee is liable to make payment of the said bill. For non-payment, legal action may be taken against him.	In case the party accommodated continues to hold till maturity, the accommodating party shall not be liable to him for payment of the bill since the contract between them is not based on any consideration (Section 43).

Generally, accommodation bills may be drawn under the following circumstances or situations:

1. When the bill is drawn for the accommodation of drawer only

ILLUSTRATION 16.17   On April 1, 2008, Gautam approached his friend Sanjeev for a loan of Rs. 6,000. Sanjeev was not in a position to provide the loan but accepted a bill for three months for the said amount for accommodation. Gautam acts accordingly and discounts the bill with his banker immediately at 12% p.a. On the due date, Gautam remits his obligation to Sanjeev and the bill was duly honoured.

Pass necessary entries in the books of Gautam and Sanjeev.

Solution

In the Books of Gautam

Date	Particulars		L.F.	Amount Dr. (Rs.)	Amount Cr. (Rs.)
2008 April 1	Bills Receivable A/c To Sanjeev A/c (Being the acceptance received for three months)	Dr.		6,000	6,000
1	Bank A/c Discount A/c To Bills Receivable A/c (Being the bill discounted with the bank @ 12% p.a.)	Dr. Dr.		5,820 180	6,000
July 4	Sanjeev A/c To Bank A/c (Being the obligation paid to Sanjeev on the due date)	Dr.		6,000	6,000

In the Books of Sanjeev

Date	Particulars	L.F.	Amount Dr. (Rs.)	Amount Cr. (Rs.)
2008 April 1	Gautam A/c Dr. To Bills Payable A/c (Being the acceptance given for the accommodation of drawer payable after two months)		6,000	6,000
July 4	Cash A/c Dr. To Gautam A/c (Being the cash received from Gautam on account on the due date)		6,000	6,000
July 4	Bills Payable A/c Dr. To Bank A/c (Being payment of the accommodation bill made at maturity)		6,000	6,000

2. When the bill is drawn for the accommodation of both the drawer and the drawee

ILLUSTRATION 16.18 On March 4, 2008, Zafar draws a bill of Rs. 9,000 on Ikbal at two months for mutual accommodation of both. After acceptance, Zafar discounts the bill at Rs. 8,700 and shares the proceeds in the ratio of 2:1 on that date. On the due date, Zafar remits his obligation to Ikbal and the bill was honoured.

Give journal entries in the books of both the parties.

Solution

In the Books of Zafar

Date	Particulars	L.F.	Amount Dr. (Rs.)	Amount Cr. (Rs.)
2008 March 4	Bills Receivable A/c Dr. To Ikbal A/c (Being the acceptance received for two months)		9,000	9,000
4	Bank A/c Dr. Discount A/c Dr. To Bills Receivable A/c (Being the bill discounted with the bank)		8,700 300	9,000
4	Ikbal A/c Dr. To Bank A/c To Discount A/c (Being one-third of the proceeds sent and proportionate discount charges charged)		3,000	2,900 100
May 7	Ikbal A/c Dr. To Bank A/c (Being the obligation paid on the due date)		6,000	6,000

In the Books of Ikbal

Date	Particulars	L.F.	Amount Dr. (Rs.)	Amount Cr. (Rs.)
2008 March 4	Zafar A/c Dr. To Bills Payable A/c (Being the acceptance given for mutual accommodation payable after two months)		9,000	9,000
4	Cash A/c Dr. Discount A/c Dr. To Zafar A/c (Being one-third of the proceeds of the bills received in cash and discount charges charged by Zafar proportionately)		2,900 100	3,000
May 7	Cash A/c Dr. To Zafar A/c (Being the cash received from Zafar on account on the due date)		6,000	6,000
7	Bills Payable A/c Dr. To Bank A/c (Being payment of the accommodation bill made at maturity)		9,000	9,000

3. When a bill is drawn by both the parties for their accommodation (i.e., each party is the drawer of one bill and the acceptor of another bill)

ILLUSTRATION 16.19   On January 1, 2008, Vikram drew a bill of Rs. 6,000 on Kailash for three months for mutual accommodation. On that date, it was discounted by Vikram at Rs. 5,800 and remitted two-fifths of the proceeds to Kailash immediately.

On the same day, Kailash drew another bill for the same purpose for three months on Vikram for Rs. 6,000. He then discounted the same with his bank at Rs. 5,880 and remitted two-fifths of the proceeds to Vikram forthwith. At maturity both the bills were honoured.

Give journal entries in the books of both the parties.

Solution

In the Books of Vikram

Date	Particulars		L.F.	Amount Dr. (Rs.)	Amount Cr. (Rs.)
2008 Jan. 1	Bills Receivable A/c 　To Kailash A/c (Being the acceptance for 3 months received for mutual accommodation)	Dr.		6,000	6,000
1	Bank A/c Discount A/c 　To Bills Receivable A/c (Being the bill discounted with the bank)	Dr. Dr.		5,800 200	6,000
1	Kailash A/c 　To Bank A/c 　To Discount A/c (Being two-fifths of the proceeds sent and proportionate discount charges charged)	Dr.		2,400	2,320 80
1	Kailash A/c 　To Bills Payable A/c (Being the acceptance given for mutual accommodation payable after three months)	Dr.		6,000	6,000
1	Cash A/c Discount A/c 　To Kailash A/c (Being two-fifths of the proceeds of the bills received in cash and discount charges charged by Kailash proportionately)	Dr. Dr.		2,352 48	2,400
April 4	Bills Payable A/c 　To Bank A/c (Being payment of the accommodation bill made at maturity)	Dr.		6,000	6,000

In the Books of Kailash

Date	Particulars		L.F.	Amount Dr. (Rs.)	Amount Cr. (Rs.)
2008 Jan. 1	Vikram A/c 　To Bills Payable A/c (Being the acceptance given for mutual accommodation payable after three months)	Dr.		6,000	6,000
1	Cash A/c Discount A/c 　To Vikram A/c (Being one-third of the proceeds of the bills received in cash and discount charges charged by Vikram proportionately)	Dr. Dr.		2,320 80	2,400
1	Bills Receivable A/c 　To Vikram A/c (Being the acceptance for three months received for mutual accommodation)	Dr.		6,000	6,000

(Contd.)

Date	Particulars	L.F.	Amount Dr. (Rs.)	Amount Cr. (Rs.)
1	Bank A/c Dr.		5,880	
	Discount A/c Dr.		120	
	To Bills Receivable A/c			6,000
	(Being the bill discounted with the bank)			
1	Vikram A/c Dr.		2,400	
	To Bank A/c			2,352
	To Discount A/c			48
	(Being two-fifths of the proceeds sent and proportionate discount charges charged)			
April 4	Bills Payable A/c Dr.		6,000	
	To Bank A/c			6,000
	(Being payment of the accommodation bill made at maturity)			

ILLUSTRATION 16.20   On April 11, 2008, Anupam drew a bill of Rs. 6,000 on Jivan at three months for mutual accommodation of both. After acceptance, Anupam discounted the bill at Rs. 5,760 and shared the proceeds in the ratio of 2:1 forthwith. On the same day, Jivan draws another bill for Rs.9,000 on Anupam for three months. He then discounted the same with his bank at Rs. 8,600 and remitted two-fifths of the proceeds to Anupam forthwith. On the due date, Jivan remits his obligation to Anupam and the bills were duly honoured.

Give journal entries in the books of both the parties.

Solution

In the Books of Anupam

Date	Particulars	L.F.	Amount Dr. (Rs.)	Amount Cr. (Rs.)
2008 April 11	Bills Receivable A/c Dr.		6,000	
	To Jivan A/c			6,000
	(Being the acceptance for three months received for mutual accommodation)			
11	Bank A/c Dr.		5,760	
	Discount A/c Dr.		240	
	To Bills Receivable A/c			6,000
	(Being the bill discounted with the bank)			
11	Jivan A/c Dr.		2,000	
	To Bank A/c			1,920
	To Discount A/c			80
	(Being one-third of the proceeds sent and proportionate discount charges charged)			
11	Jivan A/c Dr.		9,000	
	To Bills Payable A/c			9,000
	(Being the acceptance given for mutual accommodation payable after three months)			
11	Cash A/c Dr.		3,440	
	Discount A/c Dr.		160	
	To Jivan A/c			3,600
	(Being two-fifths of the proceeds of the bills received in cash and discount charges charged by Jivan proportionately)			
July 14	Cash A/c Dr.		1,400	
	To Jivan A/c			1,400
	(Being the cash received on account at maturity)			
14	Bills Payable A/c Dr.		9,000	
	To Bank A/c			9,000
	(Being payment of the accommodation bill made at maturity)			

In the Books of Jivan

Date	Particulars		L.F.	Amount Dr. (Rs.)	Amount Cr. (Rs.)
April 11	Anupam A/c	Dr.		6,000	
	To Bills Payable A/c				6,000
	(Being the acceptance given for mutual accommodation payable after three months)				
11	Cash A/c	Dr.		1,920	
	Discount A/c	Dr.		80	
	To Anupam A/c				2,000
	(Being one-third of the proceeds of the bills received in cash and discount charges charged by Anupam proportionately)				
11	Bills Receivable A/c	Dr.		9,000	
	To Anupam A/c				9,000
	(Being the acceptance for three months received for mutual accommodation)				
11	Bank A/c	Dr.		8,600	
	Discount A/c	Dr.		400	
	To Bills Receivable A/c				9,000
	(Being the bill discounted with the bank)				
11	Anupam A/c	Dr.		3,600	
	To Bank A/c				3,440
	To Discount A/c				160
	(Being two-fifths of the proceeds sent and proportionate discount charges charged)				
July 14	Anupam A/c	Dr.		1,400	
	To Bank A/c				1,400
	(Being the cash paid on account at maturity)				
11	Bills Payable A/c	Dr.		6,000	
	To Bank A/c				6,000
	(Being payment of the accommodation bill made at maturity)				

Working Note

Calculation of cash paid by Mr. Jivan to Mr. Anupam on account at maturity (i.e., July 14):

	Anupam (Rs.)	Jivan (Rs.)
First bill of Rs. 6,000 shared in the ratio of 2 : 1	4,000	2,000
Second bill of Rs. 9,000 shared in the ratio of 2 : 3	3,600	5,400
Total amount received from two bills	+ 7,600	+ 7,400
Less: First bill to be paid by Jivan		(–) 6,000
Surplus amount received by Jivan is required to be refunded to Anupam		1,400
Thus, cash paid by Jivan Rs. 1,400 to Anupam	+ 1,400	(–) 1,400
Total amount received by Anupam	+ 9,000	
Less: Second bill to be paid by Anupam	(–) 9,000	
Net effect after making the payment of two bills	–	–

4. When a bill is drawn for the accommodation of the drawer and drawee both, but one of them is declared as insolvent.

ILLUSTRATION 16.21 On May 14, 2008, Mr. Raina draws a bill of Rs. 12,000 on Mr. Pathak at three months for mutual accommodation of both. After acceptance, Mr. Raina discounts the bill at Rs. 11,600 and shares the proceeds in the ratio of 3:2 immediately. On the due date, Mr. Raina fails to remits his obligation, as he was declared bankrupt and the final dividend @ 45 paise in a rupee was realized from his estate on August 25, 2008.

Give journal entries in the books of both the parties.

Solution

In the Books of Mr. Raina

Date	Particulars		L.F.	Amount Dr. (Rs.)	Amount Cr. (Rs.)
2008 May 14	Bills Receivable A/c	Dr.		12,000	
	To Pathak A/c				12,000
	(Being the acceptance received for three months for mutual accommodation)				
14	Bank A/c	Dr.		11,600	
	Discount A/c	Dr.		400	
	To Bills Receivable A/c				12,000
	(Being the bill discounted with the bank)				
14	Pathak A/c	Dr.		4,800	
	To Cash A/c				4,640
	To Discount A/c				160
	(Being two-fifth of the proceeds sent and proportionate discount charges charged)				
August 25	Pathak A/c	Dr.		7,200	
	To Bank A/c (45% of Rs. 7,200)				3,240
	To Deficiency A/c (55% of Rs. 7,200)				3,960
	(Being the final dividend paid @ 45 paise in a rupee)				

In the Books of Mr. Pathak

Date	Particulars		L.F.	Amount Dr. (Rs.)	Amount Cr. (Rs.)
2008 May 12	Raina A/c	Dr.		12,000	
	To Bills Payable A/c				12,000
	(Being the acceptance given for mutual accommodation payable after three months)				
12	Cash A/c	Dr.		4,640	
	Discount A/c	Dr.		160	
	To Raina A/c				4,800
	(Being two-fifth of the proceeds of the bills received in cash and discount charges charged by Raina proportionately)				
August 17	Bills Payable A/c	Dr.		12,000	
	To Bank A/c				12,000
	(Being payment of the accommodation bill made at maturity)				
25	Bank A/c (45% of Rs. 7,200)	Dr.		3,240	
	Bad Debt A/c (55% of Rs. 7,200)	Dr.		3,960	
	To Raina A/c				7,200
	(Being final dividend received @ 45 paise in a rupee from Mr. Raina's estate and the balance written off as bad debt)				

Working Note

Calculation of amount receivable from Raina's estate:

	Rs.
Original bill amount	12,000
Bill amount enjoyed by Pathan (2/5th of Rs. 12,000)	4,800
Bill amount enjoyed by Raina and that is receivable from his estate	7,200

ILLUSTRATION 16.22 Rajesh and Narendra each drew a bill for Rs. 4,000 payable at three months on each other on March 1, 2008. They discounted their bills at 15% p.a. immediately. At maturity, Rajesh met his acceptance but Narendra failed to meet his acceptance, and as such, Rajesh had to take it up. Narendra then paid Rs.1,500 in cash and accepted a fresh bill for two months together with interest at 15% p.a. on the outstanding balances for the period of extension.

At maturity, the fresh bill was also dishonoured due to insolvency of Narendra and the final dividend of 30 paise in a rupee was realized from his estate 20 days after maturity.

Give necessary entries in the books of both the parties.

Solution

In the Books of Rajesh

Date	Particulars	L.F.	Amount Dr. (Rs.)	Amount Cr. (Rs.)
2008 March 1	Bills Receivable A/c .... Dr. To Narendra A/c (Being the acceptance for three months received for mutual accommodation)		4,000	4,000
2	Bank A/c .... Dr. Discount A/c .... Dr. To Bills Receivable A/c (Being the bill discounted with the bank)		3,850 150	4,000
2	Narendra A/c .... Dr. To Bills Payable A/c (Being the acceptance given for mutual accommodation payable after three months)		4,000	4,000
June 4	Bills Payable A/c .... Dr. To Bank A/c (Being payment of the accommodation bill made at maturity)		4,000	4,000
4	Narendra A/c .... Dr. To Bank A/c (Being the acceptance of Narendra paid on the due date)		4,000	4,000
4	Cash A/c .... Dr. To Narendra A/c (Being the cash received on account)		1,500	1,500
4	Narendra A/c .... Dr. To Interest A/c (Being the interest charged on the outstanding balance of Rs. 2,500 at 15% p.a. for two months)		63	63
4	Bills Receivable A/c .... Dr. To Narendra A/c (Being the acceptance for three months received)		2,563	2,563
August 7	Narendra A/c .... Dr. To Bills Receivable A/c (Being Narendra's acceptance dishonoured due to his insolvency)		2,563	2,563
27	Bank A/c (30% of Rs. 2,563) .... Dr. Bad Debt A/c (70% of Rs. 2,563) .... Dr. To Narendra A/c (Being final dividend received @ 30 paise in a rupee from Narendra's estate and the balance written off as bad debt)		769 1,794	2,563

In the Books of Narendra

Date	Particulars		L.F.	Amount Dr. (Rs.)	Amount Cr. (Rs.)
2008 March 1	Bills Receivable A/c	Dr.		4,000	
	To Rajesh A/c				4,000
	(Being the acceptance for three months received for mutual accommodation)				
1	Bank A/c	Dr.		3,850	
	Discount A/c	Dr.		150	
	To Rajesh A/c				4,000
	(Being the bill discounted with the bank)				
1	Rajesh A/c	Dr.		4,000	
	To Bills Payable A/c				4,000
	(Being the acceptance given for mutual accommodation payable after three months)				
June 4	Bills Payable A/c	Dr.		4,000	
	To Rajesh A/c				4,000
	(Being the bill dishonoured at maturity)				
4	Rajesh A/c	Dr.		1,500	
	To Bank A/c				1,500
	(Being the cash paid on account at maturity)				
4	Interest A/c	Dr.		63	
	To Rajesh A/c				63
	(Being the interest charged by Rajesh on the outstanding balance of Rs. 2,500 at 15 % p.a. for two months)				
4	Rajesh A/c	Dr.		2,563	
	To Bills Payable A/c				2,563
	(Being the acceptance given, payable after three months)				
August 7	Bills Payable A/c	Dr.		2,563	
	To Rajesh A/c				2,563
	(Being the new bill dishonoured at maturity due to insolvency)				
27	Rajesh A/c	Dr.		2,563	
	To Bank A/c (30 % of Rs. 2,563)				769
	To Deficiency A/c (70 % of Rs. 2,563)				1,794
	(Being the final dividend paid @ 30 paise in a rupee)				

ILLUSTRATION 16.23 On March 7, 2008, Srikant draws a bill of Rs. 8,000 on Ratan at three months for mutual accommodation of both. After acceptance, Srikant discounts the bill at Rs. 7,600 and shares the proceeds in the ratio of 3:2 forthwith. On the same day, Ratan drew another bill for Rs. 12,000 on Srikant for three months. He then discounted the same with his bank at Rs. 11,400 and remitted one-third of the proceeds to Srikant forthwith. On the due date, Srikant met his acceptance but Ratan failed to meet his acceptance due to his insolvency, and which was paid by Sridhar. Final dividend of 40 paise in a rupee was realized from his estate one month after maturity.

Give journal entries in the books of both the parties.

Solution

In the Books of Srikant

Date	Particulars		L.F.	Amount Dr. (Rs.)	Amount Cr. (Rs.)
2008 March 7	Bills Receivable A/c	Dr.		8,000	
	To Ratan A/c				8,000
	(Being the acceptance for three months received for mutual accommodation)				

(Contd.)

Date	Particulars		L.F.	Amount Dr. (Rs.)	Amount Cr. (Rs.)
7	Bank A/c	Dr.		7,600	
	Discount A/c	Dr.		400	
	To Bills Receivable A/c				8,000
	(Being the bill discounted with the bank)				
7	Ratan A/c	Dr.		3,200	
	To Bank A/c				3,040
	To Discount A/c				160
	(Being two-fifth of the proceeds sent and proportionate discount charges charged)				
7	Ratan A/c	Dr.		12,000	
	To Bills Payable A/c				12,000
	(Being the acceptance given for mutual accommodation payable after three months)				
7	Cash A/c	Dr.		3,800	
	Discount A/c	Dr.		200	
	To Ratan A/c				4,000
	(Being two-fifths of the proceeds of the bills received in cash and discount charges charged by Ratan proportionately)				
June 10	Bills Payable A/c	Dr.		12,000	
	To Bank A/c				12,000
	(Being payment of the accommodation bill made at maturity)				
10	Ratan A/c	Dr.		8,000	
	To Bank A/c				8,000
	(Being the acceptance of Ratan paid on the due date)				
July 10	Bank A/c (40% of Rs. 11,200)	Dr.		4,480	
	Bad Debt A/c (60% of Rs. 11,200)	Dr.		6,720	
	To Ratan A/c				11,200
	(Being final dividend received @ 40 paise in a rupee from Mr. Ratan's estate and the balance written off as bad debt)				

In the Books of Ratan

Date	Particulars		L.F.	Amount Dr. (Rs.)	Amount Cr. (Rs.)
2008 March 7	Srikant A/c	Dr.		8,000	
	To Bills Payable A/c				8,000
	(Being the acceptance given for mutual accommodation payable after three months)				
7	Cash A/c	Dr.		3,040	
	Discount A/c	Dr.		160	
	To Srikant A/c				3,200
	(Being two-fifth of the proceeds of the bills received in cash and discount charges charged by Srikant proportionately)				
7	Bills Receivable A/c	Dr.		12,000	
	To Srikant A/c				12,000
	(Being the acceptance for three months received for mutual accommodation)				
7	Bank A/c	Dr.		11,400	
	Discount A/c	Dr.		600	
	To Bills Receivable A/c				12,000
	(Being the bill discounted with the bank)				
7	Srikant A/c	Dr.		4,000	
	To Bank A/c				3,800
	To Discount A/c				200
	(Being one-third of the proceeds sent and proportionate discount charges charged)				

(Contd.)

Date	Particulars		L.F.	Amount Dr. (Rs.)	Amount Cr. (Rs.)
June 10	Bills Payable A/c To Sridhar A/c (Being the bill dishonoured at maturity)	Dr.		8,000	8,000
July 10	Srikant A/c To Bank A/c (40 % of Rs. 11,200) To Deficiency A/c (60 % of Rs. 11,200) (Being the final dividend paid @ 40 paise in a rupee)	Dr.		11,200	4,480 6,720

Working Note

Calculation of cash receivable from Ratan due to his insolvency (i.e., On June 10):

	Srikant (Rs.)	Ratan (Rs.)
First bill of Rs. 8,000 shared in the ratio of 3:2	4,800	3,200
Second bill of Rs.12,000 shared in the ratio of 1:2	4,000	8,000
Total amount received from two bills	+8,800	+11,200
Less: Both bills were paid by Srikant (Rs. 8,000 + Rs. 12,000)	(–)20,000	
Net position	(–)11,200	+11,200

Hence, total amount receivable from Ratan's estate is Rs. 11,200 due to his insolvency.

EXERCISES

I. *Multiple Choice Questions:*

1. The person who makes or prepares a bill is called
   - (a) drawer
   - (b) acceptor
   - (c) payee.
2. The person who receives the amount of bill at maturity is called
   - (a) drawee
   - (b) payee
   - (c) acceptor.
3. A bill of exchange must be
   - (a) unconditional
   - (b) conditional.
4. A bill of exchange must be
   - (a) an order in writing
   - (b) a request in writing.
5. When a bill of exchange is payable on demand, then
   - (a) no stamp is required
   - (b) a stamp has to be affixed (according to the value).
6. When a bill of exchange is payable after sometime, then
   - (a) no stamp is required
   - (b) a stamp has to be affixed (according to the value).
7. On the basis of period, bills are of two types—
   - (a) trade and accommodation bills
   - (b) demand and term bills.
8. On the basis of object or purpose, bills are classified as
   - (a) trade and accommodation bills
   - (b) demand and term bills.

9. Acceptance is not required for
   (a) hundi
   (b) promissory note
   (c) bill of exchange.
10. Promissory note is given by
    (a) a debtor to a creditor
    (b) a creditor to a debtor.
11. Bill of exchange is given by
    (a) a debtor to a creditor
    (b) a creditor to a debtor.
12. No grace period is allowed when the bill is payable
    (a) after sight
    (b) on demand or at sight
    (c) after date.
13. In case of a bill drawn 'after date', the due date or maturity date is to be calculated as follows:
    (a) Date of drawing of bill + Bill period + 3 days
    (b) Date of acceptance of bill + Bill period + 3 days.
14. In case of a bill drawn 'after sight', the due date or maturity date is to be calculated as follows:
    (a) Date of drawing of bill + bill period + 3 days.
    (b) Date of acceptance of bill + bill period + 3 days.
15. If the due date or maturity date happens to be a public holiday or Sunday, then the due date shall be
    (a) the day before maturity
    (b) the day after maturity.
16. In case of dishonour, no one can sue the other for
    (a) trade bills
    (b) accommodation bills
    (c) promissory note.
17. When the drawee of a bill is unable to meet the same on the due date, he/she may accept a fresh bill for the extended period including the interest. This is called
    (a) retirement of bill
    (b) renewal of bill.
18. When the name of another person is mentioned as the person who will accept the bill if the original drawee does not accept it, such a person is called the
    (a) holder in due course
    (b) holder
    (c) drawee in case of need.

   Ans: 1. (a); 2. (b); 3. (a); 4. (a); 5. (a); 6. (b); 7. (b); 8. (a); 9. (b); 10. (a); 11. (b); 12. (b); 13. (a); 14. (b); 15. (a); 16. (b); 17. (b); 18. (c).

II. *Short Answer Type Questions (with answer)*

1. Pass the necessary journal entries for the following cases in the books of the drawer and the drawee:
   (a) Endorsed bills receivable become dishonoured.
   (b) The bill is retained by the drawer till maturity but becomes dishonoured and noting charge is paid.
   (c) When the bill is sent to bank for collection, it becomes dishonoured and noting charge is paid.
   (d) The interest is charged for renewal of bills.

(e) In addition to the interest discount charges, other incidental charges are paid by the acceptor (in case of renewal of bills).

(f) An acceptor of a dishonoured bill becomes insolvent and nothing can be realized from his estate.

Ans: *In the books of drawer*   *In the books of drawee*

(a) Acceptor's A/c   Dr.   Bills Payable A/c   Dr.
    To Creditors A/c   To Drawer's A/c

(b) Acceptor's A/c   Dr.   Bills Payable A/c   Dr.
    To Bills Receivable A/c   Noting Charge A/c   Dr.
    To Bank A/c   To Drawer's A/c

(c) Acceptor's A/c   Dr.   Noting Charge A/c   Dr.
    To Bill for Collection A/c   To Drawer's A/c
    To Bank A/c

(d) Acceptor's A/c   Dr.   Interest A/c   Dr.
    To Interest A/c   To Drawer's A/c

(e) Cash A/c   Dr.   Interest A/c   Dr.
    To Interest A/c   Discount A/c   Dr.
    To Discount A/c   Incidental Charges A/c   Dr.
    To Incidental Charges A/c   To Cash A/c

(f) Bad debts A/c   Dr.   Drawer's A/c   Dr.
    To Acceptor's A/c   To Deficiency A/c

2. Calculate the due date or maturity date in the following cases:

(a) A bill was drawn on April 1, 1999, and was payable 70 days after sight. The bill was accepted on April 3, 1999.

(b) A bill was drawn on January 1, 1999, and was payable 80 days after date. The bill was accepted on January 3, 1999.

(c) A bill was drawn on May 1, 1999, and was payable four months after date. The bill was accepted on May 2, 1999.

(d) A bill was drawn on January 1, 1999, and was payable on demand or 'at sight' for two months.

(e) A bill was drawn on January 1, 1999, and was payable after 75 days.

(f) A bill was drawn on May 24, 1999, and was payable after 80 days.

Ans:

(a) June 15, 1999 — (27 + 31 + 12 + 3) days

(b) March 25, 1999 — (30 + 28 + 22 + 3) days

(c) September 4, 1999 — May 1, 1999 + 4 months + 3 days

(d) March 1, 1999 — (January 1, 1999 + 2 months, but no days of grace)

(e) March 19, 1999 — (30 + 29 + 16 + 3) days

(f) August 14, 1999 — (70 + 30 + 31 + 12 + 3) days. Since August 15 is a holiday, the day before the date of maturity would be the actual due date.

3. Calculate the amount of discount charges to be deducted by the bank for the following:

(a) A bill of Rs. 8,000 discounted with the bank @12% p.a. on January 18, 1999, and the due date of the said bill was on April 4, 1999.

(b) A bill of Rs. 6,000 drawn on January 1, 1999, payable after four months discounted with the bank @ 15% p.a. on February 4, 1999.

(c) A bill of Rs. 5,000 drawn on February 4, 1999, payable after 90 days was discounted with the bank @ 12% p.a., two months before the maturity.

(d) A bill of Rs. 4,000 drawn on January 17, 1999, payable 75 days after date was discounted with the bank @ 15% p.a. on February 24, 1999.

Ans: (a) Rs. 280 (for 106 days), (b) Rs. 219 (for 89 days), (c) Rs. 100 (for two months), (d) Rs. 66 (for 40 days).

4. Calculate the interest to be paid or payable for the renewal of bills from the following:
   (a) On April 18, 1999, the due date, a bill of Rs. 6,000 was dishonoured and noting charge of Rs. 50 was paid. On that date, the acceptor of the said bill paid Rs. 1,000 in cash and accepted a fresh bill for two months on the outstanding balance including an interest @12% p.a.
   (b) One month after the due date of a bill of Rs. 8,000, the acceptor paid Rs. 2,000 in cash and accepted a new bill for three months for the outstanding balance including an interest @15% p.a.
   (c) On the due date, a bill of Rs. 9,000 was dishonoured and the acceptor accepted three bills of Rs. 4,000, Rs. 3,000 and Rs. 2,000 for three months, two months and one month, respectively. The acceptor paid interest in cash @ 12% p.a. on the outstanding balance for the extended periods.

   Ans: (a) Interest Rs. 101, (b) Interest Rs. 325 (on Rs. 8,000 for one month + on Rs. 6,000 for three months), (c) Interest Rs. 200 (120 + 60 + 20).

III. *Essay Type Questions*

1. What do you mean by a bill of exchange? What are its chief features?
2. What do you mean by the essentials of a bill of exchange or parts of bills of exchange?
3. How could you classify a bill of exchange? Give a specimen of a bill of exchange.
4. What do you mean by endorsement? Explain the different types of endorsements in brief.
5. Describe the advantages of a bill of exchange.
6. What do you mean by acceptance? What are the different types of acceptances?
7. Distinguish between bill of exchange and a cheque.
8. Distinguish between a bill of exchange and a promissory note.
9. What do you mean by date of maturity or due date? How it is calculated? What is the effect of a public holiday while calculating the due date?
10. What do you mean by dishonour of a bill of exchange? What is the effect of a dishonour under different situations in the books of a drawer?
11. Distinguish between a trade bill and an accommodation bill.
12. Write short notes on:
    (a) Endorsement
    (b) Noting and protesting
    (c) Holder in due course
    (d) Discounting of bill of exchange
    (e) Retiring of a bill
    (f) Renewal of a bill
    (g) Parties to a bill of exchange
    (h) Dishonour of bill of exchange
    (i) Accommodation bill
    (j) 'after date'
    (k) 'after sight'.

IV. *Problems*

1. Kumar sold goods to Swaroop on April 1, 2004, for Rs. 11,000. On the above date, Kumar drew two bills for Rs. 4,000 and Rs. 7,000 for three months and four months, respectively, 'after date' on Swaroop. The said bills were duly accepted by Swaroop on April 2, 2004. At maturity, both the bills were honoured which were retained by the drawer till maturity.

   Pass necessary journal entries in the books of Kumar and Swaroop.

2. Ravi sold goods to Kamal on February 20, 2006, for Rs. 20,000. On February 24, Kamal issued a cheque of Rs. 6,000 in favour of Ravi and accepted a bill for the balance amount on March 1, 2006, for three months drawn by Ravi. At maturity, the said bill was duly honoured.

   Give necessary entries in the books of Ravi and Kamal.

3. Mr. Dutt sold goods to Mr. Bhaduri on March 14, 2004, for Rs. 15,000. On March 18, Mr. Bhaduri returned the goods for Rs. 3,000 to Mr. Dutt. On April 1, Mr. Dutt drew a bill of Rs. 12,000 on Mr. Bhaduri for four months. On the same day, Mr. Bhaduri accepted the bill and duly returned the same. At maturity, the above bill was duly honoured.

   Pass the necessary journal entries in the books of Mr. Dutt and Mr. Bhaduri.

4. Mr. Rao accepted a bill of Rs. 8,000 on April 1, 2004 for three months drawn by Mr. Saxena for goods sold to him during the last month. At maturity, Mr. Rao duly honoured the bill by paying cash of Rs. 6,000 and a bank draft of Rs. 2,000.

   Show the journal entries in the books of both the parties.

5. Vishnu drew two bills of Rs. 5,000 and Rs. 4,000 on Govind for two months and three months, respectively, on January 1, 2006. Govind accepted the first bill on January 2, 2006, and returned the other as the said bill was not properly prepared. On January 10, 2006, Vishnu drew a fresh bill of Rs. 4,000 for three months and received Govind's acceptance on the same date. Both the bills were duly honoured.

   Show the necessary entries and Ledger Accounts in the books of both the parties.

6. On March 1, 2003, S. Laha sold goods to D. Sinha For Rs. 8,000 subject to 10% Trade Discount. On March 10, S. Laha paid cash of Rs.2,000 and issued a cheque of Rs. 3,000 in favour of Mr. Laha. On April 1, 2003, Mr. Laha drew a bill on Mr. Sinha for the balance amount due for two months. Mr. Laha accepted the said bill duly and returned the same to him on that date. At maturity, all the bills were duly honoured.

   Pass journal entries in the books of Mr. Laha and Mr. Sinha.

7. On March 15, 2007, P sells goods to Q for Rs. 15,000 and drew upon the latter two bills for Rs. 9,000 and Rs. 6,000, both payable two months and three months after date. At maturity, the acceptor duly met both the bills.

   Show P's account in the books of Q and show Q's Account in the books of P.

8. On April 1, 2005, G accepted a bill of exchange for Rs. 7,000 after sight payable at three months and paid Rs. 2,800 in cash to H in full settlement of his account of Rs. 10,000. On the due date, the bill was honoured.

   Give necessary entries in the books of H and show H's account in the books of G.

9. On January 1, 2007, Ram sold goods to Rahim for Rs. 10,000 and allowed 10% Trade Discount. On January 15, 2007, Ram drew a bill of Rs. 6,000 payable at three months after sight as per the advice of Rahim. Rahim accepted the same on January 18, 2007, and returned the bill. At maturity, the bill was honoured.

   Give the necessary Ledger Accounts of Ram and the journal entries in the books of Rahim.

10. Ashoke sold goods to Anup on March 1, 2003, for Rs. 6,200. On that date, Ashoke drew a bill of Rs. 5,000 on Anup for three months after sight. Anup accepted the same on April 3, 2003, and returned it to Ashoke. On April 20, 2003, Anup paid Rs.1,050 in cash to Ashoke for the balance amount due in full settlement of his dues. On the due date, the bill was honoured.

    Give journal entries and Ledger Accounts in the books of Ashoke.

Discounting of Bill with the Bank

11. G. Prasad received an acceptance of Rs. 6,000, payable at three months from S. Ghosh on April 1, 2004. On May 1, 2004, Mr. Prasad discounted the above bill with his bank at 12% discount p.a. At maturity, the said bill was duly honoured.

    Show journal entries in the books of both the parties.

    Ans: Discount Charges Rs. 120.

12. On January 1, 2007, N. Yadav drew two bills of Rs. 4,500 and Rs. 6,000 for three months and four months, respectively, on P. Singh. On January 15, 2007, Mr. Yadav discounted the first bill with his banker @ 10% p.a. and the second bill on February 1, 2007, at the same rate with his banker. Both the bills were duly honoured on the due date.

    Show journal entries in the books of both the parties.

    Ans: Discount Charges: First bill Rs. 97 (approx.) and second bill Rs. 150.

13. Manas drew three bills of Rs. 4,000, Rs. 3,000 and Rs. 2,000 for ninety days on January 10, 2008, on Varun. On the same date, Varun accepted the above bills in full settlement of his dues of Rs. 9,200. The first bill was discounted on January 28, and the drawer discounted the third bill on February 12, 2008 at the rate of 12% with the bank. The drawer retained the second bill until maturity. At maturity, all the bills were honoured.

    Give necessary entries in the books of all the parties and show Varun's account in the books of Manas.

    Ans: Discount Charges: First bill Rs. 99 (approx.) and third bill Rs. 39 (approx.); Discount Allowed to Varun: Rs. 200.

14. Mr. Todi owned money to Mr. Deol and hence accepted two bills of exchange of Rs. 5,000 and Rs. 4,000 of ninety days duration drawn on him by the latter on February 12, 2004. On March 1, 2004, the first bill was discounted by Mr. Deol with his banker @ 10% p.a. The other was also discounted at the same rate fifteen days after the first bill. On the due date, both the bills were honoured.

    Give journal entries in the books of Mr. Deol and the necessary Ledger Accounts in the books of Mr. Todi.

    Ans: Discount Charges: First bill Rs. 103 (approx.) and second bill Rs. 66.

15. Swaraj sold goods to Pratap for Rs. 8,400 on January 1, 2008. On February 1, 2008, Pratap paid Rs. 1,400 in cash and accepted a bill for three months on that date drawn by Swaraj for the balance amount due. Subsequently the said bill was discounted by Swaraj with the Bank @ 12% p.a. and the bank charged discount of Rs. 138 on it. At maturity, the bill was duly honoured. Give necessary journal entries in the books of Swaraj.

    Ans: The bill was discounted on March 5, 2008 (i.e., 60 days before the maturity), because bank charges discount charges for 60 days. Note: Discount charges for full year (i.e., 365 days) @ 12% on Rs. 7,000 is equal to Rs. 840. Hence, discount charges of Rs.138 is paid for 60 days (365/840 × 138 = 60).

Endorsement of Bill to Creditors

16. B.T. Traders purchased goods from Bombay Variety for Rs. 12,000 on March 1, 2004. On that date, B.T. Traders accepted two bills of Rs. 8,000 and Rs.4,000 for three months drawn by Bombay Variety. On March 15, Bombay Variety endorsed the second bill to Kumar Bros. in full settlement of their Accounts of Rs. 4,100. On April 1, Bombay Variety endorsed the first bill in favour of G. R. Bros. together with a cash of Rs. 2,000 as a part payment of their claim. Both the bills were duly honoured.

    Show necessary entries in the books of all the parties.

    Ans: Discount allowed by Kumar Bros. Rs. 100.

17. On January 1, 2005 Ranvir sold goods to Rakesh costing Rs.7,200. On January 10, Ranvir received cash of Rs. 1,200 from Rakesh and drew a bill for the balance amount due payable four months after date on January 15. On January 17, Ranvir endorsed the bill to Suresh in full settlement of his Account of Rs. 6,200. At maturity the bill was honoured.

    Give necessary journal entries in the books of Ranvir and Rakesh. Also show Suresh's Account in the books of Ranvir.

    Ans: Discount allowed by Suresh Rs. 200.

18. Vikash drew a bill for three months on Badal for Rs.4,900 on January 1, 2006. Badal accepted the bill duly on that date.

Give the necessary journal entries in the books of Vikash under each of the following cases.
(a) Vikash retained the bill till maturity and then realized it.
(b) The bill was endorsed to Vipin in full settlement of his account of Rs. 5,000.
(c) The bill was discounted with the bank immediately at Rs. 4,690.
The said bill was duly honoured at maturity.

19. On March 1, 2004, Karan drew a bill for three months for Rs. 1,000 on Kunal against dues from him and sent it for Kunal's acceptance. Kunal accepted and returned the bill on the same date. Karan then endorsed the bill to his creditor Dilip who discounted the bill with his banker at a discount of 5% per annum on March 21, 2004. On maturity, Kunal honoured the bill duly.
    Show the journal entries in the books of all the parties.
    Ans: Discount Charges Rs. 10 (approx.).

20. Ajit bought goods from Suresh on January 6, 2004, for Rs. 8,000. He paid cash of Rs. 3,800 to Suresh on January 10, 2004, and accepted two bills of equal amount payable after two months and three months, respectively. Suresh endorsed the bill payable after three months to Amit and discounted the other bill with the bank at 6 % p.a. immediately. Both the bills were honoured on the due dates.
    Give necessary entries in the books of all the parties.

21. On January 1, 2004, Mr. Talwar purchased goods valued at Rs. 2,500 from Mr. Nigam and paid Rs.500 in cash. On January 3, 2004, Mr. Talwar sent Mr. Nigam his two acceptances, one for Rs. 1,200 at two months and the second for Rs. 800 for three months. On the next day, Mr. Nigam discounted the first bill with bankers at 9% p.a. and retained the second bill with him. At maturity, both the bills were honoured.
    Show journal entries in the books of all the parties.
    Ans: Discount Charges Rs. 18.

22. On February 1, 2007, Mr. Sen sold goods to Mr. Roy for Rs. 20,000. Mr. Sen, unable to pay the amount at present, accepted a bill for the amount due for three months. On April 3, 2007, Mr. Sen discharged the bill and was allowed a rebate of 9% p.a.
    Show the journal entries in the books of both the parties.
    Ans: Rebate allowed Rs. 150.

Bill sent to Bank for Collection

23. Mr. N. Khan sold goods to Mr. P. Shah on May 1, 2006, for Rs.16,000. On that date, Mr. Khan received two bills of Rs. 8,000 and Rs. 4,000 payable at 60 days from Mr. Shah. On May 15, he discounted the first bill with his banker @ 12% p.a. and sent the other bill for collection through bank seven days before maturity. At maturity, both the bills were honoured.
    Give necessary journal entries in the books of both the parties.
    Ans: Discount Charges Rs. 126 (approx.).

24. On January 1, 2007, Amar drew on Sashi four bills of Rs. 4,000 each payable three months after date in each case. On receiving back the bills duly accepted by Sashi, Amar discounted the first bill @ 8% p.a. on January 6, 2007, endorsed the second bill to Sunil in settlement of debt, sent the third bill to his banker for collection and decided to retain the fourth bill till its maturity. All the bills were paid on maturity.
    Show the necessary journal entries in the books of Amar and Sashi.

    [W.B.H.S., Adapted]
    Ans: Discount Charges Rs. 77 (approx.).

25. Ravi drew two bills of Rs. 3,000 and Rs. 5,000 on Raju for two months and three months, respectively, after date on April 1, 2004. Raju accepted the above bills and passed it to Ravi on April 3, 2004. Seven days before the due date, both the bills were sent to bank for collection. At maturity, both the bills were honoured and the bank charged Rs. 30 and Rs. 50, respectively, as their service charges.
    Give necessary journal entries in the books of Ravi.

Retirement of Bill

26. On January 1, 2004, Kamal received two bills of Rs. 7,000 and Rs. 3,000 payable at 90 days from Vimal after his acceptance. Kamal immediately discounted the first bill with his banker at 12% p.a. On March 4, 2004, Vimal having surplus funds paid the second bill and was allowed a rebate @ 12% p.a.

Give journal entries in the books of both the parties.

Ans: Rebate allowed Rs. 30.

27. On May 1, 2008, Pankaj accepted a bill of Rs. 4,600 drawn by Suresh, payable at three months after sight. After expiry of one month, Suresh paid the bill on request of Pankaj and was allowed a rebate @ 10% p.a.

Show Pankaj's Account and the necessary journal entries in the books of Suresh.

Ans: Rebate allowed Rs. 77 (approx.).

Dishonour of a Bill

28. Raja received on March 1, 2004, a bill for Rs. 3,000 payable after two months, accepted by Suman. He then endorsed the bill on March 4, 2004, to Rajiv. Rajiv discounted the bill with his banker on March 15, 2004, receiving Rs. 2,980 in cash. On the due date, the bill was dishonoured.

Show the necessary journal entries in the books of all the concerned parties.

[W.B.H.S., Adapted]

29. On April 1, 2004, W drew bills for Rs. 9,000, Rs. 7,000 and Rs.5,000 for three months, two months and one month, respectively, on Y. On the above date, all the bills were accepted by Y. On April 11, 2004, the first bill was endorsed to X and on May 1, 2004 the second bill was discounted with the Bank @ 12% p.a. The third bill was retained by the drawer till maturity. At maturity, all the bills were dishonoured.

Give necessary journal entries in the books of W, Y and X.

30. B sold goods to C for Rs. 8,600 on April 1, 2007. B drew two bills on C for Rs. 4,000 and Rs. 4,600, payable at three months. B discounted the first bill immediately with his banker @ 10% p.a. and retained the second bill till maturity. At maturity, both the bills were dishonoured.

Show journal entries in the books of B and C.

31. On May 1, 2008, Q received an acceptance of Rs. 6,000 from R, payable at three months. On May 12, 2008, Q endorsed the bill to S. On June 1, 2008, S then endorsed the said bill to W in full settlement of his Account of Rs. 6,100. At maturity, the bill was dishonoured.

Give necessary journal entries in the books of Q, R, S and W.

[**Note:** Discount received by S Rs.100 and the said discount is to be cancelled at maturity.]

32. Pankaj sold goods to Manas for Rs. 16,000 on January 1, 2004. Manas paid cash of Rs. 4,000, and accepted two bills of Rs 8,000 and Rs.4,000 drawn by Pankaj, payable at three months and four months, respectively. The first bill was discounted with the bank @ 10% p.a. one month before maturity and the second was sent to bank for collection, seven days before maturity. At maturity, both the bills were dishonoured.

Show necessary journal entries in the books of Pankaj and Manas.

33. On January 1, 2006, Nitin purchased goods from Vishal for Rs. 30,000 on credit. On January 4, 2006, Nitin sold the goods to Shekhar for Rs. 40,000 also on credit. For this purpose, he drew two bills on Shekhar for Rs. 20,000 each on January 5, 2006, payable after one month and two months, respectively.

On January 8, 2006, Nitin endorsed the first bill in favour of Vishal along with a cheque of Rs. 10,000 to settle the amount due to him. However, the second bill was held by him till maturity. On due dates, both the bills were dishonoured.

Show the entries in the books of Nitin and Vishal.

[W.B.H.S., Adapted]

34. On March 3, 2004, Ram drew three bills on Bharat for Rs. 4,000, Rs. 5,000 and Rs. 3,000, payable at four months, three months and two months, respectively. Bharat accepted and returned all the bills to Ram. On March 18, 2004, Ram endorsed the first bill to Ratan for discharging a debt of Rs. 3,800. Ram discounted the second bill with his banker @ 10% p.a. on April 7, 2004. Bharat paid off the third bill but failed to pay the other two bills.

Give necessary journal entries in the books of all the parties.

[**Note:** Interest paid to Ratan Rs. 200]

35. On April 1, 2007, Sunil sold goods to Rupam at Rs. 13,000 and drew two bills of exchange for Rs. 8,000 and Rs. 5,000, payable at three months and two months, respectively. Rupam duly accepted both the bills. Sunil discounted the first bill with his banker @ 12% p.a. on May 2, 2007, and endorsed the second bill in favour of Jayraj together with cash of Rs. 1,200 in order to pay off his dues of Rs. 6,400 in full settlement. Both the bills were dishonoured at maturity.

Show entries in the books of all the parties.

[**Note:** Discount received by Sunil Rs. 200 and the said discount is to be cancelled at maturity.]

36. On January 15, 2008, G received an acceptance of Rs. 7,800 from H, payable at three months. On January 28, 2008, he endorsed the said bill to T in full settlement of his dues of Rs. 8,000. T then discounted the same with his banker @ 12% p.a. on February 16, 2008. The bill was dishonoured at maturity.

Give necessary entries in the books of G, H and T.

Ans: Interest paid to T Rs. 200.

37. On April 1, 2006, Komal accepted a bill for Rs. 8,000 payable at three months drawn by Sujata. On April 4, 2008, Sujata discounted the bill with her banker @ 12% p.a. The bill was dishonoured on the due date and the bank charged Rs. 20 as expense.

Give journal entries in the books of both the parties.

38. Mr. Dalmia received a bill of Rs. 8,000 on January 1, 2007, for three months from Mr. Sharma, after his acceptance. At maturity, the said bill was dishonoured and noting charge of Rs. 40 was incurred.

Show the necessary entries in the books of Mr. Dalmia under each of the following cases:

(a) If he retains the bill until maturity.

(b) If he endorses the bill to Mr. Sen in full settlement of his Account of Rs. 8,200.

(c) If he discounts the bill with his banker @ 10% p.a.

(d) If he sends the bill to bank for collection on April 1, 2007.

39. On April 1, 2008, Sourav drew a bill on Tilak for Rs. 9,000 at three months which was duly accepted by Tilak. Sourav then endorsed the bill to Akash in full satisfaction of a claim of Rs. 9,400 on April 12, 2008. Akash then purchased goods from Aneek for Rs. 9,300 subject to 5% Trade Discount on April 15, 2008 and endorsed the said bill to Aneek in full satisfaction. At maturity, the bill was dishonoured and a noting charge of Rs. 45 was incurred.

Give the journal entries in the books of all the parties.

[**Note:** Discount received by Sourav Rs.400 and the said discount is to be cancelled at maturity. Interest charged by Aneek Rs.165 (9,000 – 8,835).]

40. Amar sold goods to Amber for Rs. 15,000 on January 10, 2007. He drew a bill on Amber on January 14, 2007, for Rs. 15,000 at three months' sight. Amber accepted the same on January 16. Amar then endorsed the bill to Kamal in payment of his dues for Rs. 14,500 in full settlement. The bill was finally dishonoured by Amber on due date. Amar had to take up the bill from Kamal on full payment together with noting charge of Rs.60.

Show the journal entries with ledger accounts in the books of Amar and Kamal.

Ans: Interest charged by Kamal Rs. 500.

41. Sreya sold goods to Uma for Rs. 7,500 on March 1, 2008. Uma accepted a bill of Rs. 5,000 for two months drawn by Sreya and paid cash of Rs, 2,500 on the same date. Sreya endorsed the bill to Rani on March 18, 2008, who discounted the same with her bank at Rs. 4,850 on April 1, 2008. At maturity, the bill was dishonoured and noting charge of Rs. 15 was incurred.

Pass journal entries in the books of all the parties.

Insolvency of the Drawee

42. Suresh received an acceptance of Rs. 3,600 for four months on June 1, 2006, from Dinesh. He then discounted the bill with his bank at 12% p.a. immediately. At maturity, the bill was dishonoured due to insolvency of Dinesh, the noting charge being Rs. 20. On October 18, 2006, he realized Rs. 1,650 from Dinesh's estate as final dividend.

Give the entries in the books of Suresh and Dinesh.

Ans: Bad Debt Rs. 1,970.

43. Rana drew a bill on Raja for Rs. 4,000 on January 1, 2004, for three months. After its acceptance, Rana discounted the bill with the bank at Rs. 3,920 on January 18, 2004. At maturity, the bill was dishonoured due to insolvency of Raja and noting charge of Rs. 20 was incurred. On May 15, 2004, Rana received a final dividend @ 40 paisa in a rupee from Raja's estate.

Pass the entries in the books of all the parties.

Ans: Bad Debt Rs. 2,412.

44. Deepak received a bill of Rs. 4,000, payable at three months from Tushar on April 1, 2007. On April 14, 2007, Deepak endorsed the said bill to Suresh. Suresh discounted the bill immediately with the bank @ 15% p.a. At maturity, the bill was dishonoured due to the insolvency of Tushar and the final dividend realized was Rs. 900 from Suresh's estate on October 12, 2007.

Give necessary entries in the books of all the parties.

Ans: Bad Debt Rs. 3,100.

45. On January 1, 2006, Mr. Roshan sold goods to Mr. Singh valuing Rs. 30,000. On January 4, 2006, Mr. Roshan received from Mr. Singh Rs. 10,000 and drew a bill payable three months after date for the balance. On the same date, Mr. Roshan endorses the accepted bill to Mr. Khan for full settlement of a debt of Rs. 21,000. On the due date, the bill was dishonoured and Mr. Singh having become insolvent, met 75% of his acceptance on May 10, 2006.

Give journal entries in the books of Mr. Roshan and Mr. Singh.

[W.B.H.S., Adapted]

Ans: Bad debt Rs. 5,000.

[**Note:** Discount received by Roshan Rs.1,000 and the said discount is to be cancelled at maturity.]

46. G sold goods worth Rs. 19,000 to K who makes a part payment of Rs. 9,000 by a cheque on January 1, 2005. K accepts a bill for three months drawn on him by G for the balance amount due. G endorsed the said bill to P in full settlement of his claim of Rs. 9,800. At maturity, the bill was dishonoured due to insolvency of K. A final dividend of 75 paisa in a rupee was realized from his estate on May 19, 2005.

Show necessary entries in the books of G, K and P. Also, show P's account in the books of G.

Ans: Bad debt Rs. 2,500; Interest charged by G Rs. 100.

47. One month before maturity, R discounted a bill of Rs. 8,000 with his banker on April 12, 2007, @ 12% p.a. At maturity, the bill was dishonoured and noting charge of Rs. 60 was paid by bank. On May 29, 2007, it was reported that Q, the acceptor of the said bill, had become insolvent and a final dividend @ 60% was realized from his estate on June 4, 2007.

Show Q's Account and the necessary entries in the books of R.

Ans: Bad debt Rs. 3,224.

48. Give journal entries in the books of H:
    (a) P's acceptance of Rs. 6,000, which had been discounted with the bank at Rs.5,800 has been returned by the bank unpaid and noting charge of Rs. 60 paid by bank.
    (b) H's acceptance for Rs. 3,200 is discharged by G's acceptance to H for a similar amount.
    (c) Q retires an acceptance of Rs. 4,200 drawn on him by H at a rebate of Rs. 150.

Renewal of Bill

49. On April 1, 2006, Arun received a bill of Rs. 4,800 from Niraj after his acceptance, payable at two months. At maturity, the bill was dishonoured. On the due date, Niraj was able to pay Rs. 1,800 in cash and accepted a fresh bill for two months for the balance amount due together with an interest of Rs. 140. At maturity, the new bill was duly honoured.
    Give necessary entries in the books of both the parties.
    Ans: New bill amount Rs. 3,140.

50. On January 1, 2008, X accepted a bill of Rs. 5,000 drawn by Y, for three months. On the due date, X approaches Y to accept an immediate cash payment of Rs. 1,000 and to draw a new bill for the balance amount due for two months together with an interest @ 15% p.a. for the extended period, by cancelling the old bill. Y acts accordingly. The new bill was duly honoured.
    Give necessary entries in the books of X and Y.
    Ans: New bill amount Rs. 4,100.

51. On March 1. 2007, G. Das received an acceptance from K. Kumar for Rs. 8,000 payable in three months. The bill was discounted by G. Das with his Bank @ 12% p.a. immediately. On the due date, the bill was dishonoured and noting charge of Rs. 60 was incurred. On the due date, K. Kumar was able to pay Rs. 2,500 in cash and accepted a new bill for the balance amount due for Rs. 5,700, payable at two months. At maturity, the new bill was honoured.
    Give journal entries in the books of both the parties.
    Ans: Interest charged on renewal of the bill Rs. 140.

52. Q accepted a bill for three months for Rs. 4,000 on January 1, 2004, drawn by P. At maturity, the bill was dishonoured and noting charge of Rs. 40 was paid. On the due date, Q was able to pay Rs. 1,000 through a bank draft and accepted a fresh bill for the balance amount due for two months together with an interest @ 12% p.a. The new bill was duly honoured
    Pass journal entries in the books of P and Q.
    Ans: Interest charged on renewal of the bill Rs. 61; new bill amount Rs. 3,101.

53. On January 18, 2007, Dinesh discounted a bill of Rs. 5,000 with his bank at Rs. 4,850. On April 4, 2007, the bill was dishonoured at maturity and noting charge of Rs. 60 was incurred. On the date Rahul, the acceptor of the above bill, paid Rs. 1,500 in cash, plus Rs. 150 for discount charges in cash and accepted a new bill for the balance amount due together with interest @ 18% p.a. for three months to Dinesh. The new bill was also dishonoured at maturity.
    Show necessary entries in the books of Dinesh and Rahul.
    Ans: Interest charged on renewal of the bill Rs. 160; new bill amount Rs. 3,720.

54. On April 15, 2006, Mahim an acceptor informed his drawer Nitish to draw a new bill at three months for Rs. 4,000, by cancelling an old bill of Rs. 5,200 and accept Rs. 1,350 in cash. Nitish acts accordingly.
    Give necessary entries in the books of Nitish.
    Ans: Interest charged on renewal of the bill Rs. 150.

55. A month before maturity of a bill of Rs. 3,900, Giri the acceptor requests Hari, the drawer to accept immediate cash payment of Rs. 900 and draw a new bill for the balance amount due for three months together with an interest @ 12% p.a. for the extended period on February 14, 2006. Hari acts accordingly.

Pass necessary journal entries in the books of Giri and Hari.

Ans: Interest charged on renewal of the bill Rs. 60 (actual extended period is two months); new bill amount Rs. 3,060.

56. On January 1, 2008, Mr. D. Dharam accepted a bill of Rs. 12,000 drawn by Mr. N. Nandalal for three months. At maturity, the bill was dishonoured, the noting charge being Rs.100. One month after maturity, Mr. D. Dharam approaches Mr. N. Nandalal to accept an immediate cash payment of Rs. 3,100 and to draw a new bill for the balance amount due for two months together with an interest @ 18% p.a. for the outstanding period. Mr. N. Nandalal acts accordingly. The new bill was duly honoured.

Give necessary entries in the books of Mr. N. Nandalal and Mr. D. Dharam.

Ans: Interest charged on renewal of the bill Rs. 452 (on Rs. 12,100 for one month and on Rs.9,000 for two months); New bill amount Rs. 9,452.

57. On April 1, 2008, Varun buys goods worth Rs. 8,000 from Gautam. Instead of paying cash, Varun agrees to accept a bill, payable at three months including interest @ 12% p.a. for an extended period. At maturity, the bill was dishonoured but Varun was able to pay Rs. 2,800 in cash and accept a fresh bill for the balance amount due for two months including an interest of Rs. 320 as per the agreement with Gautam.

Show Varun's account in the books of Gautam and the journal entries in the books of Varun.

Ans: New bill amount Rs. 5,760 (5,440 + 320).

Accommodation Bills

58. On April 1, 2006, Q agreed to accept a bill of Rs. 9,000 drawn on him for three months for accommodation in favour of R, which was duly made by Q and R. R then discounted the bill with his banker at Rs. 8,750. At maturity, R remits the amount to Q and the bill was honoured.

Give necessary journal entries in the books of Q and R.

59. On May 1, 2008, Suparna approached her friend Garima for a loan of Rs. 4,000. Garima was not in a position to provide the loan but accepted a bill for three months for the said amount for accommodation. Suparna acts accordingly and discounts the bill with her banker immediately at 12% p.a. On the due date, Suparna remits her obligation to Garima and the bill was duly honoured.

Pass necessary entries in the books of Suparna and Garima.

60. Samir draws a bill of Rs. 6,000 on Saikat at two months for mutual accommodation of both on January 1, 2007. After acceptance, Samir immediately discounted the bill at Rs. 5,880 and shared the proceeds in the ratio of 2:1. On the due date, Samir remits his obligation to Saikat and the bill was honoured.

Give journal entries in the books of both the parties.

Ans: At maturity, Samir will pay Rs.4,000 to Saikat.

61. Sujit and Somesh draw on each other bills of exchange at three months for Rs. 9,000 each for their mutual accommodation. Both of them discounted their bills with their respective bankers @ 15% p.a. At maturity, both the bills were honoured.

Give necessary entries in the books of both the parties.

62. Rupraj drew a bill on Dev for Rs. 6,000 for three months for their mutual accommodation. Rupraj discounted the same with his banker at Rs. 5,800 and shared the proceeds equally. On the same date, Dev drew another bill for Rs. 8,000 for three months for the same purpose. After acceptance, Dev discounted the bill at Rs. 7,700 and shared the proceeds equally. On the due date, Dev remits his obligation in cash in full settlement of his account with Rupraj and both the bills were duly honoured.

Pass necessary entries in the books of Rupraj and Dev.

Ans: At maturity, Dev will pay Rs.1,000 to Rupraj.

63. P and Q each draw a bill for Rs. 3,000 payable at three months on each other on January 1, 2008. They discounted their bills at 10% p.a. and 12% p.a., respectively. At maturity, P's acceptance was honoured but Q failed to meet his acceptance, and as such, P had to take it up. Q then paid cash of Rs. 1,000 and accepted a fresh bill for two months together with an interest @ 10% p.a. for the extended period for the balance amount due. The fresh bill was duly honoured at maturity.

Give necessary journal entries in the books of P and Q.

Ans: New bill amount Rs.2,033 (2,000 + 33 approx.).

64. On March 10, 2008, Mr. M. Sanyal draws a bill of Rs. 9,000 on Mr. G. Guha at three months for mutual accommodation of both and was duly accepted. Mr. M. Sanyal discounts the bill at Rs. 8,760 and shared the proceeds in the ratio of 2:1 immediately. On the due date, M. Sanyal fails to remits his obligation, as he was declared bankrupt and the final dividend @ 40 paise in a rupee was realized from his estate on July 23, 2008.

Give journal entries in the books of both the parties.

Ans: M.Sanyal's obligation at maturity was Rs. 6,000; Bad debt Rs. 3,600

65. On April 18, 2008, Kuntal draws a bill of Rs. 10,000 on Jadav at three months for mutual accommodation of both. After acceptance, Kuntal discounts the bill at Rs. 9,600 and shared the proceeds in the ratio of 3:2 forthwith. On the same day, Jadav draws another bill for Rs. 9,000 on Kuntal for three months. He then discounted the same with his bank at Rs. 8,800 and remitted two-fifth of the proceeds to Mr. Kuntal. On the due date, Kuntal met his acceptance but Jadav failed to meet his acceptance due to his insolvency, which was paid by Kuntal. Final dividend of 30 paise in a rupee was realized from his estate on August 25, 2008.

Give journal entries in the books of both the parties.

Ans: Jadav's obligation at maturity was Rs. 9,400; Bad debt Rs. 6,580

Revision Problems (Advanced)

66. Himesh sold goods to Ritesh for Rs. 12,000 on January 1, 2008. On that date, Himesh drew four bills of Rs. 3,000 each for three months, which were duly accepted by Ritesh. On January 15, 2008, Himesh endorsed the first bill for Rs. 3,000 to Naresh in full settlement of his account of Rs. 3,150. On February 1, 2,008, he discounted the second bill with the bank at 15% p.a. The third bill was retained by him till maturity and the fourth bill was sent to bank for collection on March 30, 2,008.

Show the entries for the above transactions and the necessary entries in the books of all the parties if the above bills were:

(a) honoured at maturity, and

(b) dishonoured at maturity.

67. Manas drew two bills for Rs. 5,000 and Rs. 3,000 for three months on March 1, 2007, on Tapas. Tapas duly accepted the same on that date. On March15, 2007, Manas discounted the first bill with his bank at 12% p.a. On March 19, 2007, he endorsed the second bill to Tarun in full settlement of his account of Rs. 2,850. At maturity, the second bill was honoured but the first bill was dishonoured and noting charge of Rs. 20 was incurred. On the due date, Tapas paid Rs. 1,020 to Manas and accepted a fresh bill for two months for the balance amount due together with an interest at 15% p.a. At maturity, the fresh bill was duly honoured.

Give necessary entries in the books of Manas and Tapas.

Ans: New bill amount Rs. 4,100 (4,000 + 100).

68. Rupak accepted a bill of Rs. 9,000 for three months on January 1, 1993, for goods purchased during the last month. Champak, the drawer, discounts the same with this bank at 18% p.a. on that date. At the maturity, the bill was dishonoured and noting charge incurred Rs. 45. Rupak paid Rs. 3,000 in cash for bill, noting charge in cash, interest @ 12% on the outstanding part and discount charges in cash to Champak, and accepted two bills of Rs. 4,000 and Rs. 2,000 for three months and two months, respectively. Both the bills were retained by the drawer till maturity and were honoured.

Pass entries in the books of both the parties.

[**Hint:** Interest charged on two bills Rs. 120 and Rs. 40; Discount charged by bank Rs. 405; Total cash paid by Rupak at maturity of the original bill Rs. 3,610(Rs. 3,000 + 45 + 120 + 40 + 405)]

69. Mukul sold goods to Sujit for Rs. 3,800, subject to 10% Trade Discount on April 1, 1990. Sujit endorsed an acceptance of his customer, Mr. K, amounting to Rs. 3,500 to Mukul in full settlement of his obligation for the above sale (actual) immediately.

On April 16, 1990, Mukul discounted the above bill with his bank at 12% p.a. and the discount charged by the bank was Rs. 70 for the bill. At the maturity, the said bill was dishonoured, the noting charge being Rs. 20. On July 16, 1990, Sujit paid Rs. 1,050 in cash (including the discount charges) to Mukul and accepted a fresh bill for two months for the balance amount due together with interest at 18% p.a. for the outstanding period on the outstanding balances. The new bill was retained by Mukul till the maturity and it was duly honoured.

Give journal entries in the books of Mukul and Sujit.

[**Hint:** Actual goods were sold to Sujit for Rs. 3,420 (Rs. 3,800 − 10% of 3,800). Sujit endorsed a bill for Rs. 3,500 in full settlement of his obligation. Hence, Rs. 80 paid in excess to Mukul, Rs. (3,500 − 3,420), would be considered as interest given by Sujit. On April 16, 1990, K's acceptance was discounted, discount charge being Rs. 70 @ 12% p.a. on Rs. 3,500. Therefore, discount charges paid for the period is Rs. 420 (on Rs. 3,500 @ 12% full year's discount charges). Hence, Rs. 70 is paid for [(12/420 × 70)] = 2 months. Thus, the date of maturity of the original bill was June 16, 1990 (April 16, 1990 + 2 months). Sujit paid Rs. 1,050 on July 16, 1990, i.e. one month after maturity. Hence, interest on the fresh bill is to be calculated @ 18% p.a. on Rs. 3,520 for one month and on Rs. 2,540 (3,500 + 20 + 70 − 1,050) for two months, i.e., Rs. 52.80 + 76.20 = Rs. 129. The amount of fresh bill = Rs. 2,540 + Rs. 129 = Rs. 2,669]

70. On January 1, 1993, Amit drew a bill of Rs. 5,100 on Pratap for three months for mutual accommodation of himself and Pratap. The bill was discounted by him at Rs. 4,800 on that date and send one-third of the proceeds was sent to Pratap on the next day.

On February 1, 1993, Pratap drew another bill of Rs. 3,000 on Amit for two months. The said bill was discounted with the bank at 18% p.a. by him and shared the proceeds equally immediately. At maturity, Amit was able to pay Rs. 2,100 only towards his obligation to Pratap due to financial problem. Hence, both the bills were paid by Pratap, and Pratap drew a fresh bill for one month for the balance amount due together with interest at 18% p.a. on Amit. Before the maturity, Amit became insolvent and the final dividend of Rs. 1,140 was realized from his estate.

Show the necessary entries in the books of Amit and Pratap.

[**Hint:** At the maturity, Amit's obligation was to pay (two-thirds of Rs. 5,100) + (half of Rs. 3,000) = Rs. 4,900 to Pratap, but out of that he paid Rs. 2,100 only. Hence, balance Rs. 2,800 was outstanding. The amount of new bill would be Rs. 2,800 + interest @ 18% p.a. on Rs. 2,800 for one month = Rs. 2,842]

17

Financial Statements (Final Accounts)

17.1 NATURE OF FINANCIAL STATEMENTS

The first step in the accounting process is the preparation of financial statements. Data on individual accounting events are recorded in the account books as they occur. These data are periodically aggregated and summarized and provide the basis for preparing the financial statements. Financial statements are prepared to represent financial position of an enterprise at the end of the financial year to cater to the needs of users of the accounting information. It represents the growth, present position and the prospect of the firm on the basis of the recorded facts.

At the end of a financial period after preparing the trial balance, a trader or a businessman wants to know the financial results (profit or loss) and the financial position of the business. After the preparation of an Income Statement (or Trading and profit and loss account), the results of the business come out and after preparing the balance sheet, the financial position of the business is shown.

The above two statements—the Income Statement and the Balance Sheet, are known as **Final Accounts or Financial Statements**. Owners, Investors, the Government, Management, Employees, Creditors and other interested agencies are the users of the final accounts or the financial statements.

17.2 NEED AND USES OF FINAL ACCOUNTS

At the end of the financial period, after preparing the trial balance an enterprise wants to know the financial results (profit or loss) of the business and the financial position. After the preparation of trading and profit and loss account or an income statement, the result of the business come out and by preparing the balance sheet, the financial position of the business is shown. Thus, financial statements are the end products of the accounting process.

Final accounts or financial statements are prepared in monetary terms. These are historical documents and relate to the past period.

17.3 OBJECTIVES OF PREPARING FINANCIAL STATEMENTS

The basic objectives of preparing financial statements are as follows:

1. To represent the net financial results (profit or loss) of the business.
2. The financial statements are prepared to give a 'true and fair view' of the affairs of the firm.
3. To furnish information useful in making investment and credit decisions.
4. To provide information about business resources, claims to those resources and changes in them.

Thus, the object of financial statements is to provide information about the financial position and performance of an enterprise that is useful to a wider range of users in making economic decisions.

17.4 INCOME STATEMENT

An **income statement** is a measure of financial performance between two points in time. 'Two points in time' is meant for a time period, which is a financial year. The income statement is divided into two parts. The first part is called the **trading account**. It is prepared to know the trading result of a firm, i.e., gross profit or gross loss. The second part of the income statement is called **profit and loss account**. It is opened with gross profit or loss transferred from trading account. All incomes and expenses, which are not considered in trading account (i.e., indirect incomes and expenses) and all losses should be taken into account in the profit and loss account. If credit side is greater than the debit side of the profit and loss account, the difference is called **net profit**, and in the reverse case there will be **net loss**. On the basis of accrual concept, all actual incomes and expenditures are to be taken into consideration in profit and loss account.

17.5 USERS OF FINANCIAL STATEMENTS

The chief internal and external users of financial statements are management, owners, investors, creditors, employees, labour unions, the government, researchers, tax authorities, etc. The information required for the above stated users has already been explained in Chapter 1. (Section 1.11).

17.6 CLASSIFICATION OF RECEIPTS

Receipts may be classified into two categories:

1. Capital receipts, and
2. Revenue receipts.

Capital receipts: It consists of receipts from the sale of fixed assets or any receipts from the proprietor or any additional payments made by the shareholders/debenture holders of a company to their respective companies or in connection with the raising of capital for the business. These receipts are non-recurring in nature because they are not regularly earned. Suppose, land and buildings of an enterprise is sold at Rs.120,000. Here, the receipt of Rs.120,000 is a capital receipt. When shares or debentures of a company are sold at a premium, the amount realized by way of premium is to be considered as capital receipts.

Revenue receipts: They are earned by selling goods or services. These receipts are recurring in nature. Revenue receipts are the receipts earned during the ordinary course of business. They will increase the profits of the firm. We can also say that any receipt which is not a capital receipt is a revenue receipt. Revenue receipts are not same as revenue profits. Suppose, goods costing Rs. 14,000 are sold at Rs. 18,000. Here Rs. 18,000 is revenue receipt and Rs. 4,000 is revenue profit.

17.7 CAPITAL PROFITS AND REVENUE PROFITS

Here, profits are not earned by normal trading activity. Instead, they arise in the business from certain sources which are non-recurring in nature. Thus, it is not regular in nature and arises from capital receipts. Suppose, land and buildings of an enterprise is sold at Rs. 120,000 while its book value is Rs. 80,000. Here, the receipt of Rs. 120,000 is a capital receipt and Rs. 40,000 is capital profit. Shares and debentures sold at a premium is an example of capital profit. It is usually transferred to capital reserve account or adjusted with capital losses.

Revenue profits are generally earned by selling goods or services. These receipts are recurring in nature. Revenue profits are earned during the ordinary course of business. They will increase the profit volume of the firm. Suppose, goods costing Rs. 14,000 are sold at Rs. 18,000. Here, Rs. 18,000 is revenue receipt and Rs. 4,000 is revenue profit. Revenue profits are distributed as dividends to the owners or proprietors, and for future security a part of these profits are transferred to the general reserve account.

17.8 CAPITAL EXPENDITURE

Capital expenditure refers to an outflow of funds either to acquire or to improve a fixed asset which will be used in the business or production to earn revenue for several years. It is thus incurred in an accounting year but its benefits are enjoyed by the enterprise for many years. The part of the fixed asset consumed in an accounting year in course of its use is known as **depreciation**. The fixed assets are entirely consumed over the years by rendering services. Therefore, depreciation is the permanent decrease in the value of a fixed asset and represents a part of the total cost of fixed asset used/consumed in an accounting period, and will be treated as revenue expenditure. Thus, capital expenditures include the cost of fixed assets acquired like, land and buildings, plant and machinery, furniture, cost of improving factory plant and machinery, etc., and cost of life extension or improvement of existing fixed assets, etc.

The following are the characteristic features of the capital expenditure:
1. It is incurred to acquire new fixed assets or to upgrade/improve the existing fixed assets.
2. It helps to increase the working capacity or productivity or to reduce the operating expenses of an enterprise.
3. Capital expenditure is incurred in an accounting year though its benefits are enjoyed by an enterprise over many years.
4. Here, fixed assets are not purchased for resale.
5. In addition to the cost of purchase of fixed assets, capital expenditure also includes the cost of installation, erection, registration, and carriage.

17.9 REVENUE EXPENDITURE

All those expenditures incurred in an accounting year to earn or maintain the revenue of the said year and the part of the fixed assets used/consumed in an accounting period will be treated as **revenue expenditure**. Thus, revenue expenditure is wholly consumed in an accounting year. It does not help in increasing the working capacity of an asset, instead it is incurred for running or maintaining the asset, i.e., the operating costs.

Expenses are the costs of the goods and services used up in the course of earning revenues while performing the commercial activities of an enterprise. Expenses usually include the cost of sales, other costs for running the business, and the costs of attracting and serving customers. Fixed assets such as plant and machinery are fully consumed during their life time (which is fixed). As their usefulness expires or is consumed in the operation of the business, their proportionate cost (i.e., depreciation) is allocated to expenses. If they lose their ability to generate revenue in future periods, then the concerned portion/value will be treated as expired costs. We may say that all the costs, the benefits of which have been exhausted during the accounting year are expenses.

Generally, the cost is distinguished as expired and unexpired. **Expired costs** are the ones which have help to produce revenues. Expired costs are recognized as expenses. **Unexpired costs** are those costs which still help to produce revenue in future. Such costs are recognized as assets and are to be shown in the balance sheet.

The expenses are classified mainly under two broad headings—direct expenses and indirect expenses. The expenses which are related to purchase or provide service to the customers for sale or to produce the goods for sale are known as **direct expenses** and the other costs which are incidental to run the business or to promote it are known as **indirect expenses**. Thus, expired costs or expenses are the outflow of funds in the process of earning revenue for a particular accounting period.

Table 17.1 distinguishes between revenue expenditures and capital expenditures.

TABLE 17.1 Differences between Revenue Expenditures and Capital Expenditure

Revenue expenditures	Capital expenditure
These expenditures are incurred for running the business or its day-to-day conduct in one accounting period, and its benefits are consumed in the same accounting period. For example, direct and indirect expenditure incurred for production, selling, distribution, administration, and so on.	The expenditures which are not fully consumed in an accounting period, or which increase the earning capacity or decrease the future costs and consequently, increase the profit of the business, are called capital expenditure.
Losses arise due to sale of fixed assets, depreciation of fixed assets, theft or damages by accident, and bad debt or payment of some compensation to workers or outsiders during the course of business.	These expenditures are non-recurring in nature.
Interest on loans are borrowed for the purpose of running the business.	Cost of goodwill, land and buildings, furniture and fixtures, patents, copywriters, cars, trademarks, additions to or extension of existing assets, installations, structural improvements of fixed assets, preliminary expenses, overhauling of second-hand machines, development of mines and plantation, etc., are some examples.
Expenses are incurred for the maintenance of fixed assets.	These are the expenses which are incurred for acquiring or to upgrade/improve the existing fixed assets.
Revenue expenditures include all direct and indirect expired costs.	There are no such direct and indirect costs.
Unexpired portion of revenue expenditure is known as **deferred revenue expenditure**.	Unexpired portion of capital expenditure is known as an **asset**.

17.10 DEFERRED REVENUE EXPENDITURE

There are some cases where the benefits of a revenue expenditure continues for more than one year. Such type of expenditures are known as **deferred revenue expenditure**. The total expenditure is to be written off in a number of years (subsequently), and the amount not yet written off is to be shown in the balance sheet asset side. For example, heavy expenditure incurred for advertisement. When some non-recurring expenditure, which is huge, is incurred for a particular purpose, the said amount is not fully exhausted in the accounting period in which it is incurred, because the benefit of the said expenditure will continue for number of coming years and hence, the unexhausted part is carried forward to the next year. Thus, a part of the said expenditure is adjusted yearly as revenue expenditure and the remaining portion is carried forward to the next year as deferred revenue expenditure. For example, an amount of Rs. 48,000 is expended for an advertisement campaign and it is estimated that the benefit of the said campaign will continue for six years. Under such circumstances, Rs. 8,000 will be charged yearly as revenue expenditure for six years. Hence, for the first year Rs. 8,000 will be shown as advertisement expenditure and the remaining Rs. 40,000 is to be shown as deferred revenue expenditure.

Table 17.2 shows the differences between revenue expenditure and deferred revenue expenditure, while Table 17.3 lists the points of differences between capital expenditure and deferred revenue.

TABLE 17.2 Differences between Revenue Expenditure and Deferred Revenue Expenditure

Revenue expenditures	Deferred revenue expenditure
The benefit of this expenditure is exhausted in a single accounting year.	The benefit of this expenditure lasts for more than one year.
It is a recurring expenditure.	It is a non-recurring expenditure.
It is regular.	It is not regular because it depends on the decision of the management.
The volume of this expenditure depends on the volume of the revenue income of the business.	It depends on the decision of the management to maintain the desired targeted revenue income of the business.
It arises from the regular course of business activities and depends on the nature of the business.	It arises from the huge amount incurred in revenue expenditure, but does not get exhausted in one accounting year.
It is not shown in the balance sheet.	It is shown in the balance sheet as an asset.

TABLE 17.3 Distinguish between Capital Expenditure and Deferred Revenue Expenditure

Capital expenditures	Deferred revenue expenditure
The benefit of this expenditure is not exhausted in one accounting year; it lasts for a long period.	The benefit of this expenditure is not exhausted in one accounting year, i.e., it lasts for more than one year.
It is related to an asset.	It is related to expenditure.
The impact of this expenditure will not affect the capital of the firm.	The impact of this expenditure will affect the capital of the firm.
Capital expenditure will not affect the profit of a firm directly.	Capital expenditure will affect the profit of a firm directly.
It is incurred as per the requirement and nature of the business.	It is incurred as per the requirement of a particular situation and is treated in the accounts as per the policy and decision of the management.
Capital expenditure helps to increase the earning capacity of the business.	Capital expenditure cannot help to increase the earning capacity of the business, but in some cases helps to maintain the existing profit volume.

17.11 TRADING ACCOUNT

The income statement is divided into two parts. The first part is called the **trading account**. It is prepared to find out the trading result of a firm, i.e., the gross profit or the gross loss. In the trading account, the cost of goods sold is shown on the left hand side, i.e., on the debit side, and the sales on the other side, i.e., on the credit side. When the sales are greater than the cost of goods sold, then the difference is called **gross profit**, and in the reverse case, there will be a **gross loss**. While preparing the trading account accrual concept is followed to ascertain the true profit or loss of the business. The specimen of a trading account is given in Table 17.4.

Table 17.4 The Specimen of a Trading Account

Trading Account

Dr.					Cr.
Particulars	(Rs.)	Amount (Rs.)	Particulars	(Rs.)	Amount (Rs.)
To Opening Stock			By Sales		
To Purchase			Less: Sales Returns		
Less: Purchase Return			By Closing Stock		
To Carriage inward					
To Carriage and Cartage					

for the year (or period) ended ... (date)

(Contd.)

Dr.   *Cr.*

Particulars	(Rs.)	Amount (Rs.)	Particulars	(Rs.)	Amount (Rs.)
To Wages					
To Freight					
To Customs duty					
To Dock dues					
To Import duty					
To Excise duty					
To Coal, gas and Oil					
To Motive Power or Fuel					
To Heating and Lighting					
To Octroi					
To Royalty on production					
To Gross Profit transferred to Profit and Loss A/c (Balancing figure)		****	By Gross Loss transferred to Profit and Loss A/c (Balancing figure)		****

17.11.1 Features of a Trading Account

The following features are derived from the trading account:

1. It is a nominal account and is prepared with the help of direct incomes and expenses.
2. It is prepared at the end of the financial year.
3. While preparing the trading account, accrual concept is followed.
4. It is the first part of the income statement.
5. The net result of the trading account is called **gross profit** or **gross loss,** as the case may be The said amount is then transferred to the profit and loss account.
6. All expenditures for purchasing or producing goods are shown on the debit side. All incomes by selling goods are shown on the credit side.
7. Costs of goods sold are shown on the debit side whereas the net sales are shown on the credit side.

17.11.2 Advantages of Trading Account

The following are some advantages for preparing the trading account:

1. At the end of a financial year, it is essential to know the gross profit earned or the loss suffered by a firm. From this, all the indirect expenses and losses are to be deducted to ascertain the net profit or loss of the business.
2. After calculating the gross profit, the gross profit ratio is calculated which helps the trader or the proprietor to evaluate the business performance in comparison to previous year or years.
3. It helps the management or the owner to take future action for improving the business performance. It also helps to increase or improve the sales volume under different situations.
4. Gross profit and gross profit ratio help to maintain business growth.
   (At present, everywhere there is competition which we cannot avoid and to sustain within this business world , it becomes essential to maintain a competitive price.)
5. It helps to increase the sales volume or to reduce the cost of goods sold.
6. It helps to analyse the increase or decrease in the volume of sales and other direct expenses in comparison to the previous year.

17.11.3 Gross Profit or Gross Loss

Gross profit or gross loss is the difference between the cost of goods sold and the net sale proceeds. When net sale proceeds exceeds the cost of goods sold, the difference is known as **gross profit**. When the cost of goods sold is greater than the net sale proceeds, it is known as **gross loss.** Here, sales means, goods sold during the financial year.

17.11.4 Important Items Used in Trading Account

1. Opening stock: It represents opening goods in hand, i.e., goods at the beginning of the year. In the case of a manufacturing concern it includes opening raw materials, finished goods and partly finished goods (or work in progress or semi-finished goods) at the beginning of the year. It is usually shown in the debit side of the trial balance from where it is transferred to the debit side of the trading account .

2. Purchases: Here purchase means goods or raw materials purchased during the period. It includes cash purchases, credit purchases and import of goods from foreign countries. Trading account shows the net purchases. To get the net purchases, goods returned to suppliers (or purchase returns or return outwards) are deducted form gross purchases. In some cases, goods that are distributed as free samples or those which are used by the proprietors for personal purposes (i.e., not sold during the period but used for some purpose), are to be deducted from purchases or opening stock.

3. Carriage inward or freight on purchase: Expenses incurred for carrying goods from the supplier's house to the godown are generally considered as carriage inward or freight on purchases. It is a direct expense and the trading account is debited for such expenses. If carriage is paid on purchase of some fixed assets or other items excluding goods then it is not to be considered in the trading account.

4. Wages: When wages are paid to the workers engaged in the production or in the preparation of goods for sale, then they are treated as **direct expenses** and the trading account is debited for those expenses. If wages are paid for other purposes, then such types of wages are to be considered as **indirect wages**. In some cases, wages and salaries are given. Under such circumstances, we may consider them as direct expenses. Salaries may be paid to charge men or foremen of an enterprise engaged in production, and they are to be considered as direct expenses like wages.

5. Fuel and power or gas, electricity, water, etc.: These expenses are direct expenses and the trading account is debited for such expenses. These expenses are production expenses since they are incurred for running the machineries within the factory.

6. Packing materials: When packing expenses are incurred or packing materials are used for packing the goods kept for sale without which those goods could not be sold, then they are to be treated as direct expenses. Trading Account is debited for these expenses. Again, if packing expenses are incurred for sending the goods to the customers after their sale, then they are to be considered as indirect expenses and the profit and loss account will be debited for the same.

7. Customs duty or import duty and dock charges: When goods are purchased from foreign countries, customs duty or import duty and dock charges are paid. These expenses are direct in nature. Trading account is debited for these expenses.

8. Octroi: It is a duty paid for goods purchased within the municipal limits. These expenses are direct in nature and the trading account is debited for these expenses.

9. Sales: Here, sales means goods or finished products sold during the period/the financial year. It includes cash sales, credit sales and export of goods to foreign countries. In trading account the net sales are shown. Thus, to get the net sales figure, goods returned from customers (or sales returns or return inwards) are deducted form gross sales. Sales of any fixed assets or other items wrongly included in sales are to be eliminated.

10. Closing stock: Closing stock means stock of goods or finished products that has remained unsold at the end of the year. Trading account is credited for these goods. Also, there are some other type of stock like stock of stationery, stock of postage, stock of factory consumables, etc., which are not considered as closing stock of goods. While valuing the closing stock, conservative accounting practice is generally followed. The rule is ''cost or market price, whichever is lower, should be taken into consideration''. Thus, if on the date of the balance sheet (i.e., on the closing date of the year), the market price of the inventory becomes lower than its cost, then the possible loss that may arise on sale of the same should be provided for, and accordingly, the inventory should be valued at the market price instead of at cost. On the other hand, if the market price of inventory becomes higher than its cost, the inventory should be valued at cost price. Generally, closing stock is not shown in the trial balance, however, when adjusted purchases or materials consumed are given then closing stock is shown in the trial balance.

Regarding valuation of closing stock, there are a number of methods out of which any one is followed based on the nature of goods used. The methods are explained in detail in Chapter 10. A particular method of valuation of stock is not suitable for all the firms. Thus, to select a particular method of valuation of stock, a number of factors are considered.

11. Stock turnover ratio: It is calculated by dividing the cost of goods sold for a particular period by the average stock of the said period. Stock turnover ratio is calculated as follows:

$$\text{Stock Turnover Ratio} = \frac{\text{Cost of goods sold}}{\text{Average stock}}$$

$$\text{Here, Average stock} = \frac{(\text{Opening stock} + \text{Closing stock})}{2}$$

Stock turnover ratio indicates the efficiency of the stock holding policy and performance of the business. The higher ratio indicates better performance because it shows how quickly the stock is turned over, and as a result, it automatically increases the volume of profit.

12. Gross profit ratio: It is calculated by dividing the gross profit by net sales. It expresses the result through percentage. The calculation of gross profit ratio is shown below:

$$\text{Gross Profit Ratio} = \frac{\text{Gross Profit}}{\text{Net Sales}} \times 100$$

Gross profit ratio is the indicator of profitability of the business and the efficiency of the management or the owner. Higher ratio indicates better position, as it helps to meet the other indirect expenses and losses of the business, which in turn results in a higher net profit. On the other hand, lower ratio indicates a bad position of the business. It may happen due to fall in selling price, increase in cost of goods sold or the inefficiency of the management (i.e., the resources of the business are not properly and efficiently used).

13. Balancing of trading account: The balancing figure of a trading account is either known as gross profit or gross loss. When the total of the credit side is greater than the total of the debit side, the balancing figure is considered as gross profit. On the other hand, when debit side is greater, the balancing figure is considered as gross loss. The said gross profit or gross loss is transferred to the profit and loss account.

14. Abnormal losses: Here, abnormal loss means loss of stock due to accident, theft or by fire. Thus, if such a thing happens, the trading account is credited for the entire amount (i.e., for the gross amount) for the said loss, because our purpose is to know the gross profit of the business under normal condition or situation. Suppose, goods lost by fire is worth Rs. 4,000 but the insurance company has admitted the claim to the extent of Rs. 2,600 only. Then the trading account is to be credited by Rs. 4,000.

17.12 JOURNAL ENTRIES FOR PREPARING TRADING ACCOUNT

In order to prepare trading account, the balances of some nominal accounts are closed by transferring the said balances to the trading account. The journal entries are shown as follows:

Trading Account	Dr.
To Opening Stock A/c	
To Purchases A/c	
To Carriage Inwards A/c	
To Sales Return A/c	
To Other Direct Expenses A/c	
(Being the balances transferred to trading account)	

Sales A/c	Dr.
Purchases Return A/c	Dr.
Closing Stock A/c	Dr.
To Trading A/c	
(Being the balances transferred to trading account)	

Trading A/c	Dr.
To Profit and Loss A/c	
(Being the gross profit transferred to profit and loss account)	

Profit and Loss A/c	Dr.
To Trading A/c	
(Being the gross loss transferred to profit and loss account)	

ILLUSTRATION 17.1 Prepare a trading account of M/s Gupta Bros. for the year ended March 31, 2008

	Rs.
Goods purchased	87,000
Carriage on purchase	3,500
Import duty	2,700
Freight	2,800
Wages	12,600
Customs duty	3,600
Excise duty	2,800
General expenses	4,000
Sales	179,000
Opening stock	10,500
Closing stock	14,100
Sales returns	2,100
Purchases returns	1,900
Salaries	10,600
Office rent	4,000
Purchase of furniture	21,000

Solution

M/s Gupta Bros.

Dr.   **Trading Account for the year ended March 31, 2008**   Cr.

Particulars	(Rs.)	Amount (Rs.)	Particulars	(Rs.)	Amount (Rs.)
To Opening Stock		10,500	By Sales	179,000	
To Purchase	87,000		*Less:* Sales returns	2,100	176,900
Less: Purchase return	1,900	85,100	By Closing Stock		14,100
To Carriage on purchase		3,500			
To Import Duty		2,700			
To Freight		2,800			
To Wages		12,600			

(Contd.)

Particulars	(Rs.)	Amount (Rs.)	Particulars	(Rs.)	Amount (Rs.)
To Customs duty		3,600			
To Excise duty		2,800			
To Profit and Loss A/c		67,400			
(Gross profit transfer					
– Balancing figure)					
		191,000			191,000

Working Note

All indirect expenses and asset purchases are not to be considered here, like Salaries, office rent, general expenses and purchase of furniture.

ILLUSTRATION 17.2 Prepare a trading account of M/s B. N. Bhatt for the year ended March 31, 2008:

	Rs.
Purchases	98,400
Carriage inwards	3,900
Coal, gas and oil	12,600
Heating and lighting	3,800
Freight	2,800
Advertisement	5,500
Salaries	10,700
Wages	9,600
Sales returns	4,700
Purchases returns	2,500
Octroi	1,500
Sales	174,800
Opening stock	12,800
Closing stock (Market price Rs.16,700)	20,200
Loss on sale of machine	3,600

Solution

M/s B. N. Bhatt

Dr.   **Trading Account for the year ended March 31, 2008**   Cr.

Particulars	(Rs.)	Amount (Rs.)	Particulars	(Rs.)	Amount (Rs.)
To Opening Stock		12,800	By Sales	174,800	
To Purchase	98,400		Less: Sales returns	4,700	170,100
Less: Purchase return	2,500	95,900	By Closing Stock		16,700
To Carriage Inwards		3,900			
To Coal, gas and oil		12,600			
To Heating and lighting		3,800			
To Freight		2,800			
To Wages		9,600			
To Octroi		1,500			
To Profit and Loss A/c		43,900			
(Gross profit transfer					
– Balancing figure)					
		186,800			186,800

Working Notes

1. All indirect expenses (i.e., advertisement and salaries) and loss on sale of machine are not to be considered here.

2. Closing stock is to be valued here on the basis of the market price, i.e. Rs. 16,700, because it is less than the cost price. An important example of a conservative accounting practice is the use of the inventory (stock) valuation rule —'cost or market price, whichever is lower'. If, on the date of the balance sheet, the market price of inventory becomes lower than its cost, then the possible loss that may arise on sale of the same should be provided for and accordingly, the inventory should be valued at the market price instead of at cost.

ILLUSTRATION 17.3 Prepare a trading account of Daruwala Bros. for the year ended March 31, 2008:

	Rs.
Purchases	110,700
Opening Stock:	
Raw Materials	21,500
Work in progress	32,400
Finished Goods	18,900
Sales	245,400
Carriage Inwards	7,500
Freight	2,800
Sales Returns	3,600
Wages	16,800
Factory Expenses	72,700
Purchases Returns	2,200
Closing Stock:	
Raw Materials	29,300
Work in progress	24,100
Finished Goods	27,200

Solution

Daruwala Bros.

Dr.   Trading Account for the year ended March 31, 2008   Cr.

Particulars	(Rs.)	Amount (Rs.)	Particulars	(Rs.)	Amount (Rs.)
To Opening Stock:			By Sales	245,400	
Raw Materials	21,500		*Less:* Sales returns	3,600	241,800
Work-in-progress	32,400		**Closing Stock:**		
Finished Goods	18,900	72,800	Raw Materials	29,300	
To Purchases	110,700		Work in progress	24,100	
Less: Returns	2,200	108,500	Finished Goods	27,200	80,600
To Carriage Inwards		7,500			
To Freight		2,800			
To Wages		16,800			
To Factory Expenses		72,700			
To Profit and Loss A/c					
(Gross profit transfer		41,300			
— Balancing figure)					
		322,400			322,400

17.13 PROFIT AND LOSS ACCOUNT

The second part of the income statement is called the **profit and loss account**. It is opened with the gross profit or gross loss transferred from the trading account. All the incomes and expenses which are not considered in trading account (indirect incomes and expenses) and all losses should be taken into account in the profit and loss account. All operating expenses, office expenses, marketing expenses, distribution expenses, depreciation on fixed assets, legal expenses, losses in the debit side and all incomes from other sources are to be considered on the credit side of the profit and loss account. If the credit side is greater than the debit side of the profit and loss account, the difference is called **net profit,** and in the reverse case there will be **net loss.** Net profit/loss is then transferred to the capital account. According to the accrual concept, all actual incomes and expenditures are to be taken into consideration in the profit and loss account.

Table 17.5 shows the specimen of a profit and loss account, while Tables 17.6 and 17.7 list the difference between trading account and profit and loss account, and between net profit and gross profit, respectively.

TABLE 17.5 The Specimen of a Profit and Loss Account

Profit and loss account

Dr. for the year (or period) ended ... (date) Cr.

Particulars	(Rs.)	Amount (Rs.)	Particulars	(Rs.)	Amount (Rs.)
To Trading Account (Gross loss transferred from)		—	By Trading Account (Gross profit transferred from)		—
To Selling Expenses		—	By Discount Received		—
To Carriage Outward		—	By Interest Received		—
To General Expenses		—	By Commission Received		—
To Salaries		—	By Miscellaneous Receipts		—
To Rent		—	By Rebate Received		—
To Insurance Premium		—	By Rent from Subletting		—
To Advertisement		—	By Bad debts recovered		—
To Bad debts		—	By Dividend received		—
To Audit Fees		—			
To Apprenticeship Premium		—			
To Bank Charges		—			
To Commission		—			
To Discount allowed		—			
To Electric Charges		—			
To Office Expenses		—			
To Interest paid		—			
To Law Charges		—			
To Export Duty		—			
To Loss on Sale of Assets		—			
To Packing Charges		—			
To Petty Expenses		—			
To Postage		—			
To Telephone and Internet Charges		—			
To Printing and Stationery		—			
To Rates and Taxes		—			
To Rebates Allowed		—			
To Repairs		—			
To Royalty on Sales		—			
To Samples		—			
To Sundry Expenses		—			
To Trade Expenses		—			
To Travelling Expenses		—			
To Depreciation on Fixed Assets		—			
To Net Profit transferred to Capital A/c (Balancing figure)		*****	By Net Loss transferred to Capital A/c (Balancing figure)		*****
		—			—

TABLE 17.6 Differences between Trading Account and Profit and Loss Account

Trading account	Profit and loss account
Gross profit is calculated through this account.	Net profit is calculated through this account.
It is the first part of the income statement.	It is the second part of the income statement.
Trading account is prepared with the help of direct incomes and expenses.	Trading account is prepared with the help of other incomes and expenses excluding direct incomes and expenses. For example, operating expenses, selling and distribution expenses, abnormal losses, and miscellaneous incomes.
This account does not start with any opening balance.	This account does not start with gross profit or loss of the business.
Gross profit is transferred to profit and loss account.	Net profit is transferred to capital account in case of sole proprietary business, and to the profit and loss appropriation account in case of partnership firm and companies.
It helps to assess the market strength of the business.	It helps to assess the internal management position and its effectiveness.
Trading account helps to control costs in respect of cost of goods sold only.	Profit and loss account helps to control costs in different areas like marketing, distribution, operating, and financial.

TABLE 17.7 Difference between Gross Profit and Net Profit

Gross profit	Net profit
It is the surplus of net sale of goods over cost of goods sold.	It is the surplus of gross profit plus miscellaneous incomes over all expenses and losses, excluding direct expenses.
Gross profit is transferred to profit and loss account.	Net profit is transferred to capital account in case of proprietary business, and to the profit and loss appropriation account in case of partnership firm and companies.
It is calculated through trading account.	It is calculated through profit and loss account.
It helps to control costs in respect of cost of goods sold only.	It helps to control costs in different areas like marketing, distribution, operating, and financial.
It helps to assess the market strength of the business.	It helps to assess the internal management position and its effectiveness.
Sales potentiality and its strength is measured through gross profit.	Overall business performances are measured through net profit.
Business efficiency is reflected through gross profit.	Business profitability is reflected through net profit.

17.13.1 Nature of Profit and Loss Account

It is prepared at the end of the financial year to find out the net result of the business. It may also be called a **periodic account** or a **statement**. Out of the total receipts and payments made during the current year, the incomes and payments made for the future periods are first separated and then transferred to the balance sheet. From the remaining items, the current year's incomes and expenditures are recorded or considered in the profit and loss account on the basis of accrual concept and the accepted accounting principles. Due to this reason, it is also known as an **allocation statement**.

17.13.2 Features of Profit and Loss Account

Profit and loss account has the following features:
1. It is a nominal account in nature.
2. It is prepared at the end of the financial year.
3. While preparing the profit and loss account, the accrual concept is followed.
4. It is the second part of the income statement.
5. It is prepared with the help of those items of incomes and expenditures which are not considered in the trading account, i.e., other than direct incomes and expenditures.
6. Generally, the expenditures which are considered in the profit and loss account exist in the nature of operating expenses, office expenses, marketing expenses, distribution expenses, financial, depreciation on fixed assets, legal expenses and abnormal losses.

7. Income from different sources other than sale of goods are considered here.
8. The net result of the profit and loss account is called **net profit** or **loss**, and the said amount is transferred to the capital account in case of proprietary business and to the profit and loss appropriation account in case of partnership firm and companies.

17.13.3 Advantages of Profit and Loss Account

The following are some important advantages of the profit and loss account:

1. It helps to ascertain the net profit or loss of the business at the end of the financial year.
2. With the help of the net profit and the net profit ratio, the future course of action is determined by the management.
3. It helps to ascertain the present profitability of the business.
4. Business performances are measured through the net profit and the net profit ratio in comparison to the previous year or years.
5. Different management decisions in respect of future investment proposals (both within and outside the business) are taken on the basis of the present profitability of the business.
6. On the basis of the present profitability of the business, profit and loss account helps to ascertain whether the capital of the business is maintained or not.
7. It helps to control costs in different areas like marketing, distribution, operating, financial, etc.
8. Profit and loss account also helps to fix or revise the existing selling price of the product or services.

17.13.4 Nature of the Items Used in Profit and Loss Account

Nature of the items appearing in the debit side

1. Office and administration expenses: These items are indirect in nature incurred in formulating planning policies for running the enterprise and for maintaining the offices. They are as follows:

(a) Office salaries
(b) Rent
(c) Postage and stationery
(d) Maintenance of office equipments
(e) General expenses
(f) Insurance
(g) Expenses of management
(h) Legal charges
(i) Audit fees.

2. Selling expenses: These items are also indirect in nature incurred to promote sales and to retain the existing customers. They are as follows:

(a) Advertisement
(b) Salaries and commission of salesmen
(c) Market research expenses
(d) Royalty on sales
(e) Free samples
(f) Postage and stationery
(g) Telephone and internet charges
(h) Expenses on showrooms and all other sales department expenses.

3. Distribution expenses: These expenses include all the expenditures incurred for executing orders and the cost of maintaining warehouse (warehousing and storage) of the finished products. They are as follows:

(a) Cost of packing
(b) Carriage outward or cost of transport

(c) Cost of maintaining delivery van

(d) Cost of reconditioning empty containers.

4. Financial expenses: These expenses include all the expenditures incurred for obtaining finance for running the business. They are as follows:

(a) Interest on loans

(b) Cash discount allowed

(c) Interest on capital.

5. Abnormal losses: These items include all types of abnormal losses arising due to the following factors:

(a) Goods or assets lost by fire or theft

(b) Loss on sale of fixed assets

(c) Cash stolen from office cash

(d) Expenses incurred due to accidents.

6. Maintenance and depreciation: These expenses include all expenses incurred for the following:

(a) Repairs and maintenance of buildings

(b) Machineries and equipments

(c) Furniture

(d) Depreciation charged on the fixed assets.

Profit and loss account is sometimes opened with gross loss transferred from the trading account.

Nature of the items appearing in the credit side

Profit and loss account is opened with gross profit transferred from the trading account.

Income from other sources or indirect incomes include the following:

(a) Discount received

(b) Commission received

(c) Interest on bank deposits

(d) Dividend received

(e) Interest on investments.

Abnormal gains include the following:

(a) Bad debts recovered

(b) Profit on sale of fixed assets.

ILLUSTRATION 17.4 Prepare a profit and loss account of M/s Shani Bros. for the year ended March 31, 2008:

	Rs.
Gross Profit	97,600
Carriage Outward	3,400
General Expenses	2,700
Bad debts	1,900
Insurance Premium	3,000
Advertisement	4,500
Discount allowed	3,100
Discount Received	4,200
Interest Received	6,500
Packing Charges	3,800
Salaries	14,500
Audit Fees	2,600
Interest paid	2,700
Printing and Stationary	1,100
Travelling Expenses	2,900
Depreciation on Office Equipments	4,700

Solution

M/s Shani Bros.

Dr.   Profit and Loss Account for the year ended March 31, 2008   Cr.

Particulars	(Rs.)	Amount (Rs.)	Particulars	(Rs.)	Amount (Rs.)
To Carriage Outward		3,400	By Trading Account		97,600
To General Expenses		2,700	(Gross profit transferred from)		
To Bad debts		1,900	By Discount Received		4,200
To Insurance Premium		3,000	By Interest Received		6,500
To Advertisement		4,500			
To Discount allowed		3,100			
To Packing Charges		3,800			
To Salaries		14,500			
To Audit Fees		2,600			
To Interest paid		2,700			
To Printing and Stationary		1,100			
To Travelling Expenses		2,900			
To Depreciation on Office Equipments		4,700			
To Net Profit transferred to Capital A/c (Balancing figure)		57,400			
		108,300			108,300

ILLUSTRATION 17.5 Prepare a profit and loss account of M/s G.L. Traders for the year ended March 31, 2008:

	Rs.
Gross Profit	112,700
Salaries	21,800
Discount allowed	3,100
Advertisement	5,100
Carriage Outward	4,800
Discount Received	3,900
Insurance Premium	3,300
Commission Received	2,900
Bad debts	2,700
Loss on Sale of Assets	3,600
Trade Expenses	2,400
Bank Charges	400
Rates and Taxes	1,800
Rent	6,600
Miscellaneous Receipts	4,500
Bad debts recovered	2,100
Petty Expenses	900
Legal Charges	2,200
Rent from Subletting	2,400
Depreciation on Office Furniture	3,700

Solution

M/s G.L. Traders

Dr.			Profit and Loss Account for the year ended March 31, 2008			Cr.
Particulars	(Rs.)	Amount (Rs.)	Particulars	(Rs.)	Amount (Rs.)
To Salaries		21,800	By Trading Account		112,700
To Discount allowed		3,100	(Gross profit transferred from)		
To Advertisement		5,100	By Discount Received		3,900
To Carriage Outward		4,800	By Miscellaneous Receipts		4,500
To Insurance Premium		3,300	By Bad debts Recovered		2,100
To Commission Received		2,900	By Rent from Subletting		2,400
To Bad debts		2,700			
To Loss on Sale of Assets		3,600			
To Trade Expenses		2,400			
To Bank Charges		400			
To Rates and Taxes		1,800			
To Rent		6,600			
To Petty Expenses		900			
To Legal Charges		2,200			
To Depreciation on Office Furniture		3,700			
To Net Profit transferred to Capital A/c (Balancing figure)		60,300			
		125,600			125,600

ILLUSTRATION 17.6 The following data are furnished by Kumar Trading Co. Prepare a profit and loss account of Kumar Trading Co. for the year ended March 31, 2008:

	Rs.
Gross Profit	156,800
Apprenticeship Premium paid	7,800
Electric Charges	4,700
Export Duty	5,500
Carriage Outward	7,300
Audit Fees	4,200
Insurance Premium	3,100
Discount allowed	3,700
Discount Received	2,570
Bad debts	1,600
Advertisement	8,200
Salaries	15,800
Telephone and Internet Charges	3,800
Rebate Received	2,900
Dividend received	3,400
Rent	12,500
Bad debts recovered	1,700
Rebates Allowed	1,500
Repairs	3,700
Royalty on Sales	5,700
Depreciation on Office Furniture	3,900

Solution

Kumar Trading Co.

Dr.   Profit and Loss Account for the year ended March 31, 2008   Cr.

Particulars	(Rs.)	Amount (Rs.)	Particulars	(Rs.)	Amount (Rs.)
To Apprenticeship Premium		7,800	By Trading Account		156,800
To Electric Charges		4,700	(Gross profit transferred from)		
To Export Duty		5,500	By Discount Received		2,570
To Carriage Outward		7,300	By Rebate Received		2,900
To Audit Fees		4,200	By Dividend received		3,400
To Insurance Premium		3,100	By Bad debts recovered		1,700
To Discount allowed		3,700			
To Bad debts		1,600			
To Advertisement		8,200			
To Salaries		15,800			
To Telephone and Internet		3,800			
To Rent		12,500			
To Rebates Allowed		1,500			
To Repairs		3,700			
To Royalty on Sales		5,700			
To Depreciation on Office Furniture		3,900			
To Net Profit transferred to Capital A/c					
(Balancing figure)		74,370			
		167,370			167,370

17.14 OPERATING PROFIT AND NET PROFIT

Operating profit is the excess amount of gross profit over operating expenses. In other words, it can be said that it is the difference between operating incomes (sales) minus operating expenses. Here operating expenses includes cost of goods sold, administrative expenses, selling and distribution expenses, i.e., all those expenditures incurred to maintain regular normal activity of the business.

Operating profit = Net sales
       – (Cost of goods sold, administrative expenses, selling and distribution expenses)

or

Operating profit = Gross profit (Net Sales – Cost of goods sold)
       – (Administrative expenses, selling and distribution expenses)

or

Net profit = Gross profit + All non-operating incomes – Other operating expenses
       – Non-operating expenses.

Operating profit = Net profit + Non-operating expenses – All non-operating incomes

Here, non-operating expenses include interest on loans, loss on sale of fixed assets, all types of losses, donations and charities, etc. Non-operating incomes include all indirect incomes and profits, i.e., rent received, interest received, profit on sale of fixed assets, dividend received, and so on.

ILLUSTRATION 17.7 The following data are extracted from the records of SD Bros. Calculate operating profit and net profit of the firm.

	Rs.
Gross Profit	114,600
Insurance Premium	2,400
Postage and Stationery	1,700
Lighting	2,700
Carriage Outward	3,400
Rent Paid	3,900
Bad debts	1,700
Computer Stationery	2,500
Salaries	8,700
Interest on Investments	2,900
Audit Fees	2,800
Rent Received	3,600
Dividend Received	2,600
Maintenance of Delivery Van	5,900
Travelling Expenses	4,200
General Expenses	2,600
Loss on sale of Machinery	5,700
Profit on sale of Land	10,400
Advertisement	2,900
Goods lost by fire	3,400
Charity to Blood donation Camp	1,700

Solution

In the Books of SD Bros.

	Rs.	Rs.
Gross Profit		114,600
Less: Operating Expenses:		
Office and Administration Expenses:		
Insurance Premium	2,400	
Postage and Stationery	1,700	
Lighting	2,700	
Rent Paid	3,900	
Audit Fees	2,800	
Computer Stationery	2,500	
Salaries	8,700	
General Expenses	2,600	
Selling and Distribution Expenses:		
Maintenance of Delivery Van	5,900	
Travelling Expenses	4,200	
Carriage Outward	3,400	
Bad debts	1,700	
Advertisement	2,900	45,400
		69,200
Operating Profit		
Add: Non-operating incomes:		
Interest on Investments	2,900	
Rent Received	3,600	
Dividend Received	2,600	
Profit on sale of Land	10,400	19,500
		88,700
Less: Non-operating expenses:		
Loss on sale of Machinery	5,700	
Goods lost by fire	3,400	
Charity to Blood donation Camp	1,700	10,800
Net Profit		77,900

ILLUSTRATION 17.8 The following data are extracted from the records of Dawat and Dalal Bros. Calculate operating profit and net profit by preparing a profit and loss account of Kumar Trading Co. for the year ended March 31, 2008:

	Rs.
Gross Profit	97,400
Insurance Premium	2,700
Discount allowed	3,500
Discount Received	2,900
Carriage Outward	3,100
Rent	5,600
Bad debts	1,100
Advertisement	4,800
Salaries	12,000
Interest on Investments	5,400
Repairs and Renewals	3,700
Rent Received	4,500
Received interest from bank	2,800
Postage and Stationery	780
Lighting	3,400
Travelling Expenses	5,600
Loss on sale of old Machinery	2,100
Goods lost by fire	2,400
Audit Fees	1,700

Solution

Dawat and Dalal Bros.

Profit and Loss Account for the year ended March 31, 2008

Dr.   Cr.

Particulars	(Rs.)	Amount (Rs.)	Particulars	(Rs.)	Amount (Rs.)
To Insurance Premium		2,700	By Trading Account		97,400
To Discount allowed		3,500	(Gross profit transferred from		
To Carriage Outward		3,100	Trading A/c)		
To Rent		5,600			
To Bad debts		1,100			
To Advertisement		4,800			
To Salaries		12,000			
To Repairs and Renewals		3,700			
To Postage and Stationery		780			
To Lighting		3,400			
To Travelling Expenses		5,600			
To Audit Fees		1,700			
To Operating Profit c/d		49,420			
		97,400			97,400
To Loss on sale of old Machinery		2,100	By Operating Profit b/d		49,420
To Goods lost by fire		2,400	By Discount Received		2,900
			By Interest on Investments		5,400
			By Rent Received		4,500
			By Received Interest from Bank		2,800
To Net Profit transferred to Capital A/c (Balancing figure)		60,520			
		65,020			65,020

ILLUSTRATION 17.9 Prepare a profit and loss account of M/s Sundar Traders for the year ended March 31, 2008:

	Rs.
Gross Profit	121,300
Salaries	18,000
Carriage Outward	2,600
Discount Received	2,400
Bad debts	2,600
Interest on Investments	2,100
Depreciation on Machinery	7,200
Insurance Premium	3,600
Sales Tax Paid	5,400
Rent	2,700
Travelling Expenses	6,400
Postage and Stationery	1,300
Royalty on Sales	3,500
Apprenticeship Premium	6,600

Solution

M/s Sundar Traders

Dr.　　Profit and Loss Account for the year ended March 31, 2008　　Cr.

Particulars	(Rs.)	Amount (Rs.)	Particulars	(Rs.)	Amount (Rs.)
To Carriage Outward		2,600	By Trading Account		121,300
To Bad debts		2,600	(Gross profit transferred from		
To Insurance Premium		3,600	Trading A/c)		
To Salaries		18,000	By Discount Received		2,400
To Rent		2,700	By Interest on		
To Sales Tax		5,400	Investment		2,100
To Travelling Expenses		6,400			
To Postage and Stationery		1,300			
To Royalty on Sales		3,500			
To Apprenticeship Premium		6,600			
To Depreciation on Machinery		7,200			
To Net Profit transferred to Capital A/c (Balancing figure)		65,900			
		125,800			125,800

17.15 BALANCE SHEET

It is a statement prepared at the end of a financial year to know the true financial position of a firm or business. Balance sheet is not an account but only a statement representing the closing assets and liabilities of the firm on a certain date. On the left hand side, the liabilities (owner's equity and outsiders' equity) are shown, and on the right hand side, the assets of the business are shown.

A balance sheet is the summary of the whole accounting record of a firm. It shows the liquidity and solvency position of a firm or an enterprise. The goal of the accounting system is to provide information which meets the needs of its users. There are several groups of people who vests interests in a business organization—owners, investors, managers, shareholders, employees, customers, and creditors. Thus, the purpose of preparing a balance sheet is to represent the true financial position of the firm on a certain date for the help of its users.

The specimen of a balance sheet is given below.

Balance Sheet as on ...

Liabilities		Rs.	Assets		Rs.
Capital	—		**Fixed Assets:**		
Add: Fresh Capital	—		Goodwill		—
	—		Patents and Trademarks		—
Add: Net Profit	—		Land and Building		—
	—		Freehold Premises		—
Less: Drawings	—	—	Plant and Machinery		—
(All types of Drawings:			Motor Vehicles		—
such as Cash withdrawn,			Tools and Equipments		—
goods taken and cost of			Loose Tools		—
benefits taken from the			Furniture and Fixtures		—
business)			Neon Sign		—
Long-term Loans,		—	Horses and carts		—
Reserves and Provision for any		—	Investments (Long-term)		—
Fund: (Such as National Defence			**Current Assets:**		
Fund, Draught Fund etc.)			Closing Stock		
Current Liabilities:			Raw Materials	—	
Trade Creditors		—	Work in progress	—	
Loan Creditors		—	Finished Goods	—	—
Bills Payable		—	Sundry Debtors		—
Outstanding Expenses		—	Bills Receivable		—
Income Received in advance		—	Accrued Incomes		—
Bank Overdraft		—	Prepaid Expenses		—
			Investments (Short-term)		—
			Cash at Bank		—
			Cash in Hand		—
		—			—

17.15.1 Different Views about the Balance Sheet

Three different views of a balance sheet may be represented as under:

1. The statement of remaining balances view: It is often said that a balance sheet is prepared with the help of the remaining balances left after preparing the income statement (i.e., trading and profit and loss account) through the nominal account balances from the trial balance. Thus, it is treated like a dumping ground where unused account balances are shown. Proper importance is not given to the balance sheet in this view.

2. The statement of static fund view: According to static fund view the liabilities side of the balance sheet shows different sources of funds that have been raised and the asset side shows the different items of assets where the said funds have been utilized. At the time of beginning of an enterprise, the concept of static fund may be accepted to some extent, but in case of a running business it is not acceptable because all the items in the balance sheet are changed on the basis of the nature and volume of transactions.

3. The statement of financial position view: According to this view, a balance sheet is prepared at the end of the financial year to know the financial position of a firm or a business. The balance sheet is the summary of the whole accounting record of a firm. It helps in comparing the financial position of two different periods of an enterprise. Though all the items in the balance sheet fail to represent the true or real financial position, it is prepared on the basis of some accepted accounting concepts and conventions. Thus, this view is more convincing and reliable.

17.15.2 Nature of the Balance Sheet

Balance sheet represents the financial position of an enterprise at the end of an accounting year. It is a periodic statement prepared after preparing the income statement. This statement consists of the closing balances of all assets and liabilities, and the net result (profit or loss) of an enterprise. It shows the liquidity and solvency position of a firm or an enterprise. Balance sheet is a document prepared to measure the financial status of an enterprise at the end of an accounting year. The excess of assets over the external liabilities represents the net worth or the capital of a business. The financial position of an enterprise reflected through the balance sheet is represented in terms of 'historical cost'. Thus, it does not show the actual realizable values of assets.

17.15.3 Functions of a Balance Sheet

The chief functions of the balance sheet may be represented as follows:

1. Balance sheet represents the closing value of the accumulated figure of resources and the corresponding accumulated figure of obligations of an enterprise at the end of the financial year.
2. It helps to measure working capital and capital employed by the enterprise.
3. Through the data available from a balance sheet, financial strength of an enterprise can easily be measured.
4. Balance sheet provides valuable information to its users (mainly the owner and the investors) which helps in taking decisions for their future in advance. Since through ratio analysis financial status of an enterprises may be assessed or evaluated properly.

17.15.4 Marshalling of Balance Sheet

The order in which assets and liabilities are to be shown is called **marshalling of balance sheet**. For the registered companies, there is a prescribed form of balance sheet, but no such form of balance sheet is there for a sole trader or partnership firm. However, the assets and liabilities of a firm may be shown in any of the following two orders:

1. Liquidity order, and
2. Permanency (or fixed) order.

Liquidity order

According to this arrangement the assets which are more easily convertible into liquid cash come first, and those realizable later, come next and so on. Similarly, those liabilities which are to be paid first, come first, and those payable later, come next and so on. A proforma of this order is shown below.

Proforma of a liquidity order

Liabilities	Rs.	Assets	Rs.
Current Liabilities:		**Current Assets:**	
Bank Overdraft		Cash in Hand	
Income Received in Advance		Cash at Bank	
Outstanding Expenses		Investments (Short-term)	
Bills Payable		Prepaid Expenses	
Loan Creditors		Accrued Incomes	
Trade Creditors		Bills Receivable	
Long-term Loans		Sundry Debtors	
Reserve and Surplus		Closing Stock	
Capital		Investments (Long-term)	

(Contd.)

Liabilities	Rs.	Assets	Rs.
		Fixed Assets:	
		Loose Tools	
		Furniture and Fixtures	
		Motor Vehicles	
		Tools and Equipments	
		Plant and Machinery	
		Land and Building	
		Patents and Trademarks	
		Goodwill	

Permanency (or fixed) Order

Under this arrangement the assets which are more permanent in nature will come first, the less permanent will come next, and so on. Likewise, the liabilities which are more permanent in nature will come first, the less permanent will come next, and so on. This order is just the opposite of the liquidity order.

Permanancy order

Liabilities		Rs.	Assets		Rs.
Capital			**Fixed Assets:**		
Reserve and Surplus			Goodwill		
Long-term Loans			Patents and Trademarks		
Current Liabilities:			Land and Building		
Trade Creditors			Plant and Machinery		
Loan Creditors			Tools and Equipments		
Bills Payable			Motor Vehicles		
Outstanding Expenses			Furniture and Fixtures		
Income Received in advance			Loose Tools		
Bank Overdraft			Investments (Long-term)		
			Current Assets:		
			Closing Stock		
			Sundry Debtors		
			Bills Receivable		
			Accrued Incomes		
			Prepaid Expenses		
			Investments (Short-term)		
			Cash at Bank		
			Cash in Hand		

17.15.5 Is Balance Sheet an Account?

Balance sheet is a statement prepared at the end of the financial year, but is not an account. Like an account, it has two sides. Liabilities are shown on the left hand side and assets on the right hand side, but they are not recorded as per the accounting rules of debit or credit in an account in the ledger. There are specific rules or orders for representing assets and liabilities in the balance sheet liquidity order and permanency (or fixed) order. Accounts are opened for all accounts in the ledger, but balance sheet is prepared with the help of the balances of real accounts, liabilities accounts and profit/loss balance from profit and loss account.

17.15.6 Utility of Preparing a Balance Sheet

Balance sheet is the only statement where the true financial position of a firm may be reflected if it is prepared on the basis of accepted accounting principles and guidelines. According to the objectives of accounting convention of disclosure and accrual concept, a balance sheet is needed to be prepared in such a way so that it represents a 'true and fair view' of its state of affairs as at the end of the said period.

Hence, if it is prepared in such a way, then it will fulfill the desires of its users, like owners, investors, creditors, the Government and others. Through the balance sheet, the present liquidity position, solvency position, working capital, capital employed and profitability position on capital employed of an enterprise may be estimated. On the basis of the above stated information, important business decisions may be taken by the owners and investors. In fact, the financial statements are analyses on the basis of the data provided by the balance sheet. Hence, the efficiency of the management may be estimated through the balance sheet.

17.15.7 Does the Balance Sheet Represent a 'True and Fair' Financial Position of an Enterprise? (Limitations of the Balance Sheet)

The concept of 'true and fair' is a relative matter. The object of preparing a balance sheet is to represent the true financial position of the firm on a certain date for the help of its users. The financial position of an enterprise reflected through the balance sheet is represented in terms of 'historical cost'. Hence, it does not show the actual realizable values of assets, as the effect of inflation in the economy is not at all reflected in them. Not only that, in the cases of valuation of stocks or calculation of depreciation, a number of methods are available out of which a particular one is followed by the accountant. Thus, there is every possibility of change in the figures for the same stock or the fixed assets due to the change of an accountant, as it depends on the personal judgement of the concerned person. There are some assets and liabilities which have no present value at all, but are considered based on some assumptions. However, certificates are issued by the auditors in this respect as 'true and fair' view based on their knowledge and experience, since it is the only medium by which the financial position of a firm is represented. It is suggested that if all the accepted accounting concepts and conventions are properly applied, we may expect a reliable and acceptable picture in the balance sheet of an enterprise.

17.15.8 Balance Sheet and Accounting Equation

The following fundamental accounting equation may be drawn on the basis of the principle of dual-aspect concept which is the basis of accountancy:

$$\text{Capital} + \text{Liabilities} = \text{Total assets}$$

Or Owner's equity (OE) + Outsiders equity (L) = Total assets (A)

$$A - L = OE$$

Or $$A - OE = L$$

Therefore, according to the duality concept, every transaction will affect at least two items and the outcome of such transaction will be as under:

$$\text{Total assets} = \text{Owner's equity (Capital)} + \text{Liabilities}$$

Double entry system of Bookkeeping is created with the help of this concept. For every transaction, the financial position of an enterprise will automatically change. For such a change, total assets and total liabilities will also change, though the accumulated figures of both the side would be identical. It is shown through Example 17.1.

Example 17.1

	Transactions	Total assets	Total liabilities		
			Capital	Outside liabilities	Total liabilities
		(Rs.)	(Rs.)	(Rs.)	(Rs.)
1.	Mr. X started his business with cash Rs. 75,000	75,000	75,000	0	75,000
2.	Purchased goods for Rs.10,000 from P Bros. on credit	75,000 + 10,000 (Stock)	75,000	10,000	85,000
	Net Position	85,000			85,000
3.	Purchased Office Furniture in Cash Rs. 4,000	75,000 – 4,000(Cash) + 10,000 (Stock) + 4,000 (Furniture)	75,000	10,000	85,000
	Net Position	85,000			85,000

17.15.9 Interrelation between Profit and Loss Account and Balance Sheet

The net result of all commercial activities are reflected in the profit and loss account and its effect on net worth is also reflected in the balance sheet. Income statement and the balance sheet are closely related to each other and the final financial picture of an enterprise may be obtained only when these two statements are prepared. With the help of net worth (capital) of an enterprise of two different periods (opening and closing), profit/loss may be calculated and the same profit/loss is generally reflected in the profit and loss account (after making necessary adjustments). Thus, it is said that each of these two statements serves as complementary to the other. Sometimes, it is also said that the balance sheet acts as a link between successive profit and loss accounts. In the case of some expenditures, the expired portion is shown in the profit and loss account and the unexpired portion is carried forward to the balance sheet for it's use in the future periods.

When inflow is greater than outflow, it indicates profit. Net increase in assets for a transaction, which is reflected in the balance sheet, will also be reflected in the profit and loss account by increasing the profit volume. There is another way by which their relationship or the dependence may be explained. Suppose, rent of Rs. 900 paid in advance has not been considered in the profit and loss account. As a result it decreases the current year's profit by Rs. 900. At the same time rent of Rs. 900 paid in advance will not be reflected as an asset in the balance sheet. Here lies their interdependence. In other words, it may also be said that there is a direct interrelation and inter-dependence between profit and loss account and the balance sheet.

Table 17.8 shows the list of difference between Balance Sheet and Trial Balance on the basis of their respective position and uses.

TABLE 17.8 Distinction between Balance Sheet and Trial Balance

Balance sheet	Trial balance
It is prepared to represent the financial position of an enterprise.	It is prepared to judge or check the arithmetical accuracy of the accounts maintained in the ledger.
It is prepared with the help of real and personal account balances and net profit/loss.	It is prepared with the help of real, nominal and personal account balances.
Assets and liabilities are recorded as per the rules of marshalling of balance sheet.	There is no such rule of marshalling for preparing the trial balance.
It must be prepared at the end of the financial year.	There is no particular time bound, but may be prepared any time, i.e., monthly, quarterly, half- yearly, etc.
It is prepared after preparing the Trading and profit and loss account.	It is prepared before preparing the final account.
It is prepared after considering all adjustment entries.	Ordinarily, it is prepared before considering all adjustment entries.
Liabilities are shown on the left hand side and assets on the right hand side.	Debit balances are shown on the left hand side and credit balances on the right hand side.
Auditor's signature is essential on the balance sheet in case of companies.	Auditor's signature is not essential on the trial balance in case of companies.
Closing stock appears in the balance sheet.	Closing stock generally does not appear in the trial balance. Only when adjusted purchases are given, closing stock will appear.
Opening stock does not appear in the balance sheet.	Opening stock appears in the trial balance.
Net profit/loss is reflected in the balance sheet.	Net profit/loss is reflected in the trial balance.

Table 17.9 shows the list of difference between Balance Sheet and Statement of Affairs on the basis of their respective position and presentation.

TABLE 17.9 Distinction between Balance Sheet and Statement of Affairs

Balance sheet	Statement of affairs
When books are maintained under double entry system, it is prepared after preparing the profit and loss account.	When books are maintained under single entry system it is prepared for preparing the statement of profit and loss.
It is a valuable document.	It is not a valuable document like balance sheet.
It is prepared systematically on the basis of accepted accounting rules.	It is prepared on the basis of loose documents, few accounts, statements and imaginations.
It may be detected subsequently in case of missing of any asset or a liability.	In case of missing of any asset or liability, it may not be detected subsequently.
Balances of assets and liabilities appearing in the balance sheet are reliable and verifiable.	Balances of assets and liabilities appearing in the statement of Affairs are not reliable and verifiable, as the accounts are not properly maintained.

17.16 ASSETS

The term 'assets' denotes the resources acquired by a business to get some benefit in the future. Any capitalized expenditure is treated as an asset. An expenditure is capitalized when the same is not charged against the revenue earned in the accounting or financial period in which it is incurred. As a result, the balance of the said expenditure is carried forward to the next financial year at the end of the year and these assets are usually represented by debit balances. For example, land and buildings, plant and machinery, investments, etc.

17.16.1 Classification of Assets

Fixed assets (or block capital)

Fixed assets are those assets which are purchased for a long period to be used in the business and are not for resale. These assets do not change their form like current assets. They may be divided into two types—tangible and intangible.

Tangible assets: These assets can be touched or seen and are purchased for earning revenue. For example, land and building, plant and machinery, motor vans, etc. They may further be subdivided as under:

Wasting assets. There are some assets which are exhausted completely by use and cannot be replaced by new ones within the same place. These assets are known as **wasting assets**. For example, mines, quaries, oil, etc.

Non-wasting assets. These assets are neither completely exhausted by usage nor their value is reduced due to their extensive use. For example, freehold land.

Intangible assets: These assets have no physical existence, and as such, cannot be touched or seen. They are of two types

Identifiable intangible assets: Trademark, Patents, etc.

Unidentifiable intangible assets: Goodwill.

Goodwill. It means a good name or reputation of an enterprise or a person. For acquisition of an enterprise, the excess amount paid over the value of the net asset taken over is to be considered as the value of goodwill. It's presence helps to earn extra profit in future, i.e., super profit. Thus, goodwill represents the sum paid for anticipated or expected super profit to be earned in future. According to Dr. B. K. Basu, goodwill is "the difference between a running car and a car to be started".

Patent. It is a kind of right achieved by an enterprise either by purchase or is granted by the Government. After some extensive research work by an enterprise an application is made to the Government claiming the right to manufacture a particular item exclusively in their favour. When it satisfies the Government rules in this respect, a permission is granted by the Government exclusively in favour of the said enterprise for the manufacture of that particular item. The total amount spent for the said research work or the price paid for such purchase is amortized over the period during which the benefit will be enjoyed or the right acquired.

Trademark. It is an exclusive right enjoyed by an enterprise permanently in the form of a brand name or trade symbol. These rights are also granted by the Government like patents. Sometimes they may be purchased from other firms or persons also. The total cost incurred for the said rights are recorded in the books of accounts like recording of patents.

Current assets or floating assets or circulating assets

Current assets are those assets which are acquired with the intention of converting them into cash in the ordinary course of business of an enterprise. For example, cash and bank balance, stock in trade, debtors, bills receivable and investments (short-term). Table 17.10 lists the major points of differences between fixed assets and current assets. A few current assets are described given below:

TABLE 17.10 Distinction between Fixed Assets and Current Assets

Fixed assets	Current assets
Fixed assets are those assets which are purchased to be used for a long period in the business.	Current assets are those assets which are acquired with the intention of converting then into cash in the ordinary course of business of an enterprise.
These assets are purchased to earn revenue.	These assets are acquired during the course of operating cycle of the business.
Fixed assets are valued at the end of the year by charging depreciation.	Only a few current assets are valued at the end of the year as per the rule—cost or market price, whichever is lower.
These assets are purchased entirely out of the long-term fund of the business, i.e., out of capital employed.	Current assets are purchased partly out of the short-term fund and partly from long-term fund.
Profit on sale of these assets are shown as capital profits.	Profit on sale of these assets are shown as revenue profits.
Fixed assets may be acquired on rent basis.	Current assets cannot be acquired on rent basis.

1. Cash and bank: Here, cash and bank means liquid cash at cash box or within the business in hand and at bank.

2. Stock in trade: Stock includes stock of raw materials, finished goods and partly finished goods (or work in progress). Here, stock means unused materials or unsold goods or unfinished goods. An important example of a conservative accounting practice is the use of the inventory (stock) valuation rule—cost or market price, whichever is lower. If, on the date of the balance sheet, the market price of inventory becomes lower than its cost, then the possible loss that may arise on sale of the same should be provided for, and accordingly, the inventory should be valued at the market price instead of at cost.

3. Debtors: The customers' accounts total or accumulated figure is generally shown as debtors or sundry debtors. Usually, the realizable value of the sundry debtors is shown in the balance sheet. It is based on the conservative principle (Chapter 1). For this reason some adjustments are made, like provision for bad debts, provision for discount, etc., with sundry debtors in the balance sheet.

4. Investments: Here investments include short-term securities which are convertible in cash in the current year or the financial year at any time. Sometimes, it is also valued at cost or market price, whichever is lower. When the fall in market price is purely for a few days, i.e., temporary, then no adjustment is required for such fall. It is to be valued at cost.

5. Bills receivable: A bill is complete in before law when it is duly accepted by the drawee (customer or debtor). Acceptance means writing/putting of signature by the drawee, that is, the drawee has accepted the liability. Before acceptance, a bill is called a **draft**, and when a draft is accepted it is called a **bill**. When such bills are received from the customers/debtors, **bills receivable** account is opened and is treated as an asset.

6. Accrued incomes: In some cases, certain incomes are accrued/due but not received. Such type of accrual incomes are considered in accounts and are shown as assets due to accrual or mercantile system of accounting.

7. Prepaid expenses: Certain expenses are paid in advance for the following/subsequent period. As per the accrual or mercantile system of accounting, to show the actual expenses for the current year the excess amount paid for the subsequent period is deducted from the original amount of the respective expenditure account, and the surplus portion so deducted is shown as an asset.

Fictitious assets

There are some expenditures or losses which are not charged to the profits and loss account in the year in which it actually takes place but are written off gradually in the subsequent years. As long as those items of expenditures or losses are not written off completely, they are shown in the assets. For example, discount on issue of shares and debenture, profit and loss account (Dr.) balance, underwriting commission, preliminary expenses, and so on.

Contingent assets

There are some assets whose ownership or title may or may not be achieved in future, but is dependant on the happenings or non-happenings of some future *uncertain* events. Thus, the ownership of that particular asset will be achieved only when the said uncertain event goes in favour of the enterprise in future. Suppose, a case is pending in a court of law in respect of a title of a patent; however, the ownership of the said patent will be achieved only when the judgement goes in favour of the enterprise. So long the case is pending in the court, it may be mentioned in the footnote as a contingent asset, but not in the balance sheet as an asset.

17.17 LIABILITY OR EQUITY

A claim against the assets of the business that can be enforced by law is called **equity** or **liability**. Liabilities are promises in favour of different persons for money, goods, and services. For example sundry creditors, bills payable, debentures, share capital, and outstanding expenses. Any amount received in advance for goods to be supplied in future are example of promises for goods. On the other hand, incomes received in advance are examples of promises for services. The amount of claim for which a business is liable to pay to the owner is called **internal liability** or **owner's equity**, and which is payable to the outsiders is called **external liability**. Capital, profits and reserves are the examples of promises in favour of owners.

Liabilities shown in the balance sheet may be classified as under:

Long-term or fixed liability

These liabilities are either not paid or are payable within one year. They are of two types— payable to outsiders; for example, debentures, bonds, fixed deposits received , etc.; and payable to owners.

Current liabilities

These liabilities are payable within a year or a very short period. For example, sundry creditors, bills payable, bank overdraft, outstanding expenses, etc. A few current assets described are below:

Creditors: The suppliers' accounts total or accumulated figure is generally shown as creditors or sundry creditors. Total amount payable to the suppliers for goods or services supplied by them is shown in the balance sheet as liability under the head 'sundry creditors'.

Bills Payable: When an acceptance is given in favour of a creditor or the drawer, it is known as **bills payable**. The total acceptance given in favour of the creditors is shown as bills payable in the liability side of the balance sheet.

Outstanding expenses: In some cases, certain expenses are accrued/due but not paid. For following the mercantile system of accounting, the total expenses payable for the current year is to be shown, but sometimes, a portion which is not paid in the financial year is to be shown as outstanding expenses in the balance sheet on the liability side.

Incomes received in advance: There are some cases when certain incomes are received in advance for the following/subsequent period. As per the accrual or mercantile system of accounting, to show the actual income of the current year the excess amount received for the subsequent period is deducted from the original amount of the respective income account and the surplus portion so deducted is shown as a liability.

Contingent liability

These liabilities are not actual liabilities of the business on the date of the balance sheet, but may become liabilities in the future based on the happening of any uncertain event. For example, guarantor's liability is a contingent because a guarantor is liable only when the principal debtor fails to pay his loan.

17.18 HOW TO READ A BALANCE SHEET

The object of preparing a balance sheet is to represent the true financial position of the firm on a certain date for the use of its users. Here, 'to read a balance sheet' means knowing the present liquidity position, solvency position, working capital, capital employed and profitability position on capital employed of an enterprise through a balance sheet. On the basis of the above sated information, many important business decisions may be taken by the owners and investors. Financial statements are analysis (i.e., 'to read a balance sheet') based on the data provided by the balance sheet. The calculation of the said information is shown below through an Example 17.2.

Example 17.2

Balance Sheet of Mr. S.L. Mishra
as on December 31,2007

Liabilities	Amount (Rs.)	Amount (Rs.)	Assets	Amount (Rs.)	Amount (Rs.)
Capital		250,000	Land and Building		150,000
Net Profit		57,000	Machinery		80,000
Loan from Bank (long-term)		60,000	Furniture		60,000
Creditors		25,000	Investments(long-term)		30,000
Bills Payable		15,000	Closing Stock		25,000
Outstanding Expenses		3,000	Debtors		45,000
			Prepaid Salaries		2,000
			Cash in hand		18,000
		410,000			410,000

	Rs.
Proprietor's Fund:	
Capital	250,000
Net Profit	57,000
	307,000
Current Liabilities:	
Creditors	25,000
Bills Payable	15,000
Outstanding Expenses	3,000
	43,000

(Contd.)

	Rs.
Fixed Assets:	
Land and Building	150,000
Machinery	80,000
Furniture	60,000
Investments (long-term)	30,000
	320,000
Current Assets:	
Closing Stock	25,000
Debtors	45,000
Prepaid Salaries	2,000
Cash in hand	18,000
	90,000

Working Capital

It indicates the liquidity position of an enterprise and is essential for the operating cycle.

	Rs.
Current Assets	90,000
Less: Current Liabilities	43,000
	47,000

Operating cycle of a firm is shown below.

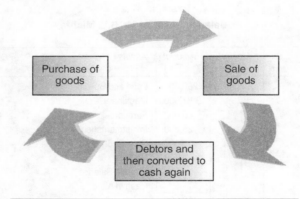

Capital Employed

	Rs.
Fixed Assets	320,000
Add: Working Capital	47,000
	367,000
Or	
Proprietor's Fund	307,000
Long-term Loan (from bank)	60,000
	367,000

Current Ratio:

$$\frac{\text{Current assets}}{\text{Current liabilities}} = \frac{90,000}{43,000} = 2.09 \text{ times}$$

Fixed Assets Ratio:

$$\frac{\text{Fixed assets}}{\text{*Long-term funds}} = \frac{320,000}{367,000} = 0.87$$

*Here, long-term funds = Capital employed

ILLUSTRATION 17.10 From the following particulars, prepare a balance sheet as at December 31, 2007:

	Rs.
Furniture and Fixtures	25,000
Investments	40,000
Land and Building	120,000
Capital	300,000
Plant and Machinery	54,000
Net Profit for the year 2007	38,000
Sundry Debtors	28,000
Cash in hand	21,000
Bills Payable	12,100
Motor Vehicles	32,000
Bank Overdraft	9,000
Goodwill	23,000
Bills Receivable	17,000
Trade Creditors	21,700
Drawings	5,300
Loan to Mr. Madan Lal	15,000
Loan from Mr.Prabhu	18,000
Closing Stock	16,000
Prepaid Expenses	2,500

Solution

Balance Sheet as at December 31, 2007

Liabilities	Rs.	Rs.	Assets	Rs.	Rs.
Capital	300,000		Goodwill		23,000
Add: Net Profit	38,000		Land and Building		120,000
	338,000		Plant and Machinery		54,000
Less: Drawings	5,300	332,700	Motor Vehicles		32,000
Bills Payable		12,100	Furniture and Fixtures		25,000
Bank Overdraft		9,000	Investments		40,000
Loan from Mr. Prabhu		18,000	Sundry Debtors		28,000
Trade Creditors		21,700	Prepaid Expenses		2,500
			Bills Receivable		17,000
			Loan to Mr. Madan Lal		15,000
			Closing Stock		16,000
			Cash in hand		21,000
		393,500			393,500

ILLUSTRATION 17.11 From the following particulars, prepare a balance sheet of Mr. Ratan Bajoria as at March 31, 2008:

		Rs.
Sundry Creditors		34,700
Bills Payable		12,600
Bills Receivable		22,400
Sundry Debtors		43,500
Cash Drawings		6,000
Net Profit for the year 2007–2008		64,800
Plant and Machinery		56,900
Cash in hand and at Bank		23,100
Closing Stock:		
Raw Materials	32,000	
Work in progress	17,500	
Finished goods	28,500	78,000
Patents and Trademarks		24,000
Land and Building		95,000
Tools and Equipments		34,000
Prepaid Rent		2,700
Outstanding Salaries		1,800
Capital		301,000
Investments		32,000
LIP of Mr. Ratan Bajoria		7,500
Income Received in Advance		2,800
Accrued Interest on Investments		3,100
Goods used by the proprietor for personal use		4,500
Loan from Bank		25,000
Income Tax paid		10,000

Solution

Balance Sheet of Mr. Ratan Bajoria as at March 31, 2008

Liabilities	Rs.	Rs.	Assets	Rs.	Rs.
Capital	301,000		Land and Building		95,000
Add: Net Profit	64,800		Plant and Machinery		56,900
	365,800		Patents and Trademarks		24,000
Less: Drawings:	28,000	337,800	Tools and Equipments		34,000
Sundry Creditors		34,700	Investments		32,000
Bills Payable		12,600	Bills Receivable		22,400
Outstanding Salaries		1,800	Sundry Debtors		43,500
Income Received		2,800	**Closing Stock:**		
in Advance			Raw Materials	32,000	
Loan from Bank		25,000	Work in progress	17,500	
			Finished goods	28,500	78,000
			Accrued Interest on Investments		3,100
			Prepaid Rent		2,700
			Cash in Hand and at Bank		23,100
		414,700			414,700

ILLUSTRATION 17.12   From the following particulars, prepare a balance sheet of Mr. Ashok Sippi as at March 31, 2008:

	Rs.
Freehold Premises	57,400
Plant and Machinery	45,000
Opening Capital	98,000
Net Profit for the year 2007–2008	76,000
Fresh Capital	50,000
Trade Creditors	30,000
Loose Tools	12,000
Closing Stock of Raw Materials	21,000
Closing Stock of Work in progress	16,000
Closing Stock of Finished goods	32,000
Neon Sign	8,000
Cash at Bank	12,000
Cash withdrawn from the business for personal use	7,000
Income Tax	9,000
Debtors	46,000
Salaries for the month of April, 2008 paid in February, 2008	4,000
Unexpired Insurance	2,000
Interest on Bank deposits due but not received	1,500
Interest on Bank Loan due but not paid	900
Bank Loan	18,000

Solution

Balance Sheet of Mr. Ashok Sippi as at March 31, 2008

Liabilities	(Rs.)	Amount (Rs.)	Assets	(Rs.)	Amount (Rs.)
Capital	98,000		Freehold Premises		57,400
Add: Fresh Capital	50,000		Plant and Machinery		45,000
	148,000		Loose Tools		12,000
Add: Net Profit	76,000		Neon Sign		8,000
	224,000		**Closing Stock:**		
Less: Drawings:			Raw Materials	21,000	
Cash withdrawn 7,000			Work in progress	16,000	
Income Tax 9,000	16,000	208,000	Finished goods	32,000	69,000
			Debtors		46,000
Trade Creditors		30,000	Unexpired Insurance	2,000	
Bank Loan		18,000	Salaries paid in advance	4,000	6,000
Outstanding interest on Bank Loan		900	Accrued interest on Bank Deposits		1,500
			Cash at Bank		12,000
		256,900			256,900

17.19   PRESENTATION OF FINANCIAL STATEMENTS

Financial statements (trading, profit and loss account and balance sheet) can be presented in any of the following two formats:

1. The horizontal format
2. The vertical format.

The horizontal format: According to this format statements are to be presented in "T" Form. Till now, all problems have been solved (all the Illustrations) in this horizontal format.

The Vertical format: According to this format, financial statements are to be presented in a single column on the right hand side of the statement.

ILLUSTRATION 17.13 From the following trial balance and information, prepare profit and loss account and balance sheet of Mr. P. Jadav in the vertical form for the year ending March 31, 2008:

Trial Balance as on March 31,2008

Dr.				Cr.
Particulars	Rs.	Particulars		Rs.
Sales Returns	2,800	Sales		265,000
Opening Inventories	12,700	Purchase Returns		3,400
Purchases	82,000	Interest on Investments		6,800
Freight and Carriage	6,700	Rent Received		4,600
Wages	12,900	Capital		240,000
Salaries	12,600	Loan from DBI		30,000
General Expenses	2,100	Sundry Creditors		28,700
Audit Fees	2,400	Bills Payable		14,300
Insurance Premium	1,800			
Rent	3,600			
Repairs and Maintenance of Equipments	1,900			
Lighting	2,900			
Carriage Outwards	4,600			
Advertising	6,900			
Bad Debts	1,400			
Travelling Expenses	4,800			
Loss on sale of Machinery	5,700			
Interest on Loan	4,900			
Drawings	21,400			
Land and Buildings	156,600			
Plant and Machinery	92,000			
Investments	45,000			
Sundry debtors	34,700			
Bills Receivable	18,100			
Cash and bank balance	52,300			
	592,800			592,800

Additional information

Closing inventories: Rs. 16,300.

Solution

Profit & Loss Account of Mr. P. Jadav
for the year ended March 31, 2008

Particulars	(Rs.)	(Rs.)	(Rs.)
A. Net Sales:			
Sales		265,000	
Less: Sales Returns		2,800	262,200
B. *Less:* **Cost of Goods Sold:**			
Opening Stock		12,700	
Purchases	82,000		
Less: Purchase Returns	3,400	78,600	
Freight and Carriage		6,700	
Wages		12,900	
		110,900	
Less: Closing Stock		16,300	94,600
C. Gross Profit (A – B)			167,600

(Contd.)

Particulars	(Rs.)	(Rs.)	(Rs.)
D. *Less:* **Operating Expenses:**			
Administrative Expenses:			
Salaries	12,600		
General Expenses	2,100		
Audit Fees	2,400		
Insurance Premium	1,800		
Rent	3,600		
Repairs and Maintenance of Equipments	1,900		
Lighting	2,900	27,300	
Selling and Distribution Expenses:			
Carriage Outwards	4,600		
Advertising	6,900		
Bad Debts	1,400		
Travelling Expenses	4,800	17,700	45,000
E. Operating Profit (C – D)			122,600
F. *Add:* **Non-Operating Incomes:**			
Interest on Investments		6,800	
Rent Received		4,600	11,400
			134,000
G. *Less:* **Non-Operating Expenses and Losses:**			
Loss on sale of Machinery		5,700	
Interest on Loan		4,900	10,600
H. Net Profit (E + F – G)			123,400
(Transferred to Capital/Proprietor's Fund)			

Balance Sheet of Mr. P. Jadav
as at March 31, 2008

Particulars	(Rs.)	(Rs.)	(Rs.)
I. **Sources of Funds**			
1. *Proprietor's funds:*			
Capital		240,000	
Add: Net Profit		123,400	
		363,400	
Less: Drawings		21,400	342,000
2. *Loan funds:*			
Loan from DBI			30,000
Total			372,000
II. Application of funds			
1. *Fixed assets:*			
(Gross block *Less:* Depreciation)			
Land and Buildings		156,600	
Plant and Machinery		92,000	248,600
2. *Investments*			45,000
3. *Current assets, loans and advances:*			
(a) Inventories	16,300		
(b) Sundry debtors	34,700		
(c) Bills Receivable	18,100		
(d) Cash and bank balance	52,300	121,400	
Less:			
Current liabilities and provisions:			
(a) Sundry Creditors	28,700		
(b) Bills Payable	14,300	43,000	78,400
Total			372,000

ILLUSTRATION 17.14 From the following trial balance of Mr. K. Madhavan, prepare a trading and profit and loss account for the year ending March 31, 2009, and a balance sheet as on that date.

Dr.		Trial Balance as on March 31, 2009	Cr.
Particulars	Amount (Rs.)	Particulars	Amount (Rs.)
Wages	6,800	Sales	166,500
Freight	6,700	Miscellaneous Receipts	3,800
Buildings	60,200	Dividend received	4,600
Heating and Lighting	5,500	Interest Received	3,600
Opening Stock	12,900	Trade Creditors	31,000
Purchase	71,500	Capital	126,400
Salaries	12,700		
Carriage Inward	3,200		
Advertisement	5,040		
Law Charges	1,660		
Drawings	2,000		
Discount allowed	2,600		
Bad debts	1,900		
Rent	4,800		
Sundry Debtors	42,000		
Cash at Bank	8,100		
Investments (Long-term)	20,000		
Petty Expenses	700		
Printing and Stationary	1,600		
Plant and Machinery	45,000		
Neon Sign	7,000		
Furniture and Fixtures	14,000		
	335,900		335,900

Adjustments:

Closing stock Rs. 24,800.

Solution

Trading and Profit and Loss Account of Mr. K. Madhavan

Dr			for the year ended March 31, 2009		Cr.
Particulars	Amount (Rs.)	Amount (Rs.)	Particulars	Amount (Rs.)	Amount (Rs.)
To Opening Stock		12,900	By Sales		166,500
To Purchases		71,500	By Closing Stock		24,800
To Heating and Lighting		5,500			
To Wages		6,800			
To Freight		6,700			
To Carriage Inwards		3,200			
To Gross Profit c/d		84,700			
		191,300			191,300
To Printing and Stationery		1,600	By Gross Profit b/d		84,700
To Advertisement		5,040	By Miscellaneous Receipts		3,800
To Petty Expenses		700	By Dividend Received		4,600
To Bad Debts		1,900	By Interest Received		3,600
To Law Charges		1,660			
To Salaries		12,700			
To Discount Allowed		2,600			
To Rent		4,800			
To Net Profit		65,700			
Transferred to Capital A/c					
		96,700			96,700

Balance sheet of Mr. K. Madhavan
as on March 31, 2009

Liabilities	Amount (Rs.)	Amount (Rs.)	Assets	Amount (Rs.)	Amount (Rs.)
Capital	126,400		Buildings		60,200
Add: Net Profit	65,700		Machinery		45,000
	192,100		Furniture and Fixtures		14,000
Less: Drawings	2,000	190,100	Neon Sign		7,000
			Investments (Long-term)		20,000
Trade Creditors		31,000	Closing Stock		24,800
			Debtors		42,000
			Cash at Bank		8,100
		221,100			221,100

EXERCISES

I. *Choose the correct alternative:*

1. A closing stock is valued at the
   - (a) cost price
   - (b) market price
   - (c) cost or market price, whichever is lower.
2. Trading account is prepared with the help of
   - (a) recurring incomes and expenditures
   - (b) direct incomes and expenditures
   - (c) indirect incomes and expenditures
3. Manufacturing account is prepared to know
   - (a) the total volume of production
   - (b) the total cost of production
   - (c) the total cost of goods sold
4. Balance sheet is prepared to know
   - (a) the true financial position of the firm
   - (b) the position of current assets and fixed assets
   - (c) the position of capital and profit
5. Marshalling of balance sheet means
   - (a) the order in which the assets and liabilities are to be shown
   - (b) how assets are classified as fixed and current
   - (c) calculation of working capital
6. Adjustments in final accounts are made to
   - (a) know the profits of the business
   - (b) know the financial position of the business
   - (c) know the true financial position on the basis of the accrual concept
7. Packing materials are to be charged to trading account when
   - (a) these materials are used for packing the goods purchased for bringing them into a suitable condition
   - (b) these materials are used after the goods are sold
8. Trade discount is calculated on the
   - (a) agreed price
   - (b) net price
   - (c) list or catalogue price

9. Actual sales/purchases price is to be calculated by
   (a) deducting the trade discount from the list price
   (b) deducting the cash discount from the list price
   (c) deducting cash discount and trade discount from the list price

10. Goodwill is a/an
    (a) fictitious asset
    (b) current asset
    (c) intangible asset

11. Mines and queries are the examples of
    (a) fictitious asset
    (b) wasting asset
    (c) current asset

12. Neon sign is a/an
    (a) current asset
    (b) fixed asset
    (c) intangible asset

13. Guarantor's liability is
    (a) a certain liability
    (b) a contingent liability
    (c) no liability at all

14. For a sole trader, income tax is a
    (a) business expense
    (b) personal expense
    (c) provision for expenses

15. When closing stock appears in the trial balance, then it will be shown
    (a) in the balance sheet
    (b) in the Trading A/c and balance sheet
    (c) in the Trading A/c only

16. The assets which are purchased for the use of the business but not for resale are known as
    (a) current assets
    (b) fixed assets
    (c) fictitious assets

17. Bad debts recovered will
    (a) increase the profits of the business
    (b) increase the Debtors' balance
    (c) will decrease the Debtors' balance

18. For abnormal loss of goods,
    (a) Profit and Loss A/c will be credited
    (b) Trading A/c will be credited
    (c) Abnormal Loss A/c will be debited and Trading A/c will be credited

19. For Set off (a particular person when included in both debtors and creditors),
    (a) bigger amount will have to be deducted from both debtors and creditors
    (b) smaller amount will have to be deducted from creditors
    (c) smaller amount will have to be deducted from both debtors and creditors

20. Loan to Mr. X is
    (a) a personal liability
    (b) a liability
    (c) an investment

21. Rent from sub-letting is
    (a) an expenditure
    (b) an income
    (c) a liability

22. A deposit received from a customer as an advance will be treated as
    (a) an income
    (b) a prepaid expenses
    (c) a liability

23. Interest on income tax paid in advance (through the business) by the proprietor will be treated as
    (a) a business income
    (b) a personal income
    (c) a personal income and will decrease the current year's drawings

Ans: 1. (c), 2. (b), 3. (b), 4. (a), 5. (a), 6. (c), 7. (a), 8. (c), 9. (a), 10. (c), 11. (b), 12. (b), 13. (b), 14. (b), 15. (a), 16. (b), 17. (a), 18. (c), 19. (c), 20. (c), 21. (b), 22. (c), 23. (c).

II. *Short Answer Type Questions (with answers)*

1. Why is final account prepared?
Ans: The final account is prepared to ascertain the results (profit or loss) of the business transactions within a given period and to ascertain the true financial position of a business concern at the end of the financial period.

or

Ans: At the end of financial period after preparing the trial balance, a trader or businessman wants to know the financial results (profit/loss) of the business and the financial position. By preparing income statement (Trading Account and Profit and Loss Account), the results of the business are found and by preparing the balance sheet, the financial position is shown. The above two statements are known as final accounts.

2. What are the different types of accounts or statements prepared within final accounts/financial statements?
Ans: Manufacturing account, trading account, profit & loss account and the balance sheet.

3. Who are the users of the financial statements?
Ans: Owners, investors, management, creditors, government, employees and researchers.

4. What is the fundamental principle for preparing the trading account and profit and loss account?
Ans: On the basis of accrual concept, all actual incomes and expenditures of a particular period/financial year are to be considered.

5. What is the nature of item of expenditures considered in trading account?
Ans: Generally, all those expenditures which are incurred for purchasing the goods or for production of goods for sale are considered in trading account.

6. Give two chief features of trading account.
    Ans: 1. It is a nominal account and is prepared with the help of direct incomes and expenses.
           2. All expenditures for purchasing goods or producing goods are shown on the debit side. All incomes by selling goods are shown on the credit side. Cost of goods sold is shown on the debit side and net sales on the credit side.

7. What is cost of goods sold ?
Ans: It is the total cost incurred for goods sold during the period but not for goods purchased during the financial year. Thus, cost of goods sold is the total direct cost incurred during the period for purchasing or producing the said quantity of goods sold.

8. What is the effect and treatment when carriage is paid for purchase of goods and for purchase of fixed assets?

   Ans: When carriage is paid for purchase of goods, it will increase the volume of direct expenditures and the trading account is debited for such expenses. However, when it is paid for purchase of fixed assets, it will increase the total value of the concerned fixed asset and will be treated as a capital expenditure.

9. Give the characters of the expenditures which are to be considered in the profit and loss account.

   Ans: Generally, the expenditures which are considered in the profit and loss account exist in the nature of operating expenses, office expenses, marketing expenses, distribution expenses, financial, depreciation on fixed assets, legal expenses and abnormal losses.

10. Give some example of incomes from other sources or indirect incomes.

    Ans: Discount received, commission received, interest on bank deposits, dividend received, interest on investments, rebate received, bad debts recovered, rent from subletting, and so on.

11. When the date of drawings are not given, then how is the amount of interest calculated on drawings?

    Ans: When date of drawings are not given then interest is to be calculated on such drawings *on average basis*. Suppose, cash withdrawn by Mr. X from his partnership firm for personal use was Rs.7,000. The rate of interest is 12% p.a. The accounts are closed on December 31, 2007. The interest on drawings is to be calculated on average basis as under:

    On Rs.7,000 for six months (on average basis) @ 12% p.a. = Rs. $7,000 \times 12/100 \times 6/12$ = Rs. 420.

12. What do you mean by 'static fund view of Balance Sheet'?

    Ans: According to static fund view, the liability side of the balance sheet shows different sources of funds that have been raised and the asset side shows the different items of assets where the said funds have been utilized. At the time of beginning of an enterprise, the concept of static fund may be accepted to some extent, but in the case of a running business it is not acceptable because all the items within the balance sheet are changed on the basis of the nature and volume of transactions.

13. Which statement represents the closing value of the accumulated figure of resources and the corresponding accumulated figure of obligations of an enterprise at the end of the financial year?

    Ans: It is the balance sheet prepared at the end of the financial year.

14. Through which statement does the present liquidity position, solvency position, working capital, capital employed and profitability position on capital employed of an enterprise estimated?

    Ans: It is the balance sheet prepared at the end of the financial year.

15. How could you establish the relationship or the dependence between profit and loss account and the balance sheet?

    Ans: There is a direct interrelation and interdependence between the profit and loss account and the balance sheet. Suppose, a rent of Rs. 900 paid in advance has not been considered in the profit and loss account. As a result, it decreases the current year's profit by Rs. 900. At the same time, a rent of Rs. 900 paid in advance will not be reflected as an asset in the balance sheet.

16. From where is the data obtained for measuring the financial strength of an enterprise income statement or the balance sheet?

    Ans: Through the data available from a balance sheet, the financial strength of an enterprise can easily be measured. Financial statements are analyses on the basis of the data provided by the balance sheet. Hence, efficiency of the management may be estimated through this balance sheet.

17. Does the balance sheet represent a 'true and fair' financial position of an enterprise?

Ans: Generally, certificates are issued by the auditors in this respect as 'true and fair' view based on their knowledge and experience, since it is the only medium by which the financial position of a firm is represented. It is suggested that if all the accepted accounting concepts and conventions are properly applied, we may expect a reliable and acceptable picture within the balance sheet of an enterprise.

18. What is the nature of item of expenditures are considered in Profit and Loss Account?

Ans: Generally, all indirect expenditures and losses incidental to a business are considered in Profit and Loss Account. Here indirect expense include all operating expenses in respect of administration, selling and distribution, and all non-operating expenses such as financial expenses and other charges.

19. How are goods lost by fire and its insurance claims are shown in final accounts?

Ans: At first, gross loss of goods by fire is to be shown in Trading A/c (Cr. side.) Then net loss of goods (gross loss − admitted insurance claim) is to be shown in Profit and Loss A/c (Dr. side) and admitted insurance claim amount is to be shown in the asset of balance sheet. If the said loss is not admitted by the insurance company or is not insured, then the entire amount of loss is to be shown in Profit and Loss A/c [after showing in Trading A/c (Cr. Side)].

20. What is balance sheet?

Ans: It is a statement prepared at the end of the financial year/period to know the true financial position of the firm. On the left hand side, all the liabilities (Owner's equity + Outsider's equity) are shown and on the right hand side, all assets are shown.

21. What is marshalling of balance sheet?

Ans: The order in which form assets and liabilities are to be shown is called *marshalling of balance sheet*. The assets and liabilities of a firm may be shown in any of the following two orders:

(a) Liquidity order

(b) Permanency (or fixed) order

22. Define the term asset.

Ans: The term *asset* denotes the resources acquired by a business to get some benefits in future, for example, land and building, plant and machinery, investments, etc.

23. How are assets classified?

Ans: Generally, assets are classified in five parts and they are as follows:

Fixed assets (or block capital), current assets, intangible assets, fictitious assets and wasting assets.

24. What are current assets?

Ans: Current assets are those assets which are acquired with the intention of converting them into cash in ordinary course of business of an enterprise, for example, debtors, stock-in-trade, investment (short term), cash and bank balances, etc.

25. What are intangible assets?

Ans: These kinds of assets cannot be seen or touched, for example, goodwill, trademark, patents, etc.

26. What are fictitious assets?

Ans: There are some expenditures or losses which are not charged to Profit and Loss Account within the year in which they actually happen, but are written off gradually in the subsequent years. So long these items of expenditures or losses are not written off completely, they are shown in the assets. Examples are Profit and Loss A/c Dr. balance, Discount on issue of shares/debentures, preliminary expenses, etc.

27. What are wasting assets?

Ans: There are some assets which are exhausted completely by use and cannot be replaced by a new one within the same place, for example, mines, queries, etc.

28. Define the term liability or equity.

Ans: A claim against the assets of a business which can be enforced by law is called *liability* or *equity*. The amount of claim for which the business is liable to pay to the owner is called *internal liability* (owner's equity) and which are payable to the outsiders is called *external liability*.

29. How are liabilities classified?

Ans: Generally, liabilities are classified in three parts and they are as follows :
   (a) Long, term or fixed liabilities
   (b) Current liabilities
   (c) Contingent liabilities

30. What are contingent liabilities?

Ans: These liabilities are not the actual liabilities of a business on the date of the balance sheet but may become in future on happening of an uncertain event. For example, guarantor's liability is a contingent liability because guarantor is liable only when the principal debtor fails to pay his loan.

31. Why are adjustments are essential in final accounts?

Ans: According to the objectives of accountancy, Convention of Disclosure and Accrual Concept is essential to prepare the final accounts in such a way that income statement and balance sheet must represent a " true and fair view " of profits earned and their state of affairs as at the end of the said period. So, in order to represent the true financial position, necessary adjustments are to be made in income statement and the balance sheet.

32. How are expenses incurred for packing materials treated in final accounts?

Ans: When Packing Materials are used for packing the goods produced for bringing them into a saleable condition are direct expenses and are to be charged to Trading Account. On the other hand if Packing Materials are used after the goods are sold, then such expenses are to be charged to Profit & Loss Account.

33. How is income tax of a sole trader is treated in final accounts?

Ans: It will be treated as a personal expenses (i.e. drawings) of the proprietor and as such, it will be deducted from capital as drawings in the balance sheet.

34. What is deferred revenue expenditure?

Ans: There are some cases, when the benefits of a revenue expenditure continue for more than a year and such type of expenditures are known as deferred revenue expenditures. Total expenditure is to be written off in number of years and the amount not yet written off is to be shown in the balance sheet asset side, for example, heavy expenditure incurred for advertisement.

35. Give a proforma of work sheet.

Ans: Proforma of work sheet

Sl. No.	Name of account	L.F.	Trial balance		Adjustments		Adjusted Trial balance		Income statement		Balance sheet	
			Dr.	Cr.	Dr.	Cr.	Dr.	Cr.	Dr.	Cr.	Asset	Liability

III. *Long Answer Type Questions*

1. What is trading account? What are the object of preparing trading account? What are its advantages?

2. What is trading account? What accounting information do we get from it?

3. What is gross profit? What is the importance of calculating gross profit?
4. What is profit and poss account? State its utilities. Explain the difference between trading account and profit and loss account.
5. Distinguish between gross profit and net profit.
6. What do you mean by balance sheet? Why is it prepared? Explain the difference between trial balance and balance sheet.
7. What are the utilities of a balance sheet? Is balance sheet an account?
8. Explain the different views about the balance sheet in brief.
9. What do you mean by 'asset' and 'liability'? How are they classified?
10. "Balance sheet may be called a second trial balance". Do you agree? Give reasons for your answers.
11. What do you mean by marshalling of assets and liabilities in a balance sheet? Describe briefly the different methods in this respect.
12. Does the balance sheet represent a 'true and fair' financial position of an enterprise?
13. Explain the interrelation between profit and loss account and balance sheet.
14. Differentiate between balance sheet and statement of affairs.
15. Write short notes on:
    Gross profit ratio; Profit and loss appropriation account; Patent; Circulating assets; Contingent assets; Tangible assets; Wasting assets; Intangible assets; Fictitious assets.

IV. *Problems*

Trading Account

1. From the following data, prepare a trading account for the year ended December 31,2008:

	Rs.		Rs.
Opening stock	12,600	Carriage inward	6,800
Purchase	98,350	Wages	7,300
Coal, gas and oil	4,100	Excise duty	1,500
Purchase return	3,150	Sales	218,600
Sales returns	3,100	Closing stock	16,300

Ans: Gross Profit Rs.104,300.

2. The following data are extracted from the records of Mr. P. Ahuja. Prepare a trading account for the year ended December 31,2008:

	Rs.		Rs.
Carriage and freight	6,100	Import duty	4,500
Purchase	172,700	Wages	5,750
Sales	336,350	Opening stock	21,950
Closing stock	27,580	Purchase return	5,400
Sales returns	5,850		

Ans: Gross Profit Rs. 152,480.

3. From the following data, prepare a trading account for the year ended March 31,2008:

	Rs.		Rs.
Opening stock	39,300	Return inwards	5,050
Closing stock	30,650	Return outwards	3,800
Purchase	186,400	Royalty on production	5,340
Sales	315,700	Motive power	6,860
Carriage inward	3,200	Wages	7,200

Ans: Gross profit Rs. 96,800.

4. From the particulars given below, prepare Trading Account for the year ended December 31, 1994:

	Rs.		Rs.
Cash in hand	366	Opening Stock	598
Credit purchases	2,000	Purchases returns	264
Cash purchases	536	Cash Sales	1,200
Credit Sales	4,312	Carraige on goods purchased	60
Sales returns	98	Carriage on goods sold	80
Railway freight and insurance	50	Wages	512
Salary	1,300	Trade charges	360
Discount on cash Purchases	70	Discount on cash Sales	20
Closing Stock	1,190		

Additional information

During the year the proprietor had taken away for his personal use goods costing Rs. 300 and cash Rs. 500 but these were not recorded in the books of the firm.

(W.B.H.S. Examination)

Ans: Gross Profit Rs. 3,412.

5. Redraft the following Trading Account prepared by and Accountant, who has no sound knowledge of Accountancy:

Trading Account for the year ended 31.12.97

		Rs.			Rs.
To Opening Stock		6,400	By Sales	1,38,200	
To Purchases	71,200		Less: Return Outwards	1,900	
Less: Return Inward	2,100	69,100		1,36,300	
To Wages		3,600	Add: Sale of scrap	800	1,37,100
To Electric charges		700	By Closing Stock	16,400	
To Carriage Inward		1,800	Add: Goods distributed	900	17,300
To Bad Debts		950	as free samples		
To Gross Profit transferred to					
P/L A/c		71,850			
		1,54,400			1,54,400

Ans: Gross Profit Rs. 72,300.

Profit & Loss Account

6. From the following data, prepare a profit and loss account for the year ended March 31,2008:

	Rs.		Rs.
Discount received	4,120	Salaries	10,800
Interest received	2,380	Rent	4,150
Gross profit	86,840	Insurance premium	2,200
Printing and stationary	1,780	Advertisement	3,600
Discount allowed	3,000	Audit fees	1,000
Electric charges	3,600	Commission received	3,800
Packing charges	5,800		

Ans: Net Profit Rs. 61,210.

7. The following data are extracted from the records of Mr.D. Sen. Prepare a profit and loss account for the year ended December 31,2008:

	Rs.		Rs.
Bad debts recovered	2,840	Interest on investment	3,500
Discount received	5,600	Rent from subletting	3,600
Salaries	16,100	Printing and stationery	2,180
Advertisement	6,500	Export duty	5,410
Insurance premium	4,390	Repairs	4,460
Bad debts	3,200	Travelling expenses	6,180
Depreciation on fixed assets	7,650	Gross profit	118,650

Ans: Net Profit Rs. 78,120.

8. From the following particulars prepare a Profit and Loss Account for the year ended 31.12.97:

Gross Profit Rs. 39,600, Salaries Rs. 4,200, Postage and Telegram Rs.600, Bad Debts Rs. 900, Wages Rs. 1,900, Carriage Rs. 1,400, Selling expenses Rs. 600, Trade expenses Rs. 750, Discount received Rs. 1,300, Commission allowed Rs. 900, Excise Duty Rs. 1,500, Fuel Rs. 300, Sale of Furniture Rs. 1,600, Loss on Sale of Furniture Rs. 380, Interest on Bank deposits Rs. 640 and Bank charges Rs. 70.

Ans: Net Profit Rs. 33,140.

9. From the following particulars prepare a Profit and Loss Account for the year ended 31st March, 1998:

	Rs.		Rs.
Advertisement	1,600	Carriage inward	1,700
Carriage outward	1,300	Gross profit	46,900
Rebate received	600	Bad debts	720
Bad debt recovered	950	Rent	1,800
Electric charges	550	Gas & oil	600
Motive power	1,300	Rent from subletting	900
Packing charges	450	Repairs	630
Samples	750	Travelling expenses	1,200
Discount allowed	480	Audit fees	390

Ans: Net Profit Rs. 39,480.

10. From the following particulars prepare a Profit and Loss Account for the year ended 31.12.1997

	Rs.		Rs.
Gross Profit	32,860	Misc. Income	4,200
Rebate received	1,600	Commission received	1,300
Selling expenses	950	Apprenticeship premium paid	1,800
Audit fees	600	Salary & Wages	4,200
Petty Expenses	520	Carriage to godown	1,400
Carriage from godown	900	insurance	1,320
Interest paid	650	Import duty	1,390
Repairs	930	Rates & Taxes	1,260
Bank charges	150	Dividend received	2,300
Heating & Lighting	1,970		

Ans: Net Profit Rs. 28,980.

Operating Profit

11. The following balances are extracted from the records of Mr. P. Jadav on December 31, 2008:

	Rs.		Rs.
Sales	290,000	Purchase Returns	1,900
Sales Returns	4,200	Closing Stock	17,800
Opening Stock	13,900	Salaries	15,600
Purchases	76,200	General Expenses	3,100
Carriage Inward	5,800	Audit Fees	4,200
Wages	12,800	Insurance Premium	6,500
Rent	7,300	Carriage Outwards	3,800
Repairs and Maintenance of Equipments	4,600	Advertising	7,600
Travelling Expenses	5,400	Bad Debts	2,100

Calculate gross profit and operating profit from the above data.

Ans: Gross profit Rs. 196,800; Operating profit Rs. 136,600.

12. The following balances are extracted from the records of Mr. G. H. Khanna on December 31, 2008:

	Rs.		Rs.
Sales	310,700	Purchase Returns	3,200
Sales Returns	4,900	Closing Stock	27,300
Opening Stock	34,000	Salaries	8,700
Purchases	123,600	General Expenses	
Carriage Inward	6,700	Postage and Stationery	2,400
Wages	18,500	Insurance Premium	6,100
Rent		Rent and Taxes	12,800
Repairs and Maintenance	6,700	Advertising and Free Sample	7,500
Carriage Outwards	4,300	Bad Debts	2,900
Lighting	5,600	Commission on Sales	5,400

Calculate gross profit and operating profit from the above data.

Ans: Gross profit Rs. 153,500; Operating profit Rs. 91,100.

Balance Sheet

13. From the following information prepare a Balance Sheet of Sri P. Sen as at 31st December 1997:

Capital Rs. 90,000, Bank Overdraft Rs. 18,000, Goodwill Rs. 21,000, Building Rs.60,000, Furniture and Fittings Rs. 19,000, Patent Rs. 10,000, Sundry Creditors Rs. 26,000, Reserve Fund Rs. 15,000, Sundry Debtors Rs. 24,000, Investment Rs. 15,000, Cash in hand Rs. 8,200, Cash at Bank Rs. 15,900, Bills Receivable Rs. 8,000, Bills Payable Rs. 6,000, Loan from Mr. X Rs. 25,000, Outstanding Expenses Rs. 1,100.

Ans: Balance Sheet Total Rs. 181,100.

14. Prepare a Balance Sheet with the following balances as on 31.12.95:

	Rs.			Rs.
Closing Stock:			Sundry Debtors	22,900
Raw Materials	12,000		Trade Mark	16,000
Work-in-progress	9,000		Sundry Creditors	15,600
Finished Goods	28,000	49,000	Bills Payable	9,400
Provision for National			Machinery	35,000
Defence Fund		8,000	Govt. Securities	20,000
Motor Van		19,000	Horse and Carts	15,000
Prepaid Expenses		1,200	Advance given to Mr. Y	1,900
Capital		130,000	Net Profit	28,000
Drawings		11,000		

Ans: Balance Sheet Total Rs. 180,000.

15. From the following particulars draft the Balance Sheet of Sri Pradip Roy as at 31st December, 1987:

	Rs.		Rs.
Sundry Debtors	51,300	Drawings	4,500
Investments	6,000	Net profit for the year	21,000
Capital	87,000	Stock-in-trade	21,300
Sundry Creditors	30,000	Bank Overdraft	12,000
Provision for Bad debts	2,100	Cash in hand	1,800
Furniture	13,800	Bills Payable	3,000
Rent Prepaid	2,100	Plant and Machinery	45,000
Outstanding Wages	900	Bills Receivable	9,000
Commission Accrued but not Received	1,200		

(W.B.H.S. 1988)

Ans: Balance Sheet Total Rs. 149,400.

16. Correct the following Balance Sheet and show the correct one:

Balance Sheet for the year ended 31st December, 1980

Liabilities	Rs.	Assets	Rs.
Capital	50,000	Sundry Debtors	40,000
Bank Overdraft	30,000	Goodwill	10,000
Bills Payable	10,000	Furniture and Fixture	20,000
Sundry Creditors	40,000	Plant and Machinery	80,000
Provision for Doubtful Debts	2,000	Stock	10,000
Profit and Loss A/c	40,000	Drawings	10,000
		Cash in hand	2,000
	172,000		172,000

(W.B.H.S. 1982)

Ans: Balance Sheet Total Rs. 160,000.

Final Accounts

17. From the following trial balance and additional information prepare trading account, profit and loss account for the year ended March 31, 2008 and the Balance Sheet as on that in the books of Mr. D. Dhikala:

Trial Balance for the year ended March 31, 2008

Dr.   Cr.

	Rs.		Rs.
Purchases	67,900	Sales	124,875
Salaries	10,700	Purchase Returns	1,400
Rent	2,500	Capital	65,000
Carriage Inward	2,100	Sundry Creditors	18,225
Insurance	2,800	Loan	21,000
Wages	4,700		
Discount Allowed	1,400		
Advertisement	4,500		
Opening Stock	7,800		
Debtors	34,900		
Cash in hand	23,600		
Machinery	45,700		
Furniture	20,300		
Bad Debts	1,600		
	230,500		230,500

Additional information: Closing stock Rs. 21,600.

Ans: Gross profit Rs. 65,375; Net profit Rs. 41,875; Balance sheet Total Rs. 146,100.

18. From the following trial balance and additional information, prepare trading account, profit and loss account for the year ended December 31,2008, and the balance sheet as on that date in the books of Mr. Sunil Chandak.

Dr.		Trial Balance for the year ended December 31, 2008		Cr.
Particulars	Rs.	Particulars	Rs.
Plant and Machinery	50,000	Sundry Creditors	21,700
Furniture and Fittings	26,000	Bills Payable	13,500
Sundry Debtors	31,200	Capital	80,000
Bills Receivable	18,700	Rent from subletting	4,300
Bad Debts	1,700	Apprenticeship Premium	
Salaries	15,100	Received	2,700
Discount Allowed	2,100	Discount Received	3,400
Rebate Allowed	1,900	Interest Received	2,700
Purchases	66,500	Sales	144,700
Cash in Hand	23,600		
Import	18,900		
Carriage Inward	2,600		
Freight	3,100		
Import Duty	3,600		
Drawings	8,000		
	273,000		273,000

Additional information: Closing stock Rs. 27,300.

Ans: Gross profit Rs. 77,300; Net profit Rs. 69,600; Balance sheet Total Rs. 176,800.

19. From the following trial balance and additional information, prepare trading account, profit and loss account for the year ended December 31, 2008, and the balance sheet as on that:

Dr.		Trial Balance for the year ended December 31, 2008		Cr.
Particulars	Rs.	Particulars	Rs.
Wages	12,800	Discount Received	2,700
Rent	3,600	Commission Received	1,500
Salaries	5,700	Capital	43,800
Carriage Inward	1,600	Miscellaneous Receipts	2,400
Insurance	2,400	Bad Debts Recovered	1,400
Bad Debts	1,900	Sales	113,400
Opening Stock	10,800	Sundry Creditors	19,800
Cash in Hand	21,700	Bills Payable	10,300
Purchases	65,000	Bank Overdraft	27,000
Plant and Machinery	40,000	Purchases Returns	1,800
Furniture and Fittings	14,000		
Sundry Debtors	29,000		
Bills Receivable	15,600		
	224,100		224,100

The stock on December 31, 2008 was valued at Rs. 17,400.

Ans: Gross profit Rs. 42,400; Net profit Rs. 36,800; Balance sheet Total Rs. 137,700.

20. The following is the Trial Balance of Mr. S. Nariman for the year ended on March 31, 2008:

Dr.		Trial Balance as on March 31, 2008		Cr.
Particulars	Amount (Rs.)	Particulars		Amount) (Rs.)
General Expenses	3,400	Sales		173,300
Salaries	10,900	Trade Creditors		26,700
Packing Charges	2,600	Loan Creditors		18,400
Petty Expenses	1,300	Rent from Subletting		3,900
Tools and Equipments	15,900	Bad debts recovered		2,100
Accrued Incomes	2,500	Purchase Returns		1,900
Prepaid Expenses	1,400	Capital		280,900
Patents and Trademarks	16,000			
Land and Building	110,000			
Insurance Premium	3,900			
Advertisement	4,800			
Bad debts	2,300			
Wages	6,800			
Freight	3,300			
Drawings	15,600			
Customs duty	2,400			
Furniture and Fixtures	21,400			
Neon Sign	10,600			
Opening Stock	7,900			
Sundry Debtors	39,800			
Cash in hand	28,300			
Purchases	91,500			
Depreciation on Machinery	12,000			
Carriage Inwards	4,100			
Machinery	86,000			
Return Inwards	2,500			
	507,200			507,200

The stock on March 31, 2008 was valued at Rs. 31,400.

Prepare Trading Account and Profit and Loss Account for the year ending March 31, 2008, and the Balance Sheet as on that date.

Ans: Gross Profit Rs. 88,100; Net Profit Rs. 52,900; Balance Sheet Total Rs. 363,300.

21. From the following trial balance and additional information, prepare Trading Account and Profit and Loss Account for the year ended December 31, 2008, and the balance sheet as on that date:

Dr.		Trial Balance as on December 31, 2008		Cr.
Particulars	Amount (Rs.)	Particulars		Amount) (Rs.)
Freehold Premises	70,500	Bills Payable		18,200
Plant and Machinery	92,600	Outstanding Expenses		3,100
Rates and Taxes	4,800	Income Received in advance		2,600
Rebates Allowed	2,700	Bank Overdraft		20,700
Trade Expenses	3,900	Interest Received		4,600
Travelling Expenses	6,100	Commission Received		1,700
Audit Fees	3,400	Capital		210,000

(Contd.)

Particulars	Amount (Rs.)	Particulars	Amount) (Rs.)
Apprenticeship Premium	2,600	Sales	167,500
Dock dues	2,300	Return Outwards	2,100
Import duty	3,100	Creditors	27,300
Selling Expenses	4,900		
Carriage Outward	3,200		
Horses and carts	20,800		
Investments (Long term)	30,000		
Royalty on Sales	3,200		
Samples	2,800		
Opening Stock	10,600		
Purchases	88,300		
Cash in hand	30,100		
Debtors	40,600		
Bills Receivable	20,800		
Drawings	10,500		
	457,800		457,800

Additional information: Closing Stock Rs. 24,600(Market Value Rs. 28,900).

Ans: Gross pofit Rs. 9,900; Net profit Rs. 58,600; Balance sheet Total Rs. 330,000.

22. The following balances are extracted from the records of Mr. Subir Ghatak on December 31, 2008:

Particulars	Rs.	Particulars	Rs.
Office Expenses	5,400	Carriage and Cartage	3,600
Interest paid	3,600	Octroi	1,400
Excise duty	2,900	Import Duty	2,600
Coal, gas and Oil	6,300	Cash in hand	30,200
Opening Stock	9,200	Sundry Creditors	19,300
Income Tax	10,800	Bills Receivable	21,600
Discount allowed	3,900	Investments (Short term)	15,000
Commission Received	4,100	Motor Vehicles	22,800
Loan from Mr. X	20,000	Import of Goods	26,000
Return Inwards	2,300	General Expenses	6,200
Life insurance premium (Proprietor)	3,400	Salaries	10,500
Rebate Received	3,600	Capital	100,000
Discount Received	2,900	Sundry Debtors	48,200
Sales	187,000	Electric Charges	2,600
Closing Stock	27,200	Purchases	98,400

Prepare trading account, profit and loss account for the year ending December 31, 2008 and the balance sheet as on that date.

Ans: Gross profit Rs. 61,500; Net profit Rs. 39,900; Balance sheet Total Rs. 165,000.

23. The following balances are extracted from the records of Mr. Bikram Bhatia on March 31, 2008:

Particulars	Rs.	Particulars	Rs.
Bills Receivable	18,400	Commission	1,900
Royalty on production	6,800	Motive Power or Fuel	3,900
Bank Charges	700	Law Charges	1,600
Capital	190,000	Goodwill	20,000
Outstanding Expenses	2,600	Cash at bank	39,200
Bills Payable	10,600	Interest from Bank	900
Export Duty	3,100	Drawings	18,100
Postage	500	Machinery	80,600
Sales:		Sundry Creditors	21,500
Local	165,400	Telephone and Internet Charges	1,900
Export	39,000	Printing and Stationery	3,100
Interest on investments	3,100	Sundry Expenses	2,600
Purchases	110,200	Carriage	4,100
Opening Stock	18,300	Debtors	48,700
Wages	15,600	Investments	30,000
Freight	3,800		
Closing Stock	29,600		

Prepare trading account, profit and loss account for the year ended March 31, 2008, and the balance sheet as on that date.

Ans: Gross profit Rs. 71,300; Net profit Rs. 59,900; Balance sheet Total Rs. 266,500.

24. From the following trial balance and additional information, prepare trading account, profit and loss account for the year ended March 31, 2008, and the balance sheet as on that date in the books of Mr. K. Nayarayan.

Dr.   **Trial Balance as on March 31, 2008**   Cr.

Particulars	Amount (Rs.)	Particulars	Amount) (Rs.)
Heating and Lighting	10,300	Dividend received	2,400
Loose Tools	18,000	Miscellaneous Receipts	1,800
Conveyance Charges	3,800	Suppliers' Balance	19,800
Loss on Sale of Assets	2,300	Bad Debts Recovered	700
Repairs	6,100	Sales	164,200
Godown Rent	8,400	Capital	210,000
Works Expenses	31,500	Out Standing Expenses	1,300
Consumers' Balance	40,700	Advance from Customers	12,100
Bad debts	1,900		
Salaries and Wages	12,600		
Motor Vehicles	30,800		
Electric Charges	3,600		
Freehold Premises	80,000		
Claim recoverable (from Railways)	4,000		
Purchases	86,400		
Investments	18,000		
Opening Stock	9,600		
Advertisement	4,600		
Carriage	3,200		
Cash in hand	26,500		
Drawings	10,000		
	412,300		412,300

The Stock on March 31, 2008 was valued at Rs. 31,600.

Ans: Gross profit Rs. 54,800; Net profit Rs. 16,400; Balance sheet Total Rs. 249,600.

25. From the following trial balance and additional information, prepare trading account, profit and loss account for the year ended March 31, 2008, and the balance sheet as on that date in the books of Mr. G. Vijayan.

Dr.		Trial Balance as on March 31, 2008	Cr.
Particulars	Amount (Rs.)	Particulars	Amount) (Rs.)
Purchases	105,600	Accounts payable	19,200
Rent	10,200	Discount received	2,600
Fire Insurance Premium	3,600	Apprentiship Premium	1,500
Leasehold Building	75,800	Commission Received	3,400
Establishment Expenses	6,600	Sales	234,000
Loan to Mr. B	18,000	Loan from Mr. G	14,000
Patents and Trademarks	20,100	Rent from Subletting	4,800
Coal, gas and Oil	6,800	Income Received in Advance	2,500
Packing Charges	6,200	Capital	127,000
Drawings	18,500		
Discount allowed	4,200		
Bad debts	1,800		
Salaries and Wages	16,200		
Export Duty	4,100		
Carriage inward	3,800		
Cash and bank	40,600		
Royalty on Sales	3,500		
Distribution expenses	7,100		
Accounts receivable	35,300		
Income Tax	10,200		
Sales Tax	10,800		
	409,000		409,000

Additional Information:

Closing stock Rs. 20,400 (Market value Rs. 18,700).

Ans: Gross profit Rs. 136,500; Net profit Rs. 74,500; Balance sheet Total Rs. 208,500.

18

Financial Statements with Adjustments

CONTENTS

- Adjustment Entries in Final Accounts
- Some Important Adjustment Entries and Their Respective Positions in the Final Accounts
- Journal Entries of Some Important Adjustment Entries and Their Respective Positions in Final Accounts
- Adjustments Given Within Trial Balance

18.1 ADJUSTMENT ENTRIES IN FINAL ACCOUNTS

According to the objectives of accounting convention of the Disclosure and Accrual concept, the Final Accounts are required to be prepared in such a way so that the Income Statement (Trading and Profit and Loss Account), and the Balance Sheet represents a 'true and fair view' of the profits earned and its true state of affairs as at the end of the said period. Adjustment means recording of the current year's transactions omitted from the books, rectification of errors, recording of internal transactions not recorded till then and adjustments regarding prepaid, accrued, received in advance, outstanding, etc. Thus, if adjustments are not made regarding the said items, the actual income and expenditure cannot be ascertained on the basis of the accepted accounting principles. As a result, the Balance Sheet will not represent the true financial position of the firm.

Therefore, in order to represent the true financial position, necessary adjustments are to be made in the Income Statement and the Balance Sheet of a firm on the basis of the accepted accounting principles, otherwise the Final Accounts cannot reveal the true state of affairs of the firm. Hence, appropriate adjustments are to be made while preparing the Final Accounts.

18.2 SOME IMPORTANT ADJUSTMENT ENTRIES AND THEIR RESPECTIVE POSITIONS IN THE FINAL ACCOUNTS

1. **Closing stock:**
   (a) When Closing Stock is not given within the Trial Balance, but is given as an information for adjustment, then its adjustment entries will be as under:

   Closing Stock A/c   Dr.
       To Trading A/c

   First, it is to be shown in the Trading A/c credit side and then in the Balance Sheet as a current asset.

   (b) When Closing Stock is given within the Trial Balance then it is to be shown only in the Balance Sheet as a current asset, but not in the Trading A/c.

Working Notes

Generally, closing stock is to be valued at cost (as long as it is less than the market price). An important example of a conservative accounting practice is the use of the inventory (stock) valuation rule —'cost or market price, whichever is lower'. If, on the date of the Balance sheet, the market price of inventory becomes lower than its cost, then the possible loss that may arise on sale of the same should be provided for, and accordingly, the inventory should be valued at the market price instead of at cost.

2. Outstanding expenses: Here, outstanding means due but not paid. There are some items of expenses whose services have been utilized but payment has not been made during the financial year. Thus, at the end of the financial year the unpaid part of the respective expenditure is to be taken into account and its journal entries will be as under:

Suppose, wages is outstanding, then

Wages A/c   Dr.

    To Outstanding Wages A/c

The outstanding amount of wages is to be added to the original wages account, in The Trading Account on the debit side, and then it is to be shown as a liability in the Balance Sheet.

3. Prepaid expenses: Prepaid expenses are expenses paid in advance, i.e., not due but paid. When a particular expense is paid for the following/subsequent period it is known as an **advance**. Thus, at the end of the financial year, the prepaid amount of the respective expenditure is to be taken into account and its journal entries will be as under:

Suppose, salaries is paid in advance, then

Prepaid salaries A/c   Dr.

    To salaries A/c

The prepaid portion of salaries is to be deducted from salaries account in the Profit and Loss A/c, and then the prepaid salaries to be shown on the asset side of the Balance Sheet.

4. Accrued income: When an income is due or accrued but not received, it is known as an **accrued income**. Suppose, interest on investment is due but not received, then the entry for the same would be as under:

Accrued Interest on Investment A/c   Dr.

    To Interest on Investment A/c

The accrued portion of the interest or income is to be added with the respective income account in the Profit and Loss A/c credit side, and then the accrued interest on investment account is to be shown on the asset side of the balance sheet.

5. Income received in advance: When an income is not due or accrued but is received, then the said income received for the subsequent year is known as **income received in advance.** Suppose, at the end of the financial year, rent is received in advance for three months. Then, the adjustment entry for the same would be as under:

Rent received A/c   Dr.

    To rent received in advance account

First, the amount of advance is to be deducted from the rent received or respective income account, and then the said advance portion is to be shown as liability in the Balance Sheet.

6. Goods used by the proprietor for personal use: When goods are used by the proprietor for private/personal use then they will be treated as drawings of the proprietor. The adjustment entry would be as under:

Drawings A/c   Dr.

    To Opening Stock/Purchases A/c

The amount of goods used by the proprietor is to be deducted from the opening stock/purchases account, and then it is to be deducted as drawings from the capital account in the balance sheet.

7. Goods distributed as free sample: When goods are distributed as free samples, they are treated as advertisement of the business. The adjustment entry would be as under:

Free sample A/c   Dr.

    To opening stock/purchases A/c

At first it is to be deducted from the opening stock/purchases A/c in the Trading A/c and then added to the advertisement A/c in the Profit and Loss A/c.

8. Goods lost by fire: It generally takes place under three different situations as under:
  (a) Goods lost by fire and not admitted by the insurance company.
  (b) Goods lost by fire and fully admitted by the insurance company.
  (c) Goods lost by fire and partially admitted by the insurance company.
       At first, the entire amount of loss of goods is to be shown on the credit side of the Trading Account as Goods lost by fire:
       Goods Lost by Fire A/c   Dr.
         To Trading A/c
       (For the original/gross loss)
       Then, the treatments would be as under for the above three situations:
  (a) Goods lost by fire and not admitted by the insurance company:
       The entire amount of loss is to be shown in the debit side of the Profit and Loss A/c
       Profit and Loss A/c   Dr.
         To goods lost by fire A/c
  (b) Goods lost by fire and fully admitted by the insurance company:
       The entire amount of loss is to be shown in the Balance Sheet asset side as 'Admitted Insurance Claim'.
       Admitted insurance claim A/c   Dr.
         To goods lost by fire A/c
  (c) Goods lost by fire and partially admitted by the insurance company:
       Net goods lost by fire (Original/entire amount of loss – Amount admitted by the insurance company) is to be shown in the debit side of the Profit and Loss A/c and then the amount admitted by the insurance company is to be shown in the asset side of the Balance Sheet as 'Admitted Insurance Claim'.
       Admitted Insurance Claim A/c   Dr. (Admitted portion)
       Profit and Loss A/c   Dr. (Net loss)
         To Goods Lost by fire A/c

9. Royalty on production/sales: Usually, the owners of certain assets (like patents, mines, quaries, copyright, etc.), earn revenues from the users of the said assets for allowing or granting them permission to use the said assets. The amount paid by the users for such use is known as **royalty.** The treatment of royalties would be as under:

  (a) If it is paid or payable for production, then the entire amount of royalty will be treated as direct expenses and will be debited to the Trading Account.
  (b) If it is paid or payable for sale of goods, then the entire amount of royalty will be treated as indirect expenses and will be debited to the Profit and Loss Account.

10. Bad debts: Bad debts are irrecoverable debts. Bad debts are those debts which cannot be recovered in future. Now a question may be raised that how does a bad debt arise? Generally, goods are sold on credit to increase the volume of sales. Out of these debtors, some fail to pay the whole or a part of their dues or obligations in future which becomes a business loss. These types of losses are known as bad debts.

  When a debt is declared bad or irrecoverable, then that amount is written off from the debtors as bad debts. Usually, all the debtors of the current year are not realized in future within the credit period, because some debtors fail to pay their obligation. Such debtors are written off as bad debts in future. When a debtor is declared as insolvent, then also a part of the receivable amount is lost and the said unrealized portion is known as bad debts.

  The accounting entries would be as under:
  (a) For writing off the bad debts:
       Bad Debts A/c   Dr.
         To Debtor's/Customer's A/c

(b) For transferring bad debts account to Profit and Loss A/c or Provision for Bad and Doubtful Debts account at the end of the year:

Profit and Loss A/c/Provision for Bad and Doubtful Debts A/c   Dr.

    To Bad Debts A/c

When bad debts account appears in the trial balance, the said bad debts account is only to be shown/transferred to the Profit and Loss Account, i.e., the above journal entry is already passed. Thus, no further entry is required. However, when it is considered as an adjustment entry, then only the above journal entry is required and this new bad debt is shown/transferred to Profit and Loss Account, i.e., to be added with old bad debts, if any.

Bad Debts Recovery. Sometimes, a part or whole of a bad debt is recovered from the concerned debtor written off as bad debt. Such recovery is known as **bad debts recovered.** For bad debts, Profit and Loss A/c is debited as a loss, and thus, bad debts recovery should be considered as an income/profit and hence, Profit and loss Account will be credited for the same. The following entries should be shown:

(a) When cash is realized:

Cash/Bank A/c   Dr.

    To Bad Debts Recovery A/c

(b) For transferring the Bad Debts Recovery A/c to Profit and Loss A/c:

Bad Debts Recovery A/c   Dr.

    To Profit and Loss A/c

11. Provision for bad and doubtful debts: Usually, all the debtors of the current year are not realized later on within the credit period as some debtors fail to pay their obligations. Such debtors are written off as bad debts in the future. This anticipated loss cannot be ascertained accurately in the current year; it can only be estimated on the basis of the past experiences. With the help of this estimated amount, a provision is created out of the current year's profit or revenue which is known as the **provision for bad and doubtful debts.**

It is a practice to adjust all the actual and the estimated current year's losses from the current year's revenues. In order to follow this practice, a Provision for Bad and Doubtful Debts is created. Any of the following three methods is used. Treatments under different situations are shown below:

(a) When there is no old Provision for Bad and Doubtful Debts, it will not appear in the Trial Balance:

Entry for creating new Provision for Bad and Doubtful Debts will be as follows:

Profit & Loss A/c   Dr.

    To Provision for Bad and Doubtful Debts A/c

The amount of actual closing debtors is calculated; then the amount of provision on such debtors is calculated with the help of the given percentage. First, the amount of Provision for Bad and Doubtful Debts is to be shown in the debit side of the Profit & Loss Account, and then is deducted from the debtors in the asset side of the Balance Sheet.

(b) Whenever there is old Provision for Bad and Doubtful Debts, it will appear in the Trial Balance:

Entry for creating new Provision for Bad and Doubtful Debts will be as follows:

(i) When old Provision for Bad and Doubtful Debts is less than the new provision

Profit & Loss A/c   Dr. (Net amount)*

    To Provision for Bad and Doubtful Debts A/c.

*The net amount of provision is to be calculated as under:

Amount of new Provision for Bad and Doubtful Debts   ...

[to be calculated as (a) above]

    Less: Amount of old Provision for Bad and Doubtful Debts   ...

(Amount appearing in the Trial Balance)

Net amount to be charged to Profit & Loss A/c   ...

The net amount charged to the Profit and Loss A/c is to be shown on the debit side of the Profit and Loss A/c and the amount of new Provision for Bad and Doubtful Debts be deducted from Debtors on the asset side of the Balance Sheet.

(ii) When old Provision for Bad and Doubtful Debts is greater than the new provision
(For transferring surplus amount old Provision to Profit & Loss A/c)

Provision for Bad and Doubtful Debts A/c   Dr.**
   To Profit & Loss A/c

**The amount of surplus old provision will be calculated as under:

Amount of old Provision for Bad and Doubtful Debts   ...
Less: Amount of new Provision for Bad and Doubtful Debts   ...
Surplus amount of old provision   ...

Surplus amount of old provision is to be shown in the credit side of the Profit & Loss A/c, and then the amount of new Provision for Bad and Doubtful Debts is deducted from the debtors on the asset side of the Balance Sheet.

12. Provision for discount on debtors: Cash discount is allowed to encourage the debtors, if the debts are paid within the credit period. The total goods sold in an accounting period cannot be realized in the said period, because a part of the debtors is realized in the next accounting period, and at the same time, a cash discount is allowed. Though the discount is allowed in the next year, it is actually considered as the expenditure of the previous year, i.e., the discount allowed should be charged to the period in which the related sales were actually achieved. Hence, considering this point of view, a provision is created on the basis of the past experience at a fixed percentage on the debtors. This provision is known as the **provision for discount on debtors.**

It is desirable that the debtors appearing in the Balance Sheet should reflect such an amount which is expected to be realized later. In the Balance Sheet, the 'provision for discount on debtors' should be deducted from the gross figure of the debtors after deducting the Provision for Bad and Doubtful Debts to show the net realizable value, otherwise the Balance sheet will not represent the true financial position of an enterprise (Chapter 11 Reserves and Provisions).

Treatments under different situations are shown below:

(a) When there is no old provision for discount on debtors, it will not appear in the Trial Balance:
Entry for creating new provision for discount on debtors will be as follows:

Profit & Loss A/c   Dr.
   To Provision for Discount on Debtors A/c

The amount of actual closing debtors is calculated and thereafter, the amount of Provision for Bad and Doubtful Debts is calculated upon such debtors with the help of the given percentage. Then, after deducting the Provision for Bad and Doubtful Debts from the debtors the amount of provision for discount on debtors is calculated as per the given percentage.

Calculation of provision for discount on debtors is done as under:

Actual Closing Debtors   ...
Less: Provision for Bad and Doubtful Debts   ...
Remaining Debtors   ...

$$\text{Provision for discount on debtors} = \frac{\%}{100} \times \text{Remaining debtors}$$

First, the provision for discount on debtors is shown on the debit side of the Profit and Loss Account, and then it is deducted from the debtors (i.e., Actual Closing Debtors–Provision for Bad and Doubtful Debts–Provision for Discount on Debtors) on the asset side of the Balance Sheet.

(b) When old provision for discount on debtors is greater than the new provision:
(For transferring surplus amount old provision to Profit & Loss A/c)

Provision for Discount on Debtors A/c   Dr. **
   To Profit & Loss A/c

** The amount of surplus old provision will be calculated as under:

Amount of old Provision for Discount on Debtors   ...
Less: Amount of new Provision for Discount on Debtors ...
Surplus Amount of old Provision   ...

The surplus amount of old provision is shown on the credit side of the Profit & Loss A/c. The amount of new Provision for Discount on Debtors is then deducted from the Debtors in the asset side of the Balance Sheet.

13. Provision for discount on creditors: Generally, cash discount is received for making prompt payment to the creditors. However, it has been found that the current year's outstanding creditors are paid in the next year, and as a practice, some amount of the discount is also received on such creditors (which are paid within the credit period). The said discount (which may be received in the next year) should be considered in the current year's account as an income because it is calculated or based on the current year's creditors. Hence, a reserve is created on the basis of the current year's creditors at some agreed percentage known as **reserve for discount on creditors.** For creating reserve for discount on creditors, the following entry is made:

    Reserve for Discount on Creditors A/c   Dr.
      To Profit and Loss A/c

The said reserve will be deducted from the current year's creditors while preparing the Balance Sheet. At the end of the next year, the actual discount received will be transferred to this 'Provision for Discount on Creditors Account', and again, a new amount of provision is created on the closing balance of the creditors, and so on.

Accounting treatments and adjustments regarding the discount received from creditors and provision for discount on creditors:

 (a) For adjustment of discount received from creditors through Provision for Discount on Creditors A/c

    Discount Received A/c   Dr.
      To Reserve/Provision for Discount on Creditors A/c

 (b) For creation of new provision for discount on creditors when old provision is less than the total amount of discount received and the new provision

    Reserve/Provision for Discount on Creditors A/c   Dr.
      To Profit and Loss A/c

    (Net amount required on balancing the amount of Provision for Discount on Creditors Account)

 (c) When old provision is greater than the discount received plus the new provision, the surplus amount is to be transferred to Profit and Loss A/c

    Profit and Loss A/c   Dr.
      To Reserve/Provision for Discount on Creditors A/c

Table 18.1 gives distinction between provision for discount on debtors and reserve for discount on creditors.

TABLE 18.1 Distinction Between Provision for Discount on Debtors and Reserve for Discount on Creditors

Provision for discount on debtors	*Reserve for discount on creditors*
It is created on debtors.	It is created on creditors.
This provision is related to cash discount allowed to debtors.	This provision is related to cash discount received from creditors.
For creating this provision profit of the firm is decreased.	For creating this provision profit of the firm is increased.
Its favourable balance is credit.	Its favourable balance is debit.
It is deducted from debtors in the Balance Sheet to show the net realizable amount of debtors.	It is deducted from creditors in the Balance Sheet to show the net amount payable to the creditors.
To follow the convention of conservatism this provision is created.	It is created to increase the profit on the basis of anticipation which is just the reverse of the convention of conservatism.

14. Depreciation on fixed assets: Depreciation is the permanent decrease in the value of a fixed asset and represents a part of the total cost of fixed asset used/consumed in an accounting period. Thus, it is an expired cost of a fixed asset considered as an expenditure in the process of its useful life in an accounting year.

Thus, it can be said that the historical cost of the fixed asset is spread over its effective life on the basis of some accepted rules or methods by way of depreciation and is charged against the revenue of each financial year [Chapter 9 Depreciation Accounting].

Accounting entries for charging depreciation would be as under:

(a) When fixed asset accounts are maintained on written down on value basis:

    (i) For charging depreciation

        Depreciation A/c   Dr.

          To Asset A/c

    (ii) For transferring depreciation to Profit and Loss A/c

        Profit and Loss A/c   Dr.

          To depreciation A/c

        Depreciation is to be shown on the debit side of the Profit & Loss A/c. It will then be deducted from the respective Asset A/c in the balance sheet.

(b) When fixed asset accounts are maintained at its cost price:

    (i) For charging depreciation

        Depreciation A/c   Dr.

          To Provision for Depreciation A/c

    (ii) For transferring depreciation to the Profit and Loss A/c

        Profit and Loss A/c   Dr.

          To Depreciation A/c

        Depreciation is shown on the debit side of the Profit and Loss A/c and the Provision for Depreciation is shown on the Balance Sheet liability side. The Fixed Asset Account will maintain its cost in the Balance Sheet. Alternatively, the accumulated depreciation (i.e., total of the Provision for Depreciation A/c balance) may be deducted from the fixed asset in the Balance Sheet.

15. Interest on investments: Interest on investment is an indirect income. When such income is due or accrued but not received, then the amount of such income is shown in the Profit &Loss A/c credit side, and thereafter, in the Balance Sheet asset side as an accrued income. Accounting entries for accrued interest on investment would be as under:

(a) Accrued Interest on Investment A/c   Dr.

        To Interest on Investment A/c

    (When interest on investment is due)

(b) Interest on Investment A/c   Dr.

        To Profit & Loss A/c

    (For transferring interest on investment)

16. Interest on loans: Interest on loan is an indirect expenditure. When such an expenditure is due or accrued but not paid, then the amount of such expenditure is shown in the Profit and Loss A/c debit side, and thereafter, in the liability side of the Balance Sheet as an outstanding liability. Accounting entries for outstanding interest on loan would be as under:

(a) Interest on Loan A/c   Dr.

        To Outstanding Interest on Loan A/c

    (For charging interest)

(b) Profit & Loss A/c   Dr.

        To Interest on Loan A/c

    (For transferring interest on loan)

17. Interest on capital: Interest on capital is not a business expenditure because it is an appropriation of profit payable to the proprietor or to the partners. Accounting entries for interest on capital would be as under:

For Sole Proprietorship Firm

(a) Profit & Loss A/c   Dr.

     To Interest on capital A/c

     (For charging interest)

For a Partnership Firm

(i) Profit & Loss Appropriation A/c   Dr.

       To Interest on capital A/c

       (For charging interest)

(ii) Interest on capital A/c   Dr.

       To Partners' Capital/Current A/c

       (For transferring interest on capital)

18. Interest on drawings: Cash is the blood of a business. Excess cash drawings by the partners may affect the working capital of the business. Interest on drawings is not a business income; however in some cases it is charged on drawings in a partnership firm to control the cash drawings of the partners. Accounting entries for interest on drawings would be as under:

(a) Interest on Drawings capital A/c   Dr.

     To Profit & Loss Appropriation A/c

     (For charging interest on drawings)

(b) Partners' Capital/Current A/c   Dr.

     To Interest on Drawings capital A/c

     (For transferring interest on drawings)

19. Income tax: Income tax is not a business expenditure in case of Sole Proprietorship Firm or a Partnership Firm. It is a personal expenditure. Hence, it should be treated as a drawing and is deducted from the capital. Thus, when it is paid from the business and appears in the Trial Balance it should be treated as under:

Drawings A/c   Dr.

     To Income Tax A/c

20. Mutual indebtedness: There are some cases when a debtor of a firm may be a creditor at the same time due to certain business transaction. Suppose, raw materials are purchased by D.K. Traders from X & Co. for Rs. 2,000. Because of this transaction, X & Co. becomes a creditor for that period. Now, if the finished products are also sold by D.K. Traders to X & Co. for Rs. 3,000, then X & Co. would be a debtor in the books of D.K. Traders. Thus, X & Co. becomes both a debtor and a creditor in the books of D.K. Traders at the same time. However, as per the accounting principles and practices we cannot represent a particular firm or a party both as a debtor and a creditor. It can either be a debtor or a creditor. Therefore, as per given example, X & Co. would be a debtor of Rs. 1,000 (3,000 – 2,000) of D.K. Traders. The lesser amount is deducted from both the debtor and the creditor as set off in the Balance Sheet. The adjustment entry for the same would be as under:

Creditors A/c   Dr. (As per our example the Lesser amount of Rs. 2,000)

     To Debtors A/c

21. Dishonour of cheque/bill receivable but no entry has been made in the books: There are some cases where a cheque or a bill is dishonoured but no entry has been made in the books for such dishonour before the preparation of the Trial Balance. Under such circumstances, the adjustment entry for the same would be as under:

Debtor's A/c   Dr.

     To Bank/Bills Receivable A/c

Thus, the amount of dishonoured cheque/bills receivable is added to the Debtors A/c, and the same amount is deducted from the Bank/Bills Receivable A/c in the Balance Sheet.

22. Goods purchased on credit but not recorded in the books: It will increase the volume of the Purchases A/c in the Trading Account and the amount of Creditors in the Balance Sheet. The adjustment entry for the same would be as under:

Purchases A/c   Dr.
     To Creditors A/c

Thus, it is added to the Purchases A/c in the Trading A/c and to the creditors in the Balance Sheet. Here, it is to be assumed that stocks are properly recorded, but if stocks are not properly recorded, then it is to be added to the value of Closing Stock.

23. Wages includes installation charges of a Machine: Generally, wages are direct expenses However, when such wages are expended for installation of machines, it will be treated as a capital expenditure. Thus, at first, it is to be deducted from the Wages A/c in the Trading A/c and then added to the Machineries A/c in the Balance Sheet. The adjustment entry for the same would be as under:

Machineries A/c   Dr.
     To Wages A/c

24. Purchase of fixed assets passed through the purchase day books: The adjustment entry for the same would be as under:

Fixed Assets A/c   Dr.
     To Purchases A/c

Thus, the purchase price of a fixed asset is deducted from the Purchases A/c in the Trading Account, and then added to the Fixed Assets A/c in the Balance Sheet.

25. Carriage includes carriage paid for purchase of assets: Carriage Inward is ordinarily a direct expense, but when such Carriage is expended for the purchase of a machine, it will be treated as a capital expenditure. Thus, at first it is deducted from Carriage A/c in the Trading Account, and then added to the Fixed Assets A/c in the Balance Sheet. The adjustment entry for the same would be as under:

Fixed Assets A/c   Dr.
     To Carriage A/c

26. Goods sent on approval basis: There are some cases where goods are sent to customers on a condition that within a certain period of time they may accept the said goods or reject the goods. This facility is given to the prospective buyers or old customers to increase the sales volume and this arrangement is known as **goods sent on approval basis.** When such goods are sent to customers, it is not a case of sale; instead it is transfer of goods only (ownership of the goods is not transferred), and becomes sales when such goods are retained or approved by the buyer within the stipulated time.

At the end of the year when goods are lying with customers but are not approved by them till then (because the time stipulated for sending approval had still then not expired), or when goods are rejected (not approved) by the customers, the adjustment entry for the same would be as under:

(a)   Sales A/c   Dr. (At selling price)
        To Customer's A/c
        (For cancellation of sale)

(b)   Stock with customer's A/c   Dr. (At cost price or market price, whichever is lower)
        To Trading A/c

For recording stock with customers, goods are included in stock at cost price, or market price whichever is lower (though such goods remain with the customer even after rejection).

18.3 JOURNAL ENTRIES OF SOME IMPORTANT ADJUSTMENT ENTRIES AND THEIR RESPECTIVE POSITIONS IN FINAL ACCOUNTS

Journal entries of some important adjustment entries and their respective portions in Final A/cs are shown below:

Adjustment entries	Journal entries	To be shown in Trading or Profit and Loss A/c	To be shown in balance sheet
1. Closing stock	Closing Stock A/c Dr. To Trading A/c	In Trading A/c (Cr. side)	Asset side
2. Outstanding expenses	Expenses A/c Dr. To Outstanding Expenses A/c	Direct expenses to be shown in Trading A/c (Dr. side); Indirect expenses in P/L A/c (Dr. side)	Liability side
3. Accrued income	Accrued Income A/c Dr. To Income A/c	P/L A/c (Cr. side)	Asset side
4. Prepaid expenses	Prepaid Expenses A/c Dr. To Expenses A/c	For direct expenses to be deducted from actual expenses in Trading A/c (Dr. side) and for indirect expenses P/L A/c (Dr. side)	Asset side
5. Goods used by the proprietor for personal purposes	Drawings A/c Dr. To Purchases or Opening Stock A/c	To be deducted from opening stock or purchases in Trading A/c	To be included in Drawings A/c and then to be deducted from Capital A/c
6. Goods distributed as free sample	Advertisement A/c Dr. To opening stock or Purchase A/c	To be deducted from opening stock on purchases in Trading A/c and then to be included with Advertisement A/c in P/L A/c	—
7. Asset purchased but wrongly included in Purchases A/c	Asset A/c Dr. To Purchase A/c	To be deducted from Purchases in Trading A/c	To be included with respective assets
8. Goods purchased on credit but not recorded in the books.	Purchase A/c Dr. To Creditors A/c	To be added with Purchases A/c and closing stock in Trading A/c.	To be added to creditors in liabilities side
9. Wages include wages paid for installation of plant	Plant A/c Dr. To Wages A/c	To be deducted from wages in Trading A/c	To be added to Plant A/c on asset side
10. Wages include wages for construction of building.	Building A/c Dr. To Wages A/c	— do —	To be added to Building A/c on asset side
11. Profit or loss on sale of fixed assets	(a) In case of loss: (i) Loss on Sale of Assets A/c Dr. To Asset A/c. (ii) P/L A/c Dr. To Loss on Sale of Asset A/c	P/L A/c (debit side)	To be deducted from the assets
	(b) In case of profit: (i) Asset A/c Dr. To Profit on Sale of Asset A/c (ii) Profit on Sale of Asset A/c Dr. To Capital Reserve A/c (for actual sale price the entry is: Bank A/c Dr. To Asset A/c)	No entry	Book value of the asset sold to be deducted from the assets and profits to be shown on liabilities side as capital reserve

(Contd.)

Adjustment entries	Journal entries	To be shown in Trading or Profit and Loss A/c	To be shown in balance sheet
12. Depreciation on assets	(i) Depreciation A/c Dr. 　　To Asset A/c (ii) P/L A/c Dr. 　　To Depreciation A/c	P/L A/c (debit side)	To be deducted from assets
13. Bad debts to be written off	(i) Bad debts A/c Dr. 　　To Debtor's A/c (ii) P/L A/c Dr. 　　To Bad debt A/c	To be added to Bad debts A/c in P/L A/c debit side	To be deducted from debtors
14. Purchase of assets passed through the Purchase day book	Asset A/c Dr. 　　To Purchase A/c	To be deducted from Purchase A/c in Trading A/c (Dr. side)	To be added to assets
15. Sales include sale of assets	Sales A/c Dr. 　　To Assets A/c	To be deducted from sales in Trading A/c	To be deducted from assets
16. Provision for doubtful debts	(a) When old provision is nil or is less than the New provision: Profit and Loss A/c Dr. 　　To Provision for Doubtful Debts A/c (New provision – Old provision)	Net amount in Profit and Loss A/c Dr. side	New provision for doubtful debts is to be deducted from sundry debtors
	(b) When old provision is greater than the new provision: Provision for Doubtful Debts A/c Dr. 　　To Profit and Loss A/c (Old provision – New provision)	Net amount in Profit and Loss A/c Cr. side	— do —
17. Provision for discount on debtors	(a) — do — Profit and Loss A/c Dr. 　　To Provision for Discount on debtors A/c (New provision – Old provision)	— do —	New provision for discount on debtors is to be deducted from debtors
	(b) — do —	— do —	— do —
18. Provision for discount on creditors	Provision for Discount on Creditors A/c Dr. 　　To profit and Loss A/c	Profit and Loss A/c (Cr. side)	To be deducted from creditors
19. Goods lost by fire or abnormal loss.	(i) Abnormal Loss/ Goods lost by Fire A/c Dr. 　　To Trading A/c	Trading A/c (Cr. side) full loss	
	(ii) Then: (a) If insured fully and admitted by the insurance company Insurance Claim A/c Dr. 　　To Abnormal Loss	No entry	Admitted claim in asset side
	(b) When admitted by the Insurance company partially: Insurance Claim A/c Dr. Profit and Loss A/c Dr. 　　To Abnormal Loss A/c	Net loss to be shown in Profit and Loss A/c Dr. side	Asset side

(Contd.)

Adjustment entries	Journal entries	To be shown in Trading or Profit and Loss A/c	To be shown in balance sheet
	(c) When not admitted by the insurance company or not insured Profit and Loss A/c Dr. To Abnormal Loss A/c	Profit and Loss A/c (Dr. side) full loss	—
20. Proprietor's life insurance premium included in insurance A/c	Drawings A/c Dr. To Insurance A/c	To be deducted from the Insurance in Profit and Loss A/c (Dr. side)	To be deducted from Capital A/c as drawings
21. Net profit transfered to general reserve or any other fund	Profit and Loss Appropriation A/c Dr. To General Reserve/ special Fund A/c	In Profit and Loss Appropriation (Dr. side)	Liabilities side
22. To create provision for manager's commission	Profit and Loss A/c Dr. To Provision for manager Commission A/c	Profit and Loss A/c (Dr. side)	Liabilities side
23. Interest on capital	Profit and Loss Appropriation A/c Dr. To interest on capital A/c	Profit and Loss Appropriation A/c (Dr. side)	To be added to Capital A/c on the liabilities side
24. Interest on drawings	Interest on Drawing A/c Dr. To Profit and Loss Appropriation A/c	Profit and Loss Appropriation A/c Cr.	To be added to drawings and then to be deducted from Capital A/c
25. Carriage includes carrying of an asset	Asset A/c Dr. To Carriage A/c	To be deducted from Carriage in Trading A/c	To be added to relevant assets
26. Wages include wages paid for repairing	Repairing A/c Dr. To Wages A/c	To be deducted from wages in Trading A/c and to be added to Repairing A/c in P/L A/c	—
27. Set off—A person both as a debtor and a creditor	Creditors A/c Dr. To Debtors A/c (Entry is for the smaller of the two amounts.)	—	Smaller amount to be deducted from both debtors and creditors
28. Bill receivable includes a dishonoured bill	Debtors A/c Dr. To Bills Receivable A/c	—	To be deducted from bills receivable and to be added to Debtors A/c

ILLUSTRATION 18.1   Trial Balance of Mr. Anubhav Sharma as on December 31, 2007 is given below:

Dr.   **Trial Balance as on December 31, 2007**   Cr.

Particulars	Amount (Rs.)	Particulars	Amount (Rs.)
Opening Stock	8,600	Rent Received	4,300
Purchases	67,300	Capital	78,000
Wages	4,800	Sundry Creditors	28,400
Return Inwards	2,900	Sales	132,600
Drawings	3,500	Discount Received	3,200
Salaries	5,100	Provision for Doubtful	
Carriage Inwards	2,600	Debts	2,600
Machinery	42,800		
Discount Allowed	2,400		
Cash at Bank	21,900		
Insurance Premium	2,400		
Advertisement	3,700		
Sundry Debtors	39,500		
General Expenses	1,600		
Buildings	40,000		
	249,100		249,100

Adjustments

1. Closing Stock Rs. 32,700.
2. Goods lost by fire worth Rs. 1,900 (not insured).
3. Depreciate Machinery by 10% and Buildings by 5%.
4. Unexpired insurance Rs. 500.
5. Provision for doubtful debts @ 5% on debtors.
6. Debtors include Rs. 850 due from a customer Mr. K. Kutty who has become insolvent and nothing could be realized from his estate.

Prepare Trading and Profit and Loss Account for the year ended on December 31, 2007, and Balance Sheet as on that date.

Solution

Trading and Profit & Loss Account of Mr. Anubhav Sharma

Dr. For the year ended December 31, 2007 Cr.

Particulars	Amount (Rs.)	Amount (Rs.)	Particulars	Amount (Rs.)	Amount (Rs.)
To Opening Stock		8,600	By Sales	132,600	
To Purchases		67,300	Less: Return Inwards	2,900	129,700
To Wages		4,800	By Closing Stock		32,700
To Carriage Inwards		2,600	By Goods lost by fire		1,900
To Gross Profit c/d		81,000			
		164,300			164,300
To Insurance	2,400		By Gross Profit b/d		81,000
Less: Unexpired	500	1,900	By Discount Received		3,200
To Advertisement		3,700	By Rent Received		4,300
To General Expenses		1,600	By Provision for		
To Salaries		5,100	Doubtful Debts	2,600	
To Goods lost by fire		1,900	Less: New Provision for		
To Discount Allowed		2,400	Doubtful Debts	1,933	667
To Bad Debts		850			
To Depreciation on:					
Buildings	2,000				
Machinery	4,280	6,280			
To Net Profit transferred					
(to Capital A/c)		65,437			
		89,167			89,167

Balance Sheet of Mr. Anubhav Sharma as on December 31, 2007

Liabilities	Amount (Rs.)	Amount (Rs.)	Assets	Amount (Rs.)	Amount (Rs.)
Capital	78,000		Buildings	40,000	
Add: Net Profit	65,437		Less: Depreciation	2,000	38,000
	143,437		Machinery	42,800	
Less: Drawings	3,500	139,937	Less: Depreciation	4,280	38,520
Sundry Creditors		28,400	Closing Stock		32,700
			Debtors	39,500	
			Less: Bad Debts	850	
				38,650	
			Less: Provision for		
			Doubtful Debts	1,933	36,717
			Unexpired insurance		500
			Cash at Bank		21,900
		168,337			168,337

Working Note

An amount of Rs. 850 receivable from Mr. K. Kutty is to be considered here as a bad debt, as he has been declared insolvent and nothing could be realized from his estate.

ILLUSTRATION 18.2   From the following trial balance of Mr. Sanjay Kumbley, prepare a Trading and Profit and Loss Account for the year ending December 31, 2007, and a balance sheet as on that date.

Dr.		Trial Balance as on December 31, 2007	Cr.
Particulars	Amount (Rs.)	Particulars	Amount (Rs.)
Wages	6,800	Sales	166,500
Freight	6,700	Miscellaneous Receipts	3,800
Buildings	60,200	Dividend received	4,600
Heating and Lighting	5,500	Interest Received	3,600
Opening Stock	12,900	Provision for Doubtful Debts	1,400
Purchase	71,500	Trade Creditors	31,000
Salaries	12,700	Capital	125,000
Carriage Inward	3,200		
Advertisement	5,040		
Law Charges	1,660		
Drawings	2,000		
Discount allowed	2,600		
Bad debts	1,900		
Rent	4,800		
Sundry Debtors	42,000		
Cash at Bank	8,100		
Investments (Long-term)	20,000		
Petty Expenses	700		
Printing and Stationary	1,600		
Plant and Machinery	45,000		
Neon Sign	7,000		
Furniture and Fixtures	14,000		
	335,900		335,900

Adjustments

1. Closing Stock Rs. 24,800.
2. Debtors include Rs. 900 due from Mr. Q and creditors include Rs. 500 due to Mr. Q.
3. Goods lost by fire is worth Rs. 890 and the insurance company admitted the claim to the extent of Rs. 720.
4. Outstanding expenses—salaries Rs. 400 and carriage inwards Rs. 350.
5. Make a provision for doubtful debts @ 5% on debtors.
6. A cheque of Rs. 370 deposited in the bank became dishonoured, no entry has been made in the cash book for such dishonour.
7. Depreciations are to be provided as under:
   On Plant and Machinery   10%
   On Furniture and Fixtures   5%
   On Buildings   2%

Solution

Trading and Profit & Loss Account of Mr. Sanjay Kumbley

Dr   for the year ended December 31, 2007   Cr.

Particulars	Amount (Rs.)	Amount (Rs.)	Particulars	Amount (Rs.)	Amount (Rs.)
To Opening Stock		12,900	By Sales		166,500
To Purchases		71,500	By Closing Stock		24,800
To Heating & Lighting		5,500	By Goods lost by fire		890
To Wages		6,800			
To Freight		6,700			
To Carriage Inwards	3,200				
Add: Outstanding	350	3,550			
To Gross Profit c/d		85,240			
		192,190			192,190
To Printing and Stationery		1,600	By Gross Profit b/d		85,240
To Advertisement		5,040	By Miscellaneous Receipts		3,800
To Petty Expenses		700	By Dividend received		4,600
To Bad Debts		1,900	By Interest Received		3,600
To Law Charges		1,660			
To Salaries	12,700				
Add: Outstanding	400	13,100			
To Goods lost by fire	890				
Less: Admitted claim	720	170			
To Discount Allowed		2,600			
To Rent		4,800			
To Provision for					
Doubtful Debts	2,094				
Less: Old Provision	1,400	694			
To Depreciation on:					
Buildings	1,204				
Machinery	4,500				
Furniture and Fixtures	700	6,404			
To Net Profit					
transferred to Capital A/c		58,572			
		97,240			97,240

Balance Sheet of Mr. Sanjay Kumbley
as at December 31, 2007

Liabilities	Amount (Rs.)	Amount (Rs.)	Assets	Amount (Rs.)	Amount (Rs.)
Capital	125,000		Buildings	60,200	
Add: Net Profit	58,572		Less: Depreciation	1,204	58,996
	183,572		Machinery	45,000	
Less: Drawings	2,000	181,572	Less: Depreciation	4,500	40,500
Trade Creditors	31,000		Furniture and Fixtures	14,000	
Less: Set off (Mr. Q)	500	30,500	Less: Depreciation	700	13,300
Outstanding expenses:			Neon Sign		7,000
Carriage inwards	350		Investments (Long-term)		20,000
Salaries	400	750	Closing Stock		24,800
			Debtors	42,000	
			Less: Set off (Mr. Q)	500	
				41,500	
			Add: Cheque dishonoured	370	
				41,870	
			Less: Provision for		
			Doubtful Debts	2,094	39,776
			Admitted Insurance Claim		720
			Cash at Bank	8,100	
			Less: Cheque dishonoured	370	7,730
		212,822			212,822

ILLUSTRATION 18.3 Following is the trial balance of Mr. Simon Pitter for the year ended March 31, 2008:

Dr.   **Trial Balance as on March 31, 2008**   *Cr.*

Particulars	Amount (Rs.)	Particulars	Amount (Rs.)
Furniture	20,000	Capital	152,000
Royalty on Sales	3,700	Sales	134,800
Travelling Expenses	3,900	Purchase Returns	2,700
Plant and Machinery	36,000	Bad Debts Recovered	900
Salaries	12,700	Commission Received	2,600
Office Expenses	2,400	Discount Received	3,400
Audit Fees	3,300	Creditors	26,200
Sundry Debtors	38,500	Provision for Doubtful Debts	1,400
Patents and Trademarks	21,000		
Purchases	62,000		
Motor Vehicles	30,600		
Cash at Bank	25,000		
Fixed Deposits at Bank	24,000		
Printing and Stationery	3,400		
Rent	2,400		
Sales Returns	3,000		
Wages	9,800		
Telephone and Internet Charges	3,600		
Repairs	5,600		
Coal, gas and Oil	6,200		
Sundry Expenses	2,400		
Carriage and Cartage	4,500		
	324,000		324,000

Adjustments

1. Closing stock Rs. 18,400 (market price Rs. 16,900).
2. Stock worth Rs. 850 used for private purpose and worth Rs. 900 is used as free samples.
3. Accrued interest on bank deposit is Rs. 700.
4. Depreciation to be provided @ 10% on machinery, @ 20% on motor vehicles and @ 5% on furniture.
5. Rent paid during the year was for eight months.
6. Purchase invoices aggregating to Rs. 2,500 were omitted to be entered in the purchase day book.
7. A sum of Rs. 4,000 paid for purchase of some furniture on July 1, 2007 has been wrongly debited to the Purchase A/c.

From the above information, prepare a Trading & Profit and Loss A/c for the year ended March 31, 2008 and a balance sheet as on that date.

Solution

Trading and Profit & Loss Account of Mr. Simon Pitter

Dr.   **For the year ended March 31, 2008**   *Cr.*

Particulars	Amount (Rs.)	Amount (Rs.)	Particulars	Amount (Rs.)	Amount (Rs.)
To Purchases	62,000		By sales	134,800	
Less: Private use	850		*Less:* Sales Returns	3,000	131,800
	61,150		By Closing Stock		16,900
Less: Free samples	900				
	60,250				

(Contd.)

Particulars	Amount (Rs.)	Amount (Rs.)	Particulars	Amount (Rs.)	Amount (Rs.)
Add: Omitted from books	2,500				
	62,750				
Less: Furniture purchase	4,000				
	58,750				
Less: Purchase Returns	2,700	56,050			
To Coal, gas and Oil		6,200			
To Wages		9,800			
To Carriage and Cartage		4,500			
To Gross Profit c/d		72,150			
		148,700			148,700
To Printing and Stationery		3,400	By Gross Profit b/d		72,150
To Telephone and Internet Charges		3,600	By Discount Received		3,400
To Repairs		5,600	By Bad debts recovered		900
To Royalty on Sales		3,700	By Interest on bank deposit		700
To Travelling Expenses		3,900	By Commission Received		2,600
To Office Expenses		2,400			
To Audit Fees		3,300			
To Salaries		12,700			
To Rent	2,400				
Add: Outstanding (for 4 months)	1,200	3,600			
To Sundry Expenses		2,400			
To Free samples		900			
To Depreciation on:					
Motor Vehicles	6,120				
Machinery	3,600				
Furniture and Fixtures	1,150	10,870			
To Net Profit transferred (to Capital A/c)		23,380			
		79,750			79,750

Balance Sheet of Mr. Simon Pitter as at March 31, 2008

Liabilities	Amount (Rs.)	Amount (Rs.)	Assets	Amount (Rs.)	Amount (Rs.)
Capital	152,000		Plant and Machinery	36,000	
Add: Net Profit	23,380		Less: Depreciation	3,600	32,400
	175,380		Motor Vehicles	30,600	
Less: Drawings	850	174,530	Less: Depreciation	6,120	24,480
(Private use of stock)			Furniture and Fixtures	20,000	
Trade Creditors	26,200		Add: Purchase	4,000	
Add: Omitted from books	2,500	28,700		24,000	
Outstanding expenses:			Less: Depreciation	1,150	22,850
Rent		1,200	Patents and Trademarks		21,000
			Fixed Deposits at Bank		24,000
			Closing Stock		16,900
			Debtors	38,500	
			Less: Provision for Doubtful Debts	1,400	37,100
			Accrued interest on bank deposit		700
			Cash at Bank		25,000
		204,430			204,430

18.4 ADJUSTMENTS GIVEN WITHIN TRIAL BALANCE

There are some adjustments or items whose treatments have to be made on the basis of data available from the Trial Balance or adjustments already made in the Trial Balance, whereas posting is required to be made in final accounts. These positions in the Trial Balance are shown below, and necessary treatments or steps to be taken for the adjustments are also explained in the Trial Balance (see Example 18.1)

Example 18.1

Sl.No.	Particulars	Amount Dr. (Rs.)	Amount Cr. (Rs.)
1.	12% Investments (was made on 1.5.07)	50,000	
2.	Interest on investments received		2,700
3.	10% Loan (was taken on 1.6.07)		40,000
4.	Interest on paid	1,800	
5.	Machinery	56,000	
6.	Depreciation on Machinery	4,000	
7.	Salaries	6,700	
8.	Outstanding Salaries		900
9.	Rent	4,700	
10.	Rent Prepaid/Rent Paid in advance	1,400	
11.	Annual Insurance Premium paid (commencing from 1.5.07)	6,000	
12.	Patent (to be written off in 10 years)	20,000	
13.	Unexpired Wages (1.1.07)	600	
14.	Wages Paid (including unexpired wages balance on 31.12.07 Rs. 700)	5,900	

Treatments or steps to be taken for the above stated adjustments are as follows:

Sl.No. 1 and 2 Investment was made on 1.5.07. Thus, interest on investment is receivable for eight months on Rs. 50,000 @ 12 %, i.e., Rs. 4,000, and interest received Rs. 2,700. Hence, actual amount receivable is Rs. 1,300 (4,000 – 2,700). Therefore, Rs. 1,300 to be added with Interest on Investments Received A/c in Profit & Loss A/c credit side and Rs. 1,300 again to be shown in asset side of the Balance Sheet as 'Accrued Interest on Investment'. Their position in Profit & Loss A/c and Balance Sheet would be as under:

Profit & Loss Account of...

Dr. For the year ended December 31, 2007 Cr.

Particulars	Amount (Rs.)	Amount (Rs.)	Particulars	Amount (Rs.)	Amount (Rs.)
			By Interest on investments	2,700	
			Add: Accrued interest	1,300	4,000

Balance Sheet of...
as on December 31, 2007

Liabilities	Amount (Rs.)	Amount (Rs.)	Assets	Amount (Rs.)	Amount (Rs.)
			12% Investments		50,000
			Accrued interest		1,300

Sl.No. 3 and 4 Loan was taken on 1.6.07 and as such, interest is required to be paid for seven months @ 10% p.a. on Rs. 40,000, i.e., Rs. 2,333. Interest paid during the year Rs. 1,800. Balance Rs. 533 to be added with Interest on loan A/c in Profit & Loss A/c debit side and again to be shown as outstanding in the Balance Sheet as a liability. Their position in Profit & Loss A/c and Balance Sheet would be as under:

Profit & Loss Account of...

Dr.   For the year ended December 31, 2007   Cr.

Particulars	Amount (Rs.)	Amount (Rs.)	Particulars	Amount (Rs.)	Amount (Rs.)
To Interest on loan Add: Outstanding	1,800 533	2,333			

Balance Sheet of... as on December 31, 2007

Liabilities	Amount (Rs.)	Amount (Rs.)	Assets	Amount (Rs.)	Amount (Rs.)
10 % Loan Outstanding Interest on loan		40,000 533			

Sl.No. 5 and 6 Depreciation on Machinery Rs. 4,000 is to be shown in the Profit & Loss A/c debit side only. No further deduction is required to be made in Balance Sheet, as it is already deducted from Machinery A/c.

Sl.No. 7 and 8 Outstanding Salaries of Rs. 900 is already added with Salary A/c, as adjustment entry has already been passed. Thus, no further adjustment is required to be shown in the Profit & Loss A/c. It is to be shown in the Balance Sheet liability side as a liability.

Sl.No. 9 and 10 Rent Prepaid Rs. 1,400 is already deducted from rent, as adjustment entry has already been passed. Hence, no further adjustment is required to be shown in the Profit & Loss A/c. It is to be shown in the Balance Sheet asset side as an asset.

Sl.No. 11 Annual Insurance Premium paid Rs. 6,000. It is effective for 12 months from 1.5.07. Thus, it is paid advance for four months, i.e., Rs. 2,000. Hence, this advance of Rs. 2,000 is required to be deducted from Insurance Premium A/c in the Profit & Loss A/c debit side, and then as an asset in the Balance Sheet. Their position in Profit & Loss A/c and Balance Sheet would be as under:

Profit & Loss Account of ...

Dr.   For the year ended December 31, 2007   Cr.

Particulars	Amount (Rs.)	Amount (Rs.)	Particulars	Amount (Rs.)	Amount (Rs.)
To Insurance Premium Less: Paid advance	6,000 2,000	4,000			

Balance Sheet...of as on December 31, 2007

Liabilities	Amount (Rs.)	Amount (Rs.)	Assets	Amount (Rs.)	Amount (Rs.)
			Prepaid insurance		2,000

Sl.No. 12 Patent is to be written off in ten years. Thus, Rs. 2,000 is required to be written off yearly from the Patent. Their position in Profit & Loss A/c and Balance Sheet would be as under:

Profit & Loss Account of ...

Dr.   For the year ended December 31, 2007   Cr.

Particulars	Amount (Rs.)	Amount (Rs.)	Particulars	Amount (Rs.)	Amount (Rs.)
To Patent Written off		2,000			

Balance Sheet of... as at December 31, 2007

Liabilities	Amount (Rs.)	Amount (Rs.)	Assets	Amount (Rs.)	Amount (Rs.)
			Patent Less: Written off	20,000 2,000	18,000

Sl.No. 13 and 14 Unexpired Wages A/c balance on 1.1.07 is Rs. 600. It is paid in last year for the current year. Thus, it is to be added with Wages A/c of Rs. 5,900 in the Trading A/c and therefrom current year's unexpired amount of Rs. 700 is to be deducted. This Rs. 700 is shown as an asset in the Balance Sheet. Their position in Trading A/c and Balance Sheet would be as under:

Trading Account of ...

Dr.			**For the year ended December 31, 2007**		Cr.
Particulars	Amount (Rs.)	Amount (Rs.)	Particulars	Amount (Rs.)	Amount (Rs.)
To Wages	5,900	2,000			
Add: Unexpired Wages (on 1.1.07)	600				
	6,500				
Less: Unexpired Wages (on 31.12.07)	700	5,800			

Balance Sheet of... as on December 31, 2007

Liabilities	Amount (Rs.)	Amount (Rs.)	Assets	Amount (Rs.)	Amount (Rs.)
			Unexpired Wages		700

ILLUSTRATION 18.4 Following is the trial balance of Mr. Pritam Batra for the year ended December 31, 2007:

Dr.		**Trial Balance as on December 31,2007**	Cr.
Particulars	Amount (Rs.)	Particulars	Amount (Rs.)
Insurance	4,000	Rent from Subletting	3,600
Audit Fees	1,500	Discount Received	2,800
Opening Stock	17,400	Capital	120,000
Packing Charges	4,600	Sundry Creditors	26,000
Carriage Inward	3,800	Miscellaneous Receipts	3,900
Trade Expenses	4,200	10% Loan from Mr.C. Thakur	30,000
Sundry Debtors	44,300	Interest on investments	1,800
Carriage Outward	3,700	Sales	165,600
Machinery	54,000		
Rent and Rates	4,800		
Cash in hand and cash at Bank	49,400		
Drawings	3,000		
Discount allowed	1,900		
Furniture	20,000		
12% Investments	30,000		
Bad debts	2,600		
Salaries and Wages	9,200		
Goodwill	24,000		
Freight	3,000		
Purchase	68,300		
	353,700		353,700

Prepare a Trading and Profit and Loss Account for the year ended December 31, 2007, and a Balance Sheet as on that date. You are given the following information:

1. Make Provision for doubtful debts @ 5% and provision for discounts on debtors @ 2% on debtors.
2. Rent outstanding Rs. 350 and Rates prepaid Rs. 500.
3. Investment was made on May 1, 2007 and the loan was taken from Mr. C. Thakur two years before.
4. Closing stock is Rs. 20,450.

5. Bad debts of the current year have increased to Rs. 3,000.
6. Furniture of book value of Rs. 1,900 has been sold for Rs. 1,150, and the sale proceeds are credited to Furniture A/c.
7. Depreciate Machinery and Furniture @ 10% p.a.

Solution

Trading and Profit & Loss Account of Mr. Pritam Batra

Dr. For the year ended December 31,2007 Cr.

Particulars	Amount (Rs.)	Amount (Rs.)	Particulars	Amount (Rs.)	Amount (Rs.)
To Opening Stock		17,400	By Sales		165,600
To Purchases		68,300	By Closing Stock		20,450
To Freight		3,000			
To Carriage Inwards		3,800			
To Gross Profit c/d		93,550			
		186,050			186,050
To Insurance		4,000	By Gross Profit b/d		93,550
To Audit Fees		1,500	By Discount Received		2,800
To Bad Debts	2,600		By Interest on investments	1,800	
Add: Written off(New)	400	3,000	Add: Accrued	600	2,400
To Packing Charges		4,600	By Rent from Subletting		3,600
To Salaries and Wages		9,200	By Miscellaneous Receipts		3,900
To Trade Expenses		4,200			
To Discount allowed		1,900			
To Carriage Outward		3,700			
To Rent and Rates	4,800				
Add: Outstanding Rent	350				
	5,150				
Less: Rates Prepaid	500	4,650			
To Loss on sale of Furniture		750			
To Provision for Doubtful Debts		2,195			
To Provision for Discounts		834			
To Interest on loan		3,000			
To Depreciation on:					
Machinery	5,400				
Furniture	1,925	7,325			
To Net Profit transferred to Capital A/c		55,396			
		106,250			106,250

Balance Sheet of Mr. Pritam Batra
as on December 31, 2007

Liabilities	Amount (Rs.)	Amount (Rs.)	Assets	Amount (Rs.)	Amount (Rs.)
Capital	120,000		Goodwill		24,000
Add: Net Profit	55,396				
	175,396		Machinery	54,000	
Less: Drawings	3,000	172,396	Less: Depreciation	5,400	48,600
			Furniture	20,000	
Trade Creditors		26,000	Less: Loss on sale	750	
				19,250	
			Less: Depreciation	1,925	17,325
Loan from Mr. C. Thakur		30,000	12% Investments		30,000
			Accrued Interest on Investments		600
					(Contd.)

Liabilities	Amount (Rs.)	Amount (Rs.)	Assets	Amount (Rs.)	Amount (Rs.)
Outstanding expenses:			Closing Stock		20,450
Rent	350		Debtors	44,300	
Interest on loan	3,000	3,350	Less: Bad Debts	400	
				43,900	
			Less: Provision for Doubtful Debts	2,195	
				41,705	
			Less: Provision for Discounts	834	40,871
			Prepaid Rates		500
			Cash in hand and at Bank		49,400
		231,746			231,746

Working Notes

1. Calculation of Provision for Doubtful Debts:
   5% on Rs. 43,900 = Rs. 2,195.
2. Calculation of Provision for Discounts Debtors:
   2% on Rs. 41,705 = Rs. 834.
3. Calculation of accrued interest on investments:

   Total interest receivable on investment was   Rs. 2,400
   (12% on Rs. 30,000 for eight months)

      Less: Interest on Investments Received   Rs. 1,800

   Accrued Interest on Investments   Rs. 600
4. Calculation of interest on loan:
   10% Loan from Mr. C. Thakur was taken two years before, but no interest had been paid during the year. Thus, the entire amount of interest is outstanding, i.e., Rs. 3,000 (10% of 30,000).

ILLUSTRATION 18.5   Following is the trial balance of Mr. S. Baruah for the year ended December 31, 2007:

Dr.   **Trial Balance as on December 31, 2007**   Cr.

Particulars	Amount (Rs.)	Particulars	Amount (Rs.)
General Expenses	5,400	Creditors	27,400
Sundry Debtors	43,700	Discount Received	3,200
Rebates Allowed	2,600	Capital	115,000
Loan to Mr. K. Gupta	20,000	Interest from Mr. K. Gupta	1,200
Advertisement	6,600	Sales	167,900
Purchases	84,000	Purchase Returns	3,800
Salaries	14,300		
Car Expenses	3,600		
Drawings	4,000		
Insurance	2,400		
Import Duty	2,100		
Motor Vehicles	37,500		
Wages	12,800		
Plant and Machinery	50,000		
Carriage and Cartage	3,600		
Cash at Bank	14,200		
Printing and Stationery	2,500		
Sales Returns	3,400		
Travelling Expenses	5,800		
	318,500		318,500

Adjustments

1. One-third of the car expenses and depreciation on car should be charged to Mr. S. Baruah's A/c for private use of car.
2. Depreciations on Motor Vehicles and Plant and Machinery are to be provided at 10% p.a.
3. Insurance is paid for 12 months, commencing from June 1, 2007.
4. Debtors include Rs. 1,500 due from the proprietor.
5. Make Provision for doubtful debts @ 5% on debtors.
6. An amount of Rs. 950 received from a debtor was wrongly credited to Sales A/c.
7. Closing stock Rs. 13,600.

Prepare a Trading and Profit and Loss Account for the year ended December 31, 2007, and a Balance Sheet as on that date.

Solution

Trading and Profit & Loss Account of Mr. S. Baruah

Dr. For the year ended December 31, 2007 Cr.

Particulars	Amount (Rs.)	Amount (Rs.)	Particulars	Amount (Rs.)	Amount (Rs.)
To Purchases	84,000		By Sales	167,900	
Less: Purchase Returns	3,800	80,200	Less: Sales Returns	3,400	
To Wages		12,800		164,500	
To Import Duty		2,100	Less: Received from Debtors	950	163,550
To Carriage and Cartage		3,600	By Closing Stock		13,600
To Gross Profit c/d		78,450			
		177,150			177,150
To General Expenses		5,400	By Gross Profit b/d		78,450
To Rebates Allowed		2,600	By Discount Received		3,200
To Printing and Stationary		2,500	By Interest from Mr. K. Gupta		1,200
To Travelling Expenses		5,800			
To Salaries		14,300			
To Advertisement		6,600			
To Car Expenses	3,600				
Less: Drawings	1,200	2,400			
(private use of car)					
To Insurance	2,400				
Less: Prepaid (For five months)	1,000	1,400			
To Provision for					
Doubtful Debts		2,063			
To Depreciation on:					
Machinery	5,000				
Motor Vehicles	2,500	7,500			
To Net Profit					
transferred to Capital A/c		32,287			
		82,850			82,850

Balance Sheet of Mr. S. Baruah

As on December 31, 2007

Liabilities	Amount (Rs.)	Amount (Rs.)	Assets	Amount (Rs.)	Amount (Rs.)
Capital	115,000		Plant and Machinery	50,000	
Add: Net Profit	32,287		Less: Depreciation	5,000	45,000
	147,287		Motor Vehicles	37,500	
Less: Drawings	7,950	139,337	Less: Depreciation	3,750	33,750
			Loan to Mr. K. Gupta		20,000
			Closing Stock		13,600

(Contd.)

Liabilities	Amount (Rs.)	Amount (Rs.)	Assets	Amount (Rs.)	Amount (Rs.)
Creditors		27,400	Debtors	43,700	
			Less: Drawings	1,500	
				42,200	
			Less: Received from Debtors	950	
				41,250	
			Less: Provision for Doubtful Debts	2,063	39,187
			Prepaid Insurance		1,000
			Cash at Bank		14,200
		166,737			166,737

Working Notes

Calculation of Drawings:	Rs.
One-third of Car Expenses	1,200
One-third of Depreciation on Car	1,250
Drawings	4,000
Debtors (include Rs. 1,500 due from proprietor)	1,500
Total Drawings	7,950

ILLUSTRATION 18.6 From the following particulars extracted from the books of Mr. Bhupali, prepare a Trading and Profit and Loss Account, and a Balance sheet as on December 31, 2007 after making the necessary adjustments:

Dr.   **Trial Balance as on December 31, 2007**   Cr.

Particulars	Amount (Rs.)	Particulars	Amount (Rs.)
Purchases	76,400	Capital	161,000
Cash in Hand	45,600	Interest on Bank Deposits	2,200
Furniture	16,000	Bills Payable	15,800
Opening Stock	11,900	Sales	132,700
Plant and Machinery	60,800	Return Outwards	2,800
Return Inwards	1,400	Commission Received	1,900
Wages	7,600	Sundry Creditors	38,000
Carriage Inwards	4,500		
Advertisement	8,000		
Cash at Bank	17,400		
Debtors	43,000		
Drawings	4,000		
General Expenses	3,200		
Investments	35,000		
Insurance	3,400		
Printing & Stationery	1,200		
Travelling Expenses	2,700		
Bad debts	1,600		
Salaries	10,700		
	354,400		354,400

Adjustments

1. Sundry creditors include Rs. 4,000 taken as loan from Mr. K. Khurana on August 1, 2007, bearing an interest @ 12% p.a.
2. An advance of Rs. 700 paid to an employee against his salary in January 2008 has been debited to the Salary A/c.
3. Sundry creditors included a sum of Rs. 1,500 recovered from a customer whose account was written off in the previous year.

4. Travelling includes the proprietor's personal travelling for which he is to be charged Rs. 750.
5. Closing Stock Rs. 21,200.
6. Depreciation to be provided 10% on machinery and 5% on furniture.
7. Advertisement includes Rs. 4,000 towards cost of a campaign run during the year. It is expected that the effect of this campaign will be felt for at least four years.

Solution

Trading and Profit & Loss Account of Mr. Bhupali

Dr.   For the year ended December 31, 2007   Cr.

Particulars	Amount (Rs.)	Amount (Rs.)	Particulars	Amount (Rs.)	Amount (Rs.)
To Opening Stock		11,900	By Sales	132,700	
To Purchases	76,400		Less: Return Inwards	1,400	131,300
Less: Return Outwards	2,800	73,600	By Closing Stock		21,200
To Wages		7,600			
To Carriage Inwards		4,500			
To Gross Profit c/d		54,900			
		152,500			152,500
To Insurance		3,400	By Gross Profit b/d		54,900
To General Expenses		3,200	To Commission Received		1,900
To Printing and Stationery		1,200	By Interest on Bank Deposits		2,200
To Bad debts		1,600	By Bad debts recovered		1,500
To Salaries	10,700				
Less: Prepaid	700	10,000			
To Advertisements	8,000				
Less: Deferred revenue expenses	3,000	5,000			
To Travelling Expenses	2,700				
Less: Personal Travelling	750	1,950			
To Interest on loan		200			
To Depreciation on:					
Machinery	6,080				
Furniture	800	6,880			
To Net Profit					
transferred to Capital A/c		27,070			
		60,500			60,500

Balance Sheet of Mr. Bhupali

As on December 31, 2007

Liabilities	Amount (Rs.)	Amount (Rs.)	Assets	Amount (Rs.)	Amount (Rs.)
Capital	161,000		Machinery	60,800	
Add: Net Profit	27,070		Less: Depreciation	6,080	54,720
	188,070		Furniture	16,000	
Less: Drawings	4,750	183,320	Less: Depreciation	800	15,200
(4,000 + 750)			Investments		35,000
Sundry Creditors	38,000		Closing Stock		21,200
Less: Loan(Mr. K. Khurana)	4,000		Debtors		43,000
	34,000		Prepaid Salaries		700
Less: Bad debts Recovered	1,500	32,500	Deferred revenue expenses		3,000
Bills Payable		15,800	Cash at Bank		17,400
Loan (Mr. K. Khurana)		4,000	Cash in hand		45,600
Outstanding expenses:					
Interest on loan		200			
		235,820			235,820

Working Note

Advertisement includes Rs. 4,000 towards cost of a campaign run during the year and it is expected that the effect of this campaign will be felt for at least four years. Hence, three years' proportionate expenditure is to be considered as deferred revenue expenditure, i.e., Rs. 3,000 (4,000/4 × 3).

ILLUSTRATION 18.7 From the following particulars extracted from the books of Mr. Vikram Mehra, prepare a Trading and Profit and Loss Account and a Balance sheet as on March 31, 2008 after making the necessary adjustments:

Dr.		Trial Balance as on March 31, 2008	Cr.
Particulars	*Amount (Rs.)*	*Particulars*	*Amount (Rs.)*
General Expenses	4,600	**Sales:**	
Export Duty	5,100	Local	136,700
Carriage inward	4,900	Export	56,500
Purchase	87,200	Miscellaneous Receipts	7,500
Royalty on Sales	4,900	Rebate Received	2,700
Travelling Expenses	3,600	Interest Received	3,400
Salaries	12,700	Trade Creditors	22,800
Printing and Stationery	3,700	Loan Creditors	20,000
Wages and Salaries	10,200	Capital	145,000
Electric Charges	3,100		
Freehold Premises	60,000		
Furniture and Fixtures	21,000		
Cash in hand	12,500		
Opening Stock	10,900		
Goodwill	18,000		
Loose Tools	14,000		
Plant and Machinery	57,000		
Sundry Debtors	39,500		
Bills Receivable	15,000		
Drawings	6,700		
	394,600		394,600

Adjustments

1. Closing stock Rs. 11,000.
2. Stationery of Rs. 480 was consumed by the family members of the proprietor.
3. Closing stock includes goods costing Rs. 1,200 returned by a customer on March 29, 2008 but no entry has been passed in the books for such return. The said goods are sold at 25% profit on cost.
4. An amount of Rs. 1,400 received in respect of a private loan advanced by the proprietor was wrongly credited to Sundry Debtors A/c.
5. Depreciate Plant and Machinery and Furniture and Fixtures by 10%. The estimated value of loose tools on March 31, 2008, was Rs. 7,800.

Solution

Trading and Profit & Loss Account of Mr. Vikram Mehra

Dr.			For the year ended March 31, 2008		Cr.
Particulars	*Amount (Rs.)*	*Amount (Rs.)*	*Particulars*	*Amount (Rs.)*	*Amount (Rs.)*
To Opening Stock		10,900	**By Sales:**		
To Purchases		87,200	Local	136,700	
To Wages and Salaries		10,200	Export	56,500	
To Carriage Inwards		4,900		193,200	
			Less: Sales Return	1,500	191,700

(Contd.)

Particulars	Amount (Rs.)	Amount (Rs.)	Particulars	Amount (Rs.)	Amount (Rs.)
To Gross Profit c/d		89,500	By Closing Stock		11,000
		202,700			202,700
To General Expenses		4,600	By Gross Profit b/d		89,500
To Export Duty		5,100	By Miscellaneous Receipts		7,500
To Printing and Stationery	3,700		By Rebate Received		2,700
Less: Drawings	480	3,220	By Interest Received		3,400
To Salaries		12,700			
To Royalty on Sales		4,900			
To Electric Charges		3,100			
To Travelling Expenses		3,600			
To Depreciation on:					
Machinery	5,700				
Loose Tools	6,200				
Furniture and Fixtures	2,100	14,000			
To Net Profit transferred					
to Capital A/c		51,880			
		103,100			103,100

Balance Sheet of Mr. Vikram Mehra
as on March 31, 2008

Liabilities	Amount (Rs.)	Amount (Rs.)	Assets	Amount (Rs.)	Amount (Rs.)
Capital	145,000		Goodwill		18,000
Add: Net Profit	51,880		Freehold Premises		60,000
	196,880		Plant and Machinery	57,000	
Less: Drawings	7,180		Less: Depreciation	5,700	51,300
(Rs. 6,700 + Rs. 480)	189,700		Furniture and Fixtures	21,000	
Add: Fresh Capital	1,400	191,100	Less: Depreciation	2,100	18,900
(Private loan realized)			Loose Tools	14,000	
			Less: Depreciation	6,200	7,800
Trade Creditors		22,800	Bills Receivable		15,000
Loan Creditors		20,000	Closing Stock		11,000
			Debtors	39,500	
			Less: Sales Return	1,500	
				38,000	
			Add: Wrongly credited	1,400	39,400
			(Private loan realized)		
			Cash in hand		12,500
		233,900			233,900

Working Notes

1. Closing stock includes goods costing Rs. 1,200 returned by a customer sold at 25% profit on cost.

   Hence, amount of sales return comes out to be Rs. 1,500 (1,200 + 25 % of 1,200).

2. Private loan realized Rs. 1,400 and the said amount is kept within the business. Hence, it is to be treated as fresh Capital.

ILLUSTRATION 18.8 The Trial Balance of Mr. Ratan Agarwal as on December 31, 2007 is given below.

Dr.   **Trial Balance as on December 31, 2007**   Cr.

Particulars	Amount (Rs.)	Particulars	Amount (Rs.)
General Expenses	4,600	Purchase Returns	2,800
Travelling Expenses	5,200	Sales	135,800

(Contd.)

Particulars	Amount (Rs.)	Particulars	Amount (Rs.)
Sales Returns	3,500	Interest Received	5,000
Purchases	67,300	Capital	127,000
Telephone and Internet Charges	3,700	Sundry Creditors	26,400
Prepaid Salaries	1,500	Outstanding Rent	2,000
Bills Receivable	14,000	Bank Overdraft	17,100
Wages	8,400	Miscellaneous receipts	900
Investments	25,000		
Sundry Debtors	42,600		
Salaries	9,200		
Audit Fees	2,700		
Petty Expenses	1,200		
Freight	3,600		
Cash in hand	44,760		
Furniture	19,200		
Bad debts	540		
Plant and Machinery	60,000		
	317,000		317,000

Additional information:

1. The manager is to get a commission of 10% on net profits after charging his commission.
2. Depreciate machinery and furniture by 10% and 5%, respectively.
3. Miscellaneous receipts represent the sale proceeds of old furniture, the written-down value of which was Rs. 1,700.
4. Bad debts increased by Rs. 780.
5. Two-thirds of the wages were for preparing goods for sale.
6. Closing stock Rs. 20,600.

Prepare a Trading and Profit and Loss Account for the year ended December 31, 2007, and a Balance sheet as on that date from the above information.

Solution

Trading and Profit & Loss Account of Mr. Ratan Agarwal

Dr.   For the year ended December 31, 2007   Cr.

Particulars	Amount (Rs.)	Amount (Rs.)	Particulars	Amount (Rs.)	Amount (Rs.)
To Purchases	67,300		By Sales	135,800	
Less: Purchase Returns	2,800	64,500	Less: Sales Returns	3,500	132,300
To Wages	8,400		By Closing Stock		20,600
Less: Indirect Wages	2,800	5,600			
To Freight		3,600			
To Gross Profit c/d		79,200			
		152,900			152,900
To General Expenses		4,600	By Gross Profit b/d		79,200
To Travelling Expenses		5,200	By Interest Received		5,000
To Bad Debts	540				
Add: Written off (New)	780	1,320			
To Salaries		9,200			
To Audit Fees		2,700			
To Telephone and Internet Charges		3,700			
To Indirect Wages		2,800			
To Loss on sale of furniture		800			
To Petty Expenses		1,200			
To Depreciation on:					
Machinery	6,000				
Furniture	875	6,875			

(Contd.)

Particulars	Amount (Rs.)	Amount (Rs.)	Particulars	Amount (Rs.)	Amount (Rs.)
To Net profit before charging manager's commission		45,805			
		84,200			84,200
To Manager's commission (10/110 × 45,805)		4,164	By Net profit before charging manager's commission		45,805
To Net profit transferred to Capital A/c		41,641			
		45,805			45,805

Balance Sheet of Mr. Ratan Agarwal
As on December 31, 2007

Liabilities	Amount (Rs.)	Amount (Rs.)	Assets	Amount (Rs.)	Amount (Rs.)
Capital	127,000		Plant and Machinery	60,000	
Add: Net Profit	41,641	168,641	Less: Depreciation	6,000	54,000
			Furniture	19,200	
Bank Overdraft		17,100	Less: Sale of Furniture	1,700	
Sundry Creditors		26,400		17,500	
Outstanding Rent		2,000	Less: Depreciation	875	16,625
Outstanding Manager's commission		4,164	Investments		25,000
			Bills Receivable		14,000
			Closing Stock		20,600
			Debtors	42,600	
			Less: Bad Debts	780	41,820
			Prepaid Salaries		1,500
			Cash in hand		44,760
		218,305			218,305

Working Note

Wages was Rs. 8,400 and two-thirds of the wages were for preparing goods for sale. Thus, two-third of the wages is considered as direct expenses and remaining one-third as indirect expenses, i.e., Rs. 2,800 (8,400/3). Indirect wages is shown in Profit & Loss A/c.

ILLUSTRATION 18.9 From the following trial balance of Mr. K. Kulkarni, prepare a Trading and Profit and Loss Account for the year ending December 31, 2007, and the Balance sheet as on that date.

Dr.   **Trial Balance as on December 31, 2007**   Cr.

Particulars	Amount (Rs.)	Particulars	Amount (Rs.)
Sundry Debtors	38,000	Outstanding Insurance	1,200
Carriage Outward	2,900	Discount Received	2,400
Cash in hand and cash at Bank	12,000	Capital	97,000
Drawings	4,700	Sundry Creditors	24,800
Carriage Inward	4,300	Sales	138,100
Trade Expenses	7,600	Interest on investments	1,620
Discount allowed	3,200	Provision for Doubtful Debts	1,900
Furniture	18,000		
Machinery	45,000		
12% Investments (From 1.4.07)	18,000		
Bad debts	700		
Salaries	10,600		
Freight	1,800		
Prepaid Salaries (1.1.07)	500		
Insurance	4,700		

(Contd.)

Particulars	Amount (Rs.)	Particulars	Amount (Rs.)
Purchase	67,400		
Rent and Rates	7,200		
Opening Stock	10,200		
Wages	7,900		
Accrued Interest on investments	1,620		
Prepaid Rent	700		
	267,020		267,020

Adjustments

1. Debtors include:
   (a) Rs. 1,000 due from Mr. D considered definitely good.
   (b) Rs. 400 due from Mr. W considered definitely bad.
   (c) Rs. 700 due from Mr. H considered very much doubtful.
   Make provision for doubtful debts at 5% on debtors.
2. A machine which stood in the books for Rs. 3,900 on January 1, 2007, was sold for Rs. 2,150 in exchange for a new machine costing Rs. 6,400 on June 1, 2007. The net invoice of Rs. 4,250 was passed through the inward invoice book. Depreciate Machinery and Furniture by 10%.
3. Closing stock Rs. 13,800.
4. Prepaid Salaries on December 31, 2007 amounting to Rs. 900.

Solution

Trading and Profit & Loss Account of Mr. K. Kulkarni

Dr. For the year ended December 31, 2007 Cr.

Particulars	Amount (Rs.)	Amount (Rs.)	Particulars	Amount (Rs.)	Amount (Rs.)
To Opening Stock		10,200	By Sales		138,100
To Purchases	67,400		By Closing Stock		13,800
Less: Machinery purchase	4,250	63,150			
To Wages		7,900			
To Carriage Inward		4,300			
To Freight		1,800			
To Gross Profit c/d		64,550			
		151,900			151,900
To Trade Expenses		7,600	By Gross Profit b/d		64,550
To Discount Allowed		3,200	By Discount Received		2,400
To Bad Debts	700		By Interest on investments		1,620
Add: Bad debts (W)	400	1,100			
To Salaries	10,600				
Add: Prepaid (on 1.1.07)	500				
	11,100				
Less: Prepaid (on 31.12.07)	900	10,200			
To Insurance		4,700			
To Rent and Rates		7,200			
To Carriage Outward		2,900			
To Loss on sale of Machinery		1,750			
To Provision for Doubtful Debts	2,495				
Less: Old Provision	1,900	595			
To Depreciation on:					
Machinery	4,750				
Furniture	1,800	6,550			
To Net profit transferred to Capital A/c		22,775			
		68,570			68,570

Balance Sheet of Mr. K. Kulkarni
As on December 31, 2007

Liabilities	Amount (Rs.)	Amount (Rs.)	Assets	Amount (Rs.)	Amount (Rs.)
Capital	97,000		Machinery	45,000	
Add: Net Profit	22,775		Less: Sale of machinery	3,900	
	119,775			41,100	
Less: Drawings	4,700	115,075	Add: New Purchase	6,400	
Sundry Creditors		24,800		47,500	
Outstanding Insurance		1,200	Less: Depreciation	4,750	42,750
			Furniture	18,000	
			Less: Depreciation	1,800	16,200
			12% Investments		18,000
			Prepaid Expenses:		
			Rent	700	
			Salaries	900	1,600
			Closing Stock		13,800
			Debtors	38,000	
			Less: Bad Debts	400	
				37,600	
			Less: Provision for Doubtful Debts	2,495	35,105
			Accrued Interest on investments		1,620
			Cash in hand and cash at Bank		12,000
		141,075			141,075

Working Notes

1. Calculation of provision for doubtful debts:

	Rs.		Rs.
Debtors	38,000	5% provision on remaining	
Less: Bad debts (W)	400	debtors of Rs. 35,900	1,795
	37,600	Add: 100% provision for H	700
Less: Good debts (D)	1,000	Total provision for 2007	2,495
	36,600		
Less: 100% provision (H) for doubtful debts	700		
Remaining debtors (Doubtful)	35,900		

2. Calculation of Loss on sale of Machinery:

Book value of the machine sold	Rs. 3,900
Less: Selling price	Rs. 2,150
Loss on sale	Rs. 1,750

ILLUSTRATION 18.10 From the following particulars extracted from the books of Mr. Surendra, prepare a Trading and Profit and Loss Account, and a Balance sheet as on March 31, 2008, after making the necessary adjustments.

Trial Balance as on March 31, 2008

Dr.			Cr.
Particulars	Amount (Rs.)	Particulars	Amount (Rs.)
Furniture	28,000	Capital	176,000
Office Expenses	4,100	Discount Received	2,500
Audit Fees	2,800	Creditors	31,500
Plant & Machinery	120,000	Interest Received	2,300
Cash at Bank	40,200	Sales	147,000
Purchases	81,000	Purchase Returns	2,700
Printing & Stationery	2,600		
Rent	6,000		
Repairs	2,400		
			(Contd.)

Particulars	Amount (Rs.)	Particulars	Amount (Rs.)
Debtors	36,000		
Salaries	12,000		
Sundry Expenses	600		
Wages	9,300		
Sales Returns	2,500		
Life Insurance of Mr. Surendra	5,000		
Advertisement	4,800		
Carriage	4,700		
	362,000		362,000

Adjustments to be made

1. Closing stock Rs. 31,000.
2. Works Manager is to be given a commission of 15% on the net profit after charging the commission of General Manager and his own.
3. General Manager is to be given a commission of 10% on the net profit after charging the commission of Works Manager and his own.
4. Sales Manager is entitled to a commission of 6% on net sales and is to bear the current year's bad debts. Bad debts to be written off amounting to Rs. 1,500.
5. Provide depreciation on Machinery and Furniture at 10% p.a.
6. Salary for March 2008 amounting to Rs. 1,500 was paid in April 2008.

Prepare a Trading and Profit and Loss Account for the year ended on March 31, 2008 from the above information and a Balance sheet as on that date.

Solution

Trading and Profit & Loss Account of Mr. Surendra

Dr.   For the year ended March 31, 2008   Cr.

Particulars	Amount (Rs.)	Amount (Rs.)	Particulars	Amount (Rs.)	Amount (Rs.)
To Purchases	81,000		By Sales	147,000	
Less: Purchase Returns	2,700	78,300	Less: Sales Returns	2,500	144,500
To Wages		9,300	By Closing Stock		31,000
To Carriage		4,700			
To Gross Profit c/d		83,200			
		175,500			175,500
To Office Expenses		4,100	By Gross Profit b/d		83,200
To Audit Fees		2,800	By Interest Received		2,300
To Advertisement		4,800	By Discount Received		2,500
To Commission to Sales Manager		8,670			
To Salaries	12,000				
Add: Outstanding	1,500	13,500			
To Printing and Stationery		2,600			
To Rent		6,000			
To Sundry Expenses		600			
To Repairs		2,400			
To Depreciation on:					
Machinery	12,000				
Furniture	2,800	14,800			
To Net profit before charging		27,730			
Manager's Commission		88,000			88,000
To Works Manager's Commission		3,328	By Net profit before charging		
			Manager's Commission		27,730
To General Manager's Commission		2,218			
To Net profit transferred to Capital A/c		22,184			
		27,730			27,730

Balance Sheet of Mr. Surendra
as on March 31, 2008

Liabilities	Amount (Rs.)	Amount (Rs.)	Assets	Amount (Rs.)	Amount (Rs.)
Capital	176,000		Plant and Machinery	120,000	
Add: Net Profit	22,184		Less: Depreciation	12,000	108,000
	198,184		Furniture	28,000	
Less: Drawings	5,000	193,184	Less: Depreciation	2,800	25,200
(LIP of proprietor)			Closing Stock		31,000
Sundry Creditors		31,500	Debtors	36,000	
Outstanding Expenses:			Less: Bad Debts	1,500	34,500
Sales Manager's Commission	7,170		Cash at Bank		40,200
Works Manager's Commission	3,328				
General Manager's Commission	2,218				
Salaries	1,500	14,216			
		238,900			238,900

Working Notes

1. Calculation of Commission payable to Sales Manager:
   Commission @ 6 % on net sales of Rs. 144,500 Rs. 8,670
   Less: Bad debts adjusted   Rs. 1,500
   Net amount payable   Rs. 7,170

2. Calculation of commission payable to General Manager and Works Manager:
   Say, Works Manager's commission = X
   General Manager's commission = Y
   The equation will be as follows:

	$X = 15/115 (27,730 - Y) = 3/23 (27,730 - Y)$	...(1)
	$Y = 10/110 (27,730 - X) = 1/11 (27,730 - X)$	...(2)
	$X = 3/23 (27,730 - Y)$	...(1)
or	$23X = 83,190 - 3Y$	...(3)
or	$23X + 3Y = 83,190$	...(4)
or	$Y = 1/11 (27,730 - X$	...(2)
or	$11Y = 27,730 - X$ or $X + 11Y = 27,730$	...(5)

   Multiplying (5) by 23 we get,

	$23X + 253Y = 637,790$	...(6)
	$23X + 3Y = 83,190$	...(4)

   $$250Y = 554,600$$
   $$Y = 554,600/ 250 = 2,218.4 = 2,218 \text{ Approx.}$$
   $$23X = 83,190 - 3Y \qquad ....(3)$$
   or
   $$23X = 92,190 - (3 \times 2,218.4)$$
   $$23X = 83,190 - 6,655.2 = 76,534.8$$
   $$X = 76,534.8/23 = 3,327.6 = 3,328 \text{ Approx.}$$
   $$X = \text{Rs. } 3,328 \text{ Approx. } Y = \text{Rs. } 2,218 \text{ Approx.}$$

   So, the commission payable to Works Manager = Rs. 3,328 and the commission payable to General Manager = Rs. 2,218.

Advanced Illustrations for Revision

ILLUSTRATION 18.11 Trial Balance of Mr. G.P. Jubida as on December 31, 2007 is given below:

Dr.		Trial Balance as on December 31, 2007		Cr.
Particulars	Amount (Rs.)	Particulars		Amount (Rs.)
Opening Stock	12,000	Sales		112,400
Purchases	68,000	Creditors		14,200
Sales Return	1,500	Discount Received		1,900
Import Duty	1,600	Capital		60,000
Carriage Inwards	2,400	Provision for Doubtful Debts		600
Freight	1,800	Commission Received		900
Wages	4,600			
Insurance	2,100			
Rent	3,600			
Salaries	4,800			
Machinery	26,000			
Furniture	18,000			
Debtors	24,600			
Cash in hand	19,000			
	190,000			190,000

Adjustments

1. Closing Stock Rs. 18,000.
2. Goods lost by fire worth Rs. 1,500 and Insurance Company admitted the claim to the extent of Rs. 900.
3. Stock used for private purpose Rs. 600 and used as free sample Rs. 900.
4. Wages include Rs. 2,000 for installation of a new machine.
5. Machinery worth Rs. 8,000 purchased on April 1, 2007 wrongly included in purchases.
6. Depreciate machinery and furniture @ 10% p.a.
7. Outstanding expenses:
   Rent Rs. 400 and insurance Rs. 300.
8. Salaries paid in advance amounting to Rs. 500
9. Debtors include Rs. 500 proved as bad debt.
10. Make provision for doubtful debts @ 5% on debtors.

Prepare a Trading and Profit & Loss Account for the year ended December 31, 2007, and the Balance Sheet as on that date.

Solution

Trading and Profit & Loss Account of Mr. G.P. Jubida

Dr.			For the year ended December 31, 2007		Cr.
Particulars	Amount (Rs.)	Amount (Rs.)	Particulars	Amount (Rs.)	Amount (Rs.)
To Opening Stock	12,000		By Sales	112,400	
Less: Private Use	600		Less: Return	1,500	110,900
	11,400		By Closing Stock		18,000
Less: Free Sample	900	10,500	By Goods lost by fire		1,500
To Purchases	68,000				
Less: Machinery	8,000	60,000			
To Carriage Inwards		2,400			
To Import Duty		1,600			
To Freight		1,800			
To Wages	4,600				
Less: Installation of machinery	2,000	2,600			
To Gross Profit c/d		51,500			
		130,400			130,400

(Contd.)

Particulars	Amount (Rs.)	Amount (Rs.)	Particulars	Amount (Rs.)	Amount (Rs.)
To Insurance	2,100		By Gross Profit b/d		51,500
Add: Outstanding	300	2,400	By Discount Received		1,900
To Rent	3,600		By Commission Received		900
Add: Outstanding	400	4,000			
To Salaries	4,800				
Less: Prepaid	500	4,300			
To Goods lost by fire	1,500				
Less: Admitted					
insurance claim	900	600			
To Advertisement		900			
(Free sample)					
To Bad Debts		500			
To Provision for					
Doubtful Debts	1,205				
Less: Old Provision	600	605			
To Depreciation on:					
Machinery	3,350				
Furniture	1,800	5,150			
To Net Profit					
transferred to Capital A/c		35,845			
		54,300			54,300

Balance Sheet of Mr. G.P. Jubida
as on December 31, 2007

Liabilities	Amount (Rs.)	Amount (Rs.)	Assets	Amount (Rs.)	Amount (Rs.)
Capital	60,000		Machinery	26,000	
Add: Net Profit	35,845		*Add:* Purchase	8,000	
	95,845		*Add:* Installation		
Less: Drawings	600	95,245	Charges	2,000	
(Private use of stock)				36,000	
Creditors		14,200	*Less:* Depreciation	3,350	32,650
Outstanding Expenses:			Furniture	18,000	
Rent	400		*Less:* Depreciation	1,800	16,200
Insurance	300	700	Closing Stock		18,000
			Debtors	24,600	
			Less: Bad Debts	500	
				24,100	
			Less: Provision for		
			Doubtful Debts	1,205	22,895
			Prepaid Salaries		500
			Admitted Insurance Claim		900
			Cash in hand		19,000
		110,145			110,145

Working Note

Calculation of depreciation on machinery:	Rs.
On Rs. 26,000 for full year @ 10 %	2,600
On Rs. 10,000 for 9 months @ 10 %	750
Total	3,350

ILLUSTRATION 18.12 The Trial Balance of Mr. D.R. Singhania as on December 31, 2007 is given below.

Dr.   **Trial Balance as on December 31, 2007**   Cr.

Particulars	Amount (Rs.)	Particulars	Amount (Rs.)
Carriage Inwards	3,100	Sales	98,500
Purchases	79,000	Capital	61,000
Return Inwards	2,700	Sundry Creditors	16,000
Drawings	2,500	Interest on Bank Deposits	900
Travelling	2,400	Rent Received	2,800
Petty Expenses	900	Provision for Doubtful Debts	800
Wages	3,700		
Life Insurance Premium			
of the Proprietor	1,800		
Advertisement	2,900		
Salaries	4,500		
Machinery	31,000		
Bills Receivable	9,000		
Sundry Debtors	19,700		
Discount Allowed	1,700		
Cash at Bank	13,300		
Insurance Premium	1,800		
	180,000		180,000

Adjustments

1. Closing Stock Rs. 24,500.
2. Debtors include Rs. 900 due from the proprietor.
3. An amount of Rs. 800 received from a debtor was wrongly credited to Sales A/c.
4. Debtors include Rs. 500 due from Mr. P. Nag, a customer, and creditors include an amount Rs. 900 due to Mr. P. Nag.
5. Bills receivable include a dishonoured bill of Rs. 1,200.
6. Make provision for doubtful debts @ 5% and provision for discount on debtors @ 2%.
7. Depreciate machinery by 10%.
8. Bonus declared but not paid Rs. 1,750.
9. Salary for the year 2007 was actually Rs. 4,950.

Solution

Trading and Profit & Loss Account of Mr. D.R. Singhania

Dr.   **for the year ended December 31, 2007**   Cr.

Particulars	Amount (Rs.)	Amount (Rs.)	Particulars	Amount (Rs.)	Amount (Rs.)
To Purchases		79,000	By Sales	98,500	
To Carriage Inwards		3,100	Less: Return	2,700	
To Wages		3,700		95,800	
To Gross Profit c/d		33,700	Less: Received from Debtors	800	95,000
			By Closing Stock		24,500
		119,500			119,500
To Advertisement		2,900	By Gross Profit b/d		33,700
To Travelling		2,400	By Rent Received		2,800
To Insurance Premium		1,800	By Interest on Bank Deposits		900
To Discount Allowed		1,700			
To Salaries	4,500				
Add: Outstanding	450	4,950			

(Contd.)

Particulars	Amount (Rs.)	Amount (Rs.)	Particulars	Amount (Rs.)	Amount (Rs.)
To Petty Expenses		900			
To Bonus		1,750			
To Provision for Doubtful Debts	935				
Less: Old Provision	800	135			
To Provision for Discount on Debtors		355			
To Depreciation on Machinery		3,100			
To Net Profit transferred to Capital A/c		17,410			
		37,400			37,400

Balance Sheet of Mr. D.R. Singhania
as on December 31, 2007

Liabilities	Amount (Rs.)	Amount (Rs.)	Assets	Amount (Rs.)	Amount (Rs.)
Capital	61,000		Machinery	31,000	
Add: Net Profit	17,410		Less: Depreciation	3,100	27,900
	78,410		Bills Receivable	9,000	
Less: Drawings	2,500		Less: Bills Dishonoured	1,200	7,800
	75,910		Closing Stock		24,500
Less: Included in Debtors	900		Debtors	19,700	
	75,010		Add: Bills Dishonoured	1,200	
Less: L.I.P of Proprietor	1,800	73,210		20,900	
Sundry Creditors	16,000		Less: Due from Proprietor	900	
Less: Set Off	500	15,500		20,000	
Outstanding Expenses:			Less: Received but Included in sales	800	
Salary	450			19,200	
Bonus	1,750	2,200	Less: Set off	500	
				18,700	
			Less: Provision for Doubtful Debts	935	
				17,765	
			Less: Provision for Discount	355	17,410
			Cash at Bank		13,300
		90,910			90,910

ILLUSTRATION 18.13 Trial Balance of Mr. Kumar Basu as on December 31, 2007 is given below:

Dr.		Trial Balance as on December 31, 2007	Cr.
Particulars	Amount (Rs.)	Particulars	Amount (Rs.)
Opening Stock	9,000	Sundry Creditors	15,000
Purchases	71,000	12% Loan from P. C. Sen	18,000
Freight	2,100	(Taken on April 1, 2007)	
Wages	2,700	Capital	50,000
Advertisement	3,400	Sales	92,500
12% Loan to Mr. M.G	15,000	Apprentiship Premium	2,500
(Given on June 1, 2007)		Interest on loan to Mr. M.G	500
Plant and Machinery	24,000	Return Outwards	1,500
			(Contd.)

Particulars	Amount (Rs.)	Particulars	Amount (Rs.)
Patent	6,000		
Interest on Loan from P. C. Sen	600		
Drawings	2,500		
Salaries	3,400		
Stationery Purchased	2,850		
Sundry Debtors	21,550		
Bad Debts	600		
Cash at Bank	14,100		
Insurance	1,200		
	180,000		180,000

Adjustments

1. Closing Stock Rs. 21,000 (including stationery stock of Rs. 1,100).
2. Patent is to be written off in six years.
3. Goods lost by fire worth Rs. 600 (not insured).
4. A cheque of Rs. 600 deposited into bank, but became dishonoured and not corrected in the cash book.
5. Accrued interest on bank deposit Rs. 400.
6. Depreciate machinery @ 15%.
7. Purchase invoice aggregating to Rs. 1,500 was omitted to be entered in the Purchase Day Book.
8. Bad debts of the current year increased to Rs. 900.
9. Unexpired insurance Rs. 200.

Prepare a Trading and Profit & Loss Account for the year ended December 31, 2007, and the Balance Sheet as on that date.

Solution

Trading and Profit & Loss Account of Mr. Kumar Basu

Dr.   For the year ended December 31, 2007   Cr.

Particulars	Amount (Rs.)	Amount (Rs.)	Particulars	Amount (Rs.)	Amount (Rs.)
To Opening Stock		9,000	By Sales		92,500
To Purchases	71,000		By Closing Stock	21,000	
Add: Purchases omitted	1,500		*Less:* Stationery stock	1,100	19,900
	72,500		By Goods lost by fire		600
Less: Return	1,500	71,000			
To Wages		2,700			
To Freight		2,100			
To Gross Profit c/d		28,200			
		113,000			113,000
To Advertisement		3,400	By Gross Profit b/d		28,200
To Interest on Loan from P. C. Sen	600		By Apprentiship Premium		2,500
Add: Outstanding	1,020	1,620	By Interest on Bank Deposits		400
To Salaries		3,400	By Interest on loan to Mr. M.G	500	
To Stationery Used: Purchased	2,850		*Add:* Accrued interest	375	875
Less: Closing Stock	1,100	1,750			
To Bad Debts	600				
Add: New Bad Debt	300	900			
To Insurance	1,200				
Less: Unexpired	200	1,000			

(Contd.)

Particulars	Amount (Rs.)	Amount (Rs.)	Particulars	Amount (Rs.)	Amount (Rs.)
To Patent Written off (6,000/6)		1,000			
To Goods Lost by fire		600			
To Depreciation on Machinery		3,600			
To Net Profit transferred to Capital A/c		14,705			
		31,975			31,975

Balance Sheet of Mr. Kumar Basu
as on December 31, 2007

Liabilities	Amount (Rs.)	Amount (Rs.)	Assets	Amount (Rs.)	Amount (Rs.)
Capital	50,000		Plant & Machinery	24,000	
Add: Net Profit	14,705		Less: Depreciation	3,600	20,400
	64,705		Patent	6,000	
Less: Drawings	2,500	62,205	Less: Written off	1,000	5,000
12% Loan from P. C.Sen		18,000	12% Loan to Mr. M.G		15,000
Outstanding Expenses:			Accrued interest on Loan to Mr. M.G		375
Interest on Loan from P. C. Sen		1,020	Closing Stock		19,900
Sundry Creditors	15,000		Debtors	21,550	
Add: Purchases	1,500	16,500	Less: Bad Debts	300	
				21,250	
			Add: Cheque dishonoured	600	21,850
			Accrued Interest on Bank Deposits		400
			Stock of stationery		1,100
			Unexpired Insurance		200
			Cash at Bank	14,100	
			Less: Cheque dishonoured	600	13,500
		97,725			97,725

ILLUSTRATION 18.14   Prepare a Trading and Profit & Loss Account for the year ended March 31, 2008 of Mr. Surendra and the Balance Sheet as on that date from the following information:

1. Closing Stock Rs. 15,900.
2. Goods lost by fire worth Rs. 900 and the Insurance Company admitted the claim fully.
3. A sum of Rs. 1,200 paid for purchase of furniture on June 1, 2007 has been wrongly debited to Purchases A/c.
4. The Manager is to get a commission of 10% on net profit before charging his commission.
5. Travelling expenses include proprietor's personal travelling for which he is to be charged Rs. 700.
6. An amount of Rs. 3,000 received in respect of a private loan advanced by the proprietor which was wrongly credited to Debtor's A/c.
7. Sundry creditors included a sum of Rs. 1,200 recovered from a customer whose account was written off in the previous year.
8. Depreciate machinery at 10% p.a. and furniture by 5 %.
9. Purchases include Rs. 900 for private purchase of the proprietor.
10. Unexpired expenses:
   Rent Rs. 700 Wages Rs. 800.

Dr.	Trial Balance as on March 31, 2008			Cr.
Particulars	Amount (Rs.)	Particulars		Amount (Rs.)
Freight	1,950	Sales		116,650
Purchases	81,000	Capital		60,000
Rent	3,400	Sundry Creditors		16,000
Travelling Expenses	3,900	Bank Overdraft		9,000
Furniture	8,000	Provision for Doubtful Debts		1,700
Cash in hand	38,300	Discounts		1,400
Distribution Expenses	1,700			
Motive Power	1,200			
Wages	4,200			
Debtors	21,000			
Advertisement	1,700			
Plant & Machinery	37,000			
(Rs. 8,000 purchased on 1.6.07)				
Insurance	1,400			
	204,750			204,750

Solution

Trading and Profit & Loss Account

Dr.		For the year ended March 31, 2008			Cr.
Particulars	Amount (Rs.)	Amount (Rs.)	Particulars	Amount (Rs.)	Amount (Rs.)
To Purchases	81,000		By Sales		116,650
Less: Private purchase	900		By Closing Stock		15,900
	80,100		By Goods lost by fire		900
Less: Furniture purchase	1,200	78,900			
To Wages	4,200				
Less: Prepaid	800	3,400			
To Motive Power		1,200			
To Freight		1,950			
To Gross Profit c/d		48,000			
		133,450			133,450
To Rent	3,400		By Gross Profit b/d		48,000
Less: Prepaid	700	2,700	By Bad Debts Recovered		1,200
To Advertisement		1,700	By Discount		1,400
To Travelling Expenses	3,900				
Less: Drawings	700	3,200			
(Personal travelling)					
To Insurance		1,400			
To Distribution Expenses		1,700			
To Depreciation on:					
Machinery	3,567				
Furniture	460	4,027			
To Net profit before charging		35,873			
Manager's commission					
		50,600			50,600
To Manager's commission		3,587	By Net profit before charging		35,873
(10/100 × 35,873)			Manager's commission		
To Net profit transferred to Capital A/c		32,286			
		35,873			35,873

Balance Sheet
as on March 31, 2008

Liabilities	Amount (Rs.)	Amount (Rs.)	Assets	Amount (Rs.)	Amount (Rs.)
Capital	60,000		Plant and Machinery	37,000	
Add: Net Profit	32,286		Less: Depreciation	3,567	33,433
	92,286		Furniture	8,000	
Less: Drawings:			Add: Purchase	1,200	
Private purchase 900				9,200	
Travelling 700	1,600		Less: Depreciation	460	8,740
	90,686		Closing Stock		15,900
Add: Private loan realized	3,000	93,686	Admitted insurance claim		900
(Treated as capital)			Debtors	21,000	
Sundry Creditors	16,000		Add: Private loan realized	3,000	
Less: Bad debts recovered	1,200	14,800		24,000	
Bank Overdraft		9,000	Less: Provision for Doubtful Debts	1,700	22,300
Outstanding Manager's		3,587	**Prepaid Expenses:**		
Commission			Rent	700	
			Wages	800	1,500
			Cash in hand		38,300
		121,073			121,073

ILLUSTRATION 18.15 From the following trial balance of Mr. A. Ambuja, prepare a Trading and Profit and Loss Account for the year ended December 31, 2007, and a Balance sheet as on that date.

Dr.   **Trial Balance as on December 31, 2007**   Cr.

Particulars	Amount (Rs.)	Particulars	Amount (Rs.)
Opening Stock	9,000	Accounts Payable	13,000
Purchases	76,000	Discount Received	1,300
Land and Building	70,000	Sales	142,000
Office Equipments	12,150	Capital	90,000
Machinery	31,000		
Bad Debts	700		
Carriage	1,300		
Salaries	3,400		
Distribution Expenses	1,800		
Accounts Receivable	16,000		
Petty Expenses	600		
Cash in Hand	4,400		
Wages	1,800		
Advertisement	2,600		
Furniture	12,000		
Insurance Prepaid (January 1, 2007)	450		
Insurance Paid	3,100		
	246,300		246,300

Adjustments

1. Closing stock Rs. 14,600.
2. A fire occurred on August 9, 2007 in which a part of the office building worth Rs. 19,400 was destroyed. Rs. 7,000 was realized from the insurance company for the said loss and it was credited to building account.
3. Sales include goods worth Rs. 6,000 sent on approval basis which remained unsold till December 31, 2007. Goods are sold at 25% profit on sales.
4. A machine which stood in the books at Rs. 4,000 on January 1, 1992 was sold for Rs. 2,800 in exchange for a new machine costing Rs. 5,700 on May 1, 1992. The net invoice of Rs. 2,900 was passed through the inward invoice book. Depreciate machinery by 10%.

5. Office equipments purchased at Rs. 15,000 on January 1, 1990 were depreciated at 10% by Diminishing Balance method. It was then decided to charge depreciation at 10% on fixed installment basis, effective from January 1, 1990.
6. Unexpired Insurance of Rs. 350 on December 31, 2007.

Solution

Trading and Profit & Loss Account of Mr. A. Ambuja

Dr.   For the year ended December 31, 2007   Cr.

Particulars	Amount (Rs.)	Amount (Rs.)	Particulars	Amount (Rs.)	Amount (Rs.)
To Opening Stock		9,000	By Sales	142,000	
To Purchases	76,000		Less: Sales on approval basis	6,000	136,000
Less: Machine Purchase	2,900	73,100	By Closing Stock	14,600	
To Carriage		1,300	Add: Goods sent on		
To Wages		1,800	approval basis(at cost)	4,500	19,100
To Gross Profit c/d		69,900	(Rs. 6,000 – Profit 25%)		
		155,100			155,100
To Insurance	3,100		By Gross Profit b/d		69,900
Add: Prepaid (January 1, 2007)	450		By Discount Received		1,300
	3,550				
Less: Unexpired	350	3,200			
To Bad debts		700			
To Salaries		3,400			
To Loss on sale of machinery		1,200			
To Loss by fire (Building)		12,400			
To Distribution expenses		1,800			
To Petty expenses		600			
To Advertisement		2,600			
To Depreciation on:					
Machinery	3,270				
Office equipments	1,650	4,920			
To Net Profit transferred to					
Reserve Fund Capital A/c		40,380			
		71,200			71,200

Balance Sheet of Mr. A. Ambuja

As on December 31, 2007

Liabilities	Amount (Rs.)	Amount (Rs.)	Assets	Amount (Rs.)	Amount (Rs.)
Capital	90,000		Land and building	70,000	
Add: Net Profit	40,380	130,380	Loss by fire	12,400	57,600
Accounts Payable		13,000	Machinery	31,000	
			Less: Machine sold	4,000	
				27,000	
			Add: Purchase	5,700	
				32,700	
			Less: Depreciation	3,270	29,430
			Office Equipment	12,150	
			Less: Depreciation	1,650	10,500
			Furniture		12,000
			Closing Stock		19,100

(Contd.)

Particulars	Amount (Rs.)	Amount (Rs.)	Particulars	Amount (Rs.)	Amount (Rs.)
			Accounts receivable	16,000	
			Less: Sales on approval basis	6,000	10,000
			Unexpired Insurance		350
			Cash in hand		4,400
		143,380			143,380

Working Note

Calculation of depreciation on office equipments:

	Diminishing Balance Method (Rs.)	Fixed Installment Basis (Rs.)
Depreciation for 2005	1,500	1,500
Depreciation for 2006	1,350	1,500
	2,850	3,000

Further depreciation to be charged due to change of method Rs. 150 (3,000 – 2,850).

Depreciation for 2007   Rs. 1,500

Total Depreciation for 2007   Rs. 1,650

ILLUSTRATION 18.16   The following trial balance was extracted from the books of D. H. Bros. for the year ended December 31, 2007:

Dr.   **Trial Balance as on December 31, 2007**   **Cr.**

Particulars	Amount (Rs.)	Particulars	Amount (Rs.)
Opening Stock	14,900	Sales	118,400
Purchases	67,800	Sundry Creditors	20,600
Salaries	5,400	Discount	2,700
Sundry Debtors	32,500	Capital	80,500
Claim Recoverable (From Railway Co.)	1,950	Provision for Doubtful Debts	2,750
Stationery	2,300	Outstanding Salaries	1,100
Machinery	43,800	Returns	1,500
Furniture	12,600		
Cash in hand and at Bank	21,700		
Discount	3,200		
Returns	2,900		
Wages	6,300		
Carriage	3,100		
Advertisement	4,700		
Godown Rent	2,500		
General Expenses	1,900		
	227,550		227,550

Adjustments

1. Closing stock Rs. 23,700.
2. Rs. 4,000 to be transferred to the reserve fund out of the current year's profits, if any.
3. Closing stock includes goods costing Rs. 2,500 dispatched on January 12, 2008 but sales invoice dated December 26, 2007 was taken into account.
4. Sundry creditors include an amount of Rs. 900 received from a debtor Mr. G. Khan whose account has been written off as bad three years back.
5. Closing stock includes goods costing Rs. 1,200 returned by a customer on December 28, 2007 but no entry has been passed in the books for such return. Generally, goods are sold at 25 % profit on cost.

6. The claim recoverable from the Railways has been settled for Rs. 1,600.
7. Stationery of Rs. 540 was consumed by the family members of the proprietor.
8. Depreciate machinery and furniture by 10% and 5%, respectively.

From the above information, prepare a Trading and Profit and Loss Account for the year ended December 31, 2007 and the Balance Sheet as on that date.

Solution

Trading and Profit & Loss Account of D. H. Bros.

Dr.   For the year ended December 31, 2007   Cr.

Particulars	Amount (Rs.)	Amount (Rs.)	Particulars	Amount (Rs.)	Amount (Rs.)
To Opening Stock		14,900	By Sales	118,400	
To Purchases	67,800		Less: Return	2,900	
Less: Returns	1,500	66,300		115,500	
To Carriage		3,100	Less: Return by Customer	1,500	114,000
To Wages		6,300	(Not recorded)		
To Gross Profit c/d		44,600	By Closing Stock		21,200
			(Rs. 23,700 – Rs. 2,500)		
		135,200			135,200
To Stationery	2,300		By Gross Profit b/d		44,600
Less: Drawings	540	1,760	By Discount Received		2,700
To Claims Written off			By Bad debts Recovered		900
(Rs. 1,950 – Rs. 1,600)		350			
To Salaries		5,400			
To Advertisement		4,700			
To Godown Rent		2,500			
To General Expenses		1,900			
To Discount		3,200			
To Depreciation on:					
Machinery	4,380				
Furniture	630	5,010			
To Net Profit					
transferred to					
Reserve Fund	4,000				
Capital A/c	19,380	23,380			
		48,200			48,200

Balance Sheet of D. H. Bros.
as on December 31, 2007

Liabilities	Amount (Rs.)	Amount (Rs.)	Assets	Amount (Rs.)	Amount (Rs.)
Capital	80,500		Machinery	43,800	
Add: Net Profit	19,380		Less: Depreciation	4,380	39,420
	99,880		Furniture	12,600	
Less: Drawings	540	99,340	Less: Depreciation	630	11,970
(private use of stationery)			Closing Stock		21,200
Creditors	20,600		Debtors	32,500	
Less: Bad debts Recovered	900	19,700	Less: Return by Customer	1,500	
Outstanding Salaries		1,100		31,000	
Reserve Fund		4,000	Less: Provision for Doubtful Debts	2,750	28,250
			Claims Receivable		1,600
			Cash in hand and cash at Bank		21,700
		124,140			124,140

Working Notes

1. It is assumed here that the Provision for Doubtful Debts will continue as before.
2. Goods costing Rs. 1,200 has been returned by a customer but no entry has been passed in the books for such return. The selling price of the said goods is Rs. 1,500, (i.e., Rs. 1,200 + 25% profit on Rs. 1,200). Thus, Rs. 1,500 is to be deducted from the Sales A/c and Debtors A/c.

EXERCISES

I. Short Answer Type Questions

1. How is Closing Stock treated in Final Accounts?
2. What do you mean by Outstanding and Prepaid Expenses? How are they treated in Final Accounts?
3. What do you mean accrued income? Give an example.
4. What do you mean by Capital Expenditure and Revenue Expenditure?
5. Distinguish between Capital Expenditure and Revenue Expenditure.
6. What do you mean by Deferred Revenue Expenditure?
7. Distinguish between Capital Expenditure and Deferred Revenue Expenditure.
8. Distinguish between Deferred Revenue Expenditure and Revenue Expenditure.
9. Wages paid for installation of a Plant and Machinery, but wrongly included in wages Account. How it is treated in Final Accounts?
10. Write Short Notes on the following:
    (a) Provision for Bad and Doubtful Debts
    (b) Bad Debts Recovered
    (c) Set Off of Debtors and Creditors
    (d) Proprietor's income tax paid from business cash
    (e) Good Debtors and Doubtful Debtors.
11. How is Sales Tax/VAT shown in the Trial Balance to be treated in Final Accounts?

II. Long Answer Type Questions

1. What do you understand by Adjustment in final accounts? What are their utilities?
2. What is Provision for Bad and Doubtful Debts? How is it treated in Final Accounts under different situations?
3. How is Manager's Commission calculated? Show its treatments in Final Accounts through an example.

III. Problems

Final Accounts with adjustments

1. From the following particulars prepare Trading Account and Profit and Loss Account for the year ended 31st December, 1980 and the Balance Sheet as on that date:

Trial Balance as on 31.12.1980

	Rs.		Rs.
Purchases A/c	75,000	Capital A/c	50,000
Return Inward A/c	1,000	Sales A/c	175,000
Carriage Inward A/c	500	Creditors A/c	25,000
Carriage Outward A/c	700	Bills Payable A/c	20,000
Rent A/c	2,500	Returns Outward A/c	5,200
Stock A/c	15,000	Interest A/c	500
Debtors A/c	40,000	Provision for Doubtful Debts	2,200
Salary A/c	11,500		
Wages A/c	10,000		
Printing and Stationery A/c	300		

(Contd.)

	Rs.		Rs.
Bills Receivable A/c	11,000		
Plant and Machinery A/c	50,000		
Furniture and Fixtures A/c	10,000		
Advertisement A/c	500		
Bad Debts A/c	500		
Investment A/c	20,000		
Cash at Bank A/c	29,300		
Cash in hand A/c	100		
	277,900		277,900

   (i)   Closing Stock valued at Rs. 15,000 is to be taken into Account,
  (ii)   Plant and Machinery is to be depreciated at 10% and Furniture at 15%.
 (iii)   A further Bad Debt of Rs. 500 is to be written off.
 (iv)   Provision for Doubtful Debts is to be maintained at 4% on Sundry Debtors.
  (v)   Interest due but not received within the accounting year Rs. 500. This is to be taken into account.   (W.B.H.S. 1982)

Ans: Gross Profit Rs. 93,700, Net Profit Rs. 72,320 and Balance Sheet Total Rs. 167,320.

2.   From the following Trial Balance as on 31st December, 1985, prepare the Trading Account, Profit and Loss Account for the year ended 31st December. 1985, and the Balance Sheet as on that date:

	Rs.	Rs.
Rent, Rates and Taxes	15,000	—
Insurance Premium	5,000	—
Bad Debts	3,000	—
Sales	—	675,000
Stock (Opening)	60,000	—
Debtors	120,000	—
Travelling Expenses	6,000	—
Cash in hand	1,500	—
Purchases	300,000	—
Furniture	30,000	—
Electric Charges	4,500	—
Telephone Charges	7,500	—
Plant and Machinery	120,000	—
General Expenses	300	—
Land and Building	180,000	—
Return Outward	—	3,000
Postage and Telegram	8,700	—
Creditors	—	80,000
Wages	72,000	—
Reserves	—	40,000
Salaries	36,000	—
Capital	—	300,000
Return Inward	2,500	—
Cash at Bank	126,000	—
	1,098,000	1,098,000

The following matters are to be taken into Account:
   (i)   Closing Stock valued at Rs. 20,000.
  (ii)   Outstanding Liabilities for (a) Wages Rs. 12,000, (b) Salaries Rs. 10,000.
 (iii)   Depreciation @ 2% p.a. on Land and Buildings, @ 15% p.a. on Furniture and @ 10% p.a. on Plant and Machinery is to be provided,
 (iv)   Provision for Doubtful Debts is to be made @ 5% on Debtors.   (W.B.H.S. 1986)

Ans: Gross Profit Rs. 251,500, Net Profit Rs. 129,400 and Balance Sheet Total Rs. 571,400.

3. The Trial Balance of a trader as on 31st December, 1982 is given below:

	Rs.		Rs.
Stock	30,000	Bills Payable	5.000
Furniture	10,000	Purchases Returns	1,200
Sundry Debtors	40,000	Capital	70,000
Machinery	50,000	Discount	500
Purchases	170,000	Sales	231,000
Bills Receivable	11,000	Commission	200
Carriage Inward	1,300	Reserve	10,000
Carriage Outward	900	Sundry Creditors	30,000
Discount	700		
Sales Returns	2,000		
Wages	10,000		
Salaries	12,000		
Cash at bank	9,000		
Cash in hand	1,000		
	347,900		347,900

After the following adjustments prepare A Trading Account, Profit and Loss Account for the year ended 31st December, 1982 and a Balance Sheet as at that date:
 (i) Closing Stock Rs. 50,000.
 (ii) Outstanding Liabilities: Salaries Rs. 3,000 and Wages Rs. 500.
 (iii) Charge Depreciation on Machinery at 6% and on Furniture at 5%.
 (iv) Create Provision for Doubtful Debts at 5% on Sundry Debtors and Provision for Discount at 4% on Sundry Creditors.
 (v) Transfer 10% of Net Profit to National Defence Fund and 20% to Reserve.

(Tripura H.S. 1983)

Ans: Gross Profit Rs. 68,400, Net Profit Rs. 48,200 and Balance Sheet Total Rs. 165,500. Rs. 4,820 will be shown in the Balance Sheet as Provision for National Defence Fund (Liabilities).

4. The following Trial Balance was extracted from the books of B.K. Sen at the end of 31st December, 1996:

	Rs.		Rs.
Opening Stock	9,000	Capital	64,000
Purchases	61,000	Sales	96,000
Freight	3,000	Sundry Creditors	9,500
Gas and Water	1,700	Discount Received	1,000
Wages	4,000	Interest on Investment	900
Rent	2,900	Bank Overdraft	7,100
Petty Expenses	700		
Plant and Machinery	39,000		
Sundry Debtors	21,000		
Bad Debts	600		
Cash in hand	10,800		
Advertisement	2,300		
Salaries	4,100		
Prepaid Rent	400		
12% Investment	18,000		
	178,500		178,500

Adjustments
 (i) Closing Stock Rs. 12,700.
 (ii) Machinery worth Rs. 4,000 purchased on 1.7.96 has been wrongly included in the purchases.

(iii)   Wages includes Rs. 500 for installation of Machinery.
(iv)   Outstanding expenses: Advertisement Rs. 400 and Salaries Rs. 300.
(v)   Investment was made on 1.6.96.
(vi)   Depreciate Plant and Machinery @ 10% p.a.
(vii)   Make Provision for Doubtful Debts @ 5% on Debtors.
Ans: Gross Profit Rs. 34,500, Net profit Rs. 20,285, Balance Sheet Total Rs. 101,585.

5.   Trial Balance of Sri G.P. Healy as on 31st December, 1996 is given below:

	Rs.		Rs.
Carriage	1,700	Outstanding wages	700
Purchases	72,000	Capital	50,100
Opening Stock	3,000	Loan	10,000
Wages	5,000	Creditors	16,400
Salaries	4,800	Interest on Bank deposits	800
Motive Power	1,200	Sales	102,000
Import Duty	700		
Machinery (Addition Rs. 8,000			
was made on 1.6.96)	38,000		
Furniture	3,000		
Bad debts	900		
Discount allowed	1,200		
Distribution Expenses	1,900		
Debtors	26,000		
Travelling Expenses	1,400		
Cash in hand	7,200		
Cash at bank	12,000		
	180,000		180,000

Adjustments
(a)   Closing Stock Rs. 16,000.
(b)   Bad debts of the current year increased to Rs. 1,600.
(c)   Make Provision for Doubtful Debts @ 5% on debtors.
(d)   Depreciate Machinery and Furniture @ 10% p.a. and 5% p.a. respectively.
(e)   Travelling expenses include proprietor's personal travelling for Rs. 400.
(f)   Goods distributed as free sample Rs. 600.
Ans: Gross Profit Rs. 35,000, Net Profit Rs. 19,818, Balance Sheet Total Rs. 96,618.
Note
1.   New Bad Debts Rs. 700 and Provision for Bad Debts Rs. 1,265.
2.   Depreciation on machinery Rs. 3,467 (3000 + 467).
3.   Travelling expenses of Rs. 400 will be treated as Drawings.

6.   Sri L. M. Saha submits the following information in order to draw up his Trading and Profit & Loss Account for the year ended 31st December, 1995 and Balance Sheet as on that date:
Adjustments
(a)   Closing Stock Rs. 14,900.
(b)   A sum of Rs. 3,000 paid for purchase of some furniture on 1.4.95 has been wrongly debited to Purchase Account.
(c)   Carriage includes carriage paid on furniture purchased Rs. 200.
(d)   Rent paid during the year was for 10 months
(e)   Depreciate furniture @ 5% p.a. and delivery van by 10%.
(f)   Making Provision for Doubtful Debts @ 5% on Debtors and 2½ % for Discount on Debtors.
(g)   Unexpired insurance Rs. 600.

Trial Balance as on 31st December, 1995

	Rs.		Rs.
Carriage	3,100	Sales	102,200
Purchases	70,000	Capital	68,000
Opening Stock	6,900	Provision for Doubtful Debts	600
Wages	4,100	Return Outward	1,400
Insurance	3,200	Creditors	11,600
Furniture	12,000	Commission received	700
Debtors	18,000	Rent from subletting	1,200
Bills receivable	9,000		
Cash in hand and Cash at Bank	18,300		
Advertisement	2,600		
Return Inward	1,900		
Loan to 'X'	10,000		
Delivery Van	18,000		
Distribution expenses	4,600		
Rent	4,000		
	185,700		185,700

Ans: Gross Profit Rs. 35,700, Net Profit Rs. 19,752, Balance Sheet Total Rs. 100,152.

[Hints:
(a) Provision for discount on debtors Rs. 428.
(b) Depreciation on furniture (Rs. 600 + 120) Rs. 720.
(c) Outstanding rent Rs. 800 (for 2 months).]

7. From the following information prepare a Trading and Profit & Loss Account for the year ended 31st March, 1996 and Balance Sheet as on that date:

	Rs.		Rs.
Goodwill	10,000	Sales	91,000
Debtors	23,000	Capital	50,000
Bad Debts	800	Creditors	14,000
Opening Stock	6,400	Discounts Received	1,800
Purchases	68,500	Commission Received	1,600
Salary and Wages	6,300	Provision for Doubtful Debts	1,600
Drawings	1,650		
Equipment	8,000		
Carriage Inwards	2,100		
Stationery purchase	2,750		
Cash in hand	18,500		
Furniture	12,000		
	160,000		160,000

Adjustments
(i) Closing Stock Rs. 9,400 (Including stationery stock Rs. 600).
(ii) A cheque of Rs. 500 deposited into Bank became dishonoured, no entry has been made in the Cash Book for such dishonour,
(iii) Debtors includes Bad Debts Rs. 300.
(iv) Make Provision for Doubtful Debts @ 5% on Debtors,
(v) Depreciate Furniture and Equipment @ 10% p.a.
(vi) Unexpired Salary Rs. 300.

Ans: Gross Profit Rs. 22,800, Net Profit Rs. 15,390, Balance Sheet Total Rs. 77,740.

8. Trial Balance of Ratan Agarwal as on 31.12.96 is given below:

	Rs.		Rs.
Adjusted Purchases	72,500	Capital	80,000
Closing Stock	6,500	Sales	102,000
Life Insurance Premium of Proprietor	700	Creditors	16,000
Freehold Property	48,000	Provision for Doubtful Debts	1,200
Advertisement	4,300	Bills Payable	5,000
Salaries	12,700	Interest on Bank deposits	1,800
Prepaid Salaries	3,100	Outstanding wages	2,000
Freight	2,300		
Import Duty	1,700		
Travelling Expenses	1,900		
Cash in hand	11,400		
Cash at Bank	9,300		
Sundry debtors	18,200		
Bills Receivable	9,500		
Wages	3,900		
Rent	2,000		
	208,000		208,000

Adjustments

(i) Goods lost by fire worth Rs. 2,400 and salvage value expected to be Rs. 900. The Insurance Company admitted the claim finally Rs. 1,050 for the said loss.

(ii) Bills Receivable including a dishonoured bill of Rs. 1,500.

(iii) Accrued interest on Bank deposit Rs. 300.

(iv) The manager is to get a commission of 10% on Net profit after charging his commission,

(v) Rent @ Rs. 300 p.m. outstanding for last 2 months.

Ans: Gross Profit Rs. 24,000, Net Profit Rs. 3,773, Balance Sheet Total Rs. 107,050, Manager's Commission Rs. 377.

9. Red and Yellow are partners in a firm sharing profits and losses in the ratio of 3:2. It was agreed that each partner is entitled to 5% interest on capital and salary @ Rs. 600 and Rs. 500 p.m. Their Trial balance as on 31.12.95 is given below:

	Rs.			Rs.
Drawings:		Sales		119,900
Red	5,100	Provision for Doubtful Debts		900
Yellow	4,100	Capital:		
Machinery	31,000	Red	32,000	
Depreciation on Machinery	3,000	Yellow	18,000	18,000
Purchases	84,000	Creditors		18,000
Opening Stock	6,000			
Carriage	1,400			
Wages	3,900			
Office Expenses	2,400			
Cash in hand	11,800			
Cash at bank	7,200			
Sundry Debtors	14,600			
Bad Debts	300			
Advertisement	1,900			
	176,600			176,600

Adjustments

(a) Closing Stock Rs. 11,300.

(b) Bad debts of the current year increased by Rs. 600.

(c) Goods distributed as free sample for Rs. 700.

From the above information you are required to prepare Trading and Profit and Loss Account, Profit and Loss Appropriation Account for the year ended 31.12.95 and the Balance Sheet as on that date.

Ans: Gross Profit Rs. 36,600, Net Profit Rs. 27,700, Balance Sheet Total Rs. 74.400, Distributable Profit Rs. 12,000, Closing Adjusted Capital Red—Rs. 43,000 and Yellow—Rs. 25,600.

10. The following Trial Balance was extracted from the books of Sri M. M. Das at the end of the business on 31.12.96:

	Rs.		Rs.
Adjusted Purchases	69,500	Bank Overdraft	7,400
Closing Stock	7,500	Sales	99,200
Advertisement	3,100	Capital	50,000
Rent and Rates	2,600	Creditors	9,600
Petty Expenses	900	Discount Received	900
Wages	3,300	Outstanding Wages	1,100
Carriage	1,400		
Import Duty	1,900		
Insurance	1,800		
Drawings	2,400		
Cash in hand	14,700		
Debtors	21,400		
Plant and Machinery	34,900		
Depreciation on Machinery	2,100		
Bad Debts	700		
	168,200		168,200

Adjustments

(i) Sundry Creditors included a sum of Rs. 600 recovered from a customer whose A/c was written, off in the previous year as bad.

(ii) Make provision for Doubtful Debts @ 5% on Debtors,

(iii) Make Provision for discount on creditors @ 2% on creditors,

(iv) Outstanding Insurance Rs. 300.

(v) Interest on overdraft not taken into Account Rs. 350

From the above information prepare Trading and Profit and Loss Account for the year ended 31.12.96 and the Balance Sheet as on that date.

Ans: Gross Profit Rs. 25,000, Net Profit Rs. 11,860, Balance Sheet Total Rs. 77,430.

11. From the following Trial Balance of Mr. A, prepare a Trading and Profit and Loss Account for the year ending 31st December, 1990 and a Balance Sheet as on that date:

Dr.		**Trial Balance**	Cr.
	Rs.		Rs.
Drawings	5,275	Capital	59,700
Bills Receivable	4,750	Loan at 8% (on 1.1.90)	10,000
Machinery	14,400	Commission Received	2,820
Debtors (including X for		Creditors	29,810
dishonoured bill of Rs. 1,000)	30,000	Sales	178,215
Wages	20,485		
Return Inward	2,390		
Purchases	128,295		
Rent	2,810		
Stock (1.1.90)	44,840		
Salaries	5,500		
Travelling Expenses	945		

(Contd.)

	Rs.		Rs.
Insurance	200		
Cash	9,750		
Repairs	1,685		
Interest on Loan	500		
Discount Allowed	2,435		
Bad Debts	1,810		
Furniture	4,480		
	280,550		280,550

The following adjustments are to be made:
  (i)   Stock in shop on 31st December, 1990 was Rs. 64,480.
  (ii) Half the amount of X's bill is irrecoverable.
  (iii) Create a provision of 5% on other debtors.
  (iv) Wages include Rs. 600 for erection of new machinery.
  (v)   Depreciate Machinery by 5% and Furniture by 10%.
  (vi) Commission includes Rs. 300 being commission received in advance.

(H.S.—C.B.S.E.)

Ans: Gross Profit Rs. 47,285, Net Profit Rs. 30,472, Balance Sheet Total Rs. 125,312.

12. Given below is a Trial Balance of a business concern as on 31.12.89:

Sen & Co.
Trial Balance as on 31.12.89

	Dr. (Rs.)	Cr. (Rs.)
Goodwill	5,000	
Freehold Premises	20,000	
Salaries	7,200	
Sundry Debtors	30,000	
Stock	15,000	
Capital Account		45,000
Purchases	75,000	
Plant and Machinery	25,000	
Fixtures	5,000	
Discount	750	
Bills Receivable	3,500	
Bills Payable		5,600
Wages	16,000	
Provision for Doubtful Debts		750
Repairs	350	
Trade Charges	350	
Carriage Inward	500	
Carriage Outward	1,150	
Sundry Creditors		25,000
Cash in hand	9,100	
Cash at bank	20,000	
Sales		156,000
Commission		1,550
	233,900	233,900

Prepare (i) a Trading Account, (ii) a Profit and Loss Account for the year ending on 31.12.89 and (iii) a Balance Sheet as on that date, after making adjustments for the following:
  (i)   Closing Stock was valued at Rs. 20,000.
  (ii) Bad Debts not yet accounted for Rs. 500.
  (iii) Provide for Doubtful Debts at 5%.
  (iv) Charge interest on capital @ 5% per annum.

(v) Charge depreciation as indicated below:
On Plant and Machinery @ 6% per annum.
On Fixtures and Freehold Premises @ 2½ % per annum. (W.B.H.S.)
Ans: Gross Profit Rs. 69,500, Net Profit Rs. 57,900, Balance Sheet Total Rs. 133,500,
Net Profit after charging interest on Capital is Rs. 55,650.

13. The following balances are extracted from the books of Sri. A. N. Roy as on 31.12.90:

	Rs.		Rs.
Land and Building	130,000	Plant and Machinery	146,000
Capital	249,000	Salaries	36,000
Wages	25,600	Carriage Inward	500
Return Outward	2,700	Rent received	1,650
Purchases	76,000	Stock (1.1.90)	17,000
Insurance Premium	1,200	Sales	192,000
Sundry Debtors	17,800	Sundry Creditors	19,300
Cash in hand	200	Cash at bank	16,500
Bills Receivable	15,200	Bills Payable	17,350

The additional information are supplied:
(i) Closing Stock is valued at Rs. 23,000.
(ii) Goods purchased for Rs. 5,000 were received in Stock but no entry was made in the Invoice Book,
(iii) Rent for December, 1990 amounting to Rs. 1,500 has not yet been received.
(iv) Unexpired Insurance Premium amounts to Rs. 200
(v) Goods worth Rs. 2,000 was taken by Sri A. N. Roy for his family use.
(vi) Land and Buildings are to be depreciated @ 2½ % p.a. and Plant and Machinery @ 10% p.a.

You are required to prepare the Trading and Profit and Loss Account for the year ended 31.12.90 and the Balance Sheet as on that date. (W.B.H.S.)
Ans: Gross Profit Rs. 95,600, Net Profit Rs. 43,900, Balance Sheet Total Rs. 332,550.

14. The following are the balances of M/s Gupta and Co. as on 30th June, 1981:

Dr.			Cr.
	Rs.		Rs.
Cash in hand	540	Sales	98,780
Cash at bank	2,630	Returns Outward	500
Purchases	40,675	Capital	62,000
Return Inward	680	Sundry Creditors	6,300
Wages	8,480	Rent	9,000
Fuel and Power	4,730		
Carriage on Sales	3,200		
Carriage on Purchases	2,040		
Stock (Opening)	5,760		
Building	32,000		
Freehold Land	10,000		
Machinery	20,000		
Patents	7,500		
Salaries	15,000		
General Expenses	3,000		
Insurance	600		
Drawings	5,245		
Sundry Debtors	14,500		
	176,580		176,580

Prepare a Trading and Profit and Loss Account and a Balance Sheet as on 30th June, 1981, after taking into account the following adjustments:

(i) Stock on hand as on 30th June, 1981 is Rs. 6,800.

(ii) Machinery is to be depreciated at 10% and Patents at 20%.

(iii) Salaries for the month of June, 1981 amounting to Rs. 1,500 were unpaid,

(iv) Insurance includes a premium of Rs. 170 on a policy expiring on 31st December, 1981.

(v) Further Bad Debts Rs. 725.

(vi) Rent receivable Rs. 1,000. (H.S.—CBSE)

Ans: Gross Profit Rs. 43,715, Net Profit Rs. 26,275, Balance Sheet Total Rs. 90,830.

15. Trial Balance of S. P. Santur as on 31st March, 2009 was as follows:

Dr.   Cr.

	Rs.		Rs.
Opening Stock	18,000	Return Outward	900
Wages	11,000	Salaries Outstanding	1,400
Salaries	16,150	Provision for Doubtful Debts	2,800
Freight & Carriage	14,000	Provision for Doubtful Debts	2,800
Purchases	92,800	Provision for Doubtful Debts	2,800
Return Inward	1,200	Creditors	22,090
Wages paid in advance	1,600	Interest on Investment	300
Car	34,000	Discount	1,700
Car Expenses	3,900	Interest on Bank Deposit	800
Cash at Bank	17,800		
Distribution Expenses	2,840		
9% Investment	18,000		
(made on 1.6.2008)			
Debtors	24,000		
Machinery	64,000		
	319,290		319,290

Adjustments:

(a) Closing Stock Rs. 12,940.

(b) 1/3rd of Car Expenses and its Depreciation should be charged to proprietor's personal account for private use of car.

(c) Depreciation on Car and Machinery are to be provided at 10% p.a.

(d) A sum of Rs. 8,000 paid for purchase of Machinery on 1.9.2008 has been wrongly debited to Purchases A/c.

(e) Sundry Creditors included a sum of Rs. 1,300 recovered from a customer whose Account was written off in the previous year.

Draw up the Trading and Profit & Loss Account for the year ended 31.3.2009 and the Balance Sheet as on that date.

Ans: Gross Profit Rs. 33,240; Net Profit Rs. 7,666; Balance Sheet Total Rs. 168,323; Depreciation charged on machinery Rs. 6,867; Capital A/c balance Rs. 146,133; Drawings Rs. 2,433.

16. The Trial Balance of Mr. K. P. Sharma as on 31st March 1993 is given below.

	Rs.		Rs.
Purchases (adjusted)	78,000	Sales	101,000
Stock in trade (31.3.93)	10,200	Capital	51,000
Import Duty	900	Creditors	8,500
Freight and Insurance on Import	700	Rent Received	4,200
Wages	2,600	Outstanding Car Expenses	450
Salaries	4,800		
Bank charges	150		
Machinery (including new			
Rs. 15,000 installed on 1.10.92)	41,000		
Cash at bank	1,000		

(Contd.)

	Rs.		Rs.
Car expenses	1,800		
Prepaid salaries	600		
Bad Debts	600		
Office expenses	800		
Insurance Premium	1,800		
Prepaid Insurance (1.4.92)	200		
Sundry Debtors	20,000		
	165,150		165,150

Adjustments

(a) Unexpired insurance Rs. 380.

(b) Outstanding: Office expenses Rs. 300 and salaries Rs. 200.

(c) Depreciation to be provided on machinery at 10% p.a.

(d) An account of Rs. 1,800 received in respect of a private loan advanced by the proprietor was wrongly credited to the debtors account.

(e) Wages include Rs. 2,000 for installation of machinery.

(f) Provision for doubtful debts at 6% on debtors.

(g) The manager is to get a commission of 10% on net profits after charging his commission.

From the above information prepare Trading and Profit and Loss Account of Mr. K.P. Sharma for the year ended 31st March, 1993 and the Balance Sheet as on that date.

Working Notes:

(a) When adjusted purchase is given, then the Trading Account Closing Stock is not to be taken, because it is already adjusted with purchases. Hence, Closing Stock is to be shown in the Balance Sheet only.

(b) Private loan advanced by proprietor is considered here as fresh Capital.

Ans: Gross Profit Rs. 20,800, Net Profit Rs. 9,065, Manager's Commission Rs. 907, Balance Sheet Total Rs. 72,222.

17. Trial Balance of Sri Ratan Mohan Agarwal as on 30.6.93 is given below:

	Rs.		Rs.
Purchases	91,000	Capital	96,000
Opening Stock	4,000	Sales	121,000
Bills Receivable	12,000	Creditors	13,400
Cash at Bank	18,000	Creditors for Expenses	300
Drawings	3,000	Commission earned	1,400
Sundry Debtors	21,000	Provision for Doubtful Debts	3,100
Salaries	7,200	Bills Payable	4,000
Wages	3,600	Miscellaneous receipts	300
Carriage	1,600		
Advertisement	2,700		
Furniture	8,000		
Machinery	26,000		
Distribution Expenses	1,900		
Travelling Expenses	1,400		
Return inwards	2,100		
Freehold property	36,000		
	239,500		239,500

Adjustments

(a) Closing Stock Rs. 11,200.

(b) Miscellaneous receipts represents the sale proceeds of old furniture, written down value of which was Rs. 740.

(c) A plant which stood in the books at Rs. 4,000 on 1st Oct. 1992 was sold for Rs. 2,800 in exchange of a new machine costing Rs. 4,800. The net invoice of Rs. 2,000 was passed through the purchase day book.

(d) Depreciate machinery and furniture by 10%.

(e) Stock used for private purpose Rs. 900 and used as free sample Rs. 1,300.

(f) Make provision for doubtful debts at 5% on debtors.

(g) Creditors include Rs. 3,000, loan taken from Mr. S. K. Saraf on 1.10.92 bearing interest @ 12% p.a.

(h) An amount of Rs. 1,250 received in respect of a private loan advanced by the proprietor was wrongly credited to Debtors Account.

From the above information you are required to show the Trading and Profit and Loss Account for the year ended 30.6.93 and the Balance Sheet as on that date.

Ans: Gross Profit Rs. 34,100, Net Profit Rs. 17,661, Balance Sheet Total Rs. 128,981.

18. From the following Trial Balance of Sri Jibon Ram, prepare a Trading and Profit and Loss Account for the year ending December 31, 1992 and Balance Sheet as on that date:

Trial Balance as on 31.12.92

	Rs.		Rs.
Stock on 1.1.92	9,200	Outstanding Office Expenses	1,900
Purchases	97,000	Sales	139,000
Wages and Salaries	8,200	Capital	85,000
Carriage	3,900	Creditors	22,900
Debtors	27,000	Bills Payable	9,000
Interest	1,700		
Building	44,000		
Advertisement	6,000		
Office Expenses	9,000		
Rent	4,200		
Advance Rent	1,600		
Cash in hand	19,000		
Bills Receivable	16,000		
Furniture	11,000		
	257,800		257,800

Adjustments

(a) Closing Stock Rs. 9,940.

(b) Debtors includes a dishonoured bill for Rs. 900. 1/3rd of this is to be written off to be bad.

(c) Bills receivable includes a dishonoured bill for Rs. 700.

(d) Debtors includes an amount due from A. K. Das Rs. 600 is considered definitely good.

(e) Debtors include amount due from B. C. Sen Rs. 400 whose financial position is very doubtful.

(f) A time barred debt of Rs. 200 due from S. P. Kar was written off as bad. But now he promises to pay the amount.

(g) Debtors include Rs. 300 in respect of a insolvent whose estate is expected to realise not more than 40 Paise in a Rupee.

(h) Debtors include an item of Rs. 1,200 for goods supplied to proprietor,

(i) Make provision for doubtful debts at 5% on debtors.

[Hint:

Item no.	Bad debt	Good debt	100% provision	Doubtful debts
(b) 900	300	600	—	27,000 – 1,200 + 700 =
				(h) (c)
(d) 600	—	600	—	26,500 – 480 – 1,320
(e) 400	—	—	400	– 400 = 24,300
(g) 300	180	120	—	
	480	1320	400	

5% provision on Rs. 24,300 = 1,215. Total provision for bad debts = Rs. 1,215 + + Rs. 400 (100% Provision) = 1,615 (Provision for Bad Debts].

Ans: Gross Profit Rs. 30,640, Net Profit Rs. 7,645, Balance Sheet Total Rs, 125,245, Provision for Bad Debts Rs. 1,615.

19. X and Z are partners sharing profits and losses in the ratio of 5 : 3. It was agreed that each partner is entitled to 9% interest on Capital, but no interest is charged on Drawings.

From the following information prepare the Trading and Profit & Loss Account for the year ended 31st December, 2009 and a Balance Sheet as on that date:

Trial Balance as on 31.12.2009

Dr.			Cr.
	Rs.		**Rs.**
Purchases	80,000	Capital:	
Carriage Inward	3,200	X	52,000
Salaries and Wages	9,400	Z	36,000
Rent & Taxes	4,800	Sundry Creditors	9,500
Advertisement	3,000	Provision for Doubtful Debts	900
Drawings:		Sales	129,000
X	12,000	Discount	3,100
Z	9,000		
Sundry Expenses	2,600		
Sundry Debtors	41,000		
Van Driver's Wages	3,200		
Bad Debts	700		
Petty Cash in hand	100		
Machinery	10,000		
Electricity	600		
Furniture & Fittings	6,000		
Cash in hand	36,000		
Van Expenses	900		
Van	8,000		
	230,500		230,500

Adjustments:
(a) Stock-in-trade (31.12.2009) Rs. 12,000.
(b) Goods used by X for personal purposes Rs. 1,500 and distributed as free sample Rs. 1,600.
(c) Van driver's wages outstanding Rs. 400.
(d) Salary paid in advance Rs. 700.
(e) Depreciate Machinery including Office Equipment and Van by 10%.
(f) 2/5th of the total cost of maintaining Van was for transporting goods to the godown.

Ans: Gross Profit Rs. 58,780; Net Profit Rs. 35,100; Distributable Profits Rs. 27,180; X's share of Profit Rs. 16,987 and Z's share of Profit Rs. 10,193; Balance Sheet Total Rs. 110,500; X's Capital Rs. 60,167 and Z's Capital Rs. 40,433.

20. P and Q are partners in a firm. The Partnership Agreement provides the following:
(a) Interest on Capital at 4% p.a.
(b) Partners' salary Rs. 400 p.m. and Rs. 300 p.m. respectively.

(c) Q is entitled to a commission of 1% on net sales of the firm.

(d) The balance available profits in the ratio of 5 : 3.

The following Trial Balance was extracted from the books of P and Q on 31st December, 2009:

Dr.	Rs.		Cr. Rs.
Goodwill	12,000	Capital Accounts:	
Purchases	64,000	P	60,000
Opening Stock	19,000	Q	40,000
Return Inward	600	Current Accounts:	
Drawings:		P	3,200
P	9,000	Q	1,200
Q	6,000	Loan – P (1.1.2009)	18,000
Debtors	18,500	Creditors	10,000
Cash in hand	14,000	Discount	2,200
Wages	6,000	Sales	115,000
Carriage	4,200	Provision for Doubtful Debts	600
Travelling expenses	1,800		
Advertisement	2,100		
12% Loan to D. Sen (1.1.09)	10,000		
Trade expenses	2,600		
Insurance	3,200		
Furniture	9,000		
Machinery	68,200		
	250,200		250,200

Adjustments:

(a) Closing Stock Rs. 16,400.

(b) Depreciate Machinery and Furniture by 10%.

(c) Purchases invoice aggregating Rs. 3,600 were omitted to be entered in Purchase Day Book.

(d) Provision for Doubtful Debts to be increased to Rs. 1,250.

You are required to prepare Trading and Profit and Loss Account for the year ended 31st December, 2009 and a Balance Sheet as on that date, taking into account the above information.

Ans: Gross Profit Rs. 34,000; Net Profit Rs. 18,250; P's share of profit Rs. 2,941, Q's share of profit Rs. 1,765; P's Current Account balance Rs. 5,421, Q's Current Account balance Rs. 3,309; Balance Sheet Total Rs. 140,330; Commission Rs. 1,144 (1% of 115,000 – 600).

21. From the following information prepare the Trading and Profit & Loss Account of Sri M. K. Kanthal for the year ended 31st December, 2009 and Balance Sheet as on that date:

Dr.	Trial Balance as on 31.12.2009		Cr.
	Rs.		Rs.
Purchases	68,000	Account Payable	14,000
Wages	9,000	Rent from sub-letting	3,800
Salaries	7,200	Bills Payable	9,000
Carriage	6,000	Sales	106,400
Distribution Expenses	3,800	Capital	71,500
Bad Debts	1,900		
Account Receivable	24,000		
Rent	7,900		
Bills Receivable	11,400		
L.I.P. of Proprietor	1,600		
Goodwill	16,000		
Printing and Stationery	1,840		
Machinery	21,000		
Furniture	9,260		

	Rs.		Rs.
Cash in hand	11,200		
Insurance	2,600		
Depreciation on Machinery	2,000		
	204,700		204,700

Adjustments:

(a) Closing Stock Rs. 7,200.

(b) There was a sale against Bills Receivable on 29.12.2009; but since the goods were not delivered, no entry was passed Rs. 2,800. The goods were also wrongly included in the Closing Stock.

(c) Goods lost by fire worth Rs. 3,200 and salvage value expected to be Rs. 600. The insurance company admitted the claim finally for Rs. 1,450 for the said loss.

(d) Carriage includes Rs. 1,050 towards outward charges.

(e) Bad Debts increased to Rs. 2,100.

(f) Bills Receivable includes a dishonoured bill of Rs. 850.

(g) Purchase invoice aggregating Rs. 4,100 were omitted to be entered in Purchase Day Book.

Ans: Gross Profit Rs. 30,750; Net Profit Rs. 4,910; Balance Sheet Total Rs. 101,910.

22. From the following information prepare Trading and Profit and Loss Account of Mr. Prasant Kapoor for the year ended 31st March, 2010 and Balance Sheet as on that date:

Dr.   **Trial Balance as on 31.3.2010**   *Cr.*

	Rs.		Rs.
Goodwill	15,000	Sales	1,12,900
Cash in hand	11,900	Capital	50,000
Cash at Bank	12,800	Creditors	13,600
Furniture	13,000	12% Loan	12,000
Equipment	8,000		
Discount Received	100		
Carriage Outwards	1,300		
Carriage Inwards	1,900		
Freight	800		
Debtors	22,600		
Interest on Loan	300		
Petty Expenses	500		
Salary & Wages	4,600		
Stationery Purchases	2,800		
Purchases	79,000		
Opening Stock	9,400		
Drawings	1,800		
L.I.P. of Proprietor	900		
Insurance	2,000		
	188,600		188,600

Adjustments:

(a) Closing Stock Rs. 9,400 (including Stationery Stock Rs. 300).

(b) Opening Stock includes Rs. 600 Stationery Stock.

(c) Outstanding expenses – Salary Rs. 1,100 and Carriage Inward Rs. 700.

(d) A cheque of Rs. 600 deposited into Bank became dishonoured, no entry has been made in the Cash Book for such dishonour.

(e) Goods lost by fire worth Rs. 1,400 and insurance company admitted the claim up to the extent of Rs. 300. Salvage value of lost Stock Rs. 200.

(f) Make Provision for Doubtful Debts at 6% on debtors.

(g) Debtors include Rs. 400 due from a customer, Mr. R. Sinha, who has become insolvent and nothing shall be realized from his estate.

(h) Depreciation to be provided on equipment and furniture at 10% and 5% respectively.

Ans: Gross Profit Rs. 32,200; Net Profit Rs. 14,142; Balance Sheet Total Rs. 89,982.

19

Accounts from Incomplete Records

CONTENTS

19.1 SINGLE ENTRY SYSTEM

Small business owners who do not have any knowledge of accounting, or who do not want to follow any systematic or scientific methods of accounting, generally prefer to maintain very few accounts. They choose to prepare statements according to their desire for ascertaining profits or losses of the businesses. Recording the business transactions throughout the year are made according to the desire of the proprietor. At the end of the year with the help of these incomplete data, profits or losses of the businesses are ascertained through a system known as Single Entry System. The proprietors do not want to represent their business data analytically because they remain satisfied on receiving only a few business information like amounts payable by the business, receivable by the business, present stock position, and cash and bank balances.

The single entry system is the most unscientific method of record keeping which does not following the accepted accounting rules. It maintains only a few accounts and records according to the desire of the proprietors. The single entry system is nothing but a defective or limited use of the double entry system. Thus, there cannot be any particular system which may be called a single entry system.

Single entry system may be defined as an incomplete record of business transactions which does not follow the general accounting principles and procedures, but is done according to the desire of the trader or the owner. According to Kohler, "The single entry system is a system of book keeping in which, as a rule, only records of cash and of personal accounts are maintained, and it is always an incomplete double entry varying with circumstances." In reality in some particular areas the double entry system is followed and in others, it is not, i.e., no particular system is followed for all the transactions consistently, but it is only in some selected areas that there double entry system is followed according the desire of the owner or the proprietor.

Table 19.1 lists the major points of differences between double entry system and single entry system.

19.1.1 Types of Single Entry System

1. **Pure single entry system:** Only personal accounts are maintained.
2. **Simple single entry system:** Cash book and personal accounts are maintained.
3. **Quasi-single entry system:** Cash book, personal accounts and a few subsidiary books are maintained.

TABLE 19.1   Distinction between Double Entry System and Single Entry System

Double entry system	Single entry system
This system is based on some accepted accounting principles.	No accepted accounting principles are followed under this system.
It has a two-fold effect or a dual aspect. The receiving aspect is known as **debit** while the giving aspect is called **credit.**	There is no such two-fold effect or dual aspect in single entry system.
Arithmetical accuracy can be checked or verified through trial balance.	Arithmetical accuracy cannot be checked or verified as no trial balance is prepared due to incomplete records.
For maintaining books of accounts through this system, expert accountants are essential.	No specialized bookkeeper or accountant is required for recording the day to day transactions.
Book's maintenance cost is very high.	Book's maintenance cost is very low.
Double entry system is suitable for big firms.	Single entry system is suitable for small firms only.
Company accounts are maintained through this system.	Company accounts cannot be maintained through this system.
Gross profit and correct net profit can be ascertained easily with its help.	Gross profit and correct net profit cannot be ascertained with its help.
Trading and Profit and Loss Account can be prepared.	Due to the absence of nominal accounts, Trading and Profit and Loss Account cannot be prepared.
The true financial position can be ascertained because the Balance Sheet represents the true state of affairs of the business.	The true financial position cannot be ascertained because the statement of affairs does not represent the true state of affairs of the business.
Business performances can be measured properly and systematically.	Business performance cannot be measured properly through single entry system.
Double entry system helps to prevent frauds and misappropriations in big businesses.	Prevention of frauds and misappropriations becomes difficult in case of big businesses.

19.1.2   Salient Features of Single Entry System

1. Complete double entry system is not followed.
2. This method is followed by sole traders and partnership firms.
3. Generally, personal accounts are maintained, but nominal and real accounts (except Cash A/c) are not opened.
4. There is no uniformity in maintaining the books of accounts among traders (who follow this system). Thus, the method in which the books are maintained may differ from one firm to another.
5. This system is suitable for small firms.
6. Usually, a cash book is maintained, where both private and business transactions are recorded.
7. Instead of opening the related accounts, the original vouchers are maintained for future reference.

19.1.3   Advantages of Single Entry System

1. This method is easy to maintain. Here, transactions may be recorded according to the desire of the owner only on not having any sufficient knowledge of accounting.
2. Cost of maintaining books is very low.
3. Books may be maintained by any person having no knowledge of accounting. Thus, no specialized book keepers or accountants are required for recording the day to day transactions.
4. It helps to maintain business secrecy.
5. In case of abnormal situations like loss of accounts, destruction of books of accounts by fire or natural calamities, profit or loss of the business may be ascertain through this system.

19.1.4 Drawbacks of Single Entry System

1. Arithmetical accuracy cannot be checked or verified as no trial balance is prepared for not having complete records.
2. Due to the absence of nominal accounts, Trading and Profit and Loss Account cannot be prepared. As a result, gross profit and correct net profit cannot be ascertained.
3. As the books are not maintained properly, the information obtained from such records cannot be relied upon.
4. If the firm is big, then prevention of frauds and misappropriations would become a great problem.
5. The true financial position cannot be ascertained because the statement of affairs does not represent the true state of affairs of the business.
6. As the facts and figures supplied cannot be relied upon, proper planning for the future cannot be made, and taking important decisions in case of any critical situations becomes difficult.
7. Business performances can neither be measured properly nor compared with the performances of other periods or other similar firms systematically.

19.2 CALCULATION OF PROFIT

The profit of a particular accounting year can be computed by any of the two methods:

1. Net worth method
2. Alternative method for ascertainment of profit or loss
3. Conversion method.

19.2.1 Net Worth Method

We know that all business transactions are recorded as per the desire of the proprietors without following the accepted accounting rules or principles. As a result, it is not possible to prepare Trading and Profit and Loss Accounts to know the Gross Profits or the Net Profits of the businesses without having sufficient data. Thus, net results of the businesses are calculated without preparing Trading and Profit and Loss Accounts. According to the **Net Worth Method**, profit of a business or a firm is calculated with the help of the net worth (or capital) of two periods—opening and closing capital of the business. The basic concept of this method is that if the inflow is greater than the outflow, it indicates profit. Suppose, Rs. 100 is invested in a business, and at the end of the year, the said amount increases to Rs. 180. Here, the increase in amount of Rs. 80 is to be considered as a surplus or profit.

Considering the above stated principle, the following steps should be followed for calculating the profit or loss of a business:

1. At first, two statements of affairs are to be prepared for calculating the opening and closing capital (or net worth) of a firm (if not given). A statement of affairs is prepared with the help of assets and liabilities similar to the balance sheet. The balancing figure of this statement (liability side) is known as **capital** or **net worth** or **excess of assets over liabilities**. A statement of affairs is to be prepared as under:

Statement of Affairs as on ...

Liabilities	Amount (Rs.)	Assets	Amount (Rs.)
Capital (Being the excess of assets over liabilities) Loan (from Bank or others) Creditors Bills Payable Outstanding Expenses Income Received in Advance		Land and Buildings Plant and Machineries Furniture and Fittings Investments Stock-in-trade Debtors Bills Receivable Accrued Incomes Prepaid Expenses Cash at Bank Cash in Hand	

2. Then, a statement of profit and loss is to be prepared as follows for calculating the net profit or loss of the firm:

Statement of Profit and Loss
for the year ended ...

	Rs.	Rs.
Closing capital (as per the statement of affairs)		XXXXX
Add: Drawings:		
(Here drawing means cash withdrawn from the business by the proprietor for personal purpose, or any personal expenses paid from business cash and goods used for personal or household purpose)		XXXX
		XXXXX
Less: Additional capital or fresh capital introduced during the year *		XXXXX
		XXXXX
Less: **Opening capital:**		XXXX
Trading profit/profit before adjustment		XXXXX
Less: **Adjustments:**		
Depreciation on fixed assets		
Provision for doubtful debts		
Interest on loan		
Interest on capital (In case of sole proprietorship)		XXXXX
Net profit (net loss for negative balance)		XXXXX

*Here, additional capital or fresh capital means personal cash or any kind of assets introduced or brought in by the proprietor or used within the business during the year. Suppose that personal land of the proprietor was sold and the sale proceeds was introduced by the proprietor or personal NSC was cashed and the amount was brought into the business.

3. After preparing the statement of profit and loss, the final or revised statement of affairs is prepared with the help of closing assets and liabilities such as balance sheet. A final or revised statement of affairs is to be prepared as under:

Final or Revised Statement of Affairs as on ... (Closing date)...

Liabilities	Amount (Rs.)		Assets	Amount (Rs.)
Capital (opening)	XXXX		Land and Buildings *	
Add: Net profit	XXXX		Plant and Machineries *	
	XXXX		Furniture and Fittings *	
Less: Drawings	XXXX	XXXX	Investments	
Loan (from Bank or others)			Stock-in-trade	
Creditors			Debtors	
Bills Payable			Bills Receivable	
Outstanding Expenses			Accrued Incomes	
Income Received in Advance			Prepaid Expenses	
			Cash at bank	
			Cash in hand	

*(After charging depreciation for the period/year)

Differences between Balance Sheet and Statement of Affairs is given in Table 19.2.

TABLE 19.2 Differences between Balance Sheet and Statement of Affairs

Balance Sheet	Statement of Affairs
It is prepared with the help of Ledger Account balance of assets and liabilities (or real and personal accounts).	It is prepared with the help of some account balances as well as relevant information from the list of vouchers and other documents.
It is the true and fair view of the state of affairs of a firm.	A Statement of Affairs represents a list of assets and liabilities only.
Balance Sheet is not prepared to ascertain the capital of the firm.	It is prepared to ascertain the capital or the net worth of the business.
With the help of Balance Sheet, business performance can be measured properly and can be compared with other firms.	It cannot be done through the Statement of Affairs, because the facts and figures supplied by the Statement of Affairs cannot be relied upon.

Table 19.3 shows the differences between Profit and Loss Account and Statement of Profit and Loss.

TABLE 19.3 Differences between Profit and Loss Account and Statement of Profit and Loss

Profit and Loss Account	Statement of Profit and Loss
Accrual concept is followed for preparing the Profit and Loss Account.	Here, Net Worth Method is followed for preparing the statement of profit and loss.
According to the accrual concept, all actual incomes and expenditures (i.e., received or not and paid or not) of the financial year are to be taken into consideration in this account.	According to the Net Worth Method, profit of the business or the firm is to be calculated with the help of the net worth (or capital) of two periods, i.e., opening and closing capital of the business.
Here, incomes and expenditures are divided into two parts—direct and indirect. Matching principle is then applied for calculating the true revenue of the firm.	Matching principle is net followed for calculating the result of the business. The basic concept of the statement of Profit and Loss is that if the inflow is greater than the outs flow, it indicates profit.
It helps to ascertain the gross profit and the net profit of the firm.	Only net profit is calculated here.
Profit and Loss Account helps to ascertain the business income and the income earned from other sources.	No such allocation is possible here.
Business performances can be measured properly and systematically.	Business performance cannot be measured properly in the statement of Profit and Loss.
As the accounting principles and conventions are followed consistently, Profit and Loss Account helps its users in taking important decisions in case of critical situations and also in deciding future course of action.	As the facts and figures supplied cannot be relied upon, proper planning for the future cannot be made by its users.

ILLUSTRATION 19.1 Mr. J.J. Arora maintained his books under Single Entry System. He started his business with a capital of Rs. 96,000 in cash on January 1, 2007, and his capital (excess of assets over liabilities) was Rs. 142,000 on December 31, 2007 before considering the following points:

1. He withdrew Rs. 2,000 from the business for his personal use at the end of each quarter.
2. His house rent and electricity charges amounting to Rs. 450 p.m. were paid from the business cash.
3. He brought some household furniture costing Rs. 3,000 which was used in the business.
4. Goods costing Rs. 1,700 were used by him for personal purpose.
5. He cashed his NSC amounting to Rs.7,500 and brought that money into the business.
6. He gave a loan of Rs. 5,000 to his brother from the business cash.
7. Depreciation to be charged on fixed assets Rs. 4,200, and a Provision for Doubtful Debts is to be created on debtors Rs. 1,100.

Prepare a statement of profit and loss for the year ended on December 31, 2007.

Solution

In the books of Mr. J.J. Arora
Statement of Profit and Loss
for the year ended December 31, 2007

	Rs.	Rs.
Closing capital as on December 31, 2007		142,000
Add: Drawings:		
Cash withdrawn Rs. 2,000 at the end of per quarter (2,000 × 4)	8,000	
House rent and electricity charges Rs. 450 p.m. (450 × 12)	5,400	
Goods used for personal purposes.	1,700	
Loan to brother from the business cash	5,000	20,100
		162,100
Less: Fresh capital:		
NSC cashed and the amount brought into business	7,500	
Household furniture used in the business	3,000	10,500
		151,600
Less: Opening capital		96,000
Trading Profit/Profit before adjustments		55,600
Less: Adjustments:		
Depreciation on Fixed Assets	4,200	
Provision for doubtful debts	1,100	5,300
Net Profit		50,300

ILLUSTRATION 19.2 Mr. Sanjay Yadav does not maintain a complete double entry system. He started his business with cash of Rs. 165,000. He submits the following particulars of his business as on December 31, 2007:

	Rs.
Machinery	65,000
Furniture	22,000
Debtors	21,800
Creditors	16,400
Closing Stock	30,700
Prepaid Expenses	1,600
Outstanding Expenses	800
Cash in hand	23,700
Cash at Bank	21,000
Investments	20,000

The following adjustments are to be made:

1. Mr. Yadav cashed his NSC amounting to Rs. 10, 000 and brought the money into business on May 1, 2007.
2. He withdrew Rs. 8,000 from his business cash for his personal expenses.
3. Depreciate Machinery and Furniture @ 10% p.a.
4. His house rent and school fees of his son amounting to Rs. 2,400 p.m. were paid from the business cash.
5. Make provision on doubtful debts @ 5% on debtors.

From the above information, ascertain his profit or loss for the year ended December 31, 2007, and prepare his statement of affairs as on that date.

Solution

In the books of Mr. Sanjay Yadav
Statement of Affairs as December 31, 2007

Liabilities	Amount (Rs.)	Assets	Amount (Rs.)
Capital (Being the excess of assets over liabilities)	188,600	Machinery	65,000
		Furniture	22,000
Creditors	16,400	Debtors	21,800
Outstanding expenses	800	Investments	20,000
		Closing stock	30,700
		Prepaid expenses	1,600
		Cash at Bank	21,000
		Cash in hand	23,700
	205,800		205,800

Statement of Profit and Loss
for the year ended December 31, 2007

	Rs.	Rs.
Capital as per statement of affairs on December 31, 2007		188,600
Add: Drawings:		
Cash withdrawn for personal use	8,000	
House rent and school fees Rs.2,400 p.m. paid out of business cash	28,800	36,800
		225,400
Less: Fresh capital (NSC cashed and the amount brought into the business)		10,000
		215,400
Less: Opening capital		165,000
Trading Profit / Profit Before Adjustments		50,400
Less: Adjustments:		
Depreciation on Machinery	3,250	
Depreciation on Furniture	1,100	
Provision for Doubtful Debts	1,090	5,440
Net Profit		44,960

Final or Revised Statement of Affairs as December 31, 2007

Liabilities	(Rs.)	(Rs.)	Assets	(Rs.)	(Rs.)
Capital:	165,000		Machinery	65,000	
Add: Fresh capital	10,000		*Less:* Depreciation	3,250	61,750
Add: Net Profit	44,960		Furniture	22,000	
	219,960		*Less:* Depreciation	1,100	20,900
Less: Drawings	36,800	183,160	Investment		20,000
Creditors		16,400	Debtors	21,800	
Outstanding Expenses		800	*Less:* Provision for Doubtful		
			Debts	1,090	20,710
			Closing Stock		30,700
			Prepaid Expenses		1,600
			Cash at bank		21,000
			Cash in hand		23,700
		200,360			200,360

Working Note

Calculation of depreciation on Machinery and Furniture:

As the date of purchase of the above assets is not given, depreciation is to be charged on average basis, i.e. for six months.

Depreciation on Machinery: 10% on Rs. 65, 000 for ½ year = Rs. 3,250.

Depreciation on Furniture: 10% on Rs. 22, 000 for ½ year = Rs. 1,100.

ILLUSTRATION 19.3 Mr. Dhillon keeps his books under single entry system. His financial position on January 1, and December 31, 2007 were given below:

	January 1, 2007 (Rs.)	December 31, 2007 (Rs.)
Cash in hand	12,800	31,400
Cash at bank	26,000	19,500
Prepaid expenses	900	1,200
Debtors	43,800	56,300
Creditors	16,300	19,700
Investments	30,000	30,000
Outstanding expenses	500	800
Closing Stock	15,900	23,100
Land and Buildings	125,000	105,000
Machinery	55,000	75,000
Furniture	24,000	34,000

Additional information

1. Machinery and furniture are to be depreciated @ 10% p.a.
2. Cash withdrawn by Mr. Dhillon Rs. 900 p.m. from the business cash regularly.
3. Make provision for doubtful debts @ 5% on debtors.
4. Proprietor's house rent Rs. 1,000 p.m. was paid from the business cash regularly.
5. Accrued interest on investment Rs. 700.
6. He sold his personal jewellery and brought that money in the business Rs. 18,000.

Prepare a statement of profit and loss for the period ended December 31, 2007, and draw a statement of affairs as on that date.

Solution

In the Books of Mr. Dhillon
Statement of Affairs as on

Liabilities	2007, Jan. 1 (Rs.)	2007, Dec. 31 (Rs.)	Assets	2007, Jan. 1 (Rs.)	2007, Dec. 31 (Rs.)
Capital (Being the excess of assets over liabilities)	316,600	355,700	Land and Buildings	125,000	105,000
			Machinery	55,000	75,000
Creditors	16,300	19,700	Furniture	24,000	34,000
Outstanding expenses	500	800	Investments	30,000	30,000
			Debtors	43,800	56,300
			Prepaid expenses	900	1,200
			Accrued interest on investment	—	700
			Closing Stock	15,900	23,100
			Cash at bank	26,000	19,500
			Cash in hand	12,800	31,400
	333,400	376,200		333,400	376,200

Statement of Profit and Loss
for the year ended on December 31, 2007

	Rs.	Rs.
Capital as per statement of affairs on December 31, 2007		355,700
Add: Drawings:		
Cash withdrawn for personal use (900 × 12)	10,800	
House rent Rs. 1,000 p.m. paid out of business cash	12,000	22,800
		378,500
Less: Fresh capital (Personal jewellery sold and the amount brought in the business)		18,000
		360,500
Less: Opening capital		316,600
Trading Profit/Profit before adjustments		43,900
Less: Adjustments		
Depreciation on Machinery	6,500	
Depreciation on Furniture	2,900	
Provision for Doubtful Debts (5% of 56,300)	2,815	12,215
Net profit		31,685

Final or Revised Statement of Affairs as on December 31, 2007

Liabilities	Rs.	Rs.	Assets	Rs.	Rs.
Capital :	316,600		Land and Buildings	125,000	
Add: Fresh Capital	18,000		*Less:* Depreciation	20,000	105,000
Add: Net Profit	31,685		Machinery	75,000	
	366,285		*Less:* Depreciation	6,500	68,500
Less: Drawings	22,800	343,485	Furniture	34,000	
Creditors		19,700	*Less:* Depreciation	2,900	31,100
Outstanding expenses		800	Investment		30,000
			Debtors	56,300	
			Less: Provision for Doubtful Debts	2,815	53,485
			Closing Stock		23,100
			Prepaid expenses		1,200
			Accrued interest on investment		700
			Cash at bank		19,500
			Cash in-hand		31,400
		363,985			363,985

Working Note

Calculation of depreciation on Machinery and Furniture:

(When the date of purchase of the fixed assets is not given, depreciation is to be charged on average basis, i.e., for six months)

Depreciation on Machinery: 10% on Rs. 55,000 for full year   Rs. 5,500

10% on Rs. 20,000 for ½ year   Rs. 1,000   6,500.

Depreciation on Furniture: 10% on Rs. 24,000 for full year   Rs. 2,400

10% on Rs. 10,000 for ½ year   Rs. 500   2,900.

ILLUSTRATION 19.4 Mr. J. Karuna Nidhi does not maintain a complete double entry system. He started his business with cash of Rs. 44,000, furniture Rs. 32,000, stock Rs.18,000, and machinery Rs. 60,000 on January 1, 2007. His position on December 31, 2007 was as under:

(a) Stock in trade Rs. 27,000 (b) Cash in hand Rs. 22,600 (c) Debtors Rs. 42,000 (d) Creditors Rs. 23,000 (e) Loan from H.P. Dua Rs.14,000 (f) Computer Rs. 25,000 (g) Stationery Stock Rs. 1,400.

Additional information

1. Machinery of Rs. 26,000 and furniture of Rs. 18,000 (excluding household furniture) were purchased during the year on April 1, 2007 and on July 31, 2007, respectively. Depreciation @ 10% p.a. is to be charged on the above assets.
2. A bank loan of Rs. 28,000 was taken on April 1, 2007, for purchasing various fixed assets. Interest charged by the bank for the said loan amounting to Rs. 980 not yet paid.
3. Out of the debtors, Rs. 1,600 is to be written off as bad debt and provision for bad debt is to be created @ 5% on debtors.
4. Cash withdrawn from the business for personal use Rs. 20,000.
5. Household furniture was purchased for Rs. 4,000 but payment was made through business cash.
6. LIP of the proprietor matured and the amount was brought into business Rs. 25,000.

Prepare a statement of Profit and Loss for the period ending December 31, 2007, and a statement of affairs as on that date.

Solution

In the Books of Mr. J. Karuna Nidhi
Statement of Affairs as on December 31, 2007

Liabilities	(Rs.)	Assets	(Rs.)
Capital (Being the excess of assets over liabilities)	189,000	Machinery (Rs. 60,000 + Rs. 26,000)	86,000
		Furniture (Rs. 32,000 + Rs. 18,000)	50,000
Creditors	23,000	Debtors	42,000
Loan from H.P. Dua	14,000	Computer	25,000
Bank loan	28,000	Closing Stock	27,000
		Stationery stock	1,400
		Cash in hand	22,600
	254,000		254,000

Statement of Profit and Loss
for the year ended December 31, 2007

	Rs.	Rs.
Capital as per statement of affairs on December 31, 2007		189,000
Add: Drawings:		
Household furniture purchased	4,000	
Cash withdrawn for personal use	20,000	24,000
		213,000
Less: Fresh capital (LIP matured and brought that amount into the business)		25,000
		188,000
Less: Opening capital: (Cash of Rs. 44,000, Furniture Rs. 24,000, Stock Rs. 18,000, and Machinery Rs. 60,000 = Rs. 146,000)		146,000
Trading Profit/Profit before adjustments		42,000
Less: **Adjustments:**		
Interest on loan	980	
Bad debts	1,600	
Provision for bad debt @ 5% of Rs. 40,400 (42,000 – 1,600)	2,020	
Depreciation on Machinery	7,950	
Depreciation on Furniture	3,950	16,500
Net Profit		25,500

Final or Revised Statement of Affairs as on December 31, 2007

Liabilities	Rs.	Rs.	Assets	Rs.	Rs.
Capital	146,000		Machinery	86,000	
Add: Fresh capital	25,000		Less: Depreciation	7,950	78,050
Add: Net Profit	25,500		Furniture	50,000	
	196,500		Less: Depreciation	3,950	46,050
Less: Drawings	24,000	172,500	Computer		25,000
Loan from H.P. Dua		14,000	Debtors	42,000	
Bank loan		28,000	Less: Bad debts	1,600	
Creditors		23,000		40,400	
Outstanding expenses:			Less: Provision for Doubtful Debts	2,020	38,380
Interest on loan		980	Closing stock		27,000
			Stationery Stock		1,400
			Cash in hand		22,600
		238,480			238,480

Working Note

Calculation of depreciation on Machinery and Furniture:

Depreciation on Machinery:	10% on Rs. 60,000 for full year	Rs. 6,000	
	10% on Rs. 26,000 for nine months	Rs. 1,950	7,950.
Depreciation on Furniture:	10% on Rs. 32,000 for full year	Rs. 3,200	
	10% on Rs. 18,000 for five months	Rs. 750	3,950.

ILLUSTRATION 19.5 Mr. R.K. Jalan started his business with cash of Rs. 90,000 on April 1, 2007. He keeps his books on single entry system. The following data are available from his cash book for the year ended March 31, 2008:

	Rs.
Purchase of Furniture (on May 1, 2007)	21,000
Purchase of Machinery (on June 30, 2007)	65,000
Cash sales	36,000
Cash purchases	19,600
Received from customers	42,000
Paid to suppliers	37,800
Sundry expenses	11,200
Drawings	17,000
Sale of personal Land	39,000
Cashed personal NSC	10,000
Deposit in UBI fixed deposit account	25,000
Received interest from UBI fixed deposit account	2,400
His position on March 31, 2008 was as under:	
Debtors	34,900
Creditors	12,400
Closing stock	11,700
Outstanding expenses	3,000
Prepaid expenses	1,400
Computer (Purchased on September 1, 2007 from M/s Bright Computers)	27,000

The following adjustments are to be made:

1. All fixed assets are to be depreciated @ 10% p.a.
2. Provision for Bad Debt is to be created @ 5% on debtors.

From the above information, ascertain his profit or loss for the year ended March 31, 2008 and prepare his statement of affairs as on that date.

Solution

As the closing cash in hand has not been given, a cash account is to be opened for calculating the closing cash balance.

In the books of Mr. R.K. Jalan

Dr.		Cash Account/Cash Book	Cr.
Receipts	Rs.	Payments	Rs.
To Opening Balance	90,000	By Purchases	19,600
(Capital introduced)		By Furniture	21,000
Or		By Machinery	65,000
(To Capital A/c)		By Creditors (Paid to suppliers)	37,800
To Sales	36,000	By Sundry expenses	11,200
To Debtors (Received from customers)	42,000	By Drawings	17,000
To Capital (Sale of personal Land)	39,000	By Investment (UBI fixed deposit account)	25,000
To Capital (Cashed personal NSC)	10,000	By Balance c/d	22,800
To Interest (Received from bank)	2,400		
	219,400		219,400

Statement of Affairs as on March 31, 2008

Liabilities	Rs.	Assets	Rs.
Capital	166,400	Machinery	65,000
(Being the excess of assets overliabilities)		Furniture	21,000
Creditors	12,400	Computer	27,000
Outstanding expenses	3,000	Debtors	34,900
M/s Bright Computers	27,000	Investments	25,000
		Closing Stock	11,700
		Prepaid expenses	1,400
		Cash in hand	22,800
	208,800		208,800

Statement of Profit and Loss
for the year ended on March 31, 2008

	Rs.	Rs.
Capital as per statement of affairs at March 31, 2008		166,400
Add: Drawings		17,000
		183,400
Less: **Fresh Capital:**		
Sale of personal Land	39,000	
Cashed personal NSC	10,000	49,000
		134,400
Less: Opening Capital		90,000
Trading Profit / Profit Before Adjustments		44,400
Less: **Adjustments:**		
Depreciation on Machinery (30.6.07 to 31.3.08, i.e., for nine months)	4,875	
Depreciation on Furniture (1.05.07 to 31.3.08, i.e., for eleven months)	1,925	
Depreciation on Computer (1.09.07 to 31.3.08, i.e., for seven months)	1,575	
Provision for Doubtful Debts (5% of Rs. 34,900)	1,745	10,120
Net Profit		34,280

Final or Revised Statement of Affairs as on March 31, 2008

Liabilities	Rs.	Rs.	Assets	Rs.	Rs.
Capital:	90,000		Machinery	65,000	
Add: Fresh Capital	49,000		Less: Depreciation	4,875	60,125
Add: Net Profit	34,280		Furniture	21,000	
	173,280		Less: Depreciation	1,925	19,075
Less: Drawings	17,000	156,280	Computer	27,000	
Creditors		12,400	Less: Depreciation	1,575	25,425
Outstanding expenses		3,000	Investment		25,000
M/s Bright Computers		27,000	Debtors	34,900	
			Less: Provision for Bad Debts	1,745	33,155
			Closing Stock		11,700
			Prepaid expenses		1,400
			Cash in hand		22,800
		198,680			198,680

ILLUSTRATION 19.6 Mr. Patel, a trader, keeps his books by the single entry system. His financial position on April 1, 2007 was as under:

Statement of Affairs as on April 1, 2007

Liabilities	Rs.		Assets		Rs.
Capital	163,000		Machinery		60,000
Loan	40,000		Furniture		24,000
Creditors	23,700		Debtors		42,000
Outstanding expenses	2,300		12% Investments		30,000
			Closing stock		12,000
			Prepaid expenses		2,000
			Cash in hand and cash at bank		59,000
	229,000				229,000

His position on March 31, 2008 was as under:

	Rs.
Machinery	80,000
Furniture	32,000
Debtors	45,200
Creditors	27,300
Closing stock	16,900
Prepaid expenses	1,900
Cash in hand and cash at bank	43,700

Additional information

1. Accrued interest on investment for five months.
2. Personal shares of Rs. 10,000 sold at Rs.18,500 was introduced into the business on August 10, 2007.
3. During the year, 50% loan was repaid. Interest on loan is payable Rs.1,900.
4. Mr. Patel's son took a calculator costing Rs. 2,400 from the business showroom for his personal use.
5. Shop rent @ Rs. 2,100 p.m. has not been paid for the last two months.
6. Mr. Patel had withdrawn Rs. 1,500 p.m. at the beginning of every month during the year.
7. Depreciate Machinery and Furniture by 10%.

You are required to ascertain Profit or Loss for the period ended March 31, 2008 and a statement of affairs as on that data of Mr. Patel.

Solution

In the Books of Mr. Patel
Statement of Affairs as on March 31, 2008

Liabilities	Rs.	Assets	Rs.
Capital	197,800	Machinery	80,000
(Being the excess of assets over liabilities)		Furniture	32,000
Creditors	27,300	Debtors	45,200
Outstanding expenses:		12% investments	30,000
Shop rent	4,200	Closing stock	16,900
Interest on loan	1,900	Prepaid expenses	1,900
Loan (50% loan repaid)	20,000	Accrued interest on investment	1,500
		Cash in hand and cash at bank	43,700
	251,200		251,200

Statement of Profit and Loss
for the year ended on March 31, 2008

	Rs.	Rs.
Capital as per statement of affairs as March 31, 2008		197,800
Add: Drawings:		
Cash withdrawn Rs.1,500 p.m. (1,500 × 12)	18,000	
Calculator taken over by his son for personal use	2,400	20,400
		218,200
Less: Fresh Capital:		
Personal shares of Rs. 10,000 sold at Rs.18,500		18,500
		199,700
Less: Opening capital		163,000
Trading Profit/Profit before adjustments		36,700
Less: Adjustments:		
Depreciation on Machinery 10% of Rs. 80,000	8,000	
Depreciation on Furniture 10% of Rs. 32,000	3,200	11,200
Net Profit		25,500

Final or Revised Statement of Affairs as on March 31, 2008

Liabilities	Rs.	Rs.	Assets	Rs.	Rs.
Capital:	163,000		Machinery	80,000	
Add: Fresh Capital	18,500		*Less:* Depreciation	8,000	72,000
Add: Net Profit	25,500		Furniture	32,000	
	207,000		*Less:* Depreciation	3,200	28,800
Less: Drawings	20,400	186,600	12% Investment		30,000
Creditors		27,300	Debtors		45,200
Outstanding expenses:			Closing stock		16,900
Shop rent	4,200		Prepaid expenses		1,900
Interest on loan	1,900	6,100	Accrued interest on investment		1,500
Loan (50% loan repaid)		20,000	Cash-in-hand and cash at bank		43,700
		240,000			240,000

Working Note

Calculation of depreciation on Machinery and Furniture:
Here depreciation has been calculated for full years since 'by 10%' is given. Thus, no time factor has been considered. Time factors are to be considered under the following situations:

1. 'by ... % p.a.' is given, or
2. 'at ... % ' is given, or
3. 'at ... % p.a.' is given.

ILLUSTRATION 19.7 Mr. H. Hemant Rao does not maintain a complete double entry system. He started his business with cash of Rs.140,000 on April 1, 2007. He submits the following particulars of his business as on March 31, 2008:

	Rs.
Machinery	80,000
Furniture (Excluding the household furniture)	26,000
Debtors	39,000
Creditors	21,800
Closing stock	22,700
Cash in hand and cash at bank	32,600
10% loan	18,000
12% investments	30,000

The following adjustments are to be made:

1. Mr. Rao withdrew Rs. 300 per week regularly from his business cash and also withdrew goods of worth Rs. 2,900 for his personal use.
2. He transferred some of his household furniture to the business at an agreed valuation of Rs. 4,000.
3. Allow interest on capital @ 8% p.a. on its opening balance.
4. Insurance paid for 12 months amounting to Rs.1,800, commencing from August 1, 2007.
5. Stock on March 31, 2008 was overvalued by Rs. 1,860.
6. Interest on loan outstanding for last four months.
7. Interest on investments due but not received for the last quarter year.
8. Depreciate all fixed assets by 10%.

From the above information, you are required to ascertain his Profit or Loss for the year ended March, 31, 2008 and prepare his statement of affairs as on that data.

Solution

In the Books of Mr. H. Hemant Rao
Statement of Affairs as on March 31, 2008

Liabilities	Rs.	Assets	Rs.
Capital (Being the excess of assets over liabilities)	193,540	Machinery	80,000
		Furniture (Rs. 26,000 + Rs. 4,000)	30,000
Creditors	21,800	Debtors	39,000
Outstanding expenses:		12 % investments	30,000
Interest on loan	600	Closing stock (Rs. 22,700 – Rs. 1,860)	20,840
10% Loan	18,000	Prepaid insurance (For 4 months)	600
		Accrued interest on investment	900
		[(30,000 × 12/100 × 3/12),i.e., for three months]	
		Cash in hand and cash at bank	32,600
	233,940		233,940

Statement of Profit and Loss
for the year ended March 31, 2008

	Rs.	Rs.
Capital as per statement of affairs as on March 31, 2008		193,540
Add: Drawings:		
Cash withdrawn Rs. 300 per week (300 × 52)	15,600	
Goods worth Rs. 2,900 taken for his personal use	2,900	18,500
		212,040
Less: Fresh capital:		
Transferred some of his household furniture to the business		4,000
		208,040
Less: Opening capital		140,000
Trading Profit / Profit before adjustments		68,040
Less: Adjustments:		
Depreciation on Machinery 10% of Rs. 80,000	8,000	
Depreciation on Furniture 10% of Rs. 30,000	3,000	
Interest on capital (8% of Rs.140,000)	11,200	22,200
Net Profit		45,840

Final or Revised Statement of Affairs as on March 31, 2008

Liabilities	Rs.	Rs.	Assets	Rs.	Rs.
Capital:	140,000		Machinery	80,000	
Add: Fresh capital	4,000		Less: Depreciation	8,000	72,000
Add: Net Profit	45,840		Furniture	30,000	
Add: Interest on capital	11,200		Less: Depreciation	3,000	27,000
	201,040		12% Investment		30,000
Less: Drawings	18,500	182,540	Debtors		39,000
Creditors		21,800	Closing stock		20,840
Outstanding expenses:			Prepaid insurance		600
Interest on loan		600	Accrued interest on investment		900
10% Loan		18,000	Cash in hand and cash at bank		32,600
		222,940			222,940

Working Note

Calculation of depreciation on Machinery and Furniture:

Here depreciation has been calculated for full years since 'by 10%' is given. Thus, no time factor has been considered.

ILLUSTRATION 19.8 Mr. M. Madhavan after retirement from service started a business of fancy goods with capital of Rs.115,000 out of his gratuity receipts on April 1, 2007. He keeps his books under single entry system. He submits the following particulars of his business as on December 31, 2007:

	Rs.
Furniture	18,000
Machinery	24,000
10% Investments	21,000
Debtors	34,000
Creditors	19,000
Closing stock	20,600
Cash in hand	11,700
Balance as per pass book	20,400

The following adjustments are to be made:
1. An advance of Rs. 700 paid to an employee against his salary at January 2008 has now been identified.
2. Investment was made on May 1, 2007 and interest not yet received.
3. Business travelling included the proprietor's personal travelling for which he is to be charged Rs. 1,750.
4. Stationery of Rs. 1,480 was consumed by the family members of the proprietor.
5. Cheques amounting to Rs. 1,900 drawn in favour of suppliers, but not yet presented for payment.
6. An amount of Rs. 28,000 was withdrawn by Mr. Madhavan from the business for his personal use, but out of the said fund he purchased a computer at Rs.15,000 for his business use.
7. Depreciate Machinery and Furniture by Rs. 2,500 and Rs. 1,400, respectively.
8. Out of the debtors, Rs. 900 is to be written off as bad debt, and Provision for Bad Debt is to be created @ 5% on debtors.

Show the statement of Profit and Loss for the year ending December 31, 2007 and the final statement of affairs as on that date.

Solution

In the Books of Mr. M. Madhavan
Statement of Affairs as on December 31, 2007

Liabilities	Rs.	Assets	Rs.
Capital (Being the excess of assets over liabilities)	145,000	Machinery	24,000
Creditors	19,000	Furniture	18,000
		Computer	15,000
		10% Investments	21,000
		Debtors (Rs. 34,000 – Rs. 900)	33,100
		Closing stock	20,600
		Accrued interest on investment	1,400
		Prepaid Salaries	700
		Cash at bank (Rs. 20,400 – Rs. 1,900)	18,500
		Cash in hand	11,700
	164,000		164,000

Statement of Profit and Loss
for the year ended December 31, 2007

	Rs.	Rs.
Capital as per statement of affairs as at December 31, 2007		145,000
Add: Drawings:		
Cash withdrawn Rs. 28,000		
Less: Computer purchase for business Rs.15,000	13,000	
Proprietor's personal travelling	1,750	
Stationery consumed by the family members of the proprietor	1,480	16,230
		161,230
Less: Opening capital		115,000
Trading Profit/Profit before adjustments		46,230
Less: Adjustments:		
Depreciation on Machinery	2,500	
Depreciation on Furniture	1,400	
Provision for Bad Debt @ 5% on Debtors	1,655	5,555
Net Profit		40,675

Final or Revised Statement of Affairs as on December 31, 2007

Liabilities	Rs.	Rs.	Assets	Rs.	Rs.
Capital:	115,000		Machinery	24,000	
Add: Net Profit	40,675		*Less:* Depreciation	2,500	21,500
	155,675		Furniture	18,000	
Less: Drawings	16,230	139,445	*Less:* Depreciation	1,400	16,600
Creditors		19,000	Computer		15,000
			10% Investment		21,000
			Debtors	33,100	
			Less: Provision for Bad Debt	1,655	31,445
			Closing stock		20,600
			Accrued interest on investment		1,400
			Prepaid Salaries		700
			Cash at bank		18,500
			Cash in hand		11,700
		158,445			158,445

Working Notes

1. Interest on investment is due but not received for eight months (May to December). Amount receivable = $21,000 \times 10/100 \times 8/12$ = Rs. 1,400.
2. Balance as per passbook is given, and as such, bank balance as per cash book has been calculated by adjusting the unpresented cheques amounting to Rs.1,900 as under:

Balance as per pass book	Rs. 20,400
Less: Unpresented cheques	Rs. 1,900
Bank balance as per cash book	Rs. 18,500

ILLUSTRATION 19.9 Mr. Anil Saxena started his business on January 1, 2007 with a capital of Rs. 72,000. His position on December 31, 2007 was as under:

Debtors Rs. 24,000, Stock in trade Rs. 16,000, Machinery Rs. 30,000, Cash at bank Rs. 18,000, Cash in hand Rs. 6,000 and Creditors Rs. 9,000.

He has submitted the following further information for necessary adjustments:

1. He withdrew cash Rs. 500 p.m. at the end of each month from the business for personal use.
2. His house rent of Rs. 8,000 was paid from business cash.
3. He sold his personal jewellery and the amount brought into business Rs. 5,000 on September 1, 2007.
4. Goods costing Rs. 900 were taken over by him for personal use.
5. Depreciate Machinery by 10%.
6. Interest on capital @ 10% p.a.
7. Provision for Doubtful Debts @ 5% on debtors.

Prepare a statement of Profit and Loss for the period ending December 31, 2007 and a statement of affairs as on that date.

Solution

In the books of Mr. Anil Saxena
Statement of Affairs as on December 31, 2007

Liabilities	Rs.	Assets	Rs.
Capital	85,000	Machinery	30,000
(being the excess of assets over liabilities)		Debtors	24,000
Creditors	9,000	Closing stock	16,000
		Cash at bank	18,000
		Cash in hand	6,000
	94,000		94,000

Statement of Profit and Loss
for the year ended December 31, 2007

	Rs.	Rs.
Capital as per statement of affairs at December 31, 2007		85,000
Add: Drawings:		
Cash withdrawn for personal use Rs. 500 p.m. (500 × 12)	6,000	
House Rent	8,000	
Goods taken over	900	14,900
		99,900
Less: Fresh capital (sale of personal jewellery and the amount brought into business)		5,000
		94,900
Less: Opening capital		72,000
Trading Profit/Profit before adjustments		22,900
Less: Adjustments:		
Interest on capital	7,367	
Provision for bad debt @ 5% of Rs. 24,000	1,200	
Depreciation on Machinery	3,000	11,567
Net Profit		11,333

Final or Revised Statement of Affairs as on December 31, 2007

Liabilities	Rs.	Rs.	Assets	Rs.	Rs.
Capital	72,000		Machinery	30,000	
Add: Fresh Capital	5,000		*Less:* Depreciation	3,000	27,000
Add: Net Profit	11,333		Closing stock		16,000
Add: Interest on capital	7,367		Debtors	24,000	
	95,700		*Less:* Provision for		
Less: Drawings	14,900	80,800	doubtful debts	1,200	22,800
Creditors		9,000	Cash at bank		18,000
			Cash in hand		6,000
		89,800			89,800

Working Notes

1. Calculation of depreciation on Machinery:
   Depreciation on Machinery is to be charged for full year since 'by 10%' is given.
2. Calculation of interest on capital: Rs.
   On Rs. 72,000 for full year @ 10% 7,200
   On Rs. 5,000 for four months @ 10% 167
     7,367

Single entry system applied to partnership firm

After calculating the net profit of a partnership firm through the statement of Profit and Loss, it is essential to distribute the said profit according to the partnership agreement between/among the partners. Generally, appropriations are given in the form of partners' salaries, commission, bonus, distributable profits or losses, etc. However, the adjustment of interest on drawings (if any) are to be made after calculating the net profit. When there is no written agreement, there cannot be any kind of adjustment or distribution of appropriations, only the net profit will be distributed between/among the partners equally. Under such circumstances, the Partnership Act and its provisions must be followed.

Calculation of interest on drawings under different situations

1. When date of drawings are given
2. When date of drawings are not given

3. When cash is withdrawn at the end of each month
4. When cash is withdrawn at the beginning of each month
5. When cash is withdrawn at the middle of each month
6. When cash is withdrawn at the end of each quarter year
7. When cash is withdrawn at the beginning of each quarter year

1. When date of drawings are given: Interest is to be charged on actual basis.

2. When date of drawings are not given: The interest on drawings is to be calculated **on average basis**, i.e. for 6 months.

3. When cash is withdrawn at the end of each month: Interest is to be charged for **5.5 months**

4. When cash is withdrawn at the beginning of each month: Interest is to be charged for **6.5 months**

5. When cash is withdrawn at the middle of each month: Interest is to be charged for **6 months**.

ILLUSTRATION 19.10   Mukesh and Sunil are equal partners in a firm in which books are kept under single entry system. Their position on January 1, 2007 and December 31, 2007 was as under :

	January 1, 2007 (Rs.)	December 31, 2007 (Rs.)
Machinery	40,000	60,000
10% Investment	18,000	18,000
Debtors	20,000	24,000
Bills Receivable	3,000	2,000
Bills Payable	4,000	4,500
Stock-in-trade	6,000	8,500
Cash in hand	16,000	22,500
Creditors	7,000	9,000

The following adjustments are to be considered:

1. Mukesh took a loan of Rs. 15,000 from UBI at 12% p.a. on which interest of half year is outstanding.
2. Mukesh had withdrawn Rs. 500 p.m. at the beginning of every month during the year, and Sunil drew Rs. 1,500 at the end of each quarter during the year.
3. Interest @ 5% on capital would be given on their initial capitals (they contributed equally) and interest @ 6% p.a. on drawings would be charged.
4. Depreciate machinery @ 10% p.a.
5. Accrued interest on investment for three months.

Show the statement of Profit and Loss for the year ended December 31, 2007 and the final statement of affairs as on that date.

Solution

In the Books of Mukesh and Sunil
Statement of Affairs as on December 31, 2007

Liabilities	1.1.07	31.12.07	Assets	1.1.07	31.12.07
Combined Capital	92,000	106,050	Machinery	40,000	60,000
(Balancing figure)			10% Investment	18,000	18,000
Creditors	7,000	9,000	Debtors	20,000	24,000
12% Loan (UBI)		15,000	Stock-in-trade	6,000	8,500
Outstanding interest			Bills Receivable	3,000	2,000
Bills Payable	4,000	4,500	Accrued interest on		
On loan		900	investment		450
			Cash in hand	16,000	22,500
	103,000	135,450		103,000	135,450

Statement of Profit and Loss
for the year ended December 31, 2007

	Rs.	Rs.
Combined capital as at December 31, 2007		106,050
Add: Drawings:		
Mukesh: Rs. 500 p.m.(Rs. 500 × 12)	6,000	
Sunil : Rs. 1,500 per quarter (Rs.1,500 × 4)	6,000	12,000
		118,050
Less: Combined Opening Capital		92,000
Trading Profit / Profit before adjustments		26,050
Less: Adjustments:		
Depreciation on Machinery	5,000	5,000
Net Profit		21,050
Less: Interest on Capital:		
Mukesh 5% on Rs. 46,000	2,300	
Sunil 5% on Rs. 46,000	2,300	4,600
		16,450
Add: Interest on Drawings		
Mukesh		
Sunil	195	
	135	330
Distributable profit		16,780
Mukesh's share of profit (Half of Rs.16,780)	8,390	
Sunil's share of profit (Half of Rs.16,780)	8,390	

Final or Revised Statement of Affairs as on December 31, 2007

Liabilities	Rs.	Rs.	Assets	Rs.	Rs.
Capital			Machinery	60,000	
Mukesh	46,000		Less: Depreciation	5,000	55,000
Add: Interest on Capital	2,300		10% Investment		18,000
Add: Share of Profit	8,390		Debtors		24,000
	56,690		Stock-in-trade		8,500
Less: Drawings	6,000		Bills Receivable		2,000
	50,690		Accrued interest on investment		450
Less: Interest on Drawings	195	50,495	Cash in hand		22,500
Sunil	46,000				
Add: Interest on Capital	2,300				
Add: Share of Profit	8,390				
	56,690				
Less: Drawings	6,000				
	50,690				
Less: Interest on Drawings	135	50,555			
Creditors		9,000			
12% Loan(UBI)		15,000			
Outstanding interest					
On loan		900			
Bills Payable		4,500			
		130,450			130,450

Working Notes

1. Calculation of interest on drawings under 'Product Method':
   Mukesh withdrew Rs. 500 p.m. at the beginning of each month.

	Product	Rs.
Amount withdrawn on January 1	Rs. 500 for 12 months	6,000
Amount withdrawn on February 1	Rs. 500 for 11 months	5,500
Amount withdrawn on March 1	Rs. 500 for 10 months	5,000
Amount withdrawn on April 1	Rs. 500 for 9 months	4,500
Amount withdrawn on May1	Rs. 500 for 8 months	4,000
Amount withdrawn on June 1	Rs. 500 for 7 months	3,500
Amount withdrawn on July 1	Rs. 500 for 6 months	3,000
Amount withdrawn on August 1	Rs. 500 for 5 months	2,500
Amount withdrawn on September 1	Rs. 500 for 4 months	2,000
Amount withdrawn on October 1	Rs. 500 for 3 months	1,500
Amount withdrawn on November 1	Rs. 500 for 2 months	1,000
Amount withdrawn on December 1	Rs. 500 for 1 month	500
	Total product	39,000

Interest @ 6% p.a. on Rs. 39,000 for one month under product method
= $39,000 \times 6/100 \times 1/12$ = Rs. 195.

Sunil withdrew Rs. 1,500 at the end of each quarter (Product method):

Interest on.	Rs.
1st Quarter Rs. 1,500 for 9 months	13,500
2nd Quarter Rs. 1,500 for 6 months	9,000
3rd Quarter Rs. 1,500 for 3 months	4,500
4th Quarter Rs. 1,500 for 0 months	0
	27,000

Interest @ 6% p.a. on Rs. 27,000 for one month under product method = $27,000 \times 6/100 \times 1/12$ = Rs. 135.

2. Calculation of depreciation on Machinery:

	Rs.	
On Rs. 40,000 at 10% for full year	4,000	
On Rs. 20,000 at 10% for half year	1,000	(As the date of purchase is not given)
Total Depreciation	5,000	

ILLUSTRATION 19.11 Mr. Madhav and Mr. Keshav are partners in a firm sharing profits and losses in the ratio of 3 : 2. They keep their books under single entry system. Their statement of affairs as on January 1, 2007 was as under:

Statement of Affairs as on January 1, 2007

Liabilities		Rs.	Assets	Rs.
Capital accounts:			Machinery	46,000
Mr. Madhav	80,000		Motor Car	38,000
Mr. Keshav	60,000	140,000	Debtors	31,000
Current Account: Mr. Madhav		6,000	Closing stock	27,800
Reserve Fund		8,100	Cash in hand	23,700
Creditors		14,900	**Current Account:** Mr. Keshav	2,500
		169,000		169,000

On December 31, 2007, their position was as under:
Debtors Rs. 42,000; Closing stock Rs. 32,000; Cash in hand Rs.36,000; Creditors Rs. 16,000; and Unexpired insurance Rs. 700.

The following adjustments are agreed upon:
1. Depreciate Machinery and Motor Car by 10%.
2. Provision for Bad Debt to be made @ 5% on debtors.

3. Interest on capital @ 5% p.a. and on drawings @ 15% p.a. in excess of Rs. 6,000 and Rs. 5,000 drawn by Mr. Madhav and Mr. Keshav, respectively.
4. Mr. Madhav is entitled to a salary of Rs. 4,000 p.a. and Mr. Keshav is entitled to a commission of Rs. 2,500 p.a.
5. The drawings of Mr. Madhav and Mr. Keshav were Rs.16,000 and Rs. 9,000, respectively.

Prepare a statement of Profit and Loss for the year ending December 31, 2007, and the final statement of affairs as on that date. Also, show the Current Account of the partners.

Solution

In the Books of Mr. Madhav and Mr. Keshav
Statement of Affairs as on December 31, 2007

Liabilities	Rs.	Assets	Rs.
Combined Capital	170,600	Machinery	46,000
(Balancing figure)		Motor Car	38,000
Reserve Fund	8,100	Debtors	42,000
Creditors	16,000	Closing stock	32,000
		Unexpired insurance	700
		Cash in hand	36,000
	194,700		194,700

Statement of Profit and Loss
for the year ended December 31, 2007

	Rs.	Rs.
Combined Capital as per statement of affairs as at December 31, 2007		170,600
Add: Drawings:		
Mr. Madhav	16,000	
Mr. Keshav	9,000	25,000
		195,600
Less: Opening Capital:		
Mr. Madhav	80,000	
Mr. Keshav	60,000	140,000
		55,600
Less: Opening Current Account Balance:		
Mr. Madhav (Credit balance)	6,000	
Mr. Keshav (Debit balance)	(−) 2,500	3,500
Trading Profit/Profit before adjustments		52,100
Less: Adjustments:		
Depreciation on Machinery 10% of Rs. 46,000	4,600	
Depreciation on Motor Car 10% of Rs. 38,000	3,800	
Provision for Bad Debt	2,100	10,500
Net Profit		41,600
Less: Interest on Capital:		
Mr. Madhav	4,000	
Mr. Keshav	3,000	7,000
		34,600
Less: Partners' Salary: Mr. Madhav		4,000
		30,600
Less: Commission: Mr. Keshav		2,500
		28,100
Add: Interest on Drawings:		
Mr. Madhav	750	
Mr. Keshav	300	1,050
Distributable Profit		29,150
Mr. Madhav's share of Profit (3/5th of Rs. 29,150)	17,490	
Mr. Keshav's share of Profit (2/5th of Rs. 29,150)	11,660	

Dr.			Current Account		Cr.
	Madhav (Rs.)	Keshav (Rs.)		Madhav (Rs.)	Keshav (Rs.)
2007 Jan. 1			2007 Jan. 1		
To Balance b/d	—	2,500	By Balance b/d	6,000	—
2007 Dec. 31			2007 Dec. 31		
To Drawings	16,000	9,000	By Interest on Capital	4,000	3,000
To Interest on Drawings	750	300	By Partners' Salary	4,000	—
To Balance c/d	14,740	5,360	By Commission	—	2,500
			By Share of Profit	17,490	11,660
	31,490	17,160		31,490	17,160

Final or Revised Statement of Affairs as on December 31, 2007

Liabilities	Rs.	Rs.	Assets	Rs.	Rs.
Capital Accounts:			Machinery	46,000	
Mr. Madhav	80,000		Less: Depreciation	4,600	41,400
Mr. Keshav	60,000	140,000	Motor car	38,000	
Current Accounts:			Less: Depreciation	3,800	34,200
Mr. Madhav	14,740		Debtors	42,000	
Mr. Keshav	5,360	20,100	Less: Provision for Bad Debt	2,100	39,900
Reserve fund		8,100	Stock-in-trade		32,000
Creditors		16,000	Unexpired insurance		700
			Cash in hand		36,000
		184,200			184,200

Working Note

Calculation of interest on drawings:

Interest on drawings is calculated on average basis, i.e., for half year, because the date of drawings are not given.

Mr. Madhav (Rs. 16,000 – Rs. 6,000) = Rs. $10,000 \times 15/100 \times \frac{1}{2}$ = Rs. 750.

Mr. Keshav (Rs. 9,000 – Rs. 5,000) = Rs. $4,000 \times 15/100 \times \frac{1}{2}$ = Rs. 300.

ILLUSTRATION 19.12 Karim, Subal and Abhik are partners in a firm sharing profits and losses in the ratio of 4 : 3 : 2, respectively. They keep their accounts under Single Entry System. Their statement of affairs as on January 1, 2007 was as under:

Liabilities		Rs.	Assets	Rs.
Capital Accounts:			Land and Building	50,000
Karim	63,000		Machinery	35,000
Subal	52,000	115,000	Furniture	15,000
Creditors		31,000	Debtors	16,000
			Closing stock	18,000
			Cash in hand	2,000
			Capital Account:	
			Abhik	10,000
		146,000		146,000

On December 31, 2007, their position was as under:

Machinery Rs. 50,000 (additions were made on 1.3.07), Furniture Rs. 20,000 (additions were made on 1.4.07), Debtors Rs. 28,000, Stock-in-trade Rs. 19,000, Cash Rs. 16,800, Creditors Rs. 34,000, Prepaid rent Rs. 700 and Outstanding Expenses Rs. 300.

The following adjustments are agreed upon:

1. Provision for Doubtful Debts @ 5% on debtors is to be made.
2. Depreciate all fixed assets @ 10% p.a.

3. The drawings of Karim, Subal and Abhik were Rs.18,000, Rs.12,000 and Rs. 6,000, respectively.
4. Interest on capitals @ 5% p.a., on drawings @ 24% p.a. and on overdrawn capital @ 10% p.a.
5. Subal is entitled to a salary of Rs. 3,000 p.a. and Abhik is entitled to a bonus of Rs. 4,000 p.a.

Show the statement of Profit and Loss for the year ended December 31, 2007, and the final statement of affairs as on that date.

Solution

In the Books of Karim, Subal and Abhik
Statement of Affairs as on December 31, 2007

Liabilities	Rs.	Assets	Rs.
Combined capital	150,200	Land and Building	50,000
(Being the excess of assets over liabilities)		Machinery	50,000
Creditors	34,000	Furniture	20,000
Outstanding expenses	300	Debtors	19,000
		Closing stock	28,000
		Cash in hand	16,800
		Prepaid Rent	700
	184,500		184,500

Statement of Profit and Loss
for the year ended December 31, 2007

	Rs.	Rs.
Combined capital as per statement of affairs as at December 31, 2007		150,200
Add: Drawings:		
Karim	18,000	
Subal	12,000	
Abhik	6,000	36,000
		186,200
Less: Opening Capital:		
Karim	63,000	
Subal	52,000	
	115,000	
Less: Abhik's Overdrawn Capital	10,000	105,000
Trading Profit/Profit before adjustments		81,200
Less: Adjustments:		
Provision for Doubtful Debts	1,400	
Depreciation on Machinery	4,750	
Depreciation on Furniture	1,875	8,025
Net Profit		73,175
Less: Interest on Capital:		
Karim (5% of Rs. 63,000)	3,150	
Subal (5% of Rs. 52,000)	2,600	5,750
		67,425
Add: Interest on Overdrawn Capital : Abhik (10% of Rs.10,000)		1,000
		68,425
Add: Interest on Drawings:		
Karim (24% of Rs.18,000 for ½ year)	2,160	
Subal (24% of Rs.12,000 for ½ year)	1,440	
Abhik (24% of Rs. 6,000 for ½ year)	720	4,320
		72,745
Less: Partner's Salary: Subal		3,000
		69,745
Less: Bonus: Abhik		4,000
		65,745
Distributable Profit:		
Karim's share of Profit (4/9 of Rs. 65,745)	29,220	
Subal's share of Profit (3/9 of Rs. 65,745)	21,915	
Abhik's share of Profit (2/9 of Rs. 65,745)	14,610	

Final or Revised Statement of Affairs as on December 31, 2007

Liabilities	Rs.	Rs.	Assets	Rs.	Rs.
Capital Accounts:			Land and Building		50,000
Karim	63,000		Machinery	50,000	
Add: Interest on Capital	3,150		*Less:* Depreciation	4,750	45,250
Add: Share of Profit	29,220		Furniture	20,000	
	95,370		*Less:* Depreciation	1,875	18,125
Less: Drawings	18,000		Stock-in-trade		19,000
	77,370		Debtors	28,000	
Less: Interest on drawings	2,160	75,210	*Less:* Provision for Bad		
			Debts	1,400	26,600
Subal	52,000		Prepaid Rent		700
Add: Interest on Capital	2,600		Cash in hand		16,800
Add: Share of Profit	21,915				
Add: Salary	3,000				
	79,515				
Less: Drawings	12,000				
	67,515				
Less: Interest on Drawings	1,440	66,075			
Abhik					
Share of Profit	14,610				
Add: Bonus	4,000				
	18,610				
Less: Overdrawn Capital	10,000				
	8,610				
Less: Drawings	6,000				
	2,610				
Less: Interest on Drawings	720				
	1,890				
Less: Interest on Overdrawn Capital	1,000	890			
Creditors		34,000			
Outstanding Expenses		300			
		176,475			176,475

Working Notes

1. Calculation of depreciation on Machinery and Furniture:
   Depreciation on Machinery: 10% on Rs. 35,000 for full year = Rs. 3,500
   10% on Rs. 15,000 for ten months = Rs. 1,250 4,750
   Depreciation on Furniture: 10% on Rs. 15,000 for full year = Rs. 1,500
   10% on Rs. 5,000 for nine months = Rs. 375 1,875

2. Interest on drawings are calculated @ 24% p.a. Here, interest is calculated for ½ year only (on average basis), as the date of drawings are not given.

ILLUSTRATION 19.13 Mr. Sahara and Mr. Sundaram are partners in a firm sharing profits and losses in the ratio of 3 : 2. They keep their books under Single Entry System. Their statement of affairs as on April 1, 2007 was as under:

Statement of Affairs as on April 1, 2007

Liabilities	Rs.	Assets	Rs.
Capital Accounts:		Machinery	32,000
Mr. Sahara	90,000	Furniture	16,000
Reserve Fund	26,400	Debtors	37,000
Creditors	25,600	Closing stock	21,000
		Cash in hand	24,000
		Capital Account:	
		Mr. Sundaram	12,000
	142,000		142,000

On March 31, 2008 their position was as under:

Machinery Rs. 42,000, Furniture Rs. 26,000, Debtors Rs. 46,000, Creditors Rs. 31,000, Closing Stock Rs. 29,000 and Cash in hand Rs. 43,000.

The following adjustments are agreed upon:

1. Transfer Rs. 3,000 out of the divisible profit to the reserve fund.
2. 20% of the net profit will be distributed between the partners as bonus in the ratio of 4:3.
3. Cash withdrawn by Mr. Sahara and Mr. Sundaram were Rs. 12,000 and Rs. 10,000, respectively.
4. Life Insurance Premium of Mr. Sundaram was paid from business cash Rs. 2,500 and Income Tax of Mr. Sahara was also paid from the business fund Rs. 3,000.
5. No interest is allowed on capitals, but will be charged on overdrawn capital @ 12% p.a.
6. Mr. Sahara advanced Rs. 20,000 to the firm on September 1, 2007, but there was no specific agreement in this respect.
7. Depreciate Machinery and Furniture by Rs. 3,500 and Rs. 2,100, respectively.

Prepare a statement of Profit and Loss for the year ended March 31, 2008, and the final statement of affairs as on that date.

Solution

The books of Mr. Sahara and Mr. Sundaram
Statement of Affairs as on March 31, 2008

Liabilities	Rs.	Assets	Rs.
Combined Capital	108,600	Machinery	42,000
(Being the excess of assets over liabilities)		Furniture	26,000
Reserve Fund	26,400	Debtors	46,000
Creditors	31,000	Closing Stock	29,000
Mr. Sahara's Loan A/c	20,000	Cash in hand	43,000
	186,000		186,000

Statement of Profit and Loss
for the year ended March 31, 2008

	Rs.	Rs.
Combined Capital as per statement of affairs as at March 31, 2008		108,600
Add: Drawings:		
Mr. Sahara (Cash withdrawn Rs.12,000 + LIP Rs. 2,500)	14,500	
Mr. Sundaram (Cash withdrawn Rs.10,000 + Income Tax Rs. 3,000)	13,000	27,500
		136,100
Less: Opening Capital:		
Mr. Sahara	90,000	

(Contd.)

	Rs.	Rs.
Less: Mr. Sundaram's Overdrawn Capital	12,000	78,000
Trading Profit/Profit Before Adjustments		58,100
Less: Adjustments:		
Depreciation on Machinery	3,500	
Depreciation on Furniture	2,100	
Interest on loan of Mr. Sahara	700	6,300
Net Profit		51,800
Add: Interest on overdrawn capital: Mr. Sundaram (12% of Rs. 12,000)		1,440
		53,240
Less: Transfer to the reserve fund		3,000
		50,240
Less: Bonus : (20% of Net Profit Rs. 51,800 = Rs. 10,360)		
Mr. Sahara's Share (4/7 of Rs. 10,360)	5,920	
Mr. Sundaram's Share (3/7 of Rs. 10,360)	4,440	10,360
Distributable Profit		39,880
Mr. Sahara's Share of Profit (3/5 of Rs. 39,880)	23,928	
Mr. Sundaram's Share of Profit (2/5 of Rs. 39,880)	15,952	

Final or Revised Statement of Affairs as on March 31, 2008

Liabilities	Rs.	Rs.	Assets	Rs.	Rs.
Capital Accounts:			Machinery	42,000	
Mr. Sahara	90,000		*Less:* Depreciation	3,500	38,500
Add: Bonus	5,920		Furniture	26,000	
Add: Share of Profit	23,928		*Less:* Depreciation	2,100	23,900
Add: Interest on Loan	700		Stock-in-trade		29,000
	120,548		Debtors		46,000
Less: Drawings	14,500	106,048	Cash in hand		43,000
Mr. Sundaram's overdrawn Capital	(–) 12,000		Mr. Sundaram's overdrawn Capital		6,048
Add: Bonus	4,440				
Add: Share of Profit	15,952				
	8,392				
Less: Interest on overdrawn Capital	1,440				
	6,952				
Less: Drawings	13,000				
[Shown on the asset side]	(–) 6,048				
Reserve Fund (Rs. 26,400 + Rs. 3,000)		29,400			
Creditors		31,000			
Mr. Sahara's Loan A/c		20,000			
		186,448			186,448

Working Notes
1. In the absence of any agreement, interest on loan is to be given @ 6% p.a. (According to the Partnership Act). It is a charge against profit and hence is shown as a business expenditure but not as an appropriation. Thus, Mr. Sahara is given seven months interest on Rs. 20,000 @ 6% (Rs. 20,000 × 6/100 × 7/12 = Rs. 700).
2. Mr. Sundaram's capital balance shown as an overdrawn balance after making all adjustments regarding appropriations and drawings, and hence shown on the asset side of the final statement of affairs again.

ILLUSTRATION 19.14 Mr. Zafar and Mr. Kumar are partners in a firm sharing profits and losses in the ratio of 4 : 3. Their books are kept under single entry system. Their statement of affairs as on April 1, 2007 was as under:

Statement of Affairs as on April 1, 2007

Liabilities		Rs.	Assets	Rs.
Capital Accounts:			Machinery	45,000
Mr. Zafar	62,000		Furniture	14,000
Mr. Kumar	48,000	110,000	Debtors	43,000
Current Account:			Closing stock	27,500
Mr. Zafar	8,000		Cash in hand	13,300
Mr. Kumar	3,000	11,000		
Creditors		21,800		
		142,800		142,800

On March 31, 2008 their position was as under:

Machinery Rs. 60,000, Furniture Rs. 26,000, Loan Rs. 20,000, Debtors Rs. 28,000, Closing stock Rs. 16,000, Cash-in-hand Rs. 18,000, Creditors Rs. 39,600.

The following adjustments are agreed upon:

1. Interest on capital @ 4% p.a. and on drawings @ 12% p.a. in excess of Rs. 9,000 and Rs. 7,000 drawn by Mr. Zafar and Mr. Kumar, respectively.
2. Mr. Zafar is entitled to a salary of Rs. 6,000 p.a. and Mr. Kumar is entitled to a commission of Rs. 3,000 p.a.
3. The drawings of Mr. Zafar and Mr. Kumar were Rs. 14,000 and Rs. 15,000, respectively.
4. Depreciate all fixed assets @ 10% p.a.
5. Provision for Bad Debts is to be made @ 5% on debtors.
6. Shop rent for the month of March, 2008 still remain unpaid Rs.1,200.

Show the statement of Profit and Loss for the year ending March 31, 2008, and the final statement of affairs as on that date.

Solution

In the Books of Mr. Zafar and Mr. Kumar
Statement of Affairs as on March 31, 2008

Liabilities	Rs.	Assets	Rs.
Combined Capital	87,200	Machinery	60,000
(Balancing figure)		Furniture	26,000
Loan	20,000	Debtors	28,000
Outstanding Shop Rent	1,200	Closing stock	16,000
Creditors	39,600	Cash-in-hand	18,000
	148,000		148,000

Statement of Profit and Loss
for the year ended March 31, 2008

	Rs.	Rs.
Combined Capital as per statement of affairs as at March 31, 2008		87,200
Add: Drawings:		
Mr. Zafar	14,000	
Mr. Kumar	15,000	29,000
		116,200
Less: Opening Capital:		
Mr. Zafar	62,000	
Mr. Kumar	48,000	110,000
		6,200

(Contd.)

	Rs.	Rs.
Less: Opening Current Account Balance:		
Mr. Zafar	8,000	
Mr. Kumar	3,000	11,000
Trading Loss/Loss before adjustments		4,800
Add: Adjustments:		
Depreciation on Machinery	5,250	
Depreciation on Motor Car	2,000	
Provision for Bad Debt @ 5% of Rs. 28,000	1,400	8,650
Net Loss		13,450
Add: Interest on Capital:		
Mr. Zafar	2,480	
Mr. Kumar	1,920	4,400
		17,850
Add: Partners' Salary: Mr. Zafar		6,000
		23,850
Add: Commission: Mr. Kumar		3,000
		26,850
Less: Interest on Drawings:		
Mr. Zafar	300	
Mr. Kumar	480	780
Distributable Loss		26,070
Mr. Zafar 's share of Loss (4/7 th of Rs. 26,070)	14,897	
Mr. Kumar's share of Loss (3/7 th of Rs. 26,070)	11,173	

Dr.			Current Account			Cr.
	Zafar (Rs.)	Kumar (Rs.)		Zafar (Rs.)	Kumar (Rs.)	
2008 March 31			2007 April 1			
To Drawings	14,000	15,000	By Balance b/d	8,000	3,000	
To Interest on drawings	300	480	2008 March 31			
To Share of loss	14,897	11,173	By Interest on capital	2,480	1,920	
			By Partners' Salary	6,000	–	
			By Commission	–	3,000	
			By Balance c/d	12,717	18,733	
	29,197	26,653		29,197	26,653	

Final or Revised Statement of Affairs as on March 31, 2008

Liabilities	Rs.	Rs.	Assets	Rs.	Rs.
Capital Accounts:			Machinery	60,000	
Mr. Zafar	62,000		*Less:* Depreciation	5,250	54,750
Mr. Kumar	48,000	110,000	Furniture	26,000	
Loan		20,000	*Less:* Depreciation	2,000	24,000
Outstanding Shop Rent		1,200	Debtors	28,000	
Creditors		39,600	*Less:* Provision for Bad Debt	1,400	26,600
			Stock-in-trade		16,000
			Cash in hand		18,000
			Current Accounts:		
			Mr. Zafar	12,717	
			Mr. Kumar	18,733	31,450
		170,800			170,800

Working Notes

1. Calculation of interest on drawings:

   Interest on drawings is calculated on average basis, i.e., for half year, because the date of drawings is not given.

   Mr. Zafar (Rs. 14,000 – Rs. 9,000) = Rs. 5,000 × 12/100 × ½ = Rs. 300.

   Mr. Kumar (Rs. 15,000 – Rs. 7,000) = Rs. 8,000 × 12/100 × ½ = Rs. 480.

2. Calculation of depreciation on Machinery and Furniture:

    Depreciation on Machinery: 10% on Rs. 45,000 for full year = Rs. 4,500

                                                10% on Rs. 15,000 for ½ year = Rs.   750   5,250.

    Depreciation on Furniture: 10% on Rs. 14,000 for full year = Rs. 1,400

                                                10% on Rs. 12,000 for ½ year = Rs.   600   2,000.

19.2.2 Alternative Method for Ascertainment of Profit or Loss

According to this alternative method, profit or loss of a business is calculated by preparing only a Statement of Profit and Loss at the end of the year. No further Statement of Affairs are required to be prepared for calculating the closing and opening capital of the business. Thus, by preparing only a Statement of Profit and Loss, the closing and opening capitals are calculated first and then the profit or loss of the business is ascertained. A specimen of the said Statement of Profit and Loss is shown below:

Statement of Profit and Loss
for the year ended ...

Liabilities	Rs.	Assets	Rs.
All Closing Liabilities:		**All Closing Assets:**	
Closing Capital (Balancing figure)	*****	Machinery	—
Or		Furniture	—
Closing Net Assets		Investment	—
Creditors	—	Debtors	—
Outstanding Expenses	—	Stock-in-trade	—
		Prepaid Expenses	—
		Cash in hand	—
	—		—
All Opening Liabilities:		**All Opening Assets:**	
Opening Capital (Balancing figure)	*****	Machinery	—
Or		Furniture	—
Opening Net Assets		Investment	—
Creditors	—	Debtors	—
Outstanding Expenses	—	Stock-in-trade	—
		Prepaid Expenses	—
		Cash in hand	—
	—		—
Opening Capital (Balancing figure)	*****	Closing Capital (Balancing figure)	*****
Or		Or	
Opening Net Assets		Closing Net Assets	
Capital introduced/New Capital	—	Drawings	—
Trading Profit/Profit Before Adjustments	****		
(Balancing figure)	—		
Adjustments:		Trading Profit / Profit before adjustments	****
Depreciation on Fixed Assets	—		
Provision for Doubtful Debts	—		
Other adjustments if any	—		
Net Profit (Balancing figure)	****		
	—		—
All Appropriations:		Net Profit	****
Interest on Capital	—	**Interest on Drawings:**	
Partners' Salaries	—	Partner X	—
Commission	—	Partner Z	—
Bonus	—		
Transfer to Reserve Fund	—		
Share of Profit:			
Partner X: ——			
Partner Z: ——			
	—		—

From the above statement it is clear that the first part shows the calculation of the closing capital, the second part shows the calculation of the opening capital (where opening capital is given, the second part need not to be shown; after completing the first part, go straight to the third part), the third part shows the calculation of trading profit/profit before adjustments and the fourth part shows the calculation of the net profit. In case of partnership, the fifth part is required to be shown.

ILLUSTRATION 19.15   Taking the data from the Illustration 19.11, a statement of Profit and Loss as per the alternative method is shown below.

Statement of Profit and Loss
for the year ended December 31, 2007

Liabilities		Rs.	Assets		Rs.
All Closing Liabilities:			**All Closing Assets:**		
Closing Capital (Balancing figure)		178,700	Machinery		46,000
Or			Motor Car		38,000
Closing Net Assets			Debtors		42,000
Creditors		16,000	Closing stock		32,000
			Unexpired insurance		700
			Cash in hand		36,000
		194,700			194,700
Opening Capital		140,000	Closing Capital		178,700
Reserve Fund		8,100	**Drawings:**		
Opening Current Account Balance:			Mr. Madhav	16,000	
Mr. Madhav	6,000		Mr. Keshav	9,000	25,000
Mr. Keshav	(–) 2,500	3,500			
Trading Profit/Profit before					
adjustments (Balancing figure)		52,100			
		203,700			203,700
Adjustments:			Trading Profit/Profit before		
Depreciation on Machinery		4,600	adjustments		52,100
Depreciation on Motor Car		3,800			
Provision for Bad Debts		2,100			
Net Profit (Balancing figure)		41,600			
		52,100			52,100
Appropriations:			Net Profit		41,600
Interest on Capital			**Interest on Drawings:**		
Mr. Madhav	4,000		Mr. Madhav	750	
Mr. Keshav	3,000	7,000	Mr. Keshav	300	1,050
Partners' Salaries: Mr. Madhav		4,000			
Commission: Mr. Keshav		2,500			
Share of Profit:					
Mr. Madhav	17,490				
Mr. Keshav	11,660	29,150			
		42,650			42,650

ILLUSTRATION 19.16   Taking the data from the Illustration 19.3 prepare a statement of Profit and Loss for the period ended December 31, 2007, and draw up a final statement of affairs as on that date as per the alternative method.

In the Books of Mr. Dhillon
Statement of Profit and Loss
For the year ended December 31, 2007

	Rs.		Rs.
All Closing Liabilities:		**All Closing Assets:**	
Closing Capital (Balancing figure)	355,700	Land and Buildings	105,000
Or		Machinery	75,000
Closing Net Assets		Furniture	34,000
Creditors	19,700	Investments	30,000
Outstanding Expenses	800	Debtors	56,300
		Prepaid expenses	1,200
		Accrued interest on investment	700
		Closing stock	23,100
		Cash at Bank	19,500
		Cash in hand	31,400
	376,200		376,200
All Opening Liabilities:		**All Opening Assets:**	
Opening Capital (Balancing figure)	316,600	Land and Buildings	125,000
Or		Machinery	55,000
Opening Net Assets		Furniture	24,000
Creditors	16,300	Investments	30,000
Outstanding Expenses	500	Debtors	43,800
		Prepaid expenses	900
		Closing stock	15,900
		Cash at bank	26,000
		Cash in hand	12,800
	333,400		333,400
Opening Capital	316,600	Closing Capital (Balancing figure)	355,700
Capital introduced	18,000	**Drawings:**	
Trading Profit/Profit before adjustments	43,900	Cash withdrawn Rs. 900 p.m. 10,800	
Adjustments (Balancing figure)		House rent Rs. 1,000 p.m. 12,000	22,800
	378,500		378,500
Adjustments:		Trading Profit/Profit before adjustments	43,900
Depreciation on Machinery	6,500		
Depreciation on Furniture	2,900		
Provision for Doubtful Debts	2,815		
Net Profit (Balancing figure)	31,685		
	43,900		43,900

Final or Revised Statement of Affairs as on December 31, 2007

Liabilities	Rs.	Rs.	Assets	Rs.	Rs.
Capital:	316,600		Land and Buildings	125,000	
Add: Fresh Capital	18,000		Less: Depreciation	20,000	105,000
Add: Net Profit	31,685		Machinery	75,000	
	366,285		Less: Depreciation	6,500	68,500
Less: Drawings	22,800	343,485	Furniture	34,000	
Creditors		19,700	Less: Depreciation	2,900	31,100
Outstanding expenses		800	Investment		30,000
			Debtors	56,300	
			Less: Provision for Doubtful Debts	2,815	53,485
			Closing stock		23,100
			Prepaid expenses		1,200
			Accrued interest on investment		700
			Cash at bank		19,500
			Cash in hand		31,400
		363,985			363,985

19.2.3 Conversion Method

From the discussions that we have had in the previous sections, it can be observed that small business owners who do not have any knowledge of accounting or do not want to follow any systematic or scientific methods of accounting, prefer to maintain very few accounts. There is no uniformity in maintaining the books of accounts among such traders. Thus, the way in which the books are maintained may differ from one firm to another. They generally want to prepare statements according to their desire for ascertaining profits or losses of the neither businesses. Business performances can be measured properly nor compared with the performances of other periods or other similar firms systematically. Due to the absence of nominal accounts, Trading and Profit and Loss Account cannot be prepared. As a result, gross profit and correct net profit cannot be ascertained. As the facts and figures supplied cannot be relied upon, proper planning for the future cannot be made, and taking important decisions in case of any critical situations become difficult.

In order to overcome the above stated difficulties, sometimes businessmen like to convert such a set of books, which are not based on the double entry system, into the main stream of accounting, by which Financial Statements may be prepared. For preparing the Financial Statements, i.e., the Trading Account, Profit and Loss Account and the balance sheet, certain steps are required to be taken. The application of those steps to convert the set of books maintained under single entry system into the double entry system is generally known as **conversion method**.

Here, conversion from single entry system to double entry system does not mean the preparation of journal, ledger, trial balance, etc., but the purpose is only to collect such information or data which will help to prepare the final accounts (i.e., Trading, and Profit and Loss Account and the balance sheet). The following steps are to be taken for preparing final accounts under this method:

1. A statement of affairs is to be prepared for calculating the opening capital, if not given.
2. Prepare a cash book or cash account, if not prepared. While preparing the cash book, there may be some difference (of amount) on the debit or credit side. For the said missing figure, the following items may be considered depending on the circumstances of the cases:

For debit side	For credit side
(a) Cash balance	(a) Cash purchase
(b) Sale of fixed assets	(b) Purchase of fixed assets
(c) Fresh capital	(c) Drawings
(d) Miscellaneous income	(d) Miscellaneous expenses

3. For calculation of credit sales and purchase, Total Debtors A/c, Bills Receivable A/c, Total Creditors A/c, and Bills Payable A/c are to be prepared.
4. Fixed Assets Account may be opened, if not clearly mentioned. The opening balance is to be collected from the opening balance sheet, any purchase or sale from the cash book and depreciation on the basis of additional information, or it would be the balancing figure if the closing balance is given.
5. Opening stock and closing stock are usually given, and if any one of them is missing, then prepare a memorandum trading account with the help of the available data and the balancing figure would be the missing data.
6. After considering the above steps, all the necessary information may be collected, by which final accounts may be prepared.

ILLUSTRATION 19.17 From the following information, calculate credit sales and purchases for the year 2007:

1. Balance on January 1, 2007: Debtors Rs. 18,000, Creditors Rs. 9,900, Bills Receivable Rs. 4,800, Bills Payable Rs. 3,100.
2. Total cash and cheque received from customers: Rs. 76,000 (Excluding cash sales Rs. 16,000).
3. Total cash and cheque paid to suppliers: Rs. 46,200 (Excluding cash purchases Rs. 9,700).
4. Bills receivable honoured during the year: Rs. 8,600.

5. Bills receivable endorsed to suppliers during the year: Rs. 2,600.
6. Bills receivable dishonoured during the year: Rs. 1,900.
7. Discount allowed to customers: Rs. 1,900; Discount allowed by suppliers: Rs. 950.
8. Goods returned by customers: Rs. 1,600; Goods returned to suppliers: Rs. 780.
9. Bad debts written off: Rs. 760; Bad debts recovered: Rs. 900.
10. Rebate allowed by suppliers: Rs. 600.
11. Interest charged to customers: Rs. 300; customer's cheque dishonoured: Rs. 860.
12. Issued cheque dishonoured: Rs.1,100; Cash paid against bills payable: Rs. 8,200.
13. Bills payable dishonoured during the year: Rs. 1,600; Cash refund to debtors: Rs. 250.
14. Total bills receivable amounting to Rs. 4,200 were discounted with the bank at Rs. 4,050.
15. Balance on December 31, 2007: Debtors Rs. 6,700; Creditors Rs. 5,400; Bills Receivable: Rs. 2,700; Bills Payable: Rs. 1,860.

Solution

Dr.   **Bills Payable Account**   Cr.

Date	Particulars	Amount (Rs.)	Date	Particulars	Amount (Rs.)
2007	To Cash	8,200	2007 Jan. 1	By Balance b/d	3,100
	To Creditors	1,600		By Creditors/Suppliers	8,560
	(Issued bill dishonoured)			(Bills issued during the year)	
2007 Dec. 31	To Balance c/d	1,860		– Balancing figure	
		11,660			11,660
			2008 Jan. 1	By Balance b/d	1,860

Dr.   **Creditors Account**   Cr.

Date	Particulars	Amount (Rs.)	Date	Particulars	Amount (Rs.)
2007	To Cash and Bank	46,200	2007 Jan. 1	By Balance b/d	9,900
	To Discount Received	950		By Bank	1,100
	To Purchases Returns	780		(Issued cheque dishonoured)	
	To Rebate Received	600		By Bills Payable	1,600
	To Bills Receivable	2,600		(Issued Bill dishonoured)	
	(Endorsed)			By Purchases	52,490
	To Bills Payable	8,560		(Credit purchases during	
	(Bills issued during the year)			the year – Balancing figure)	
2007 Dec. 31	To Balance c/d	5,400			
		65,090			65,090
			2008 Jan. 1	By Balance b/d	5,400

Dr.   **Bills Receivable Account**   Cr.

Date	Particulars	Amount (Rs.)	Date	Particulars	Amount (Rs.)
2007 Jan. 1	To Balance b/d	4,800	2007	By Cash and Bank	8,600
	To Debtors	15,200		(Honoured during the year)	
	(Bills received during the year			By Creditors (Endorsed)	2,600
	– Balancing figure)			By Debtors (Dishonoured)	1,900
				By Bank (Bill discounted)	4,050
				By Discount (Bill discounted)	150
			2007 Dec. 31	By Balance c/d	2,700
		20,000			20,000
2007 Jan. 1	To Balance b/d	2,700			

Dr.   Debtors Account   Cr.

Date	Particulars	Amount (Rs.)	Date	Particulars	Amount (Rs.)
2007 Jan. 1	To Balance b/d	18,000	2007	By Cash and Bank	76,000
	To Bills Receivable	1,900		By Bills Receivable	15,200
	(Dishonoured)			By Discount Allowed	1,900
	To Interest	300		By Sales Returns	1,600
	(Charged to customers)			By Bad Debts	760
	To Bank(Cheque dishonoured)	860			
	To Cash	250			
	(refund to customers)				
	To Sales – Balancing figure	80,850			
	(Credit sales during the year)		2007 Dec. 31	By Balance c/d	6,700
		102,160			102,160
2008 Jan. 1	To Balance b/d	6,700			

Total sales during the year :   Rs.
   Cash Sales 16,000
   Credit Sales 80,850 96,850.

Total purchases during the year: Rs.
   Cash Purchases 9,700
   Credit Purchases 52,490 62,190.

Note: Bad debts recovered are not to be considered here.

ILLUSTRATION 19.18 Mr. Jindal is a business man who keeps his books of account under single entry system. The following data are available from the records of his business for the year 2007:

	Rs.		Rs.
Capital introduced	12,000	Paid to creditors	29,400
Cash sales	31,700	Drawings	7,600
Cash Purchases	19,800	Purchase Returns	1,400
Carriage Inwards	2,700	Salaries	7,700
Received from customers	47,600	Discount Received	1,700
Discount Allowed	1,600	Rent	3,600
Wages	3,200	Sales Returns	1,100
Bad Debts	1,300	Advertisement	2,900

Additional information

	2007 Jan. 1 Rs.	2007 Dec. 31 Rs.
Stock-in-trade	12,800	16,700
Debtors	27,900	32,400
Creditors	17,800	22,500
Office Equipments	16,000	14,000
Cash-in-hand	23,900	?

From the above data, prepare a Trading Account, a Profit and Loss Account for the year ended December 31, 2007, and the Balance Sheet as on that date.

Solution

In the Books of Mr. Jindal

Dr. **Cash Account** Cr.

	Rs.		Rs.
To Balance b/d	23,900	By Purchases (Cash)	19,800
To Sales (Cash)	31,700	By Carriage Inwards	2,700
To Received from customers	47,600	By Wages	3,200
To Capital introduced	12,000	By Salaries	7,700
		By Rent	3,600
		By Advertisement	2,900
		By Paid to creditors	29,400
		By Drawings	7,600
		By Balance c/d	38,300
	115,200		115,200

Dr. **Debtors Account** Cr.

	Rs.		Rs.
To Balance b/d	27,900	By Cash (Received from customers)	47,600
To Sales (Balancing figure)	56,100	By Discount Allowed	1,600
		By Bad Debts	1,300
		By Sales Returns	1,100
		By Balance c/d	32,400
	84,000		84,000

Dr. **Creditors Account** Cr.

	Rs.		Rs.
To Cash (Paid to creditors)	29,400	By Balance b/d	17,800
To Discount Received	1,700	By Purchases (Balancing figure)	37,200
To Purchase Returns	1,400		
To Balance c/d	22,500		
	55,000		55,000

Balance Sheet as at January 1, 2007

Liabilities	Rs.	Assets	Rs.
Capital	62,800	Office Equipments	16,000
(Balancing figure)		Stock-in-trade	12,800
Creditors	17,800	Debtors	27,900
		Cash-in-hand	23,900
	80,600		80,600

Trading Account and Profit and Loss Account

Dr. for the year ended December 31, 2007 Cr.

		Rs.			Rs.
To Opening Stock		12,800	By Sales:		
To Purchases:			Cash	31,700	
Cash	19,800		Credit	56,100	
Credit	37,200			87,800	
	57,000		Less: Sales Returns	1,100	86,700
Less: Purchase Returns	1,400	55,600			

(Contd.)

	Rs.		Rs.
To Carriage Inwards	2,700	By Closing Stock	16,700
To Wages	3,200		
To Gross Profit c/d	29,100		
	103,400		103,400
To Salaries	7,700	By Gross Profit b/d	29,100
To Rent	3,600	By Discount Received	1,700
To Advertisement	2,900		
To Discount Allowed	1,600		
To Bad Debts	1,300		
To Depreciation on:			
Office Equipments	2,000		
To Net Profit	11,700		
(Transferred to Capital A/c)			
	30,800		30,800

Balance Sheet as on December 31, 2007

Liabilities		Rs.	Assets	Rs.
Capital	62,800		Office Equipments	14,000
Add: Fresh capital	12,000		Stock-in-trade	16,700
Add: Net profit	11,700		Debtors	32,400
	86,500		Cash in hand	38,300
Less: Drawings	7,600	78,900		
Creditors		22,500		
		101,400		101,400

Working Notes

1. When opening capital is not given, then the opening Balance Sheet is required to be prepared to calculate the amount of opening capital.
2. For calculating the amount of credit sales and purchases, Debtors and Creditors accounts are opened.
3. Generally, for decrease in the value of fixed assets (when closing value of any fixed asset is less than that of its opening value), the amount so decreased is to be considered as depreciation. Thus, the amount of depreciation charged on the office equipments is Rs. 2,000 (16,000 – 14,000).
4. When Cash Account is not given, it is suggested that we prepare a Cash Account to calculate the closing balance. However, if the closing cash balance is given, even then the Cash Account is to be prepared to know whether there is any missing item (Debit or Credit side) or not.

ILLUSTRATION 19.19 Ms. Reddy who keeps her books under single entry system submits the following data of her business for the year 2007:

	Rs.		Rs.
Cash sales	34,400	Discount Allowed	1,100
Cash Purchases	32,700	Discount Received	780
Carriage Inwards	2,600	Bad Debts	800
Carriage Outwards	1,800	Bad Debts Recovered	350
Wages	2,900	Received from customers	56,800
Salaries	3,400	Paid to creditors	39,300
Rent	2,400	Drawings	6,900
Sales Returns	2,300	Miscellaneous Income	4,300
Purchase Returns	1,700	Capital introduced	8,000
Furniture purchased	5,000	Computer purchased	22,000

Additional information

	2007 Jan. 1 Rs.	2007 Dec. 31 Rs.
Machinery	75,000	70,000
Furniture	24,000	26,500
Stock-in-trade	16,800	20,400
Debtors	32,600	41,100
Creditors	19,700	22,300
Cash in hand	20,900	5,750

From the above data, prepare a Trading Account, and a Profit and Loss Account for the year ending December 31, 2007, and the Balance Sheet as on that date.

Solution

In the Books of Ms. Reddy

Dr.   **Cash Account**   Cr.

	Rs.		Rs.
To Balance b/d	20,900	By Cash (Purchases)	32,700
To Cash sales	34,400	By Carriage Inwards	2,600
To Received from customers	56,800	By Carriage Outwards	1,800
To Bad Debts Recovered	350	By Wages	2,900
To Miscellaneous Income	4,300	By Salaries	3,400
To Capital introduced	8,000	By Rent	2,400
		By Furniture (Purchased)	5,000
		By Paid to creditors	39,300
		By Drawings	6,900
		By Computer (Purchased)	22,000
		By Balance c/d	5,750
	124,750		124,750

Dr.   **Debtors Account**   Cr.

	Rs.		Rs.
To Balance b/d	32,600	By Received from customers	56,800
To Sales (Balancing figure)	69,500	By Discount Allowed	1,100
		By Bad Debts	800
		By Sales Returns	2,300
		By Balance c/d	41,100
	102,100		102,100

Dr.   **Creditors Account**   Cr.

	Rs.		Rs.
To Paid to creditors	39,300	By Balance b/d	19,700
To Discount Received	780	By Purchases (Balancing figure)	44,380
To Purchase Returns	1,700		
To Balance c/d	22,300		
	64,080		64,080

Dr.   **Furniture Account**   Cr.

	Rs.		Rs.
To Balance b/d	24,000	By Depreciation	2,500
To Cash (Purchase)	5,000	(Balancing figure)	
		By Balance c/d	26,500
	29,000		29,000

Dr.		Machinery Account		Cr.
	Rs.			Rs.
To Balance b/d	75,000	By Depreciation		5,000
		(Balancing figure)		
		By Balance c/d		70,000
	75,000			75,000

Balance Sheet as at January 1, 2007

Liabilities	Rs.	Assets	Rs.
Capital	149,600	Machinery	75,000
(Balancing figure)		Furniture	24,000
Creditors	19,700	Stock-in-trade	16,800
		Debtors	32,600
		Cash in hand	20,900
	169,300		169,300

Trading Account and Profit and Loss Account
Dr.   **for the year ended December 31, 2007**   Cr.

		Rs.			Rs.
To Opening Stock		16,800	By Sales:		
To Purchases:			Cash	34,400	
Cash	32,700		Credit	69,500	
Credit	44,380			103,900	
	77,080		Less: Sales Returns	2,300	101,600
Less: Purchase Returns	1,700	75,380	By Closing Stock		20,400
To Carriage Inwards		2,600			
To Wages		2,900			
To Gross Profit c/d		24,320			
		122,000			122,000
To Carriage Outwards		1,800	By Gross Profit b/d		24,320
To Salaries		3,400	By Bad Debts Recovered		350
To Rent		2,400	By Miscellaneous Income		4,300
To Discount Allowed		1,100	By Discount Received		780
To Bad Debts		800			
To Depreciation on:					
Machinery	5,000				
Furniture	2,500	7,500			
To Net Profit		12,750			
(Transferred to Capital A/c)					
		29,750			29,750

Balance Sheet as at December 31, 2007

Liabilities	Rs.	Assets	Rs.
Capital	149,600	Machinery	70,000
Add: Fresh capital	8,000	Furniture	26,500
Add: Net Profit	12,750	Computer	22,000
	170,350	Stock-in-trade	20,400
Less: Drawings	6,900	163,450	Debtors	41,100
Creditors		22,300	Cash in hand	5,750
		185,750		185,750

ILLUSTRATION 19.20 M/s Kapoor Bros. keep their books under the single entry system. The summary of their Cash Account for 2007 was as under.

Dr.		Cash Account	Cr.
	Rs.		Rs.
To Balance b/d	19,700	By Paid to creditors	37,100
To Capital introduced	15,000	By Drawings	7,300
To Received from customers	65,800	By Rent	3,900
To Cash sales	29,400	By Wages	4,200
To Miscellaneous Income	3,700	By Salaries	5,800
To Interest Received	2,400	By Furniture Purchased	12,000
		By Purchases (Cash)	22,300
		By Carriage Inwards	3,400
		By Audit Fees	2,500
		By Commission	1,800
		By Balance c/d	35,700
	136,000		136,000

Additional information

	Rs.		Rs.
Discount Allowed	1,900	**Opening Balances:**	
Bad Debts	760	Stock	19,600
Discount Received	1,480	Machinery	48,000
Sales Returns	2,600	Furniture	24,000
Purchase Returns	2,100	Debtors	32,800
Credit Sales	72,600	Creditors	20,600
Credit Purchases	43,200	Closing Stock	22,100

The following adjustments are to be made:
1. Depreciate all fixed assets @ 10% p.a.
2. Make Provision for Bad Debts @ 5% on debtors.
3. Salary outstanding Rs.1,700.
4. Rent paid in advance Rs.600.

Prepare a Trading Account and a Profit and Loss Account of M/s Kapoor Bros. for the year ended December 31, 2007 and the Balance Sheet as on that date.

Solution

In the books of M/s Kapoor Bros.
Balance Sheet as at January 1, 2007

Liabilities	Rs.	Assets	Rs.
Capital	123,500	Machinery	48,000
(Balancing figure)		Furniture	24,000
Creditors	20,600	Debtors	32,800
		Stock	19,600
		Cash in hand	19,700
	144,100		144,100

Dr.		**Debtors Account**		Cr.
	Rs.			Rs.
To Balance b/d	32,800	By Cash (Received from customers)		65,800
To Sales	72,600	By Discount Allowed		1,900
		By Bad Debts		760
		By Sales Returns		2,600
		By Balance c/d		34,340
	105,400			105,400

Dr.		**Creditors Account**		Cr.
	Rs.			Rs.
To Cash (Paid to creditors)	37,100	By Balance b/d		20,600
To Discount Received	1,480	By Purchases		43,200
To Purchase Returns	2,100			
To Balance c/d	23,120			
	63,800			63,800

Trading Account and Profit and Loss Account
for the year ended December 31, 2007

Dr.					Cr.
		Rs.			Rs.
To Opening Stock		19,600	By Sales:		
To Purchases:			Cash	29,400	
Cash	22,300		Credit	72,600	
Credit	43,200			102,000	
	65,500		Less: Sales Returns	2,600	99,400
Less: Purchase Returns	2,100	63,400	By Closing Stock		22,100
To Carriage Inwards		3,400			
To Wages		4,200			
To Gross Profit c/d		30,900			
		121,500			121,500
To Discount Allowed		1,900	By Gross Profit b/d		30,900
To Salaries	5,800		By Discount Received		1,480
Add: Outstanding	1,700	7,500	By Miscellaneous Income		3,700
To Rent	3,900		By Interest Received		2,400
Less: Paid in advance	600	3,300			
To Audit Fees		2,500			
To Commission		1,800			
To Bad Debts		760			
To Provision for Bad Debts		1,717			
To Depreciation on:					
Machinery	4,800				
Furniture	3,000	7,800			
To Net Profit		11,203			
(Transferred to Capital A/c)					
		38,480			38,480

Balance Sheet as on December 31, 2007

Liabilities		Rs.	Assets		Rs.
Capital	123,500		Machinery	48,000	
Add: Fresh capital	15,000		*Less:* Depreciation	4,800	43,200
Add: Net Profit	11,203		Furniture(Rs. 24000 + Rs. 12,000)	36,000	
	149,703		*Less:* Depreciation	3,000	33,000
Less: Drawings	7,300	142,403	Stock-in-trade		22,100
Outstanding Salaries		1,700	Debtors	34,340	
Creditors		23,120	*Less:* Provision for Bad Debts	1,717	32,623
			Prepaid Rent		600
			Cash in hand		35,700
		167,223			167,223

Working Note

1. Calculation of depreciation on Machinery and Furniture:

   Depreciation on Machinery: 10% on Rs. 48,000 for full year   = Rs. 4,800

   Depreciation on Furniture: 10% on Rs. 24,000 for full year   = Rs. 2,400

   10% on Rs. 12,000 for six months   = Rs.   600   3,000.

2. Here, Debtors and Creditors Accounts are opened to ascertain the closing balance of the said two accounts. It is essential to prepare the closing balance sheet.

ILLUSTRATION 19.21   Mr. Sachin Talwar, who keeps his books of account under single entry system, submits the following information about his business for the year 2007–2008:

	Rs.		Rs.
Personal NSC cashed	14,000	Purchase of Machinery	20,000
Sale of Furniture	3,800	Purchase of Furniture	15,000
Received from customers	61,300	Purchase Returns	2,650
Carriage Inwards	3,200	Wages	4,250
Paid to creditors	45,100	Discount Received	2,150
Discount Allowed	1,750	Rent	4,400
Cash Purchases	21,400	Sales Returns	2,270
Bad Debts	850	Sundry Expenses	5,200
Salaries	6,200	Cash sales	34,900
Drawings	8,000	Depreciation of Furniture	3,500

Additional information

	2007 Apr. 1 Rs.	2008 Mar. 31 Rs.
Stock-in-trade	19,600	43,800
Debtors	28,000	31,750
Creditors	23,400	27,500
Machinery	47,000	52,000
Furniture	21,500	26,800
Cash in hand	44,800	31,400

From the above data, prepare a Trading Account, and a Profit and Loss Account for the year ended March 31, 2008 and the Balance Sheet as on that date.

Solution

In the Books of Mr. Sachin Talwar

Dr.		Cash Account			Cr.
	Rs.		Rs.		
To Balance b/d	44,800	By Cash (Purchases)	21,400		
To NSC cashed	14,000	By Carriage Inwards	3,200		
To Received from customers	61,300	By Wages	4,250		
To Furniture	3,800	By Machinery	20,000		
To Cash sales	34,900	By Salaries	6,200		
To Miscellaneous Income	5,350	By Furniture	15,000		
(Balancing figure assumed as		By Rent	4,400		
Miscellaneous income)		By Sundry Expenses	5,200		
		By Paid to creditors	45,100		
		By Drawings	8,000		
		By Balance c/d	31,400		
	164,150		164,150		

Dr.		Debtors Account			Cr.
	Rs.		Rs.		
To Balance b/d	28,000	By Cash (Received from customers)	61,300		
To Sales (Balancing figure)	69,920	By Discount Allowed	1,750		
		By Bad Debts	850		
		By Sales Returns	2,270		
		By Balance c/d	31,750		
	97,920		97,920		

Dr.		Creditors Account			Cr.
	Rs.		Rs.		
To Cash (Paid to creditors)	45,100	By Balance b/d	23,400		
To Discount Received	2,150	By Purchases (Balancing figure)	54,000		
To Purchase Returns	2,650				
To Balance c/d	27,500				
	77,400		77,400		

Dr.		Furniture Account			Cr.
	Rs.		Rs.		
To Balance b/d	21,500	By Depreciation	3,500		
To Cash (Purchase)	15,000	By Cash (sale)	3,800		
		By Loss on sale	2,400		
		(Balancing figure)			
		By Balance c/d	26,800		
	36,500		36,500		

Dr.		Machinery Account			Cr.
	Rs.		Rs.		
To Balance b/d	47,000	By Depreciation	15,000		
To Cash (Purchase)	20,000	(Balancing figure)			
		By Balance c/d	52,000		
	67,000		67,000		

Balance Sheet as at April 1, 2007

Liabilities	Rs.	Assets	Rs.
Capital	137,500	Machinery	47,000
(Balancing figure)		Furniture	21,500
Creditors	23,400	Stock-in-trade	19,600
		Debtors	28,000
		Cash in hand	44,800
	160,900		160,900

Trading Account and Profit and Loss Account

Dr.   for the year ended March 31, 2008   Cr.

		Rs.		Rs.	
To Opening Stock		19,600	By Sales:		
To Purchases:			Cash	34,900	
Cash	21,400		Credit	69,920	
Credit	54,000			104,820	
	75,400		Less: Sales Returns	2,270	102,550
Less: Purchase Returns	2,650	72,750	By Closing Stock		43,800
To Carriage Inwards		3,200			
To Wages		4,250			
To Gross Profit c/d		46,550			
		146,350			146,350
To Salaries		6,200	By Gross Profit b/d		46,550
To Rent		4,400	By Discount Received		2,150
To Sundry Expenses		5,200	By Miscellaneous Income		5,350
To Discount Allowed		1,750			
To Bad Debts		850			
To Loss on sale of furniture		2,400			
To Depreciation on:					
Machinery	15,000				
Furniture	3,500	18,500			
To Net Profit		14,750			
(Transferred to Capital A/c)					
		54,050			54,050

Balance Sheet as on March 31, 2008

Liabilities	Rs.		Assets	Rs.
Capital	137,500		Machinery	52,000
Add: Fresh capital	14,000		Furniture	26,800
Add: Net Profit	14,750		Stock-in-trade	43,800
	166,250		Debtors	31,750
Less: Drawings	8,000	158,250	Cash in hand	31,400
Creditors		27,500		
		185,750		185,750

Working Notes

1. Balancing figure of the Cash A/c is considered as miscellaneous income Rs. 5,350.
2. Balancing figure of the Furniture A/c is considered as loss on sale of furniture Rs. 2,400.

ILLUSTRATION 19.22 From the following information, prepare a Trading Account and a Profit and Loss Account for the year ended December 31, 2007 of Mr. Mukbul Hussain and the Balance Sheet as on that date.

List of cash transactions for the year 2007:

	Rs.		Rs.
Sale of personal gold	7,000	Miscellaneous Income	13,900
Sale of Machinery	3,500	Advertisement	2,800
Received from customers	41,800	Purchase of Furniture (on 1.10.07)	4,000
Carriage	2,200	Wages	3,950
Paid to creditors	29,200	Sundry Expenses	8,200
Cashed personal NSC	4,000	Cash sales	16,100
Cash Purchases	12,900	Drawings	5,600
Bills Payable honoured	10,000	Bills Receivable honoured	14,000

Additional information

	2007 Jan. 1 Rs.	2007 Dec. 31 Rs.
Stock-in-trade	5,800	9,200
Debtors	15,600	12,900
Creditors	9,200	7,100
Machinery	21,000	?
Outstanding Sundry Expenses	900	1,200
Prepaid Sundry Expenses	600	800
Furniture	16,000	?
Cash in hand	18,200	35,560
Bills Payable	3,000	5,000
Bills Receivable	4,500	5,500

The following adjustments are required to be made:
1. Machinery of Rs. 4,800 was sold on July 1, 2007. Depreciate machinery by 10% and Furniture @ 10% p.a.
2. Bad debts written off during the year Rs. 1,600. A provision @ 5% on debtors is to be made for bad debts.
3. Discount Allowed Rs. 700, Discount Received Rs. 650, Sales Returns Rs. 900 and Purchase Returns Rs. 600.

Solution

In the Books of Mr. Mukbul Hussain

Dr.   **Cash Account**   Cr.

	Rs.		Rs.
To Balance b/d	18,200	By Purchases	12,900
To NSC cashed	4,000	By Carriage	2,200
To Debtors	41,800	By Wages	3,950
To Machinery (Sold)	3,500	By Furniture (1.10.07)	4,000
To Sales	16,100	By Drawings	5,600
To Sale of personal gold	7,000	By Advertisement	2,800
To Miscellaneous Income	13,900	By Sundry Expenses	8,200
To Bills Receivable A/c	14,000	By Creditors	29,200
		By Bills Payable A/c	10,000
		By Balance c/d	39,650
	118,500		118,500

Dr.		Debtors Account	Cr.
	Rs.		Rs.
To Balance b/d	15,600	By Cash (Received from customers)	41,800
To Sales (Balancing figure)	57,300	By Discount Allowed	700
		By Bad Debts	1,600
		By Sales Returns	900
		By Bills Receivable A/c	15,000
		By Balance c/d	12,900
	72,900		72,900

Dr.		Creditors Account	Cr.
	Rs.		Rs.
To Cash (Paid to creditors)	29,200	By Balance b/d	9,200
To Discount Received	650	By Purchases (Balancing figure)	40,350
To Purchase Returns	600		
To Bills Payable A/c	12,000		
To Balance c/d	7,100		
	49,550		49,550

Dr.		Bills Receivable Account	Cr.
	Rs.		Rs.
To Balance b/d	4,500	By Cash (Received from customers)	14,000
To Debtors A/c (Balancing figure)	15,000	By Balance c/d	5,500
(B/R received during the period)			
	19,500		19,500

Dr.		Bills Payable Account	Cr.
	Rs.		Rs.
To Cash (Paid to creditors)	10,000	By Balance b/d	3,000
To Balance c/d	5,000	By Creditors A/c (Balancing figure)	12,000
		(B/P issued during the period)	
	15,000		15,000

Dr.		Machinery Account	Cr.
	Rs.		Rs.
To Balance b/d	21,000	By Cash (sale)	3,500
To Cash (Purchase)		By Loss on sale	1,300
		By Depreciation	
		10% of (Rs. 21,000 – Rs. 4,800)	1,620
		By Balance c/d	14,580
	21,000		21,000

Balance Sheet as on April 1, 2007

Liabilities	Rs.	Assets	Rs.
Capital	68,600	Machinery	21,000
(Balancing figure)		Furniture	16,000
Creditors	9,200	Stock-in-trade	5,800
Outstanding Sundry Expenses	900	Debtors	15,600
Bills Payable	3,000	Prepaid Sundry Expenses	600
		Bills Receivable	4,500
		Cash in hand	18,200
	81,700		81,700

Trading Account and Profit and Loss Account

Dr. For the year ended Dec. 31, 2007 Cr.

	Rs.	Rs.		Rs.	Rs.
To Opening Stock		5,800	By Sales:		
To Purchases:			Cash	16,100	
Cash	12,900		Credit	57,300	
Credit	40,350			73,400	
	53,250		*Less:* Sales Returns	900	72,500
Less: Purchase Returns	600	52,650	By Closing Stock		9,200
To Carriage		2,200			
To Wages		3,950			
To Gross Profit c/d		17,100			
		81,700			81,700
To Advertisement		2,800	By Gross Profit b/d		17,100
To Discount Allowed		700	By Discount Received		650
To Bad Debts		1,600	By Miscellaneous Income		13,900
To Sundry Expenses	8,200				
Less: Opening Outstanding	900				
	7,300				
Add: Closing Outstanding	1,200				
	8,500				
Add: Opening Prepaid	600				
	9,100				
Less: Closing Prepaid	800	8,300			
To Provision for Doubtful Debts		645			
To Loss on sale of Machinery		1,300			
To Depreciation on:					
Machinery	1,620				
Furniture	1,700	3,320			
To Net Profit		12,985			
(Transferred to Capital A/c)					
		31,650			31,650

Balance Sheet as on December 31, 2007

Liabilities	Rs.	Rs.	Assets	Rs.	Rs.
Capital	68,600		Machinery		14,580
Add: Fresh capital:			Furniture		
NSC cashed	4,000		(Rs. 16,000 + Rs. 4,000 – Rs. 1,700)		18,300
Sale of gold	7,000		Stock-in-trade		9,200
Add: Net Profit	12,985		Debtors	12,900	
	92,585		*Less:* Provision for Doubtful Debts	645	12,255
Less: Drawings	5,600	86,985	Prepaid Sundry Expenses		800
Outstanding Sundry Expenses		1,200	Cash in hand		39,650
Bills Payable		5,000	Bills Receivable		5,500
Creditors		7,100			
		100,285			100,285

Working Note

Calculation of depreciation on Furniture:

Depreciation on Furniture: 10% on Rs. 16,000 for full year = Rs. 1,600

10% on Rs. 4,000 for three months = Rs.   100   1,700.

EXERCISES

I. *Short Answer Type Questions (with answers)*

1. What is single entry system?

    Ans: In simple words, single entry system may be defined as an incomplete record of business transactions prepared by not following the general accounting principles and procedures, but is done according to the desires of the owner. Thus, there cannot be any particular system which may be called a single entry system. Single entry system is nothing but a defective or limited use of double entry system.

2. What are the different methods of calculating profit/loss generally used under single entry system?

    Ans: Statement of affairs method and conversion method.

3. In which type of business is the single entry system followed?

    Ans: Sole traders and partnership business.

4. Can business performance be compared with other similar firms following the single entry system?

    Ans: No. As the business performance cannot be measured properly, comparison cannot be made systematically.

5. Why is it generally said that proper planning for future cannot be made under the single entry system?

    Ans: Since the facts and figures supplied cannot be relied upon, proper planning for future cannot be made under a single entry system.

6. Can the true financial position be ascertained through a statement of affairs?

    Ans: The true financial position cannot be ascertained because the statement of affairs does not represent the true state of affairs of a business. In fact, this system is nothing but a defective or limited use of a double entry system.

7. Which types of accounts are maintained under the single entry system?

    Ans: Cash book and personal Ledger Accounts (debtors and creditors) are usually maintained, ignoring nominal and real accounts, under the single entry system.

8. Are subsidiary books maintained properly under the single entry system?

    Ans: Subsidiary books are not maintained properly under the single entry system except the cash book.

9. Can arithmetical accuracy be checked under the single entry system?

    Ans: Arithmetical accuracy cannot be checked under the single entry system because Trial Balance can not be prepared.

10. Are nominal and real accounts maintained under the single entry system?

    Ans: No, only cash account is maintained.

11. What are the sources of data used in the statement of affairs?

    Ans: Statement of affairs is prepared with the help of some account balances (Cash A/c, Debtors A/c and Creditors A/c), relevant information from the list of vouchers and other documents.

12. What do you mean by statement of affairs?

    Ans: Statement of affairs is a statement prepared at the beginning and at the end of a financial period to ascertain the capital or net worth of the firm with the help of assets and liabilities, like that in a balance sheet.

13. What are the different types of single entry system?

 Ans: The different types of single entry system are pure single entry system, simple single entry system and quasi-single entry system.

14. How is profit or loss calculated through the net worth method?

 Ans: Closing capital + Drawings (cash + goods + assets) – Fresh capital – Opening capital = Profit or loss before adjustments (or trading profit/loss) – Adjustments [add adjustments for loss] = Net profit/Net loss.

15. How will the amount of interest be calculated when the specific date of drawing is not given?

 Ans: When the specific date of drawing is not given, interest on drawings will be calculated on an average basis, i.e., for half a year.

16. Can the single entry system be adapted for a limited company?

 Ans: No, this system cannot be adapted for a limited company because of legal restrictions.

17. What are the different books and accounts maintained under the quasi-single entry system?

 Ans: Under the quasi-single entry system, cash book, personal accounts and a few subsidiary books are maintained.

18. What is the basis of calculation of profit under the net worth method?

 Ans: According to the net worth method, profit of a business or a firm is to be calculated with the help of the net worth (or capital) of two periods, i.e., opening and closing capital of the business. The basic concept of this method is that if the inflow is greater than the outflow, it indicates profit. Suppose, Rs.100 is invested in a business, and at the end of the year, the said amount increases to Rs.180. The increase in amount of Rs 80 is to be considered as surplus or profit.

19. What do you mean by the terms 'additional capital' or 'fresh capital' under a single entry system?

 Ans: Additional capital or fresh capital is the personal cash or assets introduced or brought in by the proprietor or used within the business during the year. Suppose, personal land of the proprietor was sold and the sale proceeds was introduced by the proprietor, or personal NSC cashed, or shares sold and the amount brought into the business.

20. When the date of purchase of any fixed asset is not given, what procedure or principle is generally followed for calculating the depreciation of the said asset?

 Ans: When the date of purchase of any fixed asset is not given, then the depreciation of the said asset is to be charged on an average basis, i.e., for six months.

21. While calculating depreciation of any fixed asset purchased at the middle or at the end of a year, when is the depreciation to be charged for full year or when is the time factor to be considered?

 Ans: When it is mentioned that depreciation is to be charged 'by ...% ', then no time factor is to be considered. Hence, depreciation has to be charged for full year though purchased at the middle or at the end of the year. Time factors are to be considered under the following situations:

 1. 'by ... % p.a.' is given, or
 2. 'at ... %' is given, or
 3. 'at ... % p.a.' is given.

22. Give the basic principles followed for calculating the interest on drawings under different situations as mentioned below:

 (a) When date of drawings are given
 (b) When date of drawings are not given
 (c) When cash is withdrawn at the end of each month
 (d) When cash is withdrawn at the beginning of each month
 (e) When cash is withdrawn at the middle of each month.

Ans: Generally, the following principles are followed for the calculation of interest on drawings under the different situations stated above:

    (a) **When the dates of drawings are given:** Interest is to be charged on actual basis.

    (b) **When the dates of drawings are not given:** The interest on drawings is to be calculated on average basis, i.e. for six months.

    (c) **When cash is withdrawn at the end of each month:** Interest is to be charged for 5.5 months.

    (d) **When cash is withdrawn at the beginning of each month:** Interest is to be charged for 6.5 months.

    (e) **When cash is withdrawn at the middle of each month:** Interest is to be charged for 6 months.

23. Suppose cash of Rs.1,500 is withdrawn at the end of each quarter year, then how can you calculate the amount of interest on drawings @ 6% p.a.?

Ans: When cash of Rs.1,500 is withdrawn at the end of each quarter, then interest is to be calculated under product method as under:

Interest on	Product (Rs.)
First quarter Rs. 1,500 for nine months	13,500
Second quarter Rs. 1,500 for six months	9,000
Third quarter Rs. 1,500 for three months	4,500
Fourth quarter Rs. 1,500 for 0 months	0
	27,000

Interest @ 6% p.a. on Rs. 27,000 for one month under product method = $27,000 \times 6/100 \times 1/12$ = Rs. 135.

24. In the absence of an agreement, how is the interest on loan provided by any partner dealt with?

Ans: In the absence of an agreement if a partner has advanced any amount to his business, he will be entitled to an interest @ 6% p.a. on his loan amount (According to the Partnership Act). It is a charge against profit, and hence, it is to be shown as a business expenditure but not as an appropriation.

25. When a partner's capital shows a negative balance and continues to show such a balance even after making all adjustments regarding appropriations and drawings, then how is it shown in the final statement of affairs?

Ans: When a partner's capital balance shows an overdrawn balance (negative balance) after making all the adjustments regarding appropriations and drawings, then such an overdrawn balance is again to be shown on the asset side of the final statement of affairs.

II. *Essay Type Questions*

    1. What is meant by the term 'single entry system' of book keeping? Give the salient features of single entry system in brief.

    2. Explain the main drawbacks of single entry system.

    3. Do you think that the single entry system of book keeping is a fool proof system of accounting? If not, then give reasons in support of your answer.

    4. What are the advantages of a single entry system?

    5. How can the profit or loss of a firm be ascertained under single entry system of book keeping?

    6. What is Net Worth Method? How is the profit or loss of a firm calculated through this method?

7. What is meant by the term 'statement of affairs'? What is the objective of preparing this statement? How is it prepared?

8. What is a statement of profit and loss? How is it prepared? Give a specimen of it.

9. Give the difference between the following:
   (a) Double entry system and single entry system.
   (b) Balance Sheet and statement of affairs.
   (c) Profit and Loss Account and Statement of Profit and Loss.

10. What do you mean by alternative method for calculating profit or loss of a firm under single entry system? Give a specimen of a statement of Profit and Loss prepared for ascertaining the profit or loss under single entry system as per alternative method.

III. *Problems*

On Net Worth or Statement of Affairs Method:

1. Mahima Prakash keeps his books of accounts under Single Entry System. He started his business on 1st January 1996 with capital of Rs. 80,000. On 31st December 1996 his position was as follows: Machinery Rs. 31,000, Furniture Rs. 14,000, Closing Stock Rs. 18,200, Debtors Rs. 28,000, Investment Rs. 8,000, Cash in hand Rs. 26,700, Creditors Rs. 12,900 and Outstanding Shop Rent Rs. 1,200.
   Ascertain the Profit or Loss made by Mahima Prakash for the year ended 31.12.96 by preparing the necessary statement.
   Ans: Net Profit Rs. 31,800.

2. P.C. Kar started his business with capital of Rs. 58,000 on 1.1.94, and his capital on 31st December 1994 stood at Rs. 63,000. He has submitted further information for consideration as follows:
   (a) He withdrew Rs. 750 p.m. from the business for his household purposes (personal use).
   (b) His house rent Rs. 600 p.m. was paid from the business cash.
   (c) He cashed his personal N.S.C. and brought that amount into the business Rs. 10,000.
   You are required to prepare the Statement of Profit and Loss for the year ended 31.12.94.
   Ans: Net Profit Rs. 11,200.

3. Mounsur Ali keeps his books under Single Entry System. His positions on January 1, 1991 and on December 31, 1991 were as follows:

	1991 Jan. 1 Rs.	1991 Dec. 31 Rs.
Machinery	30,000	30,000
Furniture	9,000	9,000
Stock	16,000	21,000
Debtors	12,500	17,500
Investment	—	12,000
Prepaid Expenses	—	1,600
Outstanding Expenses	100	600
Cash in hand	11,300	23,200
Creditors	9,000	14,300

During the year Mr. Ali used goods from the business for his personal use Rs. 300 and withdrew Rs. 500 p.m. from the business cash for his personal use. From the above information prepare a Statement of Affairs and a Statement of Profit and Loss for the year ended 31st December 1991.
Ans: Net Profit Rs. 36,000; Opening Capital Rs. 69,700: Adjusted Closing Capital Rs. 99,400.

4. Mr. Anupam Sen submits the following particulars of his business maintained under Single Entry System:

	1994 Jan. 1 Rs.	1994 Dec. 31 Rs.
Plant and Machinery	40,000	50,000
Furniture	10,000	15,000
Stock	8,600	10,400
Debtors	12,900	14,400
Creditors	10,500	13,500

Additional Informations

(a) Depreciate Plant and Machinery and Furniture @ 10% p.a. and 5% p.a. respectively.
(b) Provision for doubtful debts @ 5% on debtors.
(c) Cash withdrawn from business for personal use Rs. 12,000.
(d) Further capital introduced Rs. 6,000 during the period.

Draw up Statement of Affairs as at 31st December, 1994 and work out Profit or Loss for the year ended 31st December, 1994.

Ans: Net Profit Rs. 15,455; Opening Capital Rs. 61,000; Closing Adjusted Capital Rs. 70,455; Final Statement of Affairs Total Rs. 83,955; Trading Profit Rs. 21,300.

5. Mr. Alfa started his business with Capital Rs. 60,000 on 1.1.86 and he keeps his books under Single Entry System. His position on 31st December, 1986 was as follows:

Debtors Rs. 16,000, Machinery Rs. 24,000, Furniture Rs. 9,000, Stock Rs. 12,000, Bills Receivable Rs. 6,000, Cash at bank Rs. 16,000, Cash in hand Rs. 8,500, Creditors Rs. 11,000, Bills Payable Rs. 2,500 and Outstanding Expenses Rs. 1,200.

During the year he withdrew from his business for personal use Rs. 9,500. His house rent Rs. 500 p.m. was also paid from the business cash. The following adjustments are to be made:

(a) Interest on Capital @ 5%.
(b) Depreciate machinery and furniture @ 10%.

You are required to calculate profits of the year 1986 and Statement of Affairs at the end of the year.

Ans: Net Profit Rs. 27,650; Trading Profit Rs. 32,300; Closing Adjusted Capital Rs. 75,150; Final Statement of Affairs Total Rs. 89,850.

[**Note:** Depreciation on Assets charged for half year only.]

6. Rupa and Soma started business on 1st January 1993 with capital of Rs. 50,000 each. Their position on 31st December 1993 was as follows: Debtors Rs. 31,000, Plant and Machinery Rs. 36,000, Furniture Rs. 18,000, Stock Rs. 26,000, Investment Rs. 14,000, Cash in hand and Cash at bank Rs. 24,500, Creditors Rs. 13,900 and loan Rs. 6,000. The following adjustments are to be made:

(a) Depreciate Machinery and Furniture by 10%.
(b) Provision for Doubtful Debts @ 5% on Debtors.
(c) Interest on Capital @ 5% p.a.
(d) Rupa and Soma withdrew Rs. 1,500 p.m. and Rs. 1,000 p.m. respectively from the business.

Draw up a Statement of Profit and Loss for the year ended 31st December 1993 and also a Statement of Affairs as on that date.

Ans: Trading Profit Rs. 59,600, Net Profit Rs. 52,650, Divisible Profit Rs. 47,650 distributed equally, Closing Adjusted Capital: Rupa Rs. 58,325, Soma Rs. 64,325, Final Statement of Affairs Total Rs. 142,550.

[**Note:** Depreciation on Machinery and Furniture charged for full year, as "by" is given. Here time factor is not considered.]

7. Pushpen and Sanjib are partners sharing Profit and Losses in the ratio of 3 : 2. They keep their books under Single Entry System. The following was the Statement of Affairs as on 31st December 1995:

	Rs.	Rs.		Rs.	Rs.
Capital A/c's			Plant and Machinery		38,000
Pushpen	45,000		Furniture		16,000
Sanjib	65,000	110,000	Investment		18,000
Creditors		24,000	Debtors		32,000
Bills Payable		8,000	Prepaid Expenses		2,000
			Cash in hand		36,000
		142,000			142,000

The following was their position on 31st December 1996:

Plant and Machinery Rs. 58,000, Furniture Rs. 24,000, Investment Rs. 18,000, Debtors Rs. 36,000, Prepaid Expenses Rs. 3,000, Cash in hand Rs. 41,000, Creditors Rs. 32,000, Bills Payable Rs. 12,000 and Outstanding Expenses Rs. 1,500.

Pushpen and Sanjib withdrew Rs. 16,000 and Rs. 20,000 respectively from the business for their personal use. Sanjib also had taken goods for his personal use costing Rs. 3,000 from the business. Depreciate Machinery and Furniture @ 10% p.a. You are required to prepare a Statement of Profit and Loss for the year ended 31.12.96 and a Statement of Affairs as on that date.

Ans: Trading Profit Rs. 63,500; Net Profit Rs. 56,700; Pushpen's share of profit Rs. 34,020 and Sanjib's share of profit Rs. 22,680; Closing Statement of Affairs Total Rs. 173,200.

8. Mr. M. Parekh and G. Prasad are partners sharing Profits and Losses in the ratio of 5 : 3. Their position on 1.1.94 and 31.12.94 was as follows:

		1994 Jan. 1 Rs.	1994 Dec. 1 Rs.		1994 Jan. 1 Rs.	1994 Dec. 1 Rs.
Capital A/c's				Machinery	32,000	42,000
M. Parekh	42,000			Stock	28,000	33,000
G. Prasad	28,000	70,000	99,000	Debtors	36,000	44,000
Creditors		30,000	36,000	Cash in hand	4,000	16,000
		100,000	135,000		100,000	135,000

The following adjustments are to be made:

(a) Depreciate machinery @ 10% p.a.
(b) Provision for Doubtful Debts @ 5% on Debtors.
(c) Interest on capitals @ 5%.
(d) Interest on drawings @ 5% p.a.
(e) During the year Mr. Parekh and Mr. Prasad withdrew from the business for private use Rs. 9,000 and Rs. 12,000 respectively.

You are required to prepare a Statement of Profit and Loss for the year ended 31st December 1994 and a Statement of Affairs as on that date.

Ans: Trading Profit Rs. 50,000; Net Profit Rs. 44,100; Distributable Profit Rs. 41,125; M. Parekh's Closing Capital Rs. 60,578; G. Prasad's Closing Capital Rs. 32,522; Closing Statement of Affairs Total Rs. 129,100.

9. M, N and O are partners sharing Profits and Losses in the ratio of Total 4:3:2. Keep their books under Single Entry System. Their Statement of Affairs as on 1st January 1991 was as follows:

	Rs.	Rs.		Rs.	Rs.
Capital A/c's			Plant and Machinery		38,000
M	60,000		Motor car		16,000
O	42,000	102,000	Furniture		12,000
Sundry Creditors		13,000	Debtors		28,000
			Stock		8,000
			Cash in hand		7,000
			Capital A/c N		6,000
		115,000			115,000

On 31st December 1991 their position was as follows:

Machinery Rs. 48,000 (additions were made on 1.4.91), Furniture Rs. 15,000, Debtors Rs. 34,000, Stock Rs. 13,000, Cash in hand Rs. 19,000, Sundry Creditors Rs. 21,000 and Loan Rs. 10,000.

The following adjustments are agreed upon:
(a) Depreciate all fixed assets @ 10% p.a.
(b) Interest on capital @ 5% p.a. and on overdrawn capital @ 10% p.a.
(c) During the year M Introduced Rs. 10,000 on 1.5.91 as fresh capital.
(d) M, N and O's drawings during the year had been Rs. 12,000, Rs. 8,000 and Rs. 4,000 respectively.

You are required to show a Statement of Profit and Loss for the year ended 31.12.91 and Final Statement of Affairs as on that date.

Ans: Trading Profit Rs. 32,000; Net Profit Rs. 25,500; Distributable Profit Rs. 20,667; Closing Capital M—Rs. 70,518, N—Rs. 42,989 and O's overdrawn Rs. 6,007; Closing Statement of Affairs Total Rs. 144,507.

[**Note:** Depreciation on machinery Rs. 4,550, on furniture Rs. 1,350 and on car Rs. 1,600.]

10. Mr. Prokash submits the followingparticulars of his business, maintained under Single Entry System:

	1976 Jan. 1 Rs.	1976 Dec. 31 Rs.
Debtors	18,900	23,600
Creditors	13,700	18,200
Cash in hand and Cash at Bank	19,200	31,000
Machinery	20,000	40,000
Investment	10,000	10,000
Stock	13,000	15,900
Prepaid expenses	1,700	2,300
Outstanding expenses	600	1,900

During the year his drawings were amounting to Rs. 7,500. He sold his household furniture at Rs. 6,000 and brought that amount into the business. He gave a personal gift of Rs. 3,000 to his brother from the business cash.

The following adjustments are to be made:
(a) Depreciate machinery @ 10% p.a.
(b) Accrued interest on investment Rs. 750.
(c) Provision for doubtful debts at 5% on debtors.

You are required to calculate profits for the year 1976 and to prepare the Statement of Affairs for the year ended 31st December 1976.

Ans: Trading Profit Rs. 39,450; Net Profit Rs. 35,270; Opening Capital Rs. 68,500; Closing Adjusted Capital Rs. 99,270; Closing Statement of Affairs Total Rs. 119,370.

11. Dark and Fade started business with capital of Rs. 50,000 and Rs. 40,000 respectively on 1.1.92, which consist of the following items: Cash Rs. 16,000, Machinery Rs. 21,000, Stock Rs. 16,000, Debtors Rs. 28,000, Furniture Rs. 9,000, 10% Investment Rs. 10,000 and Creditors Rs. 10,000.

    Their position on 31st December 1992 was as follows:

    Machinery Rs. 31,000, Stock Rs. 27,000, Debtors Rs. 31,000, Cash Rs. 19,000, Creditors Rs. 17,000 and Loan Rs. 9,000.

    The following adjustments are agreed upon:

    (a) Depreciate Machinery and Furniture at 10% p.a.
    (b) Drawings made by Dark and Fade Rs. 19,800 and Rs. 7,500 respectively.
    (c) Interest on capital at 5% p.a. and on drawings at 6% p.a.
    (d) Dark is entitled to a salary of Rs. 500 p.m.

    Ascertain Profit or Loss for the year 1992 and prepare the Statement of Affairs as on 31st December 1992.

    Ans: Trading Profit Rs. 38,300; Net Profit Rs. 34,800; Distributable Profit Rs. 25,119 (distributed equally); Closing Capital; Dark Rs. 50,665.50 and Fade Rs. 46,834.50; Closing Statement of Affairs Total Rs. 123,500.

12. Mr. A. Kapoor, a businessman, keeps his books of account under single entry system. His financial position on April 1, 2007 and March 31, 2008 were as follows:

	2007 Apr. 1 Rs.	2008 Mar. 31 Rs.
Cash	7,450	6,580
Sundry debtors	25,350	36,900
Stock	30,300	40,320
Furniture	6,900	9,000
Prepaid rent	–	400
Sundry creditors	16,500	18,600
Accrued expenses	3,500	4,300

During the year ending March 31, 2008, his drawings amounted to Rs. 15,000. He also withdrew goods worth Rs. 600 for his personal use. On July 1, 2007, Mr. Kapoor transferred some of his household furniture to the business at Rs. 2,100.

From the above information, ascertain his profit or loss for the year ending March 31, 2008, and prepare his statement of affairs as on March 31, 2008, after taking into consideration the following information:

    (a) Depreciate furniture by 10% p.a.
    (b) Create a provision for doubtful debts @ 5% on debtors.

    Ans: Opening Capital Rs.50,000. Profit before adjustments Rs.33,800. Net Profit Rs. 31,107, Closing Capital Rs. 67,607, Final statement of affairs Total Rs. 90,507.

13. A trader keeps his books by the single entry system. His financial position on January 1 and December 31, 2007 were given below:

	2007 Jan. 1 Rs.	2007 Dec. 31 Rs.
Cash in hand	750	580
Cash at bank	6,300	17,200
Stock in trade	9,600	10,420
Sundry debtors	15,000	18,900
Sundry creditors	14,500	12,700
Plant and machinery	25,000	30,000
Furniture and fixtures	3,150	4,600

He withdrew Rs. 500 from the business at the end of each month, and introduced Rs. 5,000 as further capital on July 1, 2007.

From the above information, prepare a statement of profit and loss for the year ending December 31, 2007. Also, prepare a statement of affairs as on that date after depreciating plant and machinery by 15%, and furniture and fixtures by 10%, and make a provision of 2% for bad debts.

[Tripura H.S., adapted]

Ans: Opening capital Rs. 45,300, Profit before adjustments Rs. 14,700, Net Profit Rs. 9,362, Closing capital Rs. 53,662, Final statement of affairs Total Rs. 66,362.

14. Anil and Sachin are in a partnership and share profits and losses in the ratio of 2:1. They keep their books on single entry system. On December 31, 2007, a statement of affairs was prepared which showed the following:

Liabilities	Rs.	Assets	Rs.
Capital:		Plant and Machinery	70,800
Anil	60,000	Stock	30,900
Sachin	36,000	Sundry Debtors	27,600
Loan (Anil)	12,000	Cash at bank	4,980
Sundry creditors	26,280		
	134,280		134,280

On December 31, 2007, their assets and liabilities were as follows:

	Rs.
Sundry debtors	37,200
Plant and machinery	70,800
Plant and machinery (Addition)	30,000
Sundry creditors	22,800
Bills receivable	17,280
Stock	32,700
Cash at bank	5,250

Ascertain the amount of the firm's profit or loss for the year ended December 31, 2007, and prepare a statement of affairs as on that date after taking into consideration the following:

(a) Depreciation on plant and machinery, including additions is to be provided @ 10% p.a.

(b) On September 1, 2007, Anil advanced an additional loan of Rs. 30,000 for purchasing the additional machinery which was installed on the same date.

(c) Interest on loan is payable at 9% p.a.

(d) During the year, Anil and Sachin drew Rs. 9,000 and Rs. 4000, respectively, from the business. [W.B.H.S. adapted]

Ans: Profit before Adjustments Rs. 45,430. Net Profit Rs. 37,350, Divisible Profit Rs. 35,370, Closing Capital: Anil Rs. 76,560 and Sachin Rs. 43,790, Final statement of affairs Total Rs.185,150.

15. Mr. Kumar keeps his books under single entry system. His position was as under:

	2007 Jan. 1 Rs.	2007 Dec. 31 Rs.
Building	80,000	80,000
Machinery	68,000	91,000
Furniture	14,000	22,000
Debtors	46,000	56,000
Creditors	29,000	38,000

(Contd.)

	2007 Jan. 1 Rs.	2007 Dec. 31 Rs.
Investments	40,000	60,000
Cash in hand	16,300	15,100
Cash at bank	26,400	19,800
Prepaid expenses	2,700	4,400
Outstanding expenses	1,900	1,500
Closing stock	12,500	19,700

Additional information

(a) Machinery and furniture are to be depreciated @ 10% p.a.
(b) Accrued interest on investment Rs.4,900.
(c) Make provision for doubtful debts @ 5% on debtors.
(d) Proprietor's house rent Rs.750 p.m. was paid from the business cash regularly.
(e) Cash withdrawn by Mr. Kumar Rs.900 p.m. from the business cash for personal use.
(f) Personal shares of Rs. 10,000 sold at Rs.14,600 was introduced into the business on June 15, 2007.

Prepare a statement of profit and loss for the period ending December 31, 2007, and draw up the final statement of affairs as on that date.

Ans: Opening Capital Rs. 275,000, Profit before adjustments Rs. 58,700, Net Profit Rs. 51,050. Closing Capital Rs. 320,850, Final statement of affairs Total Rs. 360,350.

16. Lox and Cox are partners in a firm, sharing profit and losses in the ration of 3 : 2. On 1.1.96 their position was as follows:

Capital A/c's		Rs.	Machinery		Rs. 30,000
Lox	40,000		Stock		23,000
Cox	30,000	70,000	Debtors	28,000	
Reserve Fund		10,000	Less: Provision		
Sundry Creditors		18,000	for Bad Debts	1,000	27,000
			Bank		18,000
		98,000			98,000

The firm did not maintain Double Entry System and their position on 31.12.96 was as follows:

Debtors Rs. 34,000, Creditors Rs. 16,000, Stock Rs. 32,000 and Bank Balance Rs. 39,000.

You are required to prepare Statement of Profit and Loss Account for the period ended 31.12.96 and the Statement of Affairs of the firm as on that date after considering the following points:

(a) Depreciate machinery at 10% p.a.
(b) Provision for Bad Debts is to be created @ 5% on debtors.
(c) Drawings of partners were:
   Lox Rs. 600 p.m. at the end of each month.
   Cox Rs. 500 p.m. at the end of each month.
(d) Interest on capital @ 5% is to be allowed.
(e) Interest on drawings @ 6% p.a. is to be charged.

Ans: Trading Profit Rs. 52,200; Net Profit Rs. 47,500; Distributable Profit Rs. 44,429; Closing capital: Lox—Rs. 61,223, Cox—Rs. 43,077; Closing Statement of Affairs Total Rs. 130,300; Interest on Drawings: Lox Rs. 234 and Cox Rs. 195.

17. The Balance Sheet of A as at 31.12.1987 and 1988 are set out below. He does not understand as to what has happened to the profit of Rs. 120,000 as disclosed by 1998 Balance Sheet as he does not find in his Bank balance. Draw up statement which will explain to him as to how the profit may be accounted for:

	31.12.87 (Rs.)	31.12.88 (Rs.)		31.12.87 (Rs.)	31.12.88 (Rs.)
Capital	230,000	230,000	Cash at bank	10,000	10,000
Add: Profit for 1988		120,000	Sundry Debtors	140,000	160,000
		350,000	Stock	60,000	100,000
Less: Drawings 1988		24,000	Motor Vehicles	20,000	16,000
	230,000	326,000	Plant (Less Dep.)	160,000	140,000
Mortgage on freehold property	160,000	120,000	Fixed Property	200,000	200,000
Sundry Creditors	200,000	180,000			
	590,000	626,000		590,000	626,000

(C.U. B. Com.—Adapted)

[**Hint:** In order to prepare a statement to prove the profits of the year 1988, the following procedures are to be followed. Comparisons are to be made between the assets and liabilities of the two years as follows:

(i) Increase in assets and decrease in liabilities indicates profit.

(ii) Decrease in assets and increase in liabilities indicates loss.

(iii) The result drawn after fulfilling the steps in (i) and (ii) has to be adjusted with drawings.
(Profit + Drawings)/(Loss – Drawings) = Net Profit

Items indicating profits:

Sundry Debtors (160,000 – 140,000)	=	20,000
Stock (100,000 – 60,000)	=	40,000
Mortgage on property (160,000 – 120,000)	=	40,000
Sundry Creditors (200,000 – 180,000)	=	20,000
		120,000

Less: Items indicating losses:

Motor vehicles (20,000 – 16,000)	=	4,000	
Plant (160,000 – 140,000)	=	20,000	24,000
			96,000
Add: Drawings (1988)			24,000
Profit for the year 1988			120,000

18. Sri Bharat, a trader, keeps his books under Single Entry Method. His financial position on 1st January, 1995 and 31st December, 1995 were as follows:

	1995 Jan. 1 Rs	1995 Dec. 31 Rs
Stock-in-trade	24,000	27,900
Furniture	7,200	9,600
Cash in hand	9,000	9,600
Creditors	14,400	21,600
Plant and Machinery	36,000	48,000
Debtors	20,400	22,800
Bank balance	7,200	10,800
		(Credit)

During the year 1995, Sri Bharat had withdrawn Rs. 600 p.m. for his household use. From the above information ascertain his profit or loss for the year and also prepare his Statement of

Affairs as on 31st December, 1995 after taking into account the following informations:
(i)   Depreciate Plant and Machinery by 15% p.a. and Furniture by 12½ % p.a.
(ii) Of the debtors Rs. 500 are bad and to be written off
(iii) Create a Provision of Bad Debts on debtors at 5%.
(iv) Allow interest on capital at 5% p.a.

(W.B.H.S. 1995)

Ans: Trading Profit Rs. 3,300; Net Loss Rs. 10,135; Closing Statement of Affairs Total Rs. 108,935; Closing Adjusted Capital Rs. 76,535.

19. Mr. Sunando Sanyal who keeps his books on Single Entry System tells you that his capital on 31.12.1980 is Rs. 18,700 and on 1st January 1980 was Rs. 19,200. He further informs you that he gave a loan of Rs. 3,500 to his brother on private account and withdrew Rs. 300 p.m. for personal purposes. He also used a flat for his personal purposes, the rent of which was Rs. 100 p.m. and electric charges Rs. 10 p.m. were paid from the business account. He sold his 7% Govt. bond of Rs. 2,000 at 3% premium and brought that money into the business. Besides this, there is no other information.

You are required to prepare the Statement of Profit for the year ended 31.12.1980.

(B.U. B. Com (Pass))

Ans: Profit Rs. 5,860, Total Drawings Rs. 8,420, New Capital Rs. 2,000 at 3% premium = 2000 × (103/100) = 2,060

20. Mr. Subrata Roy after retirement from service started a business of fancy goods with a capital of Rs.120,000 out of his Provident Fund receipts on March 1, 2007. He keeps his books under single entry system. He submits the following particulars of his business as on December 31, 2007:

Particulars	Rs.
Furniture	11,900
Closing stock	15,800
Machinery	39,000
Debtors	46,200
Creditors	12,800
Fixed Deposits (at UBI)	40,000
Cash and Bank balance	42,900
Office equipments	18,000
Outstanding Expenses	3,900
Prepaid Expenses	2,100

The following adjustments are to be made:
(a) Depreciate machinery, furniture and equipments by 10%.
(b) He purchased a delivery van at Rs. 31,000 for business use out of the cash withdrawn by him from the business for his personal use Rs. 48,600.
(c) His son took a calculator costing Rs. 1,300 from the business showroom for his personal use.

From the above information, calculate Mr. Subrata Roy's profit or loss for the first year ending on December 31, 2007 and prepare the final statement of affairs as on that date.

Ans: Profit before adjustments Rs. 129,100, Net Profit Rs. 122,210, Closing Capital Rs. 223,310. Final statement of affairs Total Rs. 240,010, Drawings Rs. 18,900.

21. Mr. D. Mishra does not maintain a complete double entry system. He started his business with Cash Rs. 26,000, Furniture Rs. 19,000, Stock Rs.12,000, and Machinery Rs. 42,000 on January 1, 2007. His position on December 31, 2007 was as under:

Debtors Rs. 31,200, Creditors Rs. 18,900, Stock in trade Rs. 15,600, Cash in hand Rs. 19,700, Bank overdraft Rs.7,000 and Stationery Stock Rs. 900.

Additional information:
(a) Machinery of Rs. 16,000 and furniture of Rs.10,000 were purchased during the year on June 1, 2007, and on August 1, 2007, respectively. Depreciation @ 10% p.a. is to be charged on the above assets.
(b) A computer costing Rs. 18,000 was purchased by taking a bank loan of Rs.10,000 for business use.
(c) Out of the debtors, Rs. 900 is to be written off as bad debt and Provision for Bad Debt is to be created @ 5% on debtors.
(d) Household furniture costing Rs. 9,000 was purchased from business cash.
(e) Cash withdrawn from the business for personal use Rs. 11,300.

Prepare a statement of Profit and Loss for the period ending December 31, 2007, and the final statement of affairs as on that date.

Ans: Opening Capital Rs. 99,000, Profit before adjustments Rs. 57,800, Net Profit Rs. 47,935, Closing Capital Rs. 126,635, Final statement of affairs Total Rs. 162,535, Depreciation on Machinery Rs. 5,133, and Furniture Rs. 2,317.

22. Mr. C. Chowla submits the following particulars of his business maintained under single entry system.

Particulars	2007 Jan. 1 Rs.	2007 Dec. 31 Rs.
Plant and Machinery	60,000	72,000
Furniture and Equipment	26,000	35,000
Stock-in-trade	31,500	39,200
Debtors	42,700	46,500
Creditors	29,100	32,400
Cash in hand	12,800	20,700
Bank balance	19,000(Dr.)	8,500(Cr.)

The following adjustments are to be made:
(a) The personal computer of Mr. Chowla costing Rs. 29,000 was sold at Rs. 15,000, and the amount was brought into the business.
(b) Depreciate all fixed assets @ 10% p.a.
(c) Shop rent of Rs. 1,700 for December 2007 not yet paid.
(d) School fees of Mr. Chowla's son of Rs. 960 p.m. was paid from business cash. Goods used for personal purpose Rs. 6,000.
(e) Salary of Rs. 2,600 for the month of January, 2008 was paid to the Sales Manager in December, 2007.

Calculate the Profit or Loss for the year 2007, and to prepare the final statement of affairs for the year ended December 31, 2007.

Ans: Opening Capital Rs. 162,900, Profit before adjustments Rs. 13,020, Net Profit Rs. 3,370, Closing Capital Rs. 163,750, Final statement of affairs Total Rs. 206,350.

23. Mr. A. J. Rahman started his business with a capital of Rs. 80,000 on January 1, 2007. He keeps his books under single entry system. His position on December 31, 2007 was as under: Machinery Rs. 45,000, Furniture Rs. 20,000, Debtors Rs. 39,000, Stock Rs. 16,000, Investment Rs. 24,000, Creditors Rs. 21,000, Loan Rs.13,000, and Cash Rs. 26,000

Additional information:
(a) Depreciate machinery and furniture @ 10%.
(b) Mr. Rahman cashed his personal NSC of Rs. 16,000 and brought the amount into business.

(c) He paid Rs. 1,200 p.m. for his daughter's hostel fees from business cash.

(d) Household furniture was purchased for Rs. 3,000 but the payment was made through business cash.

(e) A computer and its printer were purchased at Rs. 39,000 for business use from his friend's shop, and as per agreement, the payment was supposed to be made in the next year. According to the manufacture, the said computer and its printer's lives are expected to be ten years.

Calculate the Profit or Loss for the year 2007, and prepare a final statement of affairs for the year ending December 31, 2007.

Ans: Profit before adjustments Rs. 57,400, Net Profit Rs. 50,250, Closing Capital Rs. 128,850, Final statement of affairs Total Rs. 201,850, Depreciation on Machinery Rs. 2,250, Computer Rs. 3,900, and Furniture Rs. 1,000.

24. Mr. A does not maintain complete Double Entry Books of Accounts. From the following details determine the profit for the year and Statement of Affairs at the end of the year.

Rs. 1,000 (cost) furniture was sold for Rs. 5,000 on 1.1.1982; 10% depreciation is to be charged on furniture; Mr. A has drawn Rs. 1,000 per month; Rs. 2,000 was invested by Mr. A in 1982.

	1982 Jan. 1 Rs.	1982 Dec. 31 Rs.
Stock	40,000	60,000
Debtors	30,000	40,000
Cash	2,000	1,000
Bank	10,000	5,000
		(Overdraft)
Creditors	15,000	25,000
Outstanding Expenses	5,000	8,000
Furniture (Cost)	3,000	2,000

Bank balance on 1.1.82 is as per Cash Book, but the Bank overdraft on 31.12.1982 is as per Bank Statement. Rs. 2,000 cheque drawn in December, 1982 have not been encashed within the year.

(C.U. B. Com.)

Ans: Opening Capital Rs. 65,000; Closing Capital Rs. 63,000; Total Profit Rs. 7,800; Final Statement of Affairs Total = Rs. 102,800; Overdraft balance as per Cash Book Rs. 7,000.

25. Sri R. Mitra commenced business on 1st January 1980, with Rs. 20,000 as Capital. He kept his books on Single Entry System. On 31st December, 1980 his books disclosed the following position:

Sundry Creditors—Rs. 7,500; Plant—Rs. 15,000; Stock-in-trade Rs. 12,000; Debtors—Rs. 13,500; and Cash at bank—Rs. 3,000. He drew from his business at the rate of Rs. 225 at the end of each month. On 1st July, 1980 he introduced a further capital amounting to Rs. 6,000. You are required to prepare a Statement of Profit and Loss for the year ended 31.12.1980 and a Statement of Affairs as on that date after taking into consideration the following:

(i) 7½ % of Sundry Debtors proved to be Bad,

(ii) Plant suffered depreciation @ 10%

(iii) a Provision for Doubtful Debts was required to be made at 2½ % of Debtors.

(C.U. B. Com.)

Ans: Net Profit Rs. 9,875; Final Statement of Affairs Total Rs. 40,675; Adjusted Closing Capital Rs. 33,175.

26. X is a small cloth merchant who has not kept full double entry records. His position as on 1st January 1982 stood as follows:

Cash in hand Rs. 760; Balance at Bank Rs. 6,950; Stock Rs. 16,700; Sundry Debtors Rs. 6,320; Furniture Rs. 2,000; Motorbike Rs. 4,000; and Sundry Creditors Rs. 5,300.

During the year he had withdrawn Rs. 400 p.m. for his personal expenses and purchased a new motorbike for his business use for Rs. 4,000. A cheque of Rs. 1,000 issued on 29.12.1982 was presented for payment on 12.1.1983.

Prepare a Statement showing his trading result for the year ended 31st December, 1982 and a Balance Sheet as on 31st December, 1982 after (a) providing 10% depreciation on the motorbike; (b) Writing off Rs. 320 as actual Bad Debts; (c) making a 5% provision for likely Bad Debts.

(C.A. Entrance)

Ans: Capital as per Statement of Affairs as on 1.1.82 and 31.12.82 Rs. 22,500 and Rs. 29,100 respectively; Trading Profit Rs. 7,420; Net Profit Rs. 5,800; Final Statement of Affairs Total Rs. 32,800; Closing Bank balance as per Cash Book Rs. 4,930.

27. K and D are partners in a firm sharing profits and losses as K, 60 p.c. and D 40 p.c. Their Statement of Affairs as at 31st March, 1982, is given below:

Liabilities		Rs.	Assets		Rs.
Sundry Creditors		40,000	Plant		40,000
Capital Accounts:			Furniture		15,000
K	50,000		Stock		25,000
D	30,000	80,000	Debtors		30,000
			Cash		10,000
		120,000			120,000

The partners keep their books by Single Entry System. On 31st March 1983, the position of the business was as follows:

Plant Rs. 50,000; Furniture Rs. 20,000; Stock Rs. 40,000; Debtors Rs. 45,000; Cash Rs. 11,000 and Sundry Creditors Rs. 30,000.

On 30th September 1982, K and D withdrew from the business Rs. 6,000 and Rs. 4,000 respectively.

You are required to ascertain the profit made by the partners during the year-end. Draw up a Statement of Affairs as at 31st March, 1983 by taking into consideration the following further information:

Plant and Furniture are to be depreciated at 10% and 20% respectively. A bad debts reserve of 2 ½ % is to be raised against Sundry Debtors. Interest on Capital is to be allowed at 5% per annum and Interest on drawings at 12% per annum.

(C.U, B. Com.)

Ans: Net Profit Rs. 56,875; Divisible Profit Rs. 53,475; K's capital Rs. 78,225; D's capital Rs. 48,650; Final Statement of Affairs Total Rs. 156,875; Interest on drawings calculated for 6 months.

Probelms on Conversion Method

1. You are required to determine the (i) Total Sates and Total Purchases for 1995 from the following particulars:

	Rs.
Total Debtors on 1.1.95	55,252
Total Creditors on 1.1.95	39,275
Bills Receivable on 1.1.95	27,322
Bills Payable on 1.1.95	9,345

(Contd.)

	Rs.
Cash received from Debtors	23,288
(not including a sum of Rs. 325 now recovered.	
It was written off as Bad Debt last year)	
Discount earned	1,455
Return Outward	2,379
Cash Sales	3,398
Total Debtors on 31.12.95	62,500
Cash Purchases	4,245
Bills Payable on 31.12.95	14,345
Cash paid to creditors	23,532
(including a sum of Rs. 1,800 being the cost of	
a typewriter purchased)	
Cash received against Bills Receivable	27,500
Return Inward	1,156
Discount Allowed	3,049
Total Creditors on 31.12.95	33,000
Bad Debts	3,224
Payment made against Bills Payable	14,000
Total Bills Receivable on 31.12.95	32,322

(C.B.S.E. Delhi Board)

Ans: Total Sales Rs. 73,863; Total Purchases Rs. 42,536.

2. From the following information calculate the Total Sales during the year 1997:
Debtors on 1.1.97 Rs. 11,600; Bills Receivable on 1.1.97 Rs. 4,900: Cash Sales Rs. 17,200; Cash received from Debtors Rs. 49,100; Bills Receivable honoured Rs. 6,200; Bills Receivable dishonoured Rs. 2,800; Customers cheque dishonoured Rs. 1,700; Discount allowed Rs. 1,200; Goods returned from customer Rs. 2,100; Bad Debts written off Rs.900; Allowance to customers Rs. 400; Bills Receivable endorsed to creditors Rs. 1,900; Interest charged to customers Rs. 120; Bills Receivable on 31.12.97 Rs. 2,400; Debtors on 31.12.97 Rs. 9,200.
Ans: Credit Sales Rs. 55,080; Total Sales Rs. 72,280; Bills Receivable received during the year Rs. 8,400.

3. From the following facts you are required to calculate the total purchase for the year 1997:
Opening Bills Payable Rs. 2,900; Opening Creditors Rs. 13,900; Cash paid to suppliers Rs. 41,500 (including cash purchase Rs. 9,800); Cash paid against bills payable Rs. 6,400; Bills Payable dishonoured Rs. 2,400; Discount received Rs. 1,600; Purchase return Rs. 1,900; Bills Receivable endorsed to creditors Rs. 2,500; Cheque issued to suppliers dishonoured Rs. 900; Closing Bills Payable Rs. 2,100; Closing creditors Rs. 7,700.
Ans: Credit purchases Rs. 36,200; Total purchases Rs. 46,000; Bills payable issued during the year Rs. 8,000.

4. You are required to calculate the Total Sales for the year 1997 from the following particulars:
Opening Debtors Rs. 21,000; Closing Debtors Rs. 16,800; Cash and cheque received from Debtors Rs. 56,200; Bills Receivable received during the year Rs. 9,500; Discount allowed Rs. 950; Sales Return Rs.1,350; Bad Debts recovered Rs. 2,800; Bad Debts written off Rs.720; Bills Receivable dishonoured Rs. 1,400; Interest charged to customers Rs. 200; Bad Debt Reserve Rs. 2,000; Cash Sales Rs. 15.900; Sale of Fixed Assets Rs. 5,000; Customer's cheque dishonoured Rs. 500, Cash refund to customers Rs. 200.
Ans: Credit Sales Rs. 62,220; Total Sales Rs. 78,120; Items not to be taken here—Bad Debts Recovered, Sale of Assets, Bad Debt Reserve.

5. From the following data, calculate the total sales and the total purchases by opening the appropriate accounts:

Balance on January 1, 2007:

Debtors Rs. 31,900, Creditors Rs. 27,200, Bills Receivable Rs. 10,300, and Bills Payable Rs. 9,500.

Other transactions:

Total cash received from customers Rs. 72,100 (including cash sales Rs. 18,700 and sale proceeds of an old machinery at Rs. 3,300), Cash paid to Creditors Rs.39,400; Cash purchases Rs. 10,900; Bills Receivable honoured during the year Rs.12,300; Discount Received Rs. 1,300, Bills Payable honoured during the year Rs. 8,700; Discount Allowed Rs. 900; Return inwards Rs. 1,100; Return Outwards Rs. 750; Bills Receivable dishonoured Rs. 2,700; Bills payable dishonoured Rs. 1,500; Customers' cheque dishonoured Rs. 2,300; Bad Debts written off Rs. 700; and Cash refund to Debtors Rs. 950.

Balance on December 31, 2007:

Debtors Rs. 41,200, Creditors Rs.31,300, Bills Receivable Rs.12,900 and Bills Payable Rs. 8,700.

Ans: Cash Sales Rs.18,700, Credit Sales Rs.73,750, Cash Purchases Rs. 10,900, Credit Purchases Rs. 53,450, Bills Receivable received Rs.17,600 and Bills Payable issued Rs. 9,400.

6. Calculate the total sales and purchases for the year 2007 from the following particulars:

	2007 Jan. 1 Rs.	2007 Dec. 31 Rs.
Trade Debtors	28,700	31,200
Trade Creditors	17,500	12,900
Bills Receivable	7,200	8,600
Bills Payable	5,900	7,800

Cash paid to suppliers Rs. 39,500; Cash purchases Rs. 12,800; Cash paid for furniture Rs. 2,100; Cash received from customers Rs. 68,100 (including sale of furniture Rs. 2,750); Allowance to customers Rs. 1,200; Discount allowed by suppliers Rs. 700; Bad Debts written off Rs. 940; Bad Debts recovered Rs. 900; Purchases Returns Rs. 1,300; Sales Returns Rs. 750; Bills Receivable endorsed to suppliers Rs. 2,100; Bills Receivable honoured Rs. 18,100; Bills Receivable dishonoured Rs. 3,200; Bills Payable honoured Rs. 9,300; Cash refund to customers Rs. 500; Customers' cheque dishonoured Rs. 840; Interest charged upon customers Rs. 170; and Cash sales Rs. 31,900.

Ans: Cash Sales Rs. 31,900, Credit Sales Rs. 90,830, Cash Purchases Rs. 12,800, Credit Purchases Rs. 50,200, Bills Receivable received Rs. 24,800, and Bills Payable issued Rs. 11,200.

7. Mr. S. Saxena keeps his books under single entry system. He submits the following information for the year 2007 about his business:

Receipts	Rs.	Payments	Rs.
Opening Balance	18,600	Creditors	46,500
Debtors	72,100	Wages	4,500
Miscellaneous Receipts	2,400	Rent and Taxes	5,200
Sales	10,900	Advertisement	2,700
		Drawings	8,900
		Carriage Inwards	2,700
		Furniture	4,000
		Salaries	5,100
		Investment	10,000
		Closing Balance	14,400
	104,000		104,000

Additional information:

	2007 Jan. 1 Rs.	2007 Dec. 31 Rs.
Balance on		
Machinery	40,000	40,000
Furniture	16,000	?
Stock in trade	12,100	21,600
Debtors	26,800	45,200
Creditors	17,400	21,600
Loan	15,000	15,000

With the help of the above information, prepare a Trading, and Profit and Loss Account for the year ended December 31, 2007 and a Balance Sheet as on that date.

Ans: Gross Profit Rs. 53,000, Net Profit Rs.42,400, Capital: Opening Rs. 81,100 and Closing Rs. 114,600, Balance Sheet Total Rs.151,200, Credit Sales Rs. 90,500, and Credit Purchases Rs. 50,700.

8. Mr. P. Guha does not maintain his books under double entry system. He submits the following information about his business for the year ended December 31, 2007:

	2007 Jan. 1 Rs.	2007 Dec. 31 Rs.
Machinery	54,000	68,000
Furniture	21,000	21,000
Debtors	36,900	28,200
Creditors	16,200	24,100
Stock in trade	20,500	16,800
Cash in hand	14,800	?
Loan	20,000	15,000

Other transactions during the period are as under:

	Rs.
Cash received from the debtors	68,200
Cash paid to creditors	32,900
Cash Sales	29,800
Discount allowed to debtors	2,600
Discount allowed by suppliers	1,400
Bad Debts written off	600
Salaries	5,500
Freight and Carriage	3,100
Rent and Insurance	2,800
General Expenses	1,600
Drawings	10,500
Return Inwards	1,400
Return Outwards	1,900
Further Capital introduced	20,000
Depreciation to be charged:	
On Machinery	9,000
On Furniture	2,800

Prepare a Trading and Profit and Loss Account for the year ending December 31, 2007 and a Balance Sheet as on that date.

Ans: Gross Profit Rs. 43,500, Net Profit Rs. 20,000, Capital: Opening Rs. 111,000 and Closing Rs. 140,500, Balance Sheet Total Rs.179,600, Credit Sales Rs. 64,100, Credit Purchases Rs. 44,100 and Closing Cash in hand Rs. 57,400.

9. Mr. X does not maintain proper books of accounts. From the following information prepare Trading and Profit and Loss Account for the year ended 31st December 1992 and the Balance Sheet as on that date:

	1992 Jan. 1 Rs.	1992 Dec. 31 Rs.
Debtors	18,000	24,000
Creditors	8,000	12,000
Stock	6,000	9,000
Furniture	16,000	19,000
Machinery	24,000	24,000
Cash in hand	3,900	?

Details of other transactions are as follows:

	Rs.
Fresh Capital introduced	10,000
Cash Sales	16,000
Cash Purchases	9,000
Cash received from Debtors	63,000
Cash paid to Creditors	37,000
Discount allowed	3,200
Discount received	4,100
Drawings	5,800
Salaries paid	9,200
Rent and Taxes paid	3,900
Office expenses paid	12,000
Bad Debts written off	1,600
Return Inwards	1,400
Return Outwards	1,900
Carriage paid	2,100
Wages paid	2,700

Ans: Closing cash in hand Rs. 8,200; Credit Sales Rs. 75,200; Credit Purchases Rs. 47,000; Opening Capital Rs. 59,900; Gross Profit Rs. 33,900; Net Profit Rs. 8,100; B/S Rs. 84,200.

10. Mr. A who keeps his book by Single Entry submits the following information about the business for the year 1991: Receipt for the year ended 31.12.91

	Rs.
From Sundry Debtors	59,000
Cash Sales	34,000
Miscellaneous Income	4,200
Introduced by A	15,000
	112,200

Payment made in the year 31.12.91:

	Rs.
Paid to creditors	35,500
Cash purchases	21,000
Wages	2,100
Salaries	3,400
Drawings	4,600
Rent	2,700
Miscellaneous Expenses	1,400

	Rs.
Sundry Expenses	700
Advertisement	1,300
Furniture	1,500
Carriage Inwards	1,300
Carriage Outwards	930
Purchase of typewriter	3,100
Interest	670
Investments	20,000

	1990 Dec. 31 Rs.	1991 Dec. 31 Rs.
Debtors	19,000	17,500
Creditors	3,800	10,200
Machinery	18,000	16,200
Furniture	19,000	19,500
Cash	3,000	15,000
Stock	3,000	8,500

From the above data prepare Trading and Profit and Loss Account for the year ended 31.12.91 and the Balance Sheet as on that date.

Ans: Credit Purchases Rs. 41,900; Opening Capital Rs. 58,200; Credit Sales Rs. 57,500; Gross Profit Rs. 30,700; Net Profit Rs. 21,000; B/S Rs. 99,800.

11. Bose supplies you the following information:

	1972 Jan. 1 Rs.	1972 Dec. 31 Rs.
Debtors	18,100	19,300
Stock	15,000	14,000
Machinery	25,000	—
Furniture	4,000	—
Creditors	11,000	12,500

Summary of Cash transactions for 1972

Receipts	Rs.	Payments	Rs.
Opening Balance	500	Payment to Creditors	35,000
Cash Sales	6,100	Purchases	16,000
Receipt from Debtors	75,300	Salaries	5,000
Miscellaneous receipts	200	Drawings	4,000
Loan from Das	10,000	Expenses	11,000
(@ 9% on 1st July)		Machinery Purchased	9,500
		(1st July)	
		Closing Balance	11,600
	92,100		92,100

Return Inwards and Outwards were Rs. 900 and Rs. 600 respectively. Discount allowed was Rs. 700 and discount received was Rs. 800. Depreciate furniture @ 5% and machinery @ 10%.

Expenses include insurance @ Rs. 500 p.a. paid upto 31st March, 1973, Wages Rs. 2,000 are still due.

Prepare Trading and Profit and Loss Accounts for the year ended 31.12.72 and the Balance Sheet as on that date.

Ans: Credit Purchases Rs. 37,900; Gross Profit Rs. 27,000; Credit Sales Rs. 78,100; Net Profit Rs. 7,800; Opening Capital Rs. 51,600; B/S Rs. 80,350.

12. A trader keeps his book under Single Entry System. The position of his business as on 1st January 1995 was as follows:

Sundry Creditors Rs. 17,000, Sundry Debtors Rs. 20,000, Freehold Premises Rs. 50,000, Stock Rs. 25,000, Furniture Rs. 2,000.

The following is the Summary of his Cash Book:

	Rs.		Rs.
Sundry Debtors	15,000	Bank balance	10.000
Cash Sales	80,000	(overdraft 1.1.95)	
		Expenses	50,000
		Drawings	3,000
		Sundry Creditors	20,000
		Cash in hand	2,000
		Cash at Bank	10,000
	95,000		95,000

The following further information is available:

Closing Stock Rs. 30,000, Closing Debtors Rs. 25,000, Closing Creditors Rs. 12,000. Depreciate premises by 10% and furniture by 15%, Create a Bad Debts Reserve 2½% on Debtors. Expenses include Rs. 2,500 for house rent of the trader and Cash Sales include Rs. 2,000 for sale of his personal jewllery.

You are required to prepare a Trading and Profit and Loss Account for the year ended 31.12.95 and a Balance Sheet as on that date.

(C.B.S.E.—Delhi Board)

Ans: Credit Sales Rs. 20,000; Gross Profit Rs. 88,000; Credit Purchases Rs. 15,000; Net Profit Rs. 34,575; B/S Rs. 113,075.

13. Mr. V. Mehra keeps his books under single entry system. He submits the following information for the year 2007-2008 regarding his business transactions:

	2007 April 1 Rs.	2008 March 31 Rs.
Furniture	20,400	20,400
Debtors	36,900	42,000
Creditors	21,400	31,700
Stock in trade	12,700	18,500
Machinery	60,000	?
Cash in hand	19,400	?
Outstanding Rent	2,100	900
Prepaid Insurance	700	400

Summary of cash transactions for the year 2007-2008:

Receipts	Rs.	Payments	Rs.
Sales	27,100	Wages	3,100
Debtors	58,900	Freight and Duty	2,700
Loan	15,000	Purchases	11,200
Fresh Capital	20,000	Creditors	31,600
Dividend Received	4,000	Salaries	4,800
		Insurance	2,700

(Contd.)

Receipts	Rs.	Payments	Rs.
		General Expenses	1,500
		Advertisement	2,900
		Drawings	12,500
		Investments (in shares)	15,000
		Rent	5,000

Additional information:

(a) Discount allowed Rs.700; Discount Received Rs. 500; Bad Debts Rs. 200; Return Inwards Rs. 650; and Return Outwards Rs.300.

(b) Depreciate Machinery and Furniture @ 10%.

Prepare a Trading and Profit and Loss Account for the year ended March 31, 2008, and a Balance Sheet as on that date.

Ans: Gross Profit Rs.38,400, Net Profit Rs.17,960, Capital: Opening Rs.126,600 and Closing Rs.152,060; Balance Sheet Total Rs. 199,660, Credit Sales Rs.65,550, Credit Purchases Rs. 42,700 and Closing Cash in hand Rs. 51,400.

14. Mr. Zoman Kundra keeps his book under single entry system. He submits the following information about his business during the year 2007:

Cash Sales Rs. 50,000; Cash Purchases Rs. 12,400; Receipts from Debtors Rs. 60,500; Paid to Creditors Rs. 39,800; Capital introduced Rs. 25,000; Miscellaneous Income Rs. 5,600; Interest on bank deposits received Rs. 3,000; Wages Rs. 3,200; Carriage Rs. 2,500; Salaries Rs. 5,000; Drawings Rs. 10,000; Shop Rent Rs. 3,400 ; Advertisement Rs. 2,900; Purchase of Furniture for personal use Rs. 4,100; Purchase of Office Equipments Rs. 2,500; Carriage Outwards Rs. 700; Discount allowed Rs. 800; Discount Received Rs. 500; Bad Debts Rs. 650; Sundry Expenses Rs. 2,000 and Return Inwards Rs. 2,100.

	2007 Jan. 1 Rs.	2007 Dec. 31 Rs.
Stock in trade	10,000	12,600
Debtors	20,000	25,000
Creditors	9,800	12,700
Furniture	18,000	20,400
Cash in hand and cash at bank	9,000	?
Machinery	25,500	40,000
Investments (in NSC)	–	18,400

Adjustments to be made:

1. Depreciate Machinery and Furniture by 10%.
2. Make provision for Bad and Doubtful Debts @ 5% on Debtors.
3. Goods used by Mr. Kundra for his personal use Rs. 3,600.

From the above data, prepare a Trading, and Profit and Loss Account for the year ended December 31, 2007 and a Balance Sheet as on that date.

Ans: Gross Profit Rs. 61,850; Net Profit Rs. 48,210; Capital: Opening Rs. 72,700 and Closing Rs. 128,210; Balance Sheet Total Rs. 140,910; Credit Sales Rs. 69,050; Credit Purchases Rs. 43,200 and Closing Cash in hand Rs. 29,300. Depreciation is to be charged for full year.

15. Mr. Arora , who keeps his books by single entry system, submits the following information about his business for the year 2007–2008:

Receipts for the year ended March 31, 2008

	Rs.
From Sundry Debtors	62,000
Cash Sales	39,200
Miscellaneous Income	5,000
Introduced by Mr. Arora	20,100
	126,300

Payments made in the year ended March 31, 2008

	Rs.		Rs.
Paid to Creditors	38,500	Cash Purchases	24,500
Wages	3,400	Salaries	4,000
Drawings	5,100	Rent	3,100
Miscellaneous Expenses	2,000	Audit Fees	800
Advertisement	1,500	Purchase of Computer	18,500
Furniture	1,800	Interest	840
Carriage Inward	2,400	Carriage Outwards	1,000
Investments	20,500		

	2007 April. 1 Rs.	2008 March 31 Rs.
Debtors	20,500	18,000
Creditors	5,100	10,500
Machinery	24,000	20,300
Furniture	20,000	20,500
Cash	19,740	18,100
Stock-in-trade	4,800	9,200

Prepare a Trading and Profit and Loss Account for the year ended March 31, 2008, and a Balance Sheet as on that date.

Ans: Gross Profit Rs. 28,900; Net Profit Rs. 15,660; Capital: Opening Rs. 83,940 and Closing Rs. 114,600; Balance Sheet Total Rs. 125,100; Credit Sales Rs. 59,500; and Credit purchases Rs. 43,900. Depreciation on Machinery Rs. 3,700 and on Furniture Rs. 1,300.

16. Mr. D. Rajan supplies you the following information:

	2007 Jan. 1 Rs.	2007 Dec. 31 Rs.
Machinery	60,000	80,000
Furniture	18,000	30,000
Debtors	36,700	45,200
Creditors	21,500	29,800
Stock in trade	16,100	22,900

Summary of cash transactions for the year 2007:

Receipts	Rs.	Payments	Rs.
Opening Balance	19,300	Carriage inward	3,100
Debtors	56,700	Creditors	34,600
Sales (Cash)	32,500	Salaries	5,900
Loan from P. Lakshman	20,000	Rent and Taxes	12,200
(@ 12% on September 1, 2007)		Drawings	18,000
		Sundry Expenses	7,200
		Machinery (On September 1, 2007)	20,000
		Closing Balance	27,500
	128,500		128,500

Additional information:
(a) Discount allowed Rs. 19,000; Discount received Rs. 2,300; Return inward Rs. 700; Return outward Rs. 950; and Bad debt written off Rs. 500.
(b) Sundry Expenses include annual insurance paid Rs. 1,200 commencing from August 1, 2007.
(c) Depreciate Machinery and furniture @ 10% p.a.

Prepare a Trading and Profit and Loss Account for the year ended December 31, 2007, and a Balance Sheet as on that date.

Ans: Gross Profit Rs. 58,600; Net Profit Rs. 24,033; Capital: Opening Rs. 128,600 and Closing Rs. 134,633, Balance Sheet Total Rs.197,233, Credit Sales Rs. 68,300 and Credit Purchases Rs. 46,150. Depreciation on Machinery Rs. 6,667 and on Furniture to be charged for half year. Out standing interest on loan Rs. 800. Prepaid insurance Rs. 700.

[**Note:** Here it is assumed that the furniture was purchased on credit.]

17. From the information given below, prepare a Trading and Profit and Loss Account for the year ended 30th June, 1986 and Balance Sheet as at that date.

	Balance on 1.7.85 Rs.	Balance on 30.6.86 Rs.
Debtors	8,000	7,400
Creditors for Purchases	3,000	2,400
Rent Payable (outstanding)	50	30
Cash	750	3,250
Stock	7,500	8,000
Plant	5,000	6,000

Cash transactions:
Receipts: Cash Sales Rs. 500, Debtors Rs. 35,500, Payments: Purchase of Plant Rs. 1,000, Rent Rs. 620, Cash Purchases Rs. 1,000, Payment to Creditors Rs. 15,600, Salaries Rs. 10,000, Wages Rs. 3,000, Electricity Rs.1,000, (shortage in Cash Balance to be treated as Drawings) Bad Debts already written off Rs. 100. Depreciation on plant has to be provided at 10% p.a.

(C.U. B.Com.)

Ans: Credit Sales Rs. 35,000; Drawings (Balancing Amount from Cash Book) Rs. 1,280; Credit Purchases Rs. 15,000; Gross Profit Rs. 17,000; Net Profit Rs. 4,750, B/S Rs. 24,100.

18. Vijay commenced business as foodgrains merchant on 1st April, 1995 with a capital of Rs. 40,000. On the same day he purchased furniture for Rs. 8,000. From the following particulars obtained from his books, which do not conform to Double Entry Principles, you are required to prepare a Trading Account and Profit and Loss Account for the year ended 31st March, 1996 and a Balance Sheet as on that date:

Sales (including Cash Sales Rs. 20,000) Rs. 50,000, Purchases (including Cash Purchases Rs. 12,000) Rs. 40,000, Vijay's Drawings in cash Rs. 4,000, Salaries to Staff Rs. 4,800, Bad Debts written off Rs. 400, Trade Expenses Paid Rs. 1,600.

Vijay used goods worth Rs. 1,200 for private purposes during the year. On 31st March 1996 his Debtors amounted to Rs. 14,000 and Creditors Rs. 8,000. Stock on that date was worth Rs. 16,000.   (C.B.S.E.—Delhi Board)

Ans: Closing Cash in hand Rs. 25,200; G.P. Rs. 27,200; Net Profit Rs. 20,400, B/S Rs. 63,200.

[**Note:** Goods used by Vijay are to be deducted from purchases in Trading A/c.]

19. Rajesh does not maintain proper books of account. From the following particulars prepare Trading and Profit and Loss Account for the year ended 31st December, 1982 and the Balance Sheet as on that date.

	1981 Dec. 31 Rs.	1982 Dec. 31 Rs.
Debtors	9,000	12,500
Stock	4,900	6,600
Furniture	500	750
Creditors	3,000	2,250

Analysis of other transactions are as follows:

	Rs.
Cash purchases	2,500
Cash collected from debtors	30,400
Cash paid to creditors	22,000
Salaries	6,000
Rent	750
Office expenses	900
Drawings	1,500
Additional Capital introduced	1,000
Cash Sales	750
Discount received	350
Discount allowed	150
Returns inwards	500
Returns outwards	400
Bad Debts	100

He had Rs. 2,500 as Cash Balance at the beginning of the year.

(I.C.W.A. (Inter))

Ans: Credit Sales Rs. 34,650; Credit Purchases Rs. 22,000; Closing Cash Balances Rs. 750; Opening Capital Rs. 13,900; Gross Profit Rs. 12,500; Net Profit Rs. 4,950; Balance Sheet Total Rs. 20,600.

Computers in Accounting

CONTENTS

INTRODUCTION

The present age is the age of computers. Computers are everywhere. In fact, you will find it in many pretty unlikely places. In the last two decades, it has reshaped our lives. Computers have changed our world remarkably. The word 'Computer' comes from the word 'compute', i.e., to calculate. There are some people who consider it as a high speed calculator. It is a device that operates on data. A computer can store, process and retrieve data as and when desired. Thus it is also known as a **data processor**. A computer is an electronic device that processes data, converting it into information that is useful to people. Any computer regardless of its type is controlled by some programmed instructions, which give the machine a purpose and tell it what to do.

According to the International Standards Organisation (ISO),

> *A computer is a data processor that can perform substantial computations, including numerous arithmetic and logic operations, without intervention of human operator during the run.*

In a computer, the data processor may gather data from various incoming sources, merge them all, sort them according to the desired order, and finally convert them into information in the desired format. Thus, data processing consists of three sub-activities, capturing input data, manipulating the data, and managing output results as per the desired order and format.

In today's rapidly changing business environment, success of a corporate body depends on three vital tasks: planning, decision-making and control. All these involve time consuming operations requiring accurate and up-to-date information and continuous monitoring. Mechanization is the only answer to this, for which the only solution is the acceptance of computer.

20.1 CHARACTERISTICS OF A COMPUTER SYSTEM

The following are the chief characteristics of a computer:

1. **Speed:** It is a very fast electronic device. A computer can perform the volume of work in a few hours which a human does in an entire year. The speed of computers is expressed in terms of microseconds (1/1,000,000 of one second), nanoseconds (1/1,000,000,000 of one second) etc. A computer is capable of performing millions of operations in a few seconds which is beyond the capability of human beings.

2. **Automation:** A computer is an automatic machine; it works independently within its programme without human assistance. In other words, once a particular job is started, it will be completed as per the programme installed and according to the desired format without intervention of any human operator during the run.

3. **Accuracy:** Computer is not only fast, but can maintain high degree of accuracy in a consistent way. However, there may be some amount of errors occurring in a computer which may be due to the fault of the operator/programmer, i.e., due to use of improper input data. Thus, computer errors caused because of incorrect input data are commonly **GIGO (Garbage-in-Garbage-out)**.

4. **Versatility:** A computer can perform multiple jobs at the same time, and one of its greatest and wonderful features is its versatility. When a computer is engaged in preparing financial statements, it may be used for writing a letter or may be used for playing game simultaneously.

5. **Storage and power of remembering:** A computer can store a large volume of information or data in a very small physical space within its hard disk, and that stored information can be recalled as and when required. It can retain and maintain its data for as long period according to the desire of the operator/user and may recall the data exactly in the same manner as was stored by its user.

6. **Diligence:** A computer is free from tiredness, monotony or lack of concentration. Thus, it can perform its job without a break for a long time with great accuracy.

20.2 COMPONENTS OF COMPUTER SYSTEM

A computer is part of a system; it does not matter how big it is or how it is used. A computer system consists of four basic parts as under:

1. *Hardware*

Hardware refers to the physical devices of a computer. It is a mechanical electronic device which helps to control the computer's operation, input and output. Hence, input, processor, memory, storage and output devices are generally known as **hardware**.

2. *Software*

It is a set of instructions that makes the computer perform its tasks. It consists of a set of computer programs, procedures, and associated documents describing the programs, and how they are to be used. Software can be divided into two major categories as under:

    (a) System Software

    (b) Application Software

System software: It is a set of one or more programs designed to control the operation system of a computer and help it to extend its processing capability. It makes the operation of a computer system more effective and efficient. It provides support for the development and execution of application of application software, and also helps the other components to work together. Some well known system software are as under:

    (i) *Operating systems.* It takes care of the effective and efficient utilization of all hardware and software components of a computer system and it helps to run a computer more efficiently.

Some example of operating systems are Windows, the Macintosh Operating System, and Linux. Operating system acts as an interpreter between hardware, application programs and the user.

(ii) *Communication software.* In a network environment, it helps to communicate and share data across a network while controlling the network operations and overseeing the network's security.

(iii) *Utility programs.* It makes the computer system easier to use and perform the highly specialized functions. It is a set of programs that helps the user in system maintenance tasks and routine tasks.

(iv) *Programming language translator.* It helps to transform the instructions prepared by a programmer in a programming language into a form that can be interpreted and executed by a computer system.

Application software: Application software tells the computer how to accomplish a specific job for the user. For example, word processing software, railway/airline reservation software, computer games software, and payroll processing software. are application softwares. Some well-known application softwares are as under:

(i) *Word processing software.* It is designed for creating documents that consist primarily of text. It also lets us add graphics and sounds to our documents. Word processing software also provides layout features for creating brochures, newsletters, web pages, etc.

(ii) *Spreadsheet software.* It is a numeric-data an analysis tool that helps us to create a kind of computerized ledger. Thus, it is a numeric base document helping to prepare balance sheets, budgets, and so on.

(iii) *Database software.* It is for building and manipulating large sets of data, such as names, address, and phone numbers in a telephone directory.

(iv) *Education software.* It allows a computer to be used as a teaching and learning tool.

(v) *Graphics software.* These programs help in designing illustrations or manipulating photographs, movies or animation.

(vi) *Entertainment software.* It helps to allow a computer to be used as an entertainment tool.

Today, there are millions of application softwares available for a wide range of applications.

3. *Data*

Data is a piece of information or fact supplied to a computer by the user. For example, basic geometric shapes may not have much meaning by themselves, but when grouped into a blueprint or a chart, they become useful information. A computer's primary job is to convert such raw data into useful information through processing.

4. *User*

The computer operators or system analysts or the programmers are known as **users**. Even though a computer can perform its job without a person sitting in front of it, people are required to design, build program, and repair computer systems.

20.3 LIMITATIONS OF COMPUTER SYSTEM

1. **Common sense:** It has no common sense or power of analysis. It works as per the instructions of the operator and on the basis of its installed programme.

2. **Decision-making:** Computer supplies useful information and on that basis decisions are taken, but a computer independently cannot take any decision. Decision-making is a complex process and a computer cannot estimate a situation or analyse a situation, and as a result, it has to wait for the instruction from its users.

3. **No I.Q.:** A computer possesses no intelligence and its I.Q. is nil. It can perform only those jobs which are set by its user or operator.

4. **No feelings:** It can perform its job with great accuracy, but has no emotion or feeling like human beings. Though it works independently within its programme and after processing its data, converts them into information in a desired format, the programme is set by human beings.

5. **A computer is confined within its programming:** A computer's performance is limited to its installed programme, because the format of a particular information may be changed manually by the user any time but it is not possible for a computer to satisfy the varying needs of the user without changing the installed programme.

20.4 BASIC OPERATIONS OF COMPUTER SYSTEM

Generally the following five basic operations are performed by all computer systems:

1. **Inputting:** It is the process of entering data and instructions into a computer system.
2. **Storing:** It is performed by saving data and instructions to make them readily available for initial and additional processing as and when required.
3. **Processing:** It means performing arithmetic or logical operations on data to convert them into useful information.
4. **Outputting:** It is done by processing or preparing useful information for the user, through printed report or visual display.
5. **Controlling:** Directing the manner and sequence in which the above operations are performed.

20.5 BASIC COMPONENTS OF COMPUTER HARDWARE

1. **Key board:** It is the primary input device for entering text and numbers into the computer. A standard key board includes about 100 keys; each key sends different signals to the CPU.
2. **CPU or Central Processing Unit:** It is the brain of a computer system. CPU helps to control other devices of a computer in a systematic way and is also responsible for activating and controlling the operations of other units of a computer system. All types of calculations and comparisons are performed by a computer system through the CPU.
3. **Monitor:** It is the most commonly used output device on most personal computer systems for producing soft copy output. Monitor serves as both an input and output device. The keyboard is used to feed the input in a computer, while the monitor is used to display the output of the computer. The two basic types of monitors used today are Cathode Ray Tube (CRT) and Liquid Crystal Display (LCD) flat-panel.
4. **Primary storage memory:** The primary storage or the main memory of a computer system is made up of several small storage areas called **locations** or **cells**. In almost all computer systems, the primary storage units have random access property and are volatile. Therefore, the primary memory is also known as **volatile memory** or **RAM** (Random Access Memory).
5. **Secondary storage devices:** Primary storage of a computer system has some limitations for which an additional memory, called **secondary storage** or **auxiliary memory**, is used with most computer systems. Secondary storage is non-volatile and has lower cost per bit stored, but it generally has an operating speed far slower than that of the primary storage. It is used primarily to store large volume of data on permanent basis.
6. **Sound systems and sound card:** Sound systems are useful to those people who use their computers to create or use multimedia products, watch videos or listen to music, participate in online activities like distance learning or video conferences. A sound card is a circuit board that converts sounds from analog to digital form and vice versa, for recording or playback. It has both input and output functions. In the present time, any new multimedia-capable PC (Personal Computer) includes a complete sound system, with a microphone, speakers, a sound card, and a CD-ROM or DVD drive.

7. Printers: Printers are the most popular output devices used for producing hard-copy output. There are a number of printers used for the printing job through a computer as under:
   (a) Dot-Matrix Printers
   (b) Inkjet Printers
   (c) Drum Printers
   (d) Chain/Band Printers
   (e) Laser Printers
8. Mouse: A mouse is an input device which we can move around on a flat surface and control the pointer. The pointer is an object, usually an arrow that is used to select text, access menus and interact with programs, files or data that appear on the screen.

Figure 20.1 shows the position of basic components of computer hardware.

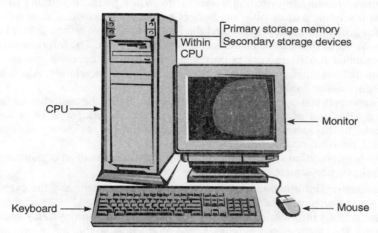

FIGURE 20.1   A computer system.

20.6 INFORMATION SYSTEM

Management needs information for planning, control and decision-making. The required information is furnished with the help of reports. Reports may be oral or written, and also, routine or special.

The term 'reporting' connotes different meanings as under:
1. Narrating some facts.
2. Reviewing certain matter with its merits and demerits and offering comments.
3. Furnishing data at regular intervals in standardized forms.
4. Submitting specific information for particular purpose on specific request/instruction.

The subject matter of information, the volume of details and method of presentation are largely determined by the type of industry, the size, power delegated to the subordinates and other characteristics of a particular undertaking and by the division and level of management to whom the information is rendered in each case. In a small unit, much of the control is exercised by personal supervision and oral reporting—the proprietor knows, by his personal knowledge, the trends of production, costs, sales and utilization of resources. The more an organization grows in size, the powers are more delegated to the subordinates and the importance of report is more felt. Reports provide means of checking a performance.

There is a good deal of difference between communication and report. The superior communicates orders to the subordinates, while the subordinate communicates results. This communication is done through reporting. In order to assist the management in taking appropriate action, information is communicated in the form of reports, statements, charts and graphs. It is essential for efficient and effective planning and control. Information through reports tells how effectively the various production, marketing and finance factors have been utilized. Efficiency of individuals and departments like purchase, sales, production and engineering may be watched through the information supplied, and responsibilities can be fixed.

An information system has inputs, processes and outputs. The creation and storage of inputs (primary collection and use of all available data, e.g., accounting data library), processing and creation and storage of outputs are the functions of an information system. The advent of mechanical processing of data and computer has allowed management to expand its horizons and expectations regarding the possibilities of information systems.

20.6.1 Accounting Information System (AIS)

The main goal of Accounting Information System is to ensure financial viability of an organization, enforce financial discipline and monitor the budget estimates. It provides such type of information through which the growth, present position and the future prospect of a firm should be clearly visible which will cater the needs of the users of the accounting information. The information contained in the accounting or financial reports is very important for its users or decision-makers. Without it, the decisions taken in different matters have a considerable degree of uncertainty. AIS is also a part of the **Management Information System (MIS)**.

Reporting is an important output of accounting function. Being the custodian of factual data about costs, production/sales and profits, an accountant provides significant information services. The management looks to the accountant for factual information for reviewing the operations for the purpose of control, decision-making, etc.

The accounting information system is the most important element of an organization's information system for the following reasons:

1. The accounting information system enables the management and the external information users to get a picture of the whole organization.
2. The accounting information system links other information systems such as marketing, personnel, R&D, stores and purchases, and production, so that the information produced by these systems can be expressed in financial terms for planning strategy to attain organizational goals.

The accounting information system is the most important subsystem as it plays the key role in managing the flow of economic data to all parts of a business, and also to the interested parties outside the business. A management information system captures data about all aspects of the company's operations, organizes them into usable information, and provides reports to the internal managers and the appropriate outside partiers. Accounting plays a key role in this function. Users of financial statements fall into two broad categories—internal and external. Management and the owners are the major **internal users**. On the other hand, investors and creditors are the chief **external users**.

Generally the following types of information are provided by the AIS:

1. Strategic
   (a) Financing methods and policy
   (b) Pricing policies
   (c) Tax planning
   (d) Investment decisions.
2. Tactical
   (a) Credit and payment status
   (b) Sale and debtors' position
   (c) Cost involvement in different areas
   (d) Variance between budgeted and actual income and expenditures
   (e) Outstanding incomes and expenditures
   (f) Impact of different taxes.

3. Operational
   (a) Expenditure incurred under different heads
   (b) Sales order processing
   (c) Payroll
   (d) Accounts payable and receivable
   (e) Inventory control
   (f) General ledger
   (g) Preparation of periodical financial statements
   (h) Budget status of different departments
   (i) Cash statements
4. Providing further data for MIS
   The position of business activity and the accounting information system is shown in the Figure 20.2.

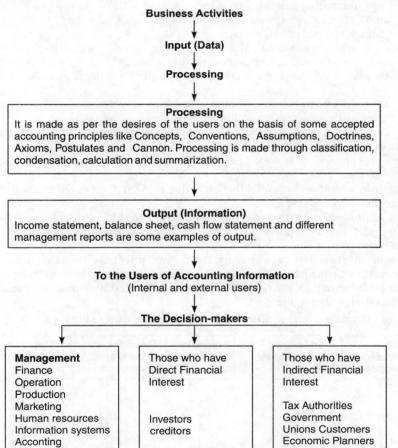

FIGURE 20.2 Relationship between business activity and accounting information system.

The chief features of accounting information system

1. It is related with business transactions only.
2. Accounting information is required for both internal and external users.

3. It uses mainly the historical data for preparing the financial statement of an enterprise.
4. The sources of data are mainly provided by the enterprise internally.
5. Business transactions are processed on the basis of accepted accounting principles, rules, Accounting Standards, and statutory obligations to protect the interest of the owners, and other users of the accounting information.

20.6.2 Data Exchange with Other Information Systems

AIS have a close and direct relationship with the other information systems. It is the objective of the management of an enterprise to provide appropriate data or information to the top management and the decision-makers to satisfy their needs for taking decisions. Thus, AIS plays a great role in fulfilling these objectives by providing appropriate information to the management. The data or information provided by different departments to AIS (Finance and Accounts Department) and the data provided by AIS to other departments are given below in brief:

1. **Data or information provided by AIS:**
   (a) **To HRD:** Total expenses incurred under the head salary, HRA, provident fund, gratuity, compensation, welfare, etc.
   (b) **To marketing:** Actual sales figure, quantity sale (area wise), bad debts, cost of advertisement, and selling and distribution cost.
   (c) **To production:** Present market demand, stock position, proposed sales target, and so on.
   (d) **To stores and purchase:** Market information, targeted production, budgeted details for stores and purchases (amount provided), etc.
   (e) **To R&D:** Amount expended till date, and amount provided for future planning.
2. **Data or information provided by HRD to AIS:** Employee details like present strength of employees, period of leave taken, promotions offered, resignations accepted, employee turnover, and so on.
3. **Data or information provided by marketing to AIS:** Cost of advertisement and proposed future plan of marketing.
4. **Data or information provided by production to AIS:** Present and future production planning, present position of production, and expenditure sanctioned for proposed investment plan, if any.
5. **Data or information provided by stores and purchase to AIS:** Amount required to execute the existing purchase proposals, budgeted amount required for future purchases, etc.
6. **Data or information provided by R&D to AIS:** Result of past and present testing and product design, and future plan.

The flow of information among different departments is shown in the Figure 20.3.

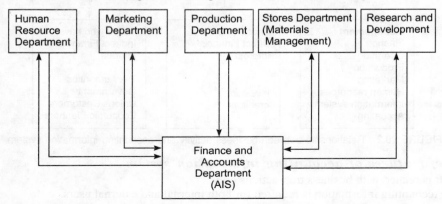

FIGURE 20.3 Flow of information among different departments of a company.

20.7 MANAGEMENT INFORMATION SYSTEM (MIS) AS DATA SOURCE

The introduction of computers and the subsequent development of management information systems have done much to provide the necessary data inputs for quantitative applications. Modern management information is nothing more than a computer which is used to provide informational inputs for management decisions. The Management Information System (MIS) generates, processes, stores, and presents data to satisfy the needs of all decision-makers in an organization.

In its simplest form, an MIS can be represented by the scheme as shown in Figure 20.4. Notice that the basic transformation in the MIS process is from data to information. Raw data enter the system and are transformed into the system's only output, information, to support decision-making.

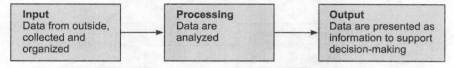

FIGURE 20.4 Management Information System (MIS).

20.7.1 Management Information System (MIS) and the Computer

In today's rapidly changing business environment, success of any corporate body depends on three vital tasks—planning, decision-making and control. All these involve time consuming operations requiring accurate and up-to-date information and continuous monitoring. Mechanization is the only answer to this for which the only solution is the acceptance of computer. Given the complexity and scope of managerial decision-making today, the need for data is so enormous that almost all organizations take the help of computers. The benefit/cost ratio is overwhelmingly in favour of using computers that manual methods can't survive.

Understanding the computer and its use in management information systems is best approached by first examining the roles of the human and the computer to see what each does best, and what each does not do well. A quick picture of human decision-makers and computers, and of the relative strengths and weaknesses of both is given below:

1. Human have imagination, creative power, judgement, and common sense. Computers do only what their programmers tell them to do in the form of certain instructions.
2. Human decision-makers can learn from their experience. Computer can only follow rules; they cannot learn deductively except in the simplest logic situations.
3. Human decision-makers are not always accurate; sometimes, their behavior is inconsistent. Computer reacts consistently and gives or takes electronic problems quite accurately.
4. Human decision-makers can see the 'overall' problem; they can then see each sub-problem as part of an overall scheme. However, even though a computer can be programmed to follow complex interacting sets of rules, but when the situation changes, it will continue to follow these rules, resulting in faulty outcomes.
5. Human decision-makers have flexibility; e.g., when the road side changes, they alter their behavior to optimize under the new situation. Computers show flexibility only if someone has programmed it; otherwise they react identically regardless of changed road signs.
6. Most humans do not have an enormous memory; they forget a lot, and are not very precise in terms of what they do remember. However, they can accommodate a wide variety of information from bits of data to complete complex thinking processes. Computers never forget; they have an enormous memory in terms of pieces of information, and they are very fast in retrieving this information.

In view of the facts stated above, it can be concluded that the computer forms the base for a management information system. The critical objective in the design of an effective MIS as a support for quantitative applications is to employ the distinct advantages of both components (the human and the electronic).

Figure 20.5 shows how a report is generated through MIS.

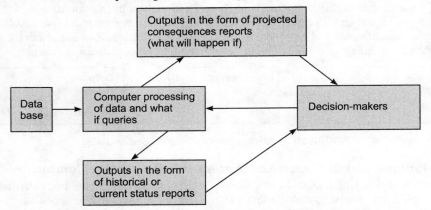

FIGURE 20.5 Report Generation Management Information System.

MIS can be explained as an all-inclusive system for providing management with information for effective planning, control and decision-making. This is a systematic process for providing reports, data or other outputs. Management information system can be conveniently categorized into the following three main areas:

1. Strategic planning information
2. Management control information
3. Operational information.

20.8 BASIC REQUISITES OF AN EFFECTIVE REPORTING SYSTEM

1. **Form:** The style and layout of a report will depend on the needs of the individual who will use it. The report may be submitted in the form of narration, statistical tabulations, graphs or charts.

2. **Contents:** Contents would depend on the subject matter being covered by the report. The report should bear a self-explanatory title, date of issue, the designation of the person issuing the report, the period to which it relates, and the designation of the recipient to whom the report is submitted. Information furnished should have a purpose, meaning and repetition should be avoided. Proper analysis and interpretation should be carried out and appropriate comments be submitted with a view to suggest a suitable course of action. There should be a uniformity in presentation, and the source from which such information is obtained should be properly defined.

3. **Timeliness:** Promptness is of paramount importance, because information delayed is information denied. The sooner the report is made, the quicker can the corrective action be taken.

4. **Relevance:** Reports should be related to the responsibilities of the recipient, as for example, Sales Manager should be provided with reports only in respect of his division and area of control.

5. **Simplicity:** The reports should be clear and presented in a simple style.

20.9 TYPES OF REPORTS

Reports may be of two types—Routine reports, and Special reports.

Routine reports: Reports which are submitted at periodical intervals on a regular basis covering routine matters are called **routine matters.** A few examples of these reports are listed below:

1. Periodical financial statements
2. General financial position and financial ratios
3. Return on capital
4. Cost statements
5. Budgets: Master budget, flexible budget and capital expenditure budget.

Special reports: Reports which are submitted on particular occasions only and that too on specific request or instruction are called **special reports**. Some of the problems on which special reports may be rendered are listed below:

1. Make or buy problems—profitability and recommendation
2. Profitability of products
3. Capital investment problem
4. Working capital
5. Cost reduction scheme
6. Reports on company's financial position
7. Feasibility study for a project.

20.10 AUTOMATION OF ACCOUNTING PROCESS

When a large volume of data requires operations and calculations of a repetitive nature, it is impractical to suggest that such operations be carried out manually. Large volume of data increases the chances of mistakes which can be very costly for an enterprise. This type of work is natural for machines which perform exactly the same way, time after time, to a given set of conditions.

All machines are devised to increase productivity. Data processing machines particularly enable to increase productivity in two ways:

1. It improves the output per hour and quality of output.
2. It presupposes the existence of planning and encourages careful, intelligent and objective planning.

Mechanical data processing is the use of machines and mechanical aids to prepare and process accounting and statistical data, and also to maintain books of accounts. This covers a wide area where large volumes of repetitive paper work are required, viz., payroll, order recording, invoice preparation, accounts receivables, loan processing in banks, and also generation of control data necessary for directing and improving the operational efficiency of the organization.

Human beings are prove to makes mistakes. Thus, under such an environment, the more the human elements could be eliminated from processing of information, the more accurate the results would be. Machines produce accurate results if the input to the machines is accurate. Great care should, therefore, be given in perfecting the source documents before they are introduced into a mechanized system. Thus, an effective control system should be enforced to obtain accurate and fruitful output.

20.11 APPLICATIONS OF COMPUTERS IN ACCOUNTING

A computer consists of devices for input, processing and output. Data collected in a coded form (known as **input**) are fed into the computer and processed at very high speed. The computer is capable of carrying out all normal arithmetical functions and has also devices for storing the data. Companies use computers for the maintenance of accounting procedures and preparing their financial statements. A computer has an inbuilt accounting system, i.e., software through which transactions are recorded in the books of accounts on the basis of the accepted accounting principles, and ledger accounts are maintained according to the desire of the users. Thus, there does not arise any problem in preparing cash book, bank statements, journal, ledger, day books, debtors ledger, creditors ledger, trial balance, and financial statements. The financial position of an enterprise may be assessed through a computer. The following accounting functions can be obtained from computer accounting:

1. Stock recording and control
2. Payroll
3. Job costing
4. Word processing
5. Integrated sales ledger:
   (a) Purchase ledger
   (b) Sales ledger
6. Financial statement
7. Reports on company's financial position.

It also helps in cost and management accounting remarkably in the following areas:

1. Budget and budgetary control
2. Working capital
3. Feasibility study for a project
4. Profitability of products
5. Make or buy problems
6. Capital investment projects
7. Cost reduction schemes.

A computer offers excellent opportunity as a tool to control the attaining of the enterprise's objectives. There is an inbuilt control system to ensure conformation to the prescribed procedure which is more efficient and effective than a manual system. The following commercial softwares are used for recording the accounting matters and storing data:

1. Word processor
2. Electronic spreadsheet
3. Database management.

Word processor: A word processing program provides tools for creating all kinds of text based documents. It helps to create, edit, view, format, store, retrieve, and print documents. A word processing package enables us to do all these on a computer system. Using a word processor, we can create long documents with separate chapters, table contents, indices, and other features.

Electronic spreadsheet: A spreadsheet program is a software tool for entering, calculating, manipulating, and analysing sets of numbers. Spreadsheets have a wide range of uses—from family budgets to corporate earnings statements. It helps us to prepare computerized ledger. A spreadsheet program offers considerable ease in performing such tasks by automating all arithmetic calculations. It also makes it easier to change certain numerical values, and helps in seeing the effect of these changes across the worksheet (ledger) immediately. A spreadsheet can be set up to show information in different ways, such as the traditional row-and-column format, or a slick report format with headings and charts.

Database management system (DBMS): Database Management System (DBMS) is a collection of programs that enables us to store, modify, and extract information from a database. A Database Management System is a software designed to gather, handle and process information. The database program manipulates the information in ways that helps us to analyse the data. A DBMS is a software tool that allows people to store, access, and process data or facts into useful information. It not only stores data, but also allows its users to easily make use of that data.

20.12 ADVANTAGES OF COMPUTERIZED ACCOUNTING SYSTEM

1. Electronic data processing system handles data promptly in the quickest possible time. Thus, for processing the voluminous data and its effective solution, computer application is the only answer.

2. Data can be processed in a better form which was not possible previously. An unlimited variety of analytical reports, returns and answers to problems may be turned out.
3. Workflow in computer data processing is smooth. Properly programmed, the computer gives uninterrupted performance for hours.
4. Time taken for performing a job in the computer is more accurately assessed and schedules are always achieved. These improve the work performance.
5. Accuracy and reliability of both input and output are ensured. The importance given to input leads to better recording of data, and there is practically no risk of any errors in the output.
6. Clerical cost is kept to the lowest possible value.
7. Computerized accounting system is particularly useful where a large number of documents like insurance premiums, bills, invoices, ledger accounts, debtors' schedules, creditors schedules, bank accounts are handled everyday.
8. Computers never forget; they have an enormous memory in terms of pieces of information, and they are very fast in retrieving this information. As a result they help remarkably in preparing cash books, bank statements, journal, ledger, day books, debtors ledger, creditors ledger, trial balance, and financial statements.
9. The books maintaining cost under computerized system is much cheaper than that of the manual system.
10. Less storage space is required for storing both data and information.
11. A computer does not suffer form tiredness or fatigue, and hence, can perform its work over and over again with the same speed and accuracy.
12. The advent of mechanical processing of data and computer has allowed management to expand its horizons and expectations regarding the possibilities of information systems.

20.13 LIMITATIONS OF COMPUTERIZED ACCOUNTING SYSTEM

1. Generally, common workers do not welcome a computer because there is a tendency to resist automation for fear of retrenchment.
2. A computer cannot function without the help of its operator and programmer. An experienced programmer is not always available everywhere.
3. In case of a breakdown, if it is not repaired or replaced immediately, the accounting work may be forced to step immediately.
4. Data may be corrupted due to viruses which may cause a lot of harm to an enterprise.
5. Due to failure of power, data may get lost from the memory.
6. The software installed today may become obsolete tomorrow. Thus, it is a costly venture and small firms cannot afford it.
7. Excessive or intensive use of computers may develop some health problems like eye problem.
8. Due to the lack of knowledge of programmers or software developers, computers may create problems, and if those technical problems are not sorted out immediately, an enterprise or a business may have to suffer for it.

20.14 COMPARISON OF ACCOUNTING PROCESS IN MANUAL AND COMPUTERIZED ACCOUNTING

A data may be processed manually or through computers. The manual method is laborious and time consuming. A manual system of data processing has the following added disadvantages:

1. Clerical errors are not ruled out.
2. It is a drudgery to handle voluminous data manually.
3. Identical data have to be copied and recopied for use in different statements.
4. Delay occurs in rendering the information.

The rapid technological advances made in the field of machine accounting over the last few decades have completely revolutionized the methods of data processing and information presentation. With the help of computers, wide fields are now covered and managerial control has been made possible to a degree that could not even be thought of earlier. The following advantages may be enjoyed if the data processing is done through the assistance of computers:

1. The chief advantage is speed, because a computer machine does work much more quickly than what could be done manually.
2. It helps to reduce clerical costs.
3. Computerized accounting helps to maintain accuracy.
4. It helps to improve managerial control through prompt reports covering aspects which would not be possible in a manual system.

20.15 SOURCING OF ACCOUNTING SOFTWARE

There are a number of accounting software packages available in the market. Any one of them may be installed and used depending on the purpose and volume of work to be rendered. Generally, accounting software packages may be classified as under:

1. Readymade or Ready-to-use software
2. Customized software
3. Tailor-made accounting system.

20.15.1 Readymade or Ready-to-use Software

This type of software is not prepared for any specific user since it is available in the open market and is able to perform some specific job. Hundreds of pre-written software packages are available and if you find a particular software package which is suitable for you, then the said software may be purchased and implemented. Tally, Busy, and Professional Accountant are some example of readymade software packages which may be used for accounting jobs. Following are the advantages of readymade software packages:

1. It is suitable for small business houses.
2. With a readymade software package, the purchaser or the user can start the planned activity almost immediately.
3. Readymade software packages usually cost less because many customers share the development and maintenance cost.
4. It is very easy to run the system efficiently.

The following are some limitations of readymade software packages:

1. The area of operation of these software packages are very limited, and hence, cannot satisfy the purpose performed by the customized software packages.
2. The security systems of these packages are not very satisfactory.
3. These packages generally do not have the facility of secondary back-up system.

20.15.2 Customized Software

Sometimes, software is designed for users who need to customize the programs they use. This special need is often met by **open-source software**. Open-source software is the software of any type whose source code is available to users. Users or other software developers can modify this code and customize it within certain guidelines set forth by the application's creator. Many kinds of open source programs are available, from standard productivity programs to high-level network administration tools. Thus, when the available pre-written software packages fail to meet the requirements of the users, then it would be a wise decision to create a customized software package. If the user has an in-house software development team, the desired software package may be developed within the business house. When there is no such in-house software development team, the desired software package is to be developed by an outside agency.

Following are the advantages and limitations of developing a customized software package:

1. It is not very expensive.
2. It is suitable for small and medium business houses.
3. Its security system is better than that of readymade or ready-to-use software packages.
4. It is easy to carry out changes in the software if an in-house software development team develops it. On the other hand, if it is developed by an outside agency, the user needs to depend always on the vendor for carrying out any kind of changes or for rectification of the system. For providing all these services, the vendor will charge separately for each occasion or visit.

20.15.3 Tailor-made Accounting System

When none of the pre-written software packages meet the specific requirements of an organization or the user, and if the organization has an in-house software development team, the organization may choose to develop customized software package in-house for its requirements.

Following are the advantages and limitations of developing a customized software package in-house rather than getting it developed by an outside party:

1. It is easy to carry out changes in the software if it has been developed in-house.
2. This software system may be linked with other information systems easily.
3. Developing software in-house means a major commitment of time, money, and resources, because an in-house software development team needs to be maintained and managed.
4. Its security system is the best, and is more protective than the previous two systems.
5. As it is developed within the in-house software development team, maximum utilization of this system is possible with great efficiency.
6. It is suitable for only big business houses.
7. Personnel engaged in operation and maintenance of this type of system must be well trained which is a very costly venture of all organizations.

20.16 FACTORS TO BE CONSIDERED BEFORE SOURCING AN ACCOUNTING SOFTWARE

The following factors are to be taken into consideration before sourcing an accounting software for its effective utilization:

1. **Cost effectiveness:** It is the most important factor to be considered before sourcing the accounting software. It includes the cost of the package, installation cost, running and maintenance cost.
2. **Size of the businesshouse:** The software package must be designed or selected according to the size of the organization and the volume of work to be done.
3. **Flexibility:** If possible there must be some provision for upgradation or modifications within the software package chosen to be installed, i.e., the software package should be flexible.
4. **Adaptability and training:** There are some software packages which can be easily operated, but others require intensive training. After completion of training the system must be run by the user efficiently. Otherwise, it may develop problem later on.
5. **Security system:** The security system of software packages are required to be considered very carefully before their selection or installation.
6. **Transfer of information:** The software package decided to be installed should have easy access of data transfer from one system to other for its effective utilization.

EXERCISES

I. *Short Answer Type Questions*

1. What are the components of a computer system?
2. What do you mean by basic operations of a computer system?
3. What do you mean by basic components of computer hardware?
4. What is CPU or Central Processing Unit?
5. What is monitor?
6. What is mouse?
7. What do you mean by information system?
8. What do you mean by Accounting Information System (AIS)?
9. What do you mean by Management Information System (MIS)?
10. What do you mean by automation of accounting process?
11. What do you mean by sourcing of accounting softwares?
12. What do you mean by readymade or ready-to-use software?
13. What do you mean by customized software?
14. What do you mean by tailor-made accounting system?

II. *Long Answer Type Questions*

1. What is a computer? Explain the basic operations of a computer system.
2. What are the limitations of a computer system?
3. What is Accounting Information System (AIS)? Explain the relationship of AIS with other information systems.
4. How could you explain Management Information System (MIS) as a data source?
5. How could you explain computer as the basis for Management Information System (MIS)?
6. What are the basic requisites of an effective reporting system? Explain the different classes of reports.
7. Explain in brief the applications of computers in accounting.
8. What are the different accounting functions that can be performed through computer accounting?
9. What are the different types of commercial softwares used for recording accounting matters and for storing data? Explain in brief.
10. Explain the advantages and limitations of computerized accounting system.
11. Compare accounting process in manual and computerized accounting.
12. What do you mean by sourcing of accounting softwares? What are the different factors which need to be considered before sourcing of accounting software?

21

Accounting and Database Management System

CONTENTS

INTRODUCTION

A database is a collection of information. Databases are used to store information that can be easily queried, sorted, and organized into reports. Data is a collection of facts which are unorganized, but databases organize them into useful information. Data can be manipulated to produce output, such as inventory report, employee payslips, etc. This output is called **information**, which helps users to take important decisions.

Processing is a series of actions or operations that converts input into useful output. In data processing, input is the data and output is the information. It consists of three sub-activities—capturing input data, manipulating it, and producing output information. A data processing system includes resources such as people, procedures and devices used to process input data for producing desirable output.

Hence, data is the raw material of information, and just as a manufacturing process transforms raw materials into finished products, data processing transforms raw data into information.

21.1 DATABASE MANAGEMENT SYSTEM

Database Management System (DBMS) is a collection of programs that enables us to store, modify, and extract information from a database. A Database Management System is software designed to gather, handle and process information. The database program manipulates the information in ways that help us to analyse the data by storing, accessing, and processing data or facts into useful information. Thus, a DBMS not only stores data, but also allows its users to easily make use of that data. Typical examples of DBMS include Oracle, DB2, Microsoft Access, Microsoft SQL Server, PostgreSQL, MySQL and FileMaker Pro. Microsoft Access, which is a part of MS Office, is a very popular Relational Database Management System (RDBMS). We see databases in everyday life; our phonebook is a database, as is the card catalog at the college library. Many large companies and organizations rely greatly on a commercial or custom DBMS to handle enormous data resources.

Thus, a database management system (DBMS) is:

1. A system whose overall purpose is to record and maintain the database of an enterprise and make it available on demand.
2. A computerized record keeping system.

DBMS is a tool which helps an enterprise organize and manage data to transform them into useful information for taking decisions.

The functional components of DBMS software are as under:

1. Data Definition Language (DDL)
2. Data Manipulation Language (DML)
3. Query Language (QL)
4. Report Generator (RG)
5. Application Generator (AG)
6. User Interface (UI).

The above functional components are represented in the Figure 21.1.

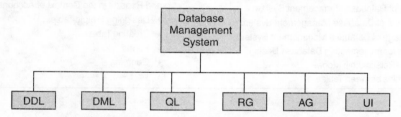

FIGURE 21.1 Functional components of DBMS.

Data Definition Language (DDL): It is used to define the contents and the structure of a database.

Data Manipulation Language (DML): It is a set of procedural commands that enables programmers to append, modify, update and retrieve data.

Query Language (QL): It is user oriented. It helps the user to make ad-hoc queries from the database.

Report Generator (RG): It helps the users to represent the reports in different form according to the demand of the situation.

Application Generator (AG): It is a DBMS package available in the fourth generation language and is a very powerful command which is helpful for developing different applications.

User Interface (UI): It is a shell that provides the environment for interaction of a user with the database.

21.2 MEANING OF DATABASE

A database is a collection of data, in an organized form, so that it can be easily accessed, managed, and updated. Some examples of databases from our daily lives are:

1. A telephone directory
2. Railway reservation system
3. Files on a computer hard drive.

Databases are commonly used to store the financial, personnel, sales, and accounting information of the companies. For example, many businesses use their order placement, invoicing, and inventory databases to foresee market trends that help them increase their efficiency and competitiveness.

21.2.1 Basic Components of Database

1. Bit [A single binary digit (0 or 1)]
2. Character [Multiple related bits are combined to form a character (byte)]
3. Field [Multiple related characters are combined to form a field]
4. Record [Multiple related fields are combined to form a record]
5. File [Multiple related records are combined to form a file]
6. Database [Multiple related files are integrated to form a database]

1. Bit or binary digit: It is the smallest item of data. Bit is a single binary digit (a bit), either a 0 or 1.

2. Byte: A byte or a character is a combination of multiple related bits.

3. Field: A field is a combination of multiple related characters. For example, if we want to process employees' data of an enterprise, we may have one field each of employee code, employee name, hours worked, tax deducted, and so on. A field is a meaningful collection of related characters.

4. Record: A record is a combination of multiple related fields. For example, an employee records have fields containing data of an employee, such as employee's code, name, and hours worked. A record is a collection of related fields treated as a single unit.

5. File: A file is a combination of multiple related records. For example, a collection of employees' records of a company forms an employee file. Similarly, a collection of all inventory records of a company forms an inventory file. Hence, a file is a number of related records treated as a unit.

6. Database: A database is an integration of multiple related files. It contains a collection of logically related data elements from multiple files. Data files are categorized according to the way an application uses them. A file management system typically supports the following types of files:

(a) *Transaction file:* A transaction file stores input data until it can be processed. For example, to prepare the monthly pay bill of employees, current month's transaction file contains all data of employees regarding hours worked, absent days, overtime hours, etc.

(b) *Master file:* A master file contains all current data relevant to an application. For example, in a payroll application, master file contains permanent details of each employee and also current data like net pay, tax deducted, and so on.

(c) *Output file:* Some applications use multiple programs for data processing. In such applications, output produced by one program is often fed as input to another program.

(d) *Report file:* A report file holds a copy of a report generated by a data processing application in computer-accessible form.

(e) *Backup file:* A backup file is a copy of a file created as a safety precaution against loss of data due to corruption or inadvertent deletion of original file. Regular creation of backup files is extremely important.

21.3 FUNCTIONS OF DATABASE MANAGEMENT SYSTEM

A database system maintains a *centralized database*, i.e., all the data is kept at one place, and any application that requires the data can access it from this central location. Any application can share data also from the central location. Though sometimes it may become necessary to duplicate the data, i.e., maintain multiple copies, the redundancy can be controlled as the DBMS is aware of the multiple copies and updates them regularly.

From the above, the functions of a database management system may be grouped as under:

1. Creating tables: The first step in building any database is to create one or more tables. To create a new database, we must first determine what kind of data will be sorted in each table. In other words, we must define each field in the table by the following three step process:

(a) Name of the field
(b) Specify the field type
(c) Specify the field size.

2. Viewing records: The way data appears on screen determines how easily users can work with it. With many DBMS products, we use the table view to create a database table and to modify field specifications. Filters are a DBMS feature for displaying a selected list or subset of records from a table. The visible records satisfy a condition that the user has set. It is called **filter**.

A DBMS also allows us to create forms for viewing records. By using forms, we can create simple, easily understood views of our data that show just one record at a time, but we can create complex forms also.

3. Sorting records: One of the most powerful features of a DBMS is the ability to sort a table data, either for a printed report or for display on the screen. Sorting arranges records according to the contents of one or more fields.

4. Creating queries: In a manner similar to entering sort conditions, we can enter expressions or criteria that

- (a) Allow the DBMS to locate records
- (b) Establish relationships or links between tables to update records
- (c) List a subset of records
- (d) Perform calculations
- (e) Delete obsolete
- (f) Perform other data management tasks.

Any of the above stated requests is called a **query**, a user-constructed statement that describes data and sets criteria so that the DBMS can gather the desired data and construct specific information.

5. Generating reports: A report is a printed information that, like a query result, is assembled by gathering data based on user-supplied criteria. Reports can range from simple lists of records to customized formats for specific purposes.

Figure 21.2 shows the designing of a database for processing accounting information through a flowchart.

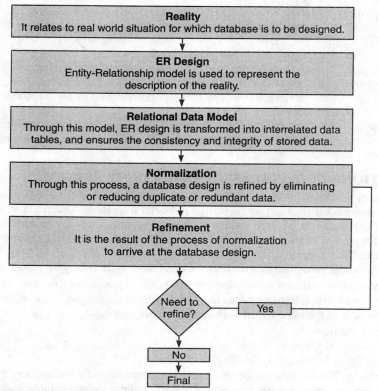

FIGURE 21.2 Process of designing database for accounting through flowchart.

21.4 THE BENEFITS OF DATABASE MANAGEMENT SYSTEM

1. Reduces redundancy: As the data is stored in one central place rather than having multiple copies of the data at multiple places, redundancy or idleness is removed. Here, duplication of data is called **data redundancy**.

2. Removes inconsistency: Storing data at one place ensures that the shared data is consistent making it easier to maintain accuracy. If we want to update shared data, we make the change in one place, and the change appears automatically in all the places wherever the data has been used. Thus, by controlling redundancy, inconsistency also gets controlled.

3. Facilitates data sharing: Sharing of data means that the same data can be shared by many users or application programs. Each user may have access to the same data, which may be used for different purposes. For example, if one salesman updates the record for a particular product, all the other salesmen would know of the change.

4. Helps enforce standards and data integrity: Data integrity implies that only valid data that meets certain rules or requirements is entered in the database.

5. Ensures security: A database management system ensures data security so that only the authorized users have access to the data. For example, some may just be able to read it, while only authorized person(s) can modify parts of the data in a database.

6. Saves resources: Storing one copy of data saves disk storage space and saves time data entry and updating.

7. Permits more information to be obtained from data: DBMS provides tools to convert the data in a form that is useful, called **information.** The said information may be used for analysing the data. For example, sales database has records of all the orders collected by the salesmen through which the highest sales in each region may be obtained.

21.5 DISADVANTAGE OF DATABASE MANAGEMENT SYSTEM

1. Lack of database expertise: Database technology or system is complex, and without having sufficient expertise, it cannot run efficiently. As a result, it is not possible for all enterprises to run it fruitfully.

2. Data security and integrity: Many users may get the opportunity to access the database and that makes the entire system insecure.

3. Cost of hardware: The entire system of database technology requires additional software packages to increase the processing capacity, and nowadays, it is one of the most costly ventures for acquiring and maintaining the system.

21.6 STRATEGIES FOR IMPLEMENTING DATABASE DESIGN

Two strategies are usually used for implementing database design: The following
1. ER Model or ER Diagram or Entity—Relationship Model
2. Normalization.
As per syllabus, only ER Model will be discussed here.

21.6.1 Entity-Relationship Model

The entity-relationship model for data uses the following three features to describe data:
1. Entities which specify distinct real-world items in an application.
2. Relationships which connect entities and represent meaningful dependencies between them.
3. Attributes which specify properties of entities and relationships.

With the help of an example, these terms are illustrated below. A vendor supplying items (products) to a company, for example, is an entity. The item he supplies is another entity. A vendor and an item are related in the sense that a vendor supplies an item. The act of supplying defines a relationship between a vendor and an item. An **entity set** is a collection of similar entities. We may thus define a vendor set and an item set. Each member of an entity set is described by some attributes. For example, a vendor may be described by the attributes like vendor code, vendor name and address. An item may be described by some attributes

[item code, items]

In the entity-relationship (ER) diagram (Figure 21.3), an entity set is represented by a rectangle and relationship set by a diamond-shaped box. We may define another entity set called **orders**, and a relationship set **'Places with'**. The statement 'Orders Placed with Vendors' is shown in the ER diagram Figure 21.4.

FIGURE 21.3 An ER diagram for vendors, items and their relation.

FIGURE 21.4 An ER diagram placed with vendors.

The interesting design problem is identifying entities which can be in a set. Only items with the same property can be in an entity set. For example, students form an entity set and course another entity set. The relationship between these entities is 'attend'. Students attend courses. Courses are held in classrooms. Classrooms is thus an entity set where the relationship is 'held in'. Once entities in an application are identified, the relationships are reasonably simple to identify.

Having identified entities and relationships, the next step is to specify their attributes. Attributes specify the properties of entities in an entity set and relationships in a relationship set. For example, the attributes of the entity 'Vendor', which describes a vendor fully, would be—(vendor identification or code, vendor name, and vendor address). The attributes of an entity are shown next to the entity box enclosed in square brackets in an ER diagram (Figure 21.5).

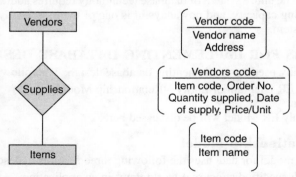

FIGURE 21.5 An ER diagram showing attributes.

Entity-relationship diagrams are a means to an end, the end being the logical design of a database. ER diagrams allow us to have an overview of the important entities for developing an information system and their relationships. Having obtained ER diagrams, the next step is to replace each entity set and relationship set by a table or a relation. Each table has a name known as the **entity name**. Each table has a number of rows and columns. Each row contains a member of the entity set, while each column corresponds to an attribute. Thus, in the ER diagram (Figure 21.5), the vendor entity is replaced by Table 21.1.

TABLE 21.1   Entity Vendor (Figure 21.5)

Vendor code	Vendor name	Address
2008	M/s DD	12, R.D. Street, Durgapur-12
2012	M/s FF	37, M.G. Road, Kolkata-9
1890	M/s GG	48, C.R. Avenue, Delhi-7
1678	M/s HH	87, Russel Street, Kolkata-27
1796	M/s KK	24, R.G.Avenue, Puri-19

Table 21.1 is also known as a **relation**. Vendor is the relation name. Each row of a relation is called **tuple**. The titles used for columns of a relation are known as **relation attributes**. Each tuple in the above example describes one vendor. Each element of a tuple gives a specific property of that vendor. Each property is identified by the title used for an attribute column. In a relation, the rows may be in any order. The columns may also be depicted in any order. No two rows can be identical.

Since it is inconvenient to show the whole table corresponding to a relation, a more concise notation is used to depict a relation. The notation consists of the relation name and its attributes. The identifier or key of the relation is shown in bold face. (We will formally define the key later in this section.) The relation of the Table 21.1 is depicted as in Figure 21.6.

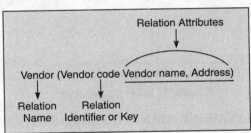

FIGURE 21.6   Relation name and its attributes.

In an accounting information system, the extended ER diagram may be drawn for each entity (transaction and accounts) and the relationship (effect) for the transaction accounts. For example, in a purchase transaction, attributes may be specified and documented as shown in Figure 21.7.

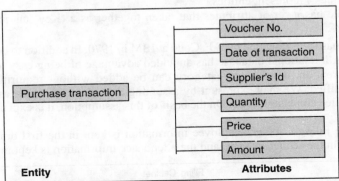

FIGURE 21.7   Extended ER diagram showing attributes in a purchase transaction.

21.7 RELATIONSHIPS BETWEEN TABLES

After setting different tables for each subject in the Microsoft Access database, we need a way of telling Microsoft Access how to bring that information back together again. The first step in this process is to define relationships between our tables. After we have done that, we can create queries, forms and reports to display the information from several tables at once.

Relationship can be

1. **One-to-one relationship:** In a one-to-one relationship, each record in Table A can have only one matching record in Table B, and vice versa.
2. **Many-to-many relationship:** In a many-to-many relationship, a record in Table A can have many matching records in Table B, and similarly, a record in Table B can have many matching records in Table A.
3. **One-to-much relationship:** In a one-to-much relationship, a record in Table A can have many matching records in Table B, but a record in Table B has only one matching record in Table A.

The coordination between different tables to accomplish certain objectives is done through relationships between tables. Many-to-many relationship is shown below in the ER diagram (Figure 21.8). Here, the attributes shown as ovals (⬭) are connected to the entities or relationships by lines.

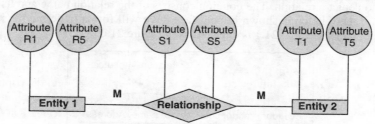

FIGURE 21.8 Entity-Relationship.

21.8 RELATIONAL DATABASE MANAGEMENT SYSTEM (RDBMS)

Relational Database Management Systems (RDBMS) have become popular, largely due to their simple data model, which is became of the following factors:

1. Data is presented as a collection of relations
2. Each relation is depicted as a table
3. Columns are attributes
4. Rows ('tuples') represent entities
5. Every table has a set of attributes that taken together as a 'Key' uniquely identifies each entity.

Relational database was invented by E.F. Codd at IBM in 1970. In addition to being relatively easy to create and access, a relational database has an added advantage of being easy to extend. After the original database creation, a new data category can be added without requiring that all existing applications be modified. We may express it by assuming a relational database as a file cabinet and each drawer of the file cabinet as a table. On the basis of this assumption, it is explained below through an example.

Here within the Filing Cabinet, employee information is kept in the first drawer, details of the payroll information in the second drawer, and the attendance information is kept in the third drawer.

Filing Cabinet	
Employee	1st Drawer
Payroll	2nd Drawer
Attendance	3rd Drawer

To connect each of these drawers (that is a 'relation'), a set piece of data from one drawer has to be present in the other drawers. For instance, in the employee drawer, the data of all the employees, i.e., the employee code, name, address, and experience details will be stored. In the attendance drawer, the employee code, and the attendance details will be stored, while in the payroll drawer, the employee code, basic pay, conveyance, house rent, and other salary details will be stored. For generating a payslip, all the three drawers are to be used. These data can be related (considering it as a relational database), and the payslip generated, based on the common information in all the drawers, i.e., the employee code.

The relational database structure is the most common in today's business organizations. In a business, a typical relational database would most likely contain separate tables with information on customers, employees, vendors, orders, and inventory.

21.9 RETRIEVAL OF ACCOUNTING INFORMATION AND BASIC QUERIES

A query is a more powerful filter that can gather information from multiple tables in a relational database. For example, a Sales Manager might create a query to list orders by a quarter. The query can include field names such as customer, city from a customers' table, and order date from the order table. To obtain the desired information, the query requires the specific data or criteria that will isolate those records from all records in both the tables. In this case, the Sales Manager includes a range of dates during which the order was shipped. Some database systems provide special windows or forms for creating queries. Such a window or form provides an area for selecting the tables the query will work with, and columns for entering the field names where the query will obtain or manipulate data.

All database management systems provide a query language enabling users to define their requirements as queries for extracting desired information from a database. For example, for an inventory database, a user may be interested in such information as 'list item description and vendor name for all items whose current inventory level is less than 20 units', or 'list stock number and item description for all items with a profit margin greater than 25%'. A query language enables proper formulation of queries for extraction of such information from a database.

Initially, queries developed for one DBMS could not be used with other DBMSs. Later on, one query language, called **SQL** Structural Query Language, (pronounced 'S-Q-L'), emerged as an industry standard. It was originally developed by IBM and was based on an earlier query language called SEQUEL, an acronym for **'Structured English Query Language'**. Today, SQL is used in many DBMSs.

SQL is a powerful tool and nearly all computer-based database management systems lane it.

The data from these two tables will be retrieved using SELECT statements of SQL

Employee Data Table

Employee ID	First name	Surname	Date of Birth	Hire Date	Salary(Rs.)	Department	Manager
2008	Anup	Gupta	02.08.74	14.09.06	24,000	03	4800
2034	Sudip	Kumar	14.09.71	19.07.07	27,000	07	4100
2056	Rupak	Singhania	23.02.69	21.05.05	29,000	09	4300
2076	Vidhan	Baxi	07.12.65	10.03.06	22,000	03	4800
2045	Sanjay	Dhali	26.11.67	03.04.08	25,000	07	4100
2078	Pradip	Kamath	11.04.73	09.07.04	24,000	06	4200
2047	Nitin	Desai	19.05.72	18.02.06	30,000	06	
2023	Suresh	Sen	27.10.68	11.08.07	22,000	07	4100
2012	Jiten	Ruia	09.07.75	17.05.05	28,000	05	4600
2033	Hari	Bhimani	12.09.71	23.06.06	21,000	09	4300
2059	Dilip	Agarwal	16.06.73	10.03.05	20,000	03	4800
2061	Siddharth	Singh	17.06.68	21.04.07	23,000	07	4100

Department Table

Department No.	Department Name	Department Manager	Location of Department
03	Marketing and Sales	4800	Kolkata
05	Finance	4600	Bangalore
06	Personnel	4200	Delhi
07	Production	4100	Durgapur
09	Accounts	4300	Jaipur

The basic symbol of **SELECT** statement is as under:

Select [Column Name]

[Table Name]

[From Where]

1. For selecting the employees of a particular department.

Query: Write a query to select the employees of the Department 03.

Select: All attributes from Employees where Department = 03.

From the Query Result, we will find that the instant query will retrieve (recover) three rows from the Employee Table because the said employees are from Department No.03.

Query Result will be as under:

EmployeeID	First Name	Surname	Date of Birth	Hire Date	Salary(Rs.)	Department
2008	Anup	Gupta	02.08.74	14.09.06	24,000	03
2076	Vidhan	Baxi	07.12.65	10.03.06	22,000	03
2059	Dilip	Agarwal	16.06.73	10.03.05	20,000	03

2. For selecting the employees of a particular department (07) and the employees drawing salary above Rs. 26,000 from the said Department.

(a) Query: Write a query to select the employees of the Department 07.

Select: All attributes from Employees where Department = 07.

From the Query Result, we will find that the instant query will retrieve (recover) four rows from the Employee Table because the said employees are from Department No.07.

Query Result will be as under:

EmployeeID	First Name	Surname	Date of Birth	Hire Date	Salary(Rs.)	Department
2034	Sudip	Kumar	14.09.71	19.07.07	27,000	07
2045	Sanjay	Dhali	26.11.67	03.04.08	25,000	07
2023	Suresh	Sen	27.10.68	11.08.07	22,000	07
2061	Siddharth	Singh	17.06.68	21.04.07	23,000	07

(b) Query: Write a query to select the employees of the Department 07 drawing salary above Rs. 26,000.

Select: First Name, Surname, Salary

From Employee Table

where Salary > Rs. 26,000.

From the Query Result, we will find that the instant query will retrieve (recover) the name of the respective employee getting salary above Rs. 26,000.

Query Result would be as under:

Employee ID	First Name	Surname	Salary(Rs.)	Department
2034	Sudip	Kumar	27,000	07

3. For selecting the employees drawing salary above Rs. 25,000

Query: Write a query to select names and salaries of those employees who are getting more than Rs. 25,000.

Select: First Name, Surname, Salary
From Employee Table
where Salary > Rs. 25,000.

From the Query Result, we will find that the instant query will retrieve (recover) the name of the respective employees getting salary above Rs. 25,000.

First Name	Surname	Salary (Rs.)
Sudip	Kumar	27,000
Rupak	Singhania	29,000
Nitin	Desai	30,000
Jiten	Ruia	28,000

4. For selecting annual salaries after increment in a particular department

Query: Write a query to select annual salaries after adding increment of Rs. 600 from Department 09.

Select: Names and (Salary + 600) × 12
From Employee Table
Department No. 09

From the Query Result, we will find that the instant query will retrieve (recover) the name of the respective employees of Department No. 09 and their annual salaries.
Query Result would be as under:

First Name	Surname	(Salary + 600) × 12 (Rs.)
Rupak	Singhania	355,200
Hari	Bhimani	259,200

5. For selecting the names and hire dates of employees of a particular period

Query: Write a query to select the names and hire dates of employees between April 01, 2005 to March 31, 2007.

Select: First Name, Surname, Hire Date
From Employee Table
where Hire Date between April 1,2005 and March 31,2007.

From the Query Result, we will find that the instant query will retrieve (recover) the name of the respective employees joined between the period from April 1,2005 to March 31,2007.
Query Result would be as under:

First Name	Surname	Hire Date
Anup	Gupta	14.09.06
Rupak	Singhania	21.05.05
Vidhan	Baxi	10.03.06
Nitin	Desai	18.02.06
Jiten	Ruia	17.05.05
Hari	Bhimani	23.06.06

21.10 DESIGNING AND CREATING SIMPLE TABLES, FORMS, QUERIES, AND REPORTS IN THE CONTEXT OF ACCOUNTING SYSTEM

21.10.1 Designing Simple Tables

A table is a collection of related data on a specific topic, such as a student's personal details, marks, competition, participation, etc. A table is organized into columns called **fields** and rows called **records**. Two or more tables can have common fields, which are used to make relations between tables. Before a table is created, it needs to be designed. Designing the table means deciding the type of data that is to be stored in the table, and based on that, deciding the fields, the type of fields and their properties.

While designing a table, the following issues need to be decided first:

1. Field name: It is the identifier of the field as it describes the data that is going to be stored in the field. The name should be short and descriptive.

2. Field type or data type: It must be decided what kind of data is going to be stored in the field. Data type dictates the type of data entered in a field.

3. Field size: We can specify the maximum length of a field. The field size can then be specified.

4. Field properties: The other properties of a field have to be decided, such as the format of data to be stored in the field or validation rules, so that only a particular type of data can be entered in the field.

5. Primary key: Decide and identify the key or field, which will be unique for each record. This will be the primary key, which identifies each record uniquely.

21.10.2 Creating Tables

A table can be created using the following three methods:

1. Create table using Design view
2. Create table by using wizard
3. Create table by entering data.

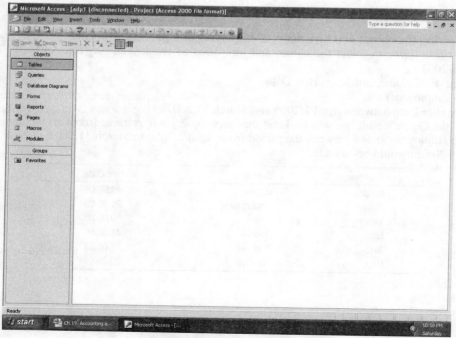

FIGURE 21.9 Database view.

1. *Create table using Design view*

The following steps are to be followed:

(a) In the database view, click on *Tables* button on the left side (see Figure 21.9).

(b) Select the first option, i.e., *Create table in Design view,* by double clicking it. Alternatively, click on *New* button on the database window toolbar. The *New Table* dialog box appears. Select *Design view* from the options. Click on *OK* button.

(c) The Table Sheet appears on the screen; enter the field name and data-type of field.

(d) Enter the field name in the first column. Then move to the second column by pressing TAB key. After that, select the data-type from the list, and enter the description in the third column (if any).

(e) Similarly, write the other fields.

2. *Create table by using wizard*

The Table Wizard helps us to create a new table. The wizard has several sample tables with many fields, from which we can select as per our requirements. To create table using the Table Wizard, follow the steps stated below:

(a) In the database window, click the *Tables* tab.

(b) Click on *New* button on the database window toolbar. The *New Table* dialog box appears.

(c) Select the *Table Wizard* option and click on *OK* button.

(d) The table wizard starts. In the first step of the wizard, click *Business* or *Personal* to choose the *Database Type.*

(e) Click on the table in the list of *Sample Tables.* Click on *Sample Fields* and then on *Move* button to select the fields. The selected fields appear on the right side list box. You can remove a field by selecting if from this list box and clicking on the *Remove* button.

(f) After selecting all the required fields for the new table, click on the *Next* button.

(g) In the second step of the Table Wizard, enter the name of the table and let MS Access set the primary key for the table or select the primary key yourself, by selecting the appropriate option button.

(h) Click on *Next* button. If you choose to enter the primary key yourself, another Wizard step appears asking you to select the field you want to assign as the primary key.

(i) Select the field and select the option buttons to specify how the data in this field is to be added. Click on *Next* button.

(j) In the last step of the Table Wizard, enter whether you want to modify the table design, add more fields, or change the data type of a field. You can also select to start entering data directly in the table or by a using a form created by the wizard. Click on the *Finish* button.

3. *Create table by entering data*

To create table by entering data, follow the steps stated below:

(a) In the Database window, select the *Tables* tab.

(b) Click the *New* button on the database window toolbar.

(c) The *New Table* dialog box appears. Select *Datasheet View* option.

(d) Click on *OK* button.

(e) A new table window appears. Double click on the field name and type the new name. Accordingly, click on other fields and rename them.

(f) Click on the *Close* button. MS Access shows a box asking whether you want to save the changes in the new table. Click on *Yes* to save changes.

(g) The *Save As* dialog box appears. Enter the *Table Name* and click on *OK* button.

(h) MS Access asks you whether you want to create a primary key. In case you want MS Access to create primary key in the table, click on *Yes* button. MS Access will create a primary key.

21.10.3 Forms

Forms are used to easily view, enter, and change data directly in a table. When you open a form, MS Access retrieves the data from one or more tables, and displays it on the screen, in a layout you choose. A form is made up of controls. A control is used to facilitate the entry of information into the table(s) that the form represents. Controls can be of various types such as text boxes, radio buttons, pull-down lists, pack lists, etc.

Designing forms

To facilitate easier data entry, forms are often designed with several special features such as:

1. A list box for a field, which lists several options on it from which the user can make a choice. For example, the form of the *Sex* field may have a box, which lists the options 'Male' and 'Female' on it, and the user simply selects the appropriate option. Depending on the user's selection option, the system automatically enters 'M' or 'F' in the *Sex* field. Similarly, the State field may have a list box, which lists all the states on it, from which the user can select the appropriate option.

2. Automatic conversion of typed characters to upper or lowercase. For example, in the form of the number 2, this feature may be used with the State field. Hence, the system will accept "mh" or "Mh", "mH" or "MH" for the state code of Maharashtra, and will automatically convert the entry to "MH". This feature can greatly ease data entry and ensure the uniformity of data.

3. Automatic formatting of certain fields. For example, in the form of the number 2, this feature can be used with the Telephone No. field to automatically display the value of this field in the specified format; that is, to enter the telephone number '(020) (5680-489)', the user only needs to type '0205680489', and the system automatically causes the form to display '(020) (5680-489)'.

21.10.4 Querying

Queries select records from one or more tables in a database so that they can be viewed, analysed, and sorted on a common datasheet. The resulting collection of records, called a **dynaset** (short for **dyn**amic sub**set**), is saved as a database object and can, therefore, be easily used in the future. The query will be updated whenever the original tables are updated.

Types of the queries are **select queries** that extract data from tables based on specified values, **find duplicate queries** that display records with duplicate values for one or more of the specified fields, and **find unmatched queries** which display records from one table that do not have corresponding values in a second table.

Create a query in design view

In order to create a new query in Design view, follow the following steps:

(a) Click the *New* button from the queries page on the database window.
(b) Then select *Design view* and click *OK*.
(c) After selecting tables and existing queries from the Tables and Queries tabs, click the *Add* button to add each one of the new query.
(d) Click *Close* when all of the tables and queries have been selected.
(e) Add fields from the tables to the new query by double clicking the field name in the table boxes or selecting the field from the Field and Table drop down menus on the query form. Specify sort orders if necessary.
(f) Enter the criteria for the query in the Criteria field.
(g) If you have selected all of the fields and tables, click the *Run* button on the toolbar.
(h) Save the query by clicking the *Save* button.

Query wizard

Access Query Wizard will easily assist you to begin creating a select query.

(a) Click the *Create query by using wizard* icon in the database window to have Access step you through the process of creating a query.

(b) From the first window, select fields that will be included in the query by first selecting the table from the drop down *Tables/Queries* menu. Select the fields by clicking the > button to move the field from the Available Fields list to Selected Fields. Click the double arrow button >> to move all of the fields to Selected Fields. Select another table or query to choose from more fields and repeat the process of moving them to the Selected Fields. Click *Next* > when all of the fields have been selected.

(c) On the Next window, enter the names for the query and click *Finish*.

Report generation

A report is an effective way to present your data in a printed format. Since you have control over the size and appearance of everything on a report; you can display the information the way you want to see it. Most of the information in a report comes from an underlying table, query or SQL statement, which is the source of report's data. Other information in the report is stored in the report's design.

A report is printed information that, like a query result, is assembled by gathering data based on user-supplied criteria. Reports can range from simple lists of records to customized formats for specific purposes.

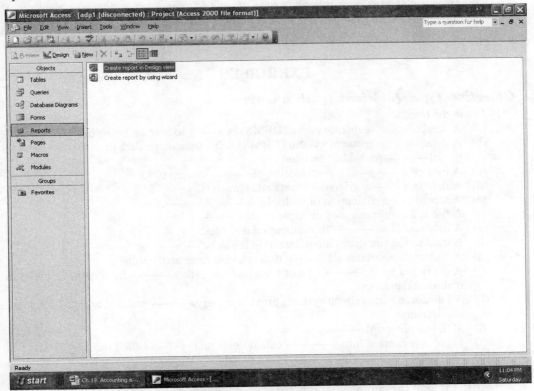

FIGURE 21.10 Report generation.

Creating a report

(a) *Creating a report by auto report:* Auto report creates a report that displays all fields and records in the underlying table or query:

1. In the Database window, click *Reports* under Objects (see Figure 21.10).
2. Click the *New* button on the Database window toolbar.
3. In the New Report dialog box, click one of the following wizards:
   - *AutoReport: Columnar.* Each field appears on a separate line with a label to its left.
   - *AutoReport: Tabular.* The fields in each record appear on one line, and the labels print once at the top of each page.
4. Click the table or query that contains the data you want to base your report on.
5. Click *OK*.

(b) *Creating a report by wizard*
   Follow the following steps:

1. In the database window, click *Reports* under *Objects*.
2. Click the *New* button on the database window toolbar.
3. In the *New Report* dialog box, click the wizard that you want to use. A description of the wizard appears on the left side of the dialog box.
4. Click the table or query that contains the data you want to base your report on.
5. Click *Ok*.
6. If you clicked *Report Wizard, Chart Wizard, or Label Wizard* in step 3, follow the directions in the wizard dialog boxes. If you click *AutoReport: Tabular* or *AutoReport: Columnar*, MS Access automatically will create your report.

EXERCISES

I. *Objective Type Questions (with answers)*

1. Fill in the blanks:
   (a) A database management system (DBMS) is a —— to help an enterprise.
   (b) A database management system (DBMS) helps to manage data to transform them into useful ——— for taking decision.
   (c) A byte or a ——— is a combination of ——— related bits.
   (d) A field is a ——— of multiple related characters.
   (e) A record is a combination of multiple ——— ———.
   (f) A file is a combination of multiple related ———.
   (g) A database is an ——— of multiple related files.
   (h) A transaction file stores input data until it can be ———.
   (i) A master file contains all ——— data relevant to an application.
   (j) A query is a more ——— type of filter that can gather ——— from multiple tables in a relational database.
   (k) All database management systems provide a query ——— enabling users to define their requirements.
   (l) SQL is a powerful ———.
   (m) Table is organized into ——— called fields and ——— called records.
   (n) The Table Wizard helps to ——— a new table.
   (o) A form is made up of ———.

   Ans: (a) tool; (b) information; (c) character, multiple; (d) combination; (e) related, fields; (f) records; (g) integration; (h) processed; (i) current; (j) powerful, information; (k) language; (l) tool; (m) columns, rows;(n) create; (o) controls.

II. *Short Answer Type Questions*

1. What do you mean by database management system?
2. What do you mean by database?
3. What are the basic components of database?
4. What do you mean by byte?
5. What is bit or binary digit?
6. What do you mean by Field?
7. What is Record?
8. What is File?
9. What do you mean by Entity Relationship Model?
10. What do you mean by Master File?
11. What do you mean by Backup File?
12. What is Relational Database Management System (RDBMS)?
13. What do you mean by basic Queries?
14. What is SQL?
15. What is designing simple tables?
16. What do you mean by Forms?

III. *Long Answer Type Questions*

1. What is Database Management System? Briefly explain its functions.
2. What do you mean by database? What are the basic components of database?
3. Explain the benefits and disadvantage of Database Management System.
4. Explain in brief the Relational Database Management System (RDBMS).
5. Explain the various ways of creating Tables using MS Access.
6. What is a Query? What are the various ways of creating a Query? Explain any one.
7. What do you mean by designing a Report? Mention different ways of creating Reports and explain any one of them.
8. Explain in brief the Entity-Relationship (ER) Model.